C000203969

WHERE to SKI
AND Snowboard 2016

Published in Great Britain by
NortonWood Publishing

tel 0844 9911 123
email w20@wheretoski.co.uk

Editors Chris Gill and Dave Watts
Editorial consultant Mandy Crook
Editorial manager Lucy Dodsworth
Assistant editors Sheila Reid, Lucy
Dodsworth, David Dalton
Admin assistant Laura Lloyd

Contributors Minty Clinch,
Alan Coulson, Nicky Holford,
James Hooke, Eric Jackson,
Tim Perry, Ian Porter, Adam Ruck,
Helena Wiesner, Fraser Wilkin

Advertising manager
Dave Ashmore

Send advertising enquiries to
publisher@wheretoski.co.uk

Design by Val Fox
Production by Guide Editors
Contents photos generally
by Snowpix.com / Chris Gill
Production manager
Sarah Carreck
Proofreader Sally Vince
Printed and bound in Italy
by Lego SpA

10 9 8 7 6 5 4 3 2 1

ISBN-13: 978-0-9558663-7-1

A CIP catalogue entry for this book
is available from the British Library.

Book trade sales are handled by
Faber Factory Plus
Bloomsbury House
74–77 Great Russell Street
London WC1B 3DA

tel 020 7927 3800
bridgetlj@faber.co.uk

**Individual copies of the book can be
bought (for delivery anywhere in the
world) at a discount price by going to
our website:
www.wheretoskiandsnowboard.com**

This edition published 2015
Copyright (text and illustrations)
© Chris Gill and Dave Watts 2015

Background images in the mountain
maps in the following chapters are
© copyright Atelier Novat:

Soldeu p80
Alpe d'Huez p196
Les Arcs p206
Chamonix p223
Les Deux-Alpes p248
Megève p269
Paradiski p303
La Plagne p305
La Rosière p321
Serre-Chevalier p327
Tignes p348
Val Cenis Vanoise p357
Val d'Isère p360
Vars p379
La Thuile p446

The right of Chris Gill and Dave
Watts to be identified as Authors of
this Work has been asserted by
them in accordance with the
Copyright, Design and Patents Act
1988.

All rights reserved. No part of this
publication may be reproduced,
stored in a retrieval system or
transmitted, in any form or by any
means, electronic, mechanical,
recording or otherwise, in any part
of the world, without the prior
permission of the publishers. All
requests for permission should be
made to the editors at this address:
publisher@wheretoski.co.uk.

Although every care has been taken
in compiling this publication, using
the most up-to-date information
available at the time of going to
press, all details are liable to change
and cannot be guaranteed. Neither
NortonWood Publishing nor the
editors accept any liability
whatsoever arising from errors or
omissions, however caused.

**Cover: Kitzbühel
© Albin Niederstrasser**

WHERE *to* SKI AND *SnoWboard* 2016

The Definitive Guide
to the 1,000 Best Winter Sports Resorts in the World

Edited by
Chris Gill
and
Dave Watts

NortonWood

1994-2014

Where to Ski

Most Improved Resort

Austria

Savour endless beauty!

KitzSki - Enjoy the outstanding variety of slopes at full length
15 runs from peak to valley - 60 in total

KitzSki - State-of-the-art cable cars with highest comfort levels
heated seats included

KitzSki calling!

BERGBAHN Kitzbühel

World's Best Ski Resort Company

Austria's Best Ski Resort

KitzSki - Fantastic skiing - overwhelming excitement on 170 km of slopes

From Kitzbühel to Land Salzburg

KitzSki - starting from November to beginning of May

150 days of skiing pleasures

THE MOUNTAIN IS CALLING

We've got all your favourites covered from the Alps to the Rockies.

Head to crystalski.co.uk or call 020 8939 0859

CRYSTAL
SKI HOLIDAYS

 ATOL protected. For info please see our booking conditions.

Contents 1

ALPBACH

PPELMAYR

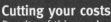

FLYBE

**That's the start of it –
turn the page for the heart of it ...**

WELCOME TO THE HOTEL POST****
THE HEART OF THE EXPERIENCE

The Hotel Post**** is St. Anton's first address. Located at the very centre of the pedestrian zone, the hotel is close to all that St. Anton has to offer; in the middle of town and up-to-the-minute since 1896. In our house, the traditional and the contemporary meet in a unique fashion: first-class service, warm hospitality, a well appointed wine cellar, outstanding cuisine, a stylish bar, friendly, generous and beautifully decorated rooms have all proven themselves to be the foundation of exceptional gastronomy for generations.

Hotel Post**** / Walter-Schuler-Weg 2
6580 St. Anton am Arlberg / Tirol / Austria
Tel.: +43 5446 22130 / Fax: +43 5446 2343
E-Mail: info@hotel-post.co.at
www.hotel-post.co.at

15313 © comdesign.net

Contents 2

Resort chapters

About this book

Dave Watts

Chris Gill

Twenty-one years ago, in 1994, we launched the first edition of this book into a highly competitive marketplace. Now, it is the only annual ski resort guidebook published in Britain. The books that we set out to compete with in 1994 have folded their tents. Other titles have appeared, but only briefly. We have managed to survive. How have we done it? Simple: by producing the book that we, as keen skiers, wanted to read.

- Every edition is the result of a thorough, painstaking process of **checking, updating and reviewing** the book's contents. We visit countless resorts every season, but even those we can't get to are reconsidered with the same care. In any one year, some chapters change hugely as a result, others hardly at all.

- The book also benefits enormously from the **hundreds of reports** that readers send us on the resorts they visit – this year, a record number of reports. Every year, we give a free copy of the book to the 100 readers who send in the best reports – and one of them wins a free week in a smart French resort apartment, courtesy of Lagrange Holidays. Read page 23.

- By making the most of technology we are able to publish at the right time while going to press late in the summer – so we can make the book **up to date for the season ahead**. Our earliest editions went to press in June; this year, it's 28 July.

- We work hard to make our information **reader-friendly**, with clearly structured text, comparative ratings and no-nonsense verdicts for the main aspects of each resort.

- We don't hesitate to express **critical views** – we learned our craft at Consumers' Association, where Chris became editor of *Holiday Which?* and Dave became editor of *Which?* itself.

- Our resort chapters give an **unrivalled level of detail** – including scale plans of each major resort, so that you get a clear idea of size – and all the facts you need.

- We use **colour printing** fully – we include not only piste maps for every major resort but also scores of photographs, carefully chosen to help you judge for yourself what the resorts are like, not just to whet your appetite for skiing and boarding.

Our ability to keep on investing in *Where to Ski and Snowboard* is largely due to the support of our advertisers, some of which have been with us since that first edition in 1994. We are extremely grateful for that support.

We are absolutely committed to helping you, our readers, to make an informed choice; and we're confident that you'll find this edition the best yet. Enjoy your skiing and riding this season.

Chris Gill and Dave Watts – Long Melford, 28 July 2015

The editorial

LET'S START WITH THE GOOD NEWS

When we went to press in late July the pound was worth around 1.4 euros. That means that local prices in France, Austria, Italy and Andorra will be around 20% lower in terms of pounds than they were two years ago and around 30% lower than when the pound almost reached parity with the euro in 2008/9. If it stays like this, or the pound goes even higher, you'll find on-the-spot prices this season lower than they have been for many years. The same cannot be said about holidays in the US or Switzerland though. Read our feature on 'Cutting your costs' on page 27.

↑ New gondola links to neighbouring ski areas will make both Saalbach-Hinterglemm and Park City the biggest ski areas in their countries

SAALBACH-HINTERGLEMM

JOINT EFFORTS

It is unprecedented in our 21 years of publishing this book to have two resorts leap ahead of their rivals to become the biggest ski areas in their respective countries. But that is happening for 2015/16.

In Austria, a new gondola and piste will link small but interesting Fieberbrunn to its better-known and much bigger neighbour Saalbach-Hinterglemm to form the biggest ski area in Austria, with 270km of slopes (as measured by independent consultant Christoph Schrahe – read our feature on piste extent on p24).

And in Utah, a new gondola and trails will link the Park City ski area to Canyons (already in the same ownership) to form the biggest ski area in the USA with 7,300 acres of skiable terrain.

13

MORE JOINT EFFORTS

Colorado has never struck us as the most liberal of American States, but it has stolen a march on California by legalizing the sale and consumption of marijuana. A reader writes: *'Staying in Aspen, we were struck by an obvious change since we last visited, just a year ago. Shops legally selling pot/marijuana have popped up all over the place, suddenly becoming almost as common as the countless art galleries – the weed, however, seeming far more attractive than the pieces of art, to judge by the numbers of customers inside the shops. Yet another interesting option to add to your 'Off the slopes' section, perhaps even granting a fifth star?'*

Well, we're resisting the fifth star, but our own 2015 tour of Colorado resorts (not including Aspen, this time) did suggest that Aspen may be well in the lead here – we spotted a shop in Steamboat, but none in the other four resorts we visited.

AND NOW THE BAD NEWS – SKI HOSTING IN DECLINE

Nearly all UK tour operators have stopped offering 'ski hosting' – guided tours of the slopes – in French resorts. That's because of an ongoing court case against chalet operator Le Ski for illegal guiding. It all started in 2012 when a ski host was stopped on the slopes by the police. The French authorities claim that the law requires anyone who is paid to show people around the slopes to be a fully

↑ Ski hosting is popular with British skiers but is in decline, mainly because of legal disputes

LE SKI

The editorial

14

qualified ski instructor. Since then there have been two court hearings which Le Ski lost (most recently in September 2014); it has appealed to the Supreme Court in Paris, but no date had been set for the hearing when we went to press in July 2015. If Le Ski loses in Paris it intends to take the case to the European court – so things could drag on for years yet. Meanwhile, this means no ski hosting for most British guests unless their tour operator hires instructors to do the guiding (which is what Skiworld is doing for two hours each Sunday in many French resorts this winter). The Ski Club of GB, which has long provided leaders (who are unpaid volunteers but get free lodgings) for its members, has also been in trouble and this season will be using Evolution 2 instructors to guide its members in 11 French resorts, charging £10 for half a day and £20 for a full day.

Andy Perrin, CEO of Hotelplan, which owns Inghams, Ski Total and Esprit Ski, said: 'It's a crying shame that this matter remains unresolved. No one gains from taking away this service that our guests thoroughly enjoyed – certainly not the ski schools, as their bookings have gone down not up as a result of this move.'

Last year some Italian resorts also clamped down on ski hosting. As a result Inghams, for example, no longer offers ski hosting in Italy or in a couple of Austrian resorts where things are difficult. And Crystal has just announced it is stopping ski hosting (or 'social skiing', to use its term) completely – saying that the service was less popular than its Ski Explorer smartphone app, which includes recommended routes for all ability levels.

OUR ANNUAL SNOW REPORT

Not a great season, for us anyway. But what does the expert think? Fraser Wilkin, of Weather to Ski, presents a more scientific analysis:

2014/15 will go down as a relatively lean but far from disastrous winter, with plenty of decent skiing on offer, especially on-piste and in the middle part of the season. Off-piste, however, was spoiled for many people by the persistently unstable snowpack.

Although there were some decent early snowfalls for the higher resorts of the south-western Alps, lower resorts – especially on the northern side of the Alps – could not have had a worse start. Some big-name resorts such as Morzine and Megève were unable to open until after Christmas.

Then, on Saturday 27 December – the busiest changeover day of the season – half a metre of snow fell in the north-western Alps, leading to unprecedented chaos on the French resort approach roads. The snow then moved east, giving Austrian resorts a happy New Year.

January saw mixed conditions, but by the middle of the season the northern side of the Alps had excellent top-to-bottom snow cover; in the southern Alps, low temperatures and artificial back-up ensured that, here too, most resorts were holding up well.

There was further snow in places towards the end of February, though eastern Italian resorts, notably the Dolomites, again missed out. Conditions in March, however, were more variable.

Overall, nearly everywhere saw below-average annual snowfall. In France, Val d'Isère managed just 4m (average 5.1m) and Avoriaz 6.1m (average 7.6m). Only a few high resorts in the south-western Alps bucked the trend. Western Italian resorts were not far off average thanks to an excellent start, but there was much less snow further east. In Switzerland, Verbier managed about average snowfall at altitude, with around 6m at Les Ruinettes. Andermatt was the stand-out Swiss resort, however, with 11m at altitude – the highest mid-mountain figure that we know of in the Alps. The highest resort-level snowfall, however, was 8.3m in Warth-Schröcken, in the notoriously snowy Austrian Vorarlberg – though still some way short of the area's super-snowy 10.6m long-term average.

Across the pond, California had a truly dismal season, with record low snowfall in many resorts. The resorts of the Pacific Northwest fared slightly better, with 6.6m at altitude in Whistler, still way below its snowy 10.5m average. Things were somewhat better inland, in both Canada and the US. Most Colorado resorts were close to par, with 8.1m in Breckenridge and 7.3m in Vail. Overall, however, it was the East Coast resorts that did best, thanks to a prolonged cold spell mid-season.

↑ Regardless of length, the Sarenne is an excellent run with fabulous views to the south

SNOWPIX.COM / CHRIS GILL

HOW LONG IS A PIECE OF PISTE?

Two years back, we ran a feature article bringing together our long-standing grumbles about exaggerated claims of piste km and the staggeringly comprehensive work of German researcher Christoph Schrahe. There's an update this year on page 24. (Executive summary: not much progress, sadly – and worrying signs of a move to quoting surface area instead of piste length.)

In our naive way, we hadn't thought that resorts' tendency to invent larger-than-life total figures would mean that they would also exaggerate the length of individual runs. But they do. Alpe-d'Huez has long claimed that its lovely Sarenne piste is the longest run in the Alps at 16km. When it failed to show up in a table of long runs published by Herr Schrahe, we looked into it; a quick map measurement and a call to Christoph leave us in no doubt that it's actually about 10km, and nothing like the longest in the Alps. The piste from the Klein Matterhorn to Zermatt, for example, is a genuine 15km. We would like at this point to trot out some more impressive examples from the Schrahe report, but his figures must be treated with care. When he measures runs to compare length, he takes the longest possible route, regardless of whether that's the route skiers take in practice. That's Christoph: scientific, objective, uncompromising.

AMERICAN DECLINE

We're as keen as ever on what US skiing has to offer, and greatly enjoyed last season's tour of Colorado. But at current exchange rates it is uncomfortably expensive in certain respects.

We said in our first editorial 21 years ago that 'There seems to be ample evidence now that America is here to stay, as it were.' Pretty perceptive, eh? It has certainly turned out to be true, although the scale of the traffic is much reduced. Back then, 11% of the reports filed by our readers were on American resorts. This year, it's 6%.

Interestingly, the flow of reader reports on Aspen seems to be holding up – surely that can't be because readers are attaching importance to our views? – while the flow on some places is drying up. Breckenridge, for example, has crashed from about ten reports a year pre-recession to only one or two in recent years.

SKI AMIS

Catered Chalets in Superb Locations

020 3411 5439
www.skiamis.com

WHAT GOES AROUND ...

We paid a brief repeat visit last winter to Val Cenis, in the wild and lovely Haute-Maurienne. The resort marketing people showed us around the hill and, naturally, showed us their preferred restaurants. It was only when we came to work on the chapter in the early summer that we began to detect references on websites to a restaurant above Termignon that we didn't visit (l'Arole) which seemed to have a highly distinctive feature: it revolves.

Motion is not one of the key characteristics we look for in a mountain restaurant, but it's certainly something we take an interest in – not least because for 20 years or so we have been spreading the message that Switzerland has a monopoly on pivoting pubs in ski resorts. (Mürren, Saas-Fee and Leysin, since you ask.) What's a bit weird is that none of the reader reports we've had on l'Arole mention its rotation. Maybe it has ground to a halt. But then the highest restaurant in the SkiWelt, the Hohe Salve above Söll, has a revolving outdoor 'panorama terrace' that no-one mentioned either.

Rotation in the interests of giving people a changing view is not confined to restaurants, of course. This year the long-awaited replacement cable car from Courmayeur to the shoulder of Mont Blanc will be open, and it is equipped with revolving cabins. Engelberg's Titlis lift is the only other one we know of in the skiing world. For many years the Titlis cabins had revolving floors, but in 2014 the cabins were replaced by ones that rotate completely.

THE EARTH MOVES IN LES DEUX-ALPES

This is a momentous year in the southern French resort of Les Deux-Alpes. At long, long last the resort is carving out what promises to be a proper intermediate piste down the steep slope above the village, where traditionally you have had a choice between a narrow, busy green track and a row of icy black mogul slopes. The photo below is evidence that it is really happening. Looks like they have got the gradient about right, at least; let's hope they've been able to create reasonable width. After 21 years of banging on about this problem, we can't wait to give the run a go. Now: come on St Anton – how about something similar from Galzig to the village?

LES DEUX-ALPES

After 21 years of us complaining, Les Deux-Alpes was hard at work this summer building a new blue piste down to resort level ↓

The editorial

16

↑ We take the editorial 4WD as much as possible when inspecting European resorts – which allows us to avoid car hire rip-offs

SNOWPIX.COM / CHRIS GILL

AND THE CAR RENTAL RIP-OFF CONTINUES

For our Colorado trip last season we were sure we had done all the right things: booked through AutoEurope (a US-based broker we've always found reliable); chosen a suitable SUV/4WD car; paid around £185 for 8 days with zero excesses and no hidden extras. Brill. So we rock up at the Dollar depot at Denver and guess what? The car is an SUV but has neither 4WD nor winter tyres. If we really want those, we can upgrade for a mere $1,000 (approx £660). We argue, we haggle. Eventually the guy asks how we flew in – we went BA. That apparently entitles us to a discount. Eventually we pay an extra $500 (£330 – almost tripling the price of the rental) to get grumpily on our way. Back in the UK, AutoEurope email us with a satisfaction survey. We let rip, and fire off a separate email. A month later, when we have given up hope, we are told they have refunded the $500 to our credit card. Result! Our faith in AutoEurope is restored. We're briefly tempted to insist on an explanation and apology from Dollar. But life's too short.

HANDS OFF THAT SPEED CONTROL KNOB, PLEASE

There's a scam going on that we'd like to stop: slow operation of fast lifts. The widespread rule now seems to be that if a detachable chair or gondola doesn't have a queue, it is wasting energy (ie money) by shifting people too quickly, and the speed should be cut until a line starts to form. As regular readers know, we are keen on fast lifts – not only because they tend to keep queues down, but also because time spent on lifts is generally time wasted. If all the 5-minute lift rides in your chosen resort become 15-minute lift rides, you can easily waste hours every day that you could spend skiing (or enjoying a more relaxed lunch).

This is a rip-off that has to be stopped, and reversed. This coming season, please pay attention to lift speed and see what you conclude. Let us know when and where you are kept dangling for longer than necessary, and we'll see what picture emerges. Ideally, whip out your smartphone and fire up a GPS app to see what your actual speed is; most detachable chairs and gondolas can operate at about 5m/s – some modern gondolas up to 6m/s.

THANKS TO YOU

We are, as ever, grateful to all the hundreds of readers who sent in reports on resorts last season – reports that are crucial to our annual updating and revision process. As usual, the most useful 100 reports have earned a free copy of this edition, and the readers' names have gone into the hat for a free week in a smart Lagrange apartment in the French Alps. And the lucky winner is ... Andrew Lawson – congratulations, Andrew. Please send in reports next season – Lagrange is again providing a prize; read page 23.

We are also indebted to the readers who make up for the inadequacy of resort picture libraries by sending in photos for publication. If we use any of your pics, you get a copy of the book – and the satisfaction of seeing your photos in print, of course. This year we have used multiple pictures provided by Tanya Booth and David Maxwell-Lees, and individual ones from Stuart McWilliam, Rod Garvey, Brian Walker, Alan Liptrot, Adrian Singleton, Simon Smith, Adrian Taylor, Alan Shepherd and Steve Solly.

Get your first issue free!

- Exclusive content
- Stunning photography
- Definitive resort & gear guides
- Plus, much more...

Download your ultimate guide
to the slopes now

 or

*Only available on iPad and Android tablets.

In this chapter we summarize major developments in ski resorts last season and those planned for 2015/16. Most resort chapters have a 'News' panel near the start; you'll find many more news items in those panels. To keep up to date, sign up for our email newsletters on our website at www.wheretoskiandsnowboard.com.

AUSTRIA

ALPBACHTAL-WILDSCHÖNAU – SKI JUWEL
2014/15: The new six-person Gmahbahn chair opened on Wiedersbergerhorn, starting much lower than the lift it replaced.

ELLMAU
2015/16: A new 10-seat gondola is planned to replace the Hartkaiser funicular. The Jochbahn quad at Brixen is due to be replaced by an eight-seater, claimed to be 'the world's fastest chairlift'.
2014/15: The Aualm quad to Zinsberg was replaced by an 8-seater.

HINTERTUX
2015/16: A new six-person chairlift will run up to Grosser Kaserer, providing a welcome alternative to the Kaserer 1 drag lift.

ISCHGL
2014/15: A 28-seat gondola replaced the old 4-seat Pardatschgrat gondola and has helped reduce morning queues.

KITZBÜHEL
2015/16: A double chair for Bichlalm to serve its area of ungroomed slopes should open in time for the season.

LECH ZÜRS
2015/16: In Zürs the Ubungshang double chair is due to be replaced by a covered six-pack.

MAYRHOFEN
2015/16: The inadequate Penken gondola from the village is being replaced by a state-of-the-art gondola with 24-seat cabins and Wi-Fi.

OBERGURGL
2015/16: In Hochgurgl the Kirchenkar draglift is due to be replaced by a 10-person gondola, with a second stage planned for 2016/17.

SAALBACH
2015/16: A new run and gondola will link with the Fieberbrunn ski area – a major expansion. A six-pack replaces the Bernkogel drags.
2014/15: An eight-seat chair replaced the Polten quad on the way to Leogang. A second gondola out of Leogang opened.

SÖLDEN
2014/15: The Wasserkar triple chair from below the Gaislachkogl gondola mid-station was replaced by a six-pack, starting much lower than the lift it replaced.

ST ANTON
2015/16: A new restaurant is to open at the top of Gampen.

ZELL AM SEE
2015/16: A two-stage 10-seat gondola will open on Kitzsteinhorn, from Alpincenter at mid-mountain to the top. The glacier area will be reconfigured, with a new nursery slope.

FRANCE

LES ARCS
2015/16: At Arc 1800 a new mini cable car will link to Le Chantel, and a six-pack will go up to Col des Frettes, above Arc 2000.

AVORIAZ-MORZINE
2014/15: The Proclou and Seraussaix chairs in the Super-Morzine area were replaced by a brace of six-packs.

CHAMONIX
2014/15: The ancient Plan Joran chair at the base of Les Grands Montets was replaced by a 10-person gondola.

CHATEL
2015/16: A new blue slope – the Forestière – has been built to link Super-Châtel to Vonnes, where last season's two new chairs meet.
2014/15: Two new fast chairs – a six-pack and a quad – were built to link the Super-Châtel and Linga ski areas.

COURCHEVEL
2015/16: The long-awaited aquatic centre below 1650 will open.
2014/15: A six-pack replaced the adjacent Aiguille du Fruit and Gravelles chairs at Praméruel between 1650 and 1850. The ancient Forêt gondola from Le Praz was replaced by a six-pack.

LES DEUX-ALPES
2015/16: The long-awaited blue Jandri run to the village is due to open in December 2015 (for more information, read the Editorial).

MEGEVE
2014/15: Both Mont Joux chairs were replaced by one fast six-pack, with a new Folie Douce (as in Val d'Isère etc) near the top.

LES MENUIRES
2015/16: A fast quad will replace the double chair towards the main resort from Le Bettex. A new wellness/pool complex has opened.

MERIBEL
2015/16: The Combes quad chair out of Mottaret will be replaced by a six-pack, and two new beginner areas are being created.
2014/15: The chair to Col de la Loze was upgraded to a fast quad.

MONTGENEVRE
2014/15: The smart Durancia leisure and wellness centre opened.

LA PLAGNE
2015/16: A 10-person gondola will replace the chairs out of Montalbert, speeding access to Plagne Centre.
2014/15: The chairlift out of Bellecôte for Plagne Centre (Colosses) was replaced by an eight-pack of huge carrying capacity.

SERRE-CHEVALIER
2014/15: The Croix de la Nore draglift on the way to Briançon from Chantemerle was replaced by a quad chair.

ST-MARTIN-DE-BELLEVILLE
2015/16: A six-pack will replace the St-Martin 2 fast quad.

VAL D'ISERE
2015/16: The former 5-star hotel Savoie will be run as a chalet hotel shared by Inghams, Ski Total and Esprit Ski.

VAL THORENS
2014/15: The fast Portette quad was replaced by a six-pack starting lower down. The slow Plan de l'Eau chair was replaced by a six-pack. A new Club Med opened at the top of the village.

ITALY

COURMAYEUR
2015/16: The new two-stage Skyway Monte Bianco cable car to Punta Helbronner at 3460m on Mont Blanc will be open.

MONTEROSA SKI
2015/16: Inghams has taken over the 3-star Champoluc hotel, right by the gondola, and will be running it as a chalet hotel.

PASSO TONALE
2015/16: A new gondola will run from Passo Paradiso to the top of the glacier, replacing the existing T-bars and chairlift. The Casola double chairlift at Ponte di Legno will be replaced by a fast quad.

SAUZE D'OULX
2014/15: A slow triple chair was built from the Capanna Mollino restaurant near Punta Rocca to Monte Triplex.

SELLA RONDA
2015/16: The La Fraina quad chair above San Cassiano will be replaced by a six-pack.
2014/15: At Corvara an eight-person gondola replaced the queue-prone Borest quad chairlift to/from Colfosco. A six-pack replaced the Pralongià triple chairlift.

SWITZERLAND

ADELBODEN
2015/16: A new fast quad chair is to be built to link the gondola station at Bergläger to the top of the neglected Chuenisbärgli sector.
2014/15: A 10-person gondola replaced the cable car out of Lenk, with a second stage up to Metschstand.

Specialists in tailor-made ski holidays, luxury ski hotels and flexible ski weekends

snow-wise
SKI HOLIDAY EXPERTS

020 3397 8450
www.snow-wise.com

ANDERMATT
2015/16: A new fast chairlift is planned to serve the pistes below Gurschen, on Gemsstock. In the separate Sedrun sector, the T-bar up from Oberalppass to Calmut will be replaced by a fast chair.

AROSA-LENZERHEIDE
2015/16: At last, the east and west sides of Lenzerheide's slopes will be connected by a new quad chairlift. The ancient triple chair from Churwalden will be replaced by a new eight-seat gondola.

CRANS-MONTANA
2014/15: A six-pack replaced the double chair to Les Violettes.

DAVOS
2014/15: The ancient Jakobshorn cable car was replaced.

LAAX
2015/16: A 10-person gondola will replace the La Siala triple chair.

ST MORITZ
2015/16: The Mandra drag-lift serving the snowpark at mid-mountain on Corvatsch is to be replaced by a quad chair.
2014/15: The Ovaverva sports centre and spa opened in Bad.

VAL D'ANNIVIERS
2015/16: A new six-pack will replace the Forêt draglift above St Luc.

ZERMATT
2015/16: The Hörnli T-bar to above Schwarzsee is due to be replaced by a new six-seat Hirli chair which will start lower down.

USA
ASPEN
2014/15: A $10 million children's centre was built at Buttermilk.

BEAVER CREEK
2014/15: The focal Centennial chairlift out of the resort was replaced by a chondola with greatly increased capacity.

BRECKENRIDGE
2014/15: Peak 8's Colorado quad chair was replaced by a six-pack.

PARK CITY/CANYONS
2015/16: A new eight-seat two-way gondola will link Canyons to the Park City slopes, creating the largest ski area in the US.

SNOWMASS
2015/16: The High Alpine chair will be replaced by a fast quad.

SQUAW VALLEY
2015/16: The Siberia Express quad is to be replaced by a six-pack.

VAIL
2015/16: The Avanti fast quad will be replaced by a six-pack.

CANADA
BANFF
2015/16: The Teepee Town double chair at Sunshine Village will be replaced by a fast quad with heated seats.

SUN PEAKS
2014/15: New trails added almost 600 acres of terrain and made Sun Peaks the second biggest ski area in Canada.

WHISTLER
2014/15: Whistler Village gondola was replaced by an eight-seater with increased capacity. Hands-free lift passes were introduced.

WHERE *to* SKI *and* SnoWboard

Send us reports on the resorts you visit!

Write a helpful resort report – the odds are you'll win a free book, plus the chance to win a week in France with Lagrange

There are too many resorts for us to visit them all every year, and too many hotels, bars and mountain restaurants for us to check them all out. So we are always keen to encourage readers to send in reports on their holiday experiences. Every year, we give 100 copies of the new edition to the writers of the best reports – and put their names into the hat to win a week in a smart Lagrange apartment.

LAGRANGE

Two of Lagrange's top properties – Les Fermes Emiguy in Les Gets and Les Chalets de l'Adet in St-Lary ↓

Your resort reports must be based on visits made during the 2015/16 season, and must be received by the end of April 2016. We much prefer to receive reports in digital form. Ideally, use our online form reached via www.wheretoskiandsnowboard.com; or you can send an email to reports@wheretoski.co.uk – but please look at the website for guidance on what we are looking for in your reports. And it's vital that you give us the date of your trip, plus your postal address (to send your book to if you win one).

The first name out of our digital hat wins a free week in a Lagrange residence. The details of your options will be made clear on our website. With the exception of Christmas/New Year and the period around February half-term, you'll be able to choose your travel dates (subject to availability).

Piste extent update

Comparable figures remain a distant hope

by **Chris Gill**

Since the start of Where to Ski and Snowboard 21 years ago, we've expressed doubts about the claimed extent of the pistes in some major Alpine resorts, and in recent years we've taken positive steps to challenge some of the figures – notably in 2010, when we said publicly that the Monterosa Ski piste total was overstated by 100%.

In 2013, German writer and consultant Christoph Schrahe started publishing the results of his own measurements of pistes, using digital techniques – first in German newspapers, and then in a detailed report published by his own consultancy. The report gave measurements of the slopes of all the big resorts, and confirmed that most of them overstated the extent of their pistes, often by surprising amounts.

In September 2013, in our 2014 edition, we brought these two strands together in a feature article which triggered media attention abroad as well as in the UK.

Some resorts are no doubt blissfully ignorant of all this, and some have no doubt decided to carry on regardless. But some have responded, as have some industry bodies, and last year we reported concrete progress towards the ideal of properly comparable piste extent figures. This year there are again some positive developments, but also a worrying development that some resorts are introducing an alternative measurement of pistes in terms of hectares, which makes comparisons with resorts that quote km impossible.

BIG NUMBERS

Claimed total / measured total / % by which these top ski areas overstate their km, according to Schrahe

Three Valleys
600 / 495 / 21%

Les Arcs-La Plagne
425 / 383 / 11%

Sella Ronda
365 / 310 / 18%

Portes du Soleil
300 / 265 / 13%
Excludes Morzine and Les Gets; this is a very complex area where there are various ways of arriving at a claimed figure

Zermatt-Cervinia
360 / 257 / 40%

Milky Way
400 / 252 / 59%

Val d'Isère-Tignes
300 / 236 / 27%

PREVIOUSLY ON 'PISTE EXTENT UPDATE'

Until we came to prepare our original feature article two years back, it had not occurred to us that there might be more than one way of measuring the length of a piste. We assumed that you would simply measure the piste down the centre line, following the curves of the piste but not deviating from that centre line. This 'centre line' approach is how Christoph Schrahe measures pistes, and it is how the FIS measures race courses.

But one of the key things we then discovered is that many resorts claim to justify their figures on the basis that what matters is the distance the skier travels. On most pistes, the thinking goes, skiers execute turns; they therefore follow a path that is longer than the centre-line length of the piste; and this longer path gives a more meaningful figure than the simple measured length. Conveniently it is also a bigger, more impressive figure.

For example, the Grand Massif area (Flaine and neighbours) assumes that your track down the mountain is a continuous series of linked semicircles. So instead of skiing 10m down the line of the piste you ski a semicircle with a diameter of 10m; the distance travelled, as any primary school pupil could tell you, is 10 x pi/2. So to get the 'linked semicircles' length the centre line length is multiplied by pi/2 or 1.57 – ie adding 57%.

We don't go along with this. Different skiers behave differently – what is a schuss to editor Watts, for example, would have many less competent skiers turning furiously. Different runs require different techniques – there are some runs that even a novice will go straight down. And if you do short turns, your feet are following a wiggly line but your head is not. We also think most skiers would intuitively expect pistes to be measured along the centre line. But the real problem is consistency: some resorts use the centre line figure, some add 57%, some add larger or smaller amounts. So comparisons between resorts are impossible.

Resorts and industry bodies are responding to the pressure for clear, sensible and comparable information about their slopes in various ways, which we'll now summarize.

THE OFFICIAL POSITION

In the wake of the publicity generated by Christoph Schrahe's work, the associations of lift companies in Austria, Switzerland and Germany reached agreement on recommendations to their members. On the fundamental question, these were clear – the length is to be measured down the centre line of the piste. These recommendations (also covering matters such as how to deal with pistes that split or join part-way down) were adopted by FIANET, the international association of ropeway operators, at its congress in October 2013. But they remain simply recommendations, which lift companies can adopt or ignore, as they choose. Broadly, they have turned out to be a waste of time.

The km total is the resort's official figure, verified by consultant Christoph Schrahe (read our feature on piste extent). It includes ski routes.

CERTIFIED SANE

Major Austrian resorts dominated the very short list of areas with claimed piste km figures that closely matched Christoph Schrahe's original measurements, and in the past year Schrahe has developed the enterprising idea of building on that by offering to 'certify' the figures published by such resorts. So far, Kitzbühel and Saalbach-Hinterglemm have signed up. We are delighted to see this happening, and we are supporting the scheme by displaying in the relevant chapters Schrahe's 'seal of approval' (shown in the margin on the left). We hope to see more resorts taking up Schrahe's offer, and not only in Austria. To be honest, right now this is the main glimmer of hope for the future.

STEPPING IN THE RIGHT DIRECTION

As we reported in our original feature two years ago, the Austrian national association of lift companies was quick to issue guidelines about piste measurement, and by the start of the 2013/14 season some resorts had taken action. The Zillertal resorts cut their claim for the whole valley from 666km to 487km; Mayrhofen cut its claim from 159km to 133km; more radically, Hochzillertal cut its claim from 181km to 88km.

Since then, disappointingly little of significance has happened. Another Austrian area, Serfaus-Fiss, which previously had claimed about 50% more than Schrahe's measurement, cut its claim radically and with 160km now almost matches the reality.

OUR FIGURES

You may find some of the numbers on the facing page don't match the ones we quote in our resort chapters. This is because Christoph Schrahe has focused on linked areas, whereas our figures will often include other local hills that are not linked.

AREA OF CONCERN

While some resorts are coming clean, others are heading in a different direction and starting to quote hectares instead of km of slopes – representing areas of piste, or areas of skiable terrain, or simply areas of ground within the lift network, skiable or not. This, of course, prevents comparisons with resorts that are sticking with km, and we view it as a backward step. It also opens up the question of how they measure their areas and yet another problem of inconsistency between resorts.

But, handily, Schrahe's new report includes the overall area of the 100 biggest linked ski areas in the world. In Europe, where ski areas do not have the boundaries that are standard in North America, this is quite tricky, but his results are very much what we would expect – the Sella Ronda in Italy and the Three Valleys in France come out way bigger than anything else.

Les Deux-Alpes already offers 415 ha of groomed slopes – a figure that is meaningless to us, and presumably to you. But on its piste map it also continues to advertise '220km of slide' – 65% more than Schrahe's figure. This season, we are told, Serre-Chevalier will not quote a km figure but will claim 410 ha of groomed pistes and a total area of 3,900 ha; Schrahe makes it 2,300 ha. Meanwhile, the latest piste map we have on file from Val d'Isère-Tignes slips in the unexplained '10,000 ha' – equivalent to a square 10km by 10km. Schrahe makes it 4,300 ha. At which point, we begin to despair.

CHOOSE YOUR OWN FIGURE

In the wake of the Schrahe report, the area shared by Austrian Ischgl and Swiss Samnaun started publishing three alternative figures based on three different measuring methods, explained with the aid of the drawing reproduced below:

238km – method a – the track a skier might follow; much like the Grand Massif figure explained earlier
172km – method b – the centre line length; the approach taken by Schrahe
163km – method c – the length as you would measure it on a map; the lowest figure, because the length measured down the slope (method b) is of course slightly more than the length measured horizontally.

This is all admirably comprehensive, but is confined to a backwater page on the Ischgl website that resort geeks will find but no one else will. When Ischgl wants to make a clear offer, it still falls back on the exaggerated 238km – now supported, on its website, by '515 ha piste area'. So you have four figures to choose from.

SORTING OUT THIS MESS

We say again: inflating the length of runs by making assumptions about how skiers behave is ludicrous. But what matters is that pistes should be measured in a standard way. Given that centre-line measurement is now recommended by the international association of ropeway operators, that's what all resorts should adopt.

This year Christoph Schrahe has produced a new and greatly expanded edition of his report, covering the top 100 ski areas and considering more aspects. Ski resort obsessives can get a copy for 99 euros – email schrahe@ski-weltweit.de.

ISCHGL FIGURES

The three ways in which Ischgl now conveys the extent of its pistes are shown in this graphic from the resort website

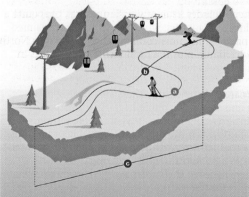

Cutting your costs

by **Chris Gill**

Our Resort Price Index figures are now an established feature of this book – our response, launched six years ago, to the weakened pound and resulting high cost of staying in a top ski resort. Despite the huge improvement in the euro exchange rate since then, we reckon holidaymakers still need a simple way to see which resorts are affordable, and which are not. That's what our RPI provides.

At the start, we based our figures on the cost of food and drink, but for some years now we have also taken into account the costs of lift passes, ski hire and lessons too. The food and drink element of the RPI, as in earlier years, is based partly on prices noted by our faithful readers. Our thanks to those who sent in prices.

£90
RESORT PRICE INDEX

£95
RESORT PRICE INDEX

£180
RESORT PRICE INDEX

LESSONS

We've used half the cost of a four-hour private lesson for two people, generally from the main school.

SKI HIRE

We've used the cost of 'performance' skis to suit an advanced or keen intermediate skier; not a beginner or top-end demo ski.

EXCHANGE RATES

We converted prices to £££ using tourist rates in June 2015:
€1.35
1.39 Swiss francs
US$1.50
CAN$1.81

In January 2009, when we were first inspired to embark on this price survey caper, it was possible at a UK airport to pay almost a pound for a euro. Parity between the currencies certainly made it easy to know what a round of drinks was costing you, but also made that cost painfully high.

Since then, the published tourist exchange rates (a bit higher than the rates at an airport bureau de change counter) have fluctuated mainly between 1.1 and 1.2 euro to the pound. A year ago, after a dip in 2013, the pound was back up to 1.2. As we prepare our RPI figures in June 2015, the rate is a giddy 1.35 euro, and still rising. We're not loading our currency cards just yet.

We have stuck to our recently adopted policy of basing our index figures on comparisons with the average cost in the main eurozone destinations – Andorra, Austria, France and Italy. These days, Swiss and North American prices are in a different league. There are panels in the margin and over the page explaining exactly what we have included in our 'basket' of items.

In margin boxes in each resort chapter we give the RPI for that resort in a colour-coded box, as shown in the margin on the left. An RPI of 100 represents the average eurozone resort. Index figures of 120 or more are coloured red, and figures of 90 or less are coloured green; ones in between are blue.

The group of resorts with roughly average blue-coded RPIs (from 95 to 115) is largely French and Austrian, with some Italian resorts. The green-coded low-cost group has eastern European countries at the bottom, but then includes a fair few Italian resorts, plus quite a few in Austria and France.

The red-coded pricey group now contains all the resorts in North America and in Switzerland, plus the most fashionable resorts in the Alps – Courchevel and Méribel in France, and Lech Zürs in Austria. In the top slot are Aspen and Beaver Creek, closely followed by Vail and Snowmass – all in Colorado.

THE PICTURE BY COUNTRY

The improvement in the value of the pound against the euro means that countries using other currencies automatically have higher RPI figures, regardless of movements in their own exchange rates.

The pound is down against the Swiss franc compared with a year ago, so Swiss prices are about 4% higher than last year to British

Alpine Weekends

Weekend ski trips, corporate events and flexible skiing holidays

020 8944 9762

www.alpineweekends.com

ALPINE
Weekends
AND FLEXIBLE BREAKS

SKI AMIS

Catered Chalets in Superb Locations

020 3411 5439
www.skiamis.com

LIFT PASSES

We have used prices for the pass you're most likely to buy – often covering other linked resorts (a Three Valleys pass, for example).

Where available, in North America we have used special passes aimed at the international market.

Six-day pass prices are given in a margin panel in most of our resort chapters. In the eurozone they range from £120 in Ste-Foy to £210 in the Three Valleys resorts. A pass in Swiss Verbier costs over £250.

holidaymakers, pushing Swiss resort RPI figures even higher. Last year, four Swiss resorts fell into our blue-coded roughly average category. Now, even the cheapest Swiss resort has a red-coded index of 125, the highest 170 (St Moritz). All Swiss resorts are expensive for eating and drinking, with budget figures, even for our very modest 'basket', ranging from £190 to £245 – that is, about £30 to £40 a day. You could easily spend £100 a day. For lift passes, too, many Swiss resorts are pricey. For lessons and ski hire, the picture is much more mixed.

The pound is down about 9% against the US$ compared with a year ago. All resorts in North America now fall well inside the pricey red-coded group, with RPI figures running from 175 to 220. But the pound is up 4% against the Canadian $, with the result that Canada now compares well with the USA – even the priciest Canadian resort, Whistler, is on a par with the cheapest American resort. North American index figures are hugely influenced by high prices for lift passes and lessons. For food and drink, a mid-market US resort is still about on the same level as major French resorts.

In the eurozone, as the table on the facing page shows, each of the Alpine countries has resorts offering relatively modest prices, although Austria and Italy are better represented at the bottom of the price league, while big French resorts tend to be a bit more expensive. But it's worth looking beyond the headline RPI figures. Compared with Austria and Italy, France is appreciably more expensive in one key respect: food and drink. There's more about this angle in the panel below the table on the facing page.

In Andorra, Soldeu comes in slightly above average, with Arinsal below. Spain costs less than average, and Slovenia appreciably less. But Bulgaria and Romania retain a firm grip on the real budget end of the market.

WAYS TO KEEP HOLIDAY COSTS UNDER CONTROL

A good way of avoiding the full impact of high resort restaurant prices is to go on a catered chalet holiday. You get afternoon tea as part of the deal, so your lunchtime needs can be minimized; some tour ops offer 'piste picnic' packed lunches at low cost; crucially, you get wine included with dinner – and you can organize your own aperitifs, or buy beer and mixers in the chalet at modest cost.

All-inclusive deals cut out spending on expensive extras. Ski 2 offers 'all-inclusive deal' options, quoting a price that includes half-board, vouchers for lunch, lift pass, and more. Club Med is a well-established operator of its own big hotels where everything is included. There are deals offered by mainstream operators, too. Inghams' Ski Inclusive offers, available in all lodgings in a couple of resorts and some lodgings in four others, includes the lift pass and equipment hire plus lunch and bar vouchers. Crystal's Ski Plus deal, also in selected resorts, includes ski/board hire and lift pass.

An obvious option is self-catering: it's now easy to find comfortable apartments with ample room to prepare meals and a dishwasher to deal with the aftermath – and with swanky spas and pools attached, in many cases. Just make sure you don't weaken and eat in restaurants every night.

Finally, think about cutting the holiday price by getting some mates together to take advantage of group discounts. Many operators offer '1 in X goes free' deals. And EurekaSKI in Serre-Chevalier is putting together special packages for groups of nine or more including special deals on lift passes, equipment hire and airport transfers.

RPI	Resort	Country	Page	RPI	Resort	C	
50	Poiana Brasov etc	Romania	665	90	La Thuile	Ita	
60	Bansko etc	Bulgaria	662	90	Valmorel	Frar	
65	Kranjska Gora etc	Slovenia	666	95	Bad Gastein	Austr	
75	Passo Tonale	Italy	422	95	Courmayeur	Italy	
80	Maurienne valley	France	265	95	Formigal etc	Spain	
80	Val Cenis Vanoise	France	357	95	Hintertux / Tux valley	Austria	109
85	Ellmau	Austria	106	95	Obertauern	Austria	150
85	Monterosa Ski	Italy	416	95	The Pyrenees	France	317
85	Ste-Foy-Tarentaise	France	336	95	Saalbach-Hinterglemm	Austria	152
85	Vars / Risoul	France	379	95	Samoëns	France	324
90	Alpbachtal-Wild'au	Austria	93	95	Schladming	Austria	158
90	Arinsal	Andorra	78	95	Sella Ronda	Italy	429
90	Brandnertal	Austria	102	95	Selva / Val Gardena	Italy	437
90	Bregenzerwald	Austria	104	95	Serre-Chevalier	France	327
90	Cervinia	Italy	391	100	Bad Kleinkirchheim	Austria	99
90	Garmisch-Partenkirchen	Germany	384	100	Châtel	France	233
90	La Grave	France	263	100	Les Carroz	France	221
90	Livigno	Italy	407	100	Les Deux-Alpes	France	248
90	Mayrhofen	Austria	138	100	Flaine	France	254
90	Montgenèvre	France	291	100	Les Gets	France	261
90	La Rosière	France	321	100	Megève	France	269
90	Sauze d'Oulx	Italy	424	100	Morzine	France	296
90	Sestriere	Italy	444	100	Stubai valley	Austria	183
90	Söll	Austria	167	100	Zell am See	Austria	185

Cutting your costs

29

Champoluc holiday prices all include lift pass and lunches

- Great value Italian resort

- Extensive range of accommodation to suit all budgets

- Book your own flights to take advantage of all the best prices

- Inclusive prices

- British ski school

- Discounts for groups

www.ski-2.com

Visit our comprehensive website,
at www.ski-2.com,
call us on **01962 713330**
or email us at **info@ski-2.com**

ABTA
The Travel Association

FOOD AND DRINK IN EUROPE

Our budget figure that feeds into the RPI calculations is for six days' modest consumption – each day, a cheap pasta or pizza lunch and four different drinks: a quarter-litre of house wine, a small beer, a Coke and a large coffee or cappuccino. This is intended to be fair to countries where one kind of drink may be more expensive than others.

Food and drink is relatively expensive in French resorts, compared to Austrian and Italian ones. In the eurozone resorts, our weekly budget figures range from £90 in the cheapest Italian resorts to £130/£140 in sporty big-name French resorts such as Val d'Isère. No Italian resort is so pricey, and in Austria only Lech Zürs. Then, at the top of the table, are Méribel and Courchevel costing even more.

But at current exchange rates even Courchevel looks cheap by comparison with Swiss resorts. Our budget figure for even a modest Swiss resort is £200, and for the top resorts such as Zermatt or St Moritz it's more like £250.

Remember, if you like good lunches or a few après-ski drinks you may spend much more than our budget figure; we certainly do.

New gear for 2016

Next season's skis on test, plus how to ski better

by **Dave Watts**

Skis get better and easier to ski every season. Here we report on the British ski industry test of all the new skis for the coming season. We also look at a recent invention designed to help you ski better.

EDITOR WATTS TRACKS DOWN THE TOP SKIS

Last March I went on a week-long test of the new skis for 2015/16 in Kühtai, at 2020m one of Austria's highest resorts. The test was organized by the trade body Snowsports Industries of Great Britain, and there were almost 900 pairs of skis available from 23 different manufacturers. I was part of the Telegraph media group test team and you can see the results of their test on their website www.telegraph.co.uk and in copies of *Telegraph Ski and Snowboard* magazine. Conditions were ideal for testing with pistes hard and firm at the start of the week and lots of snow during it (as you can see in the photo of the test site below).

The main trend seems to be skis getting lighter and lighter without losing their strength or performance. Manufacturers are doing this by using new materials and construction techniques. For example, Atomic have their Carbon Tank Mesh in their Vantage all-mountain skis, Rossignol has extended its Air Tip technology to more skis in its range and Fischer has an Air Tec wood core which is 25% lighter than its traditional core.

More and more lightweight touring skis are also being produced, many aimed not at dedicated tourers but at people who want a lightweight pair of skis for short off-piste tours that perform as well as a conventional downhill ski in the powder and crud. Almost 100 touring skis were available to test, including Salomon's new MTN range with a matching lightweight touring boot. Blizzard have a new Zero G range and Scott has its new Cascade hike and ride ski.

DAVE WATTS

The test centre at Kühtai, where almost 900 pairs of new skis were available to test
↓

The ranges of skis on test included freeride, all-mountain, on-piste, park and pipe, and big mountain. I'd advise anyone who fancies even a dabble in ungroomed terrain between pistes to go for an all-mountain ski because, in general, they work just as well as piste skis on groomed runs but are more versatile. The waists on these were generally in the 80mm to 90mm range – which is wide enough to give you a good solid platform in powder and crud as well as performing well on-piste. My favourites in the all-mountain category were the Rossignol Experience 88, Head Strong Instinct Ti, Kästle FX 85, Nordica NRG 90 and Scott The Ski.

In the freeride category (with waists generally in the 85mm to 110mm range) the Rossignol Sin 7 and Soul 7 and the Volkl 100 Eight and Mantra came out tops. And in the on-piste category the Rossignol Pursuit and Fischer Progressor ranges did well.

Women-specific skis were on test in abundance, with nearly all the major manufacturers having ranges in all the test categories. Our women testers particularly liked the K2 and Volkl ranges across the board as well as the Scott Luna and Rossignol Temptation all-mountain skis, the Atomic Vantage 95 CW and Movement Believe freeride skis, and the Atomic Cloud 9 piste ski.

FIND YOUR SWEET SPOT

Two years ago at the Kühtai ski test I also tried SkiA's new Sweetspot Ski Trainer – designed to help you improve your balance. I now have a set to use at home. When you are skiing, your centre of balance should be near the centre of the arch of your foot not, as many people think, on the balls of your feet. The idea is that the trainer gets you used to balancing correctly, and you then try to replicate the same feeling whenever you are skiing.

Emily Sarsfield & Ed Drake

SKiA SkiA Ski Trainer
Get Ready For Great Skiing

Recommended by
BASI
BRITISH ASSOCIATION OF
SNOWSPORT INSTRUCTORS

Train the skills to transform your skiing
skia.com

The trainer comes with blocks that you fix under the centre of your ski boots. You then try to balance on them on a hard surface while making various movements such as bending, stretching and tilting your legs as if edging. It is surprisingly difficult at first, but when you are in balance you can certainly feel the sweet spot. There are four pairs of blocks; you start with the widest (green) and move on to progressively narrower ones (blue, red and black – just like piste classifications of difficulty). The trainer comes with special exercises designed by Hugh Monney, founder of the British Alpine Ski School – who highly recommends it, as do other leading instructors, race coaches and competitors, including Britain's best-ever Olympic downhiller Martin Bell and current UK skicross racer Emily Sarsfield. Britain's fastest racer, speed skier Jan Farrell, is using them to help prepare for World Cup speed skiing events.

Go to www.skia.com for more details.

Short breaks

MOMENTUM SKI

Weekend and a la carte ski holiday specialists

100% Tailor-Made

Premier hotels and apartments

Flexible travel arrangements

020 7371 9111
WWW.MOMENTUMSKI.COM

32

Short-break trips to the Alps can give you three refreshing days on the snow and leave you with the feeling of having been away for ages. We love them and frequently take them. Whether you travel independently or as part of a package, short-stay trips are easier to arrange now; the choice of airlines, destination airports and onward transfers is wider than ever. Midweek trips can be even better than weekends: cheaper deals and, depending on the resort, perhaps quieter slopes.

With just a few days to enjoy, you'll need to plan your short break carefully; but that's all part of the fun. We sum up the options here, with a few handy tips to help you to maximize your slope time. Also see our Corporate ski trips chapter on page 49, which gives ideas for fun activities on a short break away.

WHERE SHALL WE GO?

Resorts closest to your arrival airport may seem the obvious choice, but travelling a bit further can avoid weekend crowds. You could also try smaller resorts that you would not go to for a week's stay.

Geneva is the classic gateway to the western Alps, with Chamonix just over an hour away, and other major French resorts such as Megève, Flaine and Morzine close by. Allow extra time for the Trois Vallées and Tarentaise resorts. You could also head into Switzerland and visit Villars or Verbier.

In Italy, Turin is a handy airport for the Aosta valley, with Courmayeur, Champoluc and La Thuile easily reached; Sauze d'Oulx and Montgenèvre in the Milky Way are even nearer.

Further east, in Switzerland, Engelberg and Andermatt are popular options easily accessible from Zürich. So is St Anton. Also in Austria, Innsbruck allows you to combine a city break with doorstep skiing. There are lots of resorts surrounding the city, and the Stubai valley with its reliable glacier is nearby. Similarly Salzburg has lots of resorts within an hour or two.

The Pyrenees offer short-break opportunities too: flights into Pau and Lourdes put you close to Cauterets, Barèges-La Mongie, Peyragudes and St-Lary-Soulan. And for a budget break, you could explore Slovenia very cheaply, with flights to Ljubljana – the nearest ski area is just 8km from the airport.

WHERE TO STAY?

The range of short-stay accommodation is improving, but can still be limited in some major resorts – places such as

ski²

www.ski-weekends.com

- Book your own low cost flights, but all of our prices include transfers to resort

- Arrive on any day of the week and stay for any number of nights

- Short transfer times

- Choice of hotels to suit all budgets

- Friendly, personal service

- Exclusive access to the Ski 2 nursery and ski school

Visit our comprehensive website, call us on 01962 713330 or email us at sales@ski-2.com

ABTA
The Travel Association

Alpine Weekends

Weekend ski trips, corporate events and flexible skiing holidays

020 8944 9762

www.alpineweekends.com

ALPINE Weekends
AND FLEXIBLE BREAKS

Discover the difference with SkiWeekends
#loveski

Prices from
£200

skiweekends.com

STC Ski

Specialists in Tailor-Made Short Breaks & Holidays

01483 771 222
www.stcski.co.uk
ski@stcski.co.uk

Chamonix, Crans-Montana and Morzine, with big summer or conference business, are easier. From Salzburg or Innsbruck you could take the daily shuttles to different resorts. If you have a rental car, valley towns such as Chur, Sion and Interlaken in Switzerland, Aosta in Italy and Moûtiers and Bourg-St-Maurice in France are cheaper bases from which you can visit different resorts nearby.

PRICING THE OPTIONS

Costs vary enormously. Tour operators have special deals with hotels and can organize the essentials to save you time.

Around 50% of Ski 2's business is short breaks to Champoluc in Italy's Monterosa ski area. Three nights' B&B in a 3-star hotel, transfers from any of six airports (meeting any flight), a three-day lift pass, first-day guiding and lunches costs from £492; you book your own flights. Stanford Skiing offers three- and four-night stays in catered chalets or self-catered apartments in Megève; prices for a catered chalet are from £310 excluding flights and transfers.

Ski Weekend is the original short-break ski specialist. A four-night B&B package to Chamonix including flights and transfers costs from £450. Don't confuse them with Skiweekends.com, which offers overnight coach travel or flight options – a four-night half-board coach package (including two nights on the coach) to Brides-les-Bains (for Méribel) giving three days of skiing costs from £209. Alpine Answers organizes a special pre-Christmas group trip to Val d'Isère from £495 for four nights B&B, lift passes and transfers – flights not included. Momentum offers flights, car hire and three nights' B&B in a 3-star hotel in Courmayeur from £399. STC Ski says three nights half-board in a Kirchberg 3-star including flights and transfers costs from £345. Hanski specializes in short breaks; a three-night late Feb/early March stay in its Les Prodains catered chalet (see Avoriaz chapter) including flights and transfers costs £355. These companies will tailor-make breaks to many resorts.

TIPS FOR THE TRIP

Unless booking at short notice, avoid low resorts (where snow may be unreliable) and high, treeless resorts (where slopes may close in bad weather). Go for early or late flights to get the most slope time, but note that Sunday evening traffic can be horrendous with locals going home. Book a transfer or rental car in advance and choose a different car hire company from the one your airline promotes to avoid queuing with others from your flight. Taxis are generally very expensive, and public transport is rarely convenient (though Switzerland has good rail links). Rather than take your skis/board, consider renting: most airlines charge hefty carriage fees.

Tailor made, long weekend and short break French Alps ski holiday specialists.

Hanski
Ski. Explore. Relax.

web: www.hanski.co.uk
tel: 01638 596373

100% Protected Holidays

Ski Weekend
the ultimate short break

we are the original
short break
ski specialists

over 25 years

01392 878 353
www.skiweekend.com

Stanford Skiing
Megève Specialists

Huge ski area
Close to Geneva
Short breaks
Chalets & hotels

01603 477471
stanfordskiing.co.uk

Short breaks

33

Luxury chalets

by **Chris Gill**

The catered chalet holiday is a uniquely British idea. The deal, in case you're new to it, is that tour operators install their own cooks and housekeepers in chalets for the season and provide half-board with wine (plus teatime cake) and, usually, travel from the UK. So you get the privacy and relaxed atmosphere of a temporary home in the mountains, without the hassle of self-catering or the cost of eating out in restaurants every night.

Chalets have come a long way since the whole thing got off the ground in the 1960s and 70s. Back then, chalets meant creaky old buildings with spartan furniture and paper-thin walls. When we first took a chalet in Méribel, in 1974, en-suite bathrooms were unheard of; they are now the norm. Spacious and plush living rooms with log fires are common (although spacious and plush bedrooms are less so). Spa facilities such as a sauna, steam room and hot tub are common too; some chalets even have a swimming pool. And all at prices we ordinary mortals can contemplate paying. It's these relatively swanky chalets that this chapter is about.

Because of the huge number of chalet holidays available, choosing the right one can be difficult. Some very helpful websites have been set up by agents, allowing you to sift out chalets that suit you best; some advertise in this chapter and elsewhere in the book.

The greatest concentration of smart chalets is found – surprise, surprise – in British-dominated **Méribel**. Ski Total has a wide range of properties here, including two with the firm's top 'Platinum' rating; they have hot tubs, of course – and a cinema and billiard room in the case of chalet Isba. Purple Ski has five top-notch and highly individual chalets – in good positions, with lovely interiors and outdoor hot tubs. Most of Alpine Action's eight properties have hot tubs. Skiworld's portfolio includes the swish Laetitia – one of its 'Signature' chalets – with hot tub, sauna and cinema room. Other companies to consider include Consensio, Meriski and VIP.

Over the hill is **Courchevel**, a resort of parts (it has recently renamed these parts but we are clinging to the old names). Courchevel 1850 is well established as the 'smartest' resort in France, with the highest prices and the swankiest hotels. So it's not surprising that the luxury chalet market is dominated by upmarket operators such as Kaluma, Consensio, Supertravel and Scott Dunn. The big UK chalet centre is Courchevel 1650, where Le Ski now has 17 chalets, sleeping from 2 (yes, two) to 22; 12 of them have sauna, steam or hot tub. And its flagship Scalottas Lodge has five apartment chalets with fabulous views, leather armchairs and sofas, solid wooden floors and hi-tech lights and heating. Skiworld has some smart-looking chalets too – the 21-bed Estrella is one of its best, with outdoor hot tub – and is

Arosa
Snowy pockets .com
Chalet Runca

Huge Luxury Chalet in Arosa for Groups & Families

Independent, Personal Service since 1995

Call Helen on
+41 (0) 798333608

www.snowypockets.com

SKI AMIS

Catered Chalets in Superb Locations

020 3411 5439
www.skiamis.com

currently revamping an existing chalet building to form three smart new smaller units. Down in Le Praz, Mountain Heaven has three chalets, including two adjoining ones that share a sauna, steam room and outdoor hot tub – Emilie (with traditional exterior but cutting-edge style within) and Jardin d'Angele (cosily traditional).

ski EXPECTATIONS 01799 531888

THE SKI HOLIDAY CONSULTANCY

with over 25 years experience
in Europe's Top Resorts, the USA & Canada

The service is friendly, the information
is accurate and the advice is free

Just one call away from your ideal holiday

01799 531888
www.skiexpectations.com

In **La Tania**, just along the road towards Méribel, Ski Amis has seven smart-looking places, all but one with outdoor hot tub and some with its Premium service.

In **Les Menuires** there are smart places on offer in the recently developed areas. In Reberty, Powder N Shine has three lovely looking chalets, all with indoor hot tub and sauna and one with an outdoor hot tub too. The firm prides itself on the quality of its food and all three chalets have chefs who have worked in Michelin-starred restaurants. Ski Amis has several chalets with outdoor hot tubs down the hill in Les Bruyères, and others with hot tubs and saunas in the hamlet of Le Bettex, down below the main village (celebrating the arrival of a new fast chairlift this year). Further down the valley near **St-Martin,** the Alpine Club (not a club) has for some time operated two luxurious chalets in the quiet hamlet of Villarabout, one newly built in traditional style with a double-height, open-plan living room and the other a beautiful 100-year-old farmhouse with spectacular views. This year it is adding a third – a 130-year-old stable being turned into a rustic but luxurious eight-bed chalet for the coming season.

Val d'Isère is the great rival to Méribel in the French chalet business. The local specialist, YSE, has several very swish places. Le Ski's chalet Angelique, in a back street of La Daille, is very different from the norm: inside it looks more like a mini stately home than a chalet (and has a steam room and gym). Kanjiroba nearby may lack the trimmings, but is a lovely chalet. Skiworld's range includes two of their top properties: Tolima, with sauna, and Madeleine, with outdoor hot tub. Crystal's range includes three of its 'Finest' properties, with saunas. The big news from the Inghams/Total/Esprit group is that this season they will jointly be operating the 5-star Savoie hotel as a chalet hotel. Ski Total has 14 other smart places, including two very swanky ones in their 'Platinum' range (one with outdoor hot tub, one with a sauna). And Inghams has a flagship 24-bed chalet hotel with sauna and hot tub up the valley in Le Fornet. Other companies include Scott Dunn and Consensio.

In **Tignes,** Skiworld's programme includes some chalets with sauna and hot tub, and a swanky chalet hotel with pool and sauna. Ski Total has some very smart places, lots with outdoor hot tub and sauna, some with pool and two in their top-of-the-market 'Platinum' range. Crystal and Inghams have some smart chalets here, too.

The other great French mega-area, Paradiski, offers lots of chalets in **La Plagne** and growing numbers at **Peisey-Vallandry**, on the Les Arcs side of the cable car from La Plagne. Few chalets stand out, but Ski Amis has a Premium service chalet in each of these resorts.

There are lots of chalets in **La Rosière**, but few notable ones.

MATTERHORN CHALETS
LUXURY CHALETS & APARTMENTS IN ZERMATT
MATTERHORNCHALETS.COM   TEL +41 (0)79 247 15 88

Mountain Heaven has two in its Premium range here, both with outdoor hot tubs: we stayed in the splendid Penthouse a couple of years back, and loved the huge living room with floor-to-ceiling windows and great views; the renovated farm-style Chez Robert is just 30m from the lifts. Crystal has a couple of places in its 'Finest' programme, with access to sauna and outdoor hot tub.

Chalets are not common in **Avoriaz**, so it's good to see that Ski Total's handful includes one of its 'Platinum' chalets, with sauna and log fire. In **Alpe-d'Huez**, Ski Total, Skiworld and Inghams all have smart places with outdoor hot tubs.

In Austria, **St Anton** is chalet central. Skiworld's flagship Monte Vera has huge bedrooms, sauna and infra-red room. Many of Ski Total's ten chalets have saunas but none qualifies for its top 'Platinum' rating. Crystal has three of its 'Finest' chalets here, including the cool 32-bed Inge, with wellness area and fabulous views. Inghams' programme includes four chalets in a stylish new building in the Gastig area, with shared spa and pool. Ski Total has three well-equipped chalet hotels (all with saunas, one with a pool) in nearby Lech. Other operators to look at are Flexiski, Kaluma, Supertravel and Scott Dunn.

Ski Total has successfully established a British presence in **Ischgl** – for many years, barely visible on the UK market – with its central 'Platinum' chalet hotel Abendrot.

Italy is not big on chalets and has never had a chalet in our luxury category, but last season Ski Total took over our favourite 4-star hotel in **Champoluc** and is running it as a chalet hotel. It is full of lovely wood beams and ceilings and has sauna, steam and hot tub. We can't wait to give it a try in its new guise.

In Switzerland, most of the larger (and lower cost) companies have pulled out of running chalets because of changes in the minimum wage legislation. But pricier plush chalets are still available. **Verbier** is the chalet capital, and there are still a few on the UK market – several good places from Ski Verbier, a couple of apartment chalets from VIP and individual swanky places from operators such as Kaluma and Scott Dunn. Over the hill in Nendaz, Skiworld has two swish chalets with outdoor hot tub, in an excellent location near the main lift.

In **Zermatt**, against the trend, Matterhorn Chalets started up last season with the very smart four-bedroom Chalet Ulysses, with a sauna; prices include the services of an instructor/guide. The company will also have two other luxury chalets for 2015/16, one with pool and sauna, the other with sauna and outdoor hot tub. VIP and Supertravel have a couple of places.

In cute little **Grimentz** (covered in our Val d'Anniviers chapter), Mountain Heaven has some smart chalets that can be booked catered or self-catered. In **Arosa** (which gets a new chapter in this edition, following its link with Lenzerheide) Snowy Pockets has a traditional 12-bed chalet with sauna and steam.

There are very few catered chalets in North America, but Skiworld has a couple of good ones in **Breckenridge** and **Vail**.

Smart apartments

Enjoy full independence in comfortable surroundings

by **Dave Watts**

Apartment holidays used to be the budget option for most people – at least on holidays to France. Shoehorn six people into a studio advertised for six and you'd have a cheap but not very comfortable time. But things have changed hugely, especially in France where lots of plush new apartment blocks ('residences', as the French say – sounds so much better) have been built in recent years. Most have dishwashers, and many share a pool, sauna, steam room and gym to add to the pampering. Some even have comfortable furniture to relax in, too. Sure, the budget option still exists, but now you can have a comfortable apartment holiday with all the other advantages that it brings (see below). We've looked for smart apartments to recommend throughout the Alps and have included them in the resort chapters.

I've been taking my annual ski holiday with my wife and a couple of friends in apartments for over 25 years. That's because we value the freedom an apartment gives you. You don't have to stick to meal times (and meals) dictated by the hotel or chalet staff and you can slob around in whatever clothes you want. And, crucially in our case, you are free to have a big lunch up the mountain without worrying about having to eat a huge half-board meal in the evening; if you don't want a big dinner, you can buy snacks such as oysters, smoked salmon, pâté and local cheeses along with a good bottle of wine or two from the supermarket. If you are hungry, you can go out to a restaurant to eat. Staying in an apartment doesn't mean having to cook big meals – not for us anyway.

When we started this apartment lark, we couldn't find the sort of thing we were looking for in tour operators' brochures (there were no websites to browse in those days) – all the apartments were of the 'cram 'em in and make it cheap' variety. So we ended up booking independently. Now, at least in France – the country that used to have the smallest, most sordid apartments – a few tour operators (including those advertising in this chapter and Erna Low,

Four-Star apartments
inc. Wifi, pools & spa

02392 839 310

PEAKRETREATS.CO.UK

◆ABTA
ABTA No.W5657

37

ERNA LOW

Some residences have comfortable communal areas like this one at Kalinda Village in Tignes 1800
→

Heavenly Skiing...
at down to earth prices

mh✳
Mountain Heaven

· Superb catered & self catered accommodation ·
· Great ski areas in the French & Swiss Alps ·
· Snow secure resorts · We only have on/near piste locations ·
· Fantastic prices & no hidden extras ·

0151 625 1921
www.mountainheaven.co.uk

Smart apartments

who provided the photos to illustrate it) offer some really smart places, mostly with leisure facilities such as pools, saunas and steam rooms. Some even have big reception areas and restaurants, just like hotels (though we'd prefer bigger rooms instead of big reception areas).

The French smart apartment concept was kick-started by places built by MGM. They now have 29 4-star residences in the Alps, managed by their sister company CGH and are the biggest provider of smart apartments. We've stayed happily in several of their places over the years.

Montagnettes was another pioneer of the concept. Now these two have been joined by other brands. PV Holidays launched its Pierre & Vacances Premium brand a few winters ago, and it now features 13 residences in 11 French resorts. Lagrange has 17 Alpine and six Pyrenean residences in its Prestige range.

So why the big change? Xavier Schouller of Peak Retreats, Ski Collection and Pyrenees Collection, which specialize in selling plush apartment holidays in French ski resorts, says, 'A lot of smart new residences have been built recently because of tax breaks for people buying them – you get the VAT back if you agree to rent them out for several years, and French residents can set costs against income tax too. This is good news for people wanting to rent an apartment for a holiday – we now have over 200 residences on our books.' Xavier's favourite residences are Ski Collection's Le Centaure in Flaine and Hameau du Kashmir in Val Thorens, and Peak Retreats' Kalinda Village in Tignes 1800.

Erna Low sells a lot of apartment holidays too and their managing director Jane Bolton says, 'We have been selling self-catering holidays for over 20 years. The widest selection is still found in France, where we now have hundreds of residences to choose from, but we also have spacious, comfortable apartments available in Switzerland, Austria, Italy, the US and Canada.'

Ski Amis is best known as a catered chalet company, but it has moved into apartments in a big way. Instead of offering big residences such as those mentioned above, it offers mostly privately owned apartments and chalets, mainly in the Tarentaise, which

ERNA LOW
Not all living rooms are as spacious and comfortable as this one at Arc 1950 looks
↓

Pools, saunas and hot tubs are the norm for new 4-star residences in France – a few with a slope-side setting like this at L'Amara in Avoriaz →

ERNA LOW

LAGRANGE
Prestige

High-standard
Self-catering
Apartments

020 7371 6111
lagrange-holidays.co.uk

includes the Trois Vallées, Paradiski and Espace Killy resorts. Mountain Heaven, which also does catered chalets, has some smart apartments in Tarentaise resorts and in Grimentz in Switzerland. Or you can rent independently; as well as contacting local rental agencies try websites such as www.holidaylettings.co.uk, www.homeaway.co.uk and www.interhome.co.uk.

WHAT TO CHECK BEFORE BOOKING
So what do you need to look for if you're booking what you hope is a smart apartment? Most importantly, you still need to check whether the space is enough to meet your expectations – and whether the number it's advertised for involves anyone sleeping in the living room, in bunk beds, on a mezzanine or in a cabin (which can mean an alcove). Also check the number of bathrooms and toilets. If the leisure facilities such as a pool, sauna, steam room and gym are important to you, check whether there is a charge for using these; sadly, there often is. And while most smart apartments come with a modern design, dishwasher and smartish furniture, we're sometimes disappointed by the lack of really comfy sofas and easy chairs (often because sofas double up as beds and are comfier to sleep in than sit on), by the size of the living rooms and, especially, the bedrooms, and by the lack of storage space – so if those are important to you, check them too.

High quality, high altitude

Four-star apartments with:
Doorstep skiing • Indoor pool & spa • Accommodation only or self-drive packages

Call our experts on
02392 890 960

ABTA
ABTA No.W5537

A WORLD-CLASS FRENCH ALPS EXPERIENCE

SKI COLLECTION
.CO.UK

A contradiction in terms?

by **Chris Gill**

I know I've said this before, but this is definitely my last contribution to the success of readers' family skiing holidays. I'm writing this more or less on the occasion of daughter Laura's 24th birthday, and some time after son Alex's 27th. It's five years since we skied together as a family – and on that occasion my main parental responsibility was payment of their unimaginably large chalet beer bill. My interest in childcare arrangements has dwindled to the point of invisibility. It's not even as if either of them shows any sign of producing grandchildren, which is a development that has got at least one skiing chum devoting most of his time to assessment of childcare facilities. So I'm definitely handing over to ... someone else.

So in this valedictory article, it's time to look back. I thought I might allow myself to reflect on what I might do differently, given my time again. Oh, and I may as well congratulate myself on one or two things I got right, as well.

GOOD CALL #1

Taking the kids skiing. Yes, I know, obvious. But to be clear: I find it difficult to imagine a more satisfactory way to spend holidays together as a family. It even works during The Kevin Years, when the teenage son essentially wants to be as far away from his parents as possible. By the simple device of skiing more quickly than them, he can achieve this for much of the day.

25 YEARS OF FAMILY SKIING

JOIN US IN THE ALPS FOR:

• **OUR EXCLUSIVE À La Carte Childcare** - provided in your own chalet. No snowy trudge to a central crèche: just pop on your skis and leave the rest to us
• **High quality well located family chalets**
• **Superb facilities and activities for children of all ages**
• **Nationwide flights, Eurostar from London direct to the Alps**
• **FREE child places and much, much more...**

Call: 01252 365495

www.skifamille.co.uk

ATOL 10863

Ski Famille

ABTOT 5141

Arosa
Snowy Pockets
.com
Chalet Runca

Huge Luxury Chalet
in Arosa
for Groups & Families

Independent, Personal
Service since 1995

Call Helen on
+41 (0) 798333608
www.snowypockets.com

MISTAKE #1

Starting Alex on skis at the age of four. It was too soon. Of course, it might have worked out better if the dinky ski school we had booked in Val d'Isère had been in operation, rather than closed by illness. Then we wouldn't have had to fall back on the ESF, which succeeded in reducing our child and most of the others to tears.

GOOD CALL #2

Going with UK chalet operators specializing in family holidays. This was the key to many relaxed trips, when the kids were young, with Esprit Ski, Mark Warner and Family Ski Co. When they were tiny, the key factor was the all-day childcare. When they were less tiny, the availability of other kids of the same age came into play.

MISTAKE #2

Being a wishy washy, caring and sharing baby boomer. I should have been a more pushy parent, and forced the kids to do more ski school lessons instead of cruising around the slopes incompetently. Alex has suffered no lasting damage, thanks to school trips and then a season working in Courchevel. But Laura never really got it, and now maybe never will.

GOOD CALL #3

The slope-side ground-floor CGH apartment above Arc 1800. OK, it wasn't really my call: friends and neighbours Richard and Jenny roped us in to a trip they had already conceived, and it was frankly the luck of the draw that resulted in our having a ground-floor apartment with patio doors opening directly on to a gentle piste.

ESPRIT
Ski
No.1 For Family Skiing

SAVE UP TO **£955 PER FAMILY**
with our Esprit Family Savers

13 TOP RESORTS in France, Austria and Italy

★ **We focus 100% on caring for your children**
★ **Dedicated Esprit Nurseries**
★ **FREE evening Baby-Listening / Child Patrol Service**
★ **Strict child care ratios**
★ **Catered chalets & Chalet Hotels**
★ Baby And Toddler Weeks

FREE infant places
Half-price Nursery Places
Half-price Skiing & Day Care for toddlers
BAT-Weeks run on 10, 17, 24, 31 Jan & 21 Feb.

Call **01483 791 900**
visit **espritski.com**

ABTA
Travel with confidence

The catered chalet holiday is as popular as ever, especially with families. Since en-suite bathrooms and solid, soundproof walls became the norm rather than the exception, the attractions of the chalet – more private and less formal than hotels – have increased considerably. Now, more people are discovering the merits of the chalet's bigger cousin, the chalet hotel.

Chalet operators have for years set the pace in childcare. It was a natural extension of hiring British gels as cooks and housekeepers to hire a few as nannies, too; then all the operator had to do was identify a suitable room in a suitable chalet, and bingo – a crèche was born. For British parents unable to handle the brutality of French nurseries, the chalet was the obvious solution.

Chalet hotels are a larger version of the same thing, with some additional advantages. Some are purpose-built, but usually they are based in buildings that have operated as normal hotels. As a result, bedrooms typically are more generous than in chalets. Facilities are often better – there is likely to be a bar (with prices below resort norms, if you're lucky), and there may be a swimming pool, spa or gym, for example. There may be a menu choice at dinner.

Two of the most long-established tour operator firms dominate the family chalet hotel market. Esprit Ski was the original family chalet specialist; its programme is still dominated by scores of standard chalets, but it now also includes seven chalet hotels – six in major French resorts plus one in Gressoney (Monterosa, Italy). Mark Warner specializes in chalet hotels, and has crèches in most (but not all) properties. The editorial Gill family took several successful holidays with these firms in the days when the kids were small.

Strikingly, these firms major on top resorts. They both have chalet hotels with childcare in Méribel, Val d'Isère and La Plagne. Esprit's flagship is the super-cool Deux Domaines at Belle-Plagne, which has a decent pool and spa – young children are not allowed in the latter – and a good ski-in/ski-out location on the lower edge of the village. The other Esprit chalet hotel resorts in France are Alpe-d'Huez and Courchevel. Mark Warner also has family-oriented properties in Tignes, Val d'Isère and Les Deux-Alpes, and in St Anton and Zell am See in Austria.

Family holidays

42

Le Ski
the chalet specialists

LE SKI
ARE CHILD
FRIENDLY!

30 CATERED CHALETS
COURCHEVEL VAL D'ISÈRE
LE SKI CRÈCHE IN LA TANIA
01484 954397 LESKI.COM

❄ Crèche exclusively for Le Ski guests
❄ Fully qualified UK nannies
❄ Civilised Sunday flights included
❄ Chalets sleeping from 2–23 guests

ski²

**The family ski specialists to the
fabulous Monterosa ski area**

• Traditional Italian alpine resort

• Our own nursery run by fully qualified
British staff

• 'Family-friendly' accommodation

• Short transfer from airport to resort

• Friendly, helpful resort staff

• British, B.A.S.I. qualified ski instructors

• Child and group discounts

www.familyskiholidays.co.uk

**Visit our comprehensive website,
call us on 01962 713330
or email us at sales@ski-2.com**

ABTA
The Travel Association

The result was that the kids probably had more fun between the lifts closing and bed-time than they did during the day.

MISTAKE #3
Failing to pray to the luggage handling gods. The most expensive skiing garment I have ever bought was (and still is) the dinky pair of salopettes I had to buy for Alex from an exclusive boutique in Val d'Isère, when our bags went to Geneva via Peking.

GOOD CALL #4
Crossing the pond. Three years on from Mistake #1, we found ourselves in New England for a week. Not only did the enthusiastic instructors in Killington get Alex skiing black runs in no time at all, but they also got four-year-old Laura launched on her skiing career. (Better instruction, or greater determination? We shall never know.)

GOOD CALL #5
CGH apartments with pools. The skiing day finishes early, and the weather isn't always conducive to tobogganing and other outdoor pursuits. To have a lovely warm pool in your apartment residence is a great advantage for families.

AND FINALLY, SOME REAL INFORMATION
In case you're convinced by Good Call #2: The firms advertising in this chapter are mostly small, specialized companies going to a small range of resorts that they know inside out. Ski 2 goes to only one resort (Champoluc), Snowy Pockets goes only to Arosa in Switzerland and Le Ski's family-oriented chalets are in a single

Family Ski ™

Perfect family skiing holidays
in high quality ski chalets with outstanding childcare

+44 (0) 1684 540 333
www.familyski.co.uk
Designed with the family in mind

ABTOT
The Association of Bonded
Travel Organisers Trust Ltd

resort too (La Tania). They are basically owner-operated, so you can expect them to be very responsive. Most operate catered chalets, where you share a house or a flat with others (you can of course fill the place if you wish). Ski 2 sell hotel and self-catering holidays.

Esprit Ski is a bit different: a chalet operator on a much bigger scale – it's one of the biggest ski holiday operators in the UK, in fact, offering chalets in 10 French resorts plus Obergurgl and St Anton in Austria and Gressoney (in the Monterosa Ski area) in Italy.

These operators provide a range of childcare options, geared to the different stages of childhood – ideally taking care of the après-ski session as well as the skiing day, and providing an early evening meal for the younger ones. Don't forget that there are mainstream operators such as Crystal that operate childcare in some of their resorts.

The list on the right shows who goes to which resorts; it covers the advertisers in this chapter and Crystal, to give you an idea of your options.

WHO GOES WHERE?

AUSTRIA
Obergurgl Esprit. **Niederau** Crystal.
St Anton Esprit.

FRANCE
Alpe-d'Huez Crystal, Esprit. **Les Arcs** Esprit.
Ardent (Avoriaz) Family Ski.
Les Coches (La Plagne) Family Ski.
Courchevel Esprit. **Les Gets** Esprit, Ski Famille.
Les Menuires Family Ski, Ski Famille.
Méribel Esprit.
Peisey-Vallandry (Les Arcs) Esprit.
La Plagne Crystal, Esprit, Ski Famille.
La Rosière Esprit. **La Tania** Le Ski.
Tignes Crystal, Esprit. **Val d'Isère** Esprit.

ITALY
Canazei Crystal. **Champoluc** Ski 2.
Claviere Crystal. **Gressoney** Esprit.

SLOVENIA
Kranjska Gora Crystal.

SWITZERLAND
Arosa Snowy Pockets.

Inspirational ski race training for youngsters in Champoluc, Italy

- Race training for 1 to 12 weeks for youngsters, aged 8 to 12

- Learn the very best in proven Italian race techniques

- Comprehensive and structured education programme

- Unrivalled resort infrastructure

- Flexible travel arrangements and good quality accommodation

www.ski2racing.com
Visit our comprehensive website,
call us on 01962 713330
or email us at info@ski-2.com

The Travel Association

SKI 2 RACING – COACHING FOR YOUR KIDS?

As well as running its own British ski school exclusively for its clients in Champoluc, Ski 2 now offers the opportunity for youngsters to train under some of the great Italian racing coaches based in the resort. Youngsters already on holiday with Ski 2 can sign up for a 6-day course, while those looking for more intense training can choose a tailor-made race programme.

The unique teaching style of the local coaches has proved successful in helping the children of Simon Brown (Ski 2's co-owner) to reach regional race finals and for Ryan Brown, Simon's son, to be invited to train with the British ski team. Although the race coaches believe that gate training is important, youngsters spend much time free skiing on and off-piste to improve dynamic balance and technique. This gives them a broader race ability, allowing them to compete well in challenging snow and weather conditions, in particular!

Prices start from £179 for those already booked on a Ski 2 holiday or £1,097 for those looking for an inclusive package with accommodation and lift pass. Check out www.ski-2.com.

Family holidays

44

Buying property

by **Dave Watts**

Buying a place in a ski resort is an ambition for lots of keen skiers and snowboarders. Buying in most of the Alps is more affordable than at any time since the £ plummeted against other currencies in 2008. In the last two years the £ has risen by around 25% against the euro, making property that much cheaper for UK buyers. Interest rates in Europe are low as well, so getting a mortgage in euros is affordable too. Sadly the £ hasn't fared as well against the Swiss franc and remains almost 40% lower than its 2008 value.

Simon Malster, managing director of Investors in Property, has been selling property in the Alps for over 25 years. He says: 'We are now selling many more properties in France. That is due not just to the strong pound but also because some superb properties have come on to the market in top resorts such as Courchevel, Méribel, Val d'Isère, Châtel and Les Menuires. Another factor is the tax break you get in France if you buy a new-build property and sign an agreement to rent it out to a specialist company on a long lease.'

With these agreements you can block out periods in which you intend to use the property yourself and the company rents it out the rest of the time and pays you a rental income of, say, 3.5% to 4% a year. The big tax advantage of doing this is that you can claim back the 20% VAT that is charged on new-build homes – which adds up to a huge saving (eg £100,000 on a £500,000 property).

'We are seeing more and more buy-to-let investors buying Alpine property to diversify their portfolio. You can get French mortgages at the moment from around 2.75% fixed for 10 years, so it makes a lot of sense. Many investors also like the idea of getting fun out of their investment by using it themselves,' says Malster.

One of Malster's favourite properties at the moment is Mammoth Lodge which is being built in Courchevel 1650 close to

INVESTORS IN PROPERTY

The Mammoth Lodge apartments in Courchevel 1650 are convenient for both the slopes and the new aqua centre ↓

45

↑ Many new-build apartments come ready-furnished or with an optional furniture package. This development is in Châtel

INVESTORS IN PROPERTY

the swanky new aqua centre and the escalator up to the main street and the lift into the slopes. This will have one- to four-bedroom apartments with underfloor heating and be built in traditional chalet-style using wood and stone. Prices start at 460,000 euros.

Investors in Property also has a smart-looking development of terraced chalets and apartments ranging from two to five bedrooms in the village of Les Allues, just below Méribel which is reached by a gondola. Prices start at around 490,000 euros and rise to over a million for the biggest places. And they are selling one- to three-bedroom apartments starting at 265,000 euros in Châtel (part of the Portes du Soleil ski area), and at 247,000 euros in the lovely old village of Samoëns (part of the Grand Massif ski area).

Erna Low Property specializes in France and has a sales office in Arc 1950 as well as London. François Marchand, the general manager, says: 'We are seeing many apartments in 1950 coming to the end their leasing agreements and being bought by people who want to use them a lot. Most of those we do sell with a rental agreement end up being promoted for holiday stays by our sister company Erna Low Travel.' A typical price for a two-bedroom resale apartment in Arc 1950 is 290,000 euros. Their London office sells properties in lots of resorts – the most popular resorts with buyers last year were Les Gets, Morzine and Châtel in the Portes du Soleil.

Marchand says that a lot of UK investors have bought Santa Terra apartments in Tignes-les-Brévières, which 'is the highest quality we have ever seen in a new-build tourist residence in France' and has a pool, sauna and steam room. Prices start at 205,000 euros for a one-bedroom apartment.

SWISS PROPERTIES STILL AVAILABLE

In 2012, the Swiss effectively voted to stop the building of second homes in ski resorts. 'But developments that already had a building permit can still be built,' says Simon Malster of Investors in Property. 'And developments which oblige owners to rent their properties out when not using them can also be permitted.'

They are selling apartments 200m from the lifts in Laax which will have 4-star hotel services such as a reception, restaurant and

Buy with the
French
Alps
specialist

02392
839 310

PEAKRETREATS.CO.UK

ABTA
ABTA No W5517

www.investorsinproperty.com
SKI PROPERTY SPECIALISTS SINCE 1986

We've Got the Alps Covered

Investors in Property are the leading ski property specialists selling ski chalets and apartments in Austria, France and Switzerland. If you are looking to buy a chalet on the slopes, a rental investment or an apartment in a luxury hotel take a look at our website.

Switzerland
- Crans-Montana
- Grimentz
- Grindelwald
- Laax
- Lenzerheide-Arosa
- Saas Fee
- Verbier ski area
- Villars
- Wengen
- Zermatt

Austria
- Bad Gastein
- Bramberg
- Ischgl
- Kitzbühel
- Lech
- Saalbach
- Seefeld
- Sölden
- St Anton
- Zell am See

France
- Chamonix
- Courchevel
- La Clusaz
- Les Arcs
- Megève
- Méribel
- Portes du Soleil
- Sainte-Foy-Tarentaise
- Samoëns
- Val d'Isère and Tignes

www.investorsinproperty.com

↑ The Courtyard Apartments in Sölden are linked to a 4-star hotel and have full use of its facilities, including a fabulous two-storey spa

INVESTORS IN PROPERTY

spa. These can be bought either outright or with a rental obligation – prices for a one-bedroom place start at 595,000 francs for the former, 465,000 for the latter. In Arosa (now with a fair-sized ski area of 225km because of a new link to neighbouring Lenzerheide) they have one- to four-bedroom apartments from 650,000 francs. And they have plots on which four- or five-bedroom detached chalets can be built to order in Les Collons (part of the same ski area as Verbier) for around 1.5 million francs.

AUSTRIAN OPTIONS TOO

Investors in Property has been selling an increasing number of properties in Austria too. In most cases, properties are available to foreigners as long as they agree to make them available for renting when not using them – this also means that you save up to 20% VAT on the purchase price. In a few rare cases, some new properties have 'second-home status' and do not have to be rented out.

Jessica Delaney says, 'We are delighted to be selling two lovely ski-in/ski-out apartments in St Anton, Austria's premier resort.' They are close to the Nasserein gondola and are priced at 700,000 euros. They also have one- to four-bedroom apartments in the centre of Sölden, linked to a 4-star hotel with use of all its facilities including restaurant and fabulous two-storey spa and wellness centre. Prices start at 290,000 euros.

CONTACTS

Investors in Property
020 8905 5511
www.investorsin
property.com

Erna Low Property
020 7590 1624
www.ernalowproperty.
co.uk

WHAT TO LOOK FOR WHEN BUYING A HOME IN THE SNOW

First, you need to decide whether you want somewhere just for the skiing or whether you want a place in a resort that is attractive in the summer as well. Many French resorts developed after the 1950s can be deadly dull in summer, whereas others are attractive for summer as well as winter use. Second, if you want the place primarily for skiing and snowboarding, you will want reliable snow. And with climate change likely to continue, that means going for somewhere with access to high, snow-sure slopes and with good snowmaking. Third, if you intend to use the place frequently yourself, you will probably want somewhere within a couple of hours of an easily accessible airport. Fourth, make sure you understand the legal and other aspects – buying and running costs, all types of taxes and any resale restrictions. It is highly advisable to get professional advice on these. Fifth, make sure you understand any arrangements that you may be offered for 'sale and leaseback' or 'guaranteed return' from renting it out – these can vary enormously and may enable you to save money on the purchase price in some circumstances. Sixth, if you are intending to rent the property out yourself, don't overestimate the income you will get from it.

Corporate ski trips

A great way to motivate your staff and clients

by **Dave Watts**

Corporate ski trips used to be big business. But in the late noughties the banking crisis and recession hit and hospitality budgets were slashed. But things are now picking up again. Three years ago we had only one advertiser in this chapter. Now we have four.

MOMENTUM SKI

Tailored Corporate Ski Events

Conferences Off-sites & Hospitality

Ski Weekends

Premier Resorts in Europe

020 7371 9111
WWW.MOMENTUMSKI.COM

Corporate ski business expert Amin Momen of Momentum Ski says, 'The market continues to improve on recent years. We find corporate clients are looking for something different rather than the usual day clay pigeon shooting or at Wimbledon.' Momen tries to think of different ideas to attract ordinary customers as well as corporate business. This season he is running the third Mountain Gourmet Ski Experience with Michelin-starred chefs Heston Blumenthal, Marcus Wareing and Sat Bains cooking for guests at mountain huts and in village restaurants (with a fourth celebrity chef to be announced in September). It is being held in Courmayeur in Italy from 8 to 11 January and includes three days' skiing. And in December Momentum is running, for the second year, a trip to Innsbruck with Amy Williams, who won the gold medal in the skeleton event at the 2010 Winter Olympics in Vancouver. Guests will get the chance to go down the modernized 1975 Olympic track at Igls as a passenger in a race bobsled and then on their own on a skeleton (after technique training from Amy).

Ski Weekend will have been going 29 years this season and was pretty much the pioneer of short-break ski holidays. About 70% of their business is to Chamonix and they know it like the back of their hand, with access to a huge range of accommodation, guides and instructors. They organize their own ski courses, off-piste adventures and heli-skiing and do a lot of corporate business with a large number of regular clients. Other activities they offer include: mini-Olympics on the mountain, dinners at private locations designed by a 3-Michelin-starred chef, skijoring, husky-sledding, a private charter train trip to dinner up the mountain in Chamonix, and a skidoo safari to a mountain refuge in Courmayeur for dinner. They also take corporate trips to a wide range of other resorts, including Morzine, La Clusaz, Cortina, Gstaad, Vail, Niseko in Japan (where they took two long-weekend groups last season along with Chamonix instructors and mountain guides) and Iceland.

Andrew Peters of STC Ski says, 'We arrange a variety of trips – from companies that simply want to invite clients for a holiday to those who want full conference facilities. We go to resorts across the Alps, such as: Zell am See, St Anton, Ischgl, Kitzbühel and Bad Gastein in Austria; Morzine, Val d'Isère and Chamonix in France.'

Tony Steward of Alpine Weekends says, 'We have worked with groups from 6 to 100, though the most frequent size is 20 to 30. And we can arrange events in any European resort but the most popular recent destinations include Morzine, Val Thorens, Chamonix, Alpe-d'Huez, Davos and Val d'Isère (where Alpine Weekends started up – as Weekends in Val d'Isère in the 1996/97 season).' Their trips are usually accompanied by an Alpine Weekends rep and they often arrange special events such as dinner up the mountain, ice driving, wine tasting and floodlit skiing.

Alpine Weekends

Weekend ski trips, corporate events and flexible skiing holidays

020 8944 9762

www.alpineweekends.com

ALPINE Weekends
AND FLEXIBLE BREAKS

Ski Weekend
the ultimate short break

we are the original
short break
ski specialists

over 25 years

01392 878 353
www.skiweekend.com

STC Ski

Specialists in Tailor-Made
Short Breaks & Holidays

01483 771 222
www.stcski.co.uk
ski@stcski.co.uk

HOW TO ORGANIZE IT

Organizing a corporate trip yourself is a real hassle. People based in different areas of the country are likely to want to fly from different airports and at different times of day. And many hotels in the Alps don't want to take bookings for just a few days, or to provide the number of single rooms that you might want. Numbers are likely to change as people drop out for various reasons. Your group is likely to have skiers and boarders of widely differing abilities and maybe some beginners or non-skiers, so you need to organize ski instructors or guides to lead different groups. You need to organize equipment (and maybe clothing) rental and lift passes. You might want to organize 'jollies' such as dinner up the mountain and a torchlit descent back or a lunchtime BBQ on the piste. And you might need rooms to hold business meetings in. But that's what you use a tour operator or event organizer for – to deal with all the hassle and organize things on your behalf. And the great thing is that they don't charge you any extra for doing all that – it's part of the business to them.

Because corporate trips tend to be short, you'll want to keep the travel time to the minimum. Transfer times from airports to resorts generally range from one to four hours, and you'll probably want to operate at the lower end of that range if you can. That's why resorts such as Courmayeur in Italy and Chamonix in France (close to Geneva airport), Engelberg in Switzerland (close to Zürich), Kitzbühel in Austria (close to Salzburg and Innsbruck) and Garmisch in Germany (close to Munich) are popular. All these resorts have hotels that are happy to offer short-break bookings too.

THE CITY SKI CHAMPIONSHIPS – VERBIER, VALAIS, 4 TO 7 FEBRUARY 2016

The Momentum Ski Festival weekend combines the City Ski Championships and the Financial Times Alpine Forum. The Forum is chaired by the FT and the focus is dependent on the panel members – last year's was largely about extremes in work and life, with panellists Marcus Wareing, Frank Gardner and Marcus Brigstocke. The debate was followed by a lively Q&A session.

There's a nightly après-ski programme of dinners, comedy and club nights. Past celebrity guests include Amy Williams, Damon Hill, Colin Jackson, Steve Redgrave, Rufus Hound, Tommy Moe, Heston Blumenthal and former British Olympic ski racers Graham Bell and Konrad Bartelski. The main hubs will be the W and Montpelier hotels in Verbier along with a prize-giving gala dinner up the mountain at the Mouton Noir restaurant on Saturday night with a top live band.

With the City Ski Championships, two races are held on the Friday: the Radar Trap Challenge (speed skiing) and the Accenture Dual Parallel Slalom. But the main event is the Saturday GS race, with live commentary by the BBC's Matt Chilton. As well as a competition for teams from City and other business firms there is one for clubs such as the Lansdowne and Queens and non-business attendees. On both days there'll be a race-side buffet and Snow+Rock will offer ski tuning, boot fitting and demo ski testing.

For more details call 020 7371 9111 or visit www.cityskichampionships.com.

MOMENTUM SKI

Flying to the snow

Flights and transfers for independent travellers

by **Sheila Reid**

There are lots of flights to the Alps and Pyrenees – including flights from quieter, queue-free regional airports. But finding your way through the minefield of routes and extra charges is hard work – and the extras can double or triple the basic cost. This brief tour of the flying business should help you navigate.

Budget airlines go to mainstream airports such as Geneva and Milan but also to smaller places, making it easier to get to many resorts in many parts of Europe, including parts of Austria, the Dolomites, the Pyrenees, Slovenia and eastern Europe. You'll find a wide choice of affordable transfers too. National carriers can be competitive, both on cost and destination, so don't ignore them when planning a trip. Note that some winter services stop operating in the spring before the ski season ends.

THE LEADING GROUP

EasyJet has a big range of flights, many to Geneva, from a broad choice of UK hubs. Other key destination airports include Zürich, Basel, Innsbruck, Salzburg, Munich, Turin, Milan, Grenoble and Lyon. From Stansted, Ljubljana is handy for Slovenia and eastern Austria. New routes for 2015/16 include Gatwick to Friedrichshafen (handy for resorts in western Austria such as St Anton and Lech).
Ryanair operates mainly from Stansted, with an increasing choice of flights from other UK airports. Routes and flight frequency change regularly, but a wide choice is offered – including Lourdes (for the western and central Pyrenees), Memmingen (Germany and western Austria), Linz (eastern Austria) and Plovdiv (Bulgaria).
Jet2.com has a dedicated ski website with flights to Geneva, Salzburg, Chambéry, Grenoble, Lyon and Turin – mainly from northern England, but also from Edinburgh and Belfast.
Flybe serves Geneva, Zürich, Salzburg, Milan, Chambéry, Nice and, unusually, Stuttgart (handy for Germany and western Austria) – mainly from Southampton but also from Exeter, Birmingham, Newcastle and Glasgow. From airports in Scotland, Flybe serves Bergen in Norway.
British Airways goes to lots of relevant airports, including Innsbruck, from a variety of UK ones.
Swiss has lots of flights to Zürich and Geneva, some to Basel.
Monarch flies to Geneva, Grenoble, Innsbruck, Friedrichshafen, Munich, Verona, Venice and Barcelona, with some flights from each of Gatwick, Manchester, Birmingham and Leeds-Bradford.

ADDING UP THE EXTRAS ...

Charges and rules for baggage and for equipment carriage vary and change frequently, so it's important to check the detail at the time you are considering a booking. But they can easily add up to much more than the basic cost of your flight (see the panel on the left).

In July 2015, on flights to Geneva EasyJet was charging £28 return for one checked bag of up to 20kg, if booked online. With the more expensive Flexi fare, one checked bag was free. Skis and/or boots (checked in online) cost another £60 return. Ryanair was

---

ONLINE BOOKING

Most budget airlines expect you to book online, and charge less if you book online such 'extras' as hold baggage and ski carriage too.

THE EXTRAS

Charges on top of basic flight costs vary between airlines and can add up alarmingly. In July 2015, we looked at Jet2, EasyJet and Flybe flights to Geneva for a week in February 2016. Basic return fares varied from £58 to £140. Extra charges included:

Checked-in 20kg bag return: £28-£50

Skis/board/boots return: £50-£60

Reserved seat return: £7-£13

Credit card payment fee: Around £4-£7: (2% to 3%)

These 'extras' can add up to much more than the original cost of the flight – almost £120 in one case.

Also, you might be offered insurance for, say, £12 (which may not cover winter sports adequately – do check) and missed flight insurance for, say, £10.

SKI AMIS

Catered Chalets in Superb Locations

020 3411 5439
www.skiamis.com

charging from £30 to £50 return for bags checked in online, depending on size; and skis/board would cost £80 return.

BA 'with-baggage' fares allow one checked-in bag up to 23kg free (there are other fares that don't); additional bags on European flights cost from £36 return. Your skis/boards will be considered your one piece of checked baggage as long as they're packed in a proper ski bag, weigh no more than 23kg and are no longer than 190cm. So you could take skis for free if you took no other checked bag. Swiss and Lufthansa will carry one set of skis and boots free, in addition to your regular baggage allowance of 23kg. Note that some airlines, Lufthansa and Flybe among them, require you to call customer services to 'register' your skis within 24 hours of making a booking.

There are other extras that inflate the price too (read the margin panel on the previous page). Airport costs such as drop-off parking fees can also add to the overall spend.

On some busy flights, EasyJet now say your carry-on bag may have to go into the hold if it exceeds dimensions of 50x40x20cm (the normal maximum for cabin bags is 56x45x25cm); they tell us you will not be charged for this.

FROM PLANE TO RESORT

Car rental can be cost-effective for a short break or a group – but, again, watch for hidden extras.

Most Swiss and Austrian airports have good public transport links to lots of resorts. Special rail passes (eg the Swiss Transfer Ticket) may be cheaper than return tickets. In Italy, buses run to the Dolomites from Verona and Innsbruck, and to the Aosta valley from Turin.

Reaching French resorts is slightly trickier, but private minibus transfers are plentiful. Tour operator Ski Amis offers a public shared minibus service on Saturdays from Geneva, Grenoble and Chambéry to the Trois Vallées, La Plagne Montalbert, La Plagne Montchavin and Peisey-Vallandry.

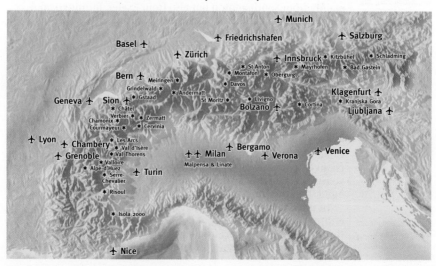

Travelling by rail

Make tracks to the snow (greener ones)

by **Sheila Reid**

Whether you're a rail enthusiast or not, rail travel has its advantages for travelling to the snow. Depending on where you start and where you plan to finish your journey, it can be very relaxed; if you live in Hampstead and ski in Les Arcs, you're in luck. And fares can be competitive, once airline baggage charges are taken into account.

There are efficient high-speed trains direct from London to the Tarentaise region of the French Alps and to Lyon (for the southern French Alps), and lots of options if you are prepared to change in Paris. Some resorts have their own railway stations and others are easily reached by onward bus or taxi transfers.

The starting point of most European rail trips is likely to be the Eurostar high-speed train from London St Pancras, Ebbsfleet or Ashford stations.

DIRECT SERVICES TO THE FRENCH ALPS

Eurostar operates weekly direct services to the Tarentaise region – to Moûtiers for the Three Valleys and to Bourg-St-Maurice (the end of the line) for Les Arcs, La Rosière, Ste-Foy, Tignes and Val d'Isère. Generally allow up to an hour or so for onward transfers. You can book bus transfers at www.altibus.com, www.transavoie.com or www.autocars-martin.com (but it's quicker – though more expensive – to book a taxi transfer).

We loved our trips on the daytime service, which operates from 19 December 2015 until 2 April 2016 (returning on 9 April). You travel on Saturday, so you get the regular six days' skiing: you leave London at 9.45am and arrive in Bourg at 6.50pm. The return service leaves Bourg at 9.34am and arrives in London at 4.13pm.

The overnight service operates from 1 January 2016 to 1 April 2016 (returning on 9 April). There are no special sleeping arrangements – you doze (or not) in your seat. You travel out over Friday night and back over Saturday night, so you get eight days on the slopes: you leave London on Friday evening at 7.45pm and arrive at Bourg at 6.16am. The return service leaves Bourg on Saturday evening at 10.12pm and arrives in London at 7.16am.

A Standard adult return costs from £149 (non-flexible). A Standard Premier ticket (non-flexible) – which gets you a bigger seat pitch and meals (hot dinner and continental breakfast for overnight travel; continental breakfast and/or afternoon tea plus hot lunch for daytime passengers) – costs from £229.

OTHER FRENCH OPTIONS

For 2015/16 there will be a new Saturday Eurostar service from London St Pancras and Ashford direct to Lyon. Change platforms there for a connection on the normal French rail network to Grenoble (around 90 minutes) and bus or taxi transfers from there to Alpe-d'Huez and Les Deux-Alpes. The train leaves London at 7.19am and arrives in Lyon at 1pm. The return journey departs at 5.25pm and arrives in London at 10.12pm.

The French rail network can get you to lots of places from both Paris and Lyon. For Chamonix, an overnight train from Paris

MAKE THE
JOURNEY
PART OF THE
HOLIDAY

Book with..

zenith holidays

0203 137 7678

zenithholidays.co.uk

ABTA
ABTA No: Y1542

Austerlitz, with a change at St-Gervais, would put you in your resort by 9.50am the next day; last season prices started at £70 return (excluding your Eurostar fare from London to Paris return). A pre-bookable taxi service to get you between the Paris stations is offered through snowcarbon.co.uk; you ring, email or book online to reserve a place, and the driver will meet your train. It costs 55 to 65 euros each way depending on the number of people.

HIGH-SPEED TO SWITZERLAND

If travelling to the Swiss Alps, you can take the Eurostar to Lille and transfer by crossing the platform to a high-speed TGV Lyria train to Geneva. This runs on Monday, Thursday, Saturday and Sunday. At Geneva you switch to normal Swiss railway services. But the timing is not ideal because the train does not arrive in Geneva till 8.16pm and it departs for the return journey at 8.30am – so it would mean a late arrival in and early departure from your resort. TGV Lyria trains from Paris also serve Geneva, Zürich and Basel, where you can change to connect with most Swiss resorts. Many resorts, such as Andermatt, Engelberg, Davos, Klosters, Grindelwald, Wengen and Zermatt, have convenient local railway stations. It's easy to get to others, such as Saas-Fee and Verbier, by train and post bus.

AUSTRIA AND GERMANY

Many Austrian resorts (such as St Anton, Zell am See, Mayrhofen and the SkiWelt) have their own stations or are easy to reach by post bus from a nearby station. But it's hard work to get there by train from the UK. The best route is to Munich via Paris or Brussels (but the Brussels service is not direct so you need to go via Frankfurt or Cologne). You change at Munich for onward connections (Garmisch-Partenkirchen in Germany is an easy hop). Sadly the City Night Line sleeper trains from Paris to Munich and on to Innsbruck have been discontinued, so you have to use daytime services.

THE ITALIAN JOB

Most Italian resorts are also hard work to reach by train. But resorts of the Val di Susa are easily reached via trains from Paris Gare de Lyon to Turin and Milan. These run four times a day and stop at Bardonecchia and Oulx – 15 minutes by bus from Sauze d'Oulx and a bit further from Sestriere. And the Dolomites are close to the line through Trento and Bolzano, reachable from Munich, from Innsbruck, or from Verona to the south.

PLANNING AND BOOKING

Rail fares have few of the extra charges that airlines make. But the cheapest fares are best secured early. Booking is normally no more than 90 days in advance, but Eurostar's direct service can be booked six months in advance and French winter services from mid-October. Main sites include: Voyages-sncf.com (www.voyages-sncf.com), Eurostar (www.eurostar.com), Swiss railways (www.sbb.ch/en) and Austrian railways (www.oebb.at/en/). Some local lines, such as Martigny to Le Châble (for Verbier) and Bex up to Villars, may have to be organized separately. Other useful websites include www.seat61.com and www.snowcarbon.co.uk.

Drive to the Alps

And ski where you please

by **Chris Gill** | **Because the Channel gets in the way, and because the British Isles are the centre of the low-cost airline business, we Brits are inclined to travel to the Alps by air, whether we are buying a package holiday or travelling independently. The French, the Germans and the Dutch, in contrast, mainly go by car. But for British skiers, too, driving to the Alps can have lots of advantages.**

Even for those going on a pretty standard week in the Alps, many people find driving is less hassle than taking flights. For families (especially those going self-catering), it simplifies the job of moving half the contents of your house to the Alps. If there are four or five people in your party, the cost can be low. If you fancy something a bit more adventurous than a standard week in one resort, taking a car opens up the exciting possibility of visiting several resorts in one trip – maybe even making up your plans as you go along, so that you go wherever the snow is looking best.

The experience of driving out can be a pleasant one. Crossing the Channel is slick and painless using the fast and frequent Eurotunnel Le Shuttle trains through the tunnel – read the feature panel below. And, although cross-Channel ferries can't compete with Le Shuttle in terms of crossing time, they are faster than they have ever been (as well as more comfortable).

EASY DOES IT WITH EUROTUNNEL LE SHUTTLE

We're now in the habit of using Eurotunnel Le Shuttle to cross the Channel if we're driving to the Alps. (Admittedly, both of the editors are based in what you might loosely call south-east England, and if we were further north we'd certainly be considering ferries across the North Sea.)

The terminal at Folkestone is very straightforward to reach. Junction 11A of the M20 takes you directly to the check-in gates. Check-in deadline is half an hour before departure. The check-in system recognizes your number plate, and without human intervention prints your boarding pass. After a quick visit to the shops in the terminal to pick up the stuff you've forgotten, it's into the marshalling yard for a few minutes before boarding the train.

If you're at the front of the queue, once on the train you drive the whole length of it before parking – and that will mean a quick exit at the other end. Within minutes of boarding you're gliding into the tunnel. If you want a quick nap while crossing, take earplugs.

You can be on the autoroute south of Calais 75 minutes after arrival at Folkestone. Overall, an early start from large parts of southern England can have you in a resort near Geneva in time for dinner without taking too many liberties with the speed limit.

EUROTUNNEL

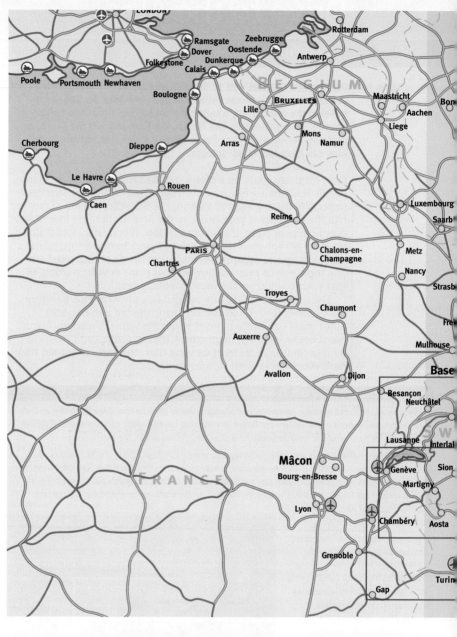

This map should help you plan your route to the Alps, at least in outline. All the main routes from the Channel and all the routes up into the mountains funnel through (or close to) three 'gateways', picked out on the map in larger type – Mâcon in France, Basel in Switzerland and Ulm in Germany (although some sat-navs will route you via Nürnberg). If you're travelling via Calais and heading for Geneva rather than Lyon/Chambéry, south of Dijon you'll want to take the motorway that passes well to the east of Mâcon, not the one that passes close on the west.

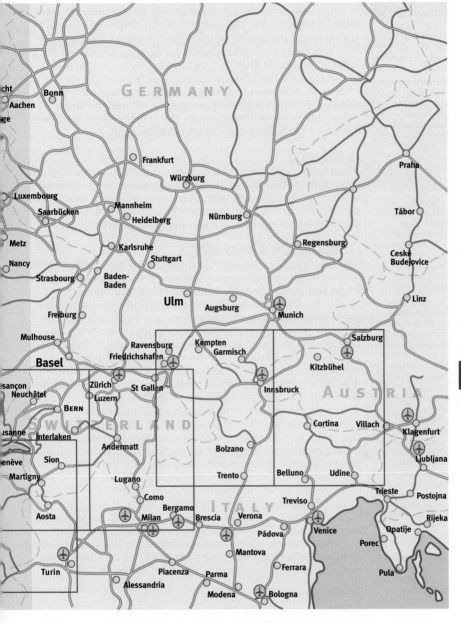

The boxes on the map correspond to the areas covered by the more detailed maps in our introductory chapters on the four main Alpine countries, starting on these pages:

Austria page 86
France page 190
Italy page 386
Switzerland page 448

ATTENTION SVP!

The UK motoring organizations say that when driving in France you must now carry:

• a warning triangle
• a reflective jacket, kept in the main compartment – not stowed in the boot
• an unused, in-date, French-certified breathalyser – the advice is to carry two, in case you want to use one.

If you have a sat-nav, it must not display speed camera locations. They say software updates are available with this data absent. A set of spare light bulbs is recommended.

For years now we have had a gadget on our windscreen that means tolls are charged to a credit card automatically – and we can bowl through autoroute toll barriers at 30kph; highly recommended. We got ours at an APRR desk in a service area for 10 euros. We pay about 2 euros for each calendar month in which we use the device. You can get a tag from a special UK website set up by the SANEF toll company – www.saneftolling.co.uk – but the costs are higher. If you can handle a French site, you can sign up cheaply at APRR's website, www.telepeagepourtous.fr.

What's more, the attractions of driving are not confined to the south of England. A reader writes: 'Living in Derbyshire we can be at Hull in just over an hour for a night crossing to Zeebrugge (for French or Swiss Alps) or Rotterdam (for Austria). After a night in a cabin and breakfast on-board, we can start the 8–10-hour journey to the Alps at 8.30am fully refreshed.' Weather permitting.

Another plus point of driving is that you can easily extend the standard six-day holiday. You can spend a full day on the slopes on the final Saturday (a blissfully quiet day in many resorts) and then drive for a few hours before stopping for the night.

AS YOU LIKE IT

If you fancy visiting several resorts, you can do it in three ways: use one resort as a base and make day trips to others; use a valley town as a base, and make resort visits from there; or go on a tour, moving on every day or two. There are some notable regional lift passes that might form the basis of a trip, in Austria especially.

AROUND THE ALPS IN SEVEN DAYS

The most rewarding approach to exploring the Alps – although the least relaxing – is to go touring, enjoying the freedom of going where you want, when you want. Out of high season there's no need to book accommodation in advance. And a touring holiday doesn't mean you'll be spending more time on the road than on the piste, provided you plan your route carefully. An hour's drive after the lifts have shut is all it need take, normally. It does eat into your après-ski time, of course. The major thing that you have to watch out for is the cost of accommodation. Checking into a resort hotel for a night or two doesn't come cheap, and can seem a rip-off. But hotels in valley towns can be very good value.

The chapter following this one has some suggestions for a trip to France. Austria offers lots of possibilities. In the west, you could take in the best skiing the country has to offer, by combining the Arlberg resorts with Ischgl, and maybe Sölden. Further east, it is easy to combine Hintertux and Mayrhofen with the SkiWelt resorts and Kitzbühel. Driving around in Austria is a doddle, because most of the resorts are low, and passes are rarely involved.

In Italy you can stay in the beautiful old city of Aosta and visit a different resort (such as Courmayeur, Cervinia and the Monterosa resorts) each day. Elsewhere in Italy, touring makes more sense.

Switzerland also offers lots of possibilities. In the west, you could combine Verbier with Val d'Anniviers and Crans-Montana. Further east, you could start in Davos/Klosters and end up in Flims.

BE PREPARED

Winter tyres make a big difference to a car's grip on cold wet roads, as well as ice and snow. These tyres are compulsory in Austria for the whole winter period. In other Alpine countries, we understand that they are not; but many 'experts' warn that if you go without them and have an incident, you could be in trouble. You may still need chains in really deep snow. But winter tyres will keep you going in pretty difficult conditions if your car also has traction control, to stop the wheels spinning. This usually forms part of the electronic stability systems now fitted to many new cars.

Cars hired in Austria and Switzerland should always be equipped with winter tyres. Cars hired elsewhere may not be.

Drive to the French Alps

To make the most of them

by **Chris Gill**

If you've read the preceding chapter, you'll have gathered that we are pretty keen on driving to the Alps in general. But we're particularly keen on driving to the French Alps. The drive is a relatively short one, whereas many of the transfers to major French resorts from Geneva airport are relatively long.

Of course, the route from the Channel to the French Alps is through France rather than Germany, which for Francophiles like us means it's a pleasant prospect rather than a vaguely off-putting one. French motorways, unlike German ones, are pleasantly low-pressure – especially those in the north-east of France, which you are likely to use when crossing the Channel to Calais. (When crossing to a Normandy port you have to tangle with Paris but also you end up on the always-busy Paris–Lyon autoroute.)

The French Alps are the number-one destination for British car-borne skiers. The journey time is surprisingly short, at least if you are starting from south-east England. From Calais, for example, you can comfortably cover the 900km/560 miles to Chamonix in about nine hours plus stops – with the exception of the final few miles, the whole journey is on motorways. And except on peak weekends, when half the population of Paris is on the move, the traffic is relatively light, if you steer clear of Paris.

With some exceptions in the southern Alps, all the resorts of the French Alps are within a day's driving range, provided you cross the Channel early in the day (or overnight). Saturday is still the main changeover day for resorts, and Saturday traffic into and out of many resorts can be heavy. This is especially true between Albertville and the Tarentaise resorts (from the Three Valleys to Val d'Isère). Things are nothing like as bad as they were 25 years ago, before road improvements for the 1992 Olympics removed some of the main bottlenecks; but the resorts have expanded further in that time, and sadly the jams are back – on peak-season Saturdays you can encounter serious queues around Moûtiers. There are traffic lights placed well away from the town, to keep the queues and associated pollution away from Moûtiers.

DAY-TRIP BASES

As we explained in the previous chapter, a car opens up different kinds of holiday for the adventurous holidaymaker – day tripping from a base resort, for example.

In the southern French Alps, Serre-Chevalier and Montgenèvre are ideal bases for day tripping. They are within easy reach of one another, and Montgenèvre is at one end of the Milky Way lift network, which includes Sauze d'Oulx and Sestriere in Italy – you can drive on to these resorts, or reach them by lift and piste. On the French side of the border, a few miles south, Vars/Risoul is an underrated area that is well worth a visit for a day. The major resorts of Alpe-d'Huez and Les Deux-Alpes are also within range, as is the cult off-piste resort of La Grave. Getting to them involves crossing the high Col du Lautaret, but it's a major route and is not allowed to close for very long in normal winter conditions.

Self-drive packages
inc. FREE Eurotunnel upgrade
02392 839 310
PEAKRETREATS.CO.UK
ABTA

SKI AMIS

Catered Chalets in Superb Locations

020 3411 5439
www.skiamis.com

The Chamonix valley is an ideal destination for day tripping. The Mont Blanc Unlimited lift pass covers all the Chamonix areas, plus Courmayeur in Italy (easily reached through the Mont Blanc tunnel) and Verbier in Switzerland (a bit of a trek, even if the intervening passes are open). Megève and Les Contamines are close by, and Flaine and its satellites are fairly accessible. You could stay in a valley town such as Cluses, to escape resort prices – but Chamonix itself is not a wildly expensive town.

In the Tarentaise region, Bourg-St-Maurice is an excellent base for visiting several resorts – Les Arcs is accessible by funicular, and La Plagne is of course linked to Les Arcs. La Rosière is only a short drive away, with a link to La Thuile. Ste-Foy is just up the valley. And at the end of the valley are Val d'Isère and Tignes. We had a great week skiing all of these resorts a few seasons ago based in a comfortable apartment in Bourg.

MOVING ON

An alternative approach in the Tarentaise region if you want to include the famous Three Valleys area is to stay in a series of different resorts for a day or two each, moving on from one to the next in the early evening; this way, you could have the trip of a lifetime (and save a lot on après-ski beers).

GETTING THERE

There are three 'gateways' to the different regions of the French Alps. For the northern Alps – Chamonix valley, Portes du Soleil, Flaine and neighbours – you want to head for Geneva. If coming from Calais or another short-crossing port, you no longer have to tangle with the busy A6 from Paris via Beaune to Mâcon and Lyon. The relatively new A39 autoroute south from Dijon means you can head for Bourg-en-Bresse, well east of Mâcon. For the central Alps – the mega-resorts of the Tarentaise, from Valmorel to Val d'Isère, and the Maurienne valley – you want to head for Chambéry. For the southern Alps – Alpe-d'Huez, Les Deux-Alpes, Serre-Chevalier – you want to head for Grenoble. And for either Chambéry or Grenoble first head for Mâcon and turn left at Lyon.

If you are taking a short Channel crossing, there are plenty of characterful towns for an overnight stop between the Channel and Dijon – Arras (our favourite), St-Quentin, Laon, Troyes, Reims. All have plenty of choice of budget chain hotels, some of them in central locations where you can easily enjoy the facilities of the town (ie the brasseries).

From the more westerly Channel ports of Le Havre or Caen, your route to Geneva or Mâcon sounds dead simple: take the A13 to Paris then the A6 south. But you have to get through or around Paris in the process. The most direct way around the city is the notorious périphérique – a hectic, multi-lane urban motorway close to the centre, with exits every few hundred yards and traffic that is either worryingly fast-moving or jammed solid. If the périphérique is jammed, getting round it takes ages. The more reliable alternative is to take a series of motorways and dual carriageways through the south-west fringes of Greater Paris. The route is not well signed, so it's a great help to have a competent navigator.

High quality, high altitude

Self-drive specialist
02392 890 960

ABTA
ABTA No JY557

SKI COLLECTION
.co.uk

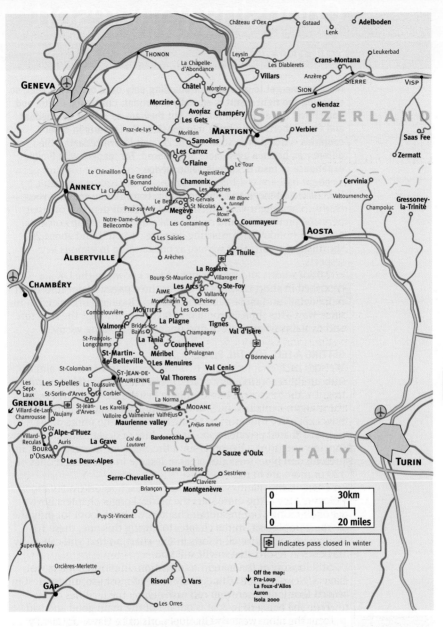

Pick the right gateway – Geneva, Chambéry or Grenoble – and you can hardly go wrong. Generally, there are no mountain passes involved. The exception is the approach to Serre-Chevalier and Montgenèvre, which involves the 2060m Col du Lautaret; the road is a major one and is ploughed frequently, but we felt the need for chains here on one occasion. Crossing the French–Swiss border between Chamonix and Verbier involves two closure-prone passes – the Montets and the Forclaz. When necessary, one-way traffic runs beside the tracks through the rail tunnel beneath the passes.

Most people get to go skiing or boarding only once or twice a year, so choosing the right resort is crucially important. Chamonix, Châtel and Courchevel are all French resorts, but they are as similar as Cheddar and Camembert. If you bring into consideration resorts in other countries – Ischgl in Austria, say, or Zermatt in Switzerland – the differences become even more pronounced. For readers with limited experience of resorts, here is some advice.

Lots of factors need to be taken into account when making your choice. The weight you attach to each of them depends on your personal preferences, and on the make-up of the group you are going on holiday with. Starting on page 71 you'll find about 20 shortlists of resorts that we rate as outstanding in various key respects.

Minor resorts and regions not widely known in the UK are described in short chapters of two or three pages. Major resorts get more detail, and more pages. Each resort chapter is organized in the same way. This short introduction takes you through the structure and explains what you will find under each heading we use.

GETTING A FEEL FOR THE PLACE

We start each chapter with a two-line verdict in which we aim to sum up the resort in a few words. If you like the sound of it, you might want to go next to our unique Resort Price Index (RPI), in the margin. Explained fully in the chapter on page 27, this tells you how expensive the resort is, taking account of the prices of lift passes, a shared private lesson or two, hire of decent skis and simple lunches and drinks; figures around the eurozone average of 100 are presented in blue, low ones of 90 or less are in green, high ones of 120 or more are in red.

Then, in the 'Ratings' section, we rate each resort from various points of view – the more stars the better. Longer chapters have a set of 19 ratings, but in shorter chapters we have room for only the 10 most important. In the chapter following this one, these 10 ratings are set out for all resorts in one chart, so that you can easily track down resorts that might suit you.

Still looking at the margin information, in most chapters we have a 'News' section; this is likely to be of most use and interest in resorts that you know from recent visits.

The next thing to look at is our list of the main good and bad points about the resort and its slopes, picked out with ➕ and ➖. This is followed by a summary in **bold type**, in which we've aimed to weigh up the pros and cons, coming off the fence and giving our view of who might like the resort. These sections should give you a good idea of whether the resort is likely to suit *you*, and whether it's worth reading our detailed analysis of it.

You'll know by now, for example, whether this is a high, hideous, convenient, purpose-built resort with superb, snow-sure, challenging slopes but absolutely no nightlife; or a pretty, traditional village with gentle wooded slopes, ideal for beginners on the rare occasions when it has some decent snow.

❄ Stanford
❄ Skiing

**Megève
Specialists**

Huge ski area
Close to Geneva
Short breaks
Chalets & hotels

01603 477471
stanfordskiing.co.uk

62

THE RESORT

In this first section of the main text, we try to sort out the character of the place for you. Later, in the 'Staying there' section, we tell you more about the hotels, restaurants, bars and so on. Resorts vary enormously in some key respects and we have separate sections for each of the following headings. These match our star ratings.

ski EXPECTATIONS 01799 531888

THE SKI HOLIDAY CONSULTANCY

with over 25 years experience in Europe's Top Resorts, the USA & Canada

The service is friendly, the information is accurate and the advice is free

Just one call away from your ideal holiday

01799 531888
www.skiexpectations.com

Village charm At the extremes of the range are the handful of really hideous modern apartment-block resorts thrown up in France in the 1960s, and the ancient, captivating mountain villages of which Switzerland has an unfair number. But it isn't simply a question of old versus new. Some purpose-built places can have a much friendlier feel than some long-established resorts with big blocky buildings. Some places are working towns. Some are full of bars, discos and shops; others are peaceful backwaters. Traffic may choke the streets; or the village may be traffic-free.

Convenience This means how easy it is to get around the resort once you are there (not how easy it is to get to the resort from the UK). Some places can be remarkably strung out, whereas others are surprisingly compact; our village plans are drawn to a standard scale, to help you gauge this. And of course proximity of lodgings to pistes determines how much walking or bussing you do.

Scenery Mountains are of course generally scenic, but there are differences, from the routinely hilly Colorado to the incredible scenery of the Italian Dolomites and the Swiss Jungfrau region.

THE MOUNTAINS

Extent of slopes Some mountains and lift networks are vast and complex, while others are much smaller and lacking variety. As last year, we have a special feature about this aspect, on page 24.

Fast lifts Gondolas and fast chairlifts travel at three times the speed of slow chairlifts – cable cars and funicular railways even faster; these lifts offer short ride times, and most of them also shift queues quickly. We summarize the kinds of lifts you'll spend your time on. On our piste maps, we use a chair symbol to identify only fast chairs; lifts not marked with a symbol are slow chairs or draglifts. (By the way: many people don't realize that many draglifts travel appreciably faster than slow chairlifts.)

Queues Monster queues are largely a thing of the past, but it still pays to avoid the resorts with the worst queues, especially in high season. Crowding on the pistes is more of a worry in many resorts, and we mention problems of this kind under this heading.

Terrain parks We summarize here the specially prepared fun parks and other terrain features most resorts now arrange for those who like to do tricks on their skis or board.

Snow reliability This is a crucial factor for many people, and one that varies enormously. In some resorts you don't have to worry at all about a lack of snow, while others are notorious for treating their paying guests to ice, mud and slush. Whether a resort is likely to have decent snow on its slopes normally depends on the height, the orientation of the slopes (north-facing good, south- and west-facing bad), its snow record and how much snowmaking it has. But bear in mind that in the Alps, high resorts tend to have rocky terrain, where the runs (and particularly the 'off-piste' terrain outside the prepared runs) will need more snow than the pasture land of lower resorts.

For experts, intermediates, beginners Most (though not all) resorts have something to offer beginners, but there are still important differences in this respect. Relatively few will keep an expert happy for a week's holiday. As for intermediates, whether a resort will suit you really depends on your skill and inclinations. Places such as Cervinia and Obergurgl are ideal for those who want easy cruising runs, but have little to offer intermediates looking for more challenge. Others, such as Sölden and Val d'Isère, may intimidate the less confident intermediate. Some areas linking several resorts, such as the Three Valleys and Portes du Soleil, have vast amounts of terrain, so you can cover different ground each day. But some other well-known names, such as Mürren and Courmayeur, have surprisingly small areas.

For boarders In earlier editions we had a special panel in longer chapters but we now deal with boarders' requirements in the main text, commenting on things like flat areas (bad) and the main types of lifts – gondolas, cable cars and chairs (all good) or draglifts (bad).

For cross-country We don't pretend that this is a guide for avid cross-country skiers. But we do try to help.

Mountain restaurants Here's a subject that arouses strong views. To some, having a decent lunch served at your table in civilized surroundings – either in the sun, enjoying amazing scenery, or in a cosy hut, sheltered from the elements – makes or breaks the holiday. Others regard a long midday stop as a waste of valuable skiing time, as well as valuable spending money. We are firmly in the former camp. We get very disheartened by places with miserable restaurants and miserable food (eg many resorts in America); and there are some resorts that we choose for our holidays partly because of the cosy huts and the food (eg Zermatt).

Schools and guides This is an area where we rely heavily on readers' reports of their own or their friends' experiences.

For families We sum up the merits of the resort for families. Again, to be of real help we need reports from people with children.

STAYING THERE

Chalets, hotels, apartments Some resorts have few hotels or few catered chalets. Note that we also have feature chapters on notably good chalets (page 34) and apartments (page 37). If there are interesting options for staying in isolation on the slopes above the resort village, or in cheap valley towns below it, we pick them out.

Eating out The range of restaurants varies widely. Even some big resorts have little choice because most visitors dine in their apartments or hotels. Most American resorts offer lots of choice.

Après-ski Tastes and styles vary enormously. Most resorts have pleasant places in which to have an immediate post-skiing beer or hot chocolate. Some then go dead. Others have noisy bars on the mountain or at the lift base, and discos until the early hours.

Off the slopes This is largely aimed at assessing how suitable a resort is for someone who doesn't intend to use the slopes, such as a non-skiing spouse. But of course it is also of interest to anyone who wants some variety of evening entertainment.

Resort ratings at a glance

We give here the ten most important ratings. Major resort chapters contain a further nine. The **Price Index figures** in the second row are explained in detail on page 27. An average eurozone resort has an RPI of 100; relatively cheap resorts have green figures, pricey ones red figures.

ANDORRA / AUSTRIA

	ARINSAL	SOLDEU		ALPBACHTAL-WILD'AU	BAD GASTEIN	BAD KLEIN-KIRCHHEIM	ELLMAU	
Page	78	80		93	96	99	106	
Price Index	90	115		90	95	100	85	
Extent	*	***		***	***	**	****	
Fast lifts	**	**		****	***	**	****	
Queues	***	***		****	***	****	****	
Snow	****	***		**	***	***	**	
Expert	*	**		**	***	**	*	
Intermediate	**	****		***	****	***	****	
Beginner	****	****		***	**	**	****	
Charm	*	*		****	***	**	***	
Convenience	***	***		***	**	***	***	
Scenery	***	***		***	***	***	***	

	HINTERTUX / TUX VALLEY	ISCHGL	KITZBÜHEL	LECH ZÜRS	MAYRHOFEN	OBERGURGL	OBERTAUERN	
Page	109	114	121	129	138	144	150	
Price Index	95	105	105	125	90	110	95	
Extent	***	****	***	***	***	**	**	
Fast lifts	***	*****	*****	****	****	*****	****	
Queues	***	****	***	****	**	*****	****	
Snow	*****	****	**	****	***	*****	****	
Expert	***	****	***	****	**	**	***	
Intermediate	***	****	****	****	***	***	****	
Beginner	**	**	**	****	**	****	***	
Charm	***	***	****	****	***	****	**	
Convenience	**	***	**	***	**	****	****	
Scenery	***	***	***	***	***	***	***	

	SAALBACH-HINTERG'M	SCHLADMING	SÖLDEN	SÖLL	ST ANTON	STUBAI VALLEY	ZELL AM SEE	
Page	152	158	162	167	174	183	185	
Price Index	95	95	110	90	110	100	100	
Extent	****	***	***	****	***	***	**	
Fast lifts	*****	****	****	****	****	***	****	
Queues	****	****	***	***	***	***	***	
Snow	**	****	****	**	****	*****	**	
Expert	**	**	***	*	*****	***	**	
Intermediate	****	****	****	****	***	***	***	
Beginner	***	***	***	**	*	**	***	
Charm	****	***	**	***	****	****	****	
Convenience	****	***	**	**	***	**	***	
Scenery	***	***	***	***	***	****	***	

The Price Index figures

The Price Index figures in the second row are explained in detail on page 27.
An average eurozone resort has an RPI of 100; relatively cheap resorts have green figures, pricey ones red figures.

FRANCE

	Alpe-d'Huez	Les Arcs	Avoriaz	Les Carroz	Chamonix	Châtel	Courchevel	
Page	196	206	216	221	223	233	238	
RPI	105	105	105	100	105	100	140	
Extent	****	***	*****	****	***	*****	*****	
Fast lifts	****	****	****	***	***	**	****	
Queues	****	***	***	***	**	***	****	
Snow	****	****	***	***	****	**	****	
Expert	****	*****	***	****	*****	***	****	
Intermediate	****	****	****	*****	**	****	*****	
Beginner	*****	***	****	****	**	***	****	
Charm	**	**	**	****	****	***	**	
Convenience	***	****	*****	***	*	**	****	
Scenery	****	***	***	****	*****	***	***	

	Les Deux-Alpes	Flaine	Les Gets	La Grave	Megève	Les Menuires	Méribel	
Page	248	254	261	263	269	276	282	
RPI	100	100	100	90	100	110	125	
Extent	***	****	*****	*	*****	*****	*****	
Fast lifts	****	***	***		**	****	*****	
Queues	***	***	****	****	****	****	****	
Snow	****	****	**	***	**	****	***	
Expert	****	****	***	*****	**	****	****	
Intermediate	**	*****	****	*	****	*****	*****	
Beginner	***	*****	****	*	***	***	****	
Charm	**	*	****	***	****	**	***	
Convenience	***	*****	***	***	**	*****	***	
Scenery	****	****	***	****	*****	***	***	

	Mont-Genèvre	Morzine	La Plagne	La Rosière	Samoëns	Serre-Chevalier	Ste-Foy-Tarentaise	
Page	291	296	305	321	324	327	336	
RPI	90	100	110	90	95	95	85	
Extent	**	*****	****	***	****	****	*	
Fast lifts	**	***	**	***	***	***	****	
Queues	****	****	**	****	****	****	*****	
Snow	****	**	****	***	***	***	***	
Expert	****	***	****	**	****	***	****	
Intermediate	****	****	*****	***	*****	****	***	
Beginner	*****	***	****	*****	**	****	**	
Charm	***	***	**	***	****	***	***	
Convenience	***	**	*****	***	*	***	****	
Scenery	***	***	***	****	****	***	***	

Want to see the full set?

Major resort chapters in the book have an additional nine ratings shown at the start of each chapter. And you can see the full set of ratings for 200+ resorts on our website.

www.wheretoskiandsnowboard.com

	St-Martin-de-B'ville	La Tania	Tignes	Val Cenis Vanoise	Val d'Isère	Valmorel	Val Thorens	Vars / Risoul
Page	339	342	348	357	360	370	372	379
RPI	110	115	115	80	110	90	115	85
Extent	★★★★★	★★★★★	★★★★★	★★★	★★★★★	★★★	★★★★★	★★★
Fast lifts	★★★★	★★★★	★★★	★★★	★★★★	★★	★★★★★	★
Queues	★★★★	★★★★	★★★★	★★★★	★★★★	★★★	★★★★	★★★★
Snow	★★★	★★★	★★★★★	★★★	★★★★★	★★	★★★★★	★★★
Expert	★★★★	★★★★	★★★★★	★★	★★★★★	★★	★★★★	★★
Intermediate	★★★★★	★★★★★	★★★★★	★★★★	★★★★★	★★★★	★★★★★	★★★★
Beginner	★★	★★★	★★	★★★★	★★★	★★★★★	★★★★	★★★★
Charm	★★★★	★★★	★	★★★	★★★	★★★★	★★	★★
Convenience	★★★	★★★★	★★★★	★★★	★★★	★★★★	★★★★★	★★★★
Scenery	★★★	★★★	★★★	★★★	★★★	★★★	★★★	★★★

GERMANY ITALY

	Garmisch-Partenk'n		Cervinia	Cortina d'Ampezzo	Courmayeur	Livigno	Madonna di Campiglio	
Page	384		391	397	402	407	411	
RPI	90		90	115	95	90	105	
Extent	★		★★★	★★	★	★★	★★★	
Fast lifts	★★★		★★★★	★★★	★★★★	★★★★	★★★★	
Queues	★★★		★★★★	★★★★	★★★★	★★★★	★★★	
Snow	★★★		★★★★★	★★★	★★★★	★★★★	★★★	
Expert	★★★★		★	★★	★★★	★★★	★★	
Intermediate	★★★		★★★★	★★★	★★★★	★★★	★★★★	
Beginner	★		★★★★★	★★★★★	★	★★★★	★★★★	
Charm	★★★		★★	★★★★	★★★★	★★★	★★★★	
Convenience	★★		★★★	★	★	★★	★★★	
Scenery	★★★★		★★★★	★★★★★	★★★★	★★★	★★★★	

	Monterosa Ski	Passo Tonale	Sauze d'Oulx	Sella Ronda	Selva / Val Gardena	Sestriere	La Thuile
Page	416	422	424	429	437	444	446
RPI	85	75	90	95	95	90	90
Extent	★★	★★	★★★★	★★★★★	★★★★★	★★★★	★★★
Fast lifts	★★★★★	★★★★	★★★	★★★★	★★★★	★★★	★★★
Queues	★★★★	★★★★	★★★	★★★	★★★	★★★	★★★★★
Snow	★★★★	★★★★	★★	★★★★	★★★★	★★★★	★★★★
Expert	★★★★	★★	★★	★★	★★★	★★★	★★
Intermediate	★★★★	★★★	★★★★	★★★★★	★★★★★	★★★★	★★★★
Beginner	★★	★★★★★	★	★★★★	★★★	★★★	★★★★
Charm	★★★	★★	★★	★★★	★★★	★	★★★
Convenience	★★★	★★★	★★	★★★	★★★	★★★	★★★
Scenery	★★★★	★★★	★★★	★★★★★	★★★★★	★★★	★★★

Resort ratings at a glance

Resort ratings at a glance

The Price Index figures

The Price Index figures in the second row are explained in detail on page 27.
An average eurozone resort has an RPI of 100; relatively cheap resorts have green figures, pricey ones red figures.

SWITZERLAND

	Adelboden	Andermatt	Arosa	Champéry	Crans-Montana	Davos
Page	454	457	459	462	465	467
RPI	140	130	145	140	155	155
Extent	***	**	****	*****	***	****
Fast lifts	***	**	****	*	*****	****
Queues	***	**	****	****	***	****
Snow	***	****	***	**	**	****
Expert	**	****	***	***	**	****
Intermediate	***	**	****	****	****	*****
Beginner	****	*	****	**	***	**
Charm	****	****	**	****	**	**
Convenience	**	***	**	*	**	**
Scenery	****	***	***	****	****	****

	Engelberg	Grindelw'd	Klosters	Laax	Mürren	Saas-Fee
Page	474	476	480	482	485	489
RPI	125	145	150	150	140	155
Extent	**	***	****	****	*	**
Fast lifts	***	****	**	*****	*****	****
Queues	**	**	**	****	***	****
Snow	***	**	****	***	***	*****
Expert	****	**	****	***	***	**
Intermediate	***	****	*****	*****	***	****
Beginner	**	***	***	****	***	****
Charm	**	****	****	***	*****	*****
Convenience	*	**	**	***	***	**
Scenery	****	*****	****	***	*****	****

	St Moritz	Val d'Anniviers	Verbier	Villars	Wengen	Zermatt
Page	494	501	505	515	517	522
RPI	170	135	160	135	140	165
Extent	*****	**	*****	***	***	****
Fast lifts	****	*	****	**	****	*****
Queues	****	****	***	***	***	***
Snow	****	****	***	**	**	****
Expert	****	****	*****	**	**	****
Intermediate	****	***	***	***	****	****
Beginner	**	***	**	****	***	**
Charm	**	*****	***	***	*****	****
Convenience	*	**	**	**	***	**
Scenery	****	****	****	***	*****	*****

Want to see the full set?

Major resort chapters in the book have an additional nine ratings shown at the start of each chapter. And you can see the full set of ratings for 200+ resorts on our website.

www.wheretoskiandsnowboard.com

USA

	CALIFORNIA Heavenly	Mammoth Mountain	Squaw Valley					
Page	539	544	549					
RPI	180	180	180					
Extent	***	***	***					
Fast lifts	****	****	***					
Queues	****	****	****					
Snow	***	****	***					
Expert	***	****	****					
Intermediate	****	****	**					
Beginner	****	****	****					
Charm	*	**	***					
Convenience	*	**	****					
Scenery	****	***	***					

	COLORADO Aspen	Beaver Creek	Breckenr'ge	Copper Mountain	Snowmass	Steamboat	Vail	Winter Park
Page	552	559	561	566	568	570	573	580
RPI	220	220	195	180	210	185	215	165
Extent	**	***	***	**	***	***	****	***
Fast lifts	****	*****	****	**	*****	****	*****	****
Queues	****	*****	****	****	****	****	**	****
Snow	*****	*****	*****	*****	*****	****	*****	*****
Expert	*****	****	****	****	*****	***	****	****
Intermediate	*****	****	****	****	*****	****	*****	****
Beginner	*****	*****	*****	****	*****	*****	***	*****
Charm	****	**	***	**	**	**	***	**
Convenience	**	****	***	****	*****	***	***	***
Scenery	***	***	***	***	****	***	***	***

	UTAH Alta	Canyons	Deer Valley	Park City	Snowbird		REST OF THE WEST Big Sky	Jackson Hole
Page	586	588	590	592	597		600	605
RPI	180	200	200	195	185		180	175
Extent	***	****	**	****	***		****	***
Fast lifts	****	****	****	****	*****		**	****
Queues	***	****	****	****	***		*****	***
Snow	*****	***	****	****	*****		*****	****
Expert	*****	****	***	****	*****		****	*****
Intermediate	***	****	****	****	***		****	**
Beginner	***	**	****	****	**		*****	***
Charm	**	**	***	***	*		**	***
Convenience	*****	****	****	**	*****		****	****
Scenery	***	***	***	***	***		***	***

Resort ratings at a glance

69

Our website has regular resort news throughout the year, and you can register for our monthly email newsletter – with special holiday offers, as well as resort news highlights.
www.wheretoskiandsnowboard.com

CANADA

	WEST							
	BANFF	BIG WHITE	FERNIE	KICKING HORSE	LAKE LOUISE			
Page	616	622	624	629	631			
RPI	160	150	155	170	160			
Extent	★★★	★★★	★★★	★★★	★★★			
Fast lifts	★★★★	★★★★	★★	★★★	★★★★			
Queues	★★★★	★★★★★	★★★★	★★★★	★★★★			
Snow	★★★★	★★★★★	★★★★	★★★★	★★★			
Expert	★★★★	★★★	★★★★★	★★★★	★★★★			
Intermediate	★★★★	★★★★	★★	★★	★★★★			
Beginner	★★★	★★★★	★★★★	★★★	★★★			
Charm	★★★	★★	★★	★★	★★★			
Convenience	★	★★★★	★★★★	★★★★	★			
Scenery	★★★★	★★★	★★★	★★★	★★★★			

					EAST		
	REVELSTOKE	SILVER STAR	SUN PEAKS	WHISTLER	TREMBLANT		
Page	636	639	641	643	653		
RPI	155	150	155	180	170		
Extent	★★★	★★★	★★★	★★★★	★		
Fast lifts	★★★★★	★★★★	★★	★★★★★	★★★★★		
Queues	★★★★★	★★★★★	★★★★★	★★	★★★		
Snow	★★★★	★★★★	★★★★	★★★★	★★★★		
Expert	★★★★★	★★★★	★★★	★★★★★	★★		
Intermediate	★★	★★★	★★★★	★★★★★	★★★		
Beginner	★★	★★★★	★★★★	★★★	★★★★		
Charm	★★	★★★	★★★	★★★	★★★★		
Convenience	★★★	★★★★★	★★★★	★★★★	★★★★		
Scenery	★★★★	★★★	★★★	★★★	★★★		

www.wheretoskiandsnowboard.com

Our website is designed to complement this book. We like to think it's one of the best in the ski business. On the site you'll find lots of interest to the keen skier/boarder:

- regular news and updates on all the major resorts in Europe and North America
- full editors' ratings for 200 resorts
- snow reports and resort weather forecasts
- links to resorts and other useful sites
- free competitions with great prizes
- special offers from leading tour operators

- blogs from the editors on their travels
- dozens of background feature articles
- forums where you can exchange views, seek advice, give vent to those grumbles
- a resort reporting system, where you can file a report and maybe win a prize
- a sign-up for monthly e-newsletters

Resort shortlists

To help you spot resorts that will suit you

To streamline the job of drawing up your own shortlist, here are some ready-made ones. Many lists we've confined to Europe, because North America has too many qualifying resorts (eg for beginners) or because they do things differently there, making comparisons between here and there invalid (eg for off-piste).

SOMETHING FOR EVERYONE
Everything from good nursery slopes to challenges for experts
Alpe-d'Huez, France 196
Les Arcs, France 206
Aspen, USA 552
Courchevel, France 238
Flaine, France 254
Mammoth Mountain, USA 544
Vail, USA 573
Val d'Isère, France 360
Whistler, Canada 643
Winter Park, USA 580

INTERNATIONAL OVERSIGHTS
Resorts that get less attention than they deserve
Alta, USA 586
Andermatt, Switzerland 457
Bad Gastein, Austria 96
Big Sky, USA 600
Laax, Switzerland 482
Monterosa Ski, Italy 416
Sella Ronda, Italy 429
Sölden, Austria 162
Val d'Anniviers, Switzerland 501
Vars / Risoul, France 379

HIGH-MILEAGE PISTE-BASHING
Extensive intermediate slopes with big, slick lift networks
Alpe-d'Huez, France 196
Les Arcs, France 206
Cervinia, Italy 391
Ellmau, Austria 106
Flaine, France 254
Kitzbühel, Austria 121
Laax, Switzerland 482
La Plagne, France 305
Portes du Soleil, France 316
Saalbach-Hinterglemm, Austria 152
Sella Ronda, Italy 429
Selva / Val Gardena, Italy 437
Söll, Austria 167
Three Valleys, France 346
Tignes, France 348
Vail, USA 573
Val d'Isère, France 360
Whistler, Canada 643
Zermatt, Switzerland 522

RELIABLE SNOW IN THE ALPS
Alpine resorts where snow is rarely in short supply
Cervinia, Italy 391
Chamonix, France 223
Courchevel, France 238
Les Deux-Alpes, France 248
Hintertux / Tux valley, Austria 109
Lech Zürs, Austria 129
Obergurgl, Austria 144
Obertauern, Austria 150
Saas-Fee, Switzerland 489
Sölden, Austria 162
Val d'Isère, France 360
Val Thorens, France 372
Zermatt, Switzerland 522

OFF-PISTE WONDERS
Alpine resorts where you can have the time of your life
Alpe-d'Huez, France 196
Andermatt, Switzerland 457
Chamonix, France 223
Davos, Switzerland 467
La Grave, France 263
Klosters, Switzerland 480
Lech Zürs, Austria 129
Monterosa Ski, Italy 416
St Anton, Austria 174
Tignes, France 348
Val d'Isère, France 360
Verbier, Switzerland 505

DRAMATIC SCENERY
Mountains that are spectacularly scenic as well as snowy
Chamonix, France 223
Cortina d'Ampezzo, Italy 397
Courmayeur, Italy 402
Grindelwald, Switzerland 476
Heavenly, USA 539
Lake Louise, Canada 631
Megève, France 269
Mürren, Switzerland 485
Sella Ronda, Italy 429
Selva / Val Gardena, Italy 437
St Moritz, Switzerland 494
Wengen, Switzerland 517
Zermatt, Switzerland 522

High quality, high altitude
Four-star apartments in world-class high altitude resorts
02392 890 960

ABTA

SKI COLLECTION
.CO.UK

Authentic
villages
in large
ski areas

02392
839 310

PEAKRETREATS.CO.UK

ABTA
ABTA No W5517

BACK-DOOR RESORTS
Cute little Alpine villages linked to big, bold ski areas
Les Brévières (Tignes), France 348
Champagny (La Plagne), France 305
Leogang (Saalbach), Austria 152
Montchavin (La Plagne), France 305
Peisey (Les Arcs), France 206
Le Pré (Les Arcs), France 206
Samoëns (Flaine), France 324
St-Martin (Trois Vallées), France 339
Stuben (St Anton), Austria 174
Vaujany (Alpe-d'Huez), France 196

VILLAGE CHARM
Traditional character – whether villages or towns
Aspen, USA 552
Champéry, Switzerland 462
Courmayeur, Italy 402
Les Gets, France 261
Kitzbühel, Austria 121
Lech Zürs, Austria 129
Megève, France 269
Mürren, Switzerland 485
Saas-Fee, Switzerland 489
Samoëns, France 324
Val d'Anniviers, Switzerland 501
Wengen, Switzerland 517
Zermatt, Switzerland 522

BLACK RUNS
Steep, mogully, lift-served slopes, protected from avalanche
Alta, USA 586
Andermatt, Switzerland 457
Aspen, USA 552
Beaver Creek, USA 559
Chamonix, France 223
Courchevel, France 238
Jackson Hole, USA 605
Snowbird, USA 597
Whistler, Canada 643
Winter Park, USA 580
Zermatt, Switzerland 522

POWDER PARADISES
Resorts with the snow and terrain for powder perfection
Alta, USA 586
Andermatt, Switzerland 457
Big Sky, USA 600
Big White, Canada 622
Fernie, Canada 624
La Grave, France 263
Jackson Hole, USA 605
Kicking Horse, Canada 629
Lech Zürs, Austria 129
Monterosa Ski, Italy 416
Revelstoke, Canada 636
Snowbird, USA 597
Ste-Foy-Tarentaise, France 336

CHOPAHOLICS
Resorts where you can have a day riding helicopters or cats
Aspen, USA 552
Courmayeur, Italy 402
Fernie, Canada 624
Lech Zürs, Austria 129
Monterosa Ski, Italy 416
Revelstoke, Canada 636
La Thuile, Italy 446
Verbier, Switzerland 505
Whistler, Canada 643
Zermatt, Switzerland 522

TOP TERRAIN PARKS
Alpine resorts with the best parks and pipes for freestyle thrills
Les Arcs, France 206
Avoriaz, France 216
Cervinia, Italy 391
Davos, Switzerland 467
Les Deux-Alpes, France 248
Ischgl, Austria 114
Laax, Switzerland 482
Lech Zürs, Austria 129
Livigno, Italy 407
Mayrhofen, Austria 138
Méribel, France 282
La Plagne, France 305
Saalbach-Hinterglemm, Austria 152
Saas-Fee, Switzerland 489
St Moritz, Switzerland 494

WEATHERPROOF SLOPES
Fairly snow-sure slopes if the sun shines, trees in case it doesn't
Les Arcs, France 206
Courchevel, France 238
Courmayeur, Italy 402
Laax, Switzerland 482
Schladming, Austria 158
Selva / Val Gardena, Italy 437
Serre-Chevalier, France 327
Sestriere, Italy 444
La Thuile, Italy 446

MOTORWAY CRUISING
Long, gentle, super-smooth pistes to bolster frail confidence
Les Arcs, France 206
Breckenridge, USA 561
Cervinia, Italy 391
Cortina d'Ampezzo, Italy 397
Courchevel, France 238
Megève, France 269
La Plagne, France 305
Snowmass, USA 568
La Thuile, Italy 446
Vail, USA 573

RESORTS FOR BEGINNERS
Gentle, snow-sure nursery slopes and easy long runs to progress to
Alpe-d'Huez, France 196
Cervinia, Italy 391
Courchevel, France 238
Flaine, France 254
Montgenèvre, France 291
Passo Tonale, Italy 422
La Plagne, France 305
La Rosière, France 321
Saas-Fee, Switzerland 489
Soldeu, Andorra 80

SPECIALLY FOR FAMILIES
Where you can easily find lodgings surrounded by snow
Les Arcs, France 206
Avoriaz, France 216
Flaine, France 254
Lech Zürs, Austria 129
Les Menuires, France 276
Montchavin, France 305
Mürren, Switzerland 485
La Plagne, France 305
La Rosière, France 321
Saas-Fee, Switzerland 489
Ste-Foy-Tarentaise, France 336
Valmorel, France 370
Vars / Risoul, France 379
Wengen, Switzerland 517

SNOW-SURE BUT SIMPATICO
High-rise slopes, but low-rise, traditional-style buildings
Andermatt, Switzerland 457
Arabba, Italy 429
Argentière, France 223
Ischgl, Austria 114
Lech Zürs, Austria 129
Monterosa Ski, Italy 416
Obergurgl, Austria 144
Saas-Fee, Switzerland 489
Sella Ronda, Italy 429
Val d'Anniviers, Switzerland 501
Zermatt, Switzerland 522

SPECIAL MOUNTAIN RESTAURANTS
Where satisfying lunches can add something extra to a holiday
Alpe-d'Huez, France 196
Cortina d'Ampezzo, Italy 397
Courmayeur, Italy 402
Kitzbühel, Austria 121
Megève, France 269
La Plagne, France 305
Saalbach-Hinterglemm, Austria 152
Sella Ronda, Italy 429
Selva / Val Gardena, Italy 437
Zermatt, Switzerland 522

MODERN CONVENIENCE
Plenty of slope-side lodgings where you can ski from the door
Les Arcs, France 206
Avoriaz, France 216
Courchevel, France 238
Flaine, France 254
Les Menuires, France 276
Obertauern, Austria 150
La Plagne, France 305
La Tania, France 342
Tignes, France 348
Val Thorens, France 372

LIVELY NIGHTLIFE
Where you'll have no difficulty finding somewhere to boogie
Chamonix, France 223
Ischgl, Austria 114
Kitzbühel, Austria 121
Mayrhofen, Austria 138
Méribel, France 282
Saalbach-Hinterglemm, Austria 152
Sauze d'Oulx, Italy 424
Sölden, Austria 162
St Anton, Austria 174
Val d'Isère, France 360
Verbier, Switzerland 505
Zermatt, Switzerland 522

OTHER AMUSEMENTS
Plenty to divert those not skiing or boarding
Bad Gastein, Austria 96
Chamonix, France 223
Cortina d'Ampezzo, Italy 397
Davos, Switzerland 467
Kitzbühel, Austria 121
Megève, France 269
St Moritz, Switzerland 494

AFFORDABLE FUN
Low in our RPI league table with good, reasonably extensive slopes
Ellmau, Austria 106
Maurienne valley, France 265
Mayrhofen, Austria 138
Monterosa Ski, Italy 416
Montgenèvre, France 291
La Rosière, France 321
Sauze d'Oulx, Italy 424
Schladming, Austria 158
Serre-Chevalier, France 327
Söll, Austria 167
La Thuile, Italy 446
Val Cenis Vanoise, France 357
Vars / Risoul, France 379

FINDING A RESORT

The bulk of the book consists of the chapters listed on the facing page, devoted to individual major resorts, plus minor resorts that share the same lift system or pass. Sometimes we devote a chapter to an area not dominated by one resort – then we use the area name (eg Monterosa Ski in Italy, Stubai valley in Austria, Val d'Anniviers in Switzerland).

Chapters are grouped by country: first, the six major European countries (including Germany); then the US and Canada (where resorts are grouped by states or regions); then minor European countries; and finally Japan. Within each group, resorts are ordered alphabetically.

Short cuts to the resorts that might suit you are provided (on the pages preceding this one) by a table of comparative **star ratings** and a series of **shortlists** of resorts with particular merits.

At the back of the book is an **index** to the resort chapters, combined with a **directory** giving basic information on hundreds of other minor resorts. Note that if the resort you are looking up is covered in a chapter devoted to a bigger resort (eg Argentière in the Chamonix chapter), the page reference will be to the start of the chapter, not to the exact page on which the minor resort is described.

There's further guidance on using our information in the chapter 'Choosing your resort', on page 62 – designed to be helpful particularly to people with little or no experience of ski resorts, who may not appreciate how big the differences between one resort and another can be.

READING A RESORT CHAPTER

There are various standard items on the first page of each resort chapter.

Prominently displayed in the left margin is our **Resort Price Index** – explained in outline on the facing page and in detail in the feature chapter on page 27.

Then come our **star ratings**, summarizing our view of the resort, including its suitability for different levels of skill. The more stars, the better. In minor resort chapters we give 10 key ratings; in major resort chapters we give an expanded set of 19 ratings.

Next comes **News** about the resort, if there is any, for the coming season and for last season, and **Key Facts** about the ski area. We now give information on **Lift Passes** in minor resort chapters as well as major resort chapters.

Our **mountain maps** show the resorts' own classification of runs. On some maps we show black diamonds to mark expert terrain without defined runs. We do not distinguish single-diamond terrain from the steeper double diamond.

We include on the map any new lifts that are definitely expected to be in place for the coming season.

MAJOR LIFTS

On our piste maps we use the following symbols to identify **fast lifts**. Slow chairlifts do not get a chair symbol.

 fast chairlift

 gondola

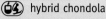 hybrid chondola

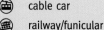 cable car

railway/funicular

THE WORLD'S BEST WINTER SPORTS RESORTS

To find a minor resort, or if you are not sure which country you should be looking under, consult the index/directory at the back of the book, which lists all resorts alphabetically.

Our resort chapters

75

RESORT PRICE INDEX BOXES

Our RPI figures show how prices in each resort compare with the average eurozone resort, taking account of food and drink, lift pass, ski hire and lessons. RPIs around the average figure of 100 are in blue boxes. RPIs of 90 or less get a green box. RPIs of 120 or more get a red box. In our chapter on 'Cutting your costs', on page 27, we explain our price survey in full, and summarize some of the results.

RPI	90
RPI	100
RPI	120

Andorra

Andorra is a tiny, almost entirely mountainous state sandwiched between France and Spain. It built its prosperity on the twin pillars of tax-haven status and low-cost tourism – particularly winter tourism, and particularly in the UK market. Andorra used to be seen primarily as a cheap and cheerful holiday destination, attracting singles and young couples looking for a good time in the duty-free bars and clubs, as well as learning to ski or snowboard. But the place has changed radically over the last 25 years and has tried to move upmarket.

LIFT PASS

Ski Andorra
The Ski Andorra pass covers all Andorran areas and allows skiing at any single one of them each day: €205 for five non-consecutive days

Soldeu, the main resort, is no longer cheap. Our price survey shows it to be more expensive than many high-profile Alpine resorts that have much more appeal. And its popularity has fallen. According to the Crystal Ski Industry Report, a decade ago Andorra's share of the UK ski market was 14%; it is now around half that.

The main resorts – **Soldeu** and **Pas de la Casa** (which share the fairly extensive Grandvalira ski area) and **Arinsal** (linked to **Pal** to form a much more modest area) – are covered in the two chapters that follow this.

The other main ski area is **Arcalis**, tucked away at the head of a long valley with no accommodation at its base. For non-beginners it makes a very worthwhile day trip, particularly from Arinsal and Pal, with which it shares a lift pass. The terrain is varied and scenic, the slopes are usually deserted except at weekends, and the snow is usually the best in Andorra. There is excellent intermediate and beginner terrain, but what marks it out is the expert terrain, including lots of off-piste – see the Arinsal chapter for a little more on this.

The capital, **Andorra la Vella**, is choked by traffic and fumes but worth a visit for its duty-free shopping and the splendid Caldea spa at Escaldes-Engordany, just outside the centre, with a fantastic array of pools, baths and treatments.

TOURIST OFFICES

Ski Andorra
www.skiandorra.ad
Arcalis
www.vallnord.com

VALLNORD TO

← Andorra's resorts lack much charm – Arinsal looks OK in this photo but it's long, narrow and the buildings don't look as good when you're down at street level

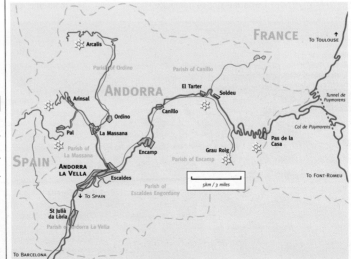

Arinsal

Lively base that suits beginners (thanks to an excellent school), with a cable car link to Pal to keep intermediates amused

£90
RESORT PRICE INDEX

TOP 10 RATINGS

Extent	★
Fast lifts	★★
Queues	★★★
Snow	★★★★
Expert	★
Intermediate	★★
Beginner	★★★★
Charm	★
Convenience	★★★
Scenery	★★★

NEWS

2014/15: There's a new Freestyle pass for the Arinsal park, which covers its lift and access lifts. The Snowbar, a new chill-out area with music, has been built at the Panoramix restaurant. At Pal a new restaurant with great views has been built at Pla de la Cot.

78

- ➕ Lively bars
- ➕ Ski school geared to British needs
- ➕ Linked to Pal and lift pass covers Arcalis (well worth an outing)
- ➕ Pretty, treelined slopes in Pal

- ➖ Arinsal slopes are bleak and very confined (though this does mean children can't stray far)
- ➖ Linear, dour village with no focus
- ➖ Poor bus link to Arcalis

Tour operators used to bring British beginners here in large numbers. Low prices and the Brit-oriented ski school were key factors; but prices are no longer that different from those in more attractive Austrian and Italian resorts.

THE RESORT

Arinsal sits near the head of a steep-sided valley north of Andorra la Vella. Pal has a more open setting in another valley. The two are linked by cable car.

The valley town of La Massana is linked by gondola to Pal's slopes, and makes a better base for those wanting to spend some time at Arcalis (read the Andorra introduction).

Village charm The resort is a long, narrow village of grey, stone-clad buildings. It's no beauty, but the atmosphere is friendly and relaxed.

Convenience The main gondola starts from the village centre and you have to ride it down as well as up; the alternative is a six-pack 1km away at Cota, with a piste to return. There are free buses linking the lift bases (but timekeeping is poor, says a reporter). You can leave kit at the top of the lift.

Scenery Shady valleys and nicely wooded slopes dominate.

THE MOUNTAINS

The slopes are in an open but extremely narrow bowl, facing east. Pal has the most densely wooded slopes in Andorra. Most face east; those down to the link with Arinsal face north. The piste map is very poor, covering distant Arcalis as well as Arinsal and Pal and showing the roads and local hamlets in more detail than the ski areas – nuts! Signposting is good but a 2015 reporter complained that black runs were marked at the top but not after that.

Slopes Arinsal's slopes consist essentially of a single, long, narrow bowl above the top gondola station at Comallempla, served by a network of chairs and drags, including a six-pack. Almost at the top is the cable car link with Pal. Pal's slopes are widely spread around the mountain, with four main lift bases, all reachable by road. The main one, La Caubella, is the

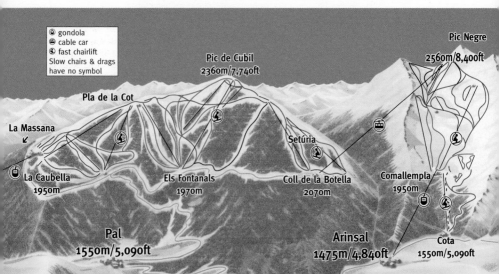

gondola
cable car
fast chairlift
Slow chairs & drags have no symbol

Pic Negre
2560m/8,400ft

Pic de Cubil
2360m/7,740ft

Pla de la Cot

La Massana

Setúria

La Caubella
1950m

Els Fontanals
1970m

Coll de la Botella
2070m

Comallempla
1950m

Pal
1550m/5,090ft

Arinsal
1475m/4,840ft

Cota
1550m/5,090ft

Virtually all Arinsal's local pistes are in the narrow, open bowl above the treeline; near the top of it is the cable car link to Pal →

KEY FACTS

Resort	1475m
	4,840ft
Slopes	1550-2560m
	5,090-8,400ft
Lifts	30
Pistes	63km
	39 miles

LIFT PASSES

Prices in €

Age	6-day
under 16	137
16 to 64	191
65 plus	90

Free Under 6, 70 plus
Beginner Limited pass €15 a day
Note Covers Pal-Arinsal and Arcalis

Alternative pass
The Ski Andorra pass covers all Andorran areas and allows skiing at any single one of them each day; €205 for five non-consecutive days

arrival point of the gondola up from La Massana.

Fast lifts Access is by gondola or fast chairlift. Other fast chairs exist, but there are still many slow lifts too.

Queues Reporters note few problems. But you may meet queues to ride the gondola down, and for the nursery moving carpets. The cable car link with Pal can be closed by high winds.

Terrain parks Arinsal's big freestyle area impressed a 2015 reporter ('excellent'); it has its own lift, 'a lovely selection' of rails and jumps, a 'fun' snowcross and a beginner zone 'ideal for a first foray into park riding'. Last season a special pass for the park and its lifts cost 30 euros.

Snow reliability With most runs above 1950m, the easterly orientation and a decent amount of snowmaking, snow is relatively assured even in poor snow years. Grooming is good.

Experts It's not a great area for experts, but there is good tree skiing in Pal. Arcalis is the best area for off-piste. It has two 'freeride exclusive' lifts and some red dotted runs marked (but not explained) on the map.

Intermediates Arinsal offers a fair range of difficulty, but competent intermediates will want to explore the much more interesting, varied and extensive Pal slopes, and perhaps make a day trip or two to Arcalis.

Beginners Around half the guests here are beginners. A special pass is available (15 euros per day), though we guess most people will book ski rental/pass/tuition packs through their tour operators. The nursery slopes are wide, gentle and set apart from the main runs and a reporter with a beginner girlfriend thought they were great. But they can get crowded. There are longer easy runs to progress to.

Snowboarding It's a fine place to learn, but over half the lifts are drags and some of them are vicious. There are some flat sections in Pal.

Cross-country There isn't any.

Mountain restaurants These are mainly uninspiring self-service snackeries, and crowded. The Igloo does 'good hearty fare from a varied menu'.

Schools and guides The school is crucial to the resort's appeal; over half the instructors are native English speakers. We've had good reports.

Families There are themed ski kindergartens for four- to eight-year-olds and nurseries for children aged one to four at both Pal and Arinsal.

Arinsal

79

STAYING THERE

Hotels The Princesa Parc is a big, glossy 4-star place near the gondola – 'great value, excellent facilities'; swanky spa and a bowling alley. Rooms in the hotel Arinsal are not large, but the hotel is ideally placed and has a pleasant bar. The 3-star Crest is at the bottom of the run to Cota, handy for the fast chair up to the slopes. The Husa Xalet Verdú is a smooth little 3-star. A 2015 reporter enjoyed the British-run Palarine in Erts, between Arinsal and La Massana ('unreliable bus service but nice, good value, themed buffets – Italian, Japanese/Chinese, Indian').

Apartments There is a reasonable choice of places.

Eating out The Sidreria Pub Herri serves traditional Basque food. Cisco's is a Tex-Mex place in a lovely wood-and-stone building. The Surf disco-pub has been recommended for its steaks.

Après-ski Arinsal has plenty of lively bars 'from full-on 18–30 drink fests to great family places'. The hotel Arinsal has good-value pints. The Derby Irish pub has a 'relaxed atmosphere, a good selection of drinks, reasonable prices and a sun trap beer garden'. For a wilder time try El Cau or Surf.

Off the slopes Activities include dog sledding, snowmobiling, snowshoeing, tobogganing, snow bikes, helicopter rides and paragliding. Andorra la Vella is half an hour away by taxi or infrequent bus. The Caldea Spa there was a 'highlight' for a 2015 reporter.

SNOWPIX.COM / CHRIS GILL

Soldeu

Our favourite place to stay in Andorra: not an attractive village, but centrally placed in the impressive Grandvalira ski area

£115
RESORT PRICE INDEX

RATINGS

The mountains

Extent	★★★
Fast lifts	★★
Queues	★★★
Terrain p'ks	★★★★
Snow	★★★
Expert	★★
Intermediate	★★★★
Beginner	★★★★
Boarder	★★★★
X-country	★
Restaurants	★★
Schools	★★★★★
Families	★★

The resort

Charm	★
Convenience	★★★
Scenery	★★★
Eating out	★★★
Après-ski	★★★★
Off-slope	★

NEWS

2014/15: More snowmaking was added and several slopes were remodelled. There is now night skiing twice a week at Pas de la Casa. Mon(t) Magic, a themed children's park, opened at El Forn.

KEY FACTS

Resort	1800m
	5,910ft

Grandvalira (Soldeu/El Tarter/Pas/Grau Roig)

Slopes	1710-2560m
	5,610-8,400ft
Lifts	64
Pistes	210km
	130 miles

➕ Rivals some serious Alpine resorts in terms of size

➕ Excellent beginner and early intermediate terrain

➕ Ski school has excellent British-run section for English-speaking visitors

➖ Village is spread along a busy through-road, lacking atmosphere

➖ Slopes can get very crowded

➖ Expensive lift pass, and beginners are charged the full cost

➖ Not much to do off the slopes

If we were planning a holiday in Andorra, it would be in Soldeu (or the isolated hotel at Grau Roig, up the road). It is best placed to explore the extensive Grandvalira area. But the village is a difficult place to like, and beginners be warned: you are forced to buy one of Europe's priciest passes.

THE RESORT

Soldeu is set on a steep hillside facing the ski area across the valley. It is on the busy road that runs down the valley from France to Andorra la Vella and on to Spain. The Grandvalira ski area is shared with several alternative bases. Chief among them is Pas de la Casa, near the French border; El Tarter, a few miles down the valley from Soldeu, also has both lifts and return pistes. Further down still, Canillo and Encamp have gondolas but no pistes. Outings to other resorts in Andorra are possible – Arcalis in particular is worth the trip, but it's easiest by car. The Ski Andorra pass covers them all.

VILLAGE CHARM ★
An urban ribbon
The village is an ever-growing ribbon of modern hotels, apartments and bars, with the occasional shop; the buildings have traditional stone cladding and mostly chalet-style roofs. Sounds OK, but it isn't; this is not a place to wander about at teatime – there is no focus or atmosphere, and traffic on the through-road can be heavy and sometimes fast.

CONVENIENCE ★★★
Over the river
A steep hillside leads down from the village to the river, and the slopes are on the opposite side. A gondola or a six-pack takes you to the heart of the slopes at Espiolets, and a wide bridge across the river forms the end of the piste home, with elevators to take you up to street level. There are ski lockers at the bottom and top of the gondola. Along the road down to El Tarter,

hotels and apartments are sold by tour operators under the Soldeu banner – so check where your proposed accommodation is if you want to avoid long walks or lots of bus rides. There is a valley bus running fairly frequently.

SCENERY ★★★
Unremarkable
Soldeu sits in a long, quite attractively wooded valley, and from the slopes there are wide mountain views, but they don't include notable drama.

THE MOUNTAINS

Soldeu's main local slopes are on open mountainsides; there are runs in the woods back to Soldeu and El Tarter, but they can be challenging, especially when conditions are not particularly good. Reporters praise signposting, but classification of the runs often overstates difficulty. The piste map is OK.

EXTENT OF THE SLOPES ★★★
Pleasantly varied but crowded
The resort claims 210km of pistes, but the Schrahe report (read our feature on piste extent) suggests that the total is around 50km less.

The village gondola rises over wooded, north-facing slopes to **Espiolets**, a broad shelf that is virtually a mini-resort – the ski school is based here, and there are extensive nursery slopes. From Espiolets, a gentle run to the east takes you to an area of long, easy runs served by a six-pack. Beyond that is an extensive area of more varied slopes that links with the Pas de la Casa area. Going west from

LIFT PASSES

Prices in €

Age	6-day
under 12	164
12 to 17	218
18 to 64	242
65 plus	162

Free Under 6, 70 plus

Beginner Pass €31 per day in Canillo, El Tarter, Grau Roig and Pas de la Casa sectors

Notes Covers all lifts in Soldeu, El Tarter, Canillo, Grau Roig and Pas de la Casa; pedestrian and half-day passes available

Alternative pass
The Ski Andorra pass covers all Andorran areas and allows skiing at any single one of them each day; €205 for five non-consecutive days

GRANDVALIRA TO

Most of the slopes in both Soldeu and Pas de la Casa are above the treeline, good when it's sunny but not when it's snowing
↓

Espiolets takes you to the open bowl of **Riba Escorxada** and the arrival point of the gondola up from El Tarter. From here, another six-pack serves sunny slopes on Tosa dels Espiolets, and a fourth goes to the high point of Tosa de la Llosada and the link with **El Forn** above Canillo.

FAST LIFTS ★★☆☆☆
Fine access but ...
Most of Grandvalira's key lifts are high-speed chairs or gondolas, but there are a lot of slow lifts too.

QUEUES ★★★☆☆
Some bottlenecks
The lift system generally copes. There can be morning queues for the gondola, but the next-door chair offers an alternative. Up the mountain, the chairlifts in both directions out of Grau Roig (pronounced 'Rosh') are the main bottleneck; the quad at Cubil and access to Tosa Espiolets can build queues. You may find crowds on some blue slopes (including lots of school classes snaking along) – the reds and blacks are much quieter.

TERRAIN PARKS ★★★★☆
There are three
The main park – Snowpark El Tarter – above Riba Escorxada has a good reputation. Features normally include a triple line of kickers, huge gap jump, jib and giant airbag. There's a great selection of rails, including a big rainbow rail and wave-box and a wall ride. For beginners there are three

small jumps, a 5m medium jump and a couple of fun boxes. A half-pipe is built when conditions permit. A draglift serves the park, and a fast chair nearby takes you slightly higher up.

Snowpark Xavi at Grau Roig is for beginners and intermediates and has kickers, jibs, rails and boxes.

The Sunset Park Peretol, above Bordes d'Envalira, caters for all levels. It has an intriguing 'street' zone that resembles a village square, they say. It is floodlit in the evenings, with music.

A park-only day pass is available.

SNOW RELIABILITY ★★★☆☆
Much better than people expect
Despite its name (Soldeu means Sun God) the slopes generally enjoy reliable snow. Most slopes are north-facing, with a good natural snow record; there's extensive snowmaking, and excellent grooming helps maintain good snow.

FOR EXPERTS ★★☆☆☆
Hope for good snow off-piste
It's a limited area for experts – on-piste, at least. The Avet black run going directly down to Soldeu deserves its grading but most of the other blacks do not. The groomed blacks on Tosa dels Espiolets, for example, are indistinguishable from the adjacent (and more direct) red and blue. Two black pistes are now marked as mogul runs on the map.

But there is plenty of off-piste potential and off-piste routes are marked on the piste map in the bowl

above Riba Escorxada and above El Forn – these are shown dotted on our map. And the ungroomed, liftless bowl between Riba Escorxada and El Forn is served by a snowcat tow. The off-piste remains untouched for days because most visitors are beginners and early intermediates. There's no explanation on the piste map of whether off-piste routes are avalanche controlled, marked or patrolled. Heli-skiing is available too.

FOR INTERMEDIATES ★★★★
Lots to explore
There is plenty to amuse intermediates. The area east of Espiolets is splendid for building confidence, and those already confident will be able to explore the whole mountain. Riba Escorxada is a fine section for mixed-ability groups.

The Canillo/El Forn sector has an easy, little-used blue run along the ridge with excellent views all the way to Pal and Arinsal and an easy black in the valley. Many of the blues and reds have short steeper sections, preceded by a 'slow' sign and netting in the middle of the piste to slow you down.

FOR BEGINNERS ★★★★
Good, but not ideal
In some respects this is an excellent place to start, particularly because of the school. But it's not ideal: you have to go up the mountain to the nursery slopes, which is not only inconvenient but also expensive. There is no special beginner pass here (unlike other base villages in the area). If you buy a ski pack through your tour operator, you may not care, of course.

Soldeu's Espiolets nursery area is vast, and there's a smaller area at Riba Escorxada, above El Tarter – each with a moving carpet. They are relatively snow-sure, and there are numerous easy pistes to move on to (though the crowds can be off-putting).

The runs to resort level can be quite challenging because of crowds and snow conditions. Near-beginners are often better off riding a lift down.

FOR BOARDERS ★★★★
Pick of the Pyrenees
Soldeu has become the home of snowboarding in the Pyrenees. This is a perfect place for beginners to learn on wide, gentle slopes that are served mainly by chairs, not drags. Just be wary of the plentiful flat spots. For the

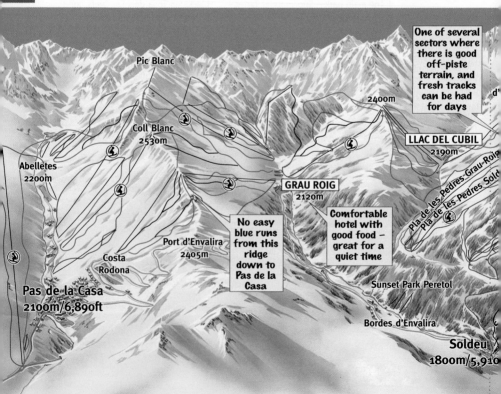

One of several sectors where there is good off-piste terrain, and fresh tracks can be had for days

Pic Blanc

LLAC DEL CUBIL
2190m

Coll Blanc
2530m

Abelletes
2200m

2400m

GRAU ROIG
2120m

Pla de les Pedres-Grau-Roig
Pla de les Pedres Sold

Comfortable hotel with good food – great for a quiet time

No easy blue runs from this ridge down to Pas de la Casa

Port d'Envalira
2405m

Costa Rodona

Sunset Park Peretol

Pas de la Casa
2100m/6,890ft

Bordes d'Envalira

Soldeu
1800m/5,910

more advanced, Soldeu offers some good off-piste and the best terrain parks in the Pyrenees.

Backcountry enthusiasts should also visit Arcalis (see Andorra introduction on page 76), which has the steepest terrain, and Pal (see Arinsal chapter on page 78), for the tree runs.

FOR CROSS-COUNTRY ★★★★★
Head for Grau Roig
The nearest loops are at Grau Roig (read the Pas de la Casa section), reachable by bus.

MOUNTAIN RESTAURANTS ★★★★★
Not a highlight
Restaurants are marked but not named on the piste map. Reports are generally lukewarm. But the table-service section of Arosseria Pi de Migdia at the top of the El Tarter gondola has been recommended. Not far away, the Riba Escorxada restaurant includes a trattoria-pizzeria with a neat little terrace – 'good-quality Italian food' says a 2015 visitor. At Espiolets, the Gall de Bosc (steakhouse) has table-service. But the best places are over towards Pas de la Casa – read that section.

SCHOOLS AND GUIDES ★★★★★
One of the best for Brits
The school is well set up to deal with Brits, with a dedicated team of mostly native English-speaking instructors led by an Englishman (named, very appropriately for a ski instructor, Gordon Standeven).

Reporters are almost all extremely positive and 2015 visitors said: 'standard of tuition was excellent for us complete beginners', 'fantastic, best I have come across in Europe'. It offers freeride and freestyle lessons as well as normal lessons.

FOR FAMILIES ★★★★★
Unconvincing
Soldeu doesn't strike us as a great place for families, with its busy through-road and remote nursery slopes. Whether skiing or not, children are looked after at the mid-mountain stations. There are nurseries and snow gardens at various points, and kids' circuits with themed runs.

A new kids' area was created last year at a cost of over a million euros: Mon(t) Magic is a themed kids' park at El Forn.

Soldeu

83

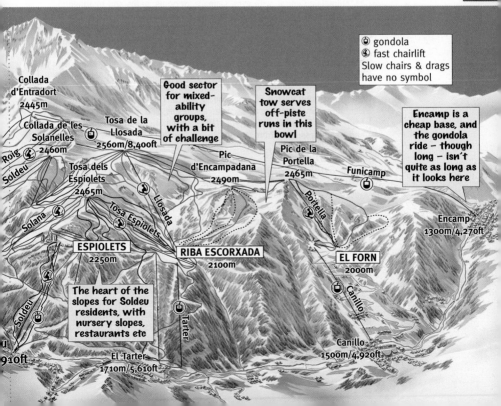

gondola
fast chairlift
Slow chairs & drags have no symbol

Collada d'Entradort 2445m

Collada de les Solanelles 2460m

Roig

Soldeu

Good sector for mixed-ability groups, with a bit of challenge

Snowcat tow serves off-piste runs in this bowl

Encamp is a cheap base, and the gondola ride – though long – isn't quite as long as it looks here

Tosa de la Llosada 2560m/8,400ft

Tosa dels Espiolets 2465m

Pic d'Encampadana 2490m

Pic de la Portella 2465m

Funicamp

Solana

Tosa Espiolets

Llosada

Portella

Encamp 1300m/4,270ft

ESPIOLETS 2250m

RIBA ESCORXADA 2100m

EL FORN 2000m

Soldeu

The heart of the slopes for Soldeu residents, with nursery slopes, restaurants etc

Tarter

Canillo

Canillo 1500m/4,920ft

910ft

El Tarter 1710m/5,610ft

↑ Don't worry: most of Grandvalira's slopes are not this steep. Sadly, they are not so deserted either
GRANDVALIRA TO

STAYING THERE

Hotels Beware hotels sold under the Soldeu name that are actually some way out of town.

*****Sport Hotel Hermitage At the foot of the slopes; all bedrooms are suites with mountain views. A huge spa is part of the hotel.

****Euro Esquí On road to El Tarter but there is a shuttle. 'Large rooms, nice pool/spa, adequate food.'

****Himàlaia Central, with gym, sauna, steam and hot tub. 'Spacious rooms, pleasant bar.'

****Piolets Park Beside the gondola, with a pool and spa.

****Sport Over the road from the other two Sports. Spa. Lively, comfortable bar and disco-bar.

****Sport Hotel Village Right by the Hermitage. Stylish public areas. Spa.

**Bruxelles Tipped for its helpful staff and cleanliness; 50m from the lift.

EATING OUT ★★★☆☆
Some atmospheric places

Most of Soldeu's restaurants are hotel-based. But we've enjoyed meals in two atmospheric old restored buildings: Fat Albert's (steaks, fish, burgers) and Borda del Rector (Andorran cuisine), nearer to El Tarter than Soldeu. A 2015 reporter recommends the family-run Merlot for its 'good-value mix of British and French food and ambience'.

APRES-SKI ★★★★☆
No shortage of live music

Lots of bars have regular or occasional live music or DJs – reader favourites include the Aspen, Fat Albert's and the Villager (with Elvis nights too).

OFF THE SLOPES ★☆☆☆☆
Head downhill

Soldeu has lots of sporting activities, including snowmobiling and dog sledding, but is otherwise not great for non-skiers. The Sport Hotel Hermitage (pricey) and Piolets Park (cheaper) both have excellent spas. Down in Canillo is the Palau de Gel (see below). Andorra la Vella, the capital of Andorra, has good shopping and the Caldea spa (an amazing array of pools, baths and treatments).

LINKED RESORT – 1710m
EL TARTER

El Tarter is rather sprawling, with no real centre, and is quiet at night. But it's otherwise a good base for the area. There are two blue runs to the resort, and a black that is an FIS (International Ski Federation)-approved downhill race course.

LINKED RESORT – 1500m
CANILLO

This acceptably pleasant spot has no runs to valley level, but has a gondola up to El Forn. The impressive Palau de Gel has lots of diversions – an Olympic ice rink plus pool, gym, sports hall etc.

LINKED RESORT – 1300m
ENCAMP

Encamp is a traffic-choked town with a long gondola to Cortals, one of the high points of the Soldeu slopes, where there is a beginner area, and onward pistes to Soldeu. There is no return piste.

Pas de la Casa 2100m

- ➕ Some conveniently placed hotels
- ➕ Andorra's liveliest nightlife
- ➕ Attractive hotel at Grau Roig
- ➖ Village an eyesore and traffic-choked
- ➖ Weekend crowds from France
- ➖ Few trees for poor-weather days

Pas has the reputation as Andorra's wildest party resort, and we don't doubt it. Having driven through it and skied down to it, we are quite happy to stay over the hill in Soldeu – or, for doorstep access to the Grandvalira slopes, at secluded Grau Roig. So are you, it seems: reports are rarely sighted.

Village charm Pas is a sizeable collection of dreary concrete-box-style apartment blocks and hotels, a product of the late 1960s and early 1970s. The central area at the base of the slopes is traffic-free, but elsewhere traffic and fumes are intrusive. By contrast, the mini-resort of Grau Roig over the ridge from Pas has an isolated hotel in an attractively wooded setting.

Convenience Most accommodation is conveniently placed near the lift base and slopes. There are plenty of shops and bars, as well as a sports centre.

Scenery Pas has a bleak position near the top of a high mountain pass, but there are fine views from the ridges.

THE MOUNTAIN

Slopes The slopes above Pas are all open, and vulnerable to bad weather. But there is some attractively wooded terrain over the ridge in the Grau Roig valley. From there a single lift goes on further west to the rest of the Grandvalira ski area. In the opposite direction out of Pas, a six-pack serving two runs heads towards another ridge and the French border. There is now night skiing twice a week.

Fast lifts Fast chairs exist, but they are outnumbered by slow ones and drags.

Queues Queues are rarely serious during the week, except at key bottlenecks. But at weekends and French school holidays some can develop, especially at Grau Roig.

Terrain parks There's a snowcross on the Pas side, and a park above Grau Roig.

Snow reliability The combination of height and lots of snowmaking means good snow reliability, but we've generally found snow quality to be better in the Soldeu sector.

Experts There are few challenges on-piste, but there seem to be plenty of off-piste slopes inviting exploration – above Grau Roig, in particular.

Intermediates The local slopes suit confident intermediates best – especially those over the ridge, above Grau Roig; more timid intermediates would be better off based in Soldeu.

Beginners There are beginner slopes in Pas and Grau Roig. The Pas area is a short but inconvenient bus ride out of town. Progression to longer runs is easier in the Grau Roig sector.

Snowboarding Boarding is popular with the young crowd that the resort attracts. Drags are usually avoidable.

Cross-country There are 8km of loops near Grau Roig.

Mountain restaurants The Rifugi dels Llacs de Pessons above Grau Roig at the head of the bowl is our favourite: a cosy, beamed table-service place with good local food; endorsed by a 2015 reporter ('absolutely superb'). The Grau Roig hotel is another good option.

Schools and guides The ski school has a high reputation, but a past reporter complained of big classes.

Families There are ski kindergartens at Pas and Grau Roig, and a non-ski one at the latter for one- to four-year-olds.

STAYING THERE

Hotels The Himàlaia-Pas is in a good position, with a pool and sauna. But the Grau Roig hotel is in a league of its own; comfortable and smart, with a spa.

Apartments Those in the Frontera Blanca are simple, but in pole position at the foot of the slopes.

Eating out It's not a resort for gourmets – but there is a wide enough choice of places to eat. Local tips include Cal Padrí (Catalan food) and KSB (Kamikaze Surf Bar) – steakhouse).

Après-ski Après-ski can be very lively, at least at peak holiday times. Popular places include Paddy's Irish Bar and the Underground.

Off the slopes You can go snowmobiling, snowshoeing, take a helicopter ride, visit the leisure centre, and take a trip to Andorra la Vella for stylish shopping and the impressive Caldea spa.

GETTING THERE

Air Toulouse 175km/110 miles (2hr30)

Rail L'Hospitalet-Près-L'Andorre (20km/ 13 miles); buses and taxis to Soldeu

TOURIST OFFICE

www.grandvalira.com

WHERE SNOW
IS AT HOME!

IT'S SNOWTIME IN OBERTAUERN FROM LATE NOVEMBER TO EARLY MAY!
- Get the fantastic holiday feeling in one of the best skiing resorts of the Alps with a snow guarantee.
- Enjoy perfect winter sports conditions in a romantic atmosphere.
- Ski in – ski out: straight from your hotel onto the slope.

OBERTAUERN AT A GLANCE:
100 km of slopes, 26 cable cars and lifts, night skiing, snowkiting school, 5 skiing and snowboarding schools, fun park for snowboarders.

ATTRACTIVE PACKAGE PERIODS:
- 18.11. – 19.12.2015: Opening Weeks
- 09.01. – 30.01.2016: Powder Snow Weeks
- 02.04. – 01.05.2016: Sun & Fun Weeks

Tourismusverband Obertauern I Pionierstraße 1
A-5562 Obertauern I tel. +43(0)6456 / 7252 I info@obertauern.com

OBERTAUERN
WWW.OBERTAUERN.COM

Austria

Austria's holiday recipe is quite distinctive. It doesn't suit everybody, but for many holidaymakers nothing else will do; in particular, French resorts will not do. Austria is the land of cute little valley villages clustered around onion-domed churches – there are no monstrous modern apartment blocks here. It's the land of prettily wooded mountains, reassuring to beginners and timid intermediates in a way that bleak snowfields and craggy peaks will never be. It's the land of friendly, welcoming people who speak good English. And it's the land of jolly, alcohol-fuelled après-ski action – in many resorts starting in mid-afternoon with dancing in mountain restaurants, and going on as long as you have the legs for it.

Back in the 1980s, Austria dominated the British skiing market. But gradually the powerful allure of the high, snow-sure French mega-resorts began to exert itself. By 1995 France had taken the lead, and it has kept it ever since. The pendulum is now swinging back: last year's Crystal Ski Industry Report showed that Austria's market share had risen over the last decade or so from 20% to 28%. But France was still well ahead, at around 33%.

There are three key factors in the revival: lift systems – these days, the most efficient lift systems in Europe are not in France but in Austria; snowmaking, which is now so widespread that you can expect reliable snow-cover even at the low altitudes typical of Austrian villages; and low on-the-spot prices. As our price survey shows, Austrian resorts are generally cheaper than the big French resorts that Brits tend to flock to – especially for eating and drinking.

Being the land of cute valley villages and friendly wooded mountains does have a downside: resorts that conform to this pattern are at low altitude, and as a result don't offer reliably good natural snow. After a few seasons of bumper snowfalls in Austria, the last two seasons were poor (especially 2013/14, when resorts like Kitzbühel and Söll received 40% less than their normal amount of snow). But it is in years like the last two that snowmaking comes into its own. Most low resorts have radically improved their snowmaking in the last 20 years. So despite the snow droughts, readers repeatedly told us they had a good time on piste (but not off): 'almost every run was open' was a typical comment about pistes in the low SkiWelt area. Of course, snow isn't simply a matter of covering the slopes: quality matters too, and it's still the case that low altitude tends to go hand in hand with slushy snow in the middle of the day and icy snow at the start and end of the day. But piste grooming has improved things greatly over the years too, and again this was reflected in comments from reporters such as: 'They did a brilliant job in difficult conditions,' said a Kitzbühel visitor.

There are some resorts that don't conform to the Austrian pattern, of course, including some excellent high-altitude ski areas – notably Obergurgl, Ischgl and Obertauern. In 2014, we had a fab morning in Ischgl on their last day of the season, 4 May, when there was no shortage of snow and even some fresh powder. There are also some excellent glacier areas in Austria, including what we reckon are the world's best, at Hintertux and in the Stubai valley.

Western Austria also has areas that get huge amounts of snow – the Lech/Zürs/Warth ski area is the snowiest corner of the Alps (the three resorts have been linked by gondola since 2013/14).

THE WORLD'S BEST LIFT SYSTEMS

The improvement in Austrian lift systems over the years comes as a surprise to many people. When we invented our 'fast lifts' rating a few years back, we certainly got some surprises. The European resorts with the highest proportions of fast lifts in their networks are Saalbach-Hinterglemm and Ischgl, both in Austria. Kitzbühel and Obergurgl also get five stars and lots of others get four stars.

SKI ROUTE CONFUSION

In many resorts you have to deal with chaotic handling of the concept of 'ski routes'. If a resort's piste map explains what a ski route is (and many don't), it often says a ski route is a run that is marked and avalanche controlled but not groomed or patrolled. Officially, we are told, the rule throughout Austria is that a ski route is 'marked, protected against avalanche hazards and can be groomed and patrolled'. In practice, many routes are groomed; they may or may not be patrolled. This is madness. If such a run is groomed *and* patrolled, it is a piste, and should be identified as such so that people skiing solo can confidently go down it. If it is groomed *but not* patrolled, it opens up the insane possibility that people skiing solo might descend it by mistake.

THE PARTY STARTS EARLY

These days, one of the things that annoys us most about Austrian skiing is the strange business of opening hours or, strictly speaking, closing hours. As spring approaches, lift closing times in the rest of the Alps, even for some high-altitude cable cars, drift towards 5pm or even later. In most Austrian resorts, basically the lifts shut at around 4pm, even if there are three hours of daylight remaining. Nuts.

You're welcome to stay on the mountain drinking, and descend at leisure, and it has crossed our minds that the lift companies may be in the pay of the breweries. Instead of skiing on, people pack into mountain restaurants well before the end of the day and gyrate in their ski boots on the dance floor, on the tables, on the bar, on the roof beams. There are open-air ice bars, umbrella bars and transparent 'igloo' bars in which to shelter from bad weather. Huge quantities of beer and schnapps are drunk, often to the accompaniment of German drinking songs or loud Europop music. In many resorts the bands don't stop playing until after darkness falls, when the happy punters slide off in the general direction of the village to find another watering hole.

After dinner (for those who pause for dinner, that is) the drinking and dancing start again and carry on in town in bars and clubs until the early hours.

Of course, not all resorts conform to this image. 'Exclusive' Lech and Zürs, for example, are full of rich, cool, 'beautiful' people enjoying the comfort of 4- or 5-star hotels. And villages such as Westendorf and Obergurgl are pretty, quiet, family resorts. But lots of big-name places with the best and most extensive slopes are also big party towns – notably St Anton, Saalbach-Hinterglemm, Ischgl and Sölden. *... continued on page 92*

TVB SAALBACH-HINTERGLEMM / DIETMAR SOCHOR

← You don't see many Austrian villages without an onion-domed church. This is Saalbach's

Introduction

89

... continued on page 92

GETTING AROUND THE AUSTRIAN ALPS

Austria presents few problems for the car-borne visitor, because practically all the resorts are valley villages, which involve neither steep, winding approach roads nor high-altitude passes.

The motorway along the Inn valley runs from Kufstein via Innsbruck to Landeck and, with one or two breaks, extends to the Arlberg pass and on to Switzerland. This key artery is relatively reliable except in exceptionally bad weather – the altitude is low, and the road is a vital link that is kept open in virtually all conditions.

The Arlberg – which divides the Tirol from Vorarlberg, but which is also the watershed between Austria and Switzerland – is one of the few areas where

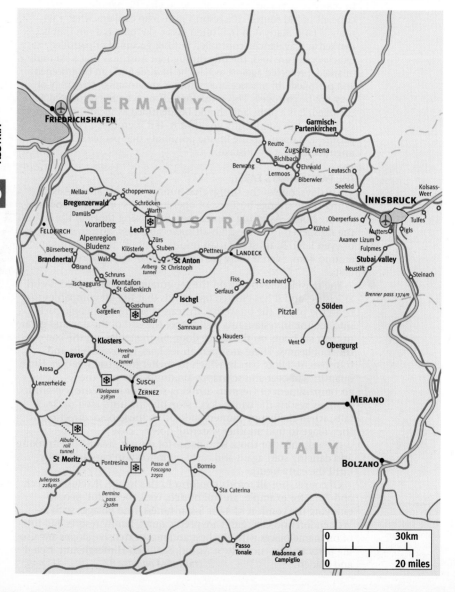

driving plans are likely to be seriously affected by snow. The east–west Arlberg pass itself has a long tunnel underneath it; this isn't cheap, and you may want to take the pass road when it's clear, through Stuben, St Christoph and St Anton. The Flexen pass road to Zürs and Lech branches off northwards, just to the west of the Arlberg summit; this is often closed by avalanche risk (sometimes for days on end) even when the Arlberg pass is open.

All cars must display a motorway toll sticker, available at petrol stations, post offices and newsagents. There's a 10-day one for 8.70 euros and a two-month one for 25.30 euros.

From 1 November to 15 April winter tyres must be fitted. Be aware that cars hired in Germany or Italy might not meet this requirement.

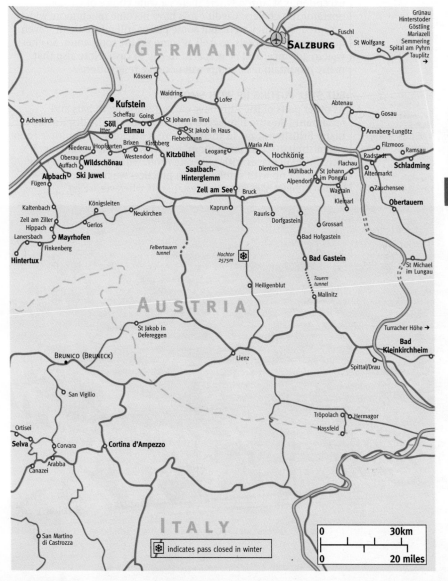

indicates pass closed in winter

✱ **Want the next edition free?**

Send us a useful report on your holiday, and you could be among those who win one of 100 free copies. Then you might become one of our 'resort observers', and get free lift passes.

Find out more at:

www.wheretoskiandsnowboard.com

Après-ski is not limited to drinking and dancing. There are lots of floodlit toboggan runs, and UK tour operator reps organize folklore, bowling, fondue, karaoke and other evenings.

GOOD-VALUE, HIGH-QUALITY LODGING

One thing that all Austrian resorts have in common is reliably comfortable accommodation – whether it's in 4- or 5-star hotels with pools, saunas and spas or in great-value, family-run guest houses, of which Austria has thousands. Catered chalets and self-catering apartments are in general much less widely available than in French resorts; a notable exception is St Anton where there's a wide choice of UK tour operator run chalets. Credit cards have become much more widely accepted than they were. But some places still refuse them – even quite upmarket hotels, as well as some ski lift companies. So check well in advance, and be prepared to pay in cash. Note also that many mountain restaurants will not take reservations.

BUT STILL PUTTING UP WITH SMOKING

As other parts of the Alps have cut out smoking in bars and restaurants, Austria has lagged behind, much to the displeasure of many British visitors. In theory, there is progress. In 'multiple room establishments' the 'main room' now has to be non-smoking. It's only in small places with only one room where you should now have to put up with smoke. But in practice, we find annoying smoke in most bars and some restaurants wherever we go.

TVB KITZBÜHEL / MICHAEL WERLBERGER

If Austria's snow was always this fresh and powdery, there would be few reasons to go elsewhere. This is Kitzbühel ↓

Alpbachtal-Wildschönau – Ski Juwel

This worthwhile new ski area brings together two small areas with a tradition of attracting British visitors

£90
RESORT PRICE INDEX

TOP 10 RATINGS

Extent	★★★
Fast lifts	★★★★
Queues	★★★★
Snow	★★
Expert	★★
Intermediate	★★★
Beginner	★★★
Charm	★★★★
Convenience	★★★
Scenery	★★★

NEWS

2015/16: Family weeks will be offered, with free lift passes for under 15s.

2014/15: The new six-person Gmahbahn chair opened on Wiedersbergerhorn, starting much lower than the lift it replaced. Snowmaking was improved.

KEY FACTS

Alpbach	1000m
	3,280ft

Ski Juwel	
Slopes	670-2025m
	2,200-6,640ft
Lifts	47
Pistes	128km
	80 miles

- ✚ Charming, traditional, relaxed villages, good for families
- ✚ Good intermediate terrain, not without challenges
- ▬ A lot of bus riding if you choose to stay in cute central Alpbach
- ▬ Long easy runs for progression are few, and not easily reached

Alpbach is an old British favourite – it even has a British ski club. The Wildschönau area is best known in Britain for the tiny resort of Niederau, although its major resort in skiing terms is Auffach. A two-stage gondola is all it took in 2012 to link Alpbach and Auffach. Reith and Oberau, like Niederau, aren't linked to the other resorts; we cover all three at the end of the chapter.

ALPBACH & AUFFACH

These resorts are linked by a two-stage gondola from Inneralpbach, at the base of the Alpbach slopes, to the top of the Auffach slopes. Together they form a fair-sized area. They are also part of the Kitzbüheler Alpen All Star pass area, including the SkiWelt (Söll, Ellmau etc) and Kitzbühel – a great base for day tripping by car.

Village charm Alpbach is a notably pretty, captivating place; hotels and guest houses in traditional woody, chalet style crowd around the church. Auffach is more diffuse, but still a pleasantly rustic, traditional place.

Convenience Inneralpbach, once a backwater hamlet, is now the obvious place to stay, with gondolas to the top of both mountains. From the more remote bits of Inneralpbach you get to the main lifts by riding a drag and skiing down. Staying in central Alpbach, you take a free shuttle-bus to and from the lifts at Inneralpbach or Achenwirt. Auffach is centred on its gondola, but it spreads quite widely, and of course it's not very handy for the Alpbach slopes. Ski-buses link the Wildschönau resorts.

Scenery The pretty valleys and low, partly wooded ridges are picture-postcard Tirol.

THE MOUNTAINS

Throughout the area, the upper slopes are open, the lower slopes wooded.

Slopes From Inneralpbach, a two-stage gondola takes you up to open, north-east-facing slopes on the pointy Wiedersbergerhorn, served by short chairs and drags. Longer runs go down into trees towards the mid and bottom

93

ALPACH SEENLAND TOURISM

Alpbach's rustic traditional style has been carefully preserved →

LIFT PASSES

Ski Juwel

Prices in €

Age	6-day
Under 16	120
16 to 18	174
19 plus	217
Free Under 6	

Note Covers Alpbach, Auffach, Kramsach, Niederau, Oberau and Reith

Alternative pass
Kitzbüheler Alpen All Star pass

stations of a second gondola, rising from Achenwirt – the usual starting point for those staying in downtown Alpbach. There is a red run back to Inneralpbach. This is also the start of the new linking gondola going in two stages to Schatzberg, the top of the Auffach slopes. There is a red run back to the mid-station of this gondola, but no piste back to Inneralpbach.

The pre-existing Auffach slopes follow much the same pattern as the Alpbach ones, but with better lifts.

Fast lifts The access lifts are all gondolas. Auffach has two six-packs serving most of its upper slopes. Alpbach gains one this year, but still has several slow lifts.

Queues The system has its weaknesses, but queues for the gondolas are confined to peak hours at peak times of the season.

Terrain parks There are parks and pipes on both mountains.

Snow reliability These resorts cannot claim great snow reliability; but the slopes all face somewhere between north and east, and the altitudes are not the lowest in the Tirol. There is extensive snowmaking.

Experts The reds and the blacks (often groomed) are not without challenge, and there are runs of 1000m vertical on both mountains when snow is good. There are one or two ski routes, and more adventurous routes including the Gern run from Schatzberg down a deserted valley to the road a little way from Auffach. The schools take the top classes off-piste.

Intermediates There is plenty of fine red-run terrain; but near-beginners wanting to build their confidence are not well catered for at Alpbach, and not catered for at all at Auffach.

Beginners Alpbach beginners love the sunny nursery slopes beside the village. Inneralpbach has a good slope at valley level, too. But we're told most people staying in Alpbach start up the mountain, where at least you have longer blues to move on to. In Auffach, beginners are confined to the nursery slopes at mid-mountain.

Snowboarding There's some good freeride terrain, plus parks.

Cross-country There are 20km of pretty cross-country trails up the valley beyond Inneralpbach.

Mountain restaurants There is an adequate supply on both mountains, all named on the piste map. Most are pleasant but unremarkable self-service places – but we've enjoyed the table-service reader favourite, Gipfö Hit at Schatzberg. On W-horn, head for Dauerstoa Alm.

Schools and guides We've had good reports on both the main Alpbach schools, 'red' and 'blue'.

Families Reporters find the compact, relaxed village and adjacent nursery slopes of Alpbach very child-friendly. The schools have excellent facilities.

STAYING THERE

Hotels There are several appealing 4-star places in central Alpbach. Readers tip the Alpbacherhof – 'fab food, excellent staff and service' – but

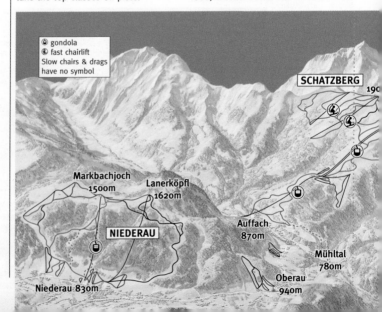

we'd be aiming for Inneralpbach and the Wiedersbergerhorn hotel. In Auffach, the Platzl and Auffacherhof are good central spots.

Apartments A reader heartily approves Haus Hislop, 'a lovely chalet run by a Yorkshire woman called Claire'. Good location in Inneralpbach.

Eating out Mostly in hotels and guest houses. In Inneralpbach, the Wiedersbergerhorn is tipped for 'fine dining', the Zirmalm for a more traditional atmosphere. In Alpbach, reader tips have included the Berghof and the Jakober (and its pizzeria, Messner's). For a change from the norm, try Flo's.

Après-ski Joe's Salettl is a lively round bar at Inneralpbach. The Post Alm in central Alpbach is popular early and later on. Here and at the Jakober there is live music some nights.

Off the slopes There are pretty walks, and tobogganing – including a 5km run at Auffach, from mid-mountain. All the gondolas have restaurants at or near the top where you can meet skiing friends for lunch. Trips to Innsbruck and Salzburg are possible.

940m
OBERAU

Oberau, 5km from Auffach, has only a tiny area of slopes nearby; but it is the main village of the Wildschönau. Its chief attraction as a base is the lovely, historic hotel Kellerwirt, in the hands of the same family for six generations.

TOURIST OFFICE

www.alpbachtal.at
www.wildschoenau.
com
www.skijuwel.com

830m
NIEDERAU

Niederau is 8km from Auffach, at the foot of a wooded mountain that rises to only 1600m. The village is not notably cute – it is quite spread out, with a cluster of restaurants and shops around the gondola station.

The main lifts are an eight-person gondola to Markbachjoch and a fast quad a few minutes' walk away, going slightly higher on Lanerköpfl. The whole area is very small – you can ski most of it in an hour or two. There are a couple of ungroomed ski routes, and three pistes to the village – an easy black, a proper red and, on skier's right, a relatively easy red. So near-beginners have to be prepared to tackle a red if they want to progress. There are excellent nursery slopes at the top and bottom, but the low ones don't get much sun in midwinter.

The 4-star Sonnschein and the 3-star Austria are central hotel tips. The village has a nice balance of après-ski – neither too noisy for families nor too quiet for the young and lively. Some bars are quite lively both at teatime and at night. Several hotel pools are open to the public.

670m
REITH IM ALPBACHTAL

Reith's mountain is basically a one-run affair, but its access lift is a modern gondola rising almost 600m, and there is a top-to-bottom toboggan run.

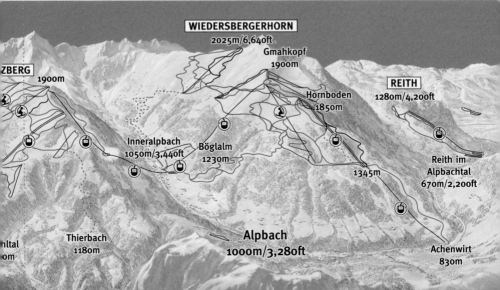

WIEDERSBERGERHORN
2025m/6,640ft
Gmahkopf
1900m
ZBERG 1900m
REITH 1280m/4,200ft
Hornboden
1850m
Inneralpbach
1050m/3,440ft
Böglalm
1230m
Reith im
Alpbachtal
670m/2,200ft
1345m
htal
om
Thierbach
1180m
Alpbach
1000m/3,280ft
Achenwirt
830m

Bad Gastein

*If you fancy 'taking the cure', there are few better resorts;
even if you don't, you're likely to be impressed by the slopes*

£95
RESORT PRICE INDEX

TOP 10 RATINGS

Extent	★★★
Fast lifts	★★★
Queues	★★★
Snow	★★★
Expert	★★★
Intermediate	★★★★
Beginner	★★
Charm	★★★
Convenience	★★
Scenery	★★★

NEWS

2014/15: A new ski route opened from the top station of the Kaserebenbahn (on skier's right of the Schlossalm sector) into Angertal. The Gasti children's park was expanded.

96

➕ Excellent, testing long runs for confident intermediates

➕ Good mix of high, open slopes and lower woodland runs

➕ Good mountain restaurants

➕ Excellent thermal spas, but ...

➖ Main resorts are spa towns, lacking the usual Austrian resort ambience

➖ Valley slopes are split into five areas, and having a car helps

➖ Lacks genuinely easy long runs for painless progression

With its essentially red-gradient mountains and spa-town resorts, the Gastein valley is a bit different from Austrian ski resort norms. We prefer spacious Bad Hofgastein to steeply tiered, rather urban Bad Gastein. But little rustic Dorfgastein, down the valley, is our favourite. All three are covered here.

THE RESORT

Bad Gastein is an old spa town near the head of the Gastein valley. At its heart is the original spa area, laid out in a compact horseshoe on steep slopes. Above this, at the level of the railway and the gondola station, is a modern suburb with more lodgings.

The Stubnerkogel slopes above the town link with Bad Hofgastein, down the valley. Further down, a separate area of slopes above Dorfgastein links with Grossarl in the next valley. Way up the valley is another separate area at Sportgastein. Various ski-bus routes and trains connect these points, and 'run as per timetable'. Lots of resorts in this region (including Schladming,

which has its own chapter) are covered by the lift pass (Ski Amadé) and are easily reached by car.

Village charm The core is a curious mix of towny buildings – some grand, some modest. Away from here, the more modern hotels and guest houses have more of a normal ski resort feel.

Convenience The higher part of the resort is handy for the Stubnerkogel gondola, but the resort as a whole spreads widely. The double chair up the separate Graukogel area is on the opposite side of town.

Scenery The resort is set in virtually a gorge, steeply tiered and wooded. The slopes are higher than many Austrian resorts (particularly at Sportgastein), with wide views as a result.

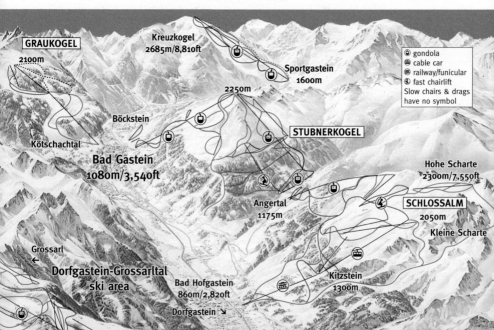

KEY FACTS

Resort	1080m
	3,540ft

The Gastein valley including Dorfgastein and Grossarl area

Slopes	840-2685m
	2,760-8,810ft
Lifts	42
Pistes	218km
	135 miles

The Gastein valley excluding Dorfgastein and Grossarl area

Slopes	860-2685m
	2,820-8,810ft
Lifts	25
Pistes	129km
	80 miles

LIFT PASSES

Prices in €

Age	6-day
under 16	121
16 to 18	181
19 plus	241

Free Under 6
Senior Free ski pass with seven nights' accommodation in low season
Beginner Day passes for individual beginner lifts

THE MOUNTAINS

Most of the pistes are on open slopes. Graukogel is wooded, and blissfully quiet in our experience. The piste map tries to cover all the areas in one view, and wastes the reverse side advertising the Ski Amadé region.

Slopes From the Stubnerkogel gondola a long blue run goes back to base, but most runs head for Angertal, which links with Bad Hofgastein.

Fast lifts There are several gondolas, but also lots of slow chairs and T-bars.

Queues The main access lifts can build queues in peak weeks of the season.

Terrain parks There is a good, varied park on Stubnerkogel.

Snow reliability The slopes go a bit higher than many Austrian rivals – Sportgastein much higher – and there is decent snowmaking.

Experts The few black runs are not severe, but many reds are long and satisfying. But there is plenty of good off-piste – by the Jungeralm chair on the shady side of Stubnerkogel, for example. Sportgastein has a ski route from top to bottom.

Intermediates Confident intermediates, will find long, leg-testing red runs in all sectors. The valley in general and Stubnerkogel in particular are not nearly so good for blue-run skiers. Sportgastein has a good range of runs, up to an easy black.

Beginners There are nursery areas near the gondola station and at Angertal – a better bet. But progression is awkward – the mountains are essentially steep. The few easy long runs are boring paths.

Snowboarding The valley hosts snowboard events, and there is good freeriding. Draglifts are dotted around.

Cross-country There are 45km of trails in the area, but most are low down.

Mountain restaurants The piste map names them, in tiny type. There are lots of pleasant huts doing decent food; but they can get crowded. We like the simple, quiet Graukogelhütte. Reader tips include Bellevue Alm, Waldgasthof and Hirschen Hütte.

Schools and guides Past reports on the school have been favourable.

Families Angertal has a snow adventure park. The town is not very child-friendly, but the swimming and skating are good.

STAYING THERE

Hotels There are lots of smart 4- and 3-star hotels with spa facilities. The Grüner Baum is a lovely retreat – 'very friendly' says a reader this year – but isolated. We enjoyed a stay in 2015 at the small, funky Miramonte – excellent food and very helpful staff.

Eating out Choice is reasonable. Steak & Mehr is 'excellent if you like a good steak'. More reports, please!

Après-ski Bars are lively at close of play, evenings more subdued – but there are places to go. Multiple reports this year tipped Lederhosen – 'superb resident band, the Naked Swedes'. Silver Bullet and Haeggbloms are among the most popular. There are a couple of discos and a casino.

Off the slopes The thermal spa/pool facilities are excellent and extensive – but expensive. There's ice climbing. There are quite a few shops, and excursions to Salzburg are possible, and worthwhile.

Bad Hofgastein 860m

+ Sunny, spacious setting
+ Lovely long runs

− Lacks ski resort ambience
− Funicular from base can be crowded

Bad Hofgastein is a sizeable, spacious, quiet spa town set on flat ground in the widest part of the valley, with funicular access to the slopes.

Village charm The pedestrianized centre is compact, and pleasant enough to stroll around, with lots of shops and restaurants. But it does feel like a town; there's little traditional Austrian rustic charm. There is a sizeable park next to the centre.

Convenience The resort spreads widely across the flat valley floor; the funicular is an efficient ski-bus ride from many lodgings. It's a longer ski-bus ride to Angertal.

Scenery Good valley views.

THE MOUNTAINS

Schlossalm is a broad, open bowl, with runs through patchy woods to both Bad Hofgastein and Angertal.

Slopes The funicular to Kitzstein is followed by a cable car to the Schlossalm slopes. These link to Stubnerkogel via Angertal.

Fast lifts Getting up the mountain can be slow, and a few old chairs remain.

↑ Open upper slopes, and densely wooded and steeper lower slopes on Stubnerkogel, seen here from Schlossalm
SNOWPIX.COM / CHRIS GILL

Queues The access lifts are queue-prone at peak times – and the cable car can be closed by wind.

Terrain parks The new Fun Slope Gastein mixes a piste and snow park, with bridges, tunnels and jumps.

Snow reliability Snowmaking is fairly extensive, but snow-cover down to the bottom is unreliable.

Experts There are no real challenges on the local pistes, but there is ample opportunity to go off-piste.

Intermediates The Schlossalm slopes offer a good range of red runs, from easy to testing; H32 into Angertal is one of the most serious reds we know. The few blues are not all entirely easy. Hohe Scharte Nord is a splendid run, away from the lifts, to the valley floor.

Beginners There is a small nursery slope at the funicular – better to catch a bus to the bigger area at Angertal. Progression options are not ideal.

Snowboarding Good freeriding. Draglifts are dotted around though.

Cross-country Bad Hofgastein makes a fine base for cross-country when its lengthy valley-floor trails have snow.

Mountain restaurants They are named, minutely, on the piste map. A clear reader favourite is Aeroplanstadl, an inviting woody place doing self-service of simple dishes. Hamburger Skihütte offers 'fast and cheerful' table-service, and one reader strongly recommends the out-of-the-way Hofgasteinerhaus ('more varied menu, uncrowded').

Schools and guides We lack recent reports.

Families The town is much more suitable than Bad Gastein.

TOURIST OFFICE

For all resorts in the Gastein valley:
www.gastein.com

STAYING THERE

Hotels We enjoyed a stay at the 4-star Bismarck – fairly central, excellent food. Reader tips include the 'friendly' Salzburgerhof and the Rauscher. Our regular reporter has switched allegiance from the St Georg to similarly well placed Klammers Kärnten – 'bigger spa, even better food'.

Apartments A 2014 reporter found the 'simple' Apartehaus Schmidt 'good value and spacious'.

Eating out There's plenty of choice. Reader tips include Piccola Italia, Salzburgerhof ('excellent steaks'), and Rudi's Klause Stüberl ('best pizza').

Après-ski Quiet by Austrian standards. At close of play Aeroplanstadl on the hill does good business, as does Gastein Alm at the base. Head to Cafe Weitmoser, a historic little castle, for cakes. There are some pleasant bars in the town; a reader found a smoke-free one, the Bolten. The Almrausch is a late-night club.

Off the slopes The huge Alpen Therme Gastein spa has excellent pools etc. Other amenities include good shops, walking and a full-size ice rink.

DOWN-VALLEY VILLAGE – 830m

DORFGASTEIN

Dorfgastein is a quiet, rustic village. It has its own extensive slopes, shared with Grossarl in the next valley, which offer some good long runs on both sides of the ridge. A two-stage gondola and alternative chairlift start a little way outside the village. There is a nursery slope here, and another at mid-mountain. Like the other sectors in the valley, the mountain is basically of red gradient, and best suits confident intermediates. On the front side there is one good long blue, but it doesn't go all the way to the valley.

There are pleasant huts. We've had consistently good reports on the 'outstanding' table-service Wengeralm since we started keeping records in 2007. Other reader tips include the Jagahütte and Harbachhütte. The ski schools get good reviews. Off-slope amenities are limited, but there's a pool with sauna and steam. Evenings are quiet. Reporters love the 4-star hotel Römerhof – 'great food, lovely spa, good value' – and our regular reporter has now stayed happily in the Gästehaus Schernthaner apartments six years running. There are two Italian restaurants, and a Spar shop.

Bad Kleinkirchheim

Large resort tucked away in Carinthia, with marvellous spa facilities and a ski area best suited to intermediates

£100
RESORT PRICE INDEX

TOP 10 RATINGS

Extent	★★
Fast lifts	★★
Queues	★★★★
Snow	★★★
Expert	★★
Intermediate	★★★
Beginner	★★
Charm	★★
Convenience	★★★
Scenery	★★★

NEWS

2014/15: Two infrared 'spa cubes' were installed on the slopes to allow skiers and boarders to step in and warm themselves up. One of them also has two chairs that will massage you.

KEY FACTS

Resort	1090m
	3,580ft
Slopes	1090-2055m
	3,580-6,740ft
Lifts	26
Pistes	103km
	64 miles

- ➕ Mainly red intermediate slopes
- ➕ Virtually 100% snowmaking
- ➕ Two superb thermal spas
- ➕ Cheap, even by Austrian standards
- ➖ Spread-out town
- ➖ Still a lot of slow chairs and T-bars
- ➖ Slopes limited in extent and variety
- ➖ Après-ski quiet

BKK, as the Brits call it, is downhill race hero Franz Klammer's favourite ski area – he learned to ski here, there's a World Cup downhill run named after him, and he skis with guests here a few times a year.

Given Klammer's endorsement, it's no surprise that the resort has some serious skiing: 75% of its slopes are classified red and suit confident intermediates best. It is perhaps a surprise that there are few real challenges for experts.

THE RESORT

BKK is tucked away on the edge of the Nock Mountain National Park in Carinthia, in the far south-east of Austria, near the Italian and Slovenian borders. The nearest airports are Klagenfurt (around 50 minutes away) and Ljubljana (90 minutes). Salzburg is less than two hours away.

The lift pass covers St Oswald, a smaller village at the far end of the shared ski area, and all the resorts in Carinthia – useful for visiting other resorts if you have a car.

BKK's spa facilities are excellent, with indoor and outdoor thermal pools, different types of sauna – including a tepidarium (which is a sauna with a lower temperature so you can sit there longer) – and steam rooms, solariums, hot tubs, massage and therapy rooms. There are also water slides, waterfalls and massage jets in the pools. The Thermal Römerbad reopened in 2007 after complete refurbishment and is set over three floors, with 13 different types of sauna and steam rooms. We tried it and thought it was superb; we could happily have spent days there. 'World class – we went for an hour and stayed all day,' says a recent reporter.

Village charm The mainly chalet-style buildings with sloping roofs are more appealing than the austere blocks of some spa resorts. But it is a sprawling place with no real centre.

Convenience The town is very spread out along the valley, and the most convenient place to stay is near one of the main lifts out. A free ski-bus links all the main lift stations, and some buses also go to St Oswald.

Scenery The scenery you gaze at from the spa pools is of gently rounded, rather than dramatic, mountains.

99

KAISERBURG
2055m/6,740ft

Strohsack
1905m

MAIBRUNN
1760m/5775ft

Priedröf
1965m/6,445ft

NOCKALM

Wieser Nock
1970m/6,460ft

Brunnach
1910m/6,270ft

1370m

1025m

1280m

St Oswald

Bad Kleinkirchheim
1090m/3,580ft

◉ gondola
◎ fast chairlift
Slow chairs & drags have no symbol

Feldkirchen ↓

FRANZ KLAMMER

Klammer is one of the most famous downhill skiers of all time and, now aged over 60, is still a national hero in Austria.

He won Olympic Gold at Innsbruck in 1976 and a record 25 World Cup Downhills. He was born near Bad Kleinkirchheim, learned to ski at BKK, and it remains his favourite resort.

A few times a year he skis with anyone who signs up for the experience. A recent reporter who joined him said it was 'brilliant, he made everyone feel special and never stopped smiling'.

LIFT PASSES

Prices in €

Age	6-day
under 15	111
15 to 18	178
19 to 64	222
65 plus	178

Free Under 5

Beginner No deals

Alternative pass
With thermal spa included

TOURIST OFFICE

www.
badkleinkirchheim.at

THE MOUNTAINS

BKK has shady home slopes and sunnier ones shared with St Oswald. They are mainly wooded and of intermediate standard (75% are red).
Slopes BKK's main home slopes are reached by lifts from two different parts of the village. A two-stage gondola goes up to the area's high point, Kaiserburg, at one end of the ski area, where a couple of T-bars serve the highest slopes. And a fast quad takes you to the other end of the mountainside at Maibrunn. Pistes go down from both peaks to the gondola mid-station, where a double chair takes you to above Maibrunn.

From the same end of the village as the Maibrunn quad, successive old double chairs and a drag take you up the other side of the valley to the Nockalm slopes, which link in with St Oswald's slopes further along the valley. This area can also be accessed by a gondola midway between BKK and St Oswald, which can be reached by ski-bus. At St Oswald a gondola goes up to Brunnach, at the far end of the shared ski area.

Three slow quads link the Nockalm and St Oswald slopes, and most of the other upper lifts are drags.
Fast lifts There are three gondolas and one fast chair but the other lifts are all slow chairs or T-bars.
Queues A recent reporter advises going to Nockalm in the morning to avoid any queues for the local slopes.
Terrain parks The park is at Nockalm and has jumps, rails and boxes.
Snow reliability In general, BKK's main home slopes are north-facing and keep their snow best. The Nockalm-St Oswald slopes are more sunny. Virtually all the pistes are covered by snowmaking. Grooming is of a 'very high standard', says a recent visitor.
Experts BKK has little to keep experts interested for a week. The best and most challenging black is the Franz Klammer World Cup run, which goes from Strohsack to the gondola base (the short top section is very steep and often closed). Off-piste tours are popular and the resort organizes three-hour guided tours.
Intermediates Virtually all the slopes are ideal for good intermediates and many are long (up to 1000m vertical). For timid intermediates, the Nockalm and St Oswald sectors are best.
Beginners The nursery slopes at the

top of the Nockalm gondola are much warmer and sunnier than the low shady BKK ones. Once off the nursery slopes, there is a long blue the length of the Nockalm gondola. But that's it - no other long, easy blues.
Snowboarding Best for experienced boarders. Beginners may struggle with the many T-bars.
Cross-country Some of the area's 42km of tracks are at 1900m at the top of the Nockalm.
Mountain restaurants There are 25 mountain restaurants and huts. We enjoyed the cosy Brentlerhütte (excellent ham) on the way down from Nockalm to the valley and Zum Poldl above St Oswald. A recent visitor recommends the Strohsack for its 'oompah band and friendly service'.
Schools and guides There are four schools to choose from, three based in BKK and one in St Oswald.
Families From 9 January to 4 March 2016 a child under 12 can ski for one euro a day if they are with an adult with a 6-day pass. The ski schools run a Bobo children's club.

STAYING THERE

Hotels Inghams is the only major tour operator to feature the resort. We stayed happily at the 4-star Trattlerhof with pool, hot tub, saunas and steam room, near the high-speed chair. The two 5-stars, the Pulverer and the Thermenhotel Ronacher, are a bit further away and have excellent spa facilities. The 4-star Almrausch is close to the chairlift to Nockalm and, says a recent reporter, is 'as good as it gets'. The 4-star Prägant is right opposite the Römerbad thermal baths and Kaiserburg gondola; pool, saunas.
Apartments There are lots of self-catering apartments to rent.
Eating out Plenty of choice. We loved the atmospheric old Loystub'n in the hotel Pulverer and the rustic Einkehr (owned by the hotel Trattlerhof).
Après-ski It is quieter than most Austrian resorts. But near the main gondola base are the Almstube, Viktoria Pub, Club MC 99 and the Take Five Dancing Club.
Off the slopes You can buy lift tickets that include the use of the thermal spas. There are 60km of walks (including the Spa Boulevard at the top of the gondola from St Oswald), a tennis centre, squash courts, outdoor ice rink, curling, snowshoeing, sleigh rides and a torchlit 4km toboggan run.

Inghams

Austria
SKI BKK
Bad Kleinkirchheim

*A picturesque ski & spa resort
in the south of Austria*

Inghams

xxx

FREE Lift Passes
For adults & children
Selected dates only

SAVE £££s with our *Inghams* PLUS deals

GROUPS - UP TO 1 IN 5 GO FREE

EARLY BOOKING DISCOUNT - SAVE UP TO £120 PER COUPLE

FREE SPA VOUCHER AT THE HOTEL ESCHENHOF | **FREE EQUIPMENT OFFER FOR CHILDREN**

FREE LIFT PASS ON SELECTED DATES | **GREAT VALUE SKI SAVER PACKS AVAILABLE**

CHOOSE FROM THREE 4 STAR HOTELS | **7 NIGHTS FROM £769 PER PERSON**

SKI WITH OLYMPIC CHAMPION & SKI LEGEND, FRANZ KLAMMER
from only £65 per person subject to availability

Franz Klammer – Abfahrt
Klammer Stich →

Terms and Conditions apply to all offers.

Call us on 01483 371 236
inghams.co.uk/bkk

100% BONDED SECURITY

ABTA
Travel with confidence
V4871

ALPENREGION BLUDENZ

Brandnertal – Vorarlberg

Small, family-friendly ski area close to the Swiss border with lots to do in addition to downhill skiing areas

£90
RESORT PRICE INDEX

NEWS

2015/16: Lift passes for more than two days will also be valid in the Montafon ski area.

KEY FACTS

Resort	890-1035m
	2,920-3,400ft
Slopes	890-2000m
	2,920-6,560ft
Lifts	14
Pistes	55km
	34 miles

+ Quiet area that suits families well
+ Plenty of activities to try other than downhill skiing
+ Affordable prices
+ Small area of slopes that suits intermediates and beginners best, but ...

− Only 55km of pistes locally
− Après-ski quiet by Austrian standards
− Still quite a few slow chairlifts and T-bars

Brandnertal is the most westerly ski area in Austria, very close to the Swiss border. Its two resorts, Brand and Bürserberg, each have their own small areas of slopes that have been linked at altitude since 2007. It doesn't add up to a huge ski area but it is popular with families and has lots of activities to amuse them as well as skiing. Keen piste-bashers will be pleased to learn that for the 2015/16 season, all lift passes for two days or more in Brandnertal will also be valid in the Montafon ski area (which is the next-door valley, has over 200km of slopes and is reachable by public transport).

Getting to the region is easy by train and bus or by car after flying in to airports such as Friedrichshafen (90km), Innsbruck (140km) or Zürich (160km).

THE RESORTS

When you enter the Brandnertal, the first ski village you come to is Bürserberg (890m). The road continues up the valley for a few km until you reach Brand (1035m), which is strung along the valley floor near its head (the south-western end) and has most of the accommodation. They

are in the province of Vorarlberg which also includes Bregenzerwald (covered in the next chapter), Montafon in the next valley, Lech-Zürs (which has its own chapter) and some other small resorts.

The Brandnertal resorts are the most westerly major ski resorts in Austria and only a few km from the border with Switzerland. There are free ski-buses. You can get to the Montafon resort of Schruns (which has a cable car into 140km of slopes) by regular bus and train in around an hour.

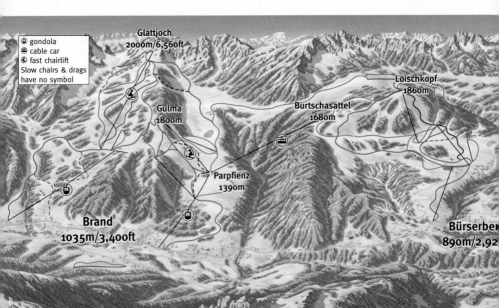

gondola
cable car
fast chairlift
Slow chairs & drags
have no symbol

Glattjoch
2000m/6,560ft

Loischkopf
1860m

Gulma
1800m

Burtschasattel
1680m

Parpfienz
1390m

Brand
1035m/3,400ft

Bürserberg
890m/2,92

↑ Accommodation is strung out along the Brandnertal, which has mainly family-friendly blue and red slopes in its ski area
ALPENREGION BLUDENZ

LIFT PASSES

Prices in €

Age	6-day
6 to 7	25
8 to 15	119
16 to 17	141
18 to 59	188
60 plus	179
Free Under 6	

Notes Pass for 2 days or more includes Montafon resorts; family discounts for more than one child

TOURIST OFFICE

www.en.alpenregion.at

THE MOUNTAINS

Eight-seat gondolas (served by free ski-buses) go up from each end of Brand into the bigger part of the ski area it shares with Bürserberg down the valley. Bürserberg has a double chairlift into its own smaller area of slopes. The two areas are linked at altitude by the 60-person Panoramabahn cable car. You can ski on an easy blue run from the Bürserberg area to the Brand area and catch the cable car the other way.

The area above Brand is served by two six-packs, a couple of short draglifts and an old double chair. One of the six-packs reaches the area's high point of 2000m. Above Bürserberg, the area is served by two double chairlifts, a quad and a couple of draglifts, one of which takes you to the blue piste linking the two areas.

Most of the runs are blue and red, though there are a few ski routes, and a solitary black run (above Bürserberg). In total there are 55km of mainly east-facing pistes that suit intermediates best; 80% of the pistes are covered by snowmaking. The area is well supplied with huts.

There's a good terrain park and a half-pipe above Brand (see www.backyards.at).

There's excellent cross-country here too, with 20km of prepared tracks including some at the top of Bürserberg and a glorious 15km circular route at 1250m.

STAYING THERE

The area goes out of its way to be family-friendly, and there's a special Kinderland area where the ski schools teach young children. Very young children ski free, and there are discounts up to age 18. When staying at certain hotels between 12 and 18 March 2016 you get a free lift pass if you book the Märzenslust package. And there are special family packages over Easter.

Hotels range from 4-stars to family-run pensions, and some have a special 'Family Friendly' accreditation. The 4-stars in Brand include the Walliserhof ('design hotel', sauna, steam room, spa), Sporthotel Beck (pool, sauna, steam room, spa) and the less central Taleu (beautiful views, pool, saunas, steam room, 'beer bath') – all available through Inghams who are featuring the resort from this winter. Apartments are plentiful too.

There are three good toboggan runs, two above Brand – one 6km long and one 3km – plus a 2km run above Bürserberg. And the area is big on dog sledding; you can learn to mush huskies (including a special course for children) and take excursions (including one where you camp overnight on the mountain). There's also snowshoeing and extensive winter walking trails that go right to the top of Bürserberg, plus ice skating on natural rinks, ice climbing, horse-riding and archery.

Bregenzerwald – Vorarlberg

An unspoiled region that is hardly heard of on the British market, with a lot of relatively small ski areas covered on one big pass

£90
RESORT PRICE INDEX

NEWS

2015/16: The old gondola out of Mellau is to be replaced by a new 10-seater.

2014/15: A red piste was opened down to Schröcken. (There is still no sign of the projected lift from the village, though.)

Bregenzerwald is tucked away at the western end of Austria in Vorarlberg, on the borders of Germany and Switzerland. It has remained remarkably unspoiled and is still primarily a farming community, famous for cheese. But it is also the snowiest region in the Alps. The resort of Warth has developed a following in the UK since it was linked to plush and pricey Lech and Zürs.

Abundant snow is a key part of the region's appeal. There is some debate about which resort gets the most snow, but the whole region gets huge amounts – about four times as much as Kitzbühel, twice as much as St Anton and Val d'Isère.

There is a ski lift in almost every village, but few of the ski areas are large. They are all covered by the 3-Valley ski pass. Having a car is useful: getting around on buses is time-consuming.

THE BIGGEST SKI AREAS

Damüls and **Mellau** share the biggest ski area entirely in Bregenzerwald (ie excluding Warth-Lech-Zürs), with 109km of runs, served by no less than seven six-packs, an eight-pack and two gondolas.

Damüls is quite high (the base area is at 1430m), and the sunny but snow-sure slopes go over 2000m. Most runs are quite short, above the treeline and of genuine red steepness, and some

of the blues are quite narrow, so it's best for adventurous rather than timid intermediates. There are quite a few ski routes; on our visit, all those we tried had been groomed – and some were busier than the pistes. Damüls has some cross-country tracks and winter walking trails. There's a good terrain park.

Mellau's ski area is reached by gondola from the edge of the village (getting a major upgrade to a 10-seater this season) and is on the more shady side of the mountain. There's a black run that merits its classification, as do the reds, and a ski route that is short but enjoyable. Most of the blues have fairly steep sections at the top – not good for timid intermediates. There's a long red through the trees right back to the village – enjoyable but narrow (it's a summer road for much of the way). There are some walking trails and extensive cross-country tracks.

Damüls has no real village centre –

104

Widderstein 2535m
Lechtal
Innsbruck
Warth 1500m
Schröcken 1260m
Schoppernau 860m
Au 800m
Damüls 1430m
Niedere 1710m
Mellau 700m
Hochhäderich 1565m
Bezau 620m
Hochälpelekopf 1465m
Schetteregg 1065m
Andelsbuch 615m
Egg 565m
Schwarzenberg 700m
Hittisau
Bödele 1140m
Riefensberg 780m
Müselbach 585m
Alberschwende 720m
Dornbirn 475m
Friedrichshafen
München
Stuttgart
BREGENZ 400m/1,310ft
Feldkirch
Zürich →

it is a series of small collections of hotels and inns, scattered along the edge of the slopes, mostly ski-in/ski-out. Mellau is much lower (690m), and a proper little village – quiet and peaceful (it's bypassed by the valley road). Even so, for the visitor it amounts to no more than a handful of hotels and inns, and a couple of bars. We enjoyed our stay at the 4-star Sonne Lifestyle – modern, minimalist, with spacious rooms, good food and spa facilities.

Warth and **Schröcken** are at opposite ends of their shared area of slopes, which are mainly between 1500m and 2000m with a lift system including five fast chairs. Warth, at the eastern end, has blue and red pistes to the village, and a fast chairlift out of it. Schröcken, at the western end, is now reached by a red piste as well as a ski route – both reportedly 'long and wonderful, with fab views' – but the nearest lift is a six-pack up the road at the Hochtannberg pass.

At the southern extremity of the area is the gondola link with Lech.

Thanks to the exceptional snowfall record and the northerly orientation of most slopes, the pistes are almost always in excellent condition, and the off-piste powder gets tracked out much less quickly than in better-known resorts.

The marked runs include several easy blacks and ski routes as well as reds and blues, and there's a terrain park with three lines from easy to pro, plus a 'funslope'. Most of the pistes are relatively quiet, and ideal for high-speed cruising. Queues are rare. Piste marking and grooming are good.

We cover the mountain restaurants in the Lech chapter.

There are modest amounts of cleared footpaths and cross-country trails, and good tobogganing.

The villages are small, pretty and unspoiled. For the moment, at least, Warth is the obvious place to stay. It spreads across the hill from the base of its chairlift – about 1km, end to end. There are several hotels close to the lift. The small Lechtalerhof wins on points – 'very good restaurant, great spa/pool'. A regular visitor has switched allegiance from the Steffisalp to the Warther Hof – 'cheaper, better spa, with a great pool'. The Walserberg is also tipped – 'top-class food'.

It's a small, quiet place, but there are bars and restaurants, mainly in hotels, in which to make merry. There are bars at the base which can be 'reasonably rowdy' at close of play. The Lechtalerhof has 'the nicest bar in the village' and runs karaoke nights.

Reports on the Warth ski school are enthusiastic – 'friendly and efficient'.

Au and **Schoppernau** are neighbouring villages sharing the **Diedamskopf** ski area. We preferred Schoppernau as a base – off the main road, on the same side as the slopes, with snow-covered lanes and chalets.

The sunny slopes totalling 40km have good views of the surrounding peaks and are popular with families. The terrain park is the biggest in the area. There's floodlit skiing.

The slopes suit good intermediates best; the blacks are quite serious, and some of the blues should be classified red. On the other hand, the reds in the Breitenalpe sector were easy and should really be classified blue. The runs are short, except for the 10km runs back to the valley station at 820m, with a vertical of over 1200m.

Children can have fun at the top of the mountain in Kids Adventure Land.

Cross-country enthusiasts will find plenty of trails; there are also lots of cleared paths and a natural ice rink.

SMALLER SKI AREAS

Andelsbuch and **Bezau** share the local **Niedere** ski area, with slopes totalling 15km. It's a family ski area but, given good snow, the ski routes offer more experienced skiers a challenge too. The top height is 1715m. Bezau has most of the lodging options.

Alberschwende has 18km of runs, and is popular with beginners. There are some cross-country tracks and an ice rink. **Riefensberg** has the tiny **Hochlitten** ski area, with just 4.4km of runs, all of which are blue. It also shares with neighbouring **Hittisau** the **Hochhäderich** ski area. This has 9km of runs (almost all blue and red). It has some cross-country tracks at altitude and some cleared paths.

Egg is the biggest village in the area, with around 3,500 inhabitants, and a small ski area at **Schetteregg**, with 10km of runs, mostly easy blue and red, between 1100m and 1400m. There are some cleared walks.

Schwarzenberg's local **Bödele** mountain has 24km of runs (mainly easy blues and reds). There are also some short cross-country tracks and rather more extensive cleared paths.

ALBIN NIEDERSTRASSER

Ellmau

A good base on the extensive SkiWelt circuit, combining charm with reasonable convenience – good value, too

£85
RESORT PRICE INDEX

TOP 10 RATINGS

Extent	★★★★
Fast lifts	★★★★
Queues	★★★★
Snow	★★
Expert	★
Intermediate	★★★★
Beginner	★★★★
Charm	★★★
Convenience	★★★
Scenery	★★★

KEY FACTS

Resort	800m
	2,620ft

Entire SkiWelt	
Slopes	620-1955m
	2,030-6,410ft
Lifts	90
Pistes	280km
	174 miles

Note The Schrahe report (read our feature on 'Piste extent') puts this area at 251km – slightly smaller than the newly expanded Saalbach-Hinterglemm area.

+ Part of the SkiWelt, one of Austria's largest linked ski areas
+ Excellent nursery slopes
+ Quiet, charming family resort – more appealing than Söll
+ Cheap, even by Austrian standards
+ Snowmaking is very extensive and well used; even so ...

− Low altitude can mean poor snow
− Main lift a bus or drag from village
− Runs on upper slopes mostly short
− Few challenges on-piste
− Limited range of nightlife
− The SkiWelt slopes can get crowded
− Piste map and signposting poor

If you like the sound of the large, undemanding SkiWelt circuit, Ellmau has a lot to recommend it as your base – as does Scheffau, also covered here. But also consider the several resorts covered in the Söll chapter.

THE RESORT

Ellmau sits at the north-eastern corner of the big SkiWelt ski area. Other parts of it are covered in our chapter on Söll. You can also progress (via Brixen) to the slopes of Kitzbühel; these and various other ski areas within reach are covered by the Kitzbüheler Alpen AllStarCard ski pass.

Village charm Although sizeable, the village remains quiet, with traditional chalet-style buildings, welcoming bars and shops, and a pretty church.

Convenience Accommodation is scattered; there is some out by the funicular to the main slopes, but we prefer to stay in the compact centre of the village. There is a bus service, but reporters complain of overcrowding. We're told that last season one of the routes 'operated two buses together serving alternate stops to ensure most people got on board'.

Scenery The village and the slopes enjoy great close-up views of the craggy Wilder Kaiser, across the valley.

THE MOUNTAINS

The piste map remains hopelessly over-ambitious in trying to show the whole SkiWelt area in a single view. Reporters also complain of poor and confusing signposting. See the Söll chapter for more on all this.

Most slopes are heavily wooded, with a mix of short runs at altitude and much longer ones to the villages.

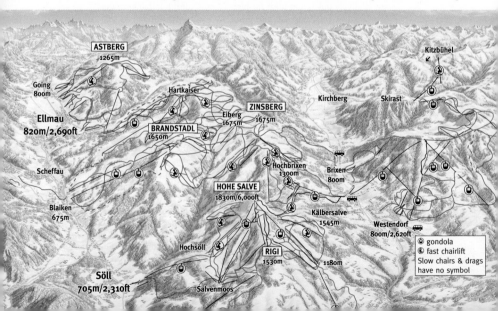

gondola
fast chairlift
Slow chairs & drags have no symbol

↑ This pic shows three of the area's key attractions: easy pistes, mountain restaurants and snowmaking

WILDER KAISER TO / CHRIS THOMAS

NEWS

2015/16: A new 10-seat gondola with a mid-station is planned to replace the Hartkaiser funicular. Carrying capacity will be doubled. The top station will have a children's restaurant and ski school and childcare facilities. The valley station is to be redeveloped with a restaurant, après-ski bar, equipment storage and underground car park for 150 cars.

The Jochbahn quad at Brixen is due to be replaced by an eight-seater which the resort claims will be 'the world's fastest chairlift'. It will be double the length of the old chair and will start much lower down the mountain.

2014/15: The Aualm quad chair up to Zinsberg was replaced by an eight-seater. The Bergkaiser mountain restaurant was refurbished and now has seating for 950. Snowmaking was increased throughout the SkiWelt area.

Slopes The old funicular railway on the edge of the village is due to be replaced by a 10-seater gondola for 2015/16. This will take you up to Hartkaiser, from where a fine long red leads down to Blaiken (Scheffau's lift base station). Here, one of two gondolas takes you up to Brandstadl. Immediately beyond Brandstadl, the slopes become rather bitty; an array of short runs and lifts link Brandstadl to Zinsberg. From Zinsberg, long, south-facing pistes lead down to Brixen, where a gondola goes up to Choralpe in Westendorf's area. Part-way down to Brixen you can head towards Söll, and if you go up Hohe Salve, you get access to a long run to Hopfgarten.

Ellmau and Going share a pleasant little area of slopes on Astberg, slightly apart from the rest of the area, and well suited to the unadventurous and to families. One piste leads to the new gondola for access to the rest of the SkiWelt. The main Astberg chair is midway between Ellmau and Going.

Fast lifts The main access lift is the new fast gondola. Fast chairs are now common on the upper slopes.

Queues Lift upgrades have greatly improved this once queue-prone area, and most reporters find few queues. But there are several bottlenecks at slow chairs around the mountain, and when snow is poor the links between Zinsberg and Eiberg get crowded.

Terrain parks The local Kaiserpark has beginner and expert options and a chill-out zone. There's a snowcross.

Snow reliability With a low average height, and important links that get a lot of sun, the snowmaking that the SkiWelt has installed is essential; the Ellmau-Going sector now claims 95% of slopes are covered and reporters have praised it. Snowmaking can, of course, be used only when temperatures are low enough. The

north-facing Eiberg area above Scheffau holds its snow well. Grooming is excellent.

Experts There is a ski route from Brandstadl down to Scheffau and a little mogul field between Brandstadl and Neualm, but the main challenges are in going off-piste.

Intermediates With good snow, the SkiWelt is a paradise for those who love easy cruising. There are lots of blue runs, and many of the reds deserve a blue classification. It is a big area, and you get a feeling of travelling around. In good snow the long red runs to the valley – down the Hartkaiser funicular, for example – are excellent. The main challenge arises when ice and slush can make even gentle lower slopes tricky. For timid intermediates Astberg is handy.

Beginners Ellmau has an array of good nursery slopes covered by snow-guns. The main ones are at the Going end, but there are some by the road to the funicular. The Astberg chair opens up a more snow-sure plateau at altitude. The Brandstadl area has a section of short easy runs.

Snowboarding Ellmau is a good place to learn as its local slopes are easy.

Cross-country The SkiWelt area has a total of 196km of trails, including long and challenging ones, but trails at altitude are lacking.

Mountain restaurants There are many small places providing good-value food in pleasant surroundings and happily marked on the piste map. The Rübezahl Alm above Ellmau is one of our favourites – a lovely old hut with good food ('excellent ribs') and lots of different rooms and areas that make it very cosy; but it gets very busy. The Tanzbodenalm near Brandstadl above Scheffau is pleasantly woody, serving delicious deer stew. Other reporter tips include: the Jägerhütte (below

LIFT PASSES

**SkiWelt Wilder
Kaiser-Brixental**

Prices in €

Age	6-day
under 16	113
16 to 17	180
18 plus	225

Free Under 7
Beginner Points cards
Note Ski-bus included
Alternative pass
Kitzbüheler Alpen
AllStarCard covers:
Schneewinkel (St
Johann), Kitzbühel,
SkiWelt, Ski Juwel,
Skicircus Saalbach-
Hinterglemm and Zell
am See-Kaprun

Hartkaiser), and the jolly Hartkaiser ('toilets accessed by escalator!'). The 'rustic' Jochstub'n has a self-service part and is 'good for an end of afternoon drink'. The table-service section at the panoramic Bergkaiser is praised this year – 'delicious, plentiful food'. It and the Blattlalm on Astberg both have great views. The 'cosy' Brenner Alm provides 'enjoyable delicacies'. Then there's the Aualm below Zinsberg for cakes and glühwein, the Brandstadl above Scheffau and, a bit lower down, the 'excellent' Bavaria.

Schools and guides There are three schools and a specialist snowboard school in Ellmau, two in Scheffau and two in Going. A reporter's beginners had problems with the Ellmauer school this year: 'Instructor refused to speak English, lacked patience, took them to slopes above their ability and they almost gave up. They were eventually moved and the second instructor really brought them on.' The Scheffau school has been praised: 'excellent, properly evaluated and put into proper groups'.

Families Ellmau is an attractive resort for families: 'Probably the best family resort I have visited – from ski school to alternative attractions,' says a reporter. Both the Ellmauer and the Top schools have their own fun parks and play areas. The leisure centre and toboggan run are popular.

STAYING THERE

Ellmau is essentially a hotel and guest house resort.

Chalets A recent reporter said Crystal's chalet Hartkaiser was 'well run, had good food, a bus stop outside and was good budget accommodation'.

Hotels The Bär is an elegant, relaxed luxury place. The Kaiserhof is another luxury option. The Sporthotel has 'comfortable rooms. gorgeous pool, fantastic food. Only downside is that smoking is allowed in the lounge/bar'. The Hochfilzer is central and well equipped (with outdoor hot tub, indoor pool, sauna, steam); the simpler Pension Claudia is under the same ownership. The Kaiserblick has good spa facilities and is right by the piste.

Apartments There is a wide variety. The Landhof apartments – with pool, sauna and steam room – have impressed a regular visitor.

Eating out The jolly Lobewein is a splendid, big, central chalet, with

cheerful service in countless rooms. The Ellmauer Alm has been tipped.

Après-ski Bettina is good for coffee and cakes. Memory is the early-evening riotous party pub. Pub 66 and Sandy's (formerly Ötzy Bar) have live music. The Ellmauer Alm has live entertainment – a 'highlight of the Ellmau après scene', says a 2015 reporter. Tour operator reps organize events such as sleigh rides and tubing, and bowling and Tirolean folklore evenings in Söll. Ski night (torchlit walk, ski instructor display, glühwein, music) has a party atmosphere each week. The toboggan run from the Astberg lift is 'great fun'.

Off the slopes A guest card conveys various discounts, including entry to the KaiserBad leisure centre. There's a pool. Excursion possibilities include Innsbruck and Salzburg. Valley walks can be spoiled by the busy main road.

LINKED RESORT – 745m

SCHEFFAU

Little Scheffau is one of the most attractive of the region's villages and is well placed for quick access to most parts of the SkiWelt area – though the village itself is not convenient for the lifts, which are a short bus ride away. You can ski down to the gondolas at Blaiken, unless of course you opt to leave your kit near the lift station. The village spreads up quite a steep slope. Reporters recommend the 3-star Alpin, the central Gasthof Weberbauer and the 'well-priced' Waldrand. Après-ski is 'non-existent', said one happy reporter, but there are a couple of bars – the Sternbar is lively after the lifts close. There's little to do off the slopes.

LINKED RESORT – 800m

GOING

Going is a tiny, attractively rustic village, ideal for families looking for a quiet time. It is well placed for the limited but quiet slopes of the Astberg and for the vast area of nursery slopes shared with Ellmau. Prices are low, but as it's at one extreme end of the SkiWelt, it's not an ideal base for covering the whole of the region on the cheap unless you have a car to speed up access to Scheffau and Söll (or you're happy to take buses). The Lanzenhof is a cosy central pension, where we have enjoyed an excellent dinner. There's an ice rink.

TOURIST OFFICES

Wilder Kaiser
(Ellmau, Söll,
Scheffau, Going)
www.wilderkaiser.
info
SkiWelt
www.skiwelt.at

Hintertux / Tux valley

Small, unspoiled, traditional villages, high snow-sure glacier slopes and lots of other areas covered by the valley lift pass

£95
RESORT PRICE INDEX

TOP 10 RATINGS

Extent	★★★
Fast lifts	★★★
Queues	★★★
Snow	★★★★★
Expert	★★★
Intermediate	★★★
Beginner	★★
Charm	★★★
Convenience	★★
Scenery	★★★

NEWS

2015/16: A new six-person chairlift will run up to Grosser Kaserer, providing a welcome alternative to the Kaserer 1 drag lift.

KEY FACTS

Resort	1500m
	4,920ft

Ziller valley
Slopes	630-3250m
	2,070-10,660ft
Lifts	178
Pistes	487km
	303 miles

Ski and Glacier World Zillertal 3000
Slopes	630-3250m
	2,070-10,660ft
Lifts	63
Pistes	193km
	120 miles

Hintertux only
Slopes	1500-3250m
	4,920-10,660ft
Lifts	21
Pistes	59km
	37 miles

➕ Hintertux has one of the best year-round glaciers in the world

➕ Lanersbach's slopes form part of an extensive area, linked to Mayrhofen

➕ Wide-ranging area lift pass

➕ Some excellent off-piste

➕ Quiet, traditional villages

➖ Not ideal for beginners or timid intermediates

➖ Not surprisingly, glacier slopes can be cold and windy

For guaranteed good snow, Hintertux is simply one of the best places to go. Its glacier is not only extensive; it is one of the two most challenging and interesting lift-served glacier areas in the Alps (along with Stubai). But the quieter, friendlier, non-glacial slopes down the valley, linked to the slopes of Mayrhofen, are also well worth exploring (read the Mayrhofen chapter too).

The Tux valley, effectively the top end of the Zillertal, offers a variety of small villages. At the end of the valley, below the glacier, is Hintertux; a few km down-valley, the main resorts are Lanersbach and Vorderlanersbach next-door. Lower down still is Finkenberg. All are covered in this chapter. There is also lodging in Juns and Madseit, between Hintertux and Lanersbach.

All the major resort villages have gondolas into the local slopes: the Lanersbach one goes to Eggalm, and you can ski to Vorderlanersbach from there; the Vorderlanersbach one goes to Rastkogel, and from there you can ski into Mayrhofen's Penken-Horberg slopes; and the Finkenberg one goes up to Penken, meeting the lifts above Mayrhofen.

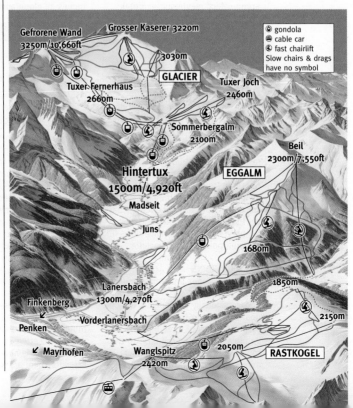

Gefrorene Wand 3250m/10,660ft

Grosser Kaserer 3220m

3030m

GLACIER

Tuxer Fernerhaus 2660m

Tuxer Joch 2460m

Sommerbergalm 2100m

Beil 2300m/7,550ft

Hintertux 1500m/4,920ft

EGGALM

Madseit

Juns

1680m

1850m

Lanersbach 1300m/4,270ft

Finkenberg

Vorderlanersbach

2150m

Penken

↙ Mayrhofen

Wanglspitz 2420m

2050m

RASTKOGEL

- 🚠 gondola
- 🚡 cable car
- 🚠 fast chairlift
- Slow chairs & drags have no symbol

↑ The runs off the glacier bring you down into this little valley, where you must ride a short six-pack back up to Sommerbergalm
WWW.TUX.AT / ROBERT REID

The higher villages are linked by frequent free ski-buses. A cheap (1.50 euros) night-bus runs until 2.30am. Finkenberg is less well served.

In general these aren't the most riotous of Austrian resorts – but there is après action to be had. At the Hintertux lift base there is a big party scene, which may result in 'drunk people fighting to get on' the mid-evening buses to lower resorts.

The Tux valley and Mayrhofen lifts form what is called the Ski and Glacier World Zillertal 3000. The Superskipass also covers other Ziller valley resorts (read the Mayrhofen chapter). The SGWZ3000 piste map is very clear, and names all mountain restaurants.

Hintertux 1500m

➕ Departure point for the excellent high glacier slopes
➕ Liveliest of the villages for après-ski

➖ Quiet later in the evening
➖ Remote setting
➖ Not much to do off the slopes

Life in Hintertux revolves around the glacier; staying here gets you up the mountain early, and means you don't have far to stagger after joining in the teatime revelry at the lift base. But later on, it may feel too quiet for some.

Village charm The resort is little more than a small collection of hotels and guest houses, in traditional style. Well, two collections actually – read on.
Convenience The main village is a 15-minute walk from the lifts, but there are also hotels at the lift base – the obvious place to stay, in our view.
Scenery There are fabulous views from the high points of the glacier.

THE MOUNTAINS
Hintertux's slopes are fairly extensive and, for a glacier, surprisingly varied and occasionally challenging. Only the final ski route to the valley is in trees.
Slopes A series of three big twin-cable gondolas goes from the base to the top of the glacier in around 30 minutes. The second and third stages are linked by a short slope at Tuxer Fernerhaus. A second smaller gondola also goes to Tuxer Fernerhaus, with a 10-seat gondola above it. From the top glacier slopes there are links across to another 1000m-vertical chain of lifts below Grosser Kaserer; from this coming season the top part will be served by a six-pack as well as two draglifts. Behind Gefrorene Wand is the area's one sunny piste, with its own triple chairlift. At Sommerbergalm a fast quad serves short, easy slopes below Tuxer Joch.

There are two runs to the valley. From Sommerbergalm there is a ski route. The second way, from Tuxer Joch down a deserted valley equipped with snowmaking, is now a red piste.
Fast lifts There are high-capacity

LIFT PASSES

Superskipass Zillertal

Prices in €	
Age	**6-day**
under 15	104
15 to 18	185
19 plus	231
Free Under 6	
Senior No deals	
Beginner No deals	
Notes 2-day and over passes include all Ziller valley lifts; part-day passes available	

gondolas all the way to the top, but the shorter lifts serving most of the slopes are T-bars and slow chairs.

Queues The gondolas make light work of any queues. But the main runs can get crowded. Traditionally the Kaserer area on skier's left has been quieter, but the new six-pack may change that. The valley run can be unpleasantly busy at the end of the day.

Terrain parks Europe's highest World Cup half-pipe is on the glacier (a popular summer hang-out), and there is a terrain park for all levels.

Snow reliability Snow does not come more reliable than this. Even off the glacier, the other slopes are high and face north. The run from Tuxer Joch to the valley has snowmaking.

Experts There is more to amuse experts here than on any other glacier, with a proper black run at glacier level and challenging slopes beneath. A lot of the off-piste is little used.

Intermediates The area particularly suits good, confident intermediates. The long runs down from Gefrorene Wand and Kaserer are fun. The runs to the valley are very satisfying. Moderate intermediates will love the top slopes on the glacier, and the Tuxer Joch area.

Beginners There is a short nursery slope at valley level, but then you're riding the gondola up to (and back from) Sommerbergalm, where there are blue runs served by drags and a chair. You'll need a full lift pass.

Snowboarding There are some great off-piste opportunities, but boarders complain about the number of T-bars.

Cross-country See Lanersbach.

Mountain restaurants For some time our favourite has been Gletscherhütte, at the top of the area – good shielded terraces with BBQ, and table-service in parts of the cosy, woody interior. But we haven't visited the ancient Spannagelhaus refuge lower down since the lift company turned it into 'an attractive table-service restaurant' with a wide-ranging menu. The 2013 renovation of Tuxer Fernerhaus 'sets the standard for self-service places', said a 2014 visitor; it also has a large table service restaurant, Wirtshaus. Tuxer Joch Haus has great views.

Schools and guides The three schools serve all the resorts in Tux, but we lack reports. Tux 3000 has guiding, touring and freeriding programmes.

Families Most of the ski schools run classes for children from age four. There's a fun area on the glacier.

STAYING THERE

Most hotels are large and comfortable and have spa facilities, but there are also more modest pensions.

Hotels We think it makes sense to stay close to the lifts. Closest is the 4-star Neuhintertux, preferred option of our regular reporter – 'food not spectacular, but spa very good'.

Apartments There are plenty of self-catering apartments.

Eating out Mainly hotel-based.

Après-ski There can be a lively après-ski scene both at mid-mountain (Sommerbergalm) and at the base, where Hohenhaus Tenne has several different bars with 'a good party atmosphere'; the Rindererhof is another popular place to gather.

Off the slopes Lots of ice activities on the glacier – climbing, natural ice palace, etc. The hotel spa facilities are excellent, including a thermal pool at the Kirchler.

Lanersbach 1300m

➕ Pleasant, compact village	➖ Village fairly quiet by Austrian
➕ Well placed for skiing the glacier	standards
and for the Mayrhofen slopes	➖ Few easy local runs for novices

Lanersbach and neighbouring Vorderlanersbach are attractive bases for accessing both the glacier and the valley resorts, with the particular attraction that you can ski home to them from the Eggalm sector.

Village charm Lanersbach is small, attractive, spacious and traditional. The quiet centre near the pretty church is delightfully unspoiled, bypassed by the busy road up to Hintertux. Vorderlanersbach is a mini version.

Convenience Lanersbach has everything you need in a resort. The centre is within walking distance of the Eggalm gondola. Vorderlanersbach has its own gondola up to Rastkogel.

Scenery These are attractive villages in a long, pretty and varied valley.

THE MOUNTAINS

Slopes The slopes of Eggalm, accessed by the gondola from Lanersbach, offer a small network of pleasantly varied intermediate pistes, usually delightfully quiet. You can descend on red or blue runs back to the village or to Vorderlanersbach, where a gondola goes up to the higher, open Rastkogel slopes; here, two fast chairlifts serve some very enjoyable long red and blue runs, and link with Mayrhofen's slopes. The linking run has red and black variants; both can get very mogulled, and many people opt to ride the jumbo cable car down; a short rope tow cuts out the need to hike up to the top station.

The lower half of the run back from Rastkogel to Eggalm is shown as a ski route on some maps but not others; it is narrow but it is effectively a piste, and it is served by snowmaking. The alternative is to ride the gondola down to Vorderlanersbach (there are no pistes) and get a bus to Lanersbach.

Fast lifts Gondolas are the access lifts, and Eggalm and Rastkogel each have two six-packs.

Queues We have no reports of any problems. Indeed, Eggalm can be delightfully quiet.

Terrain parks The nearest parks are at Mayrhofen and Hintertux.

Snow reliability Snow conditions are usually good, at least in early season; by Austrian standards these are high slopes, and snowmaking covers some runs on both Eggalm and Rastkogel. But Rastkogel is excessively sunny. The grooming is 'OK – not great'.

Experts There are no pistes to challenge experts, but there is plenty of off-piste terrain, and a fine off-piste route to the village starting a short hike from the top of Eggalm.

Intermediates The local slopes suit intermediates best, with some excellent, challenging red runs – and you have Mayrhofen's slopes to explore, too.

Beginners Lanersbach has a nursery slope (as do Madseit and Juns), but there are few ideal progression slopes on Eggalm – most of the easy runs are on the higher lifts of Rastkogel.

Snowboarding The area isn't great for novices – there are draglifts dotted around, some in key places.

Cross-country There are 28km of cross-country trails around Madseit and Vorderlanersbach.

Mountain restaurants There are quite a few rustic places doing simple food, but demand exceeds supply, and self-service is the norm. There are two table-service exceptions on Eggalm. Egger Schialm is tucked away from the main runs, so is less busy – excellent gröstl, friendly people, good prices. Lattenalm has splendid views of the Tux glacier. On Rastkogel, the self-service Heidi's Schistadl is tipped.

Schools and guides There are three schools in the valley, but we lack recent reports on them.

Families The Vorderlanersbach Playarena nursery takes all ages.

WWW.TUX.AT

The glacier is more or less central in this comprehensive shot, with the big complex of Sommerbergalm down to the left ↓

STAYING THERE

Both villages are essentially hotel-based resorts.

Hotels In central Lanersbach, the 3-star Pinzger is tipped this year – 'friendly staff, good breakfast, great value'. The Lanersbacherof is a good 4-star with a pool, sauna, steam room and hot tub close to the lifts. In Vorderlanersbach the 3-star Kirchlerhof has been recommended in the past and has a wellness area.

Apartments Plenty available locally.

Eating out Mainly hotel-based, busy, and geared to serving dinner early. Bergfriedalm does good food.

Pipasa is good for pizza, we're

Après-ski The Kleine Tenne, like its Hintertux sibling, has a 'good party atmosphere'. Bergfriedalm is an old wooden building with traditional Austrian music, 'a great place for a late drink', and judged 'best après-ski ever' by one 50-ish reporter. Gletscherspalte is a more youth-oriented disco.

Off the slopes Facilities are fairly good, and the bus service throughout the valley is extensive. Some hotels have pools and fitness rooms open to non-residents. Innsbruck and Salzburg are possible excursions.

Finkenberg 840m

+ Fast lift access to the main slopes
+ Pleasant, uncrowded village that appeals to families, but ...
- Lodging sprawls along a steep and busy main road
- No pisted runs to resort level

If you want to ski Mayrhofen's extensive area but avoid the après-ski crowds, Finkenberg makes a quieter alternative – and with direct access to the slopes. But the only way home is an itinerary (not shown on some maps).

Village charm The resort is a collection of traditional-style hotels, bars, cafes and private homes. There is a central pretty area around the church.

Convenience Most of the buildings (and hotels) are spread along the busy, steep, winding main road up to Lanersbach. Beware slippery pavements. Some hotels are within walking distance of the gondola, and many of the more distant ones run their own minibuses; there is also a village minibus service.

Scenery Steep mountains rise up on both sides.

THE MOUNTAIN

Slopes A two-stage gondola gives direct access to the Penken slopes – and in good conditions you can ski back to the village on a ski route (though it is often closed).

Fast lifts See Mayrhofen.

Queues Few problems reported. The gondola to and from the Penken may have queues at peak times.

Terrain parks The Mayrhofen park is easily accessed.

Snow reliability The local slopes are not as well endowed with snowmaking as those on Mayrhofen's side.

Experts Not much challenge, except off-piste and the Harakiri piste (read the Mayrhofen chapter).

Intermediates Lots to do. From the top of the gondola you have excellent red-gradient slopes back towards the

village, and a link to Mayrhofen's Penken and Horberg slopes – and from there, access to Rastkogel.

Beginners There is a small village slope, and further slopes up the gondola; Mayrhofen is a better bet.

Snowboarding See Mayrhofen.

Cross-country Cross-country skiers have to get a bus up to Lanersbach.

Mountain restaurants Read the Mayrhofen chapter.

Schools and guides The Finkenberg is the main one, but the Sunny and Skipower schools also operate here.

Families The Finkenberg school takes children from age four.

STAYING THERE

Hotels The 5-star Sporthotel Stock, owned by the family of 1980s downhiller Leonard Stock, has great spa facilities. There are several 4-stars, for example, the Eberl – 'excellent food more than made up for old-fashioned room' – and the Kristall, which is 150m from the gondola with good wellness/spa facilities. The 3-star B&B hotel Harpfner has been highly recommended in the past.

Eating out Mainly in hotels, notably the Eberl.

Après-ski The main après-ski spots are the lively Laterndl Pub at the foot of the gondola and Finkennest.

Off the slopes OK for the active: curling, ice skating, swimming and good local walks.

GETTING THERE

Air Innsbruck 90km/ 55 miles (1hr30); Salzburg 190km/ 120 miles (2hr30); Munich 215km/ 135 miles (3hr)

Rail Local line to Mayrhofen; regular buses from station

TOURIST OFFICE

www.tux.at

Ischgl

Ischgl is unique: high, snow-sure slopes, a superb lift system, and a traditional-style Tirolean village. Perfection? Well, not quite ...

RESORT PRICE INDEX

- ➕ Traditional-style village with a traffic-free core
- ➕ High slopes with reliable snow
- ➕ Fair-sized area of slopes linked to Samnaun in Switzerland
- ➕ Superb modern lift system
- ➕ Exceptional après-ski with a huge number of lively bars and clubs

- ➖ Village is more like a town, densely developed, with a rather urban, glitzy feel
- ➖ Not ideal for beginners or timid intermediates, for various reasons
- ➖ Few seriously steep runs
- ➖ Very little wooded terrain
- ➖ Treks to the gondolas for some

RATINGS

The mountains

Extent	★★★★
Fast lifts	★★★★★
Queues	★★★★
Terrain p'ks	★★★★★
Snow	★★★★
Expert	★★★★
Intermediate	★★★★
Beginner	★★
Boarder	★★★★★
X-country	★★★
Restaurants	★★★★
Schools	★★★
Families	★★

The resort

Charm	★★★
Convenience	★★★
Scenery	★★★
Eating out	★★★★
Après-ski	★★★★★
Off-slope	★★★

Ischgl's slopes are more like those of a purpose-built French resort than a typical Tirolean place – high, snow-sure and fab for intermediates. It can't compete with the big boys in terms of extent but it's plenty big enough for all but the keenest piste-basher for a week. And its lift system (with over 80% of them fast, including 22 fast chairs) is far better than anything in France.

But the village and vibes are most definitely Austrian – largely built in traditional chalet style and with raucous après-ski that lasts from after lunch till dawn. Two seasons ago we were there, along with 20,000 others, for the Robbie Williams end-of-season concert on the slopes, and the next day, 4 May, was one of our best ski days of the season, with wonderful fresh powder.

The place has its drawbacks – see our list of minus points above. But if you fancy something different, consider giving it a try. More and more readers are – this year we had a record number of reports on it, all singing its praises.

NEWS

2015/16: A new underground car park will open. It is part of a development including new municipal offices and a bus terminal.

2014/15: A new 28-seat gondola replaced the old 4-seat Pardatschgrat gondola and has helped reduce morning queues. The top section of the old gondola has been retained to allow skiing of the top runs without descending to the valley.

KEY FACTS

Resort	1400m	
	4,590ft	
Slopes	1400-2870m	
	4,590-9,420ft	
Lifts	45	
Pistes	163-238km	
	102-148 miles	

THE RESORT

Ischgl is a compact village tucked away south of St Anton in the long, narrow Paznaun valley on the Swiss border; the ski area is shared with Samnaun in Switzerland. The Silvretta lift pass also covers Galtür further up the valley (see the end of this chapter) and Kappl and See down the valley (covered in the resort directory, at the back). All are linked by ski-buses and worth visiting; they make cheaper, quieter bases. A car allows trips to St Anton too. But heavy snowfalls can close the valley road for days due to avalanche danger.

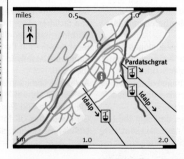

VILLAGE CHARM ★★★
More town than village

The buildings are predominantly in traditional chalet style, with one or two modern exceptions. But this is no rustic backwater – the narrow streets have a towny feel, and the style is swanky and brash rather than tasteful. There's a selection of lively bars and a better-than-usual selection of fashion shops – 'more luxury shops than Lech', said a reporter. The narrow main street plus a couple of side streets are mostly traffic-free – the valley road up to Galtür bypasses the village.

CONVENIENCE ★★★
Beware of the bypass

Choose location with care and beware of lodgings on the wrong side of the bypass road. You can leave your kit up at Idalp, Pardatschgrat and at the base lifts. Gondolas go up to mid-mountain from two points about 500m apart. The best location, overall, is on or near the main pedestrian street between the two. The eastern gondola station is separated from the main street by a low hill but is reached by an underground moving walkway.

SCENERY ★★★★★
Good at the top
The wooded flanks of the valley rise steeply from the village, which gets almost no sun in January. But above the treeline, the Silvretta range is revealed in all its glory.

THE MOUNTAINS

Practically all the slopes are above the treeline, the main exception being the steep lower slopes above the village.

The piste map is OK but we found signposting inadequate: there are no big piste maps at the top of lifts and better direction markers are needed. The run numbering is confusing: a run may have multiple tributaries, or may split part-way down, with the variants having the same number. All this means trouble navigating, especially in poor visibility. There are two varieties of ski route – plain and 'extreme' – clearly stated to be 'not monitored'.

Ischgl's narrow streets are lined by swanky Tirolean-style buildings; but the place feels more like a town than a village
↓

EXTENT OF THE SLOPES ★★★★★
Extensive cross-border cruising
Prompted, no doubt, by the Schrahe report (see our feature chapter on piste extent) Ischgl now publishes three figures for km of pistes – ranging from 238km to 163km. We

applaud this move. But whichever way you look at it, it's a fair-sized area that will keep many intermediates happy for a week.

The sunny **Idalp** plateau, reached by the 24-person Silvrettabahn or the eight-seat Fimbabahn, is the hub of the slopes. It can be very crowded around there. Pardatschgrat, reached by a fast 28-seat gondola that was new for 2014/15, is about 300m higher. From Idalp, lifts radiate to a wide variety of mainly north-west- and west-facing runs and to the Swiss border.

The red runs back down to Ischgl provoke regular complaints. Neither is easy, conditions can be tricky, and countless reckless skiers make these runs even more hazardous. Both have final stretches that probably should be black. The wide, quiet piste down the Velilltal looks better, but turns rather nasty lower down and joins the steep 'black' bottom part of run 1A. Quite a few people choose, very sensibly, to ride the gondolas down.

A short piste brings you from Idalp to the lifts serving the **Höllkar** bowl, leading to a high point at Palinkopf, from which you can go down to the Piz Val Gronda cable car at the ski area's south-western end. Runs of 800m to 900m vertical from the top of the cable car and from Palinkopf go down to the **Fimbatal**.

On the Swiss side, the hub of activity is **Alp Trida**, surrounded by south- and east-facing runs with great views. From here a scenic red run goes down to Compatsch, for buses to Ravaisch (for the cable car back up) and Samnaun. From Palinkopf there is a lovely, long red run down a beautiful valley to Samnaun – not difficult, but very sunny in parts and prone to closure by avalanche risk. There is a long flat stretch at the end.

FAST LIFTS ★★★★★
One of the best
Ischgl is near the top of our fast league table and over 80% of its main lifts are fast – mainly fast chairs. Not surprisingly, reporters praise the lifts – 'best resort I've been to in 20 years', 'exceptional', 'state of the art'.

QUEUES ★★★★★
Piste crowds more of a problem
The new Pardatschgrat gondola, which increased uplift capacity by over 1,000 people per hour, seems to have reduced peak period queues from the

LIFT PASSES

VIP Skipass

Prices in €

Age	6-day
under 17	136
17 to 59	226
60 plus	204

Free Under 8

Beginner No deals

Notes Covers Ischgl, Samnaun and local buses; family reductions; for 2-day-plus pass, guest card for staying in Ischgl/ Mathon/Samnaun needed

Alternative pass
Silvretta pass covers Ischgl, Samnaun, Galtür, Kappl and See

village. 2015 reporters tell of waits of only 10 minutes or so. Once up, there may be short queues at Idalp and returning from Alp Trida. But crowds on the runs are more of an issue, especially at Idalp, on the easier runs on the Swiss side, at the narrow start of run 40 from Palinkopf and on the valley runs at the end of the day.

TERRAIN PARKS ★★★★★
One of Europe's best
The huge 'excellent' PlayStation Vita park above Idalp is 1600m long and well maintained. It has beginner, public and pro lines, revamped each year. Last season, it had 20 kickers between 6 and 20 metres, 30 other features and an airbag jump. There is another park at Velillscharte and a small park on the Swiss side. 'My teenage sons loved them,' says a reporter this year.

SNOW RELIABILITY ★★★★☆
Very good
All the slopes apart from the runs back to the resort are above 1800m, and many on the Ischgl side are north-west-facing. So snow conditions are generally reliable; many reporters comment on excellent early/late-season conditions and we experienced no shortage in May 2014. Snowmaking covers over half the slopes, including the descents to Ischgl and Samnaun. Reporters praise the grooming.

FOR EXPERTS ★★★★☆
Plenty to do
Ischgl can't compare with St Anton for exciting slopes. But by general Tirolean standards it serves experts well. All the blacks are genuine ones and in combination with testing reds offer excellent, challenging descents. Palinkopf, Greitspitz and Pardatschgrat

gondola
cable car
fast chairlift
Slow chairs & drags have no symbol

Lovely long run, with a jolly restaurant at the end, on the outskirts of Samnaun - so a great way to end the morning or the day

Greitspitz
2870m/9,420ft

Lange Wandt

Salaas

Greitspitz

Samnaun
1840m/6,040ft

Alp Trida
Sattel
2490m

Viderjoch II

Idjoch
2760m

Idjo

Ravaisch

Pendelbahn

Luftseilbahn

Viderjoch I

Sattel

Flimjo

Velill

Laret

Compatsch

Alp Trida
2265m

Flimsattel

Velillscharte
2555m

ALP TRIDA

Muller

Vishitz

Grivalea

Grivalea
2700m

2640m

Not a slow lift in sight in this sector - or in most other sectors, actually all have some good steep blacks and the wooded lower slopes of the Fimbatal are delightful in a storm. There is plenty of off-piste, and powder doesn't get tracked out too quickly, particularly on the Swiss side. The newish Piz Val Gronda cable car has opened up a big new area of off-piste including a fabulous big bowl. We had an excellent off-piste day a few seasons ago that included exploration of the shady side of Velilltal. There are also ski routes.

FOR INTERMEDIATES ★★★★
Something for everyone
Most of the slopes are wide, forgiving and ideal for intermediates – and there are plenty of them. Our favourite runs are those from Palinkopf and Piz Val Gronda down to Gampenalp at the edge of the ski area and the beautiful isolated red run which drops 1000m

from Palinkopf down to Samnaun in Switzerland. But there are lots of other options on Palinkopf, Greitspitz and Pardatschgrat. The reds down the beautiful Velilltal and the red from Greitspitz into Switzerland are great for quiet, high-speed cruising. For easier motorway cruising, there is lots of choice, including the runs down around Alp Trida on the Swiss side – but these can get crowded.

FOR BEGINNERS ★★★★★
Up the hill with the crowds
Up the mountain at Idalp there are good, sunny, snow-sure nursery slopes served by two moving carpets, drags and two fast chairs, but there are no special deals for beginners – you must buy a full lift pass to reach them. The blue runs on the east side of the bowl and down into Switzerland offer pleasant progression but get crowded.

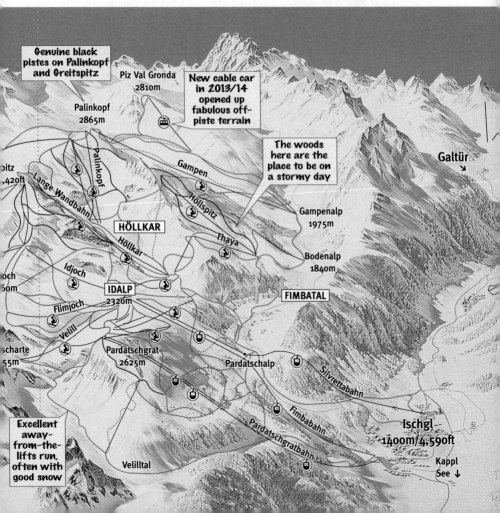

FOR BOARDERS ★★★★★
Pretty much perfect
Ischgl has long been a popular spot for snowboarders, with its long, wide, well-groomed slopes served by snowboard-friendly gondolas and fast chairlifts. The off-piste terrain is above the treeline, easily accessible and makes for great riding for most ability levels. And Ischgl is home to one of Austria's best terrain parks.

FOR CROSS-COUNTRY ★★★★★
Plenty in the valley
There are 100km of loops in the Ischgl, Galtür and Wirl area. Some trails tend to be shady, especially in early season, and are away from the main slopes, which makes meeting downhillers for lunch inconvenient.

MOUNTAIN RESTAURANTS ★★★★★
Good modern choices
Mountain restaurants generally offer good quality and choice. But they tend to be big, and despite this capacity can be stretched at peak times. They are clearly marked on the piste map.
Editors' choice On the Austrian side at Idalp, the Alpenhaus is very much a designer place, with both table-service (upstairs) and self-service areas. We're interested only in the former, although service is itself a bit slack. Food is good though and the relaxed ambience is great; recent reporters confirm our view. On the Swiss side at Alp Trida the Marmotte wins no prizes for interior design but does good food in calm and comfortable surroundings.
Worth knowing about In the Fimbatal the 'friendly' Paznauner Thaya has self-service with famously good pizza, and

table-service with good food upstairs; often with live bands or throbbing disco music. Bodenalp is a bit of a relic but some reporters like it. At Pardatschgrat, the glass-sided Pardorama is impressive, less crowded than lower places and has self- and table-service sections. A recent reporter liked the 'modern' refurbished self-service Höllboden. At the Schwarze Wand, in the Höllkar valley, you can 'watch big, tasty pizzas being made'.

On the Swiss side the woody old Alp Bella is good value for traditional food. Recent reports on the Alp Trida are favourable. The glass-sided Salaas is very stylish and spacious, but otherwise unremarkable.

SCHOOLS AND GUIDES ★★★★★
Good reports last season
The school meets up at Idalp. The beginners in a 2015 reporter's group found the 'instructors to be very good and encouraged skiers who showed aptitude'. A 2015 reporter hired a guide and had 'very good instruction – spent the whole 90 minutes in deep, fresh powder on virgin snow making my own fresh tracks – brilliant!' The school also organizes off-piste tours.

FOR FAMILIES ★★★★★
High-altitude options
Children can have lunch with their ski instructor; but small kids would be better off in Galtür or Kappl, where there are good play areas – see the end of this chapter for more on Galtür and the resort directory at the back of the book for more on Kappl.

STAYING THERE

Chalets Ski Total is the only chalet operator. They had the 58-bed chalet hotel Abendrot built for them a few years ago. On our recent visit we were impressed by the spacious, modern bedrooms and en-suite bathrooms. It is central, a few minutes from the gondolas but with no noise disturbance at night. Total also has the 22-bed Zita, near the Fimbabahn and, new for last year, the 30- to 40-bed Belmonte near the new Pardatschgrat gondola – 'very nice indeed', says a 2015 reporter. Belmonte and Abendrot have sauna and steam rooms.
Hotels There is a good selection from luxurious and pricey to simple B&Bs.
★★★★★Trofana Royal One of Austria's most luxurious hotels, with prices to

ISCHGL TO
In the foreground is the beginner area (near the buildings) and the easy blue runs that beginners progress to ↓

match. A celebrity chef runs the kitchen. Sumptuous spa facilities.

****Christine The best B&B in town? Big rooms, central location, helpful owners, good spa, pool.

****Elizabeth Newly renovated. Right by the Pardatschgrat gondola. Lively après-ski, pool, sauna and steam.

****Goldener Adler Central, traditional ambience but designer rooms; good food. Pool, sauna, spa.

****Gramaser Near the Trofana Royal. We've enjoyed staying here; friendly staff, excellent food.

****Jägerhof Friendly staff, good food, large comfortable rooms. Sauna, steam, spa.

****Madlein Convenient, chic, modern. 'Excellent' pool, sauna, spa. Nightclub.

***Alpenglühn Central, good-value B&B.

***Arnika A few minutes' walk from the Fimba gondola. 'Beautiful, gorgeous food, great staff.'

Apartments Some attractive apartments are available. The Golfais by the Pardatschgrat gondola, the apartments in the hotel Solaria (with use of its spa) and those in the Kardona hotel have been suggested.

EATING OUT ★★★★☆
Plenty of choice

Most restaurants are hotel-based. A 2015 reporter recommends the Sunnalm in the Sonne hotel for its 'salmon with honey and mustard and an excellent creamy turkey curry with rice served in a copper pot'. Two others rave about the pizzas at the Nevada. A recent visitor liked the Yscla hotel for 'fine dining'. We enjoyed excellent, varied meals at the popular Grillalm in hotel Gramaser, which also has the Steakhouse ('very good food and service'). A 2015 reporter liked Cafe Salner for its 'venison and pork steaks'. Other reporter tips include: the Nona ('pizza and Tirolean food, reasonable prices'), Allegra ('really good steaks and a pasta happy hour'), Dorf Cafe and hotel central. The Trofana Alm, which is as much a bar as a restaurant, and the Kitzloch, with its galleries over the dance floor, are good for grills and fondue.

APRES-SKI ★★★★★
Very lively

Ischgl is the liveliest resort in the Alps, we've concluded after a lot of in-depth research. The fun starts in the early afternoon – mountain restaurants such

ALPINE ANSWERS
The UK's No.1 Chalet Specialist

For choice and service look no further!

alpineanswers.co.uk
call: 020 7801 1080
ABTA

as Paznauner Thaya slide into après mode directly after lunch – and it doesn't stop; lots of people are still in ski boots late in the evening.

The obvious ports of call in the village are the Trofana Alm near the Silvrettabahn ('best après I have ever seen') and the Schatzi bar of the hotel Elizabeth by the Pardatschgratbahn – with scantily clad female dancers ('At least 500 people watching,' said a recent reporter). Next door is Freeride, with friendly staff, ski movies and dancers. Across the river the Kitzloch is one of the places for dancing on the tables in ski boots and 'conga lines'. Niki's Stadl has lively DJs. Käferalm opened last season in a new wooden building and a 2015 reporter loved it – 'amazing atmosphere with dancing on tables'. Feuer & Eis ('great atmosphere') and the basement Kuhstahl are packed all evening – the latter is one reporter's all-time favourite après bar. The Golden Eagle pub is popular with Brits looking for somewhere to sit. For a quiet drink, we (and many reporters) head for the Kiwi ('favourite spot for quiet beer or wine', 'reasonable prices', 'laid back', 'friendly staff, great music', said 2015 reporters) or for cocktails at pricey Guxa.

Later on, we've enjoyed dancing to a live band in the huge Trofana Arena – this bar also has pole dancing, as does the Coyote Ugly. Other nightclubs include Madlein (formerly Pacha), Living Room and Posthörndl, with an ancient Rome theme.

OFF THE SLOPES ★★★☆☆
No sun but a nice pool

The village gets little sun in the middle of winter, and the resort is best suited to those keen to hit the slopes. But there's no shortage of off-slope activities. There are lots of maintained paths including many at altitude (the tourist office claims over 1000km in the valley), a 7km floodlit toboggan run and a splendid sports centre with swimming pool and bowling. The outdoor ice rink has skating and curling. And you can browse upmarket shops. It's easy to get around the valley by bus, and there's a special lift pass for pedestrians.

LINKED RESORT – 1840m
SAMNAUN

Small, quiet duty-free Samnaun is in a corner of Switzerland more easily reached from Austria. We know of no UK tour operators going here, but a recent reporter reckons more Brits are finding their way to it.

There are four small components, roughly 1km apart: Samnaun-Dorf, prettily set at the head of the valley and the main focus, with some swanky hotels and duty-free shops; Ravaisch, where the cable car goes up; tiny Plan; and the hamlets of Laret and Compatsch, at the end of the main piste to the valley. We've stayed happily on the edge of Dorf in the 4-star Waldpark B&B, and a reporter recommended the Montana. Other tips: 4-star Muttler and Des Alpes. There's a smart AlpenQuell spa-pool-fitness centre.

The Schmuggler Alm at the bottom of the long run from Palinkopf is a popular lunch and après-ski spot. The Almraus (hotel Cresta) at Compatsch has been recommended for drinks. The school has a good reputation.

UP-VALLEY VILLAGE – 1585m
GALTÜR

Galtür is a charming, peaceful, traditional village clustered around a pretty little church, amid impressive scenery at the head of Ischgl's Paznaun valley. Many visitors find the resort very quiet – there are just a few shops, restaurants, and a good bakery. It is a real contrast to bustling Ischgl.

Sunnier and cheaper than Ischgl, Galtür is a good base for families and mixed-ability groups. Galtür's own slopes rise to 2295m above a lift base at Wirl, a short bus ride from the village. The free buses to Ischgl are regular and quick but overcrowded at peak times even in January. Taxis to Ischgl's nightlife are economic if shared. But a recent reporter warns that the roads even to both Wirl and Ischgl

were closed due to avalanche danger for two days, so he was unable to ski.

Galtür's Silvapark ski area has only 40km of pistes, served by two fast chairs, a gondola and some long draglifts. Queues are rare. The slopes are fairly high, so pretty snow-sure but they can be bleak in bad weather. Grooming is good.

Most runs are classified red, though some would be blue elsewhere. Run 8 is one of our favourites; a broad, long cruise with great views of the frozen dam below. The main blue piste can get crowded and has a steepish section at the top, but it is a long, pretty cruise to the valley. There are some challenges – reds and a black served by the fast Ballunspitze chair are short and steep. And there are three ski routes to try. The area on the far right of the piste map, served by a slow double chair and a T-bar, is quiet, shady and has some good off-piste in a bowl and among well-spaced trees. There's a terrain park, and a fine nursery area at the base.

The school has been praised and offers small classes. Kinderland has its own moving carpet and animal characters. There are 100km of cross-country loops in the Galtür, Ischgl and Wirl area. The cosy, wooden Wieberhimml mountain hut is a lively, sunny spot for drinks. And we had good food at the Panorama Tenne, beside the gondola. The Faulbrunnalm at the top of the gondola is 'never overcrowded'. The Addis Abeba is a hip bar near the Soppalift drag.

There are good hotels. A 2015 reporter says the 4-star Büntali 'is excellent with a great wellness centre'. The 4-star Almhof has 'excellent evening meals, every course a work of art'. A reporter this year says the Alpenhotel Tirol is 'terrific with great food and professional staff who even cooked the haggis we'd brought with us for our Burns Night supper!' Flüchthorn has a 'charming restaurant' and Tirolean atmosphere.

Off-slope facilities are limited, apart from the impressive Alpinarium, an avalanche-protection structure and exhibition centre built after the avalanche that devastated the village in 1999. Much of the information is in German only, but it's worth a visit. The sports centre has a pool, tennis and squash. There's night skiing and tobogganing on Wednesdays, hiking, ice skating and curling.

GETTING THERE

Air Innsbruck 100km/ 60 miles (1hr30); Zürich 240km/ 150 miles (3hr); Munich 300km/ 185 miles (3hr30)

Rail Landeck (30km/19 miles); buses from station

TOURIST OFFICES

Ischgl
www.ischgl.com

Samnaun
(Switzerland)
www.samnaun.ch

Galtür
www.galtuer.com

KITZBÜHEL TOURIST OFFICE

Kitzbühel

Despite the racy image, the slopes are mostly [...]
centre at the base, though, is something speci[...]

£105
RESORT PRICE INDEX

RATINGS

The mountains

Extent	★★★
Fast lifts	★★★★★
Queues	★★★
Terrain p'ks	★★★
Snow	★★
Expert	★★★
Intermediate	★★★★
Beginner	★★
Boarder	★★
X-country	★★★
Restaurants	★★★★
Schools	★★★★
Families	★

The resort

Charm	★★★★
Convenience	★★
Scenery	★★★
Eating out	★★★★
Après-ski	★★★★
Off-slope	★★★★★

NEWS

2015/16: A double chair for Bichlalm to serve its area of ungroomed slopes should open in time for the season.

2014/15: Several runs in the Ehrenbachhöhe area were remodelled.

KEY FACTS

Resort	760m
	2,490ft
Slopes	800-2000m
	2,620-6,560ft
Lifts	53
Slopes	209km
	130 miles

The km total is the resort's official figure, verified by consultant Christoph Schrahe (read our feature on piste extent). It includes ski routes.

VERIFIED
by Christoph Schrahe
PISTELENGTH.COM

+ Extensive, attractive, varied slopes offering a sensation of travel

+ Beautiful medieval town centre

+ Vibrant nightlife

+ Lots to do off the slopes

+ Hotels to suit every budget

+ Excellent mountain restaurants

− Low altitude [...]
poor low do[...]
snowmaking [...]

− Surprisingly [...] on-piste

− Mediocre resort-level nursery area

− Some crowded pistes

− Town sprawls widely

Kitzbühel's Hahnenkamm downhill race course is the most exciting on the World Cup circuit, and race weekend is one of the jolliest parties in the Alps. But the place has powerful attractions at other times too – see our + points above.

The lift system has improved hugely in the last decade and it now gets our highest ★★★★★ rating for fast lifts.

Sadly, it doesn't get the same rating for snow – for us, the great weakness of the place. It's not a matter of quantity, but of quality. Just once, we arrived in a storm and had good piste conditions to valley level. Often the snow is fine high up but not lower down. The fact is, Kitzbühel needs more altitude.

THE RESORT

Kitzbühel is a large valley town with its major ski area on one side and a couple of minor ones on the other. The major area, spreading south-west from the famous Hahnenkamm directly above the town, is reached by gondola from just outside the town centre and shared with Kirchberg, another substantial resort and covered at the end of the chapter.

The 'still great value' Kitzbüheler Alpen AllStarCard lift pass covers seven separate ski areas in the region – read 'Lift passes'. One of those – the SkiWelt – is accessible by the Ki-West gondola, a short bus ride from Skirast.

VILLAGE CHARM ★★★★
Medieval town centre

The sizeable and largely car-free medieval centre – with quaint church, cobbled streets and attractively painted buildings – is delightful and a compelling place to stay. Many visitors love the upscale, towny ambience and swanky shops and cafes. But the resort spreads widely, and busy roads surround the old town. This is no quiet little village.

CONVENIENCE ★★
Choose your spot carefully

A gondola from the edge of the town goes up to the Hahnenkamm, the start of the main area of slopes. Across town, close to the railway station but some way from the centre, another

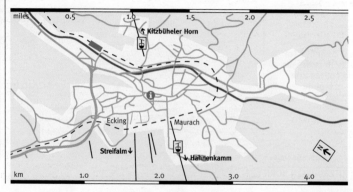

gondola accesses the much smaller Kitzbüheler Horn sector.

The size of Kitzbühel (compare the map on the previous page with other Austrian resorts, such as Ischgl) makes choice of location important. We, and many visitors, prefer to be in the centre of town and close to the Hahnenkamm gondola. Beginners should bear in mind that the Hahnenkamm nursery slopes are often lacking in snow, and then novices are taken up the Horn.

Views have varied on the free buses. The circular route and high-season crowding have led some recent reporters to walk instead, but a regular visitor rates them 'quick, efficient and uncrowded'. There are ski/boot depots at obvious points.

SCENERY ★★★☆☆
Attractive valley views
Kitzbühel is set at a junction of broad, pretty valleys, among partly wooded mountains. There are good views from

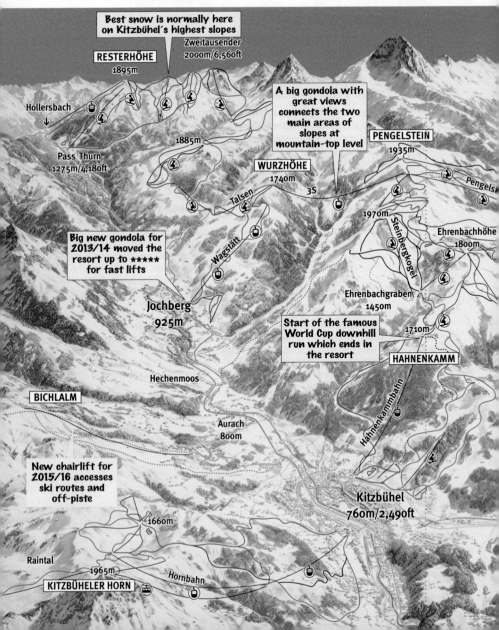

Pengelstein across both valleys (the minor peak of Gr Rettenstein is prominent) and to the SkiWelt. And it is worth riding the 3S gondola for the views alone – especially if you hit it lucky and ride in the cabin that has a glass floor. From the Resterhöhe slopes, in particular, there are great panoramic views of the high Alps to the south, including Grossvenediger directly south and Grossglockner slightly east of south.

THE MOUNTAINS

Kitzbühel's extensive main area of slopes – shared with Kirchberg and other villages – offers some open runs higher up but they soon run into patchy forest lower down. Most slopes face north-east or north-west.

The piste map is pretty clear but readers' views on signposting vary. And many readers find that run classifications exaggerate difficulty.

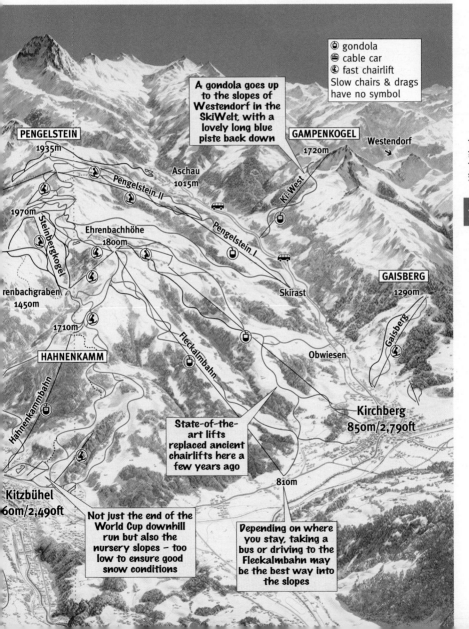

A gondola goes up to the slopes of Westendorf in the SkiWelt, with a lovely long blue piste back down

State-of-the-art lifts replaced ancient chairlifts here a few years ago

Not just the end of the World Cup downhill run but also the nursery slopes – too low to ensure good snow conditions

Depending on where you stay, taking a bus or driving to the Fleckalmbahn may be the best way into the slopes

gondola
cable car
fast chairlift
Slow chairs & drags have no symbol

Kitzbühel's Hahnenkamm Downhill race, held in mid- to late January each year (19 to 24 January in 2016), is the toughest as well as one of the most famous on the World Cup circuit. On the race weekend the town is packed, and there is a real carnival atmosphere, with bands, people in traditional costumes and huge (and loud) cowbells everywhere. The race itself starts with a steep icy section before you hit the famous Mausfalle and Steilhang, where even Franz Klammer used to get worried. The course starts near the top of the Hahnenkamm gondola and drops 860m to finish among the noise and celebrations right on the edge of town. The course is normally closed from the start of the season until the race is over, but after the race weekend ordinary mortals can try most of the course, if the snow is good enough – it's an unpisted ski route mostly. We found it steep and tricky in parts, even when going slowly – it must be terrifying at race speeds of 80mph or more.

KITZBÜHEL TOURISMUS

AUSTRIA

124

LIFT PASSES

Prices in €

Age	6-day
under 16	121
16 to 18	186
19 plus	241

Free Under 7

Senior 80+: season pass €35

Beginner Reduced pass for Gaisberg and Ganslern chairs only; six free lifts (two in Kitzbühel)

Notes Covers Kitzbühel, Kirchberg, Reith, Aurach, Jochberg, Mittersill/ Hollersbach; hourly and pedestrian tickets; 50% reduction on pool entry

Alternative passes Kitzbüheler Alpen AllStarCard covers Kitzbühel, Schneewinkel (St Johann), SkiWelt, Ski Juwel, Skicircus Saalbach, Zell-Kaprun, Fieberbrunn, Waidring; Salzburg Super Ski Card covers 22 ski areas in the Salzburg province

EXTENT OF THE SLOPES ★★★✩✩
Big but bitty
The resort claims 209km of pistes and ski routes and is one of the few to have its claim verified independently – see our feature chapter on piste extent.

The slopes can be divided into several identifiable areas. The **Hahnenkamm** gondola takes you to the bowl of Ehrenbachgraben, a major lift bottleneck in the past but, thanks to new lifts in the last few years, now a place you might want to do laps on the steep slopes of Steinbergkogel.

Beyond is the slightly lower peak of **Pengelstein**, with an eight-pack up to it from the Steinbergkogel area. Long west-facing runs go down to Skirast, where there is a gondola back up, or to Aschau. Ski-buses from these points will take you to the Ki-West gondola towards Westendorf and the SkiWelt and to Kirchberg.

Pengelstein is also the start of the impressive 30-person cross-valley 3S gondola to **Wurzhöhe** above Jochberg. This peak-to-peak link has fabulous views (especially if you hit the cabin with the partial glass floor).

Further lifts then take you to the **Resterhöhe** sector – well worth the excursion, for better snow and fewer crowds. There is a long, scenic, sunny red run to Breitmoos, mid-station of the gondola up from Hollersbach. Runs are otherwise short, but mostly served by fast chairs.

The second stage of the gondola on **Kitzbüheler Horn** leads to the sunny Trattalm bowl; or a cable car takes you up to the summit of Horn, from where a fine, solitary piste leads down into the Raintal on the east side. There's a blue piste and two ski routes back towards town.

The separate **Bichlalm** area, which last season offered guided snowcat skiing, is due to have a new double chair for 2015/16 to access the ski routes and off-piste.

FAST LIFTS ★★★★★
Rapid improvement but ...
Regular lift upgrades have resulted in Kitzbühel just squeezing into our top ★★★★★ category for fast lifts. Around 60% of lifts are gondolas or fast chairs but it still has some slow chairs and T-bars and the trip back from Resterhöhe involves one of each.

QUEUES ★★★✩✩
Much improved
Recent reporters have had few queue problems. But there can still be peak-time queues for the Hahnenkamm gondola out of the town and occasional queues up the hill, especially at the weekends. The cross-valley gondola to Wurzhöhe has relieved pressure on the slopes closer to town, by encouraging people to use the Resterhöhe slopes. But the Trattenbach chair and particularly the Gauxjoch drag you need to get back from Resterhöhe can build queues on busy afternoons.

TERRAIN PARKS ★★★☆☆
Fun for all standards
The Snowpark Hanglalm at Resterhöhe has lots for advanced riders – several kicker lines, from big to huge, as well as 35 features. Pro riders love the park's centrepiece – a huge gap jump. But it also has an area aimed at beginners and intermediates. The park on the Kitzbüheler Horn is a beginner park. Visit www.snowpark-kitzbuehel.at for more information. The park in nearby Westendorf is excellent – well worth the trip.

SNOW RELIABILITY ★★☆☆☆
More snowmaking now
The problem is that Kitzbühel's slopes have one of the lowest average heights in the Alps, and the Horn is also sunny. Even in an exceptionally good snow year some reporters complain of worn patches, ice and slush on the lower slopes. In a normal year, the lower slopes can be very tricky when slushy or more especially when icy (though the snow at the top is often OK). The expansion of snowmaking has improved matters when it's cold enough to make snow – runs down to Kitzbühel, Kirchberg, Klausen and Jochberg are covered. One reporter found conditions 'better than feared' because of this. But many slopes still remain unprotected. If snow is poor, head for Resterhöhe.

SNOWPIX.COM / CHRIS GILL

The area suits intermediates best with over 85% of the pistes classified as red or blue ↓

Reporters have found grooming 'very good in difficult conditions'.

FOR EXPERTS ★★★☆☆
Plan to go off-piste
Steep slopes – pistes and off-piste terrain – are mostly concentrated in the Steinbergkogel-Ehrenbachgraben area, equipped with three fast chairs. Direttissima is seriously steep and fabulous when groomed. The other blacks dotted around are easier. There are plenty of long, challenging reds. When conditions allow, there is plenty of gentler off-piste to be found – some of it close to pistes, some requiring a guide. The long ski routes from Pengelstein towards Jochberg and Hechenmoos are delightful in good snow. The ski routes and off-piste at Bichlalm should be served by a new double chair this season.

FOR INTERMEDIATES ★★★★☆
Lots of alternatives
The Hahnenkamm area is prime intermediate terrain but can get crowded. Good intermediates will want to do the World Cup downhill run, of course (see the feature panel opposite). And the long blues of around 1000m vertical to Klausen, Kirchberg and Skirast are satisfying. The black to Aschau is not difficult, and is a lovely way to end the day (check the bus times first).

![MOMENTUM SKI]

MOMENTUM SKI

Weekend & a la carte
ski holiday specialists

100% Tailor-made

Premier hotels
& apartments

Flexible travel
arrangements

020 7371 9111
WWW.MOMENTUMSKI.COM

The Wurzhöhe runs are good for mixed abilities, and the short, high runs at Resterhöhe are ideal if you are more timid. There are easy reds down to Pass Thurn and Jochberg. This area tends to be much quieter than Hahnenkamm and Pengelstein. Much of the Horn is good cruising, and the east-facing Raintal is excellent (but it has a slow double chair back).

FOR BEGINNERS ★★★★★
Not ideal

The Hahnenkamm nursery slopes are no more than adequate, and prone to poor snow conditions – but at least they have some free lifts. There are nursery areas with free lifts at Jochberg, Pass Thurn and Aschau, too. The Horn has a high, sunny, nursery-like section, and quick learners will soon be cruising home from there on the long Hagstein piste. There are some easy runs to progress to if the snow is OK. Day lift passes just for the Horn slopes are available. But there are better resorts to learn in.

SNOWPIX.COM / CHRIS GILL

There's no shortage of mountain restaurants: around 60 are marked on the piste map ↓

FOR BOARDERS ★★★★★
Gaining recognition

Kitzbühel was never known as a snowboarders' hub, but it is growing in popularity, year on year. There is now a good park, plus some good off-piste runs and fun natural obstacles on the Hahnenkamm and around Pengelstein. All the major lifts are gondolas or chairlifts – so the area suits beginners well. But a couple of reporters have drawn attention to the many flat linking runs, on which boarders struggle – one versatile chap ditched his board after a day, and rented skis instead.

FOR CROSS-COUNTRY ★★★★★
Plentiful but low

There are around 60km of trails scattered around. Most are at valley level and prone to lack of snow, but a reporter who got lots of snow highly recommends them.

MOUNTAIN RESTAURANTS ★★★★★
A highlight

There are many attractive restaurants, most offering table-service – one of the highlights of this resort. Around 60 are marked and named on the piste map but the useful booklet that describes them is now only in German.
Editors' choice Bärenbadalm, halfway to Resterhöhe, has a cool, modern bar area with flat-screen TVs, a roaring log fire and comfy armchairs and sofas; you can eat there or in various dining areas with a more rustic feel. We've had delicious oriental beef strip salad and crispy pork ribs here. Endorsed by reporters. But the terrace is spoiled by the adjacent lift station – not a criticism you can level at the Panoramaalm up at Resterhöhe. This has both a beautiful, intimate interior and a fine terrace including a great bar (get there early to bag a spot). Excellent food, 'efficient, friendly staff'. Seidlalm, right by the lower part of the downhill course, is quiet and delightfully rustic.
Worth knowing about In the Hahnenkamm sector we had a jolly meal a few years back at Berghaus Tyrol and a fabulous strudel at the Sonnbühel – lovely situation, sheltered and with a good view. One Kitz regular lists Hahnenkammstüberl among her favourites. Hochkitzbühel, at the top of the Hahnenkaam gondola, has been newly renovated.
On Pengelstein, Usterweis is a nice woody traditional place; Gauxerstad'l has 'a limited menu but good, friendly service and mountainous portions'. The hotel Ehrenbachhöhe at the top of

Fleckalmbahn does 'classic mountain fare with plentiful portions and efficient service', says a recent visitor.

At Wurzhöhe/Resterhöhe, try Hanglalm, Sonnalm, Bruggeralm or Berggasthaus Resterhöhe.

On the Horn, there's the Hornköpfl-Hütte and Gipfelhaus, which has 'super views'. The Adlerhütte is a favourite of a Kitzbühel regular.

On the pistes down to Kirchberg, Fleckalm and Maierlalm have been tipped by past reporters.

SCHOOLS AND GUIDES ★★★★
Plenty of choice
Of the 16 schools listed on the Kitzbühel web site, the Kitzbühel Rote Teufel (Red Devils) is the largest. A 2015 reporter was happy with Element3 – 'Excellent, very knowledgeable.' More reports please.

FOR FAMILIES ★
Not an ideal choice
It's rather a spread-out resort for family holiday purposes. Rote Teufel takes kids from age three.

STAYING THERE

Kitzbühel is essentially a hotel resort. Crystal, Inghams, Momentum and STC all have a good selection of hotels.
Chalets Crystal has two big (30 beds or so) chalets close to the Hahnenkamm gondola.
Hotels There is an enormous choice.
*****Schloss Lebenberg Modernized 'castle' with smart wellness centre; inconvenient location but free shuttle-bus. Pool.
*****Tennerhof Luxurious former farmhouse, with renowned restaurant. Beautiful panelled rooms. Relais & Châteaux. Pool, spa.
****Best Western Kaiserhof By the Hahnenkamm gondola. Spa, pool.
****Q! Hotel Maria Theresia Central. Stylish interior, sauna, steam.
****Rasmushof Right on the slopes by the race finish area, close to centre of town. We stayed here and loved it. Pool, sauna, steam.
****Schwarzer Adler Central, traditional hotel turned swanky boutique hotel. Roof-top pool, spa.
****Tiefenbrunner Central, traditional, family-run. Pool, spa. 'The standards set by the highly visible owners are impeccably high, the food is superb and the facilities faultless,' said a regular visitor last year.

STC Ski

Specialists in Tailor-Made Short Breaks & Holidays

01483 771 222
www.stcski.co.uk
ski@stcski.co.uk

***Resch Central. 'Clean, traditional rooms, good breakfast, nice sauna.'
***Strasshofer Central. 'Great location, friendly, good food – hard to beat for brilliant value,' says a regular.
**Mühlbergerhof Small, friendly pension in good position.
Apartments Many of the best are attached to hotels.

EATING OUT ★★★★
Something for everyone
There is a wide range of restaurants to suit all pockets, including pizzerias and fast-food outlets (even McDonald's) as well as gourmet dining.

The Neuwirt in the chic Schwarzer Adler hotel is regarded as one of the best in town. The Chizzo offers fine dining in one of the oldest buildings in Kitzbühel. Good, cheaper places include the traditional Huberbräu-Stüberl, Zinnkrug, Eggerwirt and, a little out of town with great views, Hagstein (traditional farm food). The Goldene Gams restaurant in the hotel Tiefenbrunner has a wide menu. Both the Centro and the Barrique are recommended for their pizzas. And the rustic Moro de Venezia serves 'simple Italian food'. For something different take a taxi to Rosi's Sonnbergstub'n. Choose the speciality lamb or duck and expect to be serenaded by Rosi herself.

Seidlalm is the place for a jolly Tirolean evening on the lower slopes. On Fridays you can dine at the top of the Hahnenkamm gondola.

APRES-SKI ★★★★
A main attraction
Nightlife is one of Kitz's attractions, and a recent reporter found 'plenty of lively bars for après-ski'. As the lifts close the town is jolly without being much livelier than many other Tirolean resorts. The Streifalm bar at the foot of the slopes is popular. The Chizzo

and Pavillon have been recommended in the past. Praxmair and Rupprechter are among the most atmospheric cafes for teatime cakes and pastries. The Centro and the 'quaint' Ursprung have been recommended for pre-dinner drinks.

The Lichtl Pub has thousands of lights hanging from the ceiling. The Londoner is a bit of an institution, appealing particularly to young Brits, but a grown-up visiting last year enjoyed it ('packed, live band until around 7pm'). The heated terrace of the Stamperl, across the road, was doing a roaring trade when we visited a few seasons ago. Highways and Take Five are discos.

OFF THE SLOPES ★★★★★
Plenty to do
The lift pass gives a 50% reduction for the pools in the Aquarena. There's skating, ice hockey matches, bowling etc at the Sportpark. Plus paragliding, tobogganing, free guided snowshoeing and hiking. There's an 'interesting' museum and a casino. The railway makes excursions easy (eg Salzburg, Innsbruck).

LINKED RESORT – 850m
KIRCHBERG

Kirchberg is a large, busy, spread-out town, with plentiful restaurants and shops and an unremarkable but pleasant centre. The road from Kitzbühel towards Innsbruck bypasses the centre, but traffic is still intrusive.

The slopes it shares with Kitzbühel are accessed via a choice of three gondolas, all requiring the use of 'regular and efficient' ski-buses or affordable taxis (unless you opt to stay at a lift base rather than in the town). The Maierlbahn goes from a station 1km from the centre, while the Fleckalmbahn goes up from Klausen beside the road to Kitzbühel about 1.5km out. The third is over 3km out at Skirast. Another 2km on from Skirast is a gondola into Westendorf's slopes. These are linked to the main SkiWelt slopes via Brixen, which can also easily be reached by train or bus – read the chapter on Söll for more on these. There is a small nursery slope at the bottom of the separate Gaisberg sector, with a free lift, but it's at low altitude, and so prone to poor snow.

A reporter had a mixed experience with the Kirchberg Aktiv school: 'I had a fantastic time in 2014 with an English instructor who taught us a lot. This year I had a 60-year-old Austrian who couldn't speak English and taught us hardly anything.'

The village has a wide choice of lodging; the 4-star Kirchberger Hof is praised this year for its 'comfortable rooms, friendly staff, tasty four-course dinners and lovely pool'. The 4-star Klausen is convenient for the Klausen gondola, and a recent visitor enjoyed the Haus Alpenblick, a five-minute walk from the centre – 'welcoming, good food, plenty of beers to try'. The 'very comfortable' Pension Hollaus 'slightly up the hill from the main road' was recommended last year. Most restaurants are hotel-based, but there are a couple of pizzerias, a Chinese ('best crispy duck') and a steakhouse.

There is some après action, both at teatime and later on. The restaurants on the home runs do good business as the lifts close. Rohrerstadl, just above Skirast, is tipped for animated après-ski with a live band. And the Boomerang was said to be the liveliest bar by a past reporter. Several places operate as discos later.

Off the slopes there's 'great' floodlit tobogganing on Gaisberg and a leisure centre, and some hotels have pools open to the public.

LINKED RESORT – 925m
JOCHBERG

Jochberg – 10km south of Kitzbühel – is not so much a village as a straggle of accommodation along a busy road – it has nothing you could call a centre. There's a church, a bank, a post office, a ski depot, a supermarket, half a dozen restaurants and a couple of bars. But if you're after accommodation close to lifts serving slopes with the best snow in the area, it's worth considering.

There's now a 10-seater gondola out of Jochberg and the cutting-edge 5-star Kempinski Hotel das Tirol a few metres away from it.

Most of the other lodgings are small pensions and apartments, but there is also the 4-star Jochbergerhof. Of the restaurants, the Alpenland was recommended by a past reporter.

GETTING THERE
Air Salzburg 75km/ 45 miles (1hr30); Innsbruck 95km/ 60 miles (1hr30); Munich 175km/ 110 miles (2hr30)

Rail Mainline station in resort

TOURIST OFFICES
Kitzbühel
www.kitzbuehel.com
Kirchberg
www.kirchberg.at

LECH TOURIST OFFICE

Lech Zürs am Arlberg

A choice of very different villages sharing exceptionally snowy slopes that saw some serious expansion in 2013/14

£125
RESORT PRICE INDEX

RATINGS

The mountains

Extent	★★★
Fast lifts	★★★★
Queues	★★★★
Terrain p'ks	★★★★
Snow	★★★★
Expert	★★★★
Intermediate	★★★★
Beginner	★★★★
Boarder	★★★★
X-country	★★★
Restaurants	★★★
Schools	★★★★
Families	★★★★★

The resort

Charm	★★★★
Convenience	★★★
Scenery	★★★
Eating out	★★★
Après-ski	★★★★
Off-slope	★★★

NEWS

2015/16: In Zürs the Ubungshang double chair is due to be replaced with a covered six-pack.

- ➕ Lech is a traditional village in a picturesque riverside setting
- ➕ Excellent snow record
- ➕ Sizeable area of slopes shared by Lech and Zürs – now enlarged by a link from Lech to humble Warth
- ➕ Access by bus to the slopes of St Anton and Stuben, on the lift pass
- ➕ Some very lovely hotels
- ➕ Lively après-ski scene in Lech

- ➖ Pricey, by Austrian standards
- ➖ Surprisingly limited shopping
- ➖ Few non-hotel bars or restaurants
- ➖ Intrusive traffic on main streets
- ➖ Hardly any challenging pistes
- ➖ Nearly all slopes above treeline
- ➖ Blue runs down to Lech are too steep for nervous novices
- ➖ Still a few slow, old lifts

Lech and linked Zürs – in Vorarlberg, but sharing a lift pass with St Anton over the Arlberg pass in Tirol – are the most fashionable resorts in Austria, each able to pull in Porsche-borne Germans by the thousand. Putting aside their 5-star hotels, though, they don't feel particularly exclusive. Lech has always been the more attractive base (to compete, Zürs needs a tunnel bypass, followed by an imaginative makeover) but the gondola link between Lech and Warth built in 2014 means there is now no contest.

Unless you are counting the pennies, Lech's combination of charm, varied slopes and good snow is difficult to beat. A wider choice of good mountain restaurants would be no bad thing, though.

THE RESORT

Lech is an old farming village set in a high valley that spent long periods of winter cut off from the outside world until the Flexen Pass road linked Zürs to Stuben at the end of the 19th century. Seriously heavy snow can close the road for days on end, marooning visitors in Lech and Zürs. There are worse problems to have.

Not far from the centre is the cable car up to Oberlech: a small, traffic-free area of 4-star hotels set on the piste.

Zug is a hamlet 3km from Lech, with a lift into the Lech slopes. It's not ideal for sampling Lech's nightlife, but there is an evening bus service.

Lech is linked by lifts and runs to higher Zürs to the south, and now by gondola (but not by piste) to Warth to

the north. Both resorts are described at the end of this chapter, although most of the detail about Warth is in our Bregenzerwald chapter. St Anton, not linked but covered by the lift pass, gets its own chapter.

The road to Warth is closed in winter. The other resorts in this area can be reached by bus, but the service is rubbish. There are free and regular ski-buses linking Lech, Zürs and Alpe Rauz for the St Anton lifts. And there are post buses to St Anton via Alpe Rauz and St Christoph. But all get seriously crowded at busy times, leaving people at the roadside at the mercy of the waiting taxi drivers. And the post buses are neither free nor frequent. It's not good enough, for big name resorts like these.

The Sonnenkopf area at Klösterle, reached by free ski-bus from Stuben, is also covered by the Arlberg pass.

VILLAGE CHARM ★★★★
Busy main street
The village is attractive, with upmarket hotels built in traditional chalet style, a gurgling river plus bridges, and a high incidence of snow on the streets. But don't expect a rustic idyll: away

KEY FACTS

Resort	1450m
	4,760ft

Arlberg region	
Slopes	1075-2650m
	3,530-8,690ft
Lifts	97
Slopes*	340km
	210 miles

For Lech-Zürs-Warth-Schröcken only	
Slopes	1450-2450m
	4,760-8,040ft
Lifts	47
Slopes*	180km
	112 miles

* pistes and ski routes

ALPINE ANSWERS
The UK's No.1 Chalet Specialist

For choice and service look no further!

alpineanswers.co.uk
call: 020 7801 1080

ABTA

slopes. Just across the river are the chairlifts for Lech's main area of slopes. Chalets, apartments and pensions are dotted around the valley, and the village spreads for 2km. Some of the cheaper accommodation is quite a walk from the lifts.

Oberlech is a tiny place with pistes where you would expect streets, and an underground tunnel system linking the hotels and cable car station – used routinely to move baggage, and by guests in bad weather. The cable car works until 1am, allowing access to the nightlife down in Lech.

SCENERY ★★★
In a bright spot

Lech is in a fairly sunny position at the junction of two attractive valleys, with adequately impressive scenery, largely thanks to the Omeshorn looming to the south. It is high and open, with very few trees. From the top slopes there are views to the Valluga above St Anton in one direction, and to Warth in the other.

from the central area the place is fairly ordinary, and the appeal is somewhat dimmed by traffic on the main street, especially at weekends when car-borne visitors arrive and depart.

CONVENIENCE ★★★
It's a long village

The heart of the village is a short stretch of the main street beside the river, with most of the main hotels, the main shop (Strolz) and the Rüfikopf cable car, for access to the Zürs

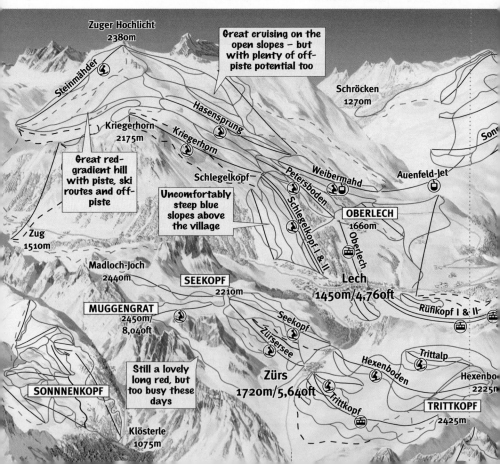

Zuger Hochlicht
2380m

Great cruising on the open slopes – but with plenty of off-piste potential too

Schröcken
1270m

Steinmähder

Hasensprung

Son

Kriegerhorn
2175m

Kriegerhorn

Schröcken

Weibermahd

Auenfeld-Jet

Great red-gradient hill with piste, ski routes and off-piste

Schlegelkopf

Petersboden

OBERLECH
1660m

Uncomfortably steep blue slopes above the village

Schlegelkopf I & II

Oberlech

Zug
1510m

Madloch-Joch
2440m

SEEKOPF
2210m

Lech
1450m/4,760ft

Rüfikopf I & II

MUGGENGRAT
2450m/
8,040ft

Seekopf

Zürsersee

Trittalp

Hexenboden

Still a lovely long red, but too busy these days

SONNNENKOPF

Zürs
1720m/5,640ft

Trittkopf

Hexenbo
2225m

TRITTKOPF
2425m

Klösterle
1075m

THE MOUNTAINS

Practically all the slopes are treeless, the main exception being the home runs just above Lech. Most are quite sunny – very few are north-facing.

The toughest runs are called 'ski routes'. The piste map says these are marked and avalanche controlled but not groomed or patrolled. We applaud the clear explanation (lacking in many resorts), but we think many of them should be patrolled pistes. Ski routes form the only ways down to Zug and Lech as part of the popular Lech-Zürs 'White Ring' circuit and are treated like pistes, as are several other ski routes. To add to the confusion, routes are sometimes groomed – we've found the Zürs to Zug route has been groomed on all our recent visits.

To judge by the latest digital version supplied to us, the Arlberg piste map will not next season show proper off-piste runs (which disappeared from the St Anton part of the map some time ago).

The piste map is too ambitious in covering the whole of the Arlberg region, including Warth, in one view: it is unclear and misleading in places – particularly around Oberlech and down from Zürs to Zug and Lech. There's a smaller separate map that shows the White Ring circuit. In Warth it's worth picking up the local map, covering its slopes much more clearly.

Piste marking is OK in general. But, confusingly, the same number is given to multiple pistes in places; there are three blue runs numbered 34a, for example. Piste classification sometimes understates difficulty.

EXTENT OF THE SLOPES ★★★
One-way traffic

The main slopes centre on **Oberlech**, 250m above Lech (just below the treeline), and can be reached by cable car or chairlifts. The wide, open pistes above here are served by a handful of chairlifts.

The newish link to the slopes of **Warth** is a 10-seat gondola which has

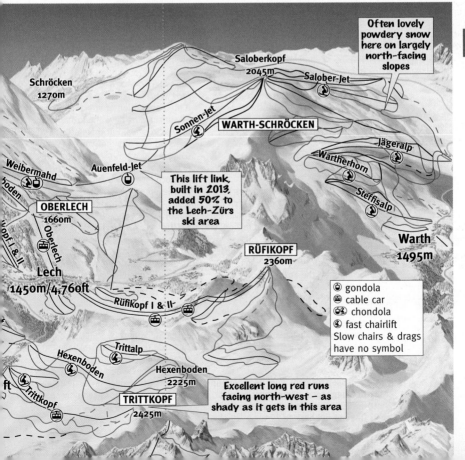

Often lovely powdery snow here on largely north-facing slopes

This lift link, built in 2013, added 50% to the Lech-Zürs ski area

Excellent long red runs facing north-west – as shady as it gets in this area

Schröcken 1270m

Saloberkopf 2045m

Salober-Jet

Sonnen-Jet

WARTH-SCHRÖCKEN

Jägeralp

Wartherhorn

Steffisalp

Warth 1495m

Weibermahd

Auenfeld-Jet

...boden

OBERLECH 1660m

Oberlech

...kopf I & II

RÜFIKOPF 2236m

Lech 1450m/4,760ft

Rüfikopf I & II

Trittalp

Hexenboden

Hexenboden 2225m

...ft

Trittkopf

TRITTKOPF 2425m

⚟ gondola
⚞ cable car
⚟⚞ chondola
⚡ fast chairlift
Slow chairs & drags have no symbol

↑ Lech enjoys a setting softened by trees, but practically all the skiing is above the treeline; Oberlech is in the trees to the right

LECH TO / SEPP MALLAUN

LIFT PASSES

Arlberg

Prices in €

Age	6-day
under 16	147
16 to 19	213
20 to 64	245
65 plus	213

Free No one; day pass €10 if under 8, €22 if over 75

Beginner Points ticket

Notes Covers St Anton, St Christoph, Stuben, Lech, Zürs and Warth, and bus linking Zürs and Lech with St Anton lifts at Alpe Rauz; also Sonnenkopf (9 lifts) at Klösterle, 7km west of Stuben; single ascent, part-day and pedestrian options

been grafted on to the Weibermahd chondola on the slopes beyond Oberlech. You ride the gondola back to Lech too – the gondola goes over flattish land. It arrives close to the bottom of red slopes on the sunny side of Saloberkopf. These red slopes aren't easily avoided, so the link is unattractive to blue run skiers who lack the confidence to tackle reds. Over the hill is a broad, shady mountainside laced with runs of all kinds, served by a mix of fast and slow chairlifts. (Strictly, some of these slopes belong to another village, Schröcken, but it is a bus ride from the lifts.)

The **Rüfikopf** cable car takes Lech residents to the start of the Lech-Zürs circuit, the White Ring, which can be done only in a clockwise direction, via the west-facing slopes of Zürs.

At the south end of these slopes is a cable car to the high point of **Trittkopf**. At the north end, chairs go up the west-facing slopes and up the east-facing mountainside to **Seekopf**. (You may find the piste map confusing at the north end of Zürs: the lift company has deliberately made it inaccurate in order to make it 'clearer'. So it's clear, but it's wrong – a spectacular piece of thinking.)

A six-pack goes from near here up to **Muggengrat** (the highest point of the Zürs area) and a long, scenic, lift-free red run back to Zürs.

From Seekopf you can ski down to the Madloch chair – slow, and liable to closure by wind – which leads to long, scenic and piste-like ski routes back to Lech or to Zug, where a slow chairlift goes up to the shoulder of Kriegerhorn above Oberlech.

FAST LIFTS ★★★★
Hot stuff
A high proportion of lifts are now fast. Seven chairlifts have the luxury bonus of heated seats. But there are still a few slow, old lifts that you can't avoid using if you want to explore the area fully (in particular, the chairs to Madloch-Joch above Zürs and from Zug to Kriegerhorn).

QUEUES ★★★★
Still a few bottlenecks
There have been significant lift improvements in recent years, and feedback is now generally positive, but there are still some bottlenecks: peak-time queues form at the Schlegelkopf fast quad out of Lech, at the crucial Madloch double chair mentioned under 'Fast lifts' above, and at the Rüfikopf cable cars to go to Zürs. The resort theoretically limits numbers on its slopes to 14,000, for safety reasons – and apparently does stop day-ticket sales on some sunny weekends. The slopes certainly seem quieter than those of St Anton (though Warth is much quieter still).

TERRAIN PARKS ★★★★
In Lech
The park, beside the Schlegelkopf chairlift, is one of the better terrain parks in Austria. There are easy, medium and pro lines with 17 features. There's also a park on the Warth slopes.

SNOW RELIABILITY ★★★★
One of Austria's best
Lech and Zürs both get a lot of snow. Lech gets an average of almost 8m of snow each season, almost twice as much as St Anton and three times as much as Kitzbühel; Zürs gets substantially more than Lech; and Warth gets an astonishing 11m. Taken together with good grooming ('perfect' said a recent reporter) and excellent snowmaking, this normally means good snow coverage until late April. But because of the sunny exposure, the lower slopes of Lech can suffer and the snow become heavy. Warth is a resort of contrasts: its main slopes are north-facing, so hold their exceptional amounts of snow very well, but the runs down to the Lech gondola are badly affected by the sun – messy in the afternoon.

FOR EXPERTS ★★★★
Off-piste is the main attraction
For the competent skier who prefers to stick to patrolled runs the area is very limited. There are no black pistes above Lech, and one short (although rewarding) one above Zürs. Warth has added many more, but they rarely approach true black gradient. But the two types of off-piste route explained earlier offer lots to enjoy. There is also plenty of other excellent off-piste, much of it accessed by long traverses; and in comparison with St Anton, fresh powder lasts well here.

Many of the best runs start from the top of the fast Steinmähder chair, which finishes just below Zuger Hochlicht. Some routes involve a short climb to access bowls of untracked powder. From the Kriegerhorn there are shorter off-piste runs down towards Lech and a very scenic long ski route down to Zug (followed by a slow chair and a rope tow to pull you along a flat area). Most runs, however, are south- or west-facing and can suffer from sun. At the end of the season, when the snow is deep and settled, the off-piste off the shoulder of the Wöstertäli from the top of the

HOTEL *Schwarzwand* ★★★★
LECH AM ARLBERG

enjoyment   harmony   freedom

Friendly service ❀ Comfortable suites and rooms ❀ Relaxing 'Oasis'

Walter Elsensohn and his team look forward to hearing from you!

A-6764 Lech am Arlberg 308
Telephone +43 5583 2469 Fax 5583 27766

www.schwarzwand.com   hotel@schwarzwand.com

SKIWORLD

Catered chalets, hotels and self catering apartments in

Europe, USA and Canada

skiworld.co.uk
08444 930 430

ABTA V2151 ATOL 2036

Rüfikopf cable car down to Lech can be superb, as can Zuger Hochlicht. There are also good runs from the Trittkopf cable car, including a tricky one down to Stuben. And there is a lot of scope for departures from the Madloch itinerary to Zug.

The Warth link has opened up some excellent off-piste opportunities. There are routes from Zuger Hochlicht to the Warth lifts, from the Warth slopes to Schröcken (bus back to the Warth lifts) and from two or three points on the Warth slopes to points down the valley from Lech.

The steeper red runs (notably on Zuger Hochlicht and both sides of Zürs) are well worth a try, as is the lovely away-from-the-lifts Langerzug ski route back to Lech on the Rüfikopf side (steep start, then a gentle cruise, flattish run-out). Heli-skiing is also available on weekdays.

FOR INTERMEDIATES ★★★★
Flattering variety for all
The pistes in the Oberlech area are nearly all immaculately groomed blue runs, the upper ones above the trees, the lower ones in wide swathes cut through them. It is ideal territory for cruisers not wanting surprises. But a regular complaint is that timid intermediates find the final blue-run descents to Lech (as opposed to Oberlech) uncomfortably steep. It's a minor disgrace that this problem has never been tackled.

Strong intermediates will want to do the circuit to Zürs and back. Whether it's wise for less confident intermediates to tackle the red ski routes from Madloch depends crucially on the conditions. They are not steep, and part or all of them may be groomed despite their non-piste status, but parts can be heavily mogulled and busy, and lots of people find the runs a struggle. Once you set off, there is no way out.

More adventurous intermediates will want to spend time on the fast Steinmähder chair on Zuger Hochlicht – a choice of satisfying pistes and ski routes, and from there take the scenic red run all the way to Zug (the latter part on an easy ski route rather than a piste, so not to be skied alone). They may even want to give the Langerzug ski route (see 'For experts') a go. The slopes of Lech are an excellent place to try skiing ungroomed snow for the first time.

Zürs has many more interesting red runs, on both sides of the village. We like the north-west-facing reds from Trittkopf and the excellent run from Muggengrat, away from the lifts.

Warth has excellent intermediate slopes to explore, of all colours. Carving down the top-to-bottom groomed black runs down the Salober-Jet chair was a highlight of our last visit – though they are not long (less than 400m vertical).

FOR BEGINNERS ★★★★
Easy slopes in all areas
There are good nursery slopes in Lech and at Oberlech. There are good, easy runs to progress to up the mountain, too, but read our remarks about the home pistes in the previous section. You can buy a points card rather than a full lift pass.

FOR BOARDERS ★★★★
Easy riders, but mind the flats
Lech's upper-crust image has not stood in the way of its snowboarding development, and it is a popular destination for freeriders. There are few draglifts to deter novices; but beware of the many flat/uphill sections on the west-facing slopes at Zürs.

FOR CROSS-COUNTRY ★★★
Picturesque valley trail
A 21km trail starts from the centre of Lech and leads through the beautiful but shady valley, along the river to Zug and back. There are three other shorter trails. In Zürs there is a 4km track to the Flexen Pass and back.

MOUNTAIN RESTAURANTS ★★★
Still not a strong point
The hotels in Oberlech have long held sway over the lunch scene here, but we're pleased to say the alternative options are slowly widening. With one or two exceptions, restaurants are clearly marked (and named in minute type) on the piste map. The ones in Oberlech aren't marked, but then they don't need to be.

Editors' choice Rud-Alpe is not far above Lech, but high enough to count as a mountain restaurant. It's a welcoming, rustic place, lovingly built using timbers from other old huts. We've had excellent lunches here, efficiently served – a couple of seasons ago, veal goulash. Endorsed by several reporters last year and this. Kriegeralpe lacks views but is great on a bad day – rustic and charming, with jolly service. It's notable for the fab Kaiserschmarrn served in giant pans late in the day – the main menu is very limited in the usual Austrian way; but we had great gröstl recently, and readers also approve ribs and gulaschsuppe.

Worth knowing about Above Zürs, we had an excellent lunch last season at Seekopf – good table-service on the huge terrace; approved by readers. Take the long, away-from-the-lifts red run from the top of that sector towards Zürs and as you approach valley level look out for Flexenhäuserl – 'a hidden gem: a tiny atmospheric hut doing good venison sausage; booking essential', says a reader.

We and reporters have also enjoyed the modern, woody Balmalp, above Zug: cool music (loud outside, quieter inside); simple food – 'excellent gulaschsuppe', ribs, 'massive pizzas to share'; good views. The Panorama restaurant at Rüfikopf is tipped for 'good food and portions, outstanding view over Lech'.

At Oberlech there are several big sunny terraces set prettily around the piste. Quite often you'll find a live band playing outside one. Reader tips include Burgwald, Petersboden, Ilga Stüble, the lovely old Alter Goldener Berg and the Mohnenfluh.

For the moment, the huts at Warth are noticeably cheaper. Dumplings are a speciality in some. Hochalp has a small, unremarkable terrace, but inside is a 'lovely space'; 'delicious food' includes 'superb rösti'. Auenfelder Hütte is a pleasant chalet doing good, simple food – but service can be stretched and, depending on snow, you may have some poling to regain a piste. Berghotel Korbersee is in a lovely spot, with 'excellent food and service', but it 'feels a bit like a hotel dining room' – which of course is exactly what it is.

SCHOOLS AND GUIDES ★★★★
Excellent in Lech
We get mainly good reports on the Lech school, although there is a dissenting voice this year complaining of 'glorified ski hosting' rather than effective teaching. Omeshorn Alpincenter and Exklusiv are alternative schools, also with guiding.

FOR FAMILIES ★★★★★
Oberlech's fine, but expensive
Oberlech makes an excellent choice for families that can afford it, particularly as its hotels are so conveniently placed for the slopes. Reporters have praised the family-friendly approach, especially to children using the lifts. There are kids' clubs in Lech, Oberlech and Zürs, and Goldener Berg has an in-house kindergarten.

LECH TO / SEPP MALLAUN

Balmalp, on the Lech slopes above Zug, enjoys a splendid position (and serves splendid pizzas) ↓

↑ Zürs is all about comfortable lodgings: 1,300 beds in four 5-star hotels, 11 4-star hotels and just one 3-star B&B
LECH TO / SEPP MALLAUN

STAYING THERE

Chalets There are a few catered chalets run by UK tour ops, including four chalet hotels by Ski Total, two with pool and all four with sauna; Elisabeth, in a riverside location close to the centre, is new this season. And Skiworld has two chalets in outlying Zug, both with sauna.

Hotels There are seven 5-stars and around 65 4-stars, but also more modest places (STC offers its tailor-made breaks in some). All the places we list are in the main village – we get few reports on Oberlech.

*****Arlberg Elegantly rustic central chalet, widely thought to be the best in Lech, but relatively unstuffy. Pool.

*****Post Lovely old Relais & Châteaux place on the main street; pool, sauna, steam. Jackets and ties at dinner, gentlemen.

****Antonius Traditional family-run B&B hotel in a quiet spot two minutes from the centre. 'Very welcoming and friendly staff, good breakfasts.' Spa.

****Haldenhof 'Lovely small hotel with very friendly owners and staff. Nearly every other guest was a returning visitor, some for many years. A short walk to the slopes.'

****Kristiania Small luxury place on outskirts; shuttle. 'Continues to impress,' says our regular reporter; 'gourmet paradise, outstanding service, but expensive.'

****Plattenhof A few minutes from the centre but near Hinterweiss drag and runs. A repeat visitor last year was very happy: 'Lovely suite, excellent food; really nice pool.'

****Schwarzwand By the separate nursery slope, so perfectly positioned for beginners. Sauna, steam room, solarium. Food, service and value for money are praised.

****Tannbergerhof Splendidly atmospheric inn on the main street, with ever-popular outdoor bar. 'Very nice rooms, good staff, good restaurant and food,' says a reporter this year. Tiny lounge, though. Steam, sauna.

***Lech Slightly out of centre towards Zürs. 'Charming, with superb staff, great food,' says a recent report.

Apartments There are lots available to independent bookers.

EATING OUT ★★★☆☆
Mainly hotel-based

There are over 50 restaurants in Lech, but nearly all of them are in hotels, and we get few reports on other places. A conspicuous and stylish exception is Skihütte Schneggarei, a big, spacious wooden building at the foot of the slopes doing a good range of modern dishes but also great pizzas from a proper oven; expect to book well ahead, or just turn up. Other authentic pizza sources are Don Enzo Due and Olympia across the road. Fux offers two options: steak or modern Asian – a refreshing change. Hûs Nr 8 is a fine old wooden chalet with a high reputation, with the result that it is booked weeks ahead.

In Zug, there are two pricey places. The Rote Wand is excellent for traditional Austrian food ('beautiful old-fashioned restaurant, attentive but not fussy service'). But one regular reporter prefers the Klösterle, 'a lovely restored farmhouse'.

APRES-SKI ★★★★☆
Good but expensive

At Oberlech, the umbrella bar of the Burg hotel is popular at close of play, as is the champagne bar in hotel Montana. Readers also like the bar of the hotel Ilga.

Down in Lech there are places for cakes and coffee, but the crowds are to be found at the outdoor bars of hotels Krone (in a lovely, sunny setting by the river) and Tannbergerhof (where there's an afternoon disco), and at the Pfefferkorn. In midwinter, at least, we prefer to head indoors, and to the cool and lively Schneggarei (read 'Eating out', above) along with many ski instructors; it's non-smoking – hooray! Later on, the K Club (hotel Krone) and Archiv Bar liven up. More mature readers like the Fux Jazzbar (with live music and a huge wine list) and the bar in the Tannbergerhof.

After 7.30pm the free resort bus becomes a pay-for bus (4.50 euros) called James, which runs until 3am.

OFF THE SLOPES ★★★☆☆
At ease

For a fashionable resort, the range of shops is surprisingly limited – there's very little apart from Strolz's plush central emporium (including a champagne bar). It's easy for pedestrians to get to Oberlech or Zug for lunch. The village outdoor bars are ideal for posing. There are 40km of prepared winter walking trails – the one along the river to Zug is particularly beautiful; the tourist office produces a good map. There's also snowshoeing and a natural ice rink. There's a sports centre (no pool, but spa, climbing, bowling).

The popular floodlit sledging run from Oberlech down to the main village is highly recommended (but beware toboggan theft – one reporter had three stolen).

Ski Total

WELCOME YOU TO

Lech

Quality chalets
Excellent value
19 resorts
across the Alps

skitotal.com
01483 791 933

But the village as a whole doesn't have much appeal – it has no real centre, few shops and a lot of intrusive traffic to/from Lech on the central through-road.

We enjoyed staying in the 5-star Zürserhof – great service, food and spa facilities – and a reader reckons the Lorunser is 'probably the most friendly and relaxed of the 5-star hotels'. We have two rave reviews this year for the hotel Erzberg – 'the best 4-star ski hotel I have ever stayed in'; 'fabulous breakfasts, 6-course dinners among the best ever; the family Schneider went out of their way to be welcoming and friendly'.

The village is quiet in the evening – 'We never found a good après-ski watering hole,' says a reader this year. Later on, Vernissage is said to be the best spot. There's a disco in the hotel Edelweiss, a piano bar in the Alpenhof.

Many of the Zürs instructors are booked up for private lessons for the entire season by regular clients.

LINKED RESORT – 1495m
WARTH

Warth is a tiny village at the east end of a broad ski area; at the west end equally small Schröcken, formerly detached from the slopes, now has a red piste to the village but for moment still lacks a lift back up.

The slopes shared by Warth and Schröcken certainly make a worthwhile addition to the Lech-Zürs area, not least because of their even better snow record and northerly orientation. There are a couple of decent mountain restaurants, too, where your euros will go further than they would in Lech.

Those restaurants are covered in this chapter, but there's more about the village and the slopes in the chapter on Bregenzerwald, the region of which is it a part.

GETTING THERE

Air Innsbruck 115km/ 70 miles (1hr30); Friedrichshafen 130km/80 miles (1hr45); Zürich 195km/120 miles (2hr15)

Rail Langen (15km/ 9 miles); regular buses from station

TOURIST OFFICES

Lech / Zürs
www.lech-zuers.at
Warth / Schröcken
www.warth-schroecken.com

LINKED RESORT – 1720m
ZÜRS

Some 10 minutes' drive towards St Anton from Lech is Zürs. Austria's first recognizable ski lift was built here in 1937. Zürs is a rare thing: a highly fashionable and expensive resort where the main occupation of visitors is skiing rather than parading. It has some excellent hotels (mainly 4-stars but including four 5-star places); once inside them, all is well with the world.

Mayrhofen

Large, lively resort with relatively reliable snow on local slopes and access to other good areas nearby, including a glacier

£90
RESORT PRICE INDEX

RATINGS

The mountains

Extent	★★★
Fast lifts	★★★★
Queues	★★
Terrain p'ks	★★★★★
Snow	★★★
Expert	★★
Intermediate	★★★
Beginner	★★
Boarder	★★★★
X-country	★★
Restaurants	★★★
Schools	★★★★
Families	★★

The resort

Charm	★★★
Convenience	★★
Scenery	★★★
Eating out	★★★
Après-ski	★★★★
Off-slope	★★★★

138

NEWS

2015/16: The inadequate Penken gondola is being replaced by a state-of-the-art gondola with 24-seat cabins (with Wi-Fi) and an increased carrying capacity of almost 3,900 people per hour.

2014/15: The fun slope on Ahorn was fully opened. The Ahorn valley run changed to black classification. A single numbering system was adopted for pistes across all local hills.

➕ Attractive, traditional village with lively après-ski

➕ High, snow-sure slopes by local standards – plus the Hintertux glacier nearby

➕ Several other worthwhile resorts nearby and on the same lift pass

➕ Good for confident intermediates who enjoy challenges, but ...

➖ Not so good for timid intermediates and near-beginners

➖ Long queues for the main gondola

➖ Buses are a key feature, and are often oversubscribed

➖ Runs mostly short

➖ Few steep pistes, although they do include Austria's steepest (possibly)

➖ No pistes to the valley locally

Mayrhofen is easy to like – a neat, polished, animated village in a pleasant rural setting – and we always enjoy our visits. In the past, we've been grateful that we've been able to dodge the Penken gondola queues by driving to other lifts; whether this will be necessary next season with the swanky new three-cable gondola in place, we shall see.

If what is attracting you is the relatively snow-sure slopes, bear in mind that you can access those slopes from quieter villages further up the valley, covered in the Hintertux chapter. Two of them, Lanersbach and Vorderlanersbach next door, also have the merit of pistes back to the village – rare in these parts.

THE RESORT

Mayrhofen is a fairly large resort sitting in the flat-bottomed, steep-sided Zillertal. Most shops, bars and restaurants are on one long street, with hotels and pensions spread over a wider area.

Free buses and trains link several different areas on the Ziller valley lift pass, including the excellent glacier at Hintertux (which has its own chapter). At the end of this chapter we cover the Zillertal Arena area, which starts at Zell am Ziller, not far away, and links to Gerlos and Königsleiten. The other major area is Hochfügen/ Hochzillertal above Kaltenbach, dealt with in the directory at the back of the book; it has a low profile in the UK, but is well worth exploring.

VILLAGE CHARM ★★★
Traditional and spacious

As the village has grown, architecture has been kept traditional, and the place merges with the surrounding fields in a rather charming way. The valley road bypasses the village and the centre is almost, but not quite, traffic-free. The steep-sided valley makes an attractive setting, but also means the village doesn't get a very long day of sun in midwinter.

CONVENIENCE ★★
Pick your spot

It's quite a big village, centred on a long main street. The church, the tourist office and the main traditional hotels are at the north end, with the bus/railway station on the nearby

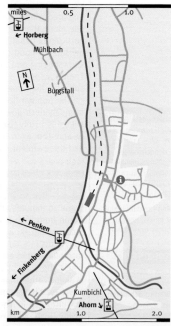

↑ Looking back from the Sun-Jet chair you get a good view of the infamous Harakiri piste and the Penken Vans mega-park

MAYRHOFEN TO / FRANK BAUER

KEY FACTS

Resort	630m
	2,070ft

Ziller valley	
Slopes	630-3250m
	2,070-10,660ft
Lifts	177
Pistes	489km
	303 miles

Mayrhofen-Lanersbach only (ie excluding Hintertux glacier)

Slopes	630-2500m
	2,070-8,200ft
Lifts	55
Pistes	134km
	83 miles

bypass; the gondola to the major Penken-Horberg sector of slopes is 700m away at the south end, with the Ahorn cable car another 200m south, over the river. You can leave kit at the lift stations (for a fee). Obvious places to stay are near the Penken gondola or near the station.

The buses serve other resorts, and there are alternatives to the Penken gondola – particularly the Horbergbahn at Mühlbach, across the valley. The bus services are comprehensive and reliable, but crowded and complex. Get the timetable leaflet (it looks intimidating to us, but readers tell us it is quite easy to use) and do some homework.

SCENERY ★★★
Views to the glacier

Mayrhofen is set between its two steep-sided mountains. From the top of each there are good views to the high peaks to the south, including the Hintertux glacier.

THE MOUNTAINS

Many of Mayrhofen's slopes are above the treeline, though there are more trees than the piste map suggests in the valley at the heart of the Penken-Horberg sector – that's the place to be in bad weather. Many of the pistes are challenging reds, and some reporters note that the blues are also often relatively tough.

Signposting is generally good, but less so in that tricky area on Penken. Last time we visited, we very nearly ended up descending to Finkenberg, with our car sitting in Mühlbach.

As elsewhere in Austria, there are unexplained 'ski routes', including the runs to the valley from Penken-Horberg. You may find some are groomed, but we presume all are unpatrolled. Take care.

EXTENT OF THE SLOPES ★★★
Fair-sized but inconvenient

Mayrhofen now measures its pistes in the Austrian standard fashion, and has cut its claimed total to 134km. Read our feature on piste extent, at the front of the book.

The larger of Mayrhofen's two areas of slopes is **Penken-Horberg**, accessed by the Penkenbahn gondola from one end of town. It is also accessible via the Horbergbahn gondola at Mühlbach and another at Finkenberg, both a bus ride away from the village. If snow-cover is good enough (it rarely is), you can ski to Finkenberg or Mühlbach on ski routes (the Finkenberg route is not on one of the two local piste maps).

A big cable car links the Penken area with the **Rastkogel** slopes above Vorderlanersbach, which is in turn linked to **Eggalm** above Lanersbach – read the Hintertux chapter. Getting back to Penken-Horberg from Rastkogel on skis means braving a busy, steep mogul field with red and

skiracer*

CHALETS, HOTELS
& APARTMENTS

Call us today

020 8600 1650

skiracer.com

Inghams

MAYRHOFEN

▸ Fun, friendly, snow-sure skiing
▸ New range of catered chalets available
▸ Free ski hosting with your Inghams Rep

inghams.co.uk 01483 371 236 ABTA V4871
ATOL 0025

AUSTRIA

140

LIFT PASSES

Superskipass Zillertal

Prices in €

Age	6-day
under 15	104
15 to 18	185
19 plus	231
Free Under 6	
Senior No deals	
Beginner No deals	

Notes 1-day pass
covers Mayrhofen
areas only; 2-day+
passes include all
Zillertal valley lifts;
part-day passes
available

black variants, but you can avoid it by
taking the cable car down.

The **Ahorn** area is pleasant but very
small, and tends to be neglected –
despite being well endowed with lifts.
It is accessed, bizarrely, by Austria's
largest cable car (carrying 160) with an
eight-pack serving the slopes at the
top. There is a lovely, long run to the
valley (about 1300m vertical), recently
changed from red to black, and in our
experience kept in good condition
regardless of natural snow shortage.

FAST LIFTS ★★★★☆
Capacity is the issue

Look at the map and you'll see that a
good proportion of the lifts are fast –
gondolas and high-speed chairs.
Readers are impressed.

QUEUES ★★☆☆☆
It's seasonal; is it fixed for now?

High-season reporters have seen waits
of 15 to 30+ minutes for the old
Penken gondola in the morning, and
more queues to ride down in the
afternoon. All kinds of tactics have
been devised to avoid these queues.
But for the coming season a new
gondola with a huge carrying capacity
is being built, and it seems reasonable
to hope that it will cope with the
demand. Up the mountain, queues are
not unknown, particularly on Horberg
– even in low season. And more of a
problem are overcrowded pistes: the
valley between Penken and Horberg
brings a lot of people together. The
run back from Rastkogel, down the
jumbo cable car, is a nightmare at the
end of the day; don't hesitate to ride
the cable car to avoid this.

TERRAIN PARKS ★★★★★
Something for everyone

Vans Penken Park is one of the finest
parks in the Alps: 'Amazing – almost
up there with Mammoth,' says an
experienced boarder reporter this year.
There's a separate kids' park and
intermediate, advanced, fun and pro
areas. There is no longer a half-pipe,
but experts should bear in mind the
World Cup pipe up the valley at

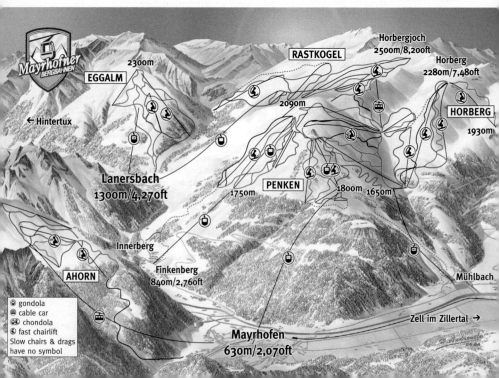

Hintertux. Ahorn now has a novice-oriented fun slope.

SNOW RELIABILITY ★★★
Good by Tirolean standards
The area is better than most Tirolean resorts for snow because the slopes are relatively high – mostly above 1500m. Snowmaking covers the whole Ahorn area (including the lovely run to the valley), all the main slopes on Penken-Horberg and some on Rastkogel and Eggalm. Hintertux is one of the best glaciers in the world. Grooming is 'impressive'.

FOR EXPERTS ★★
Commit to Harakiri
What is claimed to be one of Austria's steepest pistes, Harakiri, plunges down into the valley between Penken and Horberg. It is certainly steep for a European piste, and does offer a worthwhile challenge, particularly when it is rock-hard. (When we last skied it, it had a few cm of fresh snow on a smooth base, which was delightful.) But we don't believe the claimed average gradient of 78% (38°); it might be that steep in one or two spots. Usually, it is wonderfully quiet – surprise, surprise.

The other black runs are not steep. The long ski route to Mühlbach is quite challenging but rarely has good snow. There is, however, quite a lot of decent off-piste to be found in various parts of the area.

FOR INTERMEDIATES ★★★
On the tough side
Most of Mayrhofen's intermediate slopes are on the steep side of the usual range – great for confident intermediates; many of the runs in the main Penken-Horberg area are quite short, though, with verticals in the 300m/400m region. With access to the Lanersbach slopes, there is quite a bit of ground to cover, including lovely quiet runs on Eggalm – read the Lanersbach section of the Hintertux chapter. Don't miss Ahorn's excellent, quiet run to the valley, which doesn't merit its new black classification.

There are few really gentle blue runs, making the area less than ideal for nervous intermediates or near-beginners (and therefore for beginners, too – you don't want to be confined to the nursery slopes). Some of the best are over at Rastkogel; be sure to use the linking cable car to return, rather

STC Ski

Specialists in Tailor-Made Short Breaks & Holidays

01483 771 222
www.stcski.co.uk
ski@stcski.co.uk

than skiing back to Penken. The crowding on many runs can add to the intimidation factor. Ahorn offers a sanctuary.

FOR BEGINNERS ★★
OK if it works for you
Despite its reputation for teaching, Mayrhofen is not ideal for beginners. You have to ride up the mountain to the nursery slopes, and there are no special lift passes so you'll need the full one. The Ahorn nursery slopes are excellent – high, extensive, sunny and crowd-free. But if you are with non-beginner mates, they will want to be on Penken. There are very few easy blues to progress to.

FOR BOARDERS ★★★★
A popular hang-out
Beginners may have a hard time getting around, as the terrain tends to be relatively steep, the nursery slopes are inconvenient, and the area still has a few draglifts. Intermediates and upwards, however, will relish the abundance of good red runs and easily accessible off-piste, and the fact that 'snowboarding is embraced here', as one reporter put it. The terrain park is one of the best in Europe.

FOR CROSS-COUNTRY ★★
Head up the valley
There are 28km of trails in the area. Snow in the valley is not reliable but higher Vorderlanersbach has a much more snow-sure trail.

MOUNTAIN RESTAURANTS ★★★
Plenty of them
Most of the many mountain restaurants are attractive and are clearly marked on the piste maps. Visitors are generally impressed. **Editors' choice** Schneekar at the top of Horberg is our kind of place – beams and open fire inside, small bookable

↑ The way back from Rastkogel involves a tricky red run (you can ride the cable car instead, though); it gives another good view of Harakiri
SNOWPIX.COM / CHRIS GILL

tables on the terrace (a very rare thing in Austria), charming service, good view, excellent food – excellent onion, cheese and bacon tart. Readers endorse our view in all respects; notable Germknödel, apparently.

Worth knowing about The modern Panorahma by the draglifts down from the Finkenberg gondola is roundly recommended – 'friendly staff, wide range of tasty food, good value'. Nearby Christa's Skialm is self-service but atmospheric, with 'simple Tirolean specialities'. Also recommended recently were Grillhof Alm ('the best pizza'), Bergrast ('very comfortable and atmospheric') and Horberg. For places in the Rastkogel and Eggalm sectors, read the Hintertux chapter.

SCHOOLS AND GUIDES ★★★★☆
Excellent reputations
Mayrhofen's multiple ski schools have good reputations.

FOR FAMILIES ★★☆☆☆
Good but inconvenient
Mayrhofen majors on childcare, and the facilities are excellent. But children have to be bussed around and ferried up and down the mountain.

STAYING THERE

Chalets There are several large chalets. Skiworld has the Stoanerhof near the Ahorn cable car. Inghams' St Lukas is set in 'a very pretty copse', a short walk from the centre. Chalet Tirol, added this season, has a good position near the Penken lift.

Hotels Note that the Penken gondola is 700m from the real centre, so 'central' does not mean 'close to lifts'. There's an ice-hotel on Ahorn.

*****Elisabeth The only 5-star, slightly out of the centre.

****Gutshof Zillertal A reporter loved this place on the southern outskirts, with 'almost free' hire cars. 'Good meals, great deal.' Pool, spa.

****Neue Post An old favourite, central: 'Spacious but old-fashioned bedrooms; excellent breakfasts.' Small pool, sauna, steam.

****Neuhaus 'Well appointed, comfortable, friendly.'

****Sporthotel Manni On main street, between station and gondola. 'Large comfortable rooms, good steaks, excellent beer.'

***Edelweiss B&B. 'Good cheap option – comfy beds, plentiful breakfast, pleasant bar selling food at reasonable prices.'

Apartments Plenty available; Landhaus Gasser is central ('well equipped but in traditional style') and the Apart Mountain Lodge ('very modern') has rear garden access to the Ahorn lift.

EATING OUT ★★★★★
Wide choice

There's a wide range of restaurants, from local specialities to Chinese. We've had good, satisfying meals at the jolly, friendly Tiroler Stuben near the station. Wirtshaus zum Griena is a lovely rustic old building on the edge of town, serving 'hearty local food' – too much like a mountain restaurant for our taste, but popular with families. The set menu at the Gasthof Brücke was 'excellent quality and value'. A 2014 reporter rated the cafe attached to the Neue Post hotel as 'excellent', and a past reporter had the 'best wiener schnitzel ever' there.

APRES-SKI ★★★★★
Lively

A great selling point. It starts on the hill; the piste map helpfully identifies après spots (as if you could miss them) – Pilzbar and Elchbar at the top of the Penken gondola, and Eisbar at the top of the Horberg gondola. In the village, people pour off the gondola into the two throbbing bars nearby. Over to Robert, our key reporter this year: 'Head into the Ice Bar (hotel Strass) or the Bruck'n Stadl, where there'll be Jäger and Schnapps aplenty as well as dancing on the tables. The latter stays open until late. On the main street the Harakiri is a good spot for evening après, and Mo's is always busy with a good atmosphere as well.' Robert reckons two traditional British haunts, Piccadilly and Scotland Yard, are now the worse for wear, and favours Mike's Sportsbar. Head there or to the Movie bar to catch the big rugby matches (etc). Some of the other bars in the Strass are rocking places later on, including the Arena, with live music and dancing until 4am. For a quiet drink we head to the bars of the big traditional hotels – the Neuhaus or the Neue Post.

OFF THE SLOPES ★★★★★
Good for all

Innsbruck and other resorts are easily reached by train or bus. There are also good walks and sports amenities, including the swimming pool complex – with saunas, steam room and solarium. Pedestrians have no trouble getting up the mountain to meet friends for lunch. 'Several cafes and an ice-cream parlour make just walking the streets a very pleasant experience,' says a previous visitor.

GETTING THERE

Air Innsbruck 70km/ 45 miles (1hr15); Salzburg 170km/ 105 miles (2hr); Munich 195km/120 miles (2hr30)

Rail Local line through to resort; regular buses from station

TOURIST OFFICES

Mayrhofen
www.mayrhofen.at

Zillertal Arena
Zell im Zillertal
www.zell.at

Gerlos
www.gerlos.at

Königsleiten
www.wald-koenigsleiten.at

ZILLERTAL ARENA

The Zillertal Arena was created in 2000 by linking the slopes of Zell am Ziller, 10km down the valley from Mayrhofen, to those above the villages of Gerlos and Königsleiten. They now share an area about as big as the Mayrhofen-Lanersbach area. The slopes get a lot of sun, but they are quite high, as in Mayrhofen, and the snowmaking is very impressive – a reader who went at Christmas 2014 found the area fully open despite the lack of snowfall.

The slopes suit intermediates well, and give a real sense of travelling around: skiing from one end to the other takes you over several peaks and ridges and, according to a reporter, the return trip takes a full day with little time to deviate along the way. Most runs are short – the longest, down to Gerlos, is 4km.

Zell is the main town in the Zillertal, and a real working community. There are some good hotels, including the 4-star Zapfenhof on the outskirts (with pool) and the Brau in the centre. The town is a bus ride from the two gondolas into the ski area. These can build queues at peak times of the day. You have to ride down as well as up. Après-ski centres around a few bars near the base of the gondolas.

Gerlos has the advantage of being centrally situated in the Zillertal Arena ski area, allowing you to explore in either direction each day. It's also a better base for early intermediates than Zell, with easier slopes at the top of its main lift. It is a bustling resort that straddles the road up to the Gerlos pass; an 'efficient' bus service takes you to the gondola into the slopes. Après-ski is lively and there are several good local hotels, including the 4-star Gaspingerhof with a very smart spa.

Königsleiten is very spread out, in a scenic wooded setting above a dam, with half a dozen hotels including the 4-star Königsleiten. It has more extensive local slopes than Gerlos, on either side of the Gerlospass road, but less vertical. On the north side (reached by a gondola from the village) the runs are mostly genuine reds, radiating from the peak of Königsleitenspitze (2315m). The lower southern sector has a row of quad chairs serving easier slopes.

OBERGURGL TOURIST OFFICE

Obergurgl

A combination of high altitude and traditional Tirolean atmosphere keeps regulars going back, despite the drawbacks

£110
RESORT PRICE INDEX

RATINGS

The mountains

Extent	★★
Fast lifts	★★★★★
Queues	★★★★★
Terrain p'ks	★★
Snow	★★★★★
Expert	★★
Intermediate	★★★
Beginner	★★★★
Boarder	★★
X-country	★★
Restaurants	★★★
Schools	★★★★
Families	★★★★

The resort

Charm	★★★★
Convenience	★★★★
Scenery	★★★
Eating out	★★★
Après-ski	★★★★
Off-slope	★★

144

NEWS

2015/16: In Hochgurgl the Kirchenkar draglift is due to be replaced by a 10-person gondola. The plan is that in 2016/17 a second stage will be added to take skiers higher. At the base of the new gondola, called the Top Mountain Cross Point, there will be a table-service restaurant open for 2015/16 and a motorbike museum due to open Spring 2016.

2014/15: A new fun slope with banked bends, a tunnel, jumps and various obstacles was built above Hochgurgl.

+ Glaciers apart, one of the most snow-sure resorts in the Alps; good for a late-season holiday

+ Excellent area for beginners, timid intermediates and families

+ Queue- and crowd-free, with slick lifts in the main

+ Quiet, chalet-style village with little traffic and good hotels

+ Jolly Tirolean teatime après-ski

− Limited area of slopes, with no tough pistes (but lots of easy lift-accessed off-piste)

− Exposed setting, with very few sheltered slopes for bad weather

− Little to do outside the hotels

− Village is fragmented, and lacking a real centre

− For a small Austrian resort, hotels are rather expensive

There are, of course, other resorts with reliably good snow, or with uncrowded easy and intermediate pistes, or with traditional chalet-style architecture, or with little or no traffic, or with teatime raves on the slopes. But we're hard pressed to think of other resorts that match all of Obergurgl's attractions.

The resort attracts a lot of British visitors, many returning time after time, booking the same hotel a year in advance to avoid disappointment, and it's not difficult to see why. Many reporters stress what a good resort it is for families.

THE RESORT

Obergurgl has grown out of a traditional mountain village, set in a remote spot near the head of its valley – the highest parish in Austria and usually under a blanket of snow.

The village is small and has three main parts. First you come to a cluster of hotels near the Festkogl gondola. The road then passes another group of hotels set on a little hill (beware steep, sometimes icy walks here). Finally you reach the nearest thing to a centre – a little square with a church, a fountain, the hotel Edelweiss und Gurgl and an underground car park.

Even higher Hochgurgl, linked by a mid-mountain gondola, is little more than a handful of hotels at the foot of its own area of slopes.

The lift pass is quite pricey, for a small resort. But for any keen skier it's worth paying an extra 10 euros (at the time of buying your main pass) for a day in Sölden, a short free bus ride down the valley (buses every hour).

VILLAGE CHARM ★★★★
On the quiet side

Obergurgl has no through-traffic and few day visitors, so the place is calm and relaxed. The village 'centre' is mainly traffic-free, and entirely so at night. It's quite jolly immediately after the slopes close, but rather subdued later; most people stay in their hotels.

CONVENIENCE ★★★★
Lifts at both ends

Obergurgl is a small place, and there are lifts at both ends. The Hohe Mut gondola station is close to the 'centre', and nowhere is a long walk from a lift. But you may need to use the free shuttle-buses (eg to get to ski school) – we're told they're every 10 minutes now. Hochgurgl looks like a convenient ski-in/ski-out resort, but nearly all the hotels are separated from the snow by roads and/or stairs.

SCENERY ★★★
Panoramic peaks

There are fabulous panoramic views from the top of the lifts.

SKI-IN & SKI-OUT

Ski Straight to the Hotel Door!

EDELWEISS
GURGL
★ ★ ★ ★

NEW ROOMS
IN WINTER
15/16

★★★★HOTEL
EDELWEISS & GURGL
hospitality since 1889

Absolutely snow secure from the middle
of November until the beginning of May,
at 6,332 feet or almost 2.000 metres
above sea level. Enjoy an **outstanding
4 star hotel right at the foot of the
slopes.**
Top quality skiing in Obergurgl-Hochgurgl
– no waiting times at the ski lifts.

www.edelweiss-gurgl.com
**Hotel Edelweiss & Gurgl | Obergurgl | Tyrol
p: +43-5256-6223**

KEY FACTS

Resort	1930m
	6,330ft
Slopes	1795-3080m
	5,890-10,100ft
Lifts	24
Pistes	110km
	68 miles

LIFT PASSES

Prices in €

Age	6-day
under 16	137
16 to 18	190
18 to 59	253
60 plus	221
Free Under 9	

Beginner Limited pass covering nursery lifts

Note Covers Obergurgl and Hochgurgl, and local ski-bus

THE MOUNTAINS

Most of the slopes are very exposed. Wind and white-outs can shut the lifts, and severe cold can limit enthusiasm, especially in early season. If the weather is bad but not that bad, another problem arises: in our view, and that of many reporters, piste edge marking is dangerously slack – there are huge drop-offs that are not marked, and slopes seem to be marked either on one side only (often the uphill side) or in the middle only. Crazy. The piste map is fine – it's not a complex area – but signposting is not great. Classification of runs can overstate difficulty.

EXTENT OF THE SLOPES ★★
Limited cruising
The total area of slopes is quite limited. A gondola links the Obergurgl and Hochgurgl ski areas at mid-mountain. But it closes absurdly early at 4pm and there are no piste links.

Obergurgl is the smaller of the two linked areas. It is in two sections, with links at altitude in only one direction. The gondola from the village entrance and the Rosskar fast quad chair go to the higher **Festkogl** section. This is served by a short drag and a longer chair up to 3035m. From here you can head down to the gondola base or over to the **Hohe Mut** sector. This is also reached from the village via a gondola, which goes on to the sector high point at Hohe Mut. Lower down are slopes served by a slow quad and a six-pack.

As well as pistes, there are three or four ski routes, the status of which is not explained on the piste map.

The slopes of **Hochgurgl** consist of high, gentle bowls, with fast lifts serving the main slopes above the village and a long draglift serving a black run followed by a short one serving a red on skier's left of the mountain. From the top stations there are spectacular views to the Dolomites. A single run leads down through the woods to Untergurgl.

There's night skiing on 8km of slopes in Obergurgl once a week, and on 3km in Hochgurgl.

FAST LIFTS ★★★★★
Among the best
The system is pretty impressive. Most lifts are now high-capacity gondolas or fast chairs.

QUEUES ★★★★★
No problems
Nearly all reporters say queues are not a problem – 'fantastic'; 'not even at peak times'; 'a key reason why people return here every year'.

TERRAIN PARKS ★★
Approved by a 10-year-old
The park is on Hohe Mut. It has 17 features including rails and kickers for beginners and advanced riders. 'Good little jumps, box, trees to weave in and out of,' said a 10-year-old reporter. Visit www.snowpark-obergurgl.com for more info. A new fun slope for families was built in Hochgurgl for last season – enjoyed by a reporter and his 11-year-old son this year.

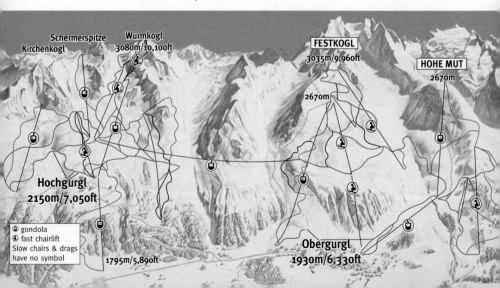

Schermerspitze
Kirchenkogl
Wurmkogl
3080m/10,100ft
FESTKOGL
3035m/9,96oft
HOHE MUT
2670m
2670m
2670m
Hochgurgl
2150m/7,05oft
Obergurgl
1930m/6,33oft
1795m/5,89oft

⊙ gondola
⚇ fast chairlift
Slow chairs & drags
have no symbol

↑ It's a small village. This is the Hohe Mut gondola; there's another gondola at the other end of the village

ÖTZTAL TOURISMUS / ALEXANDER LOHMANN

SNOW RELIABILITY ★★★★★
Excellent
Obergurgl has high slopes and is about the most snow-sure of Europe's non-glacier resorts – even without its snowmaking, which is claimed to cover 99% of the pistes. Piste grooming is good, say most reporters.

FOR EXPERTS ★★★★★
Not generally recommendable
There are few challenges on-piste – most of the blacks could easily be red, and where genuinely black it's only for short stretches (for example, at the very top of Wurmkogl). The ski routes are more challenging, particularly the one from Hohe Mut when mogulled. There is a lot of easy off-piste to be found – the top school groups often go off-piste when conditions are right. Slopes around the Kirchenkar lift (the far left of our piste map and due to be served by a new gondola from 2015/16) are good for untracked powder. And there are more serious routes – a reporter found untracked powder in the Königstal, on skier's left from Wurmkogl. In poor visibility head for the trees above David's Hütte (on the bottom right of our piste map).

FOR INTERMEDIATES ★★★★★
Good but limited
There is some perfect intermediate terrain here, made even better by the normally flattering snow conditions. The problem is, there's not much of it.

Keen piste-bashers will quickly be itching to catch the bus to Sölden.

Hochgurgl has the bigger area of easy runs, and these make good cruising. For more challenges, head to the Vorderer Wurmkogl lift, on the right as you look at the mountain.

The Obergurgl area has more red than blue runs but most offer no great challenge to a confident intermediate. There is some easy cruising around mid-mountain on Festkogl. The blue run from the top of this sector to the village, via the Hohe Mut sector, is 1100m vertical. And there's another long enjoyable run down the length of the gondola, with a scenic black run and ski route variant (neither of them very steep) in the adjoining valley.

On Hohe Mut, there are very easy runs in front of Nederhütte and back towards the village. The red from Hohe Mut is narrow and in places winding.

FOR BEGINNERS ★★★★★
You pays your money
There are two lifts that are free only to ski school pupils, and three other beginner lifts (covered by a special day pass) serving adequate slopes, at each end of Obergurgl, and just above Hochgurgl – an awkward walk from most of the hotels, but otherwise satisfactory. After that you require a full lift pass. The gentle run under the gondola from the mid-station of the Hohe Mut gondola to the village is ideal to move on to (but can be

crowded in the afternoon). The easy broad slopes served by the Bruggenboden chair are also suitable, as are the gentle blues above Hochgurgl (you can catch the ski-bus to the gondola and ride it down as well as up to avoid red runs).

FOR BOARDERS ★★☆☆☆
Lacks challenge

Beginners can access most of the slopes without having to ride draglifts. There's some good off-piste potential for more advanced riders; a recent reporter singles out the area around the Steinmann chair in the Hohe Mut sector. There's also a terrain park.

FOR CROSS-COUNTRY ★★☆☆☆
Limited but snow-sure

Three small loops, two at Obergurgl and one at Hochgurgl, amount to just 12km of trail. At Hochgurgl 1km is floodlit. All are relatively snow-sure and pleasantly situated but, like the slopes, very exposed in bad weather. Lessons are available.

MOUNTAIN RESTAURANTS ★★★☆☆
A dozen to choose from

Twelve huts are clearly marked on the map, with photos, descriptions and phone numbers – admirable.
Editors' choice Hohe Mut Alm has table-service, fabulous glacier views from the big terrace, a woody interior and good hearty food – endorsed by reporters, though one complained of slow service. But it gets packed early and doesn't take bookings.
Worth knowing about The jolly Nederhütte, not far above village level,

is hugely popular with readers and turns into the focal après-ski venue after lunch (see opposite). The Top Mountain Star at Wurmkogl looks like an air traffic control tower, has great 360º views, a varied menu and a modern bar ambience. Kirchenkarhütte by contrast is a small self-service rustic hut that serves simple food and is often crowded (but 'delicious, generous portions', 'a gem'). Other reporter tips: David's Hütte ('charming traditional chalet') and the Downhill Grill ('great burgers, huge portions').

SCHOOLS AND GUIDES ★★★★☆
Excellent reports

We have received only positive reports of the Obergurgl school and guides. 'Our daughter made great progress with her patient instructor,' says a 2015 visitor. Another recent reporter was 'very impressed' with her five-year-old's progress and her 10-year-old son 'rated his instructor highly'; 'he had technique in the mornings and fun in the afternoons'. It is advisable to book ahead during all peak periods.

FOR FAMILIES ★★★★☆
Highly rated by reporters

'Great for families and very child-friendly après-ski,' said a recent reporter. Children's ski classes start at four years and children from age three can either join Bobo Skiclub (outdoor activities) or Kindergarten (indoor/outdoor). There's lunchtime supervision for ski school and kindergarten children. Many hotels offer childcare. Esprit Ski is a family-specialist UK chalet operator here.

ÖTZTAL TOURISMUS / ANTON KLOCKER

This is Wurmkogl, the highest lift-served point in the ski area, with the Top Mountain Star restaurant ↓

STAYING THERE

Demand for rooms exceeds supply, and for once it is true that you should book early to avoid disappointment.

Chalets Ski Total has a big chalet with a sauna and, new for 2015/16, one for 6 or 8. Family specialist Esprit Ski has two chalets, including Verwall, which a 2015 reporter rates ('excellent food, nice sauna, good location'). The Chalet, at 11° East is independently run and 'superb', says a 2015 reporter.

Hotels Accommodation is of high quality: both Obergurgl and Hochgurgl have a 5-star hotel, most of the others are 4-stars, none is less than 3-star.

OBERGURGL

*****Hochfirst Five minutes from gondola. Ski-bus stop outside. Indoor/outdoor pool, spa, hot tub.

****Alpina de Luxe Big, smart; excellent children's facilities. 'Well-run, traditional hotel with exceptional food and fantastic pool/sauna/spa.'

****Austria Bellevue Family-run, 'Lovely pool and spa, food great.'

****Bergwelt 'Comfortable rooms, excellent food.' Indoor, outdoor pools and spa facilities.

****Edelweiss und Gurgl The focal hotel; on the central square, near the main lifts. 'Excellent family hotel,' says a 2015 reporter. Splendid spa with indoor and outdoor pools, hot tub, sauna, steam.

****Gotthard-Zeit Convenient for skiing, but uphill from the village. Pool, sauna, steam and hot tub.

****Vitalhotel Mühle Slightly out of town. 'Amazing spa built into old water mill, food top-notch.'

***Pension Hohenfels Opposite the Festkogl gondola. Basic, but 'food, location and service superb, couldn't fault it', says a recent visitor.

HOCHGURGL

*****Top Hotel Hochgurgl Relais & Châteaux. Good position. Pool, spa.

****Riml Ski-in/ski-out location. 'Clean, comfortable, good food.'

***Alpenglühn Beside Hochgurgl gondola. 'Run by a British woman and her ex-ski-instructor husband.'

Apartments The Lohmann residence is modern and well placed.

EATING OUT ★★★☆☆
Wide choice, limited range

Hotel à la carte dining rooms dominate almost completely. The Romantika at the hotel Madeleine ('proper Italian pizzas, friendly and efficient service';

'good value') and the Belmonte ('has a real buzz, food top-notch, doesn't take bookings, always a queue') are popular pizzerias. The Downhill Grill does 'great burgers, huge portions'. For fine dining, head for the restaurant in the Edelweiss und Gurgl. Some evenings you can eat on the hill, at Hohe Mut Alm (we've had good reports of its 'gourmet fondue') or at David's Hütte.

APRES-SKI ★★★★☆
Lively early, quiet later

Obergurgl is more animated than you might expect in the early evening. Reporters agree that it's dead later on. Nederhütte at the Hohe Mut mid-station is the place to be when the lifts close, which in practice means getting there well before then. 'The best après ever,' says a recent visitor. 'It rocks from the first anthem until the time you want to leave. Schnapps and dancing on your table/chair are obligatory – great fun!' The dancing is often enhanced by live music. You ski home afterwards (or ride down on a snowmobile). All the bars at the base of the Rosskar and Hohe Mut lifts are also popular at close of play – try the Pic-Nic.

The Josl Keller was a 2015 reporter's favourite for later on. We hear that the Krumpn's Stadl barn (with DJs and dancing) opened only on Tuesdays and Thursdays last season. Reporters have enjoyed the Tuesday ski school display/fireworks/mountain party/night ski on Festkogl and the night-time tobogganing.

Hochgurgl is very quiet at night except for live music in Toni's Almhütte bar (Sporthotel Olymp).

OFF THE SLOPES ★★☆☆☆
Very limited

There isn't much to do during the day – hardly any shops, limited facilities of other kinds. There is a natural ice rink and you can go snowshoeing and tobogganing at night in Hochgurgl. Innsbruck is over two hours away by post bus. Sölden (20 minutes away) has a leisure centre and some shops. There are buses to Längenfeld (for the Aqua Dome thermal spa). Pedestrians can ride gondolas to some of the restaurants for lunch, or walk part-way up the Hohe Mut area; there are 12km of hiking paths. The spas at the Crystal and Bergwelt hotels are open to non-residents at a cost of 30 euros.

GETTING THERE

Air Innsbruck 95km/60 miles (1hr30); Salzburg 275km/170 miles (3hr15); Munich 245km/150 miles (3hr30)

Rail Ötz 45km/28 miles; regular buses from station

TOURIST OFFICE

www.obergurgl.com

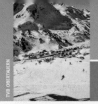

Obertauern

French-style convenience and snow-sure slopes meet Austrian après-ski – an unusual combination; great for a short break

£95
RESORT PRICE INDEX

TOP 10 RATINGS

Extent	★★
Fast lifts	★★★★
Queues	★★★★
Snow	★★★★
Expert	★★★
Intermediate	★★★★
Beginner	★★★
Charm	★★
Convenience	★★★★
Scenery	★★★

KEY FACTS

Resort	1740m
	5,710ft
Slopes	1630-2315m
	5,350-7,600ft
Lifts	26
Pistes	100km
	62 miles

150

+ Excellent snow record
+ Quite a lot of ski-in/ski-out lodging
+ Efficient modern lifts
+ Good mountain restaurants
+ Lively but not intrusive après-ski

− Village not notably charming
− Slopes limited in extent – and in vertical, in particular
− A bleak place in bad weather
− Few off-slope diversions

Obertauern's combination of attractions is unique. If you're hooked on Austrian mountain huts and après-ski but looking for a change from slush and ice at village level, moving up in the world by 1000m or so could be just the ticket. But note the minus points above.

THE RESORT

Obertauern is a mainly modern development set high on top of the Tauern pass. The slopes and lifts form a snow-sure circuit around the village.
Village charm Built in (high-rise) chalet style mixed with some stylish modern architecture, the resort is not unattractive but is not a classic Austrian charmer. Most lodgings are set along the through-road; there is traffic, but it's not heavy. The nearest thing to a central focus is a junction with a side road that has some of the best bars and smart ski shops.
Convenience Lifts go up at various points, and with care you can find ski-in/ski-out lodgings.
Scenery The setting is satisfyingly rugged, with some long views from the high points of the area.

THE MOUNTAINS

Most of the slopes are above the treeline, and bad weather can make skiing very unpleasant (as we found on one recent visit).
Slopes Lifts radiate from the village to form a piste circuit that you can ski either way in a couple of hours – which gives you an idea of the small scale of the area. Runs are short, and vertical is limited – most major lifts are in the 200m to 400m range.
Fast lifts Fast chairs dominate, and lifties reportedly manage to fill them.
Queues Crowded pistes can be more of a problem than queues. The Sonnenlift chair can build queues at ski school time; but recent reporters had few problems.
Terrain parks The Spot is a small park above the Almrausch hut, near the

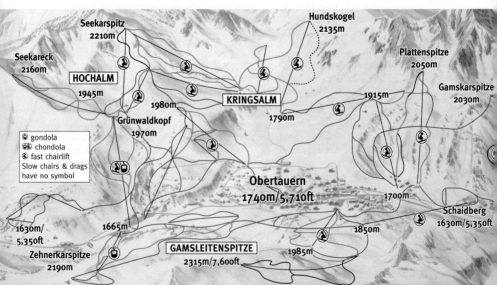

The shady side of the circuit is smaller than the sunny side, but steeper; even so, Zehnerkarspitze has a blue run down as well as multiple reds →

LIFT PASSES

Prices in €

Age	6-day
under 16	109
16 to 18	163
18 to 64	218
65 plus	207
Free Under 6	
Beginner No deals	

Note Covers Obertauern and Grosseck-Speiereck

Alternative pass
Early and late-season special weeks, 6-day (adult) €185

Kehrkopfbahn quad, on the far left on our piste map.

Snow reliability Excellent because of altitude (exceptional, for Austria) and extensive snowmaking.

Experts There are genuinely steep black pistes from the top Gamsleiten chair. Other blacks range from the just about genuine to the purely nominal. There is lots of off-piste within the lift system, and much of it is pretty safe.

Intermediates Most of the circuit is of intermediate difficulty. Stay low for easier pistes, or try the tougher runs higher up; you can't do the whole circuit without skiing reds.

Beginners There are good nursery slopes in several places, notably by the car parks at the western end of the resort. The Schaidberg chair leads to a high-altitude beginners' slope, and there are longer easy blues from there and on the lower Edelweissbahn.

Snowboarding Draglifts are optional except for beginners. Blue Tomato is a specialist school.

Cross-country 26km of trails locally.

Mountain restaurants There are lots, but they are often crowded. Last season we squeezed in to the cosy Flubachalm, only just above village level, and enjoyed a good lunch. Readers recommend the lively Hochalm, Kringsalm, Sonnhof and Edelweisshütte.

Schools and guides Past reviews of both Krallinger and Koch schools have been positive.

Families The resort isn't particularly family-oriented, and nursery slopes can be inconvenient, but most ski schools do take children. The kindergarten takes babies.

STAYING THERE

Hotels Practically all accommodation is in hotels (mostly 3-star and 4-star) and guest houses. The Steiner has been praised: 'Wonderful, faultless hotel – engaging staff, first-class food, extensive spa.' Two others are regularly tipped by readers: the Latschenhof and the Marietta. The Kindl family do an excellent B&B in their hotel Kristall, where we stayed very happily in 2015.

Apartments Apartmenthaus Steinadler is tipped this year – 'helpful staff and nice bar and spa'.

Eating out The choices are mostly hotels (the Latschenhof is highly recommended) though two gourmet places opened a few years ago. Some of the après-ski bars turn themselves into restaurants mid-evening. We've had good pizza in the modern, glass-fronted Mundwerk.

Après-ski Several huts above village level get lively as the lifts close – Hochalm and Edelweiss, for example. There are several cute woody chalets in the village that throb at teatime: Latsch'n Alm, Lürzer Alm ('dancing on the tables encouraged'), and Gruber Stadl. WeltcupSchirm is a 'superb' lively umbrella bar; Qu Bar is 'very loud'. Mundwerk is quieter. Later on, Monkey's Heaven and the People bar have dancing.

Off the slopes There's an excellent, large sports centre (no pool, but some hotel pools are open to the public). There are marked walks up to Kringsalm, and sleigh rides. Salzburg is an easy trip.

TOURIST OFFICE

www.obertauern.com

ely, noisy, traditional-style villages accessing a broad, sunny area that's about to become Austria's biggest

➕ Good intermediate area – expanded now to become Austria's largest

➕ Lift system now essentially 100% fast chairs and gondolas

➕ Saalbach is a pleasant, lively village, largely car-free in the centre

➕ Dozens of good mountain huts

➕ Extensive snowmaking, but ...

➖ The snowmaking is crucial – most slopes are sunny as well as low, and the snow suffers

➖ Limited steep terrain

➖ Both villages spread widely

➖ Boisterous evening behaviour doesn't suit everyone

RATINGS

The mountains

Extent	★★★★
Fast lifts	★★★★★
Queues	★★★★
Terrain p'ks	★★★★
Snow	★★
Expert	★★
Intermediate	★★★★
Beginner	★★★
Boarder	★★★★
X-country	★★
Restaurants	★★★★
Schools	★★★★
Families	★★★

The resort

Charm	★★★★
Convenience	★★★★
Scenery	★★★
Eating out	★★★
Après-ski	★★★★★
Off-slope	★★

This season, with a new six-pack on Bernkogel, Saalbach-Hinterglemm effectively completes its mission to abolish the slow lift. Most people holidaying here will ride nothing but gondolas and fast chairlifts. But this is overshadowed by much bigger news: a new gondola (and a new piste) this season will create a link with Fieberbrunn, to the north, making Austria's largest linked ski area.

The valley has a lot going for it in other respects, too. Sadly, reliably good snow isn't one of them. The snowmaking is good enough to make a midwinter visit here a fairly safe bet, but problems can arise as spring approaches.

THE RESORT

Saalbach and Hinterglemm are separate villages, their centres 4km apart, which have expanded along the floor of their dead-end east-west valley. They haven't quite merged, but have adopted a single marketing identity. A 'ski-circus' links the two, with lifts and runs on both sides of the valley. At the eastern end is a long-standing link to Leogang, in the next valley, and now from a point directly above Hinterglemm there will be the new link with Fieberbrunn.

Several resorts in Salzburgerland are reachable by road. Zell am See, to the south, will from this season be accessible via a new gondola from Viehhofen, only 5km down valley from the most easterly Saalbach lift. There are two regional passes to consider – read the 'Lift passes' panel.

VILLAGE CHARM ★★★★
Very appealing
Saalbach is an attractive, characterful village, with traditional-style (although mostly modern) buildings huddled together around a classic onion-domed church. Hinterglemm is less cute, with a rather featureless centre spread along a single main street. Both villages are free of through-traffic. And both are lively from mid-afternoon until the early hours. Saalbach in particular may have drunken revellers still in ski boots late in the evening.

CONVENIENCE ★★★★
Lifts near the centre
Saalbach is more convenient than most Austrian villages, with lifts into three sectors of the slopes starting close to the traffic-free village centre; the result, if staying centrally, is near to an ideal blend of Austrian charm with French convenience. Hinterglemm also has lifts and runs close to the centre, and offers quick access to some of the most interesting slopes –

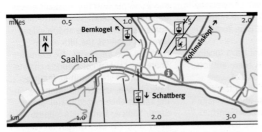

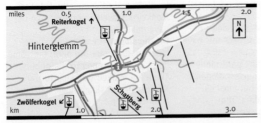

↑ Schattberg Ost, on the left, has a good black on the front face; the steeper Schattberg West has an excellent red on its flank, to Hinterglemm

WÖCKINGER / SAALBACH HINTERGLEMM

NEWS

2015/16: A new run and gondola will link with the Fieberbrunn ski area – a major expansion. A six-pack will replace the drags at Bernkogel.

2014/15: An eight-seat chair with all mod cons replaced the Polten quad on the way to Leogang. A second gondola out of Leogang was built.

KEY FACTS

Resort	1000m
	3,280ft
Slopes	830-2095m
	3,050-6,870ft
Lifts	70
Slopes	270km
	168 miles

The km total is the resort's official figure, verified by consultant Christoph Schrahe (read our feature on piste extent). It includes ski routes.

and, importantly, to most of the north-facing runs. A few reporters find walking through the villages from one side of the slopes to the other an irritant.

The valley bus service is fine, but not perfect: it finishes early, gets very busy at peak times and doesn't reach hotels or lifts in central Hinterglemm, or hotels set away from the main road. A Nightliner bus runs infrequently between the resorts in the evening.

SCENERY ★★★
Pleasant rather than dramatic
The villages are flanked by modest, broad mountain ridges. The high points give more dramatic views of the mountains to the north.

THE MOUNTAINS

The runs form a 'circus' almost entirely composed of broad slopes between swathes of forest, so this is quite a good area in bad weather. The signposting and piste map are good. But many of the blues and reds are of much the same gradient.

EXTENT OF THE SLOPES ★★★★
User-friendly circuit
On the basis of Christoph Schrahe's figures (see margin), this is now Austria's largest ski area. Travelling anticlockwise, you can make a full circuit of the valley on skis, crossing from one side to the other at Vorderglemm and Lengau – if you wish you can stick to blues almost the whole way. Clockwise, you have to do a shorter circuit through Saalbach – there is no lift at Vorderglemm – and there is more red-run skiing to do.

On the south-facing side, five sectors can be identified, each served by a lift from the valley – named on our map. The links across these slopes work well: when traversing the whole hillside you need to descend to the valley floor only once – at Saalbach, where the main street separates Bernkogel from Kohlmaiskopf.

Reiterkogel is where the new gondola and piste (3.5km long, 780m vertical) will connect with **Fieberbrunn**. Its slopes are briefly described at the end of this chapter.

The Wildenkarkogel sector connects to the slopes of **Leogang**; a small, high, open area served by fast lifts leads to a long, north-facing slope down to the base of an eight-seat gondola near Hütten, 3km from Leogang village. A new additional 10-seat access gondola starts from the nursery slope closer to Leogang.

Back in the main valley, the north-facing slopes offer two widely separated and steeper mountains, one split into twin peaks. An eight-seat gondola rises from Saalbach to Schattberg Ost, where the high, open, sunny slopes behind the peak are served by a fast quad. The slightly higher peak of Schattberg West is reached by gondola from Hinterglemm. Another gondola makes the link from Schattberg Ost. The second north-facing hill is Zwölferkogel, served by a gondola from Hinterglemm. A six-pack and draglift serve open slopes on the sunny side, and another gondola from the valley provides a link from the south-facing slopes.

The Hinterglemm nursery slopes are well used, and floodlit every evening.

FAST LIFTS ★★★★★
The world's best
Saalbach-Hinterglemm has the highest proportion of fast lifts of any major resort in the world (about 95%). But the only slow ones are in spots where they are little used.

QUEUES ★★★★
High season weaknesses
Given the fast lifts, it's not surprising that queues are few, but they do occur at peak times – you can hit queues at the Zwölferkogelbahn out of Hinterglemm, the Schattberg X-Press and Kohlmaiskopfbahn out of Saalbach. A more regular problem is the Schönleiten lifts at Vorderglemm.

TERRAIN PARKS ★★★★
Main one has its own gondola
The popular Nightpark just above Hinterglemm is served by its own heated gondola, is floodlit most evenings and has plenty of features, plus a beginner line. There are other parks below Hochalm and Kl. Asitz towards Leogang, and a snowcross and park for beginners on Bernkogel.

SNOW RELIABILITY ★★
A tale of two sides
Most slopes are below 1900m and the south-facing slopes are in the majority; they can suffer from the sun and we've often seen strips of machine-made snow amid green and brown fields –

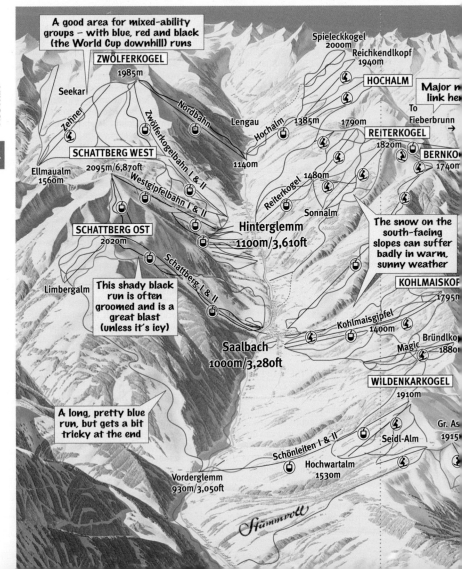

A good area for mixed-ability groups – with blue, red and black (the World Cup downhill) runs

ZWÖLFERKOGEL
1985m

Seekar

Zehner

Nordbahn

Zwölferkogelbahn I & II

Lengau

Hochalm 1385m

Spieleckkogel
2000m

Reichkendlkopf
1940m

HOCHALM

1790m

Major m link her

To Fieberbrunn →

REITERKOGEL
1820m

BERNKO
1740m

SCHATTBERG WEST
2095m/6,87oft

Ellmaualm
1560m

Westgipfelbahn I & II

1140m

Reiterkogel 1480m

SCHATTBERG OST
2020m

Schattberg I & II

Hinterglemm
1100m/3,61oft

Sonnalm

The snow on the south-facing slopes can suffer badly in warm, sunny weather

KOHLMAISKOPF
1795m

Limbergalm

This shady black run is often groomed and is a great blast (unless it's icy)

Kohlmaisgipfel
1400m

Bründlko
1880m

Magic

Saalbach
1000m/3,28oft

WILDENKARKOGEL
1910m

A long, pretty blue run, but gets a bit tricky at the end

Gr. As
1915m

Seidl-Alm

Schönleiten I & II

Hochwartalm
1530m

Vorderglemm
930m/3,05oft

Stammvoll

LIFT PASSES

Prices in €

Age	6-day
under 16	123
16 to 18	184
19 plus	245

Free Under 6

Senior No deals

Beginner Points card

Notes Covers Saalbach-Hinterglemm and Leogang, and the ski-bus; also Reiterkogel toboggan run at night; part-day and non-skier passes

Alternative passes Salzburg Super Ski Card covers 22 ski areas in the Salzburg province; Kitzbüheler Alpen AllStarCard covers Kitzbühel, Schneewinkel (St Johann), SkiWelt, Ski Juwel, Skicircus Saalbach, Zell-Kaprun

'impressive' snowmaking covers 90% of the area. The north-facing slopes keep their snow better but can get icy. The long north-facing run to Leogang – a favourite of ours – often has the best snow in the area.

FOR EXPERTS ★★★★★
Little steep stuff

There are a few challenging slopes on the north-facing side. The long (4km) Nordabfahrt run beneath the Schattberg Ost gondola is a genuine black – a fine fast bash first thing in the morning if it has been groomed and is not icy. The Zwölferkogel Nordabfahrt at Hinterglemm is less consistent, but its classification is justified by a few short, steeper pitches. The World Cup downhill run from Zwölferkogel is interesting, as is the 5km Schattberg West-Hinterglemm red (and its 'ski route' variant). Snow conditions and forest tend to limit the off-piste potential. Given decent snow, however, you can have a good time.

FOR INTERMEDIATES ★★★★★

Paradise for most. The sunny side of the area is ideal for both the mileage-hungry piste-basher and the more leisurely cruiser, although many of the blues can be quite testing. The otherwise delightful blue run from Bernkogel to Saalbach can get really crowded. For more of a challenge, the long red runs to the valley are good.

The north-facing area also has some more challenging runs, with excellent relentless reds from both Schattberg West and Zwölferkogel, and a section of relatively high, open slopes around Zwölferkogel – good for mixed-ability groups wishing to ski together. None of the black runs is beyond an adventurous intermediate, unless icy. The long, pretty blue from Schattberg to Vorderglemm gets right away from lifts – but is a bit steep and tricky towards the end, and probably should be red.

FOR BEGINNERS ★★★★★
Head for Hinterglemm

Saalbach's two sunny nursery slopes are right next to the village. The upper one is served by a short six-pack but gets a lot of through-traffic. There are short, easy runs to progress to at Bernkogel and Schattberg.

Hinterglemm's spacious nursery area is separate from the main slopes and faces north so lacks sun in midwinter but is more reliable for snow later on. Progression is aided by a gondola serving the blue slope that is also used for night skiing. There are lots of other easy blue runs to move on to, especially on the south-facing side of the valley.

FOR BOARDERS ★★★★★
Good all-rounder

Lifts are mainly chairs and gondolas, and there are pistes to appeal to beginners, intermediates and experts alike – with few flats to negotiate. For experienced boarders, there's off-piste terrain between the lifts if snow conditions permit.

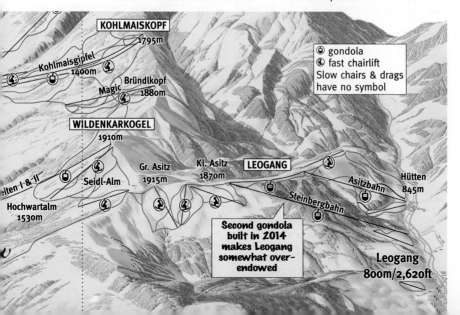

Inghams

HINTERGLEMM
▶ Extensive skiing in the picturesque Glemm Valley
▶ Chalet Hotel Pinzgauerhof NOW on sale!
▶ Additional savings for groups!

inghams.co.uk 01483 371 236 ABTA V4871 ATOL 0025

FOR CROSS-COUNTRY ★★☆☆☆
Go to Zell am See
In midwinter the 10km of valley trails get very little sun, and are not very exciting. There is a high trail on the Reiterkogel. But the area beyond nearby Zell am See is better.

MOUNTAIN RESTAURANTS ★★★★☆
Excellent quality and quantity
The area is liberally scattered with scores of huts, most of them pleasant, lively, rustic places. All are marked and named on the piste map.
Editors' choice Wieseralm, at the heart of the Hinterglemm south-facing slopes, is a welcoming woody chalet doing table-service of satisfying dishes; fine terrace; endorsed by recent reporters ('top class').
Worth knowing about Reporters regularly tip the two places at the top of the gondola from Leogang: Alte Schmiede, a lovely stone-and-wood hut that is also a kind of museum – 'ribs and pizza reliable, and service is amazing for such a big place'; and the huge, three-level Asitzbräu – no longer a brewery, but still serving excellent beer and 'superb' food.

Other tips this year include: Pfefferalm – 'really cosy, with genuine friendliness'; Breitfussalm – 'good service, quite decent food and wine'; Thurneralm – 'small, picturesque'; Maisalm – 'fantastic food, especially pizzas, reasonably priced, great terrace, very friendly staff (went there several times)'; Ellmaualm – 'great views'; Wildenkarhütte – 'very satisfying'; Winkleralm – 'excellent burgers, service seriously impressive'. We could go on.

SCHOOLS AND GUIDES ★★★★☆
More reports welcome ...
There's plenty of choice. Reports on the Fürstauer school are very good, but we lack other reports.

FOR FAMILIES ★★★☆☆
Hinterglemm tries harder
Saalbach doesn't go out of its way to sell itself to families, although it does have a ski kindergarten. Hinterglemm probably makes a better family base, with some good hotel-based nursery facilities – at the Theresia for example. And its nursery slope is better.

STAYING THERE

Chalets Inghams has a chalet hotel (with a sauna), in a prime spot right by the Reiterkogel gondola station in Hinterglemm.
Hotels Both villages have lots of hotels, mainly 3-star and 4-star. Be aware that some central hotels suffer from disco noise, and front rooms from street noise into the early hours. All the hotels we list are in Saalbach; there are plenty in Hinterglemm too (including one rather gaudy 5-star, the Alpine Palace), but they don't seem to generate many reports.
★★★★Alpenhotel Central, with countless bars and restaurants; 'high-class hotel with a good spa and food, and a nice wine list'. A bit pricey.
★★★★Herzblut Has no stars – we've awarded four. Big B&B place, built in 2011, in a quiet but convenient location. 'Excellent breakfast, spacious rooms, extremely friendly staff.' Spa.
★★★★Kendler 'Right in the centre. Good food, friendly staff and nice spa.'
★★★★Kristiania 'Charming family-run small hotel with very friendly staff and good food. Good position.'
★★★★Neuhaus Central location (insist on upper rooms to escape street noise) – 'Superb gourmet food, very accommodating staff.'
★★★★Panther Central, wellness centre, outdoor pool: 'comfortable room, excellent food'; 'staff the highlight'. Some cramped showers, though.
★★★★Saalbacher Hof Major central hotel; 'fantastic food and staff' and 'lovely ambience'. Spa and 'nice pool'.

EATING OUT ★★★☆☆
Wide choice of hotel restaurants
This is essentially a half-board resort, with strikingly few restaurants other than those in hotels. In Saalbach, we like the Kohlmais Stub'n (Aparthotel Astrid) at the foot of the slopes, but we lack recent reports from readers. La Trattoria at the Alpenhotel is 'a cut above the standard fare'. Eva,alm does 'wonderful ribs and burgers'.

APRES-SKI ★★★★★
It rocks from early on

'The best après-ski in the Alps,' claims the resort website, and it is certainly among the best. The site lists over 20 venues. Saalbach, in particular, is very lively from mid-afternoon until the early hours.

On the hill above Saalbach, the Berger Alm under the Magic chair rocks from early afternoon, with a happy hour from 3.30pm; 'Banging!' says a 57-year-old reporter. Then it's down to the rustic Hinterhag Alm, an institution – 'Everybody meets here at 4pm' they say, and that's how it seems; live bands ensure a 'totally mental' atmosphere. Then slide down to the already packed Bauer's Schi-Alm – an old cow shed with attached umbrella bars. There are alternatives: Bäckstätt Stall and the main bar of Berger's Sporthotel have dancing when the lifts close. Bobby's Pub attracts a very young crowd, is cheap, has bowling, games machines, sport on TVs. Zum Turm (a converted medieval jail) and Spitzbub (a converted garage) are loud and lively. The Ötzi bar 'is always good for a night out – good prices, friendly staff, dancing on tables'; but you have to pay for nails. Alibi is 'small but very animated at times; if you love rock music and especially AC/DC this bar is ideal … a good buzz'. There are clubs under various hotels, and several pole dancing dives.

Eva,alm offers something of a retreat – 'a wonderfully civilized bar fronting the main street'.

At Hinterglemm, the rustic goat-themed Goasstall just above the village is another institution: 'one of the great après bars in Austria – like the Mooserwirt in St Anton, but much more lively'. Crikey!

OFF THE SLOPES ★★★★★
Surprisingly little to do

The resort is not very entertaining if you're not into winter sports. There are few shops other than supermarkets and ski shops. But there is some good walking (eg up the valley beyond Lengau) including guided walks twice weekly, and the gondolas can be used. Many good restaurants are reachable by lift. At Hinterglemm a floodlit treetop walk is open all year round. There are long, fun toboggan runs above both Saalbach and Hinterglemm. Excursions to Zell am See and Salzburg are possible.

GETTING THERE

Air Salzburg 85km/ 55 miles (1hr30); Munich 220km/ 135 miles (3hr)

Rail Zell am See 18km/11 miles; hourly buses

TOURIST OFFICES

Saalbach
www.saalbach.com

Leogang
www.leogang-saalfelden.at

Saalbach-Hinterglemm

LINKED RESORT – 800m
LEOGANG

Leogang sits in a pretty valley beneath the impressive Birnhorn. It is quietly attractive but is set on a busy road leading to Fieberbrunn and St Johann.

It may seem to offer a good budget base for skiing the slopes of Saalbach-Hinterglemm, but in practice it suits best those who are content with the good, generally quiet local slopes plus the runs at the eastern end of the main circuit; getting to the best slopes at the far end of the circuit, beyond Hinterglemm, takes quite a time. The nursery slopes are good.

Lodging is widely scattered, but there are good hotels and apartments available. The new second access gondola is right next to the 4-star hotel Krallerhof, making it the obvious place to consider first. (We note that the restaurants at the top of the gondola are in the same stable; surely not all owned by the mayor, by any chance?) Restaurants are hotel-based. The rustic old chalet Kraller Alm is the focal teatime and evening rendezvous. Activities off the slopes are rather limited, but there is the mile-long Flying Fox zipwire where you whistle along at 80mph.

LINKED RESORT – 800m
FIEBERBRUNN

Fieberbrunn is a traditional village, sprawling along the valley road for 2km, but mostly set back from the road and railway. The lift base for the wooded slopes is a bus ride away from the village.

It's a small area – you could ski it in a day – but it has no less than five gondolas, plus this year's new one to Hinterglemm. From the base, one gondola serves blue slopes and links with a further gondola to the top of the local hill at 1645m. A second base gondola leads off at right angles to serve steeper red runs. Taking either route you can then take further lifts to the most challenging skiing with a top height of 2020m on Hochhörndl. It's from the bottom of this sector that the new gondola to Hinterglemm will depart. There's a popular terrain park.

Lodging in the village is in hotels; there is also lodging at the lift base.

Fieberbrunn is a good base for exploration of the Kitzbühel/SkiWelt region, too.

SCHLADMING TOURIST OFFICE

Schladming

Pleasant old valley town in Styria, with a famous racing hill directly above, links to three other mountains; plus other areas nearby

£95
RESORT PRICE INDEX

+	Ideal for intermediate cruising	−	Slopes lack variety
+	Very sheltered slopes, among trees	−	Very little to entertain experts
+	Lots of good mountain restaurants	−	Nursery slopes not central
+	Appealing town with friendly people	−	Runs to valley level are not easy

One slope may be rather like another here, but with its four linked mountains Schladming offers the keen intermediate a real sense of travelling around on the snow. And its solid valley-town ambience makes it a pleasant change from the Austrian rustic-village norm.

RATINGS

The mountains

Extent	★★★
Fast lifts	★★★★
Queues	★★★★
Terrain p'ks	★★★
Snow	★★★★
Expert	★★
Intermediate	★★★★
Beginner	★★★
Boarder	★★★
X-country	★★★★
Restaurants	★★★★
Schools	★★★
Families	★★★★

The resort

Charm	★★★
Convenience	★★★
Scenery	★★★
Eating out	★★★
Après-ski	★★★
Off-slope	★★★

158

KEY FACTS

Resort	745m
	2,440ft

Schladming's four linked mountains

Slopes	745-2015m
	2,440-6,610ft
Lifts	44
Pistes	123km
	76 miles

THE RESORT

The old town of Schladming sits at the foot of Planai, one of four linked ski mountains. It has a long skiing tradition: the town has hosted many World Cup races and in 2013 hosted the World Championships, triggering lots of new construction.

At the foot of the next mountain to the west, Hochwurzen, is Rohrmoos – a quiet, scattered satellite village set on an elevated slope that forms a giant nursery area. To the east is the small, attractively rustic village of Haus, at the foot of the highest of the four mountains, Hauser Kaibling.

Timetabled 'efficient' free ski-buses link the villages and lift bases. A night-bus runs until late (not cheap).

The multi-day lift pass also covers many other resorts in the region, easily reached by car, possibly by bus.

There are direct trains from Salzburg, so Schladming makes an excellent short break destination.

VILLAGE CHARM ★★★
Pleasant car-free centre

Most of Schladming's buildings are solid and traditional, and at its heart there's a pleasant, traffic-free main square, prettily lit at night, around which you'll find most of the shops, restaurants, bars and some appealing hotels. The ultra-modern Planet Planai area nearby at the base of the gondola is a complete contrast. The busy main road bypasses the town.

CONVENIENCE ★★★
Reasonably compact

Much of the accommodation is close to the town centre; the sports centre and tennis halls are five minutes' walk away, as is the gondola to Planai. There is also accommodation out by the Planai-Hochwurzen lift link, and further down the valley (eg Pichl).

SCENERY ★★★
Four points of view

All four mountains are broadly similar, pleasantly wooded and share decent views along the Ennstal and to the more dramatic Dachsteingruppe.

THE MOUNTAINS

Most pistes are on the wooded north-facing slopes above the main valley, with some going into the side valleys higher up; there are a few short open slopes above the trees.

Piste maps here can be confusing. The whole four-mountain area is

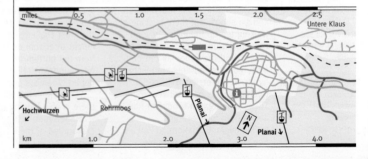

LIFT PASSES

Ski Amadé

Prices in €

Age	6-day
under 17	121
17 to 19	181
20 plus	241

Free Under 6

Senior No deals

Beginner Rohrmoos has a couple of free lifts we're told

Notes Covers the 860km of pistes and 270 lifts in five regions: Schladming-Dachstein; Gastein; Salzburger Sportwelt; Grossarl; Hochkönig

Alternative passes Schladming-Dachstein only; Salzburg Super Ski Card (all lifts in Salzburgerland, including Zell am See, Kaprun and Saalbach-Hinterglemm)

covered on one map, but the individual mountains also do their own maps (Planai and Hochwurzen do a combined one).

As in many Austrian areas, you may encounter multiple pistes identified by the same number. Add to this poor signposting, and finding your way around can be tricky.

EXTENT OF THE SLOPES ★★★
Four linked sectors

The resort claims a total of just over 120km of pistes – a modest figure, but it's enough to scrape into our ★★★ rating. Each of the sectors has a variety of runs, and you get a sensation of travelling around a lot.

Planai is the local mountain, reached directly by gondola from the edge of the town centre. It is linked to **Hauser Kaibling** at altitude via the high, wooded bowl between them. At the base of the mountain, the village of Haus has a cable car and gondola into the slopes. Links to the mountains to the west, **Hochwurzen** and **Reiteralm**, are at valley level (and the first involves riding a gondola down from Planai). Our favourite area is Reiteralm – a hi-tech lift system and nicely varied terrain, extended down into Preuneggtal a few years ago by a new gondola and runs.

Several lower runs go across poorly signposted roads – care is needed.

There are several other separate mountains nearby covered by the local lift pass – including Fageralm (only slow chairlifts and T-bars, but lovely quiet, wide, easy cruising pistes and rustic huts – a very relaxing change of pace), Galsterbergalm, the Dachstein glacier and Stoderzinken.

FAST LIFTS ★★★★
Some neglected links

Each linked sector has gondola access from the car parks at the bases, and there are now lots of fast chairs. But the slow chairlifts from Schladming to Hochwurzen and from Pichl to Reiteralm are obvious weaknesses.

QUEUES ★★★★
Not a general problem

Queues for the Planai gondola at peak times can be a problem – avoided by catching a bus to another mountain's lift station. Other bottlenecks pointed out by reporters are the slow chairs up to Rohrmoos and from Pichl up Reiteralm. But many people visiting outside high season saw no queues.

TERRAIN PARKS ★★★
Three to try

Planai has a park above Lärchkogel, with lots of features arranged in medium and pro lines. Reiteralm's park is similarly well equipped; there's also a half-pipe. Hochwurzen's park is floodlit until late.

SNOW RELIABILITY ★★★★
Excellent in cold weather

The northerly orientation of the slopes helps keep the pistes in good shape. The serious snowmaking operation makes it a good choice for early holidays; the system is put to good use. But at this altitude poor conditions on the lower slopes are a natural hazard. Grooming is good.

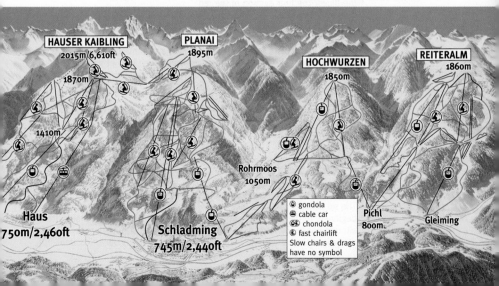

HAUSER KAIBLING
2015m/6,610ft
1870m
1410m

PLANAI
1895m

HOCHWURZEN
1850m

REITERALM
1886m

Rohrmoos
1050m

Haus
750m/2,460ft

Schladming
745m/2,440ft

Pichl
800m

Gleiming

⊚ gondola
⊜ cable car
⊛ chondola
⊕ fast chairlift
Slow chairs & drags
have no symbol

↑ Dense forest extends pretty close to the top heights. This is Hauser Kaibling

HAUSER KAIBLING

FOR EXPERTS ★★
Strictly intermediate stuff
Schladming's status as a racing venue doesn't make it macho. The steep black finish to the Men's Downhill course and the mogul runs at the top of Planai and Hauser Kaibling are the only really challenging slopes there. Reiteralm has two steep black runs (one very short) at the top and some good tree runs. Hauser Kaibling's off-piste is good, but limited; it has two itineraries, not notably steep.

FOR INTERMEDIATES ★★★★
Red runs rule
The area is ideal for intermediate cruising. The majority of runs are red but the gradient of many is similar to the blues. The final section of the red below Rohrmoos is steep though.

Newish lifts have improved access to more challenging slopes at the top of Planai and Hauser Kaibling, as well as a short but pretty blue from the high point. The black racing pistes in these sectors, and the red alternatives, are ideal for fast cruising but can get very icy and tricky on the lower sections.

Hauser Kaibling has a lovely blue running from top to bottom, and Reiteralm has some gentle blues.

FOR BEGINNERS ★★★
Good slopes but poorly sited
The ski schools generally take beginners to the extensive but low-altitude Rohrmoos nursery area, where we believe there are some free lifts –

fine if you are based there. But for residents of central Schladming, it's a bus ride. There is also a beginner slope high on Planai – a lift pass is needed. There are lots of easy runs to progress to, though getting to them can be a bit of an effort.

FOR BOARDERS ★★★
Fine for all but experts
Schladming is popular with boarders. Most lifts on the spread-out mountains are gondolas or chairs, with some short drags around. The area is ideal for beginners and intermediates, except when the lower slopes are icy, though there are few exciting challenges for expert boarders bar the off-piste tree runs.

FOR CROSS-COUNTRY ★★★★
Huge network of trails
There are almost 500km of trails in the region, and the World Championships have been held at nearby Ramsau, where there are floodlit trails in the stadium.

MOUNTAIN RESTAURANTS ★★★★
A real highlight
There are plenty of attractive rustic huts, mostly table-service and with good food. Some of the individual mountain piste maps mark them.

On Hauser Kaibling, Schoarlhütte has a real mountain-hut atmosphere and is renowned for its ribs. For a good gröstl, try Krummholzhütte.

On Planai, reporters love Onkel Willy's Hütte – 'very nice ambience, good food, fast service'. Schafalm impressed one visitor despite being packed on a snowy day.

On Hochwurzen, the 'picturesque, sweet little' Hochwurzenalm is tipped for big portions of gulaschsuppe. The large self-service Hochwurzenhütte at the top is good, too. Tauernalm, at Rohrmoos, offers 'very good food, cheerful service'.

On Reiteralm there is praise for Schnepf'n Alm, Gasselhöh Hütte and Jaga Stüberl – 'impeccable service', 'delicious crispy pizzas'.

On Fageralm, we've enjoyed the tiny Zeffererhütte, and a reporter enjoyed Unterbergalm.

SCHOOLS AND GUIDES ★★★
A good report
We had a rave review a year or two back of a private lesson with Tritscher: 'Best I've had – corrected things that have dogged me for years; brilliant.'

FOR FAMILIES ★★★★
Rohrmoos is the place
The extensive gentle slopes of Rohrmoos are ideal for building up confidence. There are Kinderlands on Planai, Reiteralm and Fageralm.

STAYING THERE

Packaged accommodation is mainly in hotels and pensions, but there are plenty of apartments for independent travellers.
Hotels Most lodging is mid-range but a few upmarket places exist.
★★★★Sporthotel Royer Big and comfortable, a few minutes from the Planai gondola. Pool, sauna, steam. We stayed here in 2013; the food was terrific and plentiful.
★★★Aqi Cool modern place, built in 2008, opposite Planai gondola. 'Helpful staff, spacious quiet room, good food, plentiful breakfast.'
★★★Kirchenwirt Off the main square. 'Quaint, rooms a good size, staff friendly, food simple but good.'
★★★Planai New three years ago, directly opposite the Planai gondola; big and bright, modern and functional; 'brilliant breakfast buffet, nice spa on top floor with views'.
★★★Pariente At Rohrmoos. 'Lovely small hotel in great piste-side location. Lovely rooms, food simple but nice and plentiful.'
Apartments A reader tips the 'spacious, excellent' Bella Vista apartments.

GETTING THERE
Air Salzburg 90km/ 55 miles (1hr15); Munich 260km/ 160 miles (3hr)
Rail Mainline station in resort

TOURIST OFFICE
www.schladming-dachstein.at
www.skiamade.com

EATING OUT ★★★
Some good places
An experienced reporter says that best in town is the cool Tischlerei – 'Exudes quality: very hospitable team, hugely impressive cooking' – endorsed by another reporter this year. The small, family-run Steakhouse Friesacher offers 'real family hospitality' and 'expertly cooked steaks'. Maria's Mexican does a roaring trade in 'spicy and delicious' Tex-Mex, amid an 'all-round feel-good ambience'. Biochi specializes in organic and vegetarian food. Many of the other good places are in hotels; tips include Johann's in the Posthotel, the Kirchenwirt and Neue Post. We liked the Lasser Cafe and the Stadttor for coffee and cakes, and the Schwalbenbräu brewery.

APRES-SKI ★★★
Hohenhaus gets lively
Some of the mountain huts have live or loud music in the afternoon. On Hochwurzen, try Tauernalm at Rohrmoos. In town, the focus is the huge Hohenhaus Tenne by the Planai gondola station, the largest après-ski bar in Europe; 'packed from 1500 – probably my favourite après bar, anywhere', says a reader this year; fabulous main bar, dance floor and regular live music. Reopens after dinner and gets packed again. Platzhirschalm (with umbrella bar) opposite also gets busy. In the main square, the Posthotel's upmarket umbrella bar Cabalou is lively, with slick service. Many of the central bars stay open until the early hours – but this isn't Ischgl. Cult and Angels are nightclubs.

OFF THE SLOPES ★★★
A few things to do
The town has a few shops, museum, pool and an ice rink. Hochwurzen has a floodlit 7km toboggan run. Some mountain restaurants are accessible to pedestrians. Trips to Salzburg are easy.

LINKED RESORT – 750m
HAUS

Haus is a fairly self-contained village, with its own ski schools, kindergartens and railway station. Hotel prices are generally lower here. The user-friendly nursery slopes are between the centre and the gondola. Excursions are easy, but off-slope activities and nightlife are very limited.

FRANK HEUER

Sölden

The resort needs a bypass tunnel, but slopes reaching glacial heights and an impressive lift system offer compensation

£110
RESORT PRICE INDEX

RATINGS

The mountains
Extent	★★★
Fast lifts	★★★★
Queues	★★★
Terrain p'ks	★★★
Snow	★★★★
Expert	★★★
Intermediate	★★★★
Beginner	★★★
Boarder	★★★★
X-country	★
Restaurants	★★★
Schools	★★★
Families	★★

The resort
Charm	★★
Convenience	★★
Scenery	★★★
Eating out	★★★
Après-ski	★★★★★
Off-slope	★★

162

NEWS

2014/15: The Wasserkar triple chair from below the Gaislachkogl gondola mid-station was replaced by a six-pack, with a new base station half a kilometre below the base of the old chair. This makes the blue and black slopes served by the chair longer and more enjoyable.

KEY FACTS

Resort	1380m
	4,530ft
Slopes	1350-3250m
	4,430-10,660ft
Lifts	33
Pistes	145km
	90 miles

+ Excellent snow reliability, with access to two glaciers and some exceptionally long runs

+ Fairly extensive network of slopes suited to adventurous intermediates

+ Impressive lift system

+ Wide choice of huts for its size

+ Very lively après-ski/nightlife

− Towny resort is spread along a road that is busy with through-traffic

− You may need a bus to the lifts

− Main runs are almost all above the trees; only a couple are sheltered

− Town centre can get rowdy (but easily avoidable, say reporters)

Sölden used to have a low profile on the UK market. But this year we received more reports on it than ever before. And its profile will be raised further because scenes from the new James Bond movie, Spectre, were shot here last season. We've always liked its snow-sure challenging red pistes and exceptionally long top-to-bottom runs. But we're less attracted to the village, with its busy road and very lively après-ski scene.

THE RESORT

Sölden is a long, towny place in the Ötz valley leading up to Obergurgl. Gondolas from opposite ends of town go up to the peak of Gaislachkogl and the lift junction of Giggijoch, with most of the shops, restaurants and hotels in between them. A road winds its way above the town through various hamlets up to Hochsölden – a group of 4-star hotels and little else.

When buying a six-day lift pass you can opt to pay 10 euros extra for a day in nearby Obergurgl (the half-hourly buses are included in the lift pass). You can also get buses down the valley to Längenfeld where there is a big thermal spa. With a car you could make trips to St Anton or Ischgl.

VILLAGE CHARM ★★
Not a strong point
Despite its traditional Tirolean buildings, a pretty church among them, Sölden is no charmer. There's a good selection of shops and bars, but the ambience is towny (prominent ads for strip clubs don't help) and lacks a central focus. More seriously, it is strung along the valley road running through it and the central strip is badly affected by traffic. The place attracts a lively crowd, and the partying can spill into the street. Across the river there's a quieter area, mainly of hotels and guest houses. Hochsölden offers splendid traffic-free isolation up the mountain.

CONVENIENCE ★★
Lifts at either end
It's a long town, and the gondola stations are almost a mile apart. So you may face a good walk to the lifts, or a ride on the free shuttle-buses. Places over the river from the main street aren't necessarily remote from the lifts. Hochsölden is ski-in/ski-out.

SCENERY ★★★
Go for the Big 3
Sölden promotes its Big 3 viewing platforms with spectacular 360° views from peaks over 3000m. But lower down things are less spectacular.

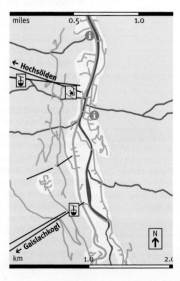

LIFT PASSES

Prices in €

Age	6-day
under 15	127
15 to 19	190
20 to 63	254
64 plus men/ 59 plus women	216
Free Under 5	

Senior 80 plus: 6-day pass €127
Beginner Limited tickets for Innerwald and Giggijoch
Notes Part-day and pedestrian options

THE MOUNTAINS

Practically all the slopes you spend your days on are above the treeline, though there are red and black runs through trees to the village.

The piste map – published in compact Z-card and a much bigger format – is adequately clear.

EXTENT OF THE SLOPES ★★★
Long run network

The ski area is not enormous. The resort claims 145km, but the Schrahe report (read our piste extent feature) puts the total at 93km, which sounds much nearer the mark to us. But it does go high and all sectors offer serious vertical and some long runs. It is 1880m vertical and a claimed 15km from the top of the glacier to the village; other long runs, including from Gaislachkogl and Hainbachjoch are 8km to 10km.

There are two similar-sized sectors above the town, linked by fast six-packs out of the intervening Rettenbachtal. At the south end of town, a gondola leads up to an impressive three-cable gondola to **Gaislachkogl**. The terrain above the mid-station is served by a fast six-pack (new last season) and a slow double. There are links south towards Gaislachalm and north towards the

Rettenbachtal. Another gondola from the north end of the resort goes to **Giggijoch**. Fast lifts from here serve wide, open slopes below Rotkogljoch, from where a series of fast chairs and gondolas (one a cross-valley affair with no piste beneath it) leads to the glaciers – first the **Rettenbach**, and then the **Tiefenbach**. It may be a long journey (at least five lifts to reach the top from the village) but with luck the reward will be quiet slopes with excellent powdery winter snow. Below Giggijoch, and reached by red and black runs, is Hochsölden, served by a slow double chair back up.

FAST LIFTS ★★★★
Well-linked system

There are still some slow lifts around – including (avoidable) T-bars on the glaciers, but most of the area is well served by fast chairs and gondolas.

QUEUES ★★★
Giggijoch's not so great

The Giggijoch gondola at one end of town still generates big queues in the morning peak. By contrast, the Gaislachkogl gondola seems to be relatively queue-free. One reporter says it's worth taking the bus to the other gondola to avoid the Giggijoch queues. Key lifts to and from the glacier, such as the Einzeiger chair and

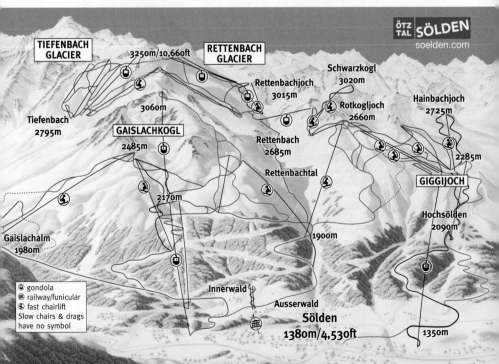

ÖTZ TAL **SÖLDEN**
soelden.com

TIEFENBACH GLACIER

3250m/10,66oft

RETTENBACH GLACIER

Rettenbachjoch 3015m

Schwarzkogl 3020m

3060m

Rotkogljoch 266om

Hainbachjoch 2725m

Tiefenbach 2795m

GAISLACHKOGL
2485m

Rettenbach 2685m

2285m

2170m

Rettenbachtal

GIGGIJOCH

Hochsölden 2009m

Gaislachalm
1980m

1900m

Innerwald

Ausserwald

Sölden
1380m/4,53oft

1350m

⊚ gondola
⊛ railway/funicular
④ fast chairlift
Slow chairs & drags have no symbol

Seiterkar chair, get busy. Both chairs to Rotkogljoch (gateway to the glaciers) are queue-prone but shift crowds fast. The slopes above Giggijoch get very busy. Weekends are especially busy because of an influx of day trippers.

TERRAIN PARKS ★★★
Sufficiently equipped
The park above Giggijoch is well established and regularly upgraded. As well as beginner, intermediate and pro kickers, there are various features and a chill-out zone. Visit www.snowpark-soelden.com for more info.

SNOW RELIABILITY ★★★★
Rarely a problem
The slopes are high and roughly east-facing; and there are two extensive glaciers. Snowmaking covers 67% of the area, including all slopes on Giggijoch. Grooming is thorough, and reportedly goes on during the day, which is unusual these days. Even in a generally poor season, you can usually count on coverage to resort level.

FOR EXPERTS ★★★
Off-piste challenges
Few of the black pistes dotted around Sölden's map are serious, and some are silly. And one recent reader was distressed by the grooming of blacks, and consequent lack of moguls. But another visitor found the black World Cup race piste (31, at the foot of the Rettenbach glacier) 'a real blast in the morning'. There are quite a few non-trivial reds, notably on Gaislachkogl – with some steeper pitches above the mid-station – and the length and vertical of some of the runs present their own challenges. There are extensive off-piste possibilities, eg into Rettenbachtal.

FOR INTERMEDIATES ★★★★
Serious verticals
Most of Sölden's main slopes are genuine red runs ideal for adventurous intermediates; there are several easy blacks, too. Keen piste-bashers will love the serious verticals and long runs to be done (notably the one from Gaislachkogl) – but after a couple of days will agree that the claimed extent of 145km is optimistic. We recommend paying the extra 10 euros when buying your lift pass to cover a day in nearby Obergurgl; reporters agree.

There are two obvious targets for less confident intermediates. The long, quiet blue run above Gaislachalm is great for cruising, and below it a gentle blue through the trees offers by far the most friendly return to the resort. And the blues above Giggijoch offer gentle gradients; but crowds, too.

The glaciers are accessible to blue-run skiers, and are almost entirely of blue-run gradient – the red runs down the Seiterkar chair offer a bit of a challenge. But beware: the busy red run (with an optional black variant) down the Rettenbachtal to the village is narrow (it's a road). You might prefer to catch a lift up and take an easier route down.

FOR BEGINNERS ★★★
Crowded nursery slopes
The beginners' slopes, served by a pair of parallel draglifts (with a special pass), are situated just above the village at Innerwald and are reached by a free funicular. Progression to longer runs usually means the blues at Giggijoch; these are wide and gentle, but very busy in places. Hochsölden is on a steep slope – avoid at all costs.

FOR BOARDERS ★★★★
Long, wide runs
Sölden is quite popular with boarders. The nursery slope involves drags, but after that draglifts can be avoided and you'll enjoy the wide, open blue runs above Giggijoch. Intermediates will relish the long runs and open terrain, and there's great freeriding for experienced boarders. There are some flat sections of piste in the Rettenbachtal and on the runs to the resort. There's a decent terrain park.

FOR CROSS-COUNTRY ★
Little to entertain
There are a couple of loops by the river to Hof (back end of town), another 5km trail to Rechenau and a 7km trail at Zwieselstein, between Sölden and Obergurgl.

MOUNTAIN RESTAURANTS ★★★
Few notable places
There are 30 huts listed, all usefully marked on the piste map and summarized in a separate leaflet. Most offer traditional food. But those in the main area can get crowded.

We like the rustic Gampe Thaya – simple food, table-service, lovely terrace, cosy interior. We've also enjoyed good käsespätzle at the

DO MORE
in
Sölden

zenith
·holidays·

0203 137 7678

zenithholidays.co.uk

⬥ABTA
ABTA No. Y1542

peaceful Heidealm above Gaislachalm (accessed via a ski route). Both places have fabulous views up the Oetztal towards Obergurgl.

A recent reporter raves about the newish Ice Q with glass walls and fabulous views at the top of Gaislachkogl – 'oozes class but at reasonable prices'. Scenes for the new James Bond film were shot here. Also on Giaslachkogl, just off blue run 2, is Löple Alm which serves 'traditional fare and has views down the valley to die for'. Hühnersteign in the Rettenbachtal is famous for its chicken (Hühner!) – it also does a 'fantastic' gröstl, says a 2015 reporter. The Stabele just below it is equally famous for its gigantic burgers. At Giggijoch a recent reporter endorses the Wirtshaus table-service option: 'excellent food, attentive service, good value'. Below Hochsölden, the 'quaint' Eugen's Obstlerhütte serves 'massive roast chicken portions and superb large ribs'. The Panorama Alm, just above town, seems a good place for an afternoon sunbathe and drink, with beanbags, deckchairs and music.

SCHOOLS AND GUIDES ★★★
Wide choice, lacking feedback
Sölden has twelve schools. Not surprisingly, we lack reports on most. A 2015 reporter was pleased with his Freeride Centre off-piste guide.

FOR FAMILIES ★★
Few special facilities
Sölden does not go out of its way to cater for families. The intrusive main

Ski Total

WELCOME YOU TO
Sölden

**Quality chalets
Excellent value
19 resorts
across the Alps**

**skitotal.com
01483 791 933**

road traffic, possibly lengthy walks to the lifts and lively après-ski detract from its family-friendliness. But there are kindergartens at two schools and children aged four to seven pay a euro per day to use all the slopes.

STAYING THERE

Chalets Ski Total has its chalet hotel Hermann (consisting of a traditional and a more modern building) above the village near the nursery slopes. A 2015 reporter said, 'Just about the best chalet hotel we've experienced. Highly recommended for quality food and fantastic hospitality.' But a couple of past reporters have been less happy with its location.

Hotels There is one 5-star hotel but most are good 3- or 4-stars. Take care if looking at very central places – there are noisy bars.

*****Central Spa Fairly central but also the biggest and best in town – the only 5-star; warmly welcoming; major spa, fitness room, pool.

ÖTZTAL TO

Hochsölden is worth considering if you want a quiet time and to hit the slopes first thing before the hordes get up the hill
↓

↑ The two glaciers (Rettenbach in the sun, Tiefenbach in the shade on the left) mean guaranteed good snow all season

****Bergland** Hip, recently built place next to the funicular to Innerwald, with big fifth-floor spa, outdoor hot tub and decent pool.

****Erhart** Across the river 500m from the Gaislachkogl gondola. 'Good, quiet location but a long walk from Giggijoch gondola,' says a 2015 reporter. Spa/fitness facilities.

****Grauer Bär** Near the Gaislachkogl lift. Comfortable rooms, good food. Wellness area.

****Hubertus** Central. 'I highly recommend it for its friendly service, superb food and good prices,' says a 2015 visitor.

****Regina** 50m from the Gaislachkogl lift. 'Incredible five-course dinner, immaculate rooms, very friendly staff, excellent spa,' says a 2015 reporter.

****Stefan** By the Giggijoch gondola. We've stayed happily here – good food. Fair-sized wellness area.

Apartments The Gaislachkogl apartments are close to the gondola, with wellness facilities.

EATING OUT ★★★☆☆
A reasonable choice
Many of the hotels have à la carte restaurants, serving traditional Austrian food. Hotel Bergland is 'one of the few places that do fondue'. Joe's Höhle in hotel Castello has been recommended for grilled steaks. We usually end up in the Tavola in the hotel Rosengarten (because it doesn't take reservations) and haven't been disappointed.

There are various pizzerias – Gusto has been praised for its huge, good-quality, good-value pizzas, but a reporter this year found the service 'not great'.

S'Pfandl, above the town at Ausserwald, makes a jolly outing for traditional Tirolean food.

APRES-SKI ★★★★★
Throbbing until late
Sölden's après-ski is justly famous. It starts up the mountain, notably at Giggijoch at Eugen's Obstlerhütte, or at Bubi's Schihütte on Gaislachkogl (with live traditional music) and progresses (possibly via Philipp's Eisbar at Innerwald) to packed bars in and around the main street.

The hotel Liebe Sonne's Schirmbar is 'the best après in town', says a seasonaire – lively and packed, usually overflowing into the road. Fire and Ice is a two-storey glass-fronted place that parties from 3pm to 3am. There are countless other places, with live bands at, er, Live, and throbbing discos, some with table dancing and/or striptease – Katapult has go-go dancers and guest DJs. And if you've any energy left, Kuhstall stays open till 5–6am. Reader tips for quieter places include Grizzly's and Die Alm.

OFF THE SLOPES ★★☆☆☆
Good spa facilities
The Freizeit leisure centre has a swimming pool, saunas, steam, gym, tennis and bowling. There's an ice rink and a 5km floodlit toboggan run. You can go snowshoeing and there are walking trails. A reporter enjoyed the Wednesday night ski show on Gaislachkogl. Trips to Innsbruck are possible. Aqua Dome is a 'beautiful' thermal spa centre at Längenfeld, reached by regular buses. There are sleigh rides up the valley at Vent.

GETTING THERE

Air Innsbruck 85km/ 50 miles (1hr15); Zürich 275km/ 170 miles (3hr15); Munich 285km/ 175 miles (3hr15)

Rail Ötz (30km/ 19 miles); buses from station

TOURIST OFFICE

www.soelden.com

SÖLL TOURIST OFFICE

Söll

The ski area is big, but the attractive village is surprisingly small and intimate; shame it is not set right by the lifts

£90
RESORT PRICE INDEX

RATINGS

The mountains

Extent	★★★★
Fast lifts	★★★★
Queues	★★★
Terrain p'ks	★★★
Snow	★★
Expert	★
Intermediate	★★★★
Beginner	★★
Boarder	★★
X-country	★★★
Restaurants	★★★
Schools	★★★
Families	★★★

The resort

Charm	★★★
Convenience	★★
Scenery	★★★
Eating out	★★
Après-ski	★★★★
Off-slope	★★

KEY FACTS

Resort	700m
	2,300ft

Entire SkiWelt	
Slopes	620-1955m
	2,030-6,410ft
Lifts	90
Pistes	280km
	174 miles

Note The Schrahe report (read our feature on 'Piste extent') puts this area at 251km – slightly smaller than the newly expanded Saalbach-Hinterglemm area.

- + Part of the SkiWelt, one of Austria's largest linked ski areas
- + Local slopes are north-facing, so they keep their snow relatively well
- + Lovely intermediate cruising runs
- + Pretty village with lively après-ski
- + Cheap, even by Austrian standards
- + Snowmaking is very extensive and well used; even so ...

- – Low altitude can mean poor snow
- – Long walk or inadequate bus service from the village to the lifts
- – Runs on upper slopes mostly short
- – Few challenges except Hohe Salve
- – Not ideal for beginners
- – The SkiWelt slopes can get crowded
- – Piste map and signposting poor

Söll has long been popular with British beginners and intermediates, attracting both youths and families looking for fun of different kinds. The resort is in fact far from ideal for beginners, but the SkiWelt can be a great area for intermediate cruising. Whether it is depends on the snow. If the weather is coming from Russia, this area can have the best snow in the Alps; but usually it isn't, and the snow may suffer from afternoon thaws and night-time frost.

Many visitors are surprised by the small size of the village (in particular, there aren't many shops) and the long trek out to the slopes. You may prefer to stay near the lifts and trek into the village in the evening. Or you may prefer, like us, to stay in one of the other SkiWelt resorts – Ellmau along the valley (which has its own chapter) or Westendorf over the hill (covered at the end of this chapter), which has quicker access to the Kitzbühel slopes.

THE RESORT

Söll is a pleasant, friendly village, bypassed by the main valley road; although its chalet-style buildings spread quite widely, the core is compact – you can explore it on foot thoroughly in a few minutes.

The resort is part of the vast SkiWelt – one of Austria's largest ski areas. You can also progress (via Brixen) to the slopes of Kitzbühel; these and various other ski areas within easy reach, such as Waidring, Fieberbrunn and St Johann, are covered by the Kitzbüheler Alpen AllStarCard ski pass.

VILLAGE CHARM ★★★☆☆
Follows tradition

Söll is quite attractive, with chalet-style buildings and a huge church near the centre (its graveyard prettily lit by candles at night).

CONVENIENCE ★★☆☆☆
Not for the slopes

The slopes are well outside the village, on the other side of a busy main road which it is best to cross by using a pedestrian tunnel. You can leave your equipment at the bottom of the gondola at Edinger sport shop for a small charge.

There is some accommodation out near the lifts, but most is in or around the village centre. From there, it's the ski-bus or a 15-minute walk to the lifts. A base on the far side of the village may mean that you board the bus before it gets too crowded. But the bus does not serve every corner. A 2015 visitor says the six euros for a taxi is 'the best option over bus and locker hire'.

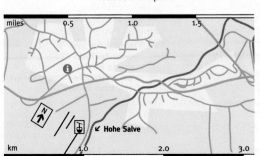

NEWS

2015/16: The slow Jochbahn quad above Brixen is due to be replaced by an eight-seater, which the resort claims will be 'the world's fastest chairlift'. It will be double the length of the old chair and will start much lower down the mountain.

2014/15: A new 1.2km red run with snowmaking was built in the Brixen area. Snowmaking was increased across the SkiWelt area. The children's Hexenkinderland at Söll was expanded.

SCENERY ★★★
Head for Hohe Salve

Söll sits in a woody valley, below the distinctive dome-shaped peak of Hohe Salve. From the top, there are good views to the whole SkiWelt and the craggy Wilder Kaiser ridges.

THE MOUNTAINS

Although there are some open slopes high up, and the prominent high point of Hohe Salve is noticeably bare, most of the slopes are heavily wooded.

The piste map is better than it was, using arrows to show which way runs go where that is in doubt. Last season, it included enlarged sections of various sectors but they don't help much (a view endorsed by a 2015 reporter: 'a good memory was more useful than the map').

We stick to the view that it is hopelessly over ambitious in trying to show the whole area in a single map; the result is simply inadequate for route finding. What's needed are separate maps for the main sectors.

Signposting is also heavily criticized by visitors; it helps once you realize that the signs point out the direction to the next lift you want and use the number of the lift to indicate the colour of the run. But a recent reporter said, 'Everyone complained about the signposting; we got lost a few times.'

EXTENT OF THE SLOPES ★★★★
Short run network

The SkiWelt is one of Austria's biggest ski areas (but we believe no longer quite the biggest – see 'Note' in Key Facts on previous page) and will easily keep an average intermediate amused for a week. In good snow there are long red runs to be done to the valley,

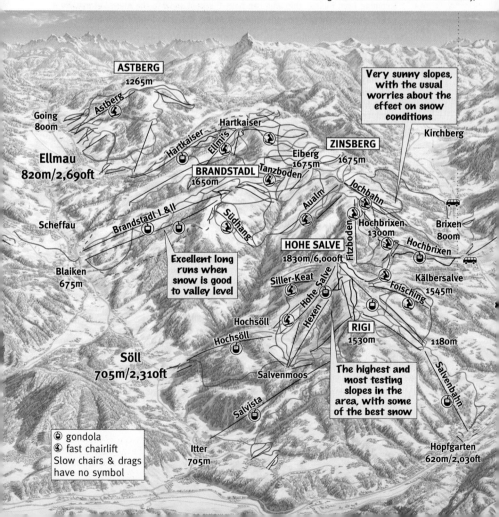

ASTBERG 1265m

Going 800m

Astberg

Hartkaiser

Hartkaiser

Ellmis

Eiberg 1675m

ZINSBERG 1675m

Kirchberg

Ellmau 820m/2,69oft

BRANDSTADL 1650m

Tanzboden

Südhang

Aualm

Jochbahn

Hochbrixen 1300m

Brixen 800m

Scheffau

Brandstadl I & II

Fitzboden

Hochbrixen

HOHE SALVE 1830m/6,000ft

Kälbersalve 1545m

Blaiken 675m

Siller-Keat

Hohe Salve

Foisching

Excellent long runs when snow is good to valley level

Hochsöll

Hexen

RIGI 1530m

1180m

Salvenbahn

Hochsöll

Söll 705m/2,310ft

Salvenmoos

The highest and most testing slopes in the area, with some of the best snow

Salvista

Very sunny slopes, with the usual worries about the effect on snow conditions

Itter 705m

Hopfgarten 620m/2,030ft

🚠 gondola
🚡 fast chairlift
Slow chairs & drags
have no symbol

but most of the skiing is on the upper slopes where most runs are very short (often less than 300m vertical).

A gondola takes all but complete beginners up to the mid-mountain shelf of Hochsöll, where there are a couple of short lifts and connections in several directions. These include an eight-seat gondola to the high point of Hohe Salve. From here there are runs to Kälbersalve, Rigi and Hopfgarten. Rigi can also be reached by chairs and runs without going to Hohe Salve – to which it is itself linked by chairs. Rigi is also the start of runs down to Itter and Hopfgarten. From Kälbersalve you can head down south-facing runs to Brixen or to Zinsberg and on towards Ellmau. From Brixen, a gondola goes up to Choralpe in Westendorf's area and a lovely north-facing red piste comes back down. From Choralpe you can also head off towards Kitzbühel.

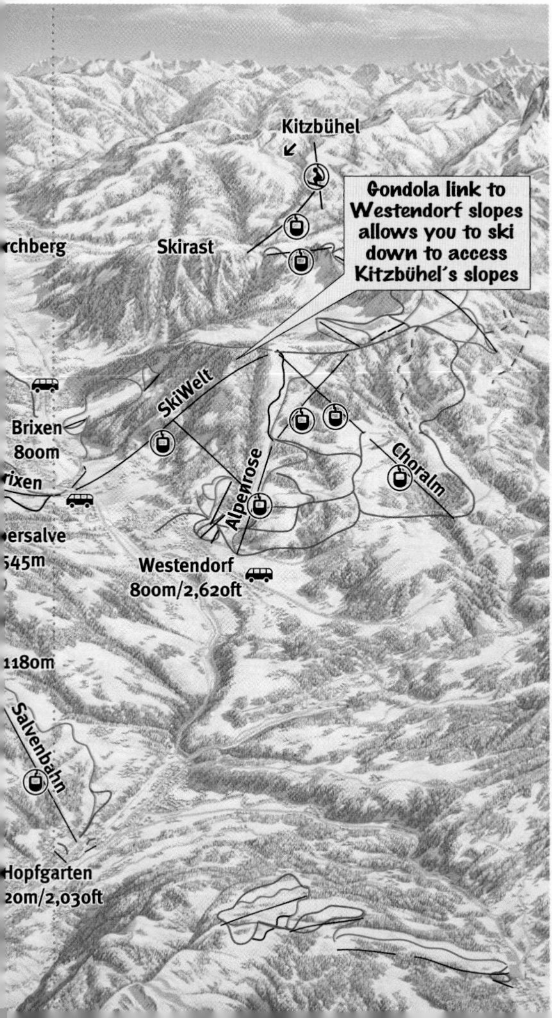

FAST LIFTS ★★★★☆
Still some slow chairs

Lifts from the valley are mainly gondolas, and there are now quite a few fast chairs on the upper slopes. But there are still some slow chairs. T-bars can generally be avoided.

QUEUES ★★★☆☆
Some high-season waits

Lift upgrades have greatly improved this once queue-prone area. In peak season getting out of Söll at ski-school time in the mornings can be a problem, and there are still some bottlenecks on the mountain. When snow is poor, the links between Zinsberg and Eiberg get crowded.

TERRAIN PARKS ★★★☆☆
Park and floodlit Funslope

Söll has its own park below Hochsöll with beginner and intermediate lines and many different features. There's also a Funslope with two lines of banked curves, jumps, boxes and a tunnel; it's floodlit for night riding four days a week.

SNOW RELIABILITY ★★☆☆☆
Erratic – but has artificial help

After a series of good seasons, with several reporters experiencing good fresh powder for much of their holidays, the last two seasons were poor for the SkiWelt (and for most of Austria).

With a low average height, and important links that get a lot of sun, the snow in the SkiWelt can suffer badly in warm weather even in good seasons. So the snowmaking that has been installed is essential. At 225km and covering over 80% of the area's pistes, it is Austria's biggest snowmaking installation. Reporters have been impressed by its use and by the grooming.

FOR EXPERTS ★☆☆☆☆
Not a lot

The black runs from Hohe Salve are challenging pistes, the steepest of them including a short pitch that locals claim is steeper than Mayrhofen's Harakiri. The black run alongside the Brixen gondola also deserves respect, especially if the snow is in poor condition because of its south-facing aspect. Those runs apart, the main challenges are gentle off-piste routes – from Brandstadl down to Scheffau, for example.

Kitzbühel

Gondola link to Westendorf slopes allows you to ski down to access Kitzbühel's slopes

chberg
Skirast
SkiWelt
Choralm
Brixen 800m
ixen
Alpenrose
rsalve 45m
Westendorf 800m/2,620ft
1180m
Salvenbahn
Hopfgarten 20m/2,030ft

↑ The SkiWelt has lots of mountain restaurants – this is the highest, at the top of Hohe Salve

SKIWELT WILDER KAISER-BRIXENTAL

FOR INTERMEDIATES ★★★★☆
Mainly easy runs

When blessed with good snow the SkiWelt is a paradise for those who love easy cruising and don't mind short runs. It is a big area, and you really get a feeling of travelling around. There are lots of blue runs and many of the reds could be blue. In general the most difficult slopes are those from the mid-stations to the valleys – to Blaiken, Brixen and Söll, for example. For more challenging reds head for Westendorf (and don't miss the excellent red down to Brixen).

FOR BEGINNERS ★★☆☆☆
Not ideal

The big area of nursery slopes between the main road and the gondola station is fine when snow is good – gentle, spacious, uncrowded and free from good skiers whizzing past. But it can get icy or slushy. In poor snow the Hochsöll area may be used. None of the lifts is free, but points cards are available. Progression to longer runs is likely to be awkward – there aren't many blue runs in this part of the SkiWelt. One is the narrow blue from Hochsöll, on which speeding skiers on their way home are a hazard.

FOR BOARDERS ★★☆☆
Great cruising

Söll is a good place to try out boarding: slopes are gentle and there are plenty of gondolas and chairs. And it has its own terrain park. For competent boarders it's more limited – the slopes of the SkiWelt are tame.

FOR CROSS-COUNTRY ★★★☆
Neighbouring villages are better

Söll has about 25km of local trails, but they are less interesting than those between Hopfgarten and Kelchsau and around and beyond Ellmau. There is a total of 196km in the SkiWelt area. Lack of snow-cover can be a problem.

MOUNTAIN RESTAURANTS ★★★☆☆
Good, but crowded

There are quite a few jolly little huts – all marked on the piste map. Our favourites in the SkiWelt are covered in the Ellmau chapter – Tanzbodenalm and Rübezahlalm.

In the Suøll area, the atmospheric converted cow shed Stöcklalm is an excellent spot. The highly rated Hohe Salve (top of the gondola) offers a large revolving terrace and good views (from the toilets as well, say reporters). Other reporter tips include the Stoagrub'nhütte and the Salvenalm above Hopfgarten. Read the Ellmau chapter, too.

SCHOOLS AND GUIDES ★★★☆☆
Good reports
Söll-Hochsöll and Knolln are the main schools. The special needs son of a 2015 reporter 'returned laughing every time with great tales of adventure' from the Söll-Hochsöll school. The beginners in the party of a recent visitor had 'excellent teachers' from it and he had a private lesson that 'pushed us and improved technique greatly – well worth it'.

FOR FAMILIES ★★★☆☆
High and low options
At the base of the gondola, Hexenkinderland is a supervised area for small kids based around a 'witches' theme and allows them to play while getting used to skis. It was enlarged this year. Monti's Kinderwelt at the gondola mid-station is well equipped with play areas and nursery slopes. Club Flocki is an option in the village.

STAYING THERE

Chalets Crystal and Inghams each have a chalet here.
Hotels There is a wide choice of simple gasthofs, pensions and B&Bs, plus better-quality hotel accommodation.
****Alpenpanorama Far from lifts but with own bus stop; wonderful views; pleasant rooms.
****Bergland Well placed between the village and lifts. Apartments as well as rooms. 'Lovely cooked breakfast.'
****Feldwebel Central, recommended for food and value.
****Greil Attractive, but on the far side of the village from the lifts. Indoor pool, five different saunas.
****Postwirt A reader favourite – attractive, central, traditional, with stube; outdoor pool, sauna, steam.
***Eggerwirt Between centre and main road, bus stop outside.
***Fuchs Far side of village from the lifts but praised by a 2015 reporter: 'Fantastic, clean, comfortable, good food, bus stop at door.'
***Hexenalm Close to the lifts, with a good spa and a popular après-ski bar.
Pension Sonnenhof 'Good-quality home cooking, spotlessly clean rooms, excellent staff.'
Apartments The central Aparthotel Schindlhaus has nice accommodation. Some of the best apartments in town are in the Bergland hotel.

EATING OUT ★★☆☆☆
A fair choice
Some of the best restaurants are in hotels – those in the Postwirt and the Feldwebel have been recommended by past reporters. The 'rustic' Dorf Stub'n offers traditional dishes and steaks – 'fantastic-value meat fondue', says a recent visitor. Rossini was recommended last year – 'excellent pizzeria'. The Whisky-Mühle is praised for its 'huge, good-value steaks'.

APRES-SKI ★★★★☆
Still some very loud bars
Söll is not as raucous as it used to be, but it's still very lively and a lot of places have live music. At teatime bars such as Moonlight and Hexenalm, close to the gondola base, are lively. So too is Salvenstadl (Cow Shed) on the edge of the village, recommended by a recent reporter. The Red Horse Pub is a 'great, lively, atmospheric bar'.
    Later on, the large, central Whisky-Mühle disco can get wild, especially after the bars close. The hotel Austria bar has been recommended by a past reporter. Rossini is good for cocktails and live music.

OFF THE SLOPES ★★☆☆☆
Toboggan runs the main attraction
There are two toboggan runs (4km and 3km) from the top of the gondola. Both are floodlit on Wednesday to Saturday, one until 10.30pm, the other until 2am. The large baroque church is worth a visit. Coach excursions go to Salzburg, Innsbruck and even Vipiteno, in Italy.

LINKED RESORT – 705m

ITTER

Itter is a tiny village halfway between Söll and Hopfgarten, with a gondola starting some way outside the village that goes up to mid-mountain. There's a hotel and half a dozen gasthofs and B&Bs. The school has a rental shop, and there are nursery slopes close to hand but few easy longer runs to progress to locally. Here, as elsewhere, the home run is red.

LINKED RESORT – 620m

HOPFGARTEN

Hopfgarten is an unspoiled, friendly, traditional resort set off the main Kitzbühel-Innsbruck road at the western extremity of the SkiWelt and with a two-stage gondola (largely queue-free, to judge by reports) from the village to the top of Hohe Salve.

When snow is good, the runs down to Hopfgarten are some of the best in the SkiWelt, but they get the damaging afternoon sun. There is a beginners' slope in the village, but it is sunny as well as low. Hopfgarten is one of the best cross-country bases in the area. There are fine trails to Kelchsau (7km) and the Itter-Grünholz loop (10km) starts nearby.

Cheap and cheerful gasthofs, pensions and little private B&Bs are the norm, and most are within five minutes' walk of the gondola. Restaurants are mostly hotel-based, but there is a pizzeria. Après-ski is generally quiet. There's a reasonable range of off-slope activities, and trains run to Kitzbühel and Innsbruck (or Salzburg).

LINKED RESORT – 800m

BRIXEN IM THALE

Brixen im Thale spreads a long way along the valley running along the south side of the SkiWelt area. It is not particularly cute, but it is traditional in style and is pretty quiet now that it is bypassed by the main valley road. From the skiing point of view it has a great location, with lifts going up both sides of the valley. On the north side, a gondola goes to Hochbrixen and the main SkiWelt slopes; lifts diverge for Hohe Salve and Söll, or Astberg and Ellmau. In the opposite direction, a gondola goes up to Choralpe above Westendorf, which links to the slopes of Kitzbühel (via a short bus ride after a long blue run down). The local slopes suit confident intermediates best, on both sides of the valley. The nursery area is secluded, but a bus ride away.

There are plenty of hotels and pensions but most restaurants are hotel-based. Après-ski is relatively quiet though there are two or three bars by the gondola base. Brixen is on the same railway line as Hopfgarten.

Westendorf 800m

➕ Pleasant, traditional village	➖ Local slopes not ideal territory for
➕ Challenging local slopes	progression from the nursery slopes
➕ Good local beginner slopes but ...	➖ Getting to main SkiWelt takes time

Westendorf is a quiet, attractive village with good local slopes for confident intermediates; it is slightly off the main SkiWelt circuit, but has easy access to Kitzbühel's area – so it is an appealing base if you plan to spend time on both.

Village charm The village is small with traditional buildings, including an attractive onion-domed church. It has a relaxed, rustic atmosphere. The quite lively late-night scene can mean a bit of noise in the streets.

Convenience The centre is close to the nursery slopes, and a five-minute walk or free ski-bus ride from the main lift. There are also regular buses to the lifts at Brixen, for quick access to the SkiWelt circuit.

Scenery The slopes here offer a bit more drama than some of the other hills nearby, and the views include the craggy Wilder Kaiser to the north.

THE MOUNTAIN

Westendorf's local slopes are separated by one valley from the main SkiWelt circuit to the north and by another valley from the Kitzbühel slopes to the east. There's a pleasant

mix of open and wooded slopes.

Slopes A two-stage gondola goes to Talkaser, one of the four minor peaks that make up the local area. From there, you can head for Choralpe and Brixen (via a splendid 5.5km-long red run of over 1000m vertical), or for Fleiding and Gampenkogel. All the local peaks have short east- or west-facing runs. A longer blue run of around 800m vertical goes from Gampenkogel to the Kitzbühel connection (which involves a short shuttle-bus ride to the Pengelstein gondola at Skirast).

Fast lifts The two gondolas make for good access but once up the mountain there are still a lot of slow lifts on the local slopes.

Queues The only report of queues is '15 minutes one afternoon for the Choralm gondola'.

Terrain parks There's an excellent park

GETTING THERE

Air Innsbruck 80km/ 50 miles (1hr); Salzburg 85km/ 55 miles (1hr30); Munich 145km/ 90 miles (2hr)

Rail Wörgl (13km/ 8 miles); Kufstein (13km/8 miles); bus to resort

↑ Westendorf is a quiet attractive village with easy access to Kitzbühel's slopes as well as the SkiWelt's

KITZBÜHELER ALPEN MARKETING GMBH

TOURIST OFFICES

WILDER KAISER
(Söll, Scheffau, Going, Ellmau)
www.wilderkaiser. info

HOHE SALVE
(Hopfgarten, Itter)
www.hohe-salve.com

KITZBÜHELER ALPEN
(Brixen, Westendorf)
www.kitzbueheler-alpen.com

SKIWELT
www.skiwelt.at

with something for all levels including jumps, boxes, kickers and rails.

Snow reliability Not a strong point of the region, because of the low altitude. But snowmaking is extensive and grooming excellent.

Experts The pistes are among the most testing in the SkiWelt area (black 112 is one of the steepest around), and there is off-piste to be explored.

Intermediates Great for confident intermediates: nearly all Westendorf's terrain is genuinely red in gradient.

Beginners The village nursery slopes are extensive and excellent. There are a couple of genuine blues to progress to on the lower mountain, but further progression can be challenging.

Snowboarding Most lifts are chairs and gondolas, and the park is great. But some runs have tedious flat sections.

Cross-country There are lots of trails, but snow-cover is unreliable.

Mountain restaurants There are good table- and self-service places. On our most recent visit we particularly liked Ki-West – good location, atmosphere and food. Alpenrosenhütte, Brechhornhaus and the Gassnerwirt are popular. Choralpe self-service is tipped by a 2014 reporter: 'Best views in SkiWelt, spacious, huge portions.'

Schools and guides There are three schools: Westendorf ('Very good,' says a reporter), Top and Snow&Co.

Families Westendorf sells itself as a family resort. The ski school kindergartens take children from the age of three.

STAYING THERE

There are plentiful hotels and guest houses.

Hotels 4-star places tipped by readers include the Jakobwirt – 'lovely food, great spa' – and Schermer. Other past recommendations: the 3-star Post and the central Pension Elisabeth. The small Glockenstuhl is a short walk away with a good spa. There are places out near the gondola.

Apartments The Schermerhof apartments are of good quality.

Eating out Most of the best restaurants are in hotels. The Wastlhof, Klingler's and Berggasthaus Stimmlach (a taxi ride out) are other possibilities.

Après-ski There are more lively spots than you might expect in a small, cute village. The Liftstüberl and Gerry's Inn are packed at close of play. Reporter recommendations include the Kibo bar near the bottom of the nursery slopes and In's Moment (aka Campbell's Bar) in the basement of the Jakobwirt hotel. The funky Moskito Cafe Bar has live music. Karat is a smart lounge bar.

Off the slopes There are excursions to Innsbruck and Salzburg, plus pretty walks and sleigh rides.

St Anton

If what you seek is dumps, bumps, boozing and bopping, there's nowhere quite like it – and with a neat Tirolean town as a bonus

£110
RESORT PRICE INDEX

RATINGS

The mountains

Extent	★★★
Fast lifts	★★★★
Queues	★★★
Terrain p'ks	★★★
Snow	★★★★
Expert	★★★★★
Intermediate	★★★
Beginner	★
Boarder	★★★★
X-country	★★
Restaurants	★★★
Schools	★★★
Families	★★★★

The resort

Charm	★★★★
Convenience	★★★
Scenery	★★★
Eating out	★★★★
Après-ski	★★★★★
Off-slope	★★

174

NEWS

2015/16: A new mountain restaurant is to open at the top of Gampen. Over in St Christoph, the Arlberg1800 contemporary art and concert hall will open this summer.

2014/15: The bottom of valley run No 1 was widened, and No 8 and No 9a were remodelled.

+ Varied terrain for experts and adventurous intermediates

+ Heavy snowfalls, lots of snow-guns

+ Car-free village centre retains solid traditional charm

+ Very lively après-ski and nightlife

+ Improved lift system has cut queues from the base areas, but ...

− Some pistes dangerously crowded

− Slopes can be tough for near-beginners and timid intermediates

− Most tough runs are unpatrolled

− Snow quality can suffer from sun

− Resort sprawls, with long treks from some lodgings to key lifts and bars

− Centre can be noisy at night

St Anton is one of the world's best resorts for competent skiers and riders, particularly those with the energy to après-ski as hard as they ski. If you want to, you can party from 3pm to 3am. Good luck!

But the place doesn't suit everyone. If you are thinking of trying an Austrian change from a major French resort, or of going up a gear from Kitzbühel or Söll, be sure that you are not going to get thrown by blues that get heavily mogulled and reds that might be black, or by runs that can be dangerously crowded. As we've been saying for years, the resort needs to create an alternative to the busy blue run down from its main mountain.

THE RESORT

St Anton is the western extremity of the Tirol, at the foot of the road up to the Arlberg pass. It is at one end of a lift network that spreads across to St Christoph and over the pass to Stuben. These two tiny villages are described at the end of the chapter.

The resort is a long, sprawling place, almost a town rather than a village, squeezed into a narrow valley. As it spreads east down the valley, it thins out before broadening again to form the suburb of Nasserein, and then the nominally distinct St Jakob. Development spreads west up the hill towards the Arlberg pass – first to Oberdorf, then Gastig, 10 minutes' walk from the centre.

The ski pass covers Lech, Zürs and Warth – now linked to Lech – and the Sonnenkopf area above Klösterle.

The nearby resorts can be reached by bus, but the service is rubbish.

There are free and regular ski-buses linking Alpe Rauz (on the edge of St Anton's slopes) with Zürs and Lech. And there are post buses from St Anton to Lech via St Christoph and Zürs. But all get seriously crowded at busy times, leaving people at the roadside to use the waiting taxis. And the post buses are neither free nor frequent. It's not good enough.

Klösterle can be reached by free ski-buses from Stuben. Serfaus, Ischgl and Sölden are feasible outings by car.

VILLAGE CHARM ★★★★
Traditional but lively
Although it is commercialized and busy, St Anton is full of character, its traffic-free main street lined by traditional-style buildings. It is a bustling place, day and night. Its shops meet everyday needs well – a well-stocked Spar, for example, and an excellent bookshop.

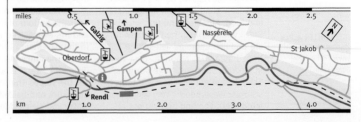

↑ Schindler Spitze is at the heart of St Anton's most famously challenging terrain; the cable car goes past it to the higher Valluga

TVB ST. ANTON AM ARLBERG / JOSEF MALLAUN

KEY FACTS

Resort	1305m
	4,280ft

Arlberg region	
Slopes	1075-2650m
	3,530-8,690ft
Lifts	97
Slopes*	340km
	211 miles

St Anton, St Christoph and Stuben	
Slopes	1305-2650m
	4,280-8,690ft
Lifts	38
Slopes*	160km
	99 miles
* pistes and ski routes	

CONVENIENCE ★★★☆☆
Not bad for a large resort
The hub of the resort is at the western end of the main street, close to the base stations of the lifts to Gampen (a fast quad chair), to Galzig and to Rendl (modern gondolas). Staying on or close to this main street is ideal to keep treks to the lifts short.

Nasserein has an eight-seater gondola up to Gampen, and makes an appealing base for a quiet time. The nightlife action is a short bus ride or 15-minute walk away. Staying between the centre and Nasserein, you can use the Fang chairlift to get to other lifts.

SCENERY ★★★☆☆
Head for the Valluga
St Anton squeezes into a narrow, partly wooded valley. The scenery becomes more impressive as you ride up the lifts, either towards the dramatic Valluga, or across the valley up to Rendl, which opens up a splendid panorama.

THE MOUNTAINS

The main slopes are essentially open: only the lower Gampen runs and the run from Rendl to the valley offer much shelter from bad weather.

St Anton vies with Val d'Isère for the title of 'resort with most underclassified slopes'. Many blue and reds seem tough for their colour. Paradoxically, none of the blacks is

seriously steep; this is because the toughest runs are called 'ski routes'. The piste map says these are marked and avalanche controlled but not groomed or patrolled. We applaud the clear explanation (lacking in many resorts), but many of these are popular runs that are treated just like pistes, and they should be patrolled pistes. To add to the confusion, some of the routes are groomed.

To judge by the latest digital version supplied to us, the Arlberg piste map will not next season show proper off-piste runs (which disappeared from the St Anton part of the map some time ago).

The piste map is designed more for marketing than navigation, covering the whole of the Arlberg region in one view. As a result, it is unclear and misleading in places. The local TV channel shows the state of the pistes and queues – very useful.

EXTENT OF THE SLOPES ★★★☆☆
Don't ignore Stuben and Rendl
St Anton's slopes fall into four main sectors, three of them linked. The major sector is that beneath the local high spot, the **Valluga**, accessed by the jumbo gondola to Galzig, then a cable car to Vallugagrat. The tiny top stage of the cable car to the Valluga summit is for sightseeing and people with a guide heading for the tricky off-piste run to Zürs. Vallugagrat gives access to St Anton's famous high,

MOMENTUM SKI

Weekend & a la carte
ski holiday specialists

100% Tailor-made

Premier hotels
& apartments

Flexible travel
arrangements

020 7371 9111
WWW.MOMENTUMSKI.COM

sunny bowls, and to the long, beautiful red/blue run to Alpe Rauz.

From here there's a six-pack, Valfagehr, to return, or you can go on to explore the rather neglected slopes of **Stuben**. The shady slow old chair from the village can be a cold ride, but blankets are available. The reward is north-facing slopes that hold powder well and some deserted off-piste. The run to Alpe Rauz and the high Valluga runs can also be accessed by riding the Schindlergrat fast triple chair, though some also involve a hike. Other runs from Galzig go to St Christoph and into the Steissbachtal.

Beyond this valley, with lift and piste links in both directions, is the **Kapall-Gampen** sector, reachable by chairlift from central St Anton or gondola from Nasserein. From Gampen at mid-mountain, pistes lead back to St Anton and Nasserein. Or you can ride a six-pack on up to Kapall to ski the treeless upper mountain.

Rendl is a separate mountain,

reached by a gondola from the centre of town. A handful of lifts serve the west-facing upper runs, and there's a good north-facing piste to the valley – the place to go in bad weather.

FAST LIFTS ★★★★
Fast access, patchy higher up
Access from the village is by smart gondolas or fast chairs. But while the Gampen and Galzig sectors have a lot of fast chairs higher up, Rendl and Stuben still have a lot of slow ones.

QUEUES ★★★☆☆
Much improved, but ...
Queues are not the problem they once were, and reporters have had few problems in recent years. But there can be queues for key lifts, including the Valluga cable car from Galzig ('15-minute wait seemed the norm,' said a March 2013 report), the alternative Schindlergrat chair to Schindler Spitze, the Zammermoos chair out of the Steissbachtal, and the

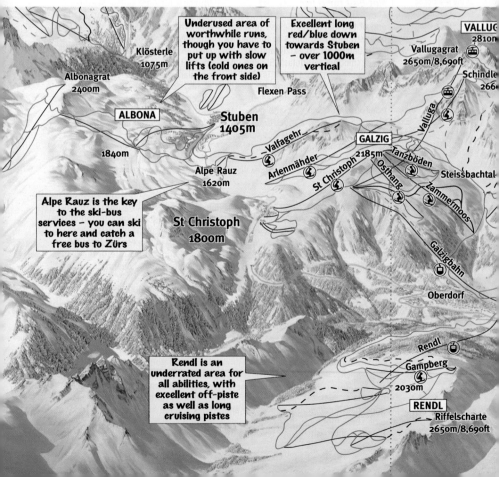

Underused area of worthwhile runs, though you have to put up with slow lifts (cold ones on the front side)

Excellent long red/blue down towards Stuben – over 1000m vertical

VALLUG
2810m

Klösterle
1075m

Vallugagrat
2650m/8,690ft

Schindle
266

Albonagrat
2400m

Flexen Pass

Schindle

ALBONA

Stuben
1405m

Valfagehr

Valluga

GALZIG
2185m

Tanzböden

1840m

Arlenmähder

St Christoph

Osthang

Steissbachtal

Alpe Rauz
1620m

Zammermoos

St Christoph
1800m

Alpe Rauz is the key to the ski-bus services – you can ski to here and catch a free bus to Zürs

Galzigbahn

Oberdorf

Rendl

Gampberg
2030m

Rendl is an underrated area for all abilities, with excellent off-piste as well as long cruising pistes

RENDL

Riffelscharte
2650m/8,690ft

LIFT PASSES	
Arlberg	
Prices in €	
Age	**6-day**
under 16	147
16 to 19	213
20 to 64	245
65 plus	213
Free No one; day pass €10 if under 8, €22 if over 75	
Beginner Points ticket	
Notes Covers St Anton, St Christoph, Stuben, Lech, Zürs and Warth, and bus linking Zürs and Lech with St Anton lifts at Alpe Rauz; also Sonnenkopf (9 lifts) at Klösterle, 7km west of Stuben; single ascent, part-day and pedestrian options	

gondola from Nasserein first thing.

But more of a worry than queues are the crowded pistes – the blues you take to get home from the upper mountain are often dangerously crowded, and the problems are compounded by recklessly fast skiers and by moguls on the lower parts.

TERRAIN PARKS ★★★☆☆
Small, but perfectly formed

The 320m-long Stanton park on Rendl, just below the top of the gondola, is pretty good – intermediate and pro lines and beginner area, all including multiple features, plus fun-cross for the kids, and chill area. There is also a Funslope on Galzig designed to amuse everyone from children and beginners to more experienced skiers/boarders.

SNOW RELIABILITY ★★★★☆
Generally very good cover

If the weather is coming from the west or north-west (as it often is), the Arlberg region gets it first, and as a

ALPINE ANSWERS
The UK's No.1 Chalet Specialist

For choice and service look no further!

alpineanswers.co.uk
call: 020 7801 1080

●ABTA

result St Anton gets heavy falls of snow – and neighbouring Lech, Zürs and Warth get even more. These resorts often have much better conditions than other resorts of a similar height, and we've had great fresh powder here as late as mid-April. But many slopes face south or south-east, causing icy or heavy conditions at times. As spring approaches, in particular, it's vital to time descents of the steeper runs off the Valluga to get

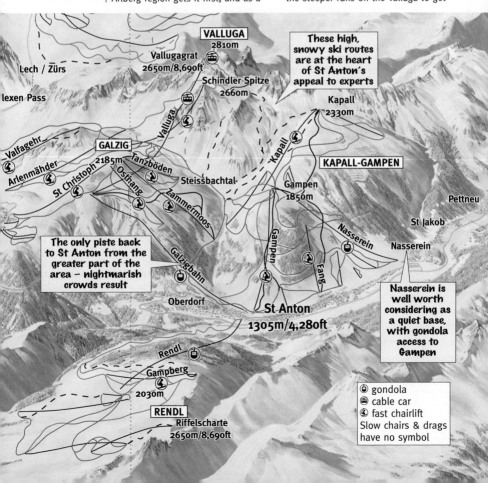

Lech / Zürs

lexen Pass

VALLUGA
2810m

Vallugagrat
2650m/8,690ft

Schindler Spitze
2660m

These high, snowy ski routes are at the heart of St Anton's appeal to experts

Kapall
2330m

Valfagehr

Valluga

GALZIG
2185m

Tanzböden

Arlenmähder

St Christoph

Osthang

Zammermoos

Steissbachtal

KAPALL-GAMPEN

Gampen
1850m

Nasserein

Pettneu

St Jakob

Nasserein

The only piste back to St Anton from the greater part of the area – nightmarish crowds result

Galzigbahn

Gampen

Fang

Nasserein is well worth considering as a quiet base, with gondola access to Gampen

Oberdorf

St Anton
1305m/4,28oft

Rendl

Gampberg
2030m

RENDL
Riffelscharte
2650m/8,690ft

ⓖ gondola
ⓒ cable car
ⓢ fast chairlift
Slow chairs & drags have no symbol

SKIWORLD

Catered chalets, hotels and self catering apartments in

Europe, USA and Canada

skiworld.co.uk

08444 930 430

ABTA V2151 ATOL 2036

decent conditions. The lower runs are well equipped with snowmaking, which generally ensures the home runs remain open. Grooming is good.

FOR EXPERTS ★★★★★
One of the world's great areas
St Anton vies with Chamonix, Val d'Isère and a handful of other resorts for the affections of experts. There are countless opportunities for going off-piste; read the feature panel for some of them. The runs in the huge bowls below the Valluga are justifiably world-famous, and immediately after a fresh snowfall you can see tracks going all over the mountain; there are ski routes in the bowls too. Lower down, there are challenging runs in many directions from both Galzig and Kapall-Gampen. These lower runs can be seriously affected by the sun.

Don't overlook the Rendl area, which has plenty of open space served by the top lifts, and several quite challenging runs. This is a great area for a mixed group and usually quieter than the main sector. The Sonnenkopf area, down-valley from Stuben, is even quieter and has several ski routes – and more serious off-piste, including an 'excellent' route to Langen. Read the Stuben section, too.

FOR INTERMEDIATES ★★★
Some real challenges
St Anton is well suited to good, adventurous intermediates. As well as lots of testing pistes, they will be able to try some of the ski routes in the Valluga bowls. The run from Schindler Spitze to Alpe Rauz is very long (over 1000m vertical), varied and ideal for good intermediates. Alternatively, turn off from this part-way down and take the Steissbachtal to the lifts back to Galzig or Gampen. The Kapall-Gampen section is also interesting, with sporty bumps among trees on the lower half. Good intermediates may enjoy the men's downhill run from the top of this sector to the town.

Timid intermediates will find St Anton less to their taste. There are few easy cruising pistes; most blue runs here would be red in most other resorts, and get bumpy, especially if there is fresh snow (the blue 1 home run often has testing moguls at the end of the day). The gentlest cruisers are the short blues on Galzig and the Steissbachtal – we skied the latter in the early morning two seasons back,

and enjoyed it for the first time ever – but they get unpleasantly crowded in the afternoon. The blue from Kapall to Gampen is wide and cruisy.

The underrated Rendl area has a variety of trails suitable for good and moderate intermediates, including the excellent long blues served by the slow chairlifts on skier's left, Riffel 1 and Salzböden. The long wooded run to the valley (over 1000m vertical from the top) is much the best place to be in the St Anton area when the visibility is poor.

FOR BEGINNERS ★
Far from ideal
The best bet for beginners is to start at Nasserein, where the nursery slope is less steep than the one close to the main lifts. There are further slopes up at Gampen and a short, gentle blue run at Rendl, served by an easy draglift. But there are no other easy, uncrowded runs for beginners to progress to. A mixed party including novices would be better off based in Lech or Zürs.

FOR BOARDERS ★★★★
Freeriding heaven
For many, St Anton is the Mecca of Austrian freeriding and expert boarders flock here. The terrain is far from ideal for beginners, but there are few T-bars to contend with.

FOR CROSS-COUNTRY ★★
A decent amount
There are 40km of easy/medium trails, and snow conditions are usually good.

MOUNTAIN RESTAURANTS ★★★
Adequate options
There are plenty of restaurants, and some of them are excellent. Most but not all are marked on the piste map, and named in ridiculously minute type. **Editors' choice** Making an exception to our preference for lunch at altitude, we've had many good lunches at the atmospheric Hospiz Alm on the fringe of St Christoph, famed for its slide down to the toilets as well as its satisfying table-service food and amazing wine cellar. Service gets stretched at times, and it can be expensive. Recent visitors approve: 'unforgettable', 'open fire, friendly service, king prawns simply excellent'.

Rodelalm is not marked on the piste map, but is on skier's far left of the Gampen slopes (reachable on blue

HOTEL MAIENSEE

FAR AWAY FROM EVERYDAY

SKI-IN SKI-OUT

ON 1800M

THE TOP OF THE

ARLBERG

ST. ANTON

ST. CHRISTOPH

6580 ST. CHRISTOPH AM ARLBERG · AUSTRIA
+43(0) 5446 2804 · STAY@MAIENSEE.COM

WWW.MAIENSEE.COM

ST. ANTON & BEYOND!

TAILOR-MADE OR ACCOMMODATION ONLY SPECIALISTS

01502 471960
info@mountainbeds.com
www.mountainbeds.com

Ski Total

WELCOME YOU TO
St Anton

Quality chalets
Excellent value
19 resorts
across the Alps

skitotal.com
01483 791 933

ESPRIT

FOR FAMILIES IN
St Anton

Family
Ski Chalets
Dedicated
Nurseries
Exclusive Ski
Classes
13 resorts
across the Alps

espritski.com
01483 791 900

TVB ST. ANTON AM ARLBERG /
WOLFGANG BURGER

St Anton lies at the head of its valley; from here you climb through St Christoph to the Arlberg pass, and the border of Tirol and Vorarlberg ↓

run 24). It has a lovely beamed interior, and we have had good traditional food here.

Worth knowing about Verwallstube on Galzig is in a class of its own – an expensive table-service place with splendid views. We've had seriously good lunches here a couple of times. Up at 2650m, the 'small and cosy' Valluga View of course has great views as well as 'simple but good-value food'. Ulmer Hütte has a 'fantastic queuing system for a small choice of quick snacks'. Just above the village, the famous Mooserwirt is not only for post-lunch boozing; with its varied menu, it surprised one visitor who chanced lunch there this year – 'genèrous portions, good prices'.

On Rendl, the spacious Rendl restaurant is about as good as self-service gets – we've had good stir fry cooked to order, and a 2014 visitor had 'hot and tasty food from the grill'. The terrace (aka Rendl Beach) has great views of the terrain park action. On the valley run there is good table-service food in the cosy Bifang-Alm, quite close to the bottom.

At Stuben there are restaurants on the hill but we reluctantly accept that the best options are the village hotels – the Post ('really good Wiener schnitzel', 'good value') or the Mondschein ('comfortable small terrace, absolutely delicious food').

The new Gampen restaurant replacing the existing building at the top of the hill for 2015/16 will have a table-service section.

SCHOOLS AND GUIDES ★★★
Good reports
The St Anton and the Arlberg schools are under the same ownership but operate separately. Recent reports have been positive. A reporter this year had 'a great week' with Arlberg Guides – 'brilliant slopes, great fun'. Other guiding outfits include Piste to Powder (run by British guide Graham Austick), St Anton Classic and Arlberg Alpin at Stuben.

FOR FAMILIES ★★★★
Nasserein 'ideal'
The youth centre attached to the Arlberg school is excellent, and the special slopes both for toddlers (at the bottom) and bigger children (at Gampen) are well done. Children's instruction is reportedly very good. At Nasserein there is a moving carpet on the baby slope. There's also a good children's area by the Gampen fast quad. Nasserein makes a good base, and family chalet specialist Esprit has its own facilities here.

The Arlberg region has lots of very varied off-piste. Here are just a few of the huge number of possibilities you could explore with a guide.

Runs from Rendl

An easy first venture away from the pistes is to go beyond the furthest lift to the rolling powder bowls of Rossfall. More serious routes take you well away from all lifts. The North Face, accessed from the Gampberg chair, offers challenging terrain for a confident off-piste skier. The Riffel chairlifts access the imposing Hinter Rendl – a gigantic bowl with a huge descent to St Anton, often in deep powder. A variant involves a climb to Rendl Scharte and a testing descent with sections of 35° to Pettneu.

Runs from Albona, above Stuben

Stuben's outstanding terrain is suited to the more experienced off-piste skier. The open treelines of the Langen forest, where the powder is regularly knee to waist deep, provide fabulous tree skiing. A 30-minute climb from Albonagrat to Maroikopfe opens up runs westwards down undulating open slopes to Langen, or eastwards down steep 40° slopes to Verwalltal ending at an old hunting lodge.

Runs from the Valluga

The runs from the summit cable car of the Valluga will make your pulse race as you trace a steep line between cliff bands in the breathtaking scenery of the Pazieltal, leading down to Zürs. Above Zürs, at the top of the Madloch chairlift and after a short climb, you can be roped down into the steep Valhalla Couloir, accessing 1200m vertical of open slopes ending at Zug, near Lech.

STAYING THERE

There's a wide range of places to stay, from quality hotels (Momentum has a good selection) to cheap and cheerful pensions and apartments.

Chalets This is, by a wide margin, Austria's catered chalet capital. Ski Total has 10 chalets ranging from 6 to 24 beds, including four smart custom-built places in one building in Nasserein, with wellness areas. Sister company Esprit, specializing in family holidays, has one large, smart chalet next to the Nasserein gondola. (At peak times of the season, Esprit also offers some of the Total properties.) Skiworld has 15 places including the flagship Monte Vera, with huge bedrooms, sauna; Crystal has half a dozen properties, including the cool 32-bed Inge; Inghams has seven, including four cool places in a stylish building in the Gastig area, with spa and pool; Supertravel has nine places.

Hotels There are dozens of 4- and 3-star places, and two 5-stars.

****Anthony's** Anthony's Life and Style, to use the full name: recently built, self-consciously 'designer' place in the centre.

****Bergschlössl** Charming 10-room B&B right by the lifts. 'Beautifully furnished, excellent value.'

****Fahrner** Up the hill. 'Unpretentious, clean rooms, friendly, first-rate food, good wine cellar.'

****Pepi's Skihotel** Stylish, modern B&B right by the Rendl lift.

****Post** Ancient place bang in the centre, with good spa and pool.

****Schwarzer Adler** Centuries-old inn on main street. Varying bedrooms. Nice pool.

Steffeler Central B&B. Simple but welcoming; good breakfasts.

Apartments There are plenty available, but few package deals. Mountain Beds has a handful of places, as well as hotels and catered chalets.

EATING OUT ★★★★
Some excellent spots

There's a lot of half-board lodging in St Anton, so the restaurant scene is not huge. Our standard port of call for a drink or two and a relaxed meal is the cool Hazienda – a basement place in the main street, with a wide-ranging menu. For more of a blowout, it's up the hill to the village museum's restaurant – excellent, sophisticated food served in elegant panelled rooms. Reader tips: Steak and Shake (American food and cocktails) and Pizza A More in Anthony's hotel; Underground on the Piste ('great steaks, great music' and 'cosy and atmospheric'), Fuhrmannstube ('lovely traditional food, friendly service; you share tables'), Skiing Buddha ('excellent Thai food, very good service'), Pomodoro ('tasty pizzas'), Fahrnerstube up the hill in Oberdorf ('pretty decor, good hearty food'), and Tenne ('good Austrian food') and Dolce Vita ('pizzas hit the spot, attentive service'), both in Nasserein.

St Anton

181

APRES-SKI ★★★★★
Throbbing till late
St Anton's bars rock from mid-afternoon until the early hours. And as our indefatigable roving bar correspondent Keith pointed out last year, 'there is plenty of variety, whether you're 16 or 60'.

It all starts in a collection of bars on the lower slopes. Heustadl is the first you come to, and still the place for 'great German cover bands' on the terrace; cosy inside. Next is Sennhütte, also with 'a lovely traditional atmosphere'. A bit lower, the formerly scruffy Krazy Kanguruh has had a complete makeover; it is now quite stylish inside, and its enlarged terrace gets packed. Next door Taps has also been smartened up and extended – whereas the famous Mooserwirt, down the hill a bit, struck Keith as living on its laurels. Griabli, opposite, is quieter; we enjoyed a live band there. All this is followed by a final slide down the piste, possibly in the dark.

The bars in town are in full swing by 4pm, too. The open-terrace Base Camp at the lift base can be 'a lot of fun' and 'attracts a mixed crowd and ski instructors'. Back up the piste slightly, Underground on the Piste is an institution, run by the eccentric Joan; 'friendly staff, large communal tables and a couple of good musicians'. Galzig Bistro, between the main lift stations, is a cool modern place we like for a drink and an emergency snack.

In the main street, the Bodega is good for pre-dinner drinks and tapas. The pubby Piccadilly is rated by Keith as 'the most animated après bar in town', with 'good entertainment, good music and efficient staff'. It gets a second wind later on, at which point Keith and others favour Bar Cuba ('crammed but a good atmosphere') and Alibi – 'convivial mix of locals and visitors'.

OFF THE SLOPES ★★★★★
Some entertainment
We and reporters love the excellent, but pricey Arlberg-well.com, a leisure centre with great indoor and outdoor pools and lots of spa options. A separate sports centre has an indoor climbing wall. There's a 4km floodlit toboggan run and a natural ice rink. Sleigh rides are also possible. It's not a place for indulgent shopping. It's easy to visit Innsbruck by train. Some

of the better mountain huts are accessible by lift or bus. There are 70km of walking trails, although a 2014 reporter says signposting was patchy.

LINKED RESORT – 1800m
ST CHRISTOPH
St Christoph is a small collection of smart hotels, restaurants and bars just down from the summit of the Arlberg pass. It does not pretend to be a village – the Arlberg pass road has no pavements, and the only shops are ski shops. Hospiz Alm (read 'Mountain restaurants') gets some business at après time, and is open (with a different menu) for dinner ('fantastic – not cheap, but worth it').

The key attractions of the place are queue-free lifts in the morning, and a crowd-free home piste with good snow at the end of the day. There are decent beginner slopes served by draglifts and a fast quad chairlift to the heart of St Anton's slopes at Galzig, but the blue back down is not an easy run to progress to. You can't miss the huge 5-star Arlberg-Hospiz. More attractive to us is the warmly welcoming 4-star Maiensee, right by the chairlift, with health and spa facilities and treatments. A couple of seasons ago we enjoyed a stay at Inghams' flagship chalet hotel here – ski-in/ski-out, with good-sized pool and sauna. Readers like it a lot, too.

Post buses to and from St Anton are free unless you foolishly offer money, but not free to Zürs and Lech.

LINKED RESORT – 1405m
STUBEN
Stuben is linked by lift and piste over the Arlberg pass to St Anton. It's a tiny, unspoiled village with an old church and a few hotels, bars and shops. Heavy snowfalls often add to the charm factor.

Stuben has sunny nursery slopes separate from the main slopes, but a lack of easy runs to progress to makes it unsuitable for beginners – less suitable than St Anton, even. We've had good reports of the school.

Evenings are quiet, but several places have a pleasant atmosphere. The charming old Post and Albona are very comfortable. The Hubertushof is 'welcoming, efficient; excellent food and facilities'.

GETTING THERE
Air Innsbruck 95km/ 60 miles (1hr15); Friedrichshafen 130km/80 miles (1hr45); Zürich 195km/120 miles (2hr15); Munich 225km/140 miles (3hr30)

Rail Mainline station in resort

TOURIST OFFICES
St Anton
www.
stantonamarlberg.com
St Christoph
www.tiscover.com/
st.christoph
Stuben
www.stuben.com

TOURISM ASSOCIATION NEUSTIFT

Stubai valley

Austria's biggest glacier area, they say, and certainly one of the best; down the valley, a string of appealing village bases

£100
RESORT PRICE INDEX

TOP 10 RATINGS

Extent	★★★
Fast lifts	★★★
Queues	★★★
Snow	★★★★★
Expert	★★★
Intermediate	★★★
Beginner	★★
Charm	★★★★
Convenience	★★
Scenery	★★★★

NEWS

2014/15: An extra lift – a rope tow – was built to serve the easier lines of the snow park at the top of the glacier area. The family fun slope on the Eisjochferner run was extended.

KEY FACTS

Resorts	935-1000m
	3,070-3,280ft
Slopes	935-3210m
	3,070-10,530ft
Lifts	47
Pistes	104km
	65 miles

✚	High, snow-sure glacier slopes plus lower bad-weather options
✚	Quiet, pretty Tirolean villages

▬	A lot of shuttling up and down the valley to and from the glacier
▬	Few challenging pistes

The Stubaier Gletscher ranks alongside Hintertux as one of the most extensive and rewarding glacier ski areas in the Alps. Neustift is the nearest major village, 20km away from the lift base. But another 5km down valley, livelier Fulpmes is at the base of the Stubaital's best low-altitude area, Schlick 2000, making it a better base for some visitors.

The 30km-long Stubai valley lies a short drive south of Innsbruck (there's also an antique tram to Fulpmes). The glacier is of course at the head of the valley. There is simple accommodation to be had in hamlets like Falbeson (10km from the glacier) or Krössbach (15km). But there are three bigger villages – Neustift, Fulpmes and Mieders – with their own wooded ski areas, covered along with the glacier (and linking buses) by the Stubai Super Skipass. These resorts, described in this chapter, amount to a sizeable area of mostly intermediate terrain. All have impressive toboggan runs – the valley has 11 in total.

The glacier offers an extensive area of runs between 3200m and 2300m. In the wake of the Schrahe report (read our feature on piste extent) the lift company now publishes a realistic total of 75km of pistes plus 29km of ski routes, making our total of 104km. But note that ski routes are 'only with ski instructor or Alpine experience' (says the piste map in German), which goes against the general rule.

Two gondolas go up from the huge car park at Mutterberg to a mid-station at Fernau, and then to the two mid-mountain stations of Eisgrat and Gamsgarten. A third gondola from Eisgrat goes to the top of the slopes. Elsewhere, there is a mix of ancient and modern chairlifts and the usual glacier drag lifts.

The slopes are broken up by rocky peaks giving more sense of variety than is normal on a glacier. There are lots of fabulous long blue and red cruising runs. The two shorter black pistes are very much at the easy end of the spectrum. The much longer Daunhill black (1.8km, 600m vertical) that opened a couple of years back is said to have a maximum gradient of 31°, so it's steeper; with its own private fast quad, it could be heavenly to do laps on. Much the toughest is the 4km Fernau-Mauer at the eastern extremity of the area – after the gentlest and widest of starts this drops steeply towards the Fernau mid-station. There is also a lovely 10km ski route (Wilde Grub'n) from Gamsgarten to the valley – start with a cruise from the top of the glacier to get a total of 1450m vertical. And there's proper off-piste to be explored – there's a special map with 11 freeride runs shown (and described in German).

There are good beginner slopes at Eisgrat and Gamsgarten, where there is also a major children's area with childcare. Higher up there is a family fun slope, extended last year.

The area is popular with snowboarders. There are lots of

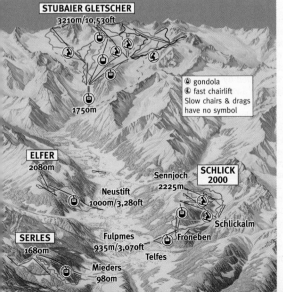

STUBAIER GLETSCHER
3210m/10,530ft

1750m

gondola
fast chairlift
Slow chairs & drags
have no symbol

ELFER
2080m

Sennjoch
2225m

SCHLICK
2000

Neustift
1000m/3,280ft

Schlickalm

SERLES
1680m

Fulpmes
935m/3,070ft

Froneben

Telfes

Mieders
980m

AUSTRIA

↑ It's a long, deep, steep-sided valley; the big smooth white bit on the horizon is the glacier
STUBAI TIROL TO

LIFT PASSES

Prices in €

Age	6-day
under 15	104
15 to 18	135
19 to 64	208
65 plus	166

Free Under 10 and over 80

Beginner No deals

Note Covers Stubaier Gletscher

Alternative pass
Super Pass covers all lifts in Stubai valley

TOURIST OFFICE

www.stubai.at

natural hits and kickers across the mountain, and a big terrain park at the top of the area which last year got an additional rope tow.

Queues are not usually a problem. The access gondolas and Eisjoch six-pack can get busy at weekends.

Gamsgarten has a huge self-service restaurant, and excellent food in the table-service Zur Goldenen Gams. Eisgrat's cool building includes the serious table-service Schaufelspitz. At Jochdohle, Austria's highest restaurant (3150m) gives good views. Dresdner Hütte is a proper climbing refuge.

Après-ski starts up the mountain in the lively Gamsgarten bar and Ice Cube (Eiswürfel) bar.

935m
FULPMES

Fulpmes (with its satellite village of Telfes) sits at the foot of Schlick 2000, the most extensive of the lower ski areas. It is an attractive, sizeable working village not dominated by skiing. The glacier is 25km away.
Uphill from the village a two-stage gondola takes you to Kreuzjoch (2135m), opening up excellent views across the Stubaital and across the Schlick slopes to the dramatic Kalkkogel range. Most of the skiing is below the top gondola station – essentially a single open slope centred on a quad chair rising 580m, plus a six-pack serving shorter runs on skier's left. It is north-facing, so keeps snow well, and grooming is good. There are about five different pistes down, mostly of red difficulty (though partly

labelled black) with some easier blue options. There is also a ski route – challenging at the best of times, very much so if snow is poor. And there is a fair amount of off-piste – 'relatively safe', notes a regular.

Below the main slopes is a long easy run-out to the gondola mid-station at Froneben (1365m). This is the location of the nursery slopes, including Big Ron's Kinderland, with moving carpets and fun features, and a couple of thumping après-ski bars. The blue run winding through woods to the village from here is good fun or tricky, depending on conditions. There is a terrain park. Queues are rare but the gondola gets busy at peak times.

There are some good huts, with table-service options at the top of the gondola and at Zirmachalm ('great gulaschsuppe'). You can be towed by snowcat to Galtalm, in woods below Kreuzjoch, for 'great food and views'.

There's a good choice of 3- and 4-star hotels, most with pools and spa facilities. The 4-star Stubaierhof is central. Café Dorfkrug, in the Dorfkrug hotel, has 'good food, friendly service'.

The nearest leisure centre is in Neustift, but Fulpmes has ice skating, snowshoeing and tobogganing.

1000m
NEUSTIFT

Neustift is the major village closest to the glacier, 20km away. It's an attractive, traditional village, with limited local slopes at Elfer.
The slopes at Elfer consist of a narrow chain of runs and lifts from Elferhütte at 2080m down to the village. The pistes are all red, and it is a quiet place for intermediates to practise. This area is north-east-facing; there is a sunny nursery slope at village level and some 40km of cross-country trails.

There is a big 5-star Relais & Châteaux hotel, and lots of 4-stars and 3-stars spread around the area. Reader tips this year are the 3-star Hoferwirt – 'brilliant staff, cracking restaurant' – and the Gasteigerhof – 'a very decent 4-star hotel with a good spa'. In the outlying hamlet of Neder, the glacier lift company runs the family-oriented 4-star Happy Stubai.

Nightlife is focused on the Dorf and Bierfassl bars and the Nachtkastl and Scala Club discos. Most restaurants are hotel-based. The big leisure centre has two pools, saunas and bowling.

ZELL AM SEE TOURIST OFFICE

Zell am See

A real one-off, this: a summer resort town in a lovely lakeside setting, with varied local slopes and an excellent glacier nearby

£100
RESORT PRICE INDEX

TOP 10 RATINGS

Extent	**
Fast lifts	****
Queues	***
Snow	**
Expert	**
Intermediate	***
Beginner	***
Charm	****
Convenience	***
Scenery	***

+ Varied, wooded slopes with fine views down to the lake

+ Charming summer resort town with lots to do off the slopes

+ Excellent glacier nearby (on the lift pass) on Kaprun's Kitzsteinhorn

− Sunny, low-altitude slopes

− Limited local slopes, especially when snow low down is poor

− Some hotels are distant from the lifts; buses can be crowded

Like St Moritz, Zell is a town beside a lake (frozen if you're lucky). The similarities end there; but Zell is a towny resort that makes a refreshing change from the Austrian norm of rustic chalet-style villages. From the skiing point of view, the appeal is greatly strengthened by having an excellent glacier just down the road at Kaprun, also covered in this chapter. Work has begun on a gondola link with Viehhofen, near Saalbach, for completion next year.

THE RESORT

Zell is a year-round resort town set between a large lake and the unusual, horseshoe-shaped mountain. There are gondolas into the slopes from here and from the suburb of Schüttdorf, about 3km south of Zell. It's a short bus ride to the glacier slopes of Kaprun, on the same lift pass. Saalbach is also easily reached by bus (read the separate chapter).

Village charm Zell has a charming, traffic-free medieval centre. The major through-road was long ago buried in a tunnel, but it's a busy little place and there is still quite a bit of local traffic passing close to the centre.

Convenience There are lodgings close to each access gondola – from the edge of town, and from Schüttdorf – and close to several lifts going up from Schmittental, in the heart of the U-shaped mountain. There are 'good bus services' serving other points.

Scenery Zell am See enjoys a pretty lakeside setting and the mountain offers good views south to the high mountains, including Kaprun's distinctive Kitzsteinhorn.

ZELL AM SEE-KAPRUN TOURISMUS GMBH / GIX MEDIA GMBH

Zell's setting is extraordinary – a horseshoe mountain on one side, a frozen lake on the other ↓

185

NEWS

2015/16: A new two-stage 10-seat gondola will open on Kitzsteinhorn, from Alpincenter at mid-mountain to the top; chairs will alternate with bubbles on the lower stage. The glacier area will be reconfigured, with a new nursery slope.

Work has started on a two-stage gondola into the Zell slopes from Viehhofen in Glemmtal, to the north (the Saalbach valley). But it will not be ready for this season.

THE MOUNTAINS

Zell's mountain is open at the top, mostly densely wooded lower down.

Slopes Above the lifts out of Zell and Schüttdorf a final gondola goes to Schmittenhöhe, meeting another gondola from Schmittental. The several lifts on the back of the hill and on the sunny slopes of the northern arm of the horseshoe mountain are accessed via Schmittenhöhe or by cable car from Schmittenhöhe. From the middle of this northern arm, a ski route descends to Viehhofen in the Glemmtal, close to Saalbach. A gondola is under construction from Viehhofen, and the ski route will in due course become a piste. And then what, we wonder?

Black runs descend from various points to Schmittental; easier runs go down the southern arm of the horseshoe to Zell and Schüttdorf. The slopes steepen as you descend – it's a red run to Schüttdorf, a black to Zell, or a winding blue path.

Fast lifts Only the sunny Sonnkogel sector now relies on slow lifts.

Queues Away from peak season there are no problems. If snow in lower resorts is poor, the queues at the Kitzsteinhorn can be 'horrendous'.

Terrain parks Schmittenhöhe has a half-pipe by the Glocknerbahn chairlift,

and there's a fun park by the Hochmaisbahn.

Snow reliability Many of Zell's slopes get a lot of sun and, although there is full snowmaking, at these altitudes there is still a danger of slush and ice. Piste grooming is 'fabulous'.

Experts Zell has several black runs, which are usually groomed. The two main ones wind through the trees into the Schmittental, offering some choice of gradient. When conditions are good they are a great blast, and when icy they present a serious challenge. The one down the Kettingbahn on the back of the hill is less steep but tends to have better snow. Off-piste terrain is limited, but there is a nice 'glade' area near the Kettingbahn and there are several ski routes in the Sonnkogel sector, including the one to Viehhofen described above.

Intermediates Good intermediates have a couple of fine, long runs, but this is not a place for high mileage. For many intermediates the most interesting sector is Sonnkogel, where there are varied runs of genuine red gradient, and space for carving. The timid can cruise the southern ridge blues.

Beginners A reporter with novice kids advises that the nursery slopes at Schüttdorf are better than those at Schmittental. Both are uncomfortably

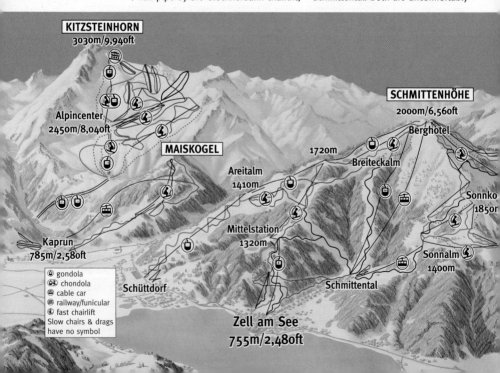

LET
THE HAPPINESS
IN!

WINTER PARADISE
WITH SNOW GUARANTEE

HIGHLIGHTS AT A GLANCE:
- Glacier skiing: high altitude, 100% snow guarantee
- Great après ski (range of bars and restaurants)
- Suitable for all abilities
- Stunning lakeside views
- Range of activities
- Peakworld 3000 at Glacier Kitzsteinhorn
- Schmittenhöhe with an incredible 360-degree view

Zell am See-Kaprun Tourismus
5700 Zell am See, phone +43 (0) 6542-770
welcome@zellamsee-kaprun.com, www.zellamsee-kaprun.com

Resort	755m
	2,480ft

Zell and Kaprun	
Slopes	755-3030m
	2,480-9,940ft
Lifts	53
Pistes	138km
	86 miles

Zell only	
Slopes	755-2000m
	2,480-6,560ft
Lifts	26
Pistes	77km
	48 miles

ZELL AM SEE-KAPRUN TOURISMUS GMBH / GIX MEDIA GMBH

The Kitzsteinhorn will look a bit different next season, with its draglifts rearranged to mesh better with the new chondola/ gondola to the top ↓

low, but there are also beginner lifts at altitude. There are lovely long easy runs to progress to.

Snowboarding Most lifts are chairs, gondolas or cable cars. Snowboard Academy is a specialist school.

Cross-country There's a total of 35km, some lit at night, and more a bus ride away around Kaprun.

Mountain restaurants Zell has quite a few welcoming huts, though demand can exceed supply. They are all named on the piste map. Last season we had a satisfying although slow-paced lunch at the cosy, beamed Hochzelleralm on the northern arm of the area (bigger than it looks – head upstairs). A reader who got around lots of the huts last year likes it too, and also favours Breiteckalm and Glocknerhaus. Pinzgauer Hütte ('wonderful venison') is secluded, away from the piste, with great views; you get a skidoo tow back – fun, but may involve queuing.

Schools and guides There are four schools; we lack recent reports.

Families Staying in Schüttdorf means you have direct gondola access to the Areitalm snow-kindergarten.

STAYING THERE

Hotels There is a broad range of hotels and guest houses. Best in town is the 5-star Salzburger Hof, complete with gourmet restaurants. The bulk are 4-stars, of which three have recently been tipped by reporters. Two rave about the Berner – 'superb', 'lovely food, ski-in/ski-out in good snow'; outdoor pool. The St Georg is 200m from the CityXPress gondola – 'great staff', 'sumptuous food'. The 'exceptionally friendly' Heitzmann is also close to the lifts.

Apartments There are lots of options bookable locally.

Eating out The Salzburger Hof takes top slot. A reader who has clearly done some dining tips the Steinerwirt ('very good cooking, panelled rooms'), the Grüner Baum hotel ('more imaginative than the norm'), Steiner Gnuss Werk ('small, funky place in an old mill') and the American-style diner Kupferkessel. Villa Crazy Daisy (read 'Après-ski') also does pizza etc.

Après-ski There are plenty of cafes and bars. Start at the top of the

LIFT PASSES

Prices in €

Age	6-day
under 15	120
15 to 17	180
18 plus	240

Free Under 5 (accompanied by parent)

Senior No deals

Beginner No deals

Note Covers Zell am See and Kaprun

Alternative passes
Kitzbüheler Alpen AllStarCard covers 10 resorts; Salzburg Super Ski Card (minimum 3 days) covers most of the Salzburg region

TOURIST OFFICE

www.zellamsee-kaprun.com

slopes at the Berghotel – where the bar has a good vibe, live music and dancing. In town, there are lots of lively bars. Pinzgauer Diele club rocks. O'Flannigan's is the main sports bar, but too cramped for our taste; one reader prefers A Bit of Irish. Ginhouse is good for a quiet drink, particularly, er, gin. Villa Crazy Daisy is 'a jumping place with a great atmosphere'; live music often.

Off the slopes There is plenty to do. In midwinter you can often walk across the frozen lake; there are marked paths up at Schmittenhöhe, too. Plus there are good sports facilities, Alpine flights, and you can watch ice hockey. Trips to Salzburg and Kitzbühel are possible and rewarding – good train service, we hear.

OUTLYING RESORT – 785m

KAPRUN

Kaprun is a pleasant and quite lively village, with a pretty church, and it's bypassed by the road up to the lifts to its Kitzsteinhorn glacier. It sprawls over a considerable area, so it's worth picking your spot with care for après-ski purposes – although you're likely to be using buses most days for skiing wherever you stay.

There is a small area of easy intermediate slopes on the outskirts of the village on the low hill of Maiskogel (top height 1675m). This has a six-pack at its core on the upper mountain serving a blue and a black/red, so it is not to be sneered at. But most people will want to spend their time on the glacier.

This is reached by a two-stage gondola to Alpincenter at 2450m, with other lifts in parallel. The main slopes are in a big bowl above Alpincenter, served by the new Gletscherjet 3 chondola and Gletscherjet 4 gondola, two six-packs and lots of T-bars; these smaller lifts are being reconfigured along with construction of the big new lifts, so our current map of the glacier is likely to be inaccurate.

There are three 'excellent' terrain parks on the glacier including one for novices, and a super-pipe.

The high black runs present no challenge to experts (they used to be red), but a black piste has been opened lower down, going to the gondola mid-station, with a claimed gradient of 32° – a proper black. In that same area, there is a set of

STC Ski

Specialists in Tailor-Made Short Breaks & Holidays

01483 771 222
www.stcski.co.uk
ski@stcski.co.uk

similarly steep itineraries (there is also one on the upper mountain) – mostly with verticals of around 500m. These runs are not explained on the piste map, but it seems that they are now operated as conventional ski routes – not prepared or patrolled, but closed if there is avalanche danger. There is also lots of genuine off-piste terrain, and the resort goes out of its way to educate visitors in safety matters.

Most pistes are mainly gentle blues and reds – great easy cruising for intermediates. One particularly entertaining red goes down to the gondola mid-station, away from the lifts. For beginners there are nursery slopes next to the village and gentle blues to progress to, both at Maiskogel and on the glacier – the latter now positioned at the mid-station of the new Gletscherjet lifts.

There are seven ski schools.

The 18km of cross-country trails on the Kaprun golf course are good, and at altitude there is one short loop.

There's a decent choice of mountain restaurants on the glacier. One of the best is the Gletschermühle at mid-mountain. Alpincenter has a large food court doing 'excellent freshly cooked food'. The Krefelder Hütte below it is a genuine mountain refuge.

Crystal has a chalet here. There's a decent choice of hotels, but we lack recent reports. A reporter this year tips three lively bars with 'an excellent atmosphere enjoyed by all', where you may find live music into the early hours: Paletti, Baumbar and Pavillon. The last also does 'hearty ribs and wings', while Dorfkrug serves 'traditional fare second to none in a fantastic setting and atmosphere'. There's a sports centre, bowling at the Sportsbar, sleigh rides and a motor museum.

Around a third of British skiers and snowboarders choose France for their holidays – more than any other country. It's not difficult to see what attracts us: France has the biggest lift and piste networks in the world, and most are at high altitude, ensuring good snow for a long season. The best of them have state-of-the-art lift systems, too – though the idea that all French lift systems are cutting-edge is a myth, going back to the days before Austria and Italy woke up to modern expectations. Another common myth is that French resort villages are all soulless, purpose-built service stations, thrown up without concern for appearance during the 1960s and 1970s. Some are, some emphatically are not.

Many French resorts are now distinctly lively in the evening – a great change over the last 20 years. And some even have the on-mountain après scene that is so common in Austria, mainly thanks to the Folie Douce chain that started in Val d'Isère and has expanded to Méribel, Val Thorens and Alpe-d'Huez – and now to Megève, even.

The big French resorts have a reputation for high prices, and in some respects it is well earned: the bars and restaurants of major resorts such as Courchevel, Méribel, Val d'Isère and Val Thorens are painfully pricey. But when you take other holiday costs into account, most French resorts are not expensive compared with their main Alpine rivals. (If you look at our RPI figures, you'll find most fall into the average band, coded blue, and some into the cheap band, coded green.) And UK tour operators do a great job in keeping catered chalet holidays affordable, with lots of food and wine included in the price. The euro exchange rate has improved in the last year, easing the pain, although not affecting comparisons with other eurozone countries, of course.

KEEPING COSTS DOWN

Chalet holidays are not the only way of economizing. Renting one of the new generation of genuinely comfortable and stylish apartments and catering for yourself is an attractive option that should keep your bar bills down – read our smart apartments chapter on page 37. Other ideas include staying in a relatively cheap valley town (such as Bourg-St-Maurice, below Les Arcs – a great place to base yourself for a week's exploration of several resorts, if you take a car) and eating packed lunches. Picnic tables are increasingly common.

ANY STYLE OF RESORT YOU LIKE

The main drawback to France, hinted at above, is the nature of some of the high-altitude purpose-built resorts. It's partly that the worst of them look hideous, but it's also that they were designed to cram in the maximum number of beds and that they are holiday camps rather than real communities. But even the worst places have learned from past mistakes, and newer developments have been built in a traditional chalet style.

If you prefer, there are genuinely old mountain villages to stay in, linked directly to the big lift networks. These are not usually as convenient for the slopes, but they give you a feel of being in

LES ARCS TO

← Arc 2000 was one of the first purpose-built resorts in France; Arc 1950 below it is quite probably the last

France rather than in a winter-holiday factory. Examples include Montchavin or Champagny for La Plagne, Vaujany for Alpe-d'Huez and St-Martin-de-Belleville for the Three Valleys (and St-Martin is actually about as convenient for the area as other bases are). There are also old villages with their own slopes that have developed as resorts while retaining at least some rustic ambience – such as Serre-Chevalier, in the southern Alps.

Two other resorts deserve a special mention. Megève is an exceptionally charming little town combining rustic style with sophistication. And then there is Chamonix, a big, bustling town sitting literally in the shadow of Mont Blanc, Europe's highest peak, and the centre of the most radical off-piste terrain in the Alps.

INSTRUCTION OR GUIDING?

Gone are the days when the Ecole du Ski Français was the only ski school in town. Most resorts now have lots of competing schools, and many are run and staffed by highly qualified British instructors.

Most experienced skiers don't want to join a school; but many do like to be shown around the slopes of an unfamiliar resort, and to be introduced to other skiers of a similar standard. So they're keen on the ski guiding/hosting services that British chalet companies have operated for many years – until 2013, when a French court ruled that the practice was illegal unless the staff member held the highest ski instructor qualification. In September 2014 Le Ski, the tour operator being prosecuted, lost its initial appeal (in the court in Chambéry) against the decision. Le Ski immediately instructed its lawyers to appeal to the supreme court in Paris; that appeal is yet to be heard. Meanwhile, tour operators have suspended their hosting services.

ANDYPARANT.COM

Tignes is one of the highest resorts, with barely a tree in sight; Tignes-le-Lac is shown in this shot – Val Claret is out of sight to the left ↓

LIVE THE GREAT OUTDOORS

les saisies

FOR THE RE-DISCOVERY OF WINTER SPORTS

WINTER 2015-2016

- 192km snow-sure pistes
- Ideal resort for beginners & intermediates
- Family Friendly
- Off-piste runs through the trees
- Views of Mont Blanc
- Close to Geneva, Lyon and Chambery airport

Book Now with Peak Retreats

02392 839 310

PeakRetreats.co.uk

Getting around the French Alps

Pick the right gateway city as your initial Continental target – Geneva, Chambéry or Grenoble – and you can hardly go wrong. The only high pass you need worry about is on the approach to Serre-Chevalier and Montgenèvre – the 2060m Col du Lauteret; but even here the road is a major one, and kept clear of snow or reopened quickly after a fall. (You can fly to Turin and avoid that pass.) Crossing the French–Swiss border between Chamonix and Verbier involves two closure-prone passes – the Montets and the Forclaz. When necessary, one-way traffic runs beside the tracks through the rail tunnel beneath the passes.

EASY PISTES

France remains unusual among European countries in rating pistes on a four-point scale. The very easiest runs are classified green; except in Val d'Isère, they are reliably gentle. This is a genuinely helpful system that helps beginners progress from the nursery slopes safe in the knowledge that there are no nasty surprises ahead (except in Val d'Isère). It ought to be used more widely. Some French resorts, sadly, don't use it – notably Les Arcs and La Plagne. And it's not that they don't have suitable slopes – many of their blue slopes could be green.

SKI AMIS

Catered Chalets in Superb Locations

020 3411 5439
www.skiamis.com

PLAT DU JOUR

Despite the high restaurant prices, France has advantages for food-lovers. Table-service in mountain restaurants is common, and most places do food (often including a plat du jour) that is varied and interesting – and, in particular, much more varied and interesting than what is served in arch-rival Austria. Most resort villages have restaurants serving good, traditional French food and regional specialities. But don't expect many options other than those – and be wary of them if they exist: we had the worst curry of all time in central Chamonix.

DRIVING AMBITION?

The French Alps are easy to get to by car from the UK. Last winter, as on many other occasions in the past, we drove from southern England via the Channel tunnel to a French resort comfortably in a day, arriving in time for dinner. On page 59 there is a chapter on driving to the French Alps. Driving is still popular, despite the growth of budget airlines; for self-caterers it has the advantage that you can stock up in good-value valley supermarkets before the final climb to your resort.

AVOID THE CROWDS

French school holidays mean crowded slopes, so they are worth avoiding. The country is divided into three zones; schools in each zone take a fortnight's holiday, with the timing staggered so that no more than two zones are on holiday at the same time. In 2016 the holidays are between 6 February and 6 March. This year Paris gets the last slot, 20 February to 6 March; in the northern mega-resorts, in particular, this is the time to avoid. Happily, it seems most English school half-term breaks will fall before the Paris fortnight.

OT ALPE-D'HUEZ / AGENCE NUTS

Alpe-d'Huez

Impressive and sunny slopes above a hotchpotch of a purpose-built village, with attractive alternative bases

£105
RESORT PRICE INDEX

RATINGS

The mountains

Extent	★★★★
Fast lifts	★★★★
Queues	★★★★
Terrain p'ks	★★★
Snow	★★★★
Expert	★★★★
Intermediate	★★★★
Beginner	★★★★★
Boarder	★★★★
X-country	★★★
Restaurants	★★★★
Schools	★★★★
Families	★★★

The resort

Charm	★★
Convenience	★★★
Scenery	★★★★
Eating out	★★★★
Après-ski	★★★★
Off-slope	★★★★

196

KEY FACTS

Resort	1860m
	6,100ft
Slopes	1100-3330m
	3,610-10,920ft
Lifts	80
Pistes	250km
	155 miles

➕ Extensive, high, sunny slopes, split interestingly into different sectors, with some very long runs

➕ Vast, gentle, sunny nursery slopes

➕ Efficient access lifts from villages

➕ Livelier than many French resorts

➕ Good, traditional alternative bases

➖ Some main intermediate runs get badly overcrowded in high season

➖ Many runs get too much sun, so slush and ice are hazards

➖ Many tough runs are high, and exposed – very few woodland runs

➖ Spread-out resort village

There are few single resorts to rival Alpe-d'Huez for extent and variety of terrain – in wintery conditions it's one of our favourites. But as the season progresses the effects of the strong southern sun become more and more of a problem.

If you don't like the look of the village, think about the smaller bases described at the end of this chapter – especially Vaujany.

THE RESORT

Alpe-d'Huez is a large, modern resort on a high, open, sunny plateau east of Grenoble. It was developed for skiing, but consists mainly of large numbers of undistinguished small buildings rather than monolithic blocks.

The resort spreads down a gentle slope in a triangular shape from the main lift station at the top corner. The main village is divided into three named 'quarters'; Vieil Alpe includes the original chalet-style part of the village, at the lower end. Outside the central triangle there are four satellite 'quarters'. The major one is Les Bergers, a second major lift base at the eastern corner of the resort; it has a chalet suburb spreading uphill.

A blue piste descends from the west side of the resort to the original (but much expanded) village of Huez, where there is lodging (and a lift to the main resort).

The lift pass gives days in some other resorts (including Les Deux-Alpes, Serre-Chevalier and Montgenèvre – see Lift passes notes in the margin). There are buses twice a week to Les Deux-Alpes, but the proper thing to do is to go by helicopter – we agree with readers that this is 'fantastic fun' (70 euros last season; three days a week). There are plans for a cross-valley lift (which, subject to permissions being granted, they hope to open by 2020).

VILLAGE CHARM ★★
Bit of a hotchpotch
The central buildings come in all styles; on the fringes there are more sizeable, modern buildings, and areas of chalets. Vieil Alpe has a trace of charm, and as a whole the resort is not unpleasant. The central Avenue des Jeux is a kind of focus, with the ice rink, indoor-outdoor swimming pool, and many of the shops, bars and restaurants.

CONVENIENCE ★★★
Choose your spot with care
Very few lodgings are ski-in/ski-out. Staying near one of the two major lift bases is the best plan – or in one of the chalets uphill of Les Bergers. The place is too big to get around on foot. There's a slow bucket-lift (with a piste beneath it) running in daytime through the centre to the main lifts. This opens a bit late (8.45am) and builds queues at peak times. There are also chairlifts across the bottom of the resort up to Les Bergers. The free ski-

miles | 0.5 | 1.0 | 1.5 | 2.0

← Signal

Pic Blanc

Marmottes

Les Bergers

L'Eclose

Signal de l'Homme

km | 1.0 | 2.0 | 3.0

2015/16: Another 33
snow-guns are
planned for the
Sarenne run, bringing
the total covering it
to over 100. The aim
is to keep this
signature run open
from December until
the end of April. At
Auris-en-Oisans, the
beginner area is due
for a revamp,
including three new
moving carpets; and
more snowmaking is
planned between
Signal de l'Homme
and the village.

2014/15: 68 snow-
guns were installed
on the Sarenne run.
A new 4-star
residence, the
Epinettes, opened.

LAURENT SALINO / ALPE D'HUEZ
TOURISME

This is the Avenue des
Jeux, with the Signal
slopes on the left and
one of the big areas
of beginner slopes on
the right ↓

bus service around the resort usually
runs to its timetable, but reporters
find the 20-minute interval between
buses too long. The satellite quarters
are a bit of a trek from the centre –
and a reader points out that there are
no proper footways – but they have
their own lifts, bars and restaurants.

SCENERY ★★★★
Splendid panoramic views
The resort has a fabulous high setting
on a sunny plateau. There are splendid
views of the Ecrins peaks.

THE MOUNTAINS

Practically all the slopes are above the
treeline, and so there may be little to
do when a storm socks in or the wind
picks up. Piste classification is rather
unreliable. There are certainly some
tough blues; but readers' views seem
to be complicated by snow conditions,
which in such a sunny resort are
naturally very variable. The piste map
is OK but has very small type; some
reporters find signposting less than
ideal.

EXTENT OF THE SLOPES ★★★★
Several well-linked areas
Alpe-d'Huez is a big-league resort,
with impressively extensive and varied
slopes. It offers many long runs, with
big verticals. It claims 250km of pistes
but last year's Schrahe report (see our
Piste Extent feature near the front of

Mega-resort skiing from a quiet
base? Check out Vaujany p205.

the book) put the total at 179km).

The slopes divide into four sectors,
with good connections between them.

The biggest sector is directly above
the village, on the slopes of **Pic Blanc**.
The huge two-stage Grandes Rousses
gondola – aka the DMC (a reference to
its technology) and marked on the
piste map just as 'first stage' and
'second stage' – goes from the top of
the village. The first stage to 2100m is
now duplicated by a state-of-the-art
chondola which can transport 3,900
people an hour.

Above the DMC, a cable car goes
up to 3330m on Pic Blanc itself – the
top of the small Sarenne glacier and
start of the eponymous run (read our
feature panel). The glacier is also
reached via the Marmottes six-pack,
then a two-stage gondola (the first
stage of which also serves lower runs
from Clocher de Macle).

The alternative from Pic Blanc is to
take a 300m tunnel through the ridge
to the front face, where a west-facing
black mogul field awaits you (closed
when we were there in March 2015).

The epic Sarenne black run ends in
a gorge that separates the main resort
area from **Signal de l'Homme**. It is
crossed by a down-and-up fast chairlift
from the Bergers part of the village.
From the top you can take excellent

Alpe-d'Huez

skitracer*

CHALETS, HOTELS
& APARTMENTS
Call us today
020 8600 1650
skitracer.com

Club Med

THE MOST COMPREHENSIVE
SKI PACKAGE ON THE MARKET

L'Alpe d'Huez La Sarenne 3

020 8313 3999
Skiline.co.uk

Skiline.co.uk

couple of chairs lower down. Runs go down the other side of the hill to Villard-Reculas. One blue run back to Alpe-d'Huez is floodlit on Thursdays.

The **Vaujany-Oz** sector consists largely of north-west-facing slopes, reached from Alpe-d'Huez via red runs. (There is blue-run access too if you are prepared to do a short stretch of easy red.) At the heart of this sector is L'Alpette, the mid-station of the cable car from Vaujany; it can also be reached by a gondola from Oz. Beyond L'Alpette, the slopes around Montfrais are blue, with the notable exception of the shady black La Fare, which plunges down to L'Enversin, just below Vaujany. The descent from Pic Blanc to L'Enversin is 2200m vertical – the second biggest in the world (beaten, as it happens, by near-neighbour Les

north-facing slopes towards the gorge, or head south to Auris or west to tiny Chatelard/La Garde.

On the other side of town from Signal de l'Homme is the small **Signal** sector, which is reached by draglifts next to the main gondola or by a

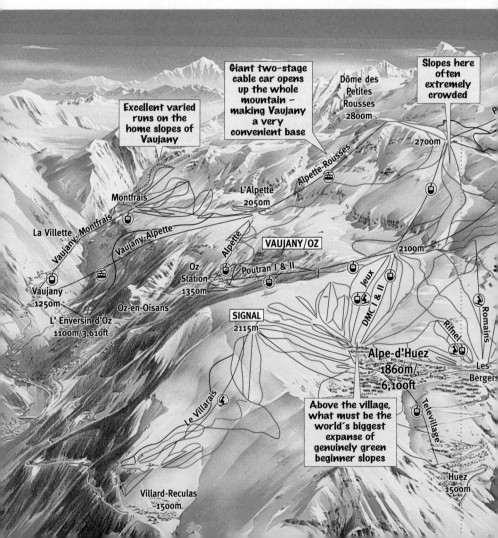

Giant two-stage cable car opens up the whole mountain – making Vaujany a very convenient base

Excellent varied runs on the home slopes of Vaujany

Slopes here often extremely crowded

Dôme des Petites Rousses 2800m

2700m

Alpette-Rousses

Montfrais

L'Alpette 2050m

Vaujany-Montfrais

La Villette

Vaujany-Alpette

Alpette

VAUJANY/OZ

2100m

Jeux

Oz Station 1350m

Poutran I & II

DMC I & II

Vaujany 1250m

Oz-en-Oisans

L' Enversin d'Oz 1100m/3,610ft

SIGNAL 2115m

Rifnel

Romains

Alpe-d'Huez 186om/ 6,100ft

Les Bergers

Le Villarais

Televillage

Above the village, what must be the world's biggest expanse of genuinely green beginner slopes

Huez 1500m

Villard-Reculas 1500m

Deux-Alpes). The links back to Alpe-d'Huez are by cable car from L'Alpette, or a second gondola from Oz. You can also reach Oz from the mid-station of the DMC at 2100m, down an excellent red with blue variant most of the way.

FAST LIFTS ★★★★
Pretty efficient overall
Gondolas and fast chairs are the main access lifts and serve most areas adequately. But there are still some old chairs and draglifts.

QUEUES ★★★★
Few problems to report
Improvements in the lifts from village level in recent years seems to have paid off and 2015 reporters mentioned few queueing problems. There can be waits for the cable car up to Pic Blanc

Mega-resort skiing from a quiet base? Check out Vaujany p205.

and the chairs serving the glacier area there – especially when snow is poor lower down. The village bucket-lift is said to generate lengthy queues first thing.

Over much of the area a greater problem than lift queues is that some pistes can be unbearably crowded. The Chamois and Couloir runs from the top of the DMC gondola are among the most crowded we've seen, anywhere, despite the laudable efforts of the lift company to divert skiers coming up the Vaujany cable car on to the Belvedere and excellent Bartavelles runs. The red Rousses run to Vaujany and Poutrans to Oz can also be

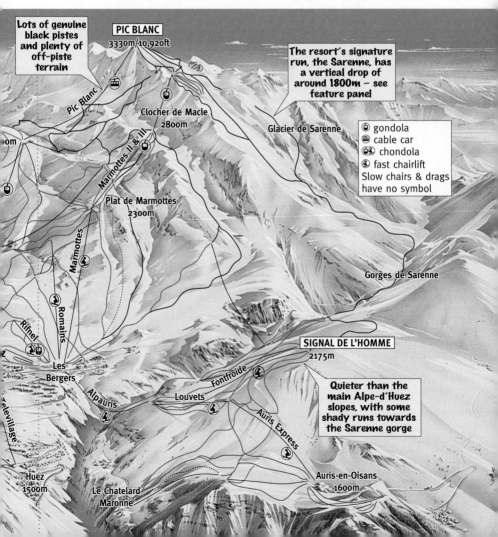

Lots of genuine black pistes and plenty of off-piste terrain

PIC BLANC
3330m/10,920ft

Pic Blanc

Clocher de Macle
2800m

Glacier de Sarenne

The resort's signature run, the Sarenne, has a vertical drop of around 1800m – see feature panel

Marmottes II & III

🚡 gondola
🚠 cable car
🚡 chondola
🚡 fast chairlift
Slow chairs & drags have no symbol

Plat de Marmottes
2300m

Marmottes

Gorges de Sarenne

Romains

Rifnel

SIGNAL DE L'HOMME
2175m

Les Bergers

Fontfroide

Quieter than the main Alpe-d'Huez slopes, with some shady runs towards the Sarenne gorge

Alpauris

Louvets

Auris Express

Huez
1500m

Le Chatelard
Maronne

Auris-en-Oisans
1600m

For years we have been repeating the resort's claim that the Sarenne run from the Pic Blanc is 16km long. But this season we skied it three times in two days and were a bit dubious. So we measured it on a topographical map and found it was roughly 10km long to the lift back up to the resort. We contacted Christophe Schrahe (see our feature chapter on Piste Extent) and he said he'd measured it as 10.5km. So we assume the 16km figure is arrived at by adding distance on for skiers' turns (see feature chapter; we asked the resort for clarification but that did not arrive before we went to press).

Whatever, the Sarenne is a long run (and around 1800m vertical). But it's a run of two halves. The bottom half is virtually flat (boarders beware), but the top half is a genuine black if you take the direct route – a demanding run (with stunning views) that any keen, competent and fit skier will enjoy. The steep mogul field near the top can be avoided by taking an easier option (or by using the Marmottes III gondola). The run gets a lot of sun, so snow conditions are highly variable; pick your time with care. Once a week (for 75 euros) you can ski the Sarenne by night: take the last lift up, watch the sun set, then ski down with guides, stopping for dinner at a mountain hut near the end.

crowded. On our March 2015 the narrow, steep part of the Sarenne before it flattens out was carnage, with crowds of people standing around afraid to turn in the slushy bumps as other whizzed past. Reporters also complain about good skiers racing through the green areas near the base far too fast.

In contrast, the slopes around Signal de l'Homme and Auris were lovely and quiet when we were there.

TERRAIN PARKS ★★★
Big and varied
A big park stretches almost all the way down the first stage of the DMC. One of our keen 'park rat' reporters says, 'It is definitely the best-placed and possibly the best-designed park I've seen. It has everything from an easy beginner line to enormous jumps and an airbag, with lots of rails too.' Other reporters praise it as well. There's also a half-pipe and a 'fast, aggressive' snowcross. And there's a beginners' park above Vaujany.

SNOW RELIABILITY ★★★★
Affected by the sun
Alpe-d'Huez is unique among major purpose-built resorts in the Alps in having mainly south- or south-west-facing slopes (and is known as 'The Island in the Sun'). The strong southern sun can affect piste conditions even in January, and late-season conditions may alternate between slush and ice on most runs. On our March 2015 visit even the high runs were slushy by mid-morning and many of the black runs were closed because they were in poor condition. The top part of the Sarenne was a welcome exception with good snow

right up to lunchtime. There are also shady slopes at Signal de l'Homme (where we enjoyed good snow and deserted pistes) and above Vaujany. Snowmaking is not comprehensive, but is now quite extensive, covering the main runs above Alpe-d'Huez, Vaujany and Oz and now the whole of the Sarenne run.

FOR EXPERTS ★★★★
Plenty of blacks and off-piste
There are long and challenging pistes as well as some serious off-piste.

The black slope beneath the Pic Blanc cable car will be on your agenda. Despite improvements to the tunnel exit, the start of the actual slope is often awkward. The slope is of ordinary black steepness, but can be very hard in the mornings (and was closed on our March 2015 visit) because it gets the afternoon sun. Get information on its condition. The long Sarenne run on the back of Pic Blanc is described in the panel above. The black Fare piste to L'Enversin is good – varied, and well away from the lifts but not steep; it faces west, and relies heavily on artificial snow.

The Marmottes II gondola serves genuine black runs and a red from Clocher de Macle; Balcons is steep and quiet, often with good snow; Clocher de Macle is easier but busier; don't miss the beautiful, long, lonely Combe Charbonnière (but there's a fairly long traverse on moderately steep ground at the start). The Lièvre Blanc chairlift serves further testing slopes – Balme, looping away from the lifts, is a black, and one or two mogully reds would be classified black in many resorts. In good snow conditions, the steep La Fuma run down to Le Chatelard (open

DO MORE
in *Alpe d'Huez*

zenith
·holidays·

0203 137 7678

zenithholidays.co.uk

⬛ ABTA
ABTA No.Y1542

Alpe-d'Huez

LIFT PASSES

Prices in €

Age	6-day
under 13	199
13 to 64	248
65 to 71	199
72 plus	75

Free Under 5

Beginner Four free lifts; Première Glisse pass covers 19 lifts

Notes Covers Alpe-d'Huez, Auris, Oz, Vaujany and Villard-Reculas; half-day passes; discounts for families; 6-day-plus passes allow one day's skiing at each of Serre-Chevalier, Puy-St-Vincent, Montgenèvre, and the Milky Way in Italy, and two days in Les Deux-Alpes; also night skiing, night tobogganing, one entry to the ice rink, to the swimming pool and to one sports centre activity during the day

Alternative passes Alpe-d'Huez only, Auris only, Oz-Vaujany only, Villard-Reculas only; pedestrian

as a piste only in good snow) is worth trying. And the Col de Cluy from Signal de l'Homme is long and gets away from all the lifts.

The off-piste possibilities are immense, and some are described in our feature panel. Some of these routes away from the lifts are shady, in contrast to the main slopes.

FOR INTERMEDIATES ★★★★
Fine selection of runs

Good intermediates have a fine selection of runs all over the area. In good snow conditions the variety of runs is difficult to beat.

Every section has some challenging red runs to test the adventurous intermediate. The Canyon run is one of the most challenging. There are lovely long runs down to Oz – the Champclotury blue from the mid-station of the gondola above Oz is a lovely, gentle run and usually quiet – and to Vaujany, with space for some serious carving. The Villard-Reculas and Signal de l'Homme sectors have long challenging reds. Those at Signal de L'Homme are quieter, so they keep their snow better. The Chamois red from the top of the gondola down to the mid-station is quite narrow, and miserable when busy and icy and/or heavily mogulled. Fearless intermediates should enjoy the long Sarenne black run (see feature panel).

For less ambitious intermediates, there are usually blue alternatives, except on the upper part of the mountain. The main Couloir blue from the top of the big gondola is a lovely run, well served by snowmaking, but like the red Chamois it does get scarily crowded at times.

There are some great cruising runs above Vaujany; but the red runs between Vaujany and Alpe-d'Huez can be too much for early intermediates. You can travel via Oz on gondolas if you are that keen to get around.

Unreliable piste classification can complicate life for early intermediates.

FOR BEGINNERS ★★★★★
Good facilities

The large networks of green runs immediately above the village and above the Les Bergers area form nursery areas as good as you will find anywhere. Sadly, these slopes carry a lot of fast through-traffic, despite being declared low-speed zones. In each area two short beginner lifts are

Mega-resort skiing from a quiet base? Check out Vaujany p205.

free, and a special lift pass covers more lifts to progress to.

FOR BOARDERS ★★★★
Suits the adventurous

The resort suits experienced boarders well – the extent and variety of the mountains mean that there's a lot of good freeriding to be had; the off-piste is vast and varied and well worth checking out with a guide. The terrain park is good, too. There are quite a few flat areas to beware of though. The nursery slopes are excellent and have fast chairlifts bottom to top.

FOR CROSS-COUNTRY ★★★
High-level and convenient

There are 50km of trails, with six loops of varying degrees of difficulty, all at around 2000m and consequently relatively snow-sure.

MOUNTAIN RESTAURANTS ★★★★
Some excellent rustic huts

There are more rustic places with table-service than is usual in high French resorts, and almost all readers are impressed – 'it's why we come here' is one emphatic view. But the restaurants in the more obvious positions get over-busy, and some charge for the toilets. The piste map does not identify restaurants. The resort's pocket guide covers 18 places, marked on a tiny piste map.

Editors' choice The cosy little Chalet du Lac Besson is an oasis of calm – tucked away on the cross-country loops north of the 2100m mid-station of the DMC gondola (and reached by a special access piste, the Boulevard des Lacs). Food and service are excellent. It's repeatedly endorsed by reporters.

Worth knowing about Immediately above the resort, the best option is Plage des Neiges, just off the Chardons green run – favourite of several reporters: 'lovely rustic bustling place', 'creamy rich tartiflette', 'very friendly'.

On the back of the hill, the cosy Bergerie above the Villard-Reculas lift base is 'very friendly with a simple but excellent menu', says a 2015 reader..

Combe Haute, at the foot of the Chalvet chair towards the end of the Sarenne run, serves 'lovely' food in 'charming, rustic surroundings'. Low

High *quality,* *high altitude*

Four-star ski apartments with spa
02392 890 960

ABTA No.W9357

SKI COLLECTION

ESPRIT
FOR FAMILIES IN
Alpe d'Huez
Family
Ski Chalets
Dedicated
Nurseries
Exclusive Ski
Classes
13 resorts
across the Alps
espritski.com
01483 791 900

Ski Total
WELCOME YOU TO
Alpe d'Huez
Quality chalets
Excellent value
19 resorts
across the Alps
skitotal.com
01483 791 933

down in the woods at Le Chatelard on the fringe of the Signal de l'Homme sector, the little Forêt de Maronne hotel is 'excellent value'.

We had a very satisfactory lunch a few seasons ago at Perce-Neige, just below the Oz-Poutran gondola mid-station. It has a wood-burning stove and a 'great snug atmosphere', with 'efficient service' and does 'terrific salads and a lovely chocolate cake'. Near the Alpette lift station, La Grange pleases readers. Down the hill slightly, Auberge de l'Alpette (aka Chez Passoud) is an unpretentious place doing good food. Further down, Airelles is a rustic hut built into the rock, with a roaring log fire; we get consistently good reports – 'excellent tartiflette'.

SCHOOLS AND GUIDES ★★★★
Masterclass worth a try
Reports on the ESF have been mixed. One recent reporter said of lessons organized by Esprit Ski: 'Our children liked their instructors and made huge improvements.' But we also heard from an adult beginner who had a 'distressing experience' as the instructor 'shouted and humiliated' her group so much she couldn't return for her remaining three lessons. A 2015 reporter 'didn't feel there was a lot of teaching' in her lesson.

Reports on British instructor Stuart Adamson's outfit Masterclass are universally positive. He 'did wonders for the lost confidence' of the woman who had the distressing ESF experience. A 2015 reporter's early intermediate wife had a 'brilliant' private lesson.

FOR FAMILIES ★★★
Plenty of choice
There's Les Intrépides day care centre for children aged six months to four years. The ESF runs the Chalets des

Enfants for children aged from two and a half to five years: this combines ski lessons with activities in a day care centre.

Family specialist Esprit operates here (read 'Chalets' in the next section) and has comprehensive childcare arrangements.

STAYING THERE

There's quite a good range of options of all kinds of lodging. There is a 364-bedroom, eight-storey Club Med in the Bergers quarter.

Chalets Skiworld's chalets include some with hot tub and sauna and a splendid looking one in their top Signature range down in Huez. Crystal has a central 34-bed chalet hotel plus four chalets ('Basic en-suite rooms, but good food and attentive staff,' says a visitor to one of them). Ski Total has five chalets, most with sauna and two with outdoor hot tubs. Inghams has two chalets (one with outdoor hot tub, one with sauna) plus a 70-bed chalet hotel ('excellent staff, good natured, good little bar'). The VIP chalets near the main lifts are also 'excellent'. Family specialist Esprit has a 60-bed chalet hotel in the old village ('Childcare top-notch, location perfect; staff were troopers') and three separate chalets using the child care facilities of the chalet hotel. Zenith has four chalets, including one very smart looking place with sauna and hot tub.

Hotels There are more than in most high French resorts.

★★★★Alpenrose On the fringe of Les Bergers – 'Possible to ski back, but a hike up to Marmottes I,' says a reporter. Spa.

★★★★Au Chamois d'Or Good facilities, modern rooms, one of the best restaurants in town and well placed for the main gondola. Spa.

★★★★Pic Blanc Across the car park from

the lifts at Les Bergers. Renovated for 2015/16 and uprated from 3- to 4-star.
****Royal Ours Blanc Heart of the village; pool, sauna, steam. 'Good food, nice staff,' said a reporter.
***Petit Prince On the Signal side of town 50m from a lift. 'Stylish and best quality for value we've had on a ski holiday,' says a 2015 visitor.
Apartments There are lots available, though few are notable. Among the smartest are those in CGH's residence Cristal de l'Alpe with pool, hot tubs, sauna, steam, fitness stuff etc, and a prime central location. The Ours Blanc has 'lovely compact rooms', but is not ideally located. Ski Collection and Erna Low offer these properties.

Some of Skiworld's chalets are available on a 'flexible catering' basis and it has the Cristal de l'Alpe too. Zenith have several chalets available catered or self-catered.

The supermarket at Les Bergers is reported to be the best in town.

EATING OUT ★★★★
Good value
Alpe-d'Huez has dozens of restaurants, some of high quality; many offer good value by ski resort standards. A pocket booklet lists over 30 of them.

We had good meals at Grenier and Passe-Montagne (both with French and Savoyard food and friendly service) on our 2015 visit and at Au P'tit Creux a few years back.

Readers' recommendations include: Genepi (French cuisine: food generally praised but service criticized), Smithy's Tavern (Tex-Mex and grills), Caribou ('very French, good menu, not known to tour op reps'), Edelweiss ('fantastic food') and Lounge 21 (good steaks).

APRES-SKI ★★★★
Plenty going on
The idea is that you now end your afternoon dancing on the tables at the newish Folie Douce. In the village there's a wide range of bars, some of which get fairly lively later on. There are several British-run bars such as the Underground in Vieil Alpe ('open mike nights and live music') and Smithy's Tavern ('great fun, lots of dancing, gets very hot'). Other places tipped by reporters include O'Bar ('beer really cheap') and the Etalon ('nice chilled-out bar run by friendly staff'). Late-night places include the Sporting, Igloo and the Caves de l'Alpe.

OFF THE SLOPES ★★★★
Good by high-resort standards
There is a wide range of facilities, praised by recent non-skiers, including a big and very popular indoor-outdoor pool ('great fun"), an Olympic-size ice rink – plus an indoor pool and a splendid sports centre. Note that a six-day-plus lift pass gets you one free visit to each of these activities.

There's also an ice-driving school and a toboggan run, and you can try paragliding, snowmobiling, snowshoeing and dog sledding. A visit to the Ice Cave at the top of the DMC

OFF-PISTE FOR ALL STANDARDS

There are vast amounts of off-piste terrain in Alpe-d'Huez, from fairly tame to seriously adventurous. Here we pick out just a few of the many runs to be explored – always with guidance, of course.

*There are lots of off-piste variants on both sides of the Sarenne run that are good for making your first turns off-piste. The **Combe du Loup**, a beautiful south-facing bowl with views over the Meije, has a black-run gradient at the top, and you end up on long, gentle slopes leading back to the Sarenne gorge. **La Chapelle Saint Giraud**, which starts at Signal de l'Homme, includes a series of small, confidence-boosting bowls, interspersed with gentle rolling terrain.*

*For more experienced and adventurous off-piste skiers, the **Grand Sablat** is a classic that runs through a magnificently wild setting on the eastern face of the Massif des Grandes Rousses. This descent of 2000m vertical includes glacial terrain and some steep couloirs. You can either ski down to the village of Clavans, where you can take a pre-booked helicopter or taxi back, or traverse above Clavans back to the Sarenne gorge. In the **Signal** sector, there are various classic routes down towards the village of Huez or to Villard-Reculas.*

*The north-facing Vaujany sector is particularly interesting for experienced off-piste enthusiasts. Route finding can be very tricky, and huge cliffs and rock bands mean this is not a place in which to get lost. From the top of Pic Blanc, a 40-minute hike takes you to Col de la Pyramide at 3250m, the starting point for the classic route **La Pyramide** with a vertical of over 2000m. Once at the bottom of the long and wide Pyramide snowfield, you can link into the Vaujany pistes.*

↑ A great view of a
small part of the ski
area – with the main
village left of centre
and the old village of
Huez below
LAURENT SALINO / ALPE D'HUEZ
TOURISME

gondola is highly recommended by
reporters. Shopping is not impressive.
The helicopter excursion to Les Deux-
Alpes is exciting and there are scenic
aeroplane flights too.

There are 35km of well-marked
local walkers' trails (map available);
and there's a special lift pass for
pedestrians. The better mountain
restaurants are widely spread, so
meetings with skiing friends may not
work well. There are 'good' weekly
organ concerts in the 'interesting
church', and there's a museum.

LINKED RESORT – 1500m

VILLARD-RECULAS

Villard-Reculas is a tiny unspoiled
village just over the hill (Signal) from
Alpe-d'Huez, and set on a small shelf
between open snowfields above and
tree-filled hillsides below. A fast quad
takes you up to Signal from Villard-
Reculas, but the return lifts are slow.

Villard-Reculas is the tiniest resort
we have stayed in: one restaurant, one
shop-cum-restaurant, two sports
shops. If you don't like ski resorts, this
is just the place. On the other hand, a
recent reporter called it 'the most
boring resort I have been to'.

Although the village is small, its
chalets are spread widely, and
practically everyone needs transport to
the lifts. There is a shuttle-bus but we
hear it gets crowded.

Accommodation is mainly self-
catering, booked either through the
tourist office or La Source – an
English-run agency. We were impressed
by the little apartment we stayed in a
few seasons ago, owned by the
community.

La Source also runs an eponymous
catered chalet – a carefully converted
stone building with a lovely, spacious,
vaulted living room at the bottom
opening on to a terrace (complete with
hot tub) giving knockout views. It is
warmly furnished with armchairs and
sofas, and a wood-burning stove. Food
is excellent, and there's a minibus to
the lifts. We have had several good
reports from readers, too.

The local slopes have something
for everyone. For beginners, it may
seem near-ideal, with several lifts
serving green runs at village level.
Sadly, these runs are mostly of blue
gradient; a recent reporter who agreed
with that assessment also pointed out
that they get icy (from afternoon sun).
The blue runs in both directions from
Signal are also not entirely easy,
especially when icy. So Villard-Reculas
is less than ideal for novices. For
confident intermediates, it's fine. And
there is challenging skiing on and off
the Forêt black piste from Signal. The
tiny branch of the ESF gave a recent
reporter 'good' lessons.

LINKED RESORT – 1350m

OZ-EN-OISANS STATION

The small purpose-built ski station
above the old village of the same
name has been built in an attractive
style, with much use of wood and
stone, and has nursery slopes, skating
rink, bars, restaurants, supermarket
and two mid-range hotels. The pool in
the Villages Club du Soleil is open to
all. But nightlife is quiet.

The slopes above Oz are about the
best in the area when snow is falling.
Two gondolas whisk you out of the
resort: one goes to L'Alpette, above
Vaujany; the other goes in two stages
to the mid-station of the DMC above
Alpe-d'Huez.

The smart Chalet des Neiges
apartments have a pool, sauna, fitness
area, bar and restaurant. Available via
Peak Retreats (who also feature
detached chalets), Lagrange and
Erna Low.

GETTING THERE

Air Grenoble, 105km/
65 miles (1hr30);
Chambéry, 130km/
80 miles (1hr45);
Lyon 155km/95 miles
(2hr); Geneva 215km/
135 miles (2hr45)

Rail Grenoble (63km/
39 miles); daily buses
from station

TOURIST OFFICE

www.alpedhuez.com

Like the resort?
You'll love our handpicked accommodation
02392 839 310
PEAKRETREATS.CO.UK
ABTA
ABTA No.W5537

Vaujany, a unique village resort with amazing amenities.

● Very affordable, less commercial than the Savoie resorts.
● Sharing world class skiing of Alpe d'Huez 3300m-1100m.
● Ski Peak are the exclusive specialists to Vaujany offering a comprehensive service and award winning accommodation.

Ski Peak   Tel: 01428 608070   www.skipeak.com

LINKED RESORT – 1600m

AURIS-EN-OISANS

Auris-en-Oisans is another small, purpose-built ski station – a series of wood-clad, chalet-style apartment blocks with a few shops, bars and restaurants set just above the treeline. Quite appealing to families. It is set to be expanded if the link to Les Deux Alpes goes ahead, because the cross-valley lift is due to start from here.

Balcons d'Aurea is new 4-star residence for 2015/16 with pool, sauna and steam room – available through Peak Retreats and Erna Low.

LINKED RESORT – 1250m

VAUJANY

Vaujany is a quiet village that has expanded over the years, perched on a sunny hillside opposite its own sector of the domain. Hydroelectricity riches have financed huge investment in infrastructure.

A 160-person two-stage cable car whisks you up into the heart of the Alpe-d'Huez lift system. Alternatively, a two-stage gondola takes you less dramatically to the local slopes at Montfrais via a mid-station below the tiny hamlet of La Villette.

Ski Peak has four luxurious catered chalets in Vaujany and La Villette, including its flagship Chalet Saskia with east and west wings with five bedrooms in each, top-notch food, panoramic views and a luxury spa including an outdoor hot tub. It also has a catered apartment some 4-star self-catered apartments with two to five bedrooms. It runs a minibus service for guests.

Peak Retreats (no relation) has a wide choice of apartments, some with pool, sauna and steam room, including the 4-star Crystal Blanc which is new for 2015/16; Erna Low features this and other apartments too.

There is a recently built complex set around a small pedestrian square, Place Centre Village, with spacious, mid-range apartments built in traditional style. There's a good ski shop, restaurants, food shops, a cafe/bar and a cavernous underground car park – and an escalator down to the nearby cable car and gondola stations. An elevator takes you further down the hill to the 'extraordinarily large' sports centre with a pool with a big slide, an ice rink and a bowling alley.

An impressive enclosed escalator goes up the hillside past chalets and farm buildings to the top of the village, where sizeable apartment buildings are grouped around the Place de la Fare – a small car-free zone with a small supermarket, a food shop, a couple of bars and a couple of restaurants. Since most of the visitor beds are up here, it is naturally the focus of evening activity.

There are no slopes leading directly to the village. But there is a 'pulse' gondola up from L'Enversin, below the village, where the Fare black run finishes (a great run and not steep – read 'For experts' earlier in this chapter), or you can take a blue to the mid-station of the Montfrais gondola and ride down the lower stage.

Beginner children are taken to a gentle roped-off area at the top of the gondola – 'suited our children' says a recent visitor – and adult beginners to the nursery slope at Alpette, the cable car mid-station. There's a self-service restaurant with sunny terrace right by the children's learning area. The ESF children's ski school has been praised ('small classes'), as has the nursery ('as good as it gets, good English spoken, not expensive'). The adult ESF got the thumbs up last year too.

The Heritage Museum displays 100 years of Vaujany's history.

TOURIST OFFICES

Villard-Reculas
www.villard-reculas.com

Oz-en-Oisans
www.oz-en-oisans.com

Auris-en-Oisans
www.auris-en-oisans.com

Vaujany
www.vaujany.com

SNOWPIX.COM / CHRIS GILL

Les Arcs

Three first-generation purpose-built villages plus a couple of attractive alternatives set among varied and extensive slopes

£105
RESORT PRICE INDEX

RATINGS

The mountains

Extent	★★★
Fast lifts	★★★★
Queues	★★★
Terrain p'ks	★★★★
Snow	★★★★
Expert	★★★★★
Intermediate	★★★★
Beginner	★★★
Boarder	★★★★
X-country	★★
Restaurants	★★★
Schools	★★★★
Families	★★★★

The resort

Charm	★★
Convenience	★★★★
Scenery	★★★
Eating out	★★★
Après-ski	★★
Off-slope	★

NEWS

2015/16: There's good news for Le Chantel (where a couple of the best residences are set). A new mini cable car will link this area to 1800. And a new six-pack will go from here up to Col des Frettes, on the ridge above Arc 2000.

2014/15: Immediately above 1800 a new activity zone was built, Mille 8, with a short gondola serving a winding piste, a fun slope and a toboggan run; a new beginner area with moving carpet and a new restaurant opened at the top; and a new kids' snow garden and an aquatic centre opened at the base.

- Varied slopes – on and off-piste
- Lots of genuinely challenging skiing
- Some excellent woodland runs
- Car-free, mainly convenient villages, including cute 1950
- Some quiet alternative bases
- Fast cable car link to La Plagne

- Arcs 1600, 1800 and 2000 lack charm, and aren't the most convenient of resorts either
- Fairly quiet nightlife
- Some flat linking runs
- Accommodation in high villages is nearly all in apartments

We've always liked Les Arcs' slopes: they offer long descents, plenty of steep stuff, plenty to keep intermediates happy, plus woods to head to in a storm. And for those who really like to travel on skis, the link to La Plagne takes the amount of skiing into the Three Valleys league.

We've never been keen on the functional main villages. We're aware that their various architectural styles are highly regarded by some; we're not among them, but our real objection is to their dreary mall-style shopping centres. Newer Arc 1950 is something else: a resort that's not only more pleasant to inhabit than the others, but also very conveniently arranged. There are attractive developments on the slopes above Arc 1800. And Peisey-Vallandry is a quiet, attractive and convenient base for exploring the La Plagne ski area as well as this one – right next to the linking cable car.

THE RESORT

Les Arcs is made up of four modern resort units, all purpose-built, traffic-free and apartment-dominated.

Arcs 1600 and 1800 stand a couple of km apart, roughly at the treeline on a broad, steepish mountainside overlooking the town of Bourg-St-Maurice (covered at the end of this chapter). Both consist mainly of large apartment blocks sitting below their slopes, with some development beside the slopes. 1600 was the first Arc, built at the top of a funicular up from Bourg. 1800 is much the largest Arc, and recently has been expanding up the hillside.

Quite separate from those two, Arcs 2000 and 1950 are close neighbours on the far side of the mountain ridge, at the bottom of a high, treeless bowl. Arc 2000 consists of half a dozen huge, linked apartment blocks, plus more recently built chalet-style blocks. Just below it and linked by a short gondola, the mini-village of Arc 1950 was built from scratch by IntraWest (of Whistler fame) in traditional style, opening its doors in 2003.

The numbers in the village names relate only loosely to their altitudes. The name 'Arc 2000' was dreamt up in the 60s to evoke the future – the distant millennium; the altitude of the village is actually over 2100m.

At the southern end of the area is

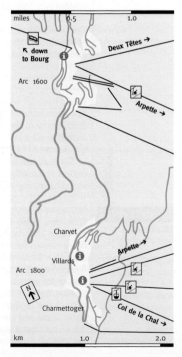

KEY FACTS

Resort	1600-2120m
	5,250-6,960ft
Slopes	1200-3225m
	3,940-10,580ft
Lifts	51
Pistes	200km
	124 miles

Paradiski area	
Slopes	1200-3250m
	3,940-10,660ft
Lifts	141
Pistes	425km
	264 miles

WWW.TRISTANSHU.COM

Much of the most challenging skiing is on the shoulders of the Aiguille Rouge, above Arc 2000 ↓

Peisey-Vallandry, from where a cable car links with La Plagne, covered by the Paradiski passes. Even from Arc 1950 you can reach this cable car in 20 minutes. Peisey-Vallandry is described at the end of the chapter. At the northern end of the ski area, at much lower altitude, is the rustic hamlet of Villaroger.

Day trips by car to Val d'Isère–Tignes are possible. La Rosière and Ste-Foy-Tarentaise are closer. If taking a car, be warned: you have to pay for parking at Arcs 1950 and 2000 – the only free parking is throughout 1600 and before the entrance to 1800. And we hear there is no longer free parking at the valley station of the funicular.

VILLAGE CHARM ★★★★★
Head for 1950
The apartment blocks of Arcs 1600 and 1800 are low-rise, and not hugely intrusive when seen from the slopes. Arc 1600 is set in the trees and has a friendly, small-scale atmosphere. Bigger Arc 1800 has three main parts. Le Charvet and Les Villards are focused on small shopping centres, mostly open-air but still seeming claustrophobic. Big apartment blocks run across and down the mountain. Charmettoger has apartment blocks, too, but also smaller, wood-clad buildings. Le Charvet has recently spread up the hill, and now has an upmarket suburb, Le Chantel.

Arc 2000 consists of futuristic large blocks with swooping roof lines, plus some large chalet-style blocks.

Arc 1950 has been designed to be cute; its smaller apartment buildings have been finished in traditional style, and they are clustered around a pleasant, traffic-free square and streets – quite lively at close of play.

Reporters repeatedly comment on the friendliness of the locals.

CONVENIENCE ★★★★★
Generally very good
Arcs 1600 and 1800 offer some very convenient lodgings a few yards from the lifts, but also some that are less convenient than they look – you can walk miles within the apartment buildings to get to (and from) the snow. The central area in Arc 1600 is good for families: uncrowded, compact, and set on even ground. Arc 1800 is more spread out, and some of the best lodgings are up the hill at Le Chantel. Highest of all is the newish Edenarc development. These high developments are a bit isolated, but a mini cable car up to this area will open for 2015/16. The main lifts depart from Les Villards. A 2013 visitor found 'the 1600/1800 buses run to a pretty strict timetable, and are generally

Les Arcs

SKIWORLD

Catered chalets, hotels and self catering apartments in

Europe, USA and Canada

skiworld.co.uk

08444 930 430

ABTA V2151 ATOL 2036

efficient, linking with the funicular timetable etc'.

Arc 2000 and Arc 1950 are compact, ski-in/ski-out places, with lifts starting below them as well as above. But getting around Arc 2000 on foot can be quite an effort and we've had reports of antiquated elevators out of action frequently. All the bits of Arc 1950 we've stayed in or looked at are genuinely ski-in/ski-out. You park directly under the apartment buildings, which is a distinct bonus at the start and end of your stay.

SCENERY ★★★☆☆
Attractively varied

Arcs 1600 and 1800, and the slopes, enjoy views across the valley to Mont Blanc. The lower villages enjoy good views along the Nancroix valley and to La Plagne's splendid north face of Bellecôte. Higher up, Arc 2000 and Arc 1950 sit beneath the Aiguille Rouge, high point of the slopes – great views from the top.

THE MOUNTAINS

Les Arcs' terrain is very varied; it has a good mixture of high, open, snow-sure slopes and lower woodland runs.

EXTENT OF THE SLOPES ★★★☆☆
Well planned and varied

Our ★★★ rating relates to just the Les Arcs area; the whole Paradiski area easily scores five stars.

Arc 1600 and Arc 1800 share a west-facing mountainside accessed by fast lifts out of each village and laced with runs down to one or the other. At the southern end is an area of woodland runs above Peisey-Vallandry, with lots of linking runs.

The new Mille 8 area at the 1800 base is a neat idea – extending the skiing day to 7.30pm in a safe and interesting area with a short winding blue piste, a 'fun slope' with obstacles and a powerful lift. It also has a toboggan run, and a new beginner area at the top.

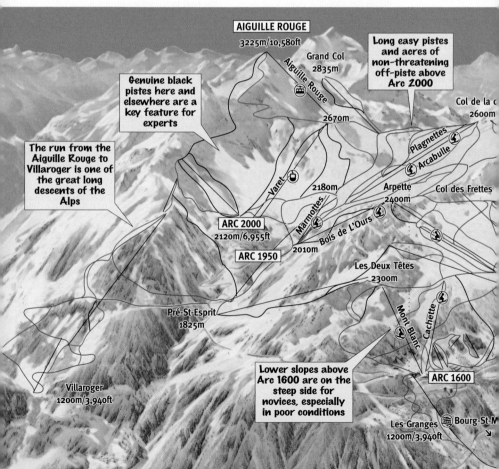

www.ski-i.com

ski independence

Call the Tailor-made Ski Specialists

0131 243 8097

Club Med

THE MOST COMPREHENSIVE
SKI PACKAGE ON THE MARKET

Arcs Extreme 3

020 8313 3999
Skiline.co.uk

Skiline co.uk

From various points on the ridge above 1600 and 1800 you can head down into the wide and mainly gentle Arc 2000 bowl. From there, lifts take you to the high points of the area, the Aiguille Rouge and the Grand Col. As well as a variety of steep runs back to Arc 2000, the Aiguille Rouge is the start of an epic black/red run (over 2000m vertical – one of the biggest anywhere – and 7km long) down to the tiny unspoiled village of Villaroger.

The resort identifies nine black runs and one red as Natur' runs which means they are never groomed – more about this later. On the lower half of the Aiguille Rouge is a speed-skiing run, used in the Albertville Olympics, which is sometimes open to the public.

On Thursdays outside high season the First Tracks scheme (10 euros) allows you up the mountain an hour early to ski deserted pistes.

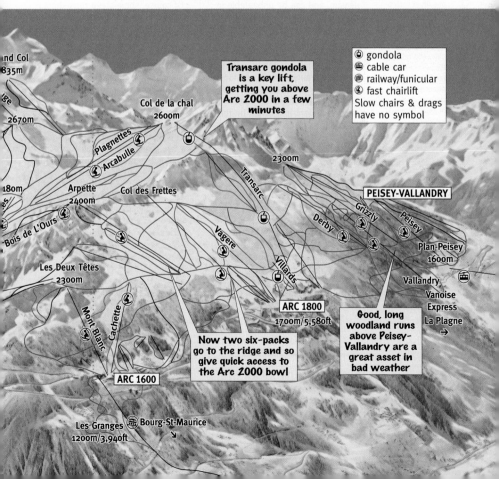

Transarc gondola is a key lift, getting you above Arc 2000 in a few minutes

Col de la chal 2600m

nd Col 835m

ge

2670m

Plagnettes
Arcabulle

180m

Arpette 2400m

Col des Frettes

Bois de L'Ours

Transarc

2300m

Vagere

Villards

PEISEY-VALLANDRY

Grizzly

Derby

Peisey

Plan-Peisey 1600m

gondola
cable car
railway/funicular
fast chairlift
Slow chairs & drags have no symbol

Les Deux Têtes 2300m

Cachette

Mont Blanc

ARC 1600

ARC 1800
1700m/5,58oft

Now two six-packs go to the ridge and so give quick access to the Arc 2000 bowl

Good, long woodland runs above Peisey-Vallandry are a great asset in bad weather

Vallandry

Vanoise Express La Plagne →

Les Granges 1200m/3,940ft

Bourg-St-Maurice

LAGRANGE Prestige

High-standard
Self-catering
Apartments

020 7371 6111
lagrange-holidays.co.uk

LIFT PASSES

Les Arcs / Peisey-Vallandry

Prices in €

Age	6-day
under 14	192
14 to 64	245
65 to 71	192

Free Under 6
Beginner Some free lifts – read the main text. Points card for one lift in each of Arcs 1600/1800/2000
Senior 72 plus: 1-15 days €7
Notes Options: half-day pass; one-day Paradiski extension; family reductions
Alternative pass Découverte pass with one-day Paradiski extension

Paradiski Unlimited

Prices in €

Age	6-day
under 14	223
14 to 64	285
65 plus	223

Free Under 6
Senior 72 plus: 1-15 days €10
Notes Covers Les Arcs and La Plagne areas; family reductions

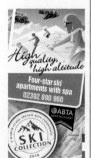

High quality, high altitude
Four-star ski apartments with spa
02392 890 960
ABTA
SKI COLLECTION

FRANCE

210

FAST LIFTS ★★★★
Generally good
Each of the four main villages and Peisey-Vallandry have fast chair or gondola access to the slopes, and most of the lifts higher up are fast, too. The main irritants now are all in the same area, on the left of the map: the slow chairs above Villaroger and the two chairs up in different directions from Pré-St-Esprit.

QUEUES ★★★
Not without problems
Queues aren't generally an issue in low season, and peak-time queues are improving. But the lifts above Arc 2000 present problems, especially on sunny days. The Varet gondola to the shoulder of the Aiguille Rouge shifts its queue quickly because it has lifties pulling people out of the queue to fill the cabins – excellent; but the waits can be non-trivial despite this. Queues for the Aiguille Rouge cable car can be serious in clear weather, even in low season, and can be unbearable in peak weeks. The lift dates from 1981, holds only 70 people and shifts only 1100 people an hour; it clearly needs to be replaced by a jumbo. The Arcabulle chair has the potential for 'five-to-ten-minute waits'. At 1800 the Transarc gondola is queue-prone, especially late in the day ('often a mega bun-fight just to get on the boarding platform'); but an alternative route is possible. At Plan-Peisey, queues for the Peisey chair (and for the Derby higher up) are not unknown, partly because of arrivals on the cable car from La Plagne.

TERRAIN PARKS ★★★★
One excellent park
The Apocalypse Parc is between Arcs 1600 and 1800, and is served by a snowboarder-friendly J-bar lift. For years, this has been one of the most advanced parks in the Alps – on a par with the main park at Avoriaz. 'It's getting better every season,' a reporter observes. But: 'all it lacks is a half-pipe', another notes.
There are snowcross runs below Col de la Chal and above Plan-Peisey.

SNOW RELIABILITY ★★★★
Good – plenty of high runs
A high percentage of the runs are above 2000m, and when necessary you can stay high by using lifts that start around that altitude. Most of the slopes face roughly west, which is not ideal. Those from the Col de la Chal and the long runs down to Villaroger are north-facing, and the blacks on the Aiguille Rouge are shady enough to keep their snow well.

FOR EXPERTS ★★★★★
Challenges on- and off-piste
Les Arcs has a lot to offer experts – at least when the high lifts are open (the Aiguille Rouge cable car, in particular, is often shut in bad weather).
The several shady black runs on the Aiguille Rouge, reached mostly from the Varet gondola, are excellent. It's a shame that a couple of other slopes reached from the cable car are no longer pistes. The runs down to Pré-St-Esprit are good, too, and merit their black classification.
Most black runs are permanently ungroomed Natur' runs, which is fine for mogul enthusiasts but in practice means that for large parts of the season few people tackle the blacks. Of course, some steep runs should remain ungroomed – perhaps most – but we think more grooming would be good (not least to give a chance of that ultimate piste delight, deep fresh snow on a steep groomed base). Other resorts strike a better balance.
Unskiable blacks naturally lead to busy reds. One of the quieter reds (and one of our favourites) is the lower part of the epic Aiguille Rouge-Villaroger run, which has remarkably varying terrain.
There is also a great deal of off-piste potential. There are steep pitches on the front face of the Aiguille Rouge and secluded runs on the back side, towards Villaroger. A short climb to the Grand Col accesses several routes, including a quite serious couloir and an easier option. From Col de la Chal there is an easy route down towards Nancroix. The wooded slopes above 1600 are another attractive possibility and there are open slopes beside the pistes all over the place.

FOR INTERMEDIATES ★★★★
Plenty for all abilities
It's an excellent intermediate area, with intimidating terrain pretty much confined to distinct slopes above Arc 2000. But Malgovert, from Les Deux Têtes towards Arc 1600, is a red Natur' piste and is tricky – it is narrow, as well as mogulled. One particular strength of the area is that most main

↑ 1800 looks like it is conveniently laid out, but some apartment blocks stretch a long way from the front de neige shown here
LES ARCS TO

routes have easy and more difficult alternatives, making it good for mixed-ability groups.

Strong intermediates shouldn't shy away from the blacks when in good condition – most are not scarily steep. The long run to Villaroger is very rewarding. The woodland runs at either end of the domain, above Peisey-Vallandry and Villaroger, and the bumpy Cachette red down to 1600, also include some challenges. We especially like the Peisey-Vallandry area: its well-groomed, treelined runs have a very friendly feel and are remarkably uncrowded much of the time, allowing great fast cruising.

The lower half of the mountainside above 1600/1800 is great for mixed-ability groups, with a choice of routes through the trees. The red runs from Arpette and Col des Frettes towards 1800 are quite steep but usually well groomed (except Clair Blanc). They get a new fast chairlift this year.

Cautious intermediates have plenty of blue cruising terrain. Many of the runs around 2000 are rather bland and prone to overcrowding. Edelweiss is more interesting, with a short red alternative, and takes you to Arc 1950 from Col des Frettes. The blues above 1800 are attractive but also crowded. A blue favourite of ours is Renard, high above Vallandry – usually with excellent snow.

And, of course, you have the whole of La Plagne's slopes to explore.

FOR BEGINNERS ★★★★★
No long greens
There are 'ski tranquille' beginner zones at each of the three main Arcs, and up the hill on the treeline above Vallandry and Plan-Peisey. There are about 10 free beginner lifts in 1800, 2000 and Villaroger; 1600, which seems to lack them, is in any case a bit steep. Additional chairs are free at weekends – you can buy a points card to use them during the week. Sadly, the resort does not use the valuable green run classification used by most other French resorts. In all sectors there are long, wide blue runs to move on to, and some are gentle enough to be green – eg Forêt down to Vallandry ('a beginner's dream'). Much of the Arc 2000 bowl is also great progression territory.

FOR BOARDERS ★★★★★
A pioneering place
Ever since 1983 when Regis Rolland introduced the sport in the cult film Apocalypse Snow, Les Arcs has been a hot spot for snowboarders. It offers excellent freeriding, and there are plenty of wide-open rolling slopes for intermediates and beginners too, especially at Vallandry and 1800. The terrain park is great and is served by a snowboarder-friendly draglift. Most other lifts are chairs and gondolas. But beware long flat areas – especially at Arc 2000 – and some linking blue runs (you may prefer the wider reds).

Ski Total

WELCOME YOU TO
Les Arcs

Quality chalets
Excellent value
19 resorts
across the Alps

skitotal.com
01483 791 933

Down at Pré-St-Esprit, the 500-year-old Belliou la Fumée is set beside a car park, but it is charmingly rustic; we get few reports. The Ferme, at Villaroger, a cosy self-service place, gets good reports – 'friendly people, huge portions'.

Above 1800, the little Blanche Murée is a simple table-service chalet praised for value and dishes such as wild boar with gratin dauphinois. Higher up, the Arpette pleases most reporters – 'mainly fast food but well cooked and big quantities'.

Above 1600, a reporter this year enjoyed the sofas at Au Sanglier qui Fume, but we lack reports on the food.

Above Plan-Peisey, the busy Cordée was endorsed again in 2014. Reports on the Enfants Terribles (the tarted up Poudreuse) are a bit mixed these days.

FOR CROSS-COUNTRY ★★★★★
Very boring locally

Short trails, mostly on roads, is all you can expect, but the pretty Nancroix valley's 40km of pleasant trails are accessible by free bus.

MOUNTAIN RESTAURANTS ★★★★★
Steadily improving

The range and quality of restaurants is gradually improving, but still can't be considered a positive feature.
Editors' choice Chalet du Solliet above Villaroger is a charming woody chalet with a warm ambience, table- or self-service of good food and great views. Readers endorse our recommendation – 'Best mountain restaurant we visited by a large margin,' said one reporter last year. 'Fantastic,' says an endorsing reporter this year.
Worth knowing about Chalets de l'Arc, just above Arc 2000, is a rustic place built in wood and stone. Recently restored to our good books after some dodgy years, it impressed one reporter this year with 'good food and service from very friendly staff'; another who thought it generally excellent had to put up with very slow service, though. La Crèche at Col de la Chal is a routine self-service place but it does have a 'fantastic terrace' as well as 'friendly staff'. The other good options in this sector are not very mountainous.

SCHOOLS AND GUIDES ★★★★★
Several, including a Brit school

British school New Generation has been consistently recommended over many years. The ESF branch here is evidently not in the forefront of the reform movement: 'On est en France, on parle Français!' was how one instructor justified his lack of English last year.

FOR FAMILIES ★★★★★
Convenient choices

Les Arcs is a good choice for families wanting convenience, with lots of slope-side lodgings. The new Mille 8 area at 1800 is a great innovation, giving kids something active to do after they've had their tea, and it has an excellent leisure pool at the base as well as skiing and tobogganing. Arc 1950 has a family-friendly layout and also has a good programme of kids' activities.

Family specialist tour op Esprit has ten chalet units in Arc 2000 and six in Peisey-Vallandry.

LES ARCS TO

Monstrous Arc 2000 represented the future when it was built; but the future turned out to be chalet-style Arc 1950, below it ↓

STAYING THERE

Most resort beds are in apartments. There is a long-established Club Med presence in Arc 2000 and there's a smarter one, built more recently in chalet style, at Peisey-Vallandry.

Chalets There are lots of catered chalets in the Peisey-Vallandry area, handy for the link to La Plagne – covered at the end of this chapter. There are also lots of apartments operated as catered chalets in smart residences with pools in Arc 2000 – operators include Ski Total, Inghams, Crystal and family specialist Esprit. Skiworld operates a couple of units, and also has a couple of proper individual chalets above 1800.

Hotels The choice of hotels in Les Arcs is not wide, but it is better than in some other purpose-built resorts. More hotel reports welcome.

****Aiguille Grive (1800) Cool wood-and-glass place just above the village, with rooms and six separate chalets.

***Arcadien (1600) Tipped by a repeat visitor – 'great: solid breakfast, big rooms, good people'.

***Cachette (1600) Two reports this year endorsing this central place – 'friendly, good value, good food and superb position'.

Apartments In the older resort units there are still plenty of cramped apartments where a family of four needs to book an apartment nominally for eight, but now there are lots of good, modern apartments available through the many operators and agents that advertise with us.

All the residences in 1950 are worth considering. The Manoir Savoie, one of the several residences operated by Radisson Blu, was tipped last year – 'excellent: cosy apartment, warm outdoor pool, nice hot tub'. Pierre & Vacances operate the other 1950 residences under their Premium brand, and we've stayed happily in several.

Above 1800, Alpages de Chantel is another Premium property with pool etc – very convenient for skiing and sledging, and now much less isolated because of the new shuttle lift linking this area to the centre of 1800. Edenarc, just above here, looks attractive, with indoor/outdoor pool, spa and fitness room.

The Roc Belle Face development in central 1600, built in tiers down the hillside, is a Lagrange Prestige property, with a small pool.

SKI AMIS

Catered Chalets in Superb Locations

020 3411 5439
www.skiamis.com

EATING OUT ★★★
Mostly uninspiring
An ad-based (therefore not comprehensive) guide is given away locally. The choice is generally uninspiring. One of the best places is Chalet de l'Arcelle on the fringe of Arc 1600; it has a warm, quirky wood and stone interior and a mouth-watering carte; and 'you can't fault them for value for money' says our latest reporter. Also in 1600, the Cairn is 'wood-panelled, with prompt, friendly service' and serves Italian as well as Savoyard dishes.

Arcs 1800 and 2000 have an adequate range of places, but none worth singling out.

Arc 1950 has a reasonable choice for a small place, but demand exceeds supply. The newish Vache Rouge offers 'very friendly staff' serving 'great food including the best ever frites'. Also tipped are Brasserie 1950 for 'good food', but erratic service, La Table des Lys and Chalet de Luigi.

APRES-SKI ★★
Arc 1800 is the place to be
Nightlife is not lively and mainly revolves around the bars. 1800 is the liveliest; some places have regular live music. The cosy Etranger is 'the place to go' and is popular with instructors says a regular. Chez Boubou at Charvet is more British and shows Premiership football matches. There are, of course, bars in the other resort units, but we get only a trickle of reports.

OFF THE SLOPES ★
Very limited
The new Mille 8 area, at the foot of the slopes at 1800, opened in December 2014. It is open in the early evening, and includes a leisure pool. Several of the newer apartment blocks have pools, and there are 'excellent' spa facilities at the Sources de Marie

Les Arcs

213

Like the resort?

You'll love our handpicked accommodation

02392 839 310

PEAKRETREATS.CO.UK

ABTA No.W5637

Club Med Ψ.

THE MOST COMPREHENSIVE
SKI PACKAGE ON THE MARKET

Peisey-Vallandry 4Ψ

020 8313 3999
Skiline.co.uk

Skiline co.uk

in Arc 1950. There's bowling at 1800 and skating at 1800 and 2000. The cinemas have English films weekly. You can visit the Beaufort cheese dairy or go shopping in Bourg-St-Maurice. The resort is 'great for hiking non-skiers', says a relieved reporter who took his non-skiing wife: 'She had a wonderful time – she could easily make it to mountain restaurants like La Crèche, and walks between the various parts of Les Arcs are plentiful.'

LINKED RESORT – 1600m
PEISEY-VALLANDRY

Plan-Peisey and Vallandry are small ski stations built in a traditional chalet style above the old village of Peisey, which has a bucket-lift up to Plan-Peisey. They sell themselves as Peisey-Vallandry, but the local cluster of villages, including one called Nancroix, is collectively known as Peisey-Nancroix. So that's clear, eh?

Both resorts have good nursery slopes high up the hill on the treeline, reached by chairlift. Of course, this means paying to get up there. The local ESF gets good reports.

The cross-valley cable car link to Montchavin and La Plagne starts from **Plan-Peisey** – one hotel, a few shops, bars and restaurants but no real focus other than the lift station. A six-pack takes you to the local slopes.

UK operator Ski Amis has a 'premium service' chalet here with a hot tub (and several self-catered chalets and apartments). Family specialist operator Esprit has six neat chalets, each with outdoor hot tub and sauna or steam room – 'brilliant location, very comfortable', said a recent reporter. The hotel Vanoise has a good location, a pool and a fitness room, and gets good reports. The Arollaie is a Lagrange Prestige apartment development, with a small pool, hot tub, spa.

For a meal out, we'd head down to the Ancolie at Nancroix – a fabulous traditional auberge with welcoming hosts and excellent food. (Beware taxi rip-offs for the short journey, though.) Of the local places, reporters like the Vache ('small and friendly, English-run') and Chez Felix ('good old-fashioned food done well, family-friendly'). The Solan is nicely rustic and has been tipped in the past. Après-ski is very quiet, but a recent visitor liked L'Armoise in Peisey ('a quiet little French bar') and Au Planté du Bâton in Plan-Peisey ('a great fun quiz night and happy hour').

There is lodging down the hill in the characterful old village of **Peisey**,

---

Selected chalet in Peisey-Vallandry   ADVERTISEMENT

SKI AMIS *www.skiamis.com*   T **0203 411 5439**

↑ CHALET SERMOZ

- Premium service chalet to sleep 14-16 people
- Outside hot-tub
- Excellent catering with full English breakfast every day, afternoon tea and four course evening meal
- Pre-dinner drinks, canapés, after dinner liqueurs
- Unlimited good quality wine
- Excellent access to Les Arcs and La Plagne

sales@skiamis.com

SKI AMIS

CHALET SERMOZ ↑

ESPRIT
FOR FAMILIES IN
Peisey-Les Arcs
Family
Ski Chalets
Dedicated
Nurseries
Exclusive Ski
Classes
13 resorts
across the Alps

espritski.com
01483 791 900

complete with fine baroque church. The other, mostly old, buildings include a few shops and a couple of bars and restaurants – a reader enjoyed the Ormelune. A 2013 reader enjoyed staying at The Goat Shed, a 'simple but welcoming' catered chalet on the outskirts run by a British couple. For this season Skiworld is adding a 22-bed chalet 10 minutes' walk from the village.

Vallandry is a few hundred metres away from Plan-Peisey and linked by shuttle-bus. A fast quad takes you into the slopes. There are lots of chalets and a small pedestrian-only square at the foot of the slopes with a small supermarket and a ski shop.

Ski Olympic has a big piste-side chalet hotel here – La Forêt; 'really good communal areas and terrace with bar and great views'. Orée des Cimes is a smart CGH apartment complex right by the Grizzly chairlift, with a pool, hot tubs and spa. Orée des Neiges is another luxury apartment development with free use of the Cimes' pool etc, 1.3km away. Both developments are available through several of our advertisers.

There are several restaurants. Newly tipped this year are La Bergerie de Raphaël, for 'fantastic posh French food, good value' and the Rilax – 'busy, friendly front-de-neige coffee and lunch place'. Le Refuge does 'good pizzas'. The Mont Blanc is a Brit bar which may have footie on the TV.

DOWN-VALLEY RESORT – 850m

BOURG-ST-MAURICE

With a funicular railway link to Arc 1600, Bourg-St-Maurice is marketed as part of Les Arcs, and does make a viable cheaper alternative to staying on the hill. Not surprisingly, it is very different – it is not a ski resort, but a real valley town, with proper everyday shops and sizeable supermarkets. It is at the end of the TGV railway line, and therefore is very appealing to rail travellers.

The funicular station is a walkable distance from the TGV platforms, but a drive or bus ride from most parts of Bourg. The advertised travel time to Arc 1600 is seven minutes, but that's for non-stop services, which in our experience are rare. In practice, staying in Bourg rather than Les Arcs costs you an hour a day in travelling time.

The plus side, of course, is that everything, from accommodation to beer, is cheaper. Depending on the time of the season and the exact comparison you make, you can rent an apartment for 30% to 60% off the cost of a similar apartment on the hill. If you plan to ski Les Arcs (and La Plagne), you simply need to balance the cost savings against that lost hour every day.

But if you fancy a bit more variety, the appeal of Bourg-St-Maurice becomes more pronounced. We spent a week here a few years back and had a fab time skiing a different resort every day, from La Plagne to Val d'Isère. The more remote resorts are best accessed by car, though there are buses. But you can easily ski La Rosière (and linked La Thuile in Italy) by taking a bus to the chairlift above Séez, which goes up into the slopes of La Rosière (and saves you a long, winding drive up the hill).

The CGH Coeur d'Or apartments, with a good pool, hot tub and spa, are close to the two major supermarkets, and a walk from the town, but a drive (or free shuttle-bus ride) from the funicular. Our regular American reporter, who normally aims a bit higher in every sense, stayed here last season and was happy in the recently renovated 2-star hotel Angival, centrally set in a quiet back street – 'small beds in small room, but very friendly staff, adequate breakfast'.

Bourg has some good, unpretentious restaurants. We've enjoyed Le Refuge in the main street; 'Delicious, great service, always packed,' said a reporter in 2013, endorsed by the aforementioned Yank this year – 'wonderfully friendly service'. But the Yank's favourite was shellfish at Bistrot Alpin. We've had excellent meals at the Tsablo (also in the main street) and the Arssiban (just outside the centre).

Les Arcs

215

GETTING THERE

Air Chambéry 130km/ 80 miles (1hr45); Geneva 165km/ 100 miles (2hr30); Grenoble 195km/ 120 miles (2hr30); Lyon 205km/ 125 miles (2hr30)

Rail Bourg-St-Maurice; frequent buses and direct funicular to resort

TOURIST OFFICES

Les Arcs
www.lesarcs.com

Peisey-Vallandry
www.peisey-vallandry. com

Bourg-St-Maurice
www.bourgsaint maurice.com

SNOWPIX.COM / CHRIS GILL

Avoriaz

Arguably the definitive purpose-built resort: conveniently arranged, usually snowy, uncompromisingly traffic-free

£105
RESORT PRICE INDEX

RATINGS

The mountains

Extent	★★★★★
Fast lifts	★★★★
Queues	★★★
Terrain p'ks	★★★★★
Snow	★★★
Expert	★★★
Intermediate	★★★★
Beginner	★★★★
Boarder	★★★★★
X-country	★★★
Restaurants	★★★★
Schools	★★★
Families	★★★★

The resort

Charm	★★
Convenience	★★★★★
Scenery	★★★
Eating out	★★★
Après-ski	★★★
Off-slope	★

NEWS

2015/16: A new slope is due to be built near the Zore run in the Super-Morzine area. More snowmaking is planned.

2014/15: In the Super-Morzine area the Proclou and Seraussaix chairs were replaced with a six-pack each. The Stash terrain park was enlarged with a new slalom course and more features. The Dromonts hotel is under new ownership and was renovated in 60s style with a smart new spa and two restaurants. It's now a 4-star. The Kouria residence has been refurbished to create 16 luxury apartments. An igloo was built on the slopes with bedrooms, bar and ice grotto.

➕ Good position on the Portes du Soleil circuit, and good local slopes

➕ Very successful design – car-free, with ski-in/ski-out lodgings

➕ Good children's facilities

➕ Snow generally good and sometimes superb, but ...

➖ Low altitudes and exposure to westerlies mean some risk of poor snow lower down, and rain

➖ Architecture doesn't suit everyone

➖ Lacks a slick bag-delivery system

➖ Can get very crowded at weekends

➖ Hardly any hotels

Of the many purpose-built resorts thrown up in France in the 1960s, Avoriaz is probably the best designed. From most points of view, it works. One particularly neat trick is that the resort is sunny but most of the local slopes are shady.

Avoriaz missed out on the smart apartment developments that transformed French self-catering a decade or so ago, but it has recently more than caught up, with some fabulous new places. Now, how about a few more hotels?

THE RESORT

Avoriaz is a purpose-built resort perched on a sloping shelf above a dramatic high cliff a few km from lower, long-established Morzine.

It is entirely free of wheeled traffic; cars are left in paid-for parks at the edge of the village – book a space underground to avoid a chaotic departure if it snows (15 euros a day).

Avoriaz is on the main lift circuit of the Portes du Soleil – for an overview, look at our separate chapter. It has links to Châtel in one direction and to Champéry in Switzerland in the other. It is linked by gondola (but not by piste) to Morzine, which shares a separate area of slopes with Les Gets. All four of these linked resorts get their own chapters, and are covered by the Portes du Soleil pass.

The hamlets of Ardent and Les Prodains are on the fringes of the Avoriaz ski area with lifts into it. Both are described in this chapter. Car trips to Flaine and Chamonix are possible.

VILLAGE CHARM ★★
One of the best modern places
The village is all angular, dark, wood-clad, high-rise buildings – almost all apartments. It's not what you would call charming, but it is at least designed coherently.

What's more, the snow-covered paths and pistes give the resort a friendly Alpine feel, and both we and reporters have enjoyed the ambience, both day and night. Family-friendly

events are laid on all season. A floodlit cliff behind the resort adds to its nocturnal charm.

CONVENIENCE ★★★★★
Ready to drag that bag?
As our scale plan suggests, it's a compact place (turn to the Chamonix chapter for a stark contrast). While you are resident, it all works well. Mostly, you can ski from close to the door, and no door is more than 500m from the central shops and bars. Although the upper part of the village is set on a steep slope, escalators and elevators (not entirely reliable) inside the buildings help you get around.

But arrival day and (particularly) departure day are something else.

If you are staying in the new Amara development, you can park your car in the basement (assuming you can face the charges). And if you are staying in the Falaise quarter, near the reception building, you can drag your luggage to your apartment on a borrowed sled.

If you are staying elsewhere, it isn't

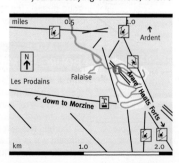

KEY FACTS

Resort	1800m
	5,910ft

Portes du Soleil

Slopes	950-2275m
	3,120-7,460ft
Lifts	196
Pistes	650km
	404 miles

Avoriaz only

Slopes	1100-2275m
	3,610-7,460ft
Lifts	36
Pistes	75km
	47 miles

AVORIAZ TO / STEVE SOLLY

Avoriaz has some of the highest, most snow-sure slopes in the Portes du Soleil. This is the Chavanette area ↓

so simple. Some lodgings are up to 800m from the drop-off point, which is a long way to drag your bags, especially if you hit deep, soft snow as we did a few winters ago. So you are probably going to need a ride on a snowcat or a horse-drawn sleigh, for which demand can exceed supply, particularly on departure day.

SCENERY ★★★☆☆
Cliff-top panorama
The village is high, and its position on a sunny balcony gives good views down across Morzine. From the high points there are great views of the Dents Blanches and the Dents du Midi.

THE MOUNTAINS

The slopes closest to Avoriaz are bleak and treeless, but fairly snow-sure.

The piste map divides the Avoriaz slopes into four sectors – beginner, family, forest and expert. We (and many reporters) think this is a nonsense – for example, the family sector includes three of the 'snowcross' runs (explained in the next sentence) and some tough reds. The map marks five runs – a blue, two reds and two blacks – as 'snowcross' runs (an unfortunate name as this is what we and many resorts now call 'boardercross' and 'skicross' courses in the interests of political correctness). These runs are marked and patrolled but ungroomed. We think the concept of red and blue runs that are never groomed is not to be encouraged; OK, leave them powdery after a snowfall but don't let huge bumps form so that intermediates avoid them. The map showing the full Portes du Soleil shows these runs as ordinary pistes.

Signposting is very good – a view endorsed by reporters.

EXTENT OF THE SLOPES ★★★★★
360° choice
The village has lifts and pistes fanning out in all directions. Facing the village are the slopes of **Arare-Hauts Forts**, and when snow is good, there are long, steep runs to Les Prodains, way below the resort, where a big gondola brings you back. To the left, lifts go off to the **Chavanette** sector on the Swiss border – a broad, undulating bowl. At the border is the infamous Swiss Wall – now an itinéraire. It's a long, steep mogul slope with a tricky start, but not the terror it is cracked up to be unless it's icy. You can ride the chair down. At the bottom is the open, gentle terrain of Champéry.

From the ridge behind Avoriaz you can descend into the prettily wooded **Lindarets-Brocheaux** valley, from where lifts go over to Châtel's Linga sector or up to Pointe de Mossettes, another way into Switzerland.

FAST LIFTS ★★★★☆
Good system here and at Linga
In the Avoriaz sector the lifts are impressively modern, as they are on the nearby Linga slopes on the way to Châtel. But beyond Châtel, and on the Swiss side of the Portes du Soleil, there are still lots of slow chairs and draglifts.

QUEUES ★★★☆☆
Still some problems
One long-standing problem – the queue to get up from Les Prodains, below the resort, when snow attracts crowds from Morzine – has been tackled by the replacement of the old cable car by a big gondola (and we mean big: cabins with 35 seats) – 'It's great, but the escalators at the Avoriaz

Inghams

AVORIAZ
▶ Spectacular family resort
▶ New catered chalet available - sleeps 10-14
▶ Fly from 12 UK airports

inghams.co.uk 01483 371 236 ABTA V4871 ATOL 0025

end don't always work,' warns a 2015 reporter. But some high-season reports speak of queues for the chairlifts from Les Lindarets (the valley between Avoriaz and Châtel) back to Avoriaz. You may also meet congestion on the runs down to Les Lindarets in the morning, especially when deep snow slows everyone down. Peak-time crowds on the pistes back to and around the village can be hazardous, too; one reporter found the concentration of kids during French holidays 'just foul'.

TERRAIN PARKS ★★★★★
Still leading the way
Avoriaz built the first terrain park in France, in 1993. It is still leading the way, and there are five parks and a super-pipe, all 'very well' maintained.

Check www.snowparkavoriaz.com for details. Park lift passes are available.

The expert park is at Arare, and the kicker and rail lines are superbly designed and shaped. It also has an airbag jump – 'The most fun I had all trip,' says a recent visitor. Beginners and intermediates should head to La Chapelle – a 500m-long park littered with jumps of all sizes and fun little boxes and rails. Parkway is great for beginners and kids. It has mini-jumps and ride-on boxes, with traffic lights for safety. The Stash, in the Lindarets valley has routes cut through the forest, and wooden and natural elements bring all-mountain riding and freestyle together; the area is great fun and was enlarged last season with a new slalom course and more features. The fifth park is the Lil'Stash – a mini version for younger kids. Just above the village is a good super-pipe. And there's a snowcross (that they call boardercross) too.

SNOW RELIABILITY ★★★☆☆
High resort, low slopes
Although Avoriaz itself is high, its slopes don't go much higher – and some parts of the Portes du Soleil circuit are much lower. But it has a good snow record; three seasons ago it got the most in the Alps – a staggering 11.8m (that's 465in, for comparison with places like Utah). And considering their altitude, the north-west-facing slopes below Hauts Forts and Chavanette hold snow well – much better than over the border on the sunnier Swiss slopes. But when snow is sparse, the smooth, grassy slopes of lower Morzine-Les Gets can deliver better conditions than the rocky ones around Avoriaz.

FOR EXPERTS ★★★☆☆
Several challenging runs
Tough terrain is scattered about. The challenging runs down from Hauts Forts to Les Prodains (including a World Cup downhill) are excellent. There is a tough red and several long, truly black runs, including one of the ungroomed so-called 'snowcross' runs we've talked about. The Swiss Wall from Chavanette (now an itinéraire) will naturally be on your agenda and there are worthwhile blacks on the Swiss side too. Châtel's Linga sector is well worth a trip. And there's plenty of good off-piste if you take a guide.

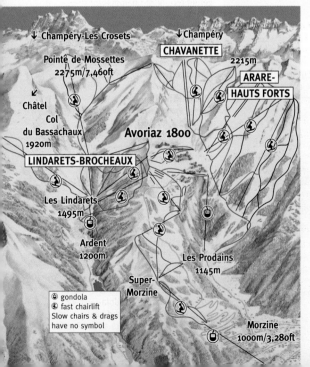

↓ Champéry-Les Crosets   ↓ Champéry

Pointe de Mossettes
2275m/7,460ft

CHAVANETTE   2215m

ARARE-HAUTS FORTS

Châtel
Col du Bassachaux
1920m

Avoriaz 1800

LINDARETS-BROCHEAUX

Les Lindarets
1495m

Ardent
1200m

Les Prodains
1145m

Super-Morzine

Morzine
1000m/3,280ft

☺ gondola
⊕ fast chairlift
Slow chairs & drags have no symbol

FOR INTERMEDIATES ★★★★
Virtually the whole area

Although some sections lack variety, the Portes du Soleil circuit through Châtel, Morgins and Champéry is excellent for all grades of intermediates, provided snow is in good supply on the lower slopes. Timid types not worried about pretty surroundings need not leave the Avoriaz sector: there are quiet and scenic blues to Les Prodains and at Super-Morzine. And the Arare and Chavanette sectors are gentle, spacious, above-the-treeline bowls. The Lindarets area is also easy, with pretty runs through the trees, but there are some long flat sections.

Further afield, Champoussin has a lot of easy runs, reached without too much difficulty via Les Crosets and Pointe de l'Au. Better intermediates have virtually the whole area at their disposal. The runs down to Pré-la-Joux and L'Essert on the way to Châtel, and those either side of Morgins, are particularly attractive – as are the long runs down to Grand-Paradis near Champéry when snow conditions allow. Pointe de Mossettes offers a less challenging route to Switzerland than the Swiss Wall itinéraire at Chavanette.

FOR BEGINNERS ★★★★
Convenient, but you pay

The nursery slopes seem small in relation to the size of the resort, but appear to cope. The slopes are sunny, yet good for snow, and link well to longer, easy runs. Our main reservation is that the pistes can be busy. There are no free lifts but there is a special beginners' lift pass.

FOR BOARDERS ★★★★★
Plenty to keep you busy all week

Avoriaz is great for intermediate and expert riders. As well as state-of-the-art 'conventional' parks, there's The Stash. For safe freeriding after a dump, head for the 'snowcross' runs. For something more extreme, the long cliff band accessed from the Arare lift is perfect for cliff drops of all sizes. It is well worth hiring a guide to exploit the off-piste riding. There are some flat sections to beware of, especially in the Lindarets valley but very few draglifts, making this a good choice for novices too.

PowderBeds.com
Ski Hotels & Apartments

FOR CROSS-COUNTRY ★★★
Varied, with some blacks

There are 38km of trails, mainly between Avoriaz and Super-Morzine, plus Lindarets and Montriond.

MOUNTAIN RESTAURANTS ★★★★
Good choice over the hill

There are some good places, marked but not named on the piste map.
Editors' choice The hamlet of Les Lindarets in the next valley consists of countless rustic restaurants – it is a popular tourist spot in summer. Our two favourites are the Terrasse on a sunny day and the jolly Crémaillière on a snowy one – the latter endorsed as 'charming; one of the best in Europe' by a reporter this year.
Worth knowing about A reporter raves about Les Alpages, just above Les Lindarets – 'ate there at least three times – huge and tasty steak with pepper sauce; such friendly service'. In the same area are the Barmettes with 'tasty crêpes and friendly service' and Mamo's Café ('very good soup', 'lovely Savoyard crêpe'). On the Super-Morzine slopes, L'Passage is 'superb, with a good atmosphere'.

SCHOOLS AND GUIDES ★★★
Positive reports

A recent reporter thought the ESF 'patient, helpful – and the cheapest'. But another observed 'classes averaging 12'. We lack up-to-date reports on the other schools.

FOR FAMILIES ★★★★
Very appealing

With snow everywhere and not a wheeled vehicle to be seen, Avoriaz has obvious appeal. Then there's the Village des Enfants, which takes children from age three. Its facilities are excellent. Check out the village of Ardent too, covered overleaf.

High quality, high altitude

Four-star ski apartments with spa
02392 890 960

ABTA

SKI COLLECTION

Catered Chalets
Morzine
9-24p

www.hostsavoie.co.uk

host savoie

Ski Total

WELCOME YOU TO
Avoriaz

Quality chalets
Excellent value
19 resorts
across the Alps

skitotal.com
01483 791 933

STAYING THERE

Alternatives to apartments are few.
Chalets Inghams has two ski-in/ski-out chalets for 12. Ski Total has four neighbouring chalets including Marie in its Platinum range. All are ski-in/ski-out and have saunas. For family-oriented places, check out Ardent.
Hotels
****Dromonts** Under new ownership and refurbished in retro (1960s) style for 2014/15. Reports welcome.
Apartments The smart, recently built Amara apartments are stylish, spacious by French standards and have a fabulous spa (but 'the pool can get busy and they charge for the outdoor hot tub' says a 2015 visitor). The Kouria apartments were rebuilt to luxury standard for last season and have pool, hot tub and steam room. The Atria Crozats places are not in the same class but are smartly furnished. Reporters have enjoyed the Saskia Falaise apartments ('nicely renovated in Alpine wood style'). Ski Collection, Inghams, Crystal, Erna Low and PowderBeds offer some or all of these. Hanski specializes in short breaks.

EATING OUT ★★★
A few interesting options
There are about 25 restaurants; but demand can exceed supply. We had an excellent dinner at the Bistro – good menu; live jazz sax. The cute, cosy old Chalet d'Avoriaz (aka Chez Lenvers) pleased one reporter: 'Nice staff, good value.' A few bars are tipped: Chapka does tapas, Tavaillon (good burgers), Intrêts ('well-priced steak').

APRES-SKI ★★★
The bars are fun
A few bars have a good atmosphere, particularly in happy hour. There's DJ-fuelled action on the terrace of the Chalet d'Avoriaz at close of play. Other top tips are Tavaillon for sports TV and Shooters. Chapka is a hip bar with TV, live music and pool. For late-night dance action, the Place has bands.

OFF THE SLOPES ★
Not much at the resort
There's not a lot to keep non-skiers interested – few shops and activities. But there's a pedestrian/cross-country skiing pass which allows access to certain lifts. Aquariaz is a smart leisure pool complex with lush vegetation and all sorts of features to amuse children, in particular. The spa (but not the pool, we're told) at the Amara development is open to non-residents. There's also bowling, dog sledding, hiking, skating outdoors snowshoeing and snowmobiling.

LINKED RESORT – 1200m

ARDENT

Ardent is a very quiet little place at the foot of the gondola up to Les Lindarets. It has the basics of life, including a bar and a ski shop. It seems ideal for families, and the Family Ski Company has nine chalets here, most with outdoor hot tub, some with sauna, none more than a short stroll from the gondola station.

LINKED RESORT – 1145m

LES PRODAINS

Les Prodains is at the foot of the cliffs on which Avoriaz sits, with a big gondola up them. The 3-star Lans is a traditional family-run hotel, 300m from the lift – a regular reporter who has stayed four times rates it highly ('simple but cosy, wonderful food'). Host Savoie has a three-bedroom chalet here and three more in Morzine. Hanski offers a converted 18th-century barn, 300m from the gondola, as a five-bedroom chalet.

GETTING THERE

Air Geneva 85km/ 55 miles (1hr45); Lyon 220km/135 miles (3hr)

Rail Cluses (44km/ 27 miles) or Thonon (46km/28 miles); bus and cable car to resort

TOURIST OFFICE

www.avoriaz.com

SNOWPIX.COM / CHRIS GILL

Les Carroz

A friendly family resort that makes a more compelling base than Flaine (or Samoëns) for the impressive Grand Massif area

£100
RESORT PRICE INDEX

TOP 10 RATINGS

Extent	★★★★
Fast lifts	★★★
Queues	★★★
Snow	★★★
Expert	★★★★
Intermediate	★★★★★
Beginner	★★★★
Charm	★★★★
Convenience	★★★
Scenery	★★★★

KEY FACTS

Resort	1120m
	3,670ft

Grand Massif ski area (Les Carroz and all linked resorts)

Slopes	700-2480m
	2,300-8,140ft
Lifts	68
Pistes	265km
	165 miles

Massif ski area (excluding Flaine)

Slopes	700-2120m
	2,300-6,700ft
Lifts	46
Pistes	125km
	78 miles

PISTE MAP

Les Carroz is covered on the Flaine map

+ Part of the big, varied Grand Massif

+ Pleasant, traditional village in a lovely balcony setting

+ Wooded slopes good in a storm

− Still lots of slow old chairlifts

− Village and local slopes are at modest altitudes

− Nightlife not a highlight

You pass through Les Carroz on the drive up to Flaine. Carry on up, if you like; these days, we prefer to make camp at the lower village. Not only is it a much more pleasant place to spend time, but also it makes more sense as a base. In a snowstorm, you can ski the excellent, wooded local slopes; when the sun comes out you can explore the exposed slopes elsewhere in the Grand Massif.

THE RESORT

Les Carroz is a traditional village that has spread widely across a sunny, wooded shelf. It claims an altitude of 1200m, but only the top fringes of the village are that high – the centre is at about 1120m. It is linked to Morillon, Samoëns and Flaine; the latter two get their own chapters.

Village charm Les Carroz has the lived-in feel of a real village, where life turns around the neat central square. Sadly, it's far from car-free: traffic on the through-road to Flaine intrudes at weekends.

Convenience Your lodgings may be some distance from the gondola or from the centre, or both; there are free ski-buses on five lines; you may find you need to use a timetable, though.

Scenery There are good views from the upper village, and the partly wooded valleys between here and Flaine are very scenic.

THE MOUNTAINS

The slopes directly above the village are densely wooded, but there are lots of open slopes towards Flaine. Some blue runs involved in the trip to Flaine have tricky steep sections.

Slopes Read the Flaine chapter for views on the extent of the Grand Massif pistes. The village gondola rises 600m, serving blue runs and launching you towards the other linked resorts.

Fast lifts Outside the Flaine bowl, there are lots of slow chairs – Tête des Saix above Samoëns has a spectacular gathering of them. More investment is needed to solve the problem.

Queues In high season the gondola may have non-trivial morning queues;

and you can expect delays and crowded pistes on the way to Flaine – and very crowded runs on the way back at the end of the day.

Terrain parks There isn't one.

Snow reliability The Les Carroz runs are west-facing and low, and can suffer from strong afternoon sun; but a few runs have snowmaking. The slopes of Morillon and Samoëns, on the other hand, are north-facing, and the latter are a bit higher, too – so the snow keeps in better condition.

Experts There are some proper black pistes above Samoëns and in the next-door Molliets valley, but the main interest is the extensive off-piste in various sectors, including the Molliets

LES CARROZ TO

There are excellent woodland runs directly above the village – great in bad weather →

milkhotel

Contemporary decor – Ski in Ski out

route des servages 74300 les carroz
tel.: +33 (0)6 17 77 70 23
www.milkhotel.fr

Like the resort?
You'll love our handpicked accommodation
02392
839 310
PEAKRETREATS.CO.UK
ABTA
ABTA No. W5937

LIFT PASSES

Grand Massif

Prices in €

Age	6-day
under 16	173
16 to 64	231
65 plus	220

Free Under 5, 75 plus
Beginner Limited pass
Note Family discounts

Alternative pass
Massif area only (Les Carroz, Samoëns, Sixt-Fer-à-Cheval, Vernant)

TOURIST OFFICE

www.lescarroz.com

and Vernant valleys between Les Carroz and Flaine. Don't miss Flaine's Combe de Gers.

Intermediates As our rating suggests, this is a great area, whether you like a challenge or not. Most people can get around the whole Grand Massif area, although the runs back from Flaine involve some blues which are rather busy and narrow.

Beginners Pretty good: the village nursery slopes are quiet and there are also good snow-sure slopes at the top of the gondola, with excellent longer blue runs to progress to.

Snowboarding Some of the linking runs at altitude are almost flat. But there are few draglifts to deal with.

Cross-country There are 25km of tracks between Morillon and Les Carroz, some quite challenging.

Mountain restaurants They are marked but not named on the resort piste map. Read the Flaine and Samoëns chapters too. The 'lovely rustic' Chalet les Molliets at the bottom of the Molliets chair always had good reports. Anfionne on the Plein Soleil home run is 'a favourite for a beer on the way home – food is good, too'. Above Morillon, we've had an excellent plat du jour at the rustic Igloo – 'great staff and excellent food'. We've had good reports on Chalet d'Clair – 'very friendly table-service', 'decent food'.

Schools and guides There is regular praise for the ESF: 'The best we've encountered,' says one visitor. Others have praised the International school: 'Kids enjoyed it and progressed well.'

Families The busy village centre is not particularly child-friendly. Pick lodgings near the lifts would be our advice.

STAYING THERE

Hotels There are half a dozen hotels, including two up beside the red home run. Servages d'Armelle is a lovely little 4-star, housed in two old chalets. The nearby Milkhotel has been highly recommended: 'friendly staff', 'good set menu'; endorsed this year by a reporter who commends its 'abundant wooden chic'. The 'really nice' Croix de Savoie, in contrast, requires use of the ski-bus that stops outside.

Apartments Les Chalets de Jouvence is an excellent CGH low-rise residence in an ideal location next to the Telecarroz draglift (for access to the gondola); we had a very spacious apartment here a couple of seasons ago; readers are impressed too – 'lovely pool', 'one of the best'. Les Fermes du Soleil is a similar Pierre & Vacances Premium residence with pool, hot tubs etc, close to the centre. Both are available through Peak Retreats.

Eating out Best in town is Aux Petits Oignons, a cosy place run by a charming couple. The Bistrot Grill du Gron is 'a carnivore delight' with its indoor BBQ equivalent. Hotel les Airelles has a cosy restaurant. Readers like La Spatule, too.

Après-ski It's pretty quiet – no beery bars at the base here. In the centre, the Marlow pub has 'a bit of a buzz', but this year CarpéDiem is reckoned to be 'liveliest'. Cave 59 is a wine bar.

Off the slopes Outdoors there's ice skating, snowshoeing, dog sledding and skijoring. There are signposted, cleared paths, and an associated map. There's a cinema. And the Aquacîme sports/spa centre has an outdoor pool.

OT CHAMONIX MONT-BLANC

Chamonix

HQ of French and arguably European mountaineering, with a magnetic attraction for tourists and off-piste thrill-seekers alike

£105
RESORT PRICE INDEX

RATINGS

The mountains

Extent	★★★
Fast lifts	★★★
Queues	★★
Terrain p'ks	★★★
Snow	★★★★
Expert	★★★★★
Intermediate	★★
Beginner	★★
Boarder	★★★
X-country	★★★
Restaurants	★★
Schools	★★★★★
Families	★★

The resort

Charm	★★★★
Convenience	★
Scenery	★★★★★
Eating out	★★★★★
Après-ski	★★★★
Off-slope	★★★★★

NEWS

2015/16: Les Houches will hold the Men's World Cup Downhill in February 2016.

2014/15: The ancient Plan Joran chair at the base of Les Grand Montets was replaced by a 10-person gondola and the cabins of the adjacent cable car were replaced. The building at the top of the cable car at Lognan was refurbished. At Les Houches, a giant slalom course of 500m vertical was built on the World Cup racing piste for anyone to try while being timed and filmed.

➕ A lot of very tough terrain, especially off-piste

➕ Amazing cable car to the Aiguille du Midi, for the famous Vallée Blanche

➕ Stunning views wherever you are

➕ Other resorts covered on extended lift pass, notably sunny Courmayeur

➕ Town steeped in Alpine tradition

➕ Lots of affordable hotels – and many will take short bookings

➖ Several separate mountains, widely separated; bad for mixed abilities

➖ Inadequate bus services

➖ Bad weather can shut the best runs

➖ Still some old lifts, and serious queues in key spots

➖ It's a busy town, with lots of road traffic; not a relaxing place

➖ Shady and cold in midwinter

Chamonix could not be more different from the archetypal high-altitude, purpose-built French resort. It hasn't been designed to deliver the smoothest possible experience to the widest possible market. It hasn't been designed.

You don't have to be an expert to enjoy the place – Editor Gill once took his blue-run-skiing wife and novice kids for a week here, and lived to tell the tale. But it is the expert and the adventurous would-be expert who really must give Chamonix a permanent place on their shortlist, despite its serious drawbacks.

THE RESORT

Chamonix is a long-established, year-round tourist town that spreads for miles along the valley in the shadow of Mont Blanc.

On either side of the centre, just within walking distance, are base stations of the cable car to the Aiguille du Midi (for the famous Vallée Blanche glacier run) and a gondola to Le Brévent. A third high-altitude area, La Flégère, is linked to Le Brévent by cable car and reached by its own cable car from the village of Les Praz.

At the top of the valley are the villages of Argentière, beneath the Grands Montets and Le Tour, at the foot of the Balme slopes (with an alternative base at Vallorcine). These villages are described at the end of the chapter, but their slopes are taken in to the main part of the chapter.

Down the valley is Les Houches, with the most sheltered slopes in the valley. This is wholly described at the end of the chapter; its lifts are not covered by the normal Chamonix pass.

Free ski-buses link all these points but can get very crowded ('even in January') and be 'infrequent and unreliable'. Don't expect additional buses to meet varying demand (eg when everyone wants to get to Les Houches in bad weather). There are also hourly trains along the valley, free with a guest card, and usually recommended by reporters.

The Mont Blanc Unlimited lift pass covers not only Les Houches but also Verbier in Switzerland and Courmayeur in Italy. The first is a major expedition; the second is of more practical use, not least because the weather can be good in Italy when it is lousy in Chamonix. And there are buses

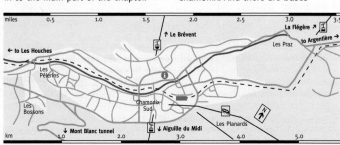

KEY FACTS

Resort	1035m
	3,400ft
Slopes	1035-3840m
	3,400-12,600ft
Lifts	42
Pistes	115km
	71 miles

through the Mont Blanc tunnel several times daily. Having a car is useful in lots of ways, and makes that outing to Verbier a more practical proposition.

VILLAGE CHARM ★★★★
Lots of atmosphere
Chamonix is a bustling place, with scores of hotels and restaurants and shops selling everything from tacky souvenirs to high-tech climbing gear. The car-free centre is full of atmosphere, with cobbled streets and squares, beautiful old buildings, a fast-running river and pavement cafes. Away from the centre, there are lots of apartment blocks. There are some disused buildings, and traffic clogs the streets at times.

CONVENIENCE ★
You don't come here for that
The obvious place to stay for the full experience is close to the centre, where you can be a short walk from the gondola to Brévent. Or you adapt to life on the buses or trains.

SCENERY ★★★★★
As dramatic as it gets
The mountains above Chamonix are not just high – the mighty Mont Blanc is the highest in Western Europe – they are also truly spectacular. The ride up the Aiguille du Midi cable car is breathtaking and at the top there's now a 'Step into the Void' glass viewing area, complete with a glass floor above a drop of 1000m.

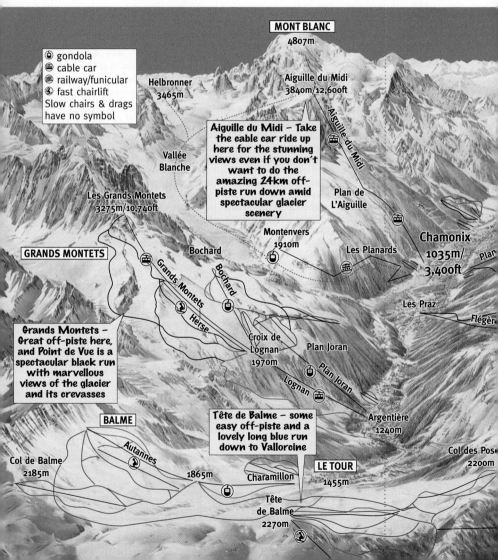

THE MOUNTAINS

Practically all the slopes – with the notable exception of Les Houches – are above the treeline. There are some runs down through woods to the valley floor but the black ones from Brévent and Flégère, in particular, are often closed due to lack of snow or poor conditions and can be unpleasantly tricky if open.

The piste map has maps for each individual area as well as the valley as a whole. Signposting and piste marking are OK. But in sectors other than Balme, the classification of runs often understates difficulty – in particular, some of the blues would be classified as reds in other resorts.

EXTENT OF THE SLOPES ★★★
Very fragmented

The gondola for **Brévent** departs a short, steep walk or bus ride from the centre. There are runs on open slopes below the arrival point, and a cable car goes on to the summit. There is a lift link to **Flégère**, also accessible via an inadequate old cable car from the village of Les Praz. These sunny areas give stunning views of Mont Blanc.

Up the valley at Argentière a cable car or a new gondola takes you up to the high slopes of **Les Grands Montets**. Chairs and a gondola serve open terrain above mid-mountain, but much of the best terrain is accessed by a further cable car of relatively low capacity, not covered by the standard

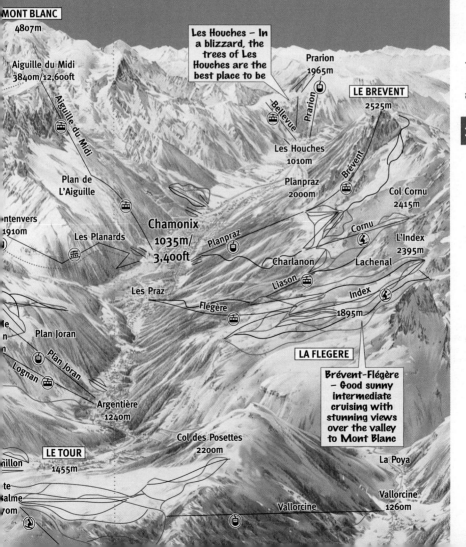

MONT BLANC
4807m

Aiguille du Midi
3840m/12,600ft

Aiguille du Midi

Plan de L'Aiguille

ntenvers
1910m

Les Planards

Chamonix
1035m/
3,400ft

Planpraz

Les Praz

Flégère

Plan Joran

Plan Joran

Lognan

Argentière
1240m

Col des Posettes
2200m

LE TOUR
1455m

nillon

te
alme
om

Les Houches – In a blizzard, the trees of Les Houches are the best place to be

Prarion
1965m

Prarion

Bellevue

Les Houches
1010m

Planpraz
2000m

Charlanon

Liason

LE BREVENT
2525m

Brévent

Col Cornu
2415m

Cornu

L'Index
2395m

Lachenal

Index
1895m

LA FLEGERE

Brévent-Flégère – Good sunny intermediate cruising with stunning views over the valley to Mont Blanc

La Poya

Vallorcine
1260m

Vallorcine

↑ Chamonix is an old mountain town with slopes rising steeply on both sides of the valley

CHAMONIX TO / MONICA DALMASSO

LIFT PASSES

Chamonix Le Pass

Prices in €

Age	6-day
under 16	205
16 to 64	241
65 plus	205

Free Under 4

Beginner No deals

Senior 75 plus: 50% of adult price

Notes Covers Brévent, Flégère, Balme, Grands Montets except top cable car, plus four small beginner areas; family reductions

Alternative pass

Mont Blanc Unlimited (MBU) covers all the above plus Les Houches, Montenvers train, Aiguille du Midi and Helbronner cable cars, Lognan-Grands Montets cable car, Courmayeur (Italy)

lift pass (read 'Lift passes'). This shady area can be very cold in early season.

A little way further up the valley, the secluded village of Le Tour sits at the foot of the broad **Balme** area. A gondola goes up to mid-mountain, with a mix of drags and chairs above. There is also a lift up from Vallorcine.

Plus there are several low beginner areas dotted along the valley.

FAST LIFTS ★★★
Not enough

Cable cars and gondolas serve each sector, but many need upgrading. The five fast chairs are widely scattered. Many reporters are scathing: 'the worst lift system I've seen', 'disgraceful'.

QUEUES ★★
Ancient lifts, serious queues

At the Grands Montets, last season's new gondola seems to have reduced the serious waiting times at the bottom. But at mid-mountain, the top cable car remains a famous bottleneck. You can book slots in advance (on the spot or online), preferably the day before, or join the 'standby' queue, which we've found to be an effective alternative.

At Flégère, the ancient 60-person cable car can have queues of an hour or more – to go down as well as up. At La Tour, there can be queues for the ancient gondola up Balme; it can be quicker to take the train to Vallorcine.

Crowded pistes and skiers travelling

too fast for the conditions can also be a problem in places – most notably on parts of the Grands Montets.

TERRAIN PARKS ★★★
A couple of options

The Summit Park on Grands Montets incorporates features for all levels and includes kickers, rails, jumps and lots of features. There's also a snowcross course. At Brévent there's an airbag jump; you can be filmed doing it to view on the internet later.

SNOW RELIABILITY ★★★★
Good high up; poor low down

The top runs on the north-facing Grands Montets slopes above Argentière generally have good snow, and the season normally lasts well into May. The risk of finding the top lift shut because of bad weather is more of a worry. There's snowmaking on the busy Bochard piste and the run to the valley. Balme has a snowy location, a good late-season record and snowmaking on the run down to the valley at Le Tour. The largely south-facing slopes of Brévent and Flégère suffer in warm weather despite quite a bit of snowmaking, and the steep black runs to the resort are often closed. Don't be tempted to try these unless you know they are in good condition – they can be very tricky. Some of the low beginners' areas have snowmaking. Piste grooming is generally OK.

FOR EXPERTS ★★★★★
One of the great resorts

Chamonix is renowned for its extensive steep terrain and deep snow. To get the best out of the area you really need to have a local guide. There is also lots of excellent terrain for ski touring on skins. Read the feature panel for some off-piste possibilities.

The Grands Montets cable car offers stunning views from the observation platform above the top station – if you've got the legs and lungs to climb the 121 steep metal steps. (But beware: it's 200 more slippery steel steps down from the cable car before you hit the snow.) The ungroomed black pistes from here – Point de Vue and Pylones – are long and exhilarating. The former sails right by some dramatic sections of glacier, with marvellous views of the crevasses.

The Bochard gondola serves a challenging red back to Lognan and a black to either the Retour Pendant chairlift or Plan Joran. Shortly after you have made a start down the black, you can head off-piste down the Combe de la Pendant bowl.

At Brévent there's more to test experts than the piste map suggests – there are a number of variations on the runs down from the summit. Some are very steep and prone to ice. The red and black runs in Combe de la Charlanon are quiet, and there is excellent off-piste if the snow is good.

At Flégère there are further challenging slopes – in the Combe Lachenal, crossed by the linking cable car, say – and a tough run back to the village when the snow permits. The short draglift above L'Index opens up a couple of good steep runs (a red and a black) plus a good area of off-piste.

Balme boasts little tough terrain on-piste, but there are off-piste routes from the high points to Le Tour, towards Vallorcine or into Switzerland.

FOR INTERMEDIATES ★★
Plenty of better resorts

Chamonix is far from ideal for intermediates unless they relish challenging slopes and trying off-piste. If what you want is mile after mile of lift-linked cruisy pistes, you should go elsewhere. For less confident intermediates, the Balme area above Le Tour is good for cruising and usually free from crowds. There are excellent shady, steeper runs, wooded lower down, on the north side of Tête

Club Med ℘.
THE MOST COMPREHENSIVE
SKI PACKAGE ON THE MARKET

Chamonix 4℘

020 8313 3999
Skiline.co.uk

Skiline co.uk

de Balme, served by a fast quad. A lovely red run goes on down to Vallorcine, but it is prone to closure.

The other areas have some blue and red runs. Even the Grands Montets has an area of blues at mid-mountain. The step up to the red terrain higher up is quite pronounced, however.

If the snow and weather are good, confident intermediates can join a guided group and do the Vallée Blanche (read our feature panel).

FOR BEGINNERS ★★
Head for Balme

Chamonix is far from ideal for beginners, too – there are countless better resorts in which to learn. There are limited but adequate nursery slopes either side of the town – Savoy, at the bottom of Brévent, and Les Planards, on the opposite side (dark and cold in midwinter). Moving on to longer runs means taking a lift up to Brévent or Flégère. La Vormaine, at Le Tour, is a much better bet: extensive, relatively high, sunny and connected to the slopes of the Balme area, where there are easy long runs to progress to. But it's 12km from Chamonix itself.

FOR BOARDERS ★★★
Leave it to the experts

The undisputed king of freeride resorts, Chamonix is a haven for advanced snowboarders who relish the steep and wild terrain, especially on the Grands Montets. This means, however, that in peak season it's crowded, and fresh snow gets tracked out very quickly. Keen riders should check out former British champion Neil McNab's excellent extreme backcountry snowboard courses at: www. mcnabsnowboarding.com.

The rough and rugged nature of the slopes means they are not best suited for beginners but rather for more adventurous riders willing to try true

THE BEST OFF-PISTE SKIING IN THE WORLD?

Chamonix is renowned as an extreme sports Mecca, with arguably some of the best off-piste skiing in the world. And while thrill-seekers and off-piste specialists are spoiled for choice, there is plenty for those looking for their first powder experience, too.

Les Houches and *Balme*, at opposite ends of the Chamonix Valley, are ideal for a first taste off the beaten track. The forested slopes of Les Houches are easy to navigate on bad-weather days, with gentle blue runs bringing you back to the valley. Balme's open slopes are perfect for a foray into deep snow in between the pistes, with firmer ground just a few reassuring metres away.

Snowboarders flock to *Flégère* after a snowfall, its array of boulders and drop-offs turning it into a massive terrain park. The open bowl of Combe Lachenal is easily accessed from the top of the Index lift, and the south-facing slopes of this ski area provide excellent spring skiing.

From the top of *Les Grands Montets* (3275m) skiing is mostly off-piste and on glacial terrain. The vast north-facing slope of the main face offers countless ways down, satisfyingly steep without being intimidating, with snow conditions that are often among the best in the valley. Off the back, there are several rewarding ways down to the Glacier d'Argentière. In the opposite direction you have access to the steep Pas de Chèvre run. Skiing under the colossal granite spire of Le Dru, with views of the Vallée Blanche, is an unforgettable experience. The Couloir du Dru and the Rectiligne are also on this face, reserved for the adventurous – with some slopes of 40° to 45°.

These are just some of the options, but the possibilities are endless. Together with heli-skiing on the Italian side of Mont Blanc and in neighbouring Switzerland, the wealth of off-piste on offer could keep you skiing for a lifetime.

THE LONGEST RUN MOST OF US WILL EVER DO – THE VALLEE BLANCHE

This is a trip you do for the stunning scenery. The views of the glacier and the spectacular rock spires beyond are simply mind-blowing. The standard run, although exceptionally long, is not steep – mostly gliding down gentle slopes (in places a bit too flat for snowboarders) with only the occasional steeper, choppy section to deal with. In the right conditions, it is well within the capability of a confident, fit intermediate. If snow is sparse, as it often is in early season, the run can be very tricky, with patches of sheet ice and exposed rocks, and narrow snow bridges over gaping crevasses. If fresh snow is abundant, different challenges may arise. Go in a guided group and check conditions before signing up at the Maison de la Montagne or other ski school offices. The trip is popular – on a busy day 2,500 people do it. To miss the crowds, go very early on a weekday, or in the afternoon if you are a good skier and can get down quickly.

The cable car takes you to 3840m and the 3842 cafeteria (claimed to be Europe's highest restaurant) – check out the amazing view of Mont Blanc from here while you adjust to the dizzying altitude. Be prepared for extreme cold, too. A tunnel delivers you to the infamous ridge-walk down to the start of the run. Except at the start of the season, the walk is well prepared, with regular steps cut in the snow and fixed ropes to hang on to. If you have a backpack capable of carrying your skis, and crampons to give some grip, it's no problem; ask for them when you book your guide. Without those items, it can be tiring and worrying. Many parties rope up to their guides.

There are variants on the classic route, of varying difficulty and danger; on our last descent we did a mixture of the Petit Envers du Plan and the Vrai Vallée Blanche in 20cm of fresh snow under a blue sky with few other people around – it was absolutely magical, with hundreds of fresh-track turns among all that stunning scenery. Lack of snow often rules out the full 24km run down to Chamonix; a steep stairway (be warned: 311 steps) leading to a slow gondola links the glacier to the station at Montenvers, for the half-hour mountain railway ride down to the town.

SNOWPIX.COM / CHRIS GILL

POW DER AMA

Ski coaching. Chamonix.
Achieve optimum results with focussed and friendly tuition.
+33(0)616871853
powderama.com

all-mountain riding. The easiest terrain is at the Balme area, though there are quite a few difficult drags here (you can avoid these if you can hack the cat tracks to take you to other lifts, says a reporter). Most lifts elsewhere are cable cars, gondolas and chairs.

If you do the Vallée Blanche, be warned: the usual route is very flat in places, so be prepared to scoot.

FOR CROSS-COUNTRY ★★★☆☆
A decent network of trails
Most of the 53km of prepared trails lie at valley level – and were highly rated by a past reporter. But the trails are shady and often icy in midwinter, and they fade fast in the spring sun. Catch the bus rather than ski between the Chamonix and Argentière areas, suggests a reporter, as the link is by 'steep and difficult trails'.

MOUNTAIN RESTAURANTS ★★☆☆☆
Mainly dull, lacking choice
Editors' choice On Brévent the Bergerie de Planpraz is a wood-and-stone building with self- and table-service sections and good food; but it gets very busy. On the Grands Montets the tiny, rustic Chalet Refuge de Lognan, off the Variante Hôtel run to the valley, has marvellous views and satisfying, simple food. Recent reporters agree.
Worth knowing about On the Grands Montets, one regular visitor rates Plan Joran 'probably the best in the valley'; it has table- and self-service, and a big terrace. Tucked away in the woods to skier's right of the home run, the Crémerie du Glacier is a cosy spot for a croûte.

On Brévent the little Panoramic at the top enjoys amazing views over to Mont Blanc, and the food is fine. On Flégère the table-service Adret is 'not outstanding, but definitely pretty good'. The Chavanne is one reader's favourite despite the 'small choice' of food – 'amazing view'. At Balme, at the top of the gondola from Le Tour, there's an adequate self-service. Ecuries de Charamillon is in a renovated farmhouse.

SCHOOLS AND GUIDES ★★★★★
The place to try something new
The schools here are particularly strong in specialist fields – off-piste, glacier and couloir skiing, ski touring, snowboarding and cross-country. English-speaking instructors and mountain guides are plentiful.

At the Maison de la Montagne are the main ESF office and the HQ of the Compagnie des Guides, which is highly rated and has taken visitors to the mountains for 150 years. We and reporters have had very good guides from here.

A 2015 reporter advises to ask for a guide with a car, so that they can drive you to and from wherever you are skiing – 'ours was good and we skied the glacier at Grands Montets'. A reporter who did the Vallée Blanche said their guide 'gave our 12-year-old lots of confidence'. Both the ESF and Compagnie des Guides offer week-long 'tours' taking clients to a different mountain or resort each day.

A recent reporter's wife went back for the second year running to Evolution 2 and found her instructor 'excellent, giving her renewed confidence to tackle steeper slopes'.

Powderama is run by British instructor Simon Halliwell and offers five-day and weekend courses plus specialized one-day clinics (off-piste, piste, moguls).

FOR FAMILIES ★★☆☆☆
Very limited
Childcare is available from some of the ski schools. Evolution 2's Panda Club is used by quite a few British visitors; reports have been enthusiastic but the Argentière base can be inconvenient. Les Houches has better facilities, with a day care centre and children's club.

STAYING THERE

There is all sorts of accommodation, and lots of it. Several weekend specialists operate here including Ski Weekend, who started up in Chamonix way back in 1987 and offer chalets, hotels, apartments and optional on- and off-piste courses. Other short-break specialists include Momentum, Hanski and Ski Weekends (not to be confused with their singular rival).
Chalets Many chalets are run by small specialist operators such as Collineige. Inghams runs the 60-bed Sapinière – overlooking the nursery slope at the bottom of Brévent and not far from the centre – as a chalet hotel: 'Comfortable, well placed, run to a very high standard,' said a reporter. They also have two central chalet apartments for six that can be combined to sleep 12. Hanski has a central 10-bedroom chalet.

Chamonix

229

Tailor made, long weekend and short break French Alps ski holiday specialists.

Hanski
Ski. Explore. Relax.

web: www.hanski.co.uk
tel: 01638 596373

tta*
100% Protected Holidays

Ski Weekend
the ultimate short break

we are the original

short break

ski specialists

over 25 years

01392 878 353
www.skiweekend.com

Hotels There's a wide choice, many modestly priced, the majority with no more than 30 rooms or so. Bookings for short stays are no problem – the peak season is summer. Club Med has three linked buildings near the centre, with sauna, steam room and outdoor pool. Out at Le Lavancher is the 'hameau hôtelier' Les Chalets de Philippe – a secluded cluster of lovingly furnished wooden chalets, most sleeping no more than three or four, with meals taken either in your own chalet or in a small central dining room.

*****Auberge du Bois Prin A small modern chalet with a big reputation; great views; bit of a hike into town (closer to Brévent). Spa.

*****Hameau Albert 1er Smart, 100-year-old chalet-style Relais & Châteaux hotel with farmhouse annexe. Pool/spa.

*****Mont-Blanc Grand 19th-century place in a central location. Refurbished a few years ago. Spa and pool.

****Jeu de Paume (Lavancher) Alpine satellite of a chic Parisian hotel: a beautifully furnished modern chalet halfway to Argentière.

****Morgane Cool modern style; good location near Aiguille de Midi cable car; pool, sauna.

****Mercure Next to the station – now a 4-star. Comfortable rooms, friendly service. Has its own ski-hire facilities.

***Alpina Striking modern place just north of centre. Much the biggest in town – 138 rooms, most with balconies and mountain views. Sauna, hot tub, steam.

***Croix-Blanche Small, simple hotel and brasserie in centre.

***Lanchers Near Flégère. Tipped repeatedly by reporters for accommodation, food and friendly service.

***Oustalet Near Aiguille de Midi cable car. 'Really helpful staff, good breakfast, spacious room, spotless.'

***Prieuré Mega-chalet on northern ring-road – handy for drivers, quite close to centre. Sauna, hot tub. 'Friendly, comfortable, good food, excellent dessert buffet.'

Le Vert In Le Gailland, a mile from town; en-suite rooms for one to six people. Lively bar, top DJs, pool table.

Apartments Many properties in UK package brochures are in convenient positions but are rather cramped if you fill them to capacity. The Ginabelle is different – a Pierre & Vacances Premium residence near the station, with pool, spa and fitness facilities, also available through Peak Retreats and Erna Low. Zenith has a wide range of self-catered chalets, sleeping from 6 to 16.

EATING OUT ★★★★★
Plenty of quality places

Chamonix offers more variety than is normal in French resorts. One or two advertising-based guides are distributed locally.

Of the hotels, Albert 1er, Auberge du Bois Prin and Morgane all have restaurants with Michelin stars.

Elsewhere, the Impossible is a favourite with us and with readers – a rustic chalet a short walk out of the centre with a varied menu. And we always enjoy the intimate Atmosphère, by the river, despite its two-sitting system – endorsed by a 2015 reporter. Alan Peru got the thumbs up last year: 'good food and relatively reasonable prices'. Café de l'Arve at the hotel de l'Arve, offers a modern, creative menu ('haute-cuisine without the haute-prices'). According to a regular reporter the Panier des 4 Saisons is 'very possibly the best restaurant in Chamonix' with its inventive modern regional French cuisine.

The 'cosy' Monchu does good Savoyard food and service at reasonable prices. The Calèche gets booked up well ahead and is short on space but does 'excellent' traditional and more adventurous dishes. Munchie offers a mix of French and Scandinavian cooking that makes a refreshing change. Maison Moustache et Filles has a varied Savoyard menu.

Value-oriented reader tips include Pitz and Neopolis (both pizza), Moö Bar (burgers), La Flambée ('good pizza, pasta, steak and local dishes') and the Poèle (calls itself an 'omeletterie' but serves other dishes too).

APRES-SKI ★★★★☆
You have to know where to go

Chamonix attracts a lot of young Brits and Scandis – blokes, mainly – wanting to après-ski hard after skiing hard. But it is not Austria, or even Méribel, and it does not have one of the rapidly expanding Folie Douce on-mountain party places. It's a big town, and you have to know where to go. One exception is an obvious place at Flégère – the Rhododendrons, which has live music.

In the town, the teatime après zone that we hear most about is beside the train station. The Swedish-run Chambre Neuf has 'good cover bands, pitchers of beer and even dancing on the tables – great fun'. Elevation 1904, opposite, is a bit quieter.

Towards the river in Rue Whymper, the Lapin Agile is a relaxed wine bar doing Italian-style appetizers. Round the corner, the Moö Bar on Ave Michel Croz has live music and a 'buzzing atmosphere'. Over the river is the central square with La Terrasse ('head upstairs – really characterful old high-ceilinged place'). To the left is Rue du Dr Paccard. The Pub gets packed with Brits. Or turn right for the key Rue des Moulins. Bar'dUp is a small, relaxed place with live music and DJs. Mix has 'big-name' DJs. Top tips for grown-ups are Privilege, a relaxed, woody, rustic-chic place with table-service and live acoustic music, and the Quartz Bar, next to the Albert 1er hotel, which is 'swanky and chic, smart dress only'. Soul Food has been recommended. In Chamonix Sud, Monkey Bar is frequented by 'those in the know'. The Jekyll does 'fun' comedy nights.

Just outside the centre, MBC is a Canadian-run microbrewery, often with live bands – 'good ambience, great beer and apparently reasonable food'.

There's a variety of nightclubs and discos. Amnesia claims to be the biggest. The Bunker (formerly White Hub) is open from 11pm to 7am; just the times we are tucked up in bed.

Real action enthusiasts may want to look at getting out of town to Le Vert ('hippest nightspot in town').

OFF THE SLOPES ★★★★★
An excellent choice
There's more off-slope activity here than in many resorts. Everyone other than those with medical issues should ride the Aiguille du Midi cable car. Excursion possibilities are endless. The Alpine Museum is 'very interesting but all in French', the library has some English language books and there's a good sports centre with a pool, sauna, steam room, hot tub, ice skating and ice hockey matches. There are 17km of walking trails and you can go snowshoeing and dog sledding.

OUTLYING VILLAGE – 1240m
ARGENTIERE

This old village is in an impressive setting towards the head of the valley, 9km from Chamonix. There's a fair bit of modern development, and the road through to Le Tour, Vallorcine and Switzerland gets uncomfortably busy, but it still has a rustic appeal.

The lifts to the Grands Montets are about 600m from the slightly elevated centre of the village. It's a fair hike, but there are buses. Readers like two central hotels: the 3-star Couronne (recommended by three recent reporters, 'cheap, comfortable, charming; friendly staff but rooms at front can be noisy') and the 2-star

Chamonix

231

STUART MCWILLIAM
Argentière has a lot of through-traffic but retains a rustic appeal and is about 600m from the Grands Montets ski area ↓

Like the resort?

You'll love our handpicked accommodation

02392 839 310

PEAKRETREATS.CO.UK

ABTA
ABTA No W5517

Dahu ('good room, excellent breakfast'; 'good value for money'). Out near the lifts are the 4-star Grands-Montets, with pool and spa ('excellent rooms and service' said a recent report) and the 4-star Montana with pool and spa.

Le Cristal d'Argentière is a smart Lagrange Prestige residence, between the centre and the lifts, with a decent pool (available through Peak Retreats and Erna Low and enjoyed by a 2015 reporter).

There's a reasonable choice of inexpensive, unpretentious restaurants and bars in the central area. An old favourite is the Office, offering a traditional Brit-pub atmosphere and menu; 'good burgers, pie and chips'; 'live music'; 'part of the reason I return to Argentière every year'. The two central hotels mentioned above both have attractive restaurants. Reader recommendations include the P'tite Verte ('excellent-value three-course dinner') and the Stone ('excellent pizzas, pasta and steak'; 'onion soup is becoming an institution').

Other tipped bars are the Savoy and the Slalom.

OUTLYING VILLAGE – 1455m
LE TOUR

Le Tour is a charming, unspoiled little village 12km from Chamonix at the foot of the Balme area. The valley's best nursery slopes are next to the village, at La Vormaine. A gondola from the edge of the village serves the Balme slopes, an area of mainly easy runs also reachable from Vallorcine.

OUTLYING VILLAGE – 1260m
VALLORCINE

Vallorcine is a small, but developing, traditional mountain village over the Col des Montets, near the Swiss border and 16km from Chamonix. The village shares with Le Tour the main valley's Balme area.

A gondola and a chairlift take you to Tête de Balme. A gentle red run leads back to the village, but it is prone to closure. There's a separate small area of local slopes at La Poya.

Accommodation is mainly in apartments. The 4-star L'Ours Bleu, with pool and spa facilities, is featured by Peak Retreats and Erna Low. There's a limited choice of restaurants and bars. The Café Comptoir at the foot of

the Forêt Verte run is 'stylish, rustic and upscale – book ahead'. The Arret Bougnete in the station specializes in local dishes and has a wide selection of drinks – 'worth a visit waiting for the train back to Chamonix', says a regular visitor.

OUTLYING VILLAGE – 1010m
LES HOUCHES

Les Houches is 6km down the valley from Chamonix. The wooded slopes are popular when bad weather closes other areas, but are not covered by the standard Chamonix pass. It has great views of the Mont Blanc massif.

It's a pleasant village, with an old core around a pretty church, but modern developments in chalet style have spread along the road at the foot of the slopes. Some developments are quite a way from the widely separated lifts going to opposite ends of the slopes – a gondola and a queue-prone cable car. On the mountain, all the lifts are slow. There are some awkward links in the network. Snow-cover on the lower slopes is not reliable, but there is a fair amount of snowmaking.

There are nursery slopes and open, gentle runs at the top of the main lifts, with long, worthwhile runs back towards the village – blue, red and a token black that is Chamonix's World Cup Downhill course – a fine intermediate run. There is a decent terrain park. But there are lots of draglifts and flat areas for boarders to avoid.

Beyond the summit ridge is a very gentle area with 10km of cross-country loops and below that some sunny woodland runs with views across to Megève.

In good weather the slopes are quiet, and the views superb from the several attractive restaurants. The 265-year-old Vieilles Luges has a 'creative menu: leek and cheese crumble, Reblochon cheesecake'.

The village is quiet – 'bring the board games' says a recent visitor; but there are some pleasant bars and restaurants – Piccolina serves 'great pizzas'. The 2-star Campanules hotel was recommended last year: 'Brilliant staff, basic but spotless rooms, cosy, shuttle-bus to slopes.'

There are some good apartments with pools, including the 4-star CGH Hameau de Pierre Blanche (available through Peak Retreats and Erna Low).

GETTING THERE

Air Geneva 90km/ 55 miles (1hr15); Lyon 220km/ 135 miles (2hr15)

Rail Station in resort, on the St-Gervais-Le Fayet/Vallorcine line

TOURIST OFFICES

Chamonix/Argentière
www.chamonix.com

Les Houches
www.leshouches.com

Châtel

A distinctively French base in the huge Portes du Soleil circuit which spans the French–Swiss border; extensive local slopes too

£100
RESORT PRICE INDEX

233

RATINGS

The mountains

Extent	★★★★★
Fast lifts	★★
Queues	★★★
Terrain p'ks	★★★
Snow	★★
Expert	★★★
Intermediate	★★★★
Beginner	★★★
Boarder	★★
X-country	★★★
Restaurants	★★★
Schools	★★★
Families	★★★

The resort

Charm	★★★
Convenience	★★
Scenery	★★★
Eating out	★★★
Après-ski	★★★
Off-slope	★★

NEWS

2015/16: A new blue slope – the Forestière – has been built to link Super-Châtel to Vonnes, where the two new chairs that opened last season meet.

2014/15: The big news is that two new fast chairs – a six-pack and a quad – were built to link the Super-Châtel and Linga ski areas. An aquatic centre, the Forme d'O, opened in the village centre. It has several indoor pools, an outdoor pool, saunas and steam rooms.

➕ Very extensive, pretty, intermediate terrain on Portes du Soleil circuit, with good local slopes

➕ Wide range of good-value accommodation including family-run 2-star and 3-star hotels

➕ Pleasant, lively, traditional, French-dominated village

➖ Low altitude and exposure to westerlies means some risk of rain and poor snow

➖ Still mainly slow lifts at Super-Châtel and over the Swiss border

➖ Few packages offered by major UK tour operators

Unlike most resorts linked to major ski areas, Châtel remains relatively unspoiled and retains a very French feel, with a life outside tourism (there are still around 30 working farms). It is also right on the huge Portes du Soleil circuit, very close to the Swiss border; and last season, at long last, its two local sectors of slopes were linked by new lifts (a fast quad and a six-pack) rather than just by bus. And for the coming season there will be a new blue piste down to those lifts from the Super-Châtel sector.

THE RESORT

Châtel is a much expanded village near the head of the wooded Dranse valley, at the north-eastern limit of the huge French-Swiss Portes du Soleil ski circuit. It has two separate sectors of slopes, one linked to its French neighbour – high, purpose-built Avoriaz – and the other linked to two resorts in Switzerland: Morgins (which is on the Portes du Soleil circuit) and Torgon (which is not on the circuit).

A few kilometres down the valley is rustic La Chapelle-d'Abondance, with lifts into the Torgon slopes – covered at the end of this chapter.

VILLAGE CHARM ★★★
Attractive chalet style
Châtel is still an attractive village, despite the inevitable expansion, and reporters remark on the friendly locals. Modern, unpretentious chalet-style hotels and apartments rub shoulders with old farms where cattle still live in winter. Life revolves around two streets that are far from traffic-free and lots of visitors take cars – but a local assures us that traffic congestion has been reduced by the two new lifts (and a car park) at Vonnes.

CONVENIENCE ★★
No perfect position
Although there is a definite centre, the village sprawls along and up the hillside from the road in from Lake Geneva. The road diverges up towards Morgins and along the valley towards the Linga and Pré-la-Joux lifts. There is a free bus service linking the sectors. Staying centrally simplifies après-ski outings – the bus finishes at around 8pm most days – and has in the past helped with catching the ski-bus to the outlying lifts before it gets very crowded. The new chairlift link makes the bus less vital now and it makes the suburb of Vonnes, where the two chairs meet, a convenient place to stay. There is accommodation out near the Linga lift, too.

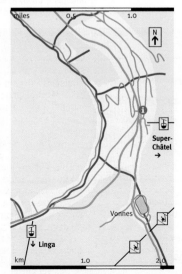

KEY FACTS

Resort	1200m
	3,940ft

Portes du Soleil	
Slopes	950-2275m
	3,120-7,460ft
Lifts	196
Pistes	650km
	404 miles

Châtel only	
Slopes	1100-2205m
	3,610-7,230ft
Lifts	43
Pistes	83km
	52 miles

LIFT PASSES

Portes du Soleil

Prices in €

Age	6-day
under 16	182
16 to 19	218
20 to 64	243
65 plus	218
Free	Under 5
Beginner	Points card
Note	Family discounts

Alternative pass
Châtel only (covers
Torgon and some of
Morgins too)

SCENERY ★★★★★
Lots of variety
Châtel's broad valley setting is very
scenic, with Linga providing a splendid
backdrop and pleasantly woody slopes
curving in both directions. The lifts
above Torgon give great views over
Lake Geneva. As you travel around the
Swiss side of the Portes du Soleil
circuit the dramatic Dents du Midi are
constantly coming into view.

THE MOUNTAINS

Châtel sits between two sectors of the
main Portes du Soleil circuit, each
offering a mix of open and wooded
slopes. For notes on the circuit read
our special chapter on it. The local
piste map is much less clear than it
used to be because they have made it
smaller. Signposting is good.

EXTENT OF THE SLOPES ★★★★★
Two sectors to choose between
Châtel has a worthwhile amount of
local skiing, in two separate sectors
which were lift-linked from last season.
    Directly above the village is **Super-
Châtel** – an area of easy, open and
lightly wooded slopes that is accessed
by a gondola or a two-stage chair.
From here you can embark on a
clockwise Portes du Soleil circuit by
heading to the Swiss resort of
Morgins. Or you can head north for the
slopes straddling a different bit of the
Swiss border, above **Torgon** (with fab
views of Lake Geneva). From this
season you will also be able to take a
new piste down to Vonnes and then
the new quad up to the **Linga** sector,

where you can start an anticlockwise
tour of the Portes du Soleil circuit.
This sector can also be reached by bus
from Châtel; if you stay on the bus it
takes you to the Pré-la-Joux/Plaine
Dranse area, closer to the link with
Avoriaz. There is night skiing at Linga
on Thursdays.

FAST LIFTS ★★★★★
Luxurious Linga
Linga and the Plaine Dranse area are
well served for fast lifts but in the
Super-Châtel sector the lifts beyond
the access gondola are almost entirely
slow chairs and drags, whether you
head for Morgins or for Torgon. Hence
our rating.

QUEUES ★★★★★
Bottlenecks have been eased
In recent years queues have been
eased throughout the Portes du Soleil
by the installation of several fast new
chairlifts. Locally Linga is no problem
but Super-Châtel is: queues form for
the gondola when school parties
gather (and you can also face queues
to get down again if the sunny home
slope is shut because of poor snow),
and reporters have also found lengthy
queues for the slow Morclan chair and
the Tour de Don, Chermeu and Chalet
Neuf draglifts at certain times of day.

TERRAIN PARKS ★★★★★
One size suits all
The Smoothpark at Super-Châtel has
lines to suit both beginners and
experienced freestylers, and they
include rails, kickers and boxes;
there's a snowcross too.

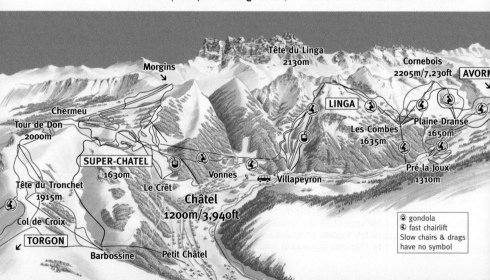

gondola
fast chairlift
Slow chairs & drags
have no symbol

↑ The Plaine Dranse and Linga sectors have fast lifts and great red- and blue-run cruising

CHATEL TO / JF VUARAND

great run from Tête du Linga over into the next (deserted) valley of La Leiche – read the special off-piste feature panel in our Morzine chapter.

FOR INTERMEDIATES ★★★★
Some great local terrain
When conditions are right the Portes du Soleil is an intermediate's paradise. Good intermediates need not go far from Châtel to find amusement: Linga and Plaine Dranse have some of the best red runs on the circuit. The moderately skilled can do the Portes du Soleil circuit without problem, and will particularly enjoy runs around Les Lindarets and Morgins. Even timid types can do the circuit, provided they take one or two short cuts and ride chairs down the trickier bits. But some blues are difficult when conditions are poor – in particular, one reporter witnessed skiers 'in tears' on the way down to Morgins from Châtel.

Visits to Avoriaz for the Hauts Forts runs are worthwhile for competent and adventurous intermediates. And note that the runs back to Plaine Dranse are real reds, and the Rochassons piste, especially, can get extremely busy at the end of the day.

Don't overlook the Torgon sector, which has some excellent slopes, including challenging ones.

FOR BEGINNERS ★★★
Three possible options
There are good beginners' areas at Pré-la-Joux (a bus ride away) and at Super-Châtel (a gondola ride above the village). And there are nursery slopes at village level if there is snow there. Reporters have praised the Super-Châtel slopes and lifts, which 'allow the beginner to progress' and 'safely practise' on gentle gradients away from the main runs. Getting up to them is a bit of an effort, though. The home run from Super-Châtel can be tricky – narrow, busy, steep at the end and often icy at the end of the day – but you can ride the gondola down. The Pré-la-Joux slopes are less varied, with some steeper draglifts.

FOR BOARDERS ★★
Best for beginners – beware drags
Avoriaz is the hard-core destination for boarders in the Portes du Soleil and has a great selection of terrain parks plus a super-pipe – see that chapter. Châtel is not a bad place to learn or to go to as a budget option. But many

SNOW RELIABILITY ★★
The main drawback
The main drawback of the Portes du Soleil as a whole is that it is low, and exposed to mild weather from the west, so snow quality can suffer when it's warm. But a lot of snowmaking has been installed at Super-Châtel and on runs down to resort level. Linga and Plaine Dranse are mainly north-facing and generally have the best local snow. The pistes to Morgins and towards Avoriaz get full sun. Grooming is 'very good' say recent reporters.

FOR EXPERTS ★★★
Some challenges
The best steep runs – on- and off-piste – are in the Linga and Pré-la-Joux area. Beneath the Linga gondola and chair there's a pleasant mix of open and wooded ground, which follows the fall line fairly directly. And there's a serious mogul field between Cornebois and Plaine Dranse. Two pistes from the Rochassons ridge are steep and kept well groomed. On the way to Torgon from Super-Châtel, the Barbossine black run is long, steep and quite narrow and tricky at the top. There's plenty of good lift-served off-piste to be explored with a guide: we did a

Like the resort?
You'll love our handpicked accommodation
02392 839 310
PEAKRETREATS.CO.UK

ABTA
ABTA No W5517

CHATEL TO / JF VUARAND

The village is attractive with chalet-style buildings. That's the Linga sector of slopes on the right ↓

lifts in the Super-Châtel sector are drags, and reporters warn that they can be a 'painful experience'. The Linga area has good, varied slopes and off-piste possibilities and more boarder-friendly chairlifts.

FOR CROSS-COUNTRY ★★★
Pretty, if low, trails
There are pretty trails (12km) along the river, around Lake Vonnes and through the woods on the lower slopes of Linga, but snow-cover can be a problem. When combined with La Chapelle-d'Abondance's trails, the total is 40km. The tourist office produces good maps.

MOUNTAIN RESTAURANTS ★★★
Some quite good local huts
Restaurants are marked but not named on the piste map.

A cluster of cosy huts can be found at Plaine Dranse. We get regular reports from a devotee of the 'camp and cosy' Vieux Chalet, aka Chez Babeth: 'The food is excellent but it has become increasingly pricey; Babeth the owner is absolutely barking.'

In the Linga area the Ferme des Pistes is a lovely cosy old barn (complete with stable-door) where a reporter enjoyed 'a huge plateful of

spud, ham and cheese'. The chapter on Avoriaz has some tips on restaurants at Les Lindarets, in the valley between the resorts.

SCHOOLS AND GUIDES ★★★
Plenty of choice
There are several schools in Châtel, including a branch of BASS (British Alpine Ski & Snowboard School) as well as the usual ESF and International schools.

A recent reporter says: 'I learned with ESF at Super-Châtel and the instructors were generally very good but their standard of English varied.'

FOR FAMILIES ★★★
Some good facilities
The ESF-run Piou Piou nursery offers indoor and outdoor activities plus getting a taste for skiing. Châtel Ski Sensations has its own nursery area with a draglift and chalet at Linga.

STAYING THERE

This is emphatically a French resort. No big UK tour operators feature it in a major way.
Chalets Some smart-looking places are available from owner-managers and small specialist tour operators.
Hotels Most are friendly 2- or 3-stars,

built in chalet-style and wooden or at least partly wood-clad.

****Macchi** Smart, modern chalet, spacious comfortable rooms, central, good food; small pool, spa.

***Belalp** Simple chalet, small rooms.

***Fleur de Neige** Woody chalet near centre, good food; spa, pool.

***Kandahar** One for peace lovers: a logis by the river, a walkable distance from the centre.

Choucas Central location.

Roitelet Basic, near the centre.

Apartments Peak Retreats offers four recently built properties that set a new standard for Châtel, all with pools and various spa facilities: Grand Lodge and Grand Ermitage (both in the Vonnes area near the new chairlifts), Chalets d'Angèle and, new for 2015/16, the Fermes de Châtel right next to the Super-Châtel gondola. Erna Low has most of these too and Crystal has Fermes de Châtel. Châtel's village supermarkets are reported to be small and overcrowded, but there is a large supermarket out in the direction of Chapelle-d'Abondance.

EATING OUT ★★★ ★★
Fair selection

There is an adequate number and range of restaurants. The Macchi and Fleur de Neige hotels both have ambitious restaurants. We've also enjoyed the Table d'Antoine restaurant of the hotel Chalet d'Alizée, though that was a few years ago. The rustic Vieux Four does ambitious dishes alongside Savoyard specialities. The fixed price menus at the 'wonderful' Poya are 'good value' says a 2015 reporter. The Pierrier and the 'friendly' Fiacre ('great pizzas and typical Savoyard mains') are more modest, everyday restaurants, good for families.

It's worth a trip to the eccentric hotel Cornettes in La Chapelle-d'Abondance (described on the right).

APRES-SKI ★★★ ★★
All down to bars

The Nazca (formerly Tunnel) bar has a happy hour and a DJ or live music every night. The Avalanche is a very popular English-style pub. The Godille – close to the Super-Châtel gondola and crowded when everyone descends at close of play – has a more French feel. The Isba is the locals' choice, and shows extreme-sports videos. The bowling alley has a good bar.

OFF THE SLOPES ★★ ★★★
Bad for meeting up

There's the new Forme d'O aqua centre. Those with a car can easily visit places such as Geneva, Thonon and Evian. There are pleasant walks, ice skating and bowling; you can visit the cheese factory or the two cinemas, or join in daily events organized by the tourist office.

The Portes du Soleil as a whole is less than ideal for non-skiers who like to meet their more active friends for lunch: they are likely to be at some distant resort – maybe in another country – at lunchtime, and even if they are not, very few lifts are accessible to pedestrians.

DOWN-VALLEY VILLAGE – 1010m
LA CHAPELLE-D'ABONDANCE

This unspoiled, rustic farming community, complete with old church and friendly locals, is 5km down the valley from Châtel. It has its own small, quiet north-facing area of easy wooded runs, and a gondola starting on the outskirts links it to slopes between Torgon in Switzerland and Super-Châtel, and so to the Portes du Soleil circuit.

The hotel Cornettes is an amazing 3-star with 4-star facilities, including an indoor pool, a sauna, a steam room and hot tubs. It has an atmospheric bar and an excellent restaurant with good-value menus. The hotel has been run by the Trincaz family since 1894. Look out for the showcases displaying their collections of puppets and dolls and for other eccentric touches, such as ancient doors that unexpectedly slide open automatically.

A regular reporter recommends L'Echo de la Corne apartments ('reasonably priced, convenient for the gondola or driving to Châtel') and chalet Montana ('spacious and comfortable apartment, French owners were lovely').

Nightlife is virtually non-existent – just a few quiet bars, a cinema and torchlit descents. You can go dog sledding and snowshoeing. The Fer Rouge is a popular microbrewery, with live music.

GETTING THERE

Air Geneva 80km/ 50 miles (1hr30)

Rail Thonon les Bains (40km/25 miles)

TOURIST OFFICES

Châtel
www.chatel.com

La Chapelle-d'Abondance
www.lachapelle74.com

Courchevel

Arguably the best of the half-dozen resorts that make up the famous Three Valleys – with a choice of four different villages

£140
RESORT PRICE INDEX

RATINGS

The mountains

Extent	★★★★★
Fast lifts	★★★★
Queues	★★★★
Terrain p'ks	★★
Snow	★★★★
Expert	★★★★
Intermediate	★★★★★
Beginner	★★★★
Boarder	★★★
X-country	★★★★
Restaurants	★★★
Schools	★★★★
Families	★★★★

The resort

Charm	★★
Convenience	★★★★
Scenery	★★★
Eating out	★★★★★
Après-ski	★★★★
Off-slope	★★★

KEY FACTS

Resort 1260-1850m
4,130-6,070ft

Three Valleys
Slopes	1260-3230m
	4,130-10,600ft
Lifts	180
Pistes	600km
	373 miles

Courchevel/
La Tania only
Slopes	1260-2740m
	4,130-8,990ft
Lifts	58
Pistes	150km
	93 miles

- ➕ Extensive, varied slopes – many visitors don't leave this valley
- ➕ Impressive snowmaking and piste grooming, and a decent lift system
- ➕ Partly wooded setting means you have options in bad weather
- ➕ Choice of four very different villages
- ➕ Some great restaurants and top-notch hotels – and plenty of non-swanky options in lower villages

- ➖ Unremarkable villages – downtown 1850 is particularly disappointing, for an upmarket resort
- ➖ Very high prices in 1850, and in all mountain restaurants
- ➖ In 1850 the French feel has been lost, with huge numbers of foreign visitors; and to some extent the ski-resort feel has been lost, too
- ➖ Not great for the indolent non-skier unless glitzy shops are your thing

Courchevel's ski area is the most compelling sector of the famous Three Valleys, the biggest linked ski area in the world; if we're heading for the 3V, more often than not we'll head for Courchevel.

But it's not one destination, it's four. Swanky 1850 catches the headlines, with its airstrip, ritzy hotels and countless Michelin-star restaurants. The other villages have none of 1850's pretensions and high prices. The village restaurants and bars are not cheap, but they are not noticeably more expensive than in other top French resorts. There are plenty of affordable catered chalet holidays on sale here, even (thanks to the miracles worked by UK tour ops) in 1850. Sadly, on the slopes there are few affordable lunches to be had.

You may notice that we're still resisting the rebranding of the component villages, explained in the box on the facing page. We'll probably adapt to it one day, but when you've been referring to 1850, 1650 and 1550 for [cough] years as we have, it's difficult to shake the habit.

THE RESORT

The numbers in the village names that were used until 2011 implied altitudes, and although they were seriously inaccurate they did give clues to altitude: 1850 is higher than 1650, etc.

What we persist in calling Courchevel 1850 was one of the first French resorts to be purpose-built after World War 2. The other villages were developed later, although they already existed as old hamlets.

1850 is big enough to have several distinguishable quarters. The main lift base and the central area around it is La Croisette; the resort spreads a long way up the hillside on the left through the chalet-filled suburbs of Cospillot and Nogentil to the altiport, the resort's famously hazardous little airstrip. Part of these suburbs is the Jardin Alpin, a forested area with some of the swankiest hotels (and more modest chalets and apartments), served by its own gondola. On the

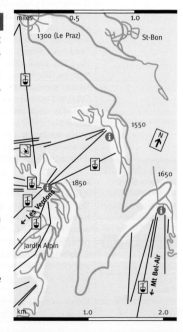

NEWS

2015/16: The long-awaited aquatic centre below 1650 will open. Women's World Cup races will be held here in December 2015. Disabled access to the lifts and pistes is being improved. Eco-friendly snowmaking is being introduced.

2014/15: A six-pack replaced the adjacent Aiguille du Fruit and Gravelles chairs at Praméruel between 1650 and 1850. The ancient Forêt gondola distinct from Le Praz was replaced by a six-pack. The Park City run has been reshaped as a blue.

opposite, right-hand side of La Croisette is another little 'downtown' area, with the suburbs of Chenus above it and Plantret below.

The other resort villages are smaller and simpler. The main part of 1650 has grown up along the road that links the resorts (though traffic is not very intrusive on weekdays); and the centre, below the lift base area, has been attractively developed and is lined with good everyday shops, restaurants and bars. Opposite the main gondola (reached by an escalator) individual chalets spread down the hill. Then there is another area of chalet development spreading up the slopes to an area known as Belvédère. 1650 has its own distinct sector of slopes, connected to 1850.

1550 is a bit of a backwater, with a few blocks and many more individual properties, directly below 1850. Le Praz is an old village on a plateau at the bottom of wooded slopes. Among its attractions is a ski shop with an exceptional range of top-quality 'demo' skis – Olympic Sports, in the centre.

With a car, Champagny (linked to La Plagne's slopes) is easily reached.

VILLAGE CHARM ★★
Not a strong point
Courchevel 1850 has most of the smart hotels and shops, and you would expect it to be a pretty smooth place in general. The reality is a let-down; when compared with other smart resorts, 1850 does not impress.

The approach has been smartened up somewhat but is still rather dreary, and at the hub of the resort, La Croisette, you are confronted by the back side of the main lift station building, complete with garage entrances. Past this point, things improve again: the streets are lined by smart shops and jolly restaurants. But the nearest thing to a central focus is where a hairpin bend on the busy road through the resort to the affluent

suburbs touches the slopes. The areas above the centre are more pleasant – in places, peacefully rustic – and of course if you are going to be closeted in a 5-star hotel in the Jardin Alpin you may not care much about village ambience.

Central 1650 is more attractive, and has a friendly traditional feel once you get away from the through-road up to 1850. 1550 is a pleasantly quiet, spacious mini-resort, bypassed by the road to 1850. Le Praz suffers from the through-traffic, but away from the road is a low-key rustic place, with a friendly atmosphere, relatively unspoiled despite expansion for the 1992 Olympics – the ski jump is a prominent legacy.

CONVENIENCE ★★★★
Varies – research your location
The villages all have lifts into the slopes, with much of the lodging close by, but in all cases you need to be careful about location if you want to avoid walks. Frequent free buses link the villages.

1850 has several pistes running through it, and a high proportion of ski-in/ski-out lodgings. Central 1650 lodgings are a short walk from the lifts; those down the hill below the centre are served by a long, three-stage covered escalator. There are slope-side lodgings at the lift base, and on skier's right as you descend to the village. 1550 is arranged along the bottom of the slopes, with lifts immediately above most of the lodgings. In Le Praz the lifts start a short walk outside the village.

SCENERY ★★★
Some good views
Most of the villages enjoy a pretty woodland setting, and from parts of them and from the slopes above there are good views to Mont Blanc and over the valley to Champagny and Bellecôte (in the La Plagne ski area).

NAME CHANGES FOR THE COURCHEVEL VILLAGES

In 2011, the villages that make up Courchevel were given new names. Courchevel 1850 is now supposed to be called Courchevel; 1650 revived the name of the old village it is based on and is now Courchevel Moriond; 1550 became Courchevel Village. Le Praz (aka 1300) is Courchevel Le Praz. Most signs on the mountain still use the old names, and for the moment, we're doing the same.

The old names were implicitly related to altitude. We revealed many years ago that the names exaggerated the altitudes – central 1850 is at about 1750m, and you have to go way up the hill to the Biollay and Coqs lifts to reach 1850m – so we should perhaps welcome the changes. But the piste map now explicitly states altitudes based on the old names, which defies belief.

LeSki
the chalet specialists

30 CATERED CHALETS
COURCHEVEL
VAL D'ISÈRE LA TANIA
01484 954397 LESKI.COM

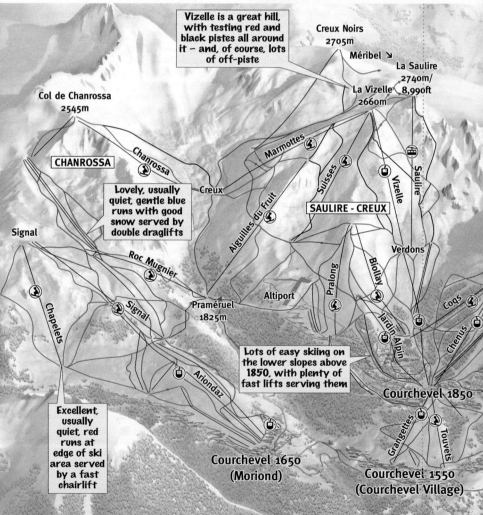

Vizelle is a great hill, with testing red and black pistes all around it – and, of course, lots of off-piste

Creux Noirs
2705m

Méribel ↘

La Saulire
2740m/
8,990ft

La Vizelle
2660m

Col de Chanrossa
2545m

Marmottes

Suisses

Vizelle

Saulire

CHANROSSA

Chanrossa

Creux

Aiguilles du Fruit

SAULIRE - CREUX

Lovely, usually quiet, gentle blue runs with good snow served by double draglifts

Signal

Roc Mugnier

Verdons

Pralong

Biollay

Chapelets

Signal

Praméruel
1825m

Altiport

Jardin Alpin

Coqs

Chenus

Lots of easy skiing on the lower slopes above 1850, with plenty of fast lifts serving them

Ariondaz

Courchevel 1850

Excellent, usually quiet, red runs at edge of ski area served by a fast chairlift

Grangettes

Touvets

Courchevel 1650
(Moriond)

Courchevel 1550
(Courchevel Village)

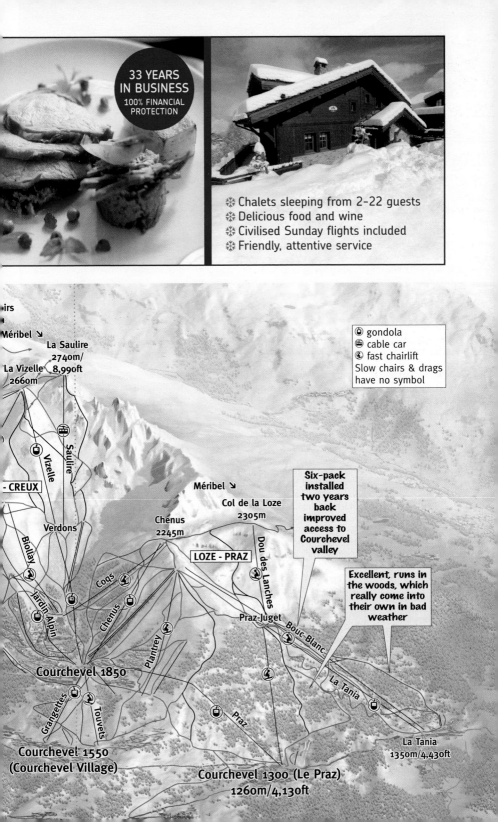

33 YEARS IN BUSINESS
100% FINANCIAL PROTECTION

❄ Chalets sleeping from 2-22 guests
❄ Delicious food and wine
❄ Civilised Sunday flights included
❄ Friendly, attentive service

🚠 gondola
🚋 cable car
🚡 fast chairlift
Slow chairs & drags have no symbol

irs
Méribel ↘
La Saulire
2740m/
8,990ft
La Vizelle
2666m

Saulire

Vizelle

- CREUX

Verdons

Biollay

Coqs

Chenus

Jardin Alpin

Plantrey

Courchevel 1850

Grangettes

Touvets

Courchevel 1550
(Courchevel Village)

Méribel ↘
Col de la Loze
2305m

Chenus
2245m

LOZE - PRAZ

Dou des Lanches

Praz-Juget

Bouc Blanc

La Tania

Praz

Courchevel 1300 (Le Praz)
1260m/4,130ft

La Tania
1350m/4,430ft

Six-pack installed two years back improved access to Courchevel valley

Excellent runs in the woods, which really come into their own in bad weather

↑ There are plenty of convenient slope-side lodgings at 1850

SNOWPIX.COM / CHRIS GILL

LIFT PASSES

Three Valleys

Prices in €

Age	6-day
under 13	228
13 to 64	283
65 plus	255

Free Under 5, 75 plus

Beginner Limited pass

Notes Covers Courchevel, La Tania, Méribel, Val Thorens, Les Menuires and St-Martin; reductions for families, duos and groups. Options: pedestrian and half-day passes

Alternative passes Courchevel/La Tania + 3V extension; Courchevel 1650 only

THE MOUNTAINS

Although there are plenty of trees around the villages, most of the slopes are essentially open, with the notable exception of the runs down to 1550 and to Le Praz, and the valley between 1850 and 1650 – both excellent areas to head for in a blizzard.

We have few complaints about the piste map or general signposting. They have stopped handing out maps of which pistes have been groomed, which we think is very regrettable, but you can now get this information on the Three Valleys smartphone app and it appears in notices posted in lift stations. They also list recommended 'pistes du jour' – a really good idea.

The long Creux piste from La Saulire was changed from red to blue classification a year or two back; we are getting used to the idea – it clearly is a borderline case, whichever classification it is given – but would still recommend timid intermediates from Méribel to access Courchevel via Col de la Loze – not least because Creux, always a popular piste, is now busier than ever.

EXTENT OF THE SLOPES ★★★★★
Huge variety to suit everyone
A network of lifts and pistes spreads out from 1850. The main axis is the **Verdons** gondola, leading to a second gondola to La Vizelle and a nearly parallel cable car up to La Saulire. These high points of the **Saulire-Creux** sector give access to a wide range of terrain above Courchevel and to Méribel and thus the whole of the Three Valleys. Next to the Verdons gondola is the Jardin Alpin gondola, which serves the hotels until 8pm and also links to lifts and pistes further up the hill.

To the right looking up, the Chenus gondola goes towards the **Loze-Praz** sector, which forms a second link with Méribel – these days you have to descend to Bouc Blanc, at mid-mountain above La Tania, to make the link. Runs also go back from here to 1850, and through the woods to La Tania, Le Praz and 1550.

The main gondola from 1650 goes to Bel Air and further lifts on into the **Chanrossa** sector. This sector has links to Saulire-Creux at two points – Praméruel and Creux.

FAST LIFTS ★★★★
Plenty of them
You will occasionally find yourself on a slow chair, but there are only a couple of places where slow lifts are not avoidable. The piste map makes the distinction between slow and fast chairs, which helps. Many of the chairs are now equipped with a system to hold the safety bar down automatically until you are very near the top – this can be quite unnerving when you first encounter it.

QUEUES ★★★★
Not a problem

The lift system is impressive, and continually being improved (two new fast chairs last season, for example). even in peak season queues are minimal. But there can be a build-up at 1850 as the ski school gets going. The Biollay chair is very popular with the ski school; it was upgraded to a six-pack a few seasons ago, but still builds queues – two March reporters had to wait '10 to 15 minutes'. At 1650, the lifts at the base can have queues. Upgrades are coming.

TERRAIN PARKS ★★
Freestyle for all the family

The Family Park below Verdons is now the main park and has lines to suit different levels, with a variety of rails, tables and obstacles – but, says an unimpressed reporter, 'essentially no jumps except the airbag jump'; there's also a snowcross. There are smaller 'fun zones' above 1650: Snake Park has a snowcross and Fun Park has large bumps. The Wood Park above 1550 has, er, wooden rails and tables.

SNOW RELIABILITY ★★★★
Very good

The combination of Courchevel's northerly orientation, its height, an abundance of snowmaking and excellent grooming usually guarantees good snow down to at least 1850 and 1650. The snow is usually much better than in Méribel, where the slopes (particularly the slopes you ski from the Courchevel ridge) get more sun. The runs to Le Praz are prone to closure in warm weather.

ALPINE ANSWERS
The UK's No.1 Chalet Specialist

For choice and service look no further!

alpineanswers.co.uk
call: 020 7801 1080   ABTA

FOR EXPERTS ★★★★
Entertaining pistes, and ...

There is plenty to interest experts, even without considering the rest of the Three Valleys. The most obvious expert runs are the shady couloirs you can see on the right as you near the top of the Saulire cable car. All three main couloirs were once black pistes (some of the steepest in Europe), but only the Grand Couloir remains a piste – the widest and easiest of the three but the trickiest to reach, via a narrow, bumpy, precipitous ridge.

The shady slopes of La Vizelle and Creux Noirs are not seriously steep, but all the runs – tough reds and not-tough blacks – offer a worthwhile challenge. If you like groomed blacks in the early morning, keep an eye on the grooming notices at lift bases/ticket offices to see when Suisses, Combe Pylones or M is groomed. Chanrossa often has the most serious bumps (and the iciest snow in late season – it gets afternoon sun). The blacks above Le Praz can be great fun, offering a vertical of almost 1000m.

There is a huge amount of off-piste

Courchevel

243

ONE OF THE BEST FOR OFF-PISTE SKIING

Courchevel's image is of upmarket luxury and pampered piste skiing. But it is a great resort for off-piste too (always go with a guide). Manu Gaidet is a Courchevel mountain guide and a ski instructor with the Courchevel ESF. He is also one of the world's top freeriders, and won the Freeride World Championship three years running. We asked him to pick out a few of the best runs.

For a first experience off-piste, the Tour du Rocher de l'Ombre is great. Access is easy from the left of the Combe de la Saulire piste, and you are never far from it. It is very quiet, the slope is very broad and easy and you get a real sense of adventure as you plan your way between the rocks. And the view of the Croix des Verdons is impressive. Keep to the left for the best snow.

The Chanrossa chairlift opens up several routes. Les Avals is one of my favourites, involving a short climb to the ridge to the south. This run is not technically difficult and is particularly beautiful in spring conditions. Another possibility is to traverse towards the Aiguille du Fruit, and pick your spot to start skiing down to Creux. And there is Plan Mugnier, a shady run with normally very good snow, but more difficult. It's for experienced off-piste skiers only and starts with a 20-minute hike.

Le Curé is in the Saulire area: this narrow gully starts under a towering rock and offers a steady 35° slope; it is only for expert skiers who don't mind climbing to the Doigt du Curé starting point.

IMPROVE YOUR SKIING
SKI WITH OTHERS
GO PLACES

SNOWORKS
snoworks.com

terrain, including lots next to the pistes. The runs off Dou des Lanches through the trees down to La Tania and off the top of Creux Noir (via a little walk) down to join up with the Creux piste are recommended. The wooded areas in general are great for bad weather. Read our feature panel on the previous page.

In good snow conditions you can ski all the way down (around 2000m vertical) from La Saulire to Bozel.

There is plenty of other off-piste terrain in this valley to try with a guide – read the feature panel.

FOR INTERMEDIATES ★★★★★
Paradise for red-run skiers

For confident intermediates, Courchevel's local slopes are simply fabulous. Every sector has long, testing red runs and easy blacks, and there is abundant easy off-piste to experiment in. There are too many excellent runs to list; every high point – Signal, Chanrossa, Vizelle, Creux Noirs, Saulire, Chenus, Loze – offers one, two, three, four notable descents.

For timid intermediates, we're not so enthusiastic. The red runs from Vizelle and Saulire can be quite testing, especially late in the day. But there are some excellent sectors to focus on. The long, narrow sector of blue slopes above 1650 is superb, and there is an array of excellent blue slopes above and below 1850 – the Biollay and Pralong fast chairs are the ones to head for here. The runs down to La Tania are long, rolling cruises, fine in good snow conditions.

FOR BEGINNERS ★★★★
Great graduation runs

There are excellent nursery slopes above both 1650 and 1850. At 1650, there are short drags right above the village. At 1850 there is a small but good beginner area in the Jardin Alpin, reachable by the gondola, and an excellent bigger one at Pralong, near the altiport. Absolute beginners have to get to this by road. There are nine free beginner lifts – at least one in each village, five in 1850. 1550 and Le Praz have small nursery areas; but the 1550 one is quite steep. There are excellent long runs to progress to.

FOR BOARDERS ★★★
Upmarket all-rounder

Despite being an upmarket resort, Courchevel has always been popular with snowboarders. There are miles of well-groomed pistes, good freeride terrain and the lifts are in general very modern and quick, with few drags. The resort's freestyle facilities are not what you would call hard-core, though.

FOR CROSS-COUNTRY ★★★★
Long wooded trails

Courchevel has around 60km of trails. Le Praz is the best village, with trails through the woods towards 1550, 1850 and Méribel. Given enough snow, there are also loops around the village.

MOUNTAIN RESTAURANTS ★★★
Fine if you can afford them

Restaurants are plentiful and pleasant, but very pricey (and not named on the piste map). Fortunately, the local lift pass permits lunch at Bouc Blanc above La Tania; of course, the 3V pass gets you to excellent spots above Les Menuires, St-Martin and Val Thorens.
Editors' choice The Bel Air, above 1650, has long stood out for its warm welcome, efficient service, good food, splendid tiered terrace, nice woody interior and (by local standards) reasonable drinks prices. But even here the food is unpleasantly pricey (23 euros for the plat du jour; even including a big salad, too much).
Worth knowing about Such is the difficulty of finding a good, affordable lunch above Courchevel that we are prepared to descend to the terrace of the hotel Courcheneige on the Bellecôte slope (and it is terrace-only, so forget it on bad days). The fixed-price three-course meal is good value, but the 'spectacular entrée buffet' is enough for many of our enthusiastic reporters. The Soucoupe at Loze is a traditional place that merits a mention, despite its typically high prices, for 'amazing ribs and the best ever gratin dauphinois'.

SCHOOLS AND GUIDES ★★★★
Plenty of choice

We've had many positive reports on New Generation (run by top British instructors), with only the occasional dissenting voice. Reporters also praise Brit-based RTM Snowboarding: 'Great backcountry coaching.' BASS, Sweet Snowsports and Supreme are other Brit-run schools. We've had positive reports on the ESF, particularly on its handling of children. Note that the Courchevel ESF is not involved in the legal action against chalet operator Le

Ski that put an end to tour operator ski guiding throughout France two seasons back.

FOR FAMILIES ★★★★
Lots of suitable options

Courchevel is a good choice for families; there is lots of convenient lodging and gentle slopes. Many of the fast chairlifts have an electro-magnet system that works in conjunction with special bibs to hold children securely onto the chairlifts. The ESF Club des Piou Piou at 1650, for kids aged three to five, is reportedly 'very well run'. Several UK chalet operators run nurseries. Family specialist Esprit Ski operates in 1850 – read 'Chalets', under 'Staying there'. The Indiens blue above 1650 with an 'exciting natural half-pipe and Indian village' was a hit with a previous reporter and family.

ESPRIT
FOR FAMILIES IN
Courchevel
Family
Ski Chalets
Dedicated
Nurseries
Exclusive Ski
Classes
13 resorts
across the Alps
espritski.com
01483 791 900

STAYING THERE

Chalets There are lots available – specialist agents list dozens of them. 1650 is UK chalet central.

Le Ski, coming up to its 34th year in Courchevel, now has an impressive 17 chalets in 1650, sleeping from 2 (yes, two) to 22; 12 of them have sauna, steam or hot tub. Its flagship Scalottas Lodge has five apartment-chalets; we've stayed in two of them, both with fabulous views, leather armchairs and sofas, solid wooden floors, a jacuzzi and hi-tech lights and heating. Crystal has two eight-person units in one building in 1650. Ski Olympic is also a 1650 specialist, with the central Avals chalet hotel.

Skiworld has four chalets in 1650, including the traditional but smooth Estrella, with hot tub, and one in 1550 – soon to be joined by three smart new units currently being formed in an existing chalet building. Inghams has four chalets and the very central 30-bedroomed chalet hotel les Anémones in 1850, and two chalets with hot tub and sauna in 1650. Ski Total has a huge chalet bang in the centre of 1650, and in 1850 a central 60-bed chalet hotel, the Coq de Bruyeres; approved again this year – 'hotel, staff, food and entertainment good'. Also six smaller chalets, one of them the 8-bed penthouse of the Coq. Also in 1850, family specialist Esprit Ski has a chalet hotel with a good pool, sauna and hot tub right next to the lifts at Pralong.

Down in Le Praz, Mountain Heaven has three chalets. We have enjoyed a very comfortable stay in the cosily traditional Jardin d'Angele. This shares an excellent little spa area (and outdoor hot tub) with the quite different Emilie – traditional exterior, but cutting-edge style within. The third chalet is a converted farmhouse in the

COURCHEVEL TOURISME / DAVID ANDRE

Take care when tackling Chanrossa – it gets afternoon sun and the snow can be tricky ↓

SKIWORLD

Catered chalets, hotels and self catering apartments in

Europe, USA and Canada

skiworld.co.uk

08444 930 430

ABTA V2151 ATOL 2036

core of the old village.

Luxury operators in 1850 include Consensio, Kaluma, Scott Dunn and Supertravel.

Hotels There are more than 40 hotels, mostly at 1850 and many of them very swanky. Two were awarded a new 'Palace' rating – the Cheval Blanc and the Airelles – to distinguish them from the 5-star standard invented only a few years back; amazingly, 15 hotels now hold 5-star status. The prices of the top places give new meaning to the word 'exorbitant' – it is possible to pay £1,000 per person per night without too much difficulty.

COURCHEVEL 1850

*****Lana Bottom of the Bellecôte piste. Pool, spa, hot tub. 'Good restaurant, very good service, rooms are small though comfortable.'

****Chabichou Distinctive white building, right on the slopes; family-run, friendly and rustic, with very good food plus the option of a restaurant with two Michelin stars.

***Courcheneige Ski-in/ski-out location on the Bellecôte piste (and a favourite lunch spot), with a rustic restaurant. 'Friendly young staff, small but comfortable rooms, top-quality food (though limited choice).'

COURCHEVEL 1650

****Portetta Neat place at foot of slopes, with steam, sauna, spa, good restaurant. 'Wonderful' boot room!

***Seizena Stylish and central (over road from the gondola).

COURCHEVEL LE PRAZ

***Peupliers Traditional, smart, good restaurant – focal place in le Praz.

Apartments If you want to self-cater in real style, take a look at the chalets in the resort literature. Returning to planet Earth ...

Ski Amis has privately owned apartments in several parts of the resort. Mountain Heaven has apartments in Le Praz. The best big residences are the Montagnettes Chalets de la Mouria in 1650 (we stayed there happily in 2013) with spa; and the Chalets du Forum in central 1850 – a Pierre & Vacances Premium residence.

EATING OUT ★★★★★
Pick your price

You can eat very well here, but in 1850 you have to watch the prices closely. A pocket restaurant guide is distributed locally – advertising-based, so non-comprehensive.

In 1850 there are no fewer than five places with two Michelin stars. (We'd like to witness the five chefs getting together to bitch about the third star awarded last year to La Bouitte, near humble Les Menuires.)

Leaving those aside ... we had an excellent and not too pricey dinner last season at the Chabotté – owned by, next to and much cheaper than the starred Chabichou. Le Génepi is reported to be 'wonderful – cosy, charming, with good food'. For the budget conscious, the Passage serves 'yummy pizzas' at 'affordable prices'. La Luge also does 'decent burgers and salads'. More reports on affordable places, please.

In 1650 two places that do pizza,

Selected chalets in Courchevel

ADVERTISEMENT

MOUNTAIN HEAVEN *www.mountainheaven.co.uk*   T **0151 625 1921**

Mountain Heaven has three wonderful catered chalets in the resort of Courchevel Le Praz, a true Savoyard village and the prettiest of the four Courchevel villages with great access to the whole of the Three Valleys. Chalet Jardin d'Angele is one of our Flagship Chalets, with eight bedrooms, and Chalet Emilie, with its architect-designed luxury interior and four bedrooms, has been nominated as one of the best new chalets in the world. Chalet Louis is our great value chalet located right in the heart of the village.

Email: info@mountainheaven.co.uk

HIGH QUALITY ACCOMMODATION ↑

It does get a bit steeper lower down, but this is the easy way to Courchevel from Méribel: the initial descent from Col de la Loze →

SNOWPIX.COM / CHRIS GILL

pasta and Savoyard dishes have been repeatedly tipped by reporters – the Petit Savoyard ('service was excellent, food superb') and La Table de Marie ('outstanding service, good food, enormous portions'). The Arc en Ciel (formerly the Eterlou) is also tipped by a reader – 'food delicious, owners very friendly'.

At 1550 the Oeil de Boeuf at the foot of the slopes is 'fantastic – meat perfectly cooked on an open fire'.

In Le Praz, the small and unpretentious Michelin-starred Azimut is much more affordable than equivalent places in 1850 (three-course menus from 28 euros), and we have had a delicious meal there. The Table de Mon Grand-Père in the hotel Peupliers has superb food and atmosphere but prices approaching 1850 levels. Bistrot du Praz is also expensive but worth it, say reporters. Cave des Lys is a vaulted wine bar that serves tapas-style snacks.

APRES-SKI ★★★★
The choice is yours

At close of play there are bars around the Croisette that are good for a relaxing drink, but reporters claim that 1850 isn't nearly as lively at close of play as it once was – 'All the bars have been turned into boutiques,' says one. KuDeTa is 'good value at happy hour' and later its disco pumps until 4am, as does the Grange – a Moroccan-style place. There are some exclusive nightclubs, such as Caves. The Mangeoire piano bar gets going late, with live music. Tremplin has karaoke. P'tit Drink specializes in wine and tapas. The bar of hotel Olympic has 'pints for 3 euros'.

In 1650 there are several lively bars

within a few yards of each other. The current reader favourite is the Boulotte – 'a must (like Austrian après)', 'great – rocking to a British band'. We like the Schuss for a quiet drink. The lively Funky Fox has pool, live music or DJs; the French Kiss disco stays open late.

In 1550 there are several bars that can develop a lively atmosphere both early and late.

In Le Praz there are lively terraces around the focal hotel Peupliers. Cave des Lys is a lovely spot for a quiet drink. l'Escorche-vel is 'good for live music'.

OFF THE SLOPES ★★★★★
Not ideal

There is quite a bit to do, but the emphasis is very much on physical activities. The lack of a swimming pool gets rectified at last this coming season with the opening of a seriously impressive aquatic centre with pool, surfing area and spa in the valley between 1550 and 1650, and below 1850. It will in due course be linked by lift to some or all of these villages.

A guide to walks is available from the tourist office. A pedestrian lift pass for the gondolas and buses in Courchevel and Méribel makes it easy for non-skiers to get up the mountain to meet others for lunch. Cinemas in 1850 and 1650 show English-speaking films. Snowshoeing among the trees and 'seriously awesome' tobogganing from 1850 to 1550 are popular. And you can take joyrides from the altiport. To make sure you miss no opportunity to go broke, there is a guide listing fashion and jewellery shops in 1850 – the prices in these shops are stratospheric and the customers mostly Russians.

GETTING THERE

Air Chambéry 110km/ 70 miles (1hr30); Geneva 150km/ 95 miles (2hr15); Grenoble 175km/ 110 miles (2hr15); Lyon 190km/ 120 miles (2hr15)

Rail Moûtiers (23km/ 14 miles); transfer by bus or taxi

TOURIST OFFICE

www.courchevel.com

Les Deux-Alpes

Sprawling resort with a high, narrow ski area that will disappoint many intermediates; popular for summer skiing and boarding

£100
RESORT PRICE INDEX

RATINGS

The mountains

Extent	★★★
Fast lifts	★★★★
Queues	★★★
Terrain p'ks	★★★★★
Snow	★★★★
Expert	★★★★
Intermediate	★★
Beginner	★★★
Boarder	★★★★
X-country	★★
Restaurants	★★★
Schools	★★★
Families	★★★★

The resort

Charm	★★
Convenience	★★★
Scenery	★★★★
Eating out	★★★★
Après-ski	★★★★
Off-slope	★★

248

NEWS

2015/16: The new blue Jandri run to the village is due to open in December 2015. A new terrain park near the Jandri gondola base is planned. Dog sledding is also planned.

2014/15: Progress Park replaced the snowcross in the Toura area.

KEY FACTS

Resort	1650m	
	5,410ft	
Slopes	1300-3570m	
	4,270-11,710ft	
Lifts	47	
Pistes	200km	
	124 miles	

+ High, snow-sure, varied slopes, including an extensive glacier

+ Lots of good off-piste terrain

+ Stunning views of the Ecrins peaks

+ Wide choice of affordable hotels

− Piste network modest by big resort standards, and congested in places

− Virtually no woodland runs

− Home runs far from ideal (but should be improved for 2015/16)

Les Deux-Alpes is a big resort, with a tall mountain. But it doesn't come from the standard major resort mould: it is not at all swanky, and good-value hotels are not hard to find. Its mountain is unusual, too: tall and narrow, offering a splendid Alpine feel, some long runs, but with pistes limited in total extent.

We've been complaining since 1994 about the dangerous home runs here – a hideously crowded green or blacks that are often mogulled and icy. So we are delighted to hear that a blue alternative has been built and is due to open in December 2015. In the meantime, a new red run back to the village opened a couple of seasons ago; we look forward to trying them both.

THE RESORT

Les Deux-Alpes is a long, narrow village sitting on a high col. It is modern, but gives the impression that its development has been unplanned.

Four sectors can be identified. As you enter from the north you pass through an area centred on the tourist office; from here, roads go off left up to Les 2 Alpes 1800; go straight on instead, and you come to the effective centre, with the major gondola stations, outdoor ice rink and lots of shops and restaurants; at this point you enter a long one-way system, and finally come to Alpe de Venosc.

The six-day pass gives two days in Alpe-d'Huez, one day in Serre-Chevalier (an hour away) and other

resorts and a reduced rate for La Grave. A car would be handy to make the most of these options. There are day-trip buses twice a week to Alpe-d'Huez, but a better plan is to splash out 70 euros on the splendid helicopter day trip (available three days a week). There are plans for a cross-valley lift (which, subject to permissions being granted, they hope to open by 2020).

VILLAGE CHARM ★★☆☆☆
Lively, but that's all
The village is a long, sprawling collection of apartments, hotels, bars and shops, most lining the two streets that form the one-way traffic system. There is a wide range of building styles, from old chalets through 1960s blocks to more sympathetic recent buildings. Alpe de Venosc has the most character and the best shops. The resort's buildings look better as you leave than when you arrive – all the balconies face south. The place has quite a buzz in the early evening.

CONVENIENCE ★★★☆☆
Fine if you pick your spot
It's a long village – well over 2km end to end – but lifts are dotted fairly evenly along it, and it's not difficult to find lodgings within walking distance of one of the major ones. We'd go for Alpe de Venosc and the newish Diable chair. Les 2 Alpes 1800 is inconvenient for shopping and nightlife. A free shuttle-bus links all parts of the resort

miles 0.5 1.0

N Mont-de-Lans

Village →

Jandri Express →

down to Venosc

Diable →

km 1.0 2.0

about every 15 minutes. A digital system at the stops lets you know how long you've got to wait.

SCENERY ★★★★
High southern peaks
The resort sits high among the southern Alps, with great views from the upper slopes of the Ecrins peaks.

THE MOUNTAINS

The main slopes are all above the treeline, though there are trees directly above the village.

The piste map includes four separate maps for different parts of the mountain – a good idea. Views vary about the logical but boring scheme of naming runs after the lift they lead to and distinguishing them by numbers (eg Fée 1, Fée 2 ... Fée 7).

A few blue runs have short steep sections and some readers complain that some should be classified red. And some runs are different colours on the map and the mountain. Reporters find the signposting OK.

EXTENT OF THE SLOPES ★★★
Surprisingly small
For a big resort, Les Deux-Alpes has a disappointingly small area of pistes. The main area goes very high but it is also very narrow.

Since our 2000 edition we have been querying the claimed extent of pistes. Last season, the piste map said '220km of slide' but that apparently includes 20km of cross-country loops. It also claimed 415 hectares of marked and groomed pistes (does that mean anything to you?). The Schrahe report discussed in our piste extent feature put the total of downhill pistes at 135km. To us, even Schrahe's figure feels too high. One reason is that the slopes just above the village on both sides of the valley don't feature highly in most people's days there.

The morning-sun side of Les Deux-Alpes, **Vallée Blanche**, is served by lifts at either end of town. It is relatively low (the top is 2100m) so has only short pistes back to town.

On the broad, gentle slope east of the resort are about 10 beginner lifts, and above them a steep slope rising to the ridge of **Les Crêtes**. Lifts go up to the ridge from four points spread along the village. To get back to base you have a choice of the long-awaited blue run for 2015/16, a long, winding, narrow green run (in past seasons, often very crowded and sometimes closed), a newish red run that we haven't skied yet and three short black runs. The blacks are usually mogulled and often icy (they get the afternoon sun). Or you can ride down.

The Crêtes ridge has lifts and gentle runs along it, and behind it lies the deep, steep Combe de Thuit. Lifts span the combe to the mid-mountain station at **Toura**, at the heart of the slopes. We seem to spend a lot of

SNOWPIX.COM / CHRIS GILL

Most of the slopes are above 2500m, which means good snow most of the time. This photo shows part of the Toura sector ↓

skitracer

CHALETS, HOTELS
& APARTMENTS
Call us today
020 8600 1650
skitracer.com

Club Med

THE MOST COMPREHENSIVE
SKI PACKAGE ON THE MARKET

Les Deux Alpes 3

020 8313 3999
Skiline.co.uk

Skiline.co.uk

the world's biggest on-piste vertical. In the opposite direction, a walk (or snowcat tow) takes you to the famously challenging slopes of La Grave (read our separate chapter).

FAST LIFTS ★★★★
Main lifts OK, but ...
Les Deux-Alpes has some impressive lifts, with fast chair alternatives to the gondolas. But there are still a few draglifts and slow chairs around.

QUEUES ★★★
Not as bad as they were
The village is large, and there can be queues in the valley in the morning – especially for the big Jandri gondola. The Diable chair at the southern end of the village, installed a couple of seasons ago, has improved the total lift capacity out of the village, and we have no reports of huge queues there.

Up the mountain there may be queues in late season for the lifts to the glacier, and the Crêtes area gets busy in peak season. The top lifts are prone to closure if it's windy, putting pressure on the lower lifts. There may be queues for the gondolas back to the village when snow is poor. Some recent reporters were concerned about crowding on the slopes even outside peak holiday periods.

time on three key fast chairlifts in this area – Bellecombes, at the top of the Combe; Glaciers, carrying on towards the glacier; and Fée, on its own slightly separate hill. The section of the mountain around and below Toura is very narrow – there is one main way down, and it gets crowded in the afternoon; but there are now three ways to avoid the worst of the crowds, so they are much less problematic than they once were.

The top **Glacier du Mont-de-Lans** section has long, easy runs with great views, served by an underground funicular and draglifts. There are steeper slopes off to the north, served by chairs. From the top you can descend all the way to Mont-de-Lans – a descent of well over 2200m that is

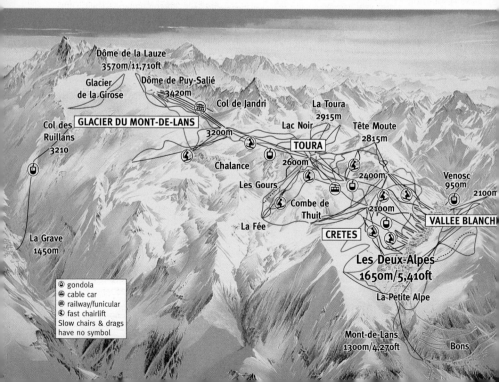

gondola
cable car
railway/funicular
fast chairlift
Slow chairs & drags
have no symbol

The off-piste routes in Les Deux-Alpes are numerous, and varied in difficulty. But never try them without the right equipment and a qualified guide.

*Both sides off the **Bellecombes** piste offer a wide range of varying terrain; it's important to take care here – there are several small cliff faces. For those keen to tackle couloirs, this descent offers small ones that are ideal for your first attempts; they can be avoided, though.*

*Traversing across the top of the black Grand Couloir piste leads to the **North Rachas** area, with off-piste faces that normally offer good snow conditions all winter. The first large valley leads to three couloirs – one fairly broad and easy, the others much narrower and steeper. Traversing further leads to a much wider descent that avoids the three couloirs.*

*Strong skiers will enjoy the famous **Chalance** run (our favourite), which starts just below the glacier and descends 1000m to join the Fée 1 piste; there are several variations, mixing wide-open slopes and rocky pitches. These faces are at times subject to quite a high avalanche risk.*

*Traversing above the north face of the Chalance leads to the couloir **Pylone Electrique** – a steep, narrow 200m-long couloir with the reward below it of an excellent wide powder field of moderate gradient. A rest on the Thuit chairlift is a must after this adrenaline-charged descent.*

*As well as these routes within the local lift network, there is a renowned descent to **St-Christophe** (you get a taxi back), and the famous **La Grave** terrain (see separate chapter) is easily accessed.*

Les Deux-Alpes

251

TERRAIN PARKS ★★★★★
Some of the best

In winter, the main terrain park is located above Toura and is split into several areas: Easy Park for beginners and families with a mini-pipe, mini-rails and tables; a new Progress Park to improve your freestyle skills; Park Avenue for jibbing; Slopestyle with a series of four tables; a Wall which is 10m long and 6m high; a Big Air jump; and a Family Snowcross for everyone. 'Brilliant,' says a 2015 reporter. The Kid Park is at Les Crêtes. On the glacier there's a competition standard half-pipe plus Slide Zones for beginner freestylers; in the summer the park here is made much bigger and includes a super-pipe. For 2015/16, a new park is planned at village level. Visit www.2alpes-snowpark.com for more information.

SNOW RELIABILITY ★★★★
Excellent on higher slopes

The snow on the higher slopes is normally very good, even in a poor winter. On a March tour that involved skiing crud in most resorts, we enjoyed packed powder most of the day here. Above 2200m most of the runs are north-facing, and the top glacier section guarantees good snow. But the runs just above the village from Les Crêtes face west, so they get afternoon sun and are often icy. Snowmaking covers some of the lower slopes – apparently including the home green run (though a 2015

reporter found it closed on his visit). On our last visit, some runs were kept closed in the morning because they were dangerously hard, and opened only once they had softened. That is an excellent scheme.

FOR EXPERTS ★★★★
Off-piste is the main attraction

The area offers excellent off-piste – read the panel above. In the past, five routes (including Chalance, described above) were identified as itinéraires, but they are no longer on the map.

There are a few black pistes. The run down the Bellecombes chair is a genuine black, with the best chance of good snow. Fée 6 from above Toura has one steep pitch at the end. Fée 5 isn't much more testing than the adjacent red. The runs down to the resort often have poor snow. The short black higher up served by the Super Diable chairlift is among the steepest.

FOR INTERMEDIATES ★★
Limited cruising

Less confident intermediates will love the quality of the snow and the gentle runs on the upper mountain. But Les Deux-Alpes can disappoint keen intermediates because of the limited extent of the pistes. Avid piste-bashers will cover them all in a couple of days. A lot are either rather tough – some of the blues could be reds – or boringly bland. The runs higher up generally have good snow, and there is some great fast cruising, especially from the

↑ The village is long and narrow, just as the mountain is high and narrow
LES DEUX ALPES TO / BRUNO LONGO

Like the resort?
You'll love our handpicked accommodation
02392 839 310
PEAKRETREATS.CO.UK

◆ABTA
ABTA No W5577

glacier to Toura and on the mainly north-facing pistes served by the chairlifts off to the sides. The chairlifts at the glacier serve great carving pistes. The Vallée Blanche area has quite testing red runs; but the snow there is often in poor condition.

FOR BEGINNERS ★★★
Good slopes
The nursery slopes beside the village are spacious and gentle, and five lifts are free. The runs along the ridge above them are excellent, too, except when crowded at the end of the day. The glacier also has a fine array of long, very easy slopes.

FOR BOARDERS ★★★★
Big appeal
Les Deux-Alpes has become a snowboard Mecca in summer when the pros descend en masse. In the winter, the limited pisted slopes aren't as off-putting to boarders as to skiers. Although the focus is on the terrain park, the freeriding is not to be underestimated, with plenty of steep challenging terrain. Beginners will find the narrow, flat crowded areas mid-mountain and the routes down to the village intimidating. Most of the lifts on the higher slopes are chairs (and so boarder-friendly). In town there is a huge airbag to get a feeling of what air-time is all about.

Needs very low-altitude snow
There are small, widely dispersed areas. Given good snow, Venosc, reached by a gondola down, has the only worthwhile picturesque ones. Total trail length is 25km.

MOUNTAIN RESTAURANTS ★★★
A few good places
The restaurants at the major lift junctions are generally unremarkable. Happily there are exceptions.
Editors' choice Diable au Coeur at the top of the Diable lift has excellent food (delicious confit de canard on our last visit) and service. Readers agree ('we ate there three times in a week it was so good'). The terrace gives good views, but sit as far as you can from the noisy adjacent chairlift machinery. The bigger Chalet la Toura, in a fine position with a big terrace at Toura in the middle of the slopes, is pleasantly woody, and serves good food – 'Best mountain restaurant we found; the lapin was delicious,' says a 2015 reporter.
Worth knowing about The Pano, also at Toura, has a wide range of daily specials but is notable mainly for its après session. There is a small table-service restaurant attached to the big self-service at the bottom of the glacier at 3200m. The Fee was rated as 'superb' by a recent reporter. The Bergerie on the Vallée Blanche slopes has been recommended in the past.

SCHOOLS AND GUIDES ★★★
Fair selection to choose from
A recent reporter was pleased with his son's progress with the ESF. But there are plenty of other schools to choose from. A 2015 reporter found Firstrax 'great for one-to-one tuition, I can't recommend Luca highly enough'. A recent visitor had 'excellent private lessons with Easiski'.
Freeride Attitude is a free off-piste safety course that sounds well organized.

FOR FAMILIES ★★★★
Fine facilities
The village nursery takes kids from six months to two years, the kindergarten from two to six years, and there are chalet-based alternatives run by UK tour operators. A recent reporter who went with Club Med said 'their childcare was second to none'.

STAYING THERE

The resort has that rarity in high French resorts: an abundance of affordable hotels. There is an eight-storey Club Med at the northern end.

Chalets Ski Total has two newly built chalets well placed at the Venosc end of the resort, each with a sauna and a heated, covered plunge pool on the terrace. Skiworld has four varied chalets including a fab looking one in its top 'signature' range with an outdoor hot tub. Crystal has six, one in its 'finest' range with a hot tub and sauna. Inghams has three chalets and Zenith has several that can be rented catered or self-catered. Mark Warner runs a chalet hotel with pool, sauna and steam room up near 1800.

Hotels There are about 30 hotels, of which the majority are 2-star or below.

****Chalet Mounier Smartly modernized. Good reputation for food. Pool, steam, sauna, hot tub. At the Venosc end of the resort.

***Côte Brune A charming woody chalet on the snow, near the Jandri Express. Comfy rooms, good food.

**Lutins Central, basic, convenient, clean and friendly.

Turan Ski-in/ski-out beside lifts. 'Good value. Hearty buffet.'

Apartments There are plenty of large apartment blocks, but most are notable chiefly for the value they offer. Peak Retreats offers lots of options including luxury residences and some cute four-bedroom chalets; some have pool, sauna etc. Erna Low has lots of apartments and individual chalets.

Out of resort Close to the final ascent to Les Deux-Alpes are two small hotels, near-ideal for anyone planning to visit Alpe-d'Huez, La Grave and Serre-Chevalier as well as Les Deux-Alpes – the Cassini at Le Freney, and Panoramique at Mizoën. An alternative is to stay in the Venosc valley, in a hamlet close to the gondola; Peak Retreats has two cute-looking chalets there with private pools and saunas.

EATING OUT ★★★★
Plenty of choice

There are about 50 restaurants, including lots of simple places. The P'tit Polyte restaurant in the hotel Chalet Mounier has a high reputation. Reader tips include La Grange, Alisier, Patate, Cloche, Crêpes à Gogo ('a lovely bar with nice snack food'), Eli's, Smokey Joes (Tex-Mex) and Etable.

Ski Total
WELCOME YOU TO
Les 2 Alpes

Quality chalets
Excellent value
19 resorts
across the Alps

skitotal.com
01483 791 933

APRES-SKI ★★★★
Not as lively as before?

Les Deux-Alpes has traditionally been one of the liveliest of French resorts, but reports seem to suggest that it has become quieter in recent years.

On the mountain, an attempt is made to deliver Austrian-style post-lunch après action at the Pano at Toura ('great après-ski, dancing on tables mandatory – take the lift down after to avoid serious injuries!' says a 2015 reporter) and Diable au Coeur. There are plenty of places to try in the village – the resort website lists about 25. Smokey Joes is a popular central sports bar and the Secret has live music and a wide choice of beers. The Red Frog has a big-screen TV and shows sports. Smithy's Tavern and Mini Bar attract the younger crowd and seasonaires. The main bar at 1800 is O'Brians. Bars favoured by reporters are the Polar Bear pub ('the pick for the 30s English crowd, with just enough space for a dance later on') and Pub le Windsor (a smaller, quieter place popular with locals). The Avalanche is a popular nightclub.

OFF THE SLOPES ★★
Limited options

The pretty valley village of Venosc is worth a visit by gondola, and you can take a scenic helicopter flight to Alpe-d'Huez. There are lots of walks, a big outdoor pool and an outdoor artificial ice rink (both free with a 6-day lift pass). The Acqua Center has a sauna, steam room and hot tub. There are three toboggan runs, snowshoeing, paragliding, bowling and, new for 2015/16, dog sledding. Several mountain restaurants are accessible to pedestrians. There is an ice cave in the glacier, complete with ice sculptures. The resort has a simulator that lets you experience what it's like to be caught in an avalanche.

GETTING THERE

Air Grenoble 110km/ 70 miles (1hr45); Chambéry 130km/ 80 miles (2hr); Lyon 160km/100 miles (2hr); Geneva 220km/ 135 miles (2hr45)

Rail Grenoble (70km/43 miles); buses from station

TOURIST OFFICE

www.les2alpes.com

OT FLAINE / PHOTOZOOM

Flaine

Still expanding, high-altitude, purpose-built resort sharing a big, broad area of varied slopes with more rustic alternatives

£100
RESORT PRICE INDEX

RATINGS

The mountains

Extent	****
Fast lifts	***
Queues	***
Terrain p'ks	*
Snow	****
Expert	****
Intermediate	*****
Beginner	*****
Boarder	***
X-country	**
Restaurants	**
Schools	***
Families	****

The resort

Charm	*
Convenience	*****
Scenery	****
Eating out	**
Après-ski	*
Off-slope	*

NEWS

2015/16: The defunct hotel Totem will reopen after a radical makeover by the top-notch Sibuet group.

2014/15: A new 'fun zone' for kids was opened in the Forêt beginner area. A new 5-star Pierre & Vacances Premium residence opened at Montsoleil.

KEY FACTS

Resort	1600m
	5,250ft

Grand Massif (Flaine, Les Carroz, Morillon, Samoëns, Sixt)

Slopes	700-2480m
	2,300-8,140ft
Lifts	69
Pistes	265km
	165 miles

For Flaine only

Slopes	1600-2480m
	5,250-8,140ft
Lifts	22
Pistes	140km
	87 miles

- ➕ Part of the big, varied Grand Massif
- ➕ Reliable snow in the main bowl
- ➕ Compact, convenient, mainly car-free village, plus traditional villages on the lower fringes of the area
- ➕ Family-friendly, in most respects

- ➖ Still some slow old chairlifts
- ➖ Original 1960s buildings block-like and austere (though newer chalet-style developments very attractive)
- ➖ Bad weather can close most runs
- ➖ Very quiet in the evening

Flaine is best known as a convenient resort catering particularly well for families, but it has a much broader appeal than that. The Grand Massif is an excellent and extensive area, with plenty to amuse anyone.

Apartments dominate here. Happily, there are some pretty good ones these days, and the other options are widening. Ski Total runs some catered chalets. And we're delighted to hear that this season Flaine will again have a proper hotel – the Totem is to reopen as the first in a planned chain of funky Terminal Neige hotels 'with an urban soul'. No, seriously – it looks very promising.

THE RESORT

Flaine was built from scratch in the 1960s at the foot of a big snowy bowl. It's high, but not super-high (it is set among trees); the road in from Les Carroz actually involves a final descent from a col some 250m higher. The architecture of the main village is distinctive and uncompromising; it has its admirers, not including us.

The road in passes two satellite mini-resorts: Hameau de Flaine – lots of small chalets plus the residence Refuge du Golf – and Montsoleil, developed by Intrawest. The main resort is tiny, as our plan shows. There are two parts: Forum, centred on a square blending with the slopes, and bigger Forêt – up the hillside, linked by two lifts (vulnerable to snow, we hear), with its own bars and shops.

With a car you can visit the Portes du Soleil, Megève or Chamonix.

VILLAGE CHARM *
Not to our taste

The concrete Bauhaus-style blocks that form the core of Flaine were supposed to exhibit 'the principle of shadow and light'. They look shocking from the approach road; from the slopes they are somewhat less obtrusive, blending into the rocky grey hillside a little.

As a place to inhabit, Flaine has an austere feel, and some buildings are now looking tatty. In contrast, the Hameau de Flaine is built in an attractive traditional chalet style, as is

Montsoleil. The main resort is largely traffic-free, and the heart of Forum is completely so, but access roads do penetrate the village.

CONVENIENCE *****
A fine example

The main resort is compact and convenient. Hameau de Flaine is about 1km from the main village, and has just a shop, a bar, and a restaurant. Montsoleil is much nearer to the mother ship (a few hundred metres' walk) and it has linking pistes. There's a 'very good' free bus service; in the evening, we are told, it is replaced by a free bookable taxi service.

SCENERY ****
Good all around the Massif

The scenery within the area is quite varied, with rocky ridges and partly wooded hillsides – the views from the dividing ridges across the Vernant and Molliets valleys are particularly lovely. To the south-west, the Aravis chain looks dramatic, while there are great views of the Mont Blanc massif from the high points.

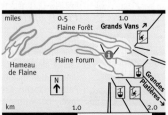

LIFT PASSES

Grand Massif

Prices in €

Age	6-day
under 16	178
16 to 64	237
65 plus	225

Free Under 5, 75 plus
Beginner Three free lifts; points card
Note Family discounts
Alternative pass Flaine area only

FLAINE TO

Flaine Forum's central plaza leads straight on to the snow. The main Platières gondola is just out of this shot, on the right ↓

THE MOUNTAINS

The slopes in the Flaine bowl are mainly open, but the lowest slopes are wooded. Outside the bowl, above the other villages (Les Carroz, Morillon, Samoëns), it's the opposite – most of the runs are below the treeline.

Piste classification is generally accurate, but the blue Tourmaline back to Flaine under the Grands Vans chair is an exception – distinctly tough (and crowded at the end of the day).

EXTENT OF THE SLOPES ★★★★
A big white playground

Grand Massif is an impressive area; but its claimed 265km of pistes is an exaggeration – measured down the fall line the total is only 170km. Read our feature chapter on piste extent. A large part of the domain lies outside the main Flaine bowl; the links are vulnerable to bad weather.

The **Grandes Platières** jumbo gondola speeds you in a single stage up the north-west-facing Flaine bowl to the high point of the Grand Massif. Both the Aup de Veran gondola and the Tête des Verds fast chair offer alternatives, linking to other fast chairs on the upper mountain. There are essentially four or five main ways down the largely treeless, rolling terrain back to Flaine. On skier's right, the much-hyped Cascades blue run

leads away from the lift system to the outskirts of Sixt, up the valley from Samoëns. It drops over 1700m and is certainly long, though nothing like the claimed 14km; having plotted it on Google Maps, we reckon it is more like 9km. The gentle/flat top half is hard work, especially for boarders, and the run is scenic rather than exciting. At the end you get a bus (often crowded) to the lifts at Samoëns.

On the near side of the Tête Pelouse, a broad catwalk leads to the experts-only **Gers** bowl.

Back at Platières, an alternative is to head down the lovely long red Méphisto (skier's left) to a quieter area of slopes beneath Tête des Lindars.

The eight-seat Grands Vans chair gives access to the extensive slopes of **Les Carroz**, **Morillon** and **Samoëns** via the wide Vernant bowl. This and the adjacent Molliets bowl have lift bases with car parks on the road between Les Carroz and Flaine.

FAST LIFTS ★★★
Gradual progress

The recent replacement of the Diamant Noir double chair in 2013 was very welcome, and effectively opened up an additional fast route to the top. But there are still some frustrating lifts inside and (especially) outside the Flaine bowl. Read the chapters on Les Carroz and Samoëns.

QUEUES ★★★☆☆
New lifts have eased problems
Hefty investment in new lifts over the last few years has paid dividends and most recent reporters have had few problems except at peak season. The exception is that short queues build for the main gondola to Platières; but it has a singles line and there are alternative ways up. In French school holidays all the major lifts can build queues at peak times – especially unavoidable link lifts between Flaine and the other villages such as Grands Vans, Vernants and Corralanche.

As much of a problem as queues is that some of the blue runs forming links between the resorts get seriously crowded, especially at the beginning and end of the day: Silice and Tourmaline on the way from Samoëns to Flaine, and Perce-Neige at Tête des Saix on the way from Flaine to Morillon and Les Carroz.

TERRAIN PARKS ★☆☆☆☆
No real park now
The only real park in the Grand Massif has been scrapped, we are told. There are now 'fun spaces' with 'slaloms, banks and a trail in the forest', but experienced boarders visiting last season pronounced them too tame.

SNOW RELIABILITY ★★★★☆
Usually keeps its whiteness
Most of the main bowl faces north-west, and keeps snow well. There is

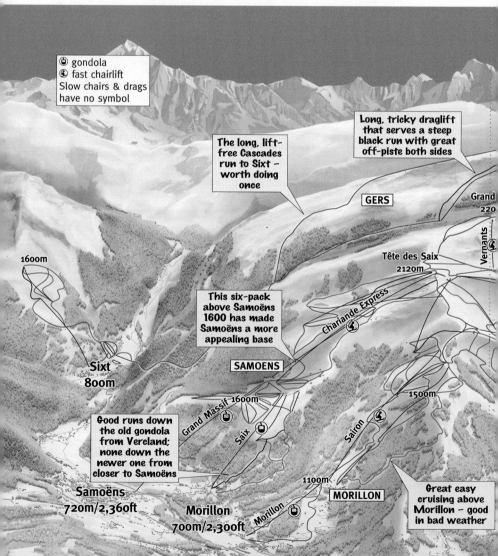

gondola
fast chairlift
Slow chairs & drags have no symbol

The long, lift-free Cascades run to Sixt – worth doing once

Long, tricky draglift that serves a steep black run with great off-piste both sides

GERS

Grand 220

Vernants

Tête des Saix
2120m

1600m

Charlande Express

This six-pack above Samoëns 1600 has made Samoëns a more appealing base

SAMOENS

Sixt
800m

1500m

Grand Massif 1600m

Saix

Sairon

Good runs down the old gondola from Vercland; none down the newer one from closer to Samoëns

1100m

Samoëns
720m/2,360ft

Morillon
700m/2,300ft

Morillon

MORILLON

Great easy cruising above Morillon – good in bad weather

snowmaking on many of the lower runs. The slopes outside the bowl are lower. Grooming is excellent.

FOR EXPERTS ★★★★
Great fun with guidance

Flaine has some seriously challenging terrain. But much of it is off-piste, and although some looks temptingly safe this impression can be mistaken. The Flaine bowl is riddled with rock crevasses and potholes, and should be treated with glacier-style caution.

All the black pistes are genuine. The Diamant Noir, close to the line of the main gondola, is tricky because of moguls, narrowness and other people, rather than great steepness; the first pitch is the steepest. To skier's left of

Diamant Noir are several short, steep off-piste routes through the crags.

The Lindars Nord chair serves a worthwhile slope that often has the best snow in the area.

The Gers draglift, outside the main bowl, serves great on- and off-piste expert terrain in a north-facing bowl (of about 550m vertical) that normally has good snow top to bottom. The Onyx piste is a proper black and nearby off-piste slopes reach 45°. There are more adventurous ways in from the Grand Vans and Véret lifts. Further serious black pistes go down from Tête des Saix towards Samoëns. A reader recommends the Corbalanche piste and the off-piste bowl to skier's right, above the little Airon lake.

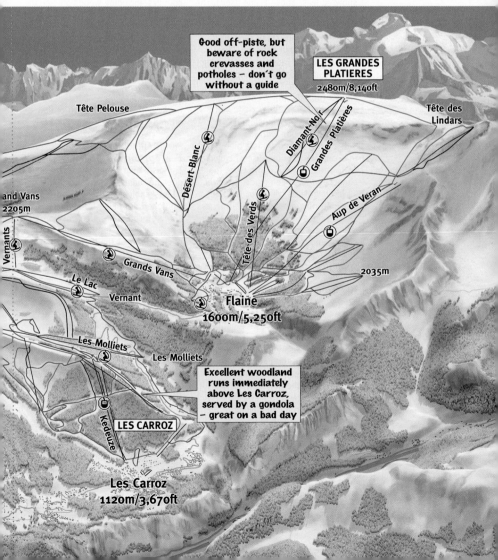

ABTA
ABTA No W5517

High quality, high altitude

Four-star luxury residence
Le Centaure in Flaine

Ski in/ski out • Great for families
Highest resort in the Grand Massif
Close to Geneva • Accommodation only
or self-drive package deals

Call us on 02392 890 960
skicollection.co.uk/Flaine

A WORLD-CLASS FRENCH ALPS EXPERIENCE
SKI COLLECTION .CO.UK

Flaine

FOR INTERMEDIATES ★★★★★
Something for everyone

Flaine is ideal for confident intermediates, with a great variety of pistes (and usually the bonus of good snow, at least above Flaine itself). The diabolically named reds that dominate the Flaine bowl tend to gain their status from short, steep sections rather than overall difficulty. The relatively direct Faust is great carving territory and Méphisto is popular with lots of reporters. There are gentler cruises from the top – Cristal, taking you to the Désert Blanc chair, and Serpentine all the way home.

The connection with the slopes outside the main bowl is a blue run that can be tricky because of crowds, narrowness or poor snow. Once the connection has been made, however, all intermediates will enjoy the long treelined runs down to Les Carroz, as long as the snow is good. (The Perce-Neige ridge-run to get to them is a bit narrow and exposed, though.) There are good, long easy-intermediate runs down to Morillon 1100.

FOR BEGINNERS ★★★★★
Two good nursery areas

There are excellent nursery slopes below Forum and across the hill from Forêt, served by free lifts, which make a pass unnecessary until you are ready to go higher up the mountain. The major Forêt area was revamped recently, with the new Balacha draglift specially designed to make life easy for novices and a remodelling of the green run. But a parent reporter complains of flat sections making life difficult for his kids on the resort-level green Epicea and on blue Serpentine – the gentle blue on skier's right of the main bowl. An alternative, given a car, is to drive over the hill to the Vernant valley where a fast chair serves the long, gentle, quiet Arolle green run.

FOR BOARDERS ★★★☆☆
Beware the draglifts

Flaine suits boarders quite well – there's lots of varied terrain and plenty of off-piste with interesting nooks and crannies, including woods outside the main bowl. The key lifts are now chairs or gondolas (but beware the draglifts marked as difficult on the piste map plus the Aujon draglift).

FOR CROSS-COUNTRY ★★☆☆☆
Very fragmented

The Grand Massif claims 64km of tracks but only about 13km of that is around Flaine itself.

MOUNTAIN RESTAURANTS ★★☆☆☆
Few options in the bowl

The piste map marks restaurants but does not name them.

Editors' choice Last season we confirmed our liking for Pente à Jules, a newish chalet in a fine position where the Faust and Almandine red runs meet, near the bottom of the woods. Friendly service, decent menu, competent cooking.

Worth knowing about We've also eaten well at the rustic Blanchot (table-service section, naturally) just above the treeline on skier's right. There is a self-service place at the top of the main gondola. At the upper nursery slopes, the Bissac has been tipped. At Forum level, across the piste from the gondola, are two attractive, woody chalets – the Michet and the fast-food-oriented Eloge ('good food, staff pleasant' said a 2014 visitor). You can of course eat in the village, at places very close to the gondola.

Outside the Flaine bowl, we have always liked the remote and cosy Gîte du Lac de Gers (0450 912076) – book in advance and use the piste-side phone to ring for a snowcat to tow you up from the Cascades run. But it recently came under new management, so please send us reports. Be aware that you have to ski on down to Sixt, and then ski back to Flaine via the Samoëns lift system.

Other places outside the Flaine bowl are covered in the Samoëns and Les Carroz chapters.

SCHOOLS AND GUIDES ★★★
Mixed reports
Reports on the schools are generally good, but one reporter this year was disappointed by the Internationale school, which amalgamated three children's classes to form one huge class of children at different stages. Very unsatisfactory.

FOR FAMILIES ★★★★
Parents' paradise?
Flaine prides itself on being a family resort, and Forum in particular is child-friendly; the number of English-speaking children around is a bonus. But there isn't a huge amount to amuse kids in the evenings – no proper toboggan run, for example. One parent notes that the ESI doesn't offer lunchtime care, which seems strange – and found the bucket lift up the resort awkward with kids in tow.

STAYING THERE
Accommodation is overwhelmingly in self-catering apartments.

Chalets Ski Total now runs three catered chalets here – 'great quality and value', says a reporter. Two are in the Refuge du Golf and have access to a pool and a spa area with sauna, steam, hot tub. The other is a proper little chalet in the Hameau de Flaine.

Hotels Terminal Neige le Totem will open its doors in December 2015 – 'latest technology, vintage furniture, wellness facilities'.

Apartments There has been a minor flood of major developments here in recent years. The CGH 4-star residence Centaure, a few metres from the gondola, is complete with spa, gym and 25m pool. The apartments are cleverly designed so that all have a south view, but a reader who thought them good value in general complains about the layout and small kitchen. Slightly outside the village in ski-in/ski-out positions at Montsoleil are the 5-star residence Terrasses d'Eos and, next door, the new Terrasses d'Hélios – both Pierre & Vacances Premium properties with pool, sauna, steam,

Flaine

TOP UK CHALET PROVIDER IN FLAINE

ABTA
Travel with confidence

Typical chalet interior

THE CHALET SPECIALIST

Ski Total

Three comfortable and well-appointed catered chalets in this high-altitude snow-sure resort.

Ski Total Savers incl. cash-back, ski pack offers & free group places | **4-course dinners** with complimentary wine
Cooked breakfast | **Free Wifi** | **Flights** from Southampton, Gatwick, Heathrow, Manchester & Edinburgh

Tel: **01483 791 933**   Book online at **skitotal.com**

Like the resort?

You'll love our handpicked accommodation

02392 839 310

PEAKRETREATS.CO.UK

ABTA
ABTA No W6537

GETTING THERE

Air Geneva 80km/ 50 miles (1hr30)

Rail Cluses (30km/ 19 miles); regular bus service

TOURIST OFFICES

Flaine
www.flaine.com
Morillon
www.ot-morillon.fr

FLAINE TO

They certainly picked a fine spot when they decided to build a resort here in the 1960s. The chalets of Le Hameau are more recent, though ↓

hot tub; both approved by readers this year. In Flaine Forêt, P&V also has the Forêt. Lagrange has several properties, including attractive chalets out at Hameau – also the location of the Refuge du Golf, with pool. Most are available through Ski Collection.

EATING OUT ★★☆☆☆
Limited choice

The choice is adequate, no more. We get most reports on the Brasserie les Cîmes in Forum: 'very friendly owners, wide menu'; 'lots of atmosphere, very good food'. The tiny Grain de Sel is 'friendly, excellent value'. Other reader tips: Michet across the piste from the gondola ('huge roaring fire, extensive gourmet-style menu') and Cascade ('will pick you up in a snowmobile').

APRES-SKI ★☆☆☆☆
Take your Kindle

'Don't go to Flaine for nightlife,' says a reporter who spent two months there. You don't have much choice of venue: 'Only two main bars really get going,' says a recent reporter: the Dutch-run Flying Dutchman in Forêt ('lively venue full of students singing Dutch songs; good-value drinks') and the White Pub, which has a big-screen TV, rock music and a happy hour; live music some nights; 'in need of refurbishment and fresh air' said a 2014 reporter. The Perdrix Noire also has a pub feel. The bar at the bowling alley is popular with families (and stays open until 3am). The Caves is a nightclub.

OFF THE SLOPES ★☆☆☆☆
Curse of the purpose-built

Flaine is not great for people who don't want to hit the slopes. But there is a fine ice-driving circuit where you can take a spin in your car or in theirs. Snowmobiling and dog sledding are popular, and there's a cinema. The full-size pool, gym and spa at the Centaure residence are open to the public. Some weeks there are concerts – classical, jazz, rock and pop. Shopping is extremely limited.

LINKED RESORT – 700m
MORILLON

Morillon is a small, quiet, traditional old village, with a few cafes, restaurants, bars, supermarket and shops spread out along the road through. Newer buildings are in chalet style and are quite attractive. There's a 3-star hotel, the Morillon, with spa. Peak Retreats offers this, a luxury chalet and good apartments.

A gondola goes up to the mid-mountain mini-resort of Morillon 1100 (aka Les Esserts), where there are slope-side apartments at the foot of lovely long, wide, gentle and treelined slopes. A choice of red and blue runs go to the valley but snow low down is not reliable, although the area as a whole is north-facing.

Morillon 1100 has the essentials of life – two ski schools, three ski shops, a bakery, a supermarket, a couple of restaurants, and the Madison pub.

Les Gets

Traditional-style village with a very French feel, providing serious competition for its larger linked neighbour, Morzine

£100
RESORT PRICE INDEX

TOP 10 RATINGS

Extent	★★★★★
Fast lifts	★★★
Queues	★★★★
Snow	★★
Expert	★★★
Intermediate	★★★★
Beginner	★★★★
Charm	★★★★
Convenience	★★★
Scenery	★★★

NEWS

2014/15: There have been several hotel revamps: the Crychar has a smart new spa; the Chasse-Montagne has been refurbished using traditional materials; and the Marmotte opened two new restaurants.

KEY FACTS

Resort	1170m
	3,840ft

Portes du Soleil

Slopes	950-2275m
	3,120-7,460ft
Lifts	196
Pistes	650km
	404 miles

Morzine-Les Gets only

Slopes	1000-2010m
	3,280-6,590ft
Lifts	49
Pistes	120km
	75 miles

Extent rating
This is for the whole Portes du Soleil area

Piste map
Refer to the map in the Morzine chapter

- ➕ Good-sized, varied and lightly wooded slopes shared with Morzine
- ➕ Attractive chalet-style village
- ➕ Usually few queues or crowds
- ➕ Part of the vast Portes du Soleil ski pass region, but ...

- ➖ It's quite a long way to the main Portes du Soleil circuit at Avoriaz
- ➖ Low altitude and exposure to westerlies mean risk of rain and poor snow
- ➖ Few challenging pistes

Les Gets is an attractive, small, family-friendly resort with a very French feel to it, partly because of appetizing food and wine shops lining the main street. The area of slopes it shares with Morzine is the most extensive local network in the region, and in some respects Les Gets is the better base for that shared area.

If you have a car, you can quite easily access the main Portes du Soleil circuit by driving to the gondola at Ardent. If you don't, the circuit is much more easily accessed from Morzine, with its quicker access to Avoriaz.

THE RESORT

Les Gets is an attractive, sunny village of traditional chalet-style buildings, on the low pass leading to Morzine. The main road over the pass bypasses the village centre.

The local pass saves a fair bit on a Portes du Soleil pass, and makes a lot of sense for many visitors.

Village charm The village has a quiet ambience that appeals to families, though it does liven up at weekends. The main street is lined with attractive food shops, other shops and restaurants. The centre is fairly pedestrian-friendly, too, and a popular and attractive outdoor ice rink adds to the charm.

Convenience Although the village has a scattered appearance, most facilities are close to the main lift station. Depending on where you stay, you may have long walks to the lifts, but there is a road-train shuttle that appeals mainly to families, and also free conventional buses around the village. Buses to Morzine cost 1.50 euros per journey. You can store skis and boots at the Perrières ski shop. And there are now ski lockers at Chavannes too.

Scenery There are good views from the high points: from Mont Chéry, in particular, you get a great panorama of the village and slopes, with Mont Blanc beyond.

THE MOUNTAINS

Slopes The main local slopes – accessed by a gondola and a fast chairlift – are shared with Morzine, and are mainly described in that chapter. On the opposite side of Les Gets is Mont Chéry, accessed by a gondola followed by a chair or drag. The slopes here include some of the most challenging in the area, and are usually very quiet. Both sectors offer wooded and open slopes.

Fast lifts The main village lifts are fast, but there are a lot of slow chairs both on Mont Chéry and in some sectors of the slopes shared with Morzine.

Queues Read the Morzine chapter. Mont Chéry is usually crowd-free.

Snow reliability The lower slopes benefit from a slightly higher elevation than Morzine, but otherwise our general reservations about the lack of altitude apply. The runs to the resort have snowmaking. The front slopes of Mont Chéry face south-east – bad news at this altitude; but the other two flanks are shadier. Grooming is good. The grassy slopes don't need much snow-cover, and in a sparse snow year you may do better here than in higher, rockier resorts such as Avoriaz.

Terrain parks The park on Mont Chéry has kickers and rails for all ability levels. There's a snowcross on Chavannes plus a mini-snowcross for kids and families.

Experts Black runs on the flank and back of Mont Chéry are quite steep

261

Like the resort?
You'll love our handpicked accommodation
02392 839 310
PEAKRETREATS.CO.UK
ABTA
ABTA No W5637

Ski Total
WELCOME YOU TO
Les Gets
Quality chalets
Excellent value
19 resorts across the Alps
skitotal.com
01483 791 933

ESPRiT
FOR FAMILIES IN
Les Gets
Family Ski Chalets
Dedicated Nurseries
Exclusive Ski Classes
13 resorts across the Alps
espritski.com
01483 791 900

LAGRANGE Prestige

High-standard Self-catering Apartments

020 7371 6111
lagrange-holidays.co.uk

FRANCE

262

LIFT PASSES

Portes du Soleil

Prices in €

Age	6-day
under 16	182
16 to 19	218
20 to 64	243
65 plus	218

Free Under 5
Beginner Lessons and lift pass packages
Note Family discounts
Alternative pass Morzine-Les Gets only

TOURIST OFFICE
www.lesgets.com

and often bumped. In good snow there's plenty to do off-piste, including some excellent wooded areas.

Intermediates High-mileage piste-bashers might prefer direct access to the main Portes du Soleil circuit, but the local slopes have a lot to offer, with excellent reds on Mont Chéry.

Beginners The village nursery slopes are convenient. At Chavannes there is a bigger and more snow-sure Mappy's area with four free lifts (you pay for a return gondola trip to reach it). There are lots of easy runs to progress to – including the Bleuets on Chavannes.

Snowboarding The local slopes are good for beginners and intermediates.

Cross-country There are 12km of good, varied loops locally.

Mountain restaurants Read the Morzine chapter for places on the shared slopes. There are two restaurants on Mont Chéry giving great views. At the top is the Grande Ourse, run by an English family, offering snacks and table-service lunches ('excellent service, good-quality food'). At mid-mountain there's the Belvedère. Over the back near the foot of the Chéry Nord lift the 'friendly' Chanterelle has been recommended for its 'tasty, traditional French food'.

Schools and guides There's a choice of schools, including at least two that are British-run. We had a good recent report on BASS: 'Our son thoroughly enjoyed himself with endlessly patient instructors.' And Les Gets Snowsports has been praised in the past. A 2015 reporter has had 'excellent top-up lessons' with 360 International.

Families This is a good resort for families. There are comprehensive facilities, including an American-Indian-themed trail area on Chavannes with tepees and various activities – the Grand Cry Territory. Major British family specialist tour operators Esprit Ski and Ski Famille have chalets here.

STAYING THERE

There is a good selection of chalets and mid-range hotels.

Chalets Families have a wide choice: Ski Famille has eight chalets, including the 'very comfortable' Chalet Marjorie, and Esprit Ski has four in one building with its own nursery. Ski Total has four chalets, all with outdoor hot tub and/ or sauna. VIP's plush Altitude Lodge, on the piste up at Les Chevannes, and private catered Chalet le Frene have been praised by reporters.

Hotels The Ferme de Montagne is small, plush and luxurious but on the edge of town; we loved our stay there. Of the 3-stars, the Crychar, at the foot of the slopes, is one of the best (and gained a smart new spa last season). The similarly convenient 4-star Marmotte has two new restaurants.

Apartments Lagrange has two prestige properties – the central Sabaudia apartments and Les Fermes Emiguy (both with pool, hot tub, sauna etc). Peak Retreats offers the latter plus other apartments and several self-catered chalets (some luxurious). Erna Low also has Les Fermes Emiguy.

Eating out The Ferme de Montagne (see 'Hotels') serves delicious food in lovely surroundings. The Tourbillon, Choucas ('good pizzas and scallops') and Outa have been recommended, as has the Fruitière for fondue and raclette. Try the Tyrol for pizza and the rustic Vieux Chêne for Savoyard food.

Après-ski Après-ski is quiet, especially on weekdays. The half a dozen bars include the Irish Pub (six home-brewed beers) and the Black Bear above it. The Bush has a 'great quiz night on Fridays'. The Igloo disco is popular.

Off the slopes There's an outdoor ice rink, bowling, some shops, a cinema, the Mechanical Music Museum, husky sled rides, snowshoeing, parapenting; also visits to Lausanne and Montreux.

SNOWPIX.COM / CHRIS GILL

La Grave

A world apart: an unspoiled mountain village beneath high, untamed off-piste slopes, some of them extreme and hazardous

£90
RESORT PRICE INDEX

TOP 10 RATINGS

Extent	★
Fast lifts	
Queues	★★★★
Snow	★★★
Expert	★★★★★
Intermediate	★
Beginner	★
Charm	★★★
Convenience	★★★
Scenery	★★★★

KEY FACTS

Resort	1450m
	4,760ft
Slopes	1450-3550m
	4,760-11,650ft
Lifts	4
Pistes	5km
	3 miles

The figures relate only to pistes; practically all the skiing – at least 90% – is off-piste

+ Legendary off-piste mountain

+ Usually crowd-free

+ Usually good snow conditions

+ Link to Les Deux-Alpes

+ Easy access by car to other resorts

– Poor weather means closure

– As a holiday base, suitable for experts only

– Through-traffic detracts from Alpine village atmosphere

– Little to do off the slopes

La Grave enjoys cult status among experts. It has around 500 visitor beds and just one serious lift serving a high, wild and almost entirely off-piste mountainside. The result: an exciting, usually crowd-free area. Strictly, you ought to have a guide, but in good weather many people go it alone.

THE RESORT

La Grave is a small, unspoiled village built along the road up to the Col du Lautaret. A car is useful for access to Les Deux-Alpes down the valley and Serre-Chevalier over the pass.

Village charm The centre has a rustic feel, some welcoming hotels and friendly inhabitants. But it is a bit plain, and traffic on the through-road can be intrusive.

Convenience The single serious lift starts a short walk below the centre.

Scenery La Grave is set on a steep hillside facing the impressive glaciers of majestic La Meije. Great views.

THE MOUNTAINS

A slow two-stage 'pulse' gondola (with an extra station at a pylon (P1) halfway up the lower stage) ascends into the slopes and finishes at 3200m. Above that, you are towed by a piste machine to access a drag serving a blue run on a glacier slope of about 350m vertical. From the top (after a walk) you can ski to Les Deux-Alpes. But the reason that people come here is to explore the legendary slopes back towards La Grave.

The slopes can be closed by bad weather or avalanche danger. If they are, a reader recommends going to the tiny resort of Le Chazelet, which has short pistes and easy off-piste served by several lifts. Assuming the Col du Lautaret was open, we would head for the lovely woods of Serre-Chevalier.

Slopes The main slopes offer no defined, patrolled, avalanche-protected pistes – but there are two marked itinéraires (with several variations). Neither is particularly steep. The Chancel route passes the eponymous refuge, and descends 1400m to the P1 station; it involves a long traverse through trees, which may consist of 'energy-sapping icy moguls'. The Vallons de la Meije offers several variants, one going the full 1750m vertical to the valley, another ending at the bottom of the upper gondola. People do take these routes without a guide or avalanche equipment, but we couldn't possibly recommend it.

There are many more demanding routes, including couloirs that range from straightforward to seriously hazardous, and long descents from the glacier to the valley road below the

Meije ...om

Dome de la Lauze
St-Christophe
↓
3550m/11,650ft
Les 2 Alpes ↘
Glacier de la Girose
Glacier du Rateau
Les Ruillans 3200m
...acier ...Meije
Brèche Pacave
Refuge Chancel
Peyrou d'Amont 2400m
Chalvachère
P1 1800m
Cascades de glace de la Grave
La Grave 1450m/4,760ft
⊕ gondola
La Lauzette

Hello La Grave

Self Catered
Apartments
Ski Coaching
+ Ski Touring
Snowshoe
Adventures
Winter Skills

eurekaski
MORE FROM YOUR MOUNTAIN HOLIDAY

eurekaski.com/lagrave

LIFT PASSES

Prices in €

Age	6-day
Student under 25	216
All others	240

Beginner No deals

Note Pass of 1+ days valid for Les Deux-Alpes

Alternative pass
Pedestrian

FRANCE

264

TOURIST OFFICE

www.lagrave-lameije.
com

village, with return by taxi, bus, or strategically parked car. You can also descend a 'spectacular' valley to St-Christophe, returning by taxi or bus and the lifts of Les Deux-Alpes.

The dangers are considerable (people die here every year), and good guidance is essential. Blindly following tracks is dangerous; they may lead to a big cliff that people have been roped down or jumped off.

Fast lifts There aren't any, and there's no need for any.

Queues The lift can build queues if conditions are very good, especially on March weekends. If there's a queue at the bottom, don't ski down to P1.

Terrain parks There aren't any.

Snow reliability The chances of powder snow on the high, north-facing slopes are good.

Experts La Grave's uncrowded off-piste slopes have earned it cult status among hard-core skiers. Only experts should contemplate a stay here.

Intermediates The itinéraires get tracked into a piste-like state, and adventurous intermediates could tackle them.

Beginners Novices tricked into coming here can go up the sunny side of the valley to the easy slopes at Le Chazelet, which has a quad chair, three drags and two snow-guns.

Snowboarding There are no special facilities for boarders, but advanced freeriders will be in their element on the open off-piste powder.

Cross-country There is a total of 20km of loops in the area.

Mountain restaurants Surprisingly, there are three. The excellent, tiny Refuge Chancel, where supplies and waste are backpacked in and out, is the pucka La Grave experience: paper plates, communal tables, good food, table-service. Les Ruillans at the top 'does a good plat du jour'.

Schools and guides There are claimed to be 30 or so guides, working through a bureau. 'Excellent' is the verdict of one of our most reliable reporters. Serre-Chevalier-based New Generation ski school is again offering two-day ProVenture off-piste guiding for 2015/16.

Families Not really a family resort, but nearby Le Chazelet is more geared up. The tourist office knows of babysitters.

STAYING THERE

Hotels There are several simple options. The Brit-run 3-star Edelweiss has quite basic rooms but they're 'comfortable', 'the food is a good standard' and there's a 'great wine list'. The Skiers Lodge/Hotel des Alpes offers all-inclusive week-long packages including guiding; a past reporter had an excellent week.

Apartments Bookable through the tourist office. EurekaSki offers a selection.

Eating out Most people eat in hotels. The Vieux Guide serves the 'best food' in the resort, says a local.

Après-ski The Castillan and Pierre Farabo are the standard teatime venues. Later on, the bars of the Skiers Lodge and Bois des Fees may have live music.

Off the slopes This isn't a resort for non-skiers, unless you are keen on ice climbing or snowshoeing.

LA GRAVE TO

← The old, unspoiled mountain village of La Grave is on the other side of the valley from its ski area of untamed off-piste slopes

SNOWPIX.COM / CHRIS GILL

Maurienne valley

*A world away from the fashionable Three Valleys just to the north –
a wide range of resorts, good for a holiday on a budget*

£80
RESORT PRICE INDEX

Ski south from Val Thorens into the 'fourth valley' of the famous Three Valleys, or off-piste from Val d'Isère's Col de l'Iseran, and you are in the Maurienne. (The river responsible for this great curving trench of a valley is the Arc; the region inherited its name from a province of Savoie.) The valley is dotted with ski resorts from St-François-Longchamp and Les Sybelles in the west to tiny Bonneval-sur-Arc in the east, at the head of the valley. They range widely in what they have to offer, but have some key things in common – low prices and a family-friendly atmosphere, free of mega-resort glitz.

The shared slopes of St-François-Longchamp and Valmorel (which is not in the Maurienne) are covered in our new chapter on Valmorel. Val Cenis Vanoise, almost at the head of the valley, gets its own chapter. This chapter covers the other resorts. We start in the west, with a destination that has a clear claim on your attention, on size grounds – Les Sybelles. Then a resort offering the best blend of civilized charm and skiing – Valloire, and its neighbour Valmeinier. Then two smaller resorts nearby that make good day trips from there – Les Karellis and Albiez. Then we continue up the valley, taking the remaining resorts in turn, and ending with Bonneval – an excellent outing from Val Cenis.

LAGRANGE
Prestige

High-standard
Self-catering
Apartments

020 7371 6111
lagrange-holidays.co.uk

SNOWPIX.COM / CHRIS GILL

Mixed message: the apartment blocks of La Toussuire on the right, the chalets beneath the sunny slopes on the left ↓

It's a valley of two halves. Off the western, lower half of the long valley are a string of resorts reached by winding roads climbing from St-Jean and St-Michel on the valley floor. Then, east of the major railway town of Modane, you climb into the Haute Maurienne – only 100m/200m higher than the lower valley, but with a wilder, more remote feel. Up here some resorts are villages on the valley floor, with no winding climbs involved. As well as the downhill resorts we cover in this chapter, Bessans has famously extensive cross-country trails of all standards, totalling 130km.

A REALLY USEFUL PASS

The Eski-Mo regional lift pass covers the five resorts directly above or to the east of Modane (ie in the Haute Maurienne): Aussois, Bonneval, La Norma, Val Cenis Vanoise and Valfréjus. They claim a total of 300km of piste, but more to the point they are all worth visiting for a day. You must spend your first one in the resort where you buy the pass; then you can do one day in each of the other four resorts. There are free shuttle-buses between all the resorts for holders of the pass. All for 170 euros.

1100–1750m
LES SYBELLES

Les Sybelles came out of nowhere in 2003, when half a dozen unknown resorts were linked by a painfully slow network of drags and old chairlifts to form an apparently impressive ski area (the current claim is 310km). Happily, there is now a sprinkling of fast lifts in key parts of the network.
The biggest resorts are La Toussuire (1750m) and Le Corbier (1550m). They're also the least attractive – La Toussuire has spacious chalet-style suburbs, but overall both are functional modern blots on the landscape. St-Sorlin-d'Arves (1600m) and St-Jean-d'Arves (1550m), in contrast, are largely unspoiled,

traditional villages that have expanded tastefully; and for our money, St-Sorlin has the best local slopes. But, being on the south side of the area, these latter resorts are less accessible – the bus from the main valley takes an hour to wind around the hill.

Les Sybelles is a fair-sized ski area but, according to Christoph Schrahe (read our feature on piste extent), the claim of 310km is one of the most extreme examples of the over-statement we keep banging on about. Schrahe's measurements give a total of 146km, or just 47% of the claimed figure. Having skied around much of the area in a leisurely day last winter, we believe Schrahe's figure.

Given the altitudes and latitude, it's slightly strange that virtually all the skiing is on open slopes. There are three main sectors, linked mainly by a spidery network of lifts and runs centred on the low peak of l'Ouillon (2430m). First, a single broad mountainside above Le Corbier, served by a six-pack and a row of slow chairs and drags; this is linked (slowly) over a ridge to a few slopes above St-Jean and via an intervening valley to the second sector, the bowl around La Toussuire. This has an array of four six-packs heading over shady slopes for l'Ouillon, while the sunny side of the bowl is slow-lift territory. And finally, two linked mountains above St-Sorlin, including the area high-point of Les Perrons (2620m); two six-packs depart from the village, and two others make the connection to pivotal l'Ouillon. There is also a rather strange leg stretching down to St-Colomban-des-Villards (1100m) which involves four slow chairs to return to l'Ouillon.

The slopes are generally easy-intermediate stuff, and a bit featureless. The St-Sorlin sector has more character and offers more challenge, with some serious reds, the occasional black and abundant varied off-piste terrain. A March visitor this year reports that the linking draglifts on l'Ouillon can build queues.

We returned to La Toussuire in 2015 after a long absence. It remains an uninspiring place, the main attraction of which is low prices; but we were comfortably accommodated in a simple but spacious apartment in Lagrange's Ecrins des Sybelles residence; and our March visitor was much impressed by their Hauts de Comborcière.

1430m

VALLOIRE

Valloire is the best known of the Maurienne resorts internationally. It is an attractive, polished village with a strong summer trade – the Tour de France normally goes through en route for the famous Col du Galibier. It shares an extensive area of slopes with Valmeinier.

It's a compact village, with its main lifts a short walk from the fine old church and central square. Naturally, modern developments spread away from this central area – pretty much all in traditional chalet style.

Gondolas go up to both local sectors of slopes. Sétaz has nursery slopes and restaurants at the mid-mountain junction of Thimel, on the treeline. Sétaz is essentially of red gradient, and blue as well as green runs have to wind their way down. There are a couple of just-genuine blacks served by a six-pack. The second sector, Crey du Quart, has a six-pack to the top height of 2535m

**LAGRANGE
Prestige**

High-standard
Self-catering
Apartments

020 7371 6111
lagrange-holidays.co.uk

LIFT PASSES

Eski-Mo pass

Prices in €

Age	6-day
under 13	141
13 to 64	170
65 plus	163

Free Under 6, 76 plus
Beginner Local passes
Note Covers Aussois, Bonneval, La Norma, Val Cenis Vanoise and Valfréjus – read the introductory text on the previous page for more details

Alternative passes
Standard passes for individual resorts

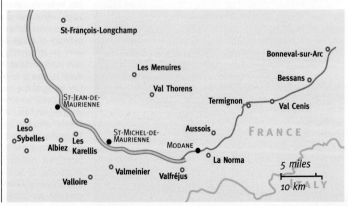

↑ The shady side of Crey du Quart, seen from the middle of the Valmeinier slopes

SNOWPIX.COM / CHRIS GILL

That's Valmeinier 1800, where most of the lodgings are to be found – mostly apartments, though there are two modest hotels. Across the hillside is the original village of Valmeinier 1500, plus assorted hamlets dotted around. The home slopes face just south of west. From 1800 a six-pack goes up about 700m serving easy intermediate slopes, while across the hillside above Valmeinier 1500 slow chairs serve more testing runs below Le Gros Crey (2595m) – there are great views from here. At 1500, a cross-valley chair connects with Valmeinier's side of Crey du Quart and so with Valloire.

1600m
LES KARELLIS

Les Karellis seems best known to readers as a good day out from bigger, more rounded Valloire, but it is a proper small resort.
Les Karellis is a modern purpose-built resort, consisting mainly of a dozen apartment blocks in an attractive setting on an open shelf in the forest. The resort claims 60km of pistes, widely spread over three identifiable mountainsides with a top height of 2520m – one of them above the more traditional village of Albanne. Drags and slow chairs dominate, but a fast chair from the village accesses two of the sectors. There is something for everyone – easy blues in one sector, wide fairly easy reds elsewhere, and a couple of short but genuine blacks served by a double drag. Cross-country trails add up to 30km. To our surprise, it has a multilingual website.

1500m
ALBIEZ

Albiez is a small, rustic, backwater village in a fine setting on the Col du Mollard, not far from St-Jean-de-Maurienne. Like Les Karellis, it makes a viable day trip from Valloire.
The ski area is a modest affair – a network of eight or nine drags and slow chairlifts from two main lift bases at around 1600m up to a top height of 2100m, with a chair off to one side reaching 2200m. It's a very small area, with no more than 35km of pistes – blue lower slopes with some reds higher up. Accommodation is in apartments and simple B&Bs. There are cross-country trails, cleared paths and snowshoeing.

above its gondola, making the link with Valmeinier and serving a much broader area of red and blue runs. At the south end of this sector, long and very gentle blue runs loop away from the lifts to take you down into the valleys that separate it from Sétaz and Valmeinier. One flank of Sétaz and most of Crey du Quart face west, and suffer from the sun. There is lots of off-piste terrain. And a terrain park.

Valloire has a good range of lodgings, and it's getting better – the 3-star Patchwork Altitude hotel, already the reader favourite, is getting a radical makeover and will reopen in December 2015 as a 4-star. There is one other 3-star and eight 2-stars. We enjoyed staying last winter in a smart and exceptionally spacious apartment in the small Chalets d'Adrien residence, in a prime central position. There are lots of highly traditional restaurants, but for lower cheese content clearly the best bet is Chez Freddy (or the hotel Patchwork). The resort is a pleasant place to spend time, and there is a reasonable range of off-slope activities, including skating and snowshoeing – but we know of no swimming pool. Market on Fridays.

1500–1800m
VALMEINIER

Valmeinier is a sharp contrast to linked Valloire: a modern apartment-based ski station – happily low-rise and in traditional chalet style, so easy on the eye.

TOURIST OFFICES
Albiez
albiez.fr

Aussois
aussois.com

Bonneval
bonneval.haute-
maurienne-vanoise.
com

Les Karellis
www.karellis.com

La Norma
www.la-norma.com

Les Sybelles
www.sybelles.com

Valfréjus
www.valfrejus.com

Valloire
www.valloire.net

Valmeinier
www.valmeinier.com

VALFREJUS
1550m

Valfréjus is built over the Fréjus road and rail tunnels from Modane to Italy (there was once fantasy-talk of a link with Bardonecchia). It's a small, purpose-built development in the forest, with most of the skiing higher up on open slopes.

The main access gondola goes to Plateau d'Arrondaz (2220m), where there are nursery slopes and short blue runs. But the heart of the skiing is the peak of Punta Bagna (2735m), with two six-packs serving slopes on the front and back – direct genuine blacks back to Plateau d'Arrondaz on the front of the hill (500m vertical), less direct reds and roundabout blues elsewhere, including a glorious long blue all the way to the resort for a vertical of almost 1200m. There are more direct blue and black ways home, too. The pistes total 70km.

The resort consists mostly of a cluster of chalet-shaped apartment blocks around the lift base, with smaller residences and individual chalets dotted around. There are cleared paths, and snowshoe outings. A chairlift of 160m vertical serves toboggan runs 3km long.

AUSSOIS
1500m

Aussois is on the sunny side of the valley, a short winding drive up from Modane (served by the TGV). It's a charming old village of stone and wood, complete with central fountain, with quite a respectable little ski area.
There are good nursery slopes next to the village. A fast and a slow chair go up from the village to the treeline, where a six-pack goes on to the top height of 2750m. Another slow chair and a drag serve the main west-facing upper slopes, red and blue, and a black goes away from the lifts to drop about 1000m before joining a green run to the village, with plentiful off-piste opportunities. There are snowshoe trails on the Aussois plateau, and more challenging ones across the hillside near Sardières, where there are also extensive cross-country trails.

The village offers a couple of B&Bs and modest hotels, as well as plenty of good-value apartments, some in slope-side locations.

LA NORMA
1350m

Across the deep Maurienne valley from Aussois, La Norma could not be more different – a modern, car-free resort in the shade of its steep, eponymous mountain. Like Aussois, it is easily reached from Modane and its TGV railway station.
The resort claims 65km of runs (or 700 ha – very fashionable). Most of the skiing, above and below the treeline, is on two flanks of that mountain – a major sector on the right accessed by a gondola and then two slow chairs to 2750m (giving an impressive vertical of 1400m), and a minor sector reached by a fast chair then two slow ones to 2500m. As you may have gathered, slow lifts dominate. There are excellent nursery slopes at village level and at both mid-mountain areas, with a long winding green track back to the base. But this is essentially a red-gradient mountain, genuinely black in places, so it is not great for timid intermediates. One reporter found lots to do off-piste from the upper lifts.

The resort is compact and family-friendly, with lodgings close to the lifts (though very little is ski-in/ski-out). A reporter who visited this year pronounced the place 'great for families on a budget'.

BONNEVAL-SUR-ARC
1850m

Bonneval is a tiny old village more or less at the head of the valley. It has an equally tiny lift system, but it serves some great off-piste terrain – a great day trip from Val Cenis.
The old village of Bonneval is a famously cute historic hamlet, well-worth a wander. On the fringes, the Glacier des Evettes is a friendly, well run 2-star hotel. There are nursery slopes beside the old village, and not far away is an area of tasteful modern development at Tralenta, where a drag serves a little nursery slope and a slow chair goes up to further beginner slopes above the treeline (2050m), with a tiny restaurant. From there, half a dozen drags and slow chairs reaching 3000m serve good but very limited intermediate pistes – but more importantly also wide and varied off-piste terrain on two flanks of the Pointe d'Andange, including runs of 1150m vertical to the valley bottom.

OT MEGÈVE

Megève

One of the traditional old winter holiday towns; best for those who enjoy relaxed cruising and spectacular views

£100
RESORT PRICE INDEX

RATINGS

The mountains

Extent	*****
Fast lifts	**
Queues	****
Terrain p'ks	***
Snow	**
Expert	**
Intermediate	****
Beginner	***
Boarder	**
X-country	****
Restaurants	****
Schools	***
Families	***

The resort

Charm	****
Convenience	**
Scenery	*****
Eating out	****
Après-ski	**
Off-slope	****

NEWS

2015/16: More snowmaking is planned for the red run from Le Bettex to St-Gervais.

2014/15: Both Mont Joux chairs were replaced by one fast six-pack. A new Folie Douce (as in Val d'Isère etc) opened at the top of Mont Joux near the top of the new chair.

KEY FACTS

Resort	1100m
	3,610ft
Slopes	850-2355m
	2,790-7,730ft
Lifts	88
Pistes	325km
	202 miles

- Extensive easy, scenic slopes
- Charming old town centre
- Some very smart hotels and shops
- Some special mountain restaurants
- Good for weekend trips
- Great in snowy weather – woodland runs with no one on them
- Plenty to do off the slopes

- Low altitude of slopes means a risk of poor snow, though the grassy terrain does not need deep cover
- Lots of slow, old lifts remain
- Three separate mountains
- Few challenging pistes
- Very muted après-ski (though it now has a Folie Douce)

Megève has a medieval heart but it was, in a way, the original purpose-built French ski resort – developed in the 1920s as a response to Switzerland's irritatingly swanky St Moritz. Although Courchevel long ago took over as France's top resort, Megève's smart hotels still attract the old money. Happily, the rest of us can enjoy it, too. And just look at that list of plus points above.

This is one of our favourite places to be in falling snow, when Megève regulars take one look and retreat to their duvets; we had a great time in mid-January 2015 making fresh tracks all morning in knee-deep powder on deserted slopes. But when the sun is out and we want to zip around the pistes, we get very frustrated by the number of slow lifts.

THE RESORT

Megève is in a lovely sunny setting and has a beautifully preserved, partly medieval centre. Visitors are mainly well-heeled French people, who come here for an all-round holiday.

The skiing divides into three sectors. One is directly accessible by lifts from close to the centre and from the southern edge of town, another from an elevated suburb or from an out-of-town lift base; these two are linked by cable car. The third involves a bus or free horse-drawn sleigh, for most people.

There are several alternative bases (which offer some good-value lodging) on the fringes of the area. St-Gervais and Le Bettex above it (described at the end of this chapter) have gondola access to the main sector. But beware slow access lifts from otherwise attractive spots. The slopes also link with La Giettaz; this has interesting local terrain, but is out on a limb and is not a sensible base.

The Evasion Mont Blanc lift pass also covers Les Contamines. Plans to create a link with this resort have existed for ages but we hear are now on hold yet again. A car is handy for outings like that, and for using the Princesse gondola, a bit out of town.

VILLAGE CHARM ****
Old France at its best

Megève's charming old centre is car-free and comes complete with open-air ice rink, horse-drawn sleighs, cobbled streets and a fine church. Lots of smart clothing, jewellery, antique, gift and food shops add to the chic atmosphere.

The main road to Albertville bypasses the centre, and there are expensive underground car parks to hide cars in. But people arrive here mainly by car, and the resulting traffic can be a problem at peak holiday times such as the French school

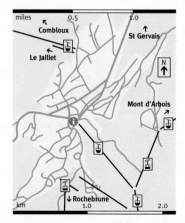

POWDERAMA

Ski coaching. Chamonix.

Achieve optimum
results with
focussed and
friendly tuition.

+33(0)616871853

powderama.com

holiday periods and New Year, particularly if you are based outside the very centre.

CONVENIENCE **
Stay close to a lift
Unless you have a car, staying close to one of the main lifts makes a lot of sense. Some hotels are close to a lift. But many lodgings depend on the free ski-buses (the two main lines run every 20 minutes – and every 10 minutes at peak times).

SCENERY *****
Beautiful town, beautiful views
The slopes are prettily wooded, but what earns Megève its five stars is the view of Mont Blanc from many of the runs – especially the red Epaule along a ridge above St-Nicolas-de-Véroce.

THE MOUNTAINS

The slopes are largely below the treeline – this is a great resort in poor weather – though there are extensive open areas, particularly higher up in the Mont d'Arbois sector.

Piste classification frequently exaggerates difficulty. The piste map could be improved, particularly in the Mont d'Arbois sector.

EXTENT OF THE SLOPES *****
More than enough for a week
Each of the three mountains has a worthwhile amount of terrain, and they add up to a great deal of skiing.

The town is most directly linked with the **Rochebrune** sector – a gondola goes up from the centre of town, and a cable car from the

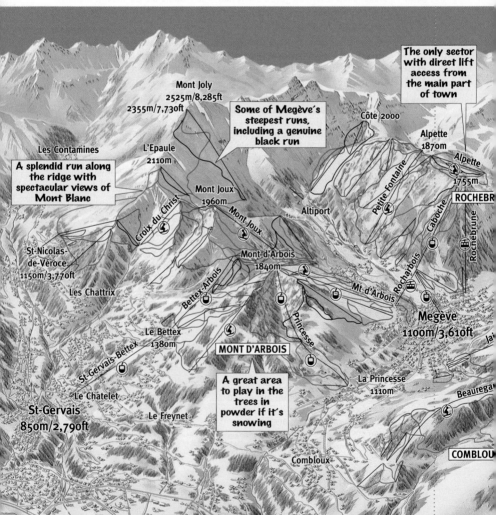

Stanford Skiing - The **Megève** Specialists

CHALETS - HOTELS - APARTMENTS - SHORT BREAKS
FLEXIBLE TRAVEL - FAMILY RUN - KNOWLEDGEABLE STAFF

Call us on 01603 477471 or visit **stanfordskiing**.co.uk

southern edge. A network of gentle, wooded, north-east-facing slopes, served by drags and mainly slow chairlifts, leads to the high point of Côte 2000, which often has the best snow but is now often used for racing, reducing the pistes available to recreational skiers.

At just above resort level the Rocharbois cable car goes across the valley to link Rochebrune to the gondola for the bigger **Mont d'Arbois** sector, starting from an elevated suburb of the resort. The Princesse

gondola starting a couple of miles north of the town (with extensive free car parking) offers another way up. A two-stage gondola comes up from St-Gervais via Le Bettex. You can work your way over to Mont Joux and up to the small Mont Joly area – Megève's highest slopes. And from there you can go to the backwater village of St-Nicolas-de-Véroce (preferably via the splendid Epaule ridge run, with wonderful views of Mont Blanc).

The third area is **Le Jaillet**, accessed by gondola from just outside the

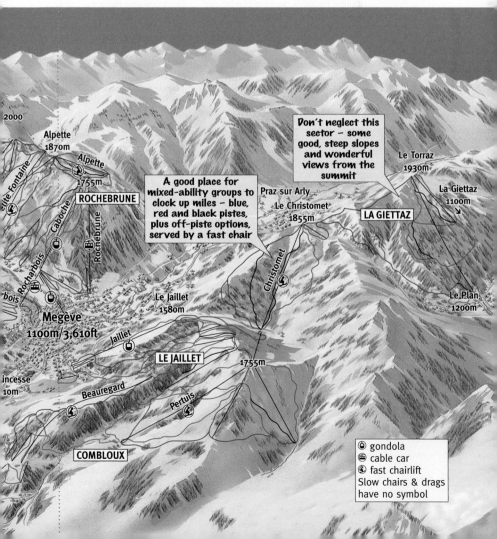

2000

Alpette
1870m

Alpette
1755m

ROCHEBRUNE

Rocharbois

Caboche

Rochebrune

bois

Megève
1100m/3,61oft

Jaillet

Le Jaillet
1580m

LE JAILLET

1755m

incesse
10m

Beauregard

Pertuis

COMBLOUX

A good place for mixed-ability groups to clock up miles – blue, red and black pistes, plus off-piste options, served by a fast chair

Praz sur Arly

Le Christomet
1855m

Christomet

Don't neglect this sector – some good, steep slopes and wonderful views from the summit

Le Torraz
1930m

La Giettaz
1100m

LA GIETTAZ

Le Plan
1200m

gondola
cable car
fast chairlift
Slow chairs & drags
have no symbol

MOMENTUM SKI

Weekend & a la carte
ski holiday specialists

100% Tailor-made

Premier hotels
& apartments

Flexible travel
arrangements

020 7371 9111
WWW.MOMENTUMSKI.COM

MEGEVE TO / JEAN-PIERRE
NOISILLIER

When there's fresh
snow on the trees and
the storm's just
clearing, it's a great
time to be on the
quiet slopes before
the Parisians venture
out ↓

north-west edge of town, or from the
separate village of Combloux. The high
point of Le Christomet is linked to the
slopes of tiny **La Giettaz** – worth the
trip, not least for spectacular views.

FAST LIFTS ★★☆☆☆
Still far too many slow ones
Megève continues to lag way behind
its rivals in the uplift business.
Gondolas and cable cars provide the
main access, and fast chairs are
dotted around – but overall three out
of four lifts are slow. The new six-pack
on Mont Joux last season was the first
new fast chair for three seasons. At
least all the slow lifts keep the pistes
uncrowded most of the time.

QUEUES ★★★★☆
Few weekday problems
During the week, Megève is relatively
queue-free and its slopes are
delightfully quiet, mostly. 'Virtually
none' and 'non-existent' were typical
2015 reporter comments on queues.
But sunny weekends (when day-
trippers from Geneva appear) and
school holidays can mean some
delays. The draglifts between Côte
2000 and the rest of the Rochebrune

slopes and the cable car that links the
Rochebrune and Mont d'Arbois slopes
can then have long queues. A 2015
reporter even found queues at the
new Mont Joux chair. Crowded pistes
at Mont Joux and Mont d'Arbois at
peak times have also been reported.
On a snowy day, even in peak season,
the slopes can be delightfully quiet as
the Parisians choose to stay in bed,
leaving the powder to you and us.

TERRAIN PARKS ★★★☆☆
Four, surprisingly
The park near the bottom of
Rochebrune was designed particularly
for beginners. There is a 500m-long
snowcross course and an airbag jump
nearby. There is also a park on Mont
d'Arbois, with good jumps for all
ability levels plus a host of rails.
Combloux also has a park and La
Giettaz a smaller park, albeit with a
real multitude of jump sizes and a few
rails; both have snowcross courses –
'great fun' says a recent visitor.

SNOW RELIABILITY ★★☆☆☆
The area's main weakness
The slopes are low, with very few runs
above 2000m, and quite sunny – the
Megève side of Mont d'Arbois gets the
afternoon sun. So in a poor snow year,
or in a warm spell, snow on the lower
slopes can suffer badly. Fortunately,
the grassy slopes don't need much
depth of snow. There is extensive
snowmaking, but that can't work in
warm weather. Grooming is very good
but read 'For experts', below.

FOR EXPERTS ★★☆☆☆
Off-piste is the main attraction
One of Megève's great advantages for
expert skiers is that there is not much
competition for the powder – many
days after a fresh dump you can often
make first tracks on good slopes. The
resort now leaves several runs
ungroomed immediately after a
snowfall, so you get to enjoy the
powder for a bit (as we experienced in
2015, when we skied knee-deep
powder all morning on red and black
pistes served by a fast chair).
  The Mont Joly and Mont Joux
sections offer the steepest slopes. The
top chair here serves a genuinely
black run, with some serious off-piste
off the back of the hill; and the
slightly lower Epaule chair has some
steep runs back down and also
accesses some good off-piste, as well

LIFT PASSES

Evasion Mont Blanc

Prices in €

Age	6-day
under 15	168
15 to 64	209
65 plus	188

Free Under 5, over 80
Beginner Three free lifts; limited passes cover a few lifts
Notes Megève, La Giettaz, Combloux, St-Gervais, St-Nicolas, plus Les Contamines; family discounts; pedestrian pass

Stanford Skiing - The **Megève** Specialists

CHALETS - HOTELS - APARTMENTS - SHORT BREAKS
FLEXIBLE TRAVEL - FAMILY RUN - KNOWLEDGEABLE STAFF

Call us on 01603 477471 or visit **stanfordskiing**.co.uk

as pistes, down to St-Nicolas. The steep area beneath the second stage of the Princesse gondola can be a play area of powder runs among the trees. Côte 2000 has a small section of steep runs, including good off-piste.

The terrain under the Christomet chair on Le Jaillet can be a good spot to develop off-piste technique, given decent snow – and a reporter recommends the extensive woods at La Giettaz.

FOR INTERMEDIATES ★★★★
Superb if the snow is good
Good intermediates will enjoy the whole area – there is so much choice it's difficult to single out any particular sectors. Keen skiers are likely to want to focus on the fast lifts, and happily several of these serve excellent terrain: the Princesse and Bettex gondolas on Mont d'Arbois, the Fontaine and Alpette chairs on Rochebrune and the Christomet chair in the Le Jaillet sector. But don't confine yourself to those – there are lots of other interesting areas, including the shady north-east-facing slopes on the back of Mont d'Arbois and Mont Joux and the front of Rochebrune, and the genuinely red/black slopes of La Giettaz. The slopes above Combloux are well worth exploring, particularly the quiet reds and black served by the Jouty chairlift. If you want to try powder, some reds and blues are left ungroomed immediately after a snowfall.

Megève is also a great area for the less confident. There are long, easy blue runs in all sectors. A number of gentle runs lead down to Le Bettex and La Princesse from Mont d'Arbois, while nearby Mont Joux accesses long, easy runs to St-Nicolas. Alpette and Côte 2000 are also suitable. As is most of Le Jaillet, especially the long easy runs down to Combloux.

FOR BEGINNERS ★★★
Good choice of nursery areas
There are beginner slopes at valley level, and more snow-sure ones at altitude on each of the main mountains. There are also plenty of very easy green runs to progress to.

FOR BOARDERS ★★
Beginner friendly
Boarding doesn't really fit with Megève's rather staid, upmarket image – there are no specialist schools – and there are quite a few flat linking runs to deal with. But freeriders will love it after snowfalls. It's a good place to try snowboarding for the first time, with plenty of fairly wide, quiet, gentle runs and a lot of chairlifts and gondolas. The draglifts are generally avoidable (except between Alpette and Côte 2000, unless you take the bus).

FOR CROSS-COUNTRY ★★★★
An excellent area
There are about 40km of varied trails spread throughout the area. Some are at altitude, making meeting with Alpine skiers for lunch simple.

MOUNTAIN RESTAURANTS ★★★★
Something for all budgets
Megève has some chic, expensive, gourmet places, but plenty of cheaper options too. Stanford Skiing's website has an absolutely essential guide to download. The piste map marks restaurants but does not name them. The tourist office restaurant guide includes huts but it is not comprehensive.

On Mont d'Arbois, La Ravière, tucked away in the woods near the Croix chair, is a tiny rustic hut that serves good food but has a limited choice (around four main courses); booking is essential and you must have at least two courses. The famously expensive Idéal 1850 is said to be excellent and Mandarines 'serves lovely food fast' says a 2015 reporter. There are several modest, small places worth seeking out. We liked Sous les Freddy's, near the Arbois chair (very good meat platter and home-made desserts) and Gouet, on the Gouet piste (tiny inside, excellent croûte and plat du jour). The tiny Refuge de Porcherey above St-Nicolas has 'lovely food and ambience'.

On Rochebrune/Côte 2000 the Alpette is the prestige place – 'good for a blowout'. We had a satisfying lunch a few years back at Javen d'en

Megève

273

Haut. Babotch near there was tipped this year and last for its 'extremely good food; try the plat du jour'. Radaz is an old farmhouse that serves 'excellent traditional food with friendly service' in several small rooms. The Terrasse has 'good food and live music'. On the back of the hill, Chalet le Forestier is an atmospheric hut.

On Le Jaillet, Face au Mont Blanc has stunning views, two-fixed price menus and a cheaper room with pasta and snacks. Auberge Bonjournal towards La Giettaz has 'fantastic views, a wood fire, good food'.

At Combloux, the Alpage de Porrez is praised by two reporters this year – 'BBQ mixed grill is superb'.

A growing number of snack bars are springing up beside the pistes, selling chips, soup, sandwiches etc – 'a good antidote to the mountain restaurants which are becoming more and more chi chi and pricey', says a local.

SCHOOLS AND GUIDES ★★★
Plenty of choice
The ESF is of course the major school. A regular visitor sees huge class sizes every season ('up to 20; though most are only just into double figures and most people we speak to seem content'). But a 2015 reporter was delighted with her private lesson with the ESF's Katie Campbell – 'can't recommend her too highly, especially for children, beginners, intermediates'. However, it has lots of competition here, not only from the International school but also from smaller French schools and some British-run outfits. A recent reporter and her friend – 'two nervous ladies from Wiltshire' – revelled in the 'idiosyncratic technique' of Megève Mike at Ski Pros; we hear that pupils love him or hate him. Powderama, based in Chamonix, offers private lessons here.

Heli-skiing (in Italy) and expeditions to the Vallée Blanche (in Chamonix) can be arranged, and mountain guides are available (we had a great morning powder skiing in the trees with Alex Périnet a few years ago).

FOR FAMILIES ★★★
Language problems
The kindergartens offer a wide range of activities. But lack of English-speaking staff could be a drawback. The slopes are family-friendly and the schools rated by reporters. There are snow gardens in the main sectors.

STAYING THERE

There is an impressive range of accommodation. Stanford is the Megève specialist. Momentum has a good range of hotels. Hanski specializes in short breaks here.

Chalets Stanford has three central chalets. We've happily stayed at two of them – the Sylvana, between the Rochebrune cable car and the centre ('great position: quiet but five minutes' walk from centre', 'good food', say recent reporters), and the Rond-Point, right by the centre. Both are cheap and cheerful former 2- or 3-star hotels and we've met happy regular guests whenever we've stayed. The bar prices must be about the cheapest in the Alps: beers at 2 euros and a good bottle of wine 8 euros. The smarter 10-bed Les Clochettes is next to the Sylvana.

Hotels Megève offers a range of exceptionally stylish hotels, mainly quite small and built in chalet style. Seven lovely but very pricey places have now been elevated to 5 stars.

*****Fer à Cheval It's rustic-chic at its best, with a lovely wood interior. Spa and pool.

*****Flocons de Sel Food-oriented eight-room place in a cluster of secluded chalets a few km out. Three Michelin stars. Spa.

****Chalet St Georges Central, close to the gondola. Warmly welcoming, with 24 rooms and suites. Read 'Eating out', below.

***Coin du Feu Mid-sized traditional rustic chalet between Rochebrune and Chamois lifts.

**Gai Soleil Simple Logis de France place. 'Good location, excellent breakfast, wonderful staff,' says a discriminating reporter.

Apartments Loges Blanches is central and smart, with restaurant and outdoor pool; bookable via Ski Collection and Erna Low. Stanford also has a couple of apartments.

EATING OUT ★★★★
Very French
The tourist office produces a pocket guide with photos. There are lots of upmarket restaurants, many of them in the better hotels and the Flocons de Sel (read 'Hotels') has the top place in town – but it also has a more modest branch, Flocons Villages, that is popular with locals and gets rave reports from readers – 'outstanding

Stanford Skiing - The **Megève** Specialists

CHALETS - HOTELS - APARTMENTS - SHORT BREAKS
FLEXIBLE TRAVEL - FAMILY RUN - KNOWLEDGEABLE STAFF

Call us on 01603 477471 or visit **stanfordskiing**.co.uk

Like the resort?
You'll love our handpicked accommodation
02392 839 310
PEAKRETREATS.CO.UK

ABTA
ABTA No.W5577

value', 'best value in town', 'miraculous lamb and veal, wonderful desserts, exceptional bread'; but a 2015 visitor was 'disappointed with the service'.

Meat, 'beautifully cooked', is a speciality at the 'superb' Table du Trappeur in the Chalet St Georges hotel. The Brasserie Centrale does precisely what brasseries were invented to do – 'good entrecôte-frites and crème brûlée'. The Vieux Megève is the place for cheesy specialities. The Café 2 la Poste is on a roundabout by the main road and 'looks like it should have plastic tablecloths but is charming, friendly, half the price of most other places'.

APRES-SKI ★★☆☆☆
Strolling and jazz

Megève's sedate image changed last season with the opening of a new Folie Douce (of Val d'Isère etc fame) at the top of Mont Joux. Reports please. That's a bizarre contrast with life in town, which we hear has remained sedate. It is a pleasant place to stroll around after the lifts close but if there are lively bars for a post-piste beer, they have so far eluded us. And those looking for loud disco-bars later may be disappointed, too. The 5 Rues is our choice – a very popular jazz club-cum-cocktail bar, open all evening, that gets some big-name musicians. It's pricey, but cocktail measures are large. The Cocoon is a Brit favourite, with live music and British sport on TV. The casino is more slot machines than blackjack tables. Palo Alto has two discos.

OFF THE SLOPES ★★★★☆
Lots to do

There is a 'fantastic' sports centre with a spa, fitness room, pool, indoor and outdoor ice rinks and cinemas. There's also snowshoeing, dog sledding, sleigh and hot air balloon rides. Shopping is a serious business and trips to Annecy and Chamonix are possible. Walks are excellent, with 50km of marked paths. Meeting friends on the slopes for lunch is easy.

LINKED RESORT – 850m
ST-GERVAIS

St-Gervais is a handsome 19th-century spa town set in a narrow river gorge, with access to the slopes shared with Megève by a gondola from the fringes. It's a pleasant place, with interesting food shops, cosy and sophisticated bars (we liked the trendy Pur bar for cocktails and posh nibbles), thermal baths and an Olympic ice rink. Prices are noticeably lower than in Megève. The resort has a train station and there are efficient bus services.

The lodgings are mostly modest. Two hotels convenient for the gondola are the Liberty Mont Blanc, a pleasantly traditional place with pool, sauna and hot tub, and the 3-star Carlina, with a small pool and sauna. The Féline Blanche is a hip boutique place with just 10 rooms done out in black and white. The basic 2-star Val d'Este has one of the best restaurants in town (Le Sérac).

Fermes de St-Gervais is a smart residence with a pool, a mile out of town; available through Peak Retreats.

The gondola from the edge of town goes to the satellite of Le Bettex. The good nursery slope here and green run above it, make it an attractive base for beginners. We enjoyed dining at the lovely rustic Chalet Rémy.

On the opposite side of St-Gervais is a rack-and-pinion railway, which in 1904 was intended to go all the way to the top of Mont Blanc. It was never completed, and terminates at the top of the ski area of Les Houches (see the Chamonix chapter); but sadly there are no lift pass sharing arrangements.

✳ **Want the next edition free?**

Send us a useful report on your holiday, and you could be among those who win one of 100 free copies. Then you might become one of our 'resort observers', and get free lift passes.

Find out more at:

www.wheretoskiandsnowboard.com

GETTING THERE

Air Geneva 90km/ 55 miles (1hr15); Chambéry 95km/ 60 miles (1hr15); Lyon 170km/ 105 miles (2hr15)

Rail Sallanches (12km/7 miles); regular buses from station

TOURIST OFFICES

Megève
www.megeve.com

St-Gervais
www.st-gervais.net

AGENCE NUIS

Les Menuires

The bargain base for the Three Valleys – with increasing amounts of stylish accommodation as well as the original dreary blocks

£110
RESORT PRICE INDEX

RATINGS

The mountains
Extent	*****
Fast lifts	****
Queues	****
Terrain p'ks	***
Snow	****
Expert	****
Intermediate	*****
Beginner	***
Boarder	****
X-country	***
Restaurants	***
Schools	***
Families	****

The resort
Charm	**
Convenience	*****
Scenery	***
Eating out	***
Après-ski	***
Off-slope	**

+ Speedy, mostly queue-free access to the huge Three Valleys area

+ Lots of slope-side accommodation, with road traffic well separated

+ Low prices by local standards

+ Distinct French atmosphere

− Big, plain blocks and gloomy indoor shopping malls in the centre

− Main intermediate and beginner slopes get a lot of sun

− Some slopes can get very crowded

Les Menuires has a better position in the Three Valleys than you might think, and we've warmed to it as better (and better-looking) lodgings have been built over recent years. As our RPI shows, it is much more affordable than more upmarket Courchevel and Méribel and we now view Les Menuires as a very attractive base – especially the bits we've christened 'Belles-Menuires'.

THE RESORT

Les Menuires is a purpose-built resort, dominated by large apartment blocks, with about 60% of the visitors French. The core of the resort is La Croisette, a horseshoe of 1960s- and 1970s-built apartment blocks plus a claustrophobic underground shopping mall with a gondola and fast chairlift into the heart of the Three Valleys slopes. Recent development has added various suburbs to the original core, and a second lift base across the mountainside at Les Bruyères.

VILLAGE CHARM **
Much improved
The original buildings that surround the main lift base are among the most uncompromising examples of the monolithic architecture of the 1960s and 1970s. They still dominate the centre of the resort; but more recent developments in the suburbs have been built in much more attractive, traditional chalet style in stone and wood, and many UK tour operators have their accommodation there. Read our Belles-Menuires feature later in the chapter for more on these.

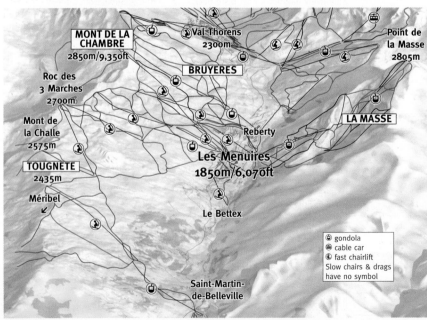

MONT DE LA CHAMBRE
2850m/9,350ft

Val Thorens
2300m

Point de la Masse
2805m

BRUYERES

Roc des 3 Marches
2700m

Mont de la Challe
2575m

LA MASSE

Reberty

Les Menuires
1850m/6,070ft

TOUGNETE
2435m

Méribel

Le Bettex

Saint-Martin-de-Belleville

○ gondola
● cable car
④ fast chairlift
Slow chairs & drags have no symbol

From La Masse you get a clear view of the layout of Les Menuires and its suburbs →

LES MENUIRES TO / P. LEBEAU

NEWS

2015/16: A fast quad (recycled from St-Martin, we hear) will replace the double chair going towards the main resort from Le Bettex, below it. A new wellness and pool complex opened at Les Bruyères.

2014/15: A new blue run opened on La Masse, making top-to-bottom descents possible on blues.

LIFT PASSES

Three Valleys

Prices in €	
Age	6-day
under 13	228
13 to 64	283
65 plus	255
Free Under 5, 75 plus	
Beginner Limited pass	

Notes Covers Courchevel, La Tania, Méribel, Val Thorens, Les Menuires and St-Martin; reductions for families, duos and groups. Options: pedestrian and half-day passes

Alternative passes
Les Menuires/St-Martin only; Vallée de Belleville only

KEY FACTS

Resort	1800m
	5,910ft

Three Valleys	
Slopes	1260-3230m
	4,130-10,600ft
Lifts	180
Pistes	600km
	373 miles

Les Menuires / St-Martin only	
Slopes	1400-2850m
	4,590-9,350ft
Lifts	34
Pistes	160km
	99 miles

CONVENIENCE ★★★★★
Easy to get around on skis
For most visitors, the resort is very conveniently arranged for skiing – a great deal of the accommodation is ski-in, and much of it ski-out.

If you stay in the central area, nothing is more than a short stroll away. If you stay in some of the outposts, it may be different. They have their own shops and bars, but if you want more choice, you are reliant on buses that are not super-frequent, especially later on in the evening.

SCENERY ★★★★★
Go up high
The scenery can be rather bleak, but there are grand views from the peaks of the ski area on both sides, especially from La Masse.

THE MOUNTAINS

Les Menuires is set just about on the treeline, with almost all the slopes above it. Piste map and signposting are good, classification reliable.

There are avalanche-controlled off-piste 'Liberty Ride' zones above the village and on La Masse. We always approve of such attempts to make powder skiing more accessible without the cost of guidance and special equipment; but it's difficult to get excited about verticals of only 200m. There's a bigger zone at St-Martin.

EXTENT OF THE SLOPES ★★★★★
Part of the huge Three Valleys
Les Menuires is well positioned for exploring the whole Three Valleys. The major part of the local area spreads across the west-facing mountainside between Les Menuires and St-Martin, with links to the Méribel valley at four points, and at the southern end links to Val Thorens. A gondola and fast chair go up from La Croisette, and the same from Les Bruyères. A gondola to the separate and unjustly neglected sector of La Masse, across the valley, starts below the village.

277

FAST LIFTS ★★★★
Good all over
The major lifts up to the peaks are now powerful gondolas or fast chairs. This year Le Bettex residents can rejoice at the news of a fast chair out of the valley bottom.

QUEUES ★★★★
Very slight
Queues are not usually a problem; most reporters comment that there are few. But the Bruyères gondola (for access to Val Thorens) is consistently mentioned by reporters ('15-minute queues at opening time'), and the Mont de la Chambre chair can also get very busy at peak times. Crowded slopes are more of a problem in general, particularly those leading down to the resort centre.

Les Belles-Menuires

DOWN THE HILL

Below the main resort centre, beside the river, is the small, recently developed suburb of Le Bettex, which this season at last gets a fast chairlift up towards the main resort.

Ski Amis has a cluster of smart chalets here with outdoor hot tubs and saunas, 150m from the piste and the Bettex chairlift. A reporter this year found Le Bettex 'charming', her Ski Amis chalet good, and meals 'absolutely first rate'.

Ski Powder Pigs has its chalet Kimberley here, too – also with hot tub.

Also in Le Bettex is the Hameaux des Airelles residence, available from Ski Collection.

There is a bar, but Le Bettex is very quiet at night, and a taxi ride from the bright lights of Les Menuires.

La Plagne has its Belle-Plagne – why shouldn't Les Menuires have its Belles-Menuires? Or should it be Beaux-Menuires? Whatever ... We've made up this name to represent the attractive, chalet-style suburbs of Les Menuires – places where Méribel habitués might be happy.

These suburbs aren't simply built in chalet style – they also contain properties where catered chalet holidays are offered. Many of them are operated by tour operators who advertise in this chapter – Ski Amis, Powder N Shine and Ski Famille – and are marked, approximately, on our map. They are concentrated up the slope in Reberty 2000, or down in Les Bruyères, a micro-resort complete with ice rink and swimming pool – and a major lift, the Bruyères gondola. The area shown also has the resort's best hotels, some smart apartment residences (read the margin panel on the right), and an excellent slope-side restaurant, the Ferme.

Down the valley, on the opposite side of the resort centre, are further traditional-style, small-scale, relatively upmarket developments where chalet holidays and self-catering apartments are offered (read the left margin panel).

Selected chalets in Les Menuires

ADVERTISEMENT

SKI AMIS *www.skiamis.com*

T **0203 411 5439**

- Chalets de Bruyeres – 5 chalets for 12-16 people – ski-in/ski-out
- Chalets de Bettaix – 4 chalets for 8-10 people
- Hot-tubs, free WIFI, satellite TV
- Excellent catering with full English breakfast every day, afternoon tea and three course evening meal
- Unlimited good quality wine

sales@skiamis.com

SKI AMIS

↑ CHALETS DE BETTAIX

CHALETS DE BRUYERES ↑

Reberty, Les Bruyères, Le Bettex

APARTMENTS

In Reberty 2000, Chalets du Soleil and Chalet Julietta are offshoots of the next-door 4-star hotel Kaya, with access to the Kaya's facilities, such as spa and restaurant.

Slightly lower down, Alpages de Reberty is a Pierre & Vacances Premium residence with pool, sauna etc.

La Sapinière includes the Montagnettes residence Hameau de la Sapinière, with sauna, steam room and hot tub, and a restaurant – and a local supermarket will deliver free of charge.

Down in Les Bruyères, Le Chalet du Mont Vallon Spa Resort has a pool, gym, sauna, steam and a serious restaurant.

Several agencies including apartment specialists Ski Collection offer these and other residences.

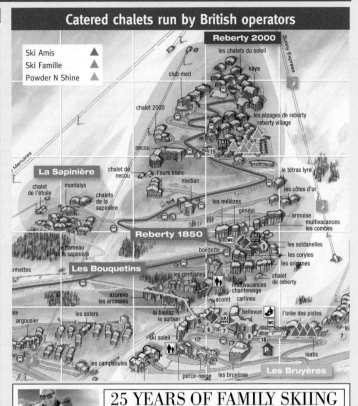

Catered chalets run by British operators

Ski Amis
Ski Famille
Powder N Shine

Reberty 2000
les chalets du soleil
kaya
club med
Sunny Express
chalet 2000
les alpages de reberty
reberty village
necou
15
La Sapinière
chalet de
necou
l'ours blanc
le tétras lyre
chalet
de l'étoile
montalys
median
les côtes d'or
chalets
de la
sapinière
les mélèzes
génépi
armoise
multivacances
les combes
le hameau
de la sapinière
Reberty 1850
WC
les soldanelles
boëdette
9
les coryles
les origanes
Les Bouquetins
les gentianes
chalet
de reberty
ermettes
multivacances
chanteneige
azureva
les arcosses
aconit
carlines
ale
argousier
les asters
la bieillaz
le sorbier
bellevue
WC
l'orée des pistes
6
6
7
2
ski soleil
9
18
P
isatis
les campanules
Les Bruyères
perce-neige
les bruyères

25 YEARS OF FAMILY SKIING
FAMILY CHALETS WITH
À LA CARTE CHILDCARE
Ski Famille
Call: 01252 365495 | www.skifamille.co.uk
ATOL 10863   ABTOT 5141

Powder N Shine
Delicious Alpine Catered Chalets
Award Winning   Ski-in/Ski-out   Excellent Service   les 3 vallées
High Altitude Accomodation   Outstanding Food & Wine

2015 Winner
tripadvisor
CERTIFICATE of EXCELLENCE

Call: +44 (0) 845 163 7596   www.powdernshine.com   info@powdernshine.com

SKI AMIS

Catered Chalets in Superb Locations

020 3411 5439
www.skiamis.com

TERRAIN PARKS ★★★
Family-friendly
The BK park near the top of the Becca chair has blue and red lines of jumps and rails plus two snowcross courses. On La Masse there's the Walibi Gliss slalom and snowcross area. There's a big airbag jump at the foot of the Slalom area.

SNOW RELIABILITY ★★★★
Coverage good, quality variable
The main west-facing slopes obviously get a great deal of strong afternoon sun. They have lots of snowmaking, but the snow lower down is often icy in the morning and slushy later on. La Masse's height and more shady orientation ensure good snow for a long season. Grooming is 'fantastic', says a 2014 visitor.

FOR EXPERTS ★★★★
Head for La Masse
The upper slopes of La Masse, served by the second stage of a fast jumbo gondola, are mostly of stiff red or easy black steepness – great fast cruises when groomed, of almost 660m vertical, and with some of the best snow in the Three Valleys. They are also usually very quiet compared with the rest of the slopes near here because La Masse is set off the busy Three Valleys 'circuit', and most people doing the circuit from Méribel, Courchevel and Val Thorens don't make the detour.

There is also a huge amount of off-piste, including the wide, sweeping, not-too-steep Vallon du Lou off the back of La Masse towards Val Thorens (this used to be a marked itinéraire and was one of our favourite runs in the whole Three Valleys). Or you could try the Liberty Rides, explained above – though they are very limited.

Read the other Three Valleys resort chapters too.

FOR INTERMEDIATES ★★★★★
600km of pistes to choose from
With good snow, the slopes above the village on the west-facing side, virtually all blue and red, have a lot to offer. Don't miss La Masse, too – now with a new blue piste on the upper slopes, as well as multiple reds.

But the real attraction is the easy access to the rest of the Three Valleys and its 600km of pistes, most of which are ideal intermediate terrain. There are lifts to four different points from which you can drop into the Méribel valley, and you can be at the far end of the Courchevel ski area in 1650 in around 90 minutes if you don't get distracted on the way. To get to Val Thorens, there's an easy blue run from the Montaulever draglift that is quieter than the main runs from the top of the Bruyères gondola.

FOR BEGINNERS ★★★
Snow quality a concern
The resort's nursery areas are pretty good, with five moving carpets that are free – but snow quality here remains a concern because of the sunny aspect. A special lift pass is available for beginners, and there is a green run to the village from the Roc des 3 Marches gondola, and lots of easy blues to progress to, but they are prone to crowds.

FOR BOARDERS ★★★★
Beware flat parts
Slushy afternoon snow on the west-facing slopes won't worry boarders as it does skiers, but the early-morning ice might. You'll still want to escape and explore the vast amount of terrain elsewhere in the Three Valleys. The local terrain park is far from hard core, but Méribel's two great parks are easy to reach. Locally, there are few draglifts but beware some flattish sections of piste.

FOR CROSS-COUNTRY ★★★
Limited and low
The 28km of trails are along the valley between St-Martin and Les Menuires.

MOUNTAIN RESTAURANTS ★★★
Affordable fare
There are some good places here charging affordable prices.
Editors' choice The Grand Lac, in a fine spot at the bottom of the Granges chair, is a big chalet where we've always had very good service and

'awesome ski chalet holidays in the Three Valleys'

SKI POWDER PIGS

Three Valleys Ski Chalet Accommodation
www.skipowderpigs.co.uk 0770 212 3883

food – endorsed by three 2015 visitors, although a fourth complains of inadequately saucey pasta.

Worth knowing about Way across the hill, we've repeatedly enjoyed the Alpage, which also keeps most visitors happy – 'service very good', 'excellent value'. We also like La Ferme, piste-side at Reberty 2000, which scrapes into the mountain restaurant category by virtue of the piste extending below it; a flood of reports this year praise food, service and value. Chez Pepe Nicolas is on our agenda: 'a tiny, charmingly rustic stone hut', off-piste below Bruyères, doing 'limited but delicious and generous food'.

The famously starry restaurant La Bouitte, in the valley near St-Martin, now has a pricey elevated offshoot here, Le Bouche à Oreille ('Word of Mouth'), obviously meant to provide a reassuringly expensive lunch spot for residents of Courchevel; sadly, we and a couple of readers have found the place incompetently run.

SCHOOLS AND GUIDES ★★★★★
Try the Ski'School
The ESF gets mixed reviews; it seems to do a lot of off-piste stuff. A group of instructors operating here and in St-Martin under the startling name of Ski'School offers only private lessons.

FOR FAMILIES ★★★★★
Lots of options
Good facilities. There are kids' 'villages' with indoor and outdoor facilities at both La Croisette and Les Bruyères. Ski Famille is a family specialist with three chalets in Reberty and its own childcare arrangements.

STAYING THERE

La Croisette consists mainly of large apartment blocks. Reberty/Les Bruyères has hotels and chalets too.
Chalets Read our Belles-Menuires feature earlier in the chapter.
Hotels There are good places on the slopes at Reberty/Les Bruyères, but we get few reports on them.
★★★★Chalet du Mont Vallon Cool place with woody suites and apartments.

Good restaurant. Spa and pool.
★★★★Kaya Smart and modern, with good spa and restaurant.
★★★★Ours Blanc Chalet style, sauna, steam, tub, good food.
★★★Isatis In chalet style, right at the Bruyères gondola – 17 suites, all with hot tubs.
★★★Neige et Ciel Slope-side family 'club' hotel with nursery and kids' club – 'great place, very good buffet meals'.
Apartments There are lots of new developments in chalet style, most of them covered by our Belles-Menuires feature. In Preyerand, just below the main resort centre, is the chalet-style 4-star residence Les Clarines, with spa and pool, run by CGH and featured by Ski Collection. Ski Amis has units in all parts of the resort. Erna Low has a good range of properties.

EATING OUT ★★★★★
Mix of gourmet and Savoyard
Several hotels have good restaurants – the Cocon des Neiges (hotel Isatis), l'Atelier (Italian, Chalet du Mont Vallon), the K (hotel Kaya). La Ferme, piste-side at Reberty, is more down to earth, reliable, jolly. Other recent tips include the Chouette at Bruyères and Belleville on the front de neige.

APRES-SKI ★★★★★
Not a lot of choice
It's pretty quiet in the evening. A reporter favourite for close-of-play beers is the Chouette at Les Bruyères. There is no shortage of bars in La Croisette, but we're not tempted by those in the claustrophobic mall. There are discos at Croisette and Bruyères.

OFF THE SLOPES ★★★★★
Great sports centre
There is an impressive sports/spa/pool/ fitness centre in the main resort, and a new one opened last season at Les Bruyères. Plus a roller-coaster, a 4km 450m vertical toboggan run from the Roc 1 gondola, mountain biking on the same hill, snowmobiling, snowshoe outings, snowscooters and paragliding. But this is basically a destination for sporty types, and not very appealing for others.

GETTING THERE

Air Chambéry 115km/ 70 miles (1hr30); Geneva 150km/ 95 miles (2hr15); Grenoble 180km/ 110 miles (2hr15); Lyon 190km/ 120 miles (2hr15)

Rail Moûtiers (25km/15 miles)

TOURIST OFFICE

www.lesmenuires.com

Les Menuires

281

SNOWPIX.COM / CHRIS GILL

Méribel

A sprawling but comfortable, upmarket chalet-style resort in the centre of the incomparable Three Valleys

£125
RESORT PRICE INDEX

RATINGS

The mountains

Extent	★★★★★
Fast lifts	★★★★★
Queues	★★★★
Terrain p'ks	★★★★
Snow	★★★
Expert	★★★★
Intermediate	★★★★★
Beginner	★★★★
Boarder	★★★★
X-country	★★★
Restaurants	★★★
Schools	★★★★
Families	★★★

The resort

Charm	★★★
Convenience	★★★
Scenery	★★★
Eating out	★★★★
Après-ski	★★★★★
Off-slope	★★★

NEWS

2015/16: At Mottaret the Combes quad chair will be replaced by a six-pack, and two new beginner areas are being created. A new sledging area is being created in Méribel.

2014/15: The Loze chair to Col de la Loze was upgraded to a fast quad, making this novice-friendly route to Courchevel much more attractive. Two new 'fun' trails were created in the woods at the beginner area at Altiport.

+ Central to the Three Valleys, the biggest lift network in the world

+ Pleasant chalet-style architecture

+ Impressive lift system

+ Very lively après-ski scene

+ Excellent piste maintenance and snowmaking; nevertheless ...

− Snow on the west-facing side suffers from afternoon sun

− Sprawling main village

− Expensive, particularly for food and drink

− Full of Brits

− Some pistes can get crowded

A loyal band of regular visitors just love Méribel, and it's not difficult to see why. For keen piste-bashers who like to rack up the miles but dislike tacky post-war resorts, it's difficult to beat: unlike other modern purpose-built resorts, Méribel has always insisted on chalet-style architecture.

But other 3V resorts have the edge in important respects. For better snow opt for Courchevel or Val Thorens; for lower prices, Les Menuires or St-Martin.

THE RESORT

Méribel was founded in 1938 by a Brit, Peter Lindsay, and has retained a strong British presence and influence.

It consists of two main resort villages. The original resort is built on a steepish west-facing hillside with the home piste running down beside it to the main lift stations in the valley bottom, slightly below the village centre. The resort now spreads widely away from the centre and the piste; various quarters can be identified – among them Mussillon, beside the road in to the resort, where many individual chalets are located.

A road winds up from the centre to the top of the main village. Then one road goes on through woods to the altiport (a snow-covered airstrip) while another goes under the home piste to the suburb of Belvedere. These higher suburbs are now known collectively as Méribel les Hauts, while the lower levels are called Méribel Centre.

The satellite resort of Méribel-Mottaret is a mile or two up the valley. The hamlet of Méribel-Village, on the road to Courchevel, has grown into a pleasant, quiet micro-resort.

A gondola links the valley-bottom spa town of Brides-les-Bains to Méribel via the village of Les Allues. They are described at the end of this chapter; both have lodgings.

A car is useful for outings to other resorts such as Les Arcs, Val d'Isère, Tignes and La Rosière; you can access La Plagne via Champagny.

VILLAGE CHARM ★★★☆☆
Built with style

Méribel is one of the most tastefully designed of French purpose-built resorts. The buildings are wood-clad, chalet-style and mainly low-rise, and they include a lot of individual chalets as well as big chalet-shaped blocks of apartments. Mottaret lacks these smaller chalets, and looks more block-

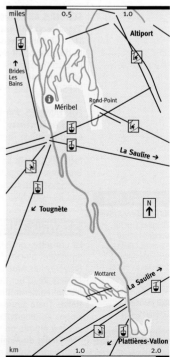

282

KEY FACTS

Resort	1400-1700m
	4,590-5,580ft

Three Valleys	
Slopes	1260-3230m
	4,130-10,600ft
Lifts	180
Pistes	600km
	373 miles

Méribel only	
Slopes	1400-2950m
	4,590-9,680ft
Lifts	41
Pistes	150km
	93 miles

MERIBEL TO
Chalets, chalets and more chalets, many of them run in catered form by British tour operators ↓

like as a result, despite wood cladding. Even so, it's more attractive than many other resorts built for slope-side convenience, but has nothing like the feel of a village.

CONVENIENCE ★★★ ★★
Shuttle to the slopes, usually
Although some lodgings are right on the piste beside the village, many depend on using free (and now 'excellent') public buses which run until midnight or private minibuses to and from the slopes. There are collections of shops and restaurants at a couple of points on the road through the resort – Altitude 1600 and Plateau de Morel.

Méribel-Village is a small place; it has some luxury chalets and apartments, but very limited amenities – a good bread shop, a small supermarket, a bar, a pizzeria and a couple of restaurants.

Mottaret has spread up both steep sides of the valley, though most of the blocks are on the east-facing side. Many lodgings are ski-in/ski-out, but not all. Both sides are served by lifts for pedestrians – but the gondola up the east-facing slope stops at 7.30.

SCENERY ★★★ ★★
Head for Vallon
The village is attractively set in woodland, below long craggy ridges – a satisfying although unspectacular scene. But there are wonderful glacial views from Mont du Vallon at the head of the valley.

THE MOUNTAINS

Most of the slopes are above the treeline, but there are some sheltered runs for bad-weather days. Piste classification is not always reliable – a problem compounded by exposure of many slopes to the sun. Signposting is excellent. The piste map is adequate; but it could be so much better if it covered the two sides of the valley separately. They have stopped handing out maps of which pistes have been groomed but you can now get this information on the Three Valleys smartphone app or on the Méribel website and it appears on small notices posted at various places.

EXTENT OF THE SLOPES ★★★★★
Centre of a huge area
Leaving aside the rest of the Three Valleys, this is a big area. Lifts go up to nine high points on the ridges above the resort: two entry points to the Courchevel valley, no fewer than six entry points to the Belleville valley (shared by St-Martin, Les Menuires and Val Thorens) and one to Mont du Vallon, a very worthwhile cul-de-sac.

On the morning-sun side, chairs go up to the first two links with St-Martin, and some relatively quiet slopes back towards Méribel. To the left, a gondola and then a six-pack go from Méribel to **Tougnète**, for both Les Menuires and St-Martin. You can also head down to **Mottaret** from here. From there, a fast chair then a drag take you to Belleville entry point number four.

High quality, high altitude

Four-star ski apartments with spa
02392 890 960

ABTA

SKI COLLECTION
.co.uk

South of Mottaret are some of the best slopes in the valley, in the **Plattières-Vallon** sector at the head of the valley. The top stage of the old Plattières gondola (the first two stages were replaced by a 10-seater) ends at the fifth entry point to the Belleville valley. To the east of this is the big stand-up gondola to the top of Mont du Vallon. The Côte Brune fast quad from near this area goes up to Mont de la Chambre, the sixth link with the next valley, and the only one giving direct access to Val Thorens.

On the afternoon-sun side, gondolas leave both Méribel and Mottaret for **Saulire**, the main link to Courchevel. The other is from the altiport – a much more attractive route now that a fast quad goes to Col de la Loze, replacing a very slow old chair.

FAST LIFTS ★★★★★
Highly efficient system
Modern chairs and gondolas serve both sides of the valley, with good links into the rest of the Three Valleys.

QUEUES ★★★★☆
3V traffic a persistent problem
The area is generally queue-free most of the time but there are a few bottlenecks. More singles lines are appearing – but the lift company could achieve a lot by employing lifties to usher people into half-empty cabins

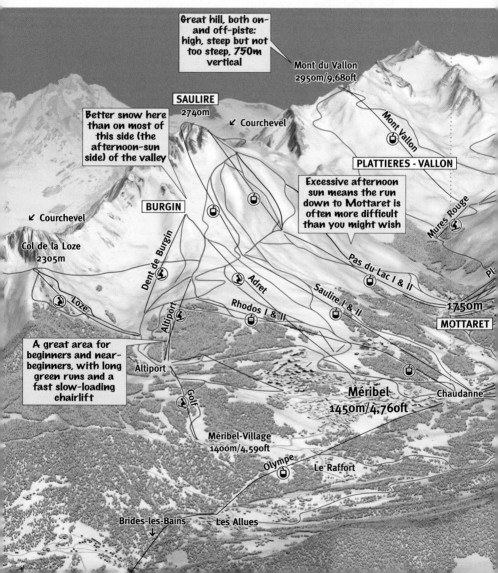

Great hill, both on- and off-piste: high, steep but not too steep, 750m vertical

Mont du Vallon
2950m/9,68oft

SAULIRE
2740m

↙ Courchevel

Mont Vallon

PLATTIERES - VALLON

Better snow here than on most of this side (the afternoon-sun side) of the valley

Mures Rouge

Excessive afternoon sun means the run down to Mottaret is often more difficult than you might wish

BURGIN

↙ Courchevel

Col de la Loze
2305m

Loze

Dent de Burgin

Adret

Pas du Lac I & II

Saulire I & II

Pl

1750m

MOTTARET

Altiport

Rhodos I & II

A great area for beginners and near-beginners, with long green runs and a fast slow-loading chairlift

Altiport

Golf

Méribel
1450m/4,76oft

Chaudanne

Méribel-Village
1400m/4,59oft

Olympe

Le Raffort

Brides-les-Bains
↓

Les Allues

and on to chairs, North American style.

We and reporters alike have found that the six-pack above the Tougnète gondola is a serious bottleneck – it comes nowhere near coping with the combination of people coming up the gondola and people descending the four good pistes above – and in spring the problem is made worse by pedestrians bringing it to a stop. A major upgrade is needed.

The recently upgraded Plattières gondola has cut queues at Mottaret but put more pressure on the old gondola third stage (which remains in place above the new lift) and the Côte Brune chair used by people heading onward to Mont de la Chambre and Val Thorens. The newish gondola from Méribel to La Saulire shifts a lot of people quickly.

In this central valley the most serious problems result from the tidal flows of people passing through in the morning (when the tide coincides with the start of ski school) and in the late afternoon, when crowds on the runs to Mottaret (returning from Val Thorens) can also be a problem.

Most people returning from Val Thorens form a queue for the Plan des Mains chair so as to avoid the flat start of the 'blue' Ours valley run. Confident skiers can by-pass Plan des Mains by traversing above it, off-piste; only with a guide, of course.

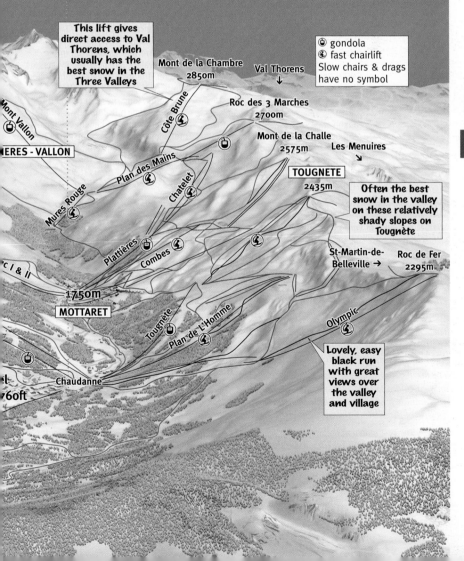

This lift gives direct access to Val Thorens, which usually has the best snow in the Three Valleys

ⓖ gondola
ⓕ fast chairlift
Slow chairs & drags have no symbol

Mont Vallon

ERES - VALLON

Mont de la Chambre
2850m

Côte Brune

Roc des 3 Marches
2700m

Val Thorens
↓

Mont de la Challe
2575m

Les Menuires
↓

Plan des Mains

Mures Rouge

Chatelet

TOUGNETE
2435m

Often the best snow in the valley on these relatively shady slopes on Tougnète

Plattières

Combes

St-Martin-de-Belleville →

Roc de Fer
2295m

c I & II

1750m

MOTTARET

Tougnète

Plan de L'Homme

Olympic

Lovely, easy black run with great views over the valley and village

Chaudanne

l

76oft

LIFT PASSES

Three Valleys

Prices in €

Age	6-day
under 13	228
13 to 64	283
65 plus	255

Free Under 5, 75 plus
Beginner Mini pass
Notes Covers
Courchevel, La Tania,
Méribel, Val Thorens,
Les Menuires and
St-Martin; reductions
for families, duos and
groups. Options:
pedestrian and half-
day passes

Alternative passes
Méribel and Méribel-
Mottaret only + 3V
extension

TERRAIN PARKS ★★★★
Two great areas
Méribel has two big parks. Moonpark
– at mid-mountain on Tougnète and
served by the Arpasson draglift –
covers over 25 acres. In charge are the
respected H05 crew. There are
beginner, intermediate and expert
lines, a snowcross and a 'chill and
grill' BBQ zone. You can be filmed and
watch the results on a big screen.

Under the Plattières gondola, the
Area 43 park was massively expanded
a couple of seasons ago to be 1200m
long with lots of features – 'excellent',
says a regular boarding reporter: 'lines
ranging from tame to terrifying', a half-
pipe at the top, snowcross and air bag
jump. You can have your run recorded
and play it back online.

Across the valley, kids get their own
mini-snowcross courses, P'tit Moon,
plus Moon Wild, an animal-themed
piste in the forest.

SNOW RELIABILITY ★★★
Not the best in the Three Valleys
Méribel's slopes aren't the highest in
the Three Valleys, and they mainly face
roughly east or west; the latter (the
runs down from Courchevel) get the
full force of the afternoon sun. In late
season you soon get into the habit of
avoiding this side in the morning,
when it is still rock-hard having frozen

overnight. Skiers coming over from
Courchevel can get a real shock. The
run down from Saulire to Mottaret is a
particular problem – often like
concrete for its whole 1000m vertical;
in our countless visits over many
years, we've only once found this run
enjoyable. The slopes above Altiport
get less direct sun and generally have
decent snow. And the morning-sun
side (the Tougnète side of the valley)
can be excellent. At the southern end
of the valley, a lot of runs are north-
facing and keep their snow well, as do
the runs on Mont du Vallon.

Snowmaking has been increased to
the point where the lower runs have
substantial cover. Lack of snow is
rarely a problem. Grooming is good.

FOR EXPERTS ★★★★
Exciting choices
The size of the Three Valleys means
experts are well catered for. In the
Méribel valley, Mont du Vallon has lots
to offer. The long, steep Combe Vallon
run here is classified red; it's a
wonderful, long, fast cruise when
groomed (which it normally is), but
presents plenty of challenge when
mogulled. And there's a beautiful off-
piste run away from the pistes, leading
back to the bottom of the gondola.

A good mogul run is down the side
of the double Roc de Tougne draglift

MERIBEL'S BEST OFF-PISTE RUNS

Méribel has a lot of very good off-piste to discover. Here, we pick out some of the best runs for skiers with at least some off-piste experience. Don't tackle them without guidance.

The run from near Roc de Fer to Le Raffort, a mid-station on the gondola from Brides-les-Bains, is an adventure with exceptional views. You ride the Olympic chairlift, go along the ridge, then ski a gentle bowl to finish among the trees.

The wide, west-facing slope above Altiport is enjoyable when the snow is fresh – varied terrain, from average to steep, some open, some wooded, reached from the Tétras black run.

There are lots of runs suitable for more accomplished off-piste skiers. One is the Cairn, from the Mouflon piste at the top of the Plattières 3 gondola; it starts in a fairly steep couloir and becomes wider, with a consistent pitch, until you reach the Sittelle piste.

The Roc de Tougne draglift accesses some challenging runs. To the right of the Lagopède red piste is an area guides call the Spot – a rather technical and steep descent to the Sittelle piste. Alternatively, a 15-minute hike brings you to the Couloir du Serail, leading to the Mouflon red piste – a favourite because of the vertical, the constant pitch and the quality of snow.

Some of the best routes in the Méribel valley are accessed from the other valleys. The Col du Fruit is a classic, far away from the lifts and resorts. You ride the Creux Noirs chairlift in Courchevel, then walk along the ridge for 15 minutes before descending through the national park to Lac de Tueda and the cross-country tracks ... 800m of flat ground from the Mottaret lifts. Some of the best snow is accessed from the 3 Vallées chairlift at Val Thorens. Ducking the rope at the top takes you into varied terrain mixing couloirs and gentle slopes, with exposures from north-east to north-west. Eventually you join the red Lac de la Chambre piste down to Plan des Mains.

SKIWORLD

Catered chalets, hotels and self catering apartments in

Europe, USA and Canada

skiworld.co.uk

08444 930 430

ABTA V2151 ATOL 2036

which leads up to Mont de la Challe. And there are steep, unrelenting runs from Tougnète back to Méribel – the upper Ecureuil piste is a black and the adjacent Combe Tougnète is a red. At the north end of the valley the Face run was created for the women's downhill race in the 1992 Olympics; served by a fast quad, it's a splendid cruise when freshly groomed.

Across the valley, the Couloir Tournier underneath the revamped Saulire gondola is seriously steep but also seriously rocky – we've never found it open, fortunately. Lower down, the Mauduit red run is quite challenging – it used to be black.

Throughout the area there are good off-piste opportunities – read our feature panel, and the other Three Valleys resort chapters.

FOR INTERMEDIATES ★★★★★
Paradise found
Méribel and the rest of the Three Valleys form something close to paradise for intermediate skiers and riders; there are few other resorts where a keen piste-basher can cover so many miles so easily and with such satisfaction. Virtually every slope has a good intermediate run down it.

For less adventurous intermediates, the Sittelle blue run down the Plattières gondola towards Mottaret is an ideal cruise – gentle and generally in good condition because of its aspect. But it can get very crowded and the lower part can get bumpy and slushy later in the day.

Even early intermediates should find the runs into the other valleys well within their capabilities, opening up vast amounts of intermediate terrain, often with better snow.

Virtually all the pistes on both sides of the Méribel valley will suit more advanced intermediates. Few of the reds are easy.

FOR BEGINNERS ★★★★
Strengths and weaknesses
Méribel continues to improve its appeal to beginners. At the core of this appeal is an excellent long green slope – gentle, wide, treelined – at Altiport, where editor Watts learned to ski [cough] years ago. New 'fun' trails in the woods were added last season. This is a lift or bus ride above the resort, which is not ideal. But the slope is served by a free draglift (and by a fast chair going higher, not free).

Meribel Chalets

01273 466535
alpineaction.co.uk

A alpineaction
quality catered chalet holidays

Central & piste locations • Fully Catered with wine Hot-tubs, Saunas & WIFI

ABTA Y5435

And there are green runs from the top and bottom of the drag back to Rond-Point, at the top of the village, where there is another free drag; beginners should take a lift or bus from there as the blue run lower down is not easy. And a green run goes from the mid-station of the Saulire gondola so that novices are able to ski from that point. The Mini lift pass gives access to a limited number of gentler slopes.

There is a small nursery slope at Rond-Point which is mainly used by the children's ski school.

At Mottaret, facilities have been less impressive, but are being improved this year, with two new nursery areas. You can graduate from the nursery slopes to an almost flat green along the valley to the main Méribel lifts (though it gets busy).

FOR BOARDERS ★★★★
Good all round
The terrain is good and varied, with a worthwhile number of tree runs. Mont du Vallon has some very good steep freeriding that stays relatively untracked. There are lots of red runs here for intermediates and gentle blues and greens for beginners. The two terrain parks are top-notch too. Most lifts are chairs or gondolas, but beware of flat sections on the main routes to and from Val Thorens – and avoid the Ours blue run down to Mottaret from Mont du Vallon, which is very hard work.

FOR CROSS-COUNTRY ★★★
Scenic routes
There are about 33km in the Méribel valley. The main area is in the forest near Altiport and is great for trying cross-country for the first time. There's also a loop around Lake Tueda, in the nature reserve at Mottaret; and for the more experienced, an 8km itinéraire from Altiport to Courchevel.

Méribel

287

IMPROVE YOUR SKIING
SKI WITH OTHERS
GO PLACES

SNOWORKS
snoworks.com

ALPINE ANSWERS
The UK's No.1 Chalet Specialist

For choice and service look no further!

alpineanswers.co.uk
call: 020 7801 1080
⊕ABTA

Discover the difference
with SkiWeekends
#loveski

Prices from
£200

skiweekends.com

MOUNTAIN RESTAURANTS ★★★☆☆
A disappointing choice

There are few places in this valley worth singling out, and there aren't enough restaurants to meet the demand. Restaurants are not named on the piste map.

The major new arrival of recent years is the Folie Douce/Fruitière complex at mid-mountain below La Saulire, part of the exploding chain that started in Val d'Isère. This year a metropolitan burger connoisseur enjoyed 'one of the best ever' at the Folie Burger Store, but we still lack reports on the proper food/table-service at La Fruitière, which we haven't yet managed to try ourselves.

We have conflicting reports this year on the table-service restaurant at Plan des Mains, of which we have fond memories; if it's quiet, expect 'great food and good service'; when busy, you may get mediocre food, long waits and no apologies. The Crêtes, on the Tougnète ridge above Les

Menuires, has a fine position and rustic interior, and was one family's favourite – 'friendly and welcoming'; 'lovely food, nicely presented' says a regular. The Coeur de Cristal, low down near Méribel Centre, is a bit 'urban and posh' in style, but has pleased visitors last year and this with 'excellent food, generous portions'.

In the absence of an Editors' choice, this is one of the few resorts in the Alps where we are easily persuaded to descend for lunch at resort level, on one of three excellent slope-side hotel terraces – the Adray Télébar or the Allodis in Méribel Centre, or the Altiport ('fabulous – best ever Savoyard meat platter').

SCHOOLS AND GUIDES ★★★★☆
Some excellent British schools

There are several British-run schools with native English-speaking instructors, which generally get good reports – including New Generation, BASS and Parallel Lines. Magic in Motion is run by an Anglo-French team and also has a number of native English-speakers.

FOR FAMILIES ★★★☆☆
A popular chalet choice

Méribel is a sensible choice for families wanting a chalet holiday. What it lacks in convenience it gains in an impressive area, with gentle beginner slopes and a couple of fun family areas (the new Inuit Village with whoops, a tunnel, banked turns and slaloms, and Moon Wild nature trail through the woods – both above Altiport).

We rarely get reports on childcare facilities – no doubt many readers use the facilities of chalet operators. Family specialist Esprit has a 60-bed chalet hotel in a good slope-side position, up at Rond-Point – 'very good', said a reader last year.

SNOWPIX.COM / CHRIS GILL

Most of the beds in Méribel-Mottaret are on the morning-sun side ↓

STAYING THERE

Club Med has two places here, both rated four 'tridents'.

Chalets Méribel has more catered chalets than any other resort. Many of them are recently built luxury places with spas, hot tubs and other fancy amenities. Many rely on minibus services to and from the lifts.

The widest choice is from Ski Total, with 11 properties in the mid-to-large size range. Two deservedly get Total's top Platinum rating: hot tubs, of course, and cinema and billiard room in the case of chalet Isba. Alpine Action has eight chalets in Méribel itself, most with hot tubs, and two in Méribel-Village. Skiworld has seven chalets of various sizes, including one swanky 'Signature' place with sauna, hot tub and cinema room.

Inghams has six chalets plus a 60-bed chalet hotel in a prime spot near the lifts at Chaudanne. Approved by a reader last year and this – 'lovely food, nice atmosphere, very helpful although inexperienced staff'. Purple Ski has five top-notch and highly individual chalets, in good positions (a couple ski-in/ski-out), with lovely interiors and hot tubs. Crystal has one of its 'finest' chalets, with sauna and hot tub. Ski Olympic has two properties at 1600. Family specialist Esprit has a 60-bed chalet hotel here – read 'For families' on the facing page.

Hotels Méribel doesn't compete with Courchevel in the fancy hotel stakes, although it does have one 5-star, Le Kaïla, well placed near Chaudanne.

Ski Total

WELCOME YOU TO

Méribel

Quality chalets
Excellent value
19 resorts
across the Alps

skitotal.com
01483 791 933

MERIBEL CENTRE
****Allodis Out of town at Belvedere, but ski-in/ski-out and excellent in every other way: seriously good restaurant, superb service, pool, sauna, nice terrace.
****Grand Coeur Our favourite almost-affordable hotel in Méribel. Just above the village centre. Welcoming, mature building with plush lounge. Huge hot tub, sauna etc.
***Adray Télébar Welcoming piste-side chalet; pretty rooms and restaurant, with good food and popular lunch terrace.
***Merilys At Rond-Point. B&B hotel plus apartments. Recommended by a regular reporter: 'Very nice room, excellent breakfast.'
MOTTARET
****Alpen Ruitor Central, with spa, hot tub. 'Very comfortable, good lounge, well worth the expense.'
***Arolles On the piste near Table Verte lift, with the 'best ever staff, food from good to superb, lovely lounge'. Pool and sauna.

Méribel

289

Selected chalets in Méribel

ADVERTISEMENT

PURPLE SKI *www.purpleski.com*   T **01885 488799**

Purple Ski are known for the extraordinary level of service, cuisine and wines we offer in our luxury chalets in Méribel. With one member of staff to every two guests, we will ensure that you have the most memorable ski holiday you have ever had.

* Professional chefs
* Personal service
* On tap Veuve Clicquot
* Domain bottled wines
* En-suite bedrooms
* Private minibus service and transfers
* Hot tubs, saunas, Sky TV and wi-fi internet access

email: michael@purpleski.com

Apartments The two most impressive larger residences are Pierre & Vacances Premium properties: Les Fermes de Méribel is a classic tasteful MGM-built development of six large chalets with the usual good pool, gym, sauna, steam in Méribel-Village (available through various agents, including Ski Collection and Skiworld); Les Crêts is a big residence up at Mottaret. Chalet Apsara is a very swanky chalet for eight in Les Allues, available through Erna Low and Ski Collection. Ski Amis has a good range of apartments.

EATING OUT ★★★★
Some good places to try

There is a reasonable selection of more modest restaurants, from pizza and pasta to ambitious French cuisine. For the best food, in plush settings, you won't beat the top hotels. The Ekrin restaurant in the swanky hotel Kaïla now has a Michelin star. The Zinc brasserie and Escale gourmet restaurant are at the highly regarded Altiport hotel. We've also enjoyed the Kouisena, with its very rustic, intimate interior and open-fire grills. For 'all French' fine food, the Orée du Bois has been recommended. The Galette is tipped for its 'great atmosphere, service and authentic raclette'. The Taverne does 'flavoursome sea bass'. In Mottaret, Table du Ruitor is 'expensive but good quality'.

In Méribel-Village, the simple Brit-run Lodge du Village (pasta, Tuscan specials) is a favourite of one regular.

APRES-SKI ★★★★★
Méribel rocks – loudly

When we checked out the newish Folie Douce at 4pm on a sunny March afternoon it was packed and rocking. With its 'spectacular dance shows' it makes a welcome upscale rival to the long-standing teatime hot spot of Rond-Point at the top of the village – entirely British, with what one reporter calls a 'youth club' feel.

In town, Meribar at Chaudanne and Jack's, not far away, are lively too, but seem to divide opinion, possibly in an age-related way. The ring of bars on the main square also do good business at teatime. One reporter this year found Barometer the bar of choice. Later on? Search us (or search the resort website – you won't find much). The once-iconic Dick's Tea Bar has been made over to become O'Sullivan's; we get no reports.

In Mottaret the bars at the foot of the pistes get packed at teatime. We hear Le Rastro is the place for dancing on the tables.

In Méribel-Village, the bar at Lodge du Village has live music at teatime a couple of nights a week.

OFF THE SLOPES ★★★
Quite a bit to do

The Olympic Centre has the ice rink where the Olympic events were held in 1992 and where you can watch regular hockey matches. It also has bowling, a climbing wall, a gym, a good public pool and a spa – these last two irritatingly separate, a reporter points out. You can take joyrides in the little planes that operate from the altiport. There are 25km of pleasant marked walks in several areas – eg between Méribel and the altiport area; down through hamlets to Les Allues (return by bus or gondola); and at Plan de Tueda, beyond Mottaret – 'gorgeous'. There's a good map of them, says a reporter. There is a pedestrian's lift pass, and accessible restaurants to meet friends for lunch. Mottaret has a cinema. Shopping is very limited.

BRIDES-LES-BAINS

Brides-les-Bains is an old spa town way down in the valley, with a gondola built to ferry athletes up to Méribel in the 1992 Olympics. It offers a quieter, cheaper alternative base, with adequate shops and restaurants, good-value apartments and some simple hotels. The Altis, five minutes from the gondola, revamped recently in a very French tarty style, is 'a very comfortable, friendly place to stay, with good food'. Skiweekends.com runs a neat-looking chalet hotel here – the Verseau – with shuttle to the gondola. There is a casino and cinema, but evenings are distinctly quiet. We have reports of one lively bar. The gondola ride is supposed to take 25 minutes, but may take 40. It arrives in Méribel at a point irritatingly short of the main lifts and closes irritatingly early, at 5pm. In good conditions you can ski off-piste to one of the mid-stations, in exceptional conditions all the way to the bottom.

Given a car, Brides makes a viable base for visiting other resorts. An obvious target is La Plagne, accessed via Champagny.

GETTING THERE

Air Chambéry 100km/60 miles (1hr15); Geneva 140km/90 miles (2hr); Grenoble 170km/ 105 miles (2hr); Lyon 180km/ 110 miles (2hr)

Rail Moûtiers (18km/11 miles); regular buses

TOURIST OFFICE

www.meribel.net

SNOWPIX.COM / CHRIS GILL

Montgenèvre

Once a bit of a backwater, this famously snowy resort is developing nicely, but urgently needs to find the cash for more new lifts

£90
RESORT PRICE INDEX

RATINGS

The mountains

Extent	★★
Fast lifts	★★
Queues	★★★★
Terrain p'ks	★★★
Snow	★★★★
Expert	★★★★
Intermediate	★★★★
Beginner	★★★★★
Boarder	★★★
X-country	★★★
Restaurants	★★
Schools	★★★
Families	★★★★

The resort

Charm	★★★
Convenience	★★★
Scenery	★★★
Eating out	★★
Après-ski	★★
Off-slope	★

NEWS

2014/15: The smart new Durancia leisure and wellness centre opened. CGH opened their new residence Napoléon, in a prime central position. The slopes on the Italian side of Colletto Verde were improved and a new blue slope was added.

KEY FACTS

Resort	1850m
	6,070ft

Montgenèvre-Monts de la Lune (Claviere)

Slopes	1760-2630m
	5,770-8,630ft
Lifts	32
Pistes	110km
	68 miles

Milky Way

Slopes	1390-2825m
	4,560-9,270ft
Lifts	75
Pistes	400km
	249 miles

➕ Varied local slopes, plus access to Italian Milky Way resorts, notably Sauze d'Oulx and Sestriere

➕ Good local snow record

➕ Suits all abilities: excellent nursery slopes, plenty of cruising and good off-piste terrain that is underused

➕ A lot of accommodation close to the slopes, some right on them

➖ Sauze and Sestriere take time to reach without road transport

➖ Lots of slow lifts, seriously undermining the resort's appeal for some (including us)

➖ Little to challenge experts on-piste

➖ Limited range of restaurants and après-ski places

Montgenèvre is right on the Italian border, at one end of the big cross-border Milky Way network, and gets much better snow than its Italian neighbours – it is set on a minor pass, a position that delivers snow whichever way the wind is blowing, but most importantly when it's blowing from the west.

The resort has made big strides in recent years, banishing through-traffic and developing modern upscale lodgings. But it now needs to prioritize investment in fast lifts – getting around the pistes can be a painfully slow-motion affair. If you're focused on the under-exploited off-piste, the slow lifts matter less.

THE RESORT

Montgenèvre is a small village sitting on a high east-west pass only 2km from the Italian border. The village is set on the sunny slope above the main street (the through-road is now buried in a tunnel) looking over the nursery slopes at the foot of the north-facing slopes of Les Gondrans. Behind the village are the south-facing slopes of Le Chalvet. Both sectors have piste links with Claviere, just over the Italian border and gateway to the other Italian resorts of the Milky Way – Sansicario, Sestriere and Sauze d'Oulx. But it takes time to get to those resorts on skis.

There are lift pass sharing arrangements with Serre-Chevalier and Puy-St-Vincent, easily reached by car, and with rather less easily reached Les Deux-Alpes and Alpe-d'Huez, which involve going over the Col du Lautaret – high, but not usually a problem.

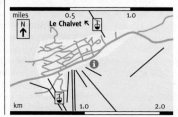

VILLAGE CHARM ★★★
Rustic and quiet

Cheap and cheerful cafes, bars and restaurants line the street running along the bottom of the nursery slopes, now carrying only local traffic. A couple of narrow parallel streets with a few bars and restaurants and a church lie behind it. The old buildings give it a rustic and lived-in feel. Friendly natives and generally good snow add to the charm factor. The Hameau de l'Obélisque development at the eastern end of the village is wood-clad in chalet style.

CONVENIENCE ★★★
Never far from a lift

It's a compact village – most of the lodgings are less than five minutes from a lift – but the main gondolas are at opposite ends, and getting from one end to the other on skis can take ages. The free bus service worked well for us. Some of the newer lodgings in Hameau de l'Obélisque are right on the slopes and a little draglift makes them ski-out as well as ski-in.

SCENERY ★★★
Look north or south

The area is broken up by rocky outcrops and woods, with good views from the higher slopes on both sides of the pass.

LIFT PASSES

Montgenèvre + Monts de la Lune

Prices in €

Age	6-day
under 15	166
15 to 64	208
65 plus	188

Free Under 6; 75 plus

Beginner Free lift in beginner area; lesson and lift deals

Notes Montgenèvre and Claviere (1-day pass is for Montgenèvre plus 10 Italian slopes only); 6-day-plus pass allows one day in the Milky Way, Alpe-d'Huez, Serre-Che, Puy-St-Vincent, Deux-Alpes; pedestrian pass

Alternative pass Via Lattea (Milky Way) International

THE MOUNTAINS

The slopes offer lots of variety – some high and open, some wooded lower down. Run classification on the local map, the Milky Way map and on the mountain are not reliably consistent. And many of the run classifications exaggerate difficulty; the black runs are not steep. Signposting is mainly adequate. The local piste map is admirably clear (but see 'Fast Lifts').

EXTENT OF THE SLOPES ★★
Nicely varied
Our stars are based on the local slopes; the Milky Way as a whole easily gets a ★★★★★ rating, although the Schrahe report discussed in our piste extent feature makes it clear that it is not quite as big as we thought.

The north-facing slopes above Montgenèvre and Claviere divide into three sectors. The high, open slopes of **Les Gondrans** are reached by the Chalmettes chondola from the west end of the village; a green run brings you back. From the same gondola or by riding a chairlift to the lower, steeper wooded peak of Le Prarial you can access the sector of **l'Aigle**, which has links at valley level and at altitude via Colletto Verde to the **Monti della Luna** slopes of Claviere.

The sunny sector behind the village of Montgenèvre – **Le Chalvet** – has long been accessed by a gondola from the east end of the village. A more recently added alternative access is the Serre Thibaud chondola, starting halfway between Montgenèvre and Claviere. This chondola has opened up new blue and black runs into the main Chalvet bowl and into the valley beyond the Col de l'Alpet. The Chalvet runs are mainly on open slopes above the gondola; there are blue and green runs back to Montgenèvre, and a blue run to Claviere – though it has a flat part that is hard work. There is also a blue run down a lift-free valley from Col de l'Alpet towards Claviere, but it doesn't reach the village.

FAST LIFTS ★★
A persistent weakness
The main lifts out of the village are a chondola and a gondola. But slow chairs and drags predominate on the upper slopes; this is a real weakness of the resort, and a regular cause of complaints from reporters. Investment is needed urgently, and there is no sign of it at present. The piste map appears to identify fast chairlifts, but actually fails to do so reliably.

QUEUES ★★★★
Not a problem
Recent reporters have found the area pretty queue-free, even in peak season – a February half term 2014 visitor found 'not a single queue', and we had much the same experience. Crowds aren't a problem, even at weekends, say reporters.

TERRAIN PARKS ★★★
Various facilities
There's a jump with an airbag to cushion landings on the lower slopes of the Gondrans sector ('kids loved it',

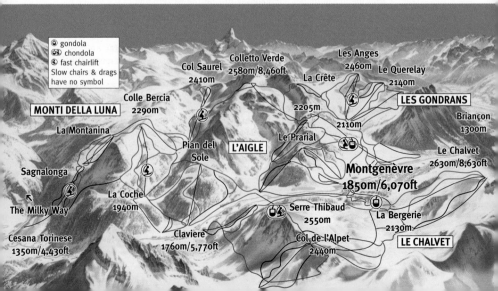

says a 2015 visitor) and snowcross runs in both main sectors ('great fun', says a reporter). There's a beginner snow park at the base area, and a regular park at Claviere with five jumps and features that are suitable for beginners – 'well maintained', but 'really needs its own short lift'.

Montgenèvre
Ski-in Ski-out
Four-star apartments with pool

02392 839 310

PEAKRETREATS.CO.UK/
MONTGENEVRE

SNOW RELIABILITY ★★★★
Excellent locally
Montgenèvre has a generally excellent snow record, receiving dumps from storms funnelling up the valleys to the east and west. The high north-facing slopes naturally keep their snow better than the south-facing area. Snow-guns now cover 55% of the area, including most lower slopes. 'Snow management is excellent,' says a recent reporter.

FOR EXPERTS ★★★★
Some excellent off-piste
The local pistes offer few challenges – the Tetras piste on Le Chalvet is steep, but the other blacks are not. There is, however, ample off-piste terrain and it is wonderfully neglected. On the Gondrans side, there's a small 'freeride zone' of ungroomed slopes that are avalanche controlled, but the real interest lies elsewhere.

We had a great day with a guide here on our last visit, getting fresh tracks down the lovely, lightly wooded east face of Serre Thibaud from the eponymous chondola, then more down Combe de Grand Charvia, accessed by a short hike from the long, slow Rocher d'Aigle chair. After lunch, a run of 1000m vertical off the back of Les Gondrans took us down the Vallon de la Vachette to the bottom of the Montgenèvre pass. We skied all of these runs without seeing any other skiers or boarders.

The Rocher de l'Aigle chair offers lots of other options, too. In addition to off-piste variants on the red runs it serves on both sides of Colletto Verde, it accesses the classic off-piste run that everybody does, with and without guidance – the Vallon de la Douare, leading down towards the Brousset chair. If you're prepared to hike, there are further slopes on La Plane, overlooking Claviere, and on Le Chenaillet, next to Les Gondrans. There are further good powder areas accessed from the top lifts on the Italian side.

Back on the Chalvet side, the remote north-east-facing bowl beyond the Col de l'Alpet is superb in good snow and has black pistes, too. Heli-skiing can be arranged in Italy.

FOR INTERMEDIATES ★★★★
Plenty of cruising terrain
The overclassified blacks (mainly concentrated in the Chalvet sector) are just right for adventurous intermediates, and there are some excellent reds – such as the pleasantly narrow treelined runs to Claviere from Pian del Sole, and from Colletto Verde back towards Montgenèvre. Average intermediates can confidently explore the whole area – few of the reds are particularly challenging. Timid intermediates have some lovely long runs on which to build confidence on both the Gondrans and Chalvet sectors – the Phare is a particularly fine long blue on the latter. The runs down to the village are easy cruises. But it would be better for encouraging timid intermediates to get around the whole area if the easiest reds were reclassified as blues.

FOR BEGINNERS ★★★★★
One of the best
'One of the best' was the verdict of one reporter last year; and others consistently praise the resort as being excellent for beginners. There is a near-perfect nursery slope area at the foot of the Gondrans sector – large, gentle, with a moving carpet and draglift, and fenced off so that you don't get speeding skiers going through it.

Progression to longer runs could not be easier, with long, very easy green runs from the top of the Les Gondrans sector all the way back to the village (around 600m vertical). Le Chalvet also has the long, easy Phare blue run.

↑ The new chalet-style Hameau de l'Obélisque development introduced a bit of class into what was a pretty plain resort
MONTGENEVRE TO / LAURIE MARTIN

FOR BOARDERS ★★★
Something for everyone
There's plenty to attract boarders to Montgenèvre. There are good local beginner slopes and long runs on varied terrain for intermediates. The only real drawback is that a fair number of the lifts are drags and there are some flat sections (especially getting to and from Sestriere). There are some excellent off-piste areas with a few natural hits for more advanced boarders and a dedicated freeride area in the Gondrans sector.

FOR CROSS-COUNTRY ★★★
Travel to the best of it
The 17km of local trails offer ample variety. But the best area is the 60km of trails in the unspoiled Clarée valley, starting an 8km drive away in Les Alberts, at the bottom of the pass road's winding descent towards Briançon.

MOUNTAIN RESTAURANTS ★★
Head for Italy
A distinct weakness, particularly on the French side of the border. Restaurants in the Montgenèvre and Claviere sectors are marked but not named on the local piste map and not even marked on the Via Lattea map.

In the Chalvet sector the table-service Bergerie gets mixed reports. At les Gondrans, les Anges is a pretty standard self-service but does 'good lasagne'. Most people eat in the village; we head over the border where there are some pleasant simple huts. All agree that Baita La Coche is

the best. It is essentially self-service, but if it's not too busy the cheerful family that run it will serve you at your table. On our last visit, we enjoyed good pasta and, to our enduring amazement, a good Barbera d'Asti for 10 euros. The nearby Montsoleil is a smoother operation, liked by recent reporters ('large, welcoming, reasonable prices'). Col Saurel, on the Gimont chair, is fine for drinks and snacks and has 'very friendly staff'.

SCHOOLS AND GUIDES ★★★
Encouraging reports
Reports on both A-Peak (aka the ESI) and the ESF are generally positive. 'ESF good, helped our beginner along,' says a 2015 reporter. One regular who put his two sons in the ESF for three years running said it was 'the most efficient school I have come across; tuition good, firm and friendly' – though the adults in his party had a mixed experience. A reporter last year had a 'helpful and informative' A-Peak instructor.

FOR FAMILIES ★★★★
Hugely improved
With intrusive main road traffic banished to a tunnel, Montgenèvre is a fine family resort – 'perfect', in the view of one recent reporter, thanks largely to the family-oriented activities available off the slopes. The excellent beginner area has the Mini-club Les Marmottes and a snow garden for young children. There is also a childcare centre. Le Chalvet has a play area up the gondola.

DO MORE
in
Montgenevre

zenith
holidays·

0203 137 7678

zenithholidays.co.uk

⬥ABTA
ABTA No.Y1542

STAYING THERE

Development of Hameau de l'Obélisque, at the east end of the resort, close to the Chalvet gondola, introduced a bit of class into what was a pretty plain resort. Last year the place took another step upmarket with the opening of the new CGH apartment complex le Napoléon.

Chalets Zenith's chalet La Clautre was refurbished in 2015 and is right by the Chalmettes lift; they have others available, catered or self-catered, too. Crystal's chalet Ourson (one of two chalets here) was approved by a reader ('economy accommodation but quiet, well located'), as was Ski Miquel's chalet hotel Ours Blanc ('fairly basic, but excellent food and friendly staff'). Pot de Miel is a B&B run on chalet lines (with optional dinners) by an Australian and her ski instructor husband; sauna and outdoor hot tub; a 2015 reporter found they were the only Brits there as all the other guests were French.

Hotels There are now two smart places in Hameau de l'Obélisque – the first two entries below (we've enjoyed stays at both).

****Chalet Blanc Very comfortable, lovely soft duvets and pillows, smart bathrooms. Spa.

***Anova Cool, relaxed, comfortable, good food. Pool, spa. Endorsed by a reporter this year ('first class').

**Alpis Cottia Budget B&B place over the Graal cafe and in the same ownership. Discouraging back-street entrance, up steep steps, but that apart we stayed here happily in 2013, in spacious rooms (although with weirdly tiny showers).

Apartments There are now three smart 4-star residences with pool and spa. Ski-in/ski-out properties at Hameau de l'Obélisque are Chalet des Dolines ('spacious, pool and sauna both clean') and the Hameau des Airelles ('nice public areas, poor ski room set-up, pool not very warm'). More central and opposite the nursery slopes is le Napoléon (which was new last season). All these properties are available through Peak Retreats, Erna Low and Zenith.

EATING OUT ** ☆☆☆
Mainly no-frills

With about 10 no-frills places in the village, the choice is no more than adequate. Jamy got the thumbs up last year as a 'high-quality dining experience'. We've had excellent pizzas at the Capitaine, which aims to corner the Italian market – endorsed by a recent reporter too ('good-quality and value Italian dishes'). We and readers have also enjoyed the Estable, a locals' favourite. Other reader tips: Graal ('good basic food'), Caesar ('friendly; one of the best pizzas ever'), Rafale ('nice food, great fire, really friendly') and Refuge ('atmospheric, friendly').

APRES-SKI ** ☆☆☆
A few bars

The range is limited – it is a quiet village. The Refuge and the Jamy are popular cafe-bars at teatime. The Graal is a friendly, 'buzzing' place with 'a good range of beers', live music and big TVs; the Ca del Sol is a cosy place with an open fire.

OFF THE SLOPES * ☆☆☆☆
Improving

The new Durancia leisure centre, with indoor and outdoor pools, saunas, steam room, massages and treatments, bar and restaurant, was highly praised by a 2015 reporter: 'kids loved it, great way to relax after skiing, had the whole complex to ourselves on Friday night'. The Monty Express 1400m-long two-seater monorail 'toboggan' run is said to be France's longest: 'Good fun, not for the faint-hearted.' A bus trip down the pass road to the beautiful old town of Briançon is possible. But it's not a great resort for non-skiers.

CLAVIERE

Claviere is a small, traditional village just down the road from Montgenèvre, and a metre or two over the Italian border. It is not chocolate-box pretty but, even more than Montgenèvre, it has been transformed by removal of through-traffic. Its single main street, lined by a few shops, restaurants and hotels, is now a pleasant place to wander about.

The two main lifts – both slow quads – are conveniently close but getting to the Montquitaine chair to Serre Thibaud is a slight uphill hike. The nursery slope is right next to the village, with a moving carpet. We've had glowing reports on the ski school's handling of kids.

GETTING THERE

Air Turin 110km/ 70 miles (1hr30); Grenoble 170km/ 105 miles (2hr45); Lyon 235km/ 145 miles (2hr45); Marseille 265km/ 165 miles (3hr15)

Rail Briançon (12km/ 7 miles) or Oulx (18km/11 miles); buses available from both

TOURIST OFFICES

Montgenèvre
www.montgenevre.
com

Claviere
www.claviere.it

OT MORZINE / P JACQUES, FOC

Morzine

A large, lively, year-round resort with its own attractive slopes and linked by lift to the main Portes du Soleil circuit

£100
RESORT PRICE INDEX

RATINGS

The mountains

Extent	★★★★★
Fast lifts	★★★
Queues	★★★★
Terrain p'ks	★★★
Snow	★★
Expert	★★★
Intermediate	★★★★
Beginner	★★★
Boarder	★★★★
X-country	★★★★
Restaurants	★★★★
Schools	★★★
Families	★★★★

The resort

Charm	★★★
Convenience	★★
Scenery	★★★
Eating out	★★★
Après-ski	★★★★
Off-slope	★★★

296

NEWS

2015/16: A new slope is due to be built near the Zore run in the Super-Morzine area (at the top of the gondola from Morzine that leads to Avoriaz).

2014/15: In the Super-Morzine area, the Proclou and Seraussaix chairs were replaced with a six-pack each.

+ Good-sized, varied, lightly wooded slopes shared with Les Gets

+ Good nightlife by French standards

+ Chalet-style town, popular in summer as well as winter

+ Few crowds on weekdays, but ...

− Sunshine brings weekend crowds

− Just off the Portes du Soleil circuit

− Some lodgings remote from lifts

− Low altitude and exposure to westerlies means risk of rain and poor snow

− Few tough pistes

Morzine is quite a large, spread out, long-established year-round resort that feels more like a town than a village. It shares with Les Gets a fairly extensive local network of gentle wooded slopes, so is a good place to be in a snowstorm (but be warned: it can, and does, rain rather than snow not infrequently). For keen piste-bashers wanting to do multiple tours of the Portes du Soleil circuit it is better positioned than Les Gets but is not ideal. But that doesn't seem to deter readers: we get reports every year from satisfied customers.

THE RESORT

Morzine is as popular in summer as in winter and sprawls along both sides of a river gorge – though with the centre emphatically on the west side, at the foot of the local slopes. These are shared with slightly higher Les Gets (covered in a separate chapter). Across town is a gondola forming the link with a chain of lifts leading to Avoriaz on the Portes du Soleil circuit.

Our view that the resort suits car drivers is widely shared. But the roads are busy and the one-way system takes some getting used to. Car trips to Flaine and Chamonix are feasible.

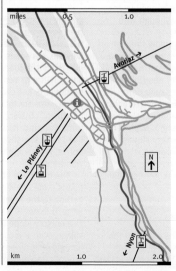

VILLAGE CHARM ★★★
Quietly attractive
The resort consists of chalet-style buildings, mostly small or mid-sized; they look cute under snow, and as that snow disappears towards spring, the village quickly takes on a spruce appearance.

Morzine is a family resort, and the village ambience tends to be fairly subdued as a result; but there are plenty of bars that get busy as the lifts close.

CONVENIENCE ★★
It's a big resort ...
Morzine is a town where getting from A to B can be tricky. The best plan is to stay in or near the centre of town, a short walk from one or both of the gondolas. Restaurants and bars line the streets up to the lifts to Le Pléney, where a busy one-way street runs along the foot of the slopes.

Accommodation is widely scattered; a multi-route bus service (including two electric buses) links all parts of the town to the lifts, including those for Avoriaz; there is a circular route, but only one way, which doesn't always suit your purposes. A recent reporter found the buses 'haphazard, not remotely running to timetable'. There are also buses to Les Gets, and to Ardent, which has a gondola into the Portes du Soleil circuit, missing out busy Avoriaz.

Extent rating
This relates to the whole Portes du Soleil area

MORZINE AVORIAZ TO / PIERRE JACQUES

Morzine feels more like a town than a village but its chalet-style buildings look pretty under a layer of snow ↓

SCENERY ★★★☆☆
Quite good from the tops
Despite their modest top heights, the local peaks of Pointe de Nyon and Chamossière are not without drama (or impressive views, including of Mont Blanc).

THE MOUNTAINS

The local slopes are mainly wooded, with some open areas higher up. The local piste map is less clear than it used to be because they have made it smaller. Signposting is good.

EXTENT OF THE SLOPES ★★★★★
Good local area, plus the PdS
Our rating is for the whole Portes du Soleil linked area, the bulk of which is reached via Avoriaz. The local area – shared with Les Gets – is a fair size.

A gondola rises from the edge of central Morzine to **Le Pléney**. Several routes return to the valley, including a run down to Les Fys – a quiet lift junction at the foot of the **Nyon-Chamossière** sector where the area's most challenging slopes are; Chamossière is served by a six-pack, but Nyon still has a slow chair. This sector can also be accessed by a cable car starting a bus ride from Morzine. A slow chair from Les Fys along with a fast one from Le Grand Pré (further up the valley) connect with the sector of **Les Chavannes**, above Les Gets. At the far end of this sector, the bowl beneath Le Ranfoilly has five chairlifts together going to different parts of the ridges.

Beyond Les Gets, **Mont Chéry** is notably quiet, and well worth a visit.

Across town from the Le Pléney sector is a gondola leading (via another couple of lifts and runs) to Avoriaz and the main Portes du Soleil circuit. You take the gondola down too – there's no piste. Alternatives are a bus ride or a short drive to either Les Prodains – for a gondola to Avoriaz or a chair into the **Hauts Forts** slopes above it – or to Ardent for a gondola to Les Lindarets, from where you can head for Châtel, Avoriaz or Champéry. There's floodlit skiing on Thursdays and a torchlit descent on Tuesdays. There are lockers at the Pléney base.

FAST LIFTS ★★★☆☆
More fast chairs needed
The main access lifts are gondolas, cable cars or fast chairs, but higher up things are not so good: some areas are equipped with fast chairs, but others rely on slow chairs and drags.

QUEUES ★★★★☆
New lifts solved most problems
The Pléney gondola was replaced a couple of seasons ago by a much more powerful lift with 10-seater cabins and double the capacity of the old one. This seems to have reduced

Tailor made, long weekend and short break French Alps ski holiday specialists.

Hanski
Ski. Explore. Relax.

web: www.hanski.co.uk
tel: 01638 596373

100% Protected Holidays

Heavenly
Skiing...
at down to earth prices

mh✱
Mountain Heaven

· Superb catered & self catered accommodation ·
· Great ski areas in the French & Swiss Alps ·
· Snow secure resorts · We only have on/near piste locations ·
· Fantastic prices & no hidden extras ·

0151 625 1921
www.mountainheaven.co.uk

TERRAIN PARKS ★★★
Lots to choose from

There is a park below Pointe de Nyon, and another park and a snowcross in Les Gets. Or you can try one of the five excellent terrain parks in Avoriaz (and the super-pipe there).

SNOW RELIABILITY ★★
A weakness at resort level

Morzine has a very low average height, and it can rain here when it is snowing higher up (almost every year reporters mention days of rain). But the grassy slopes don't need much snow-cover and in a sparse snow year you may do better here than in higher, rockier resorts such as Avoriaz. With last season's slow start to the season though, Morzine's slopes were closed till after Christmas. Snowmaking has been increased, most noticeably on the home runs. Grooming is good.

peak period queues here. However, a 2015 reporter says this means the connecting Belvedere draglift is crowded. Recent lift replacements seem to have solved most of the other long-standing problems.

Good, challenging runs both on- and off-piste

Chamossière 2000m

Le Ranfoilly 1825m

Pointe de Nyon 2010m/6,590ft

NYON-CHAMOSSIERE

Ranfoilly

Nauchets

Grains-d'

LES CHAVANNES

Tronqes

Charmiaz

Nyon 1420m

Le Grand Pré

Nyon

Les Fys

1510m

LE PLENEY

Les G 1170m/3

The gondola is a link to Avoriaz from the centre of town. But you have to catch it down too – there's no piste back

← Avoriaz

Pléney

Super Morzine

Morzine 1000m/3,280ft

Lovely easy blue run away from all the lifts

LIFT PASSES

Portes du Soleil

Prices in €

Age	6-day
under 16	182
16 to 19	218
20 to 64	243
65 plus	218

Free Under 5

Beginner Lessons and lift pass packages

Note Family discounts

Alternative pass
Morzine-Les Gets only

Catered Chalets
Morzine
9-24p
www.hostsavoie.co.uk

STC Ski

Specialists in Tailor-Made Short Breaks & Holidays

01483 771 222
www.stcski.co.uk
ski@stcski.co.uk

FOR EXPERTS ★★★
A few possibilities

The runs from Pointe de Nyon and Chamossière are quite challenging, as are the black runs down the back of Mont Chéry and the Hauts Forts blacks at Avoriaz. In bad weather the medium-altitude, lightly wooded Ranfoilly bowl is a good place to head for. Plus there is plenty of serious off-piste to try with a guide – see the feature panel overleaf.

FOR INTERMEDIATES ★★★★
Something for everyone

Good intermediates will enjoy the fine, challenging red and black down from Chamossière. Aigle Rouge on Pointe de

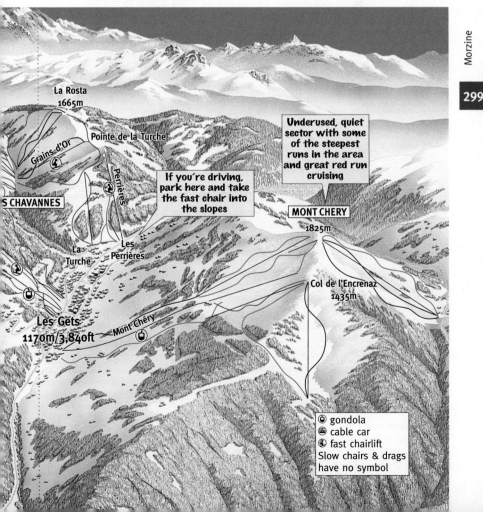

La Rosta
1665m

Grains-d'Or

Pointe de la Turche

Perrières

S CHAVANNES

If you're driving, park here and take the fast chair into the slopes

La Turche

Les Perrières

Les Gets
1170m/3,840ft

Mont Chéry

Underused, quiet sector with some of the steepest runs in the area and great red run cruising

MONT CHERY
1825m

Col de l'Encrenaz
1435m

⬤ gondola
⬤ cable car
④ fast chairlift
Slow chairs & drags have no symbol

MOMENTUM SKI

Weekend & a la carte
ski holiday specialists

100% Tailor-made

Premier hotels
& apartments

Flexible travel
arrangements

020 7371 9111
WWW.MOMENTUMSKI.COM

Discover the difference
with SkiWeekends
#loveski

Prices from
£200

skiweekends.com

ALPINE ANSWERS
The UK's No.1 Chalet Specialist

For choice and service look no further!

alpineanswers.co.uk
call: 020 7801 1080

ABTA

Nyon is not steep but is quite narrow, with great views. Mont Chéry, on the other side of Les Gets, has some fine steepish runs that are usually very quiet.

Those looking for something less challenging have a great choice. Le Pléney has a compact network of pistes that are ideal for groups with mixed abilities: there are blue and red options from every lift. One of the easiest cruises on Le Pléney is a great away-from-it-all blue (Piste B) from the top to the valley. Heading from Le Ranfoilly to Le Grand Pré on the blue is also a nice cruise.

The slopes down to Les Gets from Le Pléney are easy when conditions are right (the slopes face south). The Ranfoilly and Rosta sectors have cruisy reds and a couple of easy blacks served by fast chairs. And, of course, there is the whole of the Portes du Soleil circuit to explore via Avoriaz.

FOR BEGINNERS ★★★
Good for novices and improvers
The wide village nursery slopes are convenient, and benefit from snow-guns, though crowds are reported to be a problem. There are excellent progression runs on Le Pléney, at Nyon, and at Super-Morzine.

FOR BOARDERS ★★★★
Great for park and ride
Morzine is very popular with boarding seasonaires because of the extensive slopes, proximity to the excellent terrain parks in Avoriaz and the lower prices here. The slopes in Morzine are great for all abilities and have very few draglifts. But a reporter complained of irritating flat areas. Plenty of treelined runs make for scenic and interesting snowboarding, and the more adventurous should hire a guide to explore off-piste.

OFF-PISTE RUNS IN THE PORTES DU SOLEIL AREA

The Portes du Soleil offers a lot of great lift-served off-piste. Here is a small selection. Like all serious off-piste runs, these should not be undertaken without a guide.

Morzine – Nyon/Chamossière area
From the Chamossière chairlift, heading north brings you to two runs – one on the same north-west slope as the pistes (now marked on the piste map as a 'Zone Freeride'), the other via a col down the north-east slope to the Nyon cable car – a wild area, with a great view of Mont Blanc at first.

Avoriaz area – two suggestions
From the Fornet chairlift on the Swiss border, you head west to descend a beautiful, unspoiled bowl leading down to the village of L'Erigné. In powder snow you descend the west-facing slopes of the bowl; when there is spring snow, you traverse right to descend the south-facing slopes. Medium-pitch slopes, for skiers and snowboarders.

From the top of the Machon chairlift you traverse west, beneath the peaks of Les Hauts Forts, across Les Crozats de la Chaux – a steep, north-facing slope. You then turn north to descend through the forest to the cable car station at Les Prodains. Testing terrain, for very good skiers. And be aware that the traverse can be dangerous following a snowfall.

Châtel area
From the top of the Linga chair, head north-west to cross the ridge on your right at a col and then head down the La Leiche slope to the draglift of the same name. It's a north-facing slope, starting in a white wilderness, taking you through trees back to civilization. Steep slopes – for good skiers only.

↑ The local slopes are shared with Les Gets and suit intermediates best: almost 80% of them are classified blue or red

LES GETS TO / N JOLY

FOR CROSS-COUNTRY ★★★★
Good variety
There are around 70km of varied cross-country trails, not all at valley level. The best section is in the pretty Vallée de la Manche beside the Nyon mountain up to the Lac de Mines d'Or, where there is a good restaurant. The Pléney-Chavannes loop is pleasant and relatively snow-sure.

MOUNTAIN RESTAURANTS ★★★★
Some excellent huts
There is no shortage of good places, offering table-service in welcoming surroundings. Restaurants are marked but not named or described on the piste map.
Editors' choice We have had several very enjoyable Savoyard lunches at the rustic Chez Nannon, between Nyon and Chamossière – it is cosy inside and has a nice terrace. A regular visitor endorsed our view recently: 'A little nugget of delights.' The nearby Pointe de Nyon is a lovely spacious place where we have had excellent duck salad and ribs.
Worth knowing about La Païka, near the top of La Rosta, is a 'rustic gem' doing wood-fired grills ('the best on the mountain; fab BBQs and soups'). At Chavannes, the Croix Blanche is praised this year for its 'seriously gourmet food at a reasonable price' and the Grand Cry does 'substantial salads'. The Vaffieu above the Folliets chair 'can have slow service but the food is worth the wait'. Les Mouilles, at the top of the Crusaz chair on Pléney, does 'a fine carbonara', and has a 'cracking view'. The 2 Criquets at Grand Pré has a 'nice ambience and good food'.

SCHOOLS AND GUIDES ★★★
Two major British schools
BASS (British Alpine Ski and Snowboard School) is well established here and New Generation moved in last season – both are British-run by highly qualified and experienced instructors. Reports needed, please.
  Reports on the local ESF are generally positive: 'We were thoroughly happy; they did a first-class job with my five-year-old, and she came on in leaps and bounds.' We have had two very positive comments on Easy2Ride including a recent reporter who was 'very impressed that they moved people between groups after 30 minutes to match ability levels better; small groups too'.

FOR FAMILIES ★★★★
A fine family choice
Morzine caters well for families. On the mountain there are gentle, sheltered slopes and play areas. And there are plenty of other activities. Club des Piou Piou is run by the ESF school and takes children from three years old.

STAYING THERE

You can arrange affordable short breaks here through Ski Weekends. Hanski is a short-break specialist too.
Chalets There's a big choice, widely spread. Mountain Heaven has a good-looking modern chalet with lovely views and outdoor hot tub close to the Nyon cable car.

Inghams has three good-looking chalets, two with hot tubs and all with sauna or steam. Its 12-bed Nomis is reportedly 'a lovely place'.

Host Savoie has four 'comfortable and unpretentious' places all out of the town centre and near bus stops. Its Chery des Meuniers 'had good food, friendly and efficient staff and was good value', says a reporter. Ski Weekends runs the 'no-frills' chalet Gourmets. Hanski has four lovely-looking chalets. A reader strongly tips the chalet hotel Dents Blanches, operated by Alpine Encounters.
Hotels Part of a general drift in France, many hotels have moved up the stars scale in the past few years. There are now seven 4-stars; but 3-stars still dominate.
****Airelles Central, close to Pléney lifts. Good pool, 'great food', sauna, steam room.
****Bergerie Rustic but smart family-run B&B in centre. 'Good breakfast buffet, friendly service, thoroughly recommend it.' Outdoor pool, massage.
****Champs Fleurie Next to the Pléney lift; praised by two 2015 reporters ('excellent'; 'friendly, helpful staff').
***Alpenroc Near centre. Pool and hot tub. 'Friendly, convenient, comfortable.'
***Equipe Next to the Pléney lift with decent food and 'tiny' pool, sauna, massage, hot tub. Takes short-stay bookings.
***Tremplin At the foot of Pléney slopes. 'Rooms basic but comfortable, friendly staff, no restaurant.'
Aubergade Beside the Pléney lift. Run by British company Mountain Mavericks. Recommended by two reporters this year for its location, 'friendly staff' and 'gourmet food'.
Apartments Aiglon de Morzine has 12 luxury units and is central; sauna and steam room. Bookable through Erna Low.

GETTING THERE

Air Geneva 90km/ 55 miles (1hr30); Lyon 210km/ 130 miles (2hr30)

Rail Cluses or Thonon (30km/19 miles); regular bus connections to resort

TOURIST OFFICE

www.morzine-avoriaz. com

EATING OUT ★★★
A reasonable choice
There is a fair choice, including some fine hotel restaurants. Best in town is probably the Atelier in the hotel Samoyède, which offers traditional and modern dishes ('gourmet cuisine, stick to the set menu to keep costs under control'). Two recent reporters liked the 'stylish' Chamade for its 'tasty and beautifully presented meals', but one warned that service can be slow. Le Coup de Coeur is a crowded wine bar in the same ownership doing good tapas, pizza etc. The cassoulet at the Clin d'Oeil and the 'good Savoyard food' at the Grange get the thumbs up this year. For value, you will not beat the unpretentious, 'exceptional' Etale with its 'huge' pizzas and equally generous Savoyard dishes. Past reporter tips: Flamme, Tyrolien, Combe à Zorre and Grillion.

APRES-SKI ★★★★
One of the livelier French resorts
Morzine's après-ski is good by French resort standards. Several places around the base area get busy as the slopes empty – the Tremplin has 'live music' and 'very lively après'. The Crépu is a sports bar, pleasantly quiet early on but livening up later. Other options include the long-established Bar Robinson and the Dixie ('good atmosphere, popular with seasonaires'), with sport on TV, a cellar bar and some live music. Between the slopes and the centre, and all in the same building, are several spots: the Cavern, which is popular with seasonaires; the Coyote for arcade games and DJ; and the 'lively' Tibetan, with Asian decor and 'often a band'. The Opéra and Laury's are late-night haunts.

OFF THE SLOPES ★★★
Quite good; excursions possible
There's a cinema, an excellent ice rink, an indoor pool, lots of pretty walks and tobogganing. You can go snowshoeing, snowmobiling, paragliding and take helicopter rides. Visitors have enjoyed trips to the cheese factory and watching ice hockey. Morzine has a reasonable range of shops, relatively glitz-free. Buses run to Thonon for more shopping, and those with cars can drive to Geneva, Annecy or Montreux.

Paradiski

Les Arcs and La Plagne are pretty impressive resorts individually; the ability to explore both is the icing on the cake

KEY FACTS

Paradiski area

Slopes	1200-3250m
	3,940-10,660ft
Lifts	141
Pistes	425km
	264 miles

A decade-plus after its opening, the 200-person double-decker **Vanoise Express** cable car – which crosses a wooded valley to link Les Arcs and La Plagne, and thus form Paradiski – remains the world's biggest, as far as we know. When it opened, we were a bit sceptical. Sure, it was one of the biggest ski areas in the Alps, but weren't the two resorts quite big enough individually? Well, no. We're now quite used to staying in Arc 1950 and having lunch above Champagny. We might do this sort of thing only once or twice in a week, but we always do it.

The Vanoise Express cable car spans the 2km-wide valley between Plan-Peisey (on the edge of the Les Arcs area) and a point 300m above Montchavin (on the edge of the La Plagne area).

The linking of these two major resorts is A Good Thing for the great British piste-basher who likes to cover as much ground as possible. For those who like a bit of a challenge, getting from your home base to both far-flung outposts of the area – Villaroger in Les Arcs and Champagny in La Plagne – would make quite a full day.

The link is also good for experts. Those based in either resort can more easily tackle the north face of La Plagne's Bellecôte, finishing the run in Nancroix. Black run skiers based in La Plagne who are finding the piste skiing a bit tame can easily get across to Les Arcs' excellent Aiguille Rouge.

If you want to make the most of the link it's sensible to stay near one of the cable car stations. But it's easily accessible from many other bases too.

On the Les Arcs side, **Plan-Peisey** and nearby **Vallandry** are in pole position. They are basically small, low-rise, modern developments, built in a much more sympathetic style than the original Les Arcs resorts. They are quiet but expanding, and quite a few UK operators have chalets and apartments in them. You can also stay in the unspoiled old village of **Peisey**, 300m below and linked by bucket-lift to Plan-Peisey. These places are covered at the end of the Les Arcs chapter.

It's easy to get to the cable car station at Plan-Peisey from the main resort parts of Les Arcs. One lift and one run is all it takes to get there from **Arc 1800**, which is the biggest of the main resort units. From quieter **Arc 1600**, along the mountainside from 1800, it takes two lifts. **Arc 2000** and the stylish **Arc 1950** development seem further away, over the ridge that separates them from 1600 and 1800; but all it takes is one fast chair to the ridge and one long run down the other side. In the valley bottom beyond Arc

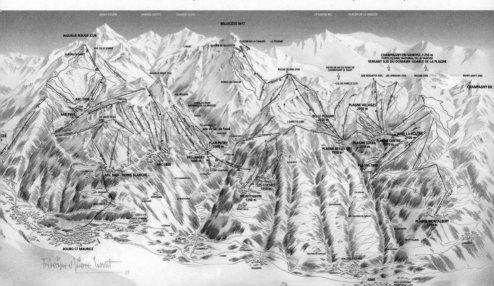

High quality, high altitude

Four-star ski apartments with spa
02392 890 960

ABTA

SKI COLLECTION
.co.uk
A WORLD CLASS FRENCH ALPS EXPERIENCE

mh✳
Mountain Heaven

Heavenly Skiing...
at down to earth prices

· Superb catered & self catered accommodation ·
· Great ski areas in the French & Swiss Alps ·
· Snow secure resorts · We only have on/near piste locations ·
· Fantastic prices & no hidden extras ·

0151 625 1921
www.mountainheaven.co.uk

LIFT PASSES

Paradiski Unlimited
Covers lifts in whole
Paradiski area.
6-day pass €285
(65 plus and under 14
€223)

Paradiski Découverte
Covers lifts in Les
Arcs area or La Plagne
area plus one-day
Paradiski extension.
6-day pass €265
(65 plus and under 14
€207)

WWW.ANDYPARANT.COM

You can make out the
slopes of Montchavin-
Les Coches in this
shot from above
Peisey-Vallandry ↓

2000, the hamlet of Villaroger is not
an ideal starting point.

On the La Plagne side, the obvious
place to stay is **Montchavin**, which is
below the Vanoise Express station.
Montchavin is a carefully developed
old village with modern additions built
in traditional style. **Les Coches**, across
the mountain from the station, is most
easily reached with the help of a lift. It
is entirely modern, but built in a
traditional style. From either village,
one lift brings you to the Vanoise
Express cable car.

The other parts of La Plagne are
some way from the cable car. But one
long lift is all it takes to get from
monolithic **Plagne Bellecôte** up to
L'Arpette, from which point it's a single
long descent. The most attractive of
the resort villages, **Belle Plagne**, is

only a short run away from Plagne
Bellecôte. From the villages further
across the bowl – **Plagne Villages**,
Plagne Soleil, dreary **Plagne Centre**,
futuristic **Plagne Aime 2000** – you
have to ride a lift to get to Bellecôte.
From **Plagne 1800**, below the bowl,
add another lift. From the villages
beyond the bowl – rustic, sunny
Champagny-en-Vanoise and expanding
Montalbert – it's going to be pretty
hard work, but it's certainly possible.

RIDING THE VANOISE EXPRESS
The cable car ride from one resort to
the other takes less than four minutes.
The system is designed to be able to
operate in high winds, so the risk of
getting stranded miles from home is
low. It can shift 2,000 people an hour,
in each direction and although end-of-
the-day crowds could be a snag in
theory, they're not in practice.

The lift company offers a six-day
pass covering the whole Paradiski
region, perhaps most likely to appeal
to people based in the villages close
to the lift. It's not cheap. But there is
also a pass (Paradiski Découverte) that
includes just one day in the other
resort during the validity of the pass.
Alternatively, you can buy a one-day
extension to a Les Arcs or a La Plagne
six-day lift pass, as and when you
fancy the outing.

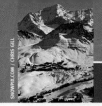

SNOWPIX.COM / CHRIS GILL

La Plagne

Villages from the rustic to the futuristic, spread over a vast area of intermediate terrain – mainly high and snow-sure

£110
RESORT PRICE INDEX

RATINGS

The mountains

Extent	★★★★
Fast lifts	★★
Queues	★★
Terrain p'ks	★★★★
Snow	★★★★
Expert	★★★★
Intermediate	★★★★★
Beginner	★★★★
Boarder	★★★
X-country	★★★★
Restaurants	★★★★
Schools	★★★
Families	★★★★

The resort

Charm	★★
Convenience	★★★★★
Scenery	★★★
Eating out	★★★
Après-ski	★★★
Off-slope	★

NEWS

2015/16: A 10-person gondola will replace the Montalbert and slow Fornelet chairs, greatly speeding access to Plagne Centre from Montalbert.

2014/15: The chairlift out of Bellecôte for Plagne Centre was replaced by an eight-pack of huge carrying capacity. The Arnica run down the Colorado chair at Centre was adapted to suit novices (but is still blue). The cable car between Centre and Aime was renovated.

+ Extensive and varied intermediate pistes, plus excellent off-piste
+ Good nursery slopes
+ High and fairly snow-sure
+ Wide choice of resort villages: high or low, convenient or cute
+ Wooded runs of lower satellite resorts are great in poor weather
+ Cable car link to Les Arcs

- Lift system still needs investment
- Pistes get very crowded in places
- Few challenging pistes
- Lower villages can have poor snow, especially sunny Champagny
- Brutal architecture in some villages
- No long green runs
- Upscale accommodation still rare

La Plagne is an intermediate's paradise, even if you don't use the link to Les Arcs. For experts, it has huge areas of off-piste that don't get skied out too quickly. We are pleased to note that last season the resort reinstated the two rewarding black pistes dropping 800m vertical from the glacier, wiped from the map a few seasons ago, but this is still an area where advanced intermediates and experts need to look off-piste for challenges.

The lift network has gradually improved over recent years (most recently with an amazingly powerful eight-pack at Plagne Bellecôte), and now seems to cause problems for our readers only at the real peaks of the season. Bigger problems these days are the number of slow chairlifts in some sectors, and the serious overcrowding on some pistes.

THE RESORT

La Plagne consists of no fewer than 11 separate 'villages'. Each is a self-sufficient mini-resort, though they vary widely in character. They divide basically into two groups: seven units purpose-built at altitude in a broad bowl, on or above the treeline; and four real villages, adapted and expanded for skiing, at lower altitude on the fringes of the area.

At the heart of the high-altitude area, Plagne Centre is aptly named: it is the focal point for shops and après-ski. Directly below Centre is the chalet-filled suburb of Plagne 1800, spread across a steep hillside. A short lift ride away from Centre are the slightly

higher units of Plagne Aime 2000 and, in the opposite direction, Plagne Soleil and Plagne Villages. Over a low ridge, beyond the last two, are Plagne Bellecôte and Belle Plagne.

Outside the main bowl, at the northern edge of the area, are Les Coches and Montchavin. At the southern edge is rustic Champagny. Beyond Plagne Aime 2000, at the western edge, is growing Montalbert. These outlying resorts are described later in the chapter.

A cable car from Montchavin links to Les Arcs via Peisey-Vallandry. Day trips by car to Val d'Isère-Tignes or the Trois Vallées resorts are possible. Staying in Champagny means quick access by car or taxi to Courchevel.

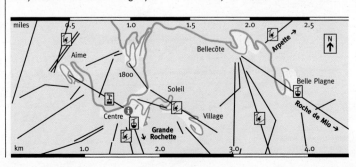

FRANCE

306

KEY FACTS	
Resort	1800-2100m
	5,900-6,890ft
La Plagne only	
Slopes	1250-3250m
	4,100-10,660ft
Lifts	90
Pistes	225km
	140 miles
Paradiski area	
Slopes	1200-3250m
	3,940-10,660ft
Lifts	141
Pistes	425km
	264 miles

SKI AMIS

**Catered Chalets
in Superb
Locations**

020 3411 5439
www.skiamis.com

VILLAGE CHARM ★★☆☆☆
Take your pick

The high-altitude villages vary quite a lot in character; our rating relates to Belle Plagne and Plagne 1800, where most Brits go. The other central resort villages would not merit two stars.

The first unit to be built, in the 1960s, was Plagne Centre. Typical of its time, it has ugly square blocks and dreary indoor 'malls' that house shops, bars and restaurants. A three-year project to improve these malls has finished, so it's time we paid another visit to see if they are less claustrophobic as a result.

More recent developments are more stylish, but they can't compete with Centre in terms of facilities. Plagne 1800 is all in chalet style, so is visually inoffensive. Plagne Aime 2000, in stark contrast, is a group of monolithic blocks given a bold chalet-roof shape. Plagne Soleil and Plagne Villages mainly consist of small-scale apartment buildings finished in traditional chalet style.

The apartment buildings of Plagne Bellecôte form a gigantic wall at the foot of the slopes leading down to it. By contrast, Belle Plagne just above it is built in a pleasant chalet style, and has a mini-resort centre, though few shops.

CONVENIENCE ★★★★★
No worries at altitude

The high-altitude villages are mostly ski-in/ski-out – but much of Plagne 1800 presents challenges because of its steep setting, which has to be negotiated on foot. At Plagne Bellecôte you'll walk further inside your apartment building than outside. Belle Plagne is now quite large, and spread over a steepish hillside that provokes the occasional complaint from our easily tired readers. Readers find Plagne Soleil convenient.

A free bus system between the core villages within the bowl runs until late, and readers seem happy with it.

SCENERY ★★★☆☆
Look to the horizon

The scenery makes an attractive and varied backdrop to the less attractive core villages. Mont Blanc looms big on the horizon, especially from Montchavin and Les Coches. And there are good views over to Courchevel from the Champagny sector. The Bellecôte glacier offers especially good views, of course.

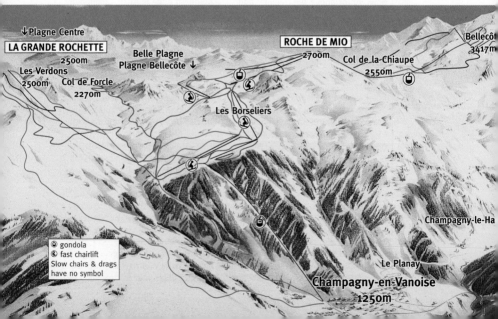

↓Plagne Centre

LA GRANDE ROCHETTE
2500m

Les Verdons
2500m   Col de Forcle
2270m

Belle Plagne
Plagne Bellecôte ↓

Les Borseliers

ROCHE DE MIO
2700m   Col de-la-Chiaupe
2550m

Bellecôt
3417m

Champagny-le-Ha

Le Planay

Champagny-en-Vanoise
1250m

ⓖ gondola
ⓕ fast chairlift
Slow chairs & drags
have no symbol

↑ From this point at
Roche de Mio you
ride a gondola down
and then up to access
the glacier, in the
background

LA PLAGNE TO

THE MOUNTAINS

The majority of the slopes in the main bowl are above the treeline, though there are trees scattered around most of the resort centres. The slopes outside the bowl are open at the top but descend into woodland – the best place to be in bad weather. So there is something to be said for choosing a base outside the bowl.

Some runs are more difficult than their classification suggests, while others are easier – note our warning in 'For intermediates'. Piste names and classification seem to alter regularly. Signposting is fine though piste marking can be a bit vague. The piste map is tricky to follow in places.

EXTENT OF THE SLOPES ★★★★
Multi-centred; can be confusing
Our ★★★★ rating relates to just the La Plagne area; the whole Paradiski area easily scores five stars.

La Plagne's pistes are spread over a wide area that can be broken down into seven sectors. From Plagne Centre you can take a lift up to **Le Biolley**, from where you can head back to Centre, to Plagne Aime 2000 or progress to **Montalbert**. The arrangements for getting back to Centre from Montalbert have changed

– you must now descend to the upgraded La Roche chairlift, via an improved blue run. The main lift out of Plagne Centre leads up to **La Grande Rochette**. From here there are good sweeping runs back down and an easier one over to Plagne Bellecôte, or you can drop over into the sunny **Champagny** sector, for excellent long runs and great views across the valley to Courchevel.

From Plagne Bellecôte and Belle Plagne, you can head up to **Roche de Mio**, and have the choice of a gondola or two successive fast chairs (the first of which also accesses Champagny). From Roche de Mio, runs spread out in all directions – towards La Plagne, Champagny or **Montchavin/Les Coches**. This sector can also be reached by taking an eight-seat chair from Plagne Bellecôte to L'Arpette. From Roche de Mio you can also take a gondola down then up to the **Bellecôte glacier**. It is prone to closure by high winds or poor weather. The top chair is often shut in winter – but if open, it offers excellent snow and stunning views.

The black piste below Col de la Chiaupe means that you can descend from the glacier on-piste to the Les Bauches chairlift without riding the gondola back up to Roche de Mio. Or you can go all the way to Montchavin (be warned: it gets very flat).

This black piste is one of a handful now marked on the piste map as Natur' (never groomed) – not popular with reporters (see 'Snow reliability'). The map also marks three draglifts (in the Montalbert/Biolley sectors) as 'difficult', and they are.

FAST LIFTS **★★**★★★
Slow progress

Many key lifts are fast, and the slopes directly above Montchavin/Les Coches are pretty much sorted, but you still find old chairs and draglifts in other areas – at the very top of the Montchavin sector; all three lifts above Les Bauches; Inversens at Roche de Mio; and the lifts out of 1800, for example. The lifts out of Montalbert are due to be replaced by a slick gondola this year. This is great news for visitors to Montalbert; it would not have been our priority for the area as a whole, but maybe Montalbert provided the funds.

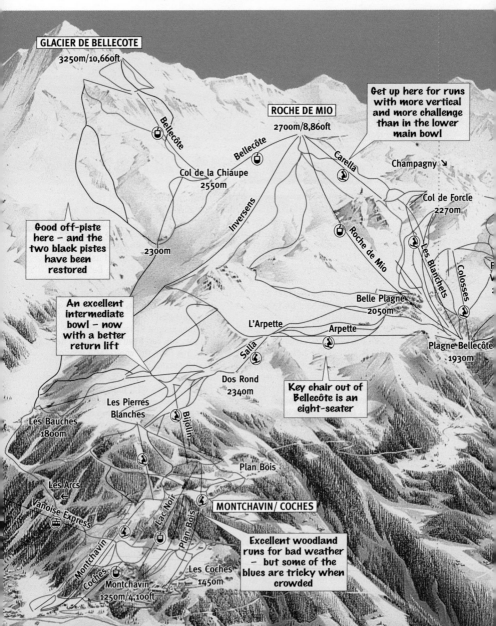

GLACIER DE BELLECOTE
3250m/10,66oft

ROCHE DE MIO
2700m/8,86oft

Get up here for runs with more vertical and more challenge than in the lower main bowl

Bellecôte

Bellecôte

Col de la Chiaupe
2550m

Carella

Champagny ↘

Col de Forcle
2270m

Inversens

Les Blanchets

Colosses

2300m

Good off-piste here – and the two black pistes have been restored

Roche de Mio

An excellent intermediate bowl – now with a better return lift

Belle Plagne
2050m

L'Arpette

Arpette

Plagne Bellecôte
1930m

Salla

Dos Rond
2340m

Key chair out of Bellecôte is an eight-seater

Les Pierres Blanches

Bijolin

Les Bauches
1800m

Plan Bois

Les Arcs

Lac Noir

Vanoise Express

Plan Bois

MONTCHAVIN/ COCHES

Excellent woodland runs for bad weather – but some of the blues are tricky when crowded

Montchavin

Coches

Les Coches
1450m

Montchavin
1250m/4,100ft

TRY THE OLYMPIC BOBSLEIGH RUN – YOU CAN EVEN DO IT SOLO

If the thrills of a day on the slopes aren't enough, you can round it off by having a go on the floodlit bobsleigh run built for the 1992 Olympic Winter Games, based in Albertville. The tightly twisting 1.5km run has 19 bends, generating centripetal forces on your body as high as 3g if your speed is high enough.

You can go in a driverless bob-raft (41 euros) reaching 50mph, which most people find quite exciting enough. Then there's the solo mono-bob (107 euros), which reaches 55mph; we found this a great thrill – we had to close our eyes on the sharper bends. Even faster is the racing-bob (115 euros), where three of you are wedged in a real four-man bob behind the driver – at speeds of up to 74mph. Be sure your physical state is up to the ride; there are minimum age limits. The run is open on certain days only, three days a week – book ahead. Additional insurance is available.

OT LA PLAGNE / J FAVRE

FRANCE

310

LIFT PASSES

La Plagne

Prices in €

Age	6-day
under 14	188
14 to 64	241
65 plus	188

Free Under 6
Beginner 10 free lifts
Senior 72 plus: 1-15 days €7
Notes La Plagne area; half-day passes; Paradiski extension

Alternative passes
Champagny only, Montchavin only, Montalbert only, Coolski for beginners; Découverte pass with one-day Paradiski extension

Paradiski Unlimited

Prices in €

Age	6-day
under 14	223
14 to 64	285
65 plus	223

Free Under 6
Senior 72 plus: 1-15 days €10
Notes Covers Les Arcs areas and La Plagne areas; family reductions

QUEUES ★★★★★
High season bottlenecks remain

When its huge bed-base is full, at New Year for example, La Plagne's lift network can't cope – in particular, at Plagne Bellecôte, the 40-year-old gondola to Roche de Mio and the relatively modern eight-seat Arpette chair for the Montchavin sector build serious queues. But for much of the season readers now report few problems; perhaps La Plagne, more so than more upmarket resorts, has been affected by the recession-inspired downturn in the French ski market. Last season another eight-pack was installed at Bellecôte: the new Colosses chair is about as powerful as a chairlift can be, shifting 4,400 people an hour towards Plagne Centre (25% more than the 10-year-old Arpette – that's progress).

The gondola to the glacier is queue-prone when snow is poor lower down – to get back to Roche de Mio as well as to get to the glacier.

The lift at the bottom of Les Bauches was upgraded to a slow quad in 2013, which seems to have dealt with the traditional queues there. We'd rather it was fast, of course.

Crowds on the pistes are now as much of a problem as lift queues. The worst-affected area is from Roche de Mio, where a single blue piste takes all the traffic from several lifts – an absolute nightmare towards the end of the day, and well worth avoiding. Some pistes converging on Bellecôte and Centre get badly crowded too, at certain times of day.

TERRAIN PARKS ★★★★★
Lots of choice

With no fewer than four terrain zones, freestylers are well catered for. There is a 90m long half-pipe at Plagne Bellecôte. Belle Plagne is home to the big park, with a separate pro area and an airbag. There's also a small park with beginner and progression obstacles above Montalbert. Then there are three snowcross courses.

SNOW RELIABILITY ★★★★★
Generally good except low down

Most of La Plagne's runs are snow-sure, being at altitudes between 2000m and 2700m on the largely north-facing open slopes above the purpose-built centres. The two sunny runs to Champagny are something else – one is often closed, the other (Les Bois) is kept open as much as possible with lots of artificial snow. Snowmaking on runs to all the villages is being improved. Grooming is good but most reporters think the Natur' runs should be groomed sometimes – unless refreshed by new snow, they can become unpleasant to ski, and then are left largely unused.

FOR EXPERTS ★★★★★
Few steep pistes; good off-piste

The two long black runs from the glacier to the Chalet chairlift below Col de la Chiaupe, closed for some years, have been reinstated. Let's hope they can be kept open more reliably than they were before the closure. The piste linking this area to Les Bauches doesn't really deserve its black status;

the Crozats black that meets it is a bit steeper, and can be tricky if snow is less than ideal.

Up on the glacier, Chiaupe merits its black status for a short stretch, but really the tough piste skiing is now confined to the Biolley sector. On the back of the hill, the Coqs and Morbleu blacks are seriously steep, Palsembleu less so. From the very top of this sector, Etroits owes its black status to a quite short pitch that is both steep and narrow, but is otherwise harmless. The long Emile Allais red down to the La Roche chair is north-facing, often quiet and great fun in good snow.

But experts will get the best out of La Plagne if they hire a guide and explore the vast off-piste potential – which takes longer to get tracked out than in more 'macho' resorts. The glacier and Biolley sectors have some excellent terrain and there are good runs from the glacier to Les Bauches (a drop of over 1400m). For the more experienced, the north face of Bellecôte presents a splendid challenge with usually excellent snow at the top. You can descend to Peisey-Nancroix (a drop of 2000m), enjoy a

PowderBeds.com

Ski Hotels & Apartments

good lunch at the charming, rustic Ancolie (a favourite of ours) and then catch a taxi or free bus to the Vanoise Express cable car. Another beautiful and out-of-the-way run starts with a climb and goes over the Cul du Nant glacier to Champagny-le-Haut.

FOR INTERMEDIATES ★★★★★
Great variety
Virtually the whole of La Plagne's area is a paradise for intermediates, with blue and red runs wherever you look. The main drawback is that some of them get very overcrowded at times.

For early intermediates there are plenty of gentle blue motorway pistes in the main La Plagne bowl, and a long, interesting (but often very crowded) run from Roche de Mio to Belle Plagne called Tunnel (going through, er, a tunnel). The blue runs either side of Arpette, on the Montchavin side of the main bowl, are glorious cruises – but beware, the blues further down towards Montchavin are quite challenging. The easiest way to and from Champagny is from the Roche de Mio-Col de Forcle area. Warning: the Mira piste from Grande Rochette and the Lanche Ronde up at Roche de Mio have steep pitches that will upset many blue-run skiers, although Mira has been widened at the top and you can avoid the moguls on the steepest section says a reporter. Verdons, nearby, is a great cruise, too.

Better intermediates have lots of delightful long red runs to try. There are challenging red mogul pitches down from Roche de Mio to Les Bauches (a drop of 900m) – the first half is a fabulous varied run with lots of off-piste diversions possible; the second half, Crozats, is classified black – read 'For experts'. The Sources red to Belle Plagne is a good run, too.

The sunny Champagny sector has a

La Plagne

LA PLAGNE TO / PHILIPPE ROYER

Plagne Aime 2000 (to use the latest of many appellations) is the highest resort unit, linked to Centre by cable car ↓

LAGRANGE Prestige

High-standard
Self-catering
Apartments

020 7371 6111
lagrange-holidays.co.uk

couple of tough reds – Kamikaze and Hara-Kiri. And the long blue cruise Bozelet has one steep section. The long Mont de la Guerre red, 1250m vertical from Les Verdons, is often closed; but when open, it's a fine away-from-all-lifts run with a decent red-gradient stretch halfway down, but long flattish tracks at the start and finish. There are further excellent red slopes in the other outlying areas.

FOR BEGINNERS ★★★★
Comprehensive facilities
La Plagne is a good place to learn, with 18 free lifts in the whole area; each village has at least one. There are good facilities for beginners, provided you go to the right bits, and generally good snow. There are

beginner areas in Centre, 1800, Soleil, Aime and Bellecôte; and in (and above) Montchavin, Les Coches and Montalbert. But here, as in Les Arcs, the usual French system of green runs is not used. Although a lot of the blue slopes are easy, you can't count on that; some, as we note above, are quite testing. The resort has 'adapted' the Arnica blue run from the Colorado chair above Centre for novices, and there is a 'Coolski' pass for beginners.

FOR BOARDERS ★★★
Something for everyone
With such a huge amount of terrain, there is something for everyone: 'One of the best for boarding,' says a recent visitor. Expert freeriders should hire a guide to explore the off-piste.

Selected chalets in La Plagne   ADVERTISEMENT

SKI AMIS *www.skiamis.com*   T 0203 411 5439

• Chalet Anniek – Montalbert – premium service, sleeps 14, close to piste, lift and village centre, indoor hot-tub and sauna

• Chalet Dolomites – Montchavin – great access to Paradiski, 8-11 people, balcony hot-tub

• Excellent catering – full English breakfast, afternoon tea, evening meal with wine

sales@skiamis.com

↑ CHALET ANNIEK   SKI AMIS   CHALET DOLOMITES ↑

MOUNTAIN HEAVEN *www.mountainheaven.co.uk*   T 0151 625 1921

Catered – Plagne 1800
* 5 catered chalets all in superb position, seconds from the piste
* Great value for money
* Fantastic food and wine

Self-catered – Plagne Montalbert
* High quality, spacious chalet apartments
* Ski in/out or within seconds of the piste
* No hidden extras
* Great value for money
* Unrivalled in resort services even for self-catered

↑ SELF-CATERED APARTMENTS – LA BERGERIE IN PLAGNE MONTALBERT

Email: info@mountainheaven.co.uk

Although this is a great place for beginners and intermediates, with huge wide-open rolling pistes, there are one or two flattish areas – for example getting across Plagne Centre, the middle of the Tunnel run and the blue run linking Les Bauches to Montchavin. Most draglifts have been replaced, and others can be avoided; the more difficult ones are marked on the map. The park caters for all levels and there are three snowcross runs.

Club Med
THE MOST COMPREHENSIVE
SKI PACKAGE ON THE MARKET

La Plagne 2100

020 8313 3999
Skiline.co.uk

Skiline.co.uk

FOR CROSS-COUNTRY ★★★★
Open and wooded trails
There are 80km of prepared cross-country trails scattered around. The most beautiful of these are the 22km of winding track set out in the sunny valley around Champagny-le-Haut, accessible to those staying in Champagny. The north-facing parts of the main ski area have more wooded trails that link the various centres.

MOUNTAIN RESTAURANTS ★★★★
A wide range of options
Mountain restaurants are an attraction of the area: numerous and varied. They are marked but not named on the piste map. Many people lunch in the satellite villages – Champagny on the south side of the area, Montchavin and Les Coches on the north side.
Editors' choice We've had several excellent meals at Chalet des Verdons Sud above Champagny; reporters agree – appetizing food and 'friendly and efficient' service, on a fine terrace or in the 'cosy, warm and welcoming' interior with a big fire. Above Montalbert, the Forperet is quite different – a simple old farm building, doing super home-made dishes (excellent tartiflette) at good prices. The rustic little Sauget, above Montchavin, is a great place to hole up in poor weather for highly traditional dishes.
Worth knowing about Most readers' tips are in the Montchavin sector, including a new one this year, Carroley – 'superb food (huge portions) and one of the best views of the area'. Other recommendations include Plan Bois Chez Laurette ('good tartiflette and salads, perfect entrecote; very nice atmosphere and well priced'); the 'lovely' Plein Soleil, also at Plan Bois ('a bit cramped inside, but excellent food', 'good crozets'); Pierres Blanches ('friendly, nice plat du jour and lovely wood-burning stove'). In a lovely spot

at Les Bauches, Chalet du Friolin pleases visitors who opt for its 'smart, cosy' table-service section.
Above Champagny, tips include Roc des Blanchets ('great views, extensive menu'), and Borseliers ('a long-standing favourite, suitable for good or bad weather'; 'huge, varied menu').

SCHOOLS AND GUIDES ★★★
Reports are mixed
Most reporters have used Oxygène in Plagne Centre and have been well satisfied, though one 2013 reporter found '14 people in the group despite the website claiming they had a maximum of 8 to 10'. Antenne Handicap offers private lessons for skiers with disabilities.

FOR FAMILIES ★★★★
Good facilities
Several UK chalet operators run childcare services. In particular, several specialist family holiday companies have chalets – Esprit in Belle Plagne, Ski Famille in 1800 and Family Ski Company in Les Coches. There are nurseries in most of the villages.

STAYING THERE

Club Med has a very visible presence in a striking red and white building up at Plagne Aime 2000.
Chalets There are lots of catered chalets. Many are in apartments, but there are lots of proper little chalets in 1800, and increasingly elsewhere.
Skiworld has over a dozen chalets dotted around several parts of the resort, including three in its 'superior' category. Ice and Fire has a ski-in/ski-out place at Plagne Villages, and two places with a sauna at 1800. Crystal will have eight chalets this season, mostly in ski-in locations in Belle Plagne, including three newly built ones in their 'finest' category.

High quality, high altitude

Four-star ski apartments with spa
02392 890 960

ABTA

SKI COLLECTION
.CO.UK

ESPRIT
FOR FAMILIES IN
Belle Plagne

Family
Ski Chalets
Dedicated
Nurseries
Exclusive Ski
Classes
13 resorts
across the Alps

espritski.com
01483 791 900

IMPROVE YOUR SKIING
SKI WITH OTHERS
GO PLACES

SNOWORKS
snoworks.com

SKIWORLD

Catered chalets, hotels and self catering apartments in

Europe, USA and Canada

skiworld.co.uk
08444 930 430

ABTA V2151 ATOL 2036

Inghams has five chalets in 1800. Mountain Heaven now has five mid-sized places in 1800, with chalet Perle being completely renovated for the coming season. Ski Olympic has a chalet hotel on the piste at Plagne Centre.

Family specialist Esprit has its flagship chalet hotel at Belle Plagne, the exceptionally cool Deux Domaines, in a great position, with good pool and spa. Approved again this year – 'superb, exceptional staff, varied food, very comfortable. Rival Ski Famille has two 20-bed properties down in 1800; its chalet Delphine was newly built last year.

Hotels There are very few.
****Carlina** Good location beside the piste below Belle Plagne. Pleasant rooms, good restaurant, pool and spa. Family-friendly. 'Especially friendly staff.' We've enjoyed our stays here in the past.
***Araucaria** At Plagne Centre; upgraded to 4-star in 2014 with a revamped wellness centre.
***Balcons** At Belle Plagne. Pool.
Apartments There is a wide choice of smart new properties, most with pools, available through the operators and agents who advertise with us. In Belle Plagne there are two good Montagnettes residences, Le Vallon and Les Cîmes. In Plagne Soleil the CGH-operated residence Granges du Soleil is very comfortable, with pool, spa and excellent views. Up at Plagne Aime 2000 is the Pierre & Vacances Premium residence Les Hauts Bois ('spacious apartments, hotel-standard spa facilities'). Lagrange has two of its Prestige residences: Aspen in Plagne Villages and Chalets Edelweiss (seven chalet-style buildings sharing a pool) – right by the lift out of 1800.

EATING OUT ★★★★★
A reasonable choice
There is a decent range of casual restaurants including pizzerias and traditional Savoyard places.

In Belle Plagne, we and readers have enjoyed meals at the hotel Carlina and the 'expensive but nice' Matafan. The Face Nord is tipped for 'excellent pierrade', among other things. La Casetta is a recommended pizzeria. La Cloche has become La Godille; reports, please.

In Plagne 1800, we had a good evening at Petit Chaperon Rouge – friendly, cosy atmosphere in a wooden chalet with reasonable prices.

At Plagne Aime 2000, the rustic old chalet Au Bon Vieux Temps on the slopes is open in the evening and is highly praised ('excellent mushroom ravioli and tarte tatin'). The 'casual, family-friendly' Montana does pizza and the 'usual Savoyard suspects'.

There are, of course, places to eat in the other resort units, but we lack recent experience or reports.

APRES-SKI ★★★★★
Bars, bars, bars
Though fairly quiet during low season, La Plagne has plenty of bars, catering particularly for the younger crowd.

In Belle Plagne, the Tête Inn and the Cheyenne are the main bars. In Plagne Centre, the Igloo has 'icy white decor' but 'is horribly expensive'. Scotty's has been known to be 'lively' (but one visitor found it often closed early) and Mouth is also tipped. La Mine is the focal point in Plagne 1800, often with live music or DJs – plus old train and mining artefacts. Mama Mia's is a fun spot, and the Bobsleigh Bar's happy hour is recommended; it also has live sport. Plagne Soleil has Monica's pub. Plagne Aime 2000 is quiet. There are discos at Centre, Belle Plagne and at Bellecôte.

OFF THE SLOPES ★★★★★
OK for the active
There are plenty of winter walks along cleared marked trails. You can ride gondolas to reach restaurants at the top. There's an ice grotto on the glacier. Plagne 1800 has bowling and tubing, and both Plagne Centre and Bellecôte have toboggan runs. The Olympic bobsleigh run is a popular evening activity (see feature box). There are cinemas at Aime, Bellecôte and Plagne Centre.

MONTCHAVIN

Montchavin is an old farming hamlet with an attractive traffic-free centre., and fruit trees dotted around its rustic front de neige. There are adequate shops, a kindergarten and a ski school. The local slopes have quite a bit to offer – pretty, sheltered runs, well endowed with snowmaking, with nursery slopes at village level, attractively surrounded by chalets and restaurants. The main blue home runs from Dos Rond can be quite tricky, though.

Après-ski is quiet, but the village doesn't lack atmosphere and has a couple of nice bars (a 2013 reporter recommends the Dos Rond bar-restaurant), a nightclub, cinema, night skiing, ice rink, and a small aquatic centre/spa, Espace Paradisio – 'nice but pricey' says a reporter.

Ski Amis has a four-bedroom chalet with outdoor hot tub – 'good location, service, food' says a reporter this year. Lagrange has a Prestige property here – Les 3 Glaciers – 'lovely rooms, great pool'. Restaurant tips include La Ferme de César ('very generous pierrade, friendly service, popular with locals') and Le Moulin à Poivre for Savoyard specialities.

LES COCHES

Les Coches is a little way above Montchavin, and shares the same slopes. It is a sympathetically designed, quiet, modern mini-resort with a traffic-free centre. The hillside setting makes for some steep walks. There are nursery slopes across the mountainside, linked by bucket-lift. It has a kindergarten, but specialist operator Family Ski Company may be a better bet, with two piste-side chalets close to the village centre; chalet David is reported to be 'basic, but good cooking and excellent childcare'. Ice and Fire has a smart-looking 24-bed chalet on the piste with a sauna – 'very warm and comfortable, with log fire'. Chalets de Wengen is a Lagrange Prestige chalet-style apartment complex sharing a pool and spa, approved by a reader this year. There is an ice rink – 'well maintained, with friendly staff', says a reporter. In 2014 'the best restaurant in town' was La Poya.

MONTALBERT

Montalbert is a traditional but much expanded village with a nice little front de neige area, with a choice of restaurant terraces. Access to the easy and wooded local slopes and to the rest of the La Plagne area will be transformed this year by construction of a powerful new gondola to the top of the local hill (a slow chair was the main impediment in the past). You then ski down to the fast Roche chair, starting well below Centre.

Restaurant choice is adequate: Abreuvoir has 'reasonable prices in happy hour', Fiftys Legend has 'prompt service', Tourmente is a popular pub with a pool table, and the Code is a 'racy but rocking' nightclub.

Ski Amis has a central seven-room chalet with all the trimmings here, and various self-catering options.

Mountain Heaven has self-catering apartments in several modern developments; the best of the apartments are notably spacious by French standards, and well furnished.

CHAMPAGNY

Champagny is a small, charming village in a pretty, wooded, sunny setting, with its modern expansion done sensitively; but it has drawbacks. It is remote from the link to Les Arcs – a reader based here this year seemed pleased to have got to the link in 'not much more than 90 minutes, in good conditions'. Its local slopes are exposed to full sun, and the red run to the village that is most reliably open is rather steep and narrow for nervous intermediates (though you can ride the gondola down). It is well placed for an outing by taxi or car to Courchevel.

There is a beginner area with free lifts at the top of the gondola, and a snowcross up beside the Rossa chair.

The Glières is a rustic old hotel with varied rooms, a friendly welcome and good food ('good set menus and classic dishes, always brilliant'). The Ancolie is smarter, with modern facilities. The Alpages de Champagny is a Lagrange Prestige property with pool and spa. The Club Alpina apartments next to the gondola have also been recommended.

The village is quiet in the evenings, but there is a cinema.

GETTING THERE

Air Chambéry 120km/ 75 miles (1hr45); Grenoble 190km/ 120 miles (2hr30); Lyon 195km/ 120 miles (2hr30); Geneva 200km/ 125 miles (2hr30)

Rail Aime (18km/ 11 miles) and Bourg-St-Maurice (35km/ 22 miles) (Eurostar service available); frequent buses from stations

TOURIST OFFICES

La Plagne
www.la-plagne.com
Montchavin-Les Coches
www.montchavin-lescoches.com
Champagny
www.champagny.com

Portes du Soleil

Low-altitude, largely intermediate circuit of slopes straddling the French-Swiss border, with a choice of contrasting resorts

KEY FACTS

Slopes	950-2275m
	3,120-7,460ft
Lifts	196
Pistes	650km
	404 miles

The Portes du Soleil seems to have quietly dropped its claim to be the biggest ski area in the world and left that to the Trois Vallées. But it remains a huge area, the central attraction of which is an extensive circular tour, straddling the French-Swiss border, taking you through one or two French resorts and several small Swiss ones – great for keen intermediates who like a sensation of travel. You can travel the circuit in either direction, no longer have to catch a bus part way round and longer or shorter variations of the circuit are possible.

We have separate chapters on the five major Portes du Soleil resorts. On the French side, high, purpose-built **Avoriaz** usually has the best snow around, and it is well placed to make the most of the slopes of Châtel and Champéry, as well as its own. Until last season you had to take a bus at the lower, traditional village of **Châtel** to bridge a gap in the circuit; but there is now a chairlift link.

On the Swiss side, **Champéry** is a classic, charming mountain village; its slopes spread across the mountainside above the tiny, purpose-built satellite stations of Champoussin and Les Crosets and lead to the traditional village of Morgins in a separate valley.

Back in France are two further traditional resorts, off the main circuit but linked by lift to Avoriaz – **Morzine** and **Les Gets**. They share the biggest area of local slopes in the region.

The lifts you ride doing the circuit vary widely. In the Avoriaz sector and in the Linga sector of Châtel the lifts are mainly modern and fast. On the far side of Châtel and on the Swiss side of the network, drags and old chairlifts dominate, and progress is slow.

The slopes are low by French standards, with top heights from 2000m to 2275m, and low points, where snow may be particularly poor, in Morgins and Châtel (1200m). In general, you can expect better snow on the north-facing French side of the circuit than on the sunnier Swiss side, particularly around Avoriaz/Champéry.

In the distant past there was a booklet-style map covering the whole of the Portes du Soleil. But now each resort has a map showing local lifts and pistes – you have to pick these up as you go. There's an overview map of the circuit on the back of each one.

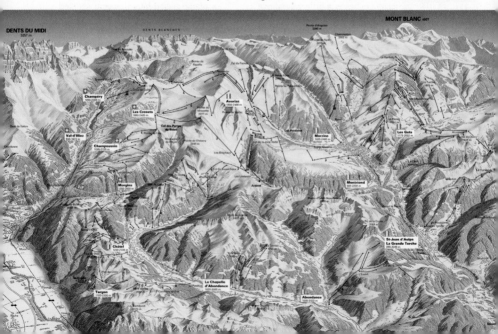

OT ST-LARY-SOULAN

The Pyrenees

An underrated region with decent skiing and boarding at lower prices than the Alps, and villages that remain distinctly French

£95
RESORT PRICE INDEX

It is certainly true that ski areas in the French Pyrenees can't compete in terms of extent with the mega-resorts of the Alps. But don't dismiss them: they have considerable attractions, including price – hotels and apartments can cost half as much as in the French Alps, and meals and drinks are cheaper. Provided the snow is good and you're not in search of steep mogul fields and wild après-ski, there is a surprising amount of variety packed into some of these smaller areas.

The Pyrenees are serious mountains, with dramatic, picturesque scenery, and are worth considering for beginners, intermediates and quiet family holidays at a lower cost. The resorts are attractively French, and many are old mountain villages that double up as spa towns. You'll also find charmless purpose-built satellites. Access has improved in the last few years, with budget airlines now using Toulouse, Pau and Lourdes airports.

The locals (including lots of Spanish) like to visit at weekends, so the slopes can get busy then. Queues are rare outside peak holidays though, and a lot of locals do cross-country rather than downhill. British visitors are still relatively few, and English is less widely spoken than in the Alps.

KEY FACTS

Resort	935m
	3,070ft
Slopes	1730-2415m
	5,680-7,920ft
Lifts	12
Pistes	36km

TOURIST OFFICE

www.cauterets.com

Cauterets

+ Charming, old spa town
+ Serious cross-country trails
− Downhill slopes very limited
− Long gondola ride to/from slopes

Cauterets is good for a short break; it's a relaxing old town, easy to reach, and its small downhill ski area suits a couple of days – try the cross-country too.

Many of Cauterets' buildings are well-preserved examples from the 19th century, and the thermal spas are a popular attraction for visitors.

There is a wide choice of hotels. The town's position at the head of a wide, sunny valley means traffic is rarely a problem, despite its appeal as a large year-round tourist destination.

The skiing takes place in a high, open and treeless bowl, the Cirque du Lys, reached by a long gondola from town; you have to ride it down as well as up. There is parking up at Le Courbet (1360m), from where a short gondola departs for the slopes.

The 36km of varied slopes radiate around the bowl, between 1730m and 2415m. The area just above the gondola top station is ideal for children and beginners; there are some gentle blue runs for progression too. But the area does get busy at weekends, as does the main restaurant – a self-service. The Oakley terrain park has an O-Rail and Stairset, unique in Europe.

Cauterets' jewel, though, is its 36.5km of cross-country, a short bus ride from town at Pont d'Espagne near the Spanish border. It's one of the best areas we've seen, set amid beautiful scenery and waterfalls. There are also 6km of snowshoe and walking trails.

Go to the french© pyrenees!

Erna Low

Short Break Ski Heaven
Call
020 7584 2841
www.ernalow.co.uk

KEY FACTS

La Mongie-Barèges	
Resort	1250-1800m
	4,100-5,910ft
Slopes	1400-2500m
	4,590-8,200ft
Lifts	34
Pistes	100km

TOURIST OFFICE

Domaine Tourmalet
www.grand-tourmalet.com

La Mongie / Barèges

+ One of the biggest Pyrenean areas
+ Contrasting villages, but ...
- Purpose-built La Mongie lacks charm
- Lots of slow chairs and drags

Nicely varied slopes and good off-piste shared by two hugely contrasting resorts – one purpose-built, the other a centuries-old spa town.

La Mongie is a purpose-built, modern resort on one side of the high Col du Tourmalet pass (closed in winter). On the other side is Barèges, with which it shares the Grand Tourmalet ski area.

The slopes span four valleys and are nicely varied with open bowls above La Mongie and a friendly treelined area above Barèges – all suitable for intermediates. The black runs are considered some of the toughest in the French Pyrenees and there is a lot of excellent off-piste including from the Pic du Midi Observatory (where you can stay the night), reached by cable car from La Mongie. There are few huts but we loved the tiny wood-panelled Etape du Berger above La Mongie – where most food comes from the owner's farm

('huge ribs of beef barbecued over a wood fire') – and the rustic Chez Louisette above Barèges.

La Mongie has little charm but is convenient, with lifts and pistes on its doorstep and good restaurant terraces from which to gaze at the scenery. As well as restaurants serving traditional French food and fondues etc the Bocadillo Cafe serves Spanish tapas in the evenings, along with live music.

On our most recent visit we enjoyed our stay at a catered chalet in Barèges run by an English couple (see www.mountainbug.com). Barèges is a small, atmospheric old spa village (with a great modern addition to its traditional old spa building) with a narrow main street a free bus ride from the slopes.

KEY FACTS

Resort	830m
	2,720ft
Slopes	1700-2515m
	5,580-8,250ft
Lifts	27
Pistes	100km

TOURIST OFFICE

www.saintlary.com

St-Lary-Soulan

+ One of the biggest Pyrenean areas
+ Attractive, traditional village
- Few challenges on-piste
- No runs back to the valley village

St-Lary combines an attractive, traditional village with one of the largest ski areas in the French Pyrenees – fine for intermediates wanting a sense of travel.

If you stay in the village, you ride a cable car or gondola both ways. Or you can stay up at purpose-built St-Lary 1700 (Pla-d'Adet).
Village charm St-Lary is pleasant with a narrow main street lined with wood and stone buildings.
Convenience Accommodation spreads from the centre along a river towards the hamlet of Soulan. Staying close to one of the two lifts is best.
Scenery The rocky ridges and open slopes give fine views including the Pyrenees National Park.

THE MOUNTAIN
The slopes cover three main sectors and most runs are above the treeline.
Slopes A cable car and gondola go up to an area of short slopes at St-Lary 1700 which is being revamped for 2015/16 with a six-pack replacing five old lifts and three new runs being created. From there you can head for 1900 and a gondola towards a more extensive area of intermediate slopes.
Fast lifts Apart from the four above, there are three other fast chairs; all other lifts are slow chairs and drags.

LAGRANGE Prestige

High-standard
Self-catering
Apartments

020 7371 6111
lagrange-holidays.co.uk

The Pyrenees are
serious mountains
with some lovely
scenery and worth
considering as an
alternative to the Alps
↓

Queues Weekends and school holidays can be busy ('horrendous queues at key lifts on Sunday', said a 2015 reporter).

Terrain parks There's a park and a snowcross.

Snow reliability Reasonable; many slopes are north-east facing and almost half have snowmaking.

Experts The few black runs are not very challenging but there's off-piste at Courne Blanque and Soum de Matte.

Intermediates Most runs are gentle cruises, with a few more challenging red runs. Best for early intermediates.

Beginners Good nursery slopes, with two covered moving carpets at 1700 and a special lift pass for 1700 only.

Snowboarding There are good cruising runs, though still some old draglifts.

Cross-country Not the best choice.

Mountain restaurants L'Oule, by a lake, is an old refuge with decent self-service food. Rustic Les 3 Guides above 1900 ('excellent charcuterie, local wine by the pichet') and tiny La Cabane on the edge of 1700 do friendly table-service.

Schools and guides The four schools offer the usual options, though good spoken English cannot be guaranteed.

Families St-Lary is a good family resort, with special kids' and family areas. The day care centre at 1700 takes children from 18 months.

STAYING THERE

Hotels We enjoyed staying at the 4-star Mercure, linked to the spa and near the gondola. The 3-star Pergola is charming with a good restaurant.

Apartments 4-stars with pool, sauna, and hot tub include l'Ardoisière (800m from the gondola) and Cami Real (central). Lagrange has the 4-star Chalets de l'Adet on the slopes. Pyrenees Collection and Erna Low have a good selection of places.

Eating out There's a fair choice, from pizzerias to grills. Our favourite is the Grange (local gourmet dishes). Other tips: the Gros Minet, Maison du Cassoule, Pergola (in old village); Myrtilles, La Cabane (at 1700).

Après-ski Nightlife is quiet, but there are a few bars. Try the Fitzroy (Irish pub), Balthazar (modern wine bar) or, at 1700, Top Ski (music and tapas).

Off the slopes There's a big spa (with pools, sauna, steam and treatments), snowmobiling, snowshoeing, dog sledding and ice skating.

QUALITY FROM £80 PP SKI APARTMENTS

Go to the french pyrenees!

A breath of French air.

ABTA
ABTA No.W5589

🏠 TRADITIONAL FAMILY FRIENDLY VILLAGE RESORTS

🎿 575 KM OF OF UNSPOILT SNOWSURE PISTES

✈ TOULOUSE, TARBES/LOURDES, PAU, CARCASSONNE, PERPIGNAN

🏃 EXTENSIVE SNOW ACTIVITIES

💧 FIRST-CLASS SPAS

CALL THE FRENCH PYRENEES SPECIALIST:
02392 890 960
pyreneescollection.co.uk
Self-drive or accommodation only packages

pyrenees COLLECTION
The French Pyrenees Specialist

KEY FACTS

Resort	1600m
	5,250ft
Slopes	1600-2400m
	5,250-7,870ft
Lifts	17
Pistes	60km

TOURIST OFFICE

www.peyragudes.com

Peyragudes

- ➕ Good for families
- ➕ Excellent spa nearby
- ➖ Few on-piste challenges for experts
- ➖ Snow can suffer from sun

Convenient purpose-built bases give easy access to a varied ski area which suits mixed-ability family groups well.

The resort has two purpose-built bases at the foot of its slopes. The largest is Peyresourde, which has lovely views over the Louron valley. A five-minute walk away, at the entrance to the village is the hamlet of Balestas and the majority of the resort's accommodation. The smaller base is Les Agudes in the next valley.

Both bases have high-speed chairs which meet at the top of the ridge that separates them. The Agudes side gets the morning sun and the Peyresourde side the afternoon sun. Both bases have fine beginner areas and there are easy blue runs to progress to.

There is good intermediate cruising (80% of the runs are blues and reds) including a couple of long top-to-bottom runs of up to 800m vertical – one on each side. For experts there

are only four black runs but there's a lot of worthwhile off-piste. A second terrain park and snowpark are planned for 2015/16.

There's one proper mountain restaurant, Cabanou, with fine panoramic views from its terrace. It's also open on Thursday evenings, when you can get a ride up by snowmobile and enjoy a tartiflette dinner.

At Peyresourde the Valnea residence opened this year with a spa open to the public.

For après-ski, don't miss the Balnea spa down in the valley. It has themed spa areas: American Indian (with totem poles and geysers), Japanese (onsen-like with a zen garden, sauna), Greco-Roman (with steam rooms, hot tubs and 'musical bath') and, new this year, Inca (with a temple, bamboos, Peruvian music).

KEY FACTS

Resort	1775m
	5,820ft
Slopes	1715-2215m
	5,630-7,270ft
Lifts	23
Pistes	58km

TOURIST OFFICE

www.font-romeu.fr

Font-Romeu

- ➕ High, fairly snow-sure slopes
- ➕ Popular family resort
- ➖ Limited in extent, with shortish runs
- ➖ Weekend crowds

With Font-Romeu you can choose from a delightful old village or a purpose-built station at the foot of the woody, cruisy slopes. Beginners are well catered for.

The old village, complete with 12th-century church and contrasting modern National Scientific Research Centre, is linked to the slopes by a gondola that you ride both ways. You can also stay at Pyrenees 2000 – a purpose-built development at the foot of the lifts, and a short bus ride away.

The slopes span three partly

wooded hills, with a good mix of runs, a terrain park and a snowcross. There are a couple of free beginner lifts and good progression to gentle greens. There is a local lift pass, but the Neiges Catalan pass also covers Les Angles (see below) and six other resorts in the region. There are 111km of cross-country tracks.

KEY FACTS

Resort	1650m
	5,410ft
Slopes	1650-2375m
	5,410-7,790ft
Lifts	19
Pistes	55km

TOURIST OFFICE

www.lesangles.com

Les Angles

- ➕ Sheltered, tree-lined slopes
- ➕ Good, gentle beginner terrain but ...
- ➖ English less widely spoken here
- ➖ Shortish runs that lack challenge

Les Angles is a small but charming stone village, complete with old church. The slopes are limited but relatively snow-sure and family-friendly.

Les Angles offers high but mainly wooded slopes that cover a broad hillside. Most runs are short and intermediate; over half are classified red, but there is a good proportion of gentler terrain. There are nursery slopes at village level and at 1800m – reached by free ski-bus. Snow coverage is helped by over 360 snow-

guns and there is a decent terrain park. 36km of cross-country and snowshoe trails are located in two areas either side of the Alpine skiing area. Font-Romeu is 16km away.

Off-slope diversions are few, but dog sledding is possible and daily entertainment is organized at the foot of the slopes.

La Rosière

A friendly, family-oriented little resort in a panoramic setting; the link to La Thuile in Italy adds much-needed interest to the skiing

SNOWPIX.COM / CHRIS GILL

£90
RESORT PRICE INDEX

TOP 10 RATINGS

Extent	★★★
Fast lifts	★★★
Queues	★★★★
Snow	★★★
Expert	★★
Intermediate	★★★
Beginner	★★★★★
Charm	★★★
Convenience	★★★
Scenery	★★★★

NEWS

2015/16: Three tracks are planned to allow you to skin up the mountain as an introduction to ski touring without danger from downhill skiers. Every Tuesday there will be 'introduction to ski touring' sessions run by the ski school (25 euros). A new tobogganing area in Les Eucherts is planned.

2014/15: A six-pack, the Plan du Repos, replaced two successive draglifts up to Le Roc Noir. A fun new children's run, the Petit St Bernard Trail, was built in the trees off the Lievre Blanc drag.

KEY FACTS

Resort	1850m
	6,070ft

Espace San Bernardo (La Rosière and La Thuile)

Slopes	1175-2610m
	3,850-8,560ft
Lifts	37
Pistes	160km
	99 miles

+ Fair-sized area of slopes if you include linked La Thuile in Italy

+ Fine panoramic views

+ Big dumps of snow when storms sock in from the west, but ...

– When storms do sock in, slopes and link to Italy can be bleak/shut

– Snow quality often affected by sun

– Local pistes limited and lack variety

– Limited village diversions

La Rosière is very different from its famous neighbours such as Val d'Isère-Tignes and Les Arcs – much smaller, quieter and sunnier. Many reporters are more impressed than we are by the skiing, which mainly consists of several runs down a single (admittedly very wide) open slope. But the link with La Thuile over the border in Italy adds another dimension.

THE RESORT

La Rosière is built in traditional chalet style high up on the road from Bourg-St-Maurice to the Petit St Bernard pass to Italy. In winter the road ends at a car park at the top of La Rosière, just below the main lifts. There's a small main village and an even smaller, newer satellite (Les Eucherts), a short bus ride – or a floodlit forest walk – to the east. This is more or less self-sufficient, but offers less choice of everything than the main village.

Village charm The resort is attractively built in chalet style; it is quiet, with a few shops and friendly locals; don't expect much lively nightlife. It is centred on the road to the lift station car park; so although there is no real through-traffic, the centre is far from traffic-free (Les Eucherts is a bit quieter but still centred on a road).

Convenience It's a small place, where you may have only a short stroll to a lift, but there's a free ski-bus.

Scenery La Rosière's sunny home slopes offer panoramic views over the Isère valley to Les Arcs and beyond.

THE MOUNTAINS

La Rosière and La Thuile in Italy share a big area of slopes called Espace San Bernardo. The link with Italy's slopes is a bit prone to closure because of high winds or heavy snow. Most slopes are above the treeline but there are few wooded runs. The two resorts produce separate maps of the whole area. La Rosière's is bigger, has the names of runs on and is easier to follow.

Slopes Two fast chairs, one at the main village and one at Les Eucherts, take you into the slopes; then you can progress across the mountain to Col de la Traversette, departure point for

321

fast chairlift
Slow chairs & drags have no symbol

La Thuile

Col du Petit
Saint Bernard
2190m

Belvedere
2610m/
8,560ft

Le Roc Noir
2330m

Col de la
Traversette
2385m

Le Gollet

La Rosière
1850m/6,070ft

Les Eucherts

1500m

Like the resort?

You'll love our handpicked accommodation

02392 839 310

PEAKRETREATS.CO.UK

ABTA
ABTA No.W5517

SKIWORLD

Catered chalets, hotels and self catering apartments in

Europe, USA and Canada

skiworld.co.uk
08444 930 430

ABTA V2151   ATOL 2036

FRANCE

Italy. West of the village is a separate sector with red and black runs through woods to the slow Ecudets chair.

Fast lifts Two recent six-packs replacing drags and a slow chair mean the resort now gets ★★★ for fast lifts. But there are still a couple of slow chairs on slopes below village level.

Queues Reporters stress the lack of queues, even at peak times. In good weather, expect some afternoon queues on the way back from Italy.

Terrain parks The main Poletta park has green, blue and red lines, including rails, other features and a big airbag. There's a snowcross course under the Fort chairlift.

Snow reliability The slopes get a lot of snow from storms coming up the valley from the south-west, but conditions can be badly affected by sun or wind. In warm sunny weather, the snow over on the north-facing slopes in Italy is often better.

Experts There are a couple of short, easy but worthwhile black runs – we particularly like Ecudets, down the eponymous chairlift. And there is an ungroomed, avalanche-controlled freeride zone (called Snowzone on the piste map but not explained). There is more serious, easily accessed off-piste terrain just outside the lift network – such as a run of almost 900m vertical on skier's left from Col de la Traversette down to the chairlift below Les Eucherts. And there's heli-skiing over the Italian border.

Intermediates The main area is a broad open mountainside offering straightforward red pistes, mostly at the easy end of the spectrum and

mostly short, with verticals in the 300m to 450m range. The exception is the Marmotte red, dropping over 800m to the chairlift below Les Eucherts. More interesting than anything on the main slope is the lovely wooded Fontaine Froide red, dropping 750m to the Ecudets chair – but it lacks snowmaking. Keen intermediates will want to make multiple trips to the more varied terrain of La Thuile.

Blue-run skiers are effectively confined to the pistes near the village. Not surprisingly, they get quite busy. The longer blues running diagonally across the main slope are just tracks from A to B, so not of much interest.

The outing to Italy involves a red run at the start, but it is not especially tricky. The two draglifts that follow are almost 3km in length – miserable in a north or east wind.

Beginners There are good nursery slopes and short lifts at both the main village and Les Eucherts; four lifts are free to use. The blue runs above are pretty good for progression, although some people find them a bit steep.

Snowboarding Most lifts are chairs, making the place good for novices. And the sunny slopes are good for gentle freeriding in soft snow.

Cross-country There are 5km of trails.

Mountain restaurants Options are limited, but we like the Antigel at the foot of the Stade de Slalom (table-service, good food, a light and spacious building). The self-service Plan du Repos in the heart of the slopes is the other main option.

Schools and guides We have had consistently good reports over many

---

Selected chalets in La Rosière

ADVERTISEMENT

MOUNTAIN HEAVEN *www.mountainheaven.co.uk*   T **0151 625 1921**

↑ THE LOUNGE/DINING AREA

We have the best selection of catered chalets and self-catered apartments in La Rosière
* Best price guarantee
* All chalets close to the piste, ski school and the village centre with ice skating rink, shops, restaurants etc.
* Amazing panoramic views
* Superb food and wine in all catered chalets
* Your money is safe as we are a fully bonded company

info@mountainheaven.co.uk

THE PENTHOUSE OFFERS STUNNING VIEWS ↑

LIFT PASSES

Espace San Bernardo

Prices in €

Age	6-day
under 5	74
5 to 12	139
13 to 64	199
65 to 74	159
75 plus	85

Free In La Rosière area only: under 5 and over 75

Beginner Four free lifts

Note Covers La Rosière and La Thuile

Alternative passes La Rosière only; non-skier

ESPRIT

FOR FAMILIES IN

La Rosière

Family Ski Chalets
Dedicated Nurseries
Exclusive Ski Classes
13 resorts across the Alps

espritski.com
01483 791 900

La Rosière

Four-star apartments close to slopes

skicollection.co.uk/La-Rosière

SKI COLLECTION .CO.UK

ABTA

years of the ESF (which is run, amazingly, by a Brit). A regular visitor has 'always been very happy' with Evolution 2. Elite Ski is a British school offering clinics and private lessons ('fantastic, an immediate improvement', says a 2015 visitor).

Families The resort caters well for children. Family specialist Esprit has its own childcare facilities here and Crystal has its own private nanny service. There is a lift pass that offers big savings to families with teenagers.

STAYING THERE

Chalets This is now a major chalet resort. Many chalets are located in Les Eucherts. The biggest operator is family specialist Esprit Ski, with 13 chalets ranging from 5 to 31 beds, plus its usual comprehensive childcare. Mountain Heaven has five chalets, most for 8 or 10 people; in 2014 we stayed in the Penthouse on the top two floors of an apartment building with a lovely big living room with floor-to-ceiling windows giving great views; comfortable bedrooms; outdoor hot tub. Skiworld has five smart mid-

sized chalet apartments in the same building (with access to sauna, steam, hot tub in a neighbouring building). Its Moet is praised this year – 'impeccable food, drink and service'. Crystal has five chalets and a recent visitor rated one of its 'Finest' properties, Cervinia, 'good value; good service'.

Hotels There are a couple of 2-star hotels in the village. Chalet Matsuzaka is a Japanese-influenced 10-room 4-star at Les Eucherts.

Apartments Many of the best places are in Les Eucherts. Mountain Heaven has a couple of good looking places with three and five bedrooms and great views. The Cîmes Blanches and Lodge Hemera residences are both very smart, with pool, hot tub, sauna and steam room – featured (along with other properties) by Peak Retreats, Ski Collection, Erna Low and Crystal.

Eating out 'Not one bad meal,' says a reporter, who tried several of the dozen or so restaurants. The best in town is probably the Genépi, where we had excellent steak in 2014 – and which reporters recommend too. Other tips: McKinley ('charming with Savoie favourites and a log fire'), Marmottes ('huge portions, good Savoyard food'), and in Les Eucherts the Kitzbühel and the Flocon ('wonderful veal escalope').

Après-ski Confined to a few bars. In the main village, Comptoir and Bar 1850 have a 'nice atmosphere' and sometimes live bands. At Les Eucherts, the Kitzbühel is the place to go for a post-slope beer and the Moo bar for late-night dancing (a reporter says there's an early-evening kids' disco too – 'our girls wanted to go every night!').

Off the slopes There's not a huge amount to amuse the non-skier – cleared walks, snowshoeing and paragliding, with ten-pin bowling and ice skating at Les Eucherts. Some hotel pools are open to the public. There is a cinema.

TOURIST OFFICE

www.larosiere.net

LA ROSIERE TO

A lot of the chalets have been built quite recently and many (like the one at the top of this pic) have fabulous views over the valley ↓

SNOWPIX.COM / CHRIS GILL

Samoëns

Characterful and charming base for the extensive and varied Grand Massif area, with its own excellent shady slopes

£95
RESORT PRICE INDEX

TOP 10 RATINGS

Extent	★★★★
Fast lifts	★★★
Queues	★★★★
Snow	★★★
Expert	★★★★
Intermediate	★★★★★
Beginner	★★
Charm	★★★★
Convenience	★
Scenery	★★★★

NEWS

2015/16: Chalets de Laÿssia, a new CGH residence in the centre, with pool and spa, should be open by Christmas 2015. A new hockey-size ice rink (with spectator seating) will open, plus a bowling alley.

324

KEY FACTS

Resort	720-1600m	
	2,360-5,250ft	

Grand Massif ski area (Samoëns and all linked resorts)

Slopes	700-2480m	
	2,300-8,140ft	
Lifts		68
Pistes		265km
		165 miles

Massif ski area (excluding Flaine)

Slopes	700-2120m	
	2,300-6,700ft	
Lifts		46
Pistes		125km
		78 miles

PISTE MAP

Samoëns is covered on the Flaine map

SAMOËNS TO / CHRISTIAN MARTELET

The village centre is exceptionally cute, centred around the market square and church →

- + Lovely historic village, with traffic-free centre and weekly market
- + Part of the big, varied Grand Massif
- + Glorious views from top heights

- − Main access lift is well outside the village, and has no return piste
- − Not the best base for beginners
- − Limited nightlife

Samoëns is the cutest of lower, traditional village bases sharing the impressive Grand Massif area with high, purpose-built Flaine; it's not the most convenient for skiing, but its fans are willing to forgive that.

THE RESORT

Samoëns is an attractive village – once a thriving centre for stonemasons, with their work much in evidence.
Village charm The resort has a small traffic-free centre of narrow streets lined by appealing food shops, and a pretty square (sadly not quite traffic-free) with a stone fountain, an ancient linden tree, a fine church and other medieval buildings. Also nearby is a nominally car-free area of modern development. The place as a whole retains the feel of 'real' rural France and makes a compelling base for families. There is a Wednesday market for your cheese supplies.
Convenience The village itself is compact, but as a skiing base it is not convenient. There are two gondolas into the slopes, both a drive or 'reliable and frequent' ski-bus ride from the village: an old one starting way across the valley at Vercland and

a newer and nearer one. You can ski down to Vercland, but only on red and black runs that can be tricky or closed; there are no runs to the new one. So at the end of the day it's a gondola then a bus; or ski to Sixt or Morillon, for a longer bus ride from there.
Scenery The village has a pretty valley setting, with attractively woody ridges and glorious views from the tops.

THE MOUNTAINS

Most of the skiing directly above Samoëns is on shady open slopes beneath the peak of Tête des Saix.
Slopes Read the Flaine chapter for an overview of the Grand Massif pistes. The two gondolas from the valley arrive at separate points on the hilly balcony of Samoëns 1600 (also reachable by road). A six-pack whisks you up to Tête des Saix, from which point you can proceed towards Flaine via a narrow, crowded piste followed by a fast chair in the Vernant bowl. Or

LIFT PASSES

Grand Massif

Prices in €

Age	6-day
under 16	173
16 to 64	231
65 plus	220

Free Under 5, 75 plus
Beginner Limited pass
Note Family discounts

Alternative pass
Massif area only (Les Carroz, Samoëns, Sixt-Fer-à-Cheval, Vernant)

you can turn right to the slopes around Morillon or Les Carroz.

Fast lifts Mountain access is now respectably quick, but the area as a whole has many slow lifts still.

Queues In general, the local lifts don't seem to present problems, though in high season you can expect delays on the way to Flaine and back. You can expect crowds on the pistes, too; any return to Samoëns involves riding one of the several lifts to Tête des Saix, which results in nightmarish crowds on the main run down in the afternoon.

Terrain parks There isn't one.

Snow reliability The slopes above Samoëns face due north, so above 1600 snow is fairly reliable. There is snowmaking around 1600.

Experts The upper pistes on Tête des Saix are among the most testing in the Grand Massif, and there is lots of good off-piste in the area. Don't miss Flaine's Combe de Gers.

Intermediates Samoëns makes a satisfactory base for all but the most timid, who will find the return from Tête des Saix pretty challenging; you might be better off in Morillon. From Tête des Saix you have a choice of good long runs in various directions.

In good snow the valley runs back to Vercland are highly enjoyable – the black can be easier than the red.

Beginners Beginners can buy a special pass and go up to 1600, where they will find gentle, snow-sure slopes of various lengths. But note our remarks under 'Intermediates'; Morillon is a better bet for progression from the nursery slopes, with its long winding green run and easy blues.

Snowboarding Not a big boarding resort, partly perhaps because there are quite a few flat linking runs.

Cross-country There are 40km of trails on the valley floor around Samoëns, including red trails up to and beyond Sixt; and there are more up at Col de Joux Plane, at 1700m.

Mountain restaurants They are not named on the piste map. There are several options at or near Samoëns 1600. For friendly service and reliable food we like Lou Caboëns, a small, modern but woody place just below the gondola station. Away from it all at the bottom of the Gouilles chair, La Luge a Téran is a cosy wooden place doing good, varied food; service is variable, in our experience. Read the chapters on Les Carroz and Flaine.

Samoëns

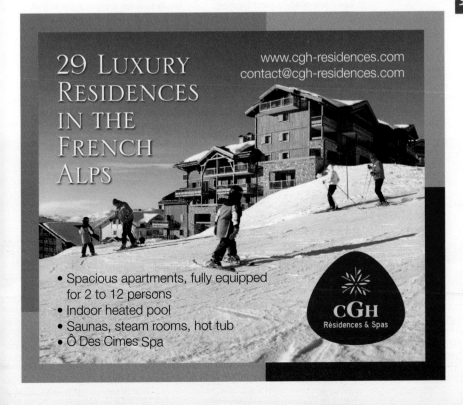

29 LUXURY RESIDENCES IN THE FRENCH ALPS

www.cgh-residences.com
contact@cgh-residences.com

- Spacious apartments, fully equipped for 2 to 12 persons
- Indoor heated pool
- Saunas, steam rooms, hot tub
- Ô Des Cimes Spa

CGH
Résidences & Spas

Tailor made, long weekend and short break French Alps ski holiday specialists.

Hanski
Ski. Explore. Relax.

web: www.hanski.co.uk
tel: 01638 596373

100% Protected Holidays

New for 15/16

peak retreats

★★★★
Les Chalets de Layssia
Samoëns, France

Brand new, centrally located residence offering 4★ apartments with luxurious spa amenities

CGH
Résidences & Spas

Call 02392 839 310
peakretreats.co.uk

ABTA
ABTA No.W5537

LAGRANGE
Prestige

High-standard
Self-catering
Apartments

020 7371 6111
lagrange-holidays.co.uk

TOURIST OFFICE

www.samoens.com

SIMON SMITH

There are excellent nursery slopes up at Samoëns 1600, but progression to the wider mountain is problematic ↓

Schools and guides We've had good reports of the ESF and the three alternatives, ZigZag, 360 International and Skisession.

Families There are nurseries and classes, of course. Bear in mind what we say under 'Convenience'.

STAYING THERE

Hanski specializes in short breaks.

Chalets Owner-run chalets dominate here. We have good reports of chalet Bezière and chalet Teresa.

Hotels There are several 2-star and 3-star places. We and readers have enjoyed the 3-star Neige et Roc, a walk from the centre. The Glaciers is 'basic' but offers 'a great location'.

Apartments Self-catering is mostly in small-scale developments or in individual chalets. Among many attractive options available through Peak Retreats are the excellent CGH residence La Reine des Prés, with pools and spa, within walking distance of the gondola and with an excellent restaurant next door; the Fermes de Samoëns, a smart Lagrange Prestige

residence; and the Ferme des Fontany. The big news this year is the opening of the new CGH residence Chalets de Laÿssia, close to the village centre.

Eating out A good selection of places. Table de Fifine, a short drive out next to the CGH residence Reine des Prés, is a fine spot, with a beautiful wooden interior and excellent cooking. 8M de Monts served one visitor last year 'about the best ski resort dinner I have had in 40 years'. Another reader tips Aux Becs à Fleu: 'excellent fixed menu – went 4 times in 3-week stay'. Monde à l'Envers and Bois de Lune are also highly regarded.

Après-ski Pré d'Oscar up at 1600 is a handy spot for a drink at the end of the day. Nightlife is quiet and there is little choice of bars; Irish pub Covey's seems to be the only one open late. The Savoie has a more French feel.

Off the slopes Samoëns offers quite a range of activities. There's dog sledding, and a reader recommends snowshoeing at Sixt. There is a sports and cultural centre, and a new ice rink opened in 2014.

SNOWPIX.COM / CHRIS GILL

Serre-Chevalier

One on its own, this – more character and less swank than you expect in a big French resort, and more woodland runs

£95
RESORT PRICE INDEX

RATINGS

The mountains

Extent	★★★★
Fast lifts	★★★
Queues	★★★★
Terrain p'ks	★★★
Snow	★★★
Expert	★★★
Intermediate	★★★★
Beginner	★★★★
Boarder	★★★★
X-country	★★★
Restaurants	★★★★
Schools	★★★★
Families	★★★

The resort

Charm	★★★
Convenience	★★★
Scenery	★★★
Eating out	★★★★
Après-ski	★★
Off-slope	★★★

NEWS

2014/15: The Croix de la Nore draglift on the way to Briançon from Chantemerle was replaced by a quad chair. And a barbecue area was installed nearby. First Tracks was started every Wednesday in Chantemerle. Electric cars were installed in each village for hire by the day or more. Snowmaking was increased.

KEY FACTS

Resort	1200-1500m
	3,940-4,920ft
Slopes	1200-2735m
	3,940-8,970ft
Lifts	61
Pistes	250km
	155 miles

➕ Big, varied mountain offering a sense of travel as you ski

➕ Lots of good woodland runs

➕ Based on old villages with character

➕ Good-value and atmospheric old hotels, restaurants and chalets

➕ Very friendly and welcoming locals

➖ Busy road through the resorts, and through the heart of Le Monêtier

➖ A lot of indiscriminate new building took place in the 1960s and 70s

➖ Still too many drags and slow chairlifts at altitude

➖ Limited nightlife

This is one of our favourite places. The modern buildings of the main resort areas are off-putting, but get into the original villages and you find the kind of ambience you might look for on a summer holiday – a sort of Provence in the snow, with small family-run hotels and restaurants in old stone buildings.

And the slopes are equally distinctive, with the trees reaching appreciably higher altitudes than the Alpine norm. This is a great place to be when it's snowing, as we have confirmed on two of our most recent visits.

THE RESORT

Serre-Chevalier is made up of a string of villages set on a valley floor, linked by a busy road.

The valley runs roughly north-west to south-east, below the north-east-facing slopes of the mountain range that gives the resort its name. From the north-west – coming over the Col du Lautaret from Grenoble – the three main villages are spread over a distance of 8km – Le Monêtier (or Serre-Che 1500), Villeneuve (1400) and Chantemerle (1350). Finally, at the extreme south-eastern end of the valley, is Briançon (1200) – not a village but a town (the highest in France). As well as the main villages there are nine smaller villages, some of which give their names to the communes: Villeneuve, for example, is in the commune of little old La Salle les Alpes. Confusing? Sure is.

The resort is not at all fashionable, and is only now developing 4-star hotels. But Serre-Che has more hotels here in the modestly priced Logis de France 'club' than any other ski resort.

This is a family resort, and it gets especially busy in the February/March French school holidays.

A six-day area pass covers a day in each of Les Deux-Alpes, Alpe-d'Huez, Puy-St-Vincent, Montgenèvre/the Milky Way, and a 25% discount on a La Grave day pass (note that to claim the discount or free day at any of these, you need to take your pass, your receipt for it, plus a ticket listing free resorts that you should be given when buying your pass). All of these outings are possible by bus, but are easier by car. Driving via Grenoble you use the Col du Lautaret, which can be closed.

VILLAGE CHARM ★★★
Some quaint old parts

Each of the parts of Serre-Chevalier is based on a simple old village, with narrow cobbled streets lined by small shops, cosy bars, hotels and traditional restaurants that give each village a very French feel. Around these older parts there is a lot more modern development ranging in style from brutal to sympathetic. It is not a smart resort in any sense; even the

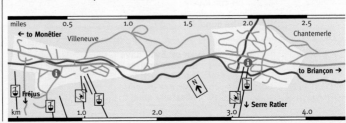

Like the resort?

You'll love our handpicked accommodation

02392 839 310

PEAKRETREATS.CO.UK

ABTA
ABTA No.W5537

older parts are roughly rustic rather than chocolate-box pretty. But when blanketed by snow the older villages do have an unpretentious charm.

Le Monêtier is the smallest, quietest and most unspoiled of the main villages, with new building mostly in sympathetic style. But the heart of the old village is bisected by the road to Grenoble. We find the traffic intrusive, but reporters don't seem to mind it.

Because the resort as a whole is so spread out, the impact of cars and buses is difficult to escape, even if you manage without them yourself.

Briançon's 17th-century fortified old town is a delight, with its traditional auberges, pâtisseries and restaurants; it is a World Heritage Site.

Every year reporters stress how friendly and welcoming the locals are.

CONVENIENCE ★★★☆☆
Good access but expect a walk
All four main resort villages have lift access, by gondola, cable car or fast chairs, to different parts of the ski area. Briançon has a gondola from the bottom of the town; your hotel could be next to it, or not. In Chantemerle the old village is quite close to the lifts, as is a lot of accommodation; but there is still a lot further away across the busy main road. Villeneuve has quite a few lodgings close to its multiple access lifts, but the old village is across the valley; to combine character with convenience, consider the nearby hamlet of Le Bez – set between two gondolas. At the top of the valley, Le Monêtier has one main access lift, reached from the centre by bus or a 10-minute walk (hilly, and tricky when ice is around). You can leave your gear at the lift base.

Local ski-buses circulate around the villages, and there are valley buses that link all the villages (running until 11.30pm). But a reporter points out that these valley buses do not visit the lift bases of Chantemerle or Villeneuve, though they stop nearby.

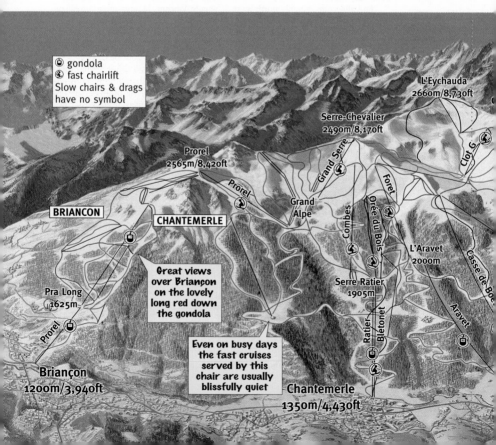

🔘 gondola
🔘 fast chairlift
Slow chairs & drags have no symbol

L'Eychauda 266om/8,73oft

Serre-Chevalier 249om/8,17oft

Prorel 2565m/8,42oft

Prorel

Grand Serre

Foret

Clot G

BRIANCON

CHANTEMERLE

Grand Alpe

Combes

Orée du Bois

L'Aravet 2000m

Casse de Bo

Pra Long 1625m

Great views over Briançon on the lovely long red down the gondola

Serre Ratier 1905m

Ratier-Bletonet

Aravet

Prorel

Even on busy days the fast cruises served by this chair are usually blissfully quiet

Briançon 1200m/3,94oft

Chantemerle 135om/4,43oft

SCENERY ★★★☆☆
Great views from the tops
The Serre-Chevalier range is not
notably dramatic seen from the valley,
though there are great views from
Briançon's old town (and of the town
on the run down to it). From the area's
high points there are fine views of the
rugged 4000m-high Ecrins massif.

THE MOUNTAINS

There are trees here up to 2200m or
more, and they cover almost two-
thirds of the mountain, providing
some of France's best bad-weather
terrain (we once had a great day here
when all the upper lifts were closed by
high winds).

Reporters are very impressed by
the improved piste signposting –
'much clearer than most resorts', said
a recent reporter. The map is not ideal,
but it is reasonably clear. Piste
classification tends to exaggerate
difficulty, most reporters agree. There's
now First Tracks on Wednesdays at
Chantemerle – you need to reserve a

place in advance, then meet at the
gondola or chair at the base at 8.15am
and get 45 minutes of skiing before
the hordes arrive.

EXTENT OF THE SLOPES ★★★★☆
Plenty for a week
Serre-Chevalier used to claim to have
250km of pistes; but the Schrahe
report (see our feature chapter on
piste extent), puts it at only 157km.
We are told that next season they will
not quote a km figure but 410
hectares of groomed pistes and 3900
hectares (39 sq km) total ski area –
does that mean anything to you?
Whatever, it is a good-sized mountain
spread across four sectors above the
four main villages, and you get a real
feeling of travel as you move around.

The sector above **Villeneuve** is the
most extensive, reaching back a good
way into the mountains and spreading
over four or five identifiable bowls.
The main mid-station is Fréjus. This
sector is linked at altitude and mid-
mountain to the slightly smaller
Chantemerle sector. The onward link

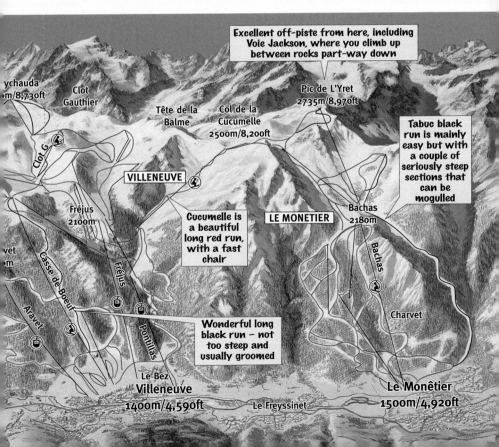

↑ Le Monêtier (aka Serre-Che 1500) is the highest, smallest and most unspoiled of the three main villages; its slopes (on the left) are a bus ride away

AGENCE ZOOM

LIFT PASSES

Prices in €

Age	6-day
under 12	191
12 to 64	238
65 plus	214

Free Under 6, over 75
Beginner Limited pass in each area: eg Villeneuve €18
Notes Briançon, Villeneuve, Chantemerle and Le Monêtier; 6+ days give one day in Les Deux-Alpes, Alpe-d'Huez, Puy-St-Vincent, Sestriere and Montgenèvre; reductions for families
Alternative passes Individual areas of Serre-Chevalier

from Chantemerle to **Briançon** is over a high, exposed col via a six-pack. In the opposite direction, the link between Villeneuve and **Le Monêtier** starts with the Vallons six-pack up the Cucumelle valley. Skiing from Le Monêtier to Villeneuve involves the red run down this valley, so timid skiers may prefer to use the bus service.

FAST LIFTS ★★★
Improvements, but slowly
A range of big lifts gets you out of the valley and progress has been made in upgrading some of the higher lifts. But there are still many old, slow lifts at altitude that hinder progress. In particular, the trio of slow chairs from Bachas at mid-mountain above Le Monêtier lead to complaints.

QUEUES ★★★★
Not normally a problem
Nearly all recent reporters have said that queues were not a problem – maybe a few minutes at the base in the morning. The main exception was a New Year holiday being 'really spoiled' by queues of 'at least 20 minutes at most big lifts'. And the Bachas area above Le Monêtier is served by three slow chairs and can get crowded. We hear that the

economic hard times have hit this resort more than most, which may have helped reduce queues; but numbers increased again last season and still no problems were reported. If the resort does get busy in the French school holidays, head for the slow Aiguillette chair at Chantemerle (see 'For intermediates').

TERRAIN PARKS ★★★
Fully featured
The Serre-Che snow park is under the Forêt chair (but has a dedicated draglift) and is easily reached from both Chantemerle and Villeneuve. It incorporates over 20 different features (plus chill-out and BBQ area) – clearly marked out in three zones for different levels. A major focus has been placed on the fabulous beginner area – 'My kids had a great time,' said a recent reporter. There's a video zone where your riding is filmed; you watch it on a screen and can download it later. The innovative Mélèzone, beside the Champcella draglift features various fun jibs built from larch wood in a wooded setting. A snowcross accessible by the Grande Serre or Combes lifts is 'fun', says a 2015 visitor. There's another near the Rocher Blanc chair above Briançon.

SNOW RELIABILITY ★★★★★
Good – especially upper slopes

Most slopes face north or north-east and so hold the snow well, especially high up (there are lots of lifts starting at altitudes above 2000m). The slopes above Le Monêtier are high and shady, and often have the best snow. The weather is different from that of the northern Alps, and even that of Les Deux-Alpes or Alpe-d'Huez, over the col to the west. Some upper lifts may be prone to closure by high winds. Snowmaking covers 75% of the pistes, including long runs to each village. Piste grooming is generally excellent.

FOR EXPERTS ★★★★★
Deep, not notably steep

There is plenty to amuse experts – except those wanting extreme steeps. Seven slopes – six black runs and one red – are left ungroomed and identified as 'brut de neige' areas.

The broad black runs down to Villeneuve (Casse du Boeuf – our favourite) and Chantemerle (Luc Alphand) are only just black in steepness. They are regularly groomed, and are great fun for a fast blast, with their gradient sustained over an impressive vertical of around 800m. A couple of years back, we had a fab run on Luc Alphand in largely untracked shin-deep powder. But one or the other may be closed for days on end for racing or training.

The rather neglected Tabuc run, sweeping around the mountain away from the lifts to Le Monêtier, has a couple of genuinely steep pitches (which may be heavily mogulled) but is mainly a cruise; great in falling snow, when it is even quieter than usual. For other steepish runs, look higher up the mountain to slopes served by the two top lifts above Le Monêtier and the two above Villeneuve. The runs beside these lifts – on- and off-piste – form a great playground in good snow.

There are huge amounts of off-piste terrain throughout the area – both high up and in the trees above Villeneuve and Chantemerle. We've enjoyed the Voie Jackson run accessed from the Yret chair above Le Monêtier, which includes a short climb between rocks to a deserted open bowl. The Cucumelle valley at the western side of the Villeneuve sector offers a huge area of gentle off-piste.

Serre-Chevalier

Photo accreditation: Agence Zoom

Ski & board from just €226pp per week inc self-catering accommodation & ski pass!*

Ski and board the secret of the French Alps

Serre Chevalier Vallée
du Galibier à Briançon

*Selected dates apply

serre-chevalier.com   Tel: +33 (0)4 92 24 98 98

LAGRANGE
Prestige

High-standard
Self-catering
Apartments

020 7371 6111
lagrange-holidays.co.uk

DO MORE
in *Serre Chevalier*

zenith holidays

0203 137 7678
zenithholidays.co.uk

ABTA
ABTA No.Y1542

There are plenty of more serious off-piste expeditions, including: Tête de Grand Pré to Villeneuve or Le Monêtier, and Couloir de Roche Corneille to Le Monêtier (both a climb from Cucumelle); off the back of L'Eychauda to Puy-St-André (isolated, beautiful, taxi ride home); l'Yret to Le Monêtier via Vallons de la Montagnolle; Tabuc also to Le Monêtier (steep at the start in a big bowl, very beautiful).

FOR INTERMEDIATES ★★★★
Ski wherever you like
Serre-Chevalier's slopes ideally suit intermediates, who can buzz around without worrying about nasty surprises on the way. On the trail map red runs far outnumber blues – but most reds are at the easy end of the scale. The broad, open bowls above Grande Alpe and Fréjus offer lots of options. The runs on skier's right on the lower slopes of Le Monêtier are gentle, quiet and wind prettily through the woods.

There's plenty for more adventurous intermediates, though. Cucumelle on the edge of the Villeneuve sector is a beautiful long red served by the Vallons fast chairlift, with opportunities to experiment off-piste on easy slopes beside it. The red runs off the little-used slow Aiguillette chair in the Chantemerle sector are worth seeking out – quiet, enjoyable fast cruises.

Other favourites include Myrtilles off the Prorel chair ('a beautiful cruise'), Le Monêtier's Aya and Clos Gaillard, and the wonderful long run from the top to the bottom of the gondola at Briançon (with great views of the town).

If the reds are starting to seem a bit tame, there is plenty more to progress to. Unless ice towards the bottom is a problem, the usually well-groomed blacks on the lower mountain should be on the agenda; try them early in the day when they are uncrowded and freshly groomed.

FOR BEGINNERS ★★★★
All four areas OK
All four sectors have their own nursery areas, and cheap daily lift passes covering a handful of lifts, including access to mid-mountain where appropriate. At Chantemerle you generally go up to Serre Ratier – rated as good by a beginner reporter. At Villeneuve there are several slopes at valley level – all 'lovely' according to a

skier having a first go at boarding recently – but also slopes up the Aravet gondola. At Le Monêtier the slopes are at the lift base – tipped by past reporters for 'better snow and fewer people' than elsewhere.

There are also easy high runs to progress to in each sector – the best are probably the green runs above the Fréjus gondola from Villeneuve. There are green paths from mid-mountain to Chantemerle and Villeneuve, though these may not be enjoyable late in the day when the runs become hard and others are speeding past.

FOR BOARDERS ★★★★
Plenty of scope for experts
The resort attracts a lot of boarders. The term 'natural playground' could quite easily have been coined in Serre-Chevalier. The slopes are littered with natural obstacles that seem made for confident snowboarders. Try the Cucumelle slope and the areas around the Rocher Blanc lift at Prorel for such terrain. For less expert boarders, the many draglifts can be a problem, as can the flat areas. There's a good terrain park for all abilities and ESI Generation in Chantemerle is a school that offers everything from beginners' lessons to freestyle courses.

FOR CROSS-COUNTRY ★★★
Excellent if the snow is good
There are 35km of tracks along the valley floor, mainly following the gurgling river between Le Monêtier and Villeneuve ('some nice trails') and going up towards the Col du Lautaret.

MOUNTAIN RESTAURANTS ★★★★
Some good places
Mountain restaurants are quite well distributed; they are marked on the piste map.
Editors' choice At Serre Ratier, Chalet Hotel de Serre Ratier has a delightful large terrace and pretty dining room, good service and delicious food. Endorsed by a reporter this year.

Two other options are more expensive. Just above the Casse du Boeuf quad from Villeneuve, the Bivouac de la Casse is an attractive chalet where we have repeatedly been impressed by both the food and service; reporters endorse our view, and recommend the 'quick' and 'good-value' self-service section too. Pi Maï in the hamlet of Fréjus is cosy on a bad day, charming on a sunny day,

CHALETS   COACHING

Spa apartments
chalets & hotels

Serre Chevalier -
a great destination
for Group ski trips

Come and stay in one of our growing number of spa
apartments, all just 150 metres from the ski lifts in
Serre Chevalier's alpine village 'Monêtier les Bains'.

For groups of 9+ guests, we have catered and self-
catered chalets, as well as hotels with pool and/or
spa facilities. Let us make your ski trip fabulous!

BEGINNER
(GET A HEAD START)
OR EXPERT
COACHING
& GUIDING

Our friends at local ski
school New Generation,
are on hand for group
ski lessons, ski guiding,
private coaching and
guided adventures

Read our online magazine at eurekaski.com - it's all about us, Serre Chevalier and Where to Stay

and offers excellent food such as steaks, tartiflette, and 'filling salads'.
Worth knowing about In the Briançon sector, the Chalet de Pra Long is a 'stunning building' at the gondola mid-station, table- and self-service sections separated by a massive fireplace; 'great views and excellent food'. The little Chalet de Serre Blanc, just down from the top of Prorel, has superb views; it gets mixed reports – but 'it's cheap and you get a coffee thrown in'.

Above Chantemerle, we and a recent visitor loved the small table-service Troll – great, good-value food and very jolly service. Cafe du Soleil became one reader's regular haunt this year. Grand Alpe self-service is spacious, and a bit cheaper than most.

Above Villeneuve, we and readers have enjoyed the Echaillon, a few metres off-piste from the blue run from Casse du Boeuf to Clot Gauthier – a lofty chalet with open fire and a table-service section: 'very good steaks'. The Bercail, near the top of the Aravet lift, impressed one discerning reporter despite using the Italian system of taking orders at the bar for delivery to your table – try the veggie noodles, advises a recent visitor. The Aravet in the same area has been recommended for thin, crispy pizzas.

Above Le Monêtier the enlarged but still tiny 'friendly' Peyra Juana near the bottom was a 'winner' with a recent visitor: 'Fantastic, hearty, generous, good food. We went there every day.' At mid-mountain there's the self-service Chapka. Both get packed on bad-weather days. But there's plenty of room at the Flocon, near the Chapka. We had an excellent table-service lunch on the terrace here a few seasons ago, but we've since had mixed reports.

SCHOOLS AND GUIDES ★★★★
Choice of good outfits
You are spoiled for choice here: we get positive reports on virtually all the schools.

The Serre-Che branch of New Generation, run by Gavin Crosby gets unstinting praise – 'very good private tuition, set us up for the week', 'superb', 'good teachers and competitively priced', 'fantastic, good value for two-hour private lessons'. Classes have a maximum size of eight. We've skied with Gavin a couple of times, and been greatly impressed. He also offers off-piste coaching from first-timer to expert levels.

Another British-run school is Ski Connections: 'Was very happy – small groups.' Private lessons with Brit Darren Turner of Insight changed one reader's skiing 'dramatically – well worth the money'.

ESI Monetier is praised this year: 'Enthusiastic Serge had our two ladies snowboarding very competently at the end of their first two-hour lesson.' The ESF was also given good feedback from three 2015 reporters ('very good beginner lessons'; 'our grandchildren were in a class of four – excellent'; 'my sister loved her lessons on Serre Ratier').

FOR FAMILIES ★★★
Facilities at each village
Serre-Chevalier is popular with French families and there are good family-friendly events and activities. For childcare, Les Schtroumpfs in Villeneuve (nine months to five years old) has been praised in the past. There is a micro-crèche (Les P'tits Loup) in Villeneuve too, taking young children. EurekaSki can arrange childcare and private nannies.

Serre-Chevalier

333

Club Med

THE MOST COMPREHENSIVE SKI PACKAGE ON THE MARKET

Serre-Chevalier 3

020 8313 3999
Skiline.co.uk

Skiline .co.uk

STAYING THERE

There is a wide choice of lodging but very little of it has any claim to luxury.

EurekaSki is a local British-run operation that can fix more or less any aspect of a holiday in Serre-Che – not only accommodation but also such things as transfers, catering, childcare, equipment, coaching and discounted lift passes. This season they are starting a special service specifically for groups such as clubs, corporate groups or just big groups of friends.

AGENCE ZOOM

The old village of Le Bez is at the foot of the slopes in the Villeneuve sector. The modern building in the background is the Club Med ↓

Chalets Several operators offer catered chalets. Zenith has the luxurious Les Clarines in Le Monêtier with pool, hot tub, steam room, sauna and the Refuge (which is being renovated for next season) in the old part of Villeneuve, plus various others which can be rented catered or self-catered. Crystal has four chalets including a converted farmhouse in its 'Finest' range in Chantemerle. Inghams has three mid-sized places in Villeneuve. EurekaSki has chalets with and without catering for 10 to 24 guests. Snowed Inn is a small Serre-Chevalier specialist offering a personal service and a varied selection of chalets – highly recommended this year by a regular reporter.

Hotels A feature of the resort is the range of simple 2- and 3-star family-run hotels – many of them members of the Logis de France consortium. There are now a few 4-star hotels too and a 350-bedroom ski-in/ski-out Club Med in the Le Bez area of Villeneuve.

LE MONETIER

*****Alliey** Charming place with well-regarded restaurant – 'Excellent food and service.'

****Europe** Simple well-run Logis in heart of old village.

VILLENEUVE

******Grand Aigle** Near the Pontillas gondola. Renovated and now a stylish 4-star with spa, sauna, hot tub.

******Rock Noir** Near the Aravets gondola. Completely renovated 'trendy' hotel with pool, sauna, hot tub. 'Smallish rooms but great food including free afternoon tea and cake,' says a 2015 reporter.

*****Christiania** Civilized, family-run hotel on main road.

***Chatelas** Prettily decorated simple chalet by river.

CHANTEMERLE

*****Plein Sud** Central. 'Basic, comfortable, terrific food and service'; 'nice pool, busy welcoming bar', say two 2015 reporters.

Apartments EurekaSki makes something of a speciality of self-catering chalets and apartments with pools and saunas.

There is an increasing supply of high-quality residences. By the slopes in Chantemerle is the 'comfortable and very well-equipped' Hameau du Rocher Blanc, in the Lagrange Prestige range (pool, gym, sauna, steam, massage); nearby is the Adret with indoor-outdoor pool; both are bookable

through Peak Retreats, Erna Low and Crystal. In Villeneuve, Pierre & Vacances' well-placed residence Alpaga has been approved by reporters. So has the Hameau du Bez. In Le Monêtier the Arts et Vie is modern, right on the slopes and good value. The hotel Alliey has apartments too. Catering company Zeste (www.zesteserrechevalier.com) will deliver homemade three-course meals to your apartment ('delicious, huge portions').

At altitude Two mountain restaurants have rooms: Pi Maïand the Chalet Hotel de Serre Ratier.

EATING OUT ★★★★
Unpretentious and traditional
In Le Monêtier, there are several good hotel-based options. At the upper end, the Maison Alliey (hotel Alliey) has a good reputation and a reporter rated it 'excellent'. The hotel Europe has reliable cooking at more modest prices. Reporter tips include the 'very friendly' Kawa ('excellent confit de canard; we ate there four times'). Up the valley at Le Casset, Chez Finette offers trips in a horse-drawn sleigh before dinner.

In Villeneuve, past reporters have raved about Eau Petit Pont. Mojo is a small, welcoming Brit-run bar-restaurant doing a good range of 'excellent-value' food.

In Chantemerle, we had an excellent dinner a few seasons ago at 34 – a cool spot with a short but wide-ranging menu. We've also enjoyed the Loup Blanc – 'Good food well presented,' says a reporter. Reporters like the 'cool' Triptyque (traditional French dishes, 'fabulous burgers and crumble to die for').

In Briançon, there are several highly regarded places in the charming old town. A recent visitor recommends the Gavroche for its 'lovely ambience, great value, generous helpings and very good service'. A local tips Plaisir d'Ambré for a 'special night out', and Pied de la Gargouille for open-fire grills. Just outside the old town, Italian-run Mamma Mia does 'excellent large pizzas at good prices'.

APRES-SKI ★★
Quiet streets and few bars
Nightlife seems to revolve around bars, scattered through the various villages, and some reporters complain that the resort is too quiet.

In Le Monêtier the British-run Bar de l'Alpen is 'about the only place to go', say two separate reports; it has live music, sports TV, free nibbles and welcoming staff. In Villeneuve, head for the Grotte at the foot of the slopes (live music, happy hour – later on it 'doubles up as a nightclub'). The newish 1420 wine bar is worth a try. The Frog is popular with Brits, while the Cocoon has been praised. In Chantemerle the Brit-run Station at the foot of the pistes is popular with Brits and 'seems to have the après all sewn up' – Sky Sports and 'sells bottled real ale'; 'live entertainment' every evening. The VSB bar on the main road gets a mention and the Triptyque serves 'great cocktails – pricey though'. The Royal is 'lively' and right by the gondola. In Briançon, there's a lively teatime scene (assisted by a happy hour) at the bar next to the gondola.

OFF THE SLOPES ★★★
Try the hot baths
The old town of Briançon is well worth a visit – there are guided tours. The Parc 1326 leisure complex has pools (25m and fun options), sauna, hot tub and steam room. There is a full-size ice rink, and Briançon has a champion ice hockey team – their games make 'a good night out'. There's also dog sledding. In Le Monêtier reporters enjoy the large thermal spa complex, Les Grands Bains ('superb tonic for tired limbs'), with indoor and outdoor pools, saunas, steam rooms, a 'chill-out' music grotto and a waterfall (some areas only for the over-18s). The hotel Alliey has a pool and spa non-residents can use if they book a treatment. There is a public swimming pool and a 4km toboggan run in Villeneuve and bowling in Chantemerle. Each of the villages has a cinema and an ice rink, and there is good walking on 25km of 'well-prepared trails'. You can learn to drive a piste-basher. Paragliding is available.

❄
Want the next edition free?

Send us a useful report on your holiday, and you could be among those who win one of 100 free copies. Then you might become one of our 'resort observers', and get free lift passes.

Find out more at:

www.wheretoskiandsnowboard.com

GETTING THERE
Air Turin 125km/ 80 miles (2hr); Grenoble 165km/ 100 miles (2hr45); Lyon 215km/ 135 miles (3hr15)

Rail Briançon (6km/ 4 miles); regular buses from station

TOURIST OFFICE
www.serre-chevalier.com

OT STE-FOY / MARK JUNAK

Ste-Foy-Tarentaise

*Tasteful, modern mini-resort appealing to families and experts –
and to motorists as a base for visiting nearby mega-resorts*

£85
RESORT PRICE INDEX

TOP 10 RATINGS

Extent	★
Fast lifts	★★★★
Queues	★★★★★
Snow	★★★
Expert	★★★★
Intermediate	★★★
Beginner	★★
Charm	★★★
Convenience	★★★★
Scenery	★★★

SAINTE FOY TARENTAISE TO / ANNE
MARMOTTAN

The resort is popular
with British families,
many of whom have
bought places here.
And the ski schools
are highly rated for
teaching kids ↓

336

➕ Safe untracked powder within the
lift system, and epic runs outside it

➕ Good base for visits to Val d'Isère/
Tignes, Les Arcs

➕ Great value (with the lowest lift
pass price in this book)

➕ Quiet most of the time, but ...

➖ Too quiet for some visitors; very
little après-ski action and very few
restaurants

➖ Very limited piste network

➖ Still two (out of four) slow chairlifts

➖ Now more British than French

**Ste-Foy is a small, attractive, unpretentious resort developed since 1990, at the
foot of what started life as a cult off-piste mountain. It remains excellent for
experts but now attracts many others, including families. Keen piste-bashers
will want to travel to big resorts nearby – easily done by car.**

THE RESORT

Ste-Foy itself is a village straddling the
busy road up from Bourg St Maurice to
Val d'Isère. Its slopes start at Ste-Foy-
Station (aka Bonconseil), which is set
4km off the main road. With a car you
can visit some excellent restaurants
close by and explore nearby resorts –
Val d'Isère, Tignes, Les Arcs, La Plagne
and La Rosière. Some tour ops
organize excursions too. With a Ste-

Foy lift pass for six days or more you
can buy day passes for these resorts
at 27 euros a day.
Village charm Ste-Foy-Station is a
complete resort in miniature, with a
limited choice of bars and restaurants
and a small supermarket; and these
are surrounded by a cluster of chalets
and chalet-style apartment blocks, all
built in the traditional Savoyard style
of wood and stone but without a real
central focus. Lots of properties have
been bought by Brits and Dutch, and
some visitors find the British
dominance of the place off-putting.
Convenience No accommodation is far
from the lifts or nursery slopes.
Scenery The Tarentaise mountains give
a dramatic backdrop to Ste-Foy's
pleasant setting among the trees.

THE MOUNTAINS

There is an attractive mix of wooded
slopes above the village and open
slopes higher up.
Slopes The newish fast quad chair out
of the village ('a massive
improvement') goes to Plan Bois at
mid-mountain and is followed by two
successive slow quad chairs. The first
goes to the treeline and the second to
the area high point of Col de l'Aiguille
at 2620m. From here there are slopes
of over 1000m vertical, almost 600m
of it above the treeline. The two
marked ungroomed black runs here
form the basis of two special off-piste
zones that are marked 'zone à theme'
on the piste map but not explained;
we're told they are avalanche
controlled and closed when conditions
aren't right. Slightly further down the

KEY FACTS

Resort	1550m
	5,090ft
Slopes	1550-2620m
	5,090-8,600ft
Lifts	6
Pistes	40km
	25 miles

NEWS

2015/16: More snowmaking is planned.

2014/15: More snowmaking was installed. Saint Germain, a new wine bar and deli, opened in the village.

hill is a less steep off-piste zone, Shaper's Paradise (it has natural terrain features, and you can build your own too), again centred on a black run.

The two lower chairs serve a few pleasant runs through trees and back to the base station. The Marquise six-pack (on the left of our piste map) serves a blue run that goes into a forested area, three reds and a black.

The red and blue pistes are 'immaculately groomed', say reporters.

Fast lifts Two out of the four chairlifts on the mountain are now fast.

Queues Despite all the new building, reporters rarely find queues at Ste-Foy – 'No significant queues even in UK and French half-term but there can be a build-up on the second chair because the first is higher capacity,' says a 2015 reporter.

Terrain parks There isn't one. But people build kickers and other features in the off-piste zones mentioned above.

Snow reliability The slopes face roughly north-west. Snow reliability can suffer on the sunnier bits, but the resort has snow-guns (over 30 from the 2015/16 season) that it uses on the runs down to the resort.

Experts Experts can have great fun on and between Ste-Foy's black and red runs, exploring lots of easily accessible off-piste and trees, including the special zones mentioned earlier. The lack of crowds means you can still make fresh tracks days after a storm.

There's more serious off-piste on offer too, for which you need a guide.

There are wonderful runs from the top of the lifts down through deserted old villages, either to the road up to Val d'Isère (you can get a bus back) or back to the base (via the deserted hamlet of Le Monal). And there's a splendid route down the north face of Foglietta in the next valley to the tiny village of Le Crot.

The ski schools run group off-piste trips, with transport back to base and perhaps with lunch in the village of Le Miroir (see 'Eating out'). Heli-skiing in Italy can be arranged, including a route that also brings you back to near Le Miroir.

Intermediates The piste skiing is limited in extent and keen piste-bashers will want to visit nearby resorts too. But you can enjoy 900m vertical of uncrowded reds and blues on the upper slopes above the top of the first chairlift. The red from the Col de l'Aiguille is a superb test for confident intermediates, who would also be up to some of the off-piste routes, especially the one back to base via Le Monal.

Beginners There are good fenced-off nursery slopes with free moving carpets in the village. You can progress to a long, easy blue run off the top of the first chairlift, then to steeper blues higher up.

Snowboarding It's a great freeriding area, with lots of trees and powder between the pistes to play in, plus the off-piste zones for building kickers and other features.

Cross-country Go elsewhere. There are no prepared trails here.

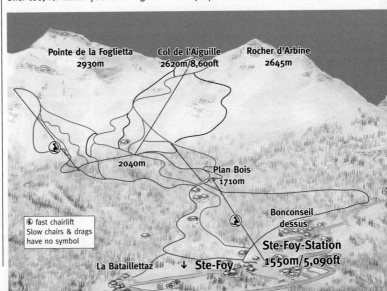

ABTA
ABTA No. V1697

Sainte-Foy Tarentaise

Four-star self-catering apartments at foot of slopes with indoor pool

02392 839 310

PEAKRETREATS.CO.UK/
SAINTE_FOY

LIFT PASSES

Prices in €	
Age	6-day
under 12	123
13 to 64	160
65 plus	123

Free Under 7, 73 plus

Beginner Free magic carpets in village

Notes Family discounts; with 6+ pass, reduced day rates at Tignes, Val d'Isere, Montchavin (for La Plagne), La Rosière, Villaroger, Peisey-Vallandry and Bourg St Maurice (for Paradiski)

TOURIST OFFICE

www.saintefoy-tarentaise.com

SAINTE FOY TARENTAISE TO / ANNE MARMOTTAN

The Tarentaise mountains form a dramatic backdrop to Ste-Foy's pretty setting in the trees ↓

Mountain restaurants Les Marquises at the foot of the La Marquise fast chair opened two seasons ago in a 'small but wonderful' restored building with a big terrace with 'stunning views' and 'delicious food including duck and homemade soups'. There are two 'rustic and charming' restaurants near the top of the first chair. Tiny Les Brevettes is cramped but cosy, with good food – while Chez Léon is much more spacious. At village level, but ski-in/ski-out, la Maison à Colonnes got mixed reviews for lunches in 2015.

Schools and guides We get good reports on the ESF ('my 10-year-old daughter spent a large part of her lesson off-piste and enjoyed it'). Evolution 2, K Spirit and Snocool ('the kids' group lessons are fantastic, they finish the day with big smiles on their faces') are alternative schools. The local guides are 'totally great', says a reporter. All the schools and guides can arrange heli-skiing.

Families Les P'tits Trappeurs takes children from age 3 to 11. UK tour operator Première Neige also runs a nursery.

STAYING THERE

Chalets Auberge sur la Montagne is an eight-room chalet in La Thuile at the bottom of the 4km access road to Ste-Foy station, with minibus shuttles; it got a rave review from a reporter last year – 'very welcoming, fantastic food, superb views (especially from hot tub)'. Première Neige's chalet The Peak was also praised – 'amazing food'.

Hotels The smartly modernized Monal down in Ste-Foy village is tipped this year for its 'good atmosphere'.

Apartments The smart CGH Fermes de Ste-Foy and Etoile des Cîmes residences are both at the foot of the slopes and have pool, hot tub, sauna, steam, fitness. La Ruitor apartments, quietly set 400m from the centre (with shuttle), also have pool, sauna and steam room. All are available through Peak Retreats and Erna Low. The tourist office website has more.

Eating out In Ste-Foy-Station the Bergerie does excellent food, the 'atmospheric' Maison à Colonnes is highly rated and L'à Coeur does 'a fantastic côte de boeuf, dinosaur size'. In the village of Le Miroir, Chez Mérie is excellent – 'the best in the Tarentaise', says a frequent visitor. In Ste-Foy village, the Monal hotel and La Grange next door are highly rated.

Après-ski Pretty quiet. Reporters have enjoyed the Iceberg piano bar. The Après is 'great for a couple of drinks; they had a live band on one night too – great for the oldies!' says a 2015 reporter. The Saint Germain wine bar and deli was new last season. The bar of the hotel Monal in Ste-Foy village can get busy, too; tastings are held in the cellar wine bar there.

Off the slopes There's little to do off the slopes, but snowshoeing and dog sledding are available. Forget shopping ('I have rarely spent so little on a ski holiday,' said a reporter).

SNOWPIX.COM / CHRIS GILL

St-Martin-de-Belleville

Explore the Three Valleys from a traditional old village – and so avoid the Méribel crowds who descend on it for lunch

£110
RESORT PRICE INDEX

TOP 10 RATINGS

Extent	★★★★★
Fast lifts	★★★★
Queues	★★★★
Snow	★★★
Expert	★★★★
Intermediate	★★★★★
Beginner	★★
Charm	★★★★
Convenience	★★★
Scenery	★★★

NEWS

2015/16: A six-pack will replace the St-Martin 2 fast quad, relieving queues at mid-mountain. Chalet operator The Alpine Club is opening a third luxury property nearby.

KEY FACTS

Resort	1400m
	4,590ft

Three Valleys	
Slopes	1260-3230m
	4,130-10,600ft
Lifts	180
Pistes	600km
	373 miles

Les Menuires / St-Martin only	
Slopes	1400-2850m
	4,590-9,350ft
Lifts	34
Pistes	160km
	99 miles

➕ Attractively developed traditional village with pretty church

➕ Quick access to Les Menuires, Méribel and the rest of the 3V

➕ Long, easy intermediate runs on rolling local slopes

➕ Extensive snowmaking keeps runs open in poor conditions, but ...

➖ Snow on runs to the resort suffers from afternoon sun, and altitude

➖ Only one run to ski if bad weather closes the top lifts

➖ No green runs for novices

➖ Some lodging a long trek from the lifts – transport needed

➖ Limited village facilities

St-Martin is a lived-in, unspoiled village with an old church (prettily lit at night), a small square and buildings of wood and stone, a few miles down the valley from Les Menuires. As a quiet, relatively inexpensive, attractive base for exploration of the Threes Valleys it's unbeatable. But it is quiet.

THE RESORT

St-Martin was a backwater farming village until the 1980s, when chairlifts linked it to the slopes of Méribel and Les Menuires.

Village charm St-Martin is a pleasant old village, set on a steep slope, with its extensive modern developments at the foot of the slopes all in traditional style. The main feature remains the lovely 16th-century church – prettily floodlit at night.

Convenience The village core is small, but some lodgings are quite a way from the lifts. The main lift is slightly away from the centre, but a draglift from above the village square accesses it. There are some good local shops and a few 'touristy' ones.

Scenery St-Martin has one of the more attractive locations in the valley, set among quiet, lightly wooded slopes.

THE MOUNTAINS

The whole of the Three Valleys can easily be explored from here. There is a safe 'Liberty Ride' off-piste zone on the upper mountain, 300m vertical.

Slopes A gondola followed by a very long chairlift– to be upgraded to a six-seater this season – take you to a

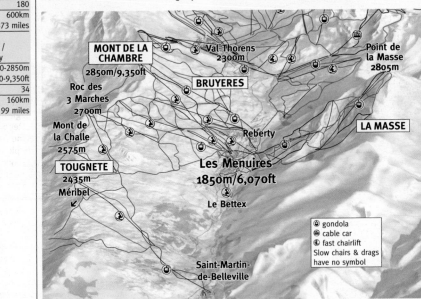

MONT DE LA CHAMBRE
2850m/9,350ft

Roc des 3 Marches 2700m

Mont de la Challe 2575m

TOUGNETE 2435m

Méribel

Val Thorens 2300m

BRUYERES

Reberty

Les Menuires 1850m/6,070ft

Le Bettex

Point de la Masse 2805m

LA MASSE

Saint-Martin-de-Belleville

🚡 gondola
🚠 cable car
🚡 fast chairlift
Slow chairs & drags have no symbol

ALAN SHEPHERD

The home run from mid-mountain is a gentle blue, with comprehensive snowmaking (which it needs) ↓

ridge from which you can access Méribel and Les Menuires. But if this lift is closed, you're stuck.

Fast lifts The main local lifts are both fast – as are most key lifts in the Three Valleys.

Queues Queues at the village gondola are not unknown, but the chairlift above it to the Méribel ridge has been the real problem – happily, about to be solved by the new six-pack.

Terrain parks None locally, but you can get to those above Les Menuires and Méribel fairly easily.

Snow reliability The local slopes get the full force of the afternoon sun, and the village is quite low. The home run is kept open by snowmaking to the bottom, but conditions are often poor.

Experts Locally there are large areas of gentle and often deserted off-piste. The descent from Roc de Fer to the village of Béranger is recommended. Or try the new Liberty Ride area. Head to La Masse for steep slopes.

Intermediates The local slopes are pleasant blues and reds, mainly of interest to intermediates. One of our favourite runs in the Three Valleys is the rolling, wide, usually quiet Jerusalem red down to the top of the

gondola from the ridge shared with Méribel. The Verdet blue from Roc de Fer is a lovely easy cruise and also usually quiet. Then, of course, there's the whole of the Three Valleys to explore.

Beginners Not ideal – there's a small nursery slope but no long green runs to progress to. The blue run down the gondola is fairly gentle, though.

Snowboarding There is some great freeriding available on the gentle slopes immediately above the village – and steeper stuff further afield.

Cross-country There are 28km of trails in the Belleville valley.

Mountain restaurants There are three atmospheric places on the home run, all generating mainly good reports: the reliable Loy, the Chardon Bleu and the Corbeleys. Not surprisingly, many people based in Méribel and Courchevel like to ski down to St-Martin for lunch – read 'Eating out'.

Schools and guides We get generally positive reports on both British-run New Generation and the ESF. One potential problem in this small village is that when demand is low you may have to go to Les Menuires to find a class of the right level.

Like the resort?

You'll love our handpicked accommodation

02392 839 310

PEAKRETREATS.CO.UK

⊕ABTA
ABTA No.W5557

Families One of our regular reporters on St-Martin has five children and seems to find it near-ideal, not least because it is so small and safe. Piou Piou club at the ESF takes children from 18 months to five years old. The tourist office has a list of babysitters.

STAYING THERE

For a small village there's a good variety of accommodation.

Chalets The Brit-run Alpine Club (not really a club) now has three luxurious chalets in the quiet hamlet of Villarabout. Two have been operated for some time – a modern property in traditional style with a double-height, open-plan living room, and a beautifully converted, 100-year-old farmhouse with spectacular views. The third is new: a 130-year-old stable to be turned into a rustic but luxurious 8-bed chalet for the coming season.

Hotels There are several 3-stars. The Alp hotel is in pole position by the gondola – 'very comfortable, good breakfast, typically French evening meals, very welcoming staff'.

Apartments There are two stylish residences in perfect piste-side locations at the top of the village, run by CGH: Chalets du Gypse follows the standard pattern – smart pool, hot tubs etc, and is available through Peak Retreats; we enjoyed a comfortable stay here in 2015 – very helpful staff. Chalet Adèle has no fancy amenities, and is booked through CGH or owners' websites. Ski Amis has an appetizing range of properties, mostly central. Erna Low has a couple of appealing places in Villarabout.

Eating out There is a good choice for a small village, no doubt due in part to the healthy lunchtime trade. The Voûte is the reader favourite, for pizza and more serious dishes – 'buzzy atmosphere', 'good food and value'. The Montagnard, just about on the snow, is an atmospheric converted barn doing a good range of dishes – but regulars complain of escalating prices. Its offspring next door, the Jardin de Joséphine, is refreshingly non-traditional in style, and also does excellent food, traditional and less so. The 'friendly, traditional' Lachenal has its supporters. The Ferme de la Choumette, slightly out of the village, is a working farm and cheesery and is often recommended. The Ferme Auberge Chantacoucou in Le Chatelard is similar. La Bouitte, a lovely rustic spot up the road in St-Marcel, now has three Michelin stars – the first such award in Savoie, we're told; yes, it is very expensive.

Après-ski Choice is limited. The Dahlia, at the bottom of the gondola, is popular for après-ski drinks. The vaulted Pourquoi Pas? near the main square is a pleasantly relaxed British-run bar (with a log fire) that's a favourite of regular visitors; it has some live music sessions.

Off the slopes Options are limited. The village has an 'excellent' museum with 'comprehensive audio guide in English' and free concerts ('high standard') in the church. And there's dog sledding, snowshoe trips, 'lovely riverside walks' and a torchlit tour of the village. Pedestrians can ride lifts to and from Méribel.

TOURIST OFFICE

www.st-martin-belleville.com

THE ALPINE CLUB *www.thealpineclub.co.uk*   helen@thealpineclub.co.uk

Sumptuous food, bespoke service, casual elegance

Individual rooms or exclusive chalet bookings

THE ALPINE CLUB
BOUTIQUE MOUNTAIN
CHALETS

THE ALPINE CLUB

La Tania

A well-placed budget base for the Courchevel and Méribel pistes – and a pleasant place, with a good choice of catered chalets

£115
RESORT PRICE INDEX

TOP 10 RATINGS

Extent	★★★★★
Fast lifts	★★★★
Queues	★★★★
Snow	★★★
Expert	★★★★
Intermediate	★★★★★
Beginner	★★★
Charm	★★★
Convenience	★★★★
Scenery	★★★

NEWS

2014/15: The ancient Forêt gondola from Le Praz was replaced by a six-pack taking a different line to a lower top station at mid-mountain, near the Bouc Blanc restaurant.

KEY FACTS

Resort	1350m
	4,430ft

Three Valleys
Slopes	1260-3230m
	4,130-10,600ft
Lifts	180
Pistes	600km
	373 miles

Courchevel/ La Tania only
Slopes	1260-2740m
	4,130-8,990ft
Lifts	58
Pistes	150km
	93 miles

+ Part of the Three Valleys, with good access to Courchevel and Méribel

+ Long runs through woods to the village: a great place in a storm

+ Attractive, compact, traffic-free village

+ Much improved snowmaking, but ...

– At this altitude, snowmaking is vital in most seasons

– Limited village facilities

– Village nursery slope gets through-traffic (but higher one does not)

– The one long green run is not genuinely easy

– No proper hotels

La Tania is a good-value, family-friendly base from which to explore the slopes of its swanky neighbours, Courchevel and Méribel. The resort was built for the 1992 Winter Olympics, and at 1350m is about the lowest purpose-built French resort you'll find; its wood-clad buildings sit comfortably in a pretty woodland setting – quite a contrast to the bleakness of many French ski stations.

THE RESORT

La Tania is set just off the minor road linking Le Praz to Méribel. Free buses go to Courchevel and there's a service to Méribel during the French school holidays.

Village charm The village has grown into a quiet, attractive, car-free collection of mainly ski-in/ski-out chalets and apartments. (It did have hotels, but they no longer operate as such.) There are a couple of lively bars and restaurants. The centre loses the sun quite early in the afternoon.

Convenience It's a small place – you can walk around the village in five minutes – but big enough to have all the basic amenities (except a pharmacy). A gondola from one end of the village leads up into the slopes, and you should be able to ski back to a point close to your doorstep. And the lower nursery slope is central.

Scenery The resort is prettily set among the trees.

THE MOUNTAINS

The slopes immediately above both La Tania and nearby Le Praz are wooded, and about the best place in the whole Three Valleys to spend time in bad weather. Above mid-mountain, the slopes are open.

Slopes The gondola out of the village goes to Praz-Juget. From below here a six-pack goes on up to the slopes above Courchevel 1850, and a fast quad goes to the link with Méribel via Col de la Loze. From all these points, varied, interesting intermediate runs can take you back into the La Tania sector.

Fast lifts Our rating is for the whole Courchevel area lift system. The lifts above La Tania have improved greatly in recent years, and last season the none-too-slick gondola from Le Praz was replaced.

Queues The slopes above La Tania are relatively crowd-free. But there may be morning queues for the gondola out of the village in peak season.

Terrain parks There is no local terrain park or half-pipe, but you can get to Courchevel's 'Family Park' fairly easily.

Snow reliability Good snow-cover down to Praz-Juget is usual all season. Snowmaking covers the green run and the whole of the blue run back to the village; if, despite this, the runs are icy in the afternoon, you have the option of riding the gondola down.

Experts The mountainside above La Tania is steep enough to be interesting without being scary. The Dou des

SKI AMIS

Catered Chalets in Superb Locations

020 3411 5439
www.skiamis.com

LIFT PASSES

Three Valleys

Prices in €

Age	6-day
under 13	228
13 to 64	283
65 plus	255

Free Under 5, 75 plus

Beginner Free lifts and limited pass

Notes Covers whole of the Three Valleys; reductions for families, duos and groups. Options: pedestrian and half-day passes

Alternative passes
Courchevel/La Tania, with optional Three Valleys extension

Lanches chairlift serves a lot of good off-piste terrain as well as an easy black piste, often groomed. The Jean Blanc and Jockeys blacks from Loze to Le Praz are challenging more because of length (and moguls) than gradient.

Intermediates There are three lovely, long, undulating intermediate runs back through the trees to La Tania. There's little difference in gradient between the blue and the red and even the green Plan Fontaine is great fun and popular. The red Murettes run to Le Praz is of genuine red steepness, winding and interesting. On the higher slopes both the red Lanches and the black Dou des Lanches pistes are excellent and challenging (the latter is often groomed and makes a great fast cruise when it is).

Beginners There is a good beginner area and free lift right in the village, and children are well catered for. But there's a lot of through-traffic on the main slope. There's now a more snow-sure area at the top of the gondola (Praz-Juget). But the Plan Fontaine green run to the village is not an ideal progression run: fairly narrow, not all that gentle, winding – and popular with better skiers, whizzing down it as if it were a race course. And the step up to the blue run back to the village is quite a big one.

Snowboarding It's easy to get around on boarder-friendly gondolas and chairlifts, avoiding drags.

Cross-country There are 67km of trails in the Courchevel/La Tania area, many of them through the woods.

33 YEARS IN BUSINESS
100% FINANCIAL PROTECTION

❄ Crèche exclusively for Le Ski guests
❄ Fully qualified UK nannies
❄ Civilised Sunday flights included
❄ Chalets sleeping from 4–23 guests

30 CATERED CHALETS
LA TANIA
COURCHEVEL VAL D'ISÈRE
01484 954397 LESKI.COM

La Tania

343

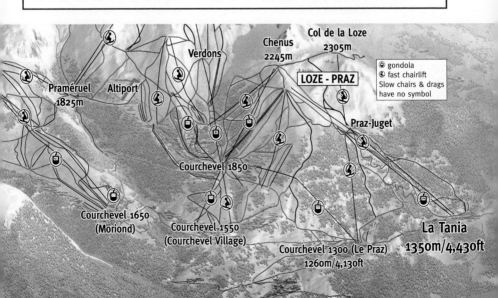

IMPROVE YOUR SKIING
SKI WITH OTHERS
GO PLACES

SNOWORKS
ALL MOUNTAIN SKI COURSES

snoworks.com

Heavenly
Skiing...
at down to earth prices

*mh**
Mountain Heaven*

· Superb catered & self catered accommodation ·
· Great ski areas in the French & Swiss Alps ·
· Snow secure resorts · We only have on/near piste locations ·
· Fantastic prices & no hidden extras ·

0151 625 1921
www.mountainheaven.co.uk

La Tania Chalets

Ski in Ski out
Fully Catered
with wine
Hot-tubs,
Saunas & WIFI

01273 466535
alpineaction.co.uk

A alpineaction
quality catered chalet holidays
ⒶABTA
Y5435

Mountain restaurants Bouc Blanc, at the heart of La Tania's slopes, is also the best place to head if you are above Courchevel and in need of a good, affordable lunch. We seem to manage a meal here most years and have never been let down, 2015 included. It has friendly table-service in two wood-clad dining rooms, good no-nonsense food (reliable plat du jour) and wine (good-value pichets) and a big terrace. Many reporters endorse our view every year, very occasionally finding service stretched.

Schools and guides Highly regarded British school New Generation gets good reports. Snoworks and Magic Snowsports are other alternatives to the ESF.

Families La Tania is popular with families looking for a quiet and convenient base, and a child-friendly atmosphere – 'excellent for our three-family group of 14, which included all ability levels'. La Tanière des Croës (formerly Chez Nounours) kindergarten takes both skiing and non-skiing children from four months to five years old. The chalets of UK tour operator Le Ski are open to family bookings, and it runs its own nursery in the resort. A list of babysitters is available from the tourist office.

STAYING THERE

Chalets There are lots, dotted around in the woods above the resort centre.

Ski Amis has seven chalets sleeping from 8 to 28, and all except one with outdoor hot tubs – we have enjoyed very comfortable stays in their premium service chalets Elliot (a splendid log-built affair) and Balkiss. Major Courchevel operator Le Ski now has four chalets here: a tiny new one next door to the firm's nursery, a mid-sized one in a great piste-side location, and two largish ones that are particularly child-friendly, with family rooms. Mountain Heaven has a 10-bed chalet, with sauna and a TV room separate from the living room. Alpine Action has four chalets, two with hot tub and two small units in a ski-in/ski-out location. Ski Total has added La Tania to its programme this year, with two well-placed mid-size places. Crystal has a 15-bed chalet. Alpine Elements runs the central 170-bed hotel Montana as a chalet hotel; pool,

SNOWPIX.COM / CHRIS GILL

The slopes of La Tania are not without challenge (seen here from the terrace of Bouc Blanc) →

↑ The home piste goes right through the traffic-free village to the gondola station

LA TANIA TO / ROBIN GARNIER

Ski Total

WELCOME YOU TO
La Tania

Quality chalets
Excellent value
19 resorts
across the Alps

skitotal.com
01483 791 933

TOURIST OFFICE

www.latania.com

sauna, steam, gym and hot tub. We've had an enthusiastic report this year on a stay with Snow Retreat.

Apartments There are no major 'smart apartment' developments. Ski Amis offers a broad range of properties, including self-catering chalets as well as regular apartments. Pierre & Vacances has the recently refurbished residences Christiania and Britania. These and other options are available from the major French specialist agencies – Peak Retreats, Erna Low and Lagrange – and from mainstream operators such as Crystal. There is a

deli, bakery and small supermarket.

Eating out If you want something between the extremes of the cheap and very cheerful Ski Lodge and the Michelin-starred Farçon – and most of us do – your best bet is the Taïga, over the road from the main village. Reports are positive without being notably enthusiastic. We have a good report this year on La Ferme, in the village, too.

Après-ski The choice is limited but it's quite lively at close of play. The central Ski Lodge 'still seems to be a focal point', says a reporter who found one 'big and strong cocktail' quite enough; 'lots of live bands', which really helps the atmosphere.

Off the slopes The place is very small and limited. However, tobogganing, snowshoeing, dog sledding, snowmobiling and paragliding are possibilities. There are some cleared paths and snowshoe routes. Non-skiers can go up the gondola or take the bus to Courchevel to meet skiing friends for lunch.

La Tania

345

Selected chalets in La Tania

ADVERTISEMENT

SKI AMIS *www.skiamis.com*   T **0203 411 5439**

- 7 chalets to sleep from 8 to 28 people – room bookings also possible
- Hot-tubs, free WIFI and satellite TV
- Excellent catering with full English breakfast every day, afternoon tea and 3 or 4 course evening meal
- Unlimited good quality wine

sales@skiamis.com

SKI AMIS

↑ CHALET ELLIOT

CHALET TITANIA ↑

COURCHEVEL / J KELAGOPIAN

The Three Valleys

With the swankiest resort in the Alps at one end, and the highest at the other: the biggest lift-linked ski area in the world

Despite competing claims, in practical terms the Three Valleys cannot be beaten for sheer quantity of lift-linked terrain. There is nowhere like it for a mileage-hungry intermediate – but it has a lot to offer beginners and experts too. What's more, the area undersells itself: it expanded years ago into a fourth valley, the Maurienne south of Val Thorens.

The Three Valleys area is dealt with in six chapters covering the four major resorts – Courchevel, Méribel, Les Menuires and Val Thorens – plus St-Martin-de-Belleville and La Tania.

None of the resorts is cheap, but of the major resorts **Les Menuires** is cheapest. The centre of the resort is an eyesore, but new developments have been built in chalet style. Les Menuires has an excellent position for exploration of the Trois Vallées.

Down the valley from Les Menuires is **St-Martin-de-Belleville**, a charming traditional village that has been expanded sympathetically. It has good-value accommodation and lift links towards Les Menuires and Méribel.

Up rather than down the Belleville

valley from Les Menuires, at 2300m **Val Thorens** is the highest resort in the Alps – and at 3230m the top of its slopes is the high point of the Trois Vallées. The snow in this area is almost always good, and it includes two glaciers where good snow is guaranteed. But the setting is bleak, and the lifts are vulnerable to closure in bad weather. It's a purpose-built resort and very convenient – and better looking than Les Menuires.

Méribel is a multi-part resort. The highest component, **Méribel-Mottaret**, is perfectly placed for access to any part of the Trois Vallées. **Méribel** itself, 200m lower, is a British favourite – the most attractive of the main resorts, built in chalet style on a steep hillside.

High quality, high altitude

Four-star ski apartments with spa
02392 890 960

ABTA

SKI COLLECTION
.CO.UK

Kaliblue

We prefer the chalet-style suburbs of Les Menuires to its functional centre →

LES MENUIRES TO / G LANSARD

SNOWPIX.COM / CHRIS GILL

A small part of Courchevel's Vizelle slopes, seen from La Saulire on the ridge between Courchevel and Méribel ↘

Parts of the resort are very convenient for the slopes and the village centre; parts are not. The growing hamlet of **Méribel-Village** has its own chairlift into the system. You can also stay in the valley town of **Brides-les-Bains**.

Courchevel has four parts, which have recently been rebranded. Courchevel (formerly Courchevel 1850) is among the most fashionable and expensive resorts in the Alps. The other parts – Le Praz, Courchevel-Village (formerly 1550) and Courchevel-Moriond (formerly 1650) – are much less expensive. Many people rate the slopes in the Courchevel valley the best in the Three Valleys.

La Tania was built for the 1992 Olympics, just off the minor road linking Courchevel to Méribel. It has now grown into an attractive, car-free collection of chalets and apartment blocks set among the trees, and is popular with families. It has good nursery slopes and good intermediate runs in the woods above.

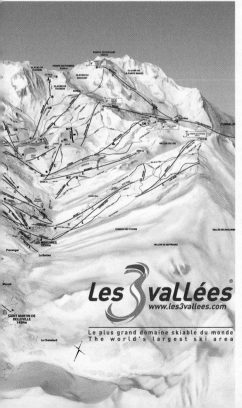

SNOWPIX.COM / CHRIS GILL

Tignes

Stark apartment blocks and a bleak, treeless setting are the prices you pay for the high, snow-sure slopes and varied terrain

£115
RESORT PRICE INDEX

RATINGS

The mountains

Extent	★★★★★
Fast lifts	★★★
Queues	★★★★
Terrain p'ks	★★★★
Snow	★★★★★
Expert	★★★★★
Intermediate	★★★★★
Beginner	★★
Boarder	★★★★★
X-country	★★★
Restaurants	★★★
Schools	★★★★
Families	★★★

The resort

Charm	★
Convenience	★★★★
Scenery	★★★
Eating out	★★★
Après-ski	★★★
Off-slope	★★

NEWS

2015/16: The new ski-in/ski-out 4-star Taos hotel and apartment building is due to open in December 2015 in Le Lac, with pool and spa. The final phase of the MGM/CGH Kalinda village at Tignes 1800 is now not due for completion until December 2016.

2014/15: The Rider Park, a new area with jumps for kids, was built at Le Lac. You can now rent electric cars for 20 euros a day.

➕	Good snow guaranteed for a long season; about the best Alpine bet
➕	One of the best areas in the world for lift-served off-piste runs
➕	Huge amount of varied terrain
➕	Lots of lodgings near the slopes
➕	Efforts to make the resort villages more welcoming are paying off

➖	Resort architecture not to everyone's taste (including ours)
➖	Bleak, treeless setting with lifts prone to closure in bad weather
➖	Still a few long, slow chairlifts
➖	Beginners need an area pass to get to long green runs

The appeal of Tignes is simple: good snow, spread over a wide area of varied terrain shared with Val d'Isère. The altitude of Tignes is crucial: a forecast of 'rain up to 2000m' means 'fresh snow down to village level in Tignes' (or at least to Tignes 2100, as they are now trying to rebrand the main resort).

We prefer to stay in Val, which is a more human place. But in many ways Tignes 2100 makes the better base: appreciably higher, more convenient, surrounded by intermediate terrain, and with quick access to the Grande Motte glacier. And the case gets stronger as the resort tries to make the place more attractive and as more traditional chalet-style buildings appear.

The lift system has improved, too, with a burst of fast chairs on the western side of the Tignes bowl a few years ago. But investment has stalled since then, and there are still a few key links that need upgrading.

THE RESORT

Tignes was created before the French discovered the benefits of making purpose-built resorts look acceptable. But things are improving, and the villages are gradually acquiring a more traditional look and feel.

Tignes-le-Lac is the hub of the resort and is itself split into two sub-resorts: Le Rosset and Le Bec-Rouge. It's at the point where these two meet – a snowy pedestrian area, with valley traffic passing through a tunnel beneath – that the lifts are concentrated: a powerful gondola towards Tovière and Val d'Isère, and a fast six-pack up the western slopes. There is also a suburb built on the lower slopes known as Les Almes. A nursery slope separates Le Rosset from the fourth component part, the group of apartment blocks called Le Lavachet, below which there are good fast lifts up both sides.

Val Claret is 2km up the valley, beyond the lake. From there, fast chairs head up towards Val d'Isère, up the western slopes opposite and to the Grande Motte. An underground funicular also serves the Grande Motte. Beside the road along the valley to

the lifts is a ribbon of development in traditional style, named Grande Motte (after the peak). Val Claret is built on two levels, which are linked by a couple of (unreliable) indoor elevators, stairs and hazardous paths.

Down the valley from the main villages (which are becoming known as Tignes 2100) are two smaller places. Tignes 1800 (which used to be called Tignes-les-Boisses) – set in the trees beside the road up – is in the

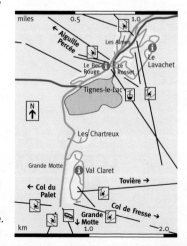

KEY FACTS

Resort	2100m
	6,890ft

Espace Killy

Slopes	1550-3455m
	5,090-11,340ft
Lifts	88
Pistes	300km
	186 miles

Tignes only

Slopes	1550-3455m
	5,090-11,340ft
Lifts	45
Pistes	150km
	93 miles

ADRIAN TAYLOR

This is a great pic of the terrain around Tignes: high, bleak, treeless and snow-sure – great when the sun is shining but not when it's snowing ↓

midst of a 150-million-euro redevelopment, with the new Kalinda Village being built by MGM. The first stage opened in December 2013, and the final stage is due to be ready for the 2016/17 season. Tignes-les-Brévières is a renovated old village at the lowest point of the slopes – a favourite lunch spot, and a friendly place to stay (but there's no bus service to the other Tignes 'villages'). Big gondolas from both these places arrive at the same point on the slopes.

VILLAGE CHARM ★
Functional, not fancy

Some of Tignes-le-Lac's smaller original eyesore buildings in the central part have been successfully revamped in chalet style. And some attractive new buildings have been added, both in the centre and on the fringes. But the blocks overlooking the lake from Le Bec-Rouge will remain monstrous until they are demolished. The buildings in the main part of Val Claret (Centre) are uncompromisingly 1960s style and set on a shelf above the valley floor.

So, if it's more charm you seek, stay in Les Brévières or 1800.

CONVENIENCE ★★★★
Good all rounder

Location isn't crucial, as a regular, free, 24-hour bus service (praised by reporters) connects all the villages except Les Brévières – but during the day the route runs along the bottom of Val Claret, leaving Val Claret Centre residents with a climb and there is no bus between Le Lac and Tignes 1800 at night.

A lift or ski run is never more than a few minutes' walk away in Le Lac. 'Convenience was the main reason we chose to go to Tignes for our holiday this year, and we were not disappointed,' said a recent reporter.

SCENERY ★★★
Great from the glacier

Tignes is in a high, bleak, treeless bowl; when the sun shines, the rugged mountain terrain is splendid, especially from the glacial heights of the Grande Motte.

THE MOUNTAINS

The area's great weakness is that it can become unusable in bad weather. There are no woodland runs except immediately above Tignes 1800 and Tignes-les-Brévières. Heavy snow produces widespread avalanche risk, and wind closes the higher chairs.

Piste classification here isn't perfect, but it is more reliable than in Val d'Isère, and signposting is clear. But we've had complaints that lift and piste closing time information is unreliable (and that sometimes information at the lift doesn't match the piste map).

We also had a complaint last year from someone who boarded a lift to

LIFT PASSES

Espace Killy

Prices in €

Age	6-day
under 14	208
14 to 64	260
65 plus	208

Free Under 5, over 75

Beginner Eight free lifts

Notes Covers Tignes and Val d'Isère; pedestrian passes; family discounts; 5-day+ passes valid for a day in the Three Valleys and a day in Paradiski (La Plagne-Les Arcs); 2-day+ pass gives one free access to pool and ice rink

Alternative pass
Tignes only

ski a blue run only to find that it was closed due to avalanche danger. The only option was a mogulled red: 'There should have been a warning sign at the bottom.'

EXTENT OF THE SLOPES ★★★★★
High, snow-sure and varied

Tignes and Val d'Isère share a huge area of slopes known as L'Espace Killy. Locally, Tignes' biggest asset is the **Grande Motte** – and the runs from, as well as on, the glacier. An underground funicular from Val Claret whizzes you up to over 3000m in seven minutes. There are blue, red and black runs to

play on up here, as well as beautiful long runs back to the resort.

The main lifts towards Val d'Isère are efficient: a high-capacity gondola from Le Lac to **Tovière**, and a fast chair from Val Claret to **Col de Fresse**. You can head back to Tignes from either lift: the return from Tovière to Tignes-le-Lac is via a steep black run, but there is an easier (though often crowded) blue run to Val Claret.

Going up the opposite side of the valley takes you to a quieter area of predominantly east-facing slopes split into two main sectors, linked in both directions – **Col du Palet** and the

At the top, the best snow in Espace Killy. Lower down, the lovely red back to Val Claret can be very crowded – try the scenic Génépy blue instead

LA GRANDE MOTTE
3455m/11,340ft

GLACIER

Col de la Leisse

3015m

COL DE FRESSE

Borsat

Val d'Isère

TOVIÈRE
2705m

Fresse

Grande Motte

Vanoise

Les Lanches

Tichot

Tommeuses

Tufs

Tovière

Bollin

Val Claret

Lavachet

Tignes-le-Lac

Daille

The only run from Tovière to Tignes-le-Lac is a black, and the blue run to Val Claret gets very busy. Accessing Tignes from Col de Fresse is more relaxing

Le Lavachet

Tignes
2100m/6,890ft

⊙ gondola
⊜ cable car
⊞ railway/funicular
⊛ fast chairlift
Slow chairs & drags have no symbol

IMPROVE YOUR SKIING
SKI WITH OTHERS
GO PLACES

SNOWORKS
snoworks.com

Aiguille Percée. Several years ago, this whole mountainside was at last given some of the fast lifts it had needed for years – but investment has stalled and some chairs still need modernizing. You can descend from the Aiguille Percée to Tignes-les-Brévières or Tignes 1800 on blue, red or black runs. There are efficient gondolas back.

FAST LIFTS ★★★☆☆
Improved but not good enough
Fast chairs and gondolas get you up the mountain from most parts of the resort. And there are some fast chairs higher up, too. But a few key slow ones remain that could do with being upgraded, including the Col des Ves chair at the south end of the Col du Palet sector and the Aiguille Percée chair above Tignes-le-Lac. The chairs above Tignes-les-Brévières and Tignes 1800 are also old and slow, and much in need of upgrading.

QUEUES ★★★★☆
Very few
Recent reporters have experienced very few queues, even in February half-term. But if snow low down is poor, the Grande Motte funicular can generate queues; the fast chairs in

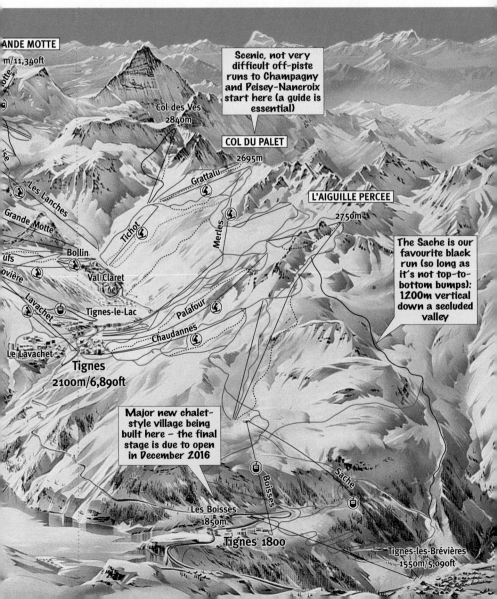

ANDE MOTTE
m/11,34oft

Scenic, not very difficult off-piste runs to Champagny and Peisey-Nancroix start here (a guide is essential)

Col des Ves
2840m

COL DU PALET
2695m

Grattalu

L'AIGUILLE PERCEE

2750m

The Sache is our favourite black run (so long as it's not top-to-bottom bumps): 1200m vertical down a secluded valley

Les Lanches

Tichot

Merles

Grande Motte

Bollin

Val Claret

Lavachet

Tignes-le-Lac

Palafour

Le Lavachet

Chaudannes

Tignes
2100m/6,89oft

Major new chalet-style village being built here – the final stage is due to open in December 2016

Boisses

Sache

Les Boisses
1850m

Tignes 1800

Tignes-les-Brévières
1550m/5,090ft

Like the resort?
You'll love our handpicked accommodation

02392
839 310

PEAKRETREATS.CO.UK

ABTA
ABTA No.W5657

Ski Total

WELCOME YOU TO

Tignes

Quality chalets
Excellent value
19 resorts
across the Alps

skitotal.com

01483 791 933

parallel with it are often quicker, despite the longer ride time. These lifts jointly shift a lot of people, with the result that the otherwise lovely Double M red run down to Val Claret can be unpleasantly crowded (the roundabout Génépy blue is a much quieter option).

The worst queues now are for the cable car on the glacier – half-hour waits are common. Of course, if higher lifts are closed by heavy snow or high winds, the lifts on the lower slopes have big queues. Otherwise there are usually very few problems. Crowded pistes can be more of an issue, and the blue Henri piste from Tovière to Val Claret and red Double M mentioned above are often unpleasantly crowded (and attract complaints from reporters).

TERRAIN PARKS ★★★★
Summer and winter options

Tignes was one of the first French resorts to build a terrain park, and it hosted four successive European Winter X Games until ESPN decided they were not financially viable. The park is beneath the Grattalu chair on Col du Palet and has rails and kickers split into XS, S, M and L levels of difficulty ('Terrific – I thoroughly enjoyed the range of obstacles,' says a 2015 visitor) and a snowcross course ('great fun'). In the summer the park doubles in size and moves up to the Grande Motte for freestyle camps. The 120m-long winter super-pipe is right at the bottom of the mountain in Val Claret, which means if it's open and you have the energy to hike, you can ride it for free. There's also an airbag jump at the bottom of Val Claret. And there's the Gliss park at town level in Le Lac with an airbag and mini-snowcross. So a day's freestyle for free is definitely an option.

29 LUXURY RESIDENCES IN THE FRENCH ALPS

• Spacious apartments, fully equipped for 2 to 12 persons
• Indoor heated pool
• Saunas, steam rooms, hot tub
• Ô Des Cimes Spa

CGH
Résidences & Spas

www.cgh-residences.com
contact@cgh-residences.com

SNOW RELIABILITY ★★★★★
Difficult to beat

Tignes has summer as well as winter skiing on its glacier area. And the resort height of 2100m generally means good snow-cover right back to base for most of the long winter season – November to May. The west-facing runs down from Col de Fresse and Tovière to Val Claret suffer from the afternoon sun, although they have serious snowmaking. Some of the lower east-facing and south-east-facing slopes on the other side of the valley can suffer late in the season, too. Grooming is generally good – 'Given the sparse snow conditions they did well,' says a 2014 visitor. But we've had a few complaints in the last couple of years: of moguls appearing on blue runs by lunchtime but not being bashed, black runs that were not 'naturides' being allowed to develop big moguls, and grooming leading to 'boilerplate conditions'.

FOR EXPERTS ★★★★★
An excellent choice

Tignes has converted many of its black runs into 'naturides', which means they are never groomed (a neat way of saving money!), but they are marked, patrolled and avalanche protected. Many of them are not especially steep (eg the Ves run – promoted from red status and now renamed after the local freeride hero Guerlain Chicherit). Perhaps the most serious challenge is the long black run from Tovière to Tignes-le-Lac, with steep, usually heavily mogulled sections (the top part, Pâquerettes, is now a naturide, but the bottom part, Trolles, is a normal black). Parts of this run get a lot of afternoon sun. Our favourite black run (still a 'normal' black) is the Sache, from the Aiguille Percée down a secluded valley to Tignes-les-Brévières. It can become very heavily mogulled, especially at the bottom – you can avoid this section by taking the red Arcosses piste option part-way down.

But it is the off-piste possibilities that make Tignes such a draw for experts, and the schools organize off-piste groups. See the feature panel overleaf for a few of the off-piste runs. The bizarre French form of heli-skiing is available here: mountaintop drops are forbidden, but from Tovière you can ski down towards the Lac du Chevril to be retrieved by chopper.

Tignes
Four-star apartments with pool and spa
skicollection.co.uk/
Tignes-Le-Lac
SKI COLLECTION
ABTA

FOR INTERMEDIATES ★★★★★
One of the best

For keen intermediate piste-bashers who like varied terrain and lots of it, the Espace Killy is one of the world's best areas.

Tignes' local slopes are ideal intermediate terrain. The runs on the Grande Motte glacier nearly always have superb snow. The runs from the top of the cable car are bizarrely classified red and black, but they are wide and mostly easy on usually fabulous snow, and could easily be blues. The Leisse run down to the chairlift of the same name is classified black and can get very mogulled, but usually has good snow. The red run all the way back to town is a delightful long cruise – though often crowded. The roundabout blue (Génépy) is much gentler and quieter.

From Tovière, the blue Henri run to Val Claret is an enjoyable cruise and generally well groomed. But, again, it can get very crowded.

There's lots to do on the other side of the valley, too, and the runs down from the Aiguille Percée to Tignes 1800 and Les Brévières are scenic and fun. There are red and blue options, and adventurous intermediates shouldn't miss the beautiful Sache black run. The runs from the Aiguille Percée to Tignes-le-Lac are gentle, wide blues.

FOR BEGINNERS ★★
Good nursery slopes, but ...

The nursery slopes of Tignes-le-Lac and Le Lavachet (which meet at the top) are excellent – convenient, snow-sure, gentle, free of through-traffic and served by a slow chair and a drag. The ones at Val Claret are less appealing: an unpleasantly steep slope within the village served by a drag, and a less convenient slope served by the fast Bollin chair. All of these lifts are free.

SKIWORLD
Catered chalets, hotels and self catering apartments in

Europe, USA and Canada

skiworld.co.uk
08444 930 430
ABTA V2151 ATOL 2036

Club Med

THE MOST COMPREHENSIVE
SKI PACKAGE ON THE MARKET

Tignes Val Claret 4♈

020 8313 3999
Skiline.co.uk

Skiline .co.uk

Although there are some fairly easy blues on the west side of Tignes, for long green runs you have to go over to the Val d'Isère sector. You need an Espace Killy pass to use them, and to get back to Tignes you have a choice between the blue run from Col de Fresse (which has a tricky start) or riding the gondola down from Tovière. And in poor weather, the high Tignes valley is an intimidatingly bleak place – enough to make any wavering beginner retreat to a bar with a book.

FOR BOARDERS ★★★★★
One of the best
Tignes has always been a popular destination for snowboarders because of easily accessible off-piste and lower prices than Val d'Isère. Quite a few top UK snowboarders make this their winter home. There are a few flat areas (avoid Génépy and Myrtilles), but the lift system relies more on chairs and gondolas than drags. There are long, wide pistes to blast down, such as Grattalu, Carline and Henri, with acres of powder between them to play in. And the backside of Col de Fresse in Val d'Isère is a natural playground. There are three specialist snowboard schools (Snocool, Rebel Alliance and Fresh Snowboarding) and a Welsh-run snowboarder chalet (www.dragonlodge.com).

FOR CROSS-COUNTRY ★★★★★
Interesting variety
There is a total of 20km of tracks on the frozen Lac de Tignes, along the valley between Val Claret and Tignes-le-Lac, at Tignes 1800 and Les Brévières and up on the Grande Motte.

MOUNTAIN RESTAURANTS ★★★★★
A couple of good places
The mountain restaurants are not a highlight. And reporters complain about charges for the toilet: 'I have never been anywhere so bad.'
Editors' choice Lo Soli at the top of the Chaudannes chair is a clear

A MECCA FOR OFF-PISTE SKIERS

Tignes is renowned for offering some of the best lift-served off-piste skiing in the world. There is a tremendous choice, with runs to suit all levels, from intermediate skiers to fearless freeriders and off-piste experts. Here's just a small selection. Don't go without a guide.

*For a first experience of off-piste, **Lognan** is ideal. These slopes – down the mountainside between the pistes to Le Lac and the pistes to Val Claret – are broad and not very difficult.*

*One of our favourite routes is the **Tour de Pramecou**. After a few minutes' walking at the bottom of the Grande Motte glacier, you pass around a big rock called Pramecou. There is then a multitude of possibilities, varying in difficulty – so routes can be found for skiers of different abilities.*

Petite Balme is a run for good skiers only – access is easy but it leads to quite challenging north-facing slopes in real high-mountain terrain, far from the pistes.

*To ski **Oreilles de Mickey** (Mickey's Ears) you start from Tovière and walk north along the ridge to the peak of Lavachet, where you get a great view of Tignes. The descent involves three long couloirs, narrow and pretty steep, that bring you back to Le Lavachet.*

*The best place to find good snow is the **Chardonnet** couloirs – they never get the sun. The route involves a 20-minute walk from the top of the Merles chairlift.*

*The **Vallons de la Sache** is one of the most famous routes – a descent of 1200m vertical down a breathtaking valley in the heart of the National Park, overlooked by the magnificent Sache glacier. Starting from the Aiguille Percée you enter a different world, high up in the mountains, far away from the ski lifts. You arrive down in Les Brévières, below the Tignes dam.*

*One of the big adventures is to go away from the Tignes ski area and all signs of civilization, starting from the Col du Palet. From there you can head for **Champagny** (linked to La Plagne's area) or **Peisey-Nancroix** (linked to Les Arcs' area) – both very beautiful runs, and not too difficult.*

favourite. From its terrace there's a superb view (shared with the adjacent self-service Alpage) of the Grande Motte. A couple of 2014 reporters were disappointed but a 2015 visitor said 'very cosy and friendly, outstanding burgers'. The table-service bit of the Panoramic at the top of the funicular competes: wonderful views, gourmet food with a wide-ranging menu; we had a good meal with charming east European service last season; endorsed by two 2015 reporters.

Worth knowing about On the nursery slope above Val Claret, the Chalet du Bollin has been recommended. So have the pizzas at the self-service at the top of Tovière ('big enough to share'); there's a good-looking table-service section too. The big Panoramic self-service at the top of the funicular gets crowded, but has great views from its huge terrace.

There are lots of easily accessible places for lunch in the resorts. One ski-to-the-door favourite of ours in Le Lac is the hotel Montana, on the left as you descend from the Aiguille Percée. Others are the Ferme des 3 Capucines, a short walk down from the bottom of the Chaudannes and Paquis chairs, and the Arbina; a recent reporter recommends Lo Terrachu; see 'Eating out' for more on these three.

In Val Claret past recommendations include: the Pignatta for quality and value, the Aspen Cafe for big portions and reasonable prices and Carline for convenience and speed.

At the extremity of the lift system, Les Brévières makes an obvious lunch stop. A short walk round the corner into the village brings you to places much cheaper than the two by the piste. Sachette (crammed with artefacts from mountain life) and Armailli have been recommended by past reporters.

SCHOOLS AND GUIDES ★★★★
Plenty of choice
There are over half a dozen schools, including three specialist snowboard schools, plus various independent instructors. Reporters advise that at busy times pre-booking is essential.

The last two reports we had on the ESF both involved children being taught mainly in French even though the instructors spoke good English; two children did not attend for their last day as a result. By contrast, a 2015 reporter and his son had lessons

Inghams

TIGNES
▶ Superb high altitude ski area-good for all skiers
▶ Exclusive Chalet Hotel Curling NOW on sale
▶ Buy 1 get 1 half price lift pass offers (terms apply)

inghams.co.uk 01483 371 236 ABTA V4871 ATOL 0025

in separate groups with Evolution 2; both had 'excellent tuition from instructors who spoke good English'.

A 2014 reporter's group thought British-run New Generation was 'fantastic', with 'patient instructors'.

Veteran British ski instruction guru Ali Ross has been running his Skiing Clinics here for decades (5-day courses; pre-booking required).

FOR FAMILIES ★★★★
Good facilities
Family specialist tour operator Esprit Ski runs chalets and comprehensive childcare here. We have had good reports in the past on the Marmottons kindergarten and British-run t4Nanny (www.t4nanny.com).

STAYING THERE

There's plenty to choose from, and more luxury options are appearing. The 229 room ski-in/ski-out Club Med in Val Claret has a pool, sauna, steam room and spa treatments.

Chalets Catered chalets run by UK tour operators are mainly in Le Lac. Skiworld has 15 chalets (some with sauna/hot tub) and the swanky 42-bed Ski Lodge Aigle with pool and sauna. Ski Total has chalet hotel Rosset (expanded for this season, including a pool, sauna and steam room) and 14 chalets, including some very smart places, lots with sauna and outdoor hot tub, one with pool, some with a steam room and two in their top-of-the-market Platinum range. Family specialist Esprit has seven chalets here, including the smart, 24-person Corniche, with sauna, steam room, hot tub and lifts to all floors.

Crystal has seven places, including two in its 'Finest' range. Inghams has four chalets (all with hot tub and/or sauna) and two chalet hotels (one in Val Claret and one in 1800).

Snowchateaux has two chalets, including Chardon, which used to be Robert Maxwell's private apartment; lovely large lounge with floor-to-ceiling windows, outdoor hot tub. And Mountainsun's chalet hotel Melezes in Tignes 1800 has a sauna and hot tub.

Hotels The few hotels are small and concentrated in Le Lac.

****Campanules** Smartly rustic chalet in upper Le Lac, with good restaurant.

****Taos** New for 2015/16. Ski-in/ski-out in Le Lac. 'New Mexico inspired decor.' Spa, pool, sauna, steam room.

****Village Montana** Stylishly woody, on east-facing slopes above Le Lac. Outdoor pool, sauna, steam, hot tub.

***Arbina** Well-run, close to the lifts in Le Lac with terrace, busy après-ski bar and one of the best restaurants.

***Diva** Biggest in town. On lower level of Val Claret. Comfortable rooms. Sauna, steam.

***Gentiana** In Le Lac. Friendly, pool, sauna, steam, hot tub. We stayed here happily a couple of seasons ago.

***Lévanna** Piste-side in Le Lac. Comfortable; big hot tub.

***Marais** Prettily furnished, simple hotel in Tignes 1800.

***Refuge** Oldest in Tignes (Le Lac).

Apartments There are lots of apartments in all price ranges. Ski Collection, Peak Retreats, Ski Amis, Erna Low, Ski Independence, PowderBeds and Skitracer have a range of options. The growing number of smart places include Jhana, Ferme du Val Claret, Nevada and Pierre & Vacances' Ecrin des Neiges in Val Claret; Taos, Télèmark and Residence Village Montana in Le Lac; and Santa Terra and Belvédère in Les Brévières. And in Tignes 1800 there's the first stage of the new MGM-built Kalinda Village apartments operated by CGH. All the above have access to pool, sauna etc, but at extra cost in some cases. Skiworld has 'flexible catered chalets' where you can choose what catering (if any) you want.

The supermarket at Le Lac is reported to be 'comprehensive but very expensive' – 'stock up in Bourg'.

EATING OUT ★★★
Few exciting options
The options in Le Lavachet are rather limited. Our favourite there is Ferme des 3 Capucines where we had a great dinner a couple of seasons ago: lovely food, reasonably priced, good service, nice rustic surroundings – endorsed

again by a recent visitor ('one to return to again and again'). And we have very positive reports of the good-value, British-run Brasero. In Le Lac, the Arbina has a very good restaurant upstairs and a simpler ground-floor brasserie which we and recent reporters have enjoyed ('great large pizzas', 'onion soup was a meal in itself'). British-run Lo Terrachu was highly recommended last year: 'Right on the lake, ridiculously good value, excellent wild boar.'

In Val Claret Pepe 2000 has 'friendly staff' and 'lovely pizzas'.

APRES-SKI ★★★
Hidden away
Reporters agree that there is plenty going on if you know where to find it. Val Claret has some early-evening atmosphere and popular happy hours. The Drop Zone has live music, a good atmosphere and a dance floor. Grizzly's log cabin is cool but pricey and has 'bears everywhere'. The Couloir has a big range of beers, wines and spirits. The Melting Pot nightclub attracts a lot of seasonaires.

Le Lac is a natural focus for après-ski drinks. The lively Loop has good DJs and live bands and a happy hour from 4pm to 6pm, while the Embuscade has 'good beer and music and attracts a slightly older crowd', said a happy 46-year-old. The bar of the hotel Arbina is our kind of spot – cosy with friendly service. It's a great place to sit outside and people-watch. The Alpaka Lodge bar is popular with Brits and a pleasant spot, especially if you manage to grab one of the sofas by the fire. Jack's is a popular late haunt (and has bowling alleys too).

OFF THE SLOPES ★★
Good leisure centre
Tignes is not a resort for those who do not want to use the slopes. And some activities get booked up quickly – a reporter said it was impossible to find a free dog sledding slot in April. The ice skating on the lake includes a 500m circuit as well as a conventional rink. This and the pools of the Lagon leisure centre (various pools, slides, wellness and fitness facilities, and praised by reporters) are free to use with a lift pass for two days or more. A reporter's kids 'really enjoyed' the bowling at Tignes-le-Lac. There's also snowmobiling, snowshowing and mountain biking on snow.

GETTING THERE

Air Chambéry 145km/ 90 miles (2hr); Geneva 225km/140 miles (2hr45); Lyon 220km/135 miles (2hr45); Grenoble 210km/130 miles (2hr45)

Rail Bourg-St-Maurice (30km/19 miles); regular buses or taxi from station

TOURIST OFFICE

www.tignes.net

L COLLINET

Val Cenis Vanoise

A fair-sized mountain above an unspoiled valley, with a row of unpretentious base villages offering attractively low prices

£80
RESORT PRICE INDEX

TOP 10 RATINGS

Extent	***
Fast lifts	***
Queues	****
Snow	***
Expert	**
Intermediate	****
Beginner	****
Charm	***
Convenience	***
Scenery	***

NEWS

2015/16: The resort's first 4-star hotel is due to open in Lanslebourg.

- + Prices well below the French norm
- + Some superb novice terrain
- + Varied terrain with fairly reliable snow – most slopes face north
- + High-quality, good-value apartments

- − Slow old lifts on upper slopes
- − Little to amuse experts on-piste
- − Quiet at night
- − Tedious long link from the westerly Termignon sector to the core sector

Val Cenis Vanoise is the ski area shared by three quiet, traditional villages in the unspoiled Haute Maurienne valley, on the Italian border south of Val d'Isère. If low prices and a low-key ambience appeal, it may be just the ticket.

The Haute Maurienne is the high eastern end of the great curving valley of the Arc. Its six main communities are marketed under the name Haute Maurienne Vanoise. Two of them – Lanslebourg and Lanslevillard – have for years used the brand name Val Cenis, and still do. And when a link was built with the slopes above distant Termignon, the resulting ski area was branded Val Cenis Vanoise. (No, we're not making this up.)

There are six main lift bases: the first resort you come to is Termignon; 6km on is Lanslebourg; then there's Les Champs, a group of apartment developments; then Lanslevillard, which has one main lift base on the outskirts and another nearer the centre; and finally its suburb, Le Haut, with the sixth lift.

There are other resorts in the Haute Maurienne, mostly covered in the Maurienne valley chapter that we have restored to the book this year. A pass is available covering days in several. And 40km down the road at Orelle is a gondola into the slopes of Val Thorens and so into the famously vast Three Valleys.

Village charm The villages are not chocolate-box pretty but solidly traditional. Lanslebourg is spread along the RN6 road, with no real focus but a range of shops and bars. Lanslevillard and Termignon are more captivating – less regularly arranged and with more character, but much quieter. The valley doesn't get a lot of sun in midwinter.

Convenience It's not difficult to find lodgings that are more-or-less ski-in,

VAL CENIS VANOISE TO / ANDRES

Pity the tourist office couldn't pick a better day to shoot pics of the Lanslevillard market ↓

KEY FACTS

Resort	1300-1460m
	4,270-4,790ft
Slopes	1300-2800m
	4,270-9,190ft
Lifts	28
Pistes	125km
	78 miles

LIFT PASSES

Prices in €

Age	6-day
under 12	140
12 to 64	170
65 to 74	153
Free Under 5, 75 plus	

Beginner One-day beginner passes available

Notes Covers Val Cenis Vanoise; Pack Tribu discount available for families or groups

Alternative pass
Eski-Mo pass also covers days in Aussois, Bonneval, La Norma and Valfréjus

ABTA
ABTA No W5537

Val Cenis
Four-star apartments at foot of slopes
02392
839 310

PEAKRETREATS.CO.UK/
VAL_CENIS

even if they are plod-out. There is a ski-bus shuttle between Lanslevillard and Lanslebourg, every 10 to 20 mins until 7pm. If staying in Les Champs, you're not within easy walking distance of either village.

Scenery The slopes are attractively wooded, and the Haute Maurienne gives a sense of unspoiled wilderness.

THE MOUNTAINS

There's a good mix of wooded lower slopes and open upper slopes.

Slopes There are three identifiable sectors. The main network of upper runs is above Lanslevillard. There are high-altitude links between this sector and the slopes around Col du Mont Cenis, above Lanslebourg. The slopes above Termignon are then reached by the long fast Turra chair followed by the slow Sources. There is a blue piste

back, but it is a pretty tedious affair; downloading on the Turra chair cuts out an interminable winding part.

Fast lifts Not a strong point: most of the lifts out of the valley are fast, but many upper ones are not.

Queues We lack recent high-season reports, but visitors in January, March and April had few problems.

Terrain parks There is a snow park and a snowcross, in theory at least. Reports welcome.

Snow reliability Most of the runs are north-facing, and there is snowmaking on the runs to each of the lift bases.

Experts The black pistes merit their colour, but don't add up to much. But there is a lot to do off-piste – routes from virtually all the upper lifts, some staying within the lift system, some ending up outside it. Sadly, most of the forest areas are out of bounds (eg the tasty glades above Termignon).

Intermediates There are intermediate runs all over the mountain, allowing for some top-to-bottom cruises of up to 1400m vertical. There are some satisfying, testing reds both above and below the treeline. Beware the Ecureuil linking run above Lanslevillard, which is a narrow nightmare when icy.

Beginners Termignon and Lanslevillard have good nursery slopes next to the villages, but the latter is much the better bet, with its lovely green runs down the length of several of the

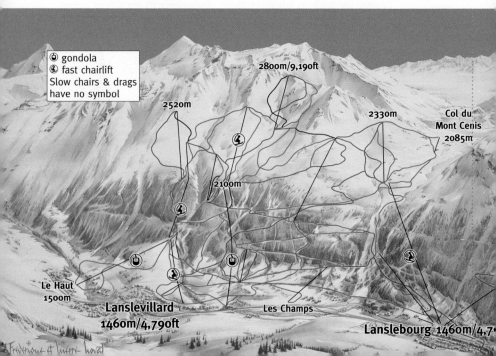

lower lifts. Then there's the splendid green from the Col du Mont Cenis to the valley, down the hairpins of the summer road to Italy.

Snowboarding Beginners should stay in Lanslevillard to avoid some long drags on the upper slopes.

Cross-country There are around 27km of trails locally, but enthusiasts will want to head 10km up the valley for the fab 130km of trails at Bessans.

Mountain restaurants Just enough places, not named on the resort piste map. We like La Ranova, near the Plan Cardinal chair – simple but good food in a cosy hut with wood stove. We skipped the Arole, above Termignon, and learned later that it is a revolver – the only one outside Switzerland.

Schools and guides We have generally good reports on the local branch of the ESF, though there are dissenting voices. Lack of good spoken English is an occasional problem.

Families 'A good resort,' says a reporter whose children particularly enjoyed the bowling in Lanslevillard.

STAYING THERE

Hotels The resort's first 4-star hotel is expected to open this season, at the foot of the slopes in Lanslebourg. That apart, the best in principle is the 3-star Moulin de Marie, also in Lanslebourg. It shares its restaurant with the next-door sister hotel, the

2-star Clé des Champs. There are half a dozen other 2-stars to choose from.

Apartments There is an excellent range of self-catering lodgings. Top of that range is the CGH residence Les Chalets de Flambeau at Les Champs; we stayed here very happily in 2015 – 'fantastic' pool, paddling pool, hot tubs, sauna and fitness. Readers also rate the Balcons de Val Cenis Village and Balcons de Val Cenis le Haut. Peak Retreats offers these and three other attractive residences.

Eating out There is a limited but adequate range of options. Last season we enjoyed a simple dinner at the Arcelle in Lanslevillard, on which occasion it was entirely filled by Brits. If you are prepared to make a bit of an effort l'Erablo, down the valley at Sollières, is worth a drive or taxi fare – very good food, charmingly served in a spacious farmhouse vault. Reader tips include Terroir Savoyard in Lanslevillard ('great – excellent food, exceptional service') and hotel des Deux Cols in Lanslebourg.

Après-ski Après-ski is quiet, but there are 'some nice bars'.

Off the slopes Lanslevillard has all the key facilities – a pool/spa complex, an artificial outdoor ice rink, a popular bowling alley with a lively bar, and a 900m toboggan run down the length of the gondola at Le Haut. Other activities include mountain biking.

TOURIST OFFICE
www.valcenis.com

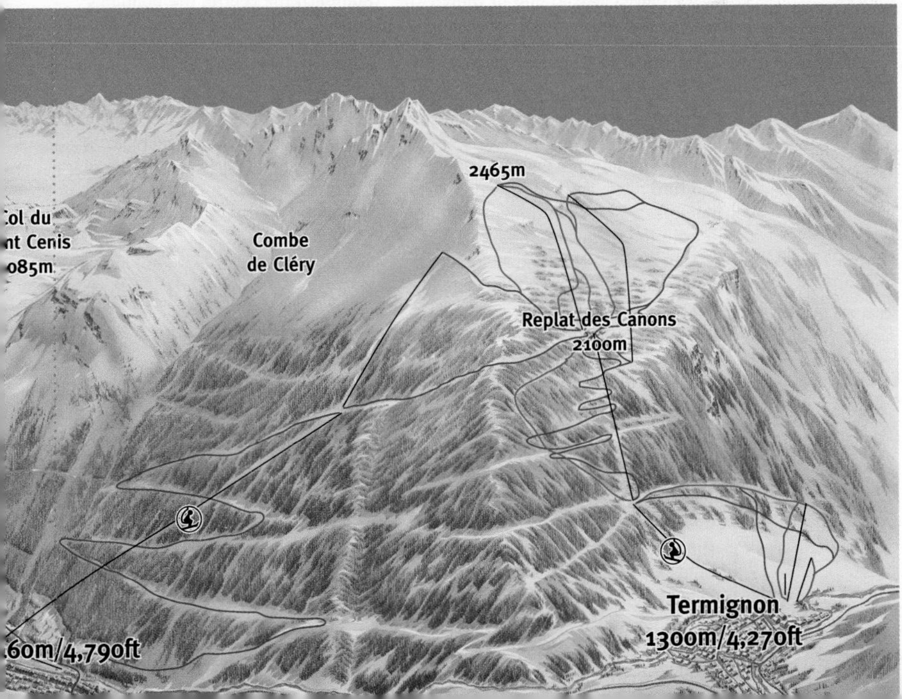

Val Cenis Vanoise

359

Col du
nt Cenis
o85m

Combe
de Cléry

2465m

Replat des Canons
2100m

Termignon
1300m/4,270ft

6om/4,79oft

OT VAL D'ISÈRE / AGENCE NUTS

Val d'Isère

One of the great high mega-resorts, particularly (though not only) for experts – with an attractive town at the base

£110
RESORT PRICE INDEX

RATINGS

The mountains

Extent	*****
Fast lifts	****
Queues	****
Terrain p'ks	***
Snow	*****
Expert	*****
Intermediate	*****
Beginner	***
Boarder	****
X-country	*
Restaurants	***
Schools	*****
Families	****

The resort

Charm	***
Convenience	***
Scenery	***
Eating out	*****
Après-ski	****
Off-slope	**

NEWS

2015/16: One new 5-star hotel is due to open – the Yule, right on the front de neige where the Grand Paradis used to be. Another, the Savoie, is to become a plush chalet hotel – see 'Staying there'.

2014/15: The Chalets du Jardin Alpin apartments were refurbished and are now 4-star with a sauna and steam room. A new après-ski bar, the Cocorico, opened as did a new nightclub, the Bunker.

+ Huge area shared with Tignes, with lots of runs for all abilities

+ One of the great resorts for lift-served off-piste runs

+ Once the snow has fallen, high altitude of slopes keeps it good

+ Wide choice of schools, especially for off-piste lessons and guiding

+ For a high Alpine resort, the town is attractive, is lively at night, and offers a good range of restaurants

+ Wide range of package holidays, including some comfortable chalets

− Some green and blue runs are too challenging, and all runs back to the village are tricky

− You're quite likely to need buses at the start and end of the day (but they are very frequent and efficient)

− Many lifts and slopes are liable to close when the weather is bad

− It can seem more British than French for much of the season

− Expensive eating and drinking; it's one of the priciest resorts in France for this – and readers complain

Val d'Isère is one of the world's best resorts for experts – who are attracted by the extent of lift-served off-piste – and for confident, mileage-hungry intermediates. You don't have to be particularly adventurous to enjoy the resort; but it would be much better for novices and timid intermediates if the piste classifications were more reliable.

The drawbacks listed above are not crucial for most people, whereas most of the plus-points weigh heavily in the balance. For a combination of seriously impressive skiing and pleasant village ambience, it is difficult to beat.

THE RESORT

Val d'Isère spreads along a remote valley that is a dead end in winter. The road in from Bourg-St-Maurice brings you dramatically through a rocky defile to La Daille – a convenient but hideous slope-side apartment complex – and the base of lifts into the major Bellevarde sector of the slopes.

Carry on into the centre of town and turn right, and you drive under the nursery slopes and major lifts up to both the Bellevarde and Solaise sectors to a lot of new development. Continue up the main valley instead, and you come first to Le Laisinant, a peaceful little outpost with a fast lift into the slopes, and then to Le Fornet, the fourth major lift station.

The developments up the side valley beyond the main lift station – in Le Châtelard and La Legettaz – are mainly attractive, and some offer ski-in/ski-out convenience. La Daille and Le Fornet have their (quite different) attractions for those less concerned about nightlife. A car is of no great value around the resort.

VILLAGE CHARM ★★★☆☆
Much improved but...

The outskirts are dreary, but as you approach the centre, the buildings become much more attractive (chalet-style, clad in wood and stone) and the central Val Village complex is traffic-free. Many first-time visitors find the resort much nicer than they expected but reporters this year complain of 'loud arrogant Brits' spoiling the place.

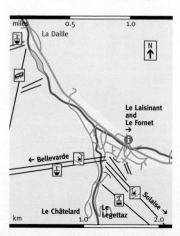

KEY FACTS

Resort	1850m
	6,070ft

Espace Killy	
Slopes	1550-3455m
	5,090-11,340ft
Lifts	88
Pistes	300km
	186 miles

Val d'Isère only	
Slopes	1785-3300m
	5,860-10,830ft
Lifts	43
Pistes	150km
	93 miles

VAL D'ISERE TO

The central area is attractive, with chalet-style buildings. The run you can see is the Face black piste coming down from Bellevarde ↓

CONVENIENCE ★★★☆☆
Mostly fine

There is a lot of traffic around, but the resort has worked hard to get cars under control and has made the centre more pedestrian-friendly. The location of your accommodation isn't crucial, unless you want to ski from the door or be close to a nursery slope. The main lift stations are served by very efficient and amazingly frequent free shuttle-buses; but in peak periods you may have to let a few full ones pass before there's space to board. After 8pm they run every 20 minutes until 2.45am.

SCENERY ★★★☆☆
Valley deep, mountain high

The resort sprawls along a steep-sided river valley, beneath a series of high and partly wooded mountain ridges. There are splendid views from the Pissaillas glacier.

THE MOUNTAINS

Although there are wooded slopes above the village on all sectors, in practice most of the runs here are on open slopes above the treeline, and a lot of lifts can close in bad weather. Signposting is good. But Val d'Isère vies with St Anton for the title of 'resort with most underclassified slopes'. Many blue and some green runs (including runs to the valley) are simply too steep, narrow and even bumpy; in other resorts they would be reds, or even blacks; we have a hefty file of complaints from readers who agree with our judgement. The local radio (96.1 FM) carries weather reports in English as well as in French.

EXTENT OF THE SLOPES ★★★★★
Vast and varied

Val d'Isère's slopes divide into three main sectors, two reachable from the village. **Bellevarde** is the mountain that is home to Val d'Isère's two famous downhill courses: the OK piste that has been used for the World Cup events and the Face piste that was used for the 1992 Winter Olympics and the 2009 World Championships. You can reach Bellevarde quickly by underground funicular from La Daille or the powerful Olympique gondola from near the centre of town. From the top you can descend to the valley, play on a variety of drags and chairs at altitude or take a choice of lifts to Tignes' slopes (see separate chapter).

Solaise is the other mountain accessible directly from the village. The Solaise fast quad takes you a few metres higher than the parallel cable car. Once up, a short drag or rope tow takes you over a plateau and down to a variety of chairs that serve this very sunny area of predominantly gentle pistes. From near the top of this area you can catch the fast Leissières chair (which climbs over a ridge and down the other side) to the third main area,

Le Ski
the chalet specialists

❄ Most chalets with outdoor hot tub
❄ Civilised Sunday flights included
❄ Delicious food and wine
❄ Genuine, friendly service

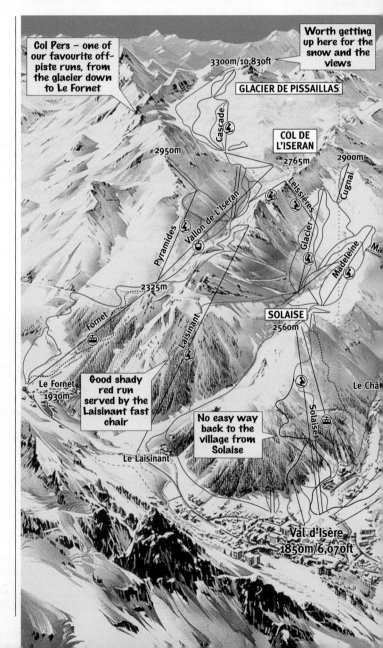

Col Pers – one of our favourite off-piste runs, from the glacier down to Le Fornet

Worth getting up here for the snow and the views

3300m/10,830ft

GLACIER DE PISSAILLAS

Cascade

2950m

COL DE L'ISERAN
2765m

2900m

Leissières

Cugnai

Pyramides

Vallon de L'Iseran

Glacier

Madeleine

Ma

2325m

SOLAISE
2560m

Fornet

Laisinant

Le Châ

Le Fornet
1930m

Good shady red run served by the Laisinant fast chair

Solaise

No easy way back to the village from Solaise

Le Laisinant

Val d'Isère
1850m/6,070ft

33 YEARS IN BUSINESS
100% FINANCIAL PROTECTION

30 CATERED CHALETS
VAL D'ISÈRE
COURCHEVEL LA TANIA
01484 954397 LESKI.COM

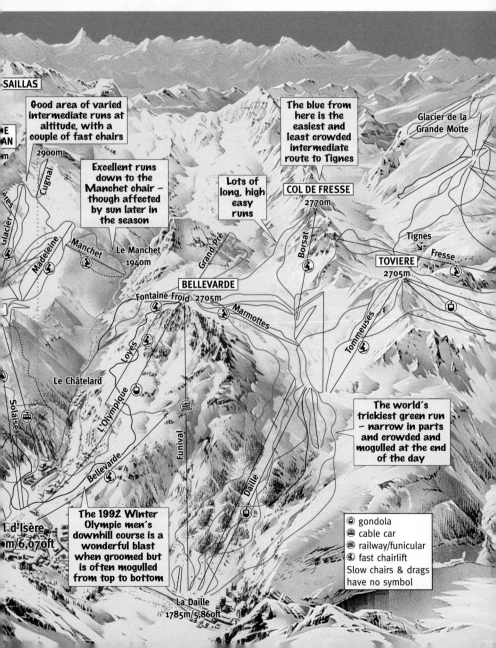

SAILLAS

Good area of varied intermediate runs at altitude, with a couple of fast chairs

2900m

Excellent runs down to the Manchet chair – though affected by sun later in the season

Lots of long, high easy runs

The blue from here is the easiest and least crowded intermediate route to Tignes

Glacier de la Grande Motte

COL DE FRESSE
2770m

Tignes

Fresse

TOVIERE
2705m

Cugnai

Madeleine

Manchet

Le Manchet
1940m

Grand Pré

Borsat

Tommeuses

BELLEVARDE

Fontaine Froid   2705m

Marmottes

Loyes

Le Châtelard

L'Olympique

The world's trickiest green run – narrow in parts and crowded and mogulled at the end of the day

Solaise

Bellevarde

Funival

Daille

l. d'Isère
m/6,07oft

The 1992 Winter Olympic men's downhill course is a wonderful blast when groomed but is often mogulled from top to bottom

La Daille
1785m/5,86oft

🚠 gondola
🚡 cable car
🚞 railway/funicular
🚠 fast chairlift
Slow chairs & drags have no symbol

LIFT PASSES

Espace Killy

Prices in €

Age	6-day
under 14	208
14 to 64	260
65 plus	208

Free under 5, over 75
Beginner Five free lifts on nursery slopes

Notes Covers Tignes and Val d'Isère; pedestrian passes; family discounts; 5-day-plus passes valid for a day in the Three Valleys and a day in Paradiski (La Plagne-Les Arcs); 2+ day pass gives one free entry to pool at Aqua Sports Centre

Alternative pass
Val d'Isère only

in the valley running up to the **Col de l'Iseran**. This area can also be reached by the fast chair from Le Laisinant or by cable car from Le Fornet. At the top here is the **Glacier de Pissaillas**.

FAST LIFTS ★★★★
Access all areas
High-capacity lifts provide good access from the valley, and there are lots of fast chairs higher up. But there are still a few slow chairs and draglifts around.

QUEUES ★★★★
Few problems
Queues to get out of the resort have been kept in check by lift upgrades and additions – but there can be a short wait at the Olympique gondola up Bellevarde. On Solaise the slow Lac chair back up to the Tête Solaise can generate queues. Crowded pistes in high season is a more common complaint than queues.

TERRAIN PARKS ★★★
Beginners and experts welcome
The park is above the La Daille gondola and served by the Mont Blanc chairlift. There are lines to suit every level from beginner to expert freestylers. There are lots of rails of all shapes and sizes, four kicker lines from easy to pro plus various features (see www.valdisere-snowpark.com).

There's also a cool zone in the middle of the park, where you can just sit back and enjoy the show. Nearby is a mini-snowcross course (P'tit cross) aimed specially at kids. 'Lots of fun jumps and mini-snowcross for the kids and me,' confirmed a recent reporter. There's a full-fledged, 800m long snowcross in the Grand Pré area. But head to Tignes for a super-pipe.

SNOW RELIABILITY ★★★★★
One of the best
In years when lower resorts have suffered, Val d'Isère has rarely been short of snow. In our experience of many late-April visits, even in poor snow years, decent skiing is still available. Once a big dump of snow has fallen, the resort's height means you can almost always get back to the village. But what's even more important is that in each sector there are lots of lifts and runs above mid-mountain, between about 2300m and 2900m. Many of the slopes face roughly north. And there is access to glaciers at Pissaillas or over in Tignes. There's substantial snowmaking too.

FOR EXPERTS ★★★★★
One of the world's best
Val d'Isère is one of the top resorts in the world for experts. The main attraction is the huge range of

---

THE BEST LIFT-SERVED OFF-PISTE IN THE WORLD?

Few resorts can rival the extent of lift-served off-piste skiing in Val d'Isère. Here is a selection of what's on offer. But don't try any of it without a guide and essential safety equipment.

*Some runs are ideal for adventurous intermediates looking to try off-piste for the first time. The **Tour du Charvet** was Editor Watts' first-ever off-piste run; it goes through glorious scenery from the top of the Grand Pré chairlift on the back of Bellevarde. For most of the way it is very gentle, with only a few steeper pitches. It ends up at the bottom of the Manchet chair up to the Solaise area. The **Pays Désert** is an easy run with superb views on the Pissaillas glacier, high above Le Fornet and reached by traversing from the top of the lift system. You end up at the Pays Désert draglift.*

*For more experienced off-piste skiers, **Col Pers** is one of our favourite runs. Again, it starts with a flat traverse from the Pissaillas glacier. You go over a pass into a big, fairly gentle bowl with glorious views and endless ways down. If there is enough snow, you drop down into the Gorges de Malpasset and ski over the frozen Isère river back to the Fornet cable car. If not, you can take a higher route.*

***Cugnai** is a wide, secluded bowl reached from the chair of the same name at the top of the Solaise sector. A steep (37 degree) slope at the far end descends beneath a sheer black rock wall and then narrows into a gully to the valley floor, leading to the Manchet chair.*

***Banane** is reached via the Face de Bellevarde piste and is a long and impressive run (37 to 40 degrees) with spectacular views over the Manchet valley. For a real challenge intrepid experts should try the **Couloir des Pisteurs,** which requires a 20-minute climb from the Tour de Charvet. The view from the top is simply stunning. A very narrow steep couloir (44 degrees) bounded by rock faces brings you out on to a wide open slope above Le Grand Pré, right opposite Bellevarde.*

Then there's the whole of Tignes' extensive off-piste to explore, of course.

CHECK OUT THE VIRTUAL TOUR ONLINE

FROM JUST
£999
PER PERSON

Proudly introducing our exclusive 5 ✦ Platinum Chalet Hotel Le Savoie, in the heart of Val d'Isère

- Substantial breakfast with a choice of cooked and continental options
- Daily afternoon tea with a selection of cakes and savouries
- 5 course dinners (6 nights per week) with a choice of menu, including pre-dinner apéritif, a choice of complimentary wines and tea/coffee & chocolates to follow
- In-house ski rental, Spa area and beauty treatments and massages
- Huge choice of rooms and suites
- Renowned **ESPRIT** Child Care available in peak weeks

ABTA
Travel with confidence

FIND OUT MORE ABOUT OUR NEW PROPERTY, ONLY AVAILABLE THROUGH:

ESPRIT Ski
No1 For Family Skiing

Inghams

THE CHALET SPECIALIST
Ski Total

espritski.com/savoie
Call 01483 791 900

inghams.co.uk/savoie
Call 01483 791 111

skitotal.com/savoie
Call 01483 791 933

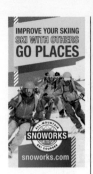

IMPROVE YOUR SKIING
SKI WITH OTHERS
GO PLACES

SNOWORKS
ALL MOUNTAIN SKI COURSES

snoworks.com

Club Med ♈

THE MOST COMPREHENSIVE
SKI PACKAGE ON THE MARKET

Val d'Isere 4 ⁛

020 8313 3999
Skiline.co.uk

Skiline.co.uk

beautiful off-piste possibilities – see the feature panel.

There may be better resorts for really steep pistes – there are certainly lots in North America – but there is plenty of on-piste action to amuse most experts, despite the small number of blacks on the piste map. And some of these have been converted to 'naturides', which means they are never groomed but they are marked, patrolled and avalanche protected. Many reds and blues are also steep enough to get mogulled.

On Bellevarde the famous Face run is the main attraction – often mogulled from top to bottom, but not worryingly steep and it's a wonderful blast if it's been groomed. Epaule is the sector's other black run; where the moguls are hit by long exposure to sun, it can be slushy or rock hard (it is prone to closure for these reasons too). Most of the blacks on Solaise and above Le Fornet are now naturides (and the proper black from Solaise to the valley is no steeper than the alternative red).

Wayne Watson of off-piste school Alpine Experience puts a daily diary of off-piste snow conditions and runs on the web at www.alpineexperience.com.

FOR INTERMEDIATES ★★★★★
Quantity and quality
Val d'Isère has just as much to offer intermediates as experts. There's enough here to keep you interested for several visits – though pistes can be crowded in high season, and the less experienced should be aware that many runs are underclassified.

The Solaise sector has a network of gentle blue runs, ideal for building confidence. And there are a couple of beautiful runs from here through the woods to Le Laisinant – ideal in bad weather, though prone to closure in times of avalanche danger.

Most of the runs in the Col de

l'Iseran sector are even easier – ideal for early and hesitant intermediates. Those marked blue and red at the top of the glacier are really very easy cruises on usually very good snow.

Bellevarde has a huge variety of runs ideally suited to intermediates of all levels. From Bellevarde itself there is a choice of green, blue and red runs of varying pitch. The World Cup downhill OK piste is a wonderful rolling cruise when groomed. The wide runs from Tovière normally offer the choice of groomed piste or moguls.

A snag for early intermediates is that runs back to the valley can be challenging. The easiest way is down to La Daille on a green run that would be classified blue or red in most resorts. It gets very crowded and mogulled by the end of the day. None of the runs from Bellevarde and Solaise back to Val itself is easy. Many early intermediates ride the lifts down.

FOR BEGINNERS ★★★★★
OK if you know where to go
The nursery slope right by the centre of town is 95% perfect; it's just a pity that the very top is unpleasantly steep. The lifts serving it are free.

Once off the nursery slopes, you have to know where to find easy runs; some of the greens should be blue, or even red (see the warning in the last paragraph of 'For intermediates' above). One local instructor admits: 'We have to have green runs on the map, even if we don't have so many green slopes – otherwise beginners wouldn't come to Val d'Isère.'

A good place for your first real runs off the nursery slopes is the Madeleine green run on Solaise, served by a six-pack. The Col de l'Iseran runs are also gentle and wide, and not overcrowded. There is good progression terrain on Bellevarde, too – though getting to it can be tricky. From all sectors, it's best to take a lift back down to the valley.

FOR BOARDERS ★★★★★
Watch out for flats
Val d'Isère's more upmarket profile attracts a different kind of holiday boarder from Tignes; the resort is, perhaps, seen as Tignes' less hard-core cousin. But the terrain here is great for freeriders. The easier slopes are suitable for beginners, and there are very few draglifts. But there are quite a few flat areas where you'll end up scooting or walking.

FOR CROSS-COUNTRY ★☆☆☆☆
Limited

There are a couple of loops in each of three areas – towards La Daille, on Solaise and out past Le Laisinant. More picturesque is the loop going from Le Châtelard (on the road past the main cable car station) to the Manchet chair. But keen cross-country enthusiasts should go elsewhere.

MOUNTAIN RESTAURANTS ★★★☆☆
Acceptable – but expensive

For such an upmarket resort, there are surprisingly few enjoyable places to eat on the mountain. The major places are self-service and at the top of lifts. Everywhere gets busy and high-season service can be poor. Reporters complain how 'hideously' expensive they are and that in many, even if you are eating there, you have to pay to use the toilets.

Editors' choice The wood-and-stone Edelweiss, above Le Fornet, is our favourite for the best food and ambience. We've had delicious lamb, duck and fish; reporters regularly send us rave reviews too. It's a bit cramped inside and, if it's a nice day, we prefer the sunny terrace. On Bellevarde, we had a superb lunch on the terrace of the Fruitière at the top of the La Daille gondola (delicious beef stew and lamb shepherd's pie, attentive service). Inside is kitted out with stuff from a dairy, but tables are very crammed in.

Worth knowing about On Bellevarde, the busy table-service Trifollet halfway down the OK run is atmospheric, reasonably priced and does a good plat du jour. The Marmottes, near the base of the chair of the same name, is one of the cheapest places to eat – an efficient self-service with a big sunny terrace, helpful staff and good food. The Peau de Vache, set between the two chairs going up Bellevarde, serves 'burgers that beat anything Soho can offer – they are truly wonderful'.

On Solaise, the Bar de L'Ouillette, at the base of the Madeleine chairlift, has a fun terrace with artificial palm trees, deck chairs and a barbecue ('lovely chicken in spicy sauce').

Above Le Fornet, the Signal at the top of the cable car is our favourite; it has self- and table-service sections and a takeaway snack bar – and reporters have recommended all three. The Cascade self-service by the foot of the chairlift with the same name is light and airy with good food.

Val d'Isère
A LA CARTE

Personalised skiing holidays in Val d'Isere from the resort specialists.

Insider knowledge of Val d'Isere. Centrally located apartments, chalets and hotels. Flexible dates available.

0033 629 89 44 57
info@skivaldisere.co.uk

www.skivaldisere.co.uk

Of course, there are lots of places in the resort villages. Arolay at Le Fornet does 'a rustic grill', and the two Michelin-starred Atelier d'Edmond (decorated like a carpenter's workshop and opposite the Fornet cable car) now has a cheaper 'gourmet bistro' open most lunchtimes with a two-course menu at 21 euros. The terrace of hotel Brussel's in Val d'Isère, right by the nursery slopes, is 'very good and has good service'. The Sun Bar at the base of the Olympique cable car is 'decent quality', as is the Tartine. At La Daille, Tufs is 'good quality at reasonable prices'. In town, the coffee shop in the Quiksilver store serves smoothies and '17 types of burger'.

SCHOOLS AND GUIDES ★★★★★
A very wide choice

There is a huge choice of schools, guides and private instructors – about 20 schools at the last count. But as they all get busy, at peak periods it's best to book in advance. Practically all the schools run off-piste groups as well as on-piste lessons.

The Development Centre (TDC) is a group of British instructors that offers intensive clinics for all levels: 'Excellent, Steve Angus was brilliant with my son, inventive, fun, engaging, made his holiday!' says a recent reporter. New Generation and Progression are other British-run schools that get good reports.

Two 2015 reporters were pleased with Evolution 2 ('both children's technique advanced and their confidence visibly grew').

A 2015 reporter had an 'excellent morning' off-piste with Snowboard Val d'Isère. Pro Snowboarding has been recommended by a past reporter too.

Alpine Experience specializes in guided off-piste groups – an excellent way to get off-piste safely without the cost of hiring a guide as an individual.

SKIWORLD

Catered chalets, hotels and self catering apartments in

Europe, USA and Canada

skiworld.co.uk

08444 930 430

ABTA V2151 ATOL 2036

ALPINE ANSWERS
The UK's No.1 Chalet Specialist

For choice and service look no further!

alpineanswers.co.uk
call: 020 7801 1080

ABTA

We have had great mornings out with them, and reporters recommend them too. Another off-piste guiding specialist is iSki. Long-standing off-piste favourites Top Ski changed ownership a few years ago. Heli-skiing trips can be arranged.

Henry's Avalanche Talks are now on demand at various venues – see www. henrysavalanchetalk.com – and are 'really impressive', says a reporter.

FOR FAMILIES ★★★★☆
Good tour op possibilities
Many people prefer to use the facilities of UK tour operators such as family specialist Esprit Ski. But there's a 'children's village' for children from 18 months to 13 years, with supervised indoor and outdoor activities on the village nursery slopes. And Petit Poucet takes children from age three and will pick them up and take them home at any time during the day.

STAYING THERE

More British tour operators go to Val (and Méribel) than anywhere else. Val d'Isère à la Carte specializes in fixing tailor-made holidays there. Club Med has a smart place with a pool, sauna and steam room: a reporter who has stayed there three times says it has 'excellent food and facilities'.
Chalets This is Planet Chalet, with properties at every level of the market. The big news for 2015/16 is that one of the top 5-star hotels, the Savoie right in the centre of the resort, with sauna, steam room, hot tub and small counter-current pool will be run as a swanky chalet hotel to be shared by sister companies Inghams, Ski Total and Esprit. In addition, Inghams has four other chalets, including one right on the nursery slope and a 24-bed chalet hotel specially built for them with sauna and hot tub in Le Fornet.

Ski Total has 14 other smart places, including two very swanky ones in their Platinum range (one with outdoor hot tub, one with a sauna) plus a chalet hotel sleeping 80 at La Daille. Esprit, the family specialist, also has a central chalet hotel with 31 bedrooms ('excellent food, friendly staff, rooms a good size'). YSE is a Val d'Isère specialist, with 20 varied chalets – from swanky apartments for four or six to proper big chalets. Le Ski has nine chalets, including two luxury places in a back street of La Daille: Chalet Angelique for 12 which inside looks more like a mini-stately home than a chalet (and has a steam room and gym) and Kanjiroba for 10, which dates from the 18th century and was totally refurbished for last season ('gorgeous chalet, beautifully restored'). Le Ski also has six splendid places grouped together just up from the main street with a big outdoor hot tub. Skiworld has 10 varied chalets from the very plush chalet Madeleine with outdoor hot tub to more modest places, plus a smart 33-bedroomed chalet hotel with sauna, steam, hot tub. Crystal has six chalets, including three smart central ones with saunas in their Finest range. There are some very luxurious chalets from operators like VIP, Consensio and Scott Dunn.
Hotels There are over 30, with increasing numbers at the luxury end: five 5-stars and six 4-stars.
★★★★★Avenue Lodge Central, fairly new. Modern decor, comfortable rooms.
★★★★★Barmes de L'Ours Near slopes and centre. Rooms are in a different style on each floor. Excellent pool.
★★★★★Blizzard Central. Comfortable. Indoor-outdoor pool, sauna, steam, hot tub. Good food and lively bar.
★★★★★Christiania Big chalet. Chic but friendly. Pool, sauna.
★★★★Aigle des Neiges Central. Pool, sauna. 'Good rooms and breakfast.'
★★★★Auberge St Hubert On main street. Family-run, friendly.
★★★★Samovar Facing the piste in La Daille. Fully renovated for last season. Small pool, sauna, steam room.
★★★★Tsanteleina On main street. Pool, hot tub, two steam rooms, sauna.
★★★Kandahar Smart building above Taverne d'Alsace on main street.
★★★Sorbiers Modern but cosy chalet, not far out.
★★Danival B&B, piste-side location.
★★Galise Central, family-run B&B.
Forêt Central, recently refurbished.

Sauna, hot tub, 'Basic rooms, very friendly staff, outstanding food.'

Apartments There are thousands of apartments available. Among the best are Chalets du Jardin Alpin at the foot of Solaise (refurbished for 2014/15), Chalets du Laisinant (at Le Laisinant) and Pierre & Vacances' Balcons de Bellevarde at La Daille and Chalets de Solaise (with outdoor pool) close to the centre. Ski Collection, Ski Amis, Ski Independence, Erna Low, Skitracer and local agency Val d'Isère Agence have good selections. Skiworld has flexible catered chalets, where you can choose what catering (if any) you want, and also apartments.

EATING OUT ★★★★★
Plenty of good places
The 70-odd restaurants offer a wide variety of cuisines; there's a free booklet covering some, but many worthwhile places are missing.

At the top end, two places have Michelin stars: L'Atelier d'Edmond at Le Fornet (see 'Mountain restaurants') has two and La Table de l'Ours, in the Barmes de l'Ours hotel, has one; but the latter got the thumbs down last year from a regular reporter ('pretentious, expensive, slow service'). The Grande Ourse, by the nursery slope, also serves top-notch meals, and we had a delicious dinner there on our last visit – endorsed by two 2015 reporters ('a real gem'). The rustic Vieille Maison ('excellent, good value') behind the main road at La Daille and Arolay at Le Fornet (see 'Mountain restaurants') are rated highly by locals.

There are plenty of pleasant mid-priced places. Perdrix Blanche was a reader favourite but, sadly, we have heard it may be closing down. Bar Jacques is regularly recommended for its excellent food and set menu ('good rib of beef' says a recent visitor). Casserole has been recommended for its 'good food and ambience'. Corniche has a lovely traditional atmosphere and is regularly praised.

Other reporter tips are: Etable d'Alain ('an old barn with farm animals on view, a 15-minute walk down the Manchet valley'); Table d'Yvonne ('simple place above 5 Frères hotel'); Casa Scara (Italian); Bar 1789 ('terrific steak, yummy potato gratin'); Chez Paolo is ('good for simple pizzas'). New last season was L'Arbre de Vie, which serves Moroccan/French dishes.

APRES-SKI ★★★★
Plenty of choice
There are lots of bars, many with happy hours and then music and dancing later on.

The Folie Douce, at the top of the La Daille gondola, has become an institution: live bands, DJs, cabarets, packed crowds and dancing on tables on the terrace every afternoon; you can ride the gondola down. It has now been replicated in four other resorts. But a local tells us that Cocorico, by the piste just above the Solaise lift, 'is fast taking over. All the live music, DJs and atmosphere without being as pretentious. Great set up.'

The Moris pub (live music at teatime and later) and Saloon (under hotel Brussel's) fill up as the slopes close. The 'friendly' Blue Note (opposite the ESF) has a 'great low-key atmosphere'. Café Face is popular, with loud music. Boubou and Bar Jacques are popular with locals. Bar Alexandra is 'atmospheric'. The Pacific Bar has sport on big-screen TVs. Baraque is a 'very trendy' wine bar with 'a great vibe, live music, with good food'. Bananas is 'fun'. The basement Taverne d'Alsace is quiet and relaxing, as are Bar XV, the first-floor bar of the hotel Blizzard, and Wine Not (er, a wine bar). The coffee shop in the Quiksilver store serves fresh smoothies. The 'great fun' Grand Marnier serves 'tempting cocktails'.

Later on, Dick's Tea Bar is the main disco (go early evening for Val's 'best-value drinking', says a reporter). Doudoune is 'more expensive but nicer'. Graal is 'usually good'. If you've any stamina left the new Bunker is open until 6am.

OFF THE SLOPES ★★
A reasonable amount to do
The sports centre (with two pools, sauna, steam, hot tub, gym, climbing wall) is consistently praised by reporters; a lift pass for two days or more gets you one free swim. There's an outdoor ice rink, ice driving, snowmobiling, snowshoeing, dog sledding, paragliding and ice climbing. The range of shops is better than in most high French resorts. There are a few mountain restaurants that are easy for pedestrians to get to. A reporter says the nature walk from Le Fornet to Pont St Charles in late season is 'fascinating'; others enjoyed the January 'polo on snow' tournament.

GETTING THERE

Air Chambéry 145km/ 90 miles (2hr); Geneva 225km/ 140 miles (2hr45); Lyon 220km/ 135 miles (2hr45); Grenoble 210km/ 130 miles (2hr45)

Rail Bourg-St-Maurice (30km/19 miles); regular buses from station

TOURIST OFFICE

www.valdisere.com

JEANNE CATTINI

Valmorel

The purpose-built resort the French got mainly right: easy on the eye, as well as convenient; sadly, they didn't pick the ideal site

£90
RESORT PRICE INDEX

TOP 10 RATINGS

Extent	★★★
Fast lifts	★★
Queues	★★★
Snow	★★
Expert	★★
Intermediate	★★★★
Beginner	★★★★★
Charm	★★★★
Convenience	★★★★
Scenery	★★★

NEWS

2014/15: A new 'Pirates Adventure' zone was created. CGH opened a new apartment residence, La Grange aux Fées.

This followed the arrival in 2012 of a very smart Club Med above the village.

- ➕ A sympathetically designed purpose-built, car-free resort
- ➕ Largely slope-side accommodation
- ➕ Extensive easy slopes linked to St-François-Longchamp
- ➕ Beginners and children particularly well catered for

- ➖ Few challenges on-piste
- ➖ Mostly low, so snow is a worry; and snowmaking is not comprehensive
- ➖ Still lots of slow lifts and drags
- ➖ Steep site, with outlying lodgings very separate from the resort core
- ➖ Few alternatives to self-catering

Built from scratch in the mid-1970s, Valmorel is unlike any of its contemporaries – its central development feels like a tiny mountain town. The resort has gone up in the world recently, in terms of accommodation; but the ski area, to be frank, is lagging some way behind – and it is never going to compete with its illustrious neighbours in the next-door Three Valleys.

THE RESORT

Valmorel is the main resort in 'Le Grand Domaine' – the ski area it shares with St-François and Longchamp, across the Madeleine pass (closed in winter). The Three Valleys resorts are within driving distance.
Village charm Le Bourg is the heart of the resort – an intimate, traffic-free street where you'll find most of the shops and restaurants. It is a pleasant and relaxing place. All the outlying developments are in chalet style.
Convenience Lodgings are widely spread over the hillside above Le Bourg in six or seven identifiable groups. Many places are ski-in/out, but some involve some plods, especially on the way out. Le Bourg is linked to the suburbs directly above it by the

Telebourg pedestrian gondola. Buses serve other parts, such as Club Med.
Scenery The resort sits among lightly wooded, hilly slopes. Although modest in height, there are good views to the Maurienne valley from the main peaks.

THE MOUNTAINS

The village is well below the treeline, but most runs are on open slopes. The resort uses the label 'snowcross' for three ungroomed but avalanche-controlled runs – two black, one red.
Slopes The pistes are spread over a number of minor valleys and ridges either side of the Col de la Madeleine. Which lift you start with will depend on where you are staying, but the basic choice is a gondola to the Pierrafort sector on the left or the fast Altispace chair towards the Madeleine

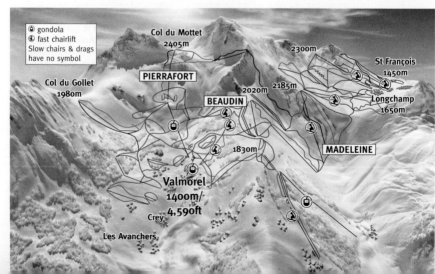

- ⊙ gondola
- Ⓕ fast chairlift
- Slow chairs & drags have no symbol

Col du Mottet 2405m

2300m

Col du Gollet 1980m

PIERRAFORT

St François 1450m

2020m 2185m

BEAUDIN

Longchamp 1650m

1830m

MADELEINE

Valmorel 1400m/ 4,590ft

Crey

Les Avanchers

↑ Most of the lodgings are separate from the resort core, spread across the hillside; Club Med is on the right here

VALMOREL TO

KEY FACTS

Resort	1400m
	4,590ft

Le Grand Domaine	
Slopes	1250-2550m
	4,100-8,370ft
Lifts	50
Pistes	152km
	94 miles

Valmorel only	
Slopes	1250-2405m
	4,100-7,890ft
Lifts	39
Pistes	95km
	59 miles

LIFT PASSES

Grand Domaine

Prices in €

Age	6-day
5 to 7	141
8 to 12	183
13 to 64	216
65 to 74	183
Free Under 5, 75 plus	
Beginner Limited pass	
Note Family discounts	

TOURIST OFFICE

www.valmorel.com

sector and the slopes of Longchamp and St-François. There are links at mid-mountain. On the left of the Valmorel slopes (looking up) is the most testing terrain, served by two slow chairs to Col du Gollet and Col du Mottet.

Fast lifts There are fast chairs on the main links, but still a lot of draglifts and slow chairs around the area.

Queues The Altispace chair may be busy in the morning rush.

Terrain parks There are two beginner parks and one intermediate-advanced, and two 'boardercross' courses.

Snow reliability The area is low by local standards, and quite sunny – not good news. There's snowmaking on the nursery slopes and the main runs back to base, but it can't be called comprehensive. (We were struck on visiting last season that the run down to the new Club Med was in much better shape than the run below it.)

Experts The black pistes are not serious, but the 'snowcross' runs provide a challenging mix of steepness and bumps. There is good off-piste that doesn't get skied out.

Intermediates The whole area – except for the steeper snowcross runs – is ideal, though the main home run can be quite daunting for the timid.

Beginners A good place to start. There are dedicated beginner areas at Creve-Coeur (one of the higher parts of the village) and at the top of the gondola, quiet green runs on the Rocher and Blanchot drags (on the extreme left of the mountain) and a network of easy blues to move on to.

Snowboarding There are decent intermediate runs; but there are lots of drags in key places.

Cross-country Trails adding up to 20km can be reached by bus.

Mountain restaurants There's just a handful. We like the Prariond, on the lower slopes of the Pierrafort sector – adequate menu, good crêpes, efficient service when lounging on terrace sofas enjoying the view of the hill.

Schools and guides The ESF appears to have a monopoly.

Families Valmorel has always gone out of its way to cater for children; there are good, gentle nursery slopes and play areas. Piou Piou club is a comprehensive childcare facility run by the ski school.

STAYING THERE

Valmorel has taken great strides in this department in recent years. Apartments still dominate, but less so than in the past. At the end of 2012 a swanky new four-trident Club Med opened high above the village, with 25 five-trident suites in The Lodge.

Hotels The hotel du Bourg is a central no-frills place, recently refurbished and upgraded to 3 stars.

Apartments A major development is that last season CGH opened a residence, La Grange aux Fées, with the usual CGH amenities – good pool, hot tubs, spa. It's bookable through Peak Retreats (as is hotel du Bourg). We hear all the Pierre & Vacances units have been refurbished recently; in the past the Athamante et Valeriane apartments have been tipped.

Eating out There's a handful of places in Le Bourg – mostly traditional fare.

Après-ski Immediate après-ski centres on the lively cafe-bars with terraces at the foot of the slopes; it's pretty quiet later on.

Off the slopes It's not a great place to hang around, but there are various activities, such as paragliding, snow-shoeing and horse sleigh rides. The spa at the CGH residence is open to the public. There's a cinema and a toboggan run.

Club Med

THE MOST COMPREHENSIVE
SKI PACKAGE ON THE MARKET

Valmorel 4

020 8313 3999
Skiline.co.uk

Skiline.co.uk

SNOWPIX.COM / CHRIS GILL

Val Thorens

Europe's highest resort, with guaranteed good snow – and other attractions, stylish lodgings and good restaurants among them

£115
RESORT PRICE INDEX

RATINGS

The mountains

Extent	★★★★★
Fast lifts	★★★★★
Queues	★★★★
Terrain p'ks	★★★★
Snow	★★★★★
Expert	★★★★
Intermediate	★★★★★
Beginner	★★★★
Boarder	★★★★
X-country	★
Restaurants	★★★★
Schools	★★★
Families	★★★

The resort

Charm	★★
Convenience	★★★★★
Scenery	★★★
Eating out	★★★★
Après-ski	★★★★
Off-slope	★★

372

NEWS

2015/16: Yet another five-star hotel is to open, Le Pashmina. A new red piste is to be added.

2014/15: The fast Portette quad was replaced by a six-pack starting at a lower point. The Boismint sector of the slopes was redesigned, with the slow Plan de l'Eau chair replaced by a six-pack finishing higher up. A new Club Med opened at the top of the village.

➕ Extensive slopes for all abilities, plus access to the Three Valleys

➕ One of the most snow-sure resorts

➕ Fastest lift system in France

➕ Compact, with ski-in/out lodgings

➕ Convenient, gentle nursery slopes

➕ Decent range of hotels and some very smart apartments

➖ Not a tree in sight

➖ Away from the front de neige, not an attractive place to walk around

➖ Not ideal for non-skiers

➖ Some very crowded pistes and dangerous intersections

➖ Queues for the justifiably popular Cime Caron cable car

Val Thorens continues its gradual drift upmarket, with a fourth 5-star hotel about to open. But it remains a top place for the enthusiast looking for the best snow available and fast lifts to whizz you around. For a late trip, in particular, it's the best base in the wonderful Three Valleys. But we normally prefer a cosier base lower down. That way, if a storm socks in, we can play in the woods; if it's scorchio, we can set off for Val Thorens.

THE RESORT

Val Thorens is a classic purpose-built resort, high above the treeline at the head of the valley it shares with Les Menuires and St-Martin. Buses to/from Les Menuires are supposed to carry just pedestrians and cross-country skiers, not downhillers – crazy!

VILLAGE CHARM ★★
Functional but pleasantly so
Seen from the slopes, the resort is not as ugly as many of its rivals, and it has quite a lively ski resort buzz. Buildings are mainly medium-rise and wood-clad; some are distinctly stylish. But many are designed with their smart 'fronts' facing the slopes, and look very dreary from behind – the walk up the road to the centre from plush lodgings in the lower part of the village is very dull. The streets are supposedly traffic-free except for loading. But workers' cars generate traffic and Saturdays can be mayhem. You're advised to book parking in advance; or look for lodgings with an underground garage.

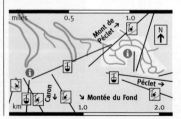

CONVENIENCE ★★★★★
Ski through the centre
It's a compact village with lots of ski-in/ski-out lodging. At its heart is the snowy Place de Caron, on the slope side rather than the street side of the central buildings, where pedestrians mix with skiers and boarders. Many of the shops and restaurants are here, along with some nice hotels; the sports and leisure centres are nearby.

The resort is divided in two by a little slope (with a moving carpet lift) that leads down from here to the broad nursery slope running the length of the village (also served by moving carpets). The upper half of the village is centred on the Place de Péclet, where there is one of two shopping malls. A road runs across the hillside from here to the chalet-style Plein Sud area, where many of the catered chalets run by UK tour operators are located. You can ski to and from some of these places, but it's often very tricky – walking can be too (we've had complaints of icy, uncleared paths).

The lower end of the village has some of the plushest lodgings, including 5-star places.

A free ski-bus runs every 20 minutes on two separate routes.

SCENERY ★★★
Panoramas on high
The resort sits on a sunny, west-facing slope. The views are merely good from the village, but fabulous from the high point at Cime de Caron.

KEY FACTS

Resort	2300m
	7,550ft

Three Valleys	
Slopes	1260-3230m
	4,130-10,600ft
Lifts	180
Pistes	600km
	373 miles

Val Thorens-Orelle only	
Slopes	1800-3230m
	5,900-10,600ft
Lifts	32
Pistes	150km
	93 miles

THE MOUNTAINS

The main disadvantage of Val Thorens is the lack of trees. Heavy snowfalls or high wind can shut practically all the lifts and slopes, and even if they don't close, poor visibility can make skiing extremely unpleasant. Some blue runs are pretty tough.

EXTENT OF THE SLOPES ★★★★★
High and snow-sure
The resort has a wide piste going right down the front of it, leading to a number of different lifts. The big **Péclet** gondola heads more or less east from the resort and rises 700m to the Péclet glacier, with a choice of red runs or a blue down. Two of these link across to a wide area of runs beneath the ridge directly south of the resort, the high point of which is the **Pointe de Thorens**. Lifts go up to three other points on the ridge. You can take very sunny red or blue runs into the 'fourth valley', the Maurienne, from the Col de Rosaël on the ridge, served by the Grand Fond jumbo gondola.

Above **Orelle** in the Maurienne valley a six-pack followed by a slow quad go up to 3230m on the flanks of Pointe du Bouchet, the highest lift-served point in the Three Valleys – stunning views.

The 150-person cable car to **Cime de Caron** is one of the great lifts of the Alps, rising 900m in no time at all. It can be reached by skiing across from mid-mountain, or via the Caron gondola that starts below the village. From the top there is a choice of red and black pistes down the front, or a black into the Maurienne. Nearby, the relatively low **Boismint** sector is underused, but it is a very respectable hill with a total vertical of 860m. It got a new fast chair last season.

Chairlifts heading north from the

Ski Total

WELCOME YOU TO

Val Thorens

Quality chalets
Excellent value
19 resorts
across the Alps

skitotal.com

01483 791 933

resort serve sunny slopes above the village and also lead to the link to the Méribel valley. Les Menuires can be reached via these lifts; the alternative Boulevard Cumin along the valley is nearly flat, and can be hard work.

FAST LIFTS ★★★★★
France's fastest lift system
Recent investment means the lift system is impressive, with jumbo gondolas and fast chairs in most of the key places. The lift upgrades last season mean that more than 80% of all major lifts are fast – many more than any other French resort.

QUEUES ★★★★☆
An increasing problem
Serious peak-time queues for the Cime Caron cable car are a continuing problem, although some reporters last year were pleased to find only short queues. The place as a whole seems to be getting busier and therefore less appealing every time we visit – but most reporters seem happy. Crowded pistes, especially around the village, are a bigger problem than queues – made worse by people going too fast. We agree with a recent reporter who suggests that it is time the resort imposed slow skiing zones around the village – and policed them.

Val Thorens

373

VAL THORENS TO / B LONGO

It's one of the best-looking purpose-built French resorts, particularly at the higher levels of the village ➔

TERRAIN PARKS ★★★★
Well designed

The terrain park on the 'Plateau' has been improving year-on-year. It is accessible via various chairlifts, is served by a dedicated draglift and has a nice open layout. There are different areas that range from beginner to pro, with all sorts of features, plus an airbag jump. There's a separate snowcross lower down.

SNOW RELIABILITY ★★★★★
One of the best

Few resorts can rival Val Thorens for reliably good snow-cover, thanks to its altitude and generally north-facing slopes. Snowmaking covers a lot of the key pistes, including the crowded south- and west-facing runs on the way from the Méribel valley and in the Orelle sector. But the terrain is rocky and needs a lot of snow – we have found the higher runs patchy in early season when snow throughout the Alps has been slow to arrive, and at times like that the off-piste terrain is inherently hazardous. 'Grooming is satisfactory,' say reporters.

FOR EXPERTS ★★★★
Lots to do off-piste

Val Thorens' local pistes are primarily intermediate terrain; many of the

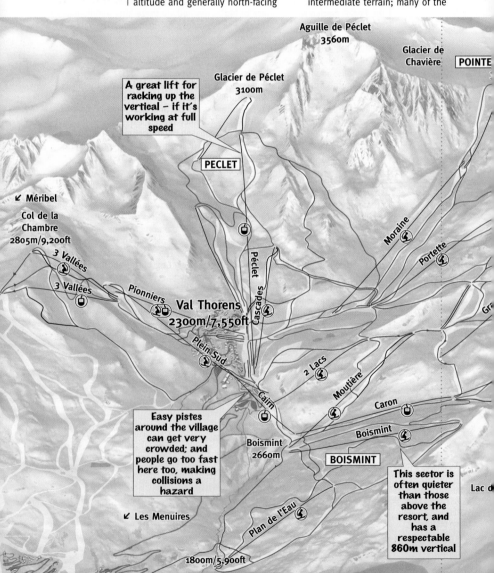

Aguille de Péclet
3560m

Glacier de Chavière

POINTE

Glacier de Péclet
3100m

A great lift for racking up the vertical – if it's working at full speed

PECLET

Moraine

Portette

Méribel

Col de la Chambre
2805m/9,200ft

3 Vallées

3 Vallées

Pionniers

Péclet

Cascades

Val Thorens
2300m/7,550ft

Plein Sud

2 Lacs

Moutière

Caron

Gr

Calm

Boismint

Easy pistes around the village can get very crowded; and people go too fast here too, making collisions a hazard

Boismint
2660m

BOISMINT

Lac d

This sector is often quieter than those above the resort, and has a respectable 860m vertical

Les Menuires

Plan de l'Eau

1800m/5,900ft

blacks could easily be classified red instead. The fast Cascades chair serves a short but steep black run that quickly gets mogulled. The pistes down from the Cime Caron cable car are challenging, but not seriously steep, and there's a good, sunny black run off the back into the fourth valley.

The Falaise and Variante runs from the Grand Fond gondola can get heavily mogulled and be challenging. The sunny Goitschel run, one of the routes from the Méribel valley, is one of the easiest blacks we've seen, but it can be icy in the morning and slushy in the afternoon.

There is a huge amount of very good off-piste terrain to explore with a guide; read our feature panel overleaf. But it does require good snowfall – note our remarks in 'Snow reliability'.

FOR INTERMEDIATES ★★★★★
Great in good weather

The scope for intermediates in the Three Valleys is enormous. A keen intermediate can get to Courchevel 1650 at the far end of the network in only 90 minutes or so, if not distracted on the way.

The local slopes in Val Thorens are some of the best intermediate terrain in the region. Most of the pistes are easy reds and blues (steeper on the

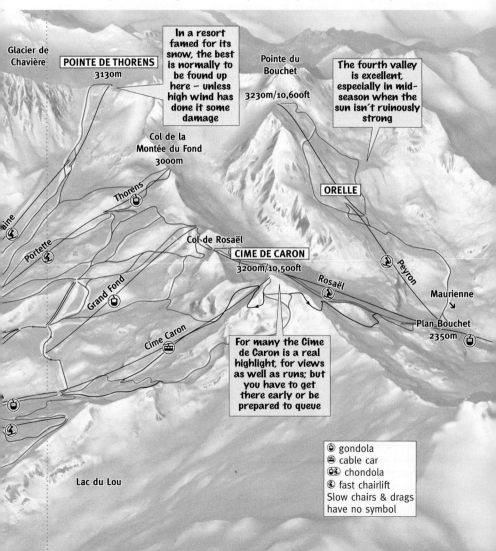

Glacier de Chavière

POINTE DE THORENS
3130m

In a resort famed for its snow, the best is normally to be found up here – unless high wind has done it some damage

Pointe du Bouchet
3230m/10,600ft

The fourth valley is excellent, especially in mid-season when the sun isn't ruinously strong

Col de la Montée du Fond
3000m

Thorens

ORELLE

Portette

Col de Rosaël

CIME DE CARON
3200m/10,500ft

Grand Fond

Rosaël

Peyron

Maurienne

Cime Caron

Plan Bouchet
2350m

For many the Cime de Caron is a real highlight, for views as well as runs; but you have to get there early or be prepared to queue

Lac du Lou

ⓖ gondola
🚠 cable car
Ⓒ chondola
Ⓕ fast chairlift
Slow chairs & drags have no symbol

SKIWORLD

Catered chalets, hotels and self catering apartments in

Europe, USA and Canada

skiworld.co.uk

08444 930 430

ABTA V2151 ATOL 2036

Club Med

THE MOST COMPREHENSIVE SKI PACKAGE ON THE MARKET

Val Thorens 4★

020 8313 3999
Skiline.co.uk

Skiline.co.uk

LIFT PASSES

Three Valleys

Prices in €

Age	6-day
under 13	228
13 to 64	283
65 plus	255

Free Under 5, 75 plus

Beginner Access to Cairn, 2 Lacs and Caron lifts for 50% of Val Thorens rate; free access to one draglift and four moving carpets

Notes Covers Courchevel, La Tania, Méribel, Val Thorens, Les Menuires and St-Martin; reductions for families, duos and groups. Options: pedestrian and half-day passes

Alternative passes Val Thorens-Orelle only; Vallée de Belleville only

top half of the mountain than the bottom) and made even more enjoyable by the excellent snow.

The snow on the red Col run is normally some of the best around. The blue Moraine below it is gentle and popular with the schools. The Grand Fond gondola serves a good variety of blue and red runs. The red and blue runs from the Péclet gondola are excellent. The Pluviomètre from the Three Valleys chair is a glorious varied blue, but is often very busy – the Mont de la Chambre from much the same area is a good alternative route to the resort, although signed for Les Menuires.

Adventurous intermediates shouldn't miss the Cime de Caron runs: the black here is very wide, usually has good snow, and is a wonderful fast cruise when freshly groomed (though reports suggest this is less likely than it was). Don't neglect the excellent, quiet Boismint area next door to Caron, either.

Blue-run skiers can now venture to the fourth valley, with the return run improved a few years back to become a blue (though not an easy one).

FOR BEGINNERS ★★★★
Good late-season choice
The slopes at the foot of the resort are very gentle and provide convenient, snow-sure nursery slopes, with four moving carpet lifts, one draglift and green runs. These are free, and there is a 50% reduction on the main lift pass for four serious lifts on the lower slopes – an excellent package. There are no long green runs to progress to, but the blues immediately above the village are easy. But it's a rather intimidating place in bad weather.

FOR BOARDERS ★★★★
Reliable all season
Val Thorens has always been popular with snowboarders; it is the highest and most snow-sure of the Three Valleys resorts, and has a younger feel compared with Courchevel and Méribel – though it's almost as pricey. There are great steep runs, gullies and groomed pistes for all levels. The terrain park is worth a visit. The lifts are mainly chairs and gondolas.

FOR CROSS-COUNTRY ★
Go to Les Menuires
There are no cross-country trails in Val Thorens. Your best bet is the 28km link between Les Menuires and St-Martin-de-Belleville.

MOUNTAIN RESTAURANTS ★★★★
Lots of choice
For a high modern resort, the choice of restaurants is good, and improving. The piste map names the restaurants – unlike the maps of the other valleys. It's such a simple thing ...
Editors' choice The self-service Folie Douce and table-service Fruitière are

FABULOUS OFF-PISTE IN VAL THORENS

Val Thorens offers a huge choice of off-piste to be explored with a guide. And because of the high altitude, the snow stays powdery longer here than in lower parts of the Three Valleys.

For those with little off-piste experience, the Pierre Lory Pass run is ideal. It is a wide and gentle slope, reached by an easy traverse on the Chavière glacier from the top of the Col chairlift and with breathtaking views of the Aiguilles d'Arves in the Maurienne valley from the top. You then ski down the glacier du Bouchet, rejoining the lift system at Plan Bouchet.

For those with more off-piste experience, the Lac du Lou is a famous off-piste run of 1400m vertical that is easily accessible via various routes from the Cime de Caron. Because many of the slopes face north or north-west it is not unusual to find good powder most of the ski season, even in late April. The views are stunning and you'll notice the quietness and vastness of the whole valley. La Combe sans Nom in the fourth valley is also accessible from the Cime de Caron and is excellent for late season spring skiing conditions.

For the more adventurous there are many options, including hiking up from the Col chairlift to a long run over the Gébroulaz glacier down to Méribel-Mottaret.

ABTA
ABTA No.W5537

High quality, high altitude

Four-star luxury residence
Koh-I Nor in Val Thorens
Door-step skiing in a quiet setting
suited to families • Based in the heart
of the Three Valleys • Accommodation
only or self-drive package deals
Call us on **02392 890 960**
skicollection.co.uk/Val-Thorens

A WORLD-CLASS FRENCH ALPS EXPERIENCE
SKI COLLECTION .CO.UK

Val Thorens

modelled on the Val d'Isère originals, the latter with an interesting menu, well executed when we last lunched there on the somewhat cramped terrace. We've had several good lunches in the rustic table-service part of the Chalet de la Marine, and it's endorsed this year by two reporters – 'lovely place, fantastic food, spacious, big tables'; 'professional but friendly staff, good value menu of two courses plus amazing dessert buffet'.

Worth knowing about After some years in the wilderness, the Caribou had good reports last year and this – 'fantastic food, good value plat du jour, superb service'. The Chalet des 2 Ours usually gets good reports and is the favourite spot of one repeat visitor, but there is one dissenting voice this year. We had a good lunch at the rustic Chalet des 2 Lacs a few seasons ago – warm, welcoming, log fire, good food – but we could do with more reports.

SCHOOLS AND GUIDES ★★★★★
Good reports

A reporter writes: 'There are various schools, including ESF, Ski Cool and Prosneige, and we have used them all over the years. They all have English-speaking instructors though you may still find yourself in a mixed class where English is not used as much as you would like.' Evolution 2, well known elsewhere, set up here last year. Prosneige is a small school that limits class sizes to 10 and gets very good reports. There are several guiding outfits.

FOR FAMILIES ★★★★★
Some facilities

There is a children's area, Espace Junior, beside the 2 Lacs chairlift, and a good family toboggan run. The tourist office produces a handy family guide to weekly activities.

STAYING THERE

Accommodation is of a higher standard than in many purpose-built resorts – more comfortable and stylish. A couple of smart recent developments blur the line between hotels and apartment residences; following the tourist office, we treat them as hotels. Club Med is well established here, too, and last year moved to a cool new development further up the hill.

Chalets There are no notably swanky places. Most catered chalets are apartments in quite big developments – mainly relatively new ones set well above the resort centre. This has the advantage that you often have the use of a pool, sauna, etc in the residence. Inghams has six of these apartment chalets. Skiworld has 17 units, from 6-bed apartments to the 24-bed 'superior' chalet Phoenix, with sauna and access to a spa. Crystal has nine units, most with use of shared sauna and pool. Ski Total has five units that are more like actual chalets – two units in one, three in another, all with shared saunas. And it has a stand-alone chalet for 24 with use of the pool and sauna at a nearby residence.

Hotels Unusually for a high, purpose-built resort, there are plenty of hotels, now including four 5-stars.

★★★★★Altapura A reporter liked the 'unfussy atmosphere' of this stylish 5-star, with 'tip-top food and service'. Indoor/outdoor pool etc.

★★★★★Koh-I Nor Rooms and suites, right at the top of the resort. Top chef. Pools, fitness, spa etc. Apartment residence next door.

★★★★Hameau du Kashmir Suites and apartments, at the resort entrance. We stayed here, and found it comfortable, but a bit cramped. Pool, spa etc.

★★★Sherpa Highly recommended by a reporter last year. Cosy, lots of wood, 'friendly, great rooms, very good food,

↑ The Val Thorens Folie Douce was the first attempt to replicate the original Val d'Isère experience

VAL THORENS TO / J SCHNEIDER

regular'), the Fondue, Auberge des Balcons, Chaumière, Cabane, Steak Club. The Blanchot is a wine bar with a simple carte. An old favourite, the Galoubet, has become La Maison Blanche – 'a traditional brasserie'.

APRES-SKI ★★★★
Livelier than you might expect
Val Thorens is more lively than most high-altitude ski stations. The action starts conspicuously up the hill at the Folie Douce, with its compulsory table dancing – the second in the ever-expanding chain. The Red Fox up at Balcons is crowded at close of play, with karaoke. The Frog and Roastbeef at the top of the village is a long-established British ghetto. The Downunder and the Saloon are lively. Quieter bars include the cosy Rhum Box Cafe (aka Mitch's). Later on, the Malaysia cellar bar rocks from 11pm until the early hours with 'top-quality' live bands and dancing.

OFF THE SLOPES ★★
OK for the active
Val Thorens is not ideal for non-skiers. But there's a sports centre with two small pools, sauna, steam, hot tubs, gym etc and a leisure centre with bowling (pricey) and pool tables. Free weekly concerts are held in the church, and there are twice-weekly street markets, a small cinema and an ice-driving course. The toboggan run (6km – the longest in France) is 'great fun'. There are four walking trails marked on the reverse of the piste map. A pedestrian lift pass covers 11 lifts, allowing access to some mountain restaurants and the Cime de Caron. There's a 'fantastic' 1.3km zipwire, Segway rides, mountain biking. Buses to St-Martin and Les Menuires run four times a day except Saturdays.

small spa – loved it'. Ski-in/ski-out.
***Val Chavière 'Excellent location for the town and the lifts, rooms good, excellent food and very friendly.'
Apartments Val Thorens now has lots of smart chalet-style developments. These and many other residences are offered by Ski Collection and other UK agents who advertise with us.

Note that the swanky Koh-I Nor and Hameau de Kashmir hotels listed above also offer apartments.

In the Plein Sud area, above the main village, there are several chalet-style residences. Among the best are Chalet Altitude and Chalet Val 2400, sharing a pool. The Balcons de Val Thorens has a 'fantastic' spa with pool. Many properties up here claim to be ski-in and possibly ski-out, but a couple of reporters have confirmed our own suspicion that access can be tricky. Down near the entrance to the resort are more very smart places, all with pool, sauna etc, including the Montana Plein Sud and Oxalys.

EATING OUT ★★★★
Star quality
Top of the range is the Jean Suplice restaurant in the Oxalys residence, with two Michelin stars. We had a delicious and very inventive meal here some years ago; expensive, but worth it. L'Epicurien now has one star. The top hotels have serious restaurants – the Koh-I Nor has a starred chef.

There are plenty of more modest places. Recent reader tips include the Petite Ferme ('prompt service, tasty traditional food'), the Chamois d'Or ('superb, varied menu, became a

GETTING THERE
Air Chambéry 120km/ 75 miles (1hr45); Geneva 160km/ 100 miles (2hr30); Grenoble 190km/ 120 miles (2hr30); Lyon 200km/ 125 miles (2hr30)

Rail Moûtiers (35km/22 miles); regular buses from station

TOURIST OFFICE
www.valthorens.com

OUTLYING RESORT – 900m
ORELLE

Set at the foot of the gondola from the fourth valley (there's no piste down), Orelle isn't a recognizable resort, but offers bargain prices. A couple of hairpins up the hill from the lift base (there's a frequent ski-bus) is Hameau des Eaux, a complex of 200 apartments in eight chalet-style buildings, sharing a spa with a decent pool – available through Peak Retreats and Zenith. It includes a small convenience store and a restaurant.

SNOWPIX.COM / CHRIS GILL

Vars / Risoul

Two high, purpose-built resorts in an attractive setting, with a traditional French atmosphere and a shared area of slopes

£85

RESORT PRICE INDEX

TOP 10 RATINGS

Extent	★★★
Fast lifts	★
Queues	★★★★
Snow	★★★
Expert	★★
Intermediate	★★★★
Beginner	★★★★
Charm	★★
Convenience	★★★★
Scenery	★★★

NEWS

2014/15: The Nevalhaia Le Chalet, a new 4-star boutique hotel with spa, opened in Vars in January 2015. And in Risoul, a new restaurant, Lo Strato, opened.

KEY FACTS

Resort	1850m
	6,070ft

The entire Forêt Blanche ski area

Slopes	1660-2750m
	5,450-9,020ft
Lifts	51
Pistes	185km
	115 miles

- ✛ Attractive, family-friendly resorts
- ✛ Reasonably snow-sure and with lots of treelined runs
- ✛ Among the cheapest resorts in the French Alps

- ▬ Still mainly draglifts and slow old chairs, though a few fast ones
- ▬ Few on-piste challenges for experts
- ▬ Little to do off the slopes
- ▬ Fairly remote location

Vars and its linked neighbour Risoul are the most southerly French resorts to get a chapter in this book. Were they nearer Geneva, they would be better known internationally; as it is, they retain a very French atmosphere (though with a strong eastern European presence at times). The slopes of their shared Forêt Blanche area are, as the name implies, attractively wooded; but they aren't hugely extensive. We went back a few seasons ago for a couple of days and loved it; a week might be too much for a keen skier or boarder though. Their shared lift system is probably the most antiquated in these pages – hence the ★ for fast lifts. They leave over 20 runs (marked on the piste map) ungroomed if there's fresh snow – a great idea that other resorts should copy.

Vars 1850m

Vars includes several small, old villages on or near the approach road, chief among them Vars-Ste-Marie. There are lifts on the fringe of this village, but the focus for most visitors is higher, purpose-built Vars-les-Claux.

Village charm Vars-les-Claux has a lot of flat-roofed apartment blocks that look much worse from up the mountain than from within the village. Reporters like the pleasant, relaxed atmosphere: 'A little gem,' said a recent reporter. Consider 'cosy' Ste-Marie, too.
Convenience It's a small place, but spread along a winding, quite steep road, with two main clusters of shops, bars, restaurants and lodgings: the original focus, at the base of the main gondola, and Point Show, 10 minutes' walk up the hill. Each of these has nursery slopes and fast lifts into the slopes. Buildings spread beyond these points, varying in convenience.
Scenery Pretty wooded slopes surround the village, and there are fine views from the high point of Pic de Chabrières at 2750m.

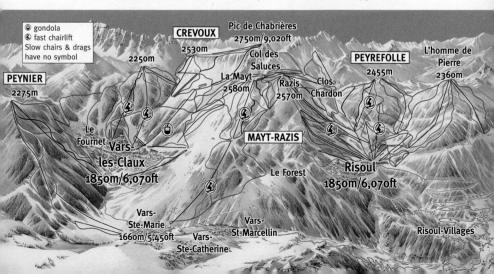

VARS TO / REMI MOREL

LIFT PASSES

Prices in €	
Age	**6-day**
under 12	152
12 to 64	190
65 plus	181
Free Under 5; 75 plus	
Beginner Limited pass	
Notes Family deals	

The area has a pretty setting with wooded lower slopes. But the slow lifts might drive you bonkers ↓

THE MOUNTAINS

There are slopes on both sides of the valley, linked by pistes and by slow double chairlifts at the lower end of Vars-les-Claux.

Some reporters have found piste classification variable and the map unclear on the links between resorts.
Slopes The wooded, west-facing Peynier area is the smaller sector, and reaches only 2275m. The main slopes are in an east-facing bowl with links to the Risoul slopes at two points. There's also a speed-skiing course. Beneath it are easy runs, open at the top but dropping into trees.
Fast lifts After the three fast lifts out of the village it's draglifts and slow chairs unless you head down to Vars-Ste-Marie or over to Risoul.
Queues Queues are rare outside the French holidays, though there is a report from a January visitor of 10-minute queues at key points. He was also concerned about crowding on the slopes, with lots of east Europeans (mainly Czech and Hungarian) skiing about in big groups.
Terrain parks There are seven freestyle areas. Your riding can be filmed at the Eyssina park.
Snow reliability Not bad: the altitudes are quite high, the orientation mostly easterly, and snowmaking is plentiful.
Experts There is little to challenge experts on-piste, but there is plenty of off-piste terrain (and great off-piste tree skiing in Risoul, too).

Intermediates These are fine intermediate slopes, with a good mix of decent reds and easy blues. Jas du Boeuf from La Mayt is a gentle cruise. The Olympique red run from the top of La Mayt to Ste-Marie delights most reporters and is a very respectable 920m vertical. If you can face the slow chairlifts and tricky drags, there are good treelined runs in the separate Peynier sector, including an easy black.
Beginners There are three free lifts on good slopes in central Vars, with lots of progression runs throughout the area and a special progression pass. Quick learners will be able to get over to Risoul by the end of the week.
Snowboarding There is good freeriding, but beginners might find the number of draglifts a problem.
Cross-country There are 10km of trails.
Mountain restaurants Most places are self-service. But the Chal Heureux table-service place is 'efficient, serves decent food and a delicious bombardino'. Cabane at the bottom of the run to Ste-Marie does 'a very good plat du jour and cheap house wine'.
Schools and guides A recent reporter had 'great' private lessons with ESF.
Families The ski school runs a nursery for children from two-and-a-half years old, and a ski kindergarten from four.

STAYING THERE

Hotels The Ecureuil is an attractive, modern B&B chalet. Ste-Marie has a Logis de France – the Vallon.

Apartments The slope-side Albane, with outdoor pool, is praised by reporters. Bookable through Ski Collection and Erna Low.
Eating out There is a choice of simple, good-value places. Après Ski at Point Show is worth a look, as is Chaudron in Ste-Marie. Escondus is said to be 'very good if a little pricey'.
Après-ski Animated at teatime; later it revolves around one or two bars.
Off the slopes There's tobogganing, ice skating, 34km of walking paths, cinema, snowmobiling, snowshoeing, dog sledding, paragliding and helicopter tours.

Risoul 1850m

Risoul 1850 is a modern ski station, purpose-built from the late 1970s onwards at the top of a winding road up from the original village of Risoul. It is a quiet, apartment-based resort, popular with families – but not exclusively so.

Village charm Many of the original resort buildings are bulky eight- or nine-storey buildings, but wood-clad with some traditional style. Newer developments are attractive and chalet-style, made of wood and stone. The busy little main street, with a small range of shops, bars and restaurants, is far from traffic-free. But the locals offer a friendly welcome.
Convenience The village meets the mountain in classic French purpose-built style, with sunny restaurant terraces facing the slopes and a compact centre. Some lodgings are a short but 'knackering' uphill walk away if you miss the last lift.
Scenery The resort is set in the woods and reporters often praise the views.

THE MOUNTAINS
The upper slopes are open, but those back to Risoul are prettily wooded, and good for bad-weather days.
Slopes The slopes, mainly north-facing, spread over several minor peaks and bowls, and connect with neighbouring Vars at two points.
Fast lifts There are three fast chairs accessing a good number of runs, but still lots of tricky 'difficile' draglifts.
Queues Queues are rare. But see the comment under Vars about crowds.
Terrain parks La Zing is aimed at beginner freestylers, with easy jumps and rails and a snowcross.
Snow reliability Snow reliability is reasonably good; the slopes are all above 1850m and mostly north-facing. Snowmaking is fairly extensive.
Experts Risoul's main top stations access a couple of steepish descents. And there's some good off-piste terrain – including excellent, widely spaced tree skiing on not very steep slopes and areas accessed through gates that are closed when there's an avalanche risk (though these are not marked or explained on the piste map).
Intermediates There are decent reds and blues in all sectors. Almost all Risoul's runs return to the village, making it difficult to get lost.
Beginners Three free lifts serve good, convenient nursery slopes. There are lots of easy pistes to move on to.
Snowboarding There is a lot of good freeriding to be done throughout the area, although beginners might not like the large proportion of draglifts.
Cross-country There are 17km of trails.
Mountain restaurants Choice is limited. The Homme de Pierre 'brings you decent dishes cooked to order'. The self-service Tetras is an attractive hut.
Schools and guides Reports on the ESF have been positive, and we had an excellent ESF guide on our visit.
Families Risoul is very much a family resort. The ESF operates a ski kindergarten.

STAYING THERE
Most visitors stay in apartments.
Hotels The Chardon Bleu is right on the slopes. You can also stay overnight up at the Tetras mountain refuge.
Apartments We enjoyed the 4-star Balcons de Sirius units – good pool, hot tub and sauna; Antarés is similar. Erna Low features these.
Eating out There's a decent choice offering fairly good value. Readers' tips: Chérine (pizza, pasta), Marmite, and Entre Pot. We tried L'Extrad, which served huge portions of hearty food.
Après-ski Nightlife is livelier than most people are expecting. There are several bars and the Reflex nightclub. Try the Babao and the Chalet or Eterlou for a quieter drink.
Off the slopes Limited. We enjoyed the guided night-time snowmobiling on adventurous terrain. There's also tobogganing, snowshoeing, skating, a zipline, paragliding and a cinema.

TOURIST OFFICES

Vars
www.vars-ski.com
Risoul
www.risoul.com

Germany

Germany isn't a big destination for UK-based skiers. Over the page is a chapter on Garmisch-Partenkirchen, by far the most important downhill resort in Germany – famously the venue for the 1936 Olympics, when downhill racing was introduced, and Adolf Hitler got the facilities built on time. Seventy-five years later it hosted the 2011 World Championships. On this page is a non-comprehensive tour of the country's main skiing regions.

Over the page is a chapter on Garmisch-Partenkirchen

WEBSITES

Allgäu
www.allgaeu.info
www.das-hoechste.de
Bavarian Alps
www.karwendelbahn.de
www.laber-bergbahn.de
www.braunecke-bergbahn.de
Black Forest
www.blackforest-tourism.com
Harz
www.harzinfo.de
Sauerland
www.wintersport-arena.de
Saxony
www.oberwiesenthal.com
www.fichtelberg-ski.de
Thüringer Wald
www.oberhof.de

THE ALPS

Allgäu This region claims 300km of downhill runs and an amazing 800km of cross-country trails. The main lift systems operate under the regional name Das Hoechste. Highest of all is Nebelhorn (2225m) reached from the nice little town of **Oberstdorf** by a two-stage cable car to the main slopes (served by two chairs), with a third stage to the top for Germany's longest on-piste descent (7.5km). Oberstdorf is probably best known as the resort that kicks off the annual Four Hills ski jumping tournament held over each New Year period. The Post hotel has been praised for 'good, substantial, reasonably priced' meals. South of Oberstdorf you enter **Kleinwalsertal**, which belongs to Austria, strangely. The Kanzelwand slopes link with Fellhorn to form Germany's biggest area, with three six-packs, two gondolas and nine other lifts. Ifen and Walmendingerhorn are smaller areas in the valley, and the Allgäu has lots of other resorts such as Oberjoch and Pfronten.

Bavarian Alps Garmisch-Partenkirchen is covered over the page. **Mittenwald** (915m) is a cute town in a spectacular setting. The cable car to Karwendel accesses an epic ski route dropping 1300m in 6km. Across the valley, Kranzbergy has seven lifts serving wooded slopes up to 1350m.

Other resorts These are on the fringes of the Alps, with less dramatic scenery. **Oberammergau** (835m and famous for its once-a-decade Passion play) is another cute town, with a gondola to Laber (1685m) that accesses a long ski route and a direct black piste; across town a chairlift serves Kolbensattel (1270m). There are more extensive slopes on Braunneck above **Lenggries** (680m) – a top height of 1710m, and 18 lifts including a gondola.

There are other small resorts, some near the infamous Berchtesgaden.

THE REST

Black Forest In the south-west corner: a lot of cross-country, but downhill too. Feldberg reaches 1500m with 31 lifts and 55km of pistes.
Harz A low mountain range, south of Hanover. A handful of small resorts, the biggest being Braunlage.
Sauerland Low mountains east of Düsseldorf. Some 500km of cross-country. Winterberg has 24 lifts, Willingen a gondola and seven drags.
Saxony On the border with the Czech Republic: a handful of low, small resorts, the most compelling at Fichtelberg above Oberwiesenthal.
Thüringer Wald North-east of Frankfurt: extensive cross-country, and a bit of easy downhill. The best-known resort is Oberhof.

GARMISCH-PARTENKIRCHEN

← Not surprisingly, Alpine Germany is indistinguishable from the Austrian Tirol

Garmisch-Partenkirchen

Twin resort towns sprawling at the foot of Germany's highest mountain, reaching glacial heights on the Austrian border

£90
RESORT PRICE INDEX

TOP 10 RATINGS

Extent	★
Fast lifts	★★★
Queues	★★★
Snow	★★★
Expert	★★★★
Intermediate	★★★
Beginner	★
Charm	★★★
Convenience	★★
Scenery	★★★★

NEWS

2015/16: Work will proceed on a big new cable car to replace the Eibsee one.

2014/15: Three new toboggan runs were created totalling 2km.

KEY FACTS

Resort	710m
	2,330ft
Slopes	720-2720m
	2,360-8,920ft
Lifts	27
Pistes	62km
	39 miles

MOMENTUM SKI

Weekend & a la carte ski holiday specialists

100% Tailor-made

Premier hotels & apartments

The No.1 Specialist in Garmisch

020 7371 9111
WWW.MOMENTUMSKI.COM

+ Weather-proof combination of a fair-sized glacier area and wooded slopes lower down

+ Some spectacular views

+ Some excellent, challenging runs

+ Good-value hotels, cheap for eating and drinking, good for short breaks

– Except on the glacier, very few long easy runs; beginners and timid intermediates beware

– Many of the best runs descend to low altitude, where conditions are rarely good

– Glacier access takes time

Garmisch is Germany's leading ski resort. It has two separate ski areas: one at low altitude with mainly tough runs, the other on a glacier with gentler terrain. It has plenty to amuse confident skiers for a couple of days, and with short transfers from Munich it makes a good short-break destination. We're getting few reports from readers; if you go, do let us know what you think.

THE RESORT

Garmisch and Partenkirchen are separate towns that have merged as they have spread to fill the broad, flat valley bottom beneath the Zugspitze, while keeping their centres distinct.

There are smaller resorts on the Austrian side of the Zugspitze. These and the Garmisch ski areas are covered by the Top Snow Card.

Village charm Each half of the resort is a sizeable town – spacious and pleasant but not notably captivating.

Convenience You'll need to use trains, buses or cars at both ends of the day. The Zugspitze railway starts next to the main station, more or less between the two town centres; it goes to the glacier via the other lift bases.

Scenery The Wetterstein massif, of which the Zugspitze is the peak, is impressive, and there are great panoramic views from the top.

THE MOUNTAINS

The glacier is quite separate from the lower slopes, which the resort calls the Classic area. In fact, the Classic area also divides into two parts, awkwardly linked – a higher, almost treeless part (Alpspitz) and a lower, heavily wooded part (Hausberg-Kreuzeck).

Slopes The **Hausberg-Kreuzeck** sector directly above the resort is accessed by two gondolas; these start a few km out of town and are served by the railway. These lower lifts have decent verticals and serve long runs; the lifts higher up are all much shorter. An inconspicuous narrow path and a rope

tow form the link between this sector and the base of the higher **Alpspitz** sector, more directly reached via the Alpspitz cable car. Although the altitude is modest, this sector feels like high-mountain terrain, with dramatic scenery – Dolomite-like on the isolated Osterfelder and Bernadein runs, on skier's right.

There are two routes to the glacier: there's the railway from town that serves the Classic area lift bases, which goes on to tunnel slowly through the mountain, emerging at the glacier; or there's the cable car from Eibsee that climbs an impressive 1950m to the Zugspitze – from there you have to ride another cable car down to the slopes.

Above the main lift junction are typical blue glacier slopes served by multiple drags. Below it and spreading across the bowl is a range of good red runs and some good off-piste terrain served by two six-packs and two drags. None of these lifts rises more than 400m vertical, but in other respects it's a good area.

Fast lifts Access lifts are fast, but after that it's mainly drags and slow chairs.

Queues Fine weekends attract crowds from Munich; but at other times we don't expect problems.

Terrain parks There's a 4,000 sqm terrain park at the Classic area. It has rails, tubes and boxes.

Snow reliability The glacier area is small and remote, so conditions lower down are important. The lower main area is shady, but some of the best runs descend to valley level – ie to

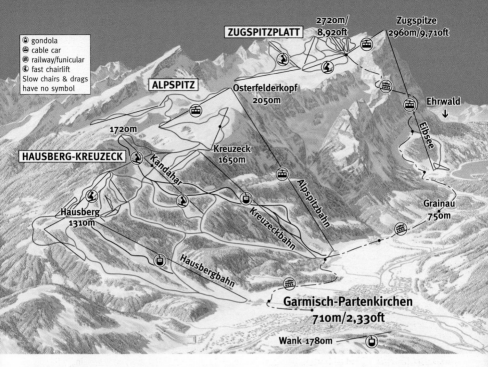

Map legend:
- gondola
- cable car
- railway/funicular
- fast chairlift
Slow chairs & drags have no symbol

ZUGSPITZPLATT
2720m/8,920ft
Zugspitze 296om/9,710ft
ALPSPITZ
Osterfelderkopf 2050m
Ehrwald ↓
1720m
Elbsee
HAUSBERG-KREUZECK
Kreuzeck 1650m
Kandahar
Alpspitzbahn
Grainau 750m
Hausberg 1310m
Kreuzeckbahn
Hausbergbahn
Garmisch-Partenkirchen 710m/2,330ft
Wank 1780m

LIFT PASSES

Prices in €

Age	6-day
under 16	117
16 to 18	204
19 plus	222

Free Under 6
Senior No deals
Beginner No deals
Note Covers all the Garmisch slopes and several resorts over the nearby border in Austria – Grainau, Ehrwald, Lermoos, Biberwier, Bichlbach, Berwang, Heiterwang

TOURIST OFFICE

www.gapa.de

720m. Despite comprehensive snowmaking, conditions at these altitudes can be poor even when there's great snow higher up, as we confirmed on one January visit.
Experts The long runs to the valley are challenging enough to amuse most experts, particularly the excellent Kandahar downhill race course. The final pitch of this takes real bottle when icy at the end of the day. Higher up, there are off-piste opportunities in the Alpspitz sector and on the glacier.
Intermediates For confident skiers it's fine, but this is not a hill where timid intermediates can build confidence.
Beginners Learn elsewhere. The nursery slopes are fine, but they're up the mountain and there is no beginner pass. And the only easy runs to move on to are busy links between Kreuzeck and Hausberg (or on the glacier).
Snowboarding There are drags in all sectors, though many can be avoided.
Cross-country There are 28km of trails along the valleys, of varying difficulty.
Mountain restaurants The glass-sided Gletschergarten on the glacier has a roof that can open on sunny days. Hochalm below Alpspitz in the Classic area does Bavarian fare. The Bayernhaus is worth a stop on the gentle blue run 6 from Hausberg.
Schools and guides There are several schools, but we lack reports.

Families The Kinderland centre at Hausberg looks good, with magic carpet and snow sculptures. There are family discounts on the lift pass.

STAYING THERE

Hotels There is one 5-star – Reindl's Partenkirchner Hof, well placed for the rail stations – and lots of 4-stars and 3-stars. Reader tips are the 3-star Garmischer Hof and Atlas Post, and the 4-star Zugspitze. Rates are low by Alpine standards.
Apartments Can be booked via the tourist office.
Eating out There's plenty of choice – these towns have a big summer trade. Gasthof Fraundorfer and the upscale Alpenhof do hearty Bavarian food.
Après-ski There are bars at the lift bases where you can enjoy waiting for the next train home, and in town there are lots of cosy bars such as Zirbel Stube, which has live music. Peaches is a lively bar with sports on TV.
Off the slopes There's lots to do, both outdoors and indoors. Walks include one through the Partnachklamm gorge and paths on the lift-served hill that is across town from the slopes – called Wank. There's an ice rink and toboggan runs – including a 5km run at Mount Hausberg that is floodlit twice a week – and three runs on the Zugspitze.

Italy

Italy has a lot going for it as a destination: it offers great value for money (over half the Italian resorts we cover have price index figures in our green category – the cheapest); the atmosphere is jolly; it offers reliably good food and wine; the scenery, especially in the Dolomites and Val d'Aosta, is simply stunning; the lift systems include some of the most modern in Europe; the snowmaking is state of the art (and they use it well); and the grooming is top-notch.

Italian resorts vary as widely in their characteristics as they do in location – and they are spread along the full length of the Italian border, from Sauze d'Oulx in the west to the Dolomites in the east. There are quaint backwater villages, fashionable towns, bleak ski stations – the choice is yours.

WEEKDAY PEACE, WEEKEND CROWDS

Many Italians based in the northern cities go skiing at weekends, and it's very noticeable that many resorts are busy only then, and become peaceful once the weekend invaders retreat. It's a great advantage for those of us who are there for the whole week, and probably skiing only one day at the weekend.

This pattern is especially noticeable at chic resorts such as Cortina, Courmayeur and Madonna, and resorts that have not yet found international fame such as those in the Monterosa region. The clearest example is La Thuile, in the Aosta valley. Even at February half-term the pistes here can be semi-deserted on weekdays. In parts of the Dolomites (such as Val Gardena) that are dominated by German visitors, the Sunday evening exodus doesn't happen – like Brits, the Germans tend to go for a week.

We may be wrong, but we also think we have detected, over the last season or two, an appreciable drop in the numbers of Italian skiers – perhaps related to the economic difficulties. On our recent February visit, Cortina offered delightfully empty pistes.

THE LONG LUNCH LIVES

Many Italians don't take their skiing or boarding too seriously. A late start, a long lunch and an early finish are common – leaving the slopes wonderfully quiet for the rest of us. Mountain restaurants are reasonably priced, and there are welcoming places almost everywhere, encouraging leisurely lunching. A persistent drag, though, is the ludicrous system in many self-service places where you have to look at what's on offer, then queue to pay at the cash desk, then queue again at the counter to collect your food or drink. Italy also has hybrid-service restaurants, where you order at the bar but are served at your table. Rather like most British pubs.

AND THE LONG EVENING

We've spent a lot of time in Italy in the last couple of years, and we've started to get the hang of après-ski in resorts where Italians are the major group of guests. In its pure form après here revolves around the aperitivo – the cocktail or Prosecco taken in a cool bar immediately before dinner – normally accompanied by some free

SNOWPIX.COM / CHRIS GILL

← Scenery doesn't get more mind-blowing than in the Dolomites. This is Sasso Lungo, looming over Piz Sella, above Selva

and delicious antipasti to nibble. You need to be in your evening finery by then, of course, and with a visit to the spa to fit in as well, there isn't much time for a protracted Austrian-style drinking session at close of play.

But there are exceptions, usually where British or German guests form a big part of the clientele, such as Sauze d'Oulx and some resorts in the Sella Ronda region – here you get quite a big early-après trade both on the mountain and in the villages.

WHO NEEDS REAL SNOW?
One thing that Italian resorts do have to contend with is erratic snowfall. While the snow in the northern Alps tends to come from the west, Italy's snow tends to come from storms arriving from the south. So Italy can have great conditions when other countries are suffering; or vice versa. But vice versa tends to apply a lot of the time. As a result, Italian resorts got into snowmaking early, and have learned how to do it well – and our observation is that they tend to use it more effectively than other Alpine countries.

A lot of Italian runs seem flatteringly easy. This is partly because grooming is immaculate and partly because piste classification often seems to overstate difficulty. Nowhere is this clearer than in the linked slopes of La Thuile (in Italy) and La Rosière (in France), where a couple of lift rides take you from Italian motorways classified red to French mogul fields classified blue.

The classification of easy runs as reds creates a real problem. In many areas – Monterosa springs to mind – the red category also

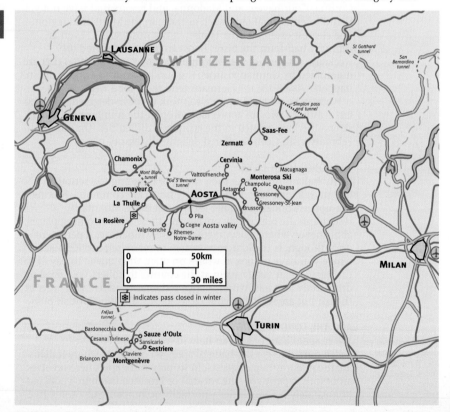

includes runs that actually are a bit challenging, and precious few runs are classed as blue. For a nervous intermediate, this is bad news – you can't know which runs you'll be comfortable on, and which ones to avoid.

OFF-PISTE CONFUSION

Many Italian areas declare it illegal to go off-piste near their pistes, or to go off-piste at all, or to go off-piste outside defined routes or without a guide or without transceiver, shovel and probe. We've tried to get to the bottom of these developments; but a prompt, clear, accurate response to a slightly technical question such as this is not a speciality of Italian tourist bodies.

Some resorts tell us there are national laws; others, that it's a regional matter; others, that it's a local matter. Of course, there is then the issue of whether the law is applied and how it is policed. Where we have a clear view of the situation in a given resort, we include that in the relevant chapter. Thankfully, we have no evidence of any interference in off-piste skiing in the Aosta valley, which is Italy's off-piste/heli-skiing HQ.

Four editions ago we were told by Livigno that off-piste without a guide was officially banned. The following season they designated half a dozen slopes in one sector as freeride routes – marking them on the piste map and guarding them with entry gates equipped with gadgets to check that your avalanche bleepers are working. Excellent, we thought. Then it turned out that you were not supposed to ski these routes without a guide. Now we are told that

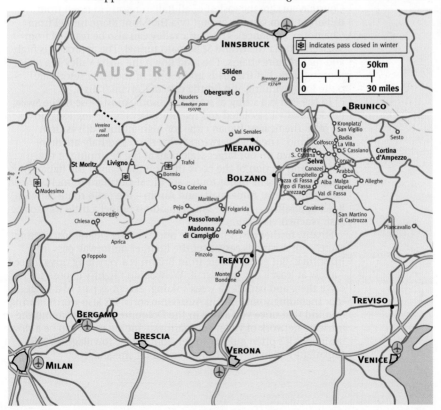

off-piste skiing is allowed everywhere with or without a guide. And heli-skiing is now promoted. So back in 2011 we were told there was a national law that banned off-piste skiing. Now we are told it is down to the local mayor to make up the rules. Bonkers!

SOME SIGHTSEEING IN VENICE?
Next time we go to the Dolomites we'll fly to Venice and get a return flight late in the day. With an early start from the resort, that will give us time to ride the water-bus to and from the city. The 'orange' line goes all the way along the Canale Grande to Santa Maria del Giglio, near San Marco. Round trip 2hr30. That would make a lovely end to a skiing trip. We had this all planned last year, but excessive snow blocking key roads out of Corvara scuppered it.

DRIVING IN THE ITALIAN ALPS
There are four main geographical groupings of Italian resorts, widely separated. Getting to some of these resorts is a very long haul, and moving from one area to another can involve very long drives (though the extensive motorway network is a great help).

The handful of resorts to the west of Turin – Bardonecchia, Sauze d'Oulx, Sestriere and neighbours in the Milky Way region – are easily reached from France via the Fréjus tunnel, or via the good road over the pass that the French resort of Montgenèvre sits on.

Further north, and somewhat nearer to Milan than Turin, are the resorts of the Aosta valley – Courmayeur, Cervinia, La Thuile and the Monterosa area are the best known. These (especially Courmayeur) are the easiest of all Italian resorts to reach from Britain or from Geneva airport (via the Mont Blanc tunnel from Chamonix in France). The Aosta valley can also be reached from Switzerland via the Grand St Bernard tunnel. The approach is high and may require chains. The road down the Aosta valley is a major thoroughfare, but the roads up to some of the other resorts are quite long, winding and (in the case of Cervinia) high.

To the east is a string of scattered resorts, most close to the Swiss border, many in isolated and remote valleys involving long drives up from the nearest Italian cities, or high-altitude drives from Switzerland. The links between Switzerland and Italy are more clearly shown on our larger-scale map at the beginning of the Switzerland section of the book than on the map of the Italian Alps included here. The major routes are the St Gotthard tunnel between Göschenen (near Andermatt) and Airolo – the main route between Basel and Milan – and the San Bernardino tunnel a little way to the east, reached via Chur.

Finally, further east still are the resorts of the Dolomites. Getting there from Austria is easy, over the Brenner motorway pass from Innsbruck. But getting there from Britain is a very long drive indeed – allow at least a day and a half. We wouldn't lightly choose to drive there and back for a week's skiing, except as part of a longer tour including some time in Austrian resorts. It's also worth bearing in mind that once you arrive in the Dolomites, getting around the intricate network of valleys on narrow, winding roads can be a slow business – it's often quicker to get from village to village on skis. Impatient Italian driving can make it a bit stressful, too.

SNOWPIX.COM / CHRIS GILL

Cervinia

One of a kind, this: for extensive, snow-sure, sunny, easy skiing, there is nowhere to match Cervinia. Good for late-season holidays

£90
RESORT PRICE INDEX

RATINGS

The mountains

Extent	★★★
Fast lifts	★★★★
Queues	★★★★
Terrain p'ks	★★★★
Snow	★★★★★
Expert	★
Intermediate	★★★★
Beginner	★★★★★
Boarder	★★★★
X-country	★
Restaurants	★★★
Schools	★★★★
Families	★★

The resort

Charm	★★
Convenience	★★★
Scenery	★★★★
Eating out	★★★★
Après-ski	★★
Off-slope	★

NEWS

2014/15:
Snowmaking was increased and the Indian terrain park was moved a bit lower down the mountain.

KEY FACTS

Resort	2050m
	6,730ft

Cervinia/Valt'nenche	
Slopes	1525-3480m
	5,000-11,420ft
Lifts	19
Pistes	160km
	100 miles

Cervinia/ Valt'nenche/ Zermatt combined	
Slopes	1525-3820m
	5,000-12,530ft
Lifts	54
Pistes	360km
	224 miles

+ Miles of long, consistently gentle runs; ideal for intermediates wary of steep slopes or bumps

+ Slopes are sunny, but high and pretty snow-sure

+ Spectacular setting beneath the towering Matterhorn

+ Excellent village nursery slope

+ Valuable link with Zermatt in Switzerland, but ...

− Bad weather (especially high winds) can close most of the higher lifts, severely limiting your options

− Very little to interest those looking for challenges

− Not a notably attractive village

− Few off-slope amenities

− Steep climb to the main gondola, although there is a more convenient chairlift alternative

If there is a better resort than Cervinia for those who like easy cruising in spring sunshine, we have yet to find it. And then there's more easy cruising on the gentlest of Zermatt's slopes just over the Swiss border.

And for the rest of us? Well, to be frank, the rest of us are better off elsewhere. In particular, those with an eye on bumps or powder over in Zermatt should stay there, not here – access to its best slopes is still time-consuming.

The village was branded Cervinia when it was developed for skiing, but these days harks back to its mountaineering roots by prefixing that with its original name, Breuil. Ever heard of that? No, quite. So we'll stick with Cervinia.

THE RESORT

Cervinia is on the Italian side of the Matterhorn (or Monte Cervino), at the head of a long valley off the Aosta valley. The resort gets a lot of Italian weekend business, and quite a lot of Russian January business. We get a good flow of reports from mainly satisfied British visitors.

The slopes link to Valtournenche further down the valley (covered by the lift pass) and at high altitude to Zermatt in Switzerland (covered by a daily supplement, or a more expensive weekly pass). Lifts at Valtournenche may be open when Cervinia's are closed due to wind – but a reporter warns the bus service is infrequent.

Day trips by car to Courmayeur, La Thuile, Pila and the Monterosa Ski resorts of Champoluc and Gressoney are not easy, but possible (and some tour operators offer excursions). A six-day lift pass covers two days in these other resorts.

VILLAGE CHARM ★★
Getting smarter?
The old climbing village grew into a ski resort in a haphazard way, and subsequent development has been no better. The result is neither pleasing to the eye nor hideous. We sense a gradual smartening up of the centre, with wood and stone taking over from concrete. The cobbled main street is traffic-free, and the place is pleasant enough to walk around in the evening. The river separating the main strip from the nursery slopes adds some charm. But ugly apartment blocks and hotels spoil the views from the slopes.

CONVENIENCE ★★★
Up or down
As our plan makes clear, this is not a big place, but location is still worth considering carefully. What used to be the main lift from the village, a gondola to Plan Maison, starts a hike up from the south end of the village – irritating for some, 'truly awful' for

[map: miles 0.5 / 1.0, N, Plan Maison, Cleloalto, km 1.0 / 2.0]

MOMENTUM SKI

Weekend & a la carte
ski holiday specialists

100% Tailor-made

Premier hotels
& apartments

Flexible travel
arrangements

020 7371 9111
WWW.MOMENTUMSKI.COM

others. The alternative of successive six-packs from the nursery slopes, next to the village centre, makes this the obvious place to stay.

There are also developments above the main village, some of them closer to the gondola. Some hotels run shuttles, and an efficient public bus serves the Cieloalto complex, high up to the south of the main village.

Footpaths can be icy and tricky.

SCENERY ★★★★
Monte Cervino rules

The Matterhorn is less special seen from the Italian rather than from the Swiss side, but Cervinia's setting close to the mountain is very impressive by normal standards, with the peak towering above the village. Driving up

in the late afternoon on our last visit, we were forced to stop and stare. There are fine views from the slopes.

THE MOUNTAINS

Cervinia's main slopes are high, open, sunny and mostly west-facing. It's an unpleasant place when the weather is bad, and some upper lifts and the link with Zermatt are often closed because of wind (sometimes for days on end), especially early in the season.

The piste map – which also covers Zermatt – and piste marking are up to scratch, and piste grooming is generally good. The high number of red runs on the map is misleading: most of them could easily be classified blue instead.

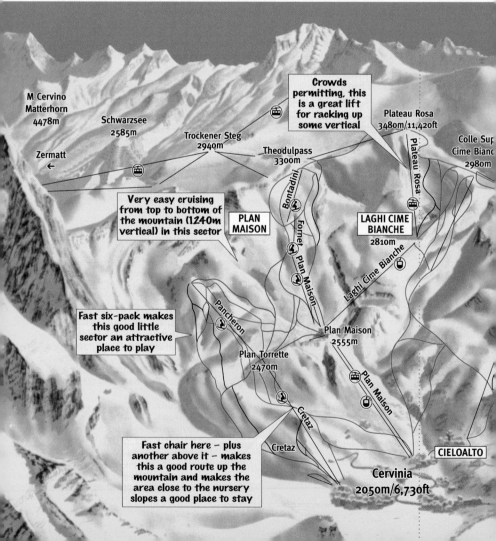

M Cervino
Matterhorn
4478m

Schwarzsee
2585m

Zermatt
←

Trockener Steg
2940m

Theodulpass
3300m

Crowds permitting, this is a great lift for racking up some vertical

Plateau Rosa
348om/11,42oft

Colle Sup
Cime Bianc
298om

Plateau Rosa

Bontadini

Fornet

Plan Maison

Very easy cruising from top to bottom of the mountain (1240m vertical) in this sector

PLAN MAISON

LAGHI CIME BIANCHE
2810m

Laghi Cime Bianche

Pancheron

Fast six-pack makes this good little sector an attractive place to play

Plan Torrette
247om

Plan Maison
2555m

Plan Maison

Cretaz

Cretaz

Fast chair here – plus another above it – makes this a good route up the mountain and makes the area close to the nursery slopes a good place to stay

CIELOALTO

Cervinia
2050m/6,73oft

EXTENT OF THE SLOPES ★★★☆☆
High, wide and easy

Cervinia has the biggest, highest, most snow-sure area of easy, well-groomed pistes we've come across. The area has Italy's highest pistes and some of its longest. At the top you are 6km as well as 1400m vertical from the village.

A deep gorge splits the slopes into two main sectors. Looking up the hill, the lifts from the village take you into the bigger left-hand sector at first.

A gondola takes you to the mid-mountain base of **Plan Maison**. We've rarely seen the parallel cable car working. A more convenient alternative for many is the six-pack from the village nursery slopes to Plan Torrette, where another six-pack serves the good slopes under the Matterhorn –

and gives quick access to Plan Maison.

Above Plan Maison, a chain of three fast quads goes on up to Theodulpass, slightly the lower of two links with the slopes of Zermatt. From Plan Maison you can instead take a gondola across to **Laghi Cime Bianche**, and the right-hand sector. From there a big cable car goes up to Plateau Rosa, the other link with Zermatt. This is also the start of the splendid, wide Ventina run back to the cable car station (or on down to the village).

Part-way down you can branch off left for **Valtournenche**. The slopes here are served by three chairlifts above a modern gondola from the village – but the final lift towards Cervinia is still a long draglift with some tricky steep sections. From top to bottom the run

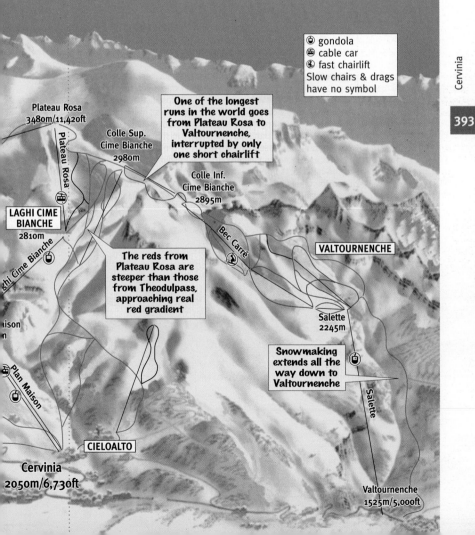

gondola
cable car
fast chairlift
Slow chairs & drags have no symbol

Plateau Rosa
3480m/11,420ft

Colle Sup.
Cime Bianche
2980m

Colle Inf.
Cime Bianche
2895m

One of the longest runs in the world goes from Plateau Rosa to Valtournenche, interrupted by only one short chairlift

LAGHI CIME BIANCHE
2810m

Bec Carré

VALTOURNENCHE

The reds from Plateau Rosa are steeper than those from Theodulpass, approaching real red gradient

Salette
2245m

Snowmaking extends all the way down to Valtournenche

Salette

CIELOALTO

Cervinia
2050m/6,730ft

Valtournenche
1525m/5,000ft

LIFT PASSES

Prices in €

Age	6-day
under 14	130
14 to 64	216
65 plus	173

Free Under 8 and 80 plus

Beginner Limited pass

Notes Covers all lifts on the Italian side, including Valtournenche; half-day passes; includes Aosta Valley extension from 3 days

Alternative passes
Valtournenche only; International (includes Zermatt); Aosta Valley

CERVINIA TO / MARCO SPATARO
Near the start of the epic 13km run down to Valtournenche – the scenery is pretty spectacular even when the Matterhorn is not in view ↓

to the valley is almost 2000m vertical and 13km long, interrupted only by a very short quad chairlift part-way.

There is also the very small, little-used **Cieloalto** area at the bottom of the Ventina run, served by a slow old chair to the south of the village. This has some of Cervinia's steeper pistes, and the only trees in the area.

FAST LIFTS ★★★★☆
Few slow lifts left
Most of Cervinia's main lifts are fast. The few slow ones left are in the Valtournenche and Cieloalto sectors.

QUEUES ★★★★☆
Very few problems
In general, neither we nor readers have complaints about queues in the main area of slopes, though the chair above Plan Maison does still get busy. Of course, the lower lifts may be busy when upper lifts are shut because of wind. The gondola station at Valtournenche has a big car park that fills up at weekends, and the lifts above the gondola can then be busy.

TERRAIN PARKS ★★★★☆
One of Italy's best
The 'Indian' terrain park was moved a bit lower down the mountain last season and is accessed by the Plan Maison or Pancheron chairlifts. It's one of the best parks in Italy, is said to be over 400m long and 100m wide and has rails and kickers for all levels;

helmets are compulsory. But there is no half-pipe. There's a special pass (30 euros a day last season) that covers the two chairlifts that access the park plus return trips on the Plan Maison gondola.

There is also a small park near the village that some of our readers have enjoyed, especially with their children.

SNOW RELIABILITY ★★★★★
A question of altitude
This is not a notably snowy corner of the Alps, and the slopes get the afternoon sun. But snow is usually good from early to late season thanks to the altitude (these slopes are among the highest in the Alps) and to good grooming and snowmaking on most key runs from top to bottom – down to Valtournenche as well as Cervinia.

FOR EXPERTS ★☆☆☆☆
Forget it
This is not a resort for experts. There are a few black runs scattered here and there, but they are not reliably open and most of them would be classified red elsewhere; we have only one sighting of moguls – on the black above Plan Torrette. Accessible off-piste terrain is limited, and high winds can play havoc with fresh snow. But of course there is some good off-piste – above Plan Torrette for example – and of course conditions can be brilliant, and you then have the advantage that

Getting to Zermatt's
classic Rothorn and
Stockhorn sectors is
much quicker than it
once was, thanks to
the Furi-Riffelberg
gondola. But you still
need four lifts after
that to get to
Stockhorn. On the
way back you may
meet long queues.
Allow plenty of time
– and beware closure
of the top lifts
because of wind.

the snow can remain untracked for ages. Heli-skiing can be arranged.

You can head over to Zermatt for more challenging slopes – look at the 'Zermatt connection' box in the margin.

FOR INTERMEDIATES ★★★★☆
Miles of long, flattering runs
Virtually the whole area can be covered comfortably by early intermediates. From top to bottom there are wide, gentle, smooth runs. Strong intermediates can find amusement at the extreme left and right of the area. The Ventina red is a particularly good fast cruise. You can use the cable car to do the top part repeatedly. The runs served by the Pancheron chair at Plan Torrette tend to be attractively quiet. But adventurous intermediates will soon be itching to be off to Zermatt.

The runs towards Valtournenche are great cruises and very popular with reporters. The 13km run all the way down is very satisfying, through splendid rocky scenery.

A reader notes that access to Zermatt via Theodulpass involves a tricky start – so early intermediates might want to go via Plateau Rosa.

FOR BEGINNERS ★★★★★
Gentle progress
A limited day pass covers the good village nursery slope, with its long moving carpet, and the adjacent chairlift. Complete beginners start there and graduate to the fine flat area around Plan Maison and the gentle blue runs above. Fast learners will be going from top to bottom of the mountain in a few days. But one reporter found many blues 'quite crowded', especially at weekends.

FOR BOARDERS ★★★★☆
Easy cruising
The wide, gentle and well-groomed slopes, generally good snow and lack of many draglifts make Cervinia pretty much ideal for beginner and early intermediate boarders. But there are some long, flat parts to beware of (notably around Plan Maison). Serious boarders will enjoy the terrain park. There's also heli-boarding.

FOR CROSS-COUNTRY ★☆☆☆☆
Hardly any
There are only two short trails (both 3km or so).

Club Med ♈

THE MOST COMPREHENSIVE
SKI PACKAGE ON THE MARKET

Cervinia 4⍩

020 8313 3999
Skiline.co.uk

Skiline .co.uk

MOUNTAIN RESTAURANTS ★★★☆☆
OK if you know where to go
There are some good places if you know where to go. They are marked but not identified on the resort piste map. Toilet facilities are a traditional cause of complaints, but several have now been improved.

Editors' choice Chalet Etoile, amid the blue runs above Plan Maison, is an old favourite. It's best on a sunny day; on a bad day it gets ridiculously crowded inside – though the atmosphere is all the jollier as a result. 'Delicious food, friendly, attentive service,' says a 2015 reporter. We had fab fish soup on our last visit. There's a self-service section too. The much simpler Rifugio Teodulo on the border at Theodulpass is another good option – excellent pasta.

Worth knowing about Reporters have tipped Plan Torrette ('good-value burgers and schnitzel', old skiing artefacts on the wall), with self- and table-service sections. The small, cosy, self-service Rifugio Guide del Cervino at Plateau Rosa has fabulous views and simple food. The Gran Sometta on run 39 has a 'nice atmosphere, good service, excellent food'. Rocce Nere at Plan Maison serves 'huge portions of everything from burgers to pork knuckles; cheap and cheerful'. Bardoney, at the bottom of the run down from Plan Maison offers 'fast table-service and fantastic goulash'. Bontadini, down from Theodulpass has 'excellent food, friendly staff'. So does Igloo at 2400m on run 7 ('good house wine, reasonable prices'); it was taken over and renovated a few years ago.

The restaurants are cheaper and less crowded in the Valtournenche sector. The Foyer des Guides on the red run to the valley is 'brilliant – lovely friendly service and excellent value'. Tips above Salette include Motta and Lo Baracon dou Tene.

SCHOOLS AND GUIDES ★★★★☆
Generally positive reports
Cervinia has three main schools. Most reports are on the Cervino school, and are positive: 'Seemed organized. Instructors spoke decent English and worked hard on technique; my friend came on in leaps and bounds.'

FOR FAMILIES ★★☆☆☆
No recent reports
The Cervino ski school runs a mini club. And there's a kindergarten area at Plan Maison.

STAYING THERE

Chalets Inghams has the 12-room chalet hotel Dragon in a great position close to the nursery slopes.
Hotels There are almost 50 hotels. Choose location with care, or look for a place with its own shuttle-bus. The Club Med has been highly praised.
*****Hermitage Small, luxurious Relais & Châteaux place just out of the village on the road to Cieloalto. Pool. Minibus to the lifts.
****Europa Near pedestrian area, with good past reports. Pool. Shuttle-bus.
****Saint Hubertus Lovely, stylish apart-hotel next to the Hermitage. Dinner served in your apartment except at weekends when the restaurant is open – excellent food, impeccable service. Spa, pool, gym.
***Breuil Central, modern. 'Comfortable, friendly and spotlessly clean,' says a reporter.
***Serenella Very Italian feel and food, good location, friendly, good value.
At altitude Two smart places just above the village were highly praised by 2015 reporters: the woody 3-star Mon Reve B&B and the chic Principe delle Nevi with indoor and outdoor pools, hot tub, sauna, steam. Both will drive you to/from town.
Apartments There are many, but few are available via UK tour ops.

EATING OUT ★★★★☆
Plenty to choose from
Cervinia's 50 or so restaurants offer plenty of choice. A long-standing reader favourite has been the Copa Pan bar's basement restaurant ('nice setting by log fire'; 'delicious venison and pasta starter and excellent steak'). Another favourite is the Falcone ('good pizza', 'cosy, welcoming, informal'). 2015 reporter tips: Sotto Zero ('75 choices of delicious, hot, thin-crust

pizzas – mainly Italian clientele'), Wood ('beautiful decor, amazing food, pricey'), Lino's at the ice rink ('welcoming, reasonably priced'), La Grotta ('wonderful shrimp pasta') and Jour et Nuit ('traditional food, friendly service – no wine list, they recommend from the owner's vineyard'). Dinner at Baita Cretaz, just above the village, makes a change ('pleasant service, good food').

APRES-SKI ★★☆☆☆
Some jolly bars
It's not a particularly lively village. 'Take a good book,' said one reporter. At teatime you can do worse than to try the cakes at the Samovar. The hotel Grivola's bars are attractively woody, friendly and lively, with free nibbles. The 'cosy' Copa Pan is lively (starting with a happy hour), with music. Lino's is rated for its happy hour, getting the last of the sun and for 'free interesting tapas-like food'. The Yeti also has a happy hour, is popular and shows English football on large screens. The bar in Inghams' chalet hotel Dragon is also popular 'but very British'. As usual in Italy, discos liven up at weekends.

OFF THE SLOPES ★☆☆☆☆
Little attraction
There is little to do for those who don't plan to hit the slopes. Amenities include hotel pools, a fitness centre and a natural ice rink. There are few diverting shops. The walks are not great. Only a few mountain restaurants are reachable by gondola or cable car, and most of these are not special.

LINKED RESORT – 1525m
VALTOURNENCHE

Some 9km down the access road and 500m below Cervinia, Valtournenche offers lower prices and a rather more traditional style. The village spreads along the busy, steep road up to Cervinia; traffic intrudes, particularly at weekends. The resort is reported to be 'not so much quiet as dead' in the evening. There's a fair selection of simple hotels; some have shuttles to the lift.

A gondola leaves from a station below the village (with a big car park). The epic run back from Plateau Rosa on the Swiss border is a great way to end the day – and has snowmaking right to the bottom.

GETTING THERE

Air Turin 120km/ 75 miles (1hr45); Milan Malpensa 185km/115 miles (2hr15); Milan Linate 205km/125 miles (2hr30); Geneva 205km/125 miles (2hr45)

Rail Châtillon (27km/17 miles); regular buses from station

TOURIST OFFICE

www.cervinia.it

Cortina d'Ampezzo

A captivating town in a truly spectacular setting; do long lunches and side trips, and you won't worry about the rather limited slopes

£115
RESORT PRICE INDEX

RATINGS

The mountains

Extent	★★
Fast lifts	★★★
Queues	★★★★
Terrain p'ks	★★
Snow	★★★
Expert	★★
Intermediate	★★★
Beginner	★★★★★
Boarder	★★★
X-country	★★★★★
Restaurants	★★★★
Schools	★★★
Families	★★

The resort

Charm	★★★★
Convenience	★
Scenery	★★★★★
Eating out	★★★★
Après-ski	★★★
Off-slope	★★★★★

NEWS

2015/16: At Tofana a big airbag jump will be available. There will also be a winter via ferrata route. At Lagazuoi the Azzurra ski school will be offering brief 'key tips' sessions for one or two people.

KEY FACTS

Resort	1225m
	4,020ft
Slopes	1225-2930m
	4,020-9,610ft
Lifts	34
Pistes	115km
	71 miles

➕ Magnificent Dolomite setting

➕ Marvellous for novices

➕ Sella Ronda area within reach, just

➕ Attractive, very Italian town

➕ Lots of off-slope diversions

➕ No crowds or queues

➖ Modest area of slopes, split into several separate areas

➖ Erratic snow record

➖ Expensive by Italian standards

➖ Still quite a few slow lifts

➖ Few tough runs

There is nowhere quite like Cortina. A famous racing town and host of the 1956 Olympics, it certainly has some serious skiing. But it is also Italy's most fashionable resort, and many visitors take their lunching and early-evening parading/shopping more seriously than their skiing. The result is that pressure on the slopes is low. No queues, no crowds, pistes rarely reduced to boilerplate by heavy traffic. We have had some of our most enjoyable piste skiing here.

And don't let this talk of fashion put you off. More of the visitors are driving Fords than Ferraris – though we concede few are driving Cortinas. And lodgings need not be expensive: there are more three-star than four-star hotels, and Inghams now run a good-value chalet hotel right on the focal Corso Italia.

The scenery is just jaw-droppingly wonderful. The town is ringed by dramatic limestone towers and cliffs, tinged pink at dawn and dusk. We were back here in 2015, and our jaws dropped once again.

Cortina is a sizeable town spread across a wide, impossibly scenic bowl. Although it runs World Cup races, it is not a hard-core ski resort – 70% of all Italian visitors don't step on to the slopes. By 5pm everybody is cruising the Corso Italia in smart gear and laden with big bags containing additional supplies of smart gear.

Cortina is pure Italy. The Veneto region has none of the Germanic culture that you'll find in parts of the Südtirol, only a few miles away. It now attracts more than a few Russians.

Within reach to the west is the Alta Badia, with Corvara at one corner of the Sella Ronda circuit – all on the Superski megapass. It can be reached by public bus, but is much easier by tour-op coach, taxi or your own car.

VILLAGE CHARM ★★★★
Bella Italia
The heart of Cortina is the cobbled Corso Italia – traffic-free thanks to the one-way ring-road system (often busy, choked at weekends). The Corso is lined by chic shops selling designer clothes, jewellery, antiques, art and furs. There is also an excellent co-op department store, but proper ski shops are to be found on the nearby

ring road, or the streets leading to it. The soaring, floodlit church campanile at the heart of the Corso adds to the atmosphere.

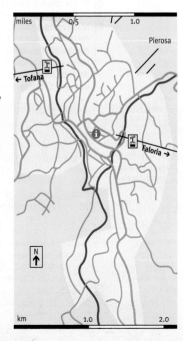

MOMENTUM SKI

Weekend & a la carte
ski holiday specialists

100% Tailor-made

Premier hotels
& apartments

Flexible travel
arrangements

020 7371 9111
WWW.MOMENTUMSKI.COM

CONVENIENCE ★☆☆☆☆
Widely scattered

Cortina is the antithesis of the modern ski-in/ski-out resort. Walks, buses and taxis are just part of life here. Relax, and you'll get used to it. It's probably best to stay close to the Corso and the Faloria cable car, so that some days, at least, you won't need the 'convenient and punctual' free ski-bus. Or stay in one of the swanky hotels in the suburbs that operate shuttles. A car can be useful, for getting to other areas such as the Sella Ronda.

SCENERY ★★★★★
Stand and admire

Cortina is surrounded by some of the most stunning mountain scenery in the skiing world – the Dolomite mountains are magnificent, with cliffs and peaks rising up from pretty wooded valleys, and tinged pink at dawn and dusk.

THE MOUNTAINS

There is a good mixture of slopes above and below the treeline.

EXTENT OF THE SLOPES ★★☆☆☆
They add up ...

With a claimed 115km of pistes (including various outlying areas), Cortina's skiing is modest in extent.

A two-stage cable car from the top of the town – an uphill 200m from the Corso – goes up to the shady, partly wooded **Faloria** area. From here you can head down to Rio Gere, and plod across the Passo Tre Croci road to reach chairlifts leading up into the limited but dramatic sunny runs beneath **Cristallo**. Quite a few people

drive out and park at Rio Gere.

The town's other access lift – another cable car – starts well to the north of the centre, near the Olympic ice rink. This goes up to **Col Drusciè**, where a second stage goes on to Ra Valles and a sector of very high, shady slopes beneath **Tofana**. There is a third stage, but for sightseeing not for skiing purposes.

A blue piste from Col Drusciè and a panoramic black one from Ra Valles lead to the largest but least clearly identified sector, which gets the morning sun. We've always called it **Pomedes**, the name of the top station (and restaurant). Resort literature may call it Pocol, after a hamlet on the edge of the sector, or Socrepes or Lacedel, at the lift base. It is a sector of two halves – serious reds and blacks at the top, glorious super-easy blues at the bottom, which remain sunny most of the day.

On the north-east fringes of the town is the little **Mietres** area.

From a point near Son del Prade, on skier's right of the Pomedes area, a shuttle-bus service takes you up the road west to the small but scenic **Cinque Torri** area. (There is said to be a long-term plan for a 5km lift link, which would be insane while the resort's main sectors remain unlinked.) This area has slopes on both sunny and shady sides of a ridge. On the sunny side, a short double chair accesses a run linking to the tiny, shady **Col Gallina** area. (After a red start which can be tricky and bumpy, this is mostly a schuss or a walk – boarders be warned.) From here you can take a blue back to Cinque Torri or

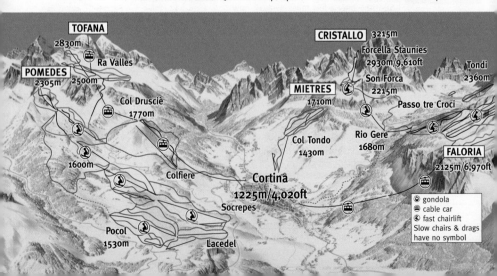

LIFT PASSES

Dolomiti Superski

Prices in €	
Age	**6-day**
under 16	189
16 to 64	270
65 plus	243

Free Under 8
Senior Must be 65 before season starts
Beginner Points cards
Note Covers 450 lifts and 1220km of pistes in the Dolomites, incl. all Cortina areas

Alternative pass
Cortina d'Ampezzo (Cortina, San Vito di Cadore, Auronzo-Misurina)

a cable car from Passo Falzarego up to **Lagazuoi** – the start of a good red run back to the base station and of the famous 'hidden valley' run (more on this in the Sella Ronda chapter).

FAST LIFTS ★★★☆☆
Some in each sector
The main access lifts are cable cars and there are fast chairs scattered throughout each sector, but a lot of slow old lifts remain.

QUEUES ★★★★☆
No problem
Generally there are few lift queues or crowds on the pistes. Queues can form for the cable car to Lagazuoi, which seems to attract more business from the Alta Badia than from Cortina.

TERRAIN PARKS ★★☆☆☆
Challenges for all
Socrepes has a 500m-long park for both beginners and intermediates. Helmets are compulsory.

SNOW RELIABILITY ★★★☆☆
Lots of artificial help
The snowfall record is erratic, depending on storms from the Adriatic to the south. But 95% of the pistes are covered by excellent snowmaking, so cover is good if temperatures are low. As so often, it's the black runs that are most vulnerable when natural snow is short – several are south-facing, and liable to closure. Grooming is 'simply excellent'.

FOR EXPERTS ★★☆☆☆
Normally rather limited
Given a decent amount of natural snow, you can find fresh tracks off-piste for days on end and good conditions on the few black pistes (some of which get a lot of sun).

There are short but genuinely black runs close to the lift line at the top of the Pomedes sector. The excellent Forcella Rossa from Tofana to Pomedes only just deserves to be black; but it faces south, so timing can be crucial. It opens up to give wonderful views of the valley. Cortina's most serious piste challenge is Forcella Staunies at the top of the Cristallo area – a south-facing couloir that we have never found open ('tougher than it looks from below', says one reporter; 'intimidating at the start', says another). This is also the launching point for some serious off-piste runs behind the hill, to the north. Locals speak highly of the ski touring possibilities, too.

FOR INTERMEDIATES ★★★☆☆
Fragmented and not extensive
Cortina is not a place for the avid mileage-hungry piste-basher. But its slopes are varied and interesting.

The high, shady runs at the top of Tofana are short but worthwhile, and normally have good snow. If tempted to descend via the easy black Forcella Rossa, check out the snow conditions first. The reds at the top of the linked Pomedes area offer good cruising and some challenges. Again, be aware that the blacks can be hard or icy.

For the best snow, head to Faloria, which has a string of excellent, shady but short (250m vertical) runs – eg Vitelli (once red, now black), curling away from the lifts. And Cristallo has a long, easy red served by a fast quad. The lower half of Staunies is a lovely easy black/serious red.

It is well worth making the trip to Cinque Torri for fast cruising – usually with excellent snow on the front, shady side. The blue and red through the woods here are indistinguishable. Do not miss the great 'hidden valley' red run from the Lagazuoi cable car.

FOR BEGINNERS ★★★★★
Wonderful progression
There are points cards for the lifts; the slopes, although a bus ride from the town, are near-perfect. The lower part of the Pomedes area has some of the biggest and best nursery slopes and progression runs we have seen. Be aware that some isolated blue runs elsewhere in the area may be much less friendly.

FOR BOARDERS ★★★★★
Wide slopes, plenty of chairs
Despite its upmarket chic, Cortina is a good resort for learning to board. The Socrepes nursery slopes are wide, gentle, served by a fast chairlift, and there are few drag lifts. There are some nice trees and hits under the top chairlift at Cinque Torri.

FOR CROSS-COUNTRY ★★★★★
One of the best
Cortina has around 70km of trails suitable for all standards, mainly up the valley at the Fiames area, where there are a cross-country centre and a school. Trails include a 30km itinerary following an old railway from Fiames to Dobbiaco, and there is a beginner area equipped with snowmaking. Passo Tre Croci offers more challenging trails, covering 10km. A Nordic area pass is available.

MOUNTAIN RESTAURANTS ★★★★★
Good, but get in early
There are some excellent spots. Many can be reached by road or lift, and in some places skiers are in the minority. Prices are high in the swishest places. The piste map doesn't identify all restaurants, but the topo map on the reverse is more helpful.

Editors' choice Close to the top of Faloria, Capanna Tondi does excellent food from a wide-ranging menu, with table-service in a series of small, cosy rooms and on a terrace with a great

SNOWPIX.COM / CHRIS GILL
Lagazuoi, seen from the run linking Cinque Torri to Col Gallina ↓

view. Rifugio Averau out at Cinque Torri comes a close second – good-humoured service from the boss, and non-routine food (try the antipasto).

Worth knowing about We've yet to try Baita Son dei Prade above Pocol, which is tipped this year for 'great authentic pasta and soups, in a spacious, modern setting, and a proper family restaurant atmosphere'. At mid-mountain at Cinque Torri, Rifugio Scoiattoli offers 'a fantastic setting and great food and wine'.

SCHOOLS AND GUIDES ★★★★★
Mixed reports
There are a number of schools but we have no recent reports – previous reviews were mixed. The Guide Alpine offers off-piste and touring.

FOR FAMILIES ★★★★★
Some good lift pass deals
Described by a 2014 reporter as being 'very safe and friendly'. There's a wide choice of lift pass deals for children and there are three snow gardens plus hotel-run nurseries. But don't count on good spoken English in this very Italian resort.

STAYING THERE

Make sure you pick up a copy of *Cortina Pocket* – a very useful guide to restaurants, bars, shops and the rest.

Hotels dominate the lodgings market but there are alternatives.
Chalets Inghams runs the ideally located Parc Hotel Victoria as a chalet hotel, and we enjoyed a stay there in 2015. Notably spacious lounge, 'friendly and efficient staff, excellent food and clean, spacious rooms'.
Hotels There's a big choice, from simple pensions to a handful of big 5-star palaces, with 3-star hotels forming the biggest group. We get very few reports from readers, which is why the list below is very limited.
★★★★★Cristallo Claims to be the best in town; 'stylish, luxurious but with friendly helpful staff – excellent shuttle service to lifts and bus station'.
★★★★Poste Charming old place, on the central Corso. Large rooms, some with spa baths.
★★★Columbia B&B hotel approved by a reader some years back, not far from the Tofana lift but a hike from town.
★★★Menardi Welcoming roadside inn where we have enjoyed staying, but a drive out of town.

★★★Olimpia Comfortable B&B hotel in the centre, near Faloria lift.
★★Montana Good value, central B&B hotel, reputedly friendly.
At altitude Rooms are available at several refuges – notably at Pomedes, Averau at Cinque Torri and at Lagazuoi, where you can have breakfast watching the sunrise.

EATING OUT ★★★★★
Wide choice
There are lots of restaurants, with some variation on local traditional cuisine. Sadly, most of the better ones are a taxi ride out of town. The word is that the very smart El Toulà, in a beautiful old barn just on the edge of town, is now overpriced. Also on the edge, Da Beppe Sello is 'a little gem, with extraordinary salad entrées and a good meat choice'. Even further out: the resort's one Michelin-starred place – Tivoli, Meloncino al Camineto, Leone e Anna (Sardinian specialities), Rio Gere (game dishes) and Baita Fraina (pasta and meats).

In and around the centre there are plenty of modest places. We like the Croda Cafè at the west end of the Corso – excellent and very popular; it claims to be the town's original pizzeria, with wood-fired oven. Birreria Vienna serves until midnight.

APRES-SKI ★★★★★
Lively in high season
Cortina is a lively social whirl in high season, with lots of well-heeled Italians staying up very late – but at other times it can be quiet, or 'very dull', to quote a January visitor.

Pasticceria Lovat is one of several high-calorie teatime spots. There are some good wine bars, often doing excellent cheese and meats too: Enoteca, La Suite and LP26 have been tipped. Bar Sport is the place for grappa. Jambo is a 'nice spot for late drinks and a dance – loud but chic'.

OFF THE SLOPES ★★★★★
A classic resort
There's much to do. There are popular walks in several sectors. Lots of upmarket shops. Activities include swimming and skating. There is a planetarium, and an observatory at Col Druscié. There are regular ice hockey matches. The Country Club spa is tipped for its 'real Scan feel'. Trips to Venice are easy. You can visit First World War tunnels at Lagazuoi.

GETTING THERE

Air Venice Marco-Polo 150km/95 miles (2hr); Treviso 140km/ 85 miles (2hr); 35-minute heli-transfers from Venice

Rail Calalzo (35km/ 22 miles) or Dobbiaco (32km/20 miles); frequent buses from station

TOURIST OFFICE
www.cortina.dolomiti. org

SNOWPIX.COM / CHRIS GILL

Courmayeur

A seductive old village on the sunny side of spectacular Mont Blanc, with a very limited area of pistes but some fab off-piste

£95
RESORT PRICE INDEX

RATINGS

The mountains

Extent	★
Fast lifts	★★★★
Queues	★★★★
Terrain p'ks	★★
Snow	★★★★
Expert	★★★
Intermediate	★★★★
Beginner	★
Boarder	★★★
X-country	★★★
Restaurants	★★★★
Schools	★★★★
Families	★★

The resort

Charm	★★★★
Convenience	★
Scenery	★★★★
Eating out	★★★★
Après-ski	★★★★
Off-slope	★★★

402

NEWS

2015/16: The new two-stage Skyway Monte Bianco cable car to Punta Helbronner at 3460m on Mont Blanc will finally be opened for the 2015/16 season. The cabins will rotate 360 degrees to make the most of the views. It will start lower than the old cable car, near Entrèves, and have a new underground car park. The third Mountain Gourmet Ski Experience arranged by Momentum Ski and Heston Blumenthal will be held from 8 to 11 January 2016.

2014/15: A new 5-star hotel, the Grand Hotel Courmayeur Mont Blanc, opened.

+ Charming old village; car-free centre with stylish shops and bars

+ Stunning views of Mont Blanc, which can be reached by a new (for 2015/16) rotating cable car

+ Some good off-piste and heli-skiing

+ Comprehensive snowmaking

+ Some great mountain restaurants

− Very small area of pistes

− Lots of drawbacks for beginners

− No really tough pistes

− No runs back to the village, only to Dolonne (where you catch a bus)

− Can get busy at weekends

Courmayeur is a great place for a short midweek break or for a day trip to escape bad weather in Megève and Chamonix – we have used it for this several times. Excellent restaurants both on and off the mountain plus village bars among the most civilized in the skiing world are important factors for us too.

The piste skiing is tricky to recommend for more than a day or two, though, because it best suits competent intermediates, who are likely to have an appetite for mileage that Courmayeur will arouse but not satisfy.

THE RESORT

Courmayeur is a traditional old mountaineering village that has retained much of its character.

La Thuile is an easy drive or bus ride away; Aosta/Pila and Chamonix are not far, and Cervinia and Monterosa are reachable; all are covered by various lift passes.

VILLAGE CHARM ★★★★☆
Attractive and sophisticated
The village has a charming traffic-free core of cobbled streets and well-preserved old buildings. As the lifts close, the central Via Roma comes alive: people pile into the many bars, or browse the tempting delis and smart clothes shops – some now have doormen to stop celebrity-spotters, and some are appointment-only at peak times, we're told; there's also a good bookshop. An Alpine museum and a statue of a long-dead mountain rescue hero add to the historical feel of the place.

Away from the centre, there are pleasant woody suburbs but also a lot of conspicuous apartment blocks.

CONVENIENCE ★☆☆☆☆
Buses to the lifts
A huge cable car on the southern edge of the village takes you to and from Plan Checrouit, at the heart of the slopes. (The cable car is open in the evening too, to serve the bars and restaurants up there.) You cannot ski back to the village, but you can ski to the base of the alternative gondola from Dolonne (across the valley); parking is much easier there, too. You can leave your gear up at Plan Checrouit. You can also access the slopes by cable car from Entrèves, a few miles from Courmayeur; the new cable car up Mont Blanc leaves from here too; and there will be a new

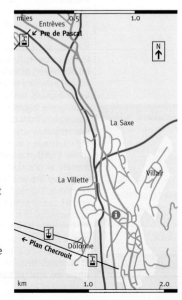

↑ The Checrouit area catches the morning sun and has mainly undemanding, wide red runs
BRIAN WALKER

KEY FACTS

Resort	1225m
	4,020ft
Slopes	1210-2755m
	3,970-9,040ft
Lifts	18
Pistes	41km
	25 miles

underground car park here for 2015/16. Buses serve all lift stations, but readers have found services 'inadequate'. Many hotels run shuttles that are welcomed by reporters.

SCENERY ★★★★☆
Mont Blanc rules
The high glacial slopes of the Mont Blanc (Monte Bianco in Italian) massif overlook Courmayeur's slopes. The views from the high points at Cresta d'Arp and Cresta Youla, especially, are stunning.

THE MOUNTAINS

The slopes above the focal point of Plan Checrouit are mainly wide open, but there are also wooded areas, particularly on the back side of the hill. The piste map now shows lift names and direction, but some reporters criticize piste signposting and marking.

EXTENT OF THE SLOPES ★☆☆☆☆
Small and variable
From the time this book started 21 years ago, we were sceptical of the resort's claimed 100km of pistes. Four seasons ago, at last, it revealed that the true extent was 36km of pistes plus 64km of off-piste runs (whatever that means). It has now adjusted the 36km figure to 41km but that is still tiny compared with most resorts in this book.

There are two distinct sectors, separated by a rocky ridge. The links between the two can be a bit confusing. Above Plan Checrouit, the east-facing **Checrouit** area, accessed mainly by the Checrouit gondola, catches the morning sun. The 20-person Youla cable car goes to the top of the pistes. A further tiny cable car to Cresta d'Arp serves only long off-piste runs.

Most people follow the sun over to the north-west-facing slopes of **Val Veny** in the afternoon. These offer a mix of open and wooded slopes, with great views of Mont Blanc and its glaciers. The Val Veny slopes are also accessible by cable car from Entrèves, a few miles outside Courmayeur.

Entrèves is also the starting point for a new cable car to Punta Helbronner, at the shoulder of **Mont Blanc**, which will be open for the 2015/16 season. This accesses the famous Vallée Blanche run to Chamonix and avoids the scary ridge walk that forms the start if you ride the cable car from Chamonix; but it also means you miss out on the chance to ski some of the more interesting and steeper variants of the run. It also accesses tougher off-piste runs on the Italian side of Mont Blanc – notably the Toula glacier run. Obviously all these glacier runs require guidance and safety equipment. There are buses back from Chamonix.

ITALY

404

LIFT PASSES

Prices in €

Age	6-day
under 14	141
14 to 64	234
65 plus	187

Free Under 8 if with adult

Beginner Three free nursery lifts (but you have to pay for the access lifts to reach them)

Notes Covers Courmayeur and the Mont Blanc cable cars; 3- or 4-hour passes; weekly passes allow two days in other Aosta valley resorts

Alternative passes
Non-skier; Mont Blanc Unlimited (includes Chamonix valley and Verbier); Valle d'Aosta (covers Aosta Valley ski areas)

FAST LIFTS ★★★★☆
A decent network
The main access lifts are cable cars or a gondola. On the hill, there are fast lifts in all the key spots.

QUEUES ★★★★☆
Much improved
Queues are generally not a problem except on busy weekends. Queues to descend at the end of the day have been eased by the evening opening of the cable car. On the back of the hill, Zerotta is a real bottleneck – we've waited 15 minutes here in March. It's worth waiting until late afternoon to ride the Youla cable car.

TERRAIN PARKS ★★☆☆☆
There is one
A park is served by the Aretù chairlift. It has a line of rails for beginners and children, another for intermediates, jumps and an airbag.

SNOW RELIABILITY ★★★★☆
Good for most of the season
Courmayeur's slopes are not high – mostly between 1700m and 2250m. Those above Val Veny face north or north-west, so they keep their snow well, but the Plan Checrouit side is too sunny for comfort in late season. There is snowmaking on most main runs, including the red run to the valley. So good coverage in early and mid season is virtually assured – we've been there in a snow drought and enjoyed decent skiing entirely on artificial snow. Grooming is good.

FOR EXPERTS ★★★☆☆
Off-piste is the challenge
Courmayeur has few challenging pistes. The black runs on the Val Veny side are not severe, but moguls are allowed to develop. If you're lucky enough to find fresh powder, you can have fantastic fun among the trees.

Classic off-piste runs go from Cresta d'Arp, at the top of the lift network, in three directions: a clockwise loop via Arp Vieille to Val Veny, with close-up views of the Miage glacier; east down a deserted valley to Dolonne or Pré-St-Didier; or south through the Youla gorge to La Balme, near La Thuile.

The off-piste possibilities on Mont Blanc are considerable, some mentioned in 'Extent of the slopes', above. A day trip to Chamonix, for both pistes and off-piste, is appealing.

(M) MOMENTUM SKI

Weekend & a la carte ski holiday specialists

100% Tailor-made

Premier hotels & apartments

The No.1 Specialist in Courmayeur

020 7371 9111
WWW.MOMENTUMSKI.COM

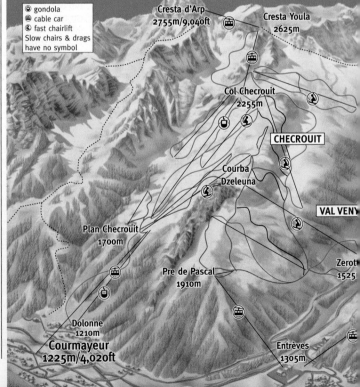

There are also heli-drops, including a wonderful 20km run from the Ruitor glacier that ends near Ste-Foy in France – you take a taxi from there to La Rosière, ride the lifts back up from there and descend to La Thuile (then take another taxi back).

FOR INTERMEDIATES ★★★★☆
Good reds, but limited extent
It's an intermediate's mountain, for sure, laced with interestingly varied, genuine red runs. But it is small; the avid piste-basher will ski it in a day. There are a few good long runs – it's 700m vertical from Col Checrouit to Zerotta, and an impressive 1400m vertical from Cresta Youla to Dolonne. On the steeper Val Veny side of the ridge there are challenges to be found – while the reds and blues cut across the mountain, a row of easy blacks go down more directly.

For the timid intermediate, on the other hand, the area is short of confidence-building blue runs. There is just one long blue on the Col Checrouit side of the ridge and a couple on the Val Veny side (which is better for the challenge-averse). Many of the reds – particularly up around Col Checrouit and down to Plan Checrouit – do have the merit that they are generally wide.

FOR BEGINNERS ★☆☆☆☆
Lots of drawbacks
To get to the free beginner lifts (at Plan Checrouit, on the ridge above there and at the top of the Val Veny cable car from Entrèves) you have the hassle and cost of getting up the mountain. The best starting point is the Val Veny cable car, which takes you to a moving carpet, and easy longer runs on the Peindeint chair. There is a clear lack of other easy longer runs to progress to.

FOR BOARDERS ★★★☆☆
Mainly intermediate fun
Courmayeur's pistes suit intermediates well, and most areas are accessible by cable cars, chairs and gondolas (though the beginner slopes have drags). For the more adventurous, there are off-piste routes.

FOR CROSS-COUNTRY ★★★☆☆
Beautiful trails
There are about 35km of trails. The best are the five covering 20km at Val Ferret, served by bus.

MOUNTAIN RESTAURANTS ★★★★☆
A very good choice
The area is well endowed with establishments ranging from rustic little huts that do table-service of delicious pizza, pasta and other dishes, to snack bars and a large self-service place – but strangely they are not marked on the piste map.

Editors' choice We and readers have had excellent meals at Chiecco by the draglift starting below Plan Checrouit – a small hut run by the very welcoming Anna; very varied menu, including fantastic chicken curry and wild boar stew; superb tiramisu. An old favourite of ours is Maison Vieille, a cosy, rustic place with jolly service; after a couple of years with lukewarm reports, a 2015 visitor loved it ('spectacular carbonara, first-class gnocchi, good house wine').

Worth knowing about Another favourite at Plan Checrouit is the Christiania (book a table downstairs to escape the crowds). Nearby, the Chaumière is family-run with good 2015 reports ('excellent pizzas, pasta and wine'), a sunny terrace with superb views; 'gourmet' restaurant downstairs, more basic 'bistrot' with limited menu upstairs. Also nearby is the rustic Chateau Branlant ('excellent local soup, barbecued meats, fine wines'). Up at Col Checrouit, Chez Croux is the place to go for cakes and hot drinks. There is another clutch of worthwhile places in Val Veny: we enjoyed the smartly rustic Grolla for steaks and salads and the Petit Mont Blanc is popular ('stunning views, spit-roasted suckling pig is fantastic').

SCHOOLS AND GUIDES ★★★★☆
Good mountain guides
We lack recent reports on both the main Monte Bianco and the Courmayeur schools; the latter has a more snowboardy and young funky image. The mountain guides' association has produced a helpful booklet showing the main off-piste possibilities; a 2015 visitor loved his day and a half with Alex. We had a couple of great days with solo guide Gianni Carbone (www.giannicarbone. com), who is patient and reassuring.

FOR FAMILIES ★★☆☆☆
Some facilities
There are children's playgrounds at Dolonne, Plan Checrouit and Val Veny, and a nursery at Plan Checrouit for children up to 10 years.

STAYING THERE

There's a wide range of packages (including some excellent weekend deals), mainly in hotels. Momentum Ski is an agent specializing in Courmayeur and can fix pretty much whatever you want here.

Chalets Mark Warner runs the central Cristallo as a chalet hotel.

Hotels There are over 50 hotels, spanning the star ratings.

*****Grand Hotel Courmayeur Mont Blanc Opened last season. Near centre, large rooms with floor-to-ceiling windows, beginner slope and moving carpet in garden; pool, steam, sauna.

*****Royal e Golf Large, grand, 200 years old, in centre. Indoor/outdoor pool, spa.

****Auberge de la Maison Small, atmospheric hotel in Entrèves; owned by the same family as Maison de Filippo (see 'Eating out').

****Villa Novecento A short walk from the centre. Elegant lobby, good food and breakfasts. Sauna, steam, hot tub.

***Bouton d'Or Small, friendly B&B hotel near main square, repeatedly recommended by reporters.

***Camosci 800m from centre: 'Not a single complaint, great minibus service to/from gondola and for après in town,' said a 2015 reporter.

***Dolonne Family-run, based in a 16th-century building. A 2015 reporter says: 'Very friendly; comfortable rooms; good food; five-minute walk from gondola.'

**Edelweiss Central, family-run 2-star B&B, 'good value with 3-star service'.

Apartments The 3-star Grand Chalet is central with spacious apartments. Hot tub, steam and sauna are also available for non-residents.

At altitude At Plan Checrouit, the 1-star Christiania has simple rooms; the 3-star Super G is smarter and has a lively après scene.

EATING OUT ★★★★☆
Jolly Italian evenings

There is a great choice of places. A handy promotional booklet describes many of them (in English). We've been impressed by the traditional Italian cuisine of the smart Cadran Solaire. La Terrazza serves classic and local cuisine plus pizzas and has been highly recommended ('superb – owners very accommodating, excellent set meal'). Other reporter tips: the Piazzetta ('very good and inexpensive',

'extremely friendly'), the very popular little Pizzeria du Tunnel ('super food, attentive service'), Ancien Casinò ('best pizza ever, and inexpensive'), Le Vieux Pommier ('great atmosphere, serves a mixture of Italian and Savoyard fare'), Aria ('very friendly, an amazing wine list') and Al Camin ('rustic yet elegant ambience, a meat lover's paradise'). In Entrèves, the touristy but very jolly Maison de Filippo is rightly famous for its fixed-price, 36-dish feast. For a gourmet treat take a taxi to the Clotze in Val Ferret (same management as Chiecco – read 'Mountain restaurants'). The cable car to Plan Checrouit now works in the evening so you can catch that up to use the restaurants there.

APRES-SKI ★★★★☆
Stylish bar-hopping

You can now stay up the mountain for après (eg at the Super G) and catch the cable car down. Down in the village there's a lively evening scene – at weekends, at least – centred on stylish bars with comfy armchairs or sofas, often serving free canapés in the early evening. We like the Privé ('great cocktails', 'reasonable prices and good service') and the back room of the Caffè della Posta ('the people-watching is superb', 'laden plates of goodies arrive with each round'). Bar Roma is an old favourite and its free antipasto buffet is back. A 2015 reporter liked the ambience of the Bar delle Guides and a recent visitor enjoyed the 'great service and very good food' at Petit Bistro. The American Bar has good live music. There are three nightclubs – Courmaclub, Jset and Shatush. Or try the branch of Shatush in Entrèves (free shuttle-bus service).

OFF THE SLOPES ★★★☆☆
Lots for non-slope users

The resort attracts many non-skiing weekenders, who focus on showing off their togs and buying more of them – so there are some tempting shops. You can go by bus to Aosta, or by cable car up to Plan Checrouit where there are countless spots to meet friends for lunch. The huge sports centre is good (but has no pool). Don't miss a visit to the thermal baths at Pré-St-Didier 6km away – with over 40 spa 'experiences', including saunas and outdoor pools. There's snowshoeing at Val Veny and on the Toula glacier with a guide. The Parco Avventura (10km from town) has a 'great' ropes course.

GETTING THERE

Air Geneva 110km/ 70 miles (1hr30); Turin 150km/95 miles (1hr45)

Rail Pré-St-Didier (5km/3 miles); regular buses from station

TOURIST OFFICE

www.courmayeur.it
www.lovevda.it

Livigno

Lowish prices and highish altitude – a tempting combination, especially when you add in a pleasant Alpine ambience

APT LIVIGNO / I. MARTINELLI

£90
RESORT PRICE INDEX

RATINGS

The mountains

Extent	★★
Fast lifts	★★★★
Queues	★★★★
Terrain p'ks	★★★★
Snow	★★★★
Expert	★★★
Intermediate	★★★
Beginner	★★★★
Boarder	★★★★
X-country	★★★★
Restaurants	★★★
Schools	★★★
Families	★★

The resort

Charm	★★★
Convenience	★★
Scenery	★★★
Eating out	★★★
Après-ski	★★★
Off-slope	★★

NEWS

2014/15: The ancient chairlift along the ridge at the top of Mottolino was dismantled. The indoor pool and gym at the Aquagranda leisure centre reopened after refurbishment but the other facilities remained closed.

KEY FACTS

Resort	1815m
	5,950ft
Slopes	1815-2795m
	5,950-9,170ft
Lifts	30
Pistes	115km
	71 miles

+ Reliable snow

+ Large choice of beginners' slopes

+ Impressive modern lift system

+ Cheap by the standards of high, snow-sure resorts

+ Lively, friendly, quite smart village with a good Alpine atmosphere

+ Long, snow-sure cross-country trails

− Few tough pistes

− Mainly above the treeline, so susceptible to white-outs

− Very long transfers from some Italian airports (Innsbruck is much quicker)

− Village is very long and straggling, with no buses later in the evening

− Nightlife can disappoint

Livigno's recipe of a fair-sized mountain, high altitude and fairly low prices is uncommon, and obviously attractive, and may be enough to get it on to your shortlist, especially if you are a beginner or unadventurous intermediate. But don't overlook the non-trivial drawbacks listed above.

After banning off-piste for several years up to 2012/13 the resort now allows it and has heli-skiing as well.

THE RESORT

Livigno is set in a wide, remote valley near the Swiss border; the airport transfers are long and winding. The Alta Valtellina lift pass covers Bormio (about an hour's bus ride – free with the lift pass) and Santa Caterina (another 20 minutes). The Livigno pass gets you half-price on one day in St Moritz – an excursion not easily done from any other major resort.

VILLAGE CHARM ★★★☆☆
Pleasant enough
At the core of the resort is a single, mainly pedestrian street that is just over 1km long and is lined by hotels, bars, specialist shops and supermarkets, with side streets linking to the parallel by-pass road. The buildings are small in scale and traditional in style, creating a pleasant atmosphere. Away from the central area, traffic can be intrusive.

CONVENIENCE ★★☆☆☆
Where you gonna stay?
It's a long, spread-out place – over 4km from one end to the other. The pedestrian core is the most attractive all-round location, but the three major lifts are out at the extremities. Unless you opt to stay near one of these, you will make heavy use of the free bus services, but they get overcrowded at peak times and they stop at around

8pm. The complex route map requires serious study, but reporters find the services 'regular' and 'efficient'. Taxis (including minibuses for groups) are affordable.

SCENERY ★★★☆☆
High and probably white
Livigno's high position and long ridges provide attractive views from both sides of the valley – but it can feel bleak and isolated.

LIFT PASSES

Prices in €

Age	6-day
under 15	151
15 to 64	219
65 plus	151

Free Under 8

Beginner Points card

Notes Half-day passes and reduced Saturday rates; 50% discount on day pass at St Moritz with a 3-day-plus pass

Alternative pass
Alta Valtellina pass covers Livigno, Bormio and Santa Caterina

The Livigno holiday experts

THE MOUNTAINS

The slopes are on either side of the valley and mainly above the treeline. It's not a good place in bad weather. Signposting is adequate, but the piste map does not name or number runs. Night skiing is available on Thursdays.

EXTENT OF THE SLOPES ★★☆☆☆
Widely spread

The slopes are more extensive than in many other budget destinations, but it's not a huge area and lots of the runs are very similar to one another.

At the north end of the village is the narrow **Costaccia** sector, reached by the two-stage Tagliede gondola (with the Cassana gondola and an adjacent six-pack offering alternative ways to the mid-station). From the top, you can cross to the Carosello sector by using two fast quads. The blue linking run back from Carosello to the top of Costaccia is flat in places and may involve energetic poling.
Carosello is more usually accessed by the optimistically named Carosello 3000 gondola at the southern end of the village, which goes up, in two stages, to almost 2800m. Most runs return towards the village, but the Federia six-pack serves west-facing slopes on the back of the mountain.
The ridge of **Mottolino** is reached

by a gondola or fast quad from Teola, across the valley from central Livigno. From the top, you can descend to fast quads on either side of the ridge.

We don't show on our map a link from the nursery drags at the bottom of Carosello to those below Costaccia; it's more of a walk than a run.

FAST LIFTS ★★★★☆
A positive attraction

The lift system is impressively modern, with fast chairs and gondolas covering both sectors – though draglifts still serve the valley nursery slopes.

QUEUES ★★★★☆
Few problems these days

Queues are generally not a problem, though delays can occur at the main gondolas at peak times. Winds can close the upper lifts, causing crowds lower down.

TERRAIN PARKS ★★★★☆
Serious facilities

The main park behind Mottolino is an impressive freestyle zone for all levels. It also hosts the World Rookie fest, which is on the Ticket to Ride calendar. It has kicker lines for all levels and is bordered by a big super-pipe. There's also a huge airbag jump – perfect for trying out backflips and other advanced tricks.

↑ The village is long and spread out. This photo is taken from Costaccia looking over to Mottolino

DAVE ASHMORE

Livigno's second park is at Carosello 3000. It also caters for all standards and includes another huge airbag jump. The three other parks, all near lifts with the same names and aimed at novices and juniors are the Amerikan and the San Rocco near the Carosello gondola and the Del Sole near the centre of town. There's a Woodpark too, with wooden obstacles. See www.livignopark.com and www.carosello3000.it.

SNOW RELIABILITY ★★★★☆
Very good, given precipitation
Livigno's slopes are high (you can spend most of your time around 2500m) and, with snow-guns on the lower slopes of Mottolino and Costaccia, the season is long. Piste grooming is 'immaculate'.

FOR EXPERTS ★★★☆☆
Off-piste is now allowed
There are a few black runs, but they are of black steepness only in places, and they are regularly groomed. The rules about off-piste have changed year by year the last few years (before 2012/13 it was banned completely). It is now allowed with or without a mountain guide or instructor. There are free avalanche awareness and equipment briefings on Sunday evenings plus daily avalanche bulletins in English posted on the resort's website. Heli-skiing is available too.

FOR INTERMEDIATES ★★★☆☆
Flattering slopes
There's nothing too demanding but good intermediates will enjoy the groomed blacks on Mottolino, as well as the wide choice of reds. The woodland black run from Carosello past Tea da Borch is narrow in places and can get mogulled and icy in the afternoon. Moderate intermediates have virtually the whole area at their disposal. The long run beneath the Mottolino gondola is one of the best, and there is also a long, varied, underused blue going less directly to the valley. Leisurely types have several long cruises available; the blue beneath the fast chair at the top of Costaccia is a splendid slope.

FOR BEGINNERS ★★★★☆
Excellent scattered slopes
There's a vast array of gentle, sunny, low-traffic nursery slopes rising from the village, with lifts concentrated in three areas: north, centre, south. For progression, there are longer blue runs at the top of Costaccia and Mottolino.

FOR BOARDERS ★★★★☆
Fun of all kinds
The pistes are generally big, wide, open and rolling motorways. The new off-piste policy and the two big parks are obvious attractions for competent boarders. Beginners be warned: practically all the nursery slopes are

serviced by drags and the runs along the ridges on both sides of the valley have some flat spots. Madness is a specialist school.

FOR CROSS-COUNTRY ★★★★☆
Good snow, bleak setting
Long snow-sure trails (30km in total) follow the valley floor, making Livigno a good choice, provided you don't mind the bleak scenery. There is a specialist school, Livigno 2000.

MOUNTAIN RESTAURANTS ★★★☆☆
No more than adequate
Our favourite is the Berghütte, in a fine position close to the bottom of Costaccia; the food is simple but satisfying, the service efficient and friendly. Up the hill at Costaccia the upstairs restaurant 'has friendly table-service and great pasta'. Carosello has a popular self-service place and a table-service wine bar and restaurant below. Tea da Borch, in the trees lower down, has a Tirolean-style atmosphere. On Mottolino, the huge M'eating Point at the top of the gondola has a self-service section that can be excessively busy but also a small, peaceful table-service section. Lower down there are rustic restaurants at Passo d'Eira and at Trepalle, on the back of the hill.

SCHOOLS AND GUIDES ★★★☆☆
Short but sweet classes
Past reports on the schools have generally been good, praising instruction and English. Classes are rated great value for money, but are mornings only (as is usual in Italy).

FOR FAMILIES ★★☆☆☆
Not bad for Italy
The schools run classes for children, and the Centrale school offers all-day non-skiing care for younger children; the staff speak English. Beware the long, winding airport transfers.

STAYING THERE

Livigno has an enormous range of hotels and a number of apartments. Ski Livigno specializes in the resort and can arrange accommodation, transfers, lift passes, ski hire etc.
Hotels There is a wide choice.
****Bivio** Welcoming chalet in centre with popular cellar bar. Good à la carte food. Pool and wellness area.
****Camana Veglia** Charming old wooden chalet. Popular restaurant

serving five-course gastro dinners. Near Cassana gondola.
****Intermonti** Modern with pool etc; on the Mottolino side of the valley.
****Lac Salin** 'Modern, stylish, with an impressive spa' and 'very friendly service, fantastic four-course menu'.
****Larice** Stylish little B&B well placed for Costaccia lifts.
***Champagne** Pleasant central B&B.
***Loredana** Modern chalet on the Mottolino side.
***Montanina** Very central, family-run.
Silvestri Comfortable place in the San Rocco area.
Apartments Available locally and from tour operators including Ski Livigno.

EATING OUT ★★★☆☆
Value for money
Livigno's restaurants are mainly traditional, unpretentious places, many hotel-based. You may have to queue to get into the Bait dal Ghet but a 2015 reporter highly recommends it ('family-run, nice big pizza for 7 or 8 euros and a whole host of shots left on the table to sample at the end of the meal'). Past recommendations include Cantina in the hotel Bivio ('excellent, with a fine choice of wines'), Paprika and Scala.

APRES-SKI ★★★☆☆
Adequately lively
The scene is quieter than some people expect – and the best places are scattered about; but we haven't found it lacking life. At teatime, Tea dal Vidal, at the bottom of Mottolino, has been recommended in the past – and things also get lively at the Stalet bar at the base of the Carosello gondola and at the central umbrella bar. Nightlife gets going after 10pm. Club Bivio under the Bivio hotel is an excellent cellar bar with live music, as is Helvetia, over the road. Daphne's and Miky's have been tipped. Cielo is the main disco.

OFF THE SLOPES ★★☆☆☆
Some distractions
The smart, modern thermal spa/wellness centre Aquagranda has a revamped gym and indoor pool. Other facilities such as saunas, steam rooms and treatment rooms were closed for refurbishment when we went to press. You can try tobogganing, skating on the open-air ice rink, dog sledding and snowmobiling. Walks are uninspiring. There's duty-free shopping, of course – and trips to Bormio and St Moritz.

GETTING THERE

Air Bolzano 135km/ 85 miles (2hr15); Innsbruck 180km/ 110 miles (2hr45); Zürich 205km/ 125 miles (3hr15); Friedrichshafen 200km/125 miles (3hr15); Bergamo 190km/120 miles (3hr30); Verona 280km/175 miles (3hr30)

Rail Tirano (73km/ 45 miles); Zernez (Switzerland, 28km/ 17 miles); regular buses from station

TOURIST OFFICE

www.livigno.eu

Madonna di Campiglio

A fashionable resort amid stunning scenery – a bit like Cortina, in other words, but with a more conveniently linked ski area

£105
RESORT PRICE INDEX

RATINGS

The mountains

Extent	★★★
Fast lifts	★★★★
Queues	★★★
Terrain p'ks	★★★★
Snow	★★★
Expert	★★
Intermediate	★★★★
Beginner	★★★★
Boarder	★★★
X-country	★★★
Restaurants	★★★
Schools	★★★
Families	★★★

The resort

Charm	★★★★
Convenience	★★★
Scenery	★★★★
Eating out	★★★
Après-ski	★★★
Off-slope	★★

NEWS

2014/15: Two new family parks were created, one at Pinzolo and one at Campo Carlo Magna including a beginners' area with five magic carpets.

KEY FACTS

Resort	1520m
	4,990ft

Madonna, Folgarida, Marilleva, Pinzolo combined area

Slopes	800-2505m
	2,620-8,220ft
Lifts	61
Pistes	150km
	93 miles

+ Splendid wooded setting in the dramatic Brenta Dolomites

+ Pleasant, stylish village, with car-free centre and a tunnel bypass

+ Extensive, varied slopes, including Folgarida, Marilleva and Pinzolo

+ Lots of long, easy runs

– Although it has a compact core, the resort spreads widely along the valley, away from the lifts

– Tough pistes are few, and widely separated around a big area – and off-piste is formally banned

– Quiet from dinner time onwards

Madonna di Campiglio has worked its way into our affections gradually, over many years; we now count it as one of our favourite Italian resorts. It may come second to Cortina d'Ampezzo for smart shops and bars – and for scenic drama – but it is nevertheless a lovely place which is attracting more and more readers.

The slopes offer plenty of variety, and a satisfying sense of travel across considerable distances – particularly since a gondola built in 2011 created a long-awaited link with Pinzolo; it's an amazing 17km from Folgarida.

THE RESORT

Campiglio is a well-established, quite fashionable resort, set near the head of a heavily wooded valley. Although the clientele is mainly Italian, the resort is now attracting Russian visitors in considerable numbers. The Skirama regional lift pass covers not only the several linked resorts but also others in the Val di Sole to the north, including Pejo and Passo Tonale (which gets its own chapter).

VILLAGE CHARM ★★★★
Smoothly traditional
Campiglio is mainly built in traditional Alpine style and has a towny, polished air, at least around the central, car-free Piazza Righi and nearby streets, where there are quite a few diverting shops. The village is bypassed by through-traffic. Near the centre is a small park and a lake, used for skating. The place doesn't go to sleep in the day, and is quite lively in the early evening.

CONVENIENCE ★★★
Good links between sectors
The centre is fairly compact: the major lifts bracket many of the main hotels, and are a 5/10-minute walk apart. Skiing links between the main slope sectors work well. But the resort sprawls about 3km down the valley, and some hotels are quite a way out; up the valley is the outlying suburb of Campo Carlo Magno, where there are further major lifts and a sizeable car

park as well as more hotels. The ski-bus service has not impressed reporters, and now costs a non-trivial 10 euros a week. We'd stay near a main lift, or at a hotel that runs a shuttle (many do).

SCENERY ★★★★
Splendid Dolomites
The resort has a splendid setting, with the dramatic cliffs of the Brenta group to the south-east.

THE MOUNTAINS

The upper slopes are open, the lower slopes attractively wooded; most major lifts go well above the treeline, so there are few entirely sheltered runs at Madonna – Folgarida is better in this respect. Many run classifications exaggerate difficulty.

EXTENT OF THE SLOPES ★★★
Plenty of variety
The extent of the pistes is not huge, but the slopes span large distances and give a great sense of travel.

Gondolas from close to the centre go west into the **Pradalago** sector – which is linked via Monte Vigo to the distant slopes of **Folgarida** and **Marilleva** – and to **Cinque Laghi**, where at mid-mountain the gondola link with **Pinzolo** starts. A bit further from the centre, another gondola goes east up to **Spinale**. The high **Grostè** sector can be reached from there or by access gondola from the outlying

MOMENTUM SKI

Weekend & a la carte
ski holiday specialists

100% Tailor-made

Premier hotels
& apartments

Flexible travel
arrangements

020 7371 9111
WWW.MOMENTUMSKI.COM

Campo Carlo Magno, where there is also a fast chairlift up to Pradalago.

FAST LIFTS ★★★★★
Some weaknesses
Most of the key lifts are fast chairs and gondolas, but moving around the area you will still meet some slow lifts. Examples include several lifts around Monte Spolverino and Monte Vigo, on Dos de la Pesa, on Monte Spinale and at Pinzolo. But at least the piste map helpfully distinguishes fast chairs.

QUEUES ★★★★★
Avoid New Year
With over a dozen reports from readers this year, we have a pretty clear view of the queue scene, and have been moved to cut a star from our rating even after discounting the one report of 'horrendous' queues at New Year. At the other extreme we have reports of no queues on one visit in January and on a Saturday in February. But we also have lots of reports of trouble spots at other times: the Grostè gondola and Fortini chair at Campo Carlo Magno; and the series of lifts between Marilleva/Folgarida and Campiglio, which get tidal flows in the morning and late afternoon. There are some piste bottlenecks in the latter area too – one reporter says the runs down the Genziana chair were 'a nightmare in the afternoon'.

LIFT PASSES

Prices in €

Age	6-day
under 8	129
8 to 15	180
16 to 64	257
65 plus	231

Free Under 8 if with family-paying adult

Beginner Day passes for the improved nursery area at Campo Carlo Magno

Note Covers, Madonna, Pinzolo, Folgarida and Marilleva

Alternative passes Madonna only; Pinzolo only; Skirama Dolomiti Adamello Brenta, covers Madonna, Pinzolo, Marilleva-Folgarida, Passo Tonale, Ponte di Legno, Andalo, Pejo, Monte Bondone and Folgaria-Lavarone

TERRAIN PARKS ★★★★☆
Serious efforts

The Ursus park, at Grostè, including snowcross and quarter-pipe, is claimed to be among the top five in the Alps and impresses all reporters who take any interest in such things. There's a special boarders' pass for the area. There is also a beginner park in the Pradalago sector.

SNOW RELIABILITY ★★★☆☆
Good snowmaking

Although many of the runs are sunny, they are at a fair altitude, and snowmaking is now claimed to cover 95% of the runs. As a result, snow reliability is reasonable, despite an erratic snowfall record. Reporters stress the immaculate grooming.

FOR EXPERTS ★★☆☆☆
Relax and enjoy the view

There are black pistes dotted around – basically, one per sector – but they only just merit the classification. The lower part of Spinale Direttissima on the front of Monte Spinale is claimed to be 35°, which is a proper black. Few of the local reds present much challenge; it's worth checking out Pinzolo and Marilleva. As in many resorts in Italy, off-piste is formally banned, but the ban is often ignored, and last year we had a report from a reader who 'had a great morning off-piste on Spinale with an instructor'. This is not an area famed for reliable powder, though. The lift company says that it leaves Spinale Direttissima and Pancugolo (on Cinque Laghi) ungroomed for a day after a snowfall.

FOR INTERMEDIATES ★★★★☆
A great area

Grostè and Pradalago have long, wide easy runs, and timid intermediates will love them, while confident skiers will need to seek out challenges. The long blue Pradalago Facile is a fabulous wide, scenic cruise. The nearby reds aren't a lot steeper, but the lovely, scenic black Amazzonia is quite testing. Grostè is both high and gentle, so has the feel of a glacier – but is entirely rock. All four runs at the very top are of blue gradient, although two are marked red. Lower down, Lame is a decent red, but the final blue to the village is 'more like XC than downhill skiing'. Next-door Monte Spinale has easy slopes on the back, linking to Grostè, but much tougher stuff on the front (read 'For experts'). Spinale Diretta (not to be confused with Spinale Direttissima) is an excellent genuine red. Cinque Laghi, Campiglio's racing mountain, has something for everyone. The long 5 Laghi is tricky at the top, but is then a lovely genuine blue run ending prettily in woods; the famous Fis 3-Tre is a good, varied red, quite steep towards the bottom.

Keen intermediates should not fail to explore the runs at Folgarida, Marilleva and Pinzolo. The Malghette red run on the way back from Monte Vigo is a favourite, with fabulous views across the valley; pity it's served by a slow lift. Most of the Pinzolo runs are relatively short, confined to the open slopes above the trees.

FOR BEGINNERS ★★★★☆
Get out of town

The main nursery slopes are up at Campo Carlo Magno, a bus ride out – now apparently with a vast range of magic carpet lifts. Day passes are available. Many people seem to start on the good slopes at the top of Pradalago, and up here you are perfectly placed for progression to longer easy runs, both in this sector and across the valley at Grostè.

FOR BOARDERS ★★★☆☆
Freeriders look elsewhere

The resort is popular with freestylers, and some major events have been held here.

FOR CROSS-COUNTRY ★★★☆☆
Respectable

There are 22km of pretty trails through the woods in a scenic setting up at Campo Carlo Magno.

MOUNTAIN RESTAURANTS ★★★☆☆
Could do better

Restaurants are named on the piste map. They are not super-numerous, and some are routine lift-station cafeterias, but there are also good table-service places with character (including mountaineering refuges).

Two of the best are on Pradalago: Rif Viviani at the top ('great views, service and food', 'friendly staff, interesting menu') and Cascina Zeledria towards the bottom ('the best – service first class, food superb').

Over on Grostè, Rif Stoppani at the top is universally liked for its fab views, and most reports on the food

↑ The close-up views of the Brenta Dolomites from the wooded slopes of Pinzolo are very impressive
FOTOTECA TRENTINO MARKETING SPA

and service are good too. The little back room at Chalet Fiat at Spinale looks like the real deal – 'great' is a reporter's verdict; the stylish self-service bit has decent food, but finding a table can be a bunfight. Lower down, the charming Malga Montagnoli pleased two reporters this year – 'good traditional food'.

High on our agenda for a visit is Malga Vigo on the way to Folgarida – in a newly renovated cow shed.

SCHOOLS AND GUIDES ★★★★★
Insist on English
There are several schools. Nazionale is the main one, and has had good reports. Some schools have minibuses; apparently some will bus you to the excellent nursery slopes at Folgarida.

FOR FAMILIES ★★★★★
Do your own thing
The ski schools offer non-ski activities as well as ski classes. But we wonder if English is reliably spoken. The central park is an attractive feature.

STAYING THERE

Zenith offers lots of hotels, and Momentum Ski can fix any kind of holiday here.
Hotels There is a wide choice of hotels – dozens of 4-star and 3-star places, and three 5-stars.
****Chalet del Brenta** Stylish place well south of the centre but strongly tipped by readers a couple of years ago – efficient shuttle, excellent food, 'very friendly staff, very good spa'.

****Lorenzetti** At southern extremity not far from the gondola for Cinque Laghi, and with timetabled shuttles. Good food, 'glorious views'.
****Oberosler** 'Design' hotel (ie bold modern decor) right next to the Spinale gondola and return piste – 'excellent food and spa', helpful staff.
***Alpen Vidi** A minor flood of testimonials this year for this central and 'first-class' family-run hotel offering 'excellent dinners', 'lovely staff' and 'large, warm rooms'.
***Ariston** On the town square, tastefully decorated and well run by an English-speaking Italian couple. 'Highly recommended.'
***Montana** 'Faultless' B&B hotel next to the 5 Laghi piste, with 'charm and atmosphere', run by a 'lovely' family. Cheap bar where you can scoff your own takeaway meals.
Apartments A reader tips the apartments at the Residence Hotel Posta, in a good central spot.

EATING OUT ★★★★★
Some good options
There are around 20 restaurants in the resort, including three with Michelin stars. Readers seem more interested in the 'excellent, reasonably priced pizzas' and 'great pasta' at Le Roi. Another modest reader tip is Antico Focolare ('spectacular ravioli in creamy nut sauce'). For a gourmet treat at sub-Michelin star prices, try the 'amazing' Alfiero at the south end of the park ('luxury, good service and food, reasonable prices') or 'superb' Zanolini in the hotel all'Imperatore.

DO MORE
in *Madonna di Campiglio*

zenith holidays·

0203 137 7678

zenithholidays.co.uk
◆ABTA
ABTA No. Y1542

APRES-SKI ★★★★★
Jolly enough at teatime

As the slopes close, people pile in to several central places – notably Caffé Campiglio and Bar Suisse, a very welcoming cafe-bar on the main square. Ober One at the bottom of Spinale is 'conveniently placed but not so popular', maybe because of the music it pumps out. Clear reader favourite, though, is the 'really lovely' little back-street bar Dolomiti – 'we went every night, which says it all'. As dinner time approaches, everyone disappears. If some of them reappear later, it's to head for Club des Alpes, Piano 54 or Cliffhanger.

OFF THE SLOPES ★★★★★
Take your Kindle

There's not a huge amount to do. Skating on the lake and snowshoeing are popular.

LINKED RESORT – 1400m
MARILLEVA

Marilleva is a modern resort consisting of several 1960s-style, ugly but functional, low-rise concrete buildings (most of them well screened by trees, thankfully) built on a mid-mountain shelf at 1400m and reached by road or gondola from the lower part of the resort at 900m, on the valley floor. A reporter this year called the lodgings here 'tired'.

The slopes above Marilleva are excellent, genuine reds served by a gondola and a six-pack (with a few blues higher up), much better for keen intermediates than Campiglio's main Pradalago slopes. And they are shady, so the snow is usually the best in the area. There's also a genuine black run on Dos de la Pesa served by a slow two-stage chairlift. Queues to get out of the village in the morning are reportedly serious if you hit the Polish spring break. The Orti mountain restaurant offers 'good food, fantastic views, reasonable prices', and Malga Panciana greatly impressed one reader this year.

LINKED RESORT – 1400m
FOLGARIDA

Folgarida is also purpose-built, but it is beside the road over to Campiglio, and is much more traditional in style than Marilleva. The resort spreads across the mountainside between two gondola stations, one right on the roadside nominally at 1400m and the other some way off the road in a much more village-like area at 1300m. This part in particular feels more upmarket than Marilleva, with smart hotels and a few shops, but there are few other amenities. The busy 4-star Park Hotel enthused one reader with its 'lavish food, good pool and gym'.

The slopes down to Folgarida are gentler than those above Marilleva, though they include an easy black. Up at Malghet Aut, where both gondolas arrive, is a beginner area that two observers rated highly last year. There are two recommended restaurants at this point: Rif Albasini is tipped for its 'fantastic hand-thrown wood-oven pizzas', Rosa Alpina for 'super food and very good local wine'.

Midway between Marilleva and Folgarida, an eight-person gondola runs from the valley village of Daolasa up to Val Mastellina, below Monte Vigo, the top section serving a long, sweeping red with lovely views.

LINKED RESORT – 770m
PINZOLO

Pinzolo is the main town of the Val Rendena, south-west of Campiglio, and 750m lower. It sells itself as a family resort, with good childcare facilities at mid-mountain.

From Pinzolo, a gondola followed by a fast chair take you, via a lively mid-mountain congregation area with nursery slopes, to the area's high point of Doss del Sabion (2100m), where there are great close-up views of the Brenta massif.

It's quite a challenging area, with genuine blacks (groomed when we have visited) and genuine reds, some at the steep end of the spectrum. Most of the runs are quite short, the notable exception being the excellent black/red run of almost 900m vertical to the valley station of a second gondola at Tulot, just outside the town. Start at Doss del Sabion and you can extend this to 1300m. Many of the slopes are quiet and shady.

Rif Doss del Sabion at the top has a calm little table-service restaurant as an alternative to the often hectic terrace and self-service. The 'very picturesque' Malga Cioca is also strongly recommended.

There are plenty of guest houses and hotels, mainly 3-star.

GETTING THERE

Air Verona 150km/ 95 miles (2hr30); Bergamo 180km/ 110 miles (2hr45); Milan Linate 220km/135 miles (3hr); Milan Malpensa 260km/160 miles (3hr30)

Rail Trento (75km/ 45 miles)

TOURIST OFFICE

www.
campigliodolomiti.it

Monterosa Ski

At last, becoming better known: three unspoiled and uncrowded valleys linked by pistes and with fab off-piste terrain

£85
RESORT PRICE INDEX

TOP 10 RATINGS

Extent	★★
Fast lifts	★★★★★
Queues	★★★★
Snow	★★★★
Expert	★★★★
Intermediate	★★★★
Beginner	★★
Charm	★★★
Convenience	★★★
Scenery	★★★★

NEWS

2015/16: UK tour op Inghams has taken over the 3-star Champoluc hotel, right by the gondola, and will be running it as a chalet hotel.

2014/15: UK tour op Ski Total has taken over one of our favourite hotels (the 4-star Breithorn) and is running it as a chalet hotel.

+ Fabulous off-piste and heli-skiing, for both intermediates and experts
+ Slopes quiet on weekdays
+ Unspoiled valleys and villages
+ Panoramic views at altitude
+ Wide variety of mountain restaurants
+ Long runs and a sensation of travel

− Extent of pistes is modest; only one main route down each valley
− Few challenges (or moguls) on-piste
− High winds can close links
− Few off-slope diversions
− Can be very busy at weekends
− Limited après-ski

Monterosa Ski's resorts – Champoluc, Gressoney and Alagna – have long been among our favourites and are popular with experts going off-piste and with Italian weekenders. Until recently they have not made much impact on the international ski market but now things are changing. Champoluc was put on the UK map on a small scale by single-resort operator Ski 2, which has been operating there for 16 years and has built a great reputation. This season Ski Total and Inghams will both have chalet hotels there. And family specialist Esprit Ski has a chalet hotel in Gressoney in the next valley.

The resorts retain a friendly, small-scale, unspoiled ambience that we (and a growing band of readers) like a lot. They share a network of pistes that is modest in size but suits intermediates well, and areas of off-piste that suit everyone from adventurous intermediates to experts (but guidance is needed).

There is one main village in each of three adjacent valleys: Champoluc in the western Val d'Ayas, Gressoney in the central valley and Alagna to the east. Champoluc and Gressoney are both reached from the Aosta valley, to the south. Alagna is more remote and isolated, and approached by a quite different route from the east.

Day trips to other resorts are hard work, but Cervinia, Courmayeur, La Thuile and Pila are reachable by car from Champoluc and Gressoney and are covered by the Aosta Valley pass.

All three villages are small-scale (Champoluc is the largest) and pleasantly rustic, without being picture-postcard pretty. Like most Italian resorts, the villages really come to life only at weekends.

KEY FACTS

Slopes	1200-3275m
	3,940-10,740ft
Lifts	25
Pistes	73km
	45 miles

TANYA BOOTH

The pistes are well groomed and usually quiet midweek – but maybe not quite as deserted as this ↓

Monterosa Ski is surrounded by a string of peaks over 4000m, and some over 4500m; the panoramic views from restaurant terraces are fabulous.

THE MOUNTAINS

Open slopes dominate, but there are woodland runs lower down. The writing, lifts and pistes on the map are ridiculously small and difficult to read. Signposting is adequate. It's a shame that many runs that could be classified blue are red, leading to uncertainty for timid intermediates.

The attraction for experts and confident intermediates is the off-piste, with great runs from the high points of the lift system and some excellent heli-skiing. The Indren cable car accesses a lovely itinerary as well as more serious routes to Alagna (a guide is essential; and when we visited on a busy weekend last season, a patroller was checking that everyone going up the cable car was wearing a transceiver). There are few black pistes and most are not steep.

There is excellent intermediate piste skiing, with some notably long runs from the ridges to the villages. The run down to Alagna is 1760m

vertical and 7km long, for example.

Although the slopes span vast distances, and give a great sense of travel, they don't add up to a huge amount of skiing. The lift company eventually accepted our view that its claimed run lengths needed, more or less, to be halved. The total for the linked area is now only 73km.

The main three-valley network is very simple: there is basically one main way down each mountainside. Champoluc and Gressoney have worthwhile local areas of pistes in addition but Alagna does not. The main lift system is vulnerable to bad weather, but both Champoluc and Gressoney have sheltered alternatives.

This is not a notably snowy area, but altitude helps, as does extensive snowmaking. Grooming is thorough – bumps on the pistes don't last long.

The important lifts are mainly fast chairs and gondolas. But sunny weekends bring crowds, and one or two queuing problems in the Champoluc and Alagna valleys.

Mountain restaurants are listed on the piste map. They are generally simple, friendly and good value, and there are some notably good ones too.

The ski holiday specialists to the acclaimed Monterosa ski area, including the three resorts of Champoluc, Gressoney and Alagna.

- Holidays of any duration for families, groups and individuals
- Ski weekends and short breaks
- Our own British ski school and nursery
- Choice of departure and arrival airports
- Quality hotels and apartments
- Swift minibus transfers

Visit our comprehensive website, at www.ski-2.com, call us on 01962 713330 or email us at sales@ski-2.com

ABTA
The Travel Association

MOMENTUM SKI

Weekend & a la carte
ski holiday specialists

100% Tailor-made

Premier hotels
& apartments

Flexible travel
arrangements

020 7371 9111
WWW.MOMENTUMSKI.COM

Champoluc 1580m

- ➕ Relaxed, traditional-style village
- ➕ Excellent beginner area at mid-mountain, but ...

- ➖ Progress to longer runs tricky
- ➖ Some tricky red runs
- ➖ Resort spread out along road

Champoluc is the largest of the resort villages and is at one end of the three-valley network. Although it has drawbacks, it's an attractive all-round base.

Champoluc is strung out along the one-way street running from the centre past various hotels to the gondola base station, where a cluster of shops and bars forms a kind of distinct micro-resort. About 3km up the valley, a short funicular goes up from Frachey (with parking right at the base).

Down-valley from Champoluc are Antagnod and Brusson. Antagnod is a good alternative for bad-weather days, and has some decent off-piste.

Village charm There is a group of bars and restaurants at the lift base but the village lacks a real focus. But we and readers like the low-key ambience.

Convenience The village is not compact, but everything is walkable. Some hotels are a 10-minute walk from the gondola base station but some have lockers near there to leave your kit in. There are free buses to and from Frachey and Antagnod. You have to pay for the Brusson bus. And Ski 2 ferries its guests around town.

THE MOUNTAINS
Slopes The gondola from Champoluc goes up to Crest, a mid-mountain nursery area with a further gondola followed by a slow quad chairlift going on to Colle Sarezza. This area is linked to the runs above Frachey via a steep, narrow, bumpy red run, commonly known as the Goat, because of the statue at the top; timid intermediates are better off starting at Frachey. From there, you ride lifts to Colle Bettaforca, for the descent to Gressoney.

Fast lifts Most lifts are fast chairs and gondolas, but the link with Frachey involves slow chairs. You can avoid these by using the Frachey funicular.

Queues Mostly blissfully queue-free. But there are two problems at Frachey. The Alpe Mandria chair above the funicular is an unavoidable bottleneck. And the old double chair that links to the home slopes of Champoluc cannot cope with afternoon demand.

Terrain parks There isn't one.

Experts Off-piste is the main draw. There are few tough on-piste runs. In bad weather, head for the excellent Mandria forest area above Frachey.

Intermediates There is a good mix of varied pistes that suit confident intermediates. But Champoluc has drawbacks for timid intermediates – as well as the Goat run, the red descent to Champoluc (excellent if you can hack it) can be too much for many. Some people find it worth going to the separate Antagnod area.

Beginners The high nursery slopes at Crest above Champoluc, served by two moving carpets, are excellent. For longer gentle runs, though, you need to go up the valley to Frachey. Or down the valley to Antagnod.

Snowboarding Great off-piste for experts but not ideal for intermediates or beginners (see above). No drag lifts to worry about though.

Cross-country There are 16km of trails in Champoluc; but Brusson, down-valley, has the best loops (30km).

Mountain restaurants There are three small, notably charming places serving excellent food in beautifully renovated old buildings. Our favourites are Rascard Frantze (where we had a lovely lunch in 2015) and l'Aroula, below and above the Champoluc mid-station respectively. They are regularly endorsed by readers ('One of the nicest mountain restaurants I have ever been to,' said an experienced reporter this year of Rascard Frantze). Stadel Soussun above Frachey is possibly the most polished of the three, but we've found service rather cool; close by is the 'quaint' Taconet with 'simple, traditional food'. We enjoyed a 2015 lunch at Campo Base at the top of the Mandria chair; modern, welcoming, good views, a rota of daily specials. La Tana del Lupo is highly praised for the warm welcome and 'good menu'.

Schools and guides We lack recent reports on the Italian ski schools but have good reports of the Ski 2 ski school ('good, friendly instructors').

Families Tour operator Ski 2 has all kinds of schemes to keep children happy. And it runs Ski 2 Racing courses for would-be Olympians (see our 'Family holidays' chapter).

LIFT PASSES

Monterosa Ski area

Prices in €

Age	6-day
Under 14	111
14 to 64	185
65 plus	148

Free Under 8 (if bought with adult pass); 80 plus

Beginner Limited passes

Alternative passes Individual areas

STAYING THERE

We've had many good reports of Champoluc specialists Ski 2 ('great from pick-up to drop-off').

Chalets Ski Total runs the lovely former 4-star hotel Breithorn as a chalet hotel. We enjoyed our 2015 stay; all bedrooms are different and wood panelled; reporters agree: 'a gem, spacious, excellent service'. Inghams will be running the former 3-star hotel Champoluc as a chalet hotel this season – perfect location right by the gondola and regularly praised by reporters when it was a hotel.

Hotels For a small place, Champoluc has a good range of attractive hotels. We've enjoyed the friendly, woody 4-star La Rouja. Reporters have enjoyed the comfortable 4-star Relais des Glaciers and the central, atmospheric, old 3-star Castor.

Three mountain restaurants have charming rooms – Stadel Soussun, Rascard Frantze ('Simply the best place I've stayed when skiing,' said a recent reporter) and l'Aroula, where we had a peaceful and comfortable stay a couple of years ago.

Eating out Most restaurants are in hotels, but there are a few stand-alone places. Osteria Il Balivo is repeatedly tipped ('truly delightful, delicious dishes') as is the Grange up at Frachey ('good freshly prepared food, lovely atmosphere and delightful').

Après-ski Near the gondola base, we and reporters have enjoyed the cosy and rustic Atelier Gourmand and the Bistrot – free antipasti at both. Golosone is a small, atmospheric, distinctly Italian wine bar; and the West Road pub in the hotel California has karaoke some nights. Tuesday is music night in the hotel Castor's bar. Later on, try Pachamama.

Off the slopes There are lovely walks up the valley. And an outdoor ice rink.

✦ Inghams

CHAMPOLUC
▸ Brand new resort for 2015/16
▸ Introduction of new Chalet Hotel de Champoluc
▸ Additional savings for groups!

inghams.co.uk 01483 371 236 ABTA V4871 ATOL 0025

Monterosa Ski

419

Back after a sold-out 2014/15 season

ABTA

THE CHALET SPECIALIST

Ski Total

Chalet Hotel Breithorn, full of character and traditional Italian charm, is ideally situated in the charming Monterosa resort of Champoluc.

Ski Total Savers incl. cash-back, ski pack offers & free group places | **Whirlpool, steam-room and sauna**
5-course dinners with complimentary wine | **Flights** from Gatwick, Birmingham or Manchester

Tel: **01483 791 933** Book online at **skitotal.com**

Gressoney la Trinité 1640m

- ⊞ Centrally placed in the three valleys
- ⊞ Some convenient lodging
- ⊞ Some good mountain restaurants
- ⊟ Access to long easy runs involves a bus ride, or lifts up and then down
- ⊟ Slow lifts on lower local slopes

If you are planning daily excursions to Passo Salati to ski Alagna or to ride the Punta Indren cable car, Gressoney is the best place to start.

Gressoney la Trinité is at the head of the long and beautiful Lys valley – a 40-minute drive from the Val d'Aosta. This is a resort of parts. The heart of the village is slightly away from the skiing, but there are skiers' satellites that have grown up at the lift bases. 500m away across the valley, at the base station of a slow chairlift into the local slopes, is a mini-resort almost as big as the village proper. The lifts for the other valleys go from a second lift base at Stafal, 5km away at the head of the valley (linked by a free but infrequent bus).

Village charm Gressoney la Trinité is a quiet, neat little village, cobbled in the centre, with an old church and wooden buildings – but many are closed up, in the winter at least. The satellites don't amount to much – a dense collection of hotels at the local lift base, a more spread-out one at Stafal.

Convenience The local lift base area is compact and convenient. Up at Stafal, walks to the lifts are a bit longer, but bearable from most lodgings.

THE MOUNTAINS

Slopes From Stafal, a cable car goes in one direction towards Colle Bettaforca and Champoluc, and a gondola goes in the other towards Passo Salati and Alagna. Down the valley at Gressoney, an old double chairlift accesses an area of wooded runs, with piste links (via another slow double chairlift) across the mountainside to the lifts from Stafal to Passo Salati.

Down the valley beyond Gressoney St Jean, at Bieltschocke, is a small but worthwhile (700m vertical) area of slopes served by a fast double chair.

Fast lifts The slow chairs in the woods at Gressoney are the main exceptions to a picture dominated by fast lifts.

Queues The queue-prone gondola from Stafal to Gabiet was upgraded a few seasons ago, but the one above it gets busy at times. And the cable car from Pianalunga above Alagna can build long queues – so, to a lesser extent, can the gondola from Alagna.

Terrain parks There's an 'excellent' park at Gabiet (Dream Park).

Experts Gressoney is well placed for access to Passo Salati and the cable car to Punta Indren, for off-piste runs. The only serious black run in the area is the short one from Punta Jolanda.

Intermediates On both sides of the valley there are fine, none-too-difficult reds above mid-mountain, with trickier runs lower down. The Moos run to Stafal on the Passo Salati side is a black, but it is not seriously steep.

Beginners There are nursery slopes with moving carpets at valley level at Gressoney itself and at Stafal. Then it's up the gondola to the short blue run at mid-mountain; or on up to the top for longer blue runs to the mid-station of the cable car from Alagna (but beware: these can close at busy times – especially weekends – to avoid queues at the cable car mid-station; watch for the 'closed' signs).

Snowboarding Great off-piste for experts, easy pistes for intermediates, no drag lifts to worry about.

Cross-country There are decent trails: 25km around Gressoney St Jean.

Mountain restaurants On the local slopes, off the main system, the woody, Punta Jolanda is a reader favourite – it does 'great pasta', 'superb wild boar' and the terrace has stunning views down to Gressoney la Trinité; but we had a report of poor service this year. Lower down, Morgenrot has also been recommended. Nearby, simple self-service Bedemie is 'excellent value – lasagne 7 euros, big beer 4 euros'. At mid-mountain on the main slope from P Salati, Rif Gabiet serves 'excellent, good-value pasta'. On the other side of the valley, 2727 at Colle della Bettaforca is 'a locals' hang-out, cheap and cheerful, good pizzas'; 'go upstairs for a superb restaurant'.

Schools and guides Three glowing reports in 2015 of children's lessons in the Gressoney school arranged by Ski Esprit. The school at Stafal is said to be short of English-speaking instructors. The guides of Guide Monterosa have consistently got good reports ('very professional') and we've been impressed with them.

ESPRIT ☀ Ski

No.1 For Family Skiing

FOR FAMILIES IN GRESSONEY

SAVE UP TO £955 PER FAMILY

with our Esprit Family Savers

★ **We focus 100% on caring for your children**

★ **Dedicated Esprit Nurseries**

★ **FREE evening Baby-Listening / Child Patrol Service**

★ **Strict child care ratios**

★ **Catered chalets & Chalet Hotels**

★ **Baby And Toddler Weeks**

Call **01483 791 900**
visit **espritski.com**

ABTA

Families Family specialist Esprit has chalet hotel Valverde here with hot tub and sauna and we've had glowing reports ('brilliant staff, good location', 'very good food', 'childcare superb').

STAYING THERE

Chalets We know of no small chalets, but see 'Families' above.

Hotels Past reporters have tipped the Jolanda Sport in the village (indoor and small outdoor pool, sauna and steam) and the 3-star Dufour at the village lift base. At Stafal, we enjoyed our stay at the modern, stylish little Nordend. The Ellex is a chalet-style eco place with 'a lovely lounge, smart bathrooms and a great spa'.

Eating out At Stafal the bar-restaurant underneath the hotel Nordend, known as the Core or Giovanni's, does excellent food, charmingly served. 2015 reporters recommended the Castore in Gressoney village ('cool vibe, excellent food, huge choice of wines') and the Faure bar/restaurant at the local lift base ('good food, fine wine selection').

Après-ski Gressoney is pretty quiet. At Stafal, head for the bar under the Nordend; at the Gressoney lift base

head for the Faure (good choice of ales and lagers on tap).

Off the slopes There's an ice rink, a sports hall and a big pool.

LINKED RESORT – 1200m

ALAGNA

Alagna is a small, remote village with a solid church and some lovely old wooden farmhouses built in the distinctive Walser style. But its local skiing is very limited; in bad weather there may be little or nothing to do. So it is difficult to recommend for a holiday booked well in advance.

The mountains above Alagna offer some of the most exciting off-piste in the area, including very steep couloirs.

In good weather, the splendid 7km (1760m vertical) descent from Passo Salati to Alagna is a highlight. At the top, the black Olen piste (once rightly classified red) is a great blast and there is good, shady, off-piste beside it. The tough red Alagna piste below it is equally rewarding – though snow on the lower sections can be poor.

ADAMELLO SKI

Passo Tonale

An unusual and attractive combination of high, snow-sure slopes (linked to lower Ponte di Legno) and the lowest prices in the Alps

£75
RESORT PRICE INDEX

TOP 10 RATINGS

Extent	★★
Fast lifts	★★★★
Queues	★★★★
Snow	★★★★
Expert	★★
Intermediate	★★★
Beginner	★★★★★
Charm	★★
Convenience	★★★
Scenery	★★★

NEWS

2015/16: A new gondola will run from Passo Paradiso to the top of the glacier, replacing the existing T-bars and chairlift. It will have a mid-station at the Capanna Presena restaurant, which will be renewed. The two-seater Casola chairlift linking Ponte di Legno to the slopes above Temù will be replaced by a quad.

KEY FACTS

Resort	1885m
	6,180ft

Whole linked area	
Slopes	1120-3015m
	3,670-9,890ft
Lifts	30
Pistes	100km
	62 miles

- ➕ Good-value mid-market lodgings
- ➕ Sunny but snow-sure slopes
- ➕ A row of uncrowded, easy runs
- ➕ Link to Ponte di Legno adds attractive, steeper, tree-lined runs

- ➖ Not much locally to amuse keen, competent intermediates
- ➖ Local slopes are all exposed
- ➖ Linear village, strung along the pass road, is no beauty

Want a reasonable range of runs and good snow, but operating on a tight budget? You'll find Passo Tonale (plus linked Ponte di Legno, over the pass to the west) difficult to beat – particularly for beginners and timid intermediates.

THE RESORT

Village charm A resort dedicated to skiing, built along a road over a high pass; many of the buildings are in chalet style, but it lacks a focus – and lacks pavements: pedestrians must compete with the traffic.
Convenience Tonale is fairly compact, with its hotels spread along the bottom of the main slope area – so all pretty convenient for the lifts.
Scenery The main slopes offer grand views of Presena, and Ponte di Legno's slopes also offer good views.

THE MOUNTAINS

The Tonale slopes are entirely above the trees, but the linked slopes of Ponte di Legno are wooded – a great combination. Thirty minutes east is Marilleva, linked to Madonna di Campiglio – see 'Lift Passes'.
Slopes Tonale's home slopes are limited in extent. The broad, gentle, sunny area north of the pass road, served by a row of chairs and drags, is

much the larger of the two sectors, but runs are short. A gondola accesses the steeper, narrower and taller north-facing sector. A new gondola is to open this season above that, going to the top of the small Presena glacier.

A blue/red run through the trees (mostly easy but with a short steeper section) descends almost 600m to a slow chair up into the Ponte di Legno slopes. This is followed by an easy black run; you can avoid this by riding the gondola down to Ponte di Legno.
Fast lifts The system is impressive, almost meriting ★★★★★.
Queues In peak season, the gondola back from Ponte di Legno can be busy. But generally there are no problems. At village level the pistes can get busy, notably at Easter.
Terrain parks The main park close to the village, with a beginners' area, can get busy, but has been much enjoyed by reporters' children.
Snow reliability In a normal season, the altitude and setting ensure good conditions, though the sunny main

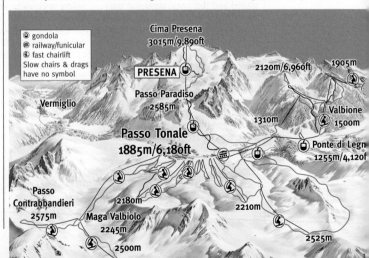

- ⓖ gondola
- 🚋 railway/funicular
- ⓕ fast chairlift
- Slow chairs & drags have no symbol

Cima Presena
3015m/9,890ft

PRESENA

2120m/6,960ft

1905m

Passo Paradiso
2585m

Vermiglio

1310m

Valbione
1500m

Passo Tonale
1885m/6,180ft

Ponte di Legno
1255m/4,120ft

Passo Contrabbandieri
2575m

2180m

2210m

Maga Valbiolo
2245m

2500m

2525m

The blue/red run down to woody Ponte di Legno is mostly easy, but one stretch is quite a bit stiffer than this section →

FOTO PINO VECLANI / ADAMELLO SKI

LIFT PASSES

Prices in €

Age	6-day
under 8	102
8 to 15	164
16 to 64	232
65 plus	209

Free Under 8 if with family-paying adult

Note Includes one day in another Skirama Dolomiti Adamello Brenta area resort

Alternative pass
Skirama Dolomiti Adamello Brenta – covers Madonna, Pinzolo, Marilleva-Folgarida, Passo Tonale, Ponte di Legno, Andalo, Pejo, Monte Bondone and Folgaria-Lavarone

TOURIST OFFICE

www.passotonale.it
www.adamelloski.com
www.valdisole.net

slopes can suffer in late season. Wind can be a problem, but the wooded slopes of Ponte di Legno offer shelter. The snowmaking is impressive.

Experts There isn't much for experts on-piste. But there is off-piste to be had in the main area, and good routes from the glacier. A reporter this year enjoyed the 10km Sgualdrina Cantiere back to Tonale, and the Pisgana takes an epic 16km to drop 1650m to PdL.

Intermediates The south-facing slopes – gentle even when labelled red – are great for the timid. Adventurous intermediates will enjoy the 4.5km Alpino piste down a deserted valley to the village, and the Presena area. The glacier runs are short and not steep. The red runs at Ponte di Legno are excellent, and correctly classified. The blacks in both sectors are not steep.

Beginners Excellent: the sunny slopes right by the village are ideal, with plenty of easy, wide blue runs too.

Snowboarding The gentle slopes and many chairlifts mean the area is good for beginners and intermediates.

Cross-country There are short trails here and down at PdL – and longer ones at Vermiglio (10km east).

Mountain restaurants A reader this year says the top place is Petit Pierre, high up at Ponte di Legno, with 'fantastic porcini ravioli' as well as great views. Lower down, we like the rustic Valbione's upstairs table-service part ('goulash recommended', 'best pasta'). On the Tonale slopes, reader tips are Bleis for 'great gulasch' and Passo Paradiso for 'delicious, hearty vegetable soup, good fries', plus 'very friendly service'. Il Faita, on the run down to Ponte di Legno, is tipped.

Schools and guides Recent reports on both main schools are enthusiastic, the Presena school drawing one reporter back for a second year.

Families The slopes suit skiing children. But there isn't much to do other than skiing, and the busy through-road is a drawback.

STAYING THERE

Hotels There are around 30, most of them 3-stars. Reporters last year and this enjoyed the 4-star Sport Hotel Vittoria ('well located, interesting food, pleasant spa'). We have good reports on two Crystal exclusive hotels – the Cielo Blu ('great staff, good food, spacious room') and the big, modern Paradiso (with pool, spa). Two other places in great locations have been tipped in recent years: the Torretta and Miramonti, with pool and spa.

Apartments There are 1,400 beds in apartments, a few on the UK market.

Eating out Mainly simple hotel restaurants; the Torretta and Miramonti are endorsed this year for pizza. Il Focolare is tipped for 'tasty steaks', and Mirandola if you are looking for 'something special'.

Après-ski Increasingly lively. The ironically named plate-glass Baracca has a 'great DJ' and a 'wild happy hour'. More our style is the 'relaxed ambience and friendly staff' at El Bait – here and at La Botte you get free après snacks. This year's star bar reporter found six other 'lively' places: Magic, Bar Heaven, Nico's, Cantuccio's, UFO and Crazy Horse. There are a couple of disco-bars.

Off the slopes There's not a lot to do – snowmobiling, snowshoeing, skating.

Sauze d'Oulx

A lively village beneath an attractive area of slopes forming part of the extensive Milky Way; but non-trivial drawbacks persist

£90
RESORT PRICE INDEX

RATINGS

The mountains

Extent	★★★★
Fast lifts	★★★
Queues	★★★
Terrain p'ks	★★
Snow	★★
Expert	★★
Intermediate	★★★★
Beginner	★
Boarder	★★
X-country	★
Restaurants	★★★
Schools	★★
Families	★★

The resort

Charm	★★
Convenience	★★
Scenery	★★★
Eating out	★★★
Après-ski	★★★★
Off-slope	★

NEWS

2014/15: A slow triple chair was built from the Capanna Mollino restaurant near Punta Rocca to Monte Triplex, restoring a route to M Fraiteve that avoids Sportinia.

KEY FACTS

Resort	1510m
	4,950ft

Milky Way	
Slopes	1390-2825m
	4,560-9,270ft
Lifts	72
Pistes	400km
	249 miles

Sauze d'Oulx-Sestriere-Sansicario

Slopes	1390-2825m
	4,560-9,270ft
Lifts	41
Pistes	300km
	186 miles

+ Extensive intermediate slopes, generally uncrowded on weekdays – great cruising

+ Mix of open and woodland runs is good for all weather conditions

+ Entertaining nightlife

+ Part of the Milky Way network, spreading across the border to Montgenèvre in France, but ...

− Getting to Montgenèvre is a time-consuming business without using a car or taxis

− Erratic snow record and far from comprehensive snowmaking

− Lift system needs improvement

− Not great for experts, and a poor choice for beginners

− Steep walks around the village

− Crowds on sunny weekends

Infamously lager-lout territory 30 years ago, Sauze still has lots of lively bars and shops festooned in English signs (and young Brits working in them); but it is a much more civilized place now, populated by grown-up Brits and Italian weekenders – this is Turin's closest major ski area. We've grown to like it.

Sauze now has a different problem: investment, lack of. It needs comprehensive snowmaking, and it needs new lifts. What the resort seems to be doing of late is reshuffling the lifts it already has. Four years ago the useful Triplex quad chair was redeployed to replace two ancient drags; now at last its vacant place has been filled – by a slow triple chair (recycled from Sansicario, we're told).

THE RESORT

Sauze d'Oulx sits on a sloping mountain shelf facing north-west to the mountains bordering France. It is a mid-sized resort – a big village rather than a town – but it spreads quite widely. Out of the bustle of the centre, there are secluded apartment blocks in quiet, wooded areas and a number of good restaurants also tucked away.

The Via Lattea (Milky Way) lift pass covers not only next-door Sansicario and Sestriere, easily reached by lift and piste, but also the more remote slopes of Claviere and Montgenèvre – more easily reached by road, but certainly possible on skis/board. Sestriere and Montgenèvre are covered in separate chapters.

VILLAGE CHARM ★★
Falling behind?

The village has an attractive old core, with narrow, cobbled streets and houses roofed with huge stone slabs. But most of the resort is modern and undistinguished, made up of block-like hotels and the occasional chalet, spreading down the steep hillside from the slopes. Smart, woody hotels and apartments are lacking.

There is a central car-free zone, but at both ends of the day the rest of the village can be congested. The roads have few pavements and can be icy.

Despite the decline in lager sales, the centre is still lively at night; the late bars are usually quite full. Noise can be a problem in the early hours. An early-season visitor found resort staff 'without exception smiling and welcoming'.

CONVENIENCE ★★
Uphill struggles

The village slopes steeply. The slow Clotes chair, for the left-hand side of the network, is at the top of the village, a short climb from the centre and 'a slog in the mornings' according to one visitor. Some hotels are above this lift, and in good snow offer ski-in/

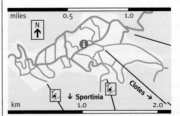

miles   0.5   1.0

↓ Sportinia   Clotes →

km   1.0   2.0

ski-out convenience – but most are not. There is a moving carpet that cuts out part of the climb. The Sportinia fast chair, the most direct way to the heart of the slopes, is a strenuous and hazardous walk (often on slippery roads) further out. There is a free ski-bus, but it can be overcrowded and not always on time. There are places to deposit skis and boots at both main lift bases.

The smaller, lower village of Jouvenceaux is worth considering as a base, with a fast lift into the slopes and a good red run back down.

SCENERY ★★★★★
Plenty of trees

The scenery is attractively woody, especially low down and along the Val di Susa. The sunny, open slopes higher up give wide panoramic views of the mountains on the French border – notably Mont Chaberton.

THE MOUNTAINS

The higher slopes are open and the lower ones pleasantly wooded. All in all, the piste system is a bit of a shambles. Piste classifications, signposting and edge marking are all erratic in the inimitable Italian way. Despite improvements, the Via Lattea piste map is still a marketing device rather than a skiing aid. Mad.

EXTENT OF THE SLOPES ★★★★★
Big and varied enough for most

Sauze's local slopes are spread across a broad wooded mountainside above the resort, ranging from west- to north-facing. This is split by woods and ravines, which gives some sensation of travel but also complicates route-finding across the mountainside.

The heart of the skiing is **Sportinia**, a sunny mid-mountain clearing in the woods, with a ring of restaurants and hotels, and a small nursery area. This is reached directly by the fast chair outside the village mentioned above, or less directly by the slow **Clotes** chair, which also accesses a worthwhile but rather neglected area of runs served by drags off to the left, on **M Moncrons**; of late this has been open only on weekdays.

A fast quad chair from Sportinia and the 'new' triple chair above Clotes access the high, open bowl that separates Sauze from Sansicario. From here you can take a steep draglift or the slow double Colo chairlift to the high point of the system – the major junction of **Monte Fraiteve**. From the peak you can go south to **Sestriere**. There are red and blue pistes all the way down, but the slope faces south and the bottom sections are rarely open – expect to ride the gondola.

Or you can go west on splendid broad, long runs to **Sansicario** – and

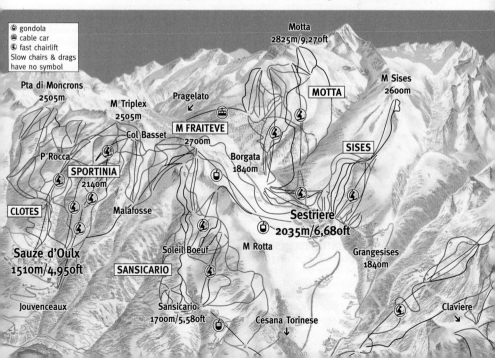

LIFT PASSES

Via Lattea

Prices in €	
Age	6-day
under 8	30
8 to 74	190
75 plus	120

Free No deals

Beginner Restricted day pass (€25)

Note Covers lifts in Sauze d'Oulx, Sestriere, Sansicario, Cesana and Claviere

Alternative pass

International (covers all the above plus Montgenèvre)

on to a two-stage gondola near **Cesana Torinese** that links with **Claviere** and then **Montgenèvre**, in France.

FAST LIFTS ★★★☆☆
Few and far between
Fast lifts are in a minority. There are still a lot of drags and old, slow chairlifts; to reach M Fraiteve you must choose one or the other. Things are improving, but too slowly.

QUEUES ★★★☆☆
Beware sunny weekends
There can be queues on sunny weekends and holidays, when the hordes from Turin flock in – crowds on the pistes can be a problem then too. But during the week the slopes are usually quiet. There can be serious congestion on the very confined peak of M Fraiteve at busy times.

TERRAIN PARKS ★★☆☆☆
Now established?
The previously unpredictable park now seems to have settled in a spot above Sportinia – and was reportedly quite large in 2015. There is a park at Sansicario too.

SNOW RELIABILITY ★★☆☆☆
Can be poor, affecting the links
The area is notorious for erratic snowfalls, suffering droughts with worrying frequency. The runs above Sansicario are affected by the afternoon sun. Snowmaking has been increased throughout the area (including the Sportinia nursery slopes); coverage is still far from complete, but great efforts are made to keep runs open. Grooming is 'the best I've seen', in one view.

FOR EXPERTS ★★☆☆☆
Head off-piste
There are black runs, but most of them do not deserve their classification. We're told the black Malafosse run is not fiercely steep, but is narrow and isolated. There are quite a few off-piste opportunities between the pistes and down lift lines.

FOR INTERMEDIATES ★★★★☆
Splendid cruising terrain
The whole area is ideal for confident intermediates who want to clock up the kilometres. The less confident are not helped by the silly classification of many easy runs as red.

There are some good long descents: red 11 is about 1000m vertical – a reader favourite, although we hear it can get busy at the end of the day.

At the higher levels, where the slopes are above the treeline, the terrain often allows a choice of route. Lower down are pretty runs through the woods, where the main complication can be route-finding.

The long runs down to Jouvenceaux are splendid, flattering intermediate terrain, as are those below Sportinia.

The Moncrons sector at the east of the area is served only by drags, but offers some wonderful, uncrowded cruising, some of it above the treeline; it is a shame it's not reliably open.

The slopes above Sansicario are also excellent, including the amiable Olympic Women's Downhill and the particularly fine red 71, away from the lifts, down to Pariol, the mid-station on the Cesana-Sansicario gondola.

FOR BEGINNERS ★☆☆☆☆
Not a good choice
Sauze presents various problems. (If you want to go to this area and you're taking a beginner, opt to stay in Sestriere.) The main nursery area up at Sportinia has only a short moving carpet, and is reached by a chairlift. There is a day pass covering these plus two other lifts, but there is no suitable longer slope to progress to. There is a slope at village level with a free moving carpet, but the slope is too steep for complete beginners. The mornings-only classes (normal in Italy, of course) don't suit everyone. Once off the nursery slopes, the main problem is erratic piste classification.

FOR BOARDERS ★★☆☆☆
Too many drags
There are inescapable draglifts in a couple of areas – notably on the way back to M Fraiteve from Sansicario; but boarders seem happy to put up with that in exchange for wide, well-groomed pistes and plentiful off-piste.

FOR CROSS-COUNTRY ★☆☆☆☆
You're on your own
There are no prepared loops in Sauze.

MOUNTAIN RESTAURANTS ★★★☆☆
Some pleasant possibilities
There are about 15 restaurants locally. They are generally pleasant, but can get very busy at weekends. Irritatingly,

↑ The village enjoys a fine balcony setting, with views of the peaks on the border with France

VIA LATTEA TO

only some are marked on the resort piste map.

There are several routine self-service places at Sportinia, plus three doing table-service, all of them worth trying – Rocce Nere (does self-service too), Orso Bianco beneath it, and Monte Triplex. In the Clotes sector there are several good bets. Clos Bourget specializes in 'large, excellent pizzas', and there are two hotels with good restaurants. The 'cosy, rustic' Ciao Pais is repeatedly recommended, whether for its 'generous, very tasty' speciality of porcini pasta or its 'picturesque out-of-the-way location'. The Naskira at the hotel Capricorno, lower down, is the place for a serious lunch; it is not cheap (hefty cover charge, for a start), and midweek it can be deserted.

Halfway down to Sansicario, the self-service Soleil Boeuf has impressed recent reporters, for both traditional atmosphere and 'great value'.

SCHOOLS AND GUIDES ★★★★★
More reports, please
Recent reports are confined to private lessons with the Sportinia school, which have been very successful.

FOR FAMILIES ★★★★
Yes and no
All the schools take children from four years, and spoken English should be OK. But note our reservations about the resort for beginners. The moving carpet just above the village is a great aid to sledging.

STAYING THERE

All the major mainstream operators offer hotel packages here.
Chalets Neilson has the catered chalet Le Valentin, set a 15-20 minute walk above the village.
Hotels Simple 2-star and 3-star hotels form the core, with a couple of 4-stars and some more basic places.
****Torre** This cylindrical landmark 200m below the centre generates mixed reports.
***Gran Baita** Central place approved by a reader: 'Decor a bit dated but superior rooms huge, excellent lounge, friendly staff, decent dinners, great value.'
***Stella Alpina** Good location above the village, between the main lifts. Well run by a friendly Anglo-Italian family.
Gran Trun This year's discovery: 'Fabulous little B&B place, full of character, right in the cobbled centre, very comfortable and run by the most welcoming host,' says a reporter.
Villa Cary Praised annually since 2007 by one regular visitor: 'Still good for people on a budget.'
Apartments Plenty are available, some through UK tour operators.
At altitude The 4-star Capricorno, up at Clotes, is the most attractive and expensive hotel in Sauze – a charming little chalet beside the piste, with only 10 bedrooms. Higher up, the more modest Ciao Pais has a high reputation too. And there are places to stay at Sportinia.

M Fraiteve gives a great view of French Mont Chaberton – and of the resort of Montgenèvre, at the far end of the Milky Way area →

VIA LATTEA TO

EATING OUT ★★★☆☆
Caters for all tastes and pockets

Sauze has over 30 restaurants. Typical Italian banquets of five or six courses can be had in places such as the Cantun. Del Falco is widely regarded as the top place – 'fabulous wines and blissful food'. We like the look of L'Ortiché, too – reports, please. Other tips this year: the Village, a conspicuous, large place near the Clotes chair offering 'huge portions of very tasty food, from steaks and hamburgers to traditional Italian specialities'; and La Griglia, which does 'fantastic pizzas from a wood-fired oven; a great atmosphere'. Paddy McGinty's steaks 'did us proud', says a reporter. Sugo's is a great place for pasta; Pizza House is 'excellent, with such a wide selection'.

APRES-SKI ★★★★☆
Suzy does it with more dignity

If cake and coffee is the order of the day, Pasticceria Gally is 'really good value' and 'a nice treat'. In most respects Sauze's bars now impress reporters, young and old – 'Classier than expected,' said one. Choice is wide, with many happy hours, and free antipasti in some places. Reporters again pick out the Grotta for the cheapest beer (well below UK prices). And our regular reporter again tips Max's Cafe ('busy for après and later') for its four-hour happy hour and live football; Mira ('probably the busiest') for sports TV; Scacco Matto for its 'popular sun terrace and big cocktail menu'; and the Scotch Bar in the hotel Stella Alpina, at the foot of the Clotes

home run, for 'relaxed atmosphere and friendly welcome'. Other tips include the Assietta, with 'generous glasses of Prosecco, and entertainment later on'; Il Lampione, underneath the hotel Chalet Faure in the old town – a 'chilled-out', 'upmarket' bar with 'excellent beer' and a 'super' range of wines; and Osteria dei Vagabondi for late-night live music.

OFF THE SLOPES ★☆☆☆☆
Go elsewhere

There are few off-slope activities. There is a sports hall, but no pool and currently, we understand, no ice rink. Shopping is limited, and there are no gondolas or cable cars to suit pedestrians. Turin and Briançon are worth visiting.

LINKED RESORT – 1700m
SANSICARIO

Sansicario, three lifts from M Fraiteve and set at the top of the down-then-up lift link for Claviere (and so Montgenèvre), is ideally placed for exploration of the whole Milky Way. It is a modern, purpose-built, self-contained but rather soulless little resort, mainly consisting of apartments grouped around the small shopping precinct – but also spreading down the steep slope. The 46-room Rio Envers is a comfortable, expensive 3-star hotel. The 4-star Majestic has a pool. Apartments to rent are 'hard to find but cheap'. Very little happens in the evening, but the Enoteca (wine bar) is 'excellent in all respects'.

GETTING THERE

Air Turin 95km/ 60 miles (1hr30)

Rail Oulx (5km/ 3 miles); frequent buses

TOURIST OFFICE

Sauze d'Oulx, Cesana Torinese (Sansicario)
www.turismotorino. org
www.vialattea.it
www.comune. sauzedoulx.to.it

APT VAL DI FASSA / STEFANO ZARDINI

Sella Ronda

Endless intermediate slopes amid spectacular scenery, and a choice of attractive valley villages with a distinctive local culture

£95
RESORT PRICE INDEX

TOP 10 RATINGS

Extent	★★★★★
Fast lifts	★★★★
Queues	★★★
Snow	★★★★
Expert	★★
Intermediate	★★★★★
Beginner	★★★★
Charm	★★★
Convenience	★★★
Scenery	★★★★★

NEWS

2015/16: The La Fraina quad chair above San Cassiano will be replaced by a six-pack.

2014/15: At Corvara an eight-person gondola replaced the queue-prone Borest quad chairlift to/from Colfosco. A six-pack replaced the Pralongià triple chairlift.

TOURIST OFFICE

www.dolomitisuperski.com
www.sella-ronda.info

LIFT PASSES

Dolomiti Superski

Prices in €

Age	6-day
under 16	189
16 to 64	270
65 plus	243
Free Under 8	
Beginner Points cards	
Note Covers 450 lifts and 1220km of pistes in the Dolomites, including all Sella Ronda resorts	

ALTA BADIA TO / FREDDY PLANINSCHEK

Col Alt above Corvara is no beauty, but its Veranda is our favourite local restaurant – and look at that view →

➕ Vast network of connected slopes – suits intermediates particularly well

➕ Stunning, unique Dolomite scenery

➕ Lots of mountain huts with good food as well as fab views

➕ Relatively low prices

➕ Extensive snowmaking – one of Europe's best systems – but ...

➖ They need it: natural snowfall is erratic in this southerly region

➖ Few tough pistes, and off-piste is very limited – in general, banned

➖ Mostly short runs with limited vertical (with notable exceptions)

➖ Crowds on the Sella Ronda circuit

➖ Some old draglifts and slow chairs

Yet another return visit in 2015 confirmed once again that this is one of our absolute favourite destinations. The landscape is the thing: the spectacular Dolomite scenery is like something Disney might have conjured up for a movie. Well, the landscape and the mountain restaurants.

The Sella Ronda is an amazing circular network of lifts and pistes around the Gruppo del Sella – a mighty limestone massif. Sheer cliffs rise out of gentle pastureland, which is where you ski mostly. The skiing is relaxing; the excitement comes from the views. This is one of the few destinations where we pray for sun; snowfalls would interfere with our scenery-gazing without bringing any real benefit – off-piste is off the agenda, and the snowmaking normally ensures reliably good piste skiing.

The scale of the area is some compensation for the lack of challenge; the distances you cover on skis are huge – in overall dimensions, the network beats even the famed Trois Vallées in France. There are three main resorts, each with its own slopes branching off from the main circuit: Selva gets its own chapter; this one covers Corvara and Arabba, plus nearby alternatives.

429

CHOOSING A BASE

For good skiers wanting challenges on hand, probably the best base is Selva – covered in the next chapter along with Santa Cristina and Ortisei, slightly further down the Val Gardena. Arabba is the other obvious option.

We're increasingly convinced that Corvara is the best all-round bet – well placed for access to Selva, Arabba, the Sella Ronda circuit, the Alta Badia area and Cortina (and the 'hidden valley' run). Colfosco is just next door. La Villa and San Cassiano are slightly off the Sella Ronda circuit.

The Dolomiti Superski pass covers dozens of resorts around this amazing region. The lift system logs your lift rides – so you can go online to check your distance and vertical.

There are countless piste maps – a dozen Superski ones in all, plus locally produced ones for some resorts. The Alta Badia one, covering Corvara and neighbours, has the advantage that restaurants are more clearly identified.

ITALY

430

KEY FACTS	
Resort	1600m
	5,250ft
Slopes	1600-3270m
	5,250-10,730ft
Lifts	27
Pistes	89km/
	55 miles

TOURIST OFFICE

www.arabba.it

Arabba

➕ Some of the best steep pistes in the Sella Ronda area – shady too
➕ Quick access to Marmolada glacier

➖ Not a good base for novices, with more blacks than blues locally
➖ Off-slope activities are limited

Arabba is a small, quiet but fast-growing village appealing particularly to people looking for more challenging terrain than this region normally offers – but also immediate access to the Sella Ronda and Alta Badia sectors.

Village charm The village is small and traditional in style, but not notably picturesque. There are a few shops, bars and restaurants, but this is not a place for lively nightlife.

Convenience It's a small place, but staying in the older part can involve an uphill walk to reach the two lifts, which are a short walk apart. A newer area of hotels and chalets has developed higher up, well placed for the lifts and slopes, though perhaps not for bars.

Scenery Arabba is beautifully positioned between the stunning Gruppo del Sella and the glacial Marmolada massif, with great views at altitude in both directions.

THE MOUNTAIN

Arabba has a good mix of open and woodland slopes.

Slopes The two-stage double-cable gondola and the cable car beside it rise from the village almost 900m vertical to the high point at Porta Vescovo (2478m). From here a choice of runs return to the village or you can head off around the clockwise Sella Ronda circuit. From the mid-station of the gondola, chairs take you to Passo Padon and onwards to the Marmolada glacier. This is an excellent outing. The views across the Gruppo del Sella from the top at 3270m are spectacular, and the 1500m vertical red run to Capanna Bill is splendid, with great snow on the top sections.

From the other side of the village, a fast quad gets you on the way to Burz, Passo di Campolongo and Corvara, and the anticlockwise circuit.

Fast lifts Key local lifts are fast, but there are slow lifts on the way to Marmolada.

Queues The outing to Marmolada can be troublesome on a busy day. The Sass de la Vegla double chair is an obvious bottleneck, but also there may be long waits for the Marmolada cable cars, especially late in the season. One late-March visitor this year waited 75 minutes.

Terrain parks There's a park above Plan Boè, on the way to Passo di Campolongo – catering best for novices, in one reporter's view.

Snow reliability Good snow is far from assured, but snowmaking is extensive and the main runs are high and shady.

Experts Arabba has steep slopes to rival those of Selva/Val Gardena. The north-facing blacks and reds from Porta Vescovo offer genuine challenges and there is some tempting off-piste terrain too – but read the off-piste feature panel in the margin.

Intermediates The local slopes suit adventurous intermediates best – most are quite challenging. But the easy Alta Badia area is nearby.

Beginners It is not a great choice for beginners. There is a nursery slope near the Burz chair, but this is red run territory. Go to Corvara or Colfosco.

Snowboarding The slopes of Porta Vescovo offer some decent challenges but there are some flat areas. The nursery slope has a draglift.

Cross-country There are no trails here.

You can ski around the huge Sella massif in either direction by following very clear coloured signs; it's easily managed in a day by even an early intermediate. The clockwise route is slightly quicker and offers more interesting slopes, but is much busier – so many reporters prefer the anticlockwise route, despite a tedious series of five lifts from Corvara. Some resort piste maps include a Sella Ronda map; most take something close to a bird's eye topographical view. (Bizarrely, at least one puts south at the top.) A very detailed topo map is available from the tourist offices (and some lift stations).

The runs total around 23km and the lifts around 14km. There is one bit where no skiing is possible: at Corvara you ride a lift both ways – a gondola which replaced a queue-prone chair for last season. The lifts take a total of about two hours (plus any queuing). We've done the circuit in just three and

a half hours excluding hut stops; five or six hours is a realistic time when things are busy.

If you set out early and make good time, you can divert from the circuit, notably at Selva and Arabba. Less confident intermediates could explore the Alta Badia area, east of Corvara.

Not everyone likes it. You may find that 'it's a bit of a slog', or it is 'too busy and crowded', and 'not a relaxing business when it's busy'. And boarders should be aware that there are quite a few flat bits.

If you pick your time – low season or a Saturday, in good weather – and start early, we reckon it's well worth doing.

Sella Ronda

431

KEY FACTS

Sella Ronda
Linked network of Val Gardena, Alta Badia, Arabba, and of Canazei and Campitello in Val di Fassa

Slopes	1005-3270m
	3,300-10,730ft
Lifts	179
Pistes	433km
	269 miles

Mountain restaurants There's lots of choice; most places are lively and welcoming, and many have great views, of course. One lift-ride from the village, Rif Burz was beautifully rebuilt in 2013 in a modern but woody style; 'good food, fast service'; there's pole dancing at après time, we hear. The lively Rif Plan Boè, nearby, has 'good food and a traditional feel', but a reporter judges the prices higher than others. Rif Fodom just below Passo Pordoi is 'bright and bustling, with good food, service and views'. The smart self-service Cesa da Fuoch at the mid-station of the Porta Vescovo gondola has excellent fresh-cooked pasta. At the top, the smart self-service Luigi Gorza reportedly has good food as well as views, and there is now a serious, very pricey table-service place there too – Viel dal Pan. On the way to Marmolada, Capanna Bill is a cosy spot with friendly service offering 'excellent value'.

Schools We have good reports on both the Arabba and Dolomites Rèba schools.

Families The ski school takes quite young children.

STAYING THERE

New accommodation has been built at the top end of the village, convenient for the lifts. We know of no catered chalets here.

Hotels There are about a dozen hotels. A 2015 visitor endorses last year's recommendation of the 'brilliant' and well-placed 4-star Sporthotel for its 'exceptional food' and 'traditional Tirolean style'. The Evaldo is 'thoroughly recommended'; the Malta too – 'central, excellent food, very spacious rooms'.

Apartments Self-catering accommodation is available.

Eating out Restaurant choice is limited. The central hotels all have busy restaurants. Recent reporters praised the hotel Pordoi restaurant for its 'good pizzas'. Also rated are Miky's Grill in the hotel Mesdì and Al Table, serving everything from simple pasta and great pizzas to well-cooked steak. The Stube Ladina in the Alpenrose hotel has been recommended in the past. You can be ferried by snowmobile up the mountain to Rif Plan Boè for dinner and dancing; or arrive at 4pm and sit tight.

Après-ski The après-ski is fairly limited. On the way back from Corvara, there is some action in the huts – Plan Boè and Burz. The 'Austrian-style' Bar Peter 'gets very busy post-ski'; Mister X is another option. Bar Heidi is more sophisticated: 'good for an early evening drink – smart, drinks served with canapés'.

Off the slopes Off-slope diversions are few. There are some shops and cafes, and there's a small ice rink. Snowmobiling and snowshoeing are available.

Corvara

KEY FACTS

Resort	1570m
	5,150ft
Slopes	1330-2530m
	4,360-8,300ft
Lifts	53
Pistes	130km/
	80 miles

➕ One of the best locations, where Alta Badia meets the Sella Ronda
➕ Pleasant, relaxed village
➕ Local slopes suit novices, but ...

➖ Few challenges locally
➖ Some walking may be involved
➖ Alta Badia still has plenty of drags and slow chairlifts

Corvara rivals Selva as a base from most points of view, the exception being that of experts, who have to travel in search of challenges; for families and novices it takes some beating – though Colfosco merits consideration too.

Village charm Although it's not notably cute, the place is lively and family-friendly, with a pleasant traditional centre. There is some through-traffic, but it does not intrude hugely.

Convenience The main shops and some hotels cluster around a small piazza at the top end of the village, close to the Col Alto gondola; but the nursery slopes are quite a walk away, across the river; so are the Sella Ronda lifts, but you can ski to them by riding the Col Alto gondola. The rest of Corvara sprawls quite a way along the valley; choose your spot with care.

Scenery The setting is superb: there are impressive rock faces and spires all around the village, notably the distinctive, towering Sassongher.

THE MOUNTAIN
Corvara is well positioned, with village lifts heading off to reasonably equidistant Selva, Arabba and San Cassiano. The local slopes are gentle and confidence-boosting.

Slopes Lifts go off in three directions. A long gondola heads south towards Boè and Arabba for the clockwise Sella Ronda circuit. A powerful gondola recently replaced the chair heading west towards Colfosco and the anticlockwise route around the circuit. The area around both lifts can get congested at peak times. Another gondola from the top of the village takes you to the slopes shared with San Cassiano and La Villa.

Fast lifts New fast lifts are gradually improving the area.

Queues Replacement of the inescapable and over-busy Borest chair between Corvara and Colfosco seems to have solved the main local problem.

Terrain parks There is a terrain park above San Cassiano, easily reached from Corvara.

Snow reliability As in the rest of the Sella Ronda area, natural snowfall is erratic, but snowmaking and grooming are excellent.

Experts Very few of Corvara's slopes offer any real challenges. The short black above Boè is really no more than a red in gradient. The much longer wooded runs down to La Villa include a genuine black, adequately tricky when icy. Otherwise, you're off

SNOWPIX.COM / CHRIS GILL

The 'hidden valley' run from Lagazuoi to Armentarola should be on your agenda ↓

ITALY

432

to Selva or Arabba. Look at the feature panel in the margin for information on off-piste opportunities.

Intermediates There's a vast network of slopes ideal for cruising and confidence-boosting. On one side is the network of rolling hills shared with San Cassiano; on the other, above Colfosco, is the more dramatically set Val Stella Alpina, off the Sella Ronda circuit, plus the long, gentle runs from Passo Gardena – essentially one long nursery slope. The red back to the village underneath the Boè cable car that goes off towards Arabba is excellent – it's usually uncrowded and retains good snow. The adventurous can head for the steeper, wooded pistes going down to La Villa.

Beginners There's a decent nursery area and lots of easy runs to progress to on both sides of the village, making this one of the best bases in the Sella Ronda area for beginners.

Snowboarding Novices can make rapid progress on gentle slopes. A few awkward draglifts remain, but most can be avoided.

Cross-country This is one of the better bases in the area. The Alta Badia area offers 35km of trails, including a 10km valley loop on the way to Colfosco.

Mountain restaurants A highlight. In the area between here and San Cassiano there are lots of good mountain restaurants marked and named clearly on the Alta Badia local piste map. Most are woody and cosy, but Las Vegas is a wild exception – cool and minimalist; the food is excellent. Our favourite is La Veranda, the very popular table-service restaurant downstairs at Col Alt. The room is nothing special, but the food is superb. Other places endorsed this year include Bamby – 'divine', 'excellent daily specials, often using organic meat from their own farm'; I Tablà – 'good atmosphere, service and menu'; Piz Arlara – '360° views, friendly, amazing food'; Punta Trieste – 'best ribs ever'; Crëp de Munt – 'great valley view, excellent ravioli'; and Bioch – 'friendly staff, delicious food'.

On the Passo Gardena side of Corvara, the regular reader favourite is Rif Jimmy, in a fabulous position above the pass; it gets extremely crowded, but we've had good lunches here, most recently in 2015. The Edelweiss above Colfosco has an 'intimate, top-notch' table-service section.

Schools There's a local branch of the Alta Badia school – reports welcome.

Sella Ronda

433

GOURMET SKIING

The Alta Badia – the area around La Villa, including Badia, San Cassiano, Corvara and Colfosco – has over recent years built up a gourmet culture. For many years, its top hotels have run excellent restaurants, but more recently the tourist office has been involving mountain restaurants, too.

In recent seasons, a dozen mountain restaurants have served special dishes conceived by 'starred' chefs from resort restaurants in the area, plus their chums from around Europe. Both we and readers have enjoyed the results. A few years ago at I Tablà, for example, we had a superb dish – knuckle of pork in honey with thyme-scented polenta and chanterelles. The following year, things changed: the emphasis was switched to a new idea, 'Slope Food'. This means appetizers or 'finger-food' rather than the main dishes of the old scheme.

At the heart of the scheme, as before, are the chefs from the three seriously good 'starred' restaurants in the Alta Badia area, all of which are in top hotels – the Rosa Alpina in San Cassiano, the Ciasa

Salares in nearby Armentarola and hotel La Perla in Corvara.

The tourist office sponsors other foodie schemes too – for example, a series of mountain restaurants between La Villa and Santa Croce, above Badia, form a 'gourmet skitour' focusing on the local Ladin cuisine, detailed in a little brochure.

These schemes encourage variety and quality in mountain nosh; we approve. Whether fancy appetizers is the right way to develop the scheme, we're not so sure.

TOURIST BOARD ALTA BADIA

ALPINE ANSWERS
The UK's No.1 Chalet Specialist

For choice and service look no further!

alpineanswers.co.uk
call: 020 7801 1080

ABTA

434

ALTA BADIA TO / FREDDY
PLANINSCHEK

Corvara is the best all-round base in this area except for black-run enthusiasts, who should check out Selva ↓

Families 'Plenty of activities for everyone,' said a 2014 visitor. School instructors are 'very good' with children – the ski school's Kinderland takes children from the age of three.

STAYING THERE

The best location is near the main square at the top end of the village. – which happens to be where the best hotels are. We know of no catered chalets here.

Hotels There are some excellent 4-star hotels. La Perla is one of our all-time favourite ski hotels, offering superb food and service in a relaxed atmosphere, lovely, individual, welcoming rooms and a perfect position at the top of the village – ski down a few yards to the Col Alto gondola. Ski back to the door. Spa and small pool. Endorsed this year by three readers – 'a real gem', 'a fabulously charming place', 'one of the best in 30 years of skiing worldwide'.

The Posta Zirm a few yards away is also reportedly 'fabulous', with 'very friendly staff, fantastic food'; pool. Down at the other end of the village, Col Alto is also praised from all points of view – rooms, service, food. We have stayed in a very comfortable, stylish room in the newish extension. Rooms in the annexe, over the road, are said to be huge. 'Superb' spa and 'huge' pool. Efficient shuttles to lifts, ski to the door (snow permitting).

Eating out There's a reasonable choice. The Stüa de Michil restaurant in hotel La Perla has a Michelin star, and greatly impressed us – superb food and a warm atmosphere. Reader tips: the Taverna in the Posta Zirm – ('good pizza, nice atmosphere'), La Fornella ('good food, great value', 'excellent pizza'), the Stube at La Tambra hotel, Pizzeria Caterina.

Après-ski The fashionable place to go at close of play these days is L'Murin, a 'jumping converted barn' next to hotel La Perla right on the home piste. The Iceberg Lounge Bar at the hotel Col Alto is 'very cool'.

Off the slopes There's a covered ice rink, indoor tennis courts, an outdoor climbing wall and snowshoeing. The Posta Zirm pool and spa is open to the public by reservation. There is a toboggan run up the road towards Arabba, at Cherz.

If you like runs in spectacular scenery well away from all signs of civilization, don't miss the easy red run from Lagazuoi, reached by cable car from Passo Falzarego. The pass is easily accessible from Armentarola, close to San Cassiano – shared taxis run a shuttle service (5 euros each) to the pass from here. There's also a bus from San Cassiano, but it is reported to be crowded and slow.

The run is one of the most beautiful we've come across, and delights most reporters. Views from the top of the cable car are splendid, and the run passes beneath sheer cliffs and frozen waterfalls. The cable car has low capacity, so the run is never crowded. We like to stop near the end at the atmospheric Rifugio Scotoni (char-grills a speciality).

At the bottom, it's a long skate to a horse-drawn sled with ropes attached, which tows you back to Armentarola (for a couple of euros). This is more of a challenge than the run – when the snow gets rutted there is some risk of pile-ups. We prefer to take the minibus alternative (there's a phone to summon it) or ride in the sled. At Armentarola there is a draglift to the run back to San Cassiano.

ALAN LIPTROT

Other resorts

LINKED RESORT – 1540m

SAN CASSIANO

San Cassiano is a pleasant, quiet village, but it is off the Sella Ronda circuit, and its main lift is well outside the village. If you prefer San Cassiano to Corvara, it's probably because you particularly like one of its smart and comfortable hotels with gourmet restaurants.

The local slopes, shared with Corvara, are mainly ideal for easy cruising on flattering, well-groomed runs and there's relatively quick access to the famous 'hidden valley' run (described in our feature panel). Read Corvara for mountain restaurants in general; but note that Malga Saraghes on the home run to San Cassiano does 'the best Kaiserschmarrn in the area'. The nursery slopes are up the valley at Armentarola.

Of the hotels the Rosa Alpina is stylish and deeply comfortable, with three good restaurants including the St Hubertus, which has two Michelin stars. The hotel Ciasa Salares, out at Armentarola, also has an excellent Michelin-star restaurant, La Siriola. The Fanes, five minutes from the centre, is tipped this year – 'excellent: large room, very good food, inside-outside pool, good staff'. Après-ski starts up the mountain with loud music at Las Vegas, but village nightlife is very limited. A reader this year tips La Siela

– 'nice trendy bar with good restaurant attached', and Da La Vedia – 'nice chilled bar'. There is a toboggan run from Piz Sorega at the top of the gondola to the village.

LINKED RESORT – 1645m

COLFOSCO

Colfosco (aka Kolfuschg – the German influence gets stronger as you move west towards Selva/Wolkenstein) is a smaller, quieter satellite of Corvara, 2km away. It has a compact centre, with a group of large chalet-style hotels spread along the road from Corvara towards Passo Gardena and Selva, enjoying splendid views of the Gruppo del Sella.

On the snow Colfosco is connected to Corvara and the clockwise Sella Ronda circuit by the new two-way gondola which replaced the queue-prone Borest chairlift last season. In the opposite direction, a gondola goes towards Passo Gardena. There are excellent nursery slopes, and the runs back from Passo Gardena, after a red start, are easy, long cruises, making this a great base for novices.

The Kolfuschgerhof hotel is 200m from the slopes (efficient shuttles) but is a 'really nice family-run hotel with fantastic food, attentive staff'. But a Sella Ronda regular trumps this by raving about the Cappella for three years in a row: 'Still absolutely superb,

OFF-PISTE

Off-piste skiing is generally prohibited in the Sella Ronda – as in many Italian areas. This doesn't stop people doing it altogether. And it doesn't rule out some spectacular routes, away from the pistes, where you can safely go with guidance.

There are well-known routes on the Sella massif, reached via the cable car from Passo Pordoi. Fairly direct descents go back to the pass (the very sunny Forcella) or down Val Lasties towards Canazei. But the classic run is Val Mesdì, a long, shady couloir down to Colfosco, reached by hiking across the massif. Marmolada, the highest peak of the Dolomites, offers some big descents.

There is a mountain guides office in Corvara (www.altabadiaguides.com).

TOURIST OFFICES

San Cassiano, Colfosco, La Villa, Badia
www.altabadia.org
Canazei, Campitello
www.fassa.com

the half-board food quite outstanding.' Excellent ski-in/ski-out location, too.

Although it's a small place, there are some restaurants. Black Hill is a popular place for 'excellent wood-fired pizza'. Mathiaskeller is tipped for après beers and 'excellent risotto'. Otherwise it's 'a sleepy village'. The Edelweiss mountain restaurant is open in the evenings, with a snowcat to ferry you up and down.

LINKED RESORT – 1435m
LA VILLA

Like San Cassiano, La Villa is a bit detached from the Sella Ronda circuit. It's a much busier place, with the road from Brunico running through it; but it is much more conveniently arranged, with lifts and pistes on both sides of the village, and nursery slopes dotted around. The local lifts can build queues at peak times. There's a bit of an après scene at the top of the lifts here. There is said to be a public swimming pool. Inghams have a chalet hotel here – Al Pigher, with 'spacious public areas, superb spa facilities, stunning views'.

LINKED RESORT – 1325m
BADIA

This small roadside village (formerly known as Pedraces) is out on a limb beyond La Villa, so it's not a great base. But some will find it more interesting because there is a free bus link with Piccolino (20 minutes), where a gondola goes into the Plan de Corones/Kronplatz ski area.

The village has its own one-run ski area with a fast quad and a slow double chair to Santa Croce (2045m), where there is a famous old rifugio with fabulous views (and a tiny church). At the mid-mountain lift station is one of our favourite restaurants in Alta Badia, Rif Lee – sheltered terrace, excellent food, friendly service. Visitors also rate Rif Nagler nearby and Rif Sponata on the slopes shared with La Villa ('warm welcome, excellent carbonara and rösti').

LINKED RESORT – 1465m
CANAZEI

Canazei is a sizeable, bustling, pretty, roadside village of narrow streets, rustic buildings and traditional hotels.

The village itself is slightly off the main Sella Ronda circuit, but its main slopes form part of it. A 12-person gondola (powerful, but queue-prone) rises 465m to Pecol, at the foot of the slopes of Belvedere. These are linked in one direction to the slopes of Passo Pordoi and Arabba, and in the other to Passo Sella and Col Rodella (above Campitello), and then on to Selva. A red run returns to Canazei, but it gets the afternoon sun and is often closed.

The Belvedere slopes are open and sunny, with modest verticals of about 450m. Almost all are graded red. This rules out the resort for timid intermediates and beginners, even if it does exaggerate difficulty. There is a nursery slope in the valley.

The grand 4-star Schloss Hotel Dolomiti in the centre is repeatedly tipped – 'central, good food, great staff, very Italian, huge room'.

There are numerous restaurants, and the après-ski is surprisingly animated. The Giardino delle Rose, Osteria and Paradis (a converted barn – 'great fun') are popular at close of play. The 'friendly' International bar and ice cream parlour is quieter. La Stua dei Ladins is an atmospheric cafe/wine bar/restaurant – 'Great,' says a reporter.

Off-slope entertainment consists of beautiful walks and shopping. There's also a pool, sauna and Turkish baths.

LINKED RESORT – 1445m
CAMPITELLO

Neighbouring Campitello is a pleasant, unremarkable village, smaller, quieter and cheaper than Canazei, and still unspoiled. A cable car starting just outside the village rises 1000m up to Col Rodella and the slopes above Passo Sella. At the start of the day this lift can build queues even in January, 'massive' ones in high season – get the bus up to Canazei's gondola. There are no pistes to the resort.

A previous reporter enjoyed the 4-star hotel Stella Montis, up a steep hill outside the village (has a shuttle): 'Excellent, good food, first-class spa.' Après-ski these days is reported to be rather quiet.

VAL GARDENA TOURIST OFFICE

Selva / Val Gardena

Pleasant village amid spectacular Dolomite scenery, well placed for skiing on and off the vast Sella Ronda lift network

£95
RESORT PRICE INDEX

RATINGS

The mountains

Extent	★★★★★
Fast lifts	★★★★
Queues	★★★
Terrain p'ks	★★★
Snow	★★★★
Expert	★★★
Intermediate	★★★★★
Beginner	★★★
Boarder	★★★
X-country	★★★★★
Restaurants	★★★★★
Schools	★★★
Families	★★

The resort

Charm	★★★
Convenience	★★★
Scenery	★★★★★
Eating out	★★★
Après-ski	★★★
Off-slope	★★★

NEWS

2014/15:
Snowmaking was improved, particularly near the Dantercëpies gondola.

KEY FACTS

Resort	1565m
	5,130ft

Sella Ronda linked network: Val Gardena, Alta Badia, Arabba, and Canazei and Campitello in Val di Fassa

Slopes	1005-3270m
	3,300-10,730ft
Lifts	179
Pistes	433km
	269 miles

Val Gardena-Alpe di Siusi only

Slopes	1005-2520m
	3,300-8,270ft
Lifts	79
Pistes	175km
	109 miles

+ A key resort of the Sella Ronda region, so good for snowmaking, extent, scenery, mountain huts

+ Spectacular, dramatic setting

+ Excellent local slopes, with big verticals by Sella Ronda standards

+ Mix of open and wooded slopes

+ Excellent nursery slopes

− Some of the minus points of the Sella Ronda region apply, too; notably: erratic natural snowfall, crowds on the main Sella Ronda circuit

− Buses or taxis are needed for access to easy long runs to suit near-beginners, at Plan de Gralba

Selva is one of three sizeable resorts near the head of Val Gardena (a name well known to ski racing fans) and one of the main bases for exploration of the unique Sella Ronda region, described in the chapter before this one. Selva is one of the best bases in the area, essentially because of the challenging local slopes, including two race courses through woods to the valley. Beginners and timid intermediates, though, are probably better off staying in Corvara or Colfosco, described in the Sella Ronda chapter.

THE RESORT

Selva is a long roadside village in a spectacular setting in Val Gardena.

For many years this area was part of Austria, and it retains a Tirolean charm. German is more widely spoken than Italian, and many visitors are German, too. Most places have two names: Selva is also known as Wolkenstein and the Gardena valley as Gröden. We do our bit for Italian unity by using the Italian place names here. The local language, Ladin, also survives – so some places have a third name. The valley is famed for wood carvings, which are widely sold.

At the end of this chapter we describe two other bases. Santa Cristina is the next village down the valley, and almost merges with Selva; lifts from both villages meet on the steep racing hill of Ciampinoi. Further down the valley is Ortisei, the main town of Val Gardena, set beneath the distinct Alpe di Siusi area. Both bases

have lifts to another distinct area, Seceda. Another possible base is the much lower village of Siusi (1005m), with a gondola up to Alpe di Siusi.

The Dolomiti Superski pass covers not only Selva and the Sella Ronda resorts but dozens of others. With a car you can reach Cortina.

VILLAGE CHARM ★★★★★
Pity about the traffic
The village has traditional Tirolean-style architecture and an attractive church, but is rather strung out along the main road and suffers a bit from through-traffic (and a lack of parking) as well as a lack of central focus. Selva is a civilized, low-key resort – relaxed and family-friendly, once you get away from the through-road.

CONVENIENCE ★★★★★
Choose your spot with care
From the village, gondolas rise in two directions. The Ciampinoi gondola goes south from near the centre of the

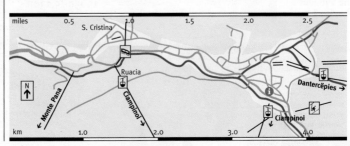

village to start the anticlockwise Sella Ronda route. The Dantercëpies gondola, for the clockwise Sella Ronda route, starts on the opposite side of the village and slightly above it, at the top of the nursery slopes (but is also accessible via a central chairlift and a short run down). The most convenient position to stay is near this chair or one of the gondolas. At various points there are lodgings on the snow, including places on the nursery slopes.

There are local buses until early evening – 9 euros for a weekly card (or free to guests at hotels in the local Tourist Association). They generate all sorts of complaints from reporters: lack of buses; not running to time; confusion between the public and the skiers' buses. There's a night bus between Selva and Ortisei. All the 4-star hotels run their own shuttles.

SCENERY ★★★★★
Pretty in pink

The village enjoys a fabulous setting under the impressive walls of Sassolungo, immediately above the slopes of Ciampinoi, and the Gruppo del Sella – a fortress-like massif 6km across that lies at the hub of the Sella Ronda circuit (described in a separate chapter). There are knockout views as you descend from Dantercëpies, for example, and from Alpe di Siusi. A Swedish reporter who has visited 62 countries rates the views here 'the most beautiful I have seen'.

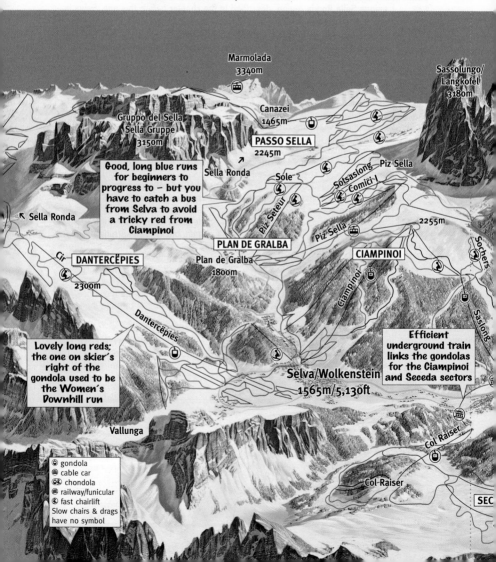

Marmolada 3340m

Sassolungo/ Langkofel 318om

Gruppo del Sella Sella Gruppe 3150m

Canazei 1465m

PASSO SELLA 2245m

Sella Ronda

Piz Sella

Sotsaslong

Comici |

Sole

Piz Seteur

Piz Sella

2255m

↖ Sella Ronda

Good, long blue runs for beginners to progress to – but you have to catch a bus from Selva to avoid a tricky red from Ciampinoi

PLAN DE GRALBA

Plan de Gralba 1800m

Sorchers

DANTERCËPIES

Cir

2300m

CIAMPINOI

Ciampinoi

Saslong

Dantercëpies

Lovely long reds; the one on skier's right of the gondola used to be the Women's Downhill run

Efficient underground train links the gondolas for the Ciampinoi and Seceda sectors

Selva/Wolkenstein 1565m/5,13oft

Vallunga

Col Raiser

gondola
cable car
chondola
railway/funicular
fast chairlift
Slow chairs & drags
have no symbol

Col Raiser

SEC

THE MOUNTAINS

Selva's own slopes cover both sides of the valley. The lower slopes are wooded, with open slopes higher up.

The local piste map exists in several confusing variations. The maps show neither names nor numbers for the runs, which strikes us as insane. Piste signing provokes some criticism.

EXTENT OF THE SLOPES ★★★★★
High-mileage excursions
The **Dantercëpies** gondola goes off eastwards to start the clockwise Sella Ronda circuit and serves lovely red runs back to Selva. On the other side of the valley, the **Ciampinoi** gondola goes south for the anticlockwise circuit via **Plan de Gralba** and accesses several shady pistes, leading back down to Selva and Santa Cristina, including the famous Downhill run.

In Santa Cristina, another gondola accesses Ciampinoi, and an underground train links the lift base to a gondola on the outskirts for the sunny **Seceda** area. In this sector, runs descend to Santa Cristina or to Ortisei – a red run of about 7km. And from Ortisei a gondola on the other side of the valley takes you to and from **Alpe di Siusi** – a gentle elevated area of quiet, easy runs, cross-country tracks and walks. You can proceed from here to the backwater **Monte Pana** (which is connected to Ciampinoi) by bus, but it's a slow affair.

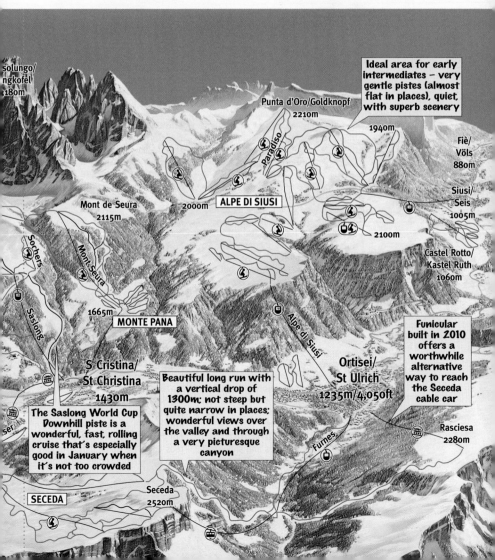

solungo/
ngkofel
180m

Punta d'Oro/Goldknopf
2210m

Paradiso

Ideal area for early intermediates – very gentle pistes (almost flat in places), quiet, with superb scenery

1940m

Fiè/
Völs
880m

Mont de Seura
2115m

2000m

ALPE DI SIUSI

Siusi/
Seis
1005m

Sorchers

Mont Seura

2100m

Castel Rotto/
Kastel Ruth
1060m

Saslong

1665m

MONTE PANA

Alpe di Siusi

S Cristina/
St Christina
1430m

Beautiful long run with a vertical drop of 1300m: not steep but quite narrow in places; wonderful views over the valley and through a very picturesque canyon

Ortisei/
St Ulrich
1235m/4,050ft

Funicular built in 2010 offers a worthwhile alternative way to reach the Seceda cable car

ser

The Saslong World Cup Downhill piste is a wonderful, fast, rolling cruise that's especially good in January when it's not too crowded

Furnes

Rasciesa
2280m

SECEDA

Seceda
2520m

↑ Alpe di Siusi is an extraordinary area, with gentle runs free of traffic, and countless good restaurants
ALAN LIPTROP

LIFT PASSES

Dolomiti Superski

Prices in €

Age	6-day
under 16	189
16 to 64	270
65 plus	243

Free Under 8

Beginner Points card

Senior Must be 65 before season starts

Note Covers 1220km of piste and 450 lifts in the Dolomites, including all Sella Ronda resorts

Alternative pass Val Gardena-Alpe di Siusi

FAST LIFTS ★★★★☆
Getting better
The main access lifts are gondolas, and there are lots of fast chairs above them, so progress can be quick. But there are still a few slow chairs and drags – an irritant on Alpe di Siusi.

QUEUES ★★★☆☆
Still some problems
The upgraded gondola seems to have dealt with the traditional morning queues at Dantercëpies, though the drags up to the gondola may hold you up. The Ciampinoi gondola builds queues in peak weeks, too – but there is a slow chair alternative. Other problems may arise on the Sella Ronda circuit – Piz Seteur for example. Doing the circuit anticlockwise from Selva has the drawback that everyone ends up on the chain of lifts from Corvara at the end of the day, in high season facing 'hideous' queues. The gondola out of Ortisei that takes you halfway to Seceda ensures that the cable car above it is over-busy.

TERRAIN PARKS ★★★☆☆
Facilities spread around
There are parks, pipes and snowcross courses in various spots. There is a mile-long park on Alpe di Siusi, with lines to suit all standards. Readers and their kids have loved the family-oriented fun park at Piz Sella, with 'plenty of easy obstacles', plus an amusing jump over a car, and other challenges for the more advanced.

SNOW RELIABILITY ★★★★☆
Excellent when it's cold
The slopes are not high – most are between 1500m and 2000m. Natural snowfalls are erratic, but the snowmaking is exceptionally good. During severe droughts we and readers have enjoyed excellent pistes here. The grooming is very good too – 'morning cruising is fantastic'. Problems arise only if it is too warm to make snow.

FOR EXPERTS ★★★☆☆
A few good runs
There are few challenges, essentially no moguls and a low likelihood of powder. There are few major off-piste routes because of the nature of the terrain, and off-piste is prohibited in places; read the off-piste panel in the Sella Ronda chapter.

The Val Gardena World Cup piste, the Saslong, is one of several steepish runs from Ciampinoi. It is open to the public much of the time – it's one of our favourite runs. There are also good reds down the same hills. The long red runs from Dantercëpies are good.

FOR INTERMEDIATES ★★★★★
Fast cruising on easy slopes
There is a huge amount of skiing to do, in several areas.

Competent intermediates will love the red and black descents from Dantercëpies and Ciampinoi to Selva (but more timid intermediates may find them too steep and/or crowded).

The blue runs in the Plan de Gralba area are gentle – great for building confidence; the red run to get there from Ciampinoi is a real obstacle – it's steep and crowded and can be icy – so you might want to go by road.

The quiet red and black runs at Mont de Seura, above Monte Pana, are worth exploring.

The gentle Alpe di Siusi above Ortisei is ideal for confidence-building. The red runs that dominate the map are mostly of blue gradient, and quiet.

The Seceda sector has good red and blue runs at altitude, and splendid runs to the valley – an easy blue/red to Santa Cristina and the beautiful red Cucasattel, passing through a natural gorge to Ortisei.

FOR BEGINNERS ★★★☆☆
Great slopes, but ...
The village nursery slopes below the Dantercëpies gondola are excellent – spacious and convenient. There are lots of gentle, long runs to progress to, but they are at Plan de Gralba and Alpe di Siusi, and reached by road. There are better places to start.

FOR BOARDERS ★★★☆☆
Limited options
Selva attracts few boarders. There's little to challenge experts, and off-piste opportunities are limited. The main valley lifts are all gondolas or chairs. There are three terrain parks and a couple of half-pipes.

FOR CROSS-COUNTRY ★★★★★
Beautiful trails
There are 115km of trails, all enjoying wonderful scenery and almost half at altitude. The 12km trail up the Vallunga valley is particularly attractive, with neck-craning views all around and has 'really good tracks for skate and classic styles', says our Swedish reporter.

MOUNTAIN RESTAURANTS ★★★★★
A real highlight
Restaurants are not identified on the main resort piste map, but they are (mostly) on the Sella Ronda map on the reverse. There are countless huts, and many of them are lively and characterful, with helpful staff, good

food and modest prices. What follows can't be considered comprehensive.

In the Dantercëpies sector, readers have tipped the Panorama near the top and the Pastura near the bottom.

On Ciampinoi, Rif Emilio Comici, set beneath the massive Sassolungo (arrive early if you want the sun), is generally tipped, notably for 'great fresh fish', but gets over-busy. Down towards Plan de Gralba, Vallongia has a cool ice bar. Piz Seteur is a lively spot with an outdoor DJ. Baita al Sole is a cute but simple place with good-value food. The revamped Gran Sas has a 'cool atmosphere' and 'even better food' than in the past. On the way to Selva, Valentini makes a good last stop – 'always friendly'.

Up at Passo Sella, Fienile Monte appears to be a recently built, upscale spot where a reporter this year had a 'fantastic lunch in the cosy downstairs wine room'. Sella Alm is a tiny hut doing 'simple, good-value food'.

In the Seceda sector there are countless options. Daniel does 'excellent, gigantic spiegeleier'. Rif Odles is one reader's favourite and another tips Sofie ('superb jumbo prawn platter'). Near the top of the long Cucasattel run, the tiny Curona is a tipped by several visitors; nearer the bottom, Val d'Anna was 'our favourite by far' for one reporter. On the S Cristina run, Pramulin offers 'friendly table-service of good meaty goulash soup'.

Alpe di Siusi alone is said to have over 40 places. We have had good reports on Floralpina – 'super-trendy, big windows, excellent pasta'; Laurin – 'superb views, very friendly service, excellent food'; Sanon – 'cosy hut, friendly service, substantial dishes'; Dibaita – 'another big terrace with fine views and service, and good Tirolean/Italian fare'. Our specialist Alpe di Siusi reporter also tips: Zallinger ('charming – a great find') and Mont Seuc – 'Perfect for watching the cliffs turn red over a last drink.'

SCHOOLS AND GUIDES ★★★☆☆
No worries
The main Selva Gardena school has been recommended by several readers. One past visitor recommended the ski safari ('took us to places we would never have dreamed of getting to') but was unhappy with the large group size and range of ability on some days.

FOR FAMILIES ★★★★★
It's all down to the detail
At first sight, in general, the village does not seem ideal for families. But make the right arrangements, and you can have very successful family holidays here. A 2014 visitor's children praised the 'fun parks, long runs and especially the food'.

STAYING THERE

Chalets A limited choice – Crystal has one 14-bed catered chalet, and Total has the 26-bed Soldanella, three minutes from the centre.

Hotels There are about 20 4-star hotels in Selva, about 40 3-stars and numerous lesser hotels. It is not a small place. Few of the best are well positioned – though they generally operate shuttle-buses.

★★★★Acadia 'Good location, ski-in/ski-out. Excellent staff, very clean, superb food,' says a reporter this year.

★★★★Gran Baita Large, luxurious sporthotel – 'excellent in every way; great food and service and a very welcome spa and pool setup'. A walk from centre and lifts but 'good shuttle' and 'ski close to the door'.

★★★★Oswald One Californian reader's Alpine favourite. 'Good rooms, fantastic food, very helpful staff.' Endorsed by another reader this year. Near ski-bus stop, and has shuttle.

★★★★Pralong By the double chair for Plan de Gralba. 'Friendly, family-run, well-equipped rooms, large comfortable bar area; food, service and cleanliness all excellent.'

★★★★Savoy Next to the 'slow but quiet' Ciampinoi chairlift. Approved again last year by our regular devotee – 'Very welcoming, great rooms, great food, lovely indoor/outdoor pool.'

★★★Armin Tipped by two readers this year: 'Place immaculate, staff all friendly, food exceptional, drinks prices non-exploitative.'

★★★Mezdi B&B hotel in good ski-in/ski-out position. 'Good breakfast, very helpful owners.'

Apartments They are available, but we have no recent reader reports.

At altitude A past reporter enjoyed a 'fabulous' stay at the hotel Sochers on Ciampinoi. Plan de Gralba on the road to Passo Sella has lodgings that are mostly ski-in/ski-out; the family-run 3-star hotel Sella is strongly tipped – 'attentive staff and excellent food'.

EATING OUT ★★★★★
Adequate choice
The better restaurants are mainly based in hotels or, ironically, B&B guest houses. Current reader favourites are La Bula ('went back three times', 'good-value, tasty pizzas') and La Stua ('great food in attractive rustic setting, friendly service'). Other

SNOWPIX.COM / CHRIS GILL

Selva's signature peak, Sasso Lungo, looms over the slopes of Ciampinoi, seen here from the slopes of Dantercëpies ↓

reader tips include: the slope-side hotel Freina ('superb seafood', 'good value and service'), the woody stube of the hotel des Alpes, Rino, and the pizzeria of the hotel Sun Valley. A taxi ride away at Plan de Gralba, a cool spot called SooChic impressed one reporter this year with its 'wonderful food, ambience and staff'.

APRES-SKI ★★★★★
Not without action
At close of play some of the mountain restaurants offer diversions. Piz Seteur, with its outdoor DJ, was as lively and fun as ever when we last visited. At the base, La Stua is a popular last stop – 'great place with delightful staff, great atmosphere and good prices' – and if you settle in for the evening, live music may arrive. The 'Tirolean' Kronestube has been tipped ('good atmosphere'). Café Mozart is 'a convivial place for a relaxed coffee'. Later on, the village streets are fairly quiet, but there are places to go. Goalies' Irish pub is 'good for a quiet drink' – it suits grown-ups with its classic rock music. The place to let your hair down is Luislkeller – 'the beer seems to come in one size – huge', 'hopping, with great craic', 'really lively, difficult to get in'. Yello's, another cellar, is a competitor. The serious nightclub is Dali, open until 3am, for 'a younger clientele'.

OFF THE SLOPES ★★★★★
Good variety
There are many spectacular walks, on Alpe di Siusi and Rasciesa, especially. There's a sports centre, snowshoeing, tobogganing and sleigh rides. 'Great night at the ice hockey,' says a repeat visitor. There are buses to Ortisei (if you don't fancy the lovely two-hour walk) and more distant Bolzano, with an excellent museum devoted to 5,000-year-old Oetzi the Ice Man, among many attractions. And there are coach excursions to Cortina and Verona. Pedestrians can reach many good mountain restaurants.

SANTA CRISTINA

A few km down-valley from Selva, at the bottom of the race course from Ciampinoi, Santa Cristina is a pleasant village well worth considering as an alternative base. It has gondolas towards Ciampinoi and Seceda (their base stations linked by an underground railway), and a slow chairlift up to a ring of nursery slopes at Monte Pana (but no piste back). There is accommodation up here, too. There's a good range of hotels in the village from 5-star down, and countless B&Bs. The restaurant of the hotel Maciaconi does 'good steaks and other local specialities'. The 'very welcoming' Villa Sella does 'very tasty pizzas and a small range of other dishes'.

ORTISEI

Ortisei is an attractive, prosperous market town with a life of its own apart from tourism. It's full of lovely buildings, pretty churches, smart shops and tempting cafes, and has an interesting museum, a large hot-spring swimming pool and an ice rink. The valley road follows the river, bypassing the centre. The local slopes offer an astonishing six toboggan runs – one from Rasciesa 6km long and accessed by funicular – as well as vast amounts of easy skiing. If you intend to spend time on the Sella Ronda circuit beyond Selva, plan on using the ski-buses.

The gondola to the Seceda slopes is easily reached from the centre by a 300m-long series of moving walkways and escalators. Alternatively, you can reach the top of that gondola, and the start of the Seceda cable car, by riding the Rasciesa funicular and descending a red piste. The gondola for Alpe di Siusi is a similar distance out, across the river – a footbridge from the centre is the best approach, going over the valley road too. Note that to move from one area to another involves quite a walk.

The nursery area, school and kindergarten are also over the river, along with a fair range of accommodation. The fine public indoor pool and ice rink are also here.

There are hotels and self-catering accommodation to suit all tastes and pockets, and many good restaurants, mainly specializing in local dishes. The 5-star Gardena is tipped for 'spacious rooms, great cuisine and friendly staff'. The 5-star Adler is also rated. The 'delightfully named' 4-star hotel Hell also gets a mention for its excellent minibus service. Après-ski is quite jolly, and many of the bars keep going till late.

Selva / Val Gardena

443

GETTING THERE
Air Bolzano 50km/ 30 miles (1hr); Innsbruck 120km/ 75 miles (1hr45); Verona 195km/ 120 miles (2hr15); Munich 320km/ 200 miles (3hr15); Milan Linate 320km/ 200 miles (3hr30)

Rail Chiusa (27km/ 17 miles); Bressanone (35km/22 miles); Bolzano (40km/ 25 miles); frequent buses from stations

TOURIST OFFICE
www.valgardena.it

SESTRIERE TOURIST OFFICE

Sestriere

Altitude is the main attraction of this, Europe's first purpose-built resort; it's a good base for exploration of the Milky Way

£90
RESORT PRICE INDEX

TOP 10 RATINGS

Extent	★★★★
Fast lifts	★★★
Queues	★★★
Snow	★★★★
Expert	★★★
Intermediate	★★★★
Beginner	★★★
Charm	★
Convenience	★★★
Scenery	★★★

KEY FACTS

Resort	2035m
	6,680ft

Milky Way	
Slopes	1390-2825m
	4,560-9,270ft
Lifts	72
Pistes	400km
	249 miles

Sestriere-Sauze d'Oulx-Sansicario	
Slopes	1390-2825m
	4,560-9,270ft
Lifts	41
Pistes	300km
	186 miles

+ Local slopes suitable for most levels – with some tough runs

+ Quick access to Sauze d'Oulx (and fairly quick to French Montgenèvre).

+ High with good snowmaking, but ...

− Erratic natural snowfall

− Village is a bit of an eyesore

− For a purpose-built resort, not conveniently arranged

− Weekend and peak-period queues

Sestriere was built for snow – high, with north-west-facing slopes; sadly, the snow on these slopes often has a large artificial component. The real drawback, though, is that the village is a difficult place to like. There are two attractive solutions: stay a bit lower down in Borgata; or stay much lower down in Pragelato (linked by cable car) where there is an appealing Club Med.

THE RESORT

Sestriere was the first purpose-built resort, developed by Fiat's Giovanni Agnelli in the 1930s. It is the best base for exploration of the Milky Way.
Village charm The resort sits on a broad, sunny and windy col. With its rows of apartments, the place doesn't look very inviting. The satellite of Borgata, a gentle blue run to the east, is quiet and traditional in style.
Convenience The village is not huge, and some lodgings are very close to the snow; but some are quite distant from the lifts, or the bars. There are buses, but you have to pay for them.
Scenery The slopes give extensive views across the part-wooded Milky Way to the peaks of the French border.

THE MOUNTAINS

The local skiing is on shady slopes, mainly open with some woodland, facing the village. The poor piste map and piste signing combine to form a small nightmare, especially on M Motta – good luck! Piste classification is erratic, too.
Slopes The local slopes, served by drags and chairs, are in two main sectors: Sises, directly in front of the village, and Motta, above Borgata; Motta is more varied and bigger, with more vertical. From a car park west of the village a gondola goes up over the opposite mountainside to M Fraiteve, for access to Sauze d'Oulx, Sansicario and the rest of the Milky Way. There are red and blue runs back from M Fraiteve – sunny, and not reliably open to the bottom. You may face a long walk from the end of the piste to the lifts or your lodgings.
Fast lifts The main lifts are modern fast ones, but there are still too many slow, old ones – both here and over in Sansicario and Sauze.
Queues The main lifts can have queues on sunny weekends. We lack high-season reports, but would expect the double chair back from Sauze to be a regular problem. At M Fraiteve the confined summit area can get seriously congested. There may be long queues for the gondola down.
Terrain parks The terrain park is by the parallel baby lifts on the village nursery slopes.
Snow reliability The Italian part of the Milky Way gets notoriously unreliable snowfalls, but Sestriere has extensive snowmaking. Add in altitude and orientation, and you can count on

Club Med 🎿

THE MOST COMPREHENSIVE
SKI PACKAGE ON THE MARKET

Pragelato 4🎿

020 8313 3999
Skiline.co.uk

Skiline.co.uk

LIFT PASSES

Prices in €

Age	6-day
under 8	30
8 to 74	190
75 plus	120

Free No deals

Beginner Restricted day pass (€25)

Note Covers lifts in Sauze d'Oulx, Sestriere, Sansicario, Cesana and Claviere

Alternative pass International (covers all the above plus Montgenèvre)

PISTE MAP

Sestriere is covered on the Sauze d'Oulx map

good cover on the pistes. Grooming is 'comprehensive' and 'excellent'.

Experts There are things to do: steep pistes – three designated as mogul fields – are served by drags at the top of both local sectors. Given good snow, there is some decent off-piste, but don't count on it; outings to snowy Montgenèvre can be very rewarding.

Intermediates Both local sectors offer something for confident intermediates – Motta especially – but they don't add up to a lot, so plan on multiple visits to other linked resorts.

Beginners There are good nursery slopes directly in front of the village, served by draglifts, but you need a lift pass (a special day pass covers five lifts). There are easy longer runs to progress to locally (the run down to Borgata is splendid) and over in Sauze.

Snowboarding The draglifts are largely avoidable except above Sansicario. There's a specialist snowboard school.

Cross-country There are three loops covering about 10km.

Mountain restaurants Not all the huts are marked on the resort piste map. We haven't made it to the place ourselves, but the woody Raggio di Sole, on skier's right at Motta, sounds like the best bet to judge by readers' reports ('tasty, filling local dishes; happy, helpful staff'). Alpette, directly above the village, has a popular terrace and is tipped for 'simple lunches, or bombardinos as the lifts close and the sun goes down'.

Schools and guides. A reporter this year had an 'absolutely fantastic experience' with the Nazionale. The other main school is the Vialattea.

Families The two main schools have mini clubs for children too young to join ski classes.

STAYING THERE

Most accommodation is in apartments, in low-rise blocks.

Hotels There are a dozen hotels, mostly 3-star or 4-star. The 3-star Biancaneve has had good reports. The ideally positioned hotel du Col – 'very friendly, lovely food' – is exclusive to Crystal; go for rooms on the snow side not the road. Just out of the village is the swanky Ròseo, with swimming pool and spa. Out at Borgata, we found a warm welcome at the Banchetta, a traditional, family-run hotel with old photos on the walls and very good food in the dining room.

Apartments The Villagio Olimpico apartments built for the 2006 Olympics are reasonably central.

Eating out There are plenty of options. A reader favourite is Last Tango – 'fab wild boar carpaccio, pork in mustard, and violet sorbet'. We can vouch for the pizzas at the popular Pinky, and a reader tips Kandahar for its cheese-burgers. Down in Borgata, the rustic Antica Spelonca has been tipped; it's in a cute vaulted cellar.

Après-ski The quietness of the place during the week disappoints some visitors. Pinky has a cafe-style bar that was packed with Brits at close of play last time we visited and reportedly has live music most nights. The bar in Crystal's hotel du Col is popular too. Readers also tip Black Pepper – 'very lively, lovely cocktails'. Tabata is the main club, with a cool bar upstairs and a big disco below.

Off the slopes There's more to do than most visitors realize. There are some smart shops, a fitness centre, an ice rink, a sports centre and pool; the dog sledding looked good to our untrained eye. Outings are possible to Turin, only 100km away by road.

SNOWPIX.COM / CHRIS GILL

← The slopes on the shady side of the resort offer more challenges than anything you'll find over in Sauze d'Oulx or Sansicario

TOURIST OFFICE

www.turismotorino.org
www.vialattea.it
www.comune.sestriere.to.it

LINKED RESORT – 1535m

PRAGELATO

A cable car at the eastern extremity of the Sestriere slopes gives access to the resort from the 500m-lower valley village of Pragelato, which hosted the ski-jump and cross-country events for the Turin 2006 Olympics. There are local lifts, which we understand now access a purely freeride area – we're not clear about the safety aspects of this. For most visitors, Pragelato means the Club Med 'village'; this is very unusual, consisting of clusters of chalets rather than the usual hotel-style setup – it looks a very civilized base from which to ski Sestriere.

La Thuile

A spread-out resort with a mix of ancient and modern parts and extensive, easy, snow-sure slopes linked with La Rosière in France

£90
RESORT PRICE INDEX

TOP 10 RATINGS

Extent	★★★
Fast lifts	★★★
Queues	★★★★★
Snow	★★★★
Expert	★★
Intermediate	★★★★
Beginner	★★★★
Charm	★★★
Convenience	★★★
Scenery	★★★

NEWS

2015/16: La Thuile will host the Women's World Cup Downhill and Super G races on 20-21 February 2016.

2014/15: Nira Montana, a new 5-star, 55-room boutique hotel with a smart spa, opened. So did Maison Musée Berton, a museum of Aosta Valley artefacts.

446

+ Fair-sized area linked to La Rosière in France

+ Strikingly crowd-free slopes

+ Excellent beginner and easy intermediate slopes

− The tough runs are low down, and most low, woodland runs are tough

− The French link is exposed to bad weather, and the return is slow

− Not the place for lively après-ski

La Thuile has a lot going for it. And if you are limited to school holidays and have had enough of the peak-season crowds over the hill in France, it could be just the job – provided a quiet village appeals to you as much as quiet slopes.

THE RESORT

La Thuile is based on an old mining village that has been expanded and restored. The attractive centre, with shops, bars and restaurants, is at the entrance, with newer developments fairly widely spread. Over the river, the modern Planibel complex, at the base of the lifts, looks a bit like a French purpose-built resort. The pass includes two days in other Val d'Aosta resorts, and buses run to nearby Courmayeur, making this an easy outing which reporters recommend.

Village charm The village centre is attractive but we, and many reporters, find the Planibel complex soulless.

Convenience The main village is a little way from the lift base and is served by a regular free bus. The Planibel complex is right by the main lift, with a few other hotels nearby.

Scenery The scenery is varied, with open bowls and lower wooded slopes overlooked by the nearby Mont Blanc massif. Good views into France.

THE MOUNTAINS

La Thuile has quite extensive slopes linked to those of La Rosière via slopes above the Petit St Bernard pass – a good sector, poorly represented on the piste map. Many runs marked red should be blues. Strong winds can close high lifts, including the link.

Slopes A gondola out of the village takes you to Les Suches and an alternative chair to 100m below it. Shady black and red runs go back to the village through the trees. Chairs take you up to Chaz Dura for access to a variety of gentle bowls and slightly more testing slopes on the back of the ridge. From there two chairs go up to the link with La Rosière.

Fast lifts Most key lifts are fast chairs.

Queues Short queues may form at the gondola first thing, but not at the chair. There are no problems once you are up the hill. Reporters regularly comment on the lack of queues: 'Non-existent, even on an Italian holiday.'

Terrain parks The Wazimu ('Madness') park is in the Les Suches area and has a line specially for younger children.

Snow reliability Most of La Thuile's slopes are north- or east-facing and above 2000m, so the snow keeps well. There's also a decent amount of snowmaking; grooming is excellent. The snow was in fine condition when we were there on a warm March visit.

Experts Black pistes 2 and 3 down through the trees from Les Suches are seriously steep, usually groomed and great fun when they are. The black slopes at the top down to the pass are easier – but there is also plenty of good off-piste here. Heli-skiing options include a 20km run from the Ruitor glacier to Ste-Foy in France, a short taxi ride from La Rosière for lifts back.

La Rosière instructors often head over to La Thuile because the snow is better and less affected by the sun →

SNOWPIX.COM / CHRIS GILL

KEY FACTS

Resort	1440m
	4,720ft

Espace San Bernardo (La Rosière and La Thuile)	
Slopes	1175-2610m
	3,850-8,560ft
Lifts	37
Pistes	160km
	99 miles

LIFT PASSES

Espace San Bernardo

Prices in €

Age	6-day
under 14	126
14 to 64	210
65 plus	168

Free Under 8

Beginner Very limited pass; points card

Note Covers La Thuile and La Rosière

Alternative pass Aosta valley

MOMENTUM SKI

Weekend & a la carte ski holiday specialists

100% Tailor-made

Premier hotels & apartments

Flexible travel arrangements

020 7371 9111
WWW.MOMENTUMSKI.COM

TOURIST OFFICE

www.lathuile.net

Intermediates The slopes above Les Suches are gentle blues and reds, ideal for cruising. There are also good long reds through the trees back to the resort. The red runs on the back of the top ridge, down towards the Petit St Bernard pass, are less gentle. The pass road forms a very gentle red run to the village, dropping a mere 600m in 11km; avoid in fresh snow.

The skiing in La Rosière is more testing – mostly genuine red runs, sometimes with moguls, and with snow more affected by sun. The route back involves at least one long draglift.

Beginners There are no free lifts, but a special day pass allows use of the moving carpet on the village nursery slope. There is also a nursery area up at Les Suches and long, easy blues to progress to. Ride the gondola down.

Snowboarding These are great slopes for learning. There are no draglifts, unless you go to La Rosière. For the more experienced there are great tree runs and good freeriding and carving runs. But there are flat sections too.

Cross-country There are 11km of loops on the valley floor and a further 20km in Arpy a few kilometres away.

Mountain restaurants Generally not great by Italian standards, but marked on the piste map. For a good lunch, we would head for the village and eat at Lo Tatà (see 'Eating out') just off the piste on skier's left – look for the sign to the path to it. Higher up, we like Off Shore, a small hut with an eclectic mix of 1960s/70s memorabilia and music and nautical/Asian/African themes – simple food that you order at the bar. Tiny Chalet de Cantamont has had glowing reviews. A 2015 visitor recommends Foyer ('great thin-crust pizza') and Roxi ('fab soups'). The remote Riondet has been tipped.

Schools and guides A recent visitor was impressed – her sons' instructor 'spoke good English and they had fun'.

Families There is a mini club and snow garden, a village kindergarten and the Birba Club for kids in the Planibel hotel. Over fives can join ski school.

STAYING THERE

Hotels The resort's first 5-star, Nira Montana, opened last season around 400m from the slopes (free shuttle); plush spa. The 4-star Planibel has a prime location at the lift base plus pools etc; but it is very impersonal. In sharp contrast, we were very impressed by the 4-star Miramonti, in

the old village – smartly renovated, free shuttle, excellent food and service, swanky spa (costs extra). Chalet Eden, a short walk from the lifts, is a 4-star eco-hotel with a big spa. The 3-star B&B hotel du Glacier, a short walk above the lifts, gets rave reviews, mainly thanks to its energetic owner Susanna. The 3-star B&B Boton D'Or was recommended by a recent reporter ('close to the lifts, superb service, comfortable rooms').

Apartments The Planibel apartments are 'noisy and ugly', but they are spacious and good value.

Eating out We had a great lunch at Lo Tatà just off the slopes at the top of the village – lovely rustic building with stone walls, wood ceilings and beams; a recent reporter who dined there endorses it too. Other reader tips include the Maison Laurent ('huge portions, charmingly chaotic'), Coppapan ('lovely pistachio-encrusted lamb cutlets') and Pepita Café ('good food, friendly service').

Après-ski 'La Cage aux Folles in the Planibel complex is the place to go at teatime and Angela's bar in town is popular with locals,' says a recent reporter. Nightlife is quiet. The Konver is open until late and has a regular DJ.

Off the slopes Not great. There are few shops; the Planibel has a pool; there are walks and dog sledding. Non-skiers can ride the gondola, but can't reach the best lunch spots. The thermal baths 10km away at Pré-St-Didier are excellent, with over 40 spa 'experiences' including saunas and outdoor pools.

Switzerland

SWISS FRANC

Back in the winter of 2007 we were getting 2.4 Swiss francs for £1. When we worked out our RPI figures for this edition the rate was 1.39 francs – about 4% less than a year ago – making everything around 75% more pricey in terms of £££ than eight years ago. Things were even worse in 2011, when the rate hit around 1.3 francs. The Swiss then decided to peg the franc to the euro, so that it would not continue to rise – but ditched this policy in January 2015.

Switzerland is home to some of our favourite resorts. Only two resorts in this book are awarded ★★★★★ for both resort charm and spectacular scenery – the essentially traffic-free Swiss villages of Mürren and Wengen – and many other Swiss resorts are not far behind in the charm and scenery stakes. Many resorts have impressive slopes, too – including some of the biggest, highest and toughest runs in the Alps – as well as a lot of good intermediate terrain. For fast, queue-free lift networks, Swiss resorts are not known as pacesetters – too many historic cable cars and mountain railways for that. But the real bottlenecks are steadily disappearing. And there are compensations – the world's best mountain restaurants, for one, and pretty reliable accommodation, too.

There's no doubt that Switzerland is expensive. Our price survey shows that food and drink now cost way more than in any other skiing country. Overall holiday costs (when you add in the cost of lifts, ski hire and lessons) are less than in most North American resorts, but way above the European norm. The main problem is the strength of the Swiss franc. As our margin panel explains, the franc has increased in value since the start of the recent recession, and has been allowed to rise even further in value against the euro this year. In comparison to France, for example, Switzerland looks more pricey than ever. Last year, the very cheapest Swiss resorts scraped into our average price category; now, all are in the pricey category. Until the exchange rate improves, most people will simply go elsewhere.

A new and regrettable development last year was that the Swiss decided to apply their minimum wage legislation to employees of foreign firms operating in Switzerland. This had a huge and immediate impact on operators of catered chalets, particularly what you might call 'affordable' chalets. Basically, such chalets are now very rare. More on this below.

Many Swiss resorts have a special relationship with the British, who invented downhill skiing in its modern form in Wengen and Mürren by persuading the locals to run their mountain railways in winter, to act as ski lifts, and by organizing the first downhill races. An indication of the continuing strength of the British presence in these resorts is that Wengen has an English church.

TRADITIONAL YEAR-ROUND RESORTS

While France is the home of the purpose-built resort, Switzerland is the home of the mountain village that has transformed itself from traditional farming community (or health retreat) into year-round holiday resort. Many of Switzerland's most famous mountain resorts are as popular in the summer as in the winter, or more so. This creates places with a more lived-in feel to them and a much more stable local community.

Not that stable local communities are entirely a good thing. Many villages are still dominated by a handful of families lucky or shrewd enough to get involved in the early development of the area, and this has its downside as well as advantages. The ruling families have been able to stifle competition and bar newcomers

JUNGFRAU REGION / JOST VON ALLMEN

← Perched on a shelf reached only by lifts, facing a row of truly spectacular peaks, Mürren is the ultimate Swiss resort

from taking a slice of their action. For example, alternative ski schools – to compete with the traditional, nationally organized school, ensuring continuing pressure to raise standards – were slower to appear here than in other Alpine countries. But this grip has been weakened over recent years, and ski school standards have risen as a result.

The quality of service throughout Switzerland is generally high. The food is almost universally of good quality, and much more varied than in Austria. Even the standard rustic dish of rösti – potatoes grated then fried – is haute cuisine compared to Austrian sausages; crucially, it comes in countless variations, which Austria's Tiroler gröstl does not. And in Switzerland you get what you pay for: the cheapest wine, for example, is not cheap – you won't find many £10 carafes – but it is reliable.

NOT ENTIRELY TRADITIONAL

Perhaps surprisingly for such a traditional, rather staid skiing nation, Switzerland has gone out of its way to attract snowboarders. Davos, for example, may hit the headlines mainly when it hosts huge economic conferences, but yards from the conference hall there are dudes getting big air on the Bolgen slope's training kickers. Little-known Laax claims one of Europe's best terrain parks and firmly targets its marketing at the youth and freestyle markets as well as families.

Switzerland, like Italy, doesn't have much time for tree-huggers who object to the impact of helicopters on wildlife. Heli-skiing is not unrestricted, but it is available – indeed, the Zermatt helipad is like a bus station at peak times, with choppers taking off every few minutes (you can even get a heli-lift to the top of the pistes, if you find conventional lifts just too ordinary). In Austria heli-skiing is confined to Lech-Zürs and in France it is largely confined to the retrieval of clients from remote spots in valleys – you can't be deposited on a peak.

THE CHALET BUSINESS UNDER PRESSURE

One way to minimize your exposure to high Swiss prices is to stay in a catered chalet. They offer very competitive package prices, and the package usually includes wine with dinner and may include other extras. So it's very regrettable that the Swiss government last year decided to apply its minimum wage legislation to the staff of these chalets, even if they are employed in the UK. The minimum wage works out at an astonishing £34,000 a year, and to cut a long story short the result is that value-conscious operators like Inghams, Ski Total and Skiworld now operate very few chalets in Swiss resorts.

GETTING AROUND BY TRAIN

The Swiss railway network is famously extensive and reliable. The trains run like clockwork to the advertised timetable – if you think a Swiss train is late, make sure your watch is right before you complain. (There is, however, some truth in the cynical view that the trains are able to run on time because the timetables incorporate long stops at stations.)

The rail network is a perfectly viable means of reaching many resorts. There are often linking cog railway services that run to the top of the mountain, doubling as ski lifts, too, sometimes accessing

The Austrians might dispute it, but Switzerland seems to do tobogganing on an unmatched scale. It isn't just the famous Cresta run at St Moritz (check out that chapter for more information); it's that so many resorts have epic runs. The longest in the world, they say, is at Grindelwald – 15km from the Faulhorn via Bussalp to the resort; it's fantastically scenic, being surrounded by famous peaks, but it does involve a 2hr30 hike from the top of the First gondola.

There are plenty of other extraordinary runs, without the hiking penalty. Fiesch in the little-known Aletsch Arena area has a 13km run, Saas-Grund below Saas-Fee has one of 11km. Even macho Verbier has a 10km run from Savoleyres, dropping 850m.

SWISS-IMAGE.CH / CHRISTIAN PERRET

high-altitude hotels. And if a resort is not on the rail network, there will usually be efficient bus services to take you to your destination from the nearest station.

There's a comprehensive array of 'rover' tickets, some of them covering every kind of public transport, not just trains. And there are special 'transfer' tickets, that get you to your resort from the airport or border, and back again.

GETTING AROUND BY CAR

Access to practically all Swiss resorts is fairly straightforward when approaching from the north – just pick your motorway. But many of the high passes that are perfectly sensible ways to get around the country in summer are closed throughout the winter, which can be inconvenient if you are planning to move around from one area to another.

There are very useful car-carrying trains in various places, crawling over impassable passes or burrowing through the mountains to cut out huge amounts of driving. One key link is between the Valais (Crans-Montana, Zermatt etc) and Andermatt via the Furka tunnel, and another is from Andermatt to the Grisons (Laax, Davos etc) via the Oberalp pass – closed to road traffic in winter but open to trains except after very heavy snowfalls. Another rail tunnel that's very handy is the Lötschberg, linking Kandersteg in the Bernese Oberland with Brig in the Valais. (The Lötschberg Base Tunnel, opened in 2007, is lower, longer and faster, but it's not relevant to travel by car – it takes only passenger and freight trains.)

St Moritz in the south-east corner of the country, close to Italy, is more awkward to get to than other major resorts. The only reliable road route is over the Julier pass. This is normally kept open, but at 2285m it is naturally prone to heavy snowfalls that can shut it for a time. The alternatives are car-carrying rail tunnels – the Albula tunnel nearby and the Vereina tunnel from near Klosters to Susch, 30km north-east of St Moritz.

These car-carrying rail services are generally painless. Often you can just turn up, sit in a queue for a bit and then drive on to the train. But carrying capacities are obviously limited, and some services (eg Oberalp between Andermatt and the Grisons) carry only a handful of cars, so booking is vital. Others (eg Furka, Lötschberg, Vereina) are much bigger operations with much greater

Introduction

451

capacity – but that's a reflection of demand, and at peak times there may be long queues – particularly for the Furka tunnel from Andermatt, which Zürich residents are inclined to use to get to the big Valais resorts.

There is a car-carrying rail tunnel linking Switzerland with Italy – the Simplon, from Brig in the Valais. But most routes to Italy are kept open by means of road tunnels. Read the Italy introduction.

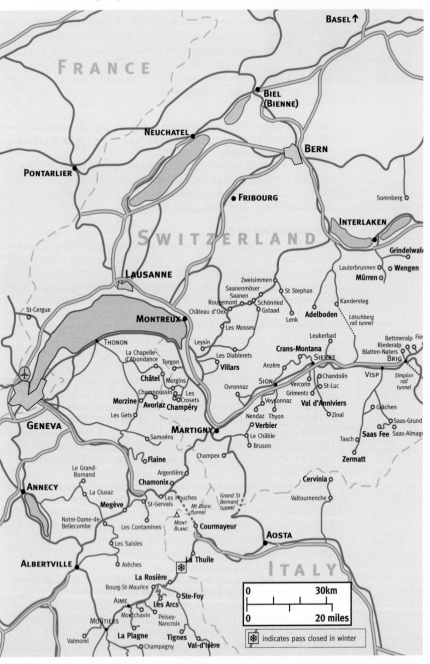

To use Swiss motorways you have to buy an annual sticker for your windscreen. These cost 40 francs, are sold at the border and are valid for 14 months – from 1 December to 31 January. If you are caught without a sticker, or if you have one but have not stuck it in place on the windscreen, you'll be fined 200 francs (in addition to being sold a sticker, of course). And 'stuck' means stuck: slipping it into a plastic holder stuck to the windscreen won't do.

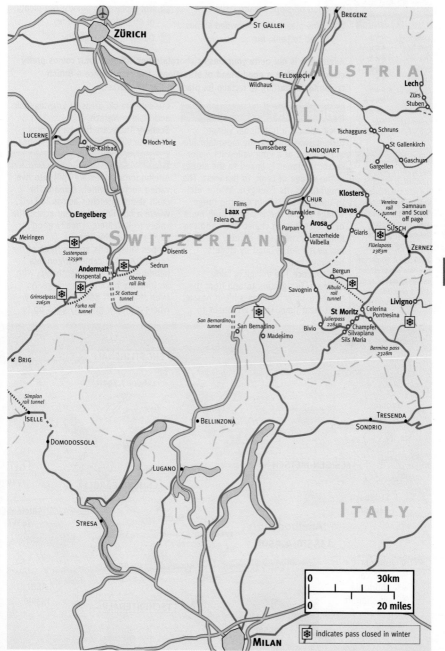

Adelboden

Traditional village with plenty to do off the snow – and with
extensive, varied and scenic slopes, also accessible from Lenk

£140
RESORT PRICE INDEX

TOP 10 RATINGS

Extent	★★★
Fast lifts	★★★
Queues	★★★
Snow	★★★
Expert	★★
Intermediate	★★★
Beginner	★★★★
Charm	★★★★
Convenience	★★
Scenery	★★★★

NEWS

2015/16: A new fast quad chair is to link the gondola station at Bergläger, below Geils in the main ski area, to the top of the rather neglected Chuenisbärgli sector.

2014/15: A 10-person gondola replaced the cable car out of Lenk, with a second stage up to Metschstand.

➕ Chalet-style mountain village in a splendid setting

➕ Good off-slope leisure facilities

➕ Some pleasantly uncrowded slopes linked to Lenk, but ...

➖ Slopes are fragmented and widely spread; access can be slow

➖ Not a place for bumps, but plenty of off-piste opportunities

➖ Quiet, limited nightlife

Adelboden is not quite your classic chocolate-box village, but it comes pretty close, and offers a good blend of attractions. The resort, once a British favourite, is starting to reclaim its place in the UK market.

THE RESORT

Adelboden is a traditional village tucked away on a sunny mountainside at the head of a long valley. Its major sector of slopes is linked to the slopes in the village of Lenk, to the west. The Jungfrau resorts (Wengen, Mürren etc) to the east are within day-trip range.

Village charm The village is built more or less entirely in chalet style, and the long main street (not entirely car-free, but nearly so) is lined by chalets housing shops.

Convenience The village is fairly compact, but getting to and from the slopes usually involves a bit of hassle, or at least time. There are buses to the satellite ski areas of Engstligenalp and Elsigen-Metsch.

Scenery There are fine panoramas from the village and from the slopes.

THE MOUNTAINS

Adelboden's slopes are split into five varied sectors, widely spread. The main sector stretches across to Lenk, where a bus link takes you across the valley to Betelberg – 'really good', says a reader this year.

Slopes Village lifts access three of the sectors. A small cable car/gondola hybrid goes up to Tschentenalp, with an itinerary back to the village. An even smaller lift goes down to Oey, where a proper gondola goes up to

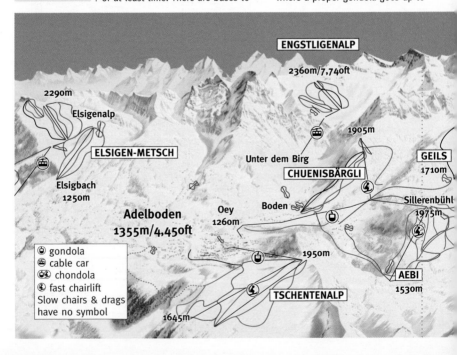

ENGSTLIGENALP

2360m/7,740ft

2290m

Elsigenalp

1905m

ELSIGEN-METSCH

Unter dem Birg

GEILS
1710m

CHUENISBÄRGLI

Elsigbach
1250m

Adelboden
1355m/4,450ft

Oey
1260m

Boden

Sillerenbühl
1975m

AEBI
1530m

🚠 gondola
🚡 cable car
🚠 chondola
🚡 fast chairlift
Slow chairs & drags have no symbol

1950m

TSCHENTENALP

1645m

ħotel
**Beau
Site**
Adelboden

ħotel
Restaurant
Fitness
Spa

Boutique Hotel
Beau-Site Fitness & Spa
Familie Markus Luder
Dorfstrasse 5, CH-3715 Adelboden
Tel. +41 (0)33 673 82 82
www.hotelbeausite.ch

← Engstligenalp is an extraordinary snowy bowl – worth a visit, despite its distance from the village

ADELBODEN TO

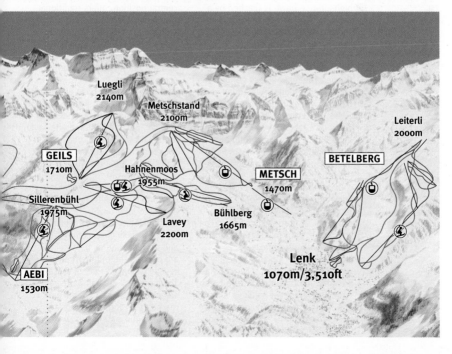

Luegli
2140m

Metschstand
2100m

Leiterli
2000m

GEILS
1710m

Hahnenmoos
1955m

METSCH
1470m

BETELBERG

Sillerenbühl
1975m

Lavey
2200m

Bühlberg
1665m

Lenk
1070m/3,510ft

AEBI
1530m

↑ Adelboden has been running World Cup slalom and GS races on Chuenisbärgli since the start in the 1960s

ADELBODEN TO

KEY FACTS

Resort	1355m
	4,450ft
Slopes	1070-2360m
	3,510-7,740ft
Lifts	57
Pistes	185km
	115 miles

LIFT PASSES

Prices in francs

Age	6-day
under 16	153
16 to 19	236
20 to 64	283
65 plus	260

Free Under 6
Beginner Passes for Engstligenalp, Tschentenalp and Elsigenalp (49-52 francs a day)
Note Covers Adelboden, Lenk and Kandersteg

TOURIST OFFICE

www.adelboden.ch

routes to Adelboden and Lenk. Engstligenalp has off-piste potential.
Intermediates All five areas deserve exploration. There is a lot of ground to be covered in the main sector; at Geils and Aebi the runs are mainly excellent wide reds, but on the sunny Metsch side there is great blue cruising.
Beginners There are good nursery slopes in the village and at the foot of nearby sectors. But progress to longer runs requires a bit of planning to avoid stressful stretches.
Snowboarding There are still lots of draglifts. Two specialist schools.
Cross-country There are trails along the valley to Engstligenalp where there is a high-altitude, snow-sure circuit. There are shorter trails (2km) through forest at Elsigbach.
Mountain restaurants There are plenty of pleasant spots. The self-service Hahnenmoos has cold and hot buffets.
Schools and guides No complaints, but we'd like more reports, please.
Families Several hotels offer childcare. There are a number of 'kids paradise' ski areas, including one at Geils. One visitor found 'many flat areas where you have to push the kids'.

STAYING THERE

There is locally bookable self-catering, and some 30 pensions and hotels.
Hotels The 4-star Beau-Site, in a good central position, offers traditional comfort and 'friendly' staff; pay the premium for the better rooms, a reader advises. In contrast, the Steinmattli and the Cambrian, with outdoor pool (even in winter), are sharply modern in style.
Eating out Readers have enjoyed the food at all the listed hotels; the hotel Bären is also tipped. A reader this year recommends the Aebi and Alte Taverne for 'great atmosphere, and steaks cooked on open fires'.
Après-ski There are several tea rooms and bars to head for at close of play, and several bars keep going into the early hours. The Alte Taverne has an 80s disco later on.
Off the slopes There's a leisure centre that has ice skating, curling, climbing and bowling, and some hotel pools are open to the public. There are several toboggan runs of up to 5km. There are well-marked paths, and some mountain restaurants are reachable on foot for lunchtime meetings; lift passes are available for walkers.

Chuenisbärgli and then, with a quick change, on via Bergläger to the major sector at Sillerenbühl (taking 15 minutes in total). Sillerenbühl has three discernible sub-sectors – Geils, Aebi and Metsch (above Lenk). There is a pretty run home to Oey.

Next season a new chairlift will link Bergläger to the top of Chuenisbärgli, which should encourage more people to make use of its worthwhile slopes.

Engstligenalp, a flat-bottomed, high-altitude bowl, is reached by a cable car from Unter dem Birg, 4km south of the resort; Elsigen-Metsch is 5km away to the north-east.
Fast lifts The main lifts are fast, but there are still a fair few slow ones.
Queues The main access gondolas get busy at peak times; Adelboden is a popular weekend destination for the Swiss. The little lift linking Oey to the centre is a real bottleneck; public and hotel buses offer a way round it.
Terrain parks The Gran Masta Park at Brenggen, near Hahnenmoos, has all the usual stuff. There are snowcross courses above Aebi, and at Elsigen.
Snow reliability Most slopes are above 1500m, so reliability is reasonable, especially at north-facing Tschentenalp and Luegli. Snowmaking is extensive, and grooming is good.
Experts The black pistes generally merit the rating, at least in parts, and are great fun unless you crave bumps – they are groomed regularly. Off-piste possibilities are good and don't get tracked out quickly; the Lavey and Luegli chairs in the Geils bowl access

Andermatt

A slow-paced, old-fashioned resort with great steep, high, snowy terrain on- and off-piste – but with major changes under way

£130
RESORT PRICE INDEX

TOP 10 RATINGS

Extent	★★
Fast lifts	★★
Queues	★★
Snow	★★★★
Expert	★★★★
Intermediate	★★
Beginner	★
Charm	★★★★
Convenience	★★★
Scenery	★★★

NEWS

2015/16: A new six-seat chair is planned to serve the pistes below Gurschen, on Gemsstock; and there is to be snowmaking on the descent to the valley. In the Sedrun sector, the T-bar up from Oberalppass to Calmut will be replaced by a fast chair. Andermatt's railway station will be moved closer to the Nätschen chair, for the convenience of rail travellers.

+ Attractive, traditional village
+ Excellent snow record
+ Some serious blacks, off-piste terrain and ski-touring opportunities

− Not great for beginners, and lousy for mileage-hungry piste skiers
− Limited off-slope diversions
− Busy at weekends

Little old Andermatt is virtually doubling in size with the construction of what amounts to a new village next to the original; the first of countless luxury hotels and apartments opened in 2013. This coming season the associated new lifts start arriving, with the last planned for 2018, linking Andermatt with Sedrun. For the moment, at least, the appeal of the tall, steep, snowy, largely off-piste Gemsstock is undiminished – but for how long?

THE RESORT

Andermatt gets a lot of weekend day-trip business; at other times, in its current form, it can seem deserted. In winter, east–west links rely on car-carrying trains. The lift pass also covers Sedrun – in line to be linked by lift, but for now reached by train.

Village charm The town is quietly attractive. Charming old houses line the main street, which runs from the central river bridge to the Gemsstock cable car. The new development is on the margins, out past the station.

Convenience The centre is compact, but the lifts are on opposite sides of the town. A free minibus shuttle runs daily throughout the ski season.

Scenery The Gemsstock peak is well defined and higher than its neighbours, with rugged steep terrain.

THE MOUNTAINS

The local skiing is split over two mountains, both limited in extent. Most slopes are above the trees.

Slopes A two-stage cable car from the edge of the village serves the open, steep, north-facing Gemsstock. The separate, sunny Nätschen area is to be linked to Sedrun by a chain of new lifts by 2018, raising the piste total to the 120+km already claimed.

Fast lifts The new fast chair on Gemsstock is an improvement, but slow lifts still predominate locally.

Queues The Gemsstock cable car can generate queues, even in low season.

Terrain parks At Gemsstock and above Sedrun, where there's a half-pipe.

Snow reliability The area has a justified reputation for reliable snow. Nätschen gets a lot of sun.

457

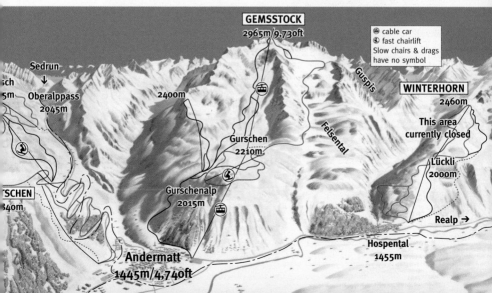

GEMSSTOCK
2965m/9,730ft

cable car
fast chairlift
Slow chairs & drags
have no symbol

Sedrun ↓

Oberalppass
2045m

2400m

Guspis

WINTERHORN
2460m

This area currently closed

Felsental

Gurschen
2210m

Lückli
2000m

Gurschenalp
2015m

Realp →

Hospental
1455m

Andermatt
1445m/4,740ft

KEY FACTS

Resort	1445m
	4,740ft
Slopes	1445-2965m
	4,740-9,730ft
Lifts	20
Pistes	86km
	54 miles

LIFT PASSES

Prices in francs

Age	6-day
under 13	132
13 to 17	198
18 plus	265
Free Under 7	
Senior 238	
Beginner No deals	

Notes Covers Andermatt, Sedrun, Oberalp, Valtgeva, Gemsstock, Nätschen and Realp; all areas can be bought separately

TOURIST OFFICE

www.andermatt.ch

ANDERMATT HOLIDAY REGION

For the moment, skiing Sedrun still involves a trip by train to Oberalppass, where a new fast chair awaits you ↓

Experts It is most definitely a resort for experts. The north-facing bowl beneath the top Gemsstock cable car is a glorious, long, steep slope (900m vertical), usually with excellent snow, down which there are off-piste routes, a ski route and a piste. Outside the bowl, Sonnenpiste is a fine, open red run away from the lifts, with more off-piste opportunities. From Gurschen to the village there is a black run, not steep but often tricky. Routes outside the bowl go down the Felsental or Guspis valleys towards Hospental, or steeply into the deserted Untertal, to the east (ending in a bit of a walk). Nätschen has black pistes, and off-piste terrain, including ski routes.

Intermediates Intermediates needn't be put off Gemsstock: the Sonnenpiste can be tackled, and at mid-mountain there are some short blues and an easy but longer black (served by a tricky draglift). Nätschen is well worth a visit, as are the red runs of Sedrun.

Beginners Not ideal; but there is one lovely blue from Gütsch to the village.

Snowboarding The cable car accesses some great freeride terrain.

Cross-country There are trails in the valley, and at Realp to the south-west.

Mountain restaurants Inadequate. The over-busy Gurschen hut has a table-service section.

Schools and guides The Swiss ski school, Andermatt Xperience and Bergschule Uri/Mountain Reality are the options, and Snowlimit is a specialist snowboard school.

Families Family passes are available.

STAYING THERE

Andermatt's accommodation is mostly in cosy 2-star and 3-star hotels, still.

Hotels The swanky 5-star Chedi opened in 2013 – 'classy but wildly OTT', in the view of one well-qualified observer. River House is a stylish, upmarket boutique B&B in a 250-year-old building. Gasthaus Sternen is an attractive central chalet. The 3-star Sonne is a lovely old place, spoilt only by farcically poor wifi, we hear.

Apartments The hotel Monopol-Metropol has apartments.

Eating out The restaurant at the River House has been well supported (meat and fish dishes with a 'modern twist'), but we lack recent reports. Reporters tip the hearty dinners at the hotel Sonne, and pizzas at the Monopol.

Après-ski We like the cosy bar Alt Apothek at River House for tea and cake (live music later on). Other possibilities include the Curva at the hotel Monopol-Metropol and the Spycher. The Piccadilly pub and De Prato liven up at weekends, while the more traditional Spycher has a bar and terrace. For the chicest après-ski in town, head to The Bar at the Chedi.

Off the slopes Toboggan run at Nätschen, snowshoeing at Gütsch and snow tubing run at Sedrun. The fitness centre at the hotel Drei Könige is open to the public. 20km of footpaths.

AROSA TOURIST OFFICE

Arosa

A classic all-round winter resort with lots of non-skiing activities, recently transformed by a trebling of its ski area

£145
RESORT PRICE INDEX

TOP 10 RATINGS

Extent	★★★★★
Fast lifts	★★★★★
Queues	★★★★★
Snow	★★★★★
Expert	★★★★★
Intermediate	★★★★★
Beginner	★★★★★
Charm	★★★★★
Convenience	★★★★★
Scenery	★★★★★

NEWS

2015/16: At last, the east and west sides of Lenzerheide's slopes will be connected by a new quad chairlift across the valley at Parpan. Until now changing sides involved a schlep or bus ride. And the ancient triple chair from Churwalden will be replaced by a new eight-seat gondola, cutting the ride time from 20 minutes to five.

KEY FACTS

Resort	1740-1820m
	5,710-5,970ft

Arosa-Lenzerheide	
Slopes	1230-2865m
	4,040-9,400ft
Lifts	42
Pistes	225km
	140 miles

- ➕ Fair-sized, largely intermediate ski area with good off-piste too
- ➕ Good nursery slopes
- ➕ Lots of cross-country loops and walking paths
- ➕ Relatively good snow reliability
- ➕ Prettily wooded setting, but …

- ➖ Block-like buildings in main village
- ➖ Spread-out village with no real focus or attractive shops
- ➖ Slopes on Arosa side are relatively short and lack variety
- ➖ Few challenging pistes for experts
- ➖ Quiet, limited après-ski

We left Arosa out of the last five editions of this book. But its attraction for keen skiers was transformed in 2014 by new lifts linking it to neighbouring Lenzerheide. This more than trebled the size of its ski area to a very respectable 225km (161km as measured by the Schrahe report – read the feature on piste extent), on a par with Ischgl and Serre-Chevalier. The resort is isolated at the head of a long, winding valley and is set by a frozen lake which hosts winter horse races and a golf tournament. Winter walking and cross-country skiing are big here as well as downhill. If this sounds like a classic all-round winter resort, it is – it's just a shame that most of the buildings in the main part of town are block-like and concrete rather than cute wooden chalets.

THE RESORT

Arosa is in a high, remote, wooded valley reached from Chur by a long, winding drive or a lovely scenic rail journey. The village spreads for 2km along the road from the lake below the lower lift base at Obersee by the railway station towards the slightly separate, rustic satellite of Inner-Arosa.

The resort attracts a loyal clientele, mostly Swiss and German, with a lot of non-skiers and families (maybe three generations holidaying together). **Village charm** The village is not unpleasant, but the block-like style of many buildings and the central layout along a pedestrian-unfriendly road detract. You can escape both, of course, notably at Inner-Arosa. There are a few everyday shops and a couple of galleries, but nothing to encourage strolling or window gazing. **Convenience** A two-stage cable car goes up from Obersee into the Weisshorn sector of the slopes. Up at Inner-Arosa are two widely separated gondolas. The one nearest town is reached from road level by two successive moving carpets and goes to the Weisshorn sector. The other, a further bus ride up the road, goes up to Hörnli and the link to Lenzerheide. Some accommodation is a long walk from the lifts and there are satellite hamlets at Maran and Prätschli; there are frequent free ski-buses, but they get crowded. **Scenery** Arosa's sheltered position at the head of a beautiful wooded valley, is in sharp contrast to the open slopes above it. There are panoramic views from the top lift stations.

THE MOUNTAINS

Arosa's slopes form a wide, open bowl, facing north-east to south-east, with all the runs returning eventually to the village at the bottom. Nearly all the slopes are above the treeline. **Slopes** The local slopes are spread over two main sectors. The **Weisshorn** sector is reachable from both Obersee and Inner-Arosa. The main access to the **Hörnli** sector is a slow gondola from Inner-Arosa. From the top here, the 150-person Urdenbahn cable car (which opened in 2014) leads to the so-called east side (west-facing runs) of Lenzerheide's slopes in the **Rothorn** sector. From the bottom of them, until now, it has been a schlep or bus ride across the valley to Lenzerheide's so-called west side (east-facing slopes) of **Stätzerhorn** and **Piz Scalottas**. But from this season they are due to be connected by a new chairlift at Parpan. **Fast lifts** The lifts from the village are fast and high-speed chairs serve most slopes in both Arosa and Lenzerheide.

Chalet Runca

Huge Luxury Chalet
in Arosa
for Groups & Families

Independent, Personal
Service since 1995

Call Helen on
+41 (0) 798333608
www.snowypockets.com

LIFT PASSES

Prices in francs

Age	6-day
under 13	111
13 to 17	221
18 to 64	332
65 plus	299
Free Under 6	
Beginner Special pass for Prätschi lift	
Note Covers entire Arosa-Lenzerheide area	

Queues We have no reports of serious queues. The Weisshorn cable car and, over in Lenzerheide, the Rothorn 2 cable car may generate short delays.

Terrain parks In Arosa, there is a park with jumps, rails and a World Cup half-pipe. And there's a jib park and a fun slope in Lenzerheide too.

Snow reliability Arosa's local slopes are quite high, but the Weisshorn sector gets a lot of sun; the shadier Hörnli slopes hold their snow better. In Lenzerheide, both sides get a lot of sun – the east side (Rothorn) in the afternoon, the west side (Stätzerhorn) in the morning, so it's best to plan your day accordingly. Grooming is good, and snowmaking extensive; we skied runs to the valley on strips of artificial snow on our recent April visit.

Experts There are few black runs in the area and most of them are short: the main exception is the long World Cup run on the Rothorn side of Lenzerheide down to Parpan. But there's some excellent and easily accessible off-piste terrain.

Intermediates Arosa's runs are mainly red and blue cruises. For more vertical and a much greater variety, head to Lenzerheide. The Rothorn sector has some good long reds, including one from Rothorn itself along a ridge with great views, followed by a tunnel – with a vertical of almost 1400m if you go all the way down to Parpan.

Beginners The easy slopes up at Tschuggen are excellent and usually have good snow. Inner-Arosa has a quieter, 'gentle' area for kids.

Snowboarding The pistes suit novice and intermediate riders and there is some great off-piste for expert riders.

T-bars are mostly avoidable except getting up the lower slopes of Lenzerheide's west side – where there are also some flat/uphill sections.

Cross-country Arosa has 30km of excellent loops and a cross-country centre at Obersee (10 francs a day).

Mountain restaurants There are eight in the Arosa sector and 30 in Lenzerheide, all clearly marked on the piste map, with photos and short descriptions (in German). In Arosa, the modern Weisshorngipfel has huge windows with stunning 360° views. The rustic Hörnli-Hütte, a short hike up from the top of the lifts, is a complete contrast, with a simple, limited menu. Reporter tips: Alpenblick, Sattelhütte and (not on the piste map but just off the piste above Inner-Arosa) Gspan.

On the Rothorn sector of Lenzerheide, the modern Scharmoin has self-service downstairs and table-service upstairs. Perched at the top of the Rothorn the Rothorngipfel has stunning views. On the opposite side of the valley the Alp Stätz has been recommended by a regular reporter. The rustic June Hütte serving local specialities has been tipped by a local.

Schools and guides Swiss and ABC are the main schools. Both will be offering free group lessons for all under 18s staying at least two nights in certain hotels and apartments for 2016/17.

Families The resort is popular with families and there is plenty to do off the slopes. There is a kindergarten at Inner-Arosa, an indoor playground for bad-weather days and a list of babysitters on the tourist office website. On the Lenzerheide side there are some dedicated family skiing areas.

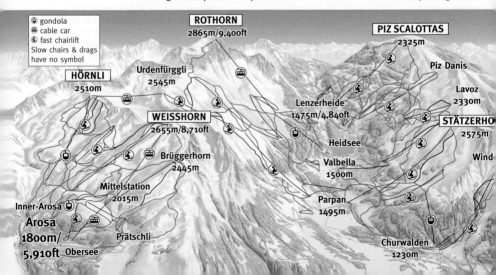

↑ The traditional chalets of Inner-Arosa are a great contrast to block-like buildings of the main part of town

AROSA TO

STAYING THERE

Chalets Snowy Pockets run a smart, traditional-style five-bedroom chalet with sauna and steam room; it can be rented catered or self-catered.

Hotels The 5-star Tschuggen Grand is in an ugly 1960s block-like building but is spectacularly ultra-modern and luxurious inside and has an award-winning spa, four restaurants and its own private train to the skiing. The 5-star Kulm has nice communal areas, stylish spa and several restaurants. The 4-star Waldhotel National with spa and modernized rooms has been recommended. So have the 3-star Vetter hotel next to the Weisshorn lift and the 3-star Hotel Streiff with spa.

Apartments Plenty available. Snowy pockets has one sleeping four.

Eating out Most restaurants are hotel-based, including the Michelin-starred La Vetta in the Tschuggen Grand. But there are many more modest places too, including Thai, Chinese, Italian and Mexican as well as Swiss.

Après-ski Not a highlight but there are some decent bars if you know where to go. Start on the slopes at the Tschuggenhutte, then in town try the Bruggli near the ski school, the Wandel in the Kurstall and Overtime opposite the Post Office. Los (lots of 60s music) and Nuts are good later on.

Off the slopes There are outdoor and indoor ice rinks used for hockey and curling matches as well as skating. Winter walkers have over 60km of cleared marked paths. You can get a pedestrian's lift pass and map.

Snowshoeing, three toboggan runs, horse-drawn sleigh rides, ballooning and paragliding are on offer. Some hotel spas are open to non-residents.

LINKED RESORT – 1475m-1500m

LENZERHEIDE-VALBELLA

These two villages lie at either end of a lake along a busy main road. There is no central focus and the place lacks a ski resort atmosphere. But there are some good 4-star hotels, such as the Lenzerhorn, Schweizerhof and the Valbella Inn (with a five-floor 'wellness tower'). For real pampering stay at the Guarda Val, out of town; made up of beautifully renovated 300-year-old barns and huts. The 3-star Dieschen is 'just above the Rothorn gondola, fairly simple, good wine list, small spa'.

A 2015 visitor was impressed with the private lessons his kids had with the Swiss school in Churwalden.

A free ski-bus travels between the ski areas looping around the lake.

Most village restaurants are in hotels. A local recommends the Heid-Stübli in the Lenzerhorn, the Tapas Lounge in the Kurhaus and the Obertorstübli in the Alpina in Parpan.

Après-ski is limited. It can get lively at the Freerider bar, in the woods near the bottom of the World Cup race piste. Otherwise it's tea and cakes in a café or a beer at a hotel bar. Later on the Cinema Music Club in the Kurhaus hotel may come to life.

Off the slopes, there's skating, curling, tobogganing, 30km of walking paths and a splendid sports centre.

Champéry

Picture-postcard village that few UK tour operators feature these days, with access to the Portes du Soleil circuit

£140
RESORT PRICE INDEX

TOP 10 RATINGS

Extent	★★★★★
Fast lifts	★
Queues	★★★★
Snow	★★
Expert	★★★
Intermediate	★★★★
Beginner	★★
Charm	★★★★
Convenience	★
Scenery	★★★★

NEWS

2015/16: Two hotels are being renovated and are due to become Champéry's first 4-stars: Le White (used to be du Parc) and the National.

2014/15: A snowcross course was built in the Foilleuse area above Champoussin.

462

+ Charmingly rustic mountain village
+ Access to Portes du Soleil circuit
+ Quiet, relaxed – yet plenty to do off the slopes

− Lift system is antiquated
− Local slopes suffer from the sun
− No runs back to the village
− Not good for beginners

Champéry is great for intermediate skiers looking for a quiet time in a lovely place if you can live with the cost and the negatives. Access to Avoriaz is fairly easy – and there may be good snow in France when the Swiss side is suffering.

THE RESORT

Champéry is on the Swiss side of the Portes du Soleil region, with fairly quick links to Avoriaz in France, and to the valley between Avoriaz and Châtel.
Village charm The village is friendly and relaxed, with classic old wooden chalets and some more substantial buildings; a charming spot.
Convenience Champéry's slopes are mainly high above the village, reached by a cable car that starts at the railway station, down a steepish hill, away from the main street. The village spreads over quite an area, but there is a free shuttle-bus.
Scenery The resort sits beneath the dramatic ridge of the Dents du Midi – impressive both from the village and the slopes.

THE MOUNTAINS

Champéry's slopes are open and sunny with the exception of two partly wooded long runs to the valley.
Slopes You reach the edge of the bowl of Planachaux via the village cable car or a fast six-seat chairlift from Grand Paradis, a short, free bus ride away. With two or three further lift rides you can get up to the French border. If snow is good, there are a couple of pistes back to Grand Paradis – one curling well away from the lift system – but no pistes back to Champéry. Some slopes are floodlit for night skiing till 10pm twice a week.
Fast lifts There are a few fast chairlifts but most lifts on the Swiss slopes are ancient draglifts and chairs.
Queues If snow is poor, you can expect end-of-day queues for the cable

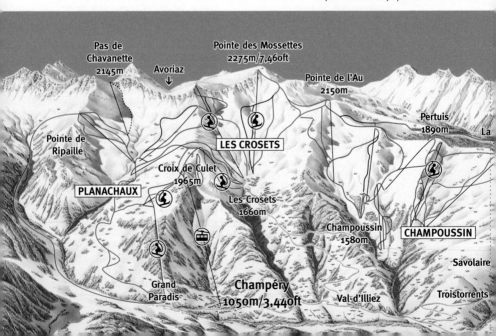

KEY FACTS

Resort	1050m
	3,440ft

Portes du Soleil	
Slopes	950-2275m
	3,120-7,460ft
Lifts	196
Pistes	650km
	404 miles

Swiss side only	
Slopes	1050-2275m
	3,440-7,460ft
Lifts	37
Pistes	100km
	62 miles

LIFT PASSES

Portes du Soleil

Prices in francs

Age	6-day
under 16	192
16 to 19	230
20 to 64	256
65 plus	230

Free Under 5
Beginner No deals
Note Family discounts

Alternative pass
Champéry-Les Crosets

car down to the village. But there are few other problems.

Terrain parks The Superpark is a good terrain park at Les Crosets (www. superpark.ch); it has everything you could want, including rails and kickers for different ability levels. There's a snowcross course near La Foilleuse. New for last season was the Micropark for beginner freestylers near the Grand Conche chair. There was also a Town Park in the village, which they are hoping to build again for 2015/16. There are other (excellent) parks easily accessible in Avoriaz.

Snow reliability The Swiss side of the mountain roughly faces south-east and so snow quality can suffer. More snowmaking would be good.

Experts The Swiss Wall, on the Champéry side of Pas de Chavanette, is usually a giant mogul field and provides great amusement to those riding the chairlift over it. It used to be classified black but is now an itinéraire. The proper blacks in the area are worthwhile and there's plenty of off-piste terrain.

Intermediates Confident intermediates have the whole Portes du Soleil at their disposal. Locally, the runs home to Grand Paradis are good when the snow conditions allow. Les Crosets is a junction of several fine runs. There are slightly tougher pistes from Mossettes and Pointe de l'Au, leisurely cruising above Champoussin, and delightful tree-lined meanders from La Foilleuse

to Morgins. From Col des Portes du Soleil a long blue run goes down a quiet, wooded valley to Morgins; but after a good descent to the rustic Tovassière restaurant the run turns into a path, dropping a mere 200m in around 4km.

Beginners Far from ideal. The Planachaux runs, where lessons are held, are steepish and small (as well as remote from the village), and there's a lack of easy longer runs to progress to – some of the local blue runs could easily be classified red.

Snowboarding Not ideal for beginners (see above), and there are several draglifts (some quite steep). There are good terrain parks in Les Crosets and Avoriaz for intermediates and experts, though, and some good powder areas to explore.

Cross-country It's advertised as 7km – not a lot – with 4km floodlit every night, and the snow is unreliable.

Mountain restaurants There are about 15 mountain restaurants between Champéry and Morgins, marked but not named on the piste map. A regular visitor reckons they are all table-service. Chez Coquoz near the Planachaux chair offers a warm welcome, a 'modern Swiss menu' and a knockout Valais wine list. The tiny Lapisa on the way to Grand Paradis is delightfully rustic – they make their own cheese and smoke their own meat on the spot.

Schools and guides The children in a recent visitor's party used the Swiss school – 'All made good progress and enjoyed their lessons.' It faces healthy competition from the Freeride Co and Redcarpet Snowsport School.

Families Champéry wouldn't be high on our shortlist for a family trip, given the lack of slopes at village level.

STAYING THERE

Hotels Champéry is due to get its first 4-stars for 2015 – see 'News'. The 2-star des Alpes was recommended by a recent reporter as 'good value, with spacious rooms and friendly staff'. A regular visitor rates the 3-star Beau Séjour very highly.

Apartments The Lodge is below the village. It has smart, modern, spacious apartments with good views.

Eating out Mitchell's is stylish and modern, and we had a good meal there on our last visit. You can 'have your steak cooked on an open fire' at the 'atmospheric' Vieux Chalet. Other

cable car
fast chairlift
Slow chairs & drags
have no symbol

La Foilleuse
1815m

Super Châtel

Châtel

Pas de Morgins

MORGINS

Morgins
1350m/4,430ft

ire

ts

reader tips are the bar of the hotel National ('good hearty food'), the Farinet, Le Pub and the 'great bistro' Le Nord, beneath the 'more sophisticated' Atelier Gourmand. Café du Centre has changed hands – reports welcome.

Après-ski The yurt at the foot of the Grand Paradis chair is popular. Mitchell's, with a fireplace and big sofas, is 'fun and lively' at teatime. The Bar des Guides in the hotel Suisse is good for a quiet drink. The Crevasse and Farinet are nightclubs.

Off the slopes The railway allows lots of excursions such as to Montreux on Lake Geneva and to Martigny for its Roman remains and art gallery. There are nice walks, snowshoeing and ice climbing on a frozen waterfall. The Palladium is a big ice sports centre with other facilities, including a pool, tennis and climbing wall.

TOURIST OFFICES

Champéry
www.champery.ch

Les Crosets / Champoussin / Val-d'Illiez
www.valdilliez.ch

Morgins
www.morgins.ch

CHAMPERY TO

The Portes du Soleil circuit has good intermediate runs but the Swiss side gets a lot of sun and has a lot of slow lifts still ↓

SWITZERLAND

LINKED RESORT – 1660m
LES CROSETS

A good base for a quiet time and slopes on the doorstep. The 3-star Télécabine hotel has 'basic rooms but extremely helpful staff, and the five-course dinner is delicious'. Mountain Lodge is a smart chalet-style hotel that impressed a recent visitor.

LINKED RESORT – 1580m
CHAMPOUSSIN

A good family choice – no through traffic, on the slopes – is the 3-star Alpadze Lou Kra (pool, sauna, steam, gym). Chez Gaby is tipped for 'Valais specialities'.

LINKED RESORT – 1350m
MORGINS

Over the hill and close to Châtel in France, Morgins is a fairly scattered, but attractive, quiet resort with a gentle nursery slope right in the village. The modern hotel Helvetia with spa was recommended last year. The 'cosy' Buvette des Sports restaurant does 'excellent' spaghetti carbonara. Black Chili was highly recommended by a recent visitor ('best restaurant in the whole of the Portes du Soleil').

DOWN-VALLEY VILLAGE – 950m
VAL-D'ILLIEZ

About 4km down the valley from Champéry, Val-d'Illiez has no lifts or slopes, but there are buses and trains up to Champéry. Down in the valley bottom is the Thermes Parc thermal spa. The hotel du Repos is comfortable, woody and British-run.

Crans-Montana

An increasingly stylish big-town base with a fabulous panoramic view and sun-soaked slopes

£155
RESORT PRICE INDEX

TOP 10 RATINGS

Extent	★★★
Fast lifts	★★★★★
Queues	★★★
Snow	★★
Expert	★★
Intermediate	★★★★
Beginner	★★★
Charm	★★
Convenience	★★
Scenery	★★★★

NEWS

2015/16: The Les Violettes gondola will be refurbished and further snowmaking will be added on the lower Piste Nationale. The Ycoor leisure centre will open in December, with skating and curling. The Mont Paisible hotel will get a 4-star makeover.

2014/15: A six-pack replaced the Cabane de Bois double chair to Les Violettes. The Cry d'Er half-pipe was 'pre-formed' – dug out of the mountain, so it needs less snowfall. The children's mini-park was enlarged.

KEY FACTS

Resort	1500m	
	4,920ft	
Slopes	1500-2925m	
	4,920-9,600ft	
Lifts	28	
Pistes	140km	
	87 miles	

- ➕ Large, varied piste area
- ➕ Splendid setting and views
- ➕ Excellent, gentle nursery slopes
- ➕ Very sunny slopes, but ...
- ➖ Snow is badly affected by the sun
- ➖ Large, busy, urban resort
- ➖ You may need a car or buses
- ➖ Few challenges except off-piste

We love Crans-Montana's wide views, its pretty slopes and some of its mountain restaurants and smart lodgings. It's just a shame that the place is more like a city than a rustic village, and that the slopes get the southern sun.

THE RESORT

Set on a broad shelf facing south across the Rhône valley, Crans and Montana are two towns, their centres a mile apart and their fringes merging. The resort can be reached by funicular railway from Sierre. There are also lodgings a mile east at the lift base of Les Barzettes (aka Les Violettes, the name of the hill) and further out at Aminona. Outings are possible – to Saas-Fee and Verbier, for example.

Village charm Both Crans and Montana are emphatically towns rather than villages, with little traditional Alpine character and a lot of traffic. But the wooded setting softens the urban feel a bit. Crans is the more upmarket part, with fancy shops, several 5-star hotels and a pedestrian-friendly centre.

Convenience The towns spread widely away from their respective gondola stations, and many visitors need to use cars or the free shuttle-bus ('infrequent' says a reader this year).

Scenery The panoramic views over the Rhône valley to the peaks bordering Italy are breathtaking.

THE MOUNTAINS

There's a pleasant mix of open and wooded runs, with few challenges. Runs are at last numbered on the piste map.

Slopes The slopes are spread over a broad mountainside, with lifts from four valley bases. Gondolas from Crans and Montana meet at Cry d'Er – an open bowl descending into patchy forest. A third gondola accesses the next sector, Les Violettes. A six-pack from the mid-station here links with Cry d'Er. Above Les Violettes, a jumbo gondola goes up to the Plaine Morte glacier. The fourth sector is served by a gondola from Aminona. Some runs down to the valley are narrow paths.

465

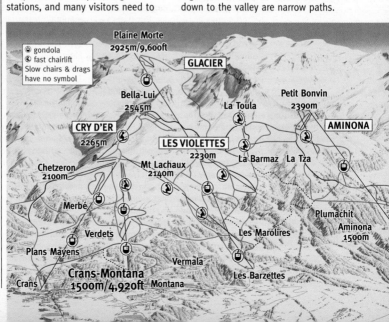

Plaine Morte
2925m/9,600ft

GLACIER

🚠 gondola
🚡 fast chairlift
Slow chairs & drags
have no symbol

Bella-Lui
2545m

La Toula

Petit Bonvin
2390m

CRY D'ER
2265m

LES VIOLETTES
2230m

La Barmaz La Tza

AMINONA

Chetzeron
2100m

Mt Lachaux
2140m

Merbé

Plumachit

Aminona
1500m

Verdets

Les Marolires

Plans Mayens

Vermala

Les Barzettes

Crans

Crans-Montana
1500m/4,920ft Montana

Avalanche Pro is a specialist shop and school. There are few draglifts.

Cross-country There are around 20km of trails, plus a glacier trail (with limited opening).

Mountain restaurants A separate map on the back of the piste map – not a user-friendly idea – marks 23 huts. The Cabane des Violettes is current reader favourite ('very pleasant staff', 'lovely rösti'). We like the traditional Merbé at mid-mountain and the smart, cool Chetzeron higher up – all steel, glass, wood and stone. A reader this year tips Mayen de la Cure, Plumachit and La Tièche (off-piste at the western extremity of the area). The restaurant on Petit Bonvin has been refurbished and is now called Vache Noir, with self-service and table-service sections – reports please. Construction has begun on yet another Folie Douce restaurant and bar at the top of Cry d'Er.

Schools and guides A 2014 reporter who had group and private lessons with the Swiss school made good progress: 'Fantastic instructor.'

Families This doesn't strike us as a natural family resort.

STAYING THERE

Hotels and apartments are plentiful.

Hotels There are some very swanky lodgings. We love two dinky little places – 5-star LeCrans, way above the town, with chalet-style suites, and Pas de l'Ours – chic but welcoming, on the edge of town. The 4-star Alpina & Savoy is 'faultless; delightful staff, the best food'. Pool, sauna. The Chetzeron mountain restaurant has stylish rooms. Readers tip the 'small but good' Olympic – 'no lounge, though'.

Eating out There is a big variety of places, from French to Lebanese to Thai. Molino is a busy Italian that is 'full of character': 'excellent food, delightful staff'.

Après-ski At close of play, Dutch-run bar/restaurant Zérodix at the Crans lift base is 'the cool place to finish the day', with 'comfy sofas'. After that, Monk'is (also a club) has been recommended, and Amadeus (at the hotel Olympic) is a lively bar. Don't expect a buzz in the streets.

Off the slopes There are swimming pools in hotels, two ice rinks, dog sledding, tubing, tobogganing, snowshoeing, 65km of walks, a cinema, casino, art galleries and model train museum. Sierre and Sion are close.

↑ The ski area is attractively rocky, and the views across the Valais are great

CRANS-MONTANA TOURISM

LIFT PASSES

Prices in francs

Age	6-day
under 17	166
18 to 60	300
60 plus	283

Free Under 6
Beginner No deals
Alternative pass 10% family discount

MOMENTUM SKI

Weekend & a la carte ski holiday specialists

100% Tailor-made

Premier hotels & apartments

Flexible travel arrangements

020 7371 9111
WWW.MOMENTUMSKI.COM

TOURIST OFFICE

www.crans-montana.ch

Fast lifts With a new six-pack last season, the resort gets ★★★★★.

Queues We know of no problems, but we lack high-season reports.

Terrain parks At Cry d'Er there's a park with features for all levels, plus a beginner park, half-pipe, airbag and snowcross.

Snow reliability The runs on the Plaine Morte glacier are very limited, and nearly all the other slopes get a lot of direct sun, with obvious effects on the snow. You may get spring snow even in January. There is snowmaking on the main runs but some runs to resort level have often been closed on our visits. Grooming is efficient.

Experts There are few steep pistes, and the only decent moguls are on the short slopes at La Toula. But there's plenty of under-utilised off-piste, particularly beneath La Toula, La Tza and Chetzeron – the best place to go in a storm. There are more adventurous routes outside the lift network – Les Faverges is a beautiful, easy valley bringing you to Aminona.

Intermediates There's a lot to do, including some notably long runs. The 12km run from Plaine Morte to Les Barzettes starts with top-of-the-world views and powder, and finishes among pretty woods. The Piste Nationale downhill course is a good fast cruise, and this season the final 2km will have additional snowmaking.

Beginners There are excellent nursery areas at resort level (on the golf course) and at mid-mountain, but no special beginner passes.

Snowboarding Despite the resort's mature image, boarding is popular.

SWISS-IMAGE / DAVOS TOURISMUS

Davos

A grey urban sprawl at the centre of a glorious Alpine playground (for skaters and langlaufers as well as downhillers)

£155
RESORT PRICE INDEX

RATINGS

The mountains

Extent	★★★★
Fast lifts	★★★★
Queues	★★★★
Terrain p'ks	★★★★
Snow	★★★★
Expert	★★★★
Intermediate	★★★★★
Beginner	★★
Boarder	★★★★★
X-country	★★★★★
Restaurants	★★★
Schools	★★★
Families	★★

The resort

Charm	★★
Convenience	★★
Scenery	★★★★
Eating out	★★★
Après-ski	★★★
Off-slope	★★★★★

KEY FACTS

Resort	1550m
	5,090ft
Slopes	810-2845m
	2,660-9,330ft
Lifts	56
Pistes	320km
	199 miles

➕ Very extensive slopes

➕ Some superb, long, and mostly easy pistes away from the lifts, with trains to bring you back to base

➕ Lots of accessible off-piste terrain, with several marked itineraries

➕ Good cross-country trails

➕ Plenty to do off the slopes

➖ Davos is a huge, busy place with dreary block-style buildings, lacking ski-resort atmosphere

➖ Five separate areas of slopes

➖ Lots of T-bars on outlying mountains

➖ The only piste back to town from the main Parsenn area is a black

One of your editors learned to ski in Davos, so it has a special place in our affections. Many return visits have confirmed the appeal of its slopes, which are both distinctive and extensive, and have revealed its considerable off-piste potential. But the town/city (it could never be called a village) does not get any easier to like. Davos may be the more convenient base for access to most of the mountains it shares with Klosters, but Klosters has the welcoming, intimate feel of a ski resort, and Davos does not.

THE RESORT

Davos is set in a high, broad, flat-bottomed valley, with its lifts and slopes either side. Arguably it was the very first place in the Alps to develop its slopes. The railway up the Parsenn was one of the first built for skiers (in 1931), and the first draglift was built on the Bolgen nursery slopes in 1934. You can reach the resort by train, but the trip from Zürich airport involves at least two changes. The Davos Express coach service is more straightforward, but runs Saturdays only.

Davos shares its slopes with the famously royal resort of Klosters,

which has its own chapter. Trips are possible by car or rail to St Moritz (via the Vereina rail tunnel) and Arosa, and by road to Laax and Lenzerheide.

VILLAGE CHARM ★★
City in the mountains
The resort is more like a city than a village, and is plagued by traffic. It started life as a health resort and many of its massive luxury hotels were built as sanatoriums. Sadly, that's just what they look like, and ski resort ambience is lacking. Davos is now well known for its conference and sporting facilities too.

CONVENIENCE ★★
Take the train
The resort has two main centres, Dorf and Platz, about 2km apart. Transport is good, with an 'excellent' bus service around the town as well as the railway linking Dorf and Platz to Klosters and other villages. It's a good idea to arm yourself with timetables. Easiest access to the main Parsenn area is from Dorf, via the funicular railway; Platz is better placed for Jakobshorn, the sports facilities, smarter shopping and the evening action.

SCENERY ★★★★
Pick your viewpoint
It's an area of grand, wide views across the broad, deep, wooded valleys from one sector of the slopes to another, and to high peaks beyond.

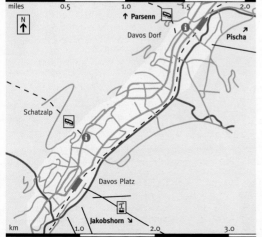

NEWS

2015/16: The new hotel Ameron, with restaurant, bar and spa, is scheduled to open in Davos Platz.

2014/15: After 31 years of service the 50-person Jakobshorn cable car from Platz was replaced by a new model twice the size.

THE MOUNTAINS

Most of the pistes are above the treeline – there are few in the woods and most are genuine blacks. Piste classification is questionable; many blue and red runs are of similar pitch, and some of the blacks barely merit the classification. The piste map generally looks clear, but tries to cover too much ground in a small space – at some points it is simply misleading, and distances are unclear. Signposting is generally fine.

EXTENT OF THE SLOPES ★★★★
Vast and varied

You could hit a different mountain around Davos nearly every day for a week. The out-of-town areas tend to be much quieter than the ones directly accessible from the resort.

The Parsennbahn funicular from Davos Dorf takes you to mid-mountain, where a choice of a six-pack or a further funicular takes you on up to the major lift junction of Weissfluhjoch, at one end of the **Parsenn**. The only run back to town is a sunny black that can have poor snow (the alternative runs to Klosters are shadier). At the other end of the wide, open Parsenn bowl is Gotschnagrat, reached by cable car from the centre of Klosters. There are exceptionally long intermediate runs down to Klosters and other villages (read the feature panel later in this chapter).

Across the valley, **Jakobshorn** is

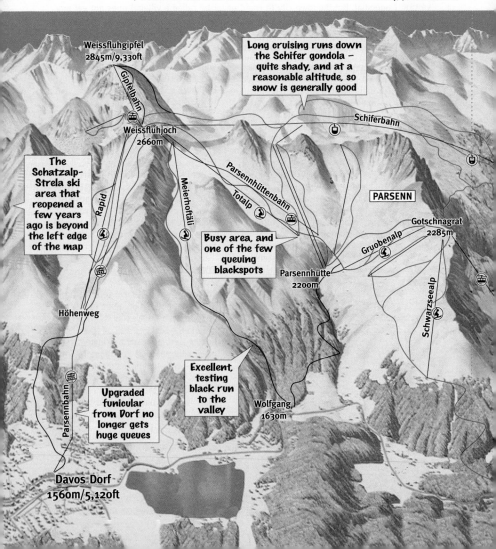

Weissfluhgipfel
2845m/9,330ft

Long cruising runs down the Schifer gondola – quite shady, and at a reasonable altitude, so snow is generally good

Gipfelbahn

Schiferbahn

Weissfluhjoch
2660m

The Schatzalp-Strela ski area that reopened a few years ago is beyond the left edge of the map

Rapid

Meierhoftäli

Parsennhüttenbahn

Totalp

PARSENN

Gotschnagrat
2285m

Busy area, and one of the few queuing blackspots

Parsennhütte
2200m

Gruobenalp

Schwarzseealp

Höhenweg

Parsennbahn

Upgraded funicular from Dorf no longer gets huge queues

Excellent testing black run to the valley

Wolfgang
1630m

Davos Dorf
1560m/5,120ft

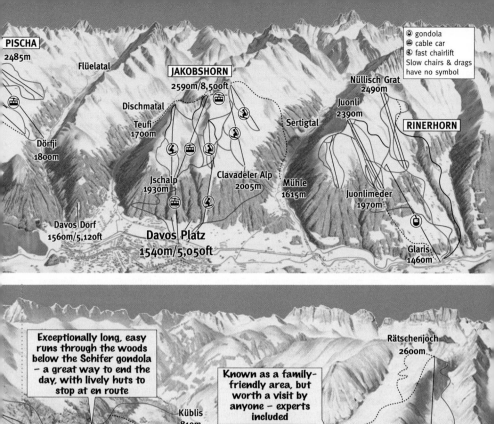

PISCHA
2485m

Flüelatal

JAKOBSHORN
2590m/8,5ooft

Dischmatal

Teufi
1700m

Dörfji
1800m

Jschalp
1930m

Davos Dorf
1560m/5,120ft

Davos Platz
1540m/5,05oft

Clavadeler Alp
2005m

Sertigtal

Mühle
1615m

Nüllisch Grat
2490m

Juonli
2390m

RINERHORN

Juonlimeder
1970m

Glaris
1460m

gondola
cable car
fast chairlift
Slow chairs & drags
have no symbol

Exceptionally long, easy runs through the woods below the Schifer gondola – a great way to end the day, with lively huts to stop at en route

Known as a family-friendly area, but worth a visit by anyone – experts included

Rätschenjoch
2600m

Schafürggli
2395m

Küblis
810m

Saas

Schifer
1560m

rat

Serneus
990m

MADRISA
1890m

Madrisabahn

Klosters' cable car is queue-prone in the mornings – more of a problem for those based here than those based in Davos

Beautiful long run away from lifts; the lower black section isn't difficult in good snow conditions (it used to be red)

Golschnabahn

Klosters Dorf
1125m

Schlappin

Klosters
1190m/3,900ft

gondola
cable car
railway/funicular
fast chairlift
Slow chairs & drags
have no symbol

LIFT PASSES

Davos/Klosters

Prices in francs

Age	6-day
under 13	133
13-17	232
18-64	332
65 plus	299

Free Under 6

Beginner No deals

Note Does not cover Schatzalp

Alternative passes
Individual areas; pedestrian single tickets

reached by an upgraded cable car or chairlift from Davos Platz; this is popular with snowboarders but good for skiers too. **Rinerhorn** and **Pischa** are separate hills reached by bus or (in the case of Rinerhorn) train.

The little **Schatzalp-Strela** area above Platz – which was closed for several years – is open again, but is not covered by the main lift pass.

Beyond the main part of Klosters, a gondola goes up from Klosters Dorf to the sunny, scenic **Madrisa** area.

FAST LIFTS ★★★★
Key ones are fine but ...

The main lifts from the valley are mostly gondolas or cable cars. Higher up, Jakobshorn is very well served by fast chairs and Parsenn reasonably so (hence the 4-star rating). But the upper lifts on Madrisa, Rinerhorn and Pischa are entirely T-bars except for one slow double chair on Madrisa.

QUEUES ★★★★
Few problems

Davos has improved its key lifts and generates relatively few complaints. But at peak times and weekends there can still be lengthy queues at the cable car out of Klosters. A high-season visitor this year reports delays for the Totalp chair on the Parsenn, the Gipfelbahn and the Jakobshorn cable car's second stage – an unsurprising consequence of upgrading the first stage; there is a chairlift alternative. Crowded pistes have raised concern – in the Parsenn sector around Weissfluhjoch especially. In contrast, the Jakobshorn is said to be quiet.

TERRAIN PARKS ★★★★
Head for Jakobshorn

The focus of the action is the big Jatz Park on Jakobshorn. At 2300m, with snowmaking to be sure, it's open from mid-November to the very end of the season, and is looked after by a small dedicated team. Four lines with lots of features provide something for everyone, with plenty for experts. Jakobshorn is also home to a super-pipe – one of Europe's largest; it is floodlit some evenings. There's also a small fun park on Rinerhorn and a kicker at Pischa. There are snowcross courses on Parsenn and Madrisa.

SNOW RELIABILITY ★★★★
Good, but not the best

Davos is high by Swiss standards. Its mountains go respectably high, too. Not many of the slopes face directly south, but Pischa does suffer from excessive sun. Snow reliability is generally good higher up. Snow-guns cover several of the upper runs on the Parsenn, most on the Jakobshorn, and the home runs from the Parsenn to Davos Dorf and Klosters. Piste grooming is generally good; but the super-long runs to the valley can become a bit neglected.

FOR EXPERTS ★★★★
Plenty to do, given snow

The appeal of this area for experts depends to a considerable degree on the snow conditions. Although there are challenges to be found at altitude, most of the rewarding runs descend through the woods to valley level, and are not reliable for snow. The black pistes include some distinctive, satisfying descents. The Meierhoftäli run to Wolfgang is a favourite – quite steep and narrow. The runs from Parsennhütte to Wolfgang and from Höhenweg to Dorf are less challenging, at least when the snow is good.

There are also some off-piste itineraries – runs that are supposedly marked but not patrolled. At one time, these runs were a key attraction for adventurous skiers not wanting to pay for guidance, but over the decade to 2005 no fewer than 10 of them disappeared from the map, including the infamous Gotschnawang run down the top stage of the Klosters cable car and its less fearsome neighbours, Drostobel and Chalbersäss. Many of these abandoned runs have had piste status at some time in the past, and are not difficult to follow if you know what you are doing. Two of the most satisfying itineraries that remain are long ones from the top of Jakobshorn, both with decent restaurants at the end. The start of the run to Mühle is not obvious, which has led more than one reporter into difficulty; once found, the run is reportedly nowhere steeper than a tough red. The run to Teufi is more often closed: it goes first down a steep 200m gully, but thereafter is easier.

There is also excellent 'proper' off-piste terrain, for which guidance is more clearly needed. Reporters have enjoyed heading away from the pistes above Serneus and Küblis. The long descent from Madrisa to St Antönien, north of Küblis, is popular, not least

↑ This dude is clearly refreshed by a proper lunch at the pricey Weissfluhgipfel, reached by the cable car

DESTINATION DAVOS KLOSTERS

for the views along the way. And there are some short tours to be done. Arosa can be reached with a bit of help from a train or taxi. From Madrisa you can make easy circular tours to Gargellen in Austria's Montafontal.

FOR INTERMEDIATES ★★★★★
A splendid variety of runs

For intermediates this is a great area. There are good cruising runs on all five mountains, so you would never get bored in a week. This variety of different slopes, taken together with the wonderful long runs to the Klosters valley, makes it a compelling area with a unique character.

As well as the epic runs described in the feature panel there is a beautiful away-from-the-lifts run to the valley from the top of Madrisa back to Klosters Dorf via the Schlappin valley (it's an easy black); there is a good restaurant en route, too.

The Jakobshorn has some genuine challenges, notably by the Brämabüel chairlift. Rinerhorn and Pischa have more gentle terrain, at altitude at least – Rinerhorn has three good runs to valley level, with a quiet gondola for the return.

FOR BEGINNERS ★★ ★★★
Platz is the more convenient

There are no free lifts but each sector offers day or half-day passes. The Bolgen nursery slope beneath the Jakobshorn is adequately spacious and gentle, and a bearable walk from the centre of Platz. Dorf-based beginners face more of a trek out to Bünda though – unless staying at the hotel of the same name. There are easy runs to progress to, spread around all the sectors. The Parsenn sector probably has the edge, with long, easy intermediate runs in the main Parsenn bowl, as well as in the valleys down from Weissfluhjoch.

FOR BOARDERS ★★★★★
Epic

Davos is a Mecca for keen snowboarders. And Jakobshorn is the favoured mountain for many of them, with its top-notch park and super-pipe. It's also a great area to learn on. Rinerhorn has trees galore and pistes like roller-coaster rides – but be aware that all except the access lifts here and at Pischa are T-bars.

Parsenn has a snowcross and night riding, and is host to international freeride competitions on the face beneath the Weissfluhgipfel, but watch out for the flats on the runs down to the Schifer gondola. And if you have a family in tow, the kids can stay out of trouble in the small terrain park at Rinerhorn.

Synergy Snowsports is a specialist school. There are several cheap hotels geared to boarders.

MOMENTUM SKI

Weekend & a la carte
ski holiday specialists

100% Tailor-made

Premier hotels
& apartments

Flexible travel
arrangements

020 7371 9111
WWW.MOMENTUMSKI.COM

FOR CROSS-COUNTRY ★★★★★
Long, scenic valley trails

Davos is a popular spot for langlauf, with a total of 122km of trails – classic and skating – running along the flat main valley and reaching well up into the side valleys of Sertigtal, Dischmatal and Flüelatal that lead away south-east. There is a cross-country ski centre on the outskirts of the town. Trails are free.

MOUNTAIN RESTAURANTS ★★★★★
Stay high or go low

Most high-altitude restaurants are dreary self-service affairs – but there are good table-service exceptions.

Weissfluhgipfel up at the very top of the Parsenn sector is a long-standing favourite with prices to match the altitude. In the main Parsenn bowl, Gruobenalp is a reader favourite offering 'efficient table-service' and a 'good atmosphere' but a very limited menu. There are several jolly, rustic 'schwendis' in the woods on the way down to the Klosters valley. Some stay open until after sunset – and sell wax torches to light your way home.

On Jakobshorn, Châlet Güggel has repeatedly impressed one visitor.

SCHOOLS AND GUIDES ★★★★★
Decent choice

We lack recent reports, but at least there is plenty of choice, with a handful of alternatives to the Swiss ski school, including some offering mainly guiding.

FOR FAMILIES ★★★★★
Not ideal

There are plenty of amusements, but Davos is a rather spread-out place in which to handle a family. The kids' ski schools operate a themed slope at Bolgen. The Top Secret school runs the Topsi ski kindergarten. Kinderland Pischa offers childcare, and there is a snow garden on Rinerhorn. But Madrisa Land at Klosters is a more comprehensive facility.

STAYING THERE

Although most beds are in apartments, hotels dominate the UK market.

Hotels A dozen 4-stars and about 30 3-stars form the core. The tourist office runs a central booking service.

★★★★Meierhof In Dorf, near Parsenn funicular. 'Spacious rooms; good pool and steam room.'

★★★★Sheraton Waldhuus Convenient for langlaufers. Quiet, modern, tasteful. 'Spacious rooms; great pool and spa facilities.'

★★★★Waldhotel In Platz. 'Looked after really well; beautiful pool,' says a recent visitor.

★★★Davoserhof Our favourite. Small, old, beautifully furnished, excellent food; in Platz.

★★Alte Post Traditional place in central Platz.

★★Ochsen Near the train station in Platz.

Fiftyone Sharp, modern, room-only hotel in Platz; online booking is best.

THE PARSENN'S SUPER-RUNS

The runs from Weissfluhjoch that head north, on the back of the mountain, make this area special for many visitors. The pistes that go down to Schifer and then on to Küblis and Serneus, and the one that curls around to Klosters, are a fabulous way to end the day, given good conditions.

The run to Saas, operated of late as an ungroomed and unpatrolled route, has rejoined the other runs which are classified red pistes. They are not steep, but the latter parts can be challenging because of the snow conditions – they get heavily skied, they are not reliably groomed, and by the end you are at low altitudes. Signposting is not always good, either. What marks these runs out is their sheer length (10-12km) and the resulting sensation of travel – plus a choice of huts in the woods at Schifer and lower down on the way to Klosters. You can descend the 1100m vertical to Schifer and take the gondola back up. Once past there, you're committed to finishing the descent.

If you are based in Davos, the return journey is by train (included in the lift pass).

ALAN SHEPHERD

↑ At least the flat-roof rule is rigorously enforced

DESTINATION DAVOS KLOSTERS

EATING OUT ★★★
Wide choice, mostly in hotels
In a town this size, you need to know where to go. For a start, get the tourist office's pocket guidebook. The more ambitious restaurants are mostly in hotels – for example, the grand, centuries-old Seehof. A reader rates its Chesa Seehof 'superb – the best we've been to in Switzerland', and its Seehofstübli has a Michelin star. Somewhat downmarket from that level, another reader this year tips a traditional Italian, Der Pate. There is plenty of variety, including some good Chinese places (again, often in hotels).

APRES-SKI ★★★
Generally quiet
At teatime, mega-calories are consumed at the Weber and Schneider's, both in the town's central Promenade. The Scala (hotel Europe) has a popular outside terrace. Nightlife is generally quiet, and to judge by reports the readers who visit have little interest in it. Nightclubs tend to be sophisticated, expensive and, during the week, lacking atmosphere. There's a casino.

OFF THE SLOPES ★★★★★
Great, apart from the buildings
Looks aside, Davos has lots to offer the non-skier. The towny resort has shops and other diversions, and transport along the valley and up on to the slopes is good – though the best of the mountain restaurants are well out of range.

The sports facilities are excellent. Europe's biggest natural ice rink is supplemented by indoor and artificial outdoor rinks. Spectator events include speed skating as well as ice hockey – a spectacle that rarely disappoints. The Eau-là-là leisure centre incorporates pools and wellness facilities. There's a Bowling-Bar-Bistro in Platz, and a climbing wall and indoor tennis courts in the Färbi sports hall.

There are lots of walks on the slopes, around the lake and along the valleys (special map available). There's tobogganing on Rinerhorn and Schatzalp (both floodlit) and from the mid-station of the cable car back to Klosters, but the best in the area is the 8.5km run from Madrisa to Saas.

A reporter recommends the local museums and galleries, and there are day trips by train to St Moritz, Scuol (for the spa) and Preda-Bergün for the 6km toboggan run.

GETTING THERE

Air Zürich 160km/ 100 miles (2hr); Friedrichshafen 155km/95 miles (2hr)

Rail Stations in Davos Dorf and Platz

TOURIST OFFICE

www.davos.ch

ENGELBERG TOURIST OFFICE

Engelberg

A high, distinctive mountain with some classic off-piste runs, above a solid valley town dominated by an ancient monastery

£125
RESORT PRICE INDEX

+	Reliable snow on high, shady slopes	−	Fragmented slopes, some poor links
+	Some classic off-piste runs	−	Ski-bus needed from most lodgings
+	Big vertical of almost 2000m	−	Limited pistes, mostly above trees

TOP 10 RATINGS

Extent	**
Fast lifts	***
Queues	**
Snow	***
Expert	****
Intermediate	***
Beginner	**
Charm	**
Convenience	*
Scenery	****

KEY FACTS

Resort	1050m
	3,440ft
Slopes	1050-3030m
	3,440-9,940ft
Lifts	25
Pistes	82km
	51 miles

MOMENTUM SKI

Weekend & a la carte
ski holiday specialists

100% Tailor-made

Premier hotels
& apartments

The No.1 Specialist
in Engelberg

020 7371 9111
WWW.MOMENTUMSKI.COM

Quick access from Zürich airport and abundant lodgings make Engelberg great for short breaks (for which we find the towny nature of the resort is worth putting up with). And Titlis is a compelling mountain, particularly for experts.

THE RESORT

The resort was named after the 12th-century Benedictine monastery (Engelberg means the mountain of the angel) that dominates the town as you look down from the lifts.

Village charm The place is more of a town than a village. Its grand Victorian hotels have been joined by chalet-style buildings, concrete blocks and new apartment buildings right next to the gondola. There is one traffic-free cobbled street in the old part.

Convenience It's a free shuttle-bus, sometimes over-busy, or longish walks to the lifts from most hotels.

Scenery There's lots of visual drama from the high, glacial slopes.

THE MOUNTAINS

The mainly treeless, shady slopes of Titlis rise almost 2000m above the town. The separate slopes of Brunni are sunnier and gently wooded.

Slopes The pistes in the main area are limited and fragmented by the glaciers and rugged terrain. There are two main sectors: Titlis-Stand and Jochpass. For the 2015/16 season a new eight-seat gondola will go to Trübsee and on to Stand, replacing the two six-seat gondolas from the village to Trübsee. An old funicular goes to Gerschnialp and a cable car goes from Gerschnialp to Trübsee. From there, there's a choice of the new gondola or an old cable car up to Stand. Then there's a further cable car (which rotates 360° on the way) to the summit of Klein Titlis. From Trübsee, you can also head for Jochpass via a two-way chairlift to Alpstübli. At Jochpass the top is served by a fast six-pack. The much smaller Brunni area is served by a cable car on the other side of town.

Fast lifts The new gondola plus high-capacity cable cars provide the main access.

Queues The new gondola's increased capacity should reduce the often big queues which have formed at village level at weekends and in peak season; reports please. The old Engstlenalp double chair below Jochpass can have queues. Pistes can also get busy.

Terrain parks There is a kicker and

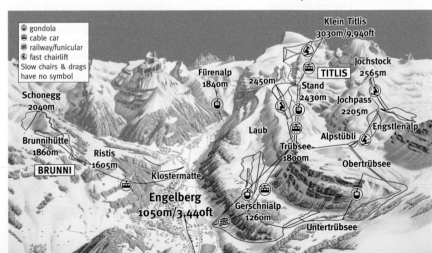

- 🚠 gondola
- 🚡 cable car
- 🚞 railway/funicular
- 🚡 fast chairlift
- Slow chairs & drags have no symbol

Klein Titlis 3030m/9,940ft

Fürenalp 1840m

2450m

Schonegg 2040m

TITLIS

Stand 2430m

Jochstock 2565m

Jochpass 2205m

Brunnihütte 1860m

Ristis 1605m

Laub

Engstlenalp

Alpstübli

BRUNNI

Klostermatte

Trübsee 1800m

Obertrübsee

Engelberg 1050m/3,440ft

Gerschnialp 1260m

Untertrübsee

↑ The town is built in a mixture of architectural styles

ENGELBERG-TITLIS TO

NEWS

2015/16: The two six-person gondolas from Engelberg and from Gerschnialp and from Gerschnialp to Trübsee are due to be replaced by an eight-person gondola going direct to Trübsee then on to Stand. This will increase capacity by 50% and the journey time to Stand will be halved to 18 minutes.

2014/15: The Rotair rotating cable car to Klein Titlis was replaced by one that gives better views. Renovation work was completed on the ski-in/ski-out Trübsee hotel. The final stage of the Titlis Resort apartment development by the lift base opened.

LIFT PASSES

Prices in francs

Age	6-day
under 16	113
16 to 19	197
20 to 63	282
64 plus	226

Free Under 6
Beginner Limited pass
Alternative passes
Brunni only; non-skier

TOURIST OFFICE

www.engelberg.ch

airbag at Jochpass where you can practise tricks.

Snow reliability The high, north-facing slopes of Titlis and Jochpass keep their snow well and have a long season. Piste grooming is 'very good'.

Experts There is lots of superb off-piste. The classic Laub run is 1000m vertical down a hugely wide, consistently steep face with great views of town. We enjoyed even more the less popular 2000m vertical Galtiberg run from the top, which ends among streams and trees, with a bus back to town – a guide is essential. The off-piste from the top of the Jochpass area to Engstlenalp has been recommended and the terrain at the top of Titlis looks great but is not without danger. There are few black pistes; the itinerary from Titlis to Stand is steep and often mogulled.

Intermediates Most runs are steep reds, and there are few easy cruises. The Jochpass area is often quieter than Titlis, with enjoyable blue and red runs, including lovely long ones down to the valley station (especially nice in the mornings when they are quiet).

Beginners There's a good isolated beginner area at Gerschnialp, smaller areas at Trübsee and Untertrübsee. You have to use lifts to and from these slopes (limited passes are available); and there are few longer easy runs to progress to – all far from ideal. Some beginners go to Brunni.

Snowboarding The beginner area is served by draglifts, so it's not ideal. But there is excellent freeriding if you hire a guide. Beware of the flat start to the runs down from Jochpass.

Cross-country One reporter's friend was very impressed with the 35km trails and loops (some at altitude).

Mountain restaurants An impressive choice. Our favourite, and that of

reporters, is Skihütte Stand, a woody table-service place beside the cable car to Titlis: 'super atmosphere'. Jochpass serves 'good Alpen macaroni'. The Untertrübsee has been tipped in the past. The Trübsee hotel 'is a good place to meet non-skiers'.

Schools and guides There is a choice of four schools. The guide office offers heli-skiing and ski touring.

Families Globi's Winterland at Brunni is best for families, with play areas and lifts. The Swiss ski school takes kids from age three, the kindergarten from two. Some hotels offer childcare; the tourist office has details of babysitters.

STAYING THERE

Hotels The 4-star Ramada Regina is 'gorgeously furnished and the spa is quite something'. The 3-star Bänklialp is 'basic, comfortable and serves good food'. The Edelweiss and the central Schweizerhof (both 3-stars) and the trendy, Scandinavian-run Ski Lodge have been recommended by past reporters.

Eating out There is a huge variety of restaurants – more than 50 – from traditional Swiss to Tex-Mex (at the Yucatan) and Chinese (Moonrise). A regular visitor's favourite is the Alpenclub ('woody, fireplace, fabulous traditional Swiss food'). We had splendid chicken/veal dishes at the hotel Central; large portions, very well presented. The Ski Lodge has been recommended. The Schweizer Haus 'is worth the 15-minute stroll from town'.

Après-ski The liveliest venue is the Chalet (bottom of the gondola) which has a popular happy hour. A recent reporter found the previously lively Yucatan (main square) 'quiet, even at happy hour'. A 2015 visitor tips the hotel Hoheneck ('cosy lounge upstairs and live music downstairs'). The Ski Lodge bar has been tipped in the past. For dancing, try the Spindle nightclub.

Off the slopes The 12th-century monastery and its cheese-making factory and shop are worth a visit. It's worth going up the cable cars for the views, the suspension bridge and the ice grotto. There are many walking and snowshoeing trails, tubing, sledging and a sports centre. Up the valley, a gondola goes up to Fürenalp for walking, tobogganing, snowshoeing. Lucerne is a possible train trip.

GRINDELWALD TOURIST OFFICE

Grindelwald

Traditional mountain village set beneath the towering Eiger and with an old cog railway still the main way up to the slopes

£145
RESORT PRICE INDEX

RATINGS

The mountains

Extent	★★★
Fast lifts	★★★★
Queues	★★
Terrain p'ks	★★★
Snow	★★
Expert	★★
Intermediate	★★★★
Beginner	★★★
Boarder	★★★
X-country	★★
Restaurants	★★★
Schools	★★★
Families	★★

The resort

Charm	★★★★
Convenience	★★
Scenery	★★★★★
Eating out	★★★
Après-ski	★★★
Off-slope	★★★★

NEWS

2015/16: Nothing for this season but there's a plan for fast new gondolas from Grund to Männlichen (an eight-seater) and to Eigergletscher (a 28-seater). They hope to receive the necessary approvals in 2016 and that the new lifts will be ready for the 2017/18 season.

- ➕ Dramatically set, beneath the north face of the Eiger
- ➕ Lots of long intermediate runs
- ➕ Pleasant old village with long mountaineering history
- ➕ Fair amount to do off the slopes, including splendid walks

- ➖ Slow, queue-prone trains and gondola to access the main slopes
- ➖ Few challenging pistes for experts
- ➖ A long trek to visit Mürren
- ➖ Natural snow-cover unreliable (but substantial snowmaking now)
- ➖ Village gets little midwinter sun

For stunning views from the resort and the slopes, there are few places to rival Grindelwald. The village is nowhere near as special as Mürren or Wengen, just over the hill, but it does provide direct access to Grindelwald's own First slopes.

The main access lifts are appalling, taking half an hour to ride even if you don't have to queue (for the gondola) or wait (for the train). Grindelwald regulars accept all this as part of the scene – though they won't have to when the planned new gondolas are in place (see 'News').

THE RESORT

Grindelwald is a long village set along a road that faces the towering north wall of the Eiger, which means that the resort gets very little sun in January. Its main slopes are shared with Wengen; and there is a separate area of sunny slopes on First. Getting to the tougher, higher slopes of Mürren on snow and lifts is a lengthy business (around three hours to the top). Trips to other resorts are not very easy.

VILLAGE CHARM ★★★★
Not in the Wengen league
The central buildings are mainly in traditional chalet style, in keeping with the resort's long mountaineering history. And the station and cog railway add to the olde-worlde charm. The village can feel very jolly at times (eg during the snow-carving festival in January, when huge sculptures are created). Although the road through goes nowhere, traffic can be intrusive.

CONVENIENCE ★★
Not a strong point
The most convenient places to stay are in the centre near the main station or at Grund, departure point of the main access lifts and arrival point of the main home piste, about 80m vertical lower. If you stay in the centre, you can also take the train up, but you need to catch it back up from Grund on the way home too. Staying near the centre means the gondola up to the First area is a walkable distance. At the foot of First are nursery slopes, ski school and kindergarten. Buses link the lift stations.

SCENERY ★★★★★
Unrivalled
The mountains in these parts are legendary among climbers – from all over the slopes there are superb views, not only of the Eiger but also of the Wetterhorn and other peaks.

THE MOUNTAINS

The major area of slopes is shared with Wengen and offers a mix of a few wooded runs and much more extensive open slopes. The smaller First area is mainly above the treeline. Several areas are designated as wildlife reserves, where you may well spot chamois. Piste marking and the piste map are poor; the Männlichen slopes, in particular, can be tricky to navigate.

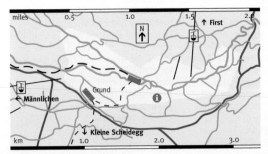

KEY FACTS		
Resort	1035m	
	3,400ft	
Jungfrau region		
Slopes	945-2970m	
	3,100-9,740ft	
Lifts		45
Pistes	213km	
	132 miles	
First-Männlichen-		
Kleine Scheidegg		
Slopes	945-2500m	
	3,100-8,200ft	
Lifts		28
Pistes	170km	
	106 miles	

EXTENT OF THE SLOPES ★★★
Broad and mainly gentle

The area shared with Wengen spreads broadly beneath the Eiger. From Grund, near the western end of town, you can get to **Männlichen** by an appallingly slow two-stage gondola, or to **Kleine Scheidegg** by an equally slow cog railway (with some trains starting in the centre of town). The slopes of the separate south-facing **First** area are reached by a long, slow gondola starting a walk or short bus ride east of the centre.

FAST LIFTS ★★★★
Better high up

Getting up into the main area from the village is seriously slow (the planned new gondolas will speed things up but not till 2017/18 at the earliest – see 'News'). But once up, you can spend most of your time on fast chairlifts.

QUEUES ★★
Can be dreadful at the bottom

These days visitors generally find few problems once they are on the mountain, but the train and the Männlichen gondola at Grund can be crowded at peak periods. Queues for the gondola can be very bad in high season, especially on Saturdays – this is the obvious entry point for residents of Bern attracted by the special family pass deals on Saturdays. And the gondola goes very slowly, too.

TERRAIN PARKS ★★★
First has it all

The White Elements Snowpark on First next to the Bärgelegg lift was redesigned last year and is 650m long, with lines for different abilities (www. white-elements.ch). There is also a snowcross near the top of the Schilt lift – 'Best fun all week,' said a recent reporter.

SNOW RELIABILITY ★★
Improved snowmaking helps

Grindelwald's low altitude means that natural snow is often in short supply or in poor condition. First is a bit higher than the Männlichen area, and may have better snow in cold midwinter; but it is sunny, and less snow-sure as spring approaches. Snowmaking has been increased recently and the resort claims that some 60% of its slopes are now covered. The last couple of times we have visited were not in bumper snow periods, but most slopes were in good condition.

FOR EXPERTS ★★
Few on-piste challenges

The area is quite limited for experts, but there is some fine off-piste if the snow is good. Heli-trips are organized. We and readers have enjoyed the splendid Bort Direct black run on First. This turns into a downhill route between Bort and town and is quite tough, especially when the snow has suffered from the sun.

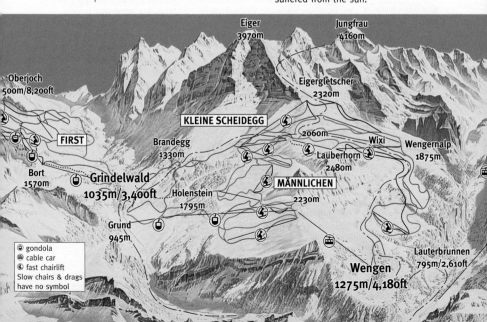

↑ Getting up the mountain on a long old gondola or cog railway is a slow business; but once up, there are plenty of fast chairs to ride
ADRIAN SINGLETON

LIFT PASSES

Jungfrau

Prices in francs

Age	6-day
under 16	170
16 to 19	271
20 to 61	339
62 plus	305

Free Under 6 (if with parent)

Beginner Points card

Note Covers trains between villages and Grindelwald ski-bus

Alternative passes
Grindelwald and Wengen only; Mürren only; non-skier pass

FOR INTERMEDIATES ★★★★
Ideal intermediate terrain
In good snow, First makes a splendid intermediate playground, though the general lack of trees makes the area less friendly than the larger Kleine Scheidegg-Männlichen area. Nearly all the runs from Kleine Scheidegg are long blues or gentle reds – great cruising terrain. On the Männlichen there's a choice of gentle but not very varied runs down to the mid-station of the gondola – and in good snow, down to the bottom. For tougher pistes, head for the top of the Lauberhorn lift and the runs to Kleine Scheidegg, or to Wixi (following the World Cup downhill course). The north-facing run from Eigergletscher served by the Eigernordwand six-pack often has the best snow late in the season.

FOR BEGINNERS ★★★
Depends where you go
The Bodmi nursery slope at the bottom of First is scenic but not particularly convenient. Snow quality can also suffer from the sun and the low altitude, and fast skiers and tobogganers racing through are off-putting. Kleine Scheidegg has a better, higher beginner area and splendid long runs to progress to, served by the railway. There are no free lifts, but a points card is available.

FOR BOARDERS ★★★
Best for intermediates
Intermediates will enjoy the area most, while experts will hanker for Mürren's steep, off-piste slopes. First is the main boarders' mountain and has the terrain park and snowcross, plus open

freeride terrain near the top. There are still a few draglifts but most are avoidable.

FOR CROSS-COUNTRY ★★
OK but shady
There are around 10km of prepared classic trails and another 10km of skating tracks. Almost all are on the valley floor, so it's shady in midwinter and may have poor snow later on.

MOUNTAIN RESTAURANTS ★★★
Wide choice
There are lots, most marked on the piste map. Read the Wengen chapter for additional options. On First we enjoyed Berghaus Bort (as did a recent reporter), where the old building houses a restaurant built in contemporary style. Reader tips include: the Genepi on First ('tasty kebabs'), Berghaus Aspen just above Grund, and Brandegg on the railway (renowned for its apple fritters and doughnuts and views).

SCHOOLS AND GUIDES ★★★
Good reports
A regular visitor recommends the 'friendly, patient and knowledgeable Paul Ashton' at the Swiss School and says, 'I've always had good experiences with this school and its various instructors at all levels.' There are several other schools but we lack reports. Altitude school offers ski touring as well as standard lessons.

FOR FAMILIES ★★
Lacks convenience
It's not a convenient place for families because of its spread-out nature.

Snowli Kids Club based at Bodmi (First) takes young kids and operates a bus from the village. Snowli Kids Club Sunshine is a nursery and play area at the top of Männlichen.

STAYING THERE

Hotels There's a 5-star, seven 4-stars and plenty of more modest places.
*****Schweizerhof Now a 5-star. Close to the station. Pool.
****Belvedere Over 100 years old, family-run, friendly, close to the station. Pool, steam, sauna, hot tub.
****Eiger 'Spacious rooms, superb friendly service, great wellness area, first-rate food.'
****Sunstar Near First gondola. Comfortable rooms, big wellness complex, conference facilities.
***Derby Right next to station; rooms and suites; several restaurants.
***Gletschergarten Out past First gondola. Friendly, good food.
***Hirschen Family-run; by nursery slopes. Good food.
***Wetterhorn Cosy, recently renovated chalet way beyond the village, with great views of the glacier.
Apartments The Eiger hotel has some.
At altitude Berghaus Bort, at the First gondola mid-station, has proper rooms and dormitories.

EATING OUT ★★★☆☆
Hotel-based
There's a wide choice of good hotel restaurants such as the Hirschen, Challistübli in the Kreuz & Post, Schmitte in the Schweizerhof, and the Alte Post. Hotel Spinne has the candlelit Rôtisserie. Onkel Tom's Hütte is an Italian and a past reporter liked the Steinbock for reasonable prices and good food including pizza cooked in a wood oven.

GETTING THERE

Air Bern 70km/ 45 miles (1hr); Zürich 155km/95 miles (2hr); Basel 175km/ 110 miles (2hr)

Rail Station in resort

TOURIST OFFICE

www.grindelwald.ch

APRES-SKI ★★★☆☆
Getting livelier
Tipirama – a wigwam at Kleine Scheidegg, sometimes with DJs and live bands – is a fun place immediately after skiing 'if not too cold'; you can catch the train down. There are various (mainly open air) bars to stop in on the way down to Grund. The liveliest are the Rancher (on run 22), attracting a young crowd, Holzerbar (on run 21) and the Aspen hotel (just below). In town, the terrace of the C&M Café und Mehr is good for coffee and cake. Later on, there's live music in several bars and hotels, such as the Challibar (hotel Kreuz & Post), but it isn't a place for bopping until dawn. The Espresso bar in the Spinne hotel seems to be the liveliest and the Gepsi Bar in the Eiger hotel is a favourite of a regular visitor. The Mescalero (in the Spinne) and Plaza (in the Sunstar) are popular clubs.

OFF THE SLOPES ★★★★☆
Plenty to do, easy to get around
There are many cleared paths with magnificent views and a special (but pricey) pedestrian lift pass. Many of the mountain huts are accessible to pedestrians. A trip to Jungfraujoch is spectacular (see feature panel below), and train trips are easy to Interlaken and Bern. Tobogganing is big here; the 70km of runs include what is claimed to be Switzerland's longest (15km) but it starts a 2hr30 walk from the top of the First gondola. First also has the First Flyer – a zip-wire affair – free if you have a ski pass. You can watch ice hockey and curling, and there is an indoor rope park and an excellent sports centre with pool. You can go snowshoeing. Scenic flights from Männlichen are spectacular.

THE JOURNEY TO THE TOP OF EUROPE

From Kleine Scheidegg you can take a train through a tunnel in the Eiger to the highest railway station in Europe – Jungfraujoch at 3450m. You stop twice on the way up to look out at magnificent views from galleries carved into the sheer north face of the Eiger. At the top is a big restaurant complex, an 'ice palace' carved out of the glacier and fabulous views of the Aletsch glacier (a UNESCO World Heritage Site). But it gets crowded with organized groups and feels rather touristy. The cost in 2014/15 was 59 francs with a Jungfrau lift pass for three days or more.

JUNGFRAU REGION MARKETING AG

KLOSTERS TOURIST OFFICE

Klosters

Ski the extensive slopes of Davos from a traditional village base – with Davos traffic happily banished to a bypass some years ago

£150
RESORT PRICE INDEX

TOP 10 RATINGS

Extent	****
Fast lifts	**
Queues	**
Snow	****
Expert	****
Intermediate	*****
Beginner	***
Charm	****
Convenience	**
Scenery	****

NEWS

2014/15: A big new mountain restaurant, Madrisahof, opened on, er, Madrisa.

KEY FACTS

Resort	1190m
	3,900ft
Slopes	810-2845m
	2,660-9,330ft
Lifts	56
Pistes	320km
	199 miles

+ Extensive slopes shared with Davos
+ Some lovely long intermediate runs
+ Lots of accessible off-piste terrain
+ Some cute mountain restaurants
+ Pleasant traditional village bypassed by valley traffic

− The slopes are spread over six widely separated areas
− Preponderance of T-bars is a problem for some visitors
− May be too quiet for some visitors

If you like the sound of the mountains around Davos but don't like the look of Davos itself, here's your solution: a traditional-style village with equally good access to the Parsenn. Jakobshorn, Rinerhorn and Pischa are distant, but Madrisa is on your doorstep.

THE RESORT

Klosters is a sizeable village with a relaxed, affluent Alpine atmosphere. **Village charm** Klosters Platz is the main focus – a collection of upmarket, traditional-style hotels around the railway station. Traffic for Davos and the Vereina rail tunnel takes a bypass – an improvement still much appreciated by old hands like us. **Convenience** The cable car up the wooded slopes of Gotschna starts in the heart of Platz. The village spreads along the valley road, fading into the countryside; then you come to the even quieter village of Klosters Dorf, and the gondola to Madrisa. Train and bus services are adequate (and free). **Scenery** The contrast between steeply wooded valleys and high, craggy peaks is impressive.

THE MOUNTAINS

Most of the runs are on open slopes above steeper woodland. **Slopes** A cable car from the railway station in Platz takes you to the Gotschnagrat end of the Parsenn area shared with Davos. These slopes are dealt with in the Davos chapter. A gondola from Dorf takes you up to the scenic Madrisa area, which we deal with here. There's also a little slope at Selfranga (floodlit some evenings), a suburb of Platz. Be aware that Madrisa closes in spring a bit earlier than the sectors around Davos. **Fast lifts** Apart from the gondola, it's T-bars and one slow chair on Madrisa. **Queues** Queues for the Gotschna cable car can be a problem at weekends and peak times, although less so with the strong franc deterring foreign visitors.

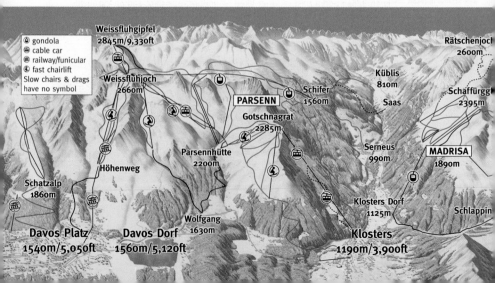

gondola
cable car
railway/funicular
fast chairlift
Slow chairs & drags have no symbol

Weissfluhgipfel 2845m/9,330ft
Rätschenjoch 2600m
Weissfluhjoch 2660m
Küblis 810m
Schifer 1560m
Schafürgg 2395m
Saas
PARSENN
Gotschnagrat 2285m
Serneus 990m
MADRISA 1890m
Parsennhütte 2200m
Höhenweg
Schatzalp 1860m
Klosters Dorf 1125m
Schlappin
Wolfgang 1630m
Davos Platz 1540m/5,050ft
Davos Dorf 1560m/5,120ft
Klosters 1190m/3,900ft

↑ Klosters, in sharp contrast to linked Davos, is a village rather than a city

DESTINATION DAVOS KLOSTERS

LIFT PASSES

Prices in francs

Age	6-day
under 13	133
13-17	232
18-64	332
65 plus	299

Free Under 6

Beginner No deals

Note Does not cover Schatzalp

Alternative passes Individual areas; pedestrian single tickets

TOURIST OFFICE

www.klosters.ch

Terrain parks Madrisa has a snowcross course.

Snow reliability It's usually good higher up. Madrisa gets a lot of sun.

Experts The lift-served off-piste possibilities are the main appeal, on Madrisa as elsewhere in the region – and on 'family-friendly' Madrisa it doesn't get skied out so quickly.

Intermediates Madrisa is not huge, but it is all excellent intermediate terrain. The black run to the valley via Schlappin is not difficult unless conditions make it so.

Beginners There is a slope between Dorf and Platz, plus Selfranga; but Madrisa's higher slopes are more appealing provided you don't mind the lift rides up and down. There are no special lift-pass deals.

Snowboarding Local slopes are good, but most boarders stay in Davos.

Cross-country There are 46km of free trails – classic and skating – and lots more up at Davos. The Swiss ski school offers lessons.

Mountain restaurants Read the Davos chapter too. On Madrisa, the new Madrisahof offers several different dining rooms. Low down on the home run, the woody Erika at Schlappin remains a reader favourite – 'great atmosphere and food'.

Schools and guides Swiss and Saas are well regarded. Adventure Skiing has been praised for private guiding.

Families Madrisa Land adventure park has lots to offer children, and access is free to infants. The kindergarten there takes babies, too.

STAYING THERE

Hotels For most people, central Platz is the best location. There's the smart Chesa Grischuna, but readers favour either the well-placed Alpina – although one report speaks of 'arrogant' service in the restaurant – or the Sunstar Albeina in Dorf. The more modest traditional British favourite, the Wynegg, is now unrecognizable after a crisp makeover under new management. The Silvretta Park seems to suit families.

Apartments Apartments are available through local agencies.

Eating out Ambitious restaurants abound, but there are few cheap and cheerful places – Al Berto (geddit?) and Fellini are pizzerias. Top of the range is the 'outstanding' Michelin-starred Walserstube in the Walserhof. Other possibilities are the restaurants of the hotels Casanna (at Platz) and Chesa Grischuna.

Après-ski Gaudy's umbrella bar at the foot of the slopes is the focal point at the end of the day. In the village, the Chesa Grischuna has a pianist. Bär's at Piz Buin is popular all day long. The Casa Antica is a small disco.

Off the slopes Klosters is an attractive base for walking (there's a special map available) and cross-country skiing. Tobogganing is popular – there is an exceptional 8.5km run from Madrisa to Saas, miles down the valley. There is an ice rink, and some hotel pools are open to the public. Read the Davos chapter for ideas for train outings.

Klosters

481

Laax

Contrasting villages beneath high, wide, sunny slopes shared by well-heeled families and trendy young freestylers

SWISS-IMAGE / MOUNTAIN MARKETING AG

£150
RESORT PRICE INDEX

TOP 10 RATINGS

Extent	★★★★
Fast lifts	★★★★★
Queues	★★★★
Snow	★★★
Expert	★★★
Intermediate	★★★★★
Beginner	★★★★
Charm	★★★
Convenience	★★★
Scenery	★★★

NEWS

2015/16: A new 10-person gondola will replace the long, slow triple chair on La Siala.

2014/15: The floodlit super-pipe was extended to the full 200m Olympic length.

482

➕ Extensive, varied slopes ideal for intermediates, shared with Flims

➕ Generally efficient lift system, although with some long ride times

➕ Some of Europe's best terrain parks and, as of last year, an Olympic-length super-pipe

➖ Sunny orientation means the snow conditions can be tricky in late season

➖ Bus rides or long walks from some lodgings to the lifts

➖ Most convenient lodgings are in bases we find difficult to like

Laax and neighbouring Flims share a ski area that is one of Switzerland's biggest, whether you look at overall dimensions or piste km. The mountain has other powerful attractions too, including altitude, but the sunny orientation is a bit of a liability when competing in the premier league. Which may be why, some years back, the resort decided to appeal to different markets by investing heavily in terrain parks, half-pipes, indoor freestyle facilities and high-profile events – and by adopting a new brand. Flims and Laax used to be marketed as Flims, and still are in the summer, when they continue to appeal to their traditional market of well-heeled Swiss and Germans.

THE RESORT

The resort has three separate main bases a few km apart by road: Laax, Flims and Falera. Laax and Flims are themselves resorts of parts. Laax Dorf is the original rustic village, a couple of km from a much newer big, busy lift base/hotel/parking complex, now called Laax. Flims Dorf is a traditional resort at the foot of the slopes; Flims Waldhaus is a leafy suburb.

Village charm Laax Dorf is pleasantly rustic, with quiet suburbs set around a lake. The lift base area called Laax is a stark contrast – sharp, modern, deliberately charm-free. Flims Dorf is traditional in style but unremarkable,

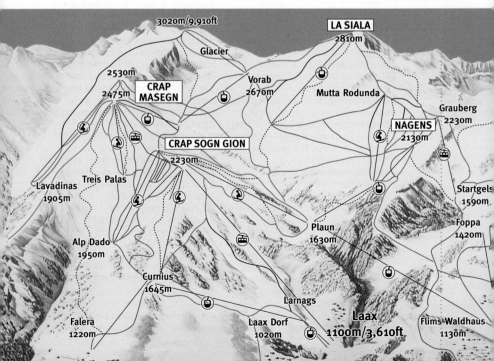

KEY FACTS

Resort	1100m
	3,610ft
Altitude	1100-3020m
	3,610-9,910ft
Lifts	29
Pistes	235km
	146 miles

LIFT PASSES

Prices in francs

Age	6-day
under 13	119
13 to 17	238
18 to 64	357
65 plus	321
Free Under 6	

Beginner One-day
tuition/pass package

spread along the road through it (though a tunnel takes the through traffic). Flims Waldhaus is wooded and more appealing, with upscale secluded hotels. Falera, once a quiet backwater hamlet, has been much expanded in traditional style.

Convenience It depends where you stay. The smart hotels in Waldhaus run shuttles, and there are 'quick and efficient' free ski-buses.

Scenery There are great panoramic views from the top of the glacier but lower down the views are less spectacular.

THE MOUNTAINS

The slopes are mostly open but there are also some quite long woodland runs. The piste map marks 'freeride runs' (dotted on our map), which are avalanche-controlled and patrolled – so they are effectively ungroomed pistes. Many of the black runs could really be classified red. A reporter who encountered thick mist last year spoke highly of the clear 'left' and 'right' piste edge marking.

Slopes There are long gondolas into the slopes from both Flims Dorf and Laax (plus a cable car of exceptional length from Laax) and a slow quad chair from Falera. Above mid-mountain, there is a complex web of lifts and runs – or, rather, two webs separated

by a deep ravine and meeting at only two points. The glacier is limited; but it accesses a superb long run to Lavadinas (an easy black).

Fast lifts The system is impressive, and scrapes into our ★★★★★ category.

Queues There may be queues for the village lifts at peak times and for the glacier drags. A reader notes that there are now priority 'Blue' lines for which you pay a hefty premium, which suggests queues can be a more general problem at times. High winds can close the upper lifts.

Terrain parks Laax is one of the top resorts in Europe for freestylers and has four parks in the Crap Sogn Gion area, catering for every standard from beginner to pro-rider. Many high-profile competitions are held here. Between them, the parks are said to have 90 obstacles; there's an airbag and two pipes (super- and mini-) plus an 'excellent' freestyle slope to Curnius. The glacier has an early-season park, too. An indoor Freestyle Academy at the base in Laax offers tuition.

Snow reliability Upper runs are fairly snow-sure. The lower ones can suffer from sun, even early in the season, and some can close (the runs from Cassons and the glacier are also prone to closure); key ones have snowmaking but more is needed.

Experts The black pistes present few challenges, but the freeride runs add a lot of excellent terrain. The sunny aspect means that timing your descents can be crucial, though, to avoid rock-hard moguls. There is a huge amount of good off-piste terrain, notably from La Siala and Cassons.

Intermediates A superb area. Reporters are often surprised by the extent, length and variety of the slopes. The bowl below La Siala is huge and gentle. For the more confident, there are plenty of reds and some easy blacks. The sheltered Grauberg valley is a good area for long and fast runs. The long black run from the glacier away from all lifts is one of our favourites; it is steep only at the top. The Downhill course from Crap Sogn Gion is also excellent. Some of the freeride runs are great for trying off-piste, but others are steep.

Beginners There are beginner areas at village level (which can suffer from the sun) and at Crap Sogn Gion, and good easy runs to progress to. A one-day pass/tuition/lunch package is available.

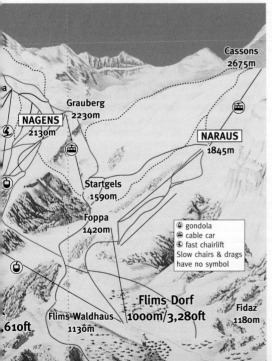

Cassons
2675m

Grauberg
2230m

NAGENS
2130m

NARAUS
1845m

Startgels
1590m

Foppa
1420m

⊙ gondola
⊜ cable car
⊄ fast chairlift
Slow chairs & drags
have no symbol

Flims Dorf
1000m/3,28oft

Fidaz
1180m

Flims Waldhaus
1130m

,610ft

↑ Why do pointy roofs look right, and flat roofs wrong? The flat roofs belong to Rocksresort

WEISSE ARENA GRUPPE

MOMENTUM SKI

Weekend & a la carte
ski holiday specialists

100% Tailor-made

Premier hotels
& apartments

Flexible travel
arrangements

020 7371 9111
WWW.MOMENTUMSKI.COM

TOURIST OFFICE

Flims, Laax and Falera
www.laax.com

Snowboarding Hugely popular. Apart from the top terrain parks, there's good freeriding. Many linking pistes have flat/uphill stretches though – 'lots of boarders struggling', says a report.

Cross-country There are 55km of trails.

Mountain restaurants Huts are taken seriously here. They are briefly described on a special Gastro Guide piste map and classified as Easy (self-service), Cosy (the majority) or Exquisite (five top spots). The two 'Exquisites' we hear most about are Ustria Startgels (aka Alpenrose) – 'by far the best: outstanding game, excellent open fire grills' – and Tegia Larnags, a 'charming' farmhouse with typically Swiss dishes. Tegia Curnius is a popular self-service ('excellent rösti'). Other table-service tips: Foppa ('very helpful staff and great views'), Runca Höhe (large heated marquee, 'good staff, fast service') and Elephant ('interesting menu, impressive toilet').

Schools and guides The school is run by the lift company, USA-style. Past reports on both adult and child instruction have been positive.

Families There are 'Wonderlands' at all three resort bases.

STAYING THERE

Hotels At Laax the 4-star 'design hotel' Signina is part of Rocksresort (see 'Apartments') and has 'excellent staff, good breakfasts, pool, wonderful indoor tennis courts'. The 4-star Laaxerhof is almost ski-in/ski-out and has large rooms, pool and sauna; its stubli has been praised. Laax Dorf offers the charming little Posta Veglia.

In Flims Dorf the cheap and cheerful Arena Lodge – with 'cool rooms, friendly and helpful staff, good restaurant and the best bar in town – suits boys' trips' (see 'Après-ski').

In Flims Waldhaus the Sunstar is over 100 years old and has been praised for its food and staff. Cresta has 'excellent food, service and top spa facilities'. The Adula is similarly praised by a regular visitor. In Falera, La Siala has traditional rooms and apartments, and a free shuttle.

Apartments At Laax, Rocksresort is uber-cool but the architecture is not to everyone's taste; you can use the facilities of the Signina hotel. The tourist office has a list of apartments.

Eating out In Laax, Rocksresort places include Nooba ('excellent Asian food, friendly staff), and the smart Grandis (fine wines and BBQ specialities). In Laax Dorf the Posta Veglia has a lovely old stube, with a plainer room behind. In Flims, a regular recommends both à la carte restaurants of the hotel Adula, and reports that the local brewery has opened a bar-restaurant in Flims.

Après-ski There are busy bars at the lift bases at close of play. Later on, clubs at the hotel Arena Lodge in Flims Dorf and the Riders Palace at Laax throb until late.

Off the slopes There's a big sports centre on the edge of Flims, with ice rink (including ice hockey), and 100km of 'really excellent' marked walks reaching high up into the slopes. Shopping is limited. Outings to historic Chur are easy.

SNOWPIX.COM / CHRIS GILL

Mürren

The dinky, car-free mountain village where the British invented downhill ski racing; stupendous views add to the charm

£140
RESORT PRICE INDEX

RATINGS

The mountains

Extent	★
Fast lifts	★★★★★
Queues	★★★
Terrain p'ks	★★
Snow	★★★
Expert	★★★
Intermediate	★★★
Beginner	★★★
Boarder	★★
X-country	★
Restaurants	★★
Schools	★★★
Families	★★★

The resort

Charm	★★★★★
Convenience	★★★
Scenery	★★★★★
Eating out	★★
Après-ski	★★
Off-slope	★★★

NEWS

2015/16: The narrow tracks at the top of the Gimmeln drag are due to be widened into a proper slope.

2014/15: Two ancient T-bars on the lower slopes were replaced by new ones and a moving carpet was installed on the village nursery slope. A new tobogganing slope from Schiltgrat opened, as did the Skyline terrain park in the Schiltgrat sector. At Birg a new Skyline Walk viewing platform was built.

miles   0.5
↑ down to
Lauterbrunnen
Allmendhubel
Schilthorn
N
↓ down to
Stechelberg
km   0.5   1.

➕ Tiny, charming, traditional village, with 'traffic-free' snowy paths

➕ Magnificent scenery, which can be admired from both village and slopes

➕ Good sports centre

➕ Good snow high up, even when the rest of the region is suffering

➖ Extent of local pistes very limited, no matter what your level of expertise

➖ Lower slopes can be in poor condition

➖ Quiet, limited nightlife

Mürren is one of our favourite resorts. There may be other mountain villages that are equally pretty, but none of them enjoys views like those from Mürren across the deep valley to the rock faces and glaciers of the Eiger, Mönch and Jungfrau: simply breathtaking. Then there's the Schilthorn run – 1300m vertical with an unrivalled combination of varied terrain and glorious views.

But our visits are normally one-day affairs; those staying for a week are likely to want to explore the extensive intermediate slopes of Wengen and Grindelwald, across the valley. And that takes time.

It was in Mürren that the British more or less invented modern skiing. Sir Arnold Lunn organized the first ever slalom race here in 1922. Some 12 years earlier his father, Sir Henry, had persuaded the locals to open the railway in winter so that he could bring the first winter package tour here. Sir Arnold's son Peter was a regular visitor for 95 years, until his death in 2011.

THE RESORT

Mürren is one of a trio of resorts set amid the fabulous scenery of the Jungfrau group. It has an amazing position, set on a shelf high above the valley floor, across from Wengen, and can be reached only by cable car from Stechelberg or from Lauterbrunnen (via Grütschalp, where you catch a train). To get to Wengen takes around an hour: you go down to Lauterbrunnen by lift or piste, and catch a cog railway up. You can then ski to Grindelwald, but getting to the First area on the far side of Grindelwald is a very long trek.

VILLAGE CHARM ★★★★★
Picturesque and peaceful
You can't fail to be struck by Mürren's beauty and tranquillity. Paths and narrow lanes weave between little wooden chalets and a handful of bigger hotel buildings – all normally blanketed by snow.

Mürren's traffic-free status has been somewhat eroded; there are now a few delivery vehicles. But it still isn't plagued by electric carts and taxis in the way that many other traditional 'traffic-free' resorts are. Even Wengen seems busy by comparison.

CONVENIENCE ★★★
Small enough not to matter
The village is tiny by general resort standards. But it's 1km from end to end and there is no transport, so it pays to plan your end-of-day return to the village with a bit of care.

SCENERY ★★★★★
Glorious panoramas
The views from the village and the slopes of the Eiger, Mönch and Jungfrau across the valley are magnificent. So are the 360° views from the top of the Schilthorn.

THE MOUNTAINS

The lower slopes are below the treeline, but it is an inhospitable area when the weather is bad.

EXTENT OF THE SLOPES ★
Small but interesting
Mürren's slopes aren't extensive. But there is something for everyone, including a vertical of some 1300m to the village. There are three connected areas. On the lower slopes, **Schiltgrat** is served by a fast quad chair at the south end of the village. A short funicular goes from the middle of the

KEY FACTS

Resort	1650m
	5,410ft

Jungfrau region	
Altitude	945-2970m
	3,100-9,740ft
Lifts	45
Pistes	213km
	132 miles

Mürren-Schilthorn only	
Slopes	1650-2970m
	5,410-9,740ft
Lifts	17
Pistes	54km
	34 miles

village to the nursery slope at **Allmendhubel** – linked by a red run and then chairlift to the slightly higher **Maulerhubel**. Runs go down from here to Winteregg and a fast quad.

The higher slopes are reached by a cable car to **Birg**. Below Birg, the fast Riggli chair serves a shady slope, and lower down two more chairs serve sunnier slopes. A further cable car goes up to the Schilthorn – check out the feature panel. In good snow you can ski from here (via a short chairlift) to Lauterbrunnen – almost 16km and 2175m vertical; below Winteregg, it's mostly narrow paths. Every January the Inferno race for amateurs is run over this route (without using the chairlift).

FAST LIFTS ★★★★★
Mostly OK
There's a draglift and a few slow chairs but most lifts are fast.

QUEUES ★★★☆☆
Generally not a problem
Mürren doesn't get as crowded as Wengen and Grindelwald, except on sunny Sundays. But there can be queues for the cable cars to Birg and Schilthorn; the top stage has only one cabin, so if you don't get on you have to wait for it to go up and back.

TERRAIN PARKS ★★☆☆☆
New one in Schiltgrat sector
A new park, the Skyline (www.skyline-snowpark.ch), opened for last season in the Schiltgrat sector with features for all abilities. There is no half-pipe.

SNOW RELIABILITY ★★★☆☆
Good on the upper slopes
We've always found Mürren has the best snow in the Jungfrau area. When Wengen-Grindelwald (and Mürren's lower slopes) have problems, the slopes up at Birg often have packed powder snow. The runs from below Engetal to Allmendhubel and parts of the lower slopes have snowmaking, as does the woodland path on down to Lauterbrunnen.

FOR EXPERTS ★★★☆☆
An attractive cocktail
The black run from the top of the Schilthorn starts with a steep but not terrifying pitch, in the past generally mogulled but now more often groomed. It flattens into a schuss to Engetal, below Birg. Then there's a wonderful, wide run with stunning views over the valley. Below the Engetal lifts you hit the Kanonenrohr (gun barrel). This is a shelf with solid rock on one side and a steep drop on

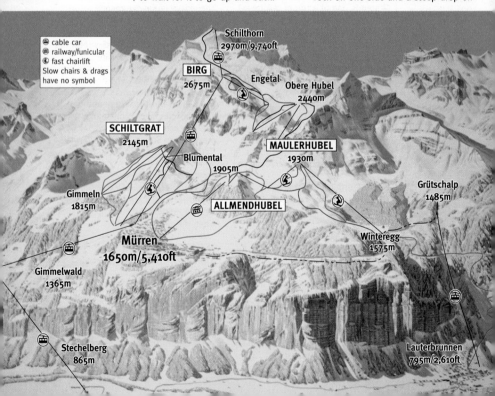

HOTEL **eiger** MÜRREN
★★★★

Perfect hideaway in the Swiss Alps.

Family run Hotel in car free Mürren

www.hoteleiger.com
Tel. +41 33 856 54 54 | info@hoteleiger.com

↑ The views across the valley are stunning. It's a pity you can't see them from this slow old chairlift

SCHILTHORN

LIFT PASSES

Jungfrau

Prices in francs

Age	6-day
under 16	170
16 to 19	271
20 to 61	339
62 plus	305

Free Under 6 (if with parent)

Beginner Points card

Note Covers trains between villages and Grindelwald ski-bus

Alternative passes Grindelwald and Wengen only; Mürren only; non-skier pass

the other – protected by nets; it is wider than it once was, and is now not seriously scary. After an open slope and scrappy zigzag path, you arrive at the 'hog's back' and can descend towards the village on either side of Allmendhubel.

There are steep mogul runs at Birg and Schiltgrat and quite a lot of off-piste potential, notably runs into the Blumental – from Schiltgrat (the north-facing Blumenlucke) and from Birg (sunnier Tschingelchrachen). And there are more adventurous runs from the Schilthorn top station.

FOR INTERMEDIATES ★★★★★
Limited, but Wengen nearby
Keen piste-bashers will want to make a few trips to the long cruising runs of Wengen-Grindelwald. The blue runs up at Engetal, below Birg and served by the Riggli chair, are good easy cruises and normally have good snow. The best easy cruising run on the lower slopes is the north-facing blue down to Winteregg. The reds on the other low slopes can get mogulled, and snow conditions can be poor.

Competent, confident intermediates can consider tackling the Schilthorn.

FOR BEGINNERS ★★★★★
Not ideal, but adequate
The main nursery slopes at Allmendhubel, up the funicular, are a little on the steep side, but secluded and quiet. You pay via points cards. From there, you have easy blue runs to graduate to in each of the sectors.

FOR BOARDERS ★★★★★
Tough going for intermediates
The major lifts are snowboard-friendly cable cars and chairlifts. The terrain above Mürren is suitable mainly for good freeriders. Intermediates will find the area tough and limited; nearby Wengen is gentler and larger.

FOR CROSS-COUNTRY ★★★★★
Forget it
There's 12km in the Lauterbrunnen valley, but snow is unreliable.

MOUNTAIN RESTAURANTS ★★★★★
Nothing outstanding
You'll want to visit the Schilthorn even if it's only for a drink – see the feature panel. Other reader tips include the cosy Schilthornhütte at Obere Hubel, the rustic, secluded Suppenalp lower down in the Blumental (which gets no

Piz Gloria revolves once an hour, displaying a fabulous 360° panorama of peaks and lakes. The ambience has improved since it was renovated and reporters have enjoyed the food. As well as admiring the views from the terrace, you can visit Bond World 007, a free exhibition based on the On Her Majesty's Secret Service *movie that was filmed here almost 50 years ago. This includes memorabilia (eg the bobsled and helicopter used in chases) and clips from the film. To get you in the mood the cable cars up occasionally play Bond theme music.*

JUNGFRAU MARKETING AG

SWITZERLAND

488

sun in January), the Schiltgrathüsi near blue run 23, and the restaurant at Winteregg. We normally lunch in the village on the rear terrace of the Bellevue hotel opposite the nursery slope – stunning views and wonderfully peaceful.

SCHOOLS AND GUIDES ★★★☆☆
No recent reports
We lack recent reports. But the school has a long tradition of teaching Brits.

FOR FAMILIES ★★★☆☆
Attractive
Mürren is attractive for a quiet family holiday, not least because of the relaxed, safe and snowy village, and the free facilities (read 'Off the slopes'). There is a good nursery slope in the village. Children as young as three can have lessons.

STAYING THERE

Hotels There are fewer than a dozen.
★★★★Eiger Chalet style; next to station. Widely recommended for good blend of efficiency and charm. Good food; pool and sauna.
★★★Alpenruh Attractively renovated chalet next to the cable car.
★★★Jungfrau Perfectly placed for families, in front of the baby slope and close to the funicular.
★★Alpenblick Simple, small, modern chalet near the station.
Apartments There are plenty for independent travellers to rent.
At altitude You can stay at the 'creaky' Suppenalp in the Blumental.

EATING OUT ★★☆☆☆
Mainly in hotels
The main alternative to hotels is the rustic Stägerstübli – a bar as well as a

restaurant, and popular with locals, serving regional dishes. The Jägerstübli in the hotel Bellevue, the Edelweiss, and the Alpenruh have been recommended by past reporters.

APRES-SKI ★★☆☆☆
Not entirely devoid of life
The tiny Stägerstübli is cosy, and the place to meet locals. The Bliemlichäller disco in the Blumental hotel caters for kids, the bar in the Eiger for a more mixed crowd.

OFF THE SLOPES ★★★☆☆
Tranquillity plus diversions
There is a very good sports centre, which was renovated a few years ago with new spa facilities. The pool and ice rink are free to those staying in Mürren with a guest card. There are lots of prepared walking trails and a signposted snowshoeing trail. Tobogganing runs and parapenting are popular. Excursions to Bern and Interlaken are easy. Skiers can easily return to the village to meet non-skiers for lunch, and non-skiers can ride the cable cars to the Schilthorn.

DOWN-VALLEY VILLAGE – 795m
LAUTERBRUNNEN

This is a good budget base, with a bit of resort atmosphere and access to both Wengen (until late) and Mürren. We've happily stayed at two hotels – the 3-star Schützen and 2-star Oberland; the 3-star Silberhorn has been highly recommended by reporters ('right by the lifts for both Mürren and Wengen and very good, price-competitive dinners'). There are bars in the hotels Horner, Steinbock and Silberhorn. Ski Miquel's chalet hotel Rosa is said to be good.

GETTING THERE
Air Bern 65km/ 40 miles (1hr); Zürich 150km/95 miles (2hr); Basel 170km/ 105 miles (2hr)

Rail Lauterbrunnen; transfer by mountain railway and cable car

TOURIST OFFICE
www.mymuerren.ch
www.muerren.ch

SNOWPIX.COM / CHRIS GILL

Saas-Fee

Some of the highest skiing in the Alps, plus a cute old village at the base; great for an early/late break

£155
RESORT PRICE INDEX

RATINGS

The mountains
Extent	★★
Fast lifts	★★★★
Queues	★★★★
Terrain p'ks	★★★★
Snow	★★★★★
Expert	★★
Intermediate	★★★★
Beginner	★★★★
Boarder	★★★★
X-country	★★★
Restaurants	★★★
Schools	★★★★
Families	★★★★

The resort
Charm	★★★★★
Convenience	★★
Scenery	★★★★
Eating out	★★★★
Après-ski	★★★★
Off-slope	★★★★

NEWS

2015/16: The Capra, Saas Fee's second 5-star hotel (opened in 2014), is adding more suites in a new building, and a new wellness centre. New pistes are planned for the separate, lower resort of Saas-Grund.

2014/15: The Aqua Allalin leisure centre and attached 168-bed youth hostel reopened in September 2014 after renovation.

KEY FACTS

Resort	1800m
	5,910ft
Slopes	1800-3500m
	5,910-11,480ft
Lifts	21
Pistes	100km
	62 miles

+ Most runs are at exceptionally high altitude, and are snow-sure
+ Great for early intermediates
+ Traditional, car-free village, with clear attractions for families
+ Dramatic setting amid high peaks and glaciers
+ Good off-slope leisure facilities

− Small area of slopes
− Mainly easy runs, with little to amuse experts (glacier limits off-piste exploration)
− Many visitors face some long walks around the village
− Shady and cold for much of winter
− Bad weather can shut the slopes

Saas-Fee is a captivating place – a sort of miniature Zermatt without the conspicuous consumption. As well as the charm factor there's the super-reliable snow: you spend most of your days here at an altitude – between 2500m and 3500m – that is unrivalled in the Alps. It's a compelling combination.

But we tend to drop in here for a day or two at a time, so the limited extent and challenge of the slopes is not a worry; if we were here for a week, we'd soon be taking trips to Saas-Grund and even Zermatt.

THE RESORT

Saas-Fee is a traditional mountain village of narrow streets lined by old chalets and free of cars, which made a recent visitor feel 'safe allowing the children to wander the streets'. It's not entirely free of traffic, though: electric minibuses, taxis and vans provoke complaints, although they're not nearly as much of a nuisance as they are in Zermatt, over the hill.

The standard lift pass also covers Saas-Almagell and Saas-Grund not far away in the valley, and the latter in particular is well worth a visit – one trusted reporter preferred it to Saas-Fee. Trips to Zermatt are time-consuming but possible.

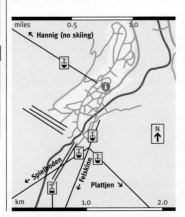

VILLAGE CHARM ★★★★★
Unpretentious rural idyll
Despite expansion, Saas-Fee still feels like a village, with cow sheds still in evidence. It doesn't have much of a central focus, but we'll forgive that; it's a charming place just to stroll around and relax in – at least when the spring sun is beating down. But it loses the sun early in the afternoon, and gets very little sun at all in midwinter.

CONVENIENCE ★★
A hike maybe
Although it's a small village, it's about 2km long, and the main slopes and most of the lifts are at one end. The bigger hotels run their own taxis. There are free but limited public minibuses and a road-train, but they are of little use – 'Very infrequent, and often full,' says a 2014 report. Most people, most of the time, just walk everywhere. The biggest lift – the Alpin Express gondola – starts from a more central location (that you can ski back to). And you can store your gear near the lifts, which helps.

SCENERY ★★★★
The Pearl of the Alps
Simply stunning, with views up to a ring of 4000-metre peaks – on a sunny day the restaurant terraces by the nursery slopes at the south end of the village are a magnet. Higher up, the views are even better.

LIFT PASSES

Saas-Fee

Prices in francs

Age	6-day
under 16	190
17 to 19	319
20 plus	370

Free Under 7

Seniors No deals

Beginner Pass for village lifts only

Notes Covers whole valley (Saas-Fee, Saas-Grund, Saas-Almagell and Saas-Balen); with 6+ day pass, day in Zermatt for additional 30 francs

Alternative passes
Passes for each of the Saastal ski areas; single and return tickets on main lifts; afternoon passes

THE MOUNTAINS

The high slopes are very exposed, and can be closed by wind or heavy snowfall, when you may find yourself resorting (along with everybody else) to the leisure centre.

Take it easy when climbing out of the top lift station at 3500m: some people can't handle the thin air.

Some of the red runs on the glacier should be classified blue, but some of the lower reds are pretty tough.

EXTENT OF THE SLOPES ★★☆☆☆
A glacier runs through it

There are two routes up to the main **Felskinn** area. The 30-person Alpin Express gondola, starting across the river from the centre of the village, takes you there via a mid-station at Morenia. The alternative is a short drag across the nursery slope at the south end of the village, and then the Felskinn cable car.

From Felskinn, the Metro Alpin underground funicular hurtles up to **Allalin**. From below here, two draglifts access the high point of the area.

Also from the south end of the village, a gondola leaves for Spielboden. This is met by a cable car that takes you up to **Längfluh**. Between Felskinn and Längfluh is an off-limits glacier area with huge crevasses. A very long draglift from Längfluh takes you to a point where you can get down to the Felskinn area.

You can descend to the village from both the Allalin and Längfluh sectors.

Another gondola from the south end of the village goes up to the small area of slopes on **Plattjen**.

FAST LIFTS ★★★★☆
Too many T-bars

The area is a strange mixture of powerful fast lifts and a lot of 'ghastly long and cold T-bars', as a recent reporter put it; there are only two chairlifts. Blame the glaciers, on which it's tricky to build chairlifts. But our rating reflects the fact that over half the lifts are fast.

QUEUES ★★★★☆
No recent problems to report

We and our readers have had largely queue-free visits throughout the season, the exceptions being at times when the altitude draws in customers. Naturally, if the upper mountain is closed by weather, the lower mountain becomes crowded.

TERRAIN PARKS ★★★★☆
Well developed

The big Morenia park has countless toys, and lines for different ability levels. Note that there is no longer a half-pipe. There's a park for beginner freestylers near the nursery slopes.

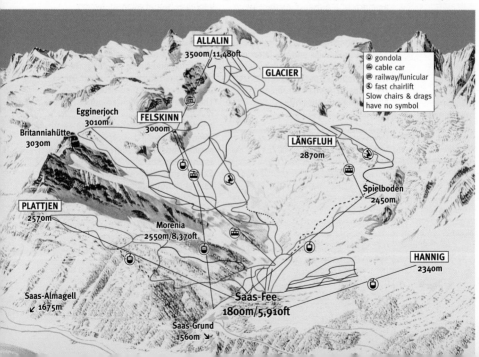

ALLALIN
3500m/11,480ft

GLACIER

⊚ gondola
⊛ cable car
⊜ railway/funicular
⊕ fast chairlift
Slow chairs & drags
have no symbol

Egginerjoch
3010m

FELSKINN
3000m

LÄNGFLUH
2870m

Britanniahütte
3030m

Spielboden
2450m

PLATTJEN
2570m

Morenia
2550m/8,370ft

HANNIG
2340m

Saas-Almagell
↙ 1675m

Saas-Fee
1800m/5,910ft

Saas-Grund
1560m ↘

The Metro Alpin underground funicular takes you to 3500m, almost at the top of the glacier; take it easy up here – the air is thin →
ROD GARVEY

SNOW RELIABILITY ★★★★★
A question of altitudes
Most of Saas-Fee's slopes face north and many are above 2500m, making this one of the most reliable resorts for snow in the Alps. The glacier is open most of the year. Lower down, on the runs back to the resort, snow quality and cover can be more patchy, but snowmaking seems adequate. Grooming is done 'very well', but takes time after a dump we hear.

FOR EXPERTS ★★★★★
Not a lot to keep your interest
There is not much steep stuff – the handful of short, sharp pitches dotted around the area just about merit their black classification – but the resort has quietly introduced a few yellow ski routes which one reporter relished this year. Where they are depends on which map you believe. The slopes around the top of Längfluh can provide good powder, and there are usually moguls above Spielboden. There is excellent tree skiing on Plattjen but it requires serious depths of snow to cover the very rocky terrain. On the main sector, crevasse danger on the glacier limits off-piste.
  Saas-Fee is a leading resort for ski touring: the extended Haute Route from Chamonix ends here.

FOR INTERMEDIATES ★★★★
Great for gentle cruising
For leisurely intermediates not looking for a lot of variety, Saas-Fee is ideal. Keen intermediates who have developed an appetite for mileage should probably look elsewhere,

though. Although there are excellent gentle blues and relatively gentle reds on the upper mountain, we get repeated views from reporters that one or two linking red runs are a bit stiff – red run 10b from the glacier to the Morenia sector, for example.
  For long cruises and usually excellent snow, head for Allalin – gentle red runs leading to even gentler blues. The reds from mid-mountain down to the village are a bit more challenging, notably from Längfluh and Spielboden. They have steepish, tricky sections and can have poor snow, and the blues here are mainly narrow paths – timid intermediates might prefer to take a lift down from mid-mountain. The descents all the way from Allalin to the village offer a leg-testing 1700m vertical.
  Don't ignore the Plattjen area, which is basically of red-run gradient.

FOR BEGINNERS ★★★★
Clear attractions
There's a superb, large, out-of-the-way nursery area at the edge of the village, as snow-sure as any you will find, and covered by a special cheap pass. One reporter judges the walk to it 'a bit of a slog'. Those ready to progress can head for the gentle blues between Felskinn and Morenia. But read 'For intermediates' too.

FOR BOARDERS ★★★★
Year-round fun
Saas-Fee has backed snowboarding from its inception and provides year-round riding. The terrain suits intermediates and beginners best;

WORLD'S HIGHEST REVOLVING LUNCH?

If you fancy 360° views during lunch, head up to Threes!xty, the world's highest revolving restaurant at Allalin, where you can get a different vista with starters, mains and pud. Only the bit of floor with the tables on it revolves; the stairs stay put (along with the windows – take care with your gloves). Switzerland has two other pivoting pubs – at Mürren and Leysin – and we rate the views there better. (There's also one in France, at Val Cenis Vanoise.) But it's an amusing novelty that most visitors enjoy, and a reader this year approves of the food. To reserve a table next to the windows phone 957 1771.

SAAS-FEE TOURISM / SWISS-IMAGE.CH

there's little to satisfy experts and the glacier limits freeriding, but carvers will find wide, well-groomed pistes to shred down. The main access lifts are gondolas, cable cars and a funicular, but nearly all the rest are T-bars. The high altitude and the glacier mean the resort is a favourite for early-season and summer riding.

FOR CROSS-COUNTRY ★★★★★
Good local trail and lots nearby
There is a nice short (6km) trail on the Hannig side of the village and 26km of trails down in the Saas valley.

MOUNTAIN RESTAURANTS ★★★★★
Huge improvements
The resort's lunch scene has been transformed in recent years. The piste map names most of the options.
Editors' choice The Spielboden restaurant was taken over and refurbished some years ago by the Fletschhorn hotel (which has a Michelin star). We haven't yet tried it, but locals rate it the best, and most reporters agree – 'Comparable with the best in Zermatt,' says one. But a reader who gave it three chances last season met very poor service; more reports, please. Berghaus Plattjen (just down from the top of Plattjen), now in the Dom hotel stable, has great Alpine atmosphere, delicious hearty food, excellent service and fab views from a tiny terrace.
Worth knowing about Reporters are keen on the Schäferstube at the top of the village nursery slope – 'excellent food, spectacular view from a large terrace, service with a smile'. Gletschergrotte is worth finding, slightly off the home run from

Spielboden (watch for signs on the left). The Rock is an interesting cool development at Längfluh. The Morenia restaurant is about as good as self-service gets, with food that impresses reporters.

For something different, a 15-minute trek from the pistes at Felskinn brings you to Britanniahütte, a real climbing refuge with great views; understandably, food is simple.

Oh, and don't overlook the revolving resto (see feature panel above).

SCHOOLS AND GUIDES ★★★★★
Good reports
We have had consistently good reports in the last few seasons on all the schools; the Swiss school, Eskimos and British-run Optimum Snowsports.

FOR FAMILIES ★★★★★
Safely suitable
The village and its gentle nursery slopes form a good environment for families, and the kids' fun park proved a 'great introduction' for one toddler. Several hotels have an in-house kindergarten. But make sure you read the 'Convenience' section. Some hotels offer childcare.

STAYING THERE

Chalets There are lots to be found with a bit of googling.
Hotels There are over 50.
*****Ferienart Central top hotel. Superb blend of comfort, service and relaxed style, with a great wellness area. Half-board food about the best we've had anywhere. Most years we get one or two endorsing reports, but this year a reader has some

reservations. Beware of rooms with a bath in the bedroom if that's not your thing. And high wine prices.

***Europa Near the Hannig gondola. Generally good reports; 'gorgeous wellness facilities'.

Fletschhorn Upmarket, elegant (Relais & Châteaux) chalet in the woods. A trek from the village and lifts, but they'll drive you; great food.

Apartments Two 2012 reporters recommended Chalet Feekatz, which has six bedrooms ('beautiful, a 10-minute walk from the centre').

EATING OUT ★★★★
Good variety

Gastronomes will want to head for the Michelin-starred and expensive Fletschhorn. We like the woody Bodmen, which has great food and a varied menu. As well as its main Cäsar Ritz restaurant, the hotel Ferienart has the traditional Swiss Art Stübli and the Italian Del Ponte, which gets good reports every year. Don Ciccio also 'serves authentic Italian food', and our regular Saas Fee reporter rates its pizzas the best in town. Other tips include the Vieux Chalet (for fondue, raclette, 'fantastic' rösti) and La Gorge ('very good Swiss food, really friendly owners').

APRES-SKI ★★★★
Lively bars and clubs

As close of play approaches, the terraces in the main street are always heaving – 'good-natured fun' at the Black Bull (eg congas) and 'a slightly more sophisticated crowd' at Zur Mühle. Lively places tipped later on include Nesti's ('love the old ski-bar ambience') and the Fee Pub ('good music, best range of draft beers'). Pic-Pic is 'a really old bar with locals drinking wine, great music', and the hotel Burgener's Skihütte is another wine-oriented bar, 'big but cosy'. The Dom Bar has live music, and is a 'lovely large space'. Popcorn ('real party place with international DJs') and Poison are popular clubs.

OFF THE SLOPES ★★★★
A mountain for pedestrians

The Hannig mountain is dedicated to walking, snowshoeing, paragliding and tobogganing. The Aqua Allalin leisure centre has a 25m pool, indoor tennis and a sunbed area. The Feeblitz 'roller-coaster-style' ride is good fun. The museums are interesting and if you like ice caves you won't want to miss the world's largest. The tourist office organizes walks every week. There are tours and tastings at the local brewery.

GETTING THERE

Air Sion 75km/ 45 miles (1hr15); Geneva 225km/ 140 miles (2hr45); Milan Malpensa 180km/110 miles (3hr); Zürich 225km/ 140 miles (3hr30)

Rail Brig (38km/ 24 miles) or Visp (27km/17 miles); regular buses from station

TOURIST OFFICE

www.saas-fee.ch

PHOTOPRESS / SAAS-FEE

The slopes above Saas Grund give a fab view of Saas-Fee's glaciers – and are well worth a visit for skiing purposes, too ↓

St Moritz

One of a kind: a panoramic high-altitude playground with as much happening off the slopes as on them

£170
RESORT PRICE INDEX

VERKEHRSVEREIN ST MORITZ

RATINGS

The mountains

Extent	★★★★★
Fast lifts	★★★★
Queues	★★★★
Terrain p'ks	★★★★
Snow	★★★★
Expert	★★★★
Intermediate	★★★★
Beginner	★★
Boarder	★★★★
X-country	★★★★★
Restaurants	★★★
Schools	★★★
Families	★★

The resort

Charm	★★
Convenience	★
Scenery	★★★★
Eating out	★★★★
Après-ski	★★★
Off-slope	★★★★★

NEWS

2015/16: The Mandra draglift serving the snowpark at mid-mountain on Corvatsch is to be replaced by a quad chair. There are also numerous other plans for the lead-up to the Alpine World Ski Championships in 2017 (to be held on Corviglia).

2014/15: The Ovaverva sports centre and spa opened in Bad, with indoor and outdoor pools, wellness area, fitness centre and restaurants.

- + Wonderful panoramic scenery
- + Extensive intermediate slopes
- + High, and fairly snow-sure
- + Off-slope diversions second to none (and a whole mountain dedicated to non-skiing activities)
- + Some good mountain restaurants, many with magnificent views

- − A sizeable town, with little traditional Alpine character and some big block buildings
- − Several unlinked mountains
- − Runs on home mountain mostly fairly easy and lacking variety
- − Can be pricey, as you'd expect from such a fashionable resort

St Moritz is Switzerland's definitive 'exclusive' winter resort: glitzy, fashionable and, above all, the place to be seen – a place for an all-round winter holiday, with an unrivalled array of wacky diversions such as cricket on snow, and countless festivals. It has long been popular with upper-crust Brits, who come for the sledging. Well, OK: for the world-famous Cresta Run, which isn't quite the same thing. But, like all such smart resorts, it makes a perfectly good destination for anyone. These days, it even has a public swimming pool.

The town of St Moritz is a bit of a blot on the landscape; but that landscape is truly spectacular. Our skiing here is regularly interrupted by the need to stand and gaze, and once installed on the right terrace we take some shifting.

THE RESORT

St Moritz is at the heart of the upper Engadin – the remote, high valley of the river En, which becomes the Austrian river Inn (as in Innsbruck). The valley bottom is filled by a chain of lakes, one of which separates the two parts of St Moritz. On a steep hillside above the lake, Dorf is the fashionable main town. Beside the lake is the more ordinary spa resort, St Moritz Bad. The skiing is in several separate sectors; only one, Corviglia, is reachable directly from the resort.

In winter the lake is used for eccentric activities including horse and greyhound racing, show jumping, polo, golf and even cricket. And there's a whole mountain (Muottas Muragl) set aside for not skiing – read 'Off the slopes' at the end of the chapter. The upper Engadin is superb for walking and cross-country skiing, which is very big here; the Engadin Ski Marathon attracts over 11,000 entries.

The Corviglia slopes are shared with Celerina, down the valley (described in this chapter). And there are other bases along the valleys.

There is a fabulously scenic railway from Zürich – a reader tips the dining car – but it's quicker to drive. A car is handy around the resort, too: the bus

service is covered by the lift pass but it gets crowded at peak times and a car greatly speeds up visits to the more distant mountains. Trips are possible to Davos and other places; you get a half-price pass in Livigno, Samnaun/Ischgl and other resorts.

Part of the attraction is that there is

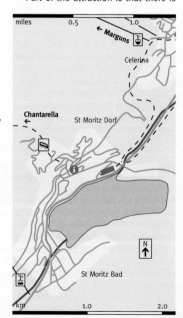

SWISS-IMAGE.CH /
CHRISTOF SONDEREGGER

↑ Muottas Muragl arguably offers the best view of the Engadin, even if it offers no skiing

KEY FACTS

Resort	1770m
	5,810ft
Slopes	1730-3305m
	5,680-10,840ft
Lifts	56
Pistes	350km
	217 miles

For Corviglia only	
Slopes	1730-3055m
	5,680-10,020ft
Lifts	22
Pistes	100km
	62 miles

a strong Italian flavour to the area – lots of Italian visitors, workers, food and wine.

VILLAGE CHARM ★★ ☆☆☆
Urban glitz instead

In the main resort centres there is little traditional Alpine character; St Moritz is very much a smooth, glitzy town rather than a cute, rustic village. Dorf has two main streets – lined with boutiques selling Rolex, Cartier, Hermes etc – a few side lanes and a small main square. Bad is less urban, and less prestigious. Many buildings in both parts are block-like.

CONVENIENCE ★ ☆☆☆☆
Bad is good – or better, at least

It's a perfectly convenient resort if you are content to ski Corviglia, stay in central Dorf and ride the funicular, or stay on the edge of Bad and use the Signal cable car. But both parts of the resort spread widely away from these lifts, and to ski other mountains transport is needed. For keen skiers, Bad is the better base – you can ski back to it from both local sectors.

SCENERY ★★★★ ☆
Fabulous panoramas

The lake-filled valley, with 4000m peaks on the Italian border, provides mesmerizing views from Corviglia, and the close-up views of Piz Bernina from Corvatsch are stunning.

THE MOUNTAINS

There are three separate areas of slopes, covered on three very clear piste maps; our maps show only the two main areas close to St Moritz (Corviglia and Corvatsch). The terrain is varied, with lots of long, wide, well-groomed runs – practically all on open slopes above the trees. There is weekly floodlit skiing.

EXTENT OF THE SLOPES ★★★★★
Three separate areas

The claimed 350km of slopes can safely be considered an exaggeration.

From St Moritz Dorf a two-stage railway goes up to **Corviglia**, a lift junction at the eastern end of a sunny and rather monotonous area of slopes facing east and south over the main valley. The peak of Piz Nair, reached from here by cable car, separates these slopes from the less sunny and more varied ones in the wide bowl above **Marguns** – and gives fabulous views across the valley to Piz Bernina. From Corviglia you can (snow permitting) head down easy paths to Dorf and Bad; at Salastrains, just above Dorf, are nursery slopes, restaurants and two hotels. There is a red run from Marguns to Celerina.

From Surlej, a few miles from St Moritz, a two-stage cable car takes you to the north-facing slopes of **Corvatsch**, which reach glacial heights.

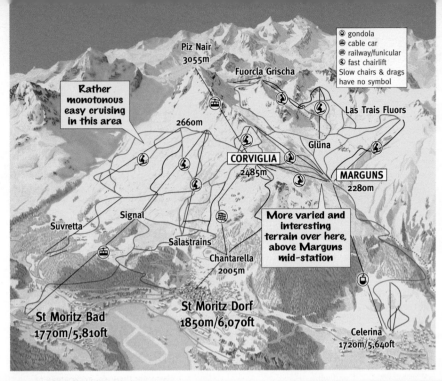

Rather monotonous easy cruising in this area

gondola
cable car
railway/funicular
fast chairlift
Slow chairs & drags have no symbol

Piz Nair
3055m

Fuorcla Grischa

Las Trais Fluors

2660m

Glüna

CORVIGLIA
2485m

MARGUNS
2280m

Signal

Suvretta

Salastrains

More varied and interesting terrain over here, above Marguns mid-station

Chantarella
2005m

St Moritz Dorf
1850m/6,07oft

St Moritz Bad
177om/5,81oft

Celerina
1720m/5,64oft

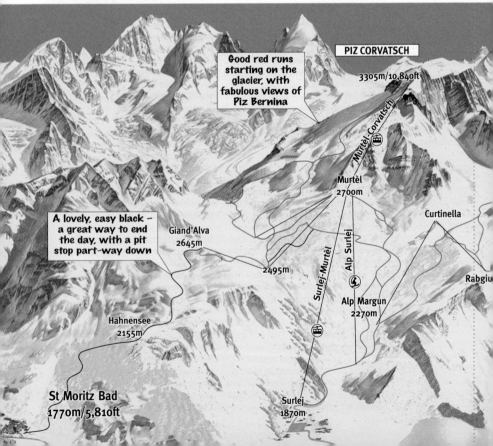

Good red runs starting on the glacier, with fabulous views of Piz Bernina

PIZ CORVATSCH

3305m/10,840ft

Murtèl-Corvatsch

Murtèl
2700m

Curtinella

Giand'Alva
2645m

A lovely, easy black – a great way to end the day, with a pit stop part-way down

2495m

Surlej-Murtèl

Alp Surlej

Rabgiu

Hahnensee
2155m

Alp Margun
2270m

St Moritz Bad
177om/5,81oft

Surlej
1870m

LIFT PASSES

Upper Engadin

Prices in francs

Age	6-day
under 13	122
13 to 17	243
18 plus	365

Free Under 6
Senior No deals
Beginner No deals

Notes Covers
Corviglia, Corvatsch,
Diavolezza-Lagalb and
Zuoz, the Engadin bus
services and stretches
of the Rhätische Bahn
railway; family
discounts

Alternative passes
Half-day and day
passes for individual
areas

From the mid-station at Murtèl you have a choice of reds to Stüvetta Giand'Alva and Alp Margun. From the latter you can work your way across the mountainside to **Furtschellas**, also reached by cable car from Sils Maria. If you're lucky with the snow, you can end the day with the splendid Hahnensee run, from the northern limit of the Corvatsch lift system at Giand'Alva down to St Moritz Bad – a black-classified run that is of red (or even blue) difficulty for 95% of its 6km length. It often opens around noon, when the snow has softened. A five-minute walk from the end of the run brings you to the cable car to Corviglia.

The third area is about 20km from St Moritz (50 minutes by bus) and consists of two peaks reached by cable cars starting from car parks (and little else) on opposite sides of the Bernina pass road to Italy. **Diavolezza** (2980m) has excellent north-facing pistes of 900m vertical. **Lagalb** (2895m) is a smaller area with quite challenging slopes – west-facing,

850m vertical. We're sorry to hear that the coming season 2015/16 may be Lagalb's last – it's a splendid place to end the afternoon. From the beginning of March the Diavolezza cable car runs until 5pm.

FAST LIFTS ★★★★
Plenty of options
St Moritz has invested heavily in upgrading lifts, especially on Corviglia and Marguns, where there are fast chairs all over the place. Corvatsch still has some T-bars, though. The area as a whole has a lot of modest-sized cable cars.

QUEUES ★★★★
Not much of a problem
A recent visitor reported short queues for the Piz Nair cable car, but most reporters have had no problems, even over Easter weekend.

TERRAIN PARKS ★★★★
World-class facilities
The park on Corviglia has countless features and multiple lines to suit every standard of freestyler. And there's a 400m family fun slope integrating easy obstacles in a snowcross course. The Freestyle Park on Corvatsch now includes a 7m half-pipe as well as big jumps, an air bag, rails and a snowcross.

SNOW RELIABILITY ★★★★
Improved by good snowmaking
This corner of the Alps has a rather dry climate, but the altitude means that any precipitation is likely to be snowy. The top runs at Corvatsch are glacial and require good snow depths to be safe. There is snowmaking in each sector, and grooming is 'magnificent – the best I've seen outside North America'.

FOR EXPERTS ★★★★
Dispersed challenges
Few of the black runs are genuinely steep; those at Lagalb and Diavolezza are the most challenging. But there is good off-piste terrain, and it doesn't get tracked out. There is an excellent north-facing slope immediately above Marguns, for example, and tough routes from Piz Nair and the Corvatsch summit. More serious expeditions can be undertaken – eg the Roseg valley from Corvatsch.

Out at Diavolezza, a very popular and spectacular off-piste glacier route

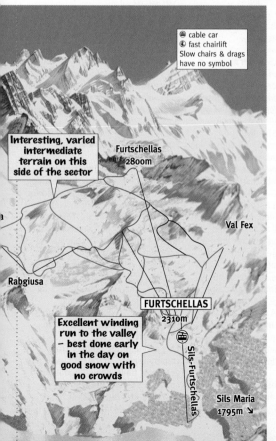

cable car
fast chairlift
Slow chairs & drags
have no symbol

Interesting, varied intermediate terrain on this side of the sector

Furtschellas
2800m

Val Fex

Rabgiusa

FURTSCHELLAS
2310m

Excellent winding run to the valley – best done early in the day on good snow with no crowds

Sils-Furtschellas

Sils Maria
1795m ↘

No trip to St Moritz is really complete without a visit to the Cresta Run. It's the last bastion of Britishness (not long ago, payment had to be made in sterling) and male chauvinism (women need an invitation from a club member). Any adult male can pay 600 Swiss francs (around £425) for five rides (helmet, boots, pads etc included). You lie on a toboggan (called a 'skeleton') and hurtle head-first down a sheet ice gully from St Moritz to Celerina. Watch out for Shuttlecock corner – that's where most of the accidents happen.

ENGADIN ST MORITZ / SWISS-IMAGE.CH / JR LARRAMAN

goes off the back beneath Piz Bernina to Morteratsch. There's a 30-minute plod at first, then it's downhill, with splendid views. It is not difficult, but may take you close to crevasses; we wouldn't do it without a guide, although of course people do. On the front of the mountain, the Gletscher chair accesses an excellent shady run down Val d'Arlas. At Lagalb, there's off-piste down the back towards La Rosa (again, a guide is needed).

There are a few firms offering heli-drops on Fuorcla Chamuotsch, for runs back to the Engadin valley.

FOR INTERMEDIATES ★★★★☆
Good but flattering
St Moritz is great for intermediates. Most pistes on Corviglia are very well groomed, easyish reds that could well have been classified blue – ideal cruising terrain or blandly monotonous, depending on your point of view. The Marguns bowl is more interesting, including some easy blacks and the pleasant Val Schattain run away from the lifts.

The Corvatsch-Furtschellas area is altogether more varied, interesting and challenging, as well as higher and wider. There are excellent red runs in both parts of the area, including the runs from the Corvatsch glacier, which give fabulous views, and descents to the two valley stations – particularly the Furtschellas one. Do these in the morning, and at the end of the day return to St Moritz Bad via the lovely Hahnensee run – an easy black. There isn't much easy skiing at Corvatsch; some of the blues (eg the lower bit of 19) should be red.

Diavolezza is mostly intermediate stuff, too. There is an easy open slope at the top, served by the Gletscher

chair, and a splendid long intermediate run back down under the lift. The link to Lagalb requires use of parts of a black run, but it is of red gradient. (Plans to improve this link seem to have stalled, and are now unlikely to be revived.) Lagalb has more challenging pistes – two reds and a genuine black.

FOR BEGINNERS ★★☆☆☆
Not ideal
Beginners start up at Salastrains or Corviglia, or slightly out of town at Suvretta. Celerina has good, broad nursery slopes at village level and a child-friendly lift. But progression from the nursery slopes to longer runs is rather awkward – there are few blue runs without a more difficult reddish section. And you have to buy a full lift pass.

FOR BOARDERS ★★★★☆
Very welcoming
The terrain in St Moritz is boarder-friendly. The great thing for freeriders is that terrain can stay untracked for days. Freeride tours are available through the ski schools. There are several draglifts on Corvatsch, but most of St Moritz's lifts are chairs, gondolas, cable cars and trains; beginners will enjoy the rolling blue runs, and intermediates will relish the red runs. There are good parks on both Corviglia and Corvatsch.

FOR CROSS-COUNTRY ★★★★★
Excellent
This is one of the premier cross-country regions in the Alps, with 200km of trails, some floodlit, amid splendid scenery and with fairly reliable snow. But the best bases are away from St Moritz.

MOUNTAIN RESTAURANTS ★★★
Some special places

Mountain restaurants are plentiful, and include some of the most glamorous in Europe. Not surprisingly, prices can be high – check the menu before you install yourself. The piste maps have pictures and phone numbers of the restaurants.

Editors' choice El Paradiso, secluded at the extreme southern end of Corviglia, has it all: breathtaking views from the big, tiered terrace, a tastefully renovated, slightly trendy interior, great service and top-notch food. Yes, it is very, very expensive. Fuorcla Surlej, on the Fuorcla run from the Corvatsch glacier, could not be more different: a remote refuge serving basic but satisfying food, sometimes very slowly. But the view of Piz Bernina and Piz Roseg from the snowy ramshackle 'terrace' is one of the best in the skiing universe; a small sample is reproduced below.

Worth knowing about On Corviglia, the top lift station houses several restaurants run under the umbrella title of Mathis Food Affairs, including the famously swanky Marmite. Not our cup of tea, but a trusted reporter recorded his 'best ever skiing lunch'

Club Med
THE MOST COMPREHENSIVE
SKI PACKAGE ON THE MARKET

Saint-Moritz Roi Soleil 4

020 8313 3999
Skiline.co.uk

Skiline.co.uk

here. Lej da la Pêsch, behind Piz Nair, is a cosy spot, better for a snowy day than a sunny one (no view). Lower down, the more atmospheric Chasellas is also recommended. On the Corvatsch side, the cosy, rustic Alpetta has been tipped in the past, and the varied menu looked good to us on our last visit. Hahnensee, on the run of that name to Bad, is a splendid place to pause in the afternoon sun. At Diavolezza, the Berghaus is tipped by a reader this year for its wide menu and reasonable prices.

SCHOOLS AND GUIDES ★★★
Internal competition

There are two main schools, Swiss and Suvretta. Past reports on both have been mainly positive. Other hotels have private instructors, too.

FOR FAMILIES ★★
Choose a hotel with a nursery

There's a kindergarten and children's restaurant at Salastrains, and we'd be inclined to stay up there if you can afford it – much more child-friendly than the towns. Some hotel nurseries are open to non-residents. Don't forget Club Med as a possibility.

STAYING THERE

There is a 'very comfortable' Club Med with 'excellent food'; it has its own mountain restaurants for lunch on the main slope sectors – a neat way to steer round the St Moritz prices. The tourist office can provide a list of apartments.

Hotels From Switzerland's highest concentration of 5-stars, we allow ourselves just one.

★★★★★**Kempinski** Unfashionable, but spacious location in Bad, and less formal than the other 5-stars.

★★★★**Crystal** Austere-looking central place with contrasting traditional rooms. Wellness facilities.

SNOWPIX.COM / BEN RILEY

One of the cheapest mountain restaurants, Fuorcla Surlej, also has the best view – one of the best you'll find anywhere ↓

****Margna** Near railway and bus stations: 'Staff could not have been more helpful.'

****Nira Alpina** Cool 'design' hotel out at Surlej, right by the Corvatsch cable-car station. 'Great food, fab bar; faultless.'

****Steffani** 'Slightly old-fashioned', family-owned hotel in the centre of Dorf. 'Plain rooms (some with lake views) but lovely modern spa/pool complex.'

***Hauser** Central in Dorf. Starkly modern after recent makeover. Tipped by a reader for B&B, but 'good-value restaurant suffers from excessive demand'. Focal après-ski bar.

***Laudinella** In Bad. Cool decor; six varied restaurants. Fitness room.

At altitude The 3-star Salastrains is on the lower slopes of Corviglia, with great views.

EATING OUT ★★★★☆
Mostly chic and expensive

A lot of restaurants here are very pricey. We like the three smooth, expensive restaurants in the Chesa Veglia (an outpost of Badrutt's hotel): 'Nice to go somewhere with Alpine atmosphere,' says a 2014 visitor. A top, world-class restaurant is Bumanns Chesa Pirani, a fine old house out of town in La Punt. A couple of years back we had an excellent dinner at the charming, polished hotel Bellavista in Surlej.

Of course, you can eat more cheaply, usually by going for basic Italian. The hotels Laudinella and Sonne, in Bad, both have wood-fired pizza ovens; the Laudinella has five other restaurants too. For something completely different and unlikely, La Baracca is a big shed in the car park of the Signal cable car doing simple but thoroughly good food in a canteen-like setting.

An evening up at Muottas Muragl offers spectacular views, a splendid sunset and dinner.

APRES-SKI ★★★☆☆
Caters for all ages

There's a big variety of après-skiing age groups here. The fur coat count is high – people come to St Moritz to be seen. For tea and good cakes head for Hanselmann's. The Roo bar terrace outside the hotel Hauser is a popular après drinking spot.

Bobby's Pub attracts a young crowd, as does the loud music of the Stübli, one of the bars in the hotel Schweizerhof: the others are the Muli, with dancing, and the chic Piano Bar. At the Steffani a 2014 visitor found the Cresta Bar 'lively but very smoky', while the Cava below it is louder and younger. We don't get many reports on the late-night scene. The jazz night at the Kulm is 'great for people-watching'. Two popular discos are Vivai and King's at Badrutt's Palace (jackets and ties required). If you need to splash even more cash, try the casino.

OFF THE SLOPES ★★★★★
Excellent variety of pastimes

Even if you lack the bravado for the Cresta Run, there is lots to do. In midwinter the snow-covered lake provides a playground for events such as polo, horse racing and cricket, but then activities are limited as the lake starts to thaw.

There's an annual 'gourmet festival', with chefs from all over the world. Of course, the shops are fantastic, for those with flexible plastic. There are 150km of well-marked walking trails (a map is available). Muottas Muragl is a mountain set aside for not skiing, with funicular access to snowshoeing and tobogganing and stunning panoramic views.

Other options are paragliding, indoor tennis and curling. A new swimming pool complex with spa and wellness facilities (Ovaverva) opened in 2014. Reporters rave about the scenic train trips north towards Chur and south to Italy.

LINKED RESORT – 1720m

CELERINA

At the bottom end of the famous Cresta Run from St Moritz Dorf, Celerina is an appealing base if you want a quiet time – it is unpretentious and villagey, but lacks a central focus (and has very few shops). It has good access to the Corviglia-Marguns sector – a gondola to Marguns. The village spreads quite widely, with a lot of second homes, many owned by Italians (the upper part is known as Piccolo Milano). There are some appealing small hotels – like the 4-star Chesa Rosatsch. The modern Inn Lodge is good value – with a mix of rooms, studios with kitchenettes and dormitories. The Freestyle School focuses on park practice.

GETTING THERE

Air Zürich 220km/ 135 miles (3hr15); Friedrichshafen 210km/130 miles (3hr15); Upper Engadin airport 5km/ 3 miles

Rail Mainline station in resort

TOURIST OFFICES

St Moritz
www.stmoritz.ch
Celerina
www.engadin.
stmoritz.ch/celerina/

Val d'Anniviers

Exceptionally cute, unspoiled villages beneath high, snow-sure slopes. Sounds perfect? Well, there are some drawbacks ...

£135
RESORT PRICE INDEX

TOP 10 RATINGS

Extent	★★
Fast lifts	★
Queues	★★★★
Snow	★★★★
Expert	★★★★
Intermediate	★★★
Beginner	★★★
Charm	★★★★★
Convenience	★★
Scenery	★★★★

NEWS

2015/16: A new six-pack will replace the Forêt draglift above St Luc, greatly improving access to the Chandolin slopes from St Luc. This second fast chair in St Luc-Chandolin comes a decade after the first.

KEY FACTS

Resorts	1340-2000m
	4,400-6,560ft
Slopes	1340-3000m
	4,400-9,840ft
Lifts	43
Pistes	220km
	137 miles

- ➕ Charming, unspoiled villages
- ➕ Four varied ski areas, linked in two pairs, plus a tiny fifth
- ➕ Excellent, extensive off-piste
- ➕ Reliable snow-cover
- ➕ No crowds or queues

- ➖ Most lifts are T-bars; few fast chairs
- ➖ Very quiet villages; dead, even
- ➖ Almost entirely open slopes
- ➖ Travelling between the two main areas is a slow business

Some people will find the slow pace of things here irritating – although there are some modern lifts in key spots (including a new cable car that links two of the four ski areas for the first time), you spend a lot of your time riding draglifts and very little time riding fast chairs. But there are compensations – most of the villages have unspoiled rustic cores, with old wooden houses lining narrow lanes. Approach the area with the right attitude and you may find it all quite a refreshing change from big-name resorts with high-speed everything.

The Val d'Anniviers runs almost due south from the Rhône valley at Sierre. The narrow road up to the resorts has in places been carved out of sheer rock faces. There are five charming main villages with lots of old wooden houses and barns, narrow paths and lanes and few shops. Some more modern development has taken place around them, but it is generally tasteful and low-rise.

On the morning-sun side of the valley, the slopes of Zinal have long been linked to those of Grimentz by a long, isolated black run, but the two resorts are now also linked by a big cable car – forming a fair-sized linked ski area, with 110km of pistes. On the afternoon-sun side, the slopes of Chandolin and St Luc are linked at high and low altitude, and offer 75km of pistes. Although these two main areas are not far apart and are served by free bus, the trip involves a change in Vissoie, and takes about an hour.

Vercorin is a smaller, separate area with just 35km of pistes, and for most visitors is irrelevant – you get there via Sierre, down in the Rhône valley. Except at Vercorin, nearly all the slopes are above the treeline and there's a lot of skiing above 2400m, which usually means good snow. All of the individual areas are small, but they add up to a decent amount.

The valley is noted for off-piste, and we have a strong recommendation this year for guiding outfit Grimentz-Zinal Backcountry Adventures, run by well-known British guide Nick Parks.

1650m / 2000m
ST LUC-CHANDOLIN

These are the sunniest of the main ski resort villages, a few km apart, and they share a well-linked area of slopes. St Luc also has the attraction of a fabulous, characterful old hotel. A funicular goes up from the edge of St Luc; from the edge of Chandolin you have a choice of a fast quad for Chandolin's home slopes and a slow triple to the edge of the St Luc slopes, meeting the new Forêt six-pack starting well above St Luc. Both main lift stations are served by the free ski-buses. The slopes face west to south-west, so the snow suffers from the sun. Apart from these three chairs, all the lifts are drags.

The pistes suit beginners and intermediates best, though there are two black runs, five short itinerary routes (including one that we reckon is the steepest marked run in the Alps) and a gnarly freeride area where competitions are held. There are some testing reds, but in general the slopes are gentle, easy cruising territory. A highlight is the long, easy red run of 1230m vertical from Bella Tola at 3000m, away from all the lifts down to a bar and ski-bus stop – a great way to end the day. There's a good beginner area and a terrain park near the top of the St Luc funicular.

There are some good mountain restaurants with fine views. Above Chandolin the tiny Illhorn has a limited menu but a cosy panelled room (and

Combe Durand

Corne de Sorebois
2895m

Sorebois
2440m

ZINAL

Zinal
1670m/5,480ft

Piste du Chamois

Mottec

Bendolla
2130m

GRIMENTZ

Grimentz
1570m/5,150ft

Roc d'Orzi
2855m

Bella Tola
3000m/
9,840ft

288

St-Jean

2770m

St Luc
1650m/5,410ft

Tignousa
218om

2470m

ST LUC-CHANDOLIN

Vissoie

Mt Major
2375m

Illhorn
2600m

VERCORIN

Chandolin
2000m/6,560ft

Vercorin
1340m/4,400ft

Chalais

To
Geneva
→

⚊ gondola
⚊ cable car
⚊ railway/funicular
⚊ fast chairlift
Slow chairs & drags
have no symbol

Sierre
560m/1,840ft

LIFT PASSES

Val d'Anniviers

Prices in francs

Age	6-day
under 16	168
16 to 64	280
65 plus	252
Free Under 6	

Notes Discounts for students and under 25. Covers St Luc-Chandolin, Zinal, Grimentz and Vercorin

Alternative pass
St Luc-Chandolin and Vercorin only

fab pear tart); the Tsapé is a smart, stark place, high up, with good local cuisine; above St Luc, the Bella Tola is a traditional, basic table-service hut.

Both Chandolin and St Luc are fairly spread out with a limited choice of places to eat. But St Luc has a cute, compact old centre with a small outdoor après-ski bar. The 4-star hotel Bella Tola is just a few strides from here. Built in 1859, it has been beautifully renovated by its current owners, with a fine spa, sunny terrace, and good restaurant. We enjoyed staying there hugely.

1670m
ZINAL

The locals 'are a highlight, with their warmth and charm', in this small and rather plain village near the head of the valley. Its local slopes have stunning views of high peaks including the Matterhorn.

A modern cable car goes to Sorebois at 2440m, the hub of the ski area. Most of the slopes face roughly east and keep their snow well.

The runs are mainly short (some only 200m or 300m vertical) but include some good reds – our favourites are those from Combe Durand at the edge of the ski area, served by a steepish draglift that also accesses a freeride area. The one fast chairlift serves wide and gentle blue runs, ideal for novices. The two short black runs are really of red steepness. There is a longer red run (with a black variant on the lower part) back to the

village. And there's great off-piste in bowls between the pistes (and, with a guide, off the back of the ski area to the Moiry dam and on to Grimentz).

From the top of the area, Piste du Chamois is a real highlight – a long, mainly easy black run of almost 1300m vertical down a shady deserted bowl with lots of accessible off-piste, ending with a woodland path to Grimentz.

Zinal is popular with families and there's a good beginner area and children's snow garden.

Zinal has a handful of hotels. The central 2-star Pointe de Zinal does excellent food and the 2-star Le Trift is 'comfortable, with adequate but small rooms and good food'. There are also several catered chalets.

A regular visitor pronounces the Alpina, Besso and Ferme his favourite village restaurants. The Bar e Vox wine bar is 'appreciated by a more mature market than Le Pub attracts along the street'.

1570m
GRIMENTZ

Grimentz has a richly deserved reputation for its extensive off-piste. Above its very cute old village is a small area of varied pistes.

The village is spread out on quite a steep slope with a lot of new building. There is a marked separation between the cute old centre – lots of tiny old barns and narrow paths – and the skiers' accommodation. Much of this is conveniently close to the gondola up to Bendolla at 2130m – but some is

---

Selected chalets in Val d'Anniviers ADVERTISEMENT

MOUNTAIN HEAVEN *www.mountainheaven.co.uk*   **T 0151 625 1921**

Mountain Heaven has a wonderful selection of self-catered chalets and apartments in Grimentz, all with WIFI and ranging from two to five bedrooms. We are financially bonded and offer all-inclusive prices with no hidden extras. Included in our portfolio are Le Lievre, a stunning apartment right by the piste, Chalet Mélèze, a detached chalet with a commanding position, Les Vieux Chalets no 2 & 7, which are right in the village centre, and Sur Les Pistes, an apartment situated on the piste itself.

Email: info@mountainheaven.co.uk

STUNNING BALCONY VIEWS ↑

↑ Grand views across
the valley from sunny
St Luc-Chandolin to
not quite so sunny
Zinal and Grimentz
SNOWPIX.COM / CHRIS GILL

less conveniently placed on the opposite side of the old village.

Bendolla has a good, roped-off beginner area and snow garden for kids, and above it are two main sectors. On the right as you look up are easy blue and red runs. On the left are steeper and quieter runs, including the long Piste Lona, which goes from the top to almost the bottom of the mountain (1300m vertical), right at the edge of the ski area; it deserves its black classification and is interestingly varied. The main run to the village is quite steep too, but you can ride the gondola down.

The real attraction for experts is the extensive off-piste. There are lots of options, including over 1500m vertical down to Vercorin, returning from there to the village of St-Jean, a bus ride from Grimentz. 'The tour from the top of the system at Orzival, down the back side all the way to the Rhône valley, is one of the most fun rides I have had,' said a 2014 reporter. 'It is quite steep with some perfect tree skiing.'

On our last visit, in poor visibility, we had a great day skiing off-piste in the trees with a guide from the International ski school. We have had positive reports on this school in the past, most recently last year.

Our favourite mountain restaurant is the rustic Etable du Marais below Grands Plans, where we have had good rösti and pasta dishes. We've also had good pasta at the self-service Orzival. The functional main Bendolla restaurant is mainly self-service, but it

also has a small table-service section where we have had an enjoyable meal.

As the lifts close, Chez Florioz on the piste just above the village is the place for a drink. The best restaurants are probably those in the main hotels. But we have also enjoyed an excellent meal at Arlequin (a pizzeria). Bar le Country is a lively sports bar.

We have had comfortable stays and good food at the two 3-star hotels – the Alpina, almost opposite the gondola, and the less convenient Cristal. The 'comfortable' and 'good-value' 2-star Becs de Bosson is run by a mountain guide.

UK tour operator Mountain Heaven has some smart chalets and apartments, which can be rented on a catered or self-catered basis. A satisfied reporter who stayed in their Sur Les Pistes apartment said: 'Perfect location, very good accommodation, well priced.'

TOURIST OFFICES

Val d'Anniviers
www.valdanniviers.ch
Grimentz
www.grimentz.ch
St Luc
www.saint-luc.ch
Vercorin
www.vercorin.ch
Zinal
www.zinal.ch
Chandolin
www.chandolin.ch

1340m

VERCORIN

The smallest area of slopes in the region (we skied virtually all the pistes in 90 minutes), and isolated from other resorts.
The pretty village of Vercorin, perched on a shelf overlooking the Rhône valley, is reached by a winding road or by a cable car from Chalais, just outside Sierre. This is followed by a free ski-bus to a revamped two-stage gondola. The slopes suit intermediates best and were deserted when we last visited.

VERBIER TOURIST OFFICE

Verbier

Big, chalet-style resort that attracts powder hounds from all over the world – and big-spending night owls from Geneva

£160
RESORT PRICE INDEX

RATINGS

The mountains

Extent	★★★★★
Fast lifts	★★★★
Queues	★★★
Terrain p'ks	★★★
Snow	★★★
Expert	★★★★★
Intermediate	★★★
Beginner	★★
Boarder	★★★
X-country	★
Restaurants	★★★
Schools	★★★★★
Families	★★★

The resort

Charm	★★★
Convenience	★★
Scenery	★★★★
Eating out	★★★★
Après-ski	★★★★★
Off-slope	★★★

NEWS

2015/16: The City Ski Championships will be held here for the first time (in early February). A new 10-room B&B hotel is due to open in Le Châble, in the valley below Verbier.

2014/15: The Etoile Rouge nightclub and supper club opened.

KEY FACTS

Resort	1500m
	4,920ft

4 Valleys area	
Slopes	1500-3330m
	4,920-10,930ft
Lifts	92
Pistes	412km
	256 miles

Verbier, Bruson and Tzoumaz/Savoleyres sectors only (covered by Verbier pass)

Slopes	1500-3025m
	4,920-9,920ft
Lifts	34
Pistes	195km
	121 miles

➕ Extensive, challenging slopes with a lot of off-piste and long bump runs
➕ Upper slopes offer a real high-mountain feel, plus great views
➕ Sizeable, animated village in a sunny, panoramic setting
➕ Lively, varied nightlife

➖ Some overcrowded areas
➖ Sunny lower slopes will always be a problem, even with snowmaking
➖ Some long walks/rides to lifts
➖ Expensive bars and restaurants
➖ The 4 Valleys network is much less wonderful than it sounds

For serious off-piste routes and for mogul fields, Verbier is one of the world's cult resorts. It has other attractions, too: for vibrant après/nightlife it is difficult to beat, and it has some lovely swanky chalets and hotels. But what if those are not the things that float your boat? In particular, what if you're basically a mileage-hungry piste skier who maybe dabbles in powder, like so many Brits? Well, Verbier doesn't measure up well against other big-name resorts.

The experience of piste skiing in Verbier has been much improved over many years – the lifts are better, the slopes have been improved and are less congested, the signs and maps are easier to follow. But there remains the question of quantity. Drawing on the work of Christoph Schrahe, discussed in our feature article on piste extent, we reckon the local slopes of Verbier amount to less than half the claimed 195km. Leaving aside the daunting itinerary runs, an energetic skier could cover these local pistes in a day.

Yes, Verbier is part of the 4 Valleys network, doubling the piste extent. But the 4 Valleys is nothing to get excited about – it's an inconveniently sprawling affair, with lots of tedious links. It's not even a continuous piste network – to get out of the Verbier area you must ski a serious mogulled itinerary route or ride a lift down to Tortin.

THE RESORT

Verbier enjoys an impressive setting on a wide, sunny balcony facing spectacular peaks. It's a fashionable, informal, very lively place that teems with cosmopolitan visitors. Most are younger than typical visitors to other big Swiss resorts.

The resort is at one end of a long, strung-out series of interconnected slopes, optimistically branded the 4 Valleys and linking Verbier to Nendaz, Veysonnaz, Thyon and other small resorts.

These other resorts have their own pros and cons. All are much less lively in the evening than Verbier, and are appreciably cheaper places to stay. Some are more sensible bases for those who plan to stick to pistes rather than venture off-piste – the Veysonnaz-Thyon sector, in particular, is much more intermediate-friendly than Verbier. As a base for exploration of the whole 4 Valleys, only tiny Siviez

is much of an advance on Verbier.

You can also stay down in the valley village of Le Châble, which has gondolas up to Verbier and to the small resort of Bruson, and makes an excellent base. There's more on all these places at the end of the chapter.

Chamonix and Champéry are within reach by car. So are a few small resorts near Orsières, about 45 minutes away: Champex-Lac, La Fouly and Vichères-Liddes (covered in our

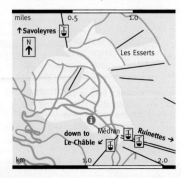

resort directory at the back of the book). But a car can be a bit of a nuisance in Verbier itself. Parking is very tightly controlled; your lodging may not have enough space for all guests' cars, which means a hike from the free parking at the sports centre – or paying for parking.

Danni Sports was praised by a recent reporter: 'Extremely helpful and friendly, good choice of equipment for hire, and they do a half-price ski-service happy hour mid-week.'

VILLAGE CHARM ★★★☆☆
Busy upmarket chalet town
The resort is an amorphous sprawl of chalet-style buildings. Most of the shops and hotels (but not chalets) are set around the Place Centrale and along the sloping streets stretching both down the hill and up to the main lift station at Médran, 500m away. At close of play this street, in particular, is buzzing with après-ski activity. These central areas get unpleasantly packed with cars at weekends.

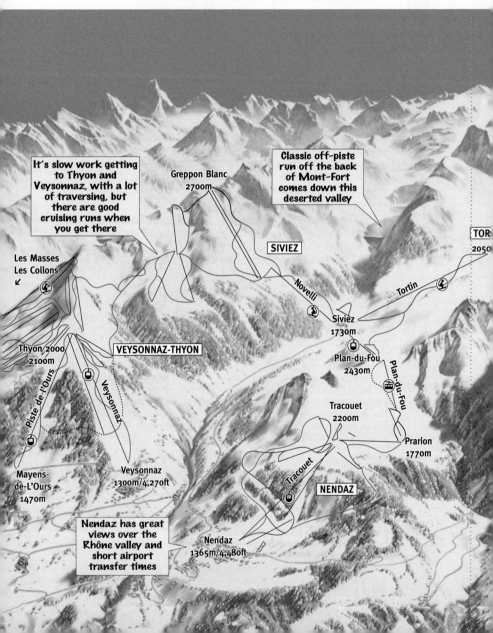

It's slow work getting to Thyon and Veysonnaz, with a lot of traversing, but there are good cruising runs when you get there

Classic off-piste run off the back of Mont-Fort comes down this deserted valley

Greppon Blanc 2700m

SIVIEZ

TOR 2050

Les Masses Les Collons

Novelli

Tortin

Siviez 1730m

Thyon 2000 2100m

VEYSONNAZ-THYON

Veysonnaz

Piste de l'Ours

Plan-du-Fou 2430m

Plan-du-Fou

Tracouet 2200m

Prarion 1770m

Mayens-de-L'Ours 1470m

Veysonnaz 1300m/4,270ft

Tracouet

NENDAZ

Nendaz has great views over the Rhône valley and short airport transfer times

Nendaz 1365m/4,480ft

CONVENIENCE ★★☆☆☆
Pick your spot

It's a sprawling resort where most people suffer some inconvenience – alleviated by the free buses, which run on several routes until 8pm. They're generally frequent and efficient, but get overcrowded at times, and some areas have quite an infrequent service. You can store your equipment at Médran, which helps you cope with the overcrowding.

The Médran lift station is a walkable distance from the Place Centrale, so staying between these two points has attractions. If nightlife is not a priority, staying somewhere near the upper fringes of the village may mean that you can almost ski to your door, though skiing from it is less likely. More chalets are built each year, with many newer properties inconveniently situated along the road to the lift base for the secondary Savoleyres area, about 1.5km from Médran.

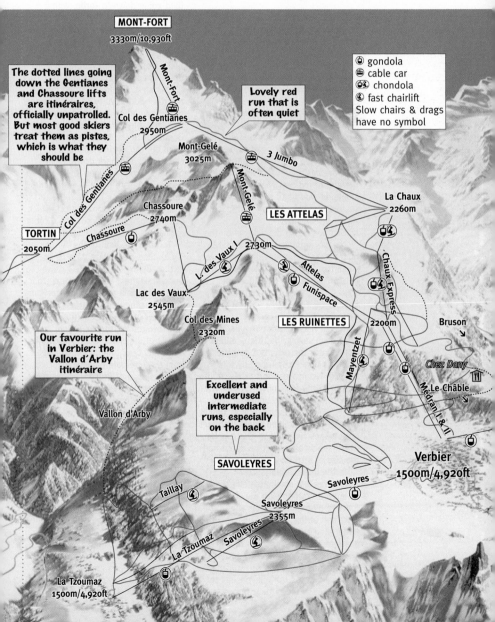

MONT-FORT
3330m/10,930ft

The dotted lines going down the Gentianes and Chassoure lifts are itinéraires, officially unpatrolled. But most good skiers treat them as pistes, which is what they should be

Col des Gentianes
2950m

Mont-Gelé
3025m

Lovely red run that is often quiet

3 Jumbo

La Chaux
2260m

Chassoure
2740m

LES ATTELAS

TORTIN
2050m

Chassoure

L. des Vaux I
2730m

Chaux Express

Attelas

Funispace

Lac des Vaux
2545m

LES RUINETTES

Col des Mines
2320m

2200m

Bruson

Mayentzet

Chez Dany

Le Châble

Our favourite run in Verbier: the Vallon d'Arby itinéraire

Médran I & II

Vallon d'Arby

Excellent and underused intermediate runs, especially on the back

SAVOLEYRES

Savoleyres

Verbier
1500m/4,920ft

Taillay

Savoleyres
2355m

La Tzoumaz

Savoleyres

La Tzoumaz
1500m/4,920ft

Legend:
- gondola
- cable car
- chondola
- fast chairlift
- Slow chairs & drags have no symbol

ALPINE ANSWERS
The UK's No.1 Chalet Specialist

For choice and service look no further!

alpineanswers.co.uk
call: 020 7801 1080
ABTA

SCENERY ★★★★
A circle of Alpine peaks
Verbier is surrounded by stunning Alpine scenery; from the top of Mont-Fort there are impressive views in all directions, including Mont Blanc to the west and the Matterhorn to the east.

THE MOUNTAINS

Essentially this is high-mountain terrain. There are wooded slopes directly above the village, but the runs here are basically just a way home at the end of the day. There is more sheltered woodland skiing in other sectors of the 4 Valleys – particularly above Veysonnaz.

Signposting to the villages on the pistes has improved, and the piste map names some runs, though in very small type. However, piste names are still not posted on the mountain.

EXTENT OF THE SLOPES ★★★★★
Smaller than claimed
Since our first edition 20 years ago we have been saying that the 4 Valleys exaggerates the extent of its pistes. This was finally confirmed by the Schrahe report (read our piste extent feature at the front of the book). The 4 Valleys has been claiming 412km, while Schrahe puts the total at 188km, or 46% of the claimed figure. Verbier's local slopes work out to about 90km, which seems about right – about half the size of Kitzbühel, for example.

In the local Verbier sector, **Savoleyres** is a small area effectively isolated from the major network, reached by a gondola from the north-west end of the village. This area is underrated and generally underused. It has open, sunny slopes on the front side, and long, pleasantly wooded, shadier runs on the back. You can take a catwalk across from Savoleyres to the foot of Verbier's main slopes.

The main slopes are served by lifts from Médran, at the opposite end of the village. Two gondolas rise to Les Ruinettes and then a gondola and chairlift continue to **Attelas**. From Attelas a small cable car goes up to Mont-Gelé, for steep off-piste runs only. If you head back down instead, you can go west to Les Ruinettes, south to La Chaux or north to Lac des Vaux. From Lac des Vaux chairs go to Attelas and Chassoure, the top of a wide, steep and shady off-piste field going down to **Tortin**, with a gondola back.

You can also ride a chondola from Les Ruinettes to the sunny, easy slopes of La Chaux. At the bottom of these slopes a jumbo cable car goes up to **Col des Gentianes** and the glacier area. The lovely, often quiet, red run back down to La Chaux is one of our favourites. A second, much smaller cable car goes up from Gentianes to the **Mont-Fort** glacier. From the top, there's only a long, steep black run back down. From Gentianes you can head down on another off-piste route to Tortin; the whole north-facing run from the top to Tortin is almost 1300m vertical, which can be moguls top to bottom. A cable car returns to Col des Gentianes.

Tortin is the limit of the Verbier lifts – you need a 4 Valleys pass to go any further. Below Tortin is the gateway to the rest of the 4 Valleys, **Siviez**. From here, a gondola takes you up to Plan-du-Fou for the long, thin **Nendaz** sector. A fast quad heads the other way towards **Veysonnaz-Thyon**, via a couple of drags and a lot of catwalks. Allow plenty of time to get to and from these remote corners.

The slopes of **Bruson**, across the valley from Verbier, are now very easy to reach via the gondola from Le Châble and are described briefly at the end of this chapter.

FAST LIFTS ★★★★
Locally fine
The main access lifts are gondolas and chairs. Further afield, more upgrades are needed to improve links throughout the 4 Valleys (especially between Siviez and Veysonnaz-Thyon).

QUEUES ★★★
Not the problem they were
Queues have been greatly eased by investment in powerful new lifts and have barely been a problem for

↑ Verbier has a lovely sunny setting on a broad shelf, with fine views to the French border

VERBIER ST BERNARD / YVES GARNEAU

LIFT PASSES

4 Vallees Ski Pass

Prices in francs

Age	6-day
under 14	178
14 to 24	302
25 to 64	355
65 plus	302

Free Under 6; over 77
Beginner Limited pass 24 francs

Notes Covers Siviez, Nendaz, Veysonnaz and Thyon; part-day passes; family reductions

Alternative passes
Local Verbier pass covering Verbier, Mont-Fort, Bruson and La Tzoumaz

reporters over the past few years. There may be queues at Médran if Sunday visitors fill the gondola from Le Châble, but they shift quickly.

Queues still occur for old lifts in the other 4 Valleys resorts ('always queues for the Greppon Blanc lifts'), and the quad at Siviez gets busy at peak times and if the weather is poor. Bruson may have queues at its old lifts if the gondola from Le Châble becomes popular. Our one reporter on Bruson last year was more concerned about the poor reliability of those lifts, which sound like they are in terminal decline.

TERRAIN PARKS ★★★
Expert and beginner options
The Swatch Snowpark, Verbier's main freestyle area, is at La Chaux. It has all the usual features, with separate lines for varying levels – blue, red and black – and a giant airbag.

SNOW RELIABILITY ★★★
Improved snowmaking
The slopes of the Mont-Fort glacier always have good snow, naturally. The runs to Tortin are normally snow-sure, too. But nearly all of this terrain is steep and mogulled, and much of it is formally off-piste. Most of Verbier's main local slopes face south or west – so they can be in poor condition at times. Snowmaking now covers the home runs from Attelas to the village, and the slopes of La Chaux. At Veysonnaz-Thyon snowmaking now covers 80% of the area. We have been

very impressed with its use on the runs down to Mayens-de-L'Ours and to Veysonnaz. Piste grooming is good.

FOR EXPERTS ★★★★★
The main attraction
Verbier has some superb tough slopes, many of them off-piste and needing a guide – read our feature panel. There are few black pistes; most steep runs are instead classified as itinéraires, which means 'marked, not maintained, not controlled' – so you should not ski them alone. They are said to be closed if unsafe, but this is not the formal position; all very unsatisfactory. The black pistes that do exist are mostly like nearby reds. The front face of Mont-Fort is an exception: a long mogul field, with a choice of gradient from steep on skier's left to intimidatingly steep on skier's right. The World Cup run (Piste de l'Ours) at Veysonnaz is a steepish red, ideal for really speeding down when in good nick, but often icy. The two most popular itinéraires to Tortin are both excellent in their different ways. The one from Chassoure starts with a rocky traverse at the top and is then normally one huge, steep, wide mogul field. The north-facing one from Gentianes is longer, less steep, but feels much more of an adventure (keep left for shallower slopes and better snow).

The improved accessibility of the Bruson slopes will encourage experts to try the great tree skiing there.

MOMENTUM SKI

Weekend & a la carte
ski holiday specialists

100% Tailor-made

Premier hotels
& apartments

Flexible travel
arrangements

020 7371 9111
WWW.MOMENTUMSKI.COM

FOR INTERMEDIATES ★★★★★
Be willing to travel

Many mileage-hungry intermediates find Verbier disappointing. The intermediate slopes in the main area are concentrated between Attelas and the village, above and below Les Ruinettes, plus the little bowl at Lac des Vaux and the sunny slopes at La Chaux. This is all excellent and varied intermediate territory, but there isn't much of it; and it is used by the bulk of the visitors staying in one of Switzerland's largest resorts. So it is often crowded, especially the lovely sweeping red from Attelas to Les Ruinettes. There is excellent easy blue run skiing at La Chaux, including a 'slow skiing' piste, but not much of it.

The underused Savoleyres area has good intermediate pistes, usually better snow and fewer people. It is also a good hill for mixed abilities, with variations of many runs. There is a blue run linking this sector to the Médran lift base, but the way down to that link from the top is not easy.

The gondola link to Bruson makes the area worth a visit. The Veysonnaz-Thyon and Nendaz sectors are also worth exploring (those not up to the itinéraires can ride the lifts down).

FOR BEGINNERS ★★★★★
OK but not ideal

There are sunny nursery slopes close to the middle of the village and at the top in Les Esserts. These are fine provided they have snow, and they are well equipped with snowmaking. Day passes covering these two areas are available. For progression, a local Verbier pass is available. Progression

to longer runs is not straightforward – there are easy blues at La Chaux and on the back of Savoleyres, but they involve a lot of lift riding.

FOR BOARDERS ★★★★★
Extreme freeride heaven

Verbier has become synonymous with extreme snowboarding and is generally seen as a freeriders' resort, with powder, cliffs, natural hits and trees all easily accessible. The final event of the Freeride world tour (see www. freerideworldtour.com) is held here every March on the Bec des Rosses. There is a lot of steep and challenging terrain to be explored with a guide, but the pistes and itinéraires will provide most riders with plenty to think about.

Chairlifts and gondolas serve the main area, with no drags. The area is far from ideal for beginners and timid intermediates, who should stick to the lower blue runs and Savoleyres. The terrain park is good.

FOR CROSS-COUNTRY ★★★★★
Little on offer

There's a 4km loop in Verbier, 10km at Les Ruinettes-La Chaux and 8km down the valley in Champsec and Lourtier.

MOUNTAIN RESTAURANTS ★★★★★
Improving, at last

Most restaurants are surprisingly uninspiring, for such an upmarket resort. But a few new openings have improved things recently.

Editors' choice In the main area, the rustic Chez Dany is an old favourite – a classic chalet in a sheltered spot in the forest, on the itinéraire on skier's

---

OFF-PISTE FOR ALL

Verbier has some of the best off-piste in the world. Here, we pick out just a few of the runs on offer. Read 'For experts' for the status of itinéraires; for the other runs here you should hire a guide.

The Col des Mines and Vallon d'Arby itinéraires, accessible from Lac des Vaux, are relatively easy, though there may be some unnerving moments on the traverse to the point where they split. The first is a long, open slope back to Verbier and the latter a very beautiful run in a steep-sided valley down to La Tzoumaz. The Eteygeon itinéraire from Greppon Blanc above Siviez is 'wonderfully varied and should not be missed', says a reporter; it ends up on a road and you catch a bus back to Les Masses.

Stairway to Heaven starts with a steep climb from near Col des Gentianes. Then you drop over the ridge into a deserted valley, and it's a long, relatively easy ski down to Tortin. The Mont-Gelé cable car offers some of the most amazing terrain accessible anywhere by lift, with long runs down to Tortin on steep but open slopes. Or go down the opposite side of the mountain through the steep rock face towards Lac des Vaux (not a route for the faint-hearted). The many couloirs from Attelas can also be fantastic. We love the runs off the back of Mont-Fort (except for the long walk out past Lac de Cleuson); it's a vast bowl and you can find fresh powder long after a snowfall; you end up at Siviez. And try the tree skiing in Bruson (described at the end of the chapter).

VERBIER & BEYOND!

TAILOR-MADE OR
ACCOMMODATION
ONLY SPECIALISTS

01502 471960
info@mountainbeds.com
www.mountainbeds.com

left of the area; we have had many good lunches here over the years.
Worth knowing about At Attelas, La Vache – run by the same team as the Farinet in town – makes a great alternative to the dreary self-service places, offering pizzas, pastas, soups and salads at prices below the Verbier norm; 'fun and stylish restaurant, great for veggies', said one reporter.

In the Mont-Fort sector, there is a big self-service at Col des Gentianes – a 'light, large space' with 'generous portions served by friendly staff'. Down the hill, off the run to La Chaux, Cabane du Mont-Fort is a proper mountain refuge and a regular reader favourite. The setting and the views are the highlights, but the food is good too – goulash soup, brownies, crepes all tipped; gets busy though. Further down at La Chaux, the table-service Dahu does 'fantastic pizza'.

Between Siviez and Thyon, Les Chottes is regularly praised – 'great atmosphere, varied menu, efficient service'. Down in Siviez, Chez Odette is an established favourite lunch spot.

There are some nice places on Savoleyres, though we rarely get reports. Namasté is tipped this year for its 'pleasant ambience, friendly service from the couple who run it and excellent food'. The Croix de Coeur and (on the fringe of the village) the Sonalon have been tipped.

SCHOOLS AND GUIDES ★★★★★
Good reports
There's no shortage of schools to choose between. New Generation, well established and a reader favourite in several top French resorts, set up its first Swiss branch in Verbier (later joined by another in Villars). Reports welcome. We were very impressed with our mountain guide from Adrenaline. European Snowsport has been praised for competitive pricing of private lessons. British instructor Warren Smith runs his Ski Academy here (five-day courses that you have to book in advance) – highly recommended by reporters this year, as last – and Powder Extreme specializes in off-piste. We have skied with both of these outfits and liked them both.

FOR FAMILIES ★★★☆☆
Good for childcare
The nursery slopes are central, and the Swiss school's facilities are good. There are considerable reductions on the lift pass price for families. The possibility of leaving very young babies at the Schtroumpfs nursery is valuable. Nanny services are offered by Chalet Services Verbier.

STAYING THERE
There are surprisingly few apartments and B&Bs, though there are inexpensive B&Bs in Le Châble. Hotels are pricey for their classifications.
Chalets Of course, the lunatic Swiss minimum wage policy has had an impact in Verbier, the chalet holiday capital of Switzerland. But Inghams continues to run the plum-central chalet hotel de Verbier ('very comfortable, newly renovated rooms', says a trusted reporter this year), and there are still some upmarket places available, eg from Ski Verbier.
Hotels Two 5-stars, five 4-stars, ten 3-stars and a few simpler places.
★★★★★Chalet d'Adrien Relais & Châteaux. A beautifully furnished 29-room chalet, with top-notch food. In a peaceful setting next to the Savoleyres lift, with great views. 'Very much worth its high prices,' says a reporter; 'superb – attentive service, good restaurant'.
★★★★★W Verbier The only ski resort hotel in the worldwide chain of self-consciously edgy W hotels – right by the slope and gondola at Médran. Take a look at the Leicester Square one to get a feel. Spa, gym and pool.
★★★★Nevaï Modern, minimalist, trendy, next to Farm Club (same ownership). Après-ski bar.
★★★★Vanessa Central, with spacious apartments as well as rooms.
★★★Farinet Central, British-owned, with a focal après-ski bar.
Apartments Mountain Beds has lots of apartments and self-catering chalets on its books.

EATING OUT ★★★★☆
Plenty of choice
There is a wide range of restaurants; many are listed in a free pocket guide.

The 5-star Chalet d'Adrien is one of the best gourmet places in town (one Michelin star). We've had good (but pricey) meals in the Nevaï and Cordée des Alpes hotels, and in the Rouge Restaurant and Club, and enjoyed sushi at the Nomad. We've also had good meals in the stylish, quiet Millénium, which is 'the place to go for top-quality venison and steaks'.

↑ The broad red run down from Attelas to Ruinettes is at the heart of the local slopes. The link to La Chaux is on the left

VERBIER ST BERNARD

An assiduous reporter identifies three 'very good' traditional places where you can expect 'a cosy Alpine atmosphere, open fires, good food and service': the Ecurie, Grange and Vieux Verbier. The ever-popular Fer à Cheval is known for its pizzas, but other dishes are also very good ('superb steak tartare').

You can be ferried by snowcat or snowmobile to various restaurants on the lower slopes, notably Chez Dany and la Marlenaz (on Savoleyres).

APRES-SKI ★★★★★
Throbbing but expensive
On the slopes, popular stops include the Rocks bar at Ruinettes, Chalet Carlsberg and the yurts of Bar 1936. In town, the Offshore at Médran is ever popular for milkshakes and cakes. Moving down the hill, we like the Fer à Cheval for a not-too-noisy drink. The central Farinet has a happy hour providing 'good deals on pitchers of beer and a live band playing on the glassed-in terrace', and the Big Ben pub is lively too. The Nevaï hotel has live music on its terraces, and the Rouge at the bottom of the golf course is packed, thanks to its popular sun deck and resident DJs.

The Pub Mont-Fort is as popular as ever with 'saisonnaires and would-be saisonnaires'. The Fer à Cheval has a 'great atmosphere from après through to the small hours'.

Crock No Name is a cool cocktail bar often with a blues band or a DJ. T-Bar is 'packed' for live rugby and football, 'best on live music nights'.

SKIWORLD
Catered chalets, hotels and self catering apartments in
Europe, USA and Canada
skiworld.co.uk
08444 930 430
ABTA V2151 ATOL 2036

The famous Farm Club is seriously pricey; we've had only one reader report, ever, and that comes from someone who doesn't sound like he's been inside it.

OFF THE SLOPES ★★★★★
A few things to do
Verbier has an excellent sports centre (with pool, saunas, hot tubs), an ice rink with curling, dog sledding between Les Ruinettes and La Chaux and some nice walks. Montreux is an enjoyable train excursion from Le Châble, and Martigny is worth a visit for the Roman remains and art gallery. Reporters have recommended the spa complex at Lavey-les-Bains. Various mountain restaurants are accessible to pedestrians – a walkers' pass covers most of the local lifts. There is a long, popular toboggan run on Savoleyres.

LINKED RESORT – 1365m
NENDAZ
Nendaz is not well known in Britain but is a major resort, with over 17,000 beds (practically all in apartments). Most of the resort is modern, built in traditional chalet style. It enjoys great views across the Rhône valley.

It's a sprawling place, and the centre is busy with traffic. The local bus services are reliable, but get over-busy at peak times. There are 100km of walks, an ice rink, fitness centre, climbing wall and squash courts.

Nendaz has its own slopes, but lots of people staying here use it as a back door to Verbier.

A 12-person gondola takes you to the top of the local slopes at Tracouet. This is a splendid, sunny little shelf with gentle slopes and long, shady red and blue runs back down to Nendaz. Getting back from Siviez was speeded up in 2013 by a gondola from Siviez to Plan-du-Fou, replacing the old chairlift. But skiing home still involves taking an itinéraire down the cable car (or riding down) followed by a black run – too tricky for many intermediates.

Neige Aventure ski school generates consistently good reports.

Currently recommended hotels are the small, simple Déserteur, a short walk from the lift, and the central 4-star Nendaz 4 Vallées – 'Utterly superb, with wonderful rooms, a magnificent spa, and probably the best ski resort breakfast I've had in 40+ years.' Skiworld has two swish chalets with outdoor hot tub, in an excellent location near the lift.

There's quite a wide choice of restaurants, offering Tex-Mex, pizzas, Thai and sushi, as well as steaks and local mountain food. The Cactus Saloon is 'lively'.

LINKED RESORT – 1730m

SIVIEZ

Siviez, a small huddle of buildings in an isolated spot, is effectively a junction of the slopes of Verbier, Nendaz and Veysonnaz-Thyon. It is the best base from which to explore the whole 4 Valleys lift network, though lodging is limited almost entirely to apartments. There are daytime buses to/from Nendaz. The long and gentle blue run through the sheltered valley from Tortin is super beginner progression territory. It is also an excellent base for doing the tough skiing of Verbier – you can end the day with a descent of 1600m vertical from Mont-Fort; no noise in the evenings; perfect.

LINKED RESORT – 1300m

VEYSONNAZ

Veysonnaz is a small, family resort, sunny in the afternoon, at the foot of an excellent, long red slope from the ridge above Thyon. A second excellent (though often icy) red, regularly used for major races, descends to the isolated lift base of Mayens-de-L'Ours.

The resort is spread widely across and down the hillside, with extensive views across the Rhône valley. The original attractive old village, complete with church, is two hairpin bends below Veysonnaz Station, the lift base and the main focus of the place for the visitor. The link up to Thyon is an eight-seat gondola, but progress from there towards Verbier is a slow business because of antique lifts. Taking a car means you can drive to Siviez for much quicker access to the Verbier slopes. Shuttle-buses serve the lifts, but they are not super-frequent and do not run on Saturdays.

Veysonnaz Station has the essential facilities – half a dozen bars and cafes, four restaurants, a disco or two and a wellness centre with swimming pool and spa facilities (closed Saturdays). There are adequate shops, including a butcher and baker.

Accommodation is mainly in apartments – substantial chalet-style buildings dotted along the road the lift base is on. There are plenty of smaller chalets, too. There are two 3-star hotels next to the gondola station: the Chalet Royal has 'stunning views', though not from all rooms, and 'generally good' food. The Magrappé has 'a bit of atmosphere' and is more the focus of lively après-ski. There are some B&Bs.

There are two schools: Swiss and Neige Aventure. And there is a children's day care centre on the mountain. A 5km cross-country trail has great views.

LINKED RESORT – 2100m

THYON 2000

Thyon 2000 is a purpose-built collection of plain, medium-rise apartment blocks just above the treeline at the hub of the Veysonnaz-Thyon sector of the 4 Valleys. The apartments are a bit of a blot on the landscape.

Thyon has the basics of resort life – supermarket, newsagent, a couple of restaurants (the Luge pizzeria was rated 'excellent, with friendly atmosphere and reasonable prices'), an indoor pool (closed Saturdays) and a disco. A free shuttle-bus runs to Les Collons. There's a fair-sized terrain park and snowcross, children's snow garden and a kindergarten, as well as a ski school. The slopes are ideal for families and beginners, with two nursery lifts close to the accommodation. The elderly lift network shared with Les Collons and Les Masses gained one new chair in 2013. Snowmaking is extensive.

LINKED RESORT – 1800m
LES COLLONS

Some 300m below Thyon, at the foot of a broad, east-facing slope, Les Collons is nothing more than a couple of strings of chalet-style buildings spread along two roads following the hillside, 50m vertical apart; a lot of building has been going on recently.

Three draglifts go up towards Thyon from the upper level of the resort, and a chairlift from the lower level takes you above Thyon. There's 6km of cross-country. A free shuttle-bus runs to Thyon.

Most accommodation is in apartments, but there are also a couple of modest hotels – including the 3-star Cambuse, just below one of the lift bases. There are a few bars and restaurants, plus a 1km toboggan run through the woods above the village. Prepared walking trails add up to a modest 8km.

LINKED RESORT – 1515m
LES MASSES

Half a dozen hairpins down the mountainside from Les Collons, Les Masses is no more than a hamlet at the base of the chairlifts that form the southern limit of the Veysonnaz-Thyon slopes. The chair out of the village was recently upgraded to a fast quad. Beware: the home run is a red. Accommodation is in apartments. There is a grocery store and a bar/restaurant.

LINKED RESORT – 1500m
LA TZOUMAZ

This tiny hamlet sits in a quiet valley on the shady, wooded side of Verbier's Savoleyres slope sector. There are a handful of small hotels, shops and restaurants, forming a very quiet place to stay and ski this underrated sector. A free bus serves the lifts. A gondola and a couple of fast chairs serve most of the slopes here. The 10km toboggan run back to the base area is one of the longest in the region; we're told by the tourist office that it is a 'professional' run, not suitable for children under seven; helmets are recommended.

LINKED RESORT – 820m
LE CHÂBLE

Le Châble is a village in the valley below Verbier, set off the main road to Italy at the bottom of the hairpin road up to Verbier. Beside the main road is a huge car park and a queue-free gondola that takes 9 minutes to Verbier and goes on (without changing cabins) to Les Ruinettes – access to the slopes can be just as quick from here as from Verbier. The gondola runs till 7.30pm; buses run later. A second gondola takes you to the heart of the slopes of Bruson. Le Châble is on the rail network (the station is near the gondolas), so you can arrive by train from Geneva.

There are several modest hotels; the 2-star Giétroz is tipped – 'comfortable, frequented by locals, good food and range of beer and wine'. Other places to eat include La Ruinette ('really good food at fairly reasonable prices and interesting wine list') and the Chat Bleu in the older part of Châble – 'pleasant, friendly place serving good food'. La Ruinette has apartments to let. The hotel de la Poste has a bar/nightclub: Manhattan.

LINKED RESORT – 1100m
BRUSON

Bruson is a small village on a shelf just above Le Châble, across the valley from Verbier. It's now reachable by a gondola from Le Châble.

The slopes above the gondola are served by a triple chair up to a ridge, on the far side of which is a short draglift serving a tight little bowl. Reports say these lifts are now unreliable. In addition to the intermediate pistes there are large areas of off-piste terrain – including tremendous skiing in well-spaced trees that is reminiscent of Canadian heli-skiing – quite steep in places. The front side of the mountain is mainly north-east facing, so it keeps its snow well. The restaurant de Moay offers 'friendly table-service of a good traditional menu'. The off-piste down the back towards Orsières is good; you return by train. Bruson can be delightfully quiet and a great contrast with Verbier, and currently seems to be staying that way despite the linking gondola (more reports, please). It would be a good place to go in white-out conditions.

GETTING THERE

Air Sion 55km/ 35 miles (1hr); Geneva 160km/ 100 miles (2hr); Zürich 280km/ 175 miles (3hr)

Rail Le Châble (7km/ 4 miles); regular buses to resort or gondola

TOURIST OFFICES

Verbier / Le Châble (Bruson) / La Tzoumaz
en.verbier.ch

Nendaz / Siviez
www.nendaz.ch

Veysonnaz
www.veysonnaz.ch

Thyon 2000 / Les Collons / Les Masses
www.thyon-region.ch

SNOWPIX.COM / CHRIS GILL

Villars

Traditional year-round resort with local low-altitude slopes, a cog railway, much improved snowmaking and a far-flung glacier

£135
RESORT PRICE INDEX

TOP 10 RATINGS

Extent	★★★
Fast lifts	★★
Queues	★★★
Snow	★★
Expert	★★
Intermediate	★★★
Beginner	★★★★
Charm	★★★
Convenience	★★
Scenery	★★★

NEWS

2014/15: 8.5 million Swiss francs (over £6 million) was invested in increased snowmaking and the resort claims that 50% of its pistes are now covered, including all the main runs to and links between the resorts.

LIFT PASSES

Prices in francs

Age	6-day
under 16	196
16 to 64	301
65 plus	271

Free Under 9, 78 plus
Beginner No deals
Note Covers Villars-Gryon, Leysin-Les Mosses, Les Diablerets, Glacier 3000

Alternative passes
SuperPass covers all the above plus Gstaad, Adelboden, Lenk; day passes for Villars-Gryon-Diablerets only

➕ Pleasant, traditional resort with a life outside skiing

➕ Fairly extensive intermediate slopes

➕ Distant access to glacier slopes beyond Les Diablerets

➕ Mountain railway is one way into the heart of the slopes

➖ Sunny slopes and modest altitudes mean snow quality can suffer – though snowmaking has recently been massively increased

➖ Short runs on the upper slopes – verticals of 200m–300m

➖ Little to amuse experts on-piste

Villars is popular with second-home owners because of its closeness to Geneva airport (a short drive down the hill puts you on the motorway for the airport). But its low altitude and the consequent risk of poor snow quality will put many keen skiers off booking far in advance. For a varied family holiday though, it has its attractions – not least the mountain railway.

THE RESORT

Villars sits on a sunny hillside looking across the Rhône valley to the Portes du Soleil. Its home slopes link to those of Les Chaux, above the rustic village of Gryon. The area pass covers the local slopes plus Les Diablerets (linked by a two-way lift), Glacier 3000 (the glacier area beyond Les Diablerets village) plus Leysin and Les Mosses (easy outings by rail or road). Getting to and from Glacier 3000 from Villars is a long, slow business – from Les Diablerets village you need to catch a bus to the glacier lift or walk 10 mins to the Isenau area to ski down to it; many instructors take clients by car or taxi. Outings to Verbier are possible.

Village charm Villars is more a town than a village, with sprawling suburbs of chalets and several international schools. The focus is a longish, traffic-filled but pleasant street.

Convenience A slow cog railway goes from the main street up to the slopes around Bretaye. A gondola from the other end of town to Roc d'Orsay is quicker. It's best to stay near one of these lifts or at a hotel with a shuttle, but there are ski-buses.

Scenery Although the local slopes lack visual drama, you can't say that of the views of glacial peaks to the east and south, and across the Rhône valley to the Dents du Midi.

SWITZERLAND

↑ Looking down to Bretaye, with the Glacier 3000 slopes in the distance – quite a long way away on skis
VILLARS TOURISM

516

KEY FACTS

Resort	1300m
	4,270ft

Villars, Gryon and Les Diablerets (excludes Glacier 3000)

Slopes	1115-2120m
	3,660-6,960ft
Lifts	34
Pistes	100km
	62 miles

MOMENTUM SKI

Weekend & a la carte
ski holiday specialists

100% Tailor-made

Premier hotels
& apartments

Flexible travel
arrangements

020 7371 9111
WWW.MOMENTUMSKI.COM

TOURIST OFFICE

www.villars.ch

THE MOUNTAINS

There's a good mix of wooded and open slopes.

Slopes The cog railway goes up to the col of Bretaye, which has intermediate slopes on either side. To the east, a gentle blue piste goes to La Rasse and the link to Les Chaux. There is also an itinerary run to La Rasse, which has a tricky section at the top that is often closed due to poor snow. From Les Chaux there are runs to Barboleuse above Gryon, with a gondola back up. The gondola from Villars takes you to Roc d'Orsay, from where you can head for Bretaye or back to Villars.

A long, painfully slow, two-way chairlift links via the peak of Meilleret to Les Diablerets, where there are further intermediate slopes. A long red run from Isenau on the other side of the village goes to Col du Pillon and meets the cable car to Glacier 3000. The glacier area has very gentle slopes at the top, but there is a splendid run down the Combe d'Audon (classified black but of red gradient) with a dramatic cliff face rising up on the right. Part-way down at Oldenegg you can catch a fast chair up to a splendid red run, or go on down to the valley.

Fast lifts Fast lifts exist, but so do old chairs and drags.

Queues The lifts at Bretaye get busy mainly at peak times. The buses and train can get overcrowded.

Terrain parks There's one at Chaux Ronde and another at Diablerets.

Snow reliability Low altitude and sunny slopes have traditionally meant poor snow reliability – though on such gentle, grassy terrain, deep snow-cover isn't needed. But last season saw a massive investment in snowmaking (the resort now claims 50% of pistes are covered), which should ensure good coverage if it's cold enough to make snow. That won't stop ice and slush forming in warm weather though.

Experts Little on-piste challenge but some good off-piste with a guide.

Intermediates The local slopes offer a good variety. Les Chaux has some steeper slopes and a lovely long cruisey blue to Barboleuse. The run from Meilleret to Les Diablerets is a delightful long cruise that can be deserted first thing in the morning.

Beginners The nursery slope behind the station is free to use. There is another at Gryon. There are gentle but often crowded runs at Bretaye.

Snowboarding There are a few tricky draglifts but good intermediate slopes.

Cross-country There are 50km of trails; those up the valley past La Rasse are long and pretty.

Mountain restaurants They are marked on the map but often oversubscribed. We like Lac des Chavonnes and the Golf Club. Above Gryon, we like the relatively quiet Restaurant 1882 at Les Chaux and Refuge Frience. The Col de Soud is tipped: 'a real sun trap'.

Schools and guides The two well-established schools here were joined last season by a new branch of British-run school New Generation.

Families La Trottinette non-ski nursery takes children up to six.

STAYING THERE

Hotels We've enjoyed staying at the 4-star central Golf – big rooms (some with fab views across the valley), spa. Nearby is the 3-star Alpe Fleurie. The 4-star Eurotel Victoria is near the gondola and 'almost ski-in'.

Eating out The Sporting serves traditional dishes/grills, and the pizzas at the Pizzeria 'take some beating'.

Après-ski The rustic Buvette d'Arrivée on the home run above the top of town is popular at close of play, as is the Sporting. Try the 'very trendy' Moon Boot Lounge for cocktails.

Off the slopes Activities include paragliding, snowshoeing, skating, tobogganing, swimming and walking (there are 30km of prepared paths). Rail excursions are another option.

SNOWPIX.COM / CHRIS GILL

Wengen

A charming old village, stunning scenery, an old cog railway and gentle intermediate slopes make for a relaxing and leisurely holiday

£140
RESORT PRICE INDEX

517

RATINGS

The mountains

Extent	★★★
Fast lifts	★★★★
Queues	★★★
Terrain p'ks	★
Snow	★★
Expert	★★
Intermediate	★★★★
Beginner	★★★
Boarder	★★
X-country	★
Restaurants	★★★
Schools	★★★
Families	★★★★

The resort

Charm	★★★★★
Convenience	★★★
Scenery	★★★★★
Eating out	★★
Après-ski	★★
Off-slope	★★★★

NEWS

Investment in lifts is on the back-burner until the proposed new gondolas from Grindelwald to Männlichen and Eigergletscher are built – see 'News' in Grindelwald chapter. They will make coming back from Grindelwald much quicker.

miles   0.5
        Männlichen

down to Lauterbrunnen

N

Kleine Scheidegg
km   0.5

+ Some of the most spectacular scenery in the Alps

+ Small, traditional, nearly traffic-free Alpine village

+ Lots of long, gentle runs, ideal for leisurely intermediates

+ Nursery slopes in heart of village

+ Calm, unhurried atmosphere

+ Good resort for families and groups that include non-skiers. It's easy to get around on mountain railways

− Limited terrain for experts and adventurous intermediates

− Natural snow unreliable (but substantial snowmaking now)

− Trains to slopes are slow and there are still a few old lifts

− Getting to/from Mürren and Grindelwald's First area are both a bit of a slog

− Subdued in the evening, with little variety of nightlife

Given the charm of the village, the friendliness of the locals and the drama of the scenery, it's easy to see why many people love Wengen – including large numbers of Brits who have been going for decades. It's great for a relaxing time, for those who don't take their skiing too seriously, for families and for mixed groups of intermediates and non-skiers.

Keen piste-bashers should not underestimate the drawbacks. If you're used to modern mega-resorts, you'll find Wengen a huge contrast, and may have difficulty adjusting. But the spectacularly scenic Jungfrau region is one that every keen skier should experience; and to experience all of it, Wengen – centrally placed between Mürren and Grindelwald – is the best base.

THE RESORT

Wengen is one of three resorts close together in the Jungfrau region. It is set on a sloping shelf above the Lauterbrunnen valley, opposite Mürren, and reached only by a cog railway, which carries on up to Kleine Scheidegg and the slopes shared with Grindelwald. Access to Mürren involves a train down to Lauterbrunnen, a cable car up and then another train (or a bus from Lauterbrunnen to a different two-stage cable car to Mürren). Access to the First area of Grindelwald is an even longer process, including skiing down to Grindelwald and crossing town – the planned new gondolas (see 'News') will speed up the return journey but not until 2017/18 at the earliest. The Jungfrau lift pass covers all three resorts. Outings further afield aren't really worth the effort.

VILLAGE CHARM ★★★★★
Almost traffic-free
The village was a farming community long before skiing arrived; it is still tiny, but dominated by sizeable hotels, mostly of Victorian origin. So it is not

exactly chocolate-box pretty, but it is charming and relaxed, and almost traffic-free. There are electric hotel taxi-trucks and a few scruffy, engine-driven taxis. (Why not electric and smart taxis like Zermatt, we wonder?)

The short main street is the hub. Lined with chalet-style shops and hotels, it also has the ice rink and village nursery slopes right next to it.

CONVENIENCE ★★★
Compact, but hilly in parts
Wengen is small, so location isn't as crucial as in many resorts. But those who don't fancy a steepish morning climb should avoid places down the hill, below the station (unless their hotel runs a shuttle service). The ridge where the slopes of Wengen meet those of Grindelwald is reached either by train or – much quicker (unless there's a long queue) – by cable car. Both stations are central. There are hotels on the home piste. You can leave skis and boots at the station (we left our rental skis at Central Sport, which is, er, central and has a big storeroom and very friendly and helpful staff).

KEY FACTS

Resort	1275m
	4,180ft

Jungfrau region	
Slopes	945-2970m
	3,100-9,740ft
Lifts	45
Pistes	213km
	132 miles

First-Männlichen-Kleine Scheidegg only	
Slopes	945-2500m
	3,100-8,200ft
Lifts	28
Pistes	170km
	106 miles

SCENERY ★★★★★
Simply the best
The views across the valley are stunning. They get even better higher up, when the famous trio of peaks comes fully into view – the Mönch (Monk) in the centre protecting the Jungfrau (Maiden) on the right from the Eiger (Ogre) on the left.

THE MOUNTAINS

Although Wengen is famous for the fearsome Lauberhorn Downhill course – the longest and one of the toughest on the World Cup circuit – its slopes are best suited to early intermediates. Most of the Downhill course is now open to the public and has excellent signs on the way explaining it. Most of Wengen's runs are gentle blues and reds, ideal for cruising.

Piste marking and piste map are poor; the Männlichen slopes, in particular, can be confusing.

EXTENT OF THE SLOPES ★★★★★
Picturesque playground
Most of the slopes are on the Grindelwald side of the mountain. From the railway station at Kleine Scheidegg you can head straight down to Grindelwald or work your way across to the top of the Männlichen. This area is served by a drag and several chairlifts, and can be reached directly from Wengen by the cable car. There are a few runs back down

towards Wengen from the top of the Lauberhorn, but there's really only one below Wengernalp.

FAST LIFTS ★★★★
OK except for the train
The fast cable car and slow train are the main access lifts; fast chairs replacing old lifts over the years have improved things higher up.

QUEUES ★★★★
Village crowds, better higher up
Both the train and the cable car can be crowded at peak periods. And queues for the cable car can be lengthy ('40 minutes to an hour queue at the cable car at 9.30am,' said a February reporter; and we waited 20 minutes in low-season March). It is best to avoid travelling up at the same time as the ski schools. Queues up the mountain have been alleviated a lot in the past few years by the installation of fast chairs, and we and reporters have experienced few problems in midweek. But weekends can be busy, especially on the Grindelwald side of the hill – the obvious entry point for residents of Bern attracted by the special family pass deals on Saturdays.

TERRAIN PARKS ★★★★★
A fair trek
There isn't one. The nearest parks are at First and Mürren – each a fair trek.

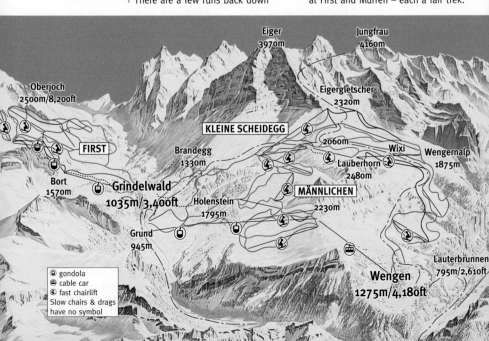

Wengen

LIFT PASSES

Jungfrau

Prices in francs

Age	6-day
under 16	170
16 to 19	271
20 to 61	339
62 plus	305

Free Under 6 (if with parent)

Beginner Points ticket

Note Covers trains between villages and ski-bus

Alternative passes
Grindelwald and Wengen only; Mürren only; non-skier pass

THE BRITISH IN WENGEN

There's a very strong British presence in Wengen. Many Brits have been returning for years to the same rooms in the same hotels in the same week, and treat the resort as a sort of second home. There is an English church with weekly services, and a British-run ski club, the DHO (Downhill Only) – so named when the Brits who colonized the resort persuaded the locals to keep the summer railway running up the mountain in winter, so that they would no longer have to climb up in order to ski down again. That greatly amused the locals, who until then had regarded skiing in winter as a way to get around on snow rather than a pastime to be done for fun. The DHO is still going strong.

SNOW RELIABILITY ★★
Improved snowmaking helps
Most slopes are below 2000m, and the few runs on the Wengen side of the ridge are sunny; the long blue run back to the village is particularly vulnerable. But a lot of snowmaking has been added recently, and some 60% of the slopes in the Kleine Scheidegg-Männlichen area are now covered. On our March 2014 visit during exceptionally hot, sunny weather, snow-cover was not a problem and most slopes were in good condition until lunchtime, when they went slushy. Several reporters have also commented on the effectiveness of the snowmaking.

FOR EXPERTS ★★
Few challenges
Wengen is quite limited for experts. The only genuine black runs in the area are parts of the Lauberhorn World Cup Downhill and a couple of pistes from Eigergletscher towards Wixi. There are some decent off-piste runs from under the north face of the Eiger and the Eigernordwand lift helps with access to these. For more challenges it's well worth going to nearby Mürren, around an hour away. Heli-trips are organized if there are enough takers.

FOR INTERMEDIATES ★★★★
Wonderful if the snow is good
Wengen and Grindelwald share superb easy intermediate slopes. Nearly all are long blue or gentle red runs (though there are genuine reds too); read the Grindelwald chapter. The run back to Wengen is a relaxing end to the day, although it can be crowded and the snow can be patchy.

For tougher pistes, head for the top of the Lauberhorn chair and then the runs to Kleine Scheidegg, or to Wixi (following the start of the Downhill course). You could also try the shady run from Eigergletscher, which often has the best snow late in the season. Or head for Mürren – well worth doing for adventurous intermediates for a day or two during a week's stay.

FOR BEGINNERS ★★★
Not ideal
There's a nursery slope in the centre of the village – convenient and gentle, but it gets afternoon sun and at this modest altitude the snow can suffer. There's a beginners' area at Wengernalp and some short beginner

lifts up at Kleine Scheidegg, but of course to use these you have to take the train down as well as up, or tackle the blue run down to the village, which can be tricky and has some flat sections. None of these areas offers free lifts, but there are alternatives to buying a full lift pass (there is a points card). There are plenty of good, long, gentle runs to progress to on the slopes above Grindelwald, reached either by train to Kleine Scheidegg or cable car to Männlichen.

FOR BOARDERS ★★
Best for beginners
Wengen is not a bad place for gentle boarding – the nursery area is not ideal, but beginners have plenty of slopes to progress to, with lots of long blue and red runs served by the train and chairlifts. Getting from Kleine Scheidegg to Männlichen means an unavoidable draglift, though. And the slope back to Wengen is narrow and almost flat in places, so you may have to scoot. For the steepest slopes and best freeriding, experts will want to head for Mürren.

FOR CROSS-COUNTRY ★
There is none
There's no cross-country in Wengen itself, which seems a shame given the nature of the resort. There are 12km of tracks down in the Lauterbrunnen valley, where the snow is unreliable.

MOUNTAIN RESTAURANTS ★★★
Plenty of variety
Editors' choice The Jungfrau hotel at Wengernalp is an old favourite of ours and a repeat visit in 2014 reinforced our view: the menu is limited, but includes possibly the best rösti in the Alps (with Gorgonzola and egg), and the view from the terrace is breathtaking. It's pricey, operates a two-sitting booking policy and doesn't take credit cards (so take plenty of cash), but we still love it.
Worth knowing about You also get magnificent views from the narrow balcony of Wengen's highest restaurant, Eigergletscher. The Bellevue hotel at Kleine Scheidegg is pricey and has a limited menu, but magnificent views from the terrace and a wonderfully old-fashioned wood-panelled dining room for bad weather days. 'Super service; expensive but worth it,' says a reporter. The 'cosy' table-service section of the restaurant

↑ Looking down to Kleine Scheidegg, with the station on the right and the Bellevue des Alpes hotel on the left

at the Männlichen top station offers a 'decent range of dishes – the star being a generous plate of dried meats and cheese'. Recent reporters have enjoyed the busy Eigernordwand restaurant which has self- and table-service sections ('good selection of reasonably priced food for Switzerland with extremely good views from the outside terrace', says a 2015 visitor. Two recent reporters endorse previous recommendations for Mary's Cafe at the bottom of the Lauberhorn ('hearty, tasty mountain food', 'excellent cake'). For restaurants above Grindelwald, read that chapter.

SCHOOLS AND GUIDES ★★★
More reports please
A 2015 reporter recommends Altitude for its private lessons ('English instructors, in a short time improved our techniques, had us skiing with more speed and control with greater confidence and comfort'). Guides are available for heli-trips and off-piste.

FOR FAMILIES ★★★★
A family favourite
It is an attractive and reassuring village for families. The nursery slope is in the centre and the Playhouse kindergarten in the tourist office nearby. There is a list of babysitters available at the tourist office. The train gives easy access to higher slopes.

STAYING THERE

Most accommodation is in hotels. Catered chalets and self-catering apartments are few.

Staying down in Lauterbrunnen will halve your accommodation costs and give faster access to Mürren.
Hotels There are about two dozen hotels, mostly 4-star and 3-star, with a handful of simpler places. There's a 207-room Club Med.
★★★★Beausite Park The best in town; reputedly very well run with good staff and food. Pool, steam, sauna, massage. Situated at the top of the nursery slopes.
★★★★Caprice Small, smartly furnished, chalet style, just above the station. Sauna and massage.
★★★★Regina Grand Victorian hotel with piano bar, sun terrace, spa and fitness room just up the hill from the station.
★★★★Silberhorn Comfortable, modern, central. 'Good food, very helpful, friendly staff.'
★★★★Sunstar Family-friendly, modern, on main street right opposite the cable car. 'Extremely welcoming, good rooms, pool a bit cool.'
★★★★Victoria Lauberhorn On main street. 'Friendly, lovely spa and pool, good food.'
★★★★Wengener Hof No prizes for style or convenience, but recommended in the past for good food, peace, helpful

staff and spacious rooms with good views.

***Alpenrose 130-year-old family-run hotel with a reputation for friendliness, service and good food; long-standing British favourite; morning shuttle service up to station.

***Belvédère Some way out, buffet-style meals, family-friendly, spacious rooms and grand art nouveau public rooms ('loved the style, worth paying extra for a south-facing room with jaw-dropping view').

***Falken A long-standing British favourite next door to the Regina.

*Bernerhof On the main street. 'Basic and clean with friendly staff and excellent food,' said a 2015 reporter.

Apartments The hotel Bernerhof's decent Résidence apartments are well positioned just off the main street, and the hotel facilities are available for guests to use. Apartments are available to book independently too – we took one for our 2014 visit.

At altitude You can stay at two points up the mountain served by the railway. At Wengernalp the Jungfrau hotel has fabulous views; a 2015 reporter said, 'Fine atmospheric hotel, excellent staff and food, not cheap but worth the money.' At Kleine Scheidegg, there are rooms in the grand and traditional Bellevue des Alpes and dormitory space above the Grindelwaldblick restaurant and the station buffet.

EATING OUT ★★☆☆☆
Mainly hotel-based

Most restaurants are in hotels and have good food and service. The Bernerhof has good-value traditional dishes. The little hotel Hirschen offers speciality steaks. There's no shortage of fondues in the village, and several bars do casual food. Da Sina is a steakhouse and pizzeria.

APRES-SKI ★★☆☆☆
It depends on what you want

People's reactions to Wengen's après-ski scene vary widely, according to their expectations and their appetites.

If you're used to raving in Kitzbühel or Les Deux-Alpes, you'll rate Wengen dead, especially for young people. If you've heard it's dead, you may be pleasantly surprised to find that there is a handful of small bars that do good business both early and late in the evening.

On the mountain, the outdoor Läger Bar, next to the Männlichen

Club Med ℣.
THE MOST COMPREHENSIVE SKI PACKAGE ON THE MARKET

020 8313 3999
Skiline.co.uk

Skiline.co.uk

chair, is good for sitting in a deckchair in the sun. Tipirama (a wigwam at Kleine Scheidegg) is a fun place immediately after skiing 'if not too cold', sometimes with DJs and live bands; you can catch the train down. The Wäsch bar at the Bumps section of the home run is a popular final-run stop-off.

In the village the tiny Pickel Bar is popular at the end of the day. The 'cosy' bar of the Silberhorn hotel got the thumbs up last year. The small, traditional Tanne has also been tipped. Sina's, a little way out of the centre, next to the Club Med, 'is probably the best night-time bar, with DJ and karaoke'. The 'lively' Rocks Bar, has plasma screens showing Sky Sports. There are discos and live music in some hotels.

OFF THE SLOPES ★★★★☆
Good for a relaxing time

With its unbeatable scenery and pedestrian-friendly trains and cable car (there's a special – but pricey – pass for pedestrians), Wengen is a superb resort for those who want a relaxing holiday. It's easy for mixed parties of skiers and non-skiers to meet up for lunch on the mountain. There are some lovely walks ('paths are superbly signposted'), and ice skating, tobogganing ('well worth doing') and curling ('great fun') are popular. There are guided snowshoeing tours. Several hotels have health spas. The cinema often shows films in English.

Excursions to Interlaken and Bern are possible by train, as is the trip up to the Jungfraujoch (see the Grindelwald chapter). From Männlichen there are scenic flights giving splendid close-up views of the mountains and glaciers, either by helicopter or much cheaper small plane.

Zermatt

A magical combination of just about everything you could hope to find in a ski resort, both on and off the slopes

£165
RESORT PRICE INDEX

RATINGS

The mountains
Extent	****
Fast lifts	*****
Queues	***
Terrain p'ks	***
Snow	****
Expert	****
Intermediate	****
Beginner	**
Boarder	***
X-country	*
Restaurants	*****
Schools	***
Families	**

The resort
Charm	****
Convenience	**
Scenery	*****
Eating out	*****
Après-ski	*****
Off-slope	****

522

NEWS

2015/16: The Hörnli T-bar to above Schwarzsee is due to be replaced by a new six-seat Hirli chair which will start lower down and make the runs here much more attractive to ski. A new wider piste following a completely new line is planned to replace the final narrow path down to town from the Rothorn-Sunnegga sector.

Throughout 2015 Zermatt is celebrating 150 years since the first ascent of the Matterhorn.

2014/15: A tricky narrow part of the run from Riffelalp to Furi was widened. Various hotels were spruced up.

➕ Wonderful, high, extensive slopes

➕ Spectacular high mountain scenery

➕ Charming but rather sprawling old village; car-free (but not traffic-free)

➕ Reliable snow at altitude

➕ World's best mountain restaurants (but not for quick pit stops)

➕ Nightlife to suit most tastes

➕ Lots to do off the slopes

➕ Linked to sunny Cervinia in Italy

➕ Extensive helicopter operation

➖ You may face long walks, crowded buses or pricey taxi rides

➖ Far from ideal for novices

➖ High prices for everything, including lift pass (one of Europe's priciest)

➖ Slow train up to Gornergrat

➖ Some lift queues at peak periods

➖ Annoying electric taxis and hotel vehicles detract from ambience

➖ Few options to ski in bad weather; can be really windy or cold too

You must try Zermatt before you die. Few places can match its combination of excellent advanced and intermediate slopes, reliable snow, magnificent scenery, Alpine charm and mountain restaurants with superb food and stunning views.

Its drawbacks are non-trivial (see the minus points above). But, for us and for virtually all our reporters, these pale into insignificance compared with its attractions. Editor Watts has taken countless holidays here. Enough said.

THE RESORT

Zermatt started life as a simple farming village, developed as a mountaineering centre in the 19th century, then became a winter resort in the late 1920s and early 1930s. Summer is still as big as winter here.

The village is car-free, but not traffic-free – electric buggies operating either as hotel shuttles or as public taxis zip around the streets. Residents and taxis can drive up to Zermatt, but the rest of us must park at Täsch (or more distant Visp) and arrive by train. At Täsch there's a big car park (14.50 francs a day), and you can wheel luggage trolleys on and off the trains. Zermatt mainly attracts a well-

heeled international clientele; the clientele is also relatively, er, mature for what is quite a sporty resort.

VILLAGE CHARM ****✫
Old and new in harmony
The resort is a mixture of ancient chalets and barns, grand 19th-century hotels and modern buildings, most in traditional style but some decidedly funky. The oldest, most charming part of the village has narrow lanes and old wooden barns with slate roofs, many of them supported on stone 'legs'. But the resort now sprawls along both sides of the river with a lot of new building at both ends and up the steep mountainsides.

Arriving at the station, it all seems very towny, especially if there is no snow on the ground. The centre doesn't have the relaxed, rustic feel of other car-free Swiss resorts, such as Wengen and Saas-Fee. The main street running away from the station is lined with luxury hotels, restaurants, banks and glitzy shops. The electric vehicles are intrusive, especially at busy times.

CONVENIENCE **✫✫✫
Lifts at opposite ends
The village is small enough to get around on foot in the evenings, but not in ski boots and carrying skis.

[Map showing: miles, 0.5, 1.0, down to Täsch, Sunnegga, N, Furi, Gornergrat, km, 1.0, 2.0]

I HAVE SIMPLE TASTES.
I'M ALWAYS SATISFIED WITH THE BEST.

Live Friday night

HOTEL ALEX — THE ONE & ONLY

Phone +41 27 966 70 70
www.hotelalexzermatt.com

ZERMATT
MATTERHORN

There is a free ski-bus service; but it is inadequate at peak times, especially from the Matterhorn area at the end of the day. Electric taxis are pricey.

You arrive at a fair-sized square at the north end of the resort, where you find ranks of electric taxis and hotel shuttles and horse-drawn sleighs.

The cog railway to the Gornergrat sector starts from near the main station. The Sunnegga underground funicular for the Rothorn sector is a few minutes' walk away, but the lifts to Furi and the other sectors (and the link to Cervinia) are over 1km away.

Staying near the lifts to Furi gives swift access to three of the four sectors. But a more central location is better for the Gornergrat and Sunnegga railways and most of the resort's shops, bars and restaurants.

Some accommodation is up the steep hill across the river in Winkelmatten, which has its own reliable bus service.

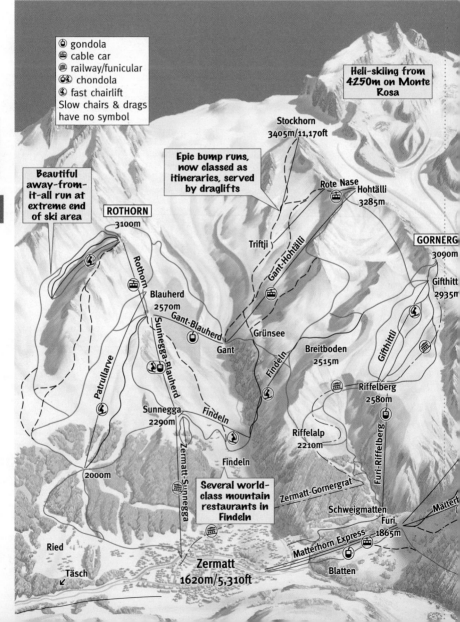

gondola
cable car
railway/funicular
chondola
fast chairlift
Slow chairs & drags have no symbol

Heli-skiing from 4250m on Monte Rosa

Stockhorn
3405m/11,170ft

Epic bump runs, now classed as itineraries, served by draglifts

Rote Nase
Hohtälli
3285m

Beautiful away-from-it-all run at extreme end of ski area

ROTHORN
3100m

GORNERG
3090m

Rothorn

Gifthitt
2935m

Triftji

Gant-Hohtälli

Blauherd
2570m

Gant-Blauherd

Grünsee

Gifthittli

Sunnegga-Blauherd

Gant

Breitboden
2515m

Patrullarve

Findeln

Riffelberg
2580m

Sunnegga
2290m

Findeln

Riffelalp
2210m

Furi-Riffelberg

Zermatt-Sunnegga

Findeln

Several world-class mountain restaurants in Findeln

Zermatt-Gornergrat

2000m

Schweigmatten

Matter

Ried

Furi
1865m

Täsch

Zermatt
1620m/5,310ft

Matterhorn Express

Blatten

SCENERY ★★★★★
On a grand scale

Zermatt's emblematic, unmistakable Matterhorn is not visible from central parts of the village – if you want the famous view from your balcony, stay on the east side of the village, or at the south end – but once you are on the slopes its unique profile dominates the views wherever you go. And the cable car trip up to the Klein Matterhorn opens up vast panoramas, as well as close-up glacier views.

THE MOUNTAINS

Practically all of the slopes are above the treeline – a run served by the Sunnegga funicular is the main exception, and once you pass below the Patrullarve chair this is mainly a path to the village.

A single piste map covers both Cervinia and Zermatt fairly clearly. Runs are numbered on the map and the ground (though only at the start). The map has a key which names runs,

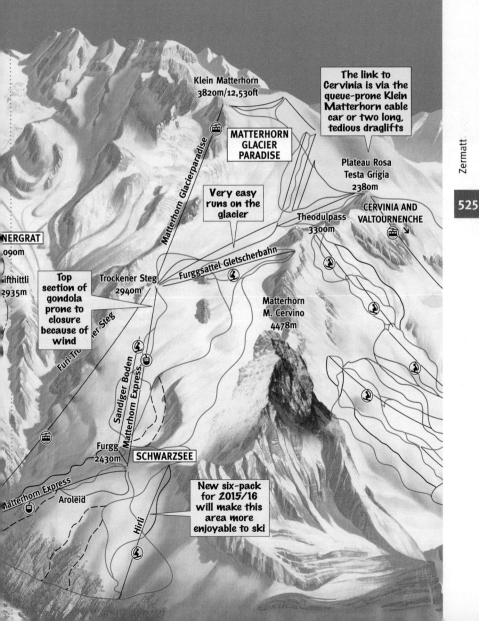

Klein Matterhorn
3820m/12,530ft

MATTERHORN
GLACIER
PARADISE

The link to
Cervinia is via the
queue-prone Klein
Matterhorn cable
car or two long,
tedious draglifts

Plateau Rosa
Testa Grigia
2380m

CERVINIA AND
VALTOURNENCHE

Very easy
runs on the
glacier

Theodulpass
3300m

Matterhorn Glacierparadise

Furggsattel Gletscherbahn

...NERGRAT
...090m

Matterhorn
M. Cervino
4478m

...ifthittli
2935m

Top
section of
gondola
prone to
closure
because of
wind

Trockener Steg
2940m

Furi-Tro... er Steg

Sandiger Boden
Matterhorn Express

Furgg
2430m

SCHWARZSEE

Matterhorn Express

Aroleïd

Hirli

New six-pack
for 2015/16
will make this
area more
enjoyable to ski

↑ The village has retained its charm despite lots of new building since the Zermatterhof hotel and the church were built in late 19th/ early 20th centuries
ZERMATT TO / LEANDER WENGER

KEY FACTS

Resort	1620m 5,310ft

Zermatt only

Slopes	1620-3820m 5,310-12,530ft
Lifts	35
Pistes	200km 124 miles

Zermatt-Cervinia-Valtournenche combined

Slopes	1525-3820m 5,000-12,530ft
Lifts	54
Pistes	360km 224 miles

but not lifts (though the Cervinia map has a key which names lifts too).

In each sector there are runs, marked in yellow on the resort map and dotted on ours, called 'itinéraires' on the Zermatt map and 'freeride' on the Cervinia one. We'll call them itineraries. These runs aren't explained on the maps but we are told they are marked and controlled for avalanche danger but are not groomed or patrolled. So don't ski these alone, particularly late in the day.

On Wednesdays and Fridays, you can get first tracks from Trockener Steg. For 42 francs you can take the lift at 7.40am, about an hour ahead of the herd, ski deserted pistes with a patroller, then jump the queue for one of the first cable cars to Klein Matterhorn and have a buffet breakfast at the restaurant there. We did this in 2015, thought it was fabulous and spent the rest of the day on Cervinia's slopes. Our routine for the rest of our stay was to take the 8am train to Gornergrat and enjoy deserted pistes there and from Hohtälli before the hordes got up there.

There are monthly moonlight descents from Rothorn with the ski patrol, including a fondue at the restaurant at the top (70.50 francs).

Over recent years, service has improved to a high standard: polite and helpful lift staff; big boards at the

bottom of each sector indicating which lifts and pistes are open in all sectors; useful announcements in English on the train and some cable cars; and free tissues at most lift stations.

EXTENT OF THE SLOPES ★★★★★
Beautiful and varied

There are four main sectors. **Rothorn** is reached by an underground funicular to Sunnegga, starting by the river, not far from the centre of the village. The main nursery area is just below Sunnegga, reached from there by a miniature funicular. A chondola goes from Sunnegga to Blauherd, where a cable car goes up to Rothorn.

The second main area, **Gornergrat**, is reached from Zermatt by cog railway trains that take around 30 minutes to the top – arrive at the bottom station early to get a seat (best on the right-hand side to enjoy fabulous views).

The Rothorn and Gornergrat sectors, separated by the Findel valley, are linked by pistes and itineraries.

The Matterhorn Express gondola from the south end of the village goes first to Furi (where you can change to another gondola to go to Riffelberg, for Gornergrat) and on to the small but worthwhile **Schwarzsee** area. The same gondola goes on up to Trockener Steg, focal point of the fourth sector, the super-high **Matterhorn glacier paradise**. The alternative jumbo cable

LIFT PASSES

Zermatt

Prices in francs

Age	6-day
under 16	190
16 to 19	323
20 plus	380

Free Under 9

Beginner Wolli Pass covers nursery area at Sunnegga

Notes Covers Swiss side of the border; half-day passes and single-ascent tickets on some lifts

Alternative passes
International for Zermatt and Cervinia; International-Aosta for Zermatt and Cervinia plus 2 days in Val d'Aosta; Peak Pass for pedestrians

car from Furi to Trockener Steg now seems to work only in very busy times or when the gondola is closed (eg because of high winds). Above Trockener Steg a cable car makes a spectacular ascent to Klein Matterhorn. At the top, you walk through a long tunnel to the highest piste in Europe. From Trockener Steg there are two ways to Cervinia (via the cable car to Klein Matterhorn or via two long successive draglifts).

There are pistes back to the village from all sectors – though some can be closed or tricky due to poor snow conditions (and crowds).

FAST LIFTS ★★★★★
Now top-notch
All Zermatt's four sectors are well connected by fast chairs, gondolas, big cable cars or mountain railways. There are of course slow lifts in places, but most can be avoided. The low speed of the Gornergrat train is something you just have to accept.

QUEUES ★★★☆☆
Still a few bottlenecks
Zermatt has improved its lift system hugely in recent years, eliminating

major bottlenecks. This year's reporters are generally positive again, but a few problems remain.

There may be queues to get up to the Matterhorn sector; and the gondola to Trockener Steg is prone to closure in high winds, in which case the alternative cable car opens but may build queues. The Klein Matterhorn cable car often has serious queues in good weather (up to an hour mid-morning; quieter in the afternoon).

A real bottleneck is Gant in the Findel valley. Half-hour waits for the old, slow gondola to Blauherd are common in high season; there are plans to replace it with a six-pack but not till the 2016/17 season. There can also be queues for the Hohtälli cable car from Gant. And the top section of piste from Hohtälli can get dangerously busy.

TERRAIN PARKS ★★★☆☆
Summer and winter
Snowpark, next to the Furggsattel six-seat chair has a variety of jumps, rails, rollers and a snowcross (but no half-pipe). A 2015 reporter 'enjoyed the big kickers and nice bumps' here but as

IN MOTION SINCE 1929.

The local swiss ski school with over 200 professional instructors

skischulezermatt.ch

Sponsored by

 Aberdeen Asset management    ACW Auto-Center Visp AG *Its BMW Partner im Oberwallis*   WENGER   TAG HEUER

Snow & Alpine Center, Bahnhofstrasse 58, +41 (0)27 966 24 66

 MATTERHORN SKI & SNOWBOARD SCHOOL ZERMATT

Zermatt offers a wide variety of off-piste runs for all abilities, from off-piste beginner to expert. And if the runs reached from the lift system aren't enough, heli-skiing is available (and popular).

Zermatt's 'itineraries' (explained under 'The mountains') open up a lot of terrain to explore without needing guidance. If you love long mogul pitches, those on the Stockhorn are the stuff of dreams. Being north-facing and high, this area keeps good snow long after a new snowfall (but it needs deep snow, and does not normally open until February; indeed, the Triftji T-bar there was closed on our March 2015 visit). The itineraries carry on down Gant, but snow quality can deteriorate on this lower part. There are excellent itineraries in other sectors, too – though again they generally need good snow-cover to be really enjoyable. Our own favourites include two wonderful runs from Rothorn (16 and 17), with spectacular views. A recent visitor particularly liked 10 from Blauherd to Findeln. The runs in the Schwarzsee sector – 58, 59 and 60 – are steeper, shadier and narrower than most.

Away from the marked runs, there are marvellous off-piste possibilities from the top lifts in each sector, but they are dangerous, because of rocky and glacial terrain; guidance is essential. Stockhorn is a great starting point; descending towards Gant, one special run goes down 'the lost valley'; going in the other direction, there is an excellent descent to the Gornergletscher, ending at Furi. Be warned: getting off the glacier may involve narrow rocky paths above long drops, or side-stepping down steep slopes, depending on snow levels (we've encountered both). In the Schwarzsee sector there are many good slopes, including 'innru waldieni', right under the Matterhorn, reached from the new Hirli lift.

Zermatt is the Alps' biggest heli-skiing centre; at times the helipad has choppers taking off every few minutes. There are only a few drop points. The classic run is from over 4250m on Monte Rosa and descends over 2300m vertical through wonderful glacier scenery to Furi; note our warning above.

another said 'it is far away and very cold if the weather is at all bad'. In the summer, the park moves up to Plateau Rosa where a crew of six shape the 600m park daily. There's a half-pipe and a good array of features.

SNOW RELIABILITY ★★★★☆
Generally good
Zermatt has rocky terrain and a relatively dry climate. But it also has some of the highest slopes in Europe. As well as the glacier, two other sectors go over 3000m, and there are loads of runs above 2500m, many of which are north-facing.

On repeated March visits we have been impressed by the snowmaking, in all four sectors, on pistes from above 3000m down to resort level. Piste grooming is generally excellent.

FOR EXPERTS ★★★★☆
Head off-piste
There is some great off-piste when conditions are right, and the off-piste itineraries include some excellent runs – read our feature panel. But Zermatt doesn't get huge snowfall, so you can't always count on good conditions, particularly early in the season. The handful of black runs are not worthy of their classification, except for the odd steep pitch such as the last part of the run from Grünsee to Findeln (which can also be icy).

FOR INTERMEDIATES ★★★★☆
Mile after mile of beautiful runs
Zermatt is ideal for adventurous intermediates. Many of the blue runs tend to be at the difficult end of their classification. Reds vary unhelpfully: some are quite tough; some ought to be classified blue. Few are really what you might call 'cruising' runs.

Among our favourites in the Gornergrat sector are the very beautiful reds down lift-free valleys from both Gornergrat (Kelle) and Hohtälli (White Hare) to Breitboden – we love these first thing in the morning, before anyone else is on them. The steepest part of Kelle is classified black, but an easier red variant bypasses it. From Breitboden you can go on down to Gant, or to the mid-station of the Findeln chairlift, or to Riffelalp on a run that includes a narrow wooded path with a sheer cliff and magnificent views to the right.

On the Rothorn sector, the 5km Kumme/Tufternkumme run – from Rothorn itself to the Patrullarve chair – also gets away from the lift system and has an interesting mix of straight-running and mogul pitches (but it gets a lot of sun and lacks snowmaking).

In the Matterhorn Glacier Paradise sector the reds served by the fast quad chair from Furgg are gloriously set at the foot of the Matterhorn. The Furggsattel chair from Trockener Steg

skitracer

CHALETS, HOTELS & APARTMENTS
Call us today
020 8600 1650
skitracer.com

serves more pistes with stunning views, notably the Matterhorn piste – blue in gradient for most of its great length, but classified red because of a short, steep pitch near the end that causes problems for many skiers.

For timid intermediates, the best runs are the blues from Blauherd on Rothorn, and above Riffelberg on Gornergrat, and in good weather the super-high runs between Klein Matterhorn and Trockener Steg. Of these, the Riffelberg area often has the best combination of good snow and easy cruising, and is understandably popular with the ski schools.

In the Matterhorn Glacier Paradise sector most of the runs, though marked red on the piste map, are very flat and include the easiest slopes Zermatt has to offer, as well as the best snow. Even an early intermediate can make the trip to Cervinia, via Theodulpass rather than the more challenging run from Plateau Rosa.

Beware the black run from Furgg to Furi at the end of the day. It is not steep, but gets chopped up, mogulled in places and very crowded. A much more relaxed alternative is the scenic Weisse Perle run from Schwarzsee (the Stafelalp variant is even more scenic but has a short uphill section). The final red run from Furi to the village gets unpleasantly crowded.

FOR BEGINNERS ★★☆☆☆
Still far from ideal
The main beginner area (with three moving carpets and two rope tows) is at Leisee, just below Sunnegga, and reached from there by a short funicular. There is the special Wolli pass to get you to and from that area and allow you to ski the blue run down to Findeln; but other than that progression to longer runs is awkward – the slopes as a whole are very challenging for near-beginners, which includes fast learners who are ready to quit the nursery slopes after a couple of days. Of course, you can learn to ski here, but we would go elsewhere.

FOR BOARDERS ★★★☆☆
Beware the flat spots
The slopes are best for experienced freeriders and the main lifts are boarder-friendly: train, funicular, gondolas, cable cars and fast chairs. There are some flat bits, including on runs 27, 44, 52 and 69.

ZERMATT TOURISM

Wherever you are on the mountain the Matterhorn always dominates the view – see the other photos in this chapter too ↓

THE WORLD'S BEST MOUNTAIN RESTAURANTS ★★★★★

The choice of restaurants is enormous, the standard (and prices) high – with the best serving food worthy of a top London restaurant. We list here only a selection. It is best to book – this is not a resort where it is always easy to just stop for a bite when you are hungry. Restaurants are marked on the piste map, but only a few places are explicitly named. The tourist office restaurant directory has photos, and clues about the style of food, but not prices. Beware: some places don't take cards.

Below Sunnegga, at Findeln, are several attractive, expensive, rustic restaurants sharing a great Matterhorn view. Our favourites are Chez Vrony where service can be stretched but is reliably friendly and the food excellent; and Findlerhof aka Franz and Heide's where we've had delicious lamb. Adler received rave reviews from two 2015 reporters ('stunning views, food seems to get better and better'); spit-roasted chicken a speciality. Further up the Findel valley, in splendid isolation, Fluhalp is another favourite; excellent food and service, often with live music on the huge terrace – endorsed by two readers this year. Up at Blauherd, Blue Lounge is a cool modern bar with sofas and a 'super gas fire', serving simple food such as tapas and 'great burgers' to jazz and other music.

Over at Riffelalp, Alphitta is 'traditional with friendly service and the least expensive place we found to eat all week', says a recent reporter. At Trockener Steg we love the Ice Pizzeria – a smart, modern table-service place with great views; delicious pizzas, as readers agree. The higher Gandegghütte is off the beaten track, has stunning views, friendly service and good, simple food. Over at Schwarzsee, we love the hotel: fab views, fairly simple and limited menu (don't miss the lamb fillets served in a snail dish) and a great band playing 60s/70s music through the afternoon. Lower down, Stafelalp was smartened up and extended a few years ago and is now a cool place in a glorious position, but be prepared to pole to get back to the main piste; fabulous lamb from its own flock of sheep.

SNOWPIX.COM / CHRIS GILL

At Furi, restaurant Furri offers a really friendly welcome, good simple food, a cosy interior and interestingly fragmented terrace. Just above Furi, Mermottes has delicious food including some from the family farm, Aroleid is recommended for rösti, and hotel Silvana has 'good pasta and good service'. Below Furi, our favourite is Zum See, a charming old hut, and one of the best (and most expensive) restaurants on the mountain. Blatten has 'delicious food' and is run by a 'nice family'.

FOR CROSS-COUNTRY ★☆☆☆☆
Down the valley
None in Zermatt but 15km of trails from Täsch to Randa (don't count on good snow at these altitudes though).

SCHOOLS AND GUIDES ★★★☆☆
Good reports
Our most recent reports on the main Swiss school have been positive ('used for snowboard lessons, good standard of instruction', 'lovely instructor, good sense of humour'). Of the other schools, Summit and European Snowsport are staffed mainly by Brits. Summit was praised this year by a reporter whose daughter had her first lessons ('we were really pleased with her progress'). We've also had reports praising European Snowsport ('professional and accommodating') and Prato Borni ('high-quality technical tuition').

FOR FAMILIES ★★☆☆☆
Good hotel nurseries
The prices, the general inconvenience of the place and the challenges facing beginners and near-beginners all work against families. But there are plenty of facilities for children, such as Snowli Kids Village and Kinderparadies, and we don't doubt that they are thoroughly well run. The tourist office has a list of babysitters. 'Choose your location with care,' advises one reader.

STAYING THERE

Chalets Most UK chalet operators pulled out of Zermatt last season because of the high minimum wage legislation. But Skiworld has the central and traditional seven-bedroom Chalet Mazot. Matterhorn Chalets started up last season with the very smart four-bedroom Chalet Ulysses with a sauna close to the Matterhorn Express gondola; prices include an instructor/guide. It will also have two other mega-luxury chalets for 2015/16, one with three-bedrooms, pool and sauna, the other with four bedrooms, sauna and outdoor hot tub. VIP has a couple of three-bedroom places.

Hotels There are over 120 hotels, mostly traditional-style 3-stars and 4-stars, but taking in the whole range. What distinguishes Zermatt is the number of 'hip' places, some of which are listed below.

*****Mont Cervin Biggest and one of the oldest in town; now a blend of traditional and modern style; pool etc.

*****Omnia Designer hotel, minimalist, central, reached by a lift in the rock, smart fitness centre and spa.

****Alex Close to train stations. An old favourite, family-run, delightfully quirky decor, good past reports of rooms and service. Large pool, saunas, steam room, indoor tennis, squash.

****Beau Site Grand place over the river with Matterhorn views – 'Service, food, facilities first class; child-friendly,' says a 2015 reporter.

****Cervo Hip place with rooms, suites, chalets for up to 10. At the end of the piste from Sunnegga.

****Europe Over the river from the church, with fab modern rooms in newish extension.

****Ginabelle Near Sunnegga lift. 'Great pool, spa, fantastic food, excellent service, great views,' says a 2015 visitor.

****Matterhorn Focus Super-stylish B&B designed by Heinz Julen, right by

ALPINE ANSWERS
The UK's No.1 Chalet Specialist

For choice and service look no further!

alpineanswers.co.uk
call: 020 7801 1080
ABTA

the Matterhorn lifts. Indoor pool, outdoor hot tub, sauna.

****Monte Rosa Well-modernized original Zermatt hotel in centre; full of climbing mementos.

****Post All rooms/suites unique and smartly modernized. Sauna, vapour-bath, hot tub. Central with several restaurants, bars, clubs.

****Sonne In quiet setting and highly praised by a regular: 'Superb spa, great food, and the staff couldn't do enough for us.'

****Walliserhof Good reports – 'convenient, very friendly, good food, spacious rooms'. Mini-spa.

***Alpenroyal Reached by elevator near Sunnegga lift. 'Really super. Clean and tidy with lovely staff – efficient, friendly and funny.'

***Romantica Central B&B in old part of town. 'We stayed in one of their "cottages" – very romantic in a converted listed hay shed!'

**Atlanta Good past reports, and tipped for 'excellent value, great staff, rooms and food'. Good position, too.

Selected chalets in Zermatt

ADVERTISEMENT

MATTERHORN CHALETS *www.matterhornchalets.com* T **0041 (0)79 247 15 88**

We are a small and personal organization dedicated to providing our guests with some of the best that Zermatt has to offer. High class accommodation in our charming, comfortable and ideally located chalets with the services of seasoned professionals who know their resort and love what they do – plus your own professional mountain guide or instructor.
book@matterhornchalets.ch

MATTERHORN
CHALETS
WWW.MATTERHORNCHALETS.COM

*Bahnhof Basic place with various forms of accommodation. No meals, but 'very clean, well-equipped kitchen for self-catering'.

Apartments There are lots. Interhome agency has a good selection and we loved the central Breithorn apartment we rented from them in 2015. Matterhorn Chalets has two mega-luxury chalets that can be rented with or without catering (see 'Chalets' above); and it has one-, two- and three-bedroom apartments.

At altitude There are several hotels on the hill, and they are not your regular mountain refuges. The pick is the 5-star Riffelalp Resort, with pool, spa and its own evening trains. At Riffelberg, the recently renovated Riffelhaus is comfortable, with a fab sauna and outdoor hot tub with Matterhorn views. We fancy staying a couple of nights at the Kulmhotel Gornergrat at the top of the mountain – the highest hotel in Switzerland.

IGLU DORF

You can stay the night at this Igloo Village near Riffelberg; dinner is fondue and there are no showers; you won't find us there ↓

EATING OUT ★★★★★
Huge choice

There are over 100 restaurants to choose from: top-quality haute cuisine, through traditional Swiss food, Chinese, Japanese and Thai, to egg and chips. There is even a McDonald's. The tourist office produces a directory, with photos. One reader reckons that you pay a lot less in restaurants at the south end of the village, well away from the centre.

At the top end of the market, Ristorante Capri (in the hotel Mont Cervin) and After Seven (part of the Vernissage/Backstage hotel complex) each have a Michelin star. A Zermatt regular who knows his food tips the cool hotel Cervo ('excellent food, very smart, nice small dining rooms, impeccable service'), Omnia ('wonderful decor, interesting food and wine') and Chez Gaby ('great grilled food, prawns, etc'). Sonnmatten has 'fantastic food, atmosphere and service – expensive, but excellent'.

At more modest prices, we've enjoyed the Schwyzer Stübli (local specialities and jolly Swiss music and dancing) and good-value Mexican and Swiss dishes at the Weisshorn. A 2015 reporter praises Sparky's for being 'one of the cheapest and good for curries and stews – vegetarian options too'. Grampi's has been tipped repeatedly for 'very good simple food, good service'.

Other reader tips include: Klein Matterhorn for fish/pasta; the Brown Cow in the hotel Post ('the best-value meal we had; great burgers in a relaxed bar environment'); Stockhorn ('generous portions, delicious venison'); the Bubble ('fantastic burgers, small, modern decor'); the 'inventive and reasonable' Thai restaurant in the hotel Helvetia; Chez Max Julen ('fantastic carvery-style meals') and the dear old Whymper-Stube. Ferdinand ('fondue/raclette/BBQ') was new last season.

APRES-SKI ★★★★★
Something for everybody

There's a good mix of sophisticated and informal fun, though it helps if you have deep pockets. Promenading the main street checking out expensive clothes and watches is a popular early-evening activity.

There are lively places to pause on the mountain. On our 2015 visit, we loved Dave and the Murpheys, who play great live 60s/70s music at Hotel

Schwarzsee – on the terrace in good weather. Lower down below Furi, Hennu Stall blasts out loud music and attracts huge crowds – live bands play most days. At the end of the piste back from Sunnegga, the funky Cervo has a popular outdoor bar with live music. In town, near the Sunnegga funicular, Caffè Snowboat is a small, modern place that looks like, er, a boat with a deck and lounge bar; and Harry's Skibar is a converted 'chicken shack' that opened last season and is recommended by a local as 'a nice mix of Swiss and Austrian après-ski'.

For a lively bar through the evening you won't beat the Papperla Pub. The long-established North Wall doesn't get many mentions in reports but still seems to be a seasonaires' favourite. Potters Bar (geddit?) is a relaxed 'perfectly nice' British pub with soccer games on TV. Gee's is a comfortable bar that replaced Grampi's bar a couple of seasons ago; mirrors on walls, live music and DJs; below it is the Cuckoo Club disco nightclub.

Elsie's famous wood-panelled bar continues to please our more mature readers ('much enjoyed for its cosy traditional ambience and excellent wine'); it gets seriously busy early and late. Other reader tips include Brit-run Sparky's, the Little Bar (crowded if there are 10 people in) and the cosy, quirky Hexen. Of the hotel bars, the Alex has comfy sofas, good service, a pool table and live music every Friday (Dave and the Murphy's – see above).

Later on, the hotel Post complex has something for everyone, from a quiet, comfortable bar (Papa Caesar's, one of our favourites) to a lively disco (Broken), live music (Pink) and various restaurants. The T-Bar draws a young crowd for dancing and bands. The Schneewittchen nightclub (at the Papperla) is very popular.

OFF THE SLOPES ★★★★☆
Considerable attractions
Zermatt is an attractive place to spend time. As well as expensive jewellery and clothes shops, there are interesting places selling food, wine, books and art. It is easy (but costly) for pedestrians to get around on the lifts and meet others for lunch, and there are some splendid walks (70km) – a special map is available.

If the weather is good, the Klein Matterhorn cable car is an experience not to be missed: there is a small self-service restaurant at the top as well as a viewing platform and an ice cave, with 'incredible carvings'. Be aware that the air is thin up there, though.

The Matterhorn Museum in the village is well worth a visit. You can take a helicopter trip around the Matterhorn. There is a cinema, and village guided tours. You can try curling or skating on the outdoor ice rink and go snowshoeing and tobogganing. For an icy experience, visit (or stay at) the Igloo Village above Riffelberg. It's easy to visit various Swiss cities by rail.

DOWN-VALLEY VILLAGE – 1450m
TÄSCH

Täsch, where visitors must leave their cars, is just a 12-minute train ride from Zermatt, so it makes a viable base. There are several 3-star hotels charging half the Zermatt price. The Täscherhof and Walliserhof have been recommended by past reporters. Täsch is very quiet in the evening, but it's no problem to spend evenings in Zermatt – trains run until late. And taxis can operate up to the edge of Zermatt.

✳ **Want the next edition free?**

Send us a useful report on your holiday, and you could be among those who win one of 100 free copies. Then you might become one of our 'resort observers', and get free lift passes.

Find out more at:

www.wheretoskiandsnowboard.com

GETTING THERE
Air Geneva 240km/ 150 miles (3hr30); Zürich 250km/ 155 miles (4hr30); Sion 80km/ 50 miles (1hr30)

Rail Station in resort

TOURIST OFFICE
www.zermatt.ch

What got the USA started in the UK market, at a time when snow in the Alps was going through a tricky phase, was its generally reliable snow, and that remains a key ingredient – along with the fact that you get access to steep ungroomed slopes that are avalanche-controlled, and don't require expensive guidance. Other factors are the relatively deserted runs ('trails' in the local parlance), spacious lodgings, excellent and varied resort restaurants, and high standards of service and courtesy. Depending on the resort, you may also be struck by the cute Wild West ambience and the superb quality of the snow.

Of course, US skiing does have disadvantages, too. Not the least of these is the cost – long-haul flights are not cheap, and the costs of lift passes and instruction are seriously high (as we go to press in the summer, higher than a year ago because of exchange rate changes).

We have organized our US chapters in regional sections – California, Colorado, Utah, Rest of the West and New England.

Most American resorts receive serious amounts of snow – typically season totals in the region of 6m to 12m (or 250 to 500 inches, as they measure it there); that's around double the 3m to 6m that resorts like Chamonix, St Anton and Val d'Isère in Europe average. The snowfalls tend to arrive more frequently than in Europe, too, so your chances of hitting fresh snow are appreciably higher. But there are wide variations in quantity and quality of snowfall. Most resorts have serious snowmaking facilities that are used well – laying down a base of snow early in the season.

The classification of trails is different from that in Europe. The colours used are combined with shapes. There are no red runs. Green circles correspond fairly closely to greens in France and easy blues in the rest of Europe. American blue squares correspond to blues and easy reds in Europe; the tougher ones are sometimes labelled as double squares, or as blue-black squares. Then there are black diamond runs, which is where things get interesting. Single diamonds correspond fairly closely to European blacks and really tough reds. But then there are multiple diamonds. Double-diamond

PATROLLED AND AVALANCHE-CONTROLLED OFF-PISTE

One of the great attractions of North American resorts is that they have patrolled and avalanche-controlled ungroomed terrain that in Europe would be classified as ski-at-your-own-risk off-piste. Each resort has a ski area boundary; this may be marked by signs on the trees bordering the trails or there may be a rope; the boundary may be moved, depending on snow conditions. Anywhere within the boundary ('in-bounds') is patrolled and avalanche-controlled. In-bounds terrain includes areas between marked and groomed trails and often big areas of ski-anywhere bowls or steep couloirs (or chutes, to use the local term). In Europe such terrain is normally off-piste, and we recommend you ski it only with a qualified local guide, which is of course expensive.

Terrain outside the ski area boundary ('backcountry') is often accessible through gates placed at various points on the boundary. In some places the official position is that you cannot cross the boundary. Backcountry terrain is not controlled or patrolled; it should be treated like European off-piste and skied only with a guide.

SNOWPIX.COM / CHRIS GILL

← Powder snow on lightly wooded, avalanche-controlled slopes – a key attraction of the USA; this is Breckenridge, last February

runs are seriously steep – usually steeper than the steepest pistes in the Alps. A few resorts have wildly steep 'extreme' terrain, which may be awarded double diamonds, or even triple diamonds.

The most obvious drawback to the US is that many resorts have slopes that are very modest in extent compared with major Alpine areas. You can compare resort size in various ways but, according to the estimable Christoph Schrahe (read our piste extent feature chapter), in overall area the biggest American areas have up to now been about a third the size of the Three Valleys in France, for example. Even the newly linked Park City and Canyons will come nowhere near the Alpine leaders.

Smaller resorts often have other resorts nearby – so if you are prepared to travel a bit, you won't get bored. Roads are good, and car hire is relatively cheap (watch out for extra insurance charges, though). But if snow is expected, you will need a 4WD or snow chains; bizarrely, you have to buy your chains – we've yet to find a US rental company that will provide them. And watch out for SUVs that look like they are 4WD motors but are not.

It's also true that in many resorts the mountains are slightly monotonous, with countless similar trails cut through the forest. You don't usually get the spectacular scenery and distinctive high-mountain runs of the Alps. But the forest runs do offer good visibility in bad weather and it's normal to be able to ski in among the trees themselves; a particular delight is lightly wooded areas they call glades. Go back a page for an example.

GREAT GROOMING AND DESERTED SLOPES

Piste grooming is taken very seriously – most US resorts set standards that only the best Alpine resorts seem to be able to match. Every morning you can expect to step out on to perfect 'corduroy' pistes. But this doesn't mean that there aren't moguls – far from it. It's just that you get moguls where the resort says you can expect moguls, not everywhere. In some resorts (notably Winter Park), virtually all the black runs are never groomed.

The slopes of most US resorts are blissfully free of crowds – a key advantage that becomes more important as the pistes of Europe become ever more congested. If you want to ski quickly and safely with less fear of collisions, head for the States.

Ski schools offer consistently high standards but work in a way that's different from the European pattern – people don't sign up for a week, only for one or two lessons as they feel the need, and you may get a different instructor every day. Prices are high. Most resorts offer free guided tours of the ski area once or twice a day (usually run by volunteers); and many have 'mountain hosts' on hand to help you find your way. Signposting is generally exemplary.

Lifts are generally efficient, and queues are orderly and short, partly because spare seats are religiously filled with the aid of cheerful, conscientious attendants. You find Americans on chairlifts expect to chat – a bit of a shock at first, but we like it. First-time visitors are surprised that some chairlifts in the States do not have safety bars; even on a chair that has a bar, you will find Americans curiously reluctant to use it. The lifts close irritatingly early – as early as 3pm in some cases (and some upper lifts might start closing as early as 1.30pm). That may explain the dearth of decent mountain restaurants. The norm is a monster (but crowded) self-service refuelling station – designed to minimize time off the slopes.

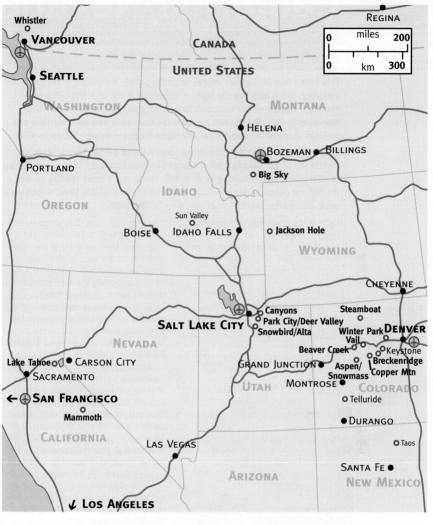

US resort towns vary widely in style and convenience, from cute restored mining towns to purpose-built monstrosities. Two common factors are high-quality, spacious accommodation and restaurants that are reliably good and varied in cuisine. Young people should be aware that the rigorously enforced legal age for drinking alcohol is 21; if you look anything near that age, carry evidence of date of birth. Sale and use of cannabis is now legal in Colorado, and you'll find it openly on sale in some resorts.

Crossing the pond is no longer cheap, and extras such as lift passes, ski hire and ski school are very expensive. Even the cheapest resorts are more expensive in these respects than the most expensive in Europe. With lift passes, you can often save huge amounts by buying in advance through tour operators or websites. Of course, a key factor is the exchange rate. As we go to press in July 2015 the rate is $1.5 – appreciably down on a year ago, and approaching its 2013 level. Local prices are over 30% higher in £££ than they were in the heady days of 2007, when we got $2 to £1.

SHOWPIX.COM / CHRIS GILL

California/Nevada

This region may conjure up images of surfing, wine, Hollywood, Disneyland and gambling. But it also has the highest mountains in the USA and some of America's biggest winter resorts. It has traditionally had reliable snow from November to May. But the last few seasons have seen very low snowfalls and we have changed our snow reliability rating for Heavenly and Squaw to ★★★.

Most visitors head for the Lake Tahoe area, mapped below. Spectacularly set high in the Sierra Nevada 320km east of San Francisco, Lake Tahoe is ringed by skiable mountains containing 14 downhill resorts and 7 cross-country centres – the highest concentration of winter sports resorts in the USA. Then, a long way south (more often reached from LA), there is Mammoth.

Each of the three major 'destination' resorts – Heavenly and Squaw Valley, at opposite ends of Lake Tahoe, and Mammoth, way off our map to the south – is covered in its own chapter

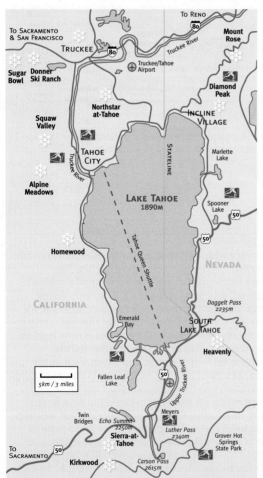

following this page. The other main Lake Tahoe resorts (shown on our map) each have an entry in the resort directory at the back of the book. Many are well worth visiting for a day or two, especially the four second-division resorts – Alpine Meadows (next door to Squaw and now in the same ownership with a shared pass), Kirkwood, Northstar- and Sierra-at-Tahoe. We have also enjoyed Sugar Bowl and Mount Rose.

As we say in the intro above, Californian resorts have had a series of poor snow years recently (to the extent that one 2015 reporter said, 'This will be my last ever visit to any California ski resort – too many bad experiences with a lack of snow.'). But in a 'normal' year the snow is fine by Alpine standards – we've had great powder days in all the major resorts.

Californian resorts don't have the traditional mountain-town ambience of many resorts in other parts of the States, particularly Colorado. The car-free plaza in South Lake Tahoe called Heavenly Village and the pedestrian Village at Mammoth – both linked to the slopes above by gondola – are not at all special. But Squaw Valley and Northstar have both developed more substantial base villages.

You could visit all the Tahoe resorts by car (best to have a 4WD) from a single base; but a two-centre holiday including some time at both ends of the lake would be better. A six-pack of lift tickets covering seven resorts around the lake is available (go to www.skilaketahoe.com).

The drives from major airports are non-trivial. Consider taking onward flights to Reno (for Tahoe) and Mammoth Yosemite.

SCOTT MARKEWITZ

Heavenly

Heavenly is unique: one of the USA's biggest mountains, with fabulous lake and 'desert' views, above a tacky casino town

£180
RESORT PRICE INDEX

RATINGS

The mountains

Extent	★★★
Fast lifts	★★★★
Queues	★★★★
Terrain p'ks	★★★★★
Snow	★★★
Expert	★★★
Intermediate	★★★★
Beginner	★★★★
Boarder	★★★★
X-country	★★
Restaurants	★
Schools	★★★★
Families	★★

The resort

Charm	★
Convenience	★
Scenery	★★★★
Eating out	★★★★
Après-ski	★★★
Off-slope	★★★

NEWS

2015/16: The Sky Deck bar and restaurant is due to be given a new look. In South Lake Tahoe various hotels are due to get an upgrade. The Château at the Village retail and restaurant complex is expanding with condominiums, a gym, pool and spa.

2014/15: Activities at Adventure Peak were expanded to include ziplines.

KEY FACTS

Resort	1900m
	6,230ft
Slopes	2000-3060m
	6,570-10,040ft
Lifts	29
Pistes	4,800 acres

HEAVENLY

Editor Gill loved the spectacular view of the lake while strutting his stuff in this half-pipe →

- ➕ Spectacular views of Lake Tahoe and the Nevada 'desert' from slopes
- ➕ Fair-sized mountain that offers a sensation of travelling around
- ➕ Large areas of widely spaced trees – fabulous in fresh powder
- ➕ Some serious challenges for experts
- ➕ Other worthwhile resorts reachable
- ➕ Good snow and snowmaking
- ➕ Unique nightlife in town at base

- ➖ If natural snow is poor, most of the challenging terrain may be closed
- ➖ Town at base, South Lake Tahoe, is a messy, traffic-ridden place
- ➖ No trail back to central SLT
- ➖ Lifts vulnerable to wind closure
- ➖ Pronounced step from easy groomed blues to mogulled blacks
- ➖ Mountain restaurants dire
- ➖ Very little traditional après-ski

With a top height of 3060m and vertical of 1060m, Heavenly is the highest and biggest of the resorts around famously deep, pure and beautiful Lake Tahoe. It has the best lake views, too. But anyone drawn by the scenic setting is likely to be dismayed by the barren base town of South Lake Tahoe, straddling busy US Highway 50. You could stay out of town, close to one of the other lift bases.

And the skiing? If your taste is for easy Alpine blacks or tough reds, just be sure you are ready to step up to ungroomed stuff (and hope that the snow is good enough) – you'll find the blues tame.

THE RESORT

South Lake Tahoe, on the shore of the lake, is primarily a summer resort. It straddles the California-Nevada border, and its economy is based on gambling, which Nevada permits. The central area is dominated by a handful of high-rise casino hotels on the Nevada side of the border.

These brash but comfortable hotels offer good-value rooms (subsidized by the gambling), swanky restaurants and various entertainments. Picking your way between the slot machines in ski gear, carrying skis or board, is weird.

Near the casino area is the small Heavenly Village, purpose-built around

the main lift base. There are other lift base areas (with lodgings) on both the California and Nevada sides of the hill.

Other resorts around the lake are easily visited, and lift passes that cover several areas are available. A car is handy to explore them (although buses, some free, are available) and to get to many of the best restaurants, but parking can be expensive.

The obvious gateway airport is San Francisco, but Reno is much closer, and the road up less likely to be affected by snow.

VILLAGE CHARM ★☆☆☆☆
The highway rules
From a distance the casinos look like a classic American downtown area, which you'd expect to be full of shops and bars. But there's hardly any of that – just the seriously busy and pedestrian-hostile Highway 50. The rest of the town spreads for miles along the road – dozens of low-rise hotels and motels, stores, wedding chapels and so on. The general effect is less dire than it might be, thanks to the camouflage of tall trees. Heavenly Village provides a downtown après-ski focus (basically just one bar), but it has little else to offer.

CONVENIENCE ★☆☆☆☆
Gamble on the gondola?
The central area close to Heavenly Village and the gondola looks the obvious place to stay, despite the lack of trails down to it. Some of the casino hotels are within five minutes' walk of the gondola, but others are a hike away. There are lodgings close to the other lift bases – California Lodge, up a heavily wooded slope 2km out of town, and the more remote Nevada bases, Boulder Lodge and Stagecoach Lodge. And there are cheaper places literally miles from a lift, used largely by people with cars. But there are free shuttle-buses.

SCENERY ★★★★☆
Splendid panoramas
The views over Lake Tahoe, ringed by snow-capped mountains, are spectacular. The casinos are a conspicuous part of those views from the lower slopes, though not from above mid-mountain; Ridge Run is good for lake views. In the other direction is arid Nevada – sufficiently arid to be classified as desert, though the Sahara it ain't.

THE MOUNTAINS

Practically all of Heavenly's slopes are cut through forest, but in many areas the forest is not dense and there is excellent tree skiing. The trail map gives a good indication of the density of trees. As elsewhere in the US, this 'off-piste' terrain is 'patrolled', but only by hollering – ineffective if you are unconscious; don't ski the trees alone.

Two days a week, am and pm, there are free and 'excellent' mountain tours led by forest rangers.

EXTENT OF THE SLOPES ★★★☆☆
Interestingly complex
The mountain is complicated, and getting from A to B requires more careful navigation than is usual on American mountains. Quite a few of the links between different sectors involve long, flat tracks.

There is a clear division between the California side of the mountain (above South Lake Tahoe) and the Nevada side. If lift closures leave you on the wrong side, it's not a big deal – the bus rides don't take long.

The gondola from South Lake Tahoe goes to one end of the California side. There is no skiing back to the town. At the other end of this side, the steep lower slopes are served by the Aerial Tramway (cable car) and Gunbarrel fast chair from California Lodge. The much more extensive upper slopes are served by four fast chairs, one going up to the Skyline trail to the Nevada side.

The Nevada side is more fragmented, but the central focus is East Peak Lodge. Above it is an excellent intermediate area, served by two fast quad chairs, with a downhill extension served by the Galaxy chair. From the fast Dipper chair back up, you can access the open terrain of Milky Way Bowl, leading to the seriously steep Mott and Killebrew Canyons, served by the slow Mott Canyon chair. Below East Peak Lodge are runs down to Nevada's two bases, Stagecoach and Boulder – the latter often quiet because its chairs are slow.

FAST LIFTS ★★★★☆
California does it better
Most people can spend practically all their time on fast chairs. The Mott Canyon chair is slow, but that's a niche market. The main weaknesses are the slow chairs up from Boulder Lodge.

LIFT PASSES

Prices in US$

Age	6-day
under 13	300
13 to 18	426
19 to 64	516
65 plus	426
Free Under 5	

Beginner Combined lesson/limited lift pass/equipment deals

Notes These are online prices for early February booked at least 3 days in advance; reduced prices to international visitors who pre-book through a UK tour operator

QUEUES ★★★★
Gondola up and down
The gondola can have queues to go up and particularly to go down – and because of this you'll see signs advising you to get back to the gondola ridiculously early. Pay no attention – have a beer or two at the top while waiting for the queue to dissipate. Or forget the gondola and head for one of the other bases, and jump on a shuttle. A couple of past reporters have found queues for the slow Groove chair and the Sky Express at the end of the day when people are returning to base. Another reported crowds around the lifts from East Peak Lodge on the Nevada side. Some lifts, including the gondola, also seem prone to closure because of wind. Most reporters have had few other problems, often commenting on uncrowded slopes.

TERRAIN PARKS ★★★★★
Splendid for all abilities
Heavenly has something for everyone – all sensibly located on the California slopes. At the top of the lifts up from California Lodge, Progression Park has mini features and is the place to try your first freestyle moves. Next to it,

Groove Park has beginner/intermediate features for riders wanting to move to the next level. Ante Up Park under the Tamarack chair has intermediate/advanced features. High Roller Park, near the top of the Canyon chair, serves expert riders. A half-pipe (5.5m high and 150m long) was built last season after a gap of four years.

SNOW RELIABILITY ★★★
Risky for experts
Heavenly claims an impressive average of 360 inches per year, but the weather here is much less consistent than further inland and the last two seasons (especially last season) have been very dry and warm. When snow is poor and temperatures are cold enough, intermediates can still have a good time thanks to impressive snowmaking and grooming. But much of the challenging ungroomed terrain can be closed when snow is poor (and was for much of last season). Lake Tahoe TV provides updates on snow conditions each day.

FOR EXPERTS ★★★
Some specific challenges
The black runs under the California base lifts – including the Face and

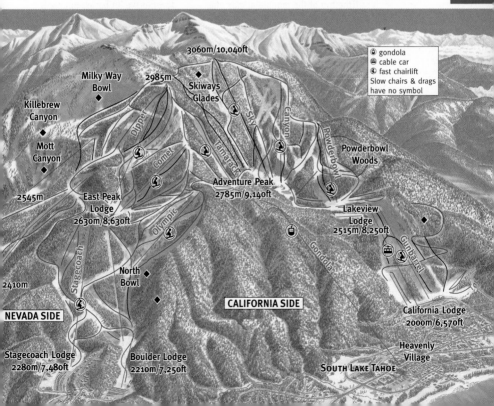

gondola
cable car
fast chairlift
Slow chairs & drags have no symbol

3060m/10,040ft

Milky Way Bowl
2985m
Skiways Glades

Killebrew Canyon

Mott Canyon

Dipper
Comet
Sky
Tamarack
Canyon
Powderbowl
Olympic
Gondola
Gunbarrel

Powderbowl Woods

2545m

East Peak Lodge
2630m/8,630ft

Adventure Peak
2785m/9,140ft

Lakeview Lodge
2515m/8,250ft

North Bowl

2410m

Stagecoach

NEVADA SIDE

CALIFORNIA SIDE

California Lodge
2000m/6,570ft

Heavenly Village

Stagecoach Lodge
2280m/7,480ft

Boulder Lodge
2210m/7,250ft

SOUTH LAKE TAHOE

↑ Those pesky high-rise casinos intrude on the views from the lower slopes. But higher up you don't notice them
HEAVENLY

Gunbarrel (often used for mogul competitions) – are seriously steep. We've seen lots of people struggling on the top-to-bottom icy bumps. Many of the single diamonds higher up are at the easy end of the range. Ellie's, at the top of the mountain, may offer continuous moguls too, but was groomed and a great fast cruise when we last skied it. Skiways Glades and the Pinnacles, to skier's right of that, offer friendly, widely spaced trees. Lower down, a trusted reader raves about Maggie's Canyon.

On the Nevada side there are some excellent single-diamond glade areas too – notably to skier's left of the slow North Bowl chair. And there is some really steep stuff. Milky Way Bowl provides a gentle single-diamond introduction to the double-diamond terrain beyond it: the chutes in the otherwise densely wooded Mott and Killebrew Canyons are seriously steep and narrow. They are accessed through roped gateways, and are not to be underestimated. The Mott Canyon chair is slow, but you may not mind. Good natural snow is needed for the Canyons to be enjoyable (or open).

FOR INTERMEDIATES ★★★★
Lots to do
The California side offers a progression from the relaxed cruising of the long Ridge Run, starting right at the top of the mountain, to more challenging

blues dropping off the ridge towards Sky Deck. More confident intermediates will want to spend time on the Nevada side, where there is more variety of terrain, more carving space and some great longer cruises down to the lift bases. But really strong intermediates looking for challenges need to be prepared to step up to the tree runs – maybe starting with Powderbowl Woods or The Pines – or to the blacks, which are often mogulled.

FOR BEGINNERS ★★★★
An excellent place to learn
There are excellent beginner areas at the top of the gondola, at California Lodge and at Boulder Lodge. On the California side there are gentle green runs to progress to at the top of the cable car. Package deals of tuition and lift ticket are worth looking into.

FOR BOARDERS ★★★★
Perfect playground – nearly
Heavenly has several terrain parks, and the resort's naturally varied terrain makes a perfect playground for advanced freeriders. Intermediates will have fun too, especially if there's powder in the trees. And there are good areas for beginners. But beware: there are many flat spots where you'll have to scoot.

FOR CROSS-COUNTRY ★★☆☆☆
A separate world

None at Heavenly but plenty at cross-country centres around the lake.

MOUNTAIN RESTAURANTS ★☆☆☆☆
Dire – but improving slowly

The on-mountain catering is grossly inadequate, especially in bad weather. Booyah's sports bar in Lakeview Lodge offers table-service, build-your-own burgers and 97 varieties of microbrews. The best of the self-service places is Tamarack Lodge at the top of the gondola. The other options are outdoor decks serving BBQs and pizzas (hugely unenjoyable in a blizzard, as we can testify) and grossly overcrowded cafeterias.

SCHOOLS AND GUIDES ★★★★☆
No recent reports

Past reports have generally been good but we lack recent ones. As usual in the US, groups tend to be small.

FOR FAMILIES ★★☆☆☆
Head for Adventure Peak

Heavenly offers various children's programmes and facilities. There's a kids' ski school building and adventure zone near the top of the gondola at Adventure Peak, which is also home to family activities such as tubing.

STAYING THERE

Accommodation in the South Lake Tahoe area is abundant and ranges from the huge casinos to small motels.
Hotels Of the main casino hotels, Harrah's and Harveys are the closest to the gondola.
★★★★Embassy Suites Luxury suites close to the gondola. Breakfast and après cocktails included.
★★★Aston Lakeland Village Wide range of lodgings from studios to five-bedroom condos. Right by the lake. Bus or drive to lifts.
★★★Avalon Lodge Small boutique hotel two blocks from the gondola.
★★★Inn by the Lake Less convenient but big rooms, some with good views. Hot tub, pool.
★★★Stardust Lodge Over the road from the gondola, tipped by two recent reporters – 'lovely apartments, friendly, great hot tub, convenient'.
★★★Station House Inn A Best Western near the gondola; approved by past reporters for comfortable rooms and good cooked breakfasts.

★★★3 Peaks Resort Convenient, with large rooms. Pool.
Apartments Plenty of choice.

EATING OUT ★★★★☆
Good value and choice

There's a huge variety, at least if you are prepared to drive (and not drink). The casino hotels' all-you-can-eat buffets offer great value and variety, and there are 'gourmet' choices too – try 19 Kitchen and Bar on the 19th floor at Harveys.

LewMarNel's at the Station House Inn serves good fish, pasta, steak and veal. The Stateline Brewery does pub fare. MacDuff's Public House, near the Inn by the Lake, is billed as a Scottish pub and has a wood-fired pizza oven and pub grub.

Other past reporter tips include Fresh Ketch at Tahoe Keys Marina, Evan's American Gourmet Cafe and the 'good-value' Applebee's. Other options include Heidi's for breakfast, Nikki's Chaat Cafe (Indian), the Blue Angel and the Driftwood Cafe.

APRES-SKI ★★★☆☆
From bars to baccarat

For years there has been a bit of late-afternoon action at the top of the gondola, to provide an alternative to queuing for the lift down. And for the last couple of seasons, there's been an organized party: 'Unbuckle at Tamarack runs from 3.30pm to 5.30pm daily, featuring live DJs, dancing, half-price drinks and the Heavenly Angel dancers on Fridays and Saturdays,' they say.

Fire+Ice at the foot of the gondola (with an outdoor seating area with open fires and heaters) gets busy. Whiskey Dick's, on the main highway, has regular live music.

Later on, the casinos have shows, occasionally with top-name entertainers, as well as endless opportunities for throwing your money away gambling.

OFF THE SLOPES ★★★☆☆
Quite a bit to entertain

If you want to get away from the bright lights, try a boat trip or a hot-air balloon ride. Pedestrians can use the cable car or the gondola to share the lake views. The expanded Adventure Peak at the top of the gondola has tubing, snow biking, tobogganing and two ziplines. There's ice skating and snowmobiling.

GETTING THERE

Air San Francisco 320km/200 miles (3hr30); Reno 90km/55 miles (1hr15); South Lake Tahoe (15min)

TOURIST OFFICE

www.skiheavenly.com

Mammoth Mountain

A big, sprawling mountain above a car-oriented, sprawling but pleasantly woody resort, a five-hour drive from Los Angeles

£180
RESORT PRICE INDEX

RATINGS

The mountains

Extent	★★★
Fast lifts	★★★★
Queues	★★★★
Terrain p'ks	★★★★★
Snow	★★★★
Expert	★★★★
Intermediate	★★★★
Beginner	★★★★
Boarder	★★★★★
X-country	★★★★
Restaurants	★
Schools	★★★★
Families	★★★★

The resort

Charm	★★
Convenience	★★
Scenery	★★★
Eating out	★★★★★
Après-ski	★★★
Off-slope	★

544

NEWS

2014/15: Rhythm Ridge, a new four-acre area of bowls, berms, banks and bumps for all levels, opened. A new bar-restaurant, 53 Kitchen and Cocktails, opened in The Village.

KEY FACTS

Resort	2425m
	7,950ft
Slopes	2425-3370m
	7,950-11,050ft
Lifts	28
Pistes	3,500 acres

- ➕ Slopes to suit all abilities
- ➕ Mix of open Alpine-style bowls and classic American wooded slopes
- ➕ Impressive snowfall record
- ➕ Uncrowded trails most of the time
- ➕ Mightily impressive terrain parks
- ➕ Good views by US standards

- ➖ Mammoth Lakes is a rather straggling place with no focus, where life revolves around cars
- ➖ Most, though not all, lodgings are miles from the slopes
- ➖ Weekend crowds in high season
- ➖ Wind can be a problem

Mammoth may not be mammoth in Alpine terms – from end to end it's less than one-third of the size of Val d'Isère-Tignes, in area more like one-sixth. But in American terms it's a decent size, with enough to keep most visitors happy.

These days there is something resembling a village to stay in – The Village, a typically careful Intrawest confection of lodgings, restaurants and shops. But most people stay elsewhere – in hotels, condos and houses spread around the vast wooded area of Mammoth Lakes – and never go near it. Pick your location carefully, and you can walk to a lift; get a car, and you open up lots of options.

THE RESORT

The mountain is set above Mammoth Lakes, a small year-round resort that spreads over a wide area of woodland and is close to Yosemite National Park (local entrance road closed in winter). The drive up from Los Angeles takes around five hours (more in poor conditions). You pass through the Santa Monica mountains close to Beverly Hills, then the San Gabriel mountains and Mojave Desert (with the world's biggest jet-plane parking lot) before reaching the Sierra Nevada.

The place is almost entirely geared to driving, with no discernible centre – hotels, restaurants and little shopping centres are scattered along the four-lane highway called Main Street and Old Mammoth Road, which crosses it.

Two lift bases are both a mile or two from most of the hotels and condos. The major one is Canyon Lodge, with a big day lodge and hotels and condos in the area below it. A green run (very flat in parts) from here goes down to The Village, a typical car-free Intrawest development that opened in 2003; there's a gondola back up to Canyon Lodge. The minor base is Eagle Lodge (aka Juniper Springs, the adjacent condos).

A road skirts the mountain to two other lift base areas: Mill Cafe, and Main Lodge, a mini-resort with a big day lodge. You can stay here, in the Mammoth Mountain Inn.

June Mountain is half an hour away from Mammoth and is covered by the lift pass; it is spectacularly underused and well worth a visit when Mammoth's slopes are crowded.

VILLAGE CHARM ★★★★★
Not an eyesore

The resort buildings are generally timber-clad in traditional style – even the McDonald's is tastefully designed – and are set among trees. So although it may be short on village ambience, the place has a pleasant enough appearance – particularly when under several feet of snow. The Village is car-free, and neatly designed.

CONVENIENCE ★★★★★
Canyon Lodge is closest

Even ignoring outlying parts, Mammoth Lakes is spread over an area roughly two miles square, so location obviously matters. If you stay at one of the lift bases, you'll have only a short walk to a lift. But out at Main Lodge you'll be four miles from the 50+ restaurants in Mammoth Lakes. With its gondola link to Canyon Lodge, The Village is also a fairly convenient base.

Reliable, frequent and free shuttle-buses run on several colour-coded routes serving the lift bases. Less frequent night buses run until midnight. But a car is useful.

LIFT PASSES

Mammoth Mountain

Prices in US$

Age	6-day
under 13	210
13 to 18	392
19 to 64	502
65 plus	425

Free Under 5, over 80

Beginner Pass for four chairs

Alternative pass
June Mountain

PETER MORNING

The Canyon Lodge area is a good place to stay: right by the slopes and not too far from downtown ↓

SCENERY ★★★
Hint of the Alpine

The resort has a wooded setting below open Alpine-style ridges. From the top there are great views north-east into Nevada, and of the jagged Minarets.

THE MOUNTAINS

The 28 lifts access an impressive area, suitable for all abilities. The high runs are open, the lower ones sheltered by trees; lightly wooded slopes at mid-mountain are great on a stormy day.

Finding your way around is not easy at first. All the chairlifts are numbered (the traditional practice), and many are also named (a relatively new practice), but the trails are rather ill defined, and signposting on the mountain could be better. The resort trail map uses six grades of difficulty instead of the usual four, of which we approve. There are free mountain tours daily plus free tours on Fridays, Saturdays and Sundays that cover the ski area's environment as well as show you around the trails.

EXTENT OF THE SLOPES ★★★
Lots for everyone

As you can see from our star ratings, Mammoth is good for every ability of skier and boarder. But it's not huge – it falls right on the borderline between our ★★ and ★★★ extent ratings and we've erred on the generous side.

From **Main Lodge** the two-stage

Panorama gondola goes via McCoy Station right to the top. From here, there are countless ways down the front of the mountain that range from steep to very steep – or vertical if the wind has created a cornice, as it often does. Or you can go off the back of the hill, down to **Outpost 14**, whence Chair 14 or Chair 13 brings you back to lower points on the ridge. The third option is to follow the ridge, which curls around and eventually brings you down to the Main Lodge area. This route brings you past an easy area served by a double chair (12), and a very easy area served by the Discovery fast quad.

McCoy Station can also be reached using the Stump Alley fast chair from **Mill Cafe**, on the road up from town. The fast Gold Rush quad, also from Mill Cafe, takes you into the more heavily wooded eastern half of the area. This has long, gentle runs served by lifts up from **Canyon Lodge** and **Eagle Lodge** and seriously steep stuff as well as some intermediate terrain served by lifts 25 and 22 and some excellent tree skiing.

FAST LIFTS ★★★★
Where it counts

The main access lifts from every base are fast chairs or gondolas. But there are still several slow old lifts. The Outpost area is the least well served for fast lifts. Usefully, the trail map lists the ride time of every lift.

QUEUES ★★★★
Normally quiet slopes

Mammoth's lifts and slopes are usually very quiet, with few queues: 'Queues? What queues?' says a reporter. But on fine peak-season weekends hordes of people may arrive from Los Angeles, and the lifts can struggle to cope. Which explains why one of the privileges of membership of the exclusive Mammoth Black club is that you get lift priority. If crowds are a problem, just head for June Mountain and ski its delightfully deserted pistes.

TERRAIN PARKS ★★★★★
World class – and lots of them

'Absolutely awesome,' is the summary of a recent reporter. Mammoth's world-class Unbound Terrain Parks offer a huge variety of challenges from elementary to mind-blowing, all looked after with artistic proficiency. There are over 50 jumps and about 100 other features plus three half-pipes in over 100 acres of freestyle territory.

Easiest are the three Unbound Playgrounds at Eagle, Canyon and Main Lodges (with small features and a 3m half-pipe beside the Canyon Playground). Forest Trail at Main Lodge is one step up. For intermediate to advanced riders South Park and Jibs Galore offer a bewildering choice of rails and kickers with a super-pipe (122m long, with 5m walls) at South Park. Alternatively, take on the X-Course snowcross run or, new for last season, Rhythm Ridge's four-acre area of bumps and other features.

Main Park, above Main Lodge, is huge; everything here is up to pro standard. The famous super-duper pipe (168m long, with 7m walls) that looms over the car park is cut daily. Main Park is serviced by a fast chairlift, allowing for a full lap time of only eight minutes.

SNOW RELIABILITY ★★★★
A long season

Mammoth has an impressive snow record – an annual average of 400 inches, which puts it ahead of major Colorado resorts (though last season was very warm and dry with only 176 inches when it closed in late May). Its slopes are appreciably higher than those of Heavenly and the other Tahoe resorts, and it has an ever-expanding array of snow-guns, so it enjoys a long season – it sometimes has slopes open on 4 July (US Independence Day). The mountain faces roughly north-east; the relatively low and slightly sunny slopes down to Eagle Lodge are affected by warm weather before others. Strong winds are not uncommon on the upper mountain, and the snow quality can be affected. But you may find powder is just shifted down the hill. Visitors continue to report 'excellent' grooming.

FOR EXPERTS ★★★★
Some very challenging terrain

The steep double-diamond chutes strung across the width of the mountaintop provide wonderful opportunities for experts. Fortunately for the rest of us, there are three or four broad single-diamond slopes,

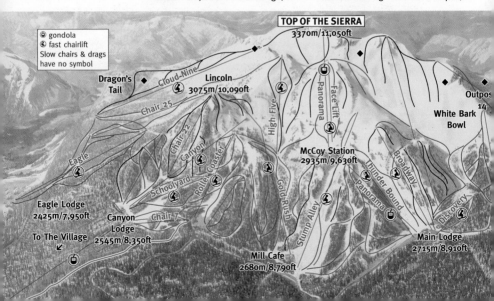

gondola
fast chairlift
Slow chairs & drags have no symbol

Dragon's Tail
Cloud-Nine
Lincoln 3075m/10,090ft
TOP OF THE SIERRA
3370m/11,050ft
Chair 25
Chair 22
High-Five
Face Lift
Panorama
Outpos
14
White Bark Bowl
Eagle
Canyon
Roller Coaster
McCoy Station 2935m/9,630ft
Thunder Bound
Broadway
Schoolyard
Gold Rush
Panorama
Discovery
Eagle Lodge 2425m/7,950ft
Canyon Lodge 2545m/8,350ft
Chair 7
To The Village
Stump Alley
Mill Cafe 268om/8,790ft
Main Lodge 2715m/8,910ft

On powder days there's plenty of gentle ungroomed terrain for intermediates to play on →

PETER MORNING

requiring rather less bottle.

There is lots of challenging terrain lower down, too, much of it lightly wooded and therefore good to ski in bad conditions; Chair 5, Chair 22 (the top of which is higher than the very top of Heavenly) and Broadway are often open in bad weather when the top is firmly shut, and their more sheltered slopes may in any case have the best snow. There are plenty of good slopes over the back, too.

Many of the steeper trails are short by Alpine standards (typically under 400m vertical), but despite this we've had some great powder days here.

FOR INTERMEDIATES ★★★★
Lots of great cruising

Although there are exceptions, most of the lower mountain, below the treeline, is intermediate cruising territory and generally flattering.

Some of the mountain's longest runs – blue-blacks served by the Cloud Nine Express and Chair 25 – are ideal for good intermediates. There are also some excellent, fairly steep woodland trails down to Mill Cafe. Most of the long runs above Eagle Lodge, and some of the shorter ones above Canyon Lodge, are easy cruises. There is a variety of terrain, including lots of gentle stuff, on skier's left of the area.

FOR BEGINNERS ★★★★
Good, gentle slopes

Chair 7 and the Schoolyard Express chair (at the Canyon Lodge base) and Discovery Chair (at Main Lodge) serve quiet, gentle green runs – perfect terrain for novices. These lifts are included in a beginner lift pass. Excellent instruction and top-notch piste maintenance usually make progress speedy, delighting reporters.

FOR BOARDERS ★★★★★
Great parks and terrain

Regularly voted one of the best snowboard resorts in the USA by *Transworld Snowboarding* magazine readers, Mammoth has encouraged snowboarding since its early days: 'We felt like we were being welcomed home here!' said a reporter. A huge amount has been spent on the terrain parks, and this tends to overshadow just how good the mountain's natural terrain really is. Largely serviced by hassle-free fast chairs and gondolas, this is a snowboarder's heaven with terrain to suit every ability level. Lower Road Runner is reportedly the only unbearably flat trail.

FOR CROSS-COUNTRY ★★★★
Very popular

The specialist Tamarack Centre has 30km of groomed trails, some going round the pretty Lakes Basin area, and provides lessons and tours. Members of a recent reporter's party had 'a wonderful time on excellent tracks'.

MOUNTAIN RESTAURANTS ★
Back to base ...

The already limited lunch options on the hill were narrowed further a few years ago. The pleasant table-service Parallax at mid-mountain is now open only to members of the exclusive Mammoth Black club. We cut our rating to ★ as a result.

McCoy Station, the plebs' self-service facility at mid-mountain, offers a wide choice ('excellent salad bar', says a 2015 visitor). Top of the Sierra is small and functional but has lovely views. A fair-weather option is the primitive outdoor BBQ at Outpost 14.

SCHOOLS AND GUIDES ★★★★
More reports needed
We have no recent reports. But adult group lessons have a maximum of four guests and there are three-day 'camps' (eg terrain park, moguls).

FOR FAMILIES ★★★★
Family favourite
Mammoth is keen to attract families. The focal points are the Mammoth Childcare centres at the Inn and at The Village, with comprehensive facilities for young children. And there are two non-skiing play zones, an Igloo ('great attraction') and a tubing park with its own lift. Kids from age three can have ski lessons, and there are four Kids Adventure zones with fun features for skiers and boarders. Three Fun Zones have mellow rollers and small spines as an introduction to a terrain park.

STAYING THERE

There's a good choice of hotels (none very luxurious or pricey) and condos. The condos tend to be out of town, near the lifts or on the road to them.
★★★★Westin Monache Resort Condo hotel near The Village gondola: restaurant, hot tubs, pool.
★★★Alpenhof Lodge Comfortable and central; shuttle-bus stop and plenty of restaurants nearby.
★★★Mammoth Mountain Inn Opposite Main Lodge, so convenient for the slopes but not the town. Outdoor pool and hot tubs.
★★★Sierra Nevada Resort Central; recently renovated. Spa. One reporter was so taken he went back again the next year: 'Nice rooms, really friendly staff, good value.'
Apartments The Village Lodge is close to many restaurants and shops; Juniper Springs Resort ('comfortable; friendly staff, its bus will pick you up at a restaurant') is near the Eagle base; both are of high quality. Other comfortable options are the Seasons 4 condos (close to The Village), the 1849 Condos (Canyon Lodge area) and the nearby Mammoth Ski and Racquet Club. Vons grocery in Mammoth Lakes

is tipped by a 2015 reporter for its 'wide variety of meals and foodstuffs'.

EATING OUT ★★★★★
Outstanding choice
Mammoth has 50+ restaurants, offering a wide choice from typical American to Japanese. There's a local menu guide covering many but not all.
The chalet-style Lakefront in the Tamarack Lodge is one of the best and was endorsed by a recent reporter ('beautiful views, great dinner and wine plus excellent service'). Rafters and the Red Lantern Chinese in the Sierra Nevada Lodge both have 'excellent cuisine and are good value, especially in happy hour', says a recent reporter who also rates the Mogul for 'the best steak in town' and Jimmy's Taverna for 'high-quality Greek food and fish dishes at decent prices'. Slocums is a popular steakhouse. Angels has typical American family food – burgers, steaks, ribs.
Other possibilities include Shogun for Japanese, Giovanni's for pizza and pasta and Gomez's for Tex-Mex. The Side Door cafe is an appealing eatery in The Village. The Parallax at McCoy Station opens for snowcat dinners up the mountain. For a hearty breakfast, try the Breakfast Club.

APRES-SKI ★★★
OK if you know where to go
At the close of play, the Yodler at Main Lodge is the liveliest spot – an old chalet (brought from Switzerland, they claim). Tusks, also at Main Lodge, and the Dry Creek bar in the Mammoth Mountain Inn across the road are other choices. Lakanuki in The Village is a 'Hawaiian-style bar that attracts a younger crowd'. Chart House was recommended last year for its 'welcoming fire and happy hour'. Grumpy's sports bar and Slocums are said to liven up at weekends.

OFF THE SLOPES ★
Mainly outdoors
Outdoor activities include skating, tubing, snowmobiling, snowshoeing, dog sledding, 'enjoyable' walks in the forest, thermal hot springs and pleasant drives. Mono Lake and the WW2 centre at Manzanar on the road to Los Angeles have been recommended. There is factory shopping nearby, too. But overall, Mammoth isn't great for non-skiers.

GETTING THERE
Air Los Angeles 515km/320 miles (5hr); Reno 275km/170 miles (3hr15)

TOURIST OFFICE
www.visitmammoth.com
www.mammothmountain.com

KENDALL

Squaw Valley

The site of the 1960 Olympics has a lot to offer novices and experts, and the little purpose-built village is worth a few days' stay

£180
RESORT PRICE INDEX

Lots of challenging terrain		Last few years have been dry
Superb beginner slopes		Not for mile-hungry intermediates
Convenient 'village' at the base		Lifts prone to closure by wind
Impressive snow record but...		Limited range of village amenities

TOP 10 RATINGS

Extent	★★★
Fast lifts	★★★
Queues	★★★★
Snow	★★★
Expert	★★★★
Intermediate	★★
Beginner	★★★★
Charm	★★★
Convenience	★★★★
Scenery	★★★

The neat little car-free base 'village' is a pleasant enough place to stay but there's not much life at night. And keen piste-bashers who like cruising groomed runs will find the ski area limited too. But Squaw now shares ownership and its lift pass with Alpine Meadows, only 15 minutes away by free shuttle-bus, which means there is quite a lot of skiing locally. Even so, we would always combine a stay in Squaw with one in another Tahoe resort.

KEY FACTS

Resort	1890m
	6,200ft
Slopes	1890-2760m
	6,200-9,050ft
Lifts	29
Pistes	3,600 acres

LIFT PASSES

Prices in US$

Age	6-day
under 13	408
13 to 22	588
23 to 64	714
65 to 75	588
76 plus	408
Free Under 5	
Beginner Combined lesson/limited lift pass/equipment deal	

THE RESORT

Squaw is the major resort at the north end of Lake Tahoe. Staying here has become more attractive since the car-free Village was built; but it is still also popular with day trippers. There are other lodgings around the lake, and at Tahoe City. The lift pass also covers neighbouring Alpine Meadows (currently a 15-minute ride by frequent free shuttle-buses; but planned to be linked by gondola in due course).
Village charm The Village is very small but works well, and older buildings next to it are not unpleasant.
Convenience The Village is at the base of the main lifts. The self-contained, luxurious, conference-oriented Resort at Squaw Creek hotel is well outside the Village, but right on the slopes.
Scenery There are fabulous views of Lake Tahoe from Squaw Peak.

THE MOUNTAINS

One of the attractions of the area is that the slopes are lightly wooded. The trail map and on-mountain signposting have been massively improved in recent years. The map covers Alpine Meadows too.
Slopes From the base, a big cable car rises 600m to High Camp and a big gondola to Gold Coast. Above them is a wide area of beginner slopes, and beyond that the three highest peaks of the area, with lifts of modest vertical; the biggest is Squaw Peak's Headwall six-pack with a vertical of just 535m.

From High Camp you can descend into a steep-sided valley from which the Silverado chair is the return.

Two other peaks are accessed directly from the Village. A fast quad serves steep KT-22; a slow triple goes to rather neglected Snow King.

Squaw's cable car runs late on selected dates to serve floodlit slopes (including a 5km run to the base).
Fast lifts There are fast lifts in each sector, but also slow old chairs.
Queues There are few problems usually, but the weather and weekend crowds are key factors. Lack of snow in the last two seasons has resulted in 10- to 15-minute waits says a reporter.
Terrain parks The Mainline park has the biggest jumps and is aimed at advanced riders. Its super-pipe wasn't built last season. The Gold Coast park has features for all standards, the Belmont park is for beginners and intermediates. There are other parks designed for kids and novices. All are

SQUAW VALLEY ALPINE MEADOWS

← The lightly wooded terrain has a lot of ungroomed slopes but not much blue cruising

NEWS

A gondola link between Squaw and Alpine Meadows has been announced. But it is subject to planning permission and no target date has been set for completion.

2015/16: The Siberia Express quad serving high intermediate runs between Squaw Peak and Emigrant is to be replaced by a six-pack.

2014/15: At the base, the SnoVentures Activity Zone was revamped to include a family lodge, more tubing and a new tubing lift. The North Face Mountain Guides offers special tours by expert guides for intermediate and advanced skiers and boarders.

TOURIST OFFICE

www.squawalpine.
com

dependent on there being enough snow and all were closed during a January 2015 reporter's stay.

Snow reliability Squaw claims an impressive 450 inches on average, plus snowmaking. But the last four seasons (especially the last two) have been unusually dry (only 216 inches last season). One Jan/Feb 2015 visitor told us: 'We were restricted to the top of the mountain and no off-piste.'

Experts The possibilities for experts on KT-22, Squaw Peak, Granite Chief and the Silverado valley are huge, with lots of steep chutes and big mogul fields; many extreme skiing and boarding movies are made here.

Intermediates Blue-run skiers have a choice of some lovely cruises in the Emigrant and Snow King sectors and a 5km run down to the Village. But there is not much more groomed cruising, so keen piste-bashers will find the area limited. There is, however, lots of steep blue and easy black terrain to test your deep-snow or mogul skills.

Beginners The SnoVentures Activities Zone at the base has a gentle slope served by a triple chairlift and three moving carpets. A First Time Lesson package, with lift pass, equipment rental and instruction began last season. There's a superb choice of easy runs to progress to at altitude, notably at High Camp.

Snowboarding This is one of the most snowboarder friendly resorts around. The higher areas are full of steep and deep gullies, cliff drops, kicker building spots and tree runs.

Cross-country There are 18km of groomed trails at Squaw Creek.

Mountain restaurants Uninspiring, except in terms of views.

Schools and guides As well as group lessons, the school runs specialist workshops – eg all-mountain, women-only clinics. A beginner this year had an 'excellent private lesson with an instructor who was great fun'. But it cost 'an eye-watering \$489'.

Families Squaw offers slope-side convenience and a children's on-slope play area at the SnoVentures Activities Zone at the base, with tubing and mini-snowmobiles. Squaw Kids takes children from three years.

STAYING THERE

Hotels The PlumpJack Inn at the base is our favourite – comfortable, stylish, central. The Red Wolf Lodge is 'comfortable' says a recent reporter. The Resort at Squaw Creek is set apart but is right on the slopes and offers luxury rooms, an outdoor pool, sauna, steam and hot tubs.

Apartments The Village has well-appointed ski-in/ski-out condos: a 2015 reporter enjoyed Squaw Valley Lodge ('spacious, well equipped').

Eating out The PlumpJack Inn has an excellent restaurant (good breakfasts too). Graham's is worth the 10-minute walk from the Village ('great chowder and tarte tatin'). More routine places include the Auld Dubliner pub, Fireside (pizza/pasta) and Mamasake (sushi).

Après-ski The Olympic House has several venues. In the Village, the places above mostly function as bars too. Uncorked at Squaw Valley is a wine bar with live music and wine tastings. Rocker@Squaw is 'friendly'.

Off the slopes High Camp has an ice rink and other activities. There's dog sledding and the Olympic Museum to visit. The Trilogy Spa offers treatments.

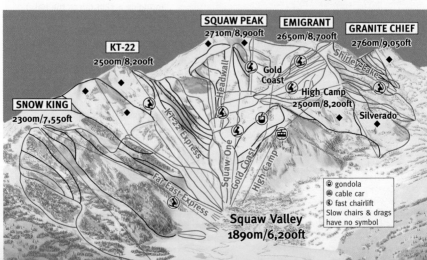

SQUAW PEAK 2710m/8,900ft

EMIGRANT 2650m/8,700ft

GRANITE CHIEF 2760m/9,050ft

KT-22 2500m/8,200ft

SNOW KING 2300m/7,550ft

Gold Coast

Shirley Lake

High Camp 2500m/8,200ft

Silverado

Headwall

KT-22 Express

Squaw One

Gold Coast

High Camp

Far East Express

Squaw Valley 1890m/6,200ft

gondola
cable car
fast chairlift
Slow chairs & drags
have no symbol

VAIL RESORTS / BOB WINSETT

Colorado

Colorado is the most popular American destination state for UK visitors, and justifiably so: it has the most alluring combination of attractive resorts, slopes to suit all abilities and excellent, reliable snow – dry enough to justify its 'champagne powder' label. It also has direct scheduled BA flights from London to Denver, which is an easy drive or shuttle transfer from many of the major resorts (less easy if it's snowing). But you may be able to save money by taking an indirect flight – and if you are going to a resort far from Denver, this makes sense because you can fly into a nearer airport.

Resorts such as Breckenridge, Vail and Winter Park are around a two-hour transfer from Denver. But Aspen and Snowmass are around four to five hours, and places such as Crested Butte and Telluride even more. For these more remote places you might want to consider an indirect flight, changing to a plane that lands at a nearby airport: Aspen, for example, has its own airport a few minutes from town. Even for Vail, you may prefer to change planes and fly into Eagle airport, only 45 minutes away.

Colorado has amazingly dry snow. Even when the snow melts and refreezes, the moisture seems to be

magically whisked away, leaving it soft and powdery. Even the artificial snow is of a quality you'll rarely find in Europe. And like most North American rivals, Colorado resorts generally have excellent, steep, ungroomed areas that you can ski safely without a guide.

The resorts vary enormously. If you want cute restored buildings from the mining boom days of the late 19th century, try the dinky old towns of Telluride and Crested Butte or the much bigger Aspen. Other resorts (such as Aspen's modern satellite, Snowmass) major on convenience. Some (such as Vail and Beaver Creek) deliberately pitch themselves upmarket, with lots of glitzy, expensive hotels, while others (such as Breckenridge and Winter Park) are much more down to earth.

You could consider renting a car and touring several resorts – maybe cutting costs by staying in valley towns rather than resorts. One regular reporter recently did a tour staying in Avon, near Beaver Creek and Vail, and then Frisco, near Breckenridge, Keystone, Copper Mountain and Arapahoe Basin.

Eight major resorts get write-ups in this section of the book. The others with blue circles on the map have entries in the resort directory at the back of the book – of these, Keystone, Crested Butte, Telluride and Durango are 'destination' resorts, with proper resort villages; the others cater more for day visitors.

Many Colorado resorts are at an extremely high altitude. As a result, visitors arriving straight from sea level are at risk of altitude sickness, which can spoil your trip. We always try to start in one of the lower resorts – or spend a night or two in Denver to acclimatize before moving on up.

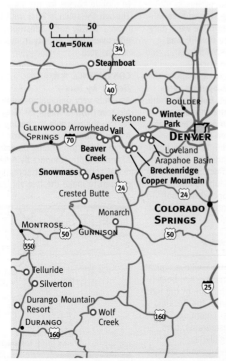

ASPEN / DOUG CHILD

Aspen

Don't be put off by the ritzy image – with a fun, historic town and quiet, extensive slopes, this is the USA's best resort

£220
RESORT PRICE INDEX

RATINGS

The mountains

Extent	★★
Fast lifts	★★★★
Queues	★★★★
Terrain p'ks	★★★★★
Snow	★★★★★
Expert	★★★★★
Intermediate	★★★★★
Beginner	★★★★★
Boarder	★★★★
X-country	★★★★
Restaurants	★★★
Schools	★★★★★
Families	★★

The resort

Charm	★★★★
Convenience	★★
Scenery	★★★
Eating out	★★★★★
Après-ski	★★★★
Off-slope	★★★★

Our extent rating excludes Snowmass. Including Snowmass would rate ★★★★

NEWS

2014/15: The Hideout, a new $10 million children's centre, was built at the base of Buttermilk. The Aspen Art Museum was extended with a new building.

- ➕ Wonderfully uncrowded slopes
- ➕ Attractive, characterful old town, with good restaurants and shops
- ➕ Excellent Aspen Highlands and Snowmass just down the road
- ➕ Convenient airport on edge of town
- ➕ Extensive slopes of all kinds, but ...

- ➖ Slopes split over four separate mountains (including Snowmass), served by efficient, free buses
- ➖ Expensive, and tending to become more so as cheap places disappear
- ➖ A bit isolated – no other major resorts within easy day-trip distance

Aspen is our favourite American resort. It has everything we look for – well, everything except convenience. Our affection depends heavily on the presence, a little way down the valley, of Aspen Highlands – and on Snowmass, much further down the valley (and covered in a separate chapter). So most days you have to ride a bus; that doesn't worry us – or you, we gather: most people who try it are captivated. Lack of crowds is part of the appeal of America in general, but in Aspen the quiet slopes are particularly impressive.

Many rich and some famous guests jet in here, and for connoisseurs of cosmetic surgery the bars of the top hotels can be fascinating places. And the place does seem to be drifting even further upmarket, with ever fewer funky bars and ever more international-brand shops. But, like all other 'glamorous' ski resorts, Aspen is actually filled by ordinary holidaymakers. Don't be put off.

THE RESORT

Aspen was built on silver-mining – in 1892 it had 12,000 inhabitants; it declined until skiing started here in the late 1930s, when there were only 700 inhabitants. The first lift was opened shortly after World War 2, and Aspen hasn't looked back.

Aspen Mountain is right above the town, its access lifts starting yards from the main street. But most of the slopes covered by the ski pass are a bus ride away. Around 3km away are Buttermilk and Aspen Highlands. Buttermilk has the Inn at Aspen hotel at the base. Highlands has a limited amount of lodging (including the very smart Ritz Carlton Club). Snowmass, 14km away, is a proper little resort beneath a big mountain that gets its own chapter.

VILLAGE CHARM ★★★★
Smart old town

Aspen's historic centre – with a typical American grid of streets – has been preserved to form the core of the most fashionable ski town in the Rockies, and one of the most charming. There's a huge variety of restaurants, bars, swanky shops and galleries.

A mixture of developments spreads out from the centre, ranging from the homes of the super-rich through surprisingly modest hotels and motels to mobile homes for the workers. Though the town is busy with traffic, it moves slowly, and pedestrians effectively have priority in much of the central area.

CONVENIENCE ★★
Better by bus

Aspen is very unusual in being a cute old town with a major lift close to the centre: the gondola to the top of Aspen Mountain is only yards from some of the top hotels. Downtown Aspen is quite compact by American resort standards, but it spreads far enough to make the free ski-bus a

KEY FACTS

Resort	2425m
	7,950ft

Aspen Mountain

Slopes	2425-3415m
	7,950-11,210ft
Lifts	8
Pistes	675 acres

Aspen Highlands

Slopes	2450-3560m
	8,040-11,680ft
Lifts	5
Pistes	1,040 acres

Buttermilk

Slopes	2400-3015m
	7,880-9,900ft
Lifts	8
Pistes	470 acres

Total with Snowmass

Slopes	2400-3815m
	7,880-12,510ft
Lifts	42
Pistes	5,517 acres

HAL WILLIAMS PHOTOGRAPHY INC.

Good views from The Cliffhouse at the top of Buttermilk – but the food hasn't impressed all our reporters ↓

necessity for some visitors staying less centrally. You also need buses to get to the other mountains, of course. Generally, they work well. But they can get crowded, and you may need to keep an eye on the timetables. You might even decide to stay near the main bus station for the easiest possible access to Snowmass etc.

SCENERY ★★★☆☆
Beautiful Bells

The views are generally unremarkable, but those from the upper part of Highlands and Buttermilk are notable – they include the distinctive Maroon Bells that appear on many postcards.

THE MOUNTAINS

Most of the slopes are in the trees. At Snowmass, free guided tours run twice a day. The ratio of acres to visitor beds is high, and the slopes are usually blissfully quiet – you get no invasions from Denver, this far west. Trail classification is generally reliable, and if the blacks on Buttermilk are a bit soft that is forgivable.

EXTENT OF THE SLOPES ★★☆☆☆
Widely dispersed

Each of the four mountains is worth a visit. Much the most extensive mountain in the area is at Snowmass – see separate chapter. Note that our ★★ extent rating excludes Snowmass;

including it would give ★★★★.

Once you are up the gondola, a series of chairs serves the ridges of **Aspen Mountain**. In general, there are long cruising blue runs along the valley floors and short, steep blacks down from the ridges.

Buttermilk is the smallest, lowest and least challenging mountain, accessed by a fast quad from the fairly primitive main base lodge. The runs fan out from the top in three directions – back to the base, down to Tiehack and down to West Buttermilk (with fast quads back from all three).

Aspen Highlands consists essentially of a single ridge served by three fast quad chairs, with easy and intermediate slopes along the ridge itself and steep black runs on the flanks – very steep ones at the top. And beyond the lift network, a free snowcat ride leads to Highland Bowl, of entirely double-black gradient.

FAST LIFTS ★★★★☆
Serving bottom to top

There are some slow lifts on Aspen mountain and Highlands, but they are relatively short, and Buttermilk has slow lifts only on the nursery slopes.

QUEUES ★★★★☆
Few problems

Major queues are rare on any of the mountains – you may hit a few during the college spring break in March. At

SKIWORLD

Catered chalets,
hotels and
self catering
apartments in

**Europe, USA
and Canada**

skiworld.co.uk
08444 930 430

ABTA V2151 ATOL 2036

GET THE BEST OF THE SNOW, ON- AND OFF-PISTE

Aspen offers special experiences for small numbers of skiers or riders.

First Tracks *The first skiers to sign up each day get to ride the gondola up Aspen Mountain at 8am the next day and get first tracks on perfect corduroy or fresh powder. Well worth doing. Free, but numbers are limited. When we did it, we took our time over the descent, to let the start-of-day queue at the bottom dissipate, but we're told you now ski in a guided group at a set pace.*

Powder Tours *Spend the day finding untracked snow in a guided group in 1,500 acres of backcountry beyond Aspen Mountain, with a 12-passenger heated snowcat as your personal lift. You're likely to squeeze in about 10 runs in all. You break for lunch at an old mountain cabin. It costs about $440 per person.*

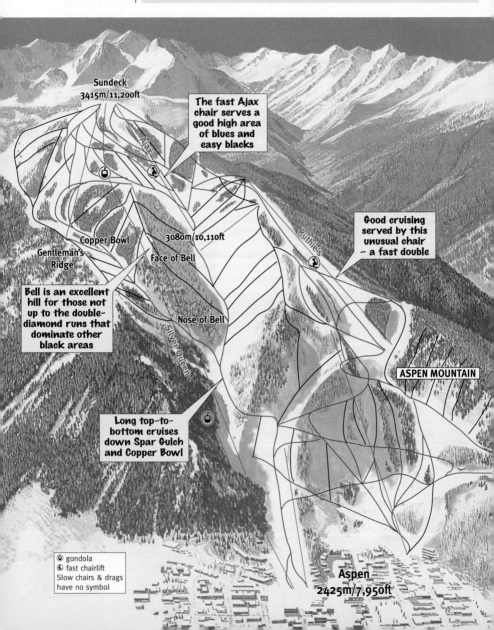

Sundeck
3415m/11,200ft

The fast Ajax chair serves a good high area of blues and easy blacks

Ajax

Copper Bowl

Gentleman's Ridge

3080m/10,110ft

Face of Bell

Ruthie's

Good cruising served by this unusual chair – a fast double

Bell is an excellent hill for those not up to the double-diamond runs that dominate other black areas

Nose of Bell

Silver Queen

ASPEN MOUNTAIN

Long top-to-bottom cruises down Spar Gulch and Copper Bowl

gondola
fast chairlift
Slow chairs & drags
have no symbol

Aspen
2425m/7,950ft

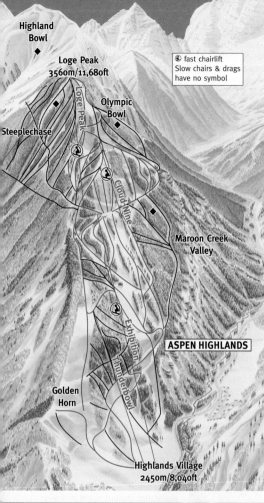

Highland Bowl ◆

Loge Peak
3560m/11,68oft

Olympic Bowl ◆

Steeplechase

Loge Peak

Cloud Nine

Maroon Creek Valley

Exhibition

Thunderbowl

Golden Horn

ASPEN HIGHLANDS

Highlands Village
2450m/8,04oft

④ fast chairlift
Slow chairs & drags have no symbol

---

④ fast chairlift
low chairs & drags
ave no symbol

West Summit
3015m/9,90oft

Cliffhouse
2955m/9,69oft

West Buttermilk

PEN HIGHLANDS

Tiehack

BUTTERMILK   West Buttermilk
2655m/8,71oft

Summit

ack
om/
4oft

Panda Hill

Main Buttermilk
2400m/788oft

Aspen Mountain, the gondola can still have delays at peak times, and we have one report of epic queues on a January powder day. You can use the slow Shadow Mountain chair, instead, with a short uphill walk to reach it. Aspen Highlands is almost always queue-free, even at peak times.

TERRAIN PARKS ★★★★★
X Games standard
Buttermilk is Aspen's pipe and park mountain. Buttermilk Park is famous as the home of the Winter X Games, and stretches over 3km from the top to the bottom of the mountain – it is said to be the longest in the world. It has over 100 features, the X Games slope-style course and a world-class super-pipe. Snowmass has a park and pipe too.

SNOW RELIABILITY ★★★★★
Rarely a problem
Aspen's mountains get an annual average of 300 inches of snow – not in the front rank, but not far behind. In addition, all areas have substantial snowmaking. Immaculate grooming adds to the quality of the pistes, and the light traffic (particularly on sectors other than Aspen mountain) can only help maintain snow quality.

FOR EXPERTS ★★★★★
Buttermilk is the only soft stuff
There's plenty to choose from – all the mountains except Buttermilk offer lots of challenges, and it is relatively easy to find untouched powder in the many gladed areas.

Aspen Mountain has a formidable array of double-black diamond runs. From the top of the gondola, Walsh's, Hyrup's and Kristi are on a lightly wooded slope and link up with Gentleman's Ridge and Jackpot to form the longest black run on the mountain. A series of steep glades drops down from Gentleman's Ridge. The central Bell ridge has less extreme single diamonds on both its flanks, including some delightful lightly wooded areas. On the opposite side of Spar Gulch is another row of double blacks, collectively called the Dumps, because mining waste was dumped here.

At Highlands there are challenging runs from top to bottom of the mountain. Consider joining a guided group as an introduction to the best of them. Highland Bowl, beyond the top lift, is superb in the right

LIFT PASSES

Four Mountain Pass

Prices in US$

Age	6-day
under 13	342
13 to 17	540
18 to 64	594
65 plus	540

Free Under 7: $5 for unlimited period

Senior Over 70: $459 for unlimited period

Beginner Included in price of lessons

Notes Includes shuttle-bus between the areas; 6-day prices are online 7 days in advance (window prices are higher); savings if you purchase in advance through certain UK tour operators and if you purchase in conjunction with lodging

DANIEL BAYER

Highland Bowl at the top of Highlands ranges from the steep to the seriously steep (the latter involving longer hikes up the ridge) ↓

conditions: a big open bowl with access gates reached by hiking (but there are usually free snowcat rides to cut out the first 20-minute walk). The trail map usefully gives key facts for each run – orientation, and average and steepest pitch, from a serious 38° to a terrifying 48°.

Left of the bowl, the Steeplechase area consists of a row of natural avalanche chutes, and their elevation means the snow keeps well. The Olympic Bowl area on the opposite flank of the mountain has great views of the Maroon Bells and some serious moguls. The Thunderbowl chair from the base serves a nice varied area that's often underused.

FOR INTERMEDIATES ★★★★★
Grooming to die for

Most intermediate runs on Highlands are concentrated above the mid-mountain Merry-Go-Round restaurant, many served by the Cloud Nine fast quad chair. But there are other good slopes – don't miss the vast, neglected expanses of Golden Horn.

Aspen Mountain has its fair share of intermediate slopes, but they tend to be on the tough side. Copper Bowl and Spar Gulch, running between the ridges, are great cruises but can get crowded. Upper Aspen Mountain, at the top of the gondola, has a dense network of well-groomed blues served by the Ajax fast chair. Ruthie's chair – a fast double, apparently installed to rekindle the romance that quads have destroyed – serves more cruising runs.

Buttermilk offers good, easy slopes to practise on, and can be quite extraordinarily quiet. For good intermediates it offers easy black runs – and it's a great place for early experiments off-piste.

Read the Snowmass chapter too.

FOR BEGINNERS ★★★★★
Can be a great place to learn

Buttermilk is superb. West Buttermilk has beautifully groomed, gentle, often deserted runs, served by a quad. The easiest slopes of all, though, are at the base of the Main Buttermilk sector – on Panda Hill. Despite its macho image, Highlands boasts the highest concentration of green runs in Aspen.

FOR BOARDERS ★★★★
Loads of scope

There is a huge amount of terrain to explore, which will satisfy all levels of boarder – especially when you include Snowmass. The hills are free of draglifts and have few flat sections. Buttermilk has a huge terrain park.

FOR CROSS-COUNTRY ★★★★
Backcountry bonanza

There are 90km of groomed trails in the Roaring Fork valley between Aspen and Snowmass – the most extensive cross-country network in the US. And the Ashcroft Ski Touring Center maintains around 35km of trails around Ashcroft, a mining ghost town. Aspen is at one end of the 370km Tenth Mountain Division Trail.

MOUNTAIN RESTAURANTS ★★★
Good by American standards

Surprisingly, macho Highlands has a good table-service place (and Snowmass has three) while Aspen Mountain doesn't.

Editors' choice At Highlands, Cloud Nine bistro is the nearest thing in the States to a cosy Alpine hut, with excellent food – thanks to an Austrian chef. Not wildly expensive, either – $45 for the daily changing set menu of two courses. We had delicious elk stew on our last visit.

Worth knowing about Another table-service option at Highlands is Willow Creek at the base – 'excellent light seafood dishes, not too expensive'.

↑ Buttermilk Park stretches 3km from top to bottom of the mountain

ASPEN

The mid-mountain Merry-Go-Round self-service has 'a comfortable bar area' with sofas as well as tables. On Aspen Mountain there's the Sundeck self-service, which is about as good as an American self-service restaurant gets – light and airy with great views across to Highland Bowl. Bonnie's self-service is another option. On Buttermilk the mountaintop Cliffhouse specializes in a Mongolian barbecue stir-fry which left at least one reporter very unimpressed.

SCHOOLS AND GUIDES ★★★★★
One of the best?
Aspen's school is highly regarded, and group classes are usually small and of a high standard: 'Maximum of three people in our lessons and the same instructor for the three days,' says a reporter. Another praises the free, full-day 'Inside Tracks' tours, run twice a week by the ski school for guests at the lift-company-owned Limelight hotel.

FOR FAMILIES ★★★★★
Choice of nurseries
Aspen caters well for families, with Buttermilk the focus for lessons. Children are bussed to and from the mountain's impressive Fort Frog, and the kids' trail map is a great idea. But Snowmass makes a better base.

STAYING THERE

Hotels There are places for all budgets, including very grand places such as the Hyatt and St Regis on which we never get reports. Most smaller hotels provide a good free après-ski cheese and wine buffet. Skiworld offers a good selection.
*****Jerome Step back a century: Victorian authenticity combined with modern-day luxury (including a spa) and a great vibe. Recently refurbed. Several blocks from the gondola.
*****Little Nell Stylish, modern hotel right by the gondola, with popular bar. Fireplaces in rooms, outdoor pool, hot tub, sauna. Smart condos, too.
***Aspen Simple but spacious, quiet rooms; pool, hot tub; on Main, 10 minutes' walk to gondola but near bus stop; 'great breakfast, fabulous après-ski food and drinks included'.
***Aspen Mountain Lodge Small, hospitable, in a quiet location. 'Very friendly, helpful staff.'
***Limelight Modern style, central. Pool, tubs. Approved for its 'massive rooms, fabulous breakfasts'. Owned by the lift company – read 'Schools and guides'. Fleet of shuttles.
***The Sky Hip, swanky New York-style hotel in a great location right by the gondola.
**Mountain Chalet Cosy lodge five minutes from the gondola. Pool, sauna, steam and fitness centre.
**St Moritz Lodge Aspen's 'youth hostel' – with a heated pool and complimentary après wine! 'Super-friendly staff' and 'mature' guests.
Apartments The standards here are high, even in US terms. Many of the smarter developments have their own free shuttle-buses. This year a reporter recommends Laurelwood – 'slope-side, couple of outdoor hot tubs'. A 2014 reporter was very happy with the 'well-appointed' Durant, close to the gondola with outdoor hot tubs. The Gant, Aspen Square and Aspen Meadows Resort have been tipped.

EATING OUT ★★★★★
Dining dilemma
Aspen has plenty of seriously good upmarket places – as our most trusted American reporter puts it, dining is 'a real highlight of staying in Aspen – there aren't that many cities in the US with better restaurants'. But there are also plenty of cheaper options, some mentioned below. Some giveaway

↑ Buttermilk offers fabulously quiet, easy trails through the trees

DANIEL BAYER

magazines include menu guides, and www.eataspen.com has listings.

Top of the range places include: Syzygy, Piñons and Element 47 in the Little Nell hotel – all with innovative American cooking; Matsuhisa (Japanese fusion); and the Rustique Bistro, Brexi Brasserie and Cache Cache (all French). Steakhouse 316 is a small steakhouse in 1920s style. The tiny Wild Fig has 'a varied, Mediterranean-influenced menu'. The underground Zocalito offers Latin American cuisine. A reporter this year strongly recommends Justice Snows ('juicy duck breast and top sirloin were by far the best dishes of our stay').

You can eat more cheaply at a lot of the smart places by eating at the bar – basically, you get smaller portions and can't book, which of course may suit you. We did this very happily on our last visit at Jimmy's (American), L'Hostaria and Campo de Fiori (both Italian). Some places include food deals in their happy hours, too – typically 4pm to 6pm.

Mid-market and cheaper choices include: 'spiffy bistro' Mezzaluna; Little Annie's; Asie (Asian fusion); Brunelleschi's (family-friendly Italian); Su Casa. Meat & Cheese does what it says on the tin, as well as Korean

GETTING THERE

Air Aspen 6km/ 4 miles (15min); Eagle 110km/70 miles (1hr30); Denver 360km/225 miles (4hr)

Rail Glenwood Springs (65km/40 miles)

TOURIST OFFICE

www.aspensnowmass. com

dishes from a Korean chef. We're delighted to hear that two affordable, lively Aspen institutions live on – the refurbished Red Onion (established 1892, they say) for 'large portions of steak, burgers and salads' and Hickory House, specializing in 'excellent ribs'.

APRES-SKI ★★★★
Lots of options

In the late afternoon, we've known Cloud Nine on Highlands to turn into an Austrian-style après-ski venue – booze-fuelled dancing on the tables in ski boots. This very un-American activity is of course terminated by the ski patrol at a very un-Austrian early hour. A few bars at the bases get busy – notably Out of Bounds and Highlands Ale House at Highlands, and Ajax Tavern and the Sky hotel in Aspen. The Little Nell is a great place for gazing at facelifts. For a sharp contrast, join the local snow bums at Zane's for its 'great atmosphere' and 'happy hour chicken wings'.

Later on, wine connoisseurs could try Victoria's Espresso & Wine Bar, while beerists should check out the 'flights' at the new Hops Culture. There is also a microbrewery, The Aspen Brewing Company. Many of the restaurants are also bars. The J-bar of the historic Jerome hotel has a great traditional feel. Aspen Billiards adjoining the fashionable Cigar Bar is an upscale venue for playing pool.

For music and dancing, head for Belly Up or the Regal Watering Hole. Or you can get a week's membership of the famous Caribou club.

OFF THE SLOPES ★★★★
Silver service

Aspen has lots to offer, especially if your credit card is in good shape. There are literally dozens of art galleries, with an impressive new building at the Aspen Art Museum which opened in 2014. As well as the predictable clothes and jewellery shops, there are plenty of shops selling affordable stuff – and an excellent bookshop. A reader notes that there are now countless marijuana shops, too. Glenwood Springs is worth a visit for its hot-spring outdoor pool. The Aspen Recreation Center at Highlands has a huge swimming complex and an indoor ice rink. Hot-air ballooning is possible. Some mountain restaurants are accessible to pedestrians.

Beaver Creek

Exclusive and very pricey modern resort with quiet, varied slopes.
Good for an indulgent stay, and a required day trip from Vail

£220
RESORT PRICE INDEX

TOP 10 RATINGS

Extent	★★★
Fast lifts	★★★★★
Queues	★★★★★
Snow	★★★★★
Expert	★★★★
Intermediate	★★★★
Beginner	★★★★★
Charm	★★
Convenience	★★★★
Scenery	★★★

NEWS

2014/15: The focal Centennial chairlift out of the resort was replaced by a chondola (a mix of chairs and gondolas) which increased carrying capacity by 35%. The plush SaddleRidge restaurant near the base opened for lunch. A new First Tracks programme started on limited dates, allowing you up the mountain an hour early followed by breakfast in Allie's Cabin. Snowmaking was increased on the Gold Dust trail and Larkspur Bowl area.

KEY FACTS

Resort	2470m
	8,100ft
Slopes	2255-3485m
	7,400-11,440ft
Lifts	24
Pistes	1,832 acres

- ➕ Slopes generally quiet on weekdays
- ➕ Mountain has it all, from superb novice runs to daunting moguls
- ➕ Fast chairlifts all over the place
- ➕ Compact, traffic-free village centre

- ➖ Lacks any Wild West atmosphere
- ➖ Very expensive
- ➖ Table-service mountain restaurants are members-only
- ➖ Not much going on at night

'Not exactly roughing it' is the ironic slogan of Vail's kid sister resort, coyly underlining its status as about the smoothest resort in the US. We don't find the exclusive resort village particularly appealing, but the mountain certainly is. If the budget is tight, consider staying down in the valley, in Avon.

THE RESORT

Beaver Creek, 16km to the west of Vail and developed in the 1980s, is unashamedly exclusive. The lift system spreads across the mountains to Bachelor Gulch, a small collection of condos and houses and a Ritz Carlton hotel, and then to Arrowhead, another slope-side hamlet. Down in the valley is the town of Avon, where you can stay much more cheaply than in Beaver Creek or Vail. There are free car parks in Avon for day visitors (parking in Beaver Creek is expensive and limited); you can take a free shuttle to the resort, or a fast chair up to Bachelor Gulch. A gondola links the Riverfront area of Avon to this chair.

Day trips to Vail, Breckenridge and Keystone, all covered by the lift pass, and Copper Mountain are possible.
Village charm The village centres on a small, smart, modern pedestrian area with upmarket shops, open-air ice rink and heated pavements.
Convenience There are top-quality hotels and condos right by the slopes, and escalators up from the centre.
Scenery The scenery is pleasantly woody rather than dramatic.

THE MOUNTAINS

All the slopes are below the treeline, though there are some more open areas. Free two-hour mountain tours run daily and there are tours just for women from Tuesday to Friday. At the top of most main lifts is a big piste map board (with lights showing which runs have been groomed – a great idea). They take 'slow skiing zones' seriously here too – with big banners across the piste warning that skier speed is monitored.
Slopes The slopes immediately above Beaver Creek divide into two sectors, each accessed by a fast quad chair – one centred on Spruce Saddle, the other on Bachelor Gulch (which links to Arrowhead). Between these are Grouse Mountain and Larkspur Bowl, again with fast quads. Off to the left is another sector, with a fast quad.

BEAVER CREEK / JACK AFFLECK

Trees galore – right up to the top of the mountains. The Centennial lift from the village goes up the mountain on the front left ➔

LIFT PASSES

Colorado

Prices in US$

Age	6-day
under 13	480
13 to 64	690
65 plus	630

Free Under 5

Beginner Included in price of lessons

Notes Covers Vail, Beaver Creek, Breckenridge, Keystone and Arapahoe Basin; prices are online rates for mid-March purchased 14 days in advance of trip; window rates in resort are considerably higher; international visitors will get best prices by pre-booking through a UK tour operator (it is not necessary to buy a complete holiday package to obtain these prices)

TOURIST OFFICE

www.beavercreek.com

Fast lifts Nearly all key lifts are fast chairs; beginners have a gondola.
Queues Not normally a problem.
Terrain parks Park 101 is a small beginners' park, Zoom Room has intermediate-level features, and Rodeo is for advanced riders. Parkology is a park and pipe programme for kids.
Snow reliability An impressive snow record (average 325 inches) and snowmaking mean you can relax. But Grouse Mountain can have thin cover (some call it Gravel Mountain).
Experts There is plenty of satisfying steep terrain. In the Birds of Prey and Grouse Mountain areas most runs are long, steep and mogulled; the downhill race course pistes are groomed periodically, making great fast cruises (but they can be closed for races or training). Grouse and Stone Creek Chutes have good steep glades.
Intermediates There are marvellous long, quiet, cruising blues everywhere you look, including top-to-bottom runs with a vertical of 1000m.
Beginners There are excellent nursery slopes at resort level – served by a short gondola – and a further large area at altitude. And there are plenty of easy long runs to progress to.
Snowboarding Good riders will love the gladed runs and quiet slopes.
Cross-country There's a splendid, mountaintop network of tracks up at McCoy Park (over 32km).
Mountain restaurants Spruce Saddle at mid-mountain is the main place – a food court in an airy log building; but it can get very busy. Mamie's Mountain Grill (outdoors at the top of Bachelor

Gulch lift) is 'fun in good weather'. Lower down, Talons has an appetizing menu. But for table-service you have to head down to the base.
Schools and guides We lack reports, but the school is doubtless excellent.
Families Small World Play School looks after non-skiing kids. At the top of the Buckaroo gondola are adventure trails and a tubing hill.

STAYING THERE

Lodgings are pricey and luxurious.
Hotels Lots of upmarket places, such as the Ritz Carlton and Park Hyatt. The Osprey, Charter and Pines Lodge combine hotel facilities with luxury condo convenience.
Apartments Slope-side condos include Elkhorn Lodge, Oxford Court, St James Place, Bear Paw and SaddleRidge.
Eating out SaddleRidge is plush and packed with photos and Wild West artefacts. A 2015 reporter enjoyed the 'fine dining' at 8100 Mountainside Bar and Grill at Park Hyatt. The Golden Eagle Inn, Dusty Boot (in St James Place) and Beaver Creek Chophouse have been recommended. You can take a sleigh ride to dine at swanky Beano's or Zach's cabins on the slopes. Or try the numerous and generally cheaper restaurants in Avon (buses run to and from there until 10pm.
Après-ski Try the Coyote Cafe, Powder 8 Kitchen and Tap (formerly McCoy's), which has live bands, and the 8100 Mountainside Bar at Park Hyatt.
Off the slopes Smart shops and galleries, an ice rink, ballooning, dog sledding, snowshoeing and concerts.

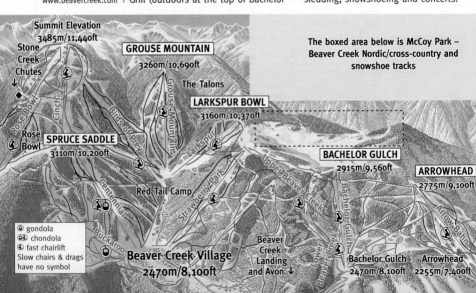

Breckenridge

A sprawling resort with a cute 'Wild West' core, beneath a wide, varied mountain; increasing amounts of slope-side accommodation

£195
RESORT PRICE INDEX

561

RATINGS

The mountains

Extent	★★★
Fast lifts	★★★★
Queues	★★★★
Terrain p'ks	★★★★★
Snow	★★★★★
Expert	★★★★
Intermediate	★★★★
Beginner	★★★★★
Boarder	★★★★★
X-country	★★★★
Restaurants	★★
Schools	★★★★★
Families	★★★★

The resort

Charm	★★★
Convenience	★★★
Scenery	★★★
Eating out	★★★★★
Après-ski	★★★
Off-slope	★★★

NEWS

2015/16: On the new Peak 6, snowmaking will be added.

2014/15: The Colorado quad chair on Peak 8 was replaced by a six-pack, increasing capacity by 30%. The restaurant at Peak 9 was revamped.

KEY FACTS

Resort		2925m
		9,600ft
Slopes	2925-3915m	
	9,600-12,840ft	
Lifts		34
Pistes		3,308 acres

Pros

- ⊞ Slopes have something for all abilities – good for mixed groups
- ⊞ Cute Victorian Main Street, with mainly sympathetic new buildings
- ⊞ Plenty of lively bars and restaurants
- ⊞ Shared lift pass covering four other worthwhile resorts nearby
- ⊞ Efficient lifts mean few queues
- ⊞ Some slope-side accommodation

Cons

- ⊟ Tougher slopes at the top very prone to closure by high winds
- ⊟ Groomed trails not very extensive, with few long runs
- ⊟ Lack of good central hotels
- ⊟ Main Street is a thoroughfare, and always busy with traffic
- ⊟ Risk of altitude sickness if going directly to 2925m from low altitude

Breckenridge has a lot going for it, but some of the flaws we list above are non-trivial. The Imperial Express may be North America's highest lift, but it was only last season that editor Gill finally got to ski it for the first time, all his previous visits having been spoiled by high winds. And on his first visit [cough] years ago, he was knocked out for 24 hours by altitude sickness. If you can, go first to a lower resort for a couple of nights – Steamboat, Aspen or Vail – to cut the risk of sickness.

With the small but worthwhile addition of Peak 6 for 2014, there are now five linked sectors to ski. Even so, if you are keen on piste mileage and variety you'll find Breck a bit limited for a week's stay – plan to visit other resorts (covered by the lift pass) by car or bus too.

THE RESORT

Breckenridge was founded in 1859 and became a booming gold-mining town. Old clapboard buildings line much of Main Street, and the streets nearby have been well renovated. Small shopping malls and other buildings have been added in similar style. But there are some (rather out-of-place) modern buildings too, especially around the base of Peak 9.

The resort is in the same ownership as Vail, Beaver Creek and Keystone. A multi-day lift ticket includes days at all these plus Arapahoe Basin. All of them plus Copper Mountain can be reached by bus (free to Keystone and A-Basin).

VILLAGE CHARM ★★★
A festive treat

The town centre is lively in the evening – particularly at weekends – with lots of people strolling around the shops on their way to or from the 100-plus restaurants and bars in and around the busy main street. Christmas lights and decorations remain throughout the season, giving the town a festive air. This is enhanced by festivals such as Ullr Fest – honouring the Norse God of Winter – and snow sculpture championships.

CONVENIENCE ★★★
Slope life or nightlife

There are a lot of slope-side lodgings, including smart recent developments at the bases of Peaks 7 and 8. But

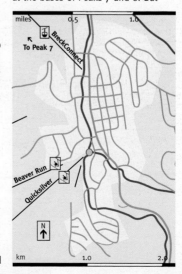

LIFT PASSES

Prices in US$

Age	6-day
under 13	402
13 to 64	672
65 plus	612

Free Under 5
Beginner Included in price of lessons
Notes Covers Breckenridge, Keystone and Arapahoe Basin, plus 3 days at Vail and Beaver Creek; prices are online rates for mid-March purchased 14 days in advance; on-the-spot rates in the resort are much higher; international visitors will get best prices by pre-booking through a UK tour operator (it is not necessary to buy a complete holiday package to obtain these prices)

there is also some inconveniently distant from both Main Street and the lift base stations. Hotels and condos are spread over a wide area and linked by regular, free shuttle-buses (less frequent in the evening – it's worth staying close to Main Street if you plan to spend much time there).

SCENERY ★★★☆☆
Peak after peak
This is high country; on a clear day above the treeline there are extensive views of Colorado's highest summits – many of which reach over 4000m.

THE MOUNTAINS

The slopes are mainly cut through the forest, but there is quite a lot of steeper skiing above the treeline, and this is prone to closure by high winds.

The resort used to have some runs classified as blue-black, particularly on Peak 10. These are now simply black runs – a real backward step.

EXTENT OF THE SLOPES ★★★☆☆
Growing but fragmented
There are now five sectors, linked by lift and piste, numbered from right to left of the trail map. Two fast chairlifts go from one end of the town up to **Peak 9**, one accessing mainly green runs on the lower half of the hill, the other mainly blue runs higher up. From there you can get to **Peak 10**, with black runs (including former blue-blacks) served by one fast quad.

The **Peak 8** area – tough stuff at

the top, easier lower down – can be reached by a fast quad from Peak 9. The base lifts of Peak 8 can also be reached by the slow Snowflake lift from the suburbs, or by gondola from a car park on the fringes of town which also accesses the six-pack serving **Peak 7**. Runs from here link across to **Peak 6**, which has a slow access lift but a fast lift serving the slopes (mainly blue unless you hike).

The higher open slopes on Peaks 7 and 8 are accessed by a T-bar – a rarity in these parts – reachable from either base, and by the Imperial fast quad at the top of the Peak 8 lift network. The resort claims a top height of 3962m, but that involves a hike up from the very top which we don't count.

FAST LIFTS ★★★★☆
Good coverage
Breckenridge's gondola and many fast chairlifts cover all five sectors and provide good access from either end of town – the slow Snowflake chair to Peak 8 in between is an obvious exception, which will be an irritant if that's the access lift you need to use.

QUEUES ★★★★☆
Peak times possibly
A previous reporter encountered 20-minute queues on President's weekend but no queues midweek. Outside peak periods, reporters confirm there are few problems. There may be queues for the old Chair 6 on a powder day and the slow Snowflake

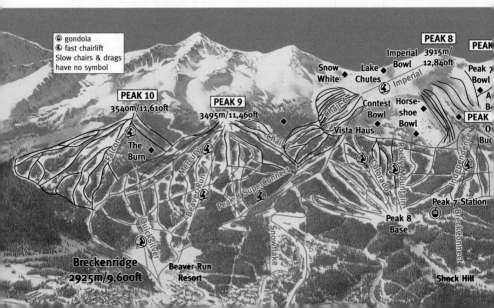

One Ski Hill Place at the base of Peak 8 is at the upper end of the condo scale →

BRECKENRIDGE

chair that gives access to Peak 8 for thousands of condo-dwellers.

TERRAIN PARKS ★★★★★
A wide choice
The main focus is Peak 8, with three parks for different ability levels. Freeway is one of the best parks in North America, and includes a super-pipe. Next to it, Park Lane offers a variety of challenging features. And Trygve's has gentle jumps and rollers for beginner freestylers. On Peak 9 are two more parks: Bonanza is a beginner progression park, and Gold King bridges the gap between Bonanza and Park Lane.

SNOW RELIABILITY ★★★★★
Normally ample quantities
With its high altitude, Breckenridge boasts a good natural snow record – annual average 300 inches. That is supplemented by substantial snowmaking (used mainly early in the season to form a good base). There are a lot of east- and north-east-facing slopes, which hold snow well. But high winds can remove or spoil the snow, notably on exposed upper runs. And there are also sunny flanks where the snow conditions may be sun-affected later in the season.

FOR EXPERTS ★★★★☆
Lots of short but tough runs
A remarkable 55% of the runs are classified black – and a good proportion are classified as 'expert'

(double diamond) or 'extreme' terrain. But most runs are short – most of the key lifts offer verticals of around 300m – and on the open upper slopes the slightest variation in route counts as another run.

Peak 8 is at the core of the tough skiing. The lightly wooded slopes served by the 6-Chair are a good place to start – picturesque and not too steep. Below, steeper runs lead further down to the junction with Peak 9. Above, the Imperial quad accesses huge amounts of above-the-treeline terrain and longer runs. You can hike up to the double-diamond Imperial Bowl, and the 'extreme' Lake Chutes and Snow White areas. Or you can traverse west towards Peak 7 and the bowl of Whale's Tail. On our 2015 visit we had a great time in fresh snow here and on the lower slopes served by the T-bar. On the lower part of Peak 8 is a worthwhile area of single diamonds.

Peak 9's wooded North Slope under Chair E is excellent – shady, sheltered and steep; we've had great runs down Devil's Crotch, Hades and Inferno. Peak 10 has easy black runs (former blue-blacks) down the central ridge, but more challenging stuff on both flanks. To skier's left is a lovely, lightly wooded area called The Burn.

The new Peak 6 area has opened up a variety of terrain. The lift serves mainly blue stuff but also the black Intuition and the Wonderland bowl – classed as double diamond but hardly

SKIWORLD

Catered chalets, hotels and self catering apartments in

Europe, USA and Canada

skiworld.co.uk

08444 930 430

ABTA V2151   ATOL 2036

SNOWPIX.COM / CHRIS GILL

Whale's Tail is a splendid snowy bowl, marked as double diamond but mostly of single-diamond steepness ↓

deserving it. Hiking and traversing takes you to some tougher stuff that looked to us like the genuine article.

FOR INTERMEDIATES ★★★★
Nice cruising, limited extent

Breckenridge has some good blue cruising runs for all intermediates. But dedicated piste-bashers are likely to find the runs short and limited in variety. Peak 9 has the easiest slopes. It is nearly all gentle, wide, blue runs at the top and almost flat, wide, green runs at the bottom.

Peak 10 has a number of easy, normally groomed, black runs that used to be classified blue-black, such as Crystal and Centennial, which make for good fast cruising. Peaks 7 and 8 both have blues on trails cut close together in the trees, which feel very similar and offer little variety. Adventurous intermediates can also try some of the high bowl runs and more gentle gladed runs such as Ore Bucket glades on the fringe of Peak 7 and the runs beneath Chair 6 on Peak 8.

Peak 6 is a good place for the more adventurous, with some challenging blue runs and glades.

FOR BEGINNERS ★★★★★
Excellent

The bottom of Peak 9 has a big, virtually flat area and some good,

gentle nursery slopes. There's then a good choice of green runs to move on to. Beginners can try Peak 8 too, with another selection of green runs and a choice of trails back to town. There is a special beginner package available (see 'Schools and guides').

FOR BOARDERS ★★★★★
One of the best

Breckenridge is pretty much ideal for all standards of boarder and hosts several major US snowboarding events. Beginners have ideal nursery slopes and greens to progress to. Intermediates have good cruising runs, all served by chairs. The powder bowls at the top of Peaks 7 and 8 make great riding and can be accessed via the Imperial quad, so avoiding the awkward T-bar. The choice of terrain parks is excellent.

FOR CROSS-COUNTRY ★★★★
Specialist centre in woods

The Nordic Center is set in the woods between the town and Peak 8 and served by shuttle-bus. It has 32km of trails and 15km of snowshoeing trails.

MOUNTAIN RESTAURANTS ★★
Improved by more base options

Of the self-service places above base level, TenMile Station, where Peak 9 meets 10, is the place we gravitate to.

Both it and the dreary Vista Haus on Peak 8 are food-court operations and get nightmarishly busy at weekends. Peak 9 restaurant has reverted to the ownership of the ski company and reopened as the Overlook. Sevens is a table-service restaurant at the Peak 7 base.

SCHOOLS AND GUIDES ★★★★★
Usual high US standard
We lack recent reports but past ones have been positive. The beginner package includes lessons, equipment rental and lift pass, and the school's special clinics include telemark.

FOR FAMILIES ★★★★
Excellent facilities
Past reports on the children's school and nursery have been full of praise. The Mountains of Discovery Program aims to combine teaching and fun on the slopes (for kids aged 3 to 13).

STAYING THERE

Chalets Skiworld has a four-bedroom house built in traditional clapboard style near Main Street with an outdoor hot tub.
Hotels There's a noticeable shortage of good places close to Main Street.
★★★★Barn on the River B&B on Main Street. Hot tub.
★★★★DoubleTree by Hilton A short walk to the slopes and a bearable walk to Main Street.
★★★★Lodge & Spa at Breckenridge Stylish luxury spa resort – renovated in summer 2014 – set out of town among 32 acres, with great views. Shuttle-bus.
★★★Beaver Run Huge, slope-side resort complex with 515 spacious rooms. Pools, hot tubs.
Apartments There is a huge choice. We were happy last winter in Mountain Thunder Lodge, a walk from the gondola station. Hyatt Main Street Station (near the Quicksilver lift) and One Ski Hill Place at Peak 8 are recommended at the luxury end.

EATING OUT ★★★★★
Over 100 restaurants
There's a wide range, from typical US food to fine dining. At peak times they get busy, and many don't take bookings. The Breckenridge Dining Guide (available online) lists the full menu of most places.
  In 2015 we had an excellent dinner

at Relish – ambitious modern dishes in a relaxed upper room. We've also enjoyed the Hearthstone – modern American cuisine in a beautiful 100-year-old house. For no-nonsense grills-and-fries in a pub ambience, we've enjoyed both the Brewery (famous for mega 'appetizers', such as buffalo wings, and splendid beers) and the Kenosha steakhouse. The Blue Moose does killer breakfasts.

APRES-SKI ★★★
The best in the area ...
There's not much teatime animation at the lift bases. The Maggie, at the base of Peak 9, 'has music on the terrace but doesn't stay open much beyond 5pm'. Park Avenue Pub, just off Main Street, and the Brewery were lively on our recent visits. Later on we've enjoyed the Gold Pan saloon (reputedly the oldest bar west of the Mississippi). Burke and Riley's is an Irish bar; Downstairs at Eric's is a disco sports bar, and Three20South has live bands.

OFF THE SLOPES ★★★
Pleasant enough
Breckenridge is a pleasant place to wander around, with souvenir and gift shops plus a museum. Silverthorne (about 30 minutes away by free bus) has bargain factory outlet stores.

FRISCO

Staying in Frisco makes sense for those touring or on a tight budget. It's a pleasant small town with bars, restaurants and good-value lodgings and is linked to resorts by a free bus. Hotel Frisco is on Main Street. Restaurants include Blue Spruce Inn ('fantastic steaks and ambience'), the Boatyard (pizzas), Food Hedz World Cafe ('good duck and steak') and Ollie's.

COPPER MOUNTAIN / BEN BLANKENBURG

Copper Mountain

Great terrain with reliable snow for all ability levels, above a small and quiet pedestrian-friendly resort

£180
RESORT PRICE INDEX

TOP 10 RATINGS

Extent	★★
Fast lifts	★★
Queues	★★★★
Snow	★★★★★
Expert	★★★★
Intermediate	★★★★
Beginner	★★★★
Charm	★★
Convenience	★★★★
Scenery	★★★

KEY FACTS

Resort	2955m
	9,700ft
Slopes	2960-3750m
	9,710-12,310ft
Lifts	23
Pistes	2,465 acres

LIFT PASSES

Prices in $

Age	6-day
under 12	348
13 to 64	454
65 plus	348

Free Under 5
Beginner Free lift in beginner area; special pass for one other lift

Notes Buying online in advance can save up to 40%; Secret! pass allows you to jump queues at seven of the busiest lifts

+ Convenient purpose-built resort

+ Fair-sized mountain, with good runs for all abilities

+ Good value by Colorado standards

+ Few queues on weekdays, but ...

− Can be long lift queues at weekends

− Risk of altitude sickness

− Village very limited

− Poor mountain restaurants

Copper's slopes are some of Colorado's best, and the modern, purpose-built village has become quite a pleasant very small resort. Great for an outing from another Colorado resort, or as a base if you want a quiet time self-catering.

THE RESORT

Intrawest (which also developed Whistler and several other resorts) owned Copper from 1997 to 2009 and did a typically thorough job developing the small, traffic-free, modern Village at Copper (aka Center Village), which is where we'd choose to stay. East Village and West Village are even quieter outposts with few facilities, a free shuttle-bus ride from Center Village. Keystone, Breckenridge and Arapahoe Basin are all nearby, and Vail and Winter Park a bit further.
Village charm Center Village's group of wood-and-stone-clad condo buildings with shops, restaurants and car-free walkways and squares, forms the heart of the resort – set just off the I-70 freeway from Denver. Although small and with limited facilities, it works well; an ice rink on a frozen lake adds to its charm. The other Villages are little more than collections of condos.
Convenience All three Villages have high-speed chairs into the slopes.
Scenery There are good views across the high, partly wooded rolling mountains that typify the Rockies.

THE MOUNTAIN

The area is medium-sized by American standards, and has great runs for all ability levels, with an attractive mix of wooded, gladed and open slopes. Free guided tours are run twice a day.
Slopes The area divides into slopes below Copper Peak and below Union Peak. In general, as you look at the

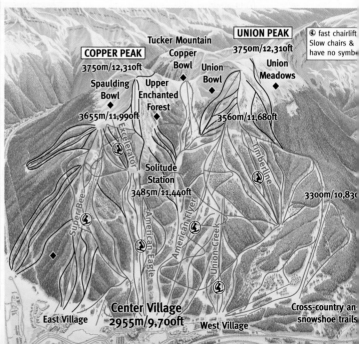

UNION PEAK
3750m/12,310ft

◉ fast chairlift
Slow chairs &
have no symbo

Tucker Mountain

COPPER PEAK
3750m/12,310ft

Copper
Bowl

Union
Bowl

Union
Meadows

Spaulding
Bowl
◆
3655m/11,990ft

Upper
Enchanted
Forest
◆

356m/11,680ft

Excelerator

Timberline

Super Bee

American Eagle

American River

Union Creek

Solitude
Station
3485m/11,440ft

3300m/10,830

Center Village
2955m/9,700ft

East Village

West Village

Cross-country an
snowshoe trails

↑ Union Meadows on the right, Copper Bowl on the left. Both have good but short ungroomed runs, with some tight trees lower down Union Meadows
SNOWPIX.COM / CHRIS GILL

WOODWARD BARN

Copper Mountain is one of the world's leading resorts for freestyle skiing and boarding. And it has a specialist indoor training centre (the Woodward Copper Barn; see www. woodwardatcopper. com) which is open year-round for anyone to learn freestyle tricks and moves under the control of coaches. You start off on trampolines and progress to jumps into huge pits with soft foam blocks to land in. We took a tour of it on our 2015 Copper visit but, sadly, didn't have time to try it. Editor Gill plans to return to learn inverted 360s next season.

TOURIST OFFICE

www.coppercolorado. com

mountain the easiest runs are on the right and it gets progressively steeper the further left you go. On the back of the hill are the high Spaulding and Copper Bowls – open slopes, in contrast to the wooded lower runs. A free snowcat operates at weekends to take you from Copper Bowl up to runs on Tucker Mountain, opposite the lift-served slopes.

Fast lifts Six of the main lifts are high-speed chairs but there are twice as many slow chairs and draglifts (including many of those to the top of the mountain).

Queues Few problems on weekdays, but crowds from Denver cause weekend queues at Center Village and the Timberline lift, in particular. The Storm King draglift can get busy at peak times. You can buy a Secret! pass which allows you to use a special entrance to jump queues at seven of the busiest lifts ($20 a day extra).

Terrain parks Copper is renowned for its freestyle facilities, which include the indoor Woodward Copper Barn training centre (see panel in margin). On the mountain there are six terrain parks with small features, one with medium and one with large features aimed at experts and pros. There's also a half-pipe with 4m walls; a huge super-pipe with walls approaching 7m is also used for major competitions.

Snow reliability Height and extensive snowmaking give Copper an early opening date and excellent reliability. Snowfall averages over 300 inches a year. The front side faces northish and keeps its snow well; the back bowls are more sun-affected and snow condition can deteriorate.

Experts There is a lot of good expert terrain. Spaulding and Copper Bowls and Tucker Mountain offer gradients ranging from moderate to seriously steep, but with limited vertical. Union Meadows at the top right side is a

great gladed area, again with limited vertical – don't ski it alone. The runs lower down the left side of the main mountain are much longer.

Intermediates There are runs to suit everyone, from top-to-bottom greens on the right of the map through similarly long blues to challenging (usually bumpy) black runs on the left.

Beginners The nursery slopes at Union Creek are excellent, and there are lots of very easy green runs to graduate to.

Snowboarding Great slopes for all abilities, plus the terrain parks.

Cross-country There are around 17km of local trails and more in the region.

Mountain restaurants Solitude Station is a dreary food court. Flyer's is a cosy little hut with a small deck. The T-Rex Grill has only outside seating. Or head for the base areas.

Schools and guides The school offers a wide variety of courses including freestyle (part in the Woodward Barn – see margin panel – part on snow).

Families The Belly Button childcare facility takes children from six months old and ski school from age three.

STAYING THERE

Hotels and condos There are no hotels. Most condos are within easy reach of a lift. In 2015 we stayed at the Tucker Mountain Lodge (with sauna, outdoor hot tub, underground car park) in Center Village and were very comfortable.

Eating out The CB Grille is supposed to be the best in town and we found the food OK (elk chop, tenderloin steak) but service poor. Other popular Center Village places include Incline Bar & Grill (wide-ranging menu), Casa Sanchez (Mexican), Storm King (sushi), Gustino's (pizza). In East Village, head for JJ's Rocky Mountain Tavern, which 'is best known for slow-smoked BBQ meats and wood-fire pizzas'.

Après-ski Weekends are lively but midweek can be pretty quiet. At close of play in Center Village, Jack's Slopeside Grill and Bar (live music sometimes), Endo's Adrenaline Cafe and Incline Bar and Grill all have happy hours, as does JJ's Rocky Mountain Tavern in East Village (live music sometimes). We are told that Mulligan's Irish Pub is the only place to stay open late (till 2am) and is popular with locals.

Off the slopes There's a good sports club with a huge pool, tubing, snowmobiling, ice skating.

ASPEN/SNOWMASS PICTURE LIBRARY

Snowmass

Aspen's modern satellite – with impressively varied and extensive slopes, and a smart new fledgling Base Village

£210
RESORT PRICE INDEX

TOP 10 RATINGS

Extent	★★★
Fast lifts	★★★★★
Queues	★★★★
Snow	★★★★★
Expert	★★★★★
Intermediate	★★★★★
Beginner	★★★★★
Charm	★★
Convenience	★★★★★
Scenery	★★★★

Our extent rating is for Snowmass alone. Including the other Aspen mountains would make it
★★★★

NEWS

2015/16: The High Alpine chair will be replaced by a fast quad; snowmaking will be installed on two existing trails; trails and glading will be improved.

+ Varied mountain, with the biggest vertical in the US – 1340m

+ Aspen accessible by free bus

+ Uncrowded slopes

+ Lots of slope-side lodgings

− Limited dining, shopping and nightlife options

− Diversions of Aspen town are a bus ride away

The slopes of Snowmass are a key part of the attraction of nearby Aspen as a destination. The skiing here is great for all standards. As a base, Snowmass has obvious appeal for families wanting easy cruising on their doorstep; but the resort is still a long way from being an entertaining place to stay.

THE RESORT

Snowmass is a modern, purpose-built resort, with low-rise buildings set next to the gentle home slope. Within these buildings is Snowmass Village Mall. A little way down the hill (with a linking gondola) is the recently added Base Village, development of which has been slowed by the recession.

Village charm Base Village has added a bit of style to what is a rather functional modern resort.

Convenience Much of the lodging is ski-in/ski-out, and Snowmass Village Mall has a small cluster of shops and restaurants. Efficient free bus services (crowded at times) link Snowmass with Aspen's mountains and town – the latter until late at night.

Scenery The views from the high-points are long but not dramatic.

THE MOUNTAINS

Most of the slopes are in the forest; higher ones are only lightly wooded.

Slopes Snowmass is big by US standards, both in area and dimensions – almost 8km across. Chairlifts and a gondola diverge from the base to go up to Elk Camp at one end of the ski area and Sam's Knob at the other. Links higher up go to the two sectors in the middle, High Alpine and Big Burn, where a draglift goes to the area high-point on The Cirque. There is a second lift-base at Two Creeks, which is nearer Aspen.

Fast lifts Most key lifts are fast, and another slow, cold chair is being replaced this winter.

Queues The home slope gets busy. The locals come out early on big powder days.

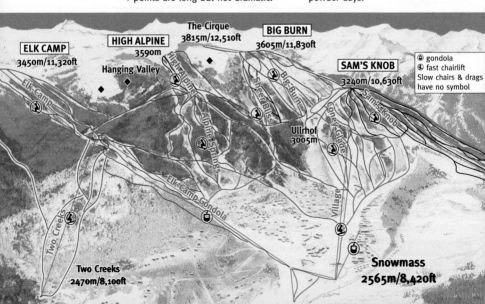

← Some of the ways in to Hanging Valley are pretty challenging – well, extreme. But there are easier ways to go
DANIEL BAYER

KEY FACTS

Resort	2565m
	8,420ft

Snowmass only	
Slopes	2470-3815m
	8,100-12,510ft
Lifts	21
Pistes	3,332 acres

See Aspen chapter for statistics on other mountains

LIFT PASSES

Four Mountain Pass

Prices in US$

Age	6-day
under 13	342
13 to 17	540
18 to 64	594
65 plus	540

Free Under 7: $5 for unlimited period
Senior Over 70: $459 for unlimited period
Beginner Included in price of lessons
Notes Includes shuttle-bus between the areas; 6-day prices are online 7 days in advance (window prices are higher); savings if you purchase in advance through certain UK tour operators and if you purchase in conjunction with lodging

TOURIST OFFICE

www.aspen
snowmass.com

Terrain parks Snowmass has a super-pipe and three parks: Lowdown (beginner) with half-pipe, Little Makaha (intermediate) and Snowmass (expert), with about 90 features including jibs, rails, boxes and jumps.
Snow reliability With 300 inches a year plus snowmaking, it's good.
Experts There's great terrain, although the steep runs tend to be short. Consider joining a guided group as an introduction. Our favourite area is around the Hanging Valley Wall and Glades – beautiful scenery and steep wooded slopes. The other seriously steep area is The Cirque, reached by draglift from Big Burn to the area's highest point. From here, the Headwall is not terrifyingly steep, but there are also narrow, often rocky, chutes – Gowdy's is one of the steepest. Try the gladed black runs mentioned under 'Intermediates' too.
Intermediates Excellent – this is the best mountain in the Aspen area for intermediates (and by far the biggest). Highlights include: the top slopes on Big Burn – a huge, varied, lightly wooded area, including the Powerline Glades for the adventurous; long, top-to-bottom cruises from Elk Camp and High Alpine; regularly groomed single-black runs from Sam's Knob. Then there are glorious runs set in the forest starting a short hike from the top of Elk Camp: these are around 5km long, end at Two Creeks and include a long-time favourite, the blue Long Shot, and three gladed black runs that were classified black only because of a narrow and quite steep traverse out.

Beginners In the heart of the resort is a broad, gentle beginners' run. An even easier slope (and less busy) is Assay Hill, at the bottom of Elk Camp. There's also a beginner area served by three lifts at the top of the Elk Camp gondola. From Sam's Knob there are long, gentle cruises back to the resort.
Snowboarding A great mountain, whatever your boarding style.
Cross-country Excellent trails between here and Aspen – see Aspen chapter.
Mountain restaurants Amazingly, there are three table-service places: long-established Gwyn's High Alpine (endorsed again by readers this year), Lynn Britt Cabin (cosy old log cabin, elegant table settings) and Sam's Smokehouse (big windows, great views, decent casual food).
Schools and guides Reports have been mixed, but predominantly positive.
Families Snowmass is a family-friendly resort. The Treehouse adventure centre at Base Village is a very impressive facility, and there are special trails (and trail maps) for children.

STAYING THERE

Most accommodation is self-catering.
Hotels Several options on or close to the home slope. The focal hotel is the plush Westin (formerly the Silvertree). The Stonebridge Inn is 'almost ski-in and out' and gets consistently good reports, again this year.
Apartments Capitol Peak has luxury condos at Base Village. Timberline condos get good reports in the main.
Eating out Eight K restaurant in the Viceroy hotel is highly recommended, especially the chef's tables where the atmosphere is 'more laid back'. Venga Venga Cantina & Tequila Bar does Mexican with an 'upscale modern feel (heavenly deep-fried Churros)'. Il Poggio (yes, it's an Italian) is 'best in town' says one reader; Base Camp Bar & Grill is good value. Stew Pot has been tipped too.
Après-ski Base Village is 'pretty dead', although Base Camp has live music. There's more of a buzz at Village Mall; Venga Venga ('excellent cocktails') is popular.
Off the slopes Snowshoe trails, snowcat rides, dog sledding plus swimming at the Recreation Center.

STEAMBOAT / LARRY PIERCE

Steamboat

The home of Champagne Powder™, with some convenient lodgings at the lift base and a lively town 10 minutes away

£185

RESORT PRICE INDEX

TOP 10 RATINGS

Extent	★★★
Fast lifts	★★★★
Queues	★★★★
Snow	★★★★
Expert	★★★
Intermediate	★★★★
Beginner	★★★★★
Charm	★★
Convenience	★★★
Scenery	★★★

NEWS

2015/16: Additional terrain will be covered by snowmaking.

KEY FACTS

Resort	2105m
	6,900ft
Slopes	2105-3220m
	6,900-10,570ft
Lifts	18
Pistes	2,965 acres

570

LIFT PASSES

Prices in US$

Age	6-day
under 13	354
13 to 17	546
18 to 69	660
70 plus	426

Free Under 6
Beginner Free lifts in beginner area
Note You can pay appreciably less by booking ahead
Alternative pass
Max Pass (adult $699) includes five days at 22 mountains

➕ Varied mountain with extensive easy runs and rightly famed gladed terrain

➕ Real town with some Western character, a drive from the slopes

➕ Fair mountain restaurants

➕ Good snow record (the home of Champagne Powder™) – but ...

➖ Low altitude by Colorado standards – snow can deteriorate quickly

➖ Modern base has little appeal except some convenient lodging developments

➖ Most lodgings are a drive from both the slopes and the town

➖ Not enough groomed runs to amuse keen intermediates for a week

➖ Rather isolated location

We dropped Steamboat from these pages a few years back, along with several other resorts that lacked support from readers. It's back because we visited in February 2015, and liked both the hill and the nearby town of Steamboat Springs more than we expected to. If it's going to stay in ... reports, please.

What we didn't like, despite recent improvements, is the mountain base area, which has been developed piecemeal over many years. Some of its lodgings are convenient for the snow (some are emphatically not), but it is devoid of life after the immediate après session. Plans to redevelop the Ski Time Square area to the left of the lift base give some hope. Meanwhile, the increasingly amusing town is only a shuttle ride away.

THE RESORT

Steamboat is a short drive from the long-established town of Steamboat Springs. It is relatively isolated – a 3-hour drive from Denver – and taking it into a trip with another resort is not very easy. The drive from Denver involves two passes which can be closed by snow. The local airport has flights from 11 hubs, so don't assume that flying into Denver is necessarily the thing to do.

Village charm The base area has little appeal. The town of Steamboat Springs combines some Wild West character with tourist appeal – it has many more interesting restaurants, shops and galleries than it did a decade ago. It's a pity that Main Street is also the busy, four-lane Highway 40.

Convenience There are hotels and condos at the lift base and up the sides of the home slopes, but many condos are a free bus (or private shuttle) ride away. A pulse gondola links one development (Trailhead) to the base area.

Scenery The slopes give long views over the wide Yampa Valley, but the scenery is not at all dramatic.

THE MOUNTAINS

Steamboat's slopes are prettily set among trees – even the highest runs offer shelter in bad weather (though a reporter found the signage not good in those conditions).

Slopes The gondola from the base rises to the low peak of Thunderhead. Beyond it are lifts to Storm Peak and Sunshine Peak – the latter offering a broad area of blue runs served by a fast quad. On the back of the hill is the Morningside Park area, with a slow chair back up to the high point of Mt Werner, also accessing some of the top runs on the front side. Below Storm Peak is a separate area served by the Pony Express fast chair. There are free daily mountain tours and you can sometimes ski with 1964 Olympic medallist Billy Kidd (Director of Skiing); 'very enjoyable' says a reporter this year. Five lower slopes are floodlit for night skiing.

Fast lifts Fast chairs serve each area, but there are still a few slow ones too.

Queues Queues form for the gondola first thing, and can be serious at times, but they can be avoided by using chairs. We now get few other complaints except about peak periods.

Terrain parks There were five last season. The 12-acre Mavericks park includes lots of obstacles and a super-pipe, while Lower Mavericks has the largest features, Rabbit Ears and Lil' Rodeo are for beginners, and Sunbeam for intermediates.

Snow reliability The term Champagne Powder™ was invented here, which may or may not reflect the true quality of the snow. Quantity is not in dispute: with a 10-year annual average of almost 350 inches, Steamboat is one of the top resorts in Colorado. But if warm weather hits the state, as it did in 2015, the relatively low altitude here can mean Alpine-style conditions.

Experts The main attraction is the challenging terrain in the glades. A great area is on Sunshine Peak below the Sundown chair. Morningside Park and the Pony Express area also have excellent gladed runs. Three steep chutes are easily accessed via the lift back from Morningside, and a short hike gets you to the tree runs of Christmas Tree Bowl. For bumps, try the runs off Four Points or the Sundown chair. Many runs are of limited vertical; try Valley View for a longer black run to the base. You can also go snowcat skiing nearby (see www.steamboatpowdercats.com).

Intermediates Much of the mountain is ideal, with long cruising blue runs. Morningside Park is a great area for easy black as well as blue slopes – and 'lovely ungroomed terrain in the trees'. The Sunshine area is mainly gentle. Some of the black runs, such as Roles and West Side, are regularly groomed, and in several sectors there are blue-black runs to help you progress to the blacks. Keen intermediates will find the mountain limited, but given fresh powder it's a great introduction to tree skiing.

Beginners There's a big nursery area, the Headwall, at the base of the mountain. Lots of easy trails offer good progression – some of the blues are quieter and more relaxing than the greens, which include many cat tracks with steep drops at the side. The Sunshine area is particularly suited to families skiing together.

Snowboarding There's a good learning area (see above), gentle slopes to progress to and you can get around using chairlifts and the gondola. For experienced riders, the glades in fresh powder are unbeatable.

Cross-country A free shuttle takes you to 15km of tracks at the Touring Center. There are five centres and a total of 166km of trails in the area.

Mt Werner
3220m/10,570ft

Morningside Park

Christmas Tree Bowl

Storm Peak 3160m

Sunshine Peak 3165m

Sunshine

Sundown

Four points

Storm Peak

Pony Express

Rendezvous Saddle

Thunderhead 2770m

Gondola

Thunderhead

Christie Peak

gondola
fast chairlift
Slow chairs & drags
have no symbol

Steamboat

Ski Time Square

Gondola base
2105m/6,900ft

Mountain restaurants There are now decent self-service food courts at three points (including the smart new Four Points Lodge) and two table-service restaurants – Hazie's at Thunderhead and Ragnar's at Rendezvous Saddle; the food is nothing special, but at least you don't have to queue for it.

Schools and guides Reports are positive: 'terrific – friendly and flexible', writes one visitor this year.

Families Arrangements are exceptional, winning awards from American magazines; there's even evening entertainment. Kids under 12 ski free with a parent or a grandparent buying a pass for at least five days. There's a similar deal for equipment rental.

STAYING THERE

Chalets There are some catered chalets run by UK tour operators.

Hotels The Steamboat Grand is a smart hotel at the base, with various kinds of accommodation; it's a plod from the snow, but has ski storage near the lifts. The Sheraton is more convenient. The town's suburbs have lots of cheap and cheerful chain hotels and motels.

Apartments There are countless condos, many with good pools and hot tubs, all on a free bus route and some with shuttles. One Steamboat Place is a swanky recent development at the base. Reporters recommend Trailhead ('high quality, wide range of facilities'; pulse gondola to the lift base) and Mountaineer ('delightful town-houses, friendly service').

Eating out There are over 70 bars and restaurants, mainly in and around the town. Pick up a dining guide booklet to check out the menus, or visit www.steamboat-dining.com. Downtown, we had an excellent tapas-style 'small plates' dinner in the funky, bare-brick-walled Laundry, and liked the look of the very popular Mahogany, for Asian fusion cuisine. The reader favourite is 8th Street Steakhouse, where 'you pick your meat at the butcher's counter and cook it yourself on a lava rock grill'. Cheap and cheerful tips this year are Cantina for 'great Tex-Mex'; Jonny B Good's Diner for 'casual burgers and fries, pies and a mingle with the locals'; and Mazzola's for pasta etc.

At the lift base, Truffle Pig in One Steamboat Place pleased one reporter with its 'varied menu and good service'. Various 'dining experiences' are offered on the mountain, some involving rides in snowcats.

Après-ski At close of play there is quite a bit of après action on the terraces of the Slopeside Grill and Bear River at the Sheraton, especially on Saturdays – live music sometimes.

Off the slopes Pedestrians can ride the gondola to meet skiers at Thunderhead. The town is quite amusing; get your Stetson at FM Light & Sons. The Strawberry Park Hot Springs are 'a great experience – lovely and relaxing'. Snowmobiling, snowshoeing, ice climbing, tubing, hot-air balloons, sleigh rides and dog sledding are also possible.

TOURIST OFFICE

www.steamboat.com

572

SNOWPIX.COM / CHRIS GILL

There are plenty of slope-side condos, but even more between the lift base and the town, seen in the distance on the far right ↓

SNOWPIX.COM / CHRIS GILL

Vail

A vast, swanky resort with some very swanky hotels at the foot of one of the biggest (but also busiest) ski areas in the States

£215
RESORT PRICE INDEX

RATINGS

The mountains

Extent	★★★★
Fast lifts	★★★★★
Queues	★★
Terrain p'ks	★★★★★
Snow	★★★★★
Expert	★★★★
Intermediate	★★★★★
Beginner	★★★
Boarder	★★★
X-country	★★★
Restaurants	★★
Schools	★★★★
Families	★★★★

The resort

Charm	★★★
Convenience	★★★
Scenery	★★★
Eating out	★★★★★
Après-ski	★★★
Off-slope	★★★

KEY FACTS

Resort	2500m
	8,200ft
Slopes	2475-3525m
	8,120-11,570ft
Lifts	31
Pistes	5,289 acres

+ One of the biggest areas in the US – especially great for confident intermediates

+ The Back Bowls are big areas of treeless terrain – unusual in the US

+ Fabulous area of ungroomed, wooded slopes at Blue Sky Basin

+ Largely traffic-free resort centres, very pleasant in parts – but ...

− Resort is a vast sprawl

− Slopes can be crowded by American standards, with serious lift queues

− Inadequate mountain restaurants

− Blue Sky Basin and Back Bowls may not be open in early season; warm weather can close much of Bowls

− Expensive, with lots of luxury lodgings but few budget options

We always enjoy skiing Vail; it's a big mountain with a decent vertical, and Blue Sky Basin's 'adventure' skiing is a key attraction. But it is far from being our favourite American mountain. In an American resort you expect the runs to be pretty much crowd-free – and in any resort you expect 20-minute lift queues to be a thing of the past. In these respects, Vail disappoints.

When the budget runs to a swanky billet in Vail Village or the Lionshead area, we're happy enough with the resort, too; it is a pleasant place to wander around. But we're not enthusiastic about Vail Village's pseudo-Tirolean style, and the rest of the huge resort lacks character. In the end, Vail can't compete with more distinctively American resorts based on old mining towns.

THE RESORT

Vail is an enormous resort, stretching almost four miles along the I-70 freeway running west from Denver. Beaver Creek, 16km away, is covered by the lift pass and is easily reached by bus. Breckenridge and Keystone – both owned by Vail Resorts and covered by the lift pass – and Copper Mountain are other possible excursions.

VILLAGE CHARM ★★★
No real identity
Standing in the centre of Vail Village, surrounded by chalets and bierkellers, you could be forgiven for thinking you were in the Tirol – which is what Vail's founder, Pete Seibert, intended back in the 1950s. But this is now just one part of a huge resort, and the rest is mostly in anonymous (although smart) modern style.

CONVENIENCE ★★★
There's always the bus
The vast village has a free and efficient bus service ('always on time'), – frequent from Lionshead to Golden Peak, less frequent to the outskirts. But the most convenient (and expensive) places to stay are in the mock-Tirolean Vail Village or at Lionshead – an area that has smart lodgings to match Vail Village; both areas have gondolas out. There is a lot of accommodation further out – some on the far side of the I-70.

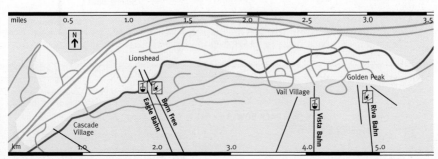

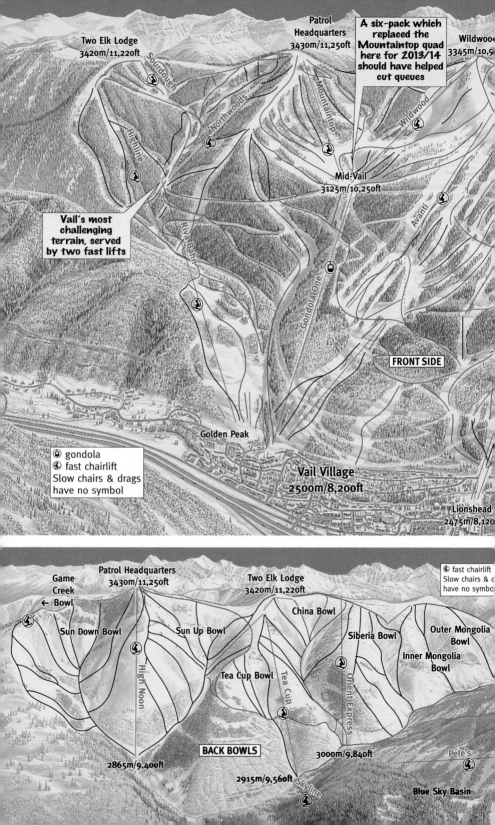

Two Elk Lodge
3420m/11,220ft

Patrol
Headquarters
3430m/11,250ft

A six-pack which
replaced the
Mountaintop quad
here for 2013/14
should have helped
cut queues

Wildwood
3345m/10,9...

Soundough

Northwoods

Mountaintop

Highline

Wildwood

Mid-Vail
3125m/10,250ft

Avanti

Vail's most
challenging
terrain, served
by two fast lifts

Riva Bahn

Gondola One

FRONT SIDE

Golden Peak

gondola
fast chairlift
Slow chairs & drags
have no symbol

Vail Village
2500m/8,200ft

Lionshead
2475m/8,120...

Game
Creek
← Bowl

Patrol Headquarters
3430m/11,250ft

Two Elk Lodge
3420m/11,220ft

fast chairlift
Slow chairs & d...
have no symbo...

Sun Down Bowl

Sun Up Bowl

China Bowl

Siberia Bowl

Outer Mongolia
Bowl

Inner Mongolia
Bowl

High Noon

Tea Cup Bowl

Tea Cup

Orient Express

BACK BOWLS

3000m/9,840ft

Pete's

2865m/9,400ft

2915m/9,560ft

Skyline

Blue Sky Basin

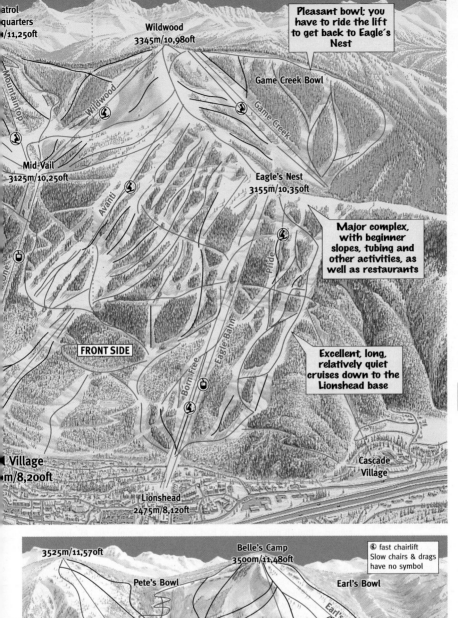

atrol
quarters
/11,250ft

Wildwood
3345m/10,980ft

Pleasant bowl: you
have to ride the lift
to get back to Eagle's
Nest

Game Creek Bowl

Game Creek

Wildwood

Mountaintop

Mid-Vail
3125m/10,250ft

Avanti

Eagle's Nest
3155m/10,350ft

Major complex,
with beginner
slopes, tubing and
other activities, as
well as restaurants

Pride

Eagle-Bahn

FRONT SIDE

Born Free

Excellent, long,
relatively quiet
cruises down to the
Lionshead base

Village
m/8,200ft

Cascade
Village

Lionshead
2475m/8,120ft

3525m/11,570ft

Belle's Camp
3500m/11,480ft

⊕ fast chairlift
Slow chairs & drags
have no symbol

Pete's Bowl

Earl's Bowl

Earl's

Pete's

Skyline

BLUE SKY BASIN

Orient Express

3000m/9,840ft

2915m/9,560ft

↑ Perfect corduroy first thing in the morning. Well worth travelling the 5,000 miles for

VAIL / JACK AFFLECK

NEWS

2015/16: The Avanti fast quad above Lionshead is due to be replaced by a six-pack, which should increase capacity by 30%.

2014/15: The renovation of the flagship Lodge at Vail (Vail's first lodging, dating from 1962 and close to the gondola from Vail Village) was completed.

Along with Beaver Creek, Vail hosted the Alpine World Ski Championships in February 2015.

SCENERY ★★★☆☆
Rolling Colorado
Like most Colorado resorts, Vail is set among rather softly contoured mountains with forest reaching to the top of the slopes. From the top you can see for miles.

THE MOUNTAINS

You get a real sense of travelling around Vail's mountains – something missing in many smaller American resorts. Run classification exaggerates the difficulty of some slopes – some of the blacks, in particular. Several runs are partly classified blue, partly black, which means fewer surprises if you study the map. Compared with most American resorts the runs are usually crowded – though nothing like as bad as in Europe. There are free mountain tours at 10.30am, with separate tours of Blue Sky Basin at 11am on Tuesday and Friday. The slopes have yellow-jacketed patrollers to stop people speeding, but they don't seem to have much effect.

EXTENT OF THE SLOPES ★★★★☆
Something for everyone
Vail's 5,289 acres of lift-linked slopes make it one of the biggest ski areas in the US (though way behind the new combined Park City-Canyons area). The slopes can be accessed via three main lifts. From Vail Village, a gondola goes up to the major mid-mountain focal point, Mid-Vail; from Lionshead, the Eagle Bahn gondola goes up to the Eagle's Nest complex; and from the

Golden Peak base area just to the east of Vail Village, the Riva Bahn fast chair goes up towards the Two Elk area.

The front face of the mountain is largely north-facing, with well-groomed trails cut through the trees. At altitude the mountainside divides into three bowls – Mid-Vail in the centre, with Game Creek to the south-west and the area below Two Elk Lodge to the north-east. Lifts reach the ridge at three points, all giving access to the **Back Bowls** (mostly ungroomed and treeless) and through them to **Blue Sky Basin** (mostly ungroomed and wooded, with a 'backcountry' feel).

FAST LIFTS ★★★★★
Plenty of them
There are lots of fast lifts on both sides of the mountain. All three of Blue Sky Basin's lifts are fast chairs.

QUEUES ★★☆☆☆
Can be bad
The front side of Vail has had some of the longest lift lines we've hit in the US, especially at weekends because of the influx from nearby Denver. A recent reporter took weekend lessons to jump the queues. And even on a mid-December visit we hit big queues. Mid-Vail is a bottleneck that is difficult to avoid; but the six-pack replacement for the Mountaintop Express a couple of years back has helped says a reporter – more reports please. The Northwoods chair, the Eagle Bahn gondola and lifts in the Back Bowls are other hot spots.

LIFT PASSES

Colorado

Prices in US$

Age	6-day
under 13	480
13 to 64	690
65 plus	630

Free Under 5

Beginner Included in price of lessons

Notes Covers Vail, Beaver Creek, Breckenridge, Keystone and Arapahoe Basin; prices are online rates for mid-March purchased 14 days in advance of trip; window rates in resort are considerably higher; international visitors will get best prices by pre-booking through a UK tour operator (it is not necessary to buy a complete holiday package to obtain these prices)

TERRAIN PARKS ★★★★★
Three to choose between

There are three parks. Beginner and intermediate freestylers will want to explore the Bwana and Pride parks, located under the Eagle Bahn gondola on Bwana run. Here, a selection of small to medium-sized features gradually become more challenging as you progress through each park.

More advanced riders will be best served at the Golden Peak Terrain Park, which got a new layout last season. Located halfway down the Riva Bahn chairlift, the park is home to various high-profile events and is often in the top ten in terrain park lists and polls. There are more than 40 features plus seven jumps ranging from extra small to large, a super-pipe and mini-pipe.

SNOW RELIABILITY ★★★★★
Excellent, except in the Bowls

As well as an exceptional natural snow record (average 354 inches), Vail has extensive snowmaking, normally needed only in early season. Grooming is excellent. Both the Back Bowls and Blue Sky Basin usually open later in the season than the front of the mountain. Blue Sky is largely north-facing (and wooded) and keeps its snow well. But the Bowls are sunny, and in warm weather snow can deteriorate (as we found on our February 2015 visit) to the point where they are closed or only a traverse is kept open to allow access to Blue Sky Basin; for the best snow, head skier's right from the top of the Game Creek chair, where the sun has least effect because the runs are east-facing.

FOR EXPERTS ★★★★
Lots of variety

Vail's Back Bowls are vast areas, served by four chairlifts and a short draglift. You can go virtually anywhere you like in the half-dozen identifiable bowls, trying the gradient and terrain of your choice. There are interesting, lightly wooded areas, as well as open slopes. The Bowls are largely classified black but are not particularly steep; they disappoint some expert reporters.

Blue Sky Basin has much better snow than the Back Bowls and some great adventure runs in the trees – some widely spaced, some very tight, some on relatively gentle terrain, some quite steep. All runs funnel into the same run-outs so you can't get lost.

www.ski-i.com

ski)))
independence

Call the Tailor-made Ski Specialists
0131 243 8097

On the front face there are some genuinely steep double-black diamond runs, which usually have great snow; they are often mogulled, but they are sometimes groomed to make wonderful fast cruising. The fast Highline lift – on the extreme east of the area – serves three black runs. Prima Cornice, served by the Northwoods Express, is one of the steepest runs on the front of the hill.

If the snow is good, try the backcountry Minturn Mile – you leave the ski area through a gate in the Game Creek area to descend a powder bowl and finish on a path by a river – ending up at the atmospheric Saloon in Minturn. You come back by bus or taxi. Go with a local guide.

FOR INTERMEDIATES ★★★★★
Ideal territory

The majority of Vail's front face is great intermediate terrain, with easy cruising runs. Above Lionshead, especially, there are excellent, long, relatively quiet blues – Bwana, Born Free and Simba all go from top to bottom. Game Creek Bowl, nearby, is excellent, too. Avanti, underneath the chair of the same name, is a nice cruise.

As well as tackling some of the easier front-face blacks, intermediates will find plenty of interest in the Back Bowls. Some of the runs are groomed and several are blue, including Silk Road, which loops around the eastern edge, with wonderful views. Some of the unpisted slopes are ideal for learning to ski powder. Confident intermediates will also enjoy Blue Sky Basin's clearly marked blue runs and the easier ungroomed runs there (Cloud 9 is a lovely gentle area of groomed glades; In the Wuides is a bit steeper but still lovely).

SKIWORLD

Catered chalets, hotels and self catering apartments in

Europe, USA and Canada

skiworld.co.uk
08444 930 430

ABTA V2151   ATOL 2036

VAIL / JACK AFFLECK

Fresh snow at the start of the day is worth getting up early for; we'd be heading over to Blue Sky Basin ↓

FOR BEGINNERS ★★★
Good but can be crowded
There are fine nursery slopes at resort level and at altitude, and easy longer runs to progress to. But they can be rather crowded, with lots of faster skiers passing through.

FOR BOARDERS ★★★
Beware of the flats
Beginners will enjoy the front side's gentle groomed pistes (but not the crowds), good for honing skills and serviced by fast chairlifts. But beware of flat areas, especially at the top of the Wildwood and Northwoods lifts, and cat tracks. The Back Bowls will keep most expert and intermediate riders busy for days. Blue Sky Basin offers acres of natural trails, gladed trees and cornices.

FOR CROSS-COUNTRY ★★★
Go for Golden
There are 17km of trails at the Nordic Center on the golf course and cross-country backcountry tours are run by the Nordic School at Golden Peak.

MOUNTAIN RESTAURANTS ★★
Improved but still poor
We have been saying for years that Vail's mountain restaurants are just inadequate for a major upscale resort. This has been proved by the popularity of the our Eds' choice...
Editors' choice The table-service 10th at Mid-Vail was built a few seasons ago and is comfortable, light, airy and very civilized compared with the alternatives. The food is fine but not outstanding. Nice bar area too. We went in 2015 and enjoyed it; endorsed

by a 2015 reporter too: 'First rate on-mountain dining experience; great food, service and wonderful views.'
Worth knowing about The only other table-service option is Bistro Fourteen at Eagle's Nest, an airy room, decent food but we much prefer the 10th.

The major self-service restaurants can be unpleasantly crowded from 11am to 2pm. The Two Elk is huge and airy, and does decent (but pricey) food – 'fresh-cooked pasta, wonderful chili' says a visitor this year; good luck finding a table. Try much smaller Wildwood for BBQs and Buffalo's for soup and sandwiches. You can cook your own food on free BBQs at Belle's Camp at the top of Blue Sky Basin (take your own booze too).

SCHOOLS AND GUIDES ★★★★
Excellent reputation, but ...
The school has an excellent reputation and past reports were usually positive. But a reporter who visited twice in the last three years has mixed feelings: 'Snowboard lesson was fantastic, hiked to get untracked powder. Brill, brill, brill.' But his wife's lesson was 'dreadful – she asked for a change of instructor for day two but was told that wasn't possible'. And in 2015 his 11-year-old son joined the top group for double-black and mogul instruction but despite being assured of this 'they only did one challenging run and spent the rest of the day on blues; the plus points were only five in the class and a late finish'. More reports, please.

You can sign up for lessons on the mountain. Full-day Adventure Sessions offer guided instruction for experts and intermediates.

↑ Vail Village is a pleasant place to stroll around but is only a small part of the sprawling resort

VAIL / CHRIS MCLENNAN

has lots of amenities. At Vail Village, Mountain Haus is central and high quality. Vail Cascade Resort and Spa is good value, including use of the hotel's leisure facilities. And Manor Vail might be a preferred family choice – it's beside the children's ski school. Good value places at Lionshead include the Lodge at Lionshead, Village Inn Plaza, Vantage Point, the Antlers, Enzian, Westwind and Vail 21.

EATING OUT ★★★★★
Endless choice
Whatever kind of food you want, Vail has it – but most of it is expensive.

Fine-dining options include Elway's (in the Lodge), the Tour (modern French) and Ludwig's (in the Sonnenalp). For Alpine ambience try Pepi's (in the hotel Gramshammer) or the Alpenrose. You can take gondolas up to The 10th at Mid-Vail or to Eagle's Nest and then be driven by snowcat to the Game Creek Club for dinner (it's a private members' club at lunchtimes).

For more moderate prices, we've found Blu's 'contemporary American' food satisfactory; Campo de Fiori is an excellent Italian. Reader tips: Pazzo's ('said to be the best pizza in Vail'), Sweet Basil (modern American), Los Amigos (Mexican), Lancelot (steaks), all in Vail Village; May Palace (Chinese) and Nozawa (Asian) in West Vail.

APRES-SKI ★★★
Fairly lively
Lionshead is quiet in the evenings; but Garfinkel's has a DJ, sun deck and happy hour. The Red Lion in Vail Village has live music, big-screen TVs and huge portions of food. The George models itself on an English-style pub. Pepi's is popular, and Los Amigos is lively at four o'clock.

OFF THE SLOPES ★★★
A lot to do
Getting around on the free bus is easy, and there are lots of activities. At Adventure Ridge at Eagle's Nest (open in the evenings too, as are bars and restaurant there) you can try tubing, ski biking, kid's snowmobiling, a zipline and snowshoeing. There's also ice skating. Pedestrians can get to Eagle's Nest or Mid-Vail for lunch by gondola; and the Eagle Bahn is free after 3.30pm. The National Mining Museum in Leadville and the factory outlets at Silverthorne are both around a 45-minute drive.

FOR FAMILIES ★★★★
Good all round
The main childcare centre is at Golden Peak, where the nursery takes kids from two months to six years. The ski school takes kids from age three. There are splendid areas with adventure trails and themed play zones, such as the Magic Forest and Chaos Canyon. There's even a special kids' cafe area at Mid Vail. There are kids' snowmobiles and trampolines at Adventure Ridge.

STAYING THERE

There's a big choice of packages to Vail (Ski Independence has a good range) and it's easy to organize your own visit, with regular airport shuttles.
Chalets Skiworld has the only UK tour op-run chalet we know of – a smart four-bedroom house with outdoor hot tub in East Vail (right by a bus stop).
Hotels Vail's hotels are nearly all upmarket and expensive. Some of the best are: Vail Cascade (with its own lift into the slopes), the plushly Bavarian Sonnenalp, the brilliantly convenient and recently revamped Lodge at Vail and the relatively new Ritz Carlton, Four Seasons and Solaris hotels. More affordable places include:
★★★★Manor Vail Lodge At Golden Peak. Suites with sitting area, fireplace, kitchen, terrace. Hot tub and pools.
★★★★Marriot Mountain Resort At Lionshead. Spa, pool, hot tub.
★★★Evergreen Lodge Between village and Lionshead. More affordable than the others. Outdoor pool, sauna and hot tub. Sports bar.
Apartments There's a wide range of condos. The Racquet Club at East Vail

Vail

579

GETTING THERE

Air Eagle 55km/ 35 miles (45min); Denver 195km/ 120 miles (2hr15)

TOURIST OFFICE

www.vail.com

WINTER PARK /
BYRON HETZLER PHOTOGRAPHY

Winter Park

A radical alternative to the run of Colorado resorts, for those more interested in snow and space than in après-ski amusements

580

£165
RESORT PRICE INDEX

RATINGS

The mountains

Extent	★★★
Fast lifts	★★★★
Queues	★★★★
Terrain p'ks	★★★★★
Snow	★★★★★
Expert	★★★★
Intermediate	★★★★
Beginner	★★★★★
Boarder	★★★
X-country	★★★★
Restaurants	★★★
Schools	★★★★★
Families	★★★★

The resort

Charm	★★
Convenience	★★★
Scenery	★★★
Eating out	★★
Après-ski	★
Off-slope	★

NEWS

2015/16: If all goes to plan, you'll be able to travel by train from Denver airport to the resort, via Denver.

2014/15: The old Lunch Rock Cafe, at the top of Mary Jane, was replaced by a smart new Lunch Rock – a food-court-style 250-seater with terrace.

KEY FACTS

Resort	2745m
	9,000ft
Slopes	2745-3675m
	9,000-12,060ft
Lifts	25
Pistes	3,081 acres

- The best snowfall record of Colorado's major resorts
- Quiet on weekdays
- Leading resort for teaching people with disabilities to ski and ride
- Largely free of ski-resort glitz
- Good terrain for all abilities, particularly mogul fans; but ...

- Nearly all steep slopes are never groomed, so always mogulled
- 'Village' at the lift base is still very limited, and dead in the evening
- Town is a bus ride away and has few shops and restaurants
- Some tough terrain is prone to closure by bad weather

Winter Park's ski area is impressive. It was developed (and is still owned) by the nearby city of Denver for the recreation of its citizens, who pour in on weekends and powder days. When Intrawest (developer of resorts such as Whistler) got involved a few years ago, there was talk of a similarly impressive 'destination' resort at the lift base, too. The base village has certainly expanded and improved, but it's still very small and quiet; there's a bit more going on, though not much, in the small town of Winter Park, a bus ride from the hill.

Winter Park's policy of grooming hardly any black runs, ever, means the step up from blue to black runs is a big one. We think the policy is a mistake.

THE RESORT

Winter Park started life in the 19th century, when the Rio Grande railway was built; workers climbed the slopes to ski down. One of its mountains, Mary Jane, is named after a legendary 'lady of pleasure' who is said to have received the land as payment for her favours. The resort (at 2745m) is one of the highest to get a chapter in this book (only Breckenridge is higher) and there is some risk of altitude sickness if you go straight there from the UK – though we survived doing exactly that in 2015.

The approach road from Denver over the Continental Divide at Berthoud Pass is spectacularly high (3450m) and Alpine in character, with very un-American hairpin bends. Driving over in the dark is not something to be done lightly if there is any sign of bad weather. Having a car permits day trips to resorts such as Copper Mountain, Keystone and Breckenridge (see separate chapters).

VILLAGE CHARM ★★
Old or new?
Most lodgings are in spacious condos scattered around either side of US Highway 40, the road that passes the lift base and goes on through the town. At night, the fairy lights and neon signs make it seem like a real ski resort town; in the cold light of day it's different – plain and very limited in what it has to offer. You have to drive to Fraser to find a proper supermarket, for example.

Stylish lodgings have been built at or near the foot of the slopes, to form a very small but pleasant, car-free mini-resort known as The Village at Winter Park. Another area of lodgings between the mountain and the town is known as Old Town.

CONVENIENCE ★★★
Walk or ride
The Village is right by the slopes. Shuttle-buses run between the town and the lift base, and hotels and condos also have their own shuttles.

SCENERY ★★★
High, but not dramatic
From the upper slopes there are wide views of the Continental Divide in one direction, and rolling hills in the other.

THE MOUNTAINS

There's a good mix of terrain – when it's all open; bad weather closures can be an issue. There are guided tours twice daily. Route finding can be tricky in places.

LIFT PASSES

Prices in US$	
Age	6-day
under 13	254
13 to 64	427
65 to 69	384

Free Under 6

Seniors Age 70+, season ticket is $350

Beginner Included in price of lessons

Notes These are 2-days-in-advance-purchase prices; window ticket prices are considerably higher; special deals for disabled skiers

EXTENT OF THE SLOPES ★★★☆☆
Interestingly divided

Winter Park's ski area is big by US standards, and quite complex – it takes a while to learn the lie of the land. The resort identifies six distinct sectors. From the main base, a fast quad takes you to the peak of the original **Winter Park** mountain. From there, you can descend in all directions. Some runs lead back towards the main base and over to the **Vasquez Ridge** area on skier's left, served by the Pioneer fast quad.

Or you can descend to the base of **Mary Jane** mountain, where four chairs up the front face serve tough runs; other chairs serve easier terrain on the flanks. Going down the back of Mary Jane you can head for the **Parsenn Bowl**, riding the Panoramic Express chair for intermediate terrain above and in the trees. From Parsenn, conditions permitting, you can hike for up to half an hour to access advanced and extreme terrain at **Vasquez Cirque**. You then have the choice of a long run-out to the base of the Vasquez Ridge area or to ride the **Eagle Wind** chair, serving its own small and quite gnarly sector and providing a return to Parsenn Bowl.

FAST LIFTS ★★★★☆
Adequately covered

Fast chairs have gradually replaced old lifts, though a few slow ones remain.

QUEUES ★★★★☆
Quiet during the week

During the week the mountain is generally very quiet; however, the Zephyr Express can get busy at peak times and there are often weekend crowds and queues ('Half an hour for Zephyr; up to 10 minutes up the mountain,' said a recent visitor).

TERRAIN PARKS ★★★★★
Parks for all standards

There are no less than six parks, ranging from beginner stuff through the flagship 1.3km-long, experts-only Rail Yard park. This includes a superpipe and the Dark Territory (the name is a railroad term, apparently), a park with such huge features that to get an access pass you have to sign a waiver and watch a safety video. Check them out at www.rlyrd.com.

↑ The base village is pleasant enough, but still has a very limited range of restaurants, bars and shops

SNOWPIX.COM / CHRIS GILL

SNOW RELIABILITY ★★★★★
Among Colorado's best
Winter Park's position, close to the Continental Divide, gives it an average yearly snowfall of 330 inches – higher than most major Colorado resorts. Snowmaking covers a lot of Winter Park mountain's runs.

FOR EXPERTS ★★★★
Some hair-raising challenges
Mary Jane has some of the steepest mogul fields, chutes and hair-raising challenges in the US; on the front side is a row of long black mogul fields that are quite steep enough for most of us. There are some good genuine blacks on Winter Park mountain, too.

Some of the best terrain is open only when there is good snow and/or weather – so it's especially unreliable early in the season. The fearsome chutes of Mary Jane's back side – all steep, narrow and bordered by rocks – need a lot of snow, are marked as 'Extreme Terrain' on the trail map and are accessed by a control gate. Parsenn Bowl has superb blue/black gladed runs and black diamond gladed runs on the back side down to the Eagle Wind chair. Vasquez Cirque, the least reliably open area, has excellent ungroomed expert terrain but you don't get much vertical before you hit the forest and the run-out.

FOR INTERMEDIATES ★★★★
Choose your challenge
From pretty much wherever you are on Winter Park mountain and Vasquez Ridge you can choose a run to suit your ability. Most blue runs are well groomed every night, giving you perfect early-morning cruising on the famous Colorado corduroy pistes. If bumps are for you, try Mary Jane's front side. If you're learning to love them, the blue/black Sleeper enables you to dip in and out.

Parsenn Bowl has grand views and several gentle cruising pistes as well as more challenging ungroomed terrain. There are blue and blue-black runs and glades here, offering a nice range of gradients – it's an ideal place to develop your powder skills. The blue-black Hughes is a great home-run thrash at close of play.

FOR BEGINNERS ★★★★★
About the best we've seen
Discovery Park is a 25-acre dedicated area for beginners, reached by a high-speed quad and served by two more chairs. As well as a nursery area and longer green runs, it has an adventure trail through trees. Sorensen Park learning zone at the base area is good too. There are lots of long green runs, but some are perilously close to flat.

SKIING AND BOARDING FOR THE DISABLED

Winter Park is home to the US National Sports Center for the Disabled (NSCD) – the world's leading centre for teaching skiing and snowboarding to people with disabilities. If you are disabled and want to learn to ski or snowboard, there's no better place to go. It's important to book ahead so that a suitably trained instructor is available. The NSCD can help with travel and accommodation arrangements. See www.nscd.org. In Winter Park itself, you can enquire at the Colorado Ski Authority in the main base station area.

FOR BOARDERS ★★★★★
Beware the moguls and flats
There is some great advanced and extreme boarding terrain and a high probability of fresh powder to ride. And the terrain parks are great. The resort is also good for beginners and intermediates, with excellent terrain for learning. But there are quite a few flat spots to beware of, and most of the steep runs have huge moguls.

FOR CROSS-COUNTRY ★★★★★
Lots of it nearby
There are several areas nearby (none actually in the resort) with over 200km of groomed trails plus backcountry tours and generally excellent snow.

MOUNTAIN RESTAURANTS ★★★★★
The news is good; well, not bad
The resort is very proud of the entirely new 250-seat Lunch Rock restaurant, at the top of Mary Jane, with heated terrace making the most of the excellent views. It's self-service, but does above-average food. The Lodge at Sunspot, at the top of Zephyr, has a welcoming (but busy) bar with a log fire and table- and self-service sections ('good soups'). And there is Snoasis, by the beginner area – 'reasonable prices' but 'overcrowded'. Otherwise, it's down to the lift bases.

SCHOOLS AND GUIDES ★★★★★
No recent reports
We have no reason to doubt the school is up to the usual high US standards. Two interesting variations on standard classes are Max Four lessons in the middle of the day (group limited to four) and Full Day Lessons that include lunch.

FOR FAMILIES ★★★★★
Some of the best facilities
The Village offers a safe and convenient environment, and has the Wee Willie's Child Care facilities, taking babies and infants. Children's classes have their own dedicated slopes.

STAYING THERE

Hotels The choice isn't wide.
★★★Iron Horse Resort Ski-in/ski-out condos a short walk south of The Village. Outdoor pool and hot tubs, steam room.
★★★Vasquez Creek Inn New for 2014/15 – a small, welcoming hotel in the middle of town, done out in a relaxed, Victorian-rustic style. Good bedrooms, pleasant bar and restaurant.
★★★Vintage Hotel Linked by the car park bucket lift to The Village. Good-value hotel with a mix of traditional rooms and studios, many with kitchenettes. Outdoor pool and tub.
Apartments The Zephyr Mountain Lodge, Fraser Crossing and Founders Pointe are all in The Village. There are a lot of comfortable condos in or on the way to town. Reader tips: Beaver Village, Sawmill Station, Red Quill, Meadowridge, Crestview Place.

EATING OUT ★★★★★
A real weakness
There isn't the range of places you get in most 'destination' resorts. The Village is particularly limited – fast food or pub grub at the Cheeky Monk ('excellent sausage and mash'). In the town, Volario's in the Vasquez Creek Inn is a welcome new addition, with the most ambitious food – good Italian dishes in a welcoming rustic setting. It's in the same ownership as the best place in the area – Devil's Thumb Ranch, 13km away, where there's Heck's and Ranch House Restaurant. We and reporters have also enjoyed Deno's (seafood, steaks etc and an amazing wine list). Other reader tips include New Hong Kong (Chinese), Fontenot's (seafood and Cajun), Hernando's (pizza/pasta) and Lime ('good Mexican food').

APRES-SKI ★★★★★
If you know where to go ...
At close of play, there's action in The Village at the Derailer Bar, Cheeky Monk (a huge selection of Belgian beers) and Doc's Roadhouse ('great atmosphere'); and at the Club Car at the base of Mary Jane. Not much happens after dinner; a reader reports that the main hot spots later on are Deno's and the Winter Park Pub in town. Moffat Station microbrewery has good beer.

OFF THE SLOPES ★★★★★
Mainly the great outdoors
Alternatives to the slopes are limited. At The Village there is free ice skating on a pond, and tubing. (From the town you also have the option of tubing at Fraser, along Highway 40 in the opposite direction.) There's also snowmobiling to the Continental Divide, ski biking and snowshoeing. Outings are possible to Denver, which has an attractive centre.

GETTING THERE

Air Denver 150km/ 95 miles (2hr15)

Rail Fraser 19km/ 12 miles

TOURIST OFFICE

www.winterparkresort. com

Utah

'The Greatest Snow on Earth' is Utah's marketing slogan. And usually it's not far from the truth. The last four seasons have been poor for snow by Utah standards, but normally the snowiest Utah resorts do get huge amounts of usually light, dry powder. If you like the steep and deep, you should at some point make the pilgrimage here (and pray you don't hit a poor snow year). And if you like an après-ski beer or two, don't be put off by the image of a 'dry' Mormon state – getting a drink is not a problem. But boarders beware: two of its top resorts don't allow snowboarding.

The biggest dumps fall at Alta (which bans boarding) and Snowbird. Their average of 500 inches of snow a year (twice as much as some Colorado resorts) has made them the powder capitals of the world.

Park City, over the hill from Alta but 45 minutes away by road, is the main 'destination' resort of the area and a sensible holiday base; this season its slopes are due to be linked to those of Canyons next door, forming the biggest ski area in the US. Deer Valley (which also bans boarding) is next door the other way. These resorts get 'only' around 350 inches of snow.

We have separate chapters on these five resorts.

Of course, you're not guaranteed fresh powder. The last four seasons have been disappointing for snow (and as one 2014 reporter said, 'It's a long way to go for 13 days of sun and blue skies'). But a few years ago we spent a week in Park City when it virtually never stopped snowing. Every day we had fresh, knee-high powder.

Other resorts worth visiting (covered in the resort directory at the end of the book) include **Brighton** and **Solitude**, in the valley that separates Park City from Alta. The snow here is almost a match for Alta/Snowbird in quantity but gets tracked out less quickly because of fewer expert visitors. The main claim to fame of **Sundance** is that it's owned by Robert Redford; it averages 320 inches of snow. **Snowbasin** (400 inches), well to the north, hosted the Olympic downhill events in 2002. **Powder Mountain** (500 inches), a bit further north, is aptly named. As well as lift-served slopes it has 3,000 acres of snowcat skiing.

Until 2009 the sale and consumption of alcohol was tightly controlled in Utah, the Mormon state. Until then, to get a drink in bars and clubs you had to jump through various hoops. These rules have now been scrapped and as long as you are over 21 (and have ID to prove it) you should have no problem.

You normally fly in to Salt Lake City, which means changing planes en route. But transfers are short (45 mins or less for the five resorts we feature).

You could consider staying in Salt Lake City and driving to a different resort each day. Two recent reporters did that and list the advantages as including: lower prices for lodging and lift passes (you can buy passes at a discount from certain sports shops), lots of choice of restaurants and bars and cultural attractions (eg concerts, the Mormon Temple, heritage sites).

PCMR

← You go to Utah to ski fresh, light, ungroomed powder. This is Jupiter Peak, which you have to hike to from the top of Park City's lifts

SNOWPIX.COM / CHRIS GILL

TOURIST OFFICE

Ski Utah
www.skiutah.com

Alta

Cult powder resort linked to Snowbird but with less brutal architecture and a friendlier, old-fashioned feel

£180
RESORT PRICE INDEX

TOP 10 RATINGS

Extent	★★★
Fast lifts	★★★★
Queues	★★★
Snow	★★★★★
Expert	★★★★★
Intermediate	★★★
Beginner	★★★
Charm	★★
Convenience	★★★★★
Scenery	★★★

NEWS

2014/15: The intermediate Corkscrew run above Wildcat Base has been remodelled to give it a consistent pitch and the run-out from the advanced Nina's Curve in the same area has been improved.

ALTA

Grooming like this is not what you go to Alta for. You go for gnarly runs down peaks like those on the left ↓

+ Steep terrain and, usually, phenomenal snow mean cult status among experts

+ Linked to Snowbird, making one of the larger ski areas in the US

+ Ski-almost-to-the-door convenience

+ No snowboarding allowed

− 'Resort' is just a scattering of lodges, so not much goes on off the slopes

− Limited groomed runs for intermediates; limited enjoyment for experts in poor snow years

− No snowboarding allowed

Alta and linked Snowbird are the powder capitals of the world, and add up to a great area for adventurous skiers. Alta has a friendlier, more personal feel than Snowbird, which gets its own chapter a few pages on.

THE RESORT

Alta sits at the craggy head of Little Cottonwood Canyon, 2km beyond Snowbird and less than an hour's drive from downtown Salt Lake City. Both the resort and the approach road are prone to avalanches and closure: visitors can be confined indoors.
Village charm Where once there was a bustling and bawdy mining town, there are now just a dozen lodges plus several parking areas.
Convenience Life revolves around the two lift base areas – Albion and Wildcat – linked by a rope tow along the valley floor. All the lodges are convenient for the lifts.
Scenery Alta is recognized for its impressively rugged scenery.

THE MOUNTAINS

Most of Alta's slopes are lightly wooded. Alta does not differentiate between single- and double-black diamond trails – regrettable, we think.
Slopes A ridge, with runs down each side, separates the area's two basins. To the left, above Albion Base, the slopes stretch away over easy green terrain towards the blue and black runs from Point Supreme and from the top of the Sugarloaf quad (also the access lift for Snowbird). To the right, above Wildcat Base, is a narrower bowl with blue runs down the middle and blacks either side. The two sectors are linked at altitude.
Fast lifts Fast chairs depart from each base; another one links to Snowbird.

KEY FACTS

Resort	2600m
	8,530ft
See Snowbird for Alta/Snowbird area	

Alta only	
Slopes	2600-3215m
	8,530-10,550ft
Lifts	11
Pistes	2,200 acres

LIFT PASSES

Prices in US$

Age	6-day
under 13	245
13 plus	474
Free 80 plus	
Beginner Limited pass	
Alternative pass	
Alta/Snowbird	

TOURIST OFFICE

www.alta.com

Queues The slopes are normally uncrowded and queues are rare. But boarding the Collins chair at the mid-station is difficult at times because of the number of people skiing to the base and getting on there.

Terrain parks There isn't one.

Snow reliability The last four seasons have seen well below average snowfalls and limited enjoyment for many experts. But the 'normal' quantity (500 inches a year on average) and quality of snow and the northerly orientation put Alta in the top rank.

Experts Alta has long held cult status among experts. There are dozens of steep slopes and chutes. But finding the best spots is tricky without local guidance and quite a lot of traversing.

Intermediates There isn't a lot of groomed terrain (more in Snowbird). But adventurous intermediates happy to try powder can have a good time.

Beginners Albion has a nursery area and gentle lower slopes, with a beginner lift pass covering three lifts.

Snowboarding Boarding is banned.

Cross-country 3km of groomed track.

Mountain restaurants There's one in each sector. Watson Shelter on the Wildcat side is light and airy with big windows, self- and table-service sections and a small coffee bar; we enjoyed the table-service Collins Grill here. Alf's on the Albion side is a standard self-service.

Schools and guides The ski school specializes in powder lessons – though there are regular classes, too.

Families Day care for children from six weeks is available at the Children's Center at Albion Base.

STAYING THERE

None of the hotels is luxurious in US terms, but most fill up with repeat visitors and, unusually for the US, offer half-board (ie dinner included).

Hotels We've twice enjoyed staying at the venerable Alta Lodge: comfortable rooms, an atmospheric bar, meals served at shared or private tables. Rustler Lodge is more luxurious, with a big outdoor pool, but impersonal. The comfortable, modern Goldminer's Daughter, the basic Peruvian Lodge, and the canyon's oldest lodge – dating from 1938 but now restored, of course – Snowpine Lodge, are cheaper.

Eating out It is possible, but eating in is the normal routine.

Après-ski The Goldminer's Daughter Saloon is the main après-ski bar; the upstairs lounge has sofas, an open fire and huge floor-to-ceiling windows.

Off the slopes There are few options other than snowshoeing, the Cliff Lodge spa down the road at Snowbird, or a sightseeing trip to Salt Lake City.

POINT SUPREME
3200m/10,500ft

East Castle

Catherine's Area

Devil's Castle

Mineral Basin/ Snowbird

3185m/10,450ft

MOUNT BALDY

3375m/11,070ft

Snowbird

Baldy Shoulder

Sugarloaf

East Greeley

Ballroom

Collins

Peruvian Ridge

Sunnyside

Collins

Wildcat Area

fast chairlift
Slow chairs & drags
have no symbol

Albion Base

Wildcat Base
2600m/8,530ft

CANYONS / HUGHES MARTIN

Canyons at Park City

Now part of the biggest ski area in the US, with a small purpose-built resort at the base, just outside Park City town

£200
RESORT PRICE INDEX

TOP 10 RATINGS

Extent	★★★★
Fast lifts	★★★★
Queues	★★★★
Snow	★★★
Expert	★★★★
Intermediate	★★★★
Beginner	★★
Charm	★★
Convenience	★★★★
Scenery	★★★

NEWS

2015/16: A new eight-seat two-way gondola from the Flatiron lift (off to the left of our map) is due to link Canyons to the Park City ski area. The joint area of 7,300 acres will be by far the largest in the US. Two new trails from the gondola mid-station will head back into the Canyons area. Red Pine Lodge will be renovated with 250 extra seats. The base area will be renamed Canyons at Park City.

+ Extensive area of slopes with new link to Park City ski area for 2015/16
+ Few lift queues (that might change with the new link though)
+ Easy access to Deer Valley ski area
+ Can stay at the base, but ...

– Village core is very small and limited with few amenities
– Snow on the many south-facing slopes is affected by sun
– Many runs are short
– Few green runs

The new gondola linking Canyons to Park City's ski area will form the biggest ski area in the USA. But although it will be bigger than Vail, its runs are nowhere near as interesting and varied. And we find the purpose-built village at Canyons base too small and dull. If we were having a holiday in the area, we'd stay in Park City to enjoy its Main Street in the evenings and we'd ski Deer Valley and Snowbird-Alta too – maybe some other Utah resorts as well.

THE RESORT

Even before the new link to Park City, Canyons had been transformed over the last 20 years or so. The local area of the slopes more than doubled in size and a small village with a car-free core was built at the base.

Village charm The village has lodgings and a few shops, restaurants and bars. It doesn't add up to much – you can stroll round it in ten minutes or so.

Convenience Staying at the base is convenient for the ski area. There are buses to Park City town. Getting to Deer Valley by bus requires one change. A recent visitor found the bus services quick and convenient.

Scenery A series of broad, long ridges are separated by valleys and most of the area is fairly densely wooded.

THE MOUNTAINS

Canyons claims that its slopes spread over nine mountains. It is certainly a complicated and extensive area.

In 2014/15 free mountain tours started daily at 10.30, and paid-for First Tracks tours ran twice a week with a guide taking you round the slopes before they officially opened.

Slopes Red Pine Lodge, at the heart of the slopes, is reached by an eight-seat gondola from the village. A fast quad reaches a higher point. From the top of both lifts you can move in either direction across a series of ridges and valleys. Runs come off both sides of each ridge and generally face north or south. Most runs are quite short (less than 500m vertical), with some long, quite flat run-outs. The new link to

588

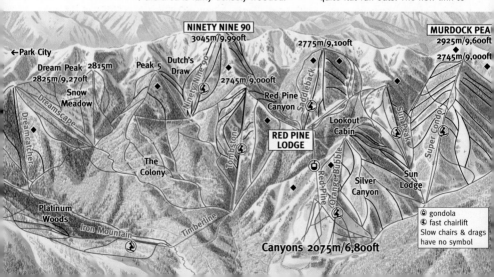

←Park City

NINETY NINE 90
3045m/9,990ft

Dream Peak 2815m
2825m/9,270ft
Peak 5
Dutch's Draw
2745m/9,000ft

2775m/9,100ft

MURDOCK PEA
2925m/9,600ft
2745m/9,000ft

Snow Meadow

Red Pine Canyon

Lookout Cabin

RED PINE LODGE

The Colony

Silver Canyon

Sun Lodge

Platinum Woods

Iron Mountain

Timberline

Canyons 2075m/6,800ft

gondola
fast chairlift
Slow chairs & drags have no symbol

↑ The village looks fairly sprawling here but the car-free core at the foot of the slopes is very small

CANYONS

KEY FACTS

Resort 2075m
6,800ft

Park City-Canyons
Slopes	2075-3050m
	6,800-10,000ft
Lifts	38
Pistes	7,300 acres

Canyons only
Slopes	2075-3045m
	6,800-9,990ft
Lifts	21
Pistes	4,000 acres

LIFT PASSES

Prices in US$
Age	6-day
under 13	282
13 to 64	444
65 plus	282

Free Under 5

Beginner Not announced when we went to press

Note Covers combined Park City/Canyons area

Alternative pass
Two Resort International Pass (see Lift Pass copy in Park City chapter for details)

TOURIST OFFICE

www.
parkcitymountain.com

Park City is off to the left of our map.

Fast lifts Most peaks are served by fast quads but the Dream Peak sector has no fast lifts.

Queues We found no queues, and reporters had no problems either.

Terrain parks There are three (one with small features, one with medium, one with large) plus a 'natural zone'.

Snow reliability The average snowfall is an impressive 355 inches. But the south-facing slopes suffer from the sun and we've never found them in good condition. Snowmaking is very limited.

Experts There is steep terrain all over the mountain. We particularly liked the north-facing runs off Ninety Nine 90, with steep double-black diamond runs plunging down through the trees. We had a great time here on our last visit, after fresh snow. A short hike from the top accesses some fine powder runs even days after a snowfall. And there is also lots of double-diamond terrain on Murdock Peak (a 20-minute hike from the Super Condor lift). Runs off the Peak 5 chair are more sheltered. And there's cat- and heli-skiing too.

Intermediates There are groomed blue runs for intermediates on all the main sectors except Ninety Nine 90. Some are quite short, but you can switch from valley to valley for added interest, or head over to Park City. From the Super Condor and Tombstone fast chairs there are excellent double-blue square runs. The Dreamscape area can be quiet, and is great for early experiments in powder.

Beginners There are good areas with moving carpets up at Red Pine Lodge. But the run you progress to is rather short and gets very busy.

Snowboarding Except for the flat run-outs from many runs, it's a great area, with lots of natural hits and half-pipes.

Cross-country None in resort. The Park City golf course has 20km and Soldier Hollow near Homestead Resort 30km.

Mountain restaurants Red Pine Lodge is a large, attractive building with a busy cafeteria and big deck. Reporters have found the Sun Lodge quieter and Cloud Dine was renovated and expanded for last season. The smart table-service Lookout Cabin has wonderful views from huge windows, and we had excellent game stew there on our last visit. The Dreamscape and Tombstone Grill snack huts offer simple food outdoors.

Schools and guides The ski school has a good reputation and classes tend to be small. A recent reporter said his son had a 'very good' lesson with only one other child in the class.

Families There's day care in the Grand Summit Hotel.

STAYING THERE

Hotels The Waldorf Astoria is the best, set below the village and served (until 5.30pm) by its own gondola. We stayed at the Grand Summit, but were disappointed with the small size of our standard King room. Silverado Lodge is the other main hotel. All have pools and/or hot tubs.

Apartments The Hyatt Escala Lodge (with pool and hot tubs) and Westgate Resort and Spa are pricey and luxurious. Of the cheaper places Timberwolf condos have been praised; other options include Bear Hollow, Hidden Creek, Red Pine and Sundial.

Eating out We had a great meal (fillet steak and buffalo osso bucco) at The Farm – the best place in town. Red Tail Grill does Tex-Mex, and Bistro offers 'modern American' kosher food. Red Pine Lodge at the top of the gondola does a BBQ on some weekends, with a C&W band and dancing. See the Park City chapter for lots of options there.

Après-ski It's generally pretty quiet. The Umbrella Bar is the main focus as the lifts close.

Off the slopes There's a great zipline tour that we enjoyed (two short training wires followed by a minute-long whizz above a deep canyon), guided snowshoeing, snowmobiling, dog sledding, horse-drawn sleigh rides. A factory outlet mall, Salt Lake City and Park City are nearby.

Deer Valley

Top of the Ivy League of US ski resorts: it promises, and delivers, the best ski and gastronomic experience – we love it

£200
RESORT PRICE INDEX

TOP 10 RATINGS

Extent	★★
Fast lifts	★★★★
Queues	★★★★
Snow	★★★★
Expert	★★★
Intermediate	★★★★
Beginner	★★★★
Charm	★★★
Convenience	★★★★
Scenery	★★★

NEWS

2014/15: The Brass Tag restaurant opened in the Lodges at Deer Valley. Snowmaking was increased.

KEY FACTS

Resort	2195m
	7,200ft
Slopes	2000-2915m
	6,570-9,570ft
Lifts	21
Pistes	2,026 acres

LIFT PASSES

Prices in US$

Age	6-day
under 5	150
5 to 12	348
13 to 64	618
65 plus	444

Free No one
Beginner Limited pass
Alternative pass
Two Resort International Pass (covers Deer Valley and Park City/Canyons) available only to international visitors and in advance of holiday departure; pedestrian pass also available

590

- ✚ Good snow and varied terrain
- ✚ Brilliant free black-diamond tours
- ✚ International visitors can buy a pass covering Park City/Canyons too
- ✚ Many fast lifts and no queues
- ✚ Good restaurants and lodgings

- ▬ Expensive, even by US standards
- ▬ Mostly short runs
- ▬ Snowboarders cannot enjoy the slopes as they are banned
- ▬ Quiet at night, though Park City is right next door

Any skier staying in the Park City area should definitely ski Deer Valley for at least a day (but snowboarding is banned). The resort prides itself on pampering its guests, with valets to unload your skis, immaculately groomed slopes, limited numbers on the mountain and gourmet dining. For most people, Park City town is the obvious base; but there are some seductive hotels at Deer Valley's mid-mountain Silver Lake area.

THE RESORT

Just a mile from the end of Park City's Main Street, Deer Valley is overtly upmarket – famed for the care and attention lavished on the slopes and the guests. But it is unpretentious.
Village charm The resort spreads along a road up the mountain but the Silver Lake area is something of a focus.
Convenience Most lodgings are right on the slopes. Free shuttles run to and from Park City.
Scenery From Bald Mountain there are extensive views to Park City and the Jordanelle reservoir. And the views of the reservoir on the run down to the Jordanelle gondola are spectacular.

THE MOUNTAINS

The slopes are varied and interesting. Deer Valley's reputation for immaculate grooming is justified, but there is also a lot of exciting tree skiing and some steep bump runs. There are free mountain tours for different standards. We have been on two three-hour black-diamond tours, and they were both brilliant, taking us through fresh powder in the trees that we would never have found on our own.

A recent reporter who was involved in two collisions on one day complains of reckless skiing and not enough fences to slow people down, especially in the Silver Lake area.
Slopes Two parallel chairs take you up Bald Eagle Mountain, just beyond which is the mid-mountain focus of Silver Lake Lodge. You can ski from here to the isolated Little Baldy Peak,

served by a gondola and a fast quad chairlift, with mainly easy runs to serve property developments there (though a local loves skiing these first thing because they are immaculately groomed and deserted, with great views). But the main skiing is on three linked peaks beyond Silver Lake Lodge – Bald Mountain, Flagstaff Mountain and Empire Canyon. The top of Empire is just a few metres from the runs of the Park City ski area but crossing the fence that divides the two is banned.
Fast lifts Fast quads rule; the three main peaks have nine.
Queues Waiting in lift lines is not something that Deer Valley wants its guests to experience, so it limits the number of lift tickets sold. But it has built four lifts ending at the same place at the top of Flagstaff – resulting in hordes of people trying to go in different directions (insane – and not what you'd expect in Deer Valley).
Terrain parks There isn't one.
Snow reliability Excellent, and there's plenty of snowmaking too.
Experts Despite the image of luxury there is excellent expert terrain on all three main mountains, including fabulous glades, bumps, chutes and bowls. And the snow doesn't get skied out quickly. The Ski Utah Interconnect Tour to Alta starts here (read about this in the Park City chapter).
Intermediates There are lots of superbly groomed blue runs.
Beginners There are nursery slopes at Silver Lake Lodge as well as the base, and gentle green runs to progress to.
Snowboarding Boarding is banned.

↑ It's late in the day. First thing you'd expect those lovely blue runs to be perfect corduroy

DEER VALLEY

TOURIST OFFICE

www.deervalley.com

a 2015 visitor), Goldener Hirsch or Royal Street Cafe (in Silver Lake Lodge).

Schools and guides The ski school is doubtless excellent; book in advance.

Families The Children's Center accepts children from two months to 12 years.

STAYING THERE

Deer Valley, Park City and Canyons are linked by efficient free shuttle-buses. But a car is useful for visiting other more distant Utah resorts (eg Alta, Snowbird).

Hotels The St Regis, Montage Deer Valley, Stein Eriksen Lodge and Goldener Hirsch Inn are some of the plushest hotels in any ski resort.

Apartments There are many luxury places to rent.

Eating out Of the gourmet restaurants, Mariposa is the best. We enjoyed the all-you-can-eat Seafood Buffet (it's not just seafood) and 'Fireside Dining' at Empire Canyon Lodge: four courses, each served at a different fireplace.

Après-ski Edgar's Beers & Spirits Lounge at the base area is the main après-ski venue, with live music at weekends. For more choice, it's not far to Main Street in Park City.

Off the slopes Park City has lots of shops and galleries etc. Salt Lake City has concerts, sights and shopping. Balloon rides, snowmobiling and snowshoeing are popular.

Cross-country There are 20km of trails on Park City golf course and 30km at Soldier Hollow near Homestead Resort.

Mountain restaurants The best in the local ski areas, with attractive wood-and-glass self-service places serving good food at Silver Lake, Empire Canyon and the base lodge. For table-service, try Stein Eriksen Lodge ('skier's buffet is recommended', says

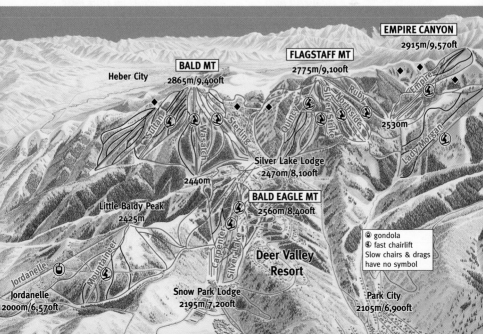

SNOWPIX.COM / CHRIS GILL

Park City

The biggest ski area in America on the doorstep of a cute and lively Main Street, with other notably snowy ski areas within reach

£195
RESORT PRICE INDEX

RATINGS

The mountains

Extent	★★★★
Fast lifts	★★★★
Queues	★★★★
Terrain p'ks	★★★★★
Snow	★★★★
Expert	★★★★
Intermediate	★★★★
Beginner	★★★★
Boarder	★★★★
X-country	★★★
Restaurants	★★
Schools	★★★★
Families	★★

The resort

Charm	★★★
Convenience	★★
Scenery	★★★
Eating out	★★★★★
Après-ski	★★★
Off-slope	★★★

NEWS

2015/16: Vail Resorts, which now owns Park City and Canyons ski areas, is spending $50 million to upgrade and link the two to create a ski area of 7,300 acres – by far the largest in the US.

KEY FACTS

Resort	2105m
	6,900ft

Park City-Canyons

Slopes	2075-3050m
	6,800-10,000ft
Lifts	38
Pistes	7,300 acres

Park City only

Slopes	2105-3050m
	6,900-10,000ft
Lifts	17
Pistes	3,300 acres

PCMR

You get great views of town if you ski back to Main Street. This snow doesn't look like the usual Utah dry powder though →

- ➕ Entertaining, historic Main Street
- ➕ Lots of bars and restaurants make nonsense of Utah's Mormon image
- ➕ Easy to ski Deer Valley as well as newly linked Canyons area

- ➖ Resort is an enormous, charmless sprawl, with most lodgings a drive from Main Street and the slopes
- ➖ Runs tend to be rather short
- ➖ Still a few slow chairlifts

The big news for 2015/16 is that Park City Mountain Resort (covered in this chapter) is to be linked to next-door Canyons (which has its own chapter) by a new gondola and new runs to form the USA's biggest linked ski area. It could easily be made even bigger by linking to neighbouring Deer Valley (which also has its own chapter), which is separated from the Park City slopes only by a fence between two pistes, and by separate ownership. Any skier holidaying in Park City should definitely spend a day or more at Deer Valley (but boarding is banned there) and international visitors can buy a pass covering days at both.

Park City's historic Main Street is a compelling place to spend time, with colourful old buildings and lively bars and restaurants. And the town is a good base for visiting other Utah resorts, including the famously powdery Snowbird and Alta (both have their own chapters), less than an hour away by car.

THE RESORT

Park City is about 45 minutes by road from Salt Lake City. It was a silver-mining boom town, and in the late 19th century it boasted a population of 10,000, a red-light area, a Chinese quarter and 27 saloons.

VILLAGE CHARM ★★★☆☆
A colourful past
Careful restoration has left the town with a splendid historic centrepiece in Main Street, now lined by a colourful

selection of bars, restaurants, galleries and shops, many quite smart, but there are touristy souvenir places too. New buildings have been tastefully designed to blend in smoothly. But most lodging is in the sprawling and characterless suburbs, a drive or bus ride from Main Street.

CONVENIENCE ★★☆☆☆
Depends on your base
The slow Town chairlift goes up from Main Street to the slopes of Park City Mountain Resort, but the main lifts are

LIFT PASSES

Prices in US$

Age	6-day
under 13	282
13 to 64	444
65 plus	282

Free Under 5

Beginner Not announced when we went to press

Note Covers combined Park City/Canyons area

Alternative pass

Two Resort International Pass (covers Park City/Canyons and Deer Valley) available only to international visitors and in advance of holiday departure

on the fringes at Resort Base; there are lodgings out there but most are a free bus ride away.

Deer Valley ski resort is on the edge of town and easily reached by a free bus. Canyons ski area will be linked to Park City's ski area from 2015/16 (and the Canyons base area will be called Canyons at Park City). Efficient free shuttle-buses run around the town and all three ski area bases until fairly late – but we've found it a pain to wait for buses in the evenings. A car is useful to avoid this, and for visiting Alta/Snowbird.

If you're not hiring a car, pick a location that's handy for Main Street and the Town chair or the free bus.

SCENERY ★★★
Gently undulating ridges

In contrast to Park City's sprawling mass, the rounded mountain ridges have a modest and gentle presence.

THE MOUNTAINS

The local area consists mostly of blue and black trails cut through the trees, with easier runs running along the ridges and the valleys between. The more interesting terrain is in the lightly wooded bowls and ridges at the top.

The 2014/15 trail map marked 13 'Signature Runs' that were groomed every night ('A great blast first thing,' says a reporter) – and five 'Adventure Alley' blue runs among the trees ('great fun'). Reporters have enjoyed the free mountain history tours of the slopes that look at the area's silver-mining heritage. A long intermediate run, a beginner run and the Three Kings terrain park were floodlit for night skiing till 8pm in 2014/15. When we went to press, it had not been confirmed whether or not the above would continue in 2015/16.

Signposting is clear.

EXTENT OF THE SLOPES ★★★★
Biggest in the USA

The ski area, when combined with Canyons, is by far the biggest in the USA. Most of the local easy and intermediate runs lie between Summit House and the base area, and are spread along the sides of a series of interconnecting ridges. Virtually all the local steep terrain is above Summit House in a series of ungroomed bowls, and accessed by the McConkey's six-pack and the old, slow Jupiter double chair. Read the Canyons chapter too.

FAST LIFTS ★★★★
Still a few slow ones

You can get around most of the area on fast chairs. But there are still a few slow ones on the upper mountain, including the 40-year-old Jupiter double which accesses a lot of expert terrain. And the lift from town is slow.

QUEUES ★★★★
Peak period crowds

It can get pretty crowded (on some trails as well as the lifts) at weekends ('massive, well-managed queues on Saturday') and in high season.

TERRAIN PARKS ★★★★★
Among the best in the world

The three terrain parks here last season suited all levels. The vast number of features and pipes are maintained daily, and rank among the best in the world. Neff Land is a great

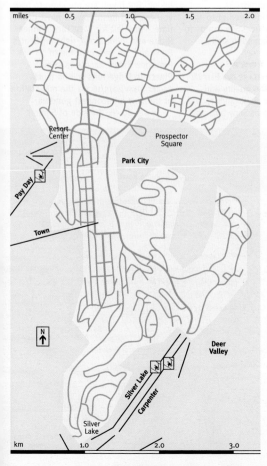

Alta, but an annual average of 355 inches is still impressive, and ahead of most Colorado figures. Snowmaking covers about 15% of the terrain.

FOR EXPERTS ★★★★
Lots of variety
There is a lot of excellent steep terrain at the top of the lift system. It is all marked as double diamond on the trail map, but many runs deserve only a single-diamond rating.

McConkey's Bowl is served by a six-pack and offers a range of open pitches and gladed terrain; we've had some great runs here on each of our visits. The slow, old Jupiter lift accesses the highest bowls, which include some serious terrain – with narrow couloirs, cliffs and cornices – as well as easier wide-open slopes. We had some enjoyable runs through fresh snow in lightly wooded terrain by heading to the right at the top of the lift, then skiing down without hiking. But if you are prepared to hike, you can find fresh powder most of the time – turn left for West Face, Pioneer Ridge and Puma Bowl, right for Scott's Bowl and the vast expanse of Pinecone Ridge. Access to some Pinecone Ridge runs will be much easier from 2015/16 via the mid-station of the new Interconnect gondola.

Lower down, the side of Summit

↑ There's good black diamond terrain in the high bowls and chutes and easy cruising lower down; but runs are mainly short

PCMR

entry-level park with a mini half-pipe. Three Kings is for all abilities and King's Crown is the park for pros, with the biggest jumps and features. The Eagle super-pipe is one of the best pipes in the world. In 2014/15, intermediate level kids aged 11 to 15 could join three-day freestyle camps to learn park and all-mountain skills.

SNOW RELIABILITY ★★★★
Not quite the greatest on Earth
Utah is famous for the quality and quantity of its snow. Park City's record doesn't match those of Snowbird and

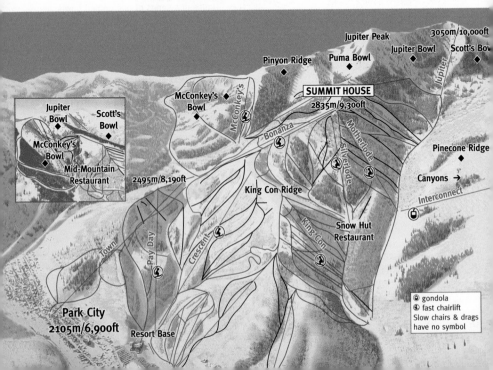

gondola
fast chairlift
Slow chairs & drags have no symbol

THE CANYONS CONNECTION

A new two-way eight-seat gondola to link the resorts is due to go from the base of the Silverlode chair to the Flatiron chair at Canyons.

A mid-station at the top of Pinecone Ridge will allow access through gates to ungroomed runs back to the Park City area and, via new groomed trails, to the Iron Mountain area at Canyons.

To avoid lift queues because of the new link, the King Con fast quad is due to be upgraded to a six-pack and the Motherlode triple to a fast quad.

A new restaurant with 500 seats will be built at the base of Silverlode chair and the new gondola. And an upgrade of Summit House restaurant is planned.

House ridge, serviced by the slow Thaynes and, for 2015/16, the revamped Motherlode chair, has some previously little-used black runs, plus a few satisfying trails in the trees. There's a zone of steep runs towards town from further round the ridge. And don't miss Blueslip Bowl near Summit House – so called because it used to be out of bounds and ski company employees caught skiing it were fired, and given their notice on a blue slip.

There's good expert terrain in the newly linked Canyons area too, so read that chapter. Skiers (no snowboarders, due to some long, flat run-outs) should consider doing the Ski Utah Interconnect Tour – see the feature panel overleaf. There's cat- and heli-skiing available too.

FOR INTERMEDIATES ★★★★
Plenty of short runs to try

There are blue runs served by all the main local lifts, apart from Jupiter. The areas around the King Con and Silverlode six-packs have a dense network of great (but fairly short) cruising runs. There are also more difficult trails close by, for those looking for a challenge. The 'Signature Runs' and 'Adventure Alleys' (see the second paragraph of 'The Mountains') are good ideas and worth trying – let's hope they continue for 2015/16.

But there are few long, fast cruising runs – most trails are 1 to 2km, and many have long, flat run-outs. The Pioneer and McConkey's chairlifts are off the main drag and serve some very pleasant, often quiet runs. The runs under the Town lift have great views of the town. And, of course, there are the linked runs of Canyons and separate area of Deer Valley to explore (read those chapters too).

FOR BEGINNERS ★★★★
A good chance for fast progress

An excellent area for beginners. Novices start on moving carpets and graduate up the hill quite quickly. The gentle three-and-a-half-mile Home Run is a lovely long green to progress to. The Town chair can be ridden down.

FOR BOARDERS ★★★★
Plenty of scope

Twenty years ago, when Park City won its Olympic bid, the resort lifted its ban on snowboarding. Since then it has steamrollered ahead to attract boarders by building some of the best terrain parks in the world. And there's some great ungroomed terrain as well: the higher bowls offer treelined powder runs and great kicker-building spots. Plus there's now the Canyons area to explore – for long a snowboarder favourite. Beginners will have no trouble on the lower slopes.

FOR CROSS-COUNTRY ★★★
Two sets of trails

There are 20km of prepared trails on the Park City golf course and 30km at Soldier Hollow just out of town.

MOUNTAIN RESTAURANTS ★★
Standard self-service stuff

The Mid-Mountain Lodge is a picturesque 19th-century mine building that was heaved up the mountain to its present location near the bottom of Pioneer chair; the food is standard self-service fare. The Summit House is due to be upgraded for 2015/16 and has good views from a big deck (with a glass surround); Snow Hut, at the base of the Silverlode lift and new Interconnect gondola, is due to be rebuilt with 500 seats; Viking Yurt is a coffee house in a tent halfway down the Bonanza chairlift; Snowed Inn has 'the cheapest food on the mountain'. There are more options down at Resort Base – the Pig Pen Saloon 'does a very good sandwich and beer'.

SCHOOLS AND GUIDES ★★★★
Good past reports

We lack recent reports, but past reviews have been very positive.

FOR FAMILIES ★★
Well organized

There are a number of licensed carers. The ski school takes children from age three and a half. Book in advance.

STAYING THERE

We prefer to stay near Main Street and its bars and restaurants, but most accommodation is in the sprawling suburbs. These, such as Kimball Junction, are relatively cheap and convenient if you have a car.

Hotels There's a wide variety, from typical chains to individual little B&Bs.

*****Park City** Swanky place on outskirts. Pool, sauna, steam, hot tub.

****Silver King** Deluxe hotel/condo complex at base of the slopes, with indoor-outdoor pool, hot tub.

****Washington School House** Historic

Good skiers prepared to do some hiking should consider this excellent guided backcountry tour that runs five days a week from Deer Valley to Snowbird. (Two days a week it runs from Snowbird, but only as far as Solitude.) When we did it (several years back, starting from Park City) we got fresh tracks in knee-deep powder practically all day. After a warm-up run to weed out weak skiers, we went

up the top chair, through a 'closed' gate in the area boundary and skied down a deserted, prettily wooded valley to Solitude. After taking the lifts to the top of Solitude we did a short traverse/walk, then skied more virgin powder towards Brighton. After more powder runs and lunch back in Solitude, it was up the lifts and a 30-minute hike up the Highway to Heaven to north-facing, treelined slopes and a great little gully down into Alta. How much of Alta and Snowbird you get to ski depends on how much time is left. The price ($325) includes guides, lunch, lift tickets and transport home.

SNOWPIX.COM / CHRIS GILL

old inn, well renovated, in a great location near Main Street.

***Best Western Landmark Inn** At Kimball Junction. Pool.

***Park City Peaks** On outskirts, large rooms, indoor-outdoor pool, indoor-outdoor hot tub. We stayed here and thought it adequate.

***Yarrow** Another adequate base, 15 mins' walk to Main Street. Pool, hot tub.

Apartments There's a big range. The Town Lift condos near Main Street and Park Avenue condos are both modern and comfortable, the latter with a pool and hot tubs. Silver Cliff condos are adjacent to the slopes and have spacious units and two outdoor hot tubs. Other ski-in/ski-out recommendations from reporters are the Lodge at the Mountain Village, Silver Star and Snow Flower. Blue Church Lodge is a well-converted 19th-century Mormon church with luxury condos and rooms.

EATING OUT ★★★★★
Lots of choice

There are over 100 restaurants. Our favourites are Wahso (Asian fusion; excellent food, but slow service on our last visit), 350 Main (new American – 'very good and excellent service') and Riverhorse (in a grand, high-ceilinged first-floor room with live music). Zoom is the old Union Pacific train depot, now a trendy restaurant owned by Robert Redford (past reports have been mixed though).

For more basic food we like the atmospheric No Name Saloon and

enjoyed their signature buffalo burgers and draft beers on our last visit. Squatters is a good microbrewery a bit out of town. Other reporter tips include Baja Cantina (Mexican), Legends (American; at the mountain), and Bandit's Grill ('basic but satisfying', 'great cowboy food'). Bear in mind the option of upscale dining at next-door Deer Valley.

APRES-SKI ★★★
Plenty around

As the slopes close, Legends is the place to head for at Resort Base. After that, go to Main Street. The Wasatch Brew Pub makes its own ale. O'Shuck's and No Name Saloon are lively, and there's usually live music and dancing at weekends. Or try Cisero's or the Black Diamond Bar at the Jupiter Bowl bowling alley.

OFF THE SLOPES ★★★
Some things of interest

At the resort there's a roller coaster style toboggan ride on rails, tubing and a zipline. Backcountry snowmobiling, balloon flights and trips to Nevada for gambling are popular. There is a bowling alley. You can try lots of activities including the Olympic bob track at the Olympic Park down the road. There is a museum on Main Street. Robert Redford's Sundance Film Festival is held each January. There are lots of shops and galleries, plus discount shopping at a factory outlet mall at Kimball Junction. Salt Lake City is easily reached and has concerts, shopping and Mormon heritage sites.

GETTING THERE

Air Salt Lake City 55km/35 miles (45mins)

TOURIST OFFICE

www.parkcitymountain.com
www.visitparkcity.com

Snowbird

A powder-pig paradise linked to neighbouring Alta; with big concrete-and-glass base buildings that remind us of Flaine

£185
RESORT PRICE INDEX

TOP 10 RATINGS

Extent	★★★
Fast lifts	★★★★★
Queues	★★★
Snow	★★★★★
Expert	★★★★★
Intermediate	★★★
Beginner	★★
Charm	★
Convenience	★★★★★
Scenery	★★★

NEWS

2015/16: A new two-storey glass building is due to open at the top of Hidden Peak offering spectacular views. It will house a self-service restaurant, coffee/pastry shop, toilets, ski patrol, private dining room and outdoor deck. Phase 1 of a revamp of the Cliff Lodge hotel is planned; all the bedrooms are due for renovation by autumn 2015.

MATT CRAWLEY

Snowbird's iconic Aerial Tram whisks you up nearly 900m to Hidden Peak (er, not in view yet) ↓

+ Unrivalled quantity and quality of powder snow in a 'normal' year; and fabulous ungroomed slopes

+ Link to Alta makes it one of the larger ski areas in the US

+ Slopes-at-the-door convenience

− Limited groomed intermediate runs; limited enjoyment for experts in poor snow years

− Tiny, claustrophobic resort 'village'

− Stark concrete architecture

− Very quiet at night

There can be few places where nature has combined the steep with the deep better than at Snowbird and next-door Alta. In a 'normal' snow year the resorts' combined area is one of the top powder-pig paradises in the world (at least for skiers – boarders are banned from Alta). So it is a shame that Snowbird's concrete, purpose-built 'base village' is so lacking in ski resort ambience.

THE RESORT

Snowbird is 40km from Salt Lake City in Little Cottonwood Canyon – just before Alta. Both the resort and the approach road are prone to avalanches and closure: visitors are sometimes confined indoors for safety.
Village charm The resort buildings are mainly block-like and lack any semblance of charm.
Convenience The resort area and the slopes are spread along the road on the south side of the narrow canyon. The focal Snowbird Center (lift base/shops/restaurants) is towards the eastern, up-canyon end. All lodgings are within walking distance, and most are ski-in/ski-out. There are free shuttle-buses, and a service to Alta.
Scenery Snowbird's setting is rugged and rather Alpine. Hidden Peak's lofty heights give impressive views.

THE MOUNTAINS

Snowbird's link with Alta (see separate chapter) forms one of the larger ski areas in the US. The stats show Snowbird and Alta's ski areas to be of fairly similar size, but Snowbird's feels much bigger to us. There are free mountain tours at 9.30 and 10.30 each morning. The nursery slopes are floodlit three evenings a week.
Slopes The north-facing slopes rear up from the edge of the resort. Six access lifts are ranged along the valley floor, the main ones being the 125-person cable car (the Aerial Tram) to Hidden Peak, the Peruvian Express quad and the Gadzoom fast quad. To the west, in Gad Valley, there are runs ranging from very tough to very easy. Mineral Basin, behind Hidden Peak and accessed from there or through a tunnel with a moving carpet at the top of the Peruvian Express chair, has 500 acres of terrain for all abilities, but it can be badly affected by sun. The Alta ski area is accessed via the Baldy Express chair in Mineral Basin.
Fast lifts All the key lifts are fast.
Queues The big problem has always been the cable car, with queues of up to an hour at times. But the Peruvian Express chair provides an alternative way up and to Mineral Basin.
Terrain parks There is one aimed at beginners and intermediates with jumps and various features.
Snow reliability The last four seasons have seen well below average snowfalls and limited enjoyment for many experts. But the 'normal' quantity and quality of snow puts

KEY FACTS

Resort	2470m
	8,100ft

For Snowbird and
Alta combined area

Slopes	2365-3350m
	7,760-11,000ft
Lifts	22
Pistes	4,700 acres

Snowbird only

Slopes	2365-3350m
	7,760-11,000ft
Lifts	11
Pistes	2,500 acres

LIFT PASSES

Prices in US$

Age	6-day
under 12	270
13 plus	460
Free Under 7	
Senior 65+: $77/day	
weekends; 70+: $48/	
day weekdays	
Beginner Limited pass	
Alternative pass	
Alta/Snowbird	

Snowbird in the top rank. Like neighbouring Alta, it averages 500 inches a year – twice as much as some Colorado resorts and around 50% more than the nearby Park City area. There's snowmaking in busy areas.

Experts The trail map is liberally sprinkled with double-black diamonds, and some of the gullies off the Cirque ridge – Silver Fox and Great Scott, for example – are exceptionally steep and frequently neck-deep in powder. Lower down lurk the bump runs, including Mach Schnell – a great run straight down the fall line through trees. There is wonderful ski-anywhere terrain in the bowl beneath the high Little Cloud chair, and the Gad 2 lift opens up attractive tree runs (and is the best place to be in a white-out). Fantastic go-anywhere terrain under the High Baldy traverse is controlled by gates. Mineral Basin has some expert terrain too. Backcountry tours and heli- and cat-skiing are also offered.

Intermediates The winding Chip's Run provides the only comfortable route from the top back to town. There's good cruising in Mineral Basin – take the narrow Path to Paradise traverse for a wide blue-black and head up the Baldy Express lift for the easiest cruises. For adventurous intermediates wanting to try powder skiing, the bowl below the Little Cloud lift is a must. There are some challenging runs through the trees off the Gad 2 lift. The groomed runs don't add up to a lot but there's more than in Alta.

Beginners There is a nursery slope next to Cliff Lodge, a ski school

Mountain Learning area part-way up the hill and a special lift pass. But progression to longer runs is not easy.

Snowboarding Good freeriders will have a wild time in the powder but there are some flat spots to beware of. Be aware that Alta bans boarders.

Cross-country No prepared trails (though there are in next-door Alta).

Mountain restaurants It's the Mid-Gad Lodge self-service or back to one of the bases – try the table-service Forklift and Rendezvous.

Schools and guides The school has a good reputation, though we lack recent reports.

Families Camp Snowbird takes children aged 12 and under. The 'kids ski free' programme allows children (six and under) to ski for free with an adult. Baby Thunder is a gentle family area.

STAYING THERE

Hotels There are several lodges and smaller condo blocks. Cliff Lodge, a huge concrete building, and The Lodge at Snowbird are both convenient and have pools and hot tubs, but they lack charm – and we lack recent reports.

Eating out Cliff Lodge and Snowbird Center are the focal points, with various options, including the 'fine dining' Aerie in the Cliff Lodge.

Après-ski Après-ski is a bit muted. The Tram Club and El Chanate Cantina are lively as the slopes close, but don't expect them to be later on.

Off the slopes There's not much to do apart from snowshoeing, snowmobiling and visiting Salt Lake City and the spas in various lodges.

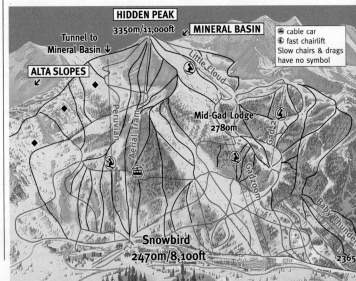

TOURIST OFFICE

www.snowbird.com

JACKSON HOLE / GORAN ASSNER

Rest of the West

This section of the book contains detailed chapters on just two resorts – Jackson Hole in Wyoming and Big Sky in Montana. Below are notes on these and various other resorts in different parts of the great chain of mountains that stretches from Washington in the north to New Mexico in the south.

The resorts of Washington state and Oregon are covered in our resort directory at the end of this book. We visited Oregon a few seasons back, when our exploration was hampered by poor early-season snow. If you want to try somewhere largely undiscovered by fellow Brits, it is worth considering. The major resorts are **Mt Hood** (which has three separate areas of slopes: Mt Hood Meadows, Mt Hood Skibowl and Timberline) and **Mt Bachelor**. These get extended entries in the resort directory.

Sun Valley, Idaho, was the USA's first purpose-built resort, developed in the 1930s by the president of the Union Pacific Railway. It quickly became popular with the Hollywood movie set and has managed to retain its stylish image and ambience; it has one of our favourite luxury hotels. Also in Idaho is the USA's newest purpose-built resort – **Tamarack**, two hours

north of Boise. The company developing the resort went bankrupt in 2009, then re-opened four days a week for some seasons, and as of last season is open continuously for a full season.

Jackson Hole in Wyoming is a resort with an impressive snow record and equally impressive steep slopes. Jackson town has a touristy Wild West cowboy atmosphere. Check out the separate chapter. A 90-minute drive from Jackson over the Teton pass (slower if you go by excursion bus) brings you to **Grand Targhee**, which gets even more snow. The west-facing slopes are usually blissfully empty, and are much easier than at Jackson. The main Fred's Mountain offers 1,500 acres and 610m vertical accessed from a central fast quad. One-third of smaller Peaked Mountain is accessed by a fast quad, while the rest – around 500 acres – is used for snowcat skiing.

About four hours north of Jackson, just inside Montana, is **Big Sky**, which absorbed neighbouring Moonlight Basin and much smaller Spanish Peaks to become the biggest ski resort in the US, only to have the crown wrested from its grip by Park City's expansion. The lack of crowds here is amazing. Check out the Big Sky chapter. From Big Sky you might also visit **Bridger Bowl**, a 90-minute drive away. It boasts broad, steep, lightly wooded slopes that offer wonderful powder descents after a fresh snowfall.

A long way south of all these resorts, **Taos** in New Mexico is the most southerly major resort in the USA, and because of its isolated location it is largely unknown on the international market. There's a small chalet-style base village with a handful of lodges; the adobe town of Taos, home to many famous artists and writers over the years, is 30km down the road. There's some good terrain for all standards, but the ski area is best known for challenging terrain, some of which involves hiking.

GLENNISS INDRELAND

This is about as busy as it gets at Big Sky, one of the USA's biggest ski areas, in a remote corner of Montana ↓

BIG SKY RESORT

Big Sky

One of the USA's biggest ski areas, with extraordinarily quiet slopes; unappealing modern resort village, though

£180
RESORT PRICE INDEX

RATINGS

The mountains

Extent	★★★★
Fast lifts	★★
Queues	★★★★★
Terrain p'ks	★★★★
Snow	★★★★★
Expert	★★★★
Intermediate	★★★★
Beginner	★★★★★
Boarder	★★★★
X-country	★★★★
Restaurants	★
Schools	★★★★
Families	★★★★

The resort

Charm	★★
Convenience	★★★★
Scenery	★★★
Eating out	★★★
Après-ski	★
Off-slope	★★

600

NEWS

2014/15: Gladed areas were extended and four new runs opened. The skiable area is now 5,800 acres. Pinnacle restaurant at the top of Andesite reopened as Everett's 8,800.

KEY FACTS

Resort	2285m
	7,500ft
Slopes	2070-3405m
	6,800-11,165ft
Lifts	29
Pistes	5,800 acres

+ It lives up to its name – easily bigger than Vail, though no longer the biggest in the States

+ By far the quietest slopes you will find in a major resort, anywhere

+ Among the cheapest resorts in the US for food and drink

+ Excellent snow record

+ Some slope-side lodgings, but ...

– Many condos are spread widely away from the lift base

– Resort amenities are limited, with little choice of nightlife and no resort-village atmosphere

– Tiny top lift accessing the most testing terrain is prone to queues

– Getting there from the UK involves at least one plane change

Big Sky is phenomenal. It has always been big, but two seasons back it acquired two adjacent mountains – small but interesting Moonlight Basin and tiny Spanish Peaks – and so overtook Vail, traditional resort-size leader in the States (now put in the shade by the new Park City / Canyons link in Utah). The area totals 5,800 acres; its lifts can carry 29,000 people an hour; but typically there are only about 3,000 people on the hill. So you get about 2 acres of snow each; or, to look at it another way .... (That's enough statistics – Ed.)

The point is, skiing Big Sky is unlike skiing anywhere else. As an experienced reporter put it last year, 'the busiest runs would be considered empty in other resorts'. The resort has other attractions too. But if you like to amble around in the evening soaking up the mountain village atmosphere, forget it.

THE RESORT

Big Sky is set amid the wide open spaces of Montana, one hour from Bozeman airport. The resort has been purpose-built at the foot of the slopes, and the main focus of development is Mountain Village, at the lift base. Bridger Bowl ski area is an easy day trip by car.

VILLAGE CHARM ★★
Some way to go
Mountain Village is a hotchpotch of buildings in different styles set vaguely around a traffic-free central plaza and bordered by car parks and unattractive service roads. There are a few hotels, a handful of bars, restaurants and shops, and some slope-side condos. The French-style enclosed Mountain Mall has further shops and gives access to many of these facilities. There are also cabins and condos around the Moonlight Basin lift base at Moonlight Lodge.

CONVENIENCE ★★★★
Generally fine
There is quite a bit of lodging at or close to the lift base. Some outlying condos and houses are served by lifts

to the slopes, but most rely on the 'comparatively poor' free bus services; a car is a better idea.

SCENERY ★★★
The lone ranger
Lone Mountain is Big Sky's signature peak, its distinctive summit rising over 1000m above the village and Andesite Mountain's wooded slopes. From the top, there are panoramic views of Montana and Yellowstone park.

THE MOUNTAINS

The formula is familiar in America: mainly steep open slopes at the top, and gentler wooded slopes lower down. There are free mountain tours. Recent visitors complain of poor signposting, especially for some black runs and gladed blues, and inconsistent trail classification.

EXTENT OF THE SLOPES ★★★★
Big – the name's right
Yes, it is big – in terms of piste extent, just outside the top ten areas in the world, and over 7km from end to end. **Lone Mountain** provides the resort's poster shot, with some seriously steep upper slopes. From Mountain Village a

↑ Lone Peak is difficult to exclude from pictures of Big Sky; it's just as steep as it looks, too

GLENNIS INDRELAND

Big Sky

601

LIFT PASSES

Prices in US$ inc tax

Age	6-day
under 11	303
11 to 17	488
18 to 69	575
70 plus	488

Free Under 6; also under 11 with lessons or if staying in resort property managed by Big Sky

Beginner First half-day lesson includes a base area pass

Notes Prices include 3% tax and are online advance purchase prices; discounts if purchased with lodging; half-day pass available

fast quad goes to mid-mountain. From there you can get to the Lone Peak triple chair, which takes you up to the Lone Peak Tram – two 15-person gondola cabins, operated as if they were a cable car. This leads to the top and fabulous 360° views. The Dakota triple chairlift serves Lone's south face and its steep bowls and glades. But a couple of reporters have found the area prone to closure due to avalanche risk. Lone Mountain's lower slopes are wooded and varied, as are those of **Andesite Mountain**, which has less vertical but three of the five fast lifts, including one from Mountain Village. At the bottom of Andesite's Southern Comfort chair is one of the two chairs on the very limited slopes of recently acquired **Spirit Mountain**, formerly Spanish Peaks. (On another flank of Andesite is part of the famously exclusive private resort, the Yellowstone Club.) From various points on Lone Mountain you can head down to the **Moonlight Basin** slopes, which start with a slow chair from Moonlight Lodge. Runs from the top of that lead to the Six Shooter fast chair, from the Madison base area, which, together with the slow Lone Tree quad, serves nearly all Moonlight's wooded, largely easy intermediate terrain. The Headwaters double chair at the top serves expert-only runs.

FAST LIFTS ★★ ☆ ☆
Needs some more

There are five fast quad chairs, but many of the chairs are still old triples and doubles.

QUEUES ★★★★★
Only for the Tram

The tiny Tram naturally builds serious queues on powder days and in peak season; but at least that means you don't get crowds on the top runs. Queues are rare otherwise: 'Even on a Saturday morning powder day, the most we stood in line was two minutes,' said one visitor. 'Queues non-existent,' said a March 2015 reporter, 'except for the Tram.'

TERRAIN PARKS ★★★★ ☆
Plenty of choice

Swifty Park on Lone Peak suits advanced riders; there are also an intermediate park, Swifty 2.0, near the village, and a beginner park by the Explorer chair. There are two natural half-pipes. The Moonlight slopes have the Zero Gravity park, and a beginner park near the base.

SNOW RELIABILITY ★★★★★
No worries here

Snowfall averages 400 inches – more than most resorts in Colorado. Grooming is 'exceptional' too.

FOR EXPERTS ★★★★ ☆
Enough to keep you amused

All of the terrain accessed from the Tram is classified black – single- or double-diamond. The steepest runs are the Big Couloir on the Big Sky side and the North Summit Snowfield on the Moonlight side. Take local advice on equipment and guidance.

There are easier ways down, though – Liberty Bowl is easiest. Marx and Lenin are a little steeper. The Dakota Territory has 212 acres of black-diamond glades, chutes and high bowls, to skier's right of Liberty Bowl – served by a triple chairlift. Lower down, the Lone Peak triple, Challenger and Shedhorn chairs also serve good steep terrain.

There are some excellent gladed runs, especially on Andesite (and more are being created). In the Moonlight sector the Headwaters is the biggest challenge – but it gets windblown and you may have to pick your way through rocks at the top. The further you hike to skier's left the steeper the couloirs. There are some good gladed runs lower down.

FOR INTERMEDIATES ★★★★
Great deserted cruising
The bulk of the terrain is of intermediate difficulty (including lots of easy blacks). The main complaint we have is that they don't seem to groom any blacks – with no traffic, they would be fabulous when groomed. But there is lots of excellent cruising on empty blue runs served by fast chairs: Ramcharger, Southern Comfort and Thunder Wolf on Andesite, Swift Current on Lone Mountain, and Six Shooter in the Moonlight sector. Several wide, gentle bowls offer a good introduction to off-piste. And there are some good easy glade runs, such as Singlejack at Moonlight and The Congo on Andesite. In general the groomed blues at

🚡 cable car
🚠 fast chairlift
Slow chairs & drags
have no symbol

Andesite has great cruising runs, although the vertical isn't huge

ANDESITE
268om/8,8ooft

Spirit Mountain lifts and slopes

Southern Comfort

Ramcharger

Thunder Wolf

Mount Villag
2285r
7,500

2070m/6,8ooft
Lone Moose Meadows

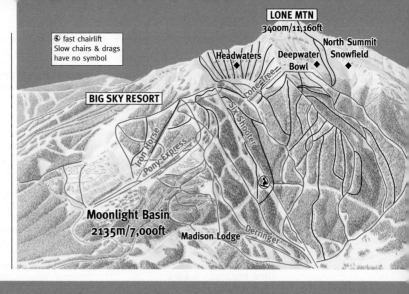

LONE MTN
3400m/11,16oft

④ fast chairlift
Slow chairs & drags
have no symbol

Headwaters ◆

Deepwater
Bowl ◆

North Summit
Snowfield ◆

Lone Tree

BIG SKY RESORT

Iron Horse

Pony Express

Six Shooter

Moonlight Basin
2135m/7,oooft

Madison Lodge

Derringer

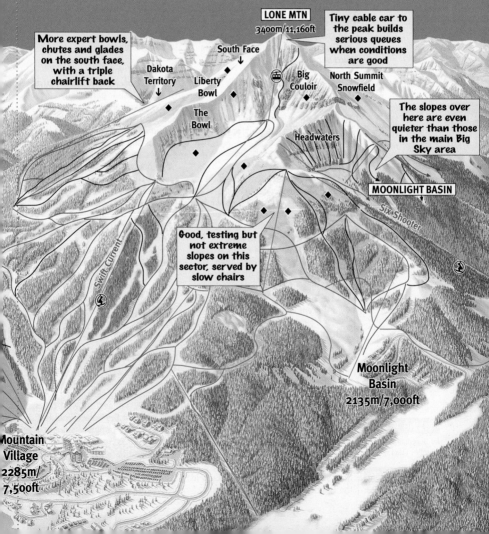

LONE MTN
3400m/11,16oft

Tiny cable car to
the peak builds
serious queues
when conditions
are good

More expert bowls,
chutes and glades
on the south face,
with a triple
chairlift back

South Face ◆

Dakota
Territory
↓

Liberty
Bowl ◆

◆

Big
Couloir

North Summit
Snowfield ◆

The
Bowl

◆

Headwaters

The slopes over
here are even
quieter than those
in the main Big
Sky area

MOONLIGHT BASIN

◆

Six Shooter

◆

◆

◆

◆

Good, testing but
not extreme
slopes on this
sector, served by
slow chairs

Swift Current

④

④

Moonlight
Basin
2135m/7,oooft

Mountain
Village
2285m/
7,5ooft

Moonlight are easier than those on Lone, especially the ones served by the Lone Tree chair. Adventurous intermediates could try Liberty Bowl from the top of the Tram; but be prepared for a rocky, windswept traverse between wooden barriers at the top to access the run.

FOR BEGINNERS ★★★★★
Ideal – lots of lovely greens
There's a good, well-developed nursery area at the base of the Explorer chair with a separate Explorer pass. There are long, deserted greens to progress to from the Explorer and Swift Current chairs, and on Andesite. The Berringer quad at the Madison base in the Moonlight sector is good, too.

FOR BOARDERS ★★★★
Something for everyone
The terrain has lots of variety, with few flats. Experts will enjoy the steeps and the glades, freestylers the good terrain parks, and novices the easy cruising runs served by chairlifts.

FOR CROSS-COUNTRY ★★★★
Head for the Ranch
There are 85km of 'excellent' trails at Lone Mountain Ranch ('helpful staff'), and more at West Yellowstone.

MOUNTAIN RESTAURANTS ★
Back to base for lunch?
The main weakness. Star attraction is the table-service Everett's 8,800, at the top of Andesite – 'refined ambience, friendly service, great terrace' says a report this year. Shedhorn Grill is a yurt on the south side of Lone Mountain, doing simple meals – 'great fun, and decent BBQ nosh'. Then there's the Black Kettle on the front of Lone Mountain – soup and snacks – and the Burrito Shack at the top of the Swift Current chairlift.

SCHOOLS AND GUIDES ★★★★
Good reputation
The Big Sky school has a good reputation. Visitors have praised the beginner snowboard classes: 'Exceptionally happy with the quality of the instruction.'

FOR FAMILIES ★★★★
Usual high US standard
Lone Peak Playhouse in the slope-side Snowcrest Lodge will take kids to and from ski school. There's a Kids' Club in the Huntley Lodge – 'very well run'

according to a 2014 visitor who put two kids in it.

STAYING THERE

Hotels There's not much choice.
★★★★Summit Central, slope-side, good rooms, outdoor hot pool, good views, and shuttle to other base areas. 'Best property here, breakfast excellent'; endorsed again this year.
★★★Huntley Lodge Big Sky's original hotel; central, part of Mountain Mall; outdoor pool, hot tubs, saunas. Our 2014 reporter was happy, but beware noisy rooms. 'Great breakfast buffet.'
★★★The Lodge at Big Sky Five minutes' walk to slopes; shuttle at peak times. Indoor pool, outdoor hot tub.
Apartments Reader tips include Stillwater, Village Center, Arrowhead, Snowcrest, Big Horn, Black Eagle and, way out of town, Powder Ridge ('fantastic accommodation', 'beautiful' said two recent reporters). Check location carefully.

EATING OUT ★★★
A fair choice for a small place
One 2014 visitor particularly enjoyed the 'excellent' Peaks restaurant in the Summit hotel – 'delicious pheasant ragout'. Andiamo Italian Grille is very popular and pleases most reporters, as does Whiskey Jack's – 'a barn-like place doing good simple food'. Other places repeatedly tipped: MR Hummers, the Cabin and (a drive down the hill) Buck's T-4 Lodge.

APRES-SKI ★
Limited
Things are generally quiet but there is live music in a couple of spots. Whiskey Jack's is the main après bar – 'good atmosphere'. Scissorbills Saloon is a 'great American bar' sometimes with live music and DJs. The plush Carabiner bar in the Summit hotel has live music most nights.

OFF THE SLOPES ★★
Mainly the great outdoors
There's snowmobiling, snowshoeing, sleigh rides, dog sledding, a floodlit tubing hill, ziplines, snowcat tours, treatments at the Solace Spa; the Huntley Lodge pool and spa are open to all for a fee. You can visit Yellowstone National Park (highly recommended by reporters); a reader also recommends the Grizzly and Wolf Discovery Center at West Yellowstone.

GETTING THERE
Air Bozeman 70km/ 45 miles (1hr15)

TOURIST OFFICE
www.bigskyresort.com

Jackson Hole

Touristy 'Wild West' town 12 miles from big, exciting slopes, and a small, modern base village with a famous après-ski saloon

£175
RESORT PRICE INDEX

RATINGS

The mountains

Extent	★★★
Fast lifts	★★★★
Queues	★★★
Terrain p'ks	★★★
Snow	★★★★
Expert	★★★★★
Intermediate	★★
Beginner	★★★
Boarder	★★★
X-country	★★★★
Restaurants	★★★
Schools	★★★★
Families	★★★★

The resort

Charm	★★★
Convenience	★★★★
Scenery	★★★
Eating out	★★★★★
Après-ski	★★★★
Off-slope	★★★

KEY FACTS

Resort	1925m
	6,310ft
Slopes	1925-3185m
	6,310-10,450ft
Lifts	13
Pistes	2,500 acres

- ➕ Lots of expert-only terrain and one of the USA's biggest verticals
- ➕ Jackson town has an entertaining Wild West ambience
- ➕ Unspoiled, remote location
- ➕ Excellent snow record
- ➕ Some unique off-slope diversions
- ➕ The airport is only minutes away

- ➖ The town is 30 minutes by bus from the slopes – though the lift base has attractive places to stay
- ➖ Low altitude and sunny orientation mean snow can deteriorate quickly
- ➖ Groomed cruising is in relatively short supply
- ➖ Getting there from the UK involves at least one plane change

When we first visited Jackson in the early 1990s, you went for its gnarly mountain, shedloads of snow and big vertical – simple as that. It had few facilities at the base or on the mountain, and an antiquated lift system.

Now, as it celebrates its 50th anniversary, Jackson has a modern (though still inadequate) cable car, a gondola, three fast chairs serving easy and intermediate terrain, a bunch of upscale hotels at the base, two table-service restaurants on the mountain – and many more beginners, intermediates and families around as a result. Some old hands hate the changes; we love them. Now, we get the best of both worlds – superb snowy steeps on the one hand, decent lunches and stylish lodgings on the other.

THE RESORT

The town of Jackson, with its wooden sidewalks, cowboy saloons and pool halls, sits on the edge of Jackson Hole – a high, flat valley surrounded by mountain ranges in Wyoming. Jackson gets many more visitors in summer than in winter, thanks to the nearby national parks. The slopes are a short drive away. At the base is Teton Village, which has developed a lot over the past few years, with an increased choice of bars, restaurants and hotels – some notably upscale.

A popular excursion by car or daily bus is over the Teton Pass to the smaller resort of Grand Targhee, which gets even more snow. Read the Rest of the West intro.

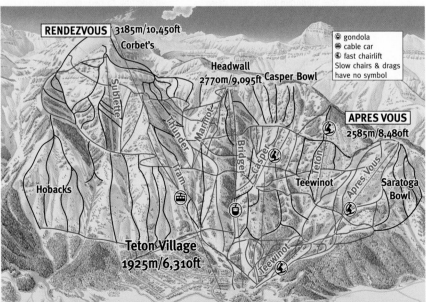

RENDEZVOUS 3185m/10,450ft
Corbet's
Headwall
2770m/9,095ft Casper Bowl

gondola
cable car
fast chairlift
Slow chairs & drags have no symbol

APRES VOUS
2585m/8,480ft

Sublette
Thunder
Marmot
Bridger
Casper
Teton
Apres Vous

Teewinot

Saratoga Bowl

Hobacks

Tram

Teton Village
1925m/6,310ft

Teewinot

JONATHAN SELKOWITZ

NEWS

2015/16: A new fast quad between the Casper and Apres Vous chairs will open up a bit of new terrain (including three short new groomed trails) but will also make laps on Moran Woods and Moran Face easier. Lunch options will be improved at Rendezvous Lodge, at the top of the Bridger gondola.

LIFT PASSES

Prices in US$

Age	6-day
under 15	305
15 to 64	503
65 plus	401

Free Under 6 (Eagle's Rest and Teewinot lifts only)

Beginner Ticket for Eagle's Rest and Teewinot lifts ($29)

Notes Prices are online advance purchase; ticket window prices are higher; afternoon ticket available

Alternative passes Grand Targhee; Snow King Mountain

VILLAGE CHARM ★★★☆☆
Cowboy or convenient
To amuse summer tourists, Jackson town cultivates a Wild West flavour – saloons with swing doors, country and western music and dancing, cowboys in Stetsons. It has lots of clothing and souvenir shops, plus upmarket galleries aimed at second-home owners. In winter it's all a bit quiet, but still quite amusing and pleasant. The friendly and helpful locals are praised by reporters. Teton Village is inoffensive, but nothing more.

CONVENIENCE ★★★★☆
Stay at the slopes
From Jackson, getting to the slopes means a $3 30-minute bus ride or a slightly quicker drive followed by payment of $15 to park close to the mountain ($5 further away). Our preferred option is to stay at the base and take the occasional bus into town.

SCENERY ★★★☆☆
You can see forever
You get great long views across the wide plain of Jackson Hole from the slopes, which rise abruptly from the valley floor.

THE MOUNTAINS

Most of the slopes are below the treeline, but most of the forest is not dense. The trail classification is pretty accurate; but some visitors reckon the toughest single diamonds would be double diamonds elsewhere. There are free mountain tours twice daily.

EXTENT OF THE SLOPES ★★★☆☆
One big mountain, one small
The main lifts out of Teton Village are the Bridger gondola and the Tram (cable car). The Tram takes you up 1260m to the summit of **Rendezvous** mountain – an exceptional vertical for the US (and an exceptional vertical anywhere for a single lift stage). It can be very cold and windy at the top, even when it's warm and calm below. To the right looking up, fast quads access **Apres Vous** mountain, with half the vertical of Rendezvous and mostly much gentler runs. Between these two, the Bridger gondola goes up over a broad mountainside split by gullies, and gives speedy access to the slow Thunder and Sublette chairs – serving some of the steepest terrain on Rendezvous – and the fast Casper

chair, from which you can traverse over to the Apres Vous area.

Snow King is a separate ski area right by Jackson town. Locals use it at lunchtime and in the evenings.

FAST LIFTS ★★★★☆
Few at mid-mountain
Fast lifts access both mountains; slow chairs rule on the upper part of Rendezvous, but a reader points out that they rise steeply, and permit a lot of vertical in a day.

QUEUES ★★★☆☆
Can be serious
Jackson now seems to attract enough visitors to stretch the lift system to breaking point. The Tram holds only 100 people, and because it was built with one epic stage it shifts under 700 people an hour – about the same as an antique double chairlift. Many people do laps on it all day long. So it generates queues, particularly when there is fresh powder or, on the other hand, in spring weather when Rendezvous is the only place high enough to retain good snow – in such conditions, a reporter this year met 'the longest queues we have seen anywhere in the last 20 years'. On the other hand, if bad weather closes the Tram, you can get non-trivial queues elsewhere. On powder days it can pay to head for Apres Vous and 'great first tracks in Saratoga Bowl'.

TERRAIN PARKS ★★★☆☆
Six plus a pipe
In addition to two terrain parks on the lower mountain with features from beginner through to advanced, there are four Burton Stash parks featuring wooden and natural obstacles. Plus there's a half-pipe; and Dick's Ditch is a 450m-long natural half-pipe.

SNOW RELIABILITY ★★★★☆
Deep snow, strong sun
The claimed average of 460 inches of snow is much more than in most Colorado (and some Utah) resorts. But the base elevation is low for the Rockies, and the slopes are sunny, facing roughly south-east (Apres Vous more south). The steep lower slopes, such as the Hobacks, may be in poor shape, or shut. On our last visit the higher slopes were frozen solid following a melt. The flanks of some ridges are more shady, and a reporter says that Saratoga Bowl keeps its

After the jump in, Corbet's Couloir is a doddle. They say
ERIC SEYMOUR

snow well. Locals claim that you can expect powder roughly half the time. Don't assume early-season conditions will be good.

FOR EXPERTS ★★★★★
Best for the brave

For the good skier or boarder who wants challenges without the expense of off-piste guides, Jackson is one of the world's best resorts. Rendezvous mountain offers virtually nothing but genuine black slopes. The routes down the main Rendezvous Bowl are not particularly fearsome; but some of the alternatives are. Go down the East Ridge at least once to stare over the lip of the notorious Corbet's Couloir. After you jump in, the slope is a mere 50°, people say.

Below Rendezvous Bowl, the wooded flanks of Cheyenne Bowl offer serious challenges, at the steep end of the single-black diamond spectrum. If instead you take the ridge run that skirts this bowl to the right, you get to the Hobacks – a huge area of open and lightly wooded slopes, gentler than those higher up, but still black and usually with big moguls; check snow conditions before tackling these.

Corbet's aside, most of the steepest slopes are more easily reached from the slightly lower quad chairs. From the Sublette chair, you have direct access to the short but seriously steep Alta chutes, and to the less severe Laramie Bowl beside them. Or you can

track over to Tensleep Bowl – pausing to inspect Corbet's from below – and on to the less extreme (and less chute-like) Expert Chutes, and the single-black Cirque and Headwall areas. Casper Bowl often has good powder, and the Crags is an area of bowls, chutes and glades reached by hiking – both are accessed through gates. Thunder chair serves steep, narrow, fairly shady chutes. Again, the lower part of the mountain here offers lightly wooded single-diamond slopes.

The gondola serves some good, underused expert terrain, particularly to skier's left of the lift, including the glades of Woolsey and Moran Woods. Even Apres Vous has serious, usually quiet, single blacks in Saratoga Bowl.

The gates into the backcountry access over 3,000 acres of amazing terrain, which should be explored only with guidance. You can stay out overnight at a backcountry yurt. There are some helicopter operations.

FOR INTERMEDIATES ★★★★★
Exciting for some

They have tried hard to improve the intermediate terrain, with fast lifts and much more grooming than in the old days. There are good cruising runs on the front face of Apres Vous from the Casper chair, and top-to-bottom quite gentle blues from the gondola. But they don't add up to a great deal of mileage, and you shouldn't consider Jackson unless you want to tackle ungroomed runs. It's then important to get guidance on steepness and snow conditions. A good number of blues are identified on the trail map as more difficult, and many of these are less frequently groomed too – these are the places to get the hang of powder. The steepest single blacks are steep, and fearsome when hard. The daily grooming map is worth consulting, but falling snow will mean moguls form.

FOR BEGINNERS ★★★
Fine, up to a point
There are good broad, gentle beginner slopes and a lift pass covering the two chairs that serve them. Progression to the blue Werner run off the Apres Vous chair is gradual enough, and the mid-mountain blues from the Casper chair are reached via the chairs from the beginner area. But few other runs will help build confidence.

FOR BOARDERS ★★★
Steep and deep thrills
Jackson Hole is a cult resort for expert snowboarders. It's not bad for novices either. But intermediates not wishing to venture off the groomed runs will find the resort limited. There's plenty for freestylers to do.

FOR CROSS-COUNTRY ★★★★
Plenty of scenic choices
The Saddlehorn Nordic Center at Teton has 17km of trails and organizes trips into the National Parks.

MOUNTAIN RESTAURANTS ★★★
Bridger blossoms
Rendezvous Lodge at the top of the Bridger gondola continues to develop, with the opening last season of the self-service Off Piste Market on the lower floor and – for this season – the table-service Piste Mountain Bistro, also on the lower floor. This takes over the casual dining role (burgers, shared plates) while the upper floor Couloir moves into gourmet territory with three-course, fixed-price meals. Couloir offers great views through big windows and now may have food that's equally impressive.

Corbet's Cabin has 'great waffles', and the Casper at the base of the Casper chairlift does a wide range of self-service food. There are simple snack bars at four other points on the mountain. There are some excellent places at the base, notably in various hotels.

SCHOOLS AND GUIDES ★★★★
Learn to tackle the steeps
The school is highly regarded and has generated favourable reports. As well as the usual lessons, there are also special camps on certain dates (pre-booking required). An experienced regular visitor recommends particularly the 'fun, great value' Elevate Women's Camp for intermediate/expert skiers.

There are excellent guiding outfits for those who want to explore the backcountry.

ERIC SEYMOUR

The Tram (cable car) climbs a huge vertical of 1260m in one stage. Skiers would be better served by a two-stage lift ↓

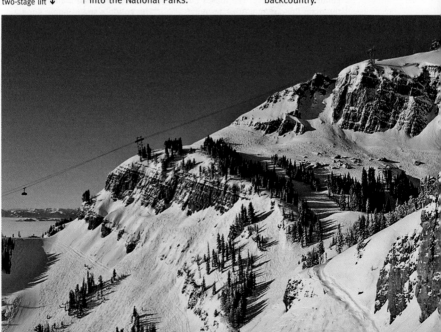

FOR FAMILIES ★★★★☆
Adventures on the Ranch
We've seen lots of kids having fun here. The 'Kids' Ranch', near the Bridger gondola, offers childcare and ski/snowboard lessons, as well as pizza parties in the evenings.

STAYING THERE

Teton Village (the lift base) is our preferred location. There are a couple of very swanky places between here and the town – Amangani and Spring Creek Ranch.
Hotels Because winter is low season, town hotel prices are low. Some town hotels are far from central.
TETON VILLAGE
*****Four Seasons Resort Stylish luxury, with art on the walls, superb skier services, health club, an exceptional outdoor pool; perfect position just above the base.
****Snake River Lodge & Spa Smartly welcoming and comfortable, with fine spa facilities.
***Alpenhof Tirolean-style, perfectly placed, with varied rooms, but 'friendly, great value, with a good buffet breakfast', according to a 2014 visitor. Good food, relaxed bar. Pool, sauna, hot tub, spa.
*Hostel Basic, good value and recommended by a reporter.
JACKSON TOWN
****Rusty Parrot Lodge Stylish, small, with a rustic feel. Hot tub, spa.
****Wort Central, above Silver Dollar Bar. Hot tub. Comfortable.
***Lodge at Jackson Hole Western-style, on outskirts. Big rooms. Free breakfast. Indoor/outdoor pools, spa, hot tub. Shuttle to the slopes.
***Parkway Inn Central. 'Decent-sized rooms. Friendly. Highly recommended.' Free breakfast. Pool, sauna, hot tubs. Shuttle to the slopes.
Apartments There is lots of choice at Teton Village and better-value places a mile or two away. Surprisingly little in and around Jackson town. Love Ridge and Snow King are 'good value'.

EATING OUT ★★★★★
A wide range of options
Jackson offers a range of excellent dining options. To check out menus, get hold of the local dining guide.
    At Teton Village, Il Villaggio Osteria at the hotel Terra has a good choice of Italian and seafood dishes. The Couloir at the top of the gondola opens on Thursday and Friday nights with a four-course gourmet menu for $95 – we had great foie gras and bison.
    In Jackson town there is a wide choice. Our regular Jackson reporter favours the 'superb' Wild Sage at the Rusty Parrot Lodge, and also rates the Gamefish at Snake River Lodge. Not to be confused with the Snake River brew-pub – 'great, happy atmosphere' and good beers – or the more upscale Snake River Grill. We loved the Asian/Japanese-fusion dishes to share at The Kitchen. Blue Lion is small and serves seafood and meat dishes. Other suggestions: the Merry Piglets (Mexican), Bubba's BBQ, Thai Me Up, which is also a brewery, and Bon Appe-Thai ('the real thing, with authentic herbs and flavours').

APRES-SKI ★★★★☆
Amusing saloons
The renowned Mangy Moose is the focus of après-ski activity at Teton Village – a big, happy place, often with live music – though it closed at 10pm midweek during our last stay. Nick Wilson's Cowboy Cafe is a popular hangout for locals and staff. In town, the Silver Dollar Bar (with 2,032 silver dollars inlaid in the counter) in the Wort hotel gets packed with locals dancing to live country music on a Saturday night. Round the corner the big Million Dollar Cowboy Bar, featuring saddles as bar stools, gets lively later and also has live music and dancing. Town Square Tavern has pool and often live music. Out of town, the Stagecoach Bar at Wilson is famously lively on Sunday nights.

OFF THE SLOPES ★★★☆☆
'Great' outdoor diversions
Yellowstone National Park is 100km to the north. You can tour the park by snowcat or snowmobile with a guide; numbers are now restricted to limit pollution. Some visitors really enjoy the park; we were underwhelmed – largely because of the noise and fumes from the snowmobiles and driving everywhere in convoy. The National Elk Refuge, with the largest elk herd in the US, is next to Jackson and across the road from the National Museum of Wildlife Art. Reporters recommend both – and walks beside the Snake river, spotting eagles and moose. In town there are some 40 galleries and museums plus Western arts and crafts shops.

AMERICAN SKIING COMPANY / NATHAN BILOW

New England

You go to Utah for the deepest snow, to Colorado for the lightest powder and swankiest resorts, to California for big mountains and relatively low prices. You go to New England for ... well, for what? Extreme cold? Rock-hard artificial snow? Mountains too limited to be of interest beyond New Jersey? Yes and no: all of these preconceptions have some basis, and in the end the East can't compete with the West. But they don't give the full picture.

Yes, it can be cold: one of our reporters recorded –27°C, with wind chill producing a perceived –73°C. Early in the season, people routinely wear face masks to prevent frostbite. It can also be warm – another reporter had a whole week of rain that washed away the early-season snow. The thing about New England's weather is that it varies – rather like old England's. The locals' favourite saying is: 'If you don't like the weather, wait two minutes.'

Many of the resorts get impressive amounts of natural snow over the season – in some years. But New England doesn't usually get much deep powder to play in. And snowmaking plays a big part in the resorts' operations. They have big snow-gun installations, designed to ensure a long season and to help the slopes to recover after a thaw. They were the pioneers of snowmaking technology; and 'farming' snow, as they put it, is something they do superbly well.

The mountains are not huge in terms of trail mileage, although Killington in particular packs in more than you would think – and in recent years has magically doubled its acreage, by tidying up forest areas to make them skiable. But several have verticals of over 800m (on a par with Colorado resorts such as Keystone), and most have over 600m, and are worth considering for a short stay, or even for a week if you like familiar runs. For more novelty, a road trip is the obvious solution.

Most resorts suit snowboarders well, and many have numerous and serious terrain parks.

You won't lack challenge – most of the double-black diamond runs are seriously steep. And you won't lack space: most American visitors stay just for a weekend, which means deserted slopes on weekdays, mostly.

It also means the resorts are keen to attract long-stay visitors, so UK package prices are low. But the big weekend and day-trip trade also means few New England resorts have developed atmospheric resort villages – just a few condos and a hotel, maybe, with places to stay further out geared to visitors with cars.

New England is easy to get to from Britain – a flight to Boston, then perhaps a three- or four-hour drive to your resort. And there are some pretty towns to visit, with their clapboard houses and big churches. You might also like to consider spending a day or two in Boston – one of America's most charming cities. Or have a shopping spree at the factory outlet stores that abound in New England.

We cover two of the most popular resorts on the UK market, Killington and Stowe, briefly on the opposite page. But there are many other small areas, too, shown on the map and covered in our index/directory.

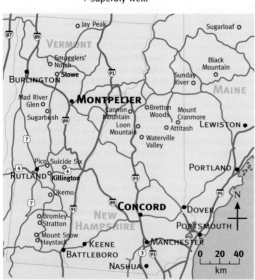

Killington

KEY FACTS

Resort	670m
	2,200ft
Slopes	355-1285m
	1,170-4,220ft
Lifts	22
Pistes	1509 acres

TOURIST OFFICE

www.killington.com

- ☐ New England's biggest ski area
- ☐ Excellent nursery slopes
- ☐ Lively après-ski and nightlife
- ☐ Widely spread lodgings, with no proper resort village
- ☐ Terminally tedious for non-skiers

Killington caters mainly for weekend visitors who drive in from the east-coast cities. There is no resort village in the usual sense.

Most of Killington's hotels and restaurants are spread along a five-mile approach road; the car is king. But there's also a free day-time shuttle-bus. The lift pass includes Pico – a separate little mountain next door.

The ski area spreads over a series of wooded peaks, with an impressive number of runs crammed into a small area. Amazingly, the Schrahe report (read our piste extent feature) reveals that they total 120km, more than some serious Alpine areas such as St Anton-Stuben. Killington Base is the main focus, with chairs radiating to three peaks. Crowds can arrive at weekends. It's a complex mountain, but the map and signing are fine. It has a good snow record (average 250 inches) and lots of snowmaking.

There are no fewer than seven terrain parks, including Burton's The Stash, an all-natural park with more than 50 features, and a super-pipe.

There are a handful of genuine double-diamond fall-line runs, many of them gladed. There are also lots of easy cruising blue and green runs all over the slopes. The resort is excellent for complete beginners too: the Snowshed base home slope is really one vast nursery slope. The Snowshed base lodge has several eating options.

Most hotels are a drive or bus ride away, but there is a wide choice of places to stay and dine. The Grand Resort at Snowshed is a swanky 4-star. Try the Santa Fe Steakhouse, or Peppino's for Italian. Killington has a well-earned reputation for a vibrant après-ski scene, led by the famous Wobbly Barn – a bar-club-steakhouse with live music.

Off the slopes? There's a tubing park plus snowmobiling and sleigh rides, but do take a car.

Stowe

KEY FACTS

Resort	475m
	1,560ft
Slopes	390-1135m
	1,280-3,720ft
Lifts	13
Pistes	485 acres

TOURIST OFFICE

www.stowe.com

- ☐ Classic, cute Vermont town
- ☐ Queue-free except at weekends
- ☐ Great children's facilities
- ☐ Slopes a bus ride from town
- ☐ Slow chairlifts in main area
- ☐ Lacks après-ski animation

Stowe is one of New England's cutest towns, with dinky clapboard shops and restaurants, and a pretty white church. The slopes have something for all.

The limited slopes of Mount Mansfield, Vermont's mainly wooded highest peak, are a 15-minute drive away. There's a good, free, day-time shuttle-bus service, but a car is useful.

The slopes span two main sectors, Mansfield and Spruce Peak, linked by the Over Easy gondola at base level. There are few queues during the week. Snowmaking is extensive, with big investments recently.

The main slopes are dominated by the famous Front Four – a row of double-black diamond runs, with genuine challenges for experts. But there is plenty of easier stuff, too. The nursery slopes at Spruce Peak are excellent, and there are splendid long green runs to progress to. There are six terrain parks, and the resort is popular with snowboarders. Children's facilities are excellent, too. There are a couple of decent eateries. The table-service Cliff House, at the top of the gondola, has impressed readers.

There is a lot of lodging along the road between the town and the slopes but there is increasing amounts at the base of Spruce Peak – swanky Stowe Mountain Lodge and the new Club Residences. Elsewhere, the Green Mountain Inn is a reader favourite. There are restaurants of every kind in the town; the Spruce Camp Base Lodge, Whip in Green Mountain Inn ('always good') and Piecasso pizzeria are reader tips. Nightlife is muted, especially later on, but the Matterhorn is 'an institution not to be missed' and the Den at Mansfield base 'still rocks'.

Stowe is a pleasant place to spend time off the slopes – at least if you like touristy shopping. There is a cinema, and snowmobiling and dog sledding too. Ben & Jerry's ice cream factory is just down the road.

In many ways Canada combines the best that the US has to offer – good service, a warm welcome, relatively quiet slopes, good lift systems with lots of fast lifts, frequent dumps of snow, great grooming and a high standard of accommodation – with more spectacular scenery. It also has the advantage that you can get direct flights to its main airports without having to change planes and go through customs part-way through your journey. But it is no longer cheap – long-haul air fares have risen and local prices are high (all Canadian resorts fall into our red category – the most expensive – for their RPI).

If Canada – well, western Canada at least – has one central attraction, it is snow. In an average year, you can expect frequent and abundant falls to provide the powder you dream of. And, as in the US, there is lots of steep terrain within resort area boundaries, which is avalanche protected and safely skiable without guidance. And there is lots of skiing among the trees – something that is very rare in Europe and is great fun, especially in fresh snow. If you really want untracked powder and are feeling flush, there is nothing to beat western Canada's heli- and snowcat-skiing operations; you can do it by the day or for a full week and stay in a luxurious lodge.

The east is completely different: expect snow and extremes of weather much like New England's. The main attraction of Québec for us is the French culture and ambience, plus the advantage of a shorter flight time. In both east and west, lifts close much earlier than in Europe – as early as 3pm in some cases (and some upper lifts might start closing as early as 1.30pm).

The Canadian people are another attraction. They share the American service culture but have a sincerity in putting it into practice that we (and our reporters) appreciate. In the west you'll also find spectacular scenery and may see impressive wildlife, especially in the Rockies and the interior of British Columbia.

The resorts obviously vary. But most have purpose-built villages (much more tastefully done than the French monstrosities of the 1960s and 70s) at the foot of the slopes – Banff and Lake Louise are notable exceptions because they are in a National Park where building is severely restricted. Whistler's village is huge but many of the others are tiny. A couple – notably Revelstoke and Fernie – have small towns nearby with decent restaurants and places to stay.

NOT AS CHEAP AS IT WAS

Canada is not as cheap a ski destination as it was. There used to be cheap charter flights but these have been dramatically reduced. At today's exchange rate, local prices for lift passes, ski school and equipment rental are all much more expensive than in Europe. And eating and drinking is no longer the bargain it once was. In many resorts you can save money by buying lift passes in advance through tour operators or websites.

Note that the legal age for buying and consuming alcohol is 18 in Alberta and Québec and 19 in British Columbia. The law is strictly enforced, so carrying your passport as evidence of age is a good idea even if you are well over the required age.

613

ROBIN O'NEILL

← Whistler has a huge 'village' at the foot of the slopes, which are the most extensive in North America

SNOWPIX.COM / CHRIS GILL

Western Canada

For international visitors to Canada, the main draw is the west. It has fabulous scenery, usually good snow and a wonderful sense of the great outdoors. Whistler attracts the highest number of British visitors. But Banff and Lake Louise have long been popular too and there are lots of good smaller resorts that more visitors are now exploring. You can have a great trip by renting a car and combining two or more of these, perhaps with a couple of days on virgin powder served by helicopters or snowcats as well.

The three big resorts mentioned above and six of the smaller ones get their own write-ups in this section.

Whistler is plenty big enough to amuse you for a whole holiday. Most visitors to Banff or Lake Louise, a half-hour drive apart, will spend time at both (and could also fit in day trips to Kicking Horse and Panorama).

But none of the other resorts has enough terrain to keep a keen piste-basher amused for a week or ten days without skiing the same runs a lot. So we'd suggest that if you want variety, you combine two or more on one

RED MOUNTAIN / FRANCOIS MARSEILLE

You don't get this very often in Europe – steep ungroomed tree runs that are avalanche controlled and patrolled ↓

holiday. Even if you don't want to drive, it is easy to combine, say, Sun Peaks with Whistler, Revelstoke, Big White or Silver Star (and the latter two with each other) using regular buses.

Several resorts that don't get a full chapter in this section are well worth considering as part of a tour.

Jasper is a low-key little town in the middle of a National Park with lots of wildlife; its small local ski area is a 30-minute drive away. The drive to Jasper from Lake Louise is one not to be missed, with spectacular views of glaciers on the Icefields Parkway.

Apex is a small, friendly rather isolated modern village with a small ski area and varied terrain that suits confident intermediates well.

Red Mountain is a cult resort for experts who can handle its steep wooded terrain; there's good cat skiing too. You can stay at the mountain or in the cute old mining town of Rossland just 4km away.

Nearby Whitewater is worth a day trip from Red and is renowned for its powder and weekend party atmosphere; or you could stay in the cute old town of Nelson nearby; there's good cat skiing near here too.

Panorama is much more of a destination resort – purpose-built on two levels at the foot of the slopes and with lots of accommodation – mainly spacious and comfortable condos. Its mountain has one of North America's biggest verticals (1220m) and there is terrain to suit all standards. There's heli-skiing direct from a heliplex in the resort and there are special three-run packages that are ideal for those who want to try heli-skiing for the first-time.

Kimberley is a former mining town that has been converted into a strange twee mixture of mock Austro-Bavarian come English Tudor architecture. It is

↑ Lovely powdery snow like this is one of western Canada's key attractions

KIMBERLEY / HENRY GEORGI

about 4km from its ski area where there is also convenient purpose-built accommodation. The ski area is fair-sized, with some good tough intermediate runs and lots of gladed terrain which really needs good snow to be enjoyable.

All these resorts have their own entries in the resort directory at the back of the book.

We once spent two weeks driving from Whistler to Banff, calling in at lots of small resorts on the way. It was a fantastic trip; for eight days in the middle it did not stop snowing, and the variety of slopes and resorts made for great contrasts. A couple of seasons ago we combined Fernie, Kicking Horse, Revelstoke and Whistler – which was an enjoyable trip, despite unseasonably warm and rainy weather.

If you fancy a day or two snowcat-skiing, there are lots of possibilities, including great operations near Fernie (see that chapter) as well as those mentioned above. Whistler and Revelstoke have both cat- and heli-skiing available.

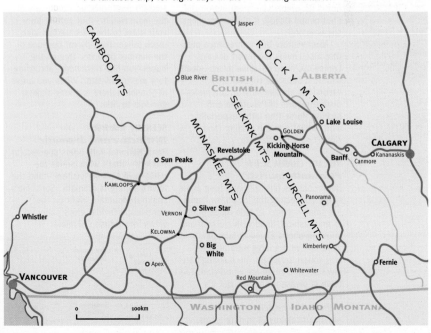

SNOWPIX.COM / CHRIS GILL

Banff

A major summer resort amid spectacular National Park scenery, with varied ski areas – including Lake Louise – nearby

£160
RESORT PRICE INDEX

RATINGS

The mountains

Extent	★★★
Fast lifts	★★★★
Queues	★★★★
Terrain p'ks	★★★★
Snow	★★★★
Expert	★★★★
Intermediate	★★★★
Beginner	★★★
Boarder	★★★★
X-country	★★★★
Restaurants	★★★
Schools	★★★★
Families	★★★★

The resort

Charm	★★★
Convenience	★
Scenery	★★★★
Eating out	★★★★★
Après-ski	★★★
Off-slope	★★★★★

616

NEWS

2015/16: The Teepee Town double chair at Sunshine Village will be replaced by a fast quad with heated seats.

2014/15: Several runs at Norquay were widened, and the tubing park was enlarged.

+ Spectacular high-mountain scenery – quite unlike the Colorado Rockies

+ Lots of touristy shops, restaurants and bars

+ Good-value lodging because winter is the area's low season

+ Excellent snow at main nearby area, Sunshine Village, but ...

− It's a 20-minute bus ride then a long gondola ride away

− You'll probably want to ski Lake Louise too, 45 minutes away

− Most lifts/runs are of limited vertical

− Can be very cold (−30°C or lower)

− Banff lacks ski resort atmosphere, though it's not an unattractive town

Banff is nothing like your typical ski resort. Even the small local hill, Norquay, is a bus ride out of town, and the daily routine is to commute to Sunshine Village or Lake Louise (which gets its own chapter). Not fun; but we enjoy its restaurants and bars, and spectacular scenery.

The alternative is to stay a few nights mid-mountain at Sunshine Village and a few at Lake Louise. Lake Louise also has the advantage of being much closer to Kicking Horse, which makes a great day trip for powderhounds.

THE RESORT

Banff is a big summer tourist town, with two ski areas nearby. Mt Norquay is a tiny area of slopes overlooking the town. Sunshine Village – whose base station is 20 minutes' drive from Banff – is a much bigger mountain; despite the name, it's not a village (it has just one hotel at mid-mountain), nor is it notably sunny (sitting on the Continental Divide, it has an excellent snow record).

Most visitors buy a three-area pass that also covers the resort of Lake Louise, 45 minutes' drive away – dealt with in a separate chapter. Bus excursions are available to the more distant resorts of Panorama and Kicking Horse (the latter especially worthwhile) and the smaller (and closer) resort of Nakiska.

VILLAGE CHARM ★★★
Pleasantly touristy
Banff consists basically of a long main street connecting the 'downtown' area – a small network of side roads built in grid fashion, lined with clothing and souvenir shops aimed at summer visitors – with a large area of hotel and condo lodgings. The buildings are low-rise, and some are wood-clad. The town is pleasant enough, but it's essentially a modern tourist town, without the character of the classic American cowboy or mining towns.

CONVENIENCE ★
Sprawling town, outlying slopes
Banff is a sprawling place, and many of the lodgings (even on the main Banff Avenue) can be quite a way from the downtown area. A car can be helpful here, especially in cold weather. But taxis are plentiful.

To get to the slopes, bus services for each mountain (free with the Tri-area lift pass) pick up from many of the main hotels – but getting from your hotel to the lift base can take much longer than by car because of the number of stops, though the buses 'run like clockwork', according to a previous visitor. When you arrive at Sunshine there is a long access gondola to ride.

SCENERY ★★★★
Distinctive and dramatic
Banff National Park offers spectacular scenery – that's what brings the millions of summer visitors – and the town's setting is dramatic. Sunshine's Lookout Mountain, right on the Continental Divide, gives panoramic views into British Columbia.

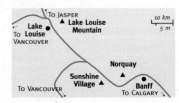

Banff

KEY FACTS

Resort	1380m
	4,530ft

Norquay, Sunshine and Lake Louise

Slopes	1630-2730m
	5,350-8,950ft
Lifts	26
Pistes	7,748 acres

Norquay only

Slopes	1630-2135m
	5,350-7,000ft
Lifts	6
Pistes	190 acres

Sunshine only

Slopes	1660-2730m
	5,440-8,950ft
Lifts	12
Pistes	3,358 acres

MOUNT NORQUAY / PAUL ZIZKA

From parts of Norquay you get a great view over the town of Banff to the distinctive Mt Rundle ↓

THE MOUNTAINS

The Sunshine Village slopes are mostly above the treeline, although there is a wooded sector, and some lightly wooded slopes higher up. Mt Norquay is a much smaller area of quiet, wooded slopes. Each area (and Lake Louise) has its own trail map, and there's another that shows all three areas. The signposting at the top of each lift is praised, but at Sunshine subsequent signs are 'small and difficult to spot', says a reporter.

There are good, free mountain tours led by friendly volunteer hosts.

EXTENT OF THE SLOPES ★★★
Lots of variety

The main slopes of **Sunshine Village** are not visible from the base station: you ride a gondola to Sunshine Village itself, with a mid-station at the base of Goat's Eye Mountain. Goat's Eye is served by a fast quad rising 580m – much the most serious lift on the mountain. Although there are some blue runs, this is basically a black mountain, with some genuine double diamonds (including extreme terrain in the Wild West area – see 'For experts').

Further up at Sunshine Village, lifts fan out in all directions, with short runs back from Mount Standish and longer ones from Lookout Mountain. From the top here you can access the more extreme terrain of Delirium Dive – read 'For experts'.

The 2.5km green run to the gondola base is a pretty cruise. Go down while the lifts are still running, and you can take the Jackrabbit chair to cut out a flat section. Alternatively, delay your descent and you'll avoid the close-of-play crowds. The Canyon trail is a fun alternative for more advanced skiers and riders. The lower part is marked black; it's just a bit narrow and twisty in places. The final option is to ride the gondola down; many people do.

The slopes at **Norquay** are served by a row of five parallel lifts and have floodlit trails twice a week.

FAST LIFTS ★★★★
Most sectors well served

At Sunshine, most sectors of the slopes have fast chairs. With the upgrade of the Teepee Town chair this year, the main weakness is the Wawa chair, and this now has a moving carpet. Norquay is so small that lift speed is hardly an issue, but it does have one fast chair.

QUEUES ★★★★
Sunshine can get busy

Many visitors are day-trippers from cities such as Calgary – so the slopes are fairly quiet during the week. Public holidays and weekends have provoked past complaints of long queues at Sunshine. But queues generally move quickly, and there are effective singles lines (well managed, as usual) you can use if in a hurry. On busy weekends, we're told the trick is to arrive at the gondola by 9am.

LIFT PASSES

Tri-area lift pass

Prices in C$

Age	6-day
under 13	162
13 to 17	444
18 to 64	498
65 plus	444

Free Under 6

Beginner Lift, lesson and rental package

Notes Covers transport between Banff, Lake Louise, Norquay and Sunshine Village; prices include 5% tax

TERRAIN PARKS ★★★★
Fun on both areas

At Sunshine, the terrain park on Lookout Mountain covers an impressive 12 acres in three sections aimed at different levels. Experts should not miss the Norquay park, which has an airbag as well as lots of terrain features. The park is floodlit some evenings.

SNOW RELIABILITY ★★★★
Excellent

Sunshine Village used to claim '100% natural snow', a neat reversal of the usual snowmaking hype. Now it has two snow-guns to tackle weak spots. In a poor snow season, some black runs can remain rocky (especially those on Goat's Eye), but the blues are usually fine. 'Three times the snow' is another slogan – a sly comparison between the impressive average snowfall here (360 to 400 inches, depending on the source) and the more modest figures at Lake Louise and Norquay. But we're told the Sunshine figures relate to Lookout, and that Goat's Eye gets less. At Norquay there is snowmaking on green and blue pistes. Late-season snow on Sunshine is usually good (we've had great April snow there).

FOR EXPERTS ★★★★
Pure pleasure

Sunshine has plenty of open runs of genuine black steepness above the treeline on Lookout, but Goat's Eye is much more compelling. It has a great area of expert double-black diamond trails and chutes, both above and below the treeline. But the slopes are rocky and need good cover, and the top can be windswept. The double-diamond runs at skier's left reportedly hold their snow better than the rest of the mountain.

Goat's Eye has some great steep terrain – single- and double-black diamond runs and an extreme zone. But it's very rocky and windswept and needs a lot of snow to be enjoyable

GOAT'S EYE
2600m/8,530ft

Goat's Eye

🚡 gondola
🚡 fast chairlift
Slow chairs & drags have no symbol

Wild West
◆ ◆

Wolverine

1660m/5,440ft

2020m/6,630ft

If it's snowing hard, visibility is usually best on the easy runs in the trees around here and on the long run down to the bottom of the gondola

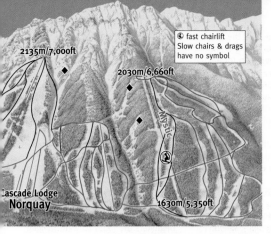

2135m/7,000ft

2030m/6,660ft

◆ fast chairlift
Slow chairs & drags
have no symbol

Mystic

Cascade Lodge
Norquay

1630m/5,350ft

ice. Also try the Shoulder on Lookout Mountain; it is sheltered, tends to accumulate powder and has been deserted whenever we've been there (probably because access to it involves a long traverse that can be tricky and is poorly marked).

A popular backcountry route follows the back of the Wawa ridge, through a river valley ('great fun – tight turns in the trees of the river bed'); a guide is essential, of course.

Real experts will want to get to grips with Delirium Dive on Lookout Mountain's north face and the Wild West area on Goat's Eye (with some narrow chutes and rock bands). For both you must have a companion, an avalanche transceiver, probes and a shovel – and a guide is recommended. It is best to book in advance and rent your equipment in Banff (you can't in Sunshine). We tried Delirium in a group with the ski patrol, who

There are short, not-too-steep black runs on Mount Standish. One more challenging novelty here is a pitch known as the Waterfall run – because you do actually ski down over a snow-covered frozen waterfall; but a lot of snow is needed to cover the waterfall

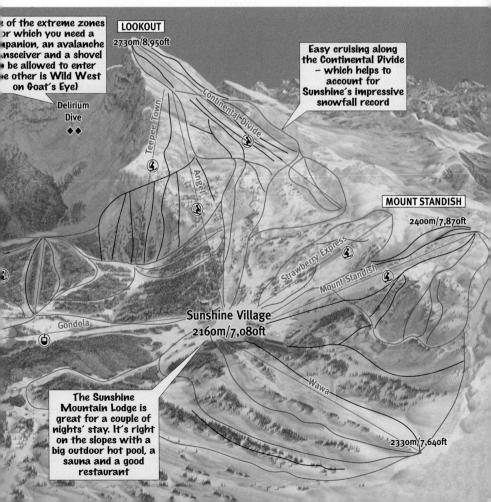

e of the extreme zones
or which you need a
mpanion, an avalanche
nsceiver and a shovel
be allowed to enter
e other is Wild West
on Goat's Eye)

Delirium
Dive
◆◆

LOOKOUT
2730m/8,950ft

Teepee Town

Continental Divide

Angel

Easy cruising along
the Continental Divide
– which helps to
account for
Sunshine's impressive
snowfall record

MOUNT STANDISH
2400m/7,870ft

Strawberry Express

Mount Standish

Sunshine Village
2160m/7,080ft

Gondola

The Sunshine
Mountain Lodge is
great for a couple of
nights' stay. It's right
on the slopes with a
big outdoor hot pool, a
sauna and a good
restaurant

Wawa

2330m/7,640ft

SKIWORLD

Catered chalets,
hotels and
self catering
apartments in

**Europe, USA
and Canada**

skiworld.co.uk
08444 930 430

ABTA V2151 ATOL 2036

620

TANYA BOOTH
If you fancy a night or
two away from the
crowds, Sunshine
Village is the place.
This isn't part of it,
it's all of it ↓

provided equipment, and the scariest
part was the walk in, along a narrow,
icy path with a sheer drop (protected
by a flimsy-looking net).

Norquay's two main lifts give only
400m vertical, but both serve black
slopes, and the North American chair
accesses a couple of serious double-
diamond runs.

Heli-skiing is available from bases
outside the National Park in British
Columbia – roughly two hours' drive.

FOR INTERMEDIATES ★★★★
Ideal runs
Half the runs on Sunshine are
classified as intermediate. Wherever
you look there are blues and greens –
and some of the greens are as
enjoyable (and pretty much as steep)
as the blues.

We particularly like the World Cup
Downhill run, from the top of Lookout
to the Village. All three chairs on
Mount Standish are excellent for
building confidence, provided you
choose a sensible route down. The
slow Wawa chair gives access to the
Wawa Bowl and Tincan Alley ('great
first blues'). This area also offers some
shelter from bad weather.

There's a delightful wooded area
under the second stage of the gondola
served by the Jackrabbit and Wolverine
chairs. The blue runs down Goat's Eye
are good cruises too, some of them
with space to indulge in fast carving.

The Mystic Express at Norquay
serves a handful of quite challenging
treelined blues and a couple of blacks
that are sometimes groomed.

FOR BEGINNERS ★★★
Pretty good terrain
Most beginners start with a package
that includes a lift pass, equipment
hire and tuition. Sunshine has a good
nursery area at the Village, served by
a moving carpet. And there are great
long green runs to progress to, served
by the fast Strawberry Express chair.

Norquay has a good small nursery
area with a moving carpet and gentle
greens to progress to, served by the
Cascade chair.

Banff is not the ideal destination
for a mixed party of beginners and
more experienced friends. The
beginners are likely to want familiar
surroundings, while the more
experienced will want to travel.

FOR BOARDERS ★★★★
A good base
Boarders will feel at home in Banff,
and there is some excellent freeriding
terrain. Natural features are part of the
appeal. But Sunshine has some flat
areas to beware of (such as the green
run to the base – read 'Extent of the
slopes'), and the blue traverse on
Goat's Eye is tedious.

FOR CROSS-COUNTRY ★★★★
High in quality and quantity
It's a good area for cross-country.
There are trails near Banff, around the
Bow River, and on the Banff Springs
golf course. But the best area is
around Lake Louise. Altogether, there
are around 80km of groomed trails
within Banff National Park.

MOUNTAIN RESTAURANTS ★★★
Quite good
With a mini-resort at mid-mountain,
Sunshine offers better options than
usual in North America. Our favourite
is the welcoming Chimney Corner
Lounge in the Sunshine Mountain
Lodge with a big open fire – endorsed
by reporters ('Tasty and good value,'
said a recent visitor). The Day Lodge
offers different styles of catering on
three floors – the table-service
Lookout Bistro has great views.

At Norquay, the big, stylish, timber-
framed Cascade Lodge is excellent – it
has table- and self-service restaurants.

SCHOOLS AND GUIDES ★★★★
Some great ideas
Each mountain has its own school. But
recognizing that visitors wanting
lessons won't want to be confined to

just one mountain, the resorts have organized an excellent Club Ski Program – three-day courses starting on Sundays and Thursdays that take you to Sunshine, Norquay and Lake Louise on different days, offering a mixture of guiding and instruction. Reporters are full of praise for these.

FOR FAMILIES ★★★★☆
Excellent choices
There are various school and activity programmes for all ages. We've had good reports of the schools in the past. All three resorts offer childcare. The Tiny Tigers Ski and Play Program at Sunshine introduces youngsters to the slopes.

STAYING THERE

A huge amount of accommodation is on offer, with a wide variety of hotels.
Hotels Summer is peak season here, with generally lower prices in winter. Skiworld offers the top hotels, plus some simpler places on which we lack reports.
★★★★★Fairmont Banff Springs A late-19th-century, castle-style property outside town (no shuttle-bus – you have to use taxis). It's a resort in itself – 2,000 beds, 17 shops, several restaurants and bars, a nightclub and a superb spa (which costs extra).
★★★★Banff Caribou Lodge On the main street, slightly out of town. Wood-clad, individually designed rooms (some small). 'Massive' hot tub; spa. Repeatedly praised by reporters ('fantastic service', 'good food').
★★★★Rimrock Spectacularly set out of town, with great views and a smart health club. Luxurious.
★★★Buffalo Mountain Lodge Slightly out of town but a 'wonderful building' in a 'beautiful location'. 'Excellent food.' Hot tub.
★★★Mount Royal Good central location, 'comfortable and reasonably priced'.
Apartments The Banff Rocky Mountain Resort is set in the woods on the edge of town, with indoor pool and hot tubs. Douglas Fir resort is a bit out of town but has a free shuttle and is popular with families; lots of facilities such as adults' and kids' swimming pools and a giant indoor playground.
At altitude The Sunshine Mountain Lodge makes a very welcoming, comfortable base at Sunshine Village – and guests can get on the slopes half an hour early. Luggage is transported

while you ski. Rooms vary in size, and include luxury loft rooms. Big outdoor hot pool. Sauna. Good restaurant.

EATING OUT ★★★★★
Lots of choice
Banff boasts over 100 restaurants, from McDonald's to the fine-dining restaurant in the Banff Springs hotel.

We've enjoyed the designer-cool Saltlik – good game, steak and fish – and a reader this year rates it the best she found. She also tips Melissa's for breakfast (and other readers have enjoyed dinner here). A recent reporter who got about a bit recommended the Keg Steakhouse in Caribou Lodge ('delicious, large portions'), Bistro Cafe de Paris ('massive and tasty wild boar shank') and particularly Buffalo Mountain Lodge a mile out of town ('magnificent meal in wonderful timber building'). Dozens of other places are worth a try.

APRES-SKI ★★★☆☆
Night on the town is best
There's little teatime après-ski because the town is a drive from the slopes. Mad Trapper's Saloon at the top of the Sunshine gondola is the place to be during the close-of-play happy hour.

In town later, the two main live music venues are the Rose & Crown and Wild Bill's. The Banff Avenue Brewing Company is the local microbrewery. The Elk and Oarsman ('a decent pub') has a lively sports bar and the St James's Gate is the local Irish pub. There are a couple of good nightclubs.

OFF THE SLOPES ★★★★★
Lots to do
Banff has lots to do off the slopes. Outdoor activities include skating, snowshoeing, dog sledding and snowmobiling. Ice canyon walks are popular – notably Johnson Canyon – and there's wildlife to see.

Shopping and soaking in the spas and hot springs are popular – the Red Earth Spa at the Caribou Lodge has the works. There are sightseeing tours and several museums – a previous visitor recommends the Whyte Museum of the Canadian Rockies and the Banff Park Museum. Many reporters have enjoyed evenings in Calgary watching the ice hockey. Banff is quite near one end of the Columbia Icefields Parkway, a three-hour drive to Jasper through spectacular national parks.

GETTING THERE

Air Calgary 140km/ 85 miles (1hr45)

TOURIST OFFICE

www.skibanff.com
www.banffnorquay. com
www.SkiBig3.com

Big White

It's a big village by Canadian standards and it's certainly white. There are few places to match it for learning to ski powder

£150
RESORT PRICE INDEX

TOP 10 RATINGS

Extent	★★★
Fast lifts	★★★★
Queues	★★★★★
Snow	★★★★★
Expert	★★★
Intermediate	★★★★
Beginner	★★★★
Charm	★★
Convenience	★★★★
Scenery	★★★

NEWS

2015/16: A new day lodge at the foot of the Black Forest chairlift is due to open.

2014/15: A new slope, the Ogopogo Adventure Trail for kids, was built.

622

+ Great for learning to ski powder

+ Slopes quiet except at weekends

+ Convenient, purpose-built village with high-quality condos and a traffic-free centre; good for families

+ Lots of non-skiing snow-based activities at Happy Valley

− Visibility can be poor, especially on the upper mountain, because of snow, cloud or freezing fog

− Ski area modest by Alpine standards

− Limited après-ski (but getting a bit livelier)

'It's the snow' says the Big White slogan. And as slogans go, it's spot on. If you want a good chance of skiing powder on reasonably easy slopes, put Big White high on the shortlist. If you want a suntan (or lively après-ski, or extensive steep terrain), look elsewhere; but if you are an intermediate looking to learn to ski powder or try gladed skiing, there can be few better places. Consider combining it with another BC resort such as Silver Star or Whistler for variety.

THE RESORT

Big White is a purpose-built resort that has more visitor beds than any other BC resort except Whistler. It's less than an hour from Kelowna airport.
Village charm The resort is rather spread out but attractively built in wood and stone, with a family-friendly traffic-free centre.
Convenience Much of the place is ski-in/ski-out smart modern condos.
Scenery Trees fill the views wherever you look; and near the top of the mountain the trees usually stay white all winter and are known as 'snow ghosts'; they make visibility tricky in a white-out but are great fun to ski between on clear days.

THE MOUNTAINS

Much of the terrain is heavily wooded. But the trees thin out towards the summits, leading to almost open slopes in the bowls at the top. There's at least one green option from the top of each lift, but the one from Gem Lake is narrow and can be tricky and busy. In general, the easiest slopes are on the right as you look at the mountain (including some very easy glade skiing) and get steeper the further left you go.
Slopes Chairs run from points below village level to above mid-mountain, serving the main area of wooded beginner and intermediate runs above and beside the village. A T-bar and

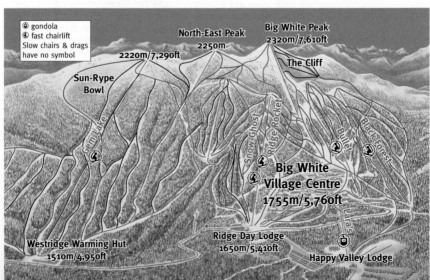

KEY FACTS

Resort	1755m
	5,760ft
Slopes	1510-2320m
	4,950-7,610ft
Lifts	16
Pistes	2,765 acres

LIFT PASSES

Prices in C$

Age	6-day
under 13	265
13 to 18	400
19 to 64	480
65 plus	400

Free Under 6

Beginner Limited pass

Notes Prices include taxes and are online advance-purchase prices

four chairs serve the higher slopes. Quite some way across the mountain is the Gem Lake fast chair, serving a range of long top-to-bottom runs; with its 710m vertical, this lift is in a different league from the others.

'Snow hosts' (highly praised by reporters) run free guided ski tours starting at 10.30 every morning. The signposting and piste map and classification are good ('excellent', says a recent visitor). There is night skiing Tuesday to Saturday on three main slopes and the terrain park.

Fast lifts The lifts from the village and the Gem Lake lift are all fast. But the other upper lifts are tediously slow.

Queues Queues are very rare.

Terrain park Served by a double chair and snowmaking, the excellent Telus park includes jumps and features for all levels, large-diameter tube rails, a half-pipe and a snowcross, and is highly praised by reporters.

Snow reliability Big White has a reputation for great powder; average snowfall is about 300 inches, which is similar to many Colorado resorts. On each of our three visits it snowed practically non-stop, the powder was excellent and we hardly saw the sun.

Experts The Cliff area at the top right of the ski area is of serious double-black diamond pitch; the runs are short, but you can ski them repeatedly using the Cliff chair. Sun-Rype bowl at the opposite edge of the ski area is more forgiving ('Excellent place to ski deep powder,' says a reporter). There are some long blacks off the Gem Lake chair and several shorter ones off the Powder and Falcon chairs. There are plenty of glades to explore.

Intermediates The resort is excellent for cruisers and families, with long blues and greens all over the hill. Good intermediates will enjoy the easier blacks and some of the gladed runs too. There is marvellous easy skiing among the trees in the Black Forest area (which we loved when it was snowing) and among the snow ghosts (see 'Scenery'), which we loved when it was clear. Some of the blues off the Gem Lake chair are quite steep, narrow and challenging.

Beginners There's a good dedicated beginner area at Happy Valley and lots of long easy runs to progress to. Every day three slopes are designated slow zones, gated and patrolled.

Snowboarding There's some excellent beginner and freeriding terrain with

boarder-friendly chairlifts and few flat areas to worry about.

Cross-country A reporter enjoyed the 25km of trails. There are free guided tours daily at 10.30am.

Mountain restaurants None up the hill – it's back to the bottom for lunch.

School and guides We have received rave reviews from reporters for both skiing and snowboarding lessons for adults and children alike.

Families The excellent day care centre takes children from 18 months to five years; a list of babysitters is available.

STAYING THERE

A good range of accommodation is featured by specialist tour operators like Frontier Ski and Ski Independence.

Hotels The choices are Chateau Big White, the White Crystal Inn and the Inn at Big White. We would prefer to stay in a smart condo.

Apartments Condo standards are high. Stonebridge and Towering Pines are both central and Copper Kettle is more secluded; all are ski-in/ski-out, with big, well-furnished rooms and private hot tubs on the balconies. Other reader tips include Black Bear, Eagles and Whitefoot Lodge.

Eating out The best restaurants here have a great selection of local Okanagan wines (there are over 130 wine producers in the valley). We had a superb meal at the 6 Degrees bistro, sharing delicious dishes (tapas-style); endorsed by a reporter this year ('brilliant seven-course taster menu'); not cheap. We've also had good meals in the Kettle Valley Steakhouse at Happy Valley but it got mixed reviews this year. Reporters have tipped the upstairs restaurant at Snowshoe Sam's for 'melt in mouth steaks' and the 'excellent' Globe (tapas-style food, theme nights). The Blarney Stone Irish Tavern is in the Inn at Big White – it's run by the people who own the Globe. The Woods is in the main square and has a patio with a firepit.

Après-ski In general, it is fairly quiet. But the ground floor of Snowshoe Sam's has a DJ and live entertainment, as do the Globe, Blarney Stone and Sessions Taphouse says a reporter.

Off the slopes Happy Valley is a great area for families, with ice skating, snowmobiling, snow biking, tubing, dog sledding, sleigh rides, 15km of snowshoeing trails and an 18m ice climbing tower. There are two spas and a shopping shuttle to Kelowna.

SHOWPIX.COM / CHRIS GILL

Fernie

Lots of snow and lots of steeps – one of our favourites, with a choice of convenient base lodging or a valley town

624

£155
RESORT PRICE INDEX

RATINGS

The mountains

Extent	★★★
Fast lifts	★★
Queues	★★★★
Terrain p'ks	★★
Snow	★★★★
Expert	★★★★★
Intermediate	★★
Beginner	★★★★
Boarder	★★★
X-country	★★★
Restaurants	★
Schools	★★★★
Families	★★★

The resort

Charm	★★
Convenience	★★★★
Scenery	★★★
Eating out	★★★
Après-ski	★★★
Off-slope	★★

KEY FACTS

Resort	1065m
	3,490ft
Slopes	1065-2135m
	3,490-7,000ft
Lifts	10
Pistes	2,500 acres

+ Good snow record, with less chance of rain than at Whistler

+ Blissfully quiet much of the time

+ Great terrain for those who like it steep, deep, and lightly wooded – including confident intermediates

+ Snowcat operations nearby

+ Some convenient on-slope accommodation available, but ...

– Mountain resort is very limited

– Access to many excellent runs is via slow lifts and long traverses

– Not a huge amount of groomed cruising to do

– After a dump it can take time to make the bowls safe (and to get the groomed trails groomed again)

– One basic mountain restaurant

Fernie has long had cult status among the residents of Calgary, and we have also had a good flow of reports from enthusiastic British visitors impressed by the adventurous skiing – it's mostly ungroomed, and much of it is steep, with a lot of lightly wooded slopes (rare in Europe). It's now quite a good resort for novices, too. The ones who will want to look elsewhere are keen but cautious, piste-only intermediates.

We find ourselves more strongly drawn to Fernie than the minus points listed above might lead you to expect. 'Hard to explain how it gets under your skin,' says a similarly smitten reporter. It is, Tanya, it is.

THE RESORT

Fernie Alpine Resort is set a little way up the mountainside from the flat Elk Valley floor and a couple of miles from the little town of Fernie. Outings to Kimberley are possible; a coach goes weekly, taking about 90 minutes.

VILLAGE CHARM ★★
Unpretentious small town
A slope-side resort has grown from very little in recent years, but there's still not much there except convenient lodging and a few restaurants, bars and sports shops. It is quiet at night. There's much more going on in the nearby town, named after the guy who discovered coal here and triggered a boom in the early 1900s. Some 'historic' buildings have survived.

Fernie town is primarily a place for locals, not tourists, but there are some lively bars, decent places to eat and a reasonable range of shops. It is down to earth rather than charming, and

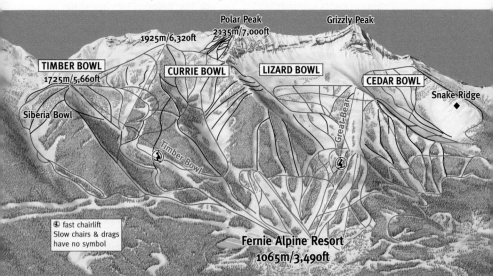

Polar Peak
2135m/7,000ft

Grizzly Peak

1925m/6,320ft

TIMBER BOWL
1725m/5,660ft

CURRIE BOWL

LIZARD BOWL

CEDAR BOWL

Snake Ridge ◆

Siberia Bowl

Timber Bowl

Great Bear

⊕ fast chairlift
Slow chairs & drags
have no symbol

Fernie Alpine Resort
1065m/3,490ft

↑ The open slopes on Polar Peak lead down into the lightly wooded slopes of Currie Bowl – one of our favourite parts of the area

TANYA BOOTH

reporters' reactions to it vary: some like staying in a 'real' town while others are put off by the highway that runs through it, close to the centre. Most stress the friendly locals.

CONVENIENCE ★★★★
Base lodging or bus ride
There is accommodation at the resort and in town. Buses between the two run hourly, stopping at some of the bigger hotels on the way and running late on Friday and Saturday.

SCENERY ★★★
The rocky ridges are impressive
Fernie's two main peaks, Grizzly and Polar, are part of the steep-sided Lizard Range. They provide an impressively rocky backdrop. There are good views across the Elk Valley too.

THE MOUNTAINS

Fernie's 2,500 acres pack in a lot of variety, from high open slopes to thick forest – but its distinctive feature is the lightly wooded glades in all the bowls. Quite a few runs go directly down the fall line.

Over the years we've been visiting, both the trail map and the signposting have improved. But you get the best out of the area with some sort of local guidance. Without it, you can end up in tight trees on slopes of double-diamond steepness. The map employs some ludicrously small type.

EXTENT OF THE SLOPES ★★★
Bowl after bowl
What you see when you arrive at the lift base is a trio of impressive mogul slopes towering above you. These excellent black runs exemplify one of the weaknesses of Fernie's lift system: to get to them you must ride lifts way off to the left or right, and then make long traverses to get to the start of the runs proper – a slow business.

The slow Deer chair serves green runs at the foot of these black slopes, but goes no further.

On the right, riding the slow Elk quad followed by the fast Great Bear quad takes you to the ridge where **Lizard Bowl** meets **Cedar Bowl**. You can traverse across the head of both of these open/lightly wooded bowls and descend pretty much wherever you like. The Haul Back T-bar brings you out of Cedar to ride the Boomerang chair. This serves a mini-bowl between Lizard and Cedar.

Off to the left, the Timber Bowl fast quad chair gives access to **Siberia Bowl** and the lower part of **Timber Bowl**. But for access to the higher slopes of Timber Bowl and to **Currie Bowl** you must take the slow White Pass quad. A long traverse from the top gets you to the steeper slopes on the far flank of Currie (our favourite area). The traverse takes you past a short, slow triple chair which accesses **Polar Peak**, the high point of the ski area – 210m higher than the White

LIFT PASSES

Prices in C$

Age	6-day
under 13	209
13 to 17	389
18 to 64	521
65 plus	419
Free Under 6	

Beginner Rental, limited pass and tuition deals

Notes Prices are advance purchase online and include taxes; half-day pass available

HENRY GEORGI

Fernie is a real town with some historic buildings – down to earth rather than notably charming. The mountain is less close than it looks ↓

Pass chair; the run from Polar Peak to the base is over 1000m vertical.

All descents of Currie or Siberia, and some in Timber Bowl, mean you have to go all the way to the lift base.

Free mountain tours are available twice a day, but 'all we learnt were some quirky facts about the resort', says a report this year.

FAST LIFTS ★★
A poor show
There are only two fast chairs, serving opposite ends of the mountain. Slow chairs and a draglift elsewhere soak up time. Then you spend more time traversing. But keen intermediates can rack up the miles doing laps on the fast chairs in Siberia and Timber bowls.

QUEUES ★★★★
Not usually a problem
Queues are generally rare unless there are weekend crowds from Calgary or heavy snow keeps part of the mountain closed. The slopes are usually very quiet; on our last March visit we skied lots of runs more or less alone.

TERRAIN PARKS ★★
Just a rail park
There is no proper park, but there is a patrolled rail park beside the Great Bear Express – you'll need a special pass (C$5 per day) and must sign a waiver to use it.

SNOW RELIABILITY ★★★★
A key part of the appeal
Fernie has an excellent snow record – with an average of 360 inches per year, it's better than practically anywhere in Colorado, for example. But the altitude is modest: rain is not unknown, and in warm weather the lower slopes can suffer. Too much snow can be a problem, with the high bowls prone to closure; the headwalls hold a lot of snow and require a lot of bombing to be made safe. As a whole, the area faces roughly north-east; but many runs are on the flanks of the ridges, facing south-east, so the sun can affect things in late season.

On our most recent visits we've been impressed by the quality of the groomed runs, despite less than ideal weather; we put it down to the very low levels of traffic on these runs. Snowmaking has been increased over recent years and now covers most of the lower runs.

FOR EXPERTS ★★★★★
Wonderful with guidance
The combination of heavy snowfalls and abundant steep terrain with the shelter of trees makes this a superb mountain for good skiers, so long as you know where you are going. If you don't, consider getting guidance, to begin with at least.

There are about a dozen identifiable faces offering genuine black or double-black slopes, each of

them with several alternative ways down and all worth exploring. Pay attention to the diamonds: the doubles are the genuine article.

Polar Peak is of limited vertical but serious double-diamond gradient; there is one single-diamond run, but even this can have a tricky entry. You can hike from here to a steep gated area where transceivers (and great care) are required.

There are a few areas where you can do laps fairly efficiently, but mostly you have to put up with a cycle of long traverse–descent–run-out–lift–lift on each lap (with a third lift to get to the Polar Peak area).

There are backcountry routes you can take with guidance (some include an overnight camp) and snowcat operations in other nearby mountains – read the feature panel overleaf. A regular reporter enjoyed exploring Fish Bowl, a short hike outside the resort boundary from Cedar Bowl.

FOR INTERMEDIATES ★★
Getting better
In recent years Fernie has made great strides to broaden its appeal. These days, the resort grooms quite a wide range of runs, including some great blue cruisers down all the bowls – but there are also quite a few blacks that get regularly groomed. And the lack of crowds makes fast skiing on these runs a real pleasure. But the groomed stuff doesn't add up to much when you compare it with many other resorts with the same sort of acreage, and after a big dump the grooming takes time. If you are not happy to try some of the easier ungroomed terrain you may find the place a bit limited. For the adventurous willing to give the powder a go, though, Fernie can be fabulous.

FOR BEGINNERS ★★★★
Surprisingly, pretty good
There's a good nursery area served by two lifts (a moving carpet and a drag), and the lower mountain served by the Deer and Elk chairs has lots of wide, smooth trails to gain confidence on. But a reader points out that these are fixed-grip chairs that novice children can find tricky.

FOR BOARDERS ★★★
Fine if you're good
Fernie is a fine place for good boarders (and there are a lot of local

experts). Lots of natural gullies, hits and endless off-piste opportunities – including some adrenaline-pumping tree runs and knee-deep powder bowls – will keep freeriders of all abilities grinning from ear to ear. But there's a lot of traversing involved to get to many of the best runs – hard work in fresh snow and bumpy later. It's not a great place for freestylers – read 'Terrain parks'.

FOR CROSS-COUNTRY ★★★
Some possibilities
There are 10km of trails in the forest adjacent to the resort. In the Fernie area as a whole there are around 50km of tracks.

MOUNTAIN RESTAURANTS ★
One tiny sit-down hut
Lost Boys Cafe is a tiny self-service place in a fine position with great views at the top of Timber Bowl, with a basic, limited menu. It gets busy even when the mountain isn't. Bear's Den at the top of the Elk chair is an open-air fast-food kiosk. Naturally, most people eat at the base; read 'Eating out'.

SCHOOLS AND GUIDES ★★★★
Highly praised
Reporters have praised the school, which seems to achieve rapid progress. We're told that class sizes are often very small, making group lessons very good value.

There are several programmes to help you get the best out of the mountain. The Steep and Deep camp has had good feedback; it is a two-day programme (C$329) where you get technique tips while exploring steep terrain – a great way to get to know at least some of the mountain. We've had good sessions being guided by some of their instructor-guides. 'First Tracks' (from C$269 for three people) is a two-hour private lesson that gets you up the mountain at 8am, before the lifts are open to others.

FOR FAMILIES ★★★
Good day care centre
There's a day care centre in the Cornerstone Lodge – 'nice staff, but few activities to occupy older children', a reporter notes. There's an adventure park with cut-outs of bears and wolves. The ski school offers a 'family' private lesson option for up to two adults and three kids.

Good skiers who relish off-piste should consider treating themselves to some cat-skiing, where you ride snowcats instead of lifts; there are several operations in this area. We've had two or three

fabulous days at Island Lake Lodge, which does all-inclusive packages in a luxury lodge (spacious rooms, big lounge, hot tubs, bar, excellent food) 10km from Fernie, reached only by snowcat, in 7,000 acres of spectacular bowls and ridges. It has 26 rooms and three cats. In a day you might do 10 to 14 powder runs averaging 500m vertical, taking in all kinds of terrain from gentle open slopes to some very Alpine adventures. You can do single days on a standby basis. Fernie Wilderness Adventures is an alternative – three cats accessing 5,000 acres.

SNOWPIX.COM / CHRIS GILL

STAYING THERE

Chalets Canadian Powder Tours has one with an outdoor hot tub in town.
Hotels There's an adequate choice.

AT THE LIFT BASE

****Lizard Creek Lodge Best ski-in/ski-out condo hotel, with good rooms and a grand, high-ceilinged lounge; spa, outdoor pool and hot tub. We've enjoyed staying here in the past.

***Alpine Lodge Chalet on edge of resort – B&B but with good attached Japanese restaurant (read 'Eating out'). 'Simple, but wonderful hosts, fantastic hot tub and very reasonable rates.'

***Cornerstone Lodge Modern condo hotel with hot tub.

***Griz Inn Sport Hotel Condo hotel at foot of slopes. Pool.

***Slopeside Lodge At base of slope. Basic but convenient. Hot tub.

NOT AT THE LIFT BASE

****Best Western Plus Fernie Mountain Lodge Next to the golf course near town. Pool, hot tub, fitness room.

***Park Place Lodge Close to centre of town, lively pub; pool bizarrely set in main lobby.

Apartments Snow Creek Lodge is 'ski in and out, well equipped, very comfy, with hot tubs and pool in a lovely slope-side location'. Timberline Lodges are very comfortable condos a shuttle ride from the lifts.

EATING OUT ★★★☆☆
Better choice in town
At the base, Lizard Creek Lodge is an attractive option. Yamagoya in the Alpine Lodge does Japanese food ('wonderful – and it's not all raw fish');

there's another branch in town. Our traditional favourite, the Corner Pocket at the Griz Inn, has become the Rusty Edge under new management, and was one reporter's regular haunt this year – 'wholesome, tasty food and good value'.

In the town of Fernie, there are quite a few options, though some places we have liked in the past have closed. On our last visit we enjoyed an excellent simple dinner at the jolly, busy Brick House (all BC wines though, which means pricey). We and reporters have also enjoyed various Asian cuisines at Curry Bowl. El Guapo does good Tex-Mex served by 'efficient but friendly staff'. Nevados is also recommended this year.

APRES-SKI ★★★☆☆
Have a beer
When the lifts close, head for the Griz Bar above the Day Lodge. During the week, the resort bars are pretty quiet later on. In town, the bars of the Royal hotel are popular with locals, as is the Park Place Lodge Pub (with pool, table-football and big-screen TVs).

OFF THE SLOPES ★★☆☆☆
Get out and about
The Arts Station has two galleries, a theatre and craft studios, and there is a walking tour of historic Fernie – you buy a C$5 self-guided booklet from the visitor information centre or retailers. Watching the local ice hockey team, the Ghostriders, is 'well worth doing – good fun'. There's a pool and gym at the Aquatic Centre in town, and this season 'fat bike' rentals for winter riding on designated trails.

GETTING THERE

Air Calgary 305km/190 miles (3hr45)

TOURIST OFFICE

www.skifernie.com

SNOWPIX.COM / CHRIS GILL

Kicking Horse

One of Canada's newest resorts: only a few lifts, but great powder at the top, and a small village at the base

£170
RESORT PRICE INDEX

+ Great terrain for experts and some for adventurous intermediates
+ Big vertical served by a gondola
+ Splendid mountaintop restaurant

− Resort village still embryonic
− Gondola needs a mid-station to make the most of the mountain
− Few groomed intermediate runs

TOP 10 RATINGS

Extent	★★★
Fast lifts	★★★
Queues	★★★★
Snow	★★★★
Expert	★★★★
Intermediate	★★
Beginner	★★★
Charm	★★
Convenience	★★★★
Scenery	★★★

KEY FACTS

Resort	1190m
	3,900ft
Slopes	1190-2445m
	3,900-8,030ft
Lifts	5
Pistes	2,825 acres

Kicking Horse was developed from a small local hill in 2000, when a long gondola was built accessing two high, powder-filled bowls – previously heli-skiing country. There were great ambitions to turn it into a major resort. But of course things have moved much more slowly than planned.

In 2011 KH was sold to Resorts of the Canadian Rockies, owner of Fernie, Kimberley and other resorts, but there is no sign of any great transformation. The lift system and the 'village' at the base remain very limited. But the place is worth incorporating in a tour, or visiting for a day from Banff or Lake Louise.

THE RESORT

Eight miles from the logging/railway town of Golden, Kicking Horse is still embryonic – it has only two main lifts and a tiny base village. Daily Powder Express buses run from Banff and Lake Louise, at reasonable cost, and it makes a great day trip.

Village charm The small resort village at the lift base has several lodges, a few restaurants and bars, a ski shop and a general store. The town of Golden has no real appeal, but there is (slightly) more going on there.
Convenience Fine if you stay at the mountain – and why not?
Scenery The scenery is not without drama – especially from the top.

THE MOUNTAINS

The lower two-thirds of the hill is wooded, with trails cut in the usual style. The upper third is a mix of open and lightly wooded slopes spread over four separate bowls, with scores of ways down for experts through the open terrain, chutes and trees.
Slopes The eight-seat Golden Eagle Express gondola rises 1150m to the peak of Eagle's Eye; it does so in a single stage, which suits summer visitors but not skiers. It serves three bowls and CPR Ridge. To the left as you ride the gondola is Bowl Over. Or take the narrow Milly Goat Traverse along a ridge towards Super Bowl – the last part of this 'traverse' is a hike up to Terminator Peak, but you can opt for an easier walk/skate around the back.
 To the right of the gondola is Crystal Bowl; you can do laps here on the slow chair to the slightly higher peak of Blue Heaven, which also accesses Feuz Bowl. From Bowl Over, Super Bowl and Feuz Bowl – and if you go below the chair in Crystal Bowl – you have to make the full descent to the base. Two chairlifts serve the lower

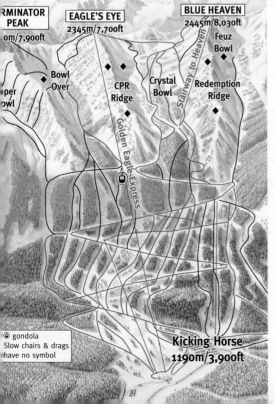

RMINATOR PEAK
om/7,900ft

EAGLE'S EYE
2345m/7,700ft

BLUE HEAVEN
2445m/8,030ft

Feuz Bowl

Bowl Over

CPR Ridge

Crystal Bowl

Redemption Ridge

Stairway to Heaven

Golden Eagle Express

per owl

Kicking Horse
1190m/3,900ft

⚉ gondola
Slow chairs & drags have no symbol

Beginners The beginner area at the base is fine, with easy slopes (but maybe poor snow) on the lower mountain for progression.

Snowboarding Freeriders will love this powder paradise.

Cross-country Dawn Mountain has loops of 30km including skating trails.

Mountain restaurants Strangely, this limited and non-swanky resort has Canada's best mountain restaurant at the top of the gondola, Eagle's Eye. Good food, service, ambience; great views. Reporters consistently agree. The Heaven's Door yurt in Crystal Bowl serves snacks. Most people lunch at the base; Slopeside Cafe does 'excellent wraps and stews'.

Schools and guides Reports are positive, classes often tiny.

Families A day-care facility at the base takes toddlers and infants. The school teaches children from the age of three.

STAYING THERE

There are smart, quite large condo-style lodges at the lift base. But we'd choose to stay in one of three much more captivating family-run places (each with about 10 rooms and outdoor hot tubs) a short walk away – described below.

Hotels The log-built Vagabond Lodge features a fabulous first-floor living room and comfortable, traditional-style rooms. Copper Horse Lodge has spacious but more austere rooms in modern styles. Winston Lodge has handmade wooden furniture, a welcoming sitting room with a floor-to-ceiling stone fireplace, a cosy, woody saloon, and a spa.

In Golden, a reader has enjoyed staying at the Auberge Kicking Horse B&B.

Apartments The Whispering Pines and the Selkirk townhomes have been recommended.

Eating out Corks in Copper Horse Lodge is under new management and is recommended – oysters, rabbit stew and elk steak. The Saloon in Winston Lodge does burgers, steaks, pizzas etc. In Golden, Kicking Horse Grill, 'bistro-style' Eleven22 and the out-of-town Cedar House are tipped. Eagle's Eye does dinner at weekends.

Après-ski There are bars at the base. In Golden, Rockwater and The Taps are lively bars.

Off the slopes There is snowmobiling, snowshoeing, tubing and an ice rink; plus a wolf centre near Golden.

↑ Unless you want to ski all the way to the base, laps on this lovely slope via the Stairway to Heaven chair are your only option

TANYA BOOTH

NEWS

2015/16: Two mid-mountain runs, Blaster and Tailspin, are being made more beginner-friendly, and there will be two new groomed pistes from the Stairway to Heaven chair. A couple of traverses are being widened.

LIFT PASSES

Prices in C$

Age	6-day
under 13	209
13 to 17	389
18 to 64	521
65 plus	419

Free Under 6

Beginner Rental, limited pass and tuition deals

Notes Prices are advance purchase online and include taxes; half-day pass available

TOURIST OFFICE

www.kickinghorse resort.com

runs that formed the original ski area here. There are free mountain tours.

Fast lifts Just the gondola.

Queues We've had reports of serious weekend queues for the gondola. During the week, though, it's quiet – 'some days, like having your own private hill', says a reporter.

Terrain park No sign of one yet.

Snow reliability The top slopes average 250 to 300 inches a year (a good but not spectacular record) and usually have light, dry powder. But the lower ones may have crud and thin cover and average only 100 inches a year; and with most of the runs you have to descend the lower slopes every time – a real drawback.

Experts From the top, you can go right into the gentle Crystal Bowl via an easy piste, or via serious chutes from CPR Ridge; or go left down pleasantly wooded single-diamond slopes into Bowl Over; or head to Super Bowl. The Stairway to Heaven chair serves further single-diamond wooded slopes. Feuz Bowl offers various challenges, not all of genuine double-diamond steepness, and gets tracked out less quickly. The lower half of the mountain has short black runs cut through the woods, some with big moguls. There is heli-skiing nearby.

Intermediates Adventurous types will have a fine time learning to play in the powder from Blue Heaven down to Crystal Bowl. Most of it is open, but you can head off into trees if you want to. The area of groomed cruising is increasing – there's a top-to-bottom 10km winding green run, but for now the timid are better off elsewhere.

Lake Louise

Stunning views and the biggest ski area in the Banff region, with some good places to stay but no real village

631

£160
RESORT PRICE INDEX

RATINGS

The mountains

Extent	★★★
Fast lifts	★★★★
Queues	★★★★
Terrain p'ks	★★★★
Snow	★★★
Expert	★★★★
Intermediate	★★★★
Beginner	★★★
Boarder	★★★
X-country	★★★★★
Restaurants	★★★
Schools	★★★★
Families	★★★★

The resort

Charm	★★★
Convenience	★
Scenery	★★★★
Eating out	★★
Après-ski	★★
Off-slope	★★★★

NEWS

2015/16: The upgraded Whitehorn Bistro will have an ambitious new chef.

2014/15: The famous après-ski dinner and torchlit descent at Whitehorn Lodge was revived. Snowmaking was improved.

KEY FACTS

Resort	1645m
	5,400ft

Sunshine, Norquay and Lake Louise	
Slopes	1630-2730m
	5,350-8,950ft
Lifts	28
Pistes	7,748 acres

Lake Louise only	
Slopes	1645-2635m
	5,400-8,650ft
Lifts	10
Pistes	4,200 acres

- ➕ Spectacular high-mountain scenery, in a largely unspoiled wilderness
- ➕ Large ski area by local standards
- ➕ Snowy Sunshine Village within reach (read the Banff chapter)
- ➕ Excellent, very scenic cross-country

- ➖ 'Village' is just a few hotels and shops, quiet in the evening
- ➖ Slopes a drive or bus ride away
- ➖ Snowfall record modest
- ➖ Can be very cold, and the chairlifts have no covers

If you care more for scenery than for après-ski action, Lake Louise is worth considering as your Rockies base. We've seen a few spectacular mountain views, and we reckon the view from the Fairmont Chateau Lake Louise hotel across frozen Lake Louise to the Victoria Glacier is one of the best.

Even if you prefer to stay in livelier Banff (read the separate chapter), you'll want to spend time at Louise. It can't compete with Sunshine Village for snow, but it's an interesting mountain, with a distant version of that stunning view.

THE RESORT

Lake Louise is small, but it's a resort of three distinct parts. First, there's the splendid lake itself overlooked by the huge Fairmont Chateau Lake Louise hotel. Then there's Lake Louise 'village' – a spacious collection of hotels, condos, petrol station and a few shops a couple of miles away in the valley. Finally, a mile or two across the valley, there's the lift base station.

Sunshine Village and Norquay ski areas (covered in our Banff chapter) are 45 minutes away by road. Buses (covered by the Tri-area lift pass) run only two days a week to each (on the days the ski school Club Ski Program goes there), so having a car helps. Bus trips also run to the more distant Kicking Horse and Panorama.

VILLAGE CHARM ★★★
Low key and relaxed
The 'village' has no focus other than a small shopping mall, but it's a quiet and relaxing place, even if the peace is disturbed by the occasional mile-long train. Up at the lake, it's all about the setting: the scenery provides the charm, and somehow the scale of the giant hotel seems appropriate.

CONVENIENCE ★
Lake or village, not slopes
Most lodging is around the 'village'. Buses run every half hour to the ski area. Staying up at the Chateau, or near it, just means a slightly longer bus ride. Taxis are said to be 'ridiculously expensive'.

SCENERY ★★★★
Splendid lakes and mountains
Lake Louise itself is in a spectacular setting beneath the Victoria Glacier. Tom Wilson, who discovered it in 1882, declared: 'As God is my judge, I never in all my exploration have seen such a matchless scene.' It can be appreciated from many rooms of the Chateau hotel on the lake shore. There are grand views from the ski area of other peaks and glaciers, including the Matterhorn lookalike, Mount Assiniboine.

THE MOUNTAINS

There's an attractive mixture of high, open slopes, low trails cut through forest and gladed slopes between the two. There are good, free guided tours daily. Some visitors find the signposting confusing. Louise is known for fiercely low temperatures; but we've generally escaped them.

EXTENT OF THE SLOPES ★★★
A wide variety
The ski area is a fair size by North American standards, but a good intermediate could ski the groomed trails in a day or two.

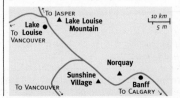

LIFT PASSES

Tri-area lift pass

Prices in C$

Age	6-day
under 13	162
13 to 17	444
18 to 64	498
65 plus	444

Free Under 6

Beginner Lift, lesson and rental package

Notes Covers transport between Banff, Lake Louise, Norquay and Sunshine Village; prices include 5% tax

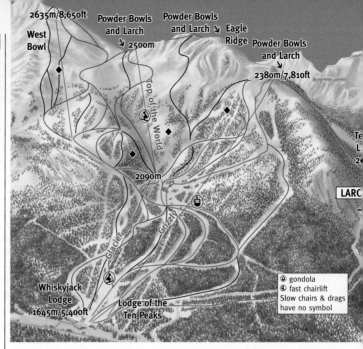

From the base area you have a choice of a fast quad to mid-mountain, followed by a six-pack to the top centre of the **Front Side** (or South Face), or a gondola direct to a slightly lower point off to the right side. From both, as elsewhere, there's a choice of green, blue or black runs (good for a group of mixed abilities who want to keep meeting up). Or you can stay on the lower part of the mountain using the chairs. From mid-mountain on the left, the long Summit draglift takes you to the high point of the area.

From here or the top chair you can go over the ridge and into the **Powder Bowls** – almost treeless, shady and mainly steep (though there are easy ways round the steep parts). From the top of the gondola, the Ptarmigan area is more wooded.

From below the bowls you can take the Paradise lift back to the top again or go on down to Temple Lodge, base station of the Ptarmigan chair to the main mountain and of a fast chair to the separate **Larch** area (just off our map). Its lift-served vertical is a modest 375m, but the sector has pretty wooded runs for all abilities. From Temple Lodge there's a long green path back to the base area.

FAST LIFTS ★★★★
Beware the cold rides
There is gondola and fast chair access to most of the slopes on the Front Side, and to Larch. The few slow lifts serve steep slopes where your descent may take some time, so the lift ride time is bearable. Reporters regularly complain of extremely cold rides.

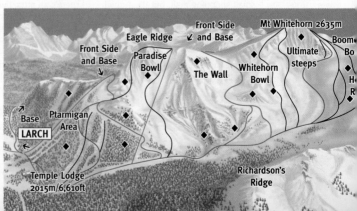

QUEUES ★★★★
Not during the week
Queues are rarely a problem midweek. But half of the area's visitors come for the day from cities such as Calgary, so there can be queues for some lifts at weekends and public holidays ('up to 45 minutes for the gondola on the Saturday'). Busy pistes can be a problem too.

TERRAIN PARKS ★★★★
Better every year
Once the snow is in good shape, an impressive park is found on the lower slopes. It is set out in clearly defined areas including progression and XL jumps, plus a snowcross and an airbag. The FIS (International Ski Federation) Snowboard Cross World Cup returned here last season.

SNOW RELIABILITY ★★★
Usually OK
Lake Louise gets an average of around 180 inches of snow a year on the Front Side, which is not a lot by North American standards, and nowhere near as much as Sunshine Village down the road (read the Banff chapter). The Front Side faces south-west, which is about the worst orientation for snow preservation; but the Powder Bowls face north-east, and Larch north. Snowmaking covers 40% of the pistes. Grooming is fine.

FOR EXPERTS ★★★★
Widespread pleasure
There are plenty of steep slopes – but bear in mind that powder is less likely here than in many other Canadian resorts. On the Front Side, as well as a score of marked black-diamond trails in and above the trees, there is the alluring West Bowl, reached from the Summit drag – a wide, open expanse of snow outside the area boundary to be explored with a guide.

Inside the boundary, the Powder Bowls area on the Back Side offers countless black mogul/powder runs, though there is no great variation in character. From the Summit drag, you can drop into The Ultimate Steeps area if it is open, directly behind the peak – a row of exceptional chutes almost 1km long. Starting from the blue Boomerang trail, you can also access much tamer, wide, open slopes in Boomerang Bowl.

The Top of the World six-pack takes you to the very popular Paradise Bowl/ Eagle Ridge area, also served by its own triple chair on the Back Side – there are endless variants here, ranging from comfortably steep single diamonds to very challenging double diamonds. The seriously steep slope served by the Ptarmigan quad chair has great gladed terrain and is a good place to escape the crowds.

The Larch area has some steep double-diamond stuff in the trees. And with good snow-cover, the open

LAKE LOUISE SKI RESORT / CHRIS MOSELEY

From the Larch area you get a good view of the chutes and glades accessed by the slow Ptarmigan chairlift →

snowfields at the top are great for those with the energy to hike up.

Heli-skiing day trips are available to bases outside the National Park.

FOR INTERMEDIATES ★★★★
Some good cruising
Almost half the runs are classified as intermediate. But from the top of the Front Side the blue runs down are little more than paths in places, and there are very few blues or greens in the Powder Bowls. Once you get part-way down the Front Side the blues are much more interesting. And when groomed, the Men's and Ladies' Downhill black runs are great fast cruises on the lower half of the mountain. Juniper, in the same area, is a varied cruise. Meadowlark is a beautiful treelined single-black run to the base area, curling away from the lifts – to find it from the Grizzly Express gondola, first follow the Eagle Meadows green.

The Larch area has some short but ideal intermediate runs – and reporters have enjoyed the natural bumps of the aptly named blue run, Rock Garden ('never had so much fun').

The adventurous should try the blue Boomerang run – which starts with a short side-step up from the top of the Summit drag – and also some of the ungroomed terrain in the Powder Bowls reachable from that run.

FOR BEGINNERS ★★★
Some long greens
Lake Louise offers first-timers a package that includes a beginner pass with tuition and equipment rental.

There is a decent nursery area near the base served by three moving carpets. You progress to the gentle, wide Wiwaxy (a designated 'learning area'), Pinecone Way and the slightly more difficult Deer Run or Eagle Meadows. The greens in the Powder Bowls and in the Larch area are worth trying for the views, though some do contain slightly steep pitches and can get busy.

FOR BOARDERS ★★★
Something for everyone
Lake Louise is a great mountain for freeriders, with plenty of challenging terrain in the bowls and glades. Beginners will have fun on the Front Side's blue and green runs. But beware of the vicious Summit button lift (top left looking at the trail map). Also avoid the long, very gentle green run through the woods from Larch back to base. This is flat in places and a nightmare for boarders. Freestylers will enjoy the varied terrain park.

FOR CROSS-COUNTRY ★★★★★
High in quality and quantity
It's a very good area for cross-country, with around 80km of groomed trails in the National Park – plenty of scenic stops needed. There are 14km of excellent trails in the local area and at Lake Louise itself. An alternative is the secluded Emerald Lake Lodge, 40km away and with some lovely trails.

MOUNTAIN RESTAURANTS ★★★
Improving facilities
There are now two table-service places – the bistro at Whitehorn Lodge on the

LAKE LOUISE SKI RESORT / CHRIS MOSELEY

There are good beginner slopes at the base, with the impressive lodges on hand ↓

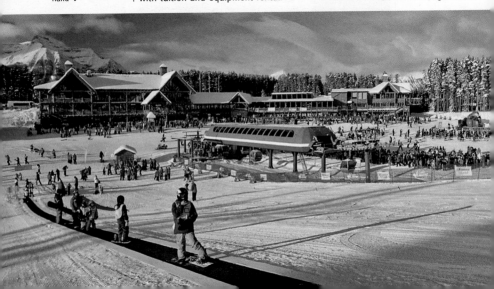

front side, which in recent years had not been operating in winter, and the long-established Sawyer's Nook in Temple Lodge behind the hill – but reports say the latter is still over-busy at times.

Most people eat at the base, where there are big-scale facilities. The Lodge of the Ten Peaks is a hugely impressive log-built affair with various eating, drinking and lounging options.

SCHOOLS AND GUIDES ★★★★
All reports positive
All past reports are positive for both adults' and children's classes, and a recent visitor was enthusiastic: 'The school is well run and the instructors are extremely professional. Probably the friendliest group of instructors we have ever come across. Excellent.' Read the Banff chapter for details of the excellent three-day, three-mountain Club Ski Program taking you to Sunshine and Norquay too. The First Tracks programme gets you on the hill half an hour early, with instruction.

FOR FAMILIES ★★★★
Good facilities
The resort has good school and childcare facilities that have been praised by reporters. Parents are lent free pagers too. The Minute Maid Wilderness Adventure Park is a kids' learning area at the base. The school gets good reviews and offers a fun programme for teenagers.

STAYING THERE

You might like to consider a two-centre holiday, combining Lake Louise with, say, Banff or Kicking Horse.
Hotels Summer is the peak season here. Prices are much lower in winter.
★★★★★Fairmont Chateau Lake Louise Huge old place with 550 rooms, countless restaurants and stunning views over frozen Lake Louise to the glacier beyond; shops, pool, hot tub, spa, steam room.
★★★★Post Small, relaxed Relais & Châteaux place in the village, with excellent restaurant (huge wine list), Stübli fondue restaurant, Outpost Pub, pool, hot tub, steam room. Avoid rooms on the railway side of the building.
★★★Deer Lodge Charming old hotel next to the Chateau. Small rooms, but helpful staff and good food. Rooftop hot tub.

★★★Lake Louise Inn Cheaper option in the village, with pool, hot tub and steam. One recent reporter has stayed there nine times.
Apartments Some are available but local shopping is limited. The Baker Creek resort is a popular retreat for a traditional 'log cabin, log fire, isolation and wildlife' experience.

EATING OUT ★★★★★
Limited choice
The Post hotel's restaurant has repeatedly impressed us and reporters with its ambitious food and excellent service. We and they have also enjoyed the simpler food and cosy ambience of its Outpost Pub. The Chateau offers half a dozen different dining experiences, including the top-notch Fairview Dining Room. Readers also like the Timberwolf Cafe (Italian) at the Lake Louise Inn, the Mountain restaurant (pasta, burgers) and Village Grill (Western/Chinese menu) for cheaper options.

APRES-SKI ★★★★★
Lively at teatime, quiet later
We're pleased to hear that après-ski dinners plus torchlit descents have been reinstated at Whitehorn Lodge. At close of play there is some action in the main base lodge, but the hub is the Kokanee Kabin, which has live music most weekends, a terrace and an outdoor fire. Later on, things are fairly quiet. Try the Glacier Saloon, in the Chateau hotel, the Explorer's Lounge in the Lake Louise Inn or the Outpost Pub in the Post hotel.

OFF THE SLOPES ★★★★
Beautiful scenery
Lake Louise makes a lovely, peaceful place to stay for someone who enjoys the great outdoors. The lake itself makes a stunning setting for walks, snowshoeing, cross-country skiing and ice skating. Reporters highly recommend the dog sledding and the Wilson Icefield discovery tour – a helicopter flight, snowshoe walk and lunch ('BBQ with superb steaks'). There are lots of attractions around Banff too (read the Banff chapter).

Lake Louise is near one end of the Columbia Icefields Parkway, a three-hour drive to Jasper through spectacular national parks.

GETTING THERE

Air Calgary 200km/ 125 miles (2hr15)

TOURIST OFFICE

www.skilouise.com
www.SkiBig3.com

Revelstoke

Recently developed resort with a ready-made reputation for steep terrain and deep snow; shame it's so remote and isolated

£155
RESORT PRICE INDEX

TOP 10 RATINGS

Extent	★★★
Fast lifts	★★★★★
Queues	★★★★★
Snow	★★★★
Expert	★★★★★
Intermediate	★★
Beginner	★★
Charm	★★
Convenience	★★★
Scenery	★★★★

KEY FACTS

Resort	510m
	1,680ft
Slopes	510-2225m
	1,680-7,300ft
Lifts	5
Pistes	3,121 acres

NEWS

2014/15: Glading was carried out to improve tree skiing.

636

➕ Fabulous steep, ungroomed terrain and an impressive snow record

➕ North America's biggest vertical, with some epic black runs going from top to bottom

➕ Great cat- and heli-skiing next door

➕ Fine views over the Columbia valley

➖ Not much intermediate groomed terrain

➖ No snowmaking on main slopes

➖ Very remote location – awkward to get to from the UK

➖ Resort base village still tiny, and Revelstoke town a drive away

Revelstoke has long been known as a heli-skiing base, but it became a ski resort for the rest of us only in 2007/8. A gondola and two fast chairs have transformed its little local ski hill into a serious resort with a vertical of over 1700m – the biggest in North America.

The resort claims over 3,000 acres of terrain – more than many Canadian and American rivals (notably Fernie and Jackson Hole) – but the quantity of defined trails is not huge. More than most places, this is a resort where you need to be happy in the trees to spend a long stay here. You might want to combine it with Kicking Horse and/or Lake Louise, both on the way from Calgary airport.

THE RESORT

Revelstoke is remote. Getting there from the UK involves two flights to get to Kelowna or Kamloops followed by a three-hour drive. Or it's a drive of five hours from Calgary, or six hours from Vancouver – and that's assuming good weather.

There is an embryonic village at the base of the slopes – one smart condo hotel, a restaurant, a coffee shop, a pub, a sports shop. Five minutes down the hill, there's a wider choice of lodging and restaurants in Revelstoke itself, a working town between the dammed Columbia river and the Trans-Canada Highway.

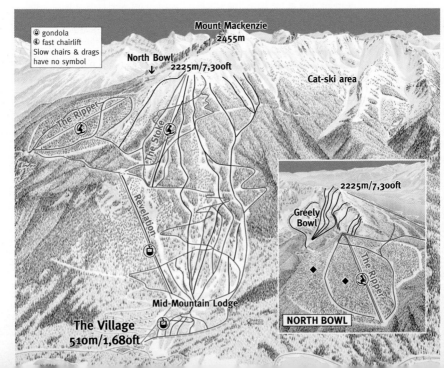

⚲ gondola
⚳ fast chairlift
Slow chairs & drags have no symbol

Mount Mackenzie
2455m

North Bowl
↓
2225m/7,300ft

Cat-ski area

The Ripper

The Stoke

Revelation

2225m/7,300ft

Greely Bowl

The Ripper

◆

◆

NORTH BOWL

Mid-Mountain Lodge

The Village
510m/1,680ft

LIFT PASSES

Prices in C$

Age	6-day
under 13	174
13 to 18	389
19 to 64	536
65 plus	389

Free Under 6
Beginner No deals
Notes Prices include sales tax; reductions for booking online

IAN HOUGHTON

There's little more to the base area than you can see here – small isn't it? ↓

Village charm At the lift base, the Village is quite polished, but it is not yet a village. The town developed on the back of forestry, mining and the railroad. There are some 'historic' brick and wooden buildings, but overall it is a rather plain, down to earth place.

Convenience The Village could not be more convenient: the access gondola is mere yards from your door. Town shuttle-buses are regular and reliable, but Village residents going out on the town in the evening are reliant on the hotel shuttle (C$5 round trip) or taxis.

Scenery There are wide views from the upper slopes over the Columbia valley and snow-capped mountains beyond.

THE MOUNTAINS

A two-stage gondola takes you from the Village to mid-mountain, from which you can reach both fast quad chairs. Be prepared for extreme cold (we once got −41°C with wind chill on a December visit).

Slopes The lift-served terrain puts Revelstoke among the biggest Canadian resorts (leaving massive Whistler aside). As we've said in our introductory summary, the quantity of defined trails is not huge, but there are top-to-bottom runs of exceptional length, three of them classified black. There is cat-skiing right next door, and vast amounts of heli-skiing on hand.

Fast lifts All three main lifts are fast.
Queues We have no reports of queues, and both we and readers have often skied trails alone.
Terrain parks A small rail park is set up during the season depending on snow conditions.
Snow reliability They claim 360 to 540 inches a year; an average mid-range figure of 450 is up there with the best. But warm weather is not unknown, and the lower slopes can suffer (and may be closed). There's snowmaking only on the lower slopes.
Experts Experts are in their element here. On skier's left, there are exceptionally long top-to-bottom black runs (not exceptionally steep), which are often groomed. On skier's right, reached by traversing and possibly hiking from the top chairlift, is the entirely ungroomed North Bowl. This has excellent steep open slopes at the top giving way to gentler woods at the bottom; for many of us the major challenge, though, is access through the band of cliffs at the top. There are about 10 identified ways in, ranging from merely tricky Meet the Neighbours to much more scary options, some now marked on the trail map as double-diamond runs.

Between the long blacks and North Bowl are several big areas of glades with nicely spaced trees. And there are

↑ North Bowl (top left) has good expert slopes but is tricky to get into because of the cliff band. The long green meandering through the trees and crossing other runs goes from top to bottom

REVELSTOKE MOUNTAIN RESORT

further wide areas of glades served by the Ripper chair, below North Bowl. The ski school runs affordable day and half-day Inside Tracks groups, to show you terrain to suit your ability – exactly what you need on this hill.

Intermediates Most blues are steepish and suit adventurous intermediates best. The Ripper chair accesses the easiest blues. And there's a 15km-long blue/green run from top to bottom. But the intermediate groomed terrain doesn't add up to much (the claimed 45% gives a misleading impression).

Beginners Moving carpets serve small beginner areas at the bottom and at the gondola mid-station. There are long, winding green runs from mid-mountain and the very top.

Snowboarding There's fabulous freeriding but lots of flats, especially getting to and from North Bowl.

Cross-country 26km of groomed trails.

Mountain restaurants The self-service mid-mountain Revelation Lodge serves OK food but gets packed. At the base pick up fresh baked goods, soups and chillies and gossip with the ski patrollers at La Baguette; for table-service, it's the smart Rockford restaurant.

Schools and guides The ski school aims to help people progress from groomed runs to the backcountry. And it runs groups to show you the terrain – read 'Experts'.

Families This is far from an ideal family resort.

TOURIST OFFICE

www.revelstoke
mountainresort.com

STAYING THERE

Hotels On our last visit we enjoyed Sutton Place, at the lift base – perfect location, exceptionally smart and well-equipped rooms, a good pool and hot tubs – endorsed by readers ('superb'). In town, we've enjoyed the friendly Courthouse Inn – great breakfast – and fancy a stay at the 'historic' Regent. Reporters have tipped Swiss Chalet motel ('comfortable, very reasonably priced'), the Inn on the River, with a panoramic rooftop hot tub, Hillcrest (slightly out of town, Selkirk-Tangiers Heliski base) and the Best Western Plus which has its own shuttle-bus.

Eating out At the Village, the Rockford is a smooth modern place doing grills and wok dishes. In town, 112 at the Regent is polished and intimate, with good gourmet food at tables or at the bar. Woolsey Creek is another gourmet option. In contrast, the Village Idiot is a lively pub-style joint doing good 'cheap' burgers and gigantic pizzas. Kawakubo has a super-high reputation for sushi. The 'good value' Paramjit's Kitchen serves Indian and German cuisine – an unusual combination.

Après-ski The Rockford at the lift base is popular. Good downtown bars are the Village Idiot, the Last Drop (sofas; in Powder Springs Inn) and River City (music, pool; in the Regent).

Off the slopes The Aquatic Centre offers pools, hot tubs, sauna and steam room. There's also tubing, snowmobiling and dog sledding.

Silver Star

Car-free, purpose-built village designed to resemble a Victorian-era mining town, with slopes for all standards

£150
RESORT PRICE INDEX

TOP 10 RATINGS
Extent	★★★
Fast lifts	★★★★
Queues	★★★★★
Snow	★★★★
Expert	★★★★
Intermediate	★★★
Beginner	★★★★
Charm	★★★
Convenience	★★★★★
Scenery	★★★

NEWS

2015/16: There are plans to develop more gladed terrain. Free winter mountain biking is being added to the lift pass. The Saloon bar and restaurant is being renovated.

2014/15: Deer Park glades – 200 acres of patrolled tree skiing – was added to the Vance Creek side. The snowcross course moved to Vance Creek from Putnam Creek.

KEY FACTS
Resort	1610m
	5,280ft
Slopes	1155-1915m
	3,790-6,280ft
Lifts	12
Pistes	3,270 acres

- ➕ Cute, colourful village
- ➕ Very family-friendly
- ➕ Some good runs for all abilities
- ➕ Excellent cross-country skiing

- ➖ Tiny village; very quiet at night
- ➖ Limited choice of accommodation (but some high-quality condos)
- ➖ Ski area not huge

This quiet, family-friendly resort has a tiny traffic-free centre resembling a 19th-century mining town. The ski area has slopes to suit everyone but it is small, so we suggest you combine a stay here with one at another BC resort such as Big White, Sun Peaks, Revelstoke or Whistler.

THE RESORT

Silver Star is a small, purpose-built resort right on the slopes.
Village charm The village has brightly painted Victorian-style buildings with wooden sidewalks and faux gas lights. It's a bit Disneyesque but works well.
Convenience The centre is compact and car-free. Ski-in/ski-out chalets are dotted in the trees too.
Scenery The views from Silver Star's summit are over gently rolling hills.

THE MOUNTAINS

The mountain has trees going right to the top and four main linked sectors.
Slopes The Vance Creek area has mainly easy intermediate runs served by the Comet six-pack, which starts below the village. From there you can ski down to the Silver Woods high-speed quad, which serves an area of mainly intermediate slopes and glades. The top of the Comet chair links to the Attridge area, which has a mix of easy runs and short, steep

blacks served by its own slow chair too. It also links to the Putnam Creek sector on the back side, which has lots of steep blacks and easier blues, all served by a fast quad. There's night skiing on Friday and Saturday.
Fast lifts There's one for each sector.
Queues During the week, no problems. But on busy weekends you may have to wait for the Comet chair and the chair in Putnam Creek (both of which had reliability problems last season, making things worse, says a reporter).
Terrain parks The 16-acre Rockstar park on Vance Creek is excellent for expert, intermediate and beginner freestylers. There's also a snowcross off the Milky Way run.
Snow reliability Silver Star gets an average of 275 inches a year – not in the top flight but not far off.
Experts Putnam Creek has a dense network of single- and double-black diamond runs plunging through the trees, many of them mogul runs. The runs to the left as you ride up the chair are north-facing and keep their

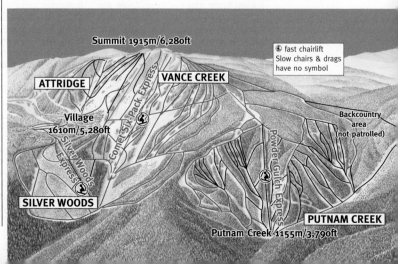

The Chute →

The Face ←

↑ As well as the cute little village centre, there are a lot of chalets blending in with the trees

SILVER STAR MOUNTAIN RESORT

LIFT PASSES

Prices in C$

Age	6-day
under 13	249
13 to 18	383
19 to 64	464
65 plus	396
Free Under 6	
Beginner Limited pass	
Note Prices include taxes	

TOURIST OFFICE
www.skisilverstar.com

snow well. There are some good short blacks in the Attridge area, too. Heli-skiing is available.

Intermediates Vance Creek has mainly easy cruising runs. Silver Woods has lovely, gentle runs cut through the trees and easy blues among the trees themselves. Putnam Creek also has excellent blue cruising. Good intermediates will appreciate the groomed black runs (they groom at least two each night – look on the boards for which ones).

Beginners There's a good nursery slope area (The Zone) by the village with a moving carpet and long easy green runs to move on to.

Snowboarding Intermediates will enjoy the blue runs and glades. But the steep bump runs in Putnam Creek are tough on a snowboard. And there are some flat areas (including the way to Putnam Creek).

Cross-country They claim 'The Best Nordic Skiing in North America' and there's over 100km of trails.

Mountain restaurants The small atmospheric table-service Paradise Camp on Putnam Creek is popular and serves good stews and soups.

Schools and guides A recent visitor's children 'improved by leaps and bounds; the instructors made the lessons fun'; and the two parents were able to 'tidy up our skills. I'd return to Silver Star for the ski school alone.'

Families Star Kids takes children aged 18 months to five years.

STAYING THERE

It is mainly specialist North American operators that come here, such as Frontier Ski and Ski Independence.

Hotels A past reporter liked the Bulldog Hotel but thought the rooms fairly basic. The Vance Creek, Lord Aberdeen and Pinnacles are other options. The Samesun Backpackers Hostel has regular rooms and dorms.

Apartments We stayed in a huge, luxurious condo with private hot tub in the Snowbird Lodge, and loved it – as have reporters. It and Firelight Lodge (ask for a condo overlooking the skating pond and tubing hill) are the best in town – both ski-in/ski-out. Other tips: Chilcoot Lodge, Creekside, Grandview and Pinnacles.

Eating out Reporters' favourite is the Bulldog Grand Cafe (Asian-influenced food). Other tips: the Silver Grill Steak & Chop House for fine dining, Long John's Pub with silver-mining theme decor. Isidore's claims to offer 'Swiss with a twist'. Bugaboos Bakery Café is good for breakfast – and for 'good home-cooked chilli and Thai curry'.

Après-ski It's very quiet. But the Saloon, Den and Lord John's Pub may be lively and have live entertainment.

Off the slopes There's a natural ice rink on a lake, tubing, snowshoeing, winter mountain biking, snowmobiling, bowling and sleigh rides; the first four are free with a lift pass (as is cross-country skiing).

Sun Peaks

Attractive car-free village at the foot of three linked mountains with varied slopes, including some unusual easy groomed glade runs

£155
RESORT PRICE INDEX

TOP 10 RATINGS

Extent	★★★
Fast lifts	★★
Queues	★★★★★
Snow	★★★★
Expert	★★★
Intermediate	★★★★
Beginner	★★★★
Charm	★★★
Convenience	★★★★
Scenery	★★★

KEY FACTS

Resort	1255m
	4,120ft
Slopes	1200-2080m
	3,930-6,820ft
Lifts	11
Pistes	4,270 acres

LIFT PASSES

Prices in C$

Age	6-day
under 13	269
13 to 18	430
19 to 64	538
65 plus	430

Free Under 6

Beginner Lesson deals including lift and rentals

Note Prices include taxes

- Great terrain for early intermediates
- Excellent glades
- Slopes very quiet during the week
- Good for families

- Village may be too small and quiet for some tastes
- Ski area modest by Alpine standards (but big by Canadian ones)

Sun Peaks has a friendly, attractive small village that has been developed since the mid-1990s. And last season's ski area expansion means that Sun Peaks is now the second biggest ski area in Canada – only Whistler is bigger. But that doesn't make it big by Alpine standards. The terrain is nicely varied but a keen skier could cover the groomed trails in a couple of days. We still suggest combining it with a stay at another resort such as Whistler.

THE RESORT

Until 1993 Sun Peaks was Tod Mountain, a local hill for the residents of nearby Kamloops. Since then the ski area has been expanded, and a small, attractive resort village has developed. There are regular transfers to other resorts such as Whistler – making a two-centre trip easy.

Village charm The low-rise pastel-coloured buildings have a vaguely Tirolean feeling to them. It's a pleasant place to stroll around and very family-friendly. The traffic-free main street is lined with lodgings, restaurants and shops, including a smart art gallery.

Convenience Much of the accommodation is ski-in/ski-out.

Scenery The slopes are pleasantly wooded and Mt Tod's modest summit gives views over gently rolling terrain.

THE MOUNTAINS

There are three linked mountains, but the links to and from Mt Morrisey from the other two are roundabout and flattish. Free guided tours are run twice a day (9.15am and 1pm), and you can ski for free with Nancy Greene (former Olympic champion, Canada's Female Athlete of the 20th Century and a Canadian senator) on Saturday and Sunday at 1pm. Don't miss it – she's great fun. At the top of each main lift there is a board showing which pistes in that area have been groomed. Each day at least one black piste is groomed.

Slopes Sun Peaks has 4,270 acres of skiable terrain – in Canada, only Whistler is bigger. But it's not huge by Alpine standards.

One lift goes from the centre of the village to mid-mountain on the resort's original ski hill, Mt Tod. This has mainly black runs, but there are easier blues and greens, too. Many of Mt Tod's steepest runs are served only by the slow Burfield quad, which takes over 20 minutes to get to the top and is frequently the subject of complaint by reporters (there's a mid-station that allows you to ski the top runs only). You can access the new Gil area from the top of the Burfield quad. The Sundance area – also reached from the village centre – has mainly blue and green cruising runs. Mt Morrisey is reached by a long green run from the top of Sundance and has a delightful network of easy blue runs with trees left uncut in the trails, effectively making them groomed glade runs that even early intermediates can try. There

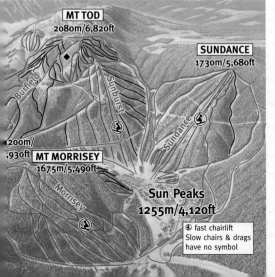

MT TOD
2080m/6,820ft

SUNDANCE
1730m/5,680ft

1200m/
,930ft

MT MORRISEY
1675m/5,490ft

Sun Peaks
1255m/4,120ft

🚡 fast chairlift
Slow chairs & drags
have no symbol

NEWS

2015/16: Additional runs will be opened in both the Gil and Morrisey areas. A new ice rink will be built capable of hosting national hockey league games as well as allowing recreational skating.

2014/15: The ski area was expanded to include the Gil area off the back of Mt Tod, with a black run and two gladed runs. And two new black runs were opened on Mt Morrisey. This development added almost 600 acres and made Sun Peaks the second biggest ski area in Canada.

TOURIST OFFICE

www.sunpeaksresort.com

are also great gladed areas for good intermediates and experts to play in where the trees are tighter (16 of them marked on the trail map – mainly on Mt Tod and Sundance).

Fast lifts The three distinct sectors are each served by a high-speed quad. The other lifts are painfully slow.

Queues Weekdays are usually very quiet; it's only at peak weekends that you might find short queues.

Terrain parks The park has advanced, intermediate and beginner areas, plus snowmaking. But there is no half-pipe.

Snow reliability Sun Peaks gets an average snowfall of 220 inches a year: not in the top league but better than some. The snow can suffer on the lower part of Mt Tod's south-facing slopes, especially later in the season.

Experts Mt Tod has most of the steep terrain, and you can ski some good (but short) steep and gladed runs without descending to the bottom by riding the Burfield quad from its mid-station and the Crystal and Elevation chairs. Some of the blacks on Mt Morrisey (such as Static Cling) have steep mogul sections, too.

Intermediates This is great terrain for early intermediates: there are the easy and charming groomed glades of Mt Morrisey, lovely swooping blues on Sundance and the long 5 Mile run from Mt Tod. More adventurous intermediates can also tackle the easier glades (such as Cahilty) and blacks (such as Peek-A-Boo).

Beginners There are nursery slopes right in the village centre, with long easy greens to progress to.

Snowboarding Boarders can explore the whole mountain. But there are flat greens to and from Mt Morrisey.

Cross-country 34km of groomed trails and 17km of backcountry trails.

Mountain restaurants Sunburst Lodge

is the only option and it gets busy; it is renowned for its cinnamon buns. It's easy to return to the village for lunch.

Schools and guides Past reports have been good, but we lack recent ones. As well as standard lessons, there are Super Groups (maximum of three people), specialist camps and freestyle sessions for children and teenagers.

Families The Sundance Kids Centre takes children from 18 months and the ski school children from three years.

STAYING THERE

Hotels Our favourites are Sun Peaks Grand (was Delta Sun Peaks until 2014) in the village centre with an 'excellent' outdoor pool and hot tub and the nearby Nancy Greene's Cahilty Lodge with indoor and outdoor hot tubs. Both are endorsed by reporters.

Apartments The Residences at the Sun Peaks Grand are luxurious, ski-in/ski-out and central. Fireside Lodge, Crystal Forest and McGillivray Creek condos have been tipped.

Eating out For a small resort, there's a good choice of restaurants. Reader tips include Powder Hounds, Steakhouse ('top-quality ribs and steaks, but need to book'), Bella Italia, Oya (Japanese), Bottom's ('great food') and Mantles (in the Sun Peaks Grand). Cahilty Creek Bar and Grill and Voyageur are other options.

Après-ski It's quiet. Bottom's and Masa's are the main après-ski bars. Morrisey's in the Sun Peaks Grand is supposed to be like a British pub. At weekends The Club in the Grand can get lively. The fondue evenings with torchlit descents are 'lots of fun'.

Off the slopes There's skating, tubing, tobogganing, snowmobiling, bungee trampolining, rides on piste-bashers, dog sledding, sleigh rides, snowshoeing and swimming.

PAUL MORRISON

Whistler

North America's biggest area of slopes, with terrain to suit every standard; plus a big, purpose-built, largely car-free village

£180
RESORT PRICE INDEX

RATINGS

The mountains

Extent	★★★★
Fast lifts	★★★★★
Queues	★★
Terrain p'ks	★★★★★
Snow	★★★★
Expert	★★★★★
Intermediate	★★★★★
Beginner	★★★
Boarder	★★★★★
X-country	★★★
Restaurants	★★
Schools	★★★★★
Families	★★★★

The resort

Charm	★★★
Convenience	★★★★
Scenery	★★★
Eating out	★★★★★
Après-ski	★★★★
Off-slope	★★★

NEWS

2015/16: There are plans to give the Rendezvous Lodge a C$5.4 million upgrade with more seating capacity and more food options. Whistler has introduced a smoke-free policy so smoking won't be allowed anywhere on Whistler-Blackcomb property, including the mountain, lifts and base areas near the lifts.

2014/15: The 26-year-old Whistler Village gondola was replaced by a new one with eight-seater cabins and increased capacity. Hands-free lift passes (rare in North America) were introduced. Four blue runs in the Crystal Ridge chair area on Blackcomb were widened or improved.

+ North America's biggest ski area

+ Excellent combination of high open bowls and woodland trails

+ Good snow record

+ Almost Alpine scenery

+ Attractive modern village, purpose-built with car-free central areas

+ Good range of village restaurants and lively après-ski

– Proximity to Pacific Ocean means a lot of cloudy weather, and rain at resort level is not unusual

– Inadequate lift system; queues can be a big problem at peak times

– Overcrowded runs also a problem

– Mountain restaurants are overcrowded and mostly no more than functional

– Resort restaurants over-busy, too

Whistler is unlike any other resort in North America. In some respects – the scale, the high bowls and glaciers, the scenery, the crowds – it is more like an Alpine resort. But like most resorts on the western side of North America, it offers the advantages of usually excellent snow and a lot of woodland runs too.

All things considered, the mountain is about the best that North America has to offer, and for us a visit here is always a highlight of the season. But we'll admit that we are generally lucky with the weather, and haven't had to put up with much rain at resort level – a real hazard (as 2015 visitors found; last season was warm and wet, with frequent heavy rain). And we try to time our visits to avoid peak periods and weekends, and therefore the worst of the crowds.

THE RESORT

Whistler Village sits at the foot of its two mountains, Whistler and Blackcomb, a scenic 135km drive from Vancouver on Canada's west coast.

Whistler started as a locals' ski area in 1966 at Creekside and is celebrating its 50th anniversary in 2016. Whistler Village, a 10-minute bus ride away, was developed in the late 1970s; Upper Village – around the base of Blackcomb Mountain and a 10-minute walk from Whistler Village – was started in the 1980s.

VILLAGE CHARM ★★★
High rise but tasteful
The three main centres are all traffic-free. The architecture is varied and, for a purpose-built resort, quite tasteful – but it is all a bit urban, with lots of blocks approaching 10 storeys high. There are also many chalet-style apartments on the hillsides. Some reporters find the central Village Square area noisy in the early hours.

CONVENIENCE ★★★★
Take your pick
The Peak 2 Peak gondola opened in 2008 and made Whistler Village, Upper Village and Creekside all equally convenient places to stay – from all you can easily access both mountains by taking a maximum of three lifts.

Whistler Village – by far the biggest and liveliest – has a gondola to each mountain. A pedestrian bridge over an access road links the main centre to newer Whistler Village North (further from the lifts), making a huge car-free area of streets lined with shops, condos, bars and restaurants.

Upper Village is much smaller and quieter. So is Creekside, which was revamped and expanded for the 2010 Winter Olympics.

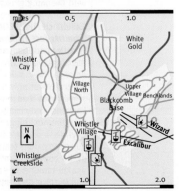

LIFT PASSES

Prices in C$	
Age	6-day
under 13	329
13 to 18	559
19 to 64	657
65 plus	591
Free Under 7	

Beginner Lift and lesson deal

Notes Prices include sales tax and are online advance-purchase price

There is a free bus between central Whistler and Upper Village, but it can be just as quick to walk. Some lodging is a long way from the centre and means taking buses (not free) or taxis. Some hotels have free buses, which will take you to and pick you up from restaurants and nightlife.

SCENERY ★★★☆☆
Almost Alpine

There are splendid views of the deep Fitzsimmons Creek valley from both mountains, and especially from the Peak 2 Peak gondola, which goes right across it – the views from the two cabins with glass floors are particularly spectacular (these cabins are painted silver rather than red). The upper slopes give good views to coastal sounds, high open bowls, glaciers and ridges.

THE MOUNTAINS

The mountains offer an excellent combination of high, open bowls and sheltered forest runs.

Many reporters enthuse about the mountain host service and the 'go slow' patrol – some find the latter over-zealous, but crowded slopes, especially on the runs home, mean they're often needed; we approve.

Signposting is generally good. Every year some reporters complain about inaccuracies on the trail map; most seem to be happy with it though. A separate Wonder Routes map has suggested tours with different themes – such as powder stashes, steeps, families and panoramic views. There's a special kids' trail map too.

One thing that annoys most people is the crazily early closing times of the lifts – 3pm or 3.30 till late February, with the top lifts closing even earlier.

EXTENT OF THE SLOPES ★★★★☆
The biggest in North America

Whistler and Blackcomb together form the biggest area of slopes in North America. They claim almost 8,200 acres (comfortably more than the 7,300 acres that the new Park City/Canyons area claims; and 50% more than the next biggest, Vail and Big Sky). Last season's Schrahe report (see our piste extent feature near the front of the book) puts Whistler's pistes at 254km (around 10% more than Vail and Big Sky and the sixth biggest in

the world, on a par with Alpine ski areas such as Zermatt-Cervinia and the Milky Way).

Whistler Mountain is accessed from Whistler Village by a gondola, which rises over 1100m to Roundhouse Lodge at mid-mountain. Or you can use two fast quads (which reporters say don't always run).

Runs down through the trees fan out from the gondola: cruises to the Emerald and Big Red chairs and longer runs to the gondola mid-station.

From Roundhouse you can see the jewel in Whistler's crown – magnificent open bowls, served by the fast Peak and Harmony chairs. The bowl beyond Harmony is served by the Symphony fast quad. The bowls are mostly go-anywhere terrain for experts, but there are groomed trails, so anyone can appreciate the views. Roundhouse is the departure point of the Peak 2 Peak gondola to Blackcomb.

A six-seat gondola from Creekside also accesses Whistler Mountain.

Access to **Blackcomb** from Whistler Village is by an eight-seat gondola, followed by a fast quad. From the base of Blackcomb you take two consecutive fast quads up to the main Rendezvous restaurant – departure point of the Peak 2 Peak gondola. From Rendezvous, on skier's right is great cruising terrain and the Glacier Express quad up to the Horstman Glacier area; on skier's left are steeper slopes, the terrain park and the traverse over to the 7th Heaven chair. The 1610m vertical from the top of 7th Heaven to the base is one of the biggest in North America. A T-bar from the Horstman Glacier brings you (with a short hike) to the Blackcomb Glacier in the next valley – away from all lifts.

Fresh Tracks is a deal that allows you to ride up Whistler Mountain (at extra cost) from 7.15am, have a buffet breakfast and get on the slopes early – very popular with many reporters. We prefer to ski first on deserted runs and breakfast later – check what time breakfast ends (9am on our March 2013 visit). Free guided tours of each mountain are offered at 11.15am.

FAST LIFTS ★★★★★
Can't cope with the crowds

While the resort has more fast lifts than any other in North America, the lift system is antiquated compared with those in the Alps and can't handle the crowds (see 'Queues').

↑ Whistler's high above-the-treeline bowls and trails are great when the sun shines (but don't count on clear weather like this)
TOURISM WHISTLER / MIKE CRANE

Gondolas provide the main access, with lots of fast quads after that. But there is only one six-pack and there are no eight-seaters, which are becoming common in Europe.

QUEUES ★★☆☆☆
A big problem
Whistler has become a victim of its own success. At peak holiday periods and weekends when people pour in from Vancouver, queues can be horrendous. There are displays of waiting times at different lifts, which readers generally find useful.

Some reporters have signed up with the ski school just to get lift priority. Others have visited Vancouver at the weekend to avoid the crowds.

The routes out of Whistler Village in the morning can be busy. Creekside is less of a problem, but gets long queues at weekends. Queues for downloading can be bad at times too (and were last season because of the lack of snow low down). Some of the chairs higher up also produce long queues (even the singles lines took 10 minutes or so on our most recent March visit); the Emerald and Peak chairs are bottlenecks – one reporter noted a 45-minute wait for the Peak chair on a Sunday in January. Reporters tell us the new six-pack Harmony chair installed for 2013/14 has reduced problems there. Another

issue is that some of the higher lifts, especially the Peak chair, are prone to open late on powder days while the ski patrol finish their avalanche control. Crowds on the slopes, especially the runs home, can be annoying, too.

TERRAIN PARKS ★★★★★
World class for all abilities
While both mountains have parks, freestylers tend to head to Blackcomb, which is home to the Olympic-standard Nintendo Super Pipe (with walls almost 7m high and shaped daily), the Mini Pipe with 5m high walls, a snowcross course ('a good laugh with friends') and three terrain parks. There's a clear rating system in place, based on feature size (S, M, L, XL). On Blackcomb, novices should begin in the Big Easy Terrain Garden. It has small features to help you get a feel for airtime and improve your control. The M-L Choker Park is vast, but is usually the busiest. It has lots of features and suits intermediate to advanced riders. Very confident freestylers should hit the XL Highest Level Park. The obstacles are huge and you have to wear a helmet. On Whistler mountain, novices should hit School Yard which has beginner rails and jumps. The Habitat Park by the Emerald chair is a 'belter' and has three lines for different skill levels.

SKIWORLD

Catered chalets,
hotels and
self catering
apartments in

**Europe, USA
and Canada**

skiworld.co.uk
08444 930 430

ABTA V2151 ATOL 2036

SNOW RELIABILITY ★★★★☆
Two poor seasons on the trot

Snow conditions at the top are usually excellent – the snowfall averages 458 inches a year (that's way more than most Colorado resorts). But the last two seasons were poor (especially last season, which some locals reckon was the worst ever, with low snowfall and lots of rain). Because the resort is low and close to the Pacific, the bottom slopes can have poor snow or slush even in a good year – leading people to 'download' from the mid-stations, especially in late season. Reporters generally praise piste maintenance. 'Groomers were out in force,' says one this year. 'Whistler did a great job under difficult conditions,' says another. However, a frequent visitor said this year that 'many pistes don't seem to be groomed for days on end'. Grooming has always been fine on our visits.

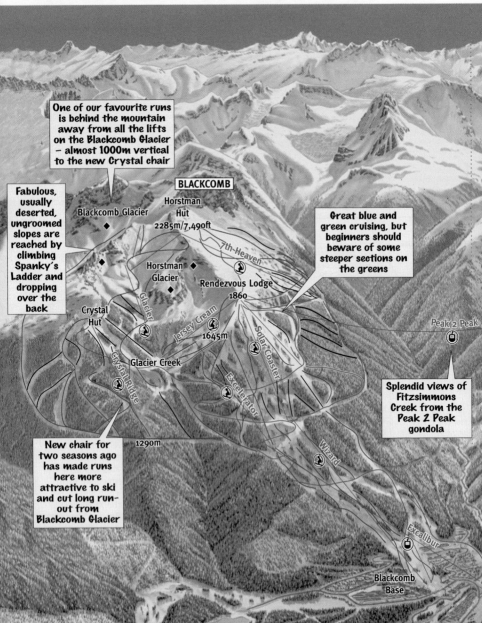

One of our favourite runs is behind the mountain away from all the lifts on the Blackcomb Glacier – almost 1000m vertical to the new Crystal chair

Fabulous, usually deserted, ungroomed slopes are reached by climbing Spanky's Ladder and dropping over the back

Great blue and green cruising, but beginners should beware of some steeper sections on the greens

Splendid views of Fitzsimmons Creek from the Peak 2 Peak gondola

New chair for two seasons ago has made runs here more attractive to ski and cut long run-out from Blackcomb Glacier

BLACKCOMB

Blackcomb Glacier

Horstman Hut
2285m/7,490ft

7th-Heaven

Horstman Glacier

Rendezvous Lodge
1860

Crystal Hut

Glacier

Jersey Cream
1645m

Solar Coaster

Crystal Ridge

Glacier Creek

Excelerator

1290m

Peak 2 Peak

Wizard

Excalibur

Blackcomb Base

FOR EXPERTS ★★★★★
Few can rival it

Whistler Mountain's bowls are enough to keep experts happy for weeks. Each has endless variations, with chutes and gullies of varied steepness and width. The biggest challenges are around Flute, Glacier, Whistler and West Bowls – you can go anywhere in these high, wide areas.

Blackcomb's steep slopes are not as extensive as Whistler's, but some are more challenging. From the top of

www.ski-i.com

ski independence

Call the Tailor-made Ski Specialists
0131 243 8097

- 🚡 gondola
- 🚟 fast chairlift
Slow chairs & drags have no symbol

There's more terrain out here at the edge of the area than this map suggests – blue runs and easy glades as well as tougher stuff in Flute Bowl

WHISTLER MOUNTAIN
2180m/7,16oft

The classic high bowls that first gave Whistler cult status among expert skiers in the 1980s and 1990s

Rhapsody Bowl

Symphony

Flute Bowl

Sun Bowl

Glacier Bowl

The Peak

Whistler Bowl

West Bowl

Bagel Bowl

Symphony

Harmony

Roundhouse Lodge
1850m

Emerald

Peak

1595m

Big Red

The 1530m vertical Peak to Creek runs are excellent in good snow

1425m

Whistler Village

Garbanzo

Raven's Nest
1300m

Take the gondola from 7.15am for uncrowded fresh tracks skiing and a buffet breakfast

1005m

Creekside

Fitzsimmons

These Creekside runs were the 2010 Olympic downhill and Super G courses

Creekside
65om/2,140ft

Whistler Village
675m/2,21oft

the 7th Heaven lift, traverse to Xhiggy's Meadow for sunny bowl runs. If you're feeling brave, go in the opposite direction and drop into the extremely steep chutes down towards Glacier Creek, including the infamous 41° Couloir Extreme (which can have massive moguls at the top), Secret Bowl and Pakalolo couloir. Our favourite runs are the less frequented but also seriously steep bowls reached by a short hike up Spanky's Ladder, after taking the Glacier Express lift. You emerge after the hike at the top of a huge deserted area with several ways down; best to have a guide.

Both mountains have challenging trails through trees. The Peak to Creek area offers 400 acres below Whistler's West Bowl to Creekside.

There's also backcountry guiding, cat-skiing and heli-skiing available by the day. One reporter had 'two incredible days' with Powder Mountain cat-skiing. Other reporters used Coast Range mountain guides ('top-quality guides and superb skiing') and found the heli-skiing 'expensive but a great experience'. We recommend the two-day Extremely Canadian clinic (see 'Schools and guides') for getting the most out of the in-bounds steeps and their one-day Backcountry Adventures.

TOURISM WHISTLER / MIKE CRANE

Whistler Village is car-free and by far the biggest and liveliest place to stay ↓

FOR INTERMEDIATES ★★★★★
Ideal and extensive terrain

Both mountains are an intermediate's paradise. In good weather, good intermediates will enjoy the easier slopes in the high bowls. One of our favourite intermediate runs is down the Blackcomb Glacier, from the top of the mountain to the Crystal chair almost 1000m below. This 5km run, away from all lifts, starts with a two-minute walk up from the top of the Showcase T-bar. Don't be put off by the 'Experts only' sign. You drop over the ridge into a wide bowl and traverse the slope to get to gentler gradients – descend too soon and you'll get a shock in the very steep double-diamond Blowhole. The tedious run-out at the end has been made a lot shorter by the newish Crystal chair.

The blue runs served by the 7th Heaven chair start above the treeline and end in it – some can get bumpy in parts. Lower down there are lots of perfect cruising runs through the trees – ideal for snowy days.

On Whistler Mountain, the ridges and bowls served by the Harmony and Symphony chairs have lots to offer – not only groomers but also excellent terrain for experiments off-piste. Symphony in particular has some very gentle and usually uncrowded terrain and widely spaced trees to play in. The Saddle run from the top of the Harmony Express lift is a favourite with many of our reporters, though it can get busy. The blue Highway 86 path, which skirts West Bowl from the Peak to Creek trail, has beautiful views over a steep valley and across to the rather phallic Black Tusk mountain. The 7km-long Peak to Creek blue run is good too, but it's rarely all groomed – check before setting off. The green Burnt Stew Trail has great views, and accesses lots of easy off-piste terrain.

Lower down the mountain there is a vast choice of groomed blue runs, with a series of fast chairs to bring you back up to the top of the gondola. It's a cruiser's paradise – especially the aptly named Ego Bowl. A great long run is the fabulous Dave Murray Downhill all the way from mid-mountain to the finish at Creekside – used as the 2010 Olympic men's downhill course. Although it is classed black, it's a wonderful fast and varied cruise when it has been groomed.

FOR BEGINNERS ★★★★★
OK if the sun shines
Whistler has excellent nursery slopes by the mid-station of the gondola, as does Blackcomb at the base. Both have facilities higher up too. There is a lift pass, lesson and rental deal on certain dates (see 'Schools and guides'), but no free lifts.

On Whistler, there are some gentle runs from the top of the gondola. Their downside is other people speeding past. On Blackcomb, there are green runs from top to bottom. The top parts are very gentle, with some steeper pitches lower down.

In general, greens can be trickier than in many North American resorts – steeper, busier and, on the lower slopes, in less good condition. Another reservation is the weather. Beginners don't get a lot out of heavy snowfalls, and rain might put them off.

FOR BOARDERS ★★★★★
Epic – winter and summer
Whistler has world-class terrain parks as well as epic terrain for freeriders: bowls with great powder, steep gullies and shedloads of natural hits, wind lips and cliffs. There are mellow groomed runs ideal for beginners and intermediates, too, and the lifts are generally snowboard-friendly; there are T-bars on the glacier, but they're not vicious. The resort has as high a reputation for summer snowboarding and camps on the glacier as for its winter boarding, and the summer Camp of Champions is hugely popular.

FOR CROSS-COUNTRY ★★★★★
Picturesque but low
There are over 28km of cross-country tracks around Lost Lake, starting by the river on the path between Whistler and Blackcomb. But it is low altitude, so conditions can be unreliable. One trail is floodlit. A specialist school, Cross-Country Connection, offers lessons and rental. Keen cross-country merchants can go to the Whistler Olympic Park and its 90km of trails (around 20 minutes away by car – there's no public bus).

MOUNTAIN RESTAURANTS ★★★★★
Overcrowded
The main restaurants sell decent food but are charmless self-service stops with long queues; most get incredibly crowded. They're huge, but not huge

Tourism BC/Randy Lincks

SKI WHISTLER

with the *luxury* tailor-made holiday experts

WHISTLER BLACKCOMB™

FrontierSki
the finest tailor-made ski holidays

AITO
HOLIDAYS WITH
100% FINANCIAL
PROTECTION

ABTA
ABTA No W3207

020 8776 8709
frontier-ski.co.uk/whistler

↑ Both Blackcomb (pictured here) and Whistler mountains have runs cut through the trees below the level of the Peak 2 Peak gondola
TOURISM WHISTLER / MIKE CRANE

enough. 'Seat-seekers' are employed to find you space, but success is not guaranteed. The piste map advises eating lunch before 11.30 (sorry?) or after 1pm. Blackcomb has the 500-seat Rendezvous (due for a revamp and increased capacity for 2015/16) and 775-seat Glacier Creek. Whistler has the 2,080-seat Roundhouse.

Editors' choice Christine's table-service restaurant in the Rendezvous building on Blackcomb is the place to go. We've had a delicious bouillabaisse and 'flight' of four different Okanagan wines with tasting notes there. Two 2015 reporters also approve.

Worth knowing about On Whistler, Steep's Grill in the Roundhouse is the table-service place ('beautiful smoked wild salmon chowder'), but we much prefer Christine's for both ambience and food. There are other smallish (self-service) places, but they get packed. On Blackcomb are two tiny huts with great views – Crystal Hut ('great waffles') and Horstman Hut. On Whistler, Raven's Nest is small and friendly, and does soups, sandwiches and BBQs; the Chic Pea ('cinnamon rolls to die for') and Harmony Snack Shack are other options.

SCHOOLS AND GUIDES ★★★★★
Very good reputation

The school limits the number in an adult group to a maximum of four. And they run Discover Whistler Days in some periods – you get a discount (25% in 2014/15) off the normal cost of lessons (and rentals and lift pass for beginners). A recent reporter who took private lessons says they were 'good quality, well planned and enjoyable'. A 2015 reporter raved about the 5-day Ride Tribe snowboard

lessons his kids had: 'The quality is so good our teenagers improved massively; the teachers are knowledgeable and really engage with teenagers – no mean feat!' The school also runs special programmes such as 3- or 4-day coaching sessions called The Camp. There's an average of six to a group and the aim is to improve your skiing in all types of terrain. Video analysis, optional race training and après-ski are included.

Extremely Canadian two-day camps run three times a week and are for those who want guiding (with a bit of coaching) in Whistler's steep and deep terrain and are a great way of finding the best steep terrain for you. We've been with them several times and been impressed (as have reporters).

Extremely Canadian also runs Backcountry Adventures day trips. Backcountry day trips or overnight touring are also available with Whistler Alpine Guides Bureau.

FOR FAMILIES ★★★★
Impressive

Blackcomb's base area has the slow-moving Magic chair to get children part-way up the mountain. Whistler's gondola mid-station has a splendid kids-only area. A reporter found the staff 'friendly, instilling confidence'. The school uses the Flaik GPS real-time tracking system so that each child's exact location is known at all times. There's a Magic Castle on Blackcomb and a Family Zone and Tree Fort on Whistler. One reporter enthused about 'climb and dine': kids combine dinner with three hours of climbing at The Core.

STAYING THERE

Whistler has every kind of lodging you might want. Ski Independence, Frontier Ski and Skiworld offer an impressive range of hotels and apartments.
Hotels There is a wide range, including a lot of top-end places.
★★★★★**Fairmont Chateau Whistler** Well run, luxurious, at the foot of Blackcomb. We and reporters love it. Excellent spa with pools and tubs.
★★★★★**Four Seasons** Luxury hotel five minutes' walk from Blackcomb base, but with ski valet service at the base. Unremarkable public areas but good service, food and fitness/spa facilities.
★★★★★**Westin Resort & Spa** Luxury all-suite hotel at the foot of Whistler

mountain. We enjoyed our 2013 stay except the pool and hot tubs were always so crowded we didn't use them. Sauna, steam.

****Crystal Lodge In Whistler Village. Pool, sauna, hot tub. Discounts in restaurants and shops in the building.

****Delta Whistler Village Suites In Whistler Village. 'Spacious family suites, friendly staff, gym, sauna, pool, two hot tubs,' says a 2015 reporter,

****Glacier Lodge In Upper Village. Large rooms.

****Pan Pacific Mountainside Luxury, all-suite, at Whistler Village base. Pool, steam, hot tub.

****Sundial Boutique In Whistler Village; one- and two-bedroom suites. Rooftop hot tubs.

****Summit Lodge Boutique In Whistler Village. Pools, sauna, hot tubs, 'free hot drinks in lobby'.

***Coast Blackcomb Suites Ski-in/ski-out in Blackcomb. 'Spacious rooms, good, plentiful, basic food,' says a 2015 reporter. Pool, hot tub.

***Tantalus Resort Lodge In Whistler Village; targets families and groups. Hot tub, sauna, pool.

Apartments There are plenty of spacious, comfortable condominiums. Price tends to be dictated by location – ski-in/ski-out condos are pricier than those a shuttle ride from the lifts.

EATING OUT ★★★★★
Good but crowded

Reporters are enthusiastic about the range, quality and value of places to eat, but there aren't enough restaurant seats to meet demand. You have to book well ahead (which may mean weeks ahead in some cases), or resign yourself to queuing for one of the places that doesn't take bookings.

At the top of the market, the Rimrock Cafe near Whistler Creek specializes in seafood and game and has several small areas rather than one big room; we have eaten very well there (last time we booked three weeks ahead); endorsed by a recent reporter who booked a month ahead.

In Whistler Village, we've enjoyed Araxi ('Brilliant, visited three times,' says a reporter), Il Caminetto di Umberto (a classy Italian) and 21 Steps (mid-market place up, er, 21 steps, where we enjoyed several delicious small plates on our most recent visit; endorsed by 2015 reporter). The pricey Ric's Grill and cheaper Keg are both parts of chains but do good seafood

and steak. Mid-market places include: Quattro and Old Spaghetti Factory ('amazing value, great service') for Italian, Bocca (modern Canadian, heated outdoor terrace), Three Below ('reasonably priced; great banana in puff pastry with caramel'), and Earl's (burgers, ribs, microbeers). In Village North, we've enjoyed Hy's Steakhouse ('good-quality steaks – but expensive', says a 2015 reporter) and the lively Brewhouse (good for steaks and ribs). There are plenty of budget places, including Fat Tony's ('tasty pizzas') and the après-ski bars below. You can also take a snowcat to the Crystal Hut for fondue and music.

APRES-SKI ★★★★☆
Something for most tastes

Whistler is very lively. We get most reviews on the Garibaldi Lift Company, which is still 'buzzing from 4pm onwards, with good live music'. Other tips are the Brewhouse ('good range of beers'), Longhorn (with a terrace), Dubh Linn Gate Irish pub ('fun', 'great live music') and Tapley's. Merlin's is the focus at Blackcomb base, with sports TV, 'great' quiz nights and music. Dusty's at Creekside has good beer and loud music.

Later on, Buffalo Bill's is lively. Tommy Africa's, Maxx Fish, Moe Joe's and Garfinkel's are the main clubs.

OFF THE SLOPES ★★★☆☆
Quite a lot to do

Meadow Park Sports Centre has fitness facilities. There are several luxurious spas and an eight-screen cinema. Reporters recommend 'lovely' walks around the lake and the climbing wall at The Core. Ziptrek Ecotours offers tours on ziplines and suspension bridges through the forest between Whistler and Blackcomb mountains – 'brilliant' says a 2015 reporter. You can also do all-terrain-vehicle/snowmobile trips and dog sledding. A reporter raves about the bobsleigh run at the Sliding Centre ('for adrenaline junkies'). Another's kids had 'multi-trampoline fun' at Bounce. A third recommends the Squamish Lil'wat Cultural Centre with its 'high-quality exhibits'. The free Sunday evening Fire & Ice show is popular. Excursions to Squamish (for eagle watching) and to Vancouver are easy. And pedestrians can get around the mountain easily (and take the Peak 2 Peak gondola for great views – see 'Scenery').

GETTING THERE

Air Vancouver 135km/85 miles (2hr15)

TOURIST OFFICE

www.whistler
blackcomb.com
www.tourismwhistler.
com

STONEHAM / JEAN VAUDREUIL

Eastern Canada

For us, the main attraction of skiing or riding in eastern Canada is the French culture and language that are predominant in the province of Québec. It really feels like a different country from the rest of Canada. And the resorts are only a 6-hour flight from the UK, compared with a 10-hour flight for western Canada.

Be prepared for variable snow conditions, including rock-hard pistes and ice; and be prepared for extreme cold in early and midwinter (February 2015 saw an average temperature in Québec City of around −18°C and a January 2015 Tremblant visitor said daytime temperatures were −25°C). But cold weather means the extensive snowmaking systems can be effective for a long season. Don't go expecting light, dry powder – if that's what you want, go west.

For people heading on holiday for a week or more, eastern Canada really means the province of Québec, its capital, Québec City, and the main destination resort Tremblant (which has its own chapter) nearer Montreal. French culture and language dominate the region. Notices, menus, trail maps and so on are usually printed in both French and English. Many ski area workers are bilingual or only French-speaking. And French cuisine abounds. The local speciality is poutine (French fries topped with a gravy-like sauce and cheese curds) – we stick with the more traditional French cuisine.

Slopes in all resorts are small, both in extent and vertical. The weather is very variable, so the snow – though pretty much guaranteed by snowmaking – varies greatly in quality. Québec City makes a good base for access to several ski areas. Old Québec, at the city's heart, is North America's only walled city and is a World Heritage site. Within the city walls are narrow, winding streets and 17th- and 18th-century houses. It is situated right on the banks of the St Lawrence river. In January/February there is a famous two-week carnival, with an ice castle, snow sculptures, dog-sled and canoe races, parades and balls. But most of the winter is low season, with good-value rooms available in big hotels.

Stoneham is the closest ski area to Québec City, around 20 minutes away. The biggest and most varied resort is Mont-Ste-Anne 30 minutes away. Le Massif is around an hour away – a cult area with locals. These three resorts have extended entries in the resort directory at the back of the book.

STONEHAM / JEAN VAUDREUIL
Slopes in Québec resorts are short, cut through the trees and rely a lot on snowmaking ↓

Tremblant

Cute, purpose-built, traffic-free village with a real French Canadian feel, at the foot of a very small area of slopes

£170
RESORT PRICE INDEX

- **+** Charming, purpose-built core village
- **+** Good snow reliability with extensive artificial backup
- **+** Some good runs for all abilities

- **–** Very limited area for piste-bashers
- **–** Can be perishingly cold in midwinter
- **–** Weekend queues and crowds

TOP 10 RATINGS

Extent	★
Fast lifts	★★★★★
Queues	★★★
Snow	★★★★
Expert	★★
Intermediate	★★★
Beginner	★★★★
Charm	★★★★
Convenience	★★★★
Scenery	★★★

Tremblant is eastern Canada's main destination resort and it attracts quite a lot of Brits. But for keen piste-bashers the limited slopes don't really match the appeal of the cute and lively little core village, built in traditional style and with typical thoroughness by Intrawest.

NEWS

2014/15: A new gladed area was opened beside the Tunnel slope on the North Side. The Tam-Tam adventure trail for kids was built on the South Side. 30km of winter mountain biking trails opened. The Westin hotel was renovated with a new gym and restaurant. The Kandahar has been refurbished and is now the Holiday Inn Express.

THE RESORT

Tremblant is eastern Canada's leading destination ski resort. It is based on a purpose-built village designed in the style of old Québec. Don't go there in midwinter unless you are prepared to put up with extreme cold (–42°C in February, said a past reporter; –25°C said a January 2015 visitor).
Village charm Buildings in vibrant colours line narrow, cobbled, traffic-free streets and squares, and it has a very French feel to it. More recent expansion on the edge is not so cute.
Convenience The village is compact but there is a regular, free ski-bus and a local town service for C$3.
Scenery There are good views over the village and a 14km lake on the South Side. The North Side overlooks National Park wilderness.

THE MOUNTAINS

The small area (less than 80km of trails) won't keep keen piste-bashers happy for more than a couple of days. But there's a good variety of pleasantly wooded terrain, from easy greens to a few steep double-black diamond runs. Usefully, the piste map shows gladed areas as well as normal trails cut through the trees.
Slopes A heated gondola from the village takes you to the top of the so-called South Side (really south-west facing and so good for the afternoon sun). From here you can drop over the back onto the North Side (which is really north-east facing and gets the morning sun). A high-speed quad brings you back and there is one other fast chair and two slow ones to play on here. Most runs on the North Side are black but there are a couple of easier top-to-bottom options. On the South Side you can go right back to town on blue or green runs, or use two high-speed quads to explore the top and bottom halves. The Versant Soleil area, served by its own fast quad, is more directly south-facing and has mainly black and tree runs with one top-to-bottom blue. Free mountain tours go each day.
Fast lifts Most of the lifts are fast.
Queues At weekends there can be queues, but they tend to move quickly. And cold days can see queues for the heated gondola – a 2015 reporter recommends using the singles line. We found crowds on the main run back to the village more of a problem.
Terrain parks On the South Side is the 30-acre Adrénaline park for advanced

653

TREMBLANT / KEVIN LEMAIRE

←The colourful purpose-built village at the foot of a small area of slopes has a very French feel

KEY FACTS

Resort	265m
	870ft
Slopes	230-875m
	750-2,870ft
Lifts	14
Pistes	662 acres

LIFT PASSES

Prices in C$

Age	6-day
under 13	265
13 to 17	320
18 to 64	453
65 plus	397
Free Under 6	
Beginner Lesson, rental and lift pass deals	
Notes Includes sales taxes	

riders (C$10 for a day pass) and the Progression park for intermediates. There's a beginner park on the North Side. Helmets are compulsory. The school offers freestyle classes.

Snow reliability Canada's east coast doesn't get as much snow as the west, but around 75% of the trails have snowmaking. Grooming is excellent.

Experts Half the runs are black, but many of them do not deserve their grading. There are steep, top-to-bottom bump runs on the North Side and good tree runs off the Edge lift. The Versant Soleil area has more black runs and some tough gladed runs. But the tree runs really need decent snow, preferably fresh, to be much fun.

Intermediates Both North and South Sides have good cruising, and we found the North Side less crowded. There are blue runs in the trees as well as on groomed trails.

Beginners The 2-acre beginner area is excellent, and there are long, easy, top-to-bottom greens to progress to. There's even a green gladed area next to the new Tam-Tam trail.

Snowboarding The slopes are good for beginners. Better boarders can't count on fresh natural snow to play in but there are good terrain parks.

Cross-country There's over 80km of trails, some at the top of the mountain, with great views.

Mountain restaurants The main Grand Manitou restaurant has good views and decent food, but can get crowded. Many people go back to town. The Refuge in the Versant Soleil area has a limited menu 'but its charm makes up for this and a guitarist plays a few times a week'.

Schools and guides Past reporters praised the school: 'good instructors and both children made progress'.

Families The Kidz Club offers day care. There's the new Tam-Tam children's adventure slope on the South Side.

STAYING THERE

Hotels and condos The luxurious Fairmont Tremblant ('one of the best hotels I have ever stayed in'), Marriott ('large, comfy rooms; very good breakfast') and the condos in the Place St Bernard, the Tour des Voyagers and the Chouette have been recommended by readers.

Eating out Try O Wok ('cosy; delicious Asian dishes'), the Forge, Ya'ooo Pizza Bar, Shack, Casey's, Spag & Co, and Windigo at the Fairmont. Fat Mardi's (steaks and seafood) has a kids' menu.

Après-ski The Forge is good as the slopes close, and the Shack brews its own beer, as does La Diable in the Residence Inn – try the seven-beer sample menu there.

Off the slopes The Aquaclub La Source pool complex resembles a lake set in a forest, but reporters complain it's expensive. For adults only, the 'excellent' Spa Scandinavie offers sauna, steam room, outdoor hot tubs, waterfalls and chill-out rooms. You can also go hiking, ice climbing, horse riding, ice skating, curling, snowshoeing, tubing, snowmobiling, dog sledding and on sleigh rides. A trip to Montreal is highly recommended by reporters, and you can take a helicopter charter with a scenic stop on top of a mountain.

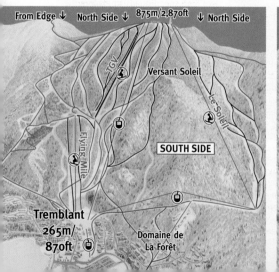

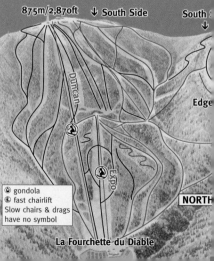

Spain

£95
RESORT PRICE INDEX

+ Vibrant Spanish culture gives a different experience from the Alps
+ Low prices for food and drink
+ Few crowds outside peak times

− Access can be difficult, with lengthy drives to reach Pyrenean resorts
− Still lots of old lifts, but improving

Spanish resorts vary enormously, so it's difficult to generalize. Nearly all the main ones, though, are benefiting from recent investment. The three we feature here have respectably sized and varied terrain that compares favourably with many smaller Alpine resorts.

Key parts of the appeal of Spanish skiing are the relatively low cost and the relaxed ambience, with a distinct emphasis on eating, partying and posing. Most resorts are in the Pyrenees. The villages are built more for convenience than charm – but they do offer a wide range of lodging set in some stunning scenery.

There is a group of worthwhile resorts in the west, between Pau and Huesca. Formigal is now the largest, and making a steady comeback on the wider market. Candanchu and Astún nearby are popular on the Spanish market. The downside is access, which can be tricky from France if snowfall closes key mountain passes. There are long drives up from Spanish airports, too, but weekly charter flights to Huesca have cut some transfer times.

The other main group of Pyrenees resorts, just east of Andorra, includes La Molina and Masella (Alp 2500). These have brief descriptions in our resort directory.

In the south of Spain is the high resort of Sierra Nevada – a quite different experience, close to Granada – a two-centre trip is tempting.

KEY FACTS

Resort	1500m
	4,920ft
Slopes	1500-2510m
	4,920-8,230ft
Lifts	33
Pistes	120km

TOURIST OFFICE

www.baqueira.es

Baqueira-Beret

+ Compact modern resort
+ Lots of good intermediate slopes

− Main village lacks atmosphere
− Still some old, slow lifts

Baqueira's village is not inspiring, but the resort has a well-linked and developing ski area that appeals to intermediates. Fine for beginners too.

Baqueira is a mainly modern development with its fair share of drab blocks in the central area, clustered below the road that runs through to the high pass of Port de la Bonaigua, with the main lift base just above it. The village is small enough for location not to matter greatly.

The slopes are split into three distinct but well-connected areas – Baqueira, Beret and Bonaigua – with long, intermediate runs, practically all of them on open, treeless slopes. Most are above 1800m, with extensive snowmaking; but afternoon sun is a problem in spring. There are increasing numbers of fast chairs dotted around, including a long six-pack. Queues are not a great problem.

Experts will find few on-piste challenges, but there is extensive off-piste terrain ('awesome', to quote one reporting dude), and three ungroomed itinerary runs (including Escornacrabes, which two recent reporters said was not for the faint-hearted). There are good nursery slopes with moving carpets at Beret, and at the top of the gondola from Baqueira. A mum with two novices in tow approves this year. The Brit-run BB Ski School is praised, not least for off-piste guiding. The mountain restaurants disappoint.

There are good hotels; reporters this year tip the big Tuc Blanc near the lift base ('comfortable, good breakfast, good restaurant') and Chalet Bassibe at the top of the resort ('lovely staff, best ever breakfasts'). Some good hotels (and restaurants) are down the valley – eg the 'very friendly' Gran Chalet at Betren, within walking distance of the 'lively and atmospheric' tapas bars and restaurants of Vielha. Some hotels have pools and spas, but there is little else for non-skiers.

KEY FACTS

Resort	1550m
	5,090ft
Slopes	1500-2250m
	4,920-7,380ft
Lifts	21
Pistes	137km

TOURIST OFFICE

www.aramon.co.uk
www.formigal.com

Formigal

- ➕ Sizeable, varied area for all abilities
- ➕ Linked valleys give sense of travel
- ➖ Traffic congestion in resort
- ➖ Wind-prone slopes, lacking trees

Formigal has the largest ski area in the Spanish Pyrenees, and varied terrain. Recent investment is slowly attracting more British visitors – reports welcome.

The resort is on the Spanish-French border at the Col de Portalet, which can be closed in heavy snowfall, preventing direct access from France.

The village – of purpose-built apartment blocks and smart hotels – is on the east side of the Tena valley. The central street is pleasant enough, with an attractive clock tower and a replica church as its focus, but it is spoiled by heavy traffic.

There are excellent free shuttles to and from the slopes, which span the west side of the valley and spread over four side-valleys. Most slopes are treeless, and prone to wind; they are north- or south-facing. Grooming is good and snowmaking extensive. Queues are rare outside holiday periods. Sextas is the nearest of the four bases to the village, with an eight-seat chair. All four have big car parks and US-style day lodges including big self-service cafeterias. There are fast chairs linking the lower parts of each valley, and runs for all standards from the tops.

Experts have three freeride areas, plus heli-skiing. Many of the black runs could be red, though. The nursery slopes are excellent. There are good

intermediate runs; the gentle blue Rio from Cantal to Sextas is ideal for the more timid. The only treelined run is a remote lovely cruise, quiet because access is by a long, slow chair.

Confident skiers can ride a snowcat above Portalet, which accesses remote runs and freeride terrain to Anayet. The huge terrain park is one of the best we've seen, and there's a kids' mini park and snowcross. We enjoyed good Italian food at the Cantal Trattoria. The school has a good reputation. They have been focusing on activities for families – well catered for with 'slow ski zones', family zones and an Indian 'village'.

There is a choice of 3- and 4-star hotels (the Aragon Hills and Abba Formigal have pools and spas), lots of apartments and over 30 restaurants, from Spanish to pizzerias. We had good gourmet food at the Vidocq. Après-ski is low-key, but the Marchica bar at Sextas is lively at close of play. Later on, there are two discos: the popular Cueva and the Tralala.

Off-slope activities include dog sledding, floodlit tobogganing and snowmobile outings up to a mountain hut. Thermal baths are nearby.

KEY FACTS

Resort	2100m
	6,890ft
Slopes	2100-3300
	6,890-10,830ft
Lifts	29
Pistes	105km

TOURIST OFFICE

www.sierranevada.es

Sierra Nevada

- ➕ Reasonably good snow record
- ➕ Fine beginner slopes
- ➖ Exposed, and prone to wind
- ➖ Crowds at weekends

In an extreme southerly position near Granada, Sierra Nevada is a high, modern resort with a decent area of slopes. It gets its own weather, of course.

Pradollano, at 2100m, is the stylish modern lift base, with shops, restaurants and bars set around traffic-free open spaces. Most of the lodgings are in older, less smart buildings along a steeply winding road above here.

Two gondolas go up in parallel to the mid-station at Borreguiles, where there are excellent nursery slopes. Fast quads go on from there to an impressive 3300m. There are four identifiable sectors, well linked, with a good range of intermediate runs, mostly easy reds, but not a lot for experts. There's a terrain park with an FIS half-pipe.

There are good views from the top of the plains and towns – and on a clear day across the Med to Africa. Weekends can be busy, and queues may develop for some of the older lifts, especially the chair up the village slope. The home run can get crowded too. Snow here may be good when it's poor in the Alps, and vice versa. Most slopes face north-west, but some get the afternoon sun. And when the wind blows, as it does, the slopes close; there are no trees.

The Sol y Nieve hotel – with spa and good kids' facilities – has had good reports in the past.

Finland

- ➕ Good for families and beginners
- ➕ Crowd-free runs, with plenty of space, for much of the season
- ➕ Ideal terrain for cross-country
- ➕ Reliable snow well into spring
- ➕ Chance of seeing Northern Lights – a key factor for some visitors

- ➖ Can be bitterly cold (and dark in the early season)
- ➖ Small ski areas, particularly lacking vertical and challenge
- ➖ Draglifts are the norm

For skiers with no appetite for the hustle and hassle of Alpine resorts in high season – especially families, perhaps – escaping to the white silence of Lapland can be an attractive alternative. Finland has the lion's share of Lapland, and a few years back we got a healthy flow of reader reports on it – but they've more or less dried up. The resorts are small but rapidly developing.

The Arctic landscape of flat and gently rolling forest, countless lakes and the occasional treeless hill is a paradise for cross-country skiing.

It also offers good beginner and intermediate downhilling, albeit on a small scale. None of the areas has significant vertical by Alpine standards, and in some cases it is seriously limited. (The two resorts on the next page offer 460m and 325m, for example.) For a time in midwinter the sun does not rise – the period depends on altitude as well as latitude. Most areas have floodlit runs. The mountains do not open fully until mid-February, when a normal skiing day is possible and Finnish schools have holidays that usually coincide with ours – making it a relatively busy time. Finland comes into its own at the end of the season, with friendlier temperatures and daylight hours longer than in the Alps. At Easter the slopes are crowded.

Conditions are usually hard-packed powder or fresh snow from the start of the season to the end (early May).

The temperature can be extremely variable, yo-yoing between 0°C and –30°C several times in a week. Fine days are the coldest, but the best for skiing: it may be 10 to 15 degrees warmer on the slopes than at valley level. 'Mild' days of cloud and wind are worse, and face masks are sold.

The staple Finnish lift is the T-bar; chairs and gondolas are rare. Pistes are wide and well maintained, as are nursery slopes. The Finns are great boarders, and consider their terrain

parks far superior to those in the Alps; super-pipes are increasingly common.

There are few mountain restaurants – but you are never far from the base, with its self-service restaurants. There are also shelters or 'kotas' – log-built tepees with an open fire – where you can warm up and cook your own food.

Ski schools are good, with English widely spoken. All ski areas have indoor playrooms for small children.

Excursions are common and generally very popular – husky sledding, snowmobile safaris, a reindeer sleigh ride and tea with the Lapp drivers in their tent. Reporters are generally very enthusiastic about these off-slope adventures.

Hotels are self-contained mini-resorts, large and practical rather than stylish, typically with a shop, a cafe, a bar with dance floor, and a pool and sauna. Hotel 'dinner' is typically served no later than seven, sometimes followed by a children's disco or dancing to a live band.

Finns usually prefer to stay in cabins, and tour operators offer the compromise of staying in a cabin but taking half-board at a nearby hotel. Cabins vary, but are mostly well equipped, with a sauna as standard.

The main resorts are Ylläs and Levi, described here, respectively close and very close to Kittilä and its airport. They are half an hour apart, and combined lift passes are sold. Three other resorts worth considering are: Ruka, Pyhä and Iso-Syöte, Finland's southernmost fell region. These are covered in our resort directory.

Yllӓs

KEY FACTS	
Resort	255m
	840ft
Slopes	255-715m
	840-2,350ft
Lifts	29
Pistes	53km

TOURIST OFFICE

www.yllas.fi

➕ Best for novices and Nordic fans
➕ Few queues and reliable late snow
➖ Slopes a bus ride from the villages
➖ Bars and restaurants not a highlight

Yllӓs is Finland's largest resort; it's a quiet family area with an increasing choice of accommodation dotted around its two villages.

Yllӓs mountain has lift systems on two sides – Sport Resort Yllӓs, with most lodging 4km away at Yllӓsjӓrvi, and Yllӓs-Ski, with lodging similarly distant at Äkӓslompolo. Development is taking place at outlying villages, and closer to the slopes too.

This is Finland's largest downhill ski area – but it has only 53km of pistes that suit novices best. Second- and third-week skiers will rapidly conquer the benign black runs. The maximum vertical is a quite respectable 460m. Grooming is 'good'. Past reports of the ski school have been positive.

The area has 330km of cross-country trails, 38km of which are floodlit; whereas a downhill skier might view the place as an awkward sprawl, for the XC fan it is a doorstep ski resort of limitless scope. There are also 15 cafes along the tracks. From the lift base, trails fan out around the mountain, across the frozen lake and away through the endless forest.

The Äkӓs cabins at Äkӓslompolo have been recommended, as has the 'comfortable' Saaga Spa hotel at Sport Resort Yllӓs, which has 'gym, pool, kids' pool, sauna, steam and hot tub, and a useful drying cabinet in the bedrooms'. (The need for drying has us rather worried, we confess.)

Eating out is slowly improving, with four restaurants at Sport Resort Yllӓs opening a few seasons ago. Tips in town include more upmarket Poro for traditional fish and meat dishes. Julie's suits families better. Tower is fairly new at Äkӓslompolo.

Off-slope activities include snowmobiling (410km of tracks), dog sledding, reindeer safaris, snowshoeing and ice fishing.

Levi

KEY FACTS	
Resort	205m
	670ft
Slopes	205-530m
	670-1,740ft
Lifts	26
Pistes	44km

TOURIST OFFICE

www.levi.fi

➕ Lodging convenient for slopes
➕ Airport transfer only 15 minutes
➖ Only one challenging piste
➖ Can be windy

Levi's convenience is its key appeal for visitors. There are good hotels and plentiful off-slope diversions too. Midwinter can be bleak on the hill, though.

Levi is a small, purpose-built village of hotels, apartments and cabins at the foot of its slopes.

The runs are mostly intermediate (only two green runs and one genuine black, plus a couple of fakes). A six-pack takes you up from the village base, but virtually all the lifts are drags. Most rise no more than 200m. The slopes can be bleak and exposed in bad weather, but the area usually has a long season. Many slopes are floodlit.

The back side of the hill, which is good for beginners, got some investment last year, including a 1.7km six-pack rising almost 300m. The main terrain park, up the hill, is 'large and varied' with 'several jumps and lots of rails'. There is also a super-pipe and snow park on the slopes at the base, with big jumps. Cross-country trails total 230km, with lots floodlit. Vilpuri Kids' Land has lifts and tobogganing areas, plus day care.

Levi's biggest hotel is the Spa Levitunturi, with a bowling alley and huge spa/pool facility. The hotel Levi Panorama is at altitude, reached by gondola. The Sokos hotel and the Levilehto apartments are tipped by readers.

There are dozens of restaurants to choose from. The Hullu Poro (Crazy Reindeer) hotel complex has several places including the 'very good and reliable' Pihvipirtti steakhouse. Panimo ('brewery') does have a brewery on one floor and a 'quite good' restaurant doing good reindeer meat among many other options.

At close of play Vinkkari at the base gets 'busy and very loud'. For a quiet drink our regular reporter favours the 'relaxed' Kota in the Holiday Club hotel. Nightlife is 'very lively', especially at holiday times – there are several nightspots.

Off-slope activities include snowmobiling, reindeer and husky safaris, snowshoeing, ice fishing and skating on the frozen lake.

Norway

NEWS

2014/15: At Hemsedal a new 4km blue run from the Skisenter down to Sentrum was created. The new Skigaarden development opened on the slopes, with apartments, shops and restaurants.

+ One of the best places in Europe for serious cross-country skiing
+ The home of telemark – plenty of opportunities to learn and practise
+ Freedom from the glitz and ill-mannered lift queues of the Alps
+ Impressive terrain parks
+ Usually reliable snow conditions throughout a long season

− Very limited downhill areas
− Very basic mountain restaurants
− Booze is prohibitively taxed
− Scenery more Pennine than Alpine
− Après-ski that is either deadly dull or irritatingly rowdy
− Short daylight hours in midwinter
− Highly changeable weather
− Limited off-slope activities

For downhillers who fancy a change from the conspicuous consumption that characterizes Alpine ski resorts, Norway could be just the place. Families with young children, in particular, will have no trouble finding junk food to please the kids – the mountain restaurants serve little else. For us, any one of our first three negatives listed above is reason to pause. Add together all the negatives, and you can count us out. We find Scotland more attractive.

We've recently detected a small surge of interest in Norway in the UK travel trade, with more tour operators entering the fray in several resorts.

There is a traditional friendship between Norway and Britain, and English is widely spoken.

For the Norwegians and Swedes, skiing is a weekend rather than a special holiday activity, and not an occasion for extravagance. So at lunchtime they haul sandwiches out of their backpacks, as we might while walking the Pennine Way, and in the evening they cook in their apartments. Don't expect tempting restaurants.

The Norwegians have a problem with alcohol. Walk into an après-ski bar at 5pm on a Saturday and you may find young men already inebriated. And this is despite incredibly high taxes on booze. In restaurants wine prices are ludicrous and the wine quality is poor – though our resident consultant on matters Norwegian says that the state liquor stores offer very good value at the top end. Other prices are generally not high by Alpine standards.

Cross-country skiing comes as naturally to Norwegians as walking; even if you're not very keen, the fact that cross-country is normal, and not a wimp's alternative to 'real' skiing, gives Norway a special appeal. Here, cross-country is both a way of getting about the valleys and a way of exploring the hills. What distinguishes Norway for the keen cross-country skier is the network of long trails across the gentle uplands, with refuges along the way where backpackers can pause for refreshment or stay overnight.

More and more Norwegians are taking to telemarking, and snowboarding is very popular – local youths fill the impressive terrain parks at weekends. For regular downhill skiing, the country isn't nearly so attractive. Despite the fact that it is able to hold downhill races, Norway's Alpine areas are of limited appeal. The most rewarding resort is Hemsedal, covered on the next page.

The other downhill resorts most widely known are Geilo and Voss, on the railway line from Bergen to Oslo. Tryvann is just 20 minutes from the centre of Oslo, on a spur of the underground system, and popular with the locals. Lillehammer is well known too, of course – it hosted the 1994 Winter Olympics; but it's a lakeside town not a downhill ski resort (the Alpine races were held some distance away). Other main resorts are Trysil, on the border with Sweden, Beitostølen in the Jotunheimen National Park, and Oppdal. All are covered in the directory at the back of the book.

KEY FACTS

Resort	640m
	2,100ft
Slopes	670-1450m
	2,200-4,760ft
Lifts	24
Pistes	47km

Hemsedal

- ✚ Convenient slope-side lodging
- ✚ Some quite challenging slopes
- ✚ Excellent children's nursery slopes
- ▬ Not much of a village
- ▬ Weekend queues
- ▬ Exposed upper mountain

Hemsedal is both an unspoiled valley and a village, the latter also referred to as Trøym and Sentrum ('Centre') – but you can also stay at the lift base or higher up in the slopes, a mile or so away.

Hemsedal is 90 minutes from Fagernes airport, served by Crystal charter flights. The lift pass also covers smaller Solheisen, up the valley.

Sentrum is a bus ride from the lift base (Skisenter) – though there is now a run to the village. It is little more than a small area of low-rise hotels and apartments, shops, a garage, a bank and a couple of cashpoints. There's a developing area of lodgings at the base, with a ski-bus linking all parts, and floodlit paths to/from the centre. You can also stay further up the hill, where there are several areas of more or less ski-in/ski-out lodgings.

Hemsedal's slopes pack a lot of variety into a small space. Fast lifts serve a high proportion of the slopes, and practically all drags can be avoided. There can be weekend crowds and queues, but during the week it is quiet. There are three terrain parks and a mini park for kids, plus ski cross, speed ski and giant slalom areas. Snowmaking covers 45% of the slopes; grooming is excellent.

The terrain is mainly easy-intermediate, but mileage-hungry piste-bashers will find the runs very limited. There are quite a few red and blue runs to play on, and splendid long green runs – but they get a lot of traffic. There is quite a bit to amuse

experts: wide areas of gentler off-piste terrain served by drags, as well as several black pistes. There is floodlit skiing several nights a week. There's a separate, gentle nursery area. The resort caters well for families; the kids' nursery slopes at the base are good.

There are 120km of prepared cross-country trails in the valley and forest, and (in late season) 90km at altitude.

The best hotel is the Skogstad in Sentrum – comfortable, with a spa; but its bar and nightclub may be noisy at weekends. The Skarsnuten, on the hill, is stylishly modern, and its attached apartments (and its restaurant) satisfied one reporter.

The dining choices are OK; the Big Horn at Fjellandsby is a popular steakhouse, and the Lodgen bar and restaurant offers Mediterranean cuisine at the Alpin Lodge. In Sentrum, a reporter tips the Hemsedal Cafe – Norwegian pierrade recommended.

Après-ski starts at the Skistua at the lift base, which has live music at the weekends. Dancing on the tables happens. The bars and clubs get rowdy at weekends and holidays, but can be very quiet midweek.

Off-slope diversions include bowling, tobogganing, ice climbing, snowmobiling and dog sledding – 'pricey but worth it'.

TOURIST OFFICE

www.hemsedal.com
www.skistar.com/hemsedal

HEMSEDAL.COM / NILS-ERIK BJØRHOLT

There are gnarly spots to be found, but the limited slopes of Hemsedal are mostly intermediate stuff ↓

Sweden

- ➕ Snow-sure from December to May
- ➕ Unspoiled, beautiful landscape
- ➕ Uncrowded pistes and lifts
- ➕ Super Nordic and off-slope activities

- ➖ Limited challenging downhill terrain
- ➖ Small areas by Alpine standards
- ➖ Lacks dramatic Alpine scenery
- ➖ Short days during the early season

Sweden appeals most to those who want an all-round winter holiday in a different environment and culture. Standards of accommodation, food and service are good, and the people are welcoming, lively and friendly, but most of the downhill areas are limited in size and challenge.

Holidaying in Sweden is a completely different experience from holidaying in the Alps. Although virtually everyone speaks good English, menus and signs are often written only in Swedish. The food is delightful, especially if you like fish and venison. And resorts are very family-friendly. It is significantly cheaper than neighbouring Norway, but reporters still complain that eating and drinking is very expensive.

Days are very short in early season. But from early February the lifts usually work from 9am to 4.30pm and by March it is light until 8.30pm. Most resorts have some floodlit pistes.

On the downside, downhill slopes are limited in both challenge and extent, and the lift systems are dominated by T-bars. There's lots of cross-country and backcountry skiing.

Après-ski is taken very seriously – with live bands from mid- to late afternoon. There is plenty to do off the slopes: snowmobile safaris, ice fishing, dog-sled rides, ice climbing, saunas galore and visiting local Sami villages.

The main resort is Åre, described below. Others include Sälen (big but fragmented) and Vemdalen. These two, plus Riksgränsen, Björkliden (both above the Arctic Circle) and tiny Ramundberget are covered in our directory at the back of the book.

KEY FACTS

Resort	380m
	1,250ft
Slopes	380-1275m
	1,250-4,180ft
Lifts	42
Pistes	100km

TOURIST OFFICE
www.skistar.com

Åre

- ➕ Good for intermediates and novices
- ➕ Excellent children's facilities

- ➖ High winds can affect snow and lifts
- ➖ Few expert challenges

Sweden's biggest ski area, with lots to do off the slopes as well as on. Not great for keen skiers but good for families wanting a change from the Alps.

The centre of this small lakeside town has old, pretty, coloured wooden buildings and some larger modern additions. Lodgings are spread out along the valley.

There are two separate areas of slopes linked by a ski-bus. In both areas, the main lifts from the valley are fast. But nearly all other lifts are drags. A new snowmaking system was installed for the Duved area in 2014/15 and pistes there have been widened.

The slopes offer mainly beginner and intermediate treelined terrain, with two windswept bowls above, which are prone to closure. Experts will find the slopes limited, especially if the high bowls are closed. But there is a lot of off-piste and guided heli-skiing was new for 2014/15. For intermediates there are steep, sometimes icy, black and red runs back to town, and lots of pretty blue runs through the trees. You get a real sense of travelling around on the main area. Beginners have good facilities in both sectors. Queues are rare.

There are three terrain parks and 88km of groomed cross-country trails. The ski school has a good reputation, and children have special areas. Kids under seven get free lift passes if they are wearing helmets. Mountain huts are good.

The best central hotel is the charming old Diplomat Åregården. There are ample apartments and cabins and lots of restaurants, from Japanese to Italian. Après-ski is lively, with the Tott, Fjällgården and Åregården busy from 3pm. Off-slope diversions are plentiful.

Bulgaria

£60
RESORT PRICE INDEX

+ Costs very low by Alpine standards
+ Good ski schools
+ Lively bars and nightlife

− Poor snow record, though snowmaking has been improved
− Small ski areas
− Cheap booze attracts 18–30 crowds

Bulgaria best suits novices and early intermediates looking for a jolly time at bargain-basement prices. Bansko's arrival on the scene years ten ago raised the bar for the country's other main resorts, which are now starting to catch up.

Bulgaria has traditionally been a place for a cheap and cheerful holiday. It is well worth considering if you are a beginner or early intermediate on a budget and want a lively time, fuelled by cheap booze. Don't expect sophistication or big ski areas. A keen piste-basher could ski even the biggest resort in a matter of hours.

But the ski schools have an excellent reputation. And Bansko has some good hotels and a modern lift system. Even Pamporovo now has a six-pack. The scenery and culture provide a very different holiday experience from the Alps.

KEY FACTS

Resort	1300m
	4,270ft
Slopes	1300-2550m
	4,270-8,370ft
Lifts	12
Pistes	58km

662

TOURIST OFFICE

www.borovets-bg.com

Borovets

+ Lively, convenient village
+ Some good intermediate slopes

− Not ideal for beginners
− Nightlife can be tacky

Borovets is a mixture of large, modern hotels and small bars, clubs and restaurants. The slopes suit intermediates best.

Most people come here on packages and stay in big hotels with their own bars, restaurants and shops within them. There is also a large selection of quirkier and lively small bars, shops and eating places. 'There must be over 40 if you include the back streets,' said a reporter, 'with touts outside most bars trying to get you in.'

Nevertheless, the resort's beautiful woodland setting gives a degree of Alpine-style charm.

A long, slow gondola rises over 1000m in 25 minutes to reach both the short, easy slopes of Markoudjik and the longer, steepish Yastrebets pistes. The runs are best for good intermediates, and include some longish reds. The resort is not ideal for novices: nursery slopes are crowded,

DAVID MAXWELL-LEES

Once you get up the mountain at Bansko queues are rare and you are whisked around on high-speed chairs →

and the step from easy blues to testing reds is a big one. There are two terrain parks, with lines for all levels. For 2014/15 night skiing was increased and is now on eight runs. There's 35km of cross-country.

Recent reporters found no big queues. Snow-guns more than doubled from 75 to 160 last season and now cover over 60% of the slopes. The ski schools are praised – a 2015 visitor says of Borosport: 'My instructor was friendly, polite, patient – I learned a great deal.'

Most reporters stay at the huge 'Soviet-style' Samokov or the Rila, which is due to be refurbished for 2015/16. Two 2015 reporters praised the Lion and another was 'very happy' with the 4-star Radina's Way – 'plush rooms, nice pool and sauna area, helpful staff'.

The Crown restaurant is praised this year – 'inauspicious exterior but good grilled meat dishes'. The Finish Line does 'good chicken kawarma (a local dish)' and service was 'efficient'. There are plenty of lively bars with 'dancing girls and live music', including the Black Tiger. Buzz is said to be one of the liveliest, and there's a night club in the Rila hotel. The Red Lion is a 'good drinking place with a real fire'. Katy's Pub 'with a guitarist in the attic' and Mamacita's Mexican restaurant and bar have been recommended in the past. There are also 'adult' bars, but they are away from the main streets, and advertising is now said to be banned, though there are plenty of touts.

Tour operator reps organize pub crawls, folklore evenings etc. Excursions to the Rila monastery or to Sofia by coach are interesting.

KEY FACTS

Resort	990m
	3,250ft
Slopes	990-2600m
	3,250-8,530ft
Lifts	14
Pistes	75km

TOURIST OFFICE

www.banskoski.com

Bansko

- ☐ Lots of fast lifts on the mountain
- ☐ Atmospheric town centre
- ☐ Friendly, helpful locals

- ☐ Long, queue-prone access gondola
- ☐ Few off-slope diversions
- ☐ Some unfinished buildings evident

Bansko is an old valley town in the scenic Pirin National Park, catapulted into the 21st century in 2004 by the construction of modern lifts and smart lodgings. Reporters like what they find, and some go back repeatedly.

The area near the base of the access gondola to the slopes has a lot of modern hotels, apartments, bars and restaurants. Some are ski-in, and many others run shuttle-buses to the lift.

The older part of town looks no great beauty on the outskirts, but the central square reveals a quiet and charming heart, and there are few outward signs of commercial tourism.

The slopes are reached by an eight-seat gondola to Bunderishka, for which there are long queues in the morning ('horrendous, took almost two hours'). Some people start queuing well before the lift opens, others take taxis up the mountain or join the ski school (which gives you priority). An alternative is to pay for a VIP card, we're told. A planned additional gondola is on hold. Queues further up the hill are rare.

There is an easy blue piste back to the town, with snowmaking and floodlighting. Most lifts are fast chairs, and successive ones take you up mainly north-facing slopes to the high point of the area. Work has begun on replacing a slow triple chair with a six-pack. You can ski down reds or blues to Shiligarnika, or a red followed by

the Tomba black to Bunderishka. Some of these are quite long and challenging. Reporters judge the piste classification accurate.

A reporter notes that small variations on the pistes and skiable trees beside them make the area add up to more skiing than you might expect. There is a small terrain park.

The nursery slopes near the top of the gondola are good, with little through-traffic. The main school – Ulen – has 'well-trained and experienced instructors with a strong focus on piste safety', says a 2015 reporter. There's a snow garden, and the kindergarten takes children from age four years.

Snow is more reliable than the Bulgarian norm and there is substantial snowmaking with 60 more snow-guns planned for 2015/16. Reporters find the grooming good.

Mountain huts are mostly self-service, and the food 'basic'. But the newly extended VIP Room at the top of the gondola serves 'top Italian cuisine in a well-designed dining room'.

Hotels near the gondola station (the obvious place to stay) include the

Bulgaria

663

↑ Most Bulgarian slopes are cut through the trees and suit intermediates best
DAVID MAXWELL-LEES

swanky Florimont with its own casino; the 5-star Kempinski Grand Arena ('spa to die for') – its Tepanyaki Japanese restaurant is 'a special experience'; and the MPM Sport ('spacious, with a good spa'). The Emerald has been recommended. The Lion has 'spacious, spotlessly clean rooms and a pool, steam and sauna'. The Grand Montana apartments are 'basic, spacious and excellent value', says a 2015 visitor.

There are some smart bars near the lift. Staying there, you are a short taxi ride from the town and its many mehanas (traditional inns) with roaring fires, real Bulgarian food and good wine. And there are lots of lively bars – readers' tips include Harry's bar near the Victoria restaurant ('a good buzz'), Happy End at the gondola base ('good bands, happy hour, mainly a British crowd'), Euphoria, Penguins, Diamonds and Amigos.

Other activities include paragliding, skating on an outside rink, snowmobiling and bowling.

KEY FACTS

Resort	1650m
	5,410ft
Slopes	1450-1935m
	4,760-6,350ft
Lifts	15
Pistes	37km

TOURIST OFFICE

www.
pamporovoresort.com

Pamporovo

➕ Pretty, tree-lined slopes
➕ Good, low-cost choice for novices

➖ Limited extent and short runs
➖ Poor piste maintenance

Pamporovo is a purpose-built village, in a pretty woodland area a short shuttle-bus ride from its easy slopes that suit beginners best.

The resort is strictly for beginners and near-beginners, with mostly easy and short runs – but some beginners find the runs rather too narrow. Keen intermediates and better will the find area too limited and lacking in challenges.

The 37km of slopes are pretty and sheltered, with pistes cutting through pine forest. For 2015/16 a new quad will replace a draglift beside the black No 3 run and will serve about 80% of the slopes, we're told. There's a

half-pipe and a terrain park.

Snow reliability is poor, but snowmaking covers 90% of the slopes. There are plenty of mountain huts, though they are not enticing.

The ski school is praised this year: 'Very friendly, well organized, incredible value.' There are 25km of cross-country trails.

A past reporter recommends the hotel Finlandia.

Romania

£50
RESORT PRICE INDEX

+ Cheap packages, and very low prices on the spot
+ Interesting excursions and friendly local people
+ Good tuition from keen instructors

− Primitive facilities, especially mountain restaurants and toilets
− Uninspiring food
− Very limited slopes

Romania sells mainly on price. On-the-spot prices, in particular, are very low. Provided you don't have unreasonably high expectations, you'll probably come back from Poiana Brasov content. It allows complete beginners to try a ski holiday at the minimum cost, and to have a jolly time in the evenings without adding substantially to that cost.

TOURIST OFFICE
www.poianabrasov.com

POIANA BRASOV
Most accommodation is scattered around a pretty wooded plateau and is a bus ride or cheap taxi ride from the slopes ↓

Romania's main resort – and the only one featuring in any UK package programme – is **Poiana Brasov** (1030m) in the Carpathian mountains. It is a short drive above the city of Brasov, about 120km (on alarmingly rough, slow roads) north-west of the capital and arrival airport, Bucharest.

The resort is purpose-built, and has the air of a spacious, pleasant holiday camp. But it is not designed for the convenience of skiers: some serious-sized hotels are right by the lifts, but most are scattered about a pretty, wooded plateau, served by regular buses and cheap taxis.

The slopes are extremely limited – 24km of pistes in total. They consist of intermediate treelined runs with a decent vertical of about 825m, roughly following the line of the main cable car and gondola, plus an open nursery area at the top. A few years ago four new slopes (two blues and two reds) opened, accessed by a quad and a six-pack. There are some nursery lifts at village level, which are used when snow permits. Night skiing is also available. The resort gets weekend crowds from Brasov and Bucharest, and queues can result, but during the week there are few problems.

A key part of the resort's appeal is the friendly and effective teaching from enthusiastic instructors.

Hotel standards are higher than you might expect. The linked 3-star Bradul and 4-star Sport hotels are handy for the lower nursery slopes and for one of the cable cars. Guests in both have use of the Sport's spa facilities. Après-ski revolves around the hotel bars and nightclubs – plus outings to rustic barns for BBQs with gypsy music and to the bars and restaurants in the nearby town of Brasov. With cheap beer and very cheap spirits on tap, things can be quite lively.

Off-slope facilities are limited: there are two good-sized pools (in hotels) and bowling. An excursion to nearby Bran Castle (Count Dracula's lair) is also popular.

Slovenia

£65
RESORT PRICE INDEX

+ Low prices
+ Beautiful, varied scenery
+ Good beginner slopes and lessons

− Limited, mostly easy slopes
− Still lots of slow, antiquated lifts
− Mountain huts not a highlight

Slovenia offers lower prices and fewer crowds than the Alps, attracting economy minded visitors from neighbouring Italy and Austria as well as Britain and the Netherlands. The ski areas are limited and a bit antiquated; most suit novices well. Some Slovenian resorts are making obvious investments but some are struggling. Sadly, one of the best, Kanin – which has Slovenia's highest terrain and cross-border skiing into Italy – has been closed for the last couple of seasons, and as we go to press we haven't heard whether it will be operational for the 2015/16 season. For information see www.boveckanin.si/en/ski-resort.

TOURIST OFFICES
www.slovenia.info
Bled
www.bled.si

WENDY KING

Slovenia is not renowned for its mountain huts but there are a few like this on Vogel's slopes
↓

Slovenia – which is bordered by Italy, Austria and Croatia – has 30 or so ski areas, the main ones concentrated in the Julian Alps in the west, dominated by its highest mountain, Mt Triglav; all are small and some are tiny. None is likely to keep the adventurous piste-basher amused for a week; but you can have an enjoyable trip touring by car or by combining several resorts from one base. EasyJet (from Stansted) and Adria (from Gatwick) fly to Ljubljana.

The season is shorter than in the Alps and the resorts low. Most slopes are below 2000m.

Prices are low, and there is a positive feel – and a warm and hospitable welcome. Standards of service and accommodation have improved – the hotels may not be particularly attractive, but many are new or modernized, complete with pools, spas and often free Wi-Fi.

Getting around is relatively easy, and most ski areas are within a 40-minute drive of each other on good roads. And the main resorts are within a two-hour bus ride of Ljubljana.

Bled, with its beautiful lake and fairly lively nightlife, is an attractive base and is featured by a few British tour operators. It has just one steepish slope. But other resorts nearby include Kranjska Gora, Krvavec, Kanin, Vogel and Kobla (the only ski area in Slovenia reachable by train).

The other main group of resorts centres on Maribor to the east, a quite different area of low-slung wooded ridges. But it has the biggest ski area in the country at 43km.

The Ski Pass Slovenia covers all resorts in Slovenia.

Most resorts fit best into the intermediate category but differ on their suitability for novices. Experts will find few black runs, but there is good off-piste when conditions permit. Lift systems are improving and queues are rare. Most Slovenians visit at weekends; midweek the slopes can be deserted. A common feature of many areas is an access lift with no runs back to valley level. One drawback for us is the lack of quality lunches: snacks and picnics are the norm, hearty menus and cute huts are rare. Ski schools are of a high quality and cheap, with good spoken English. Other winter activities are big in Slovenia, too, so there is plenty to do off the slopes.

Krvavec

KEY FACTS

Resort	1450m
	4,760ft
Slopes	1450-1970m
	4,760-6,460ft
Lifts	11
Pistes	30km

TOURIST OFFICE

www.rtc-krvavec.si

- ➕ Convenient for short breaks
- ➕ Quiet slopes midweek
- ➕ Jolly, family atmosphere

- ➖ Lacks proper resort base
- ➖ Short, mainly south-facing runs
- ➖ Not ideal for novices

Krvavec has been voted Slovenia's best ski area and is just 8km from Ljubljana airport. There's no central village, but then most visitors are locals on day trips from the city.

Krvavec has some of the country's steepest slopes, including five black runs. It is a lively place, especially at weekends. Most visitors are families on day trips. Bled is 40 minutes by daily bus (free with the lift pass). There is no resort, but there is one hotel on the slopes and some lodging in nearby Cerklje. The local lift pass also covers Rogla, near Maribor.

A gondola goes up to the slopes, which span three partly wooded hills from a high point of 1970m. The lifts include a six-pack and a quad; queues

are rare. The pistes get a lot of sun, though snowmaking is extensive and grooming good. There's a terrain park, a good nursery slope and a children's area with a fun park, moving carpet and drag lift. But there are few easy blues to progress to. The mid-mountain Plaza has picnic spots and snack bars. There are huts on the Kriska Planina area. Snowshoeing is popular, and you can try airboarding and tobogganing – floodlit on Friday and Saturday evenings.

Kranjska Gora

KEY FACTS

Resort	810m
	2,660ft
Slopes	810-1295m
	2,660-4,250ft
Lifts	18
Pistes	20km

TOURIST OFFICE

www.kranjska-gora.si/en

- ➕ Good for novices and families
- ➕ Convenient, good, slope-side hotels

- ➖ Slopes limited in extent, variety, length and vertical
- ➖ Still some old lifts, and gets busy

Despite limited slopes (most other areas are bigger), Kranjska Gora is offered by a few UK tour operators. It's a good-value, pretty and compact resort that is popular with families. Since the centre is fairly small, most facilities are near the slopes, too.

Kranjska Gora is close to the Austrian and Italian borders. Day trips to ski in resorts over the borders are possible.

The 20km of wide, treelined pistes rise to 1295m and best suit very unadventurous intermediates and novices – though there is a World Cup slalom black run. The slopes above Podkoren are quiet and gentle.

There are four quad chairlifts, but still lots of draglifts. And getting around involves tedious traversing. Queues are rare despite fairly busy slopes here. Snow reliability is poor, but snowmaking covers many pistes.

There is a terrain park and a children's area with moving carpets. Cross-country trails total 40km. It is back to base for lunch and Bedanc is a good self-service beside chair 7.

Hotels are of a high standard, most with pools and spas. For slope-side convenience, the Lek and Ramada are best. The Alpina is popular with families. We liked the Kompas, with good breakfast buffet and pool.

For eating out try the Kotnik pizzeria, or the Ostarija for finer dining. Ice skating, night tobogganing and snowshoeing are popular.

Slovenia

667

KEY FACTS

Resort	570m
	1,870ft
Slopes	1535-1800m
	5,040-5,910ft
Lifts	9
Pistes	22km

TOURIST OFFICE

www.vogel.si

Vogel

➕ Beautiful lake setting, pretty runs
➕ Good choice of huts

➖ Bus ride from most lodging
➖ Limited in extent and challenge

Vogel overlooks stunning Lake Bohinj, part of the Triglav National Park. It's tiny, but is the main ski area within commuting distance of Bled.

Vogel has the best conditions and prettiest slopes in the area. Buses arrive daily from Bled; but there are small hotels and restaurants near the base and in villages along the lakeside (served by free ski-bus).

The 22km of partly wooded slopes are reached by a cable car up from the valley. A fast quad serves a mid-mountain area, with a single-seat chair to the high point at 1800m (great views). Pistes served by another chair and three drags include a lovely gentle blue. There is a terrain park with beginner and advanced lines and a snowcross course.

There is a separate nursery slope, with snowmaking, a moving carpet and a children's area.

When conditions permit, a long red run returns to the bottom cable car station via a quiet, pretty valley. Several of the huts are nicer than the Slovenian norm.

For a change of scene Kobla, with 24km of wide, wooded runs, is a short bus ride away at Bohinjska Bistrica – the railway terminus. The 5-star Bohinj Park hotel is eco-friendly, with pool, saunas, cinema and bowling. Next door is a huge aqua park. Near Vogel, the 3-star Zlatarog is comfortable.

KEY FACTS

Resort	325m
	1,070ft
Slopes	325-1330m
	1,070-4,360ft
Lifts	21
Pistes	43km

TOURIST OFFICE

www.maribor-pohorje.si

Maribor-Pohorje

➕ Good access, close to the city
➕ Gentle, sheltered slopes for novices

➖ Mostly short runs
➖ Few challenges except the FIS run

Slovenia's second city, Maribor, is just 6km from its local slopes – where there's also limited lodging. There's some varied terrain but most runs are short and served by drag lifts running along one side of a ridge.

This is the country's biggest ski area, twice the size of better-known Kranjska Gora.

The lifts include a six-pack and a gondola to Pohorje summit. There's night skiing, and snowmaking covers 95% of the area. There are 27km of

cross-country trails. The area lift pass also covers Kranjska Gora. The Pohorje school offers a wide range of classes. There are several atmospheric old inns serving good, Hungarian-influenced food. The 4-star Arena and 3-star Videc hotels are slope-side.

WENDY KING

Most of Slovenia's runs are short and suit unadventurous intermediates best →

Scotland

➕ Easy to get to from northern Britain	➖ Weather is extremely changeable and sometimes vicious
➕ It is possible to experience perfect snow and very satisfying skiing	➖ Snowfall is erratic
➕ Midweek it's rarely crowded	➖ Slopes limited; runs mainly short
➕ Lots to do off the slopes	➖ Queues can be a problem in good weather

Scottish skiing conditions are unpredictable, to say the least. If you live nearby and can go at short notice when things look good, the several ski areas are a tremendous asset. But booking a holiday here as a replacement for your usual week in the Alps is just too risky.

Most of the slopes in most of the areas suit intermediates best. But all apart from The Lecht also offer one or two tough or very tough slopes.

For novices who are really keen to learn, Scotland could make sense, especially if you live nearby. You can book instruction via one of the excellent outdoor centres, many of which also provide accommodation. The ski schools at the ski areas themselves are also very good.

Snowboarding is popular, and all of the ski areas have some special terrain features, but maintaining these facilities in good nick is problematic. When the conditions are right, the natural terrain is good for freeriding.

CairnGorm Mountain is the best-known resort, with 11 lifts and 30km of runs. The small town of Aviemore is the main base (with a shuttle-bus to the slopes). Eateries include the Winking Owl, a 'modern gastro-pub'. The slopes are accessed by a funicular from the main car park up to Ptarmigan at 1100m. There's a 'short but impressive' terrain park.

Nevis Range is the highest Scottish resort, with 20km of groomed runs on the north-facing slopes of Aonach Mor reaching 1190m. It has 11 lifts plus a long six-seat access gondola. There are many B&Bs and hotels in and around Fort William, 10 minutes away by bus.

Glenshee is the largest ski area, with 40km of runs spread out over three minor parallel valleys served by 22 lifts, including a chairlift link to the Cairnwell cafe and the slopes in that area. It has some natural quarter-pipes. Glenshee is primarily a venue for day-trippers, though there are hotels, hostels and B&Bs in the area.

Glencoe's seven lifts and 20km of runs lie east of moody Glen Coe itself. We get a steady dribble of reports from experienced reporters impressed by the whole deal – 'A truly wonderful experience,' says one. A double chairlift and a drag go up to the main slopes, including the nursery area. The black Flypaper is 'seriously steep'. The cafe at the base serves 'traditional hearty fare'. The isolated Kings House Hotel is 2km away.

The Lecht is largely a novices' area, with 13 lifts and 20km of runs on the gentle slopes beside a high pass, with a series of parallel lifts and runs above the car parks. With a maximum vertical of only 200m, runs are short. There's extensive snowmaking, a terrain park, and a day lodge at the base. The village of Tomintoul is 10km away.

FURTHER INFORMATION

The VisitScotland organization runs an excellent website at: ski.visitscotland.com

Japan

- ➕ Reliable deep powder snow in Hokkaido resorts, lift-served
- ➕ Fabulous food
- ➕ Polite and gracious locals
- ➕ Night skiing is the norm, allowing a long ski day if you want one

- ➖ Pricey and lengthy trip; 6,000 miles and 24 hours door to door
- ➖ Lack of off-slope diversions
- ➖ Snowfall can go on for weeks in Hokkaido resorts
- ➖ Main hotels vast, modern, charmless

Although it is roughly the same size as the British Isles, Japan has hundreds of ski resorts. And places on the northern island of Hokkaido have developed something like cult status with keen skiers and riders from Australia. The reason is simple: humongous, frequent and reliable falls of powder snow.

You fly in to Sapporo (about three hours by bus to the resorts), via Tokyo or Osaka. Ski Independence says a week in Niseko and a two-night stopover in Tokyo on the way home would cost from around £1,700.

Few of the locals speak English but we were struck by how friendly, charming, polite and helpful they all were. The food is delicious – and the menus often have photos to help you.

Hokkaido has a well-deserved reputation for powder snow, which usually falls almost constantly from December to the end of February. Skiing waist-deep powder is normally an everyday occurrence. You go for

that, not for the piste skiing. The slopes are not steep, which some people are disappointed by; but there is tremendous skiing among nicely spaced trees. Strangely, off-piste is officially prohibited in many resorts and there are prominent signs saying that – but nearly everyone ignores the ban and we are told that the officials turn a blind eye to it. In Niseko, though, off-piste is allowed (except in two dangerous areas marked on the piste map) and there are gates into the backcountry. For 2014/15, Furano also installed four access points for off piste; you must fill in a form and give it to the ski patrol before heading out.

On our 2013 visit we were unlucky with the weather – it was warm and either foggy or windy most of the time. That meant avalanche danger was high and so out-of-bounds skiing was out of the question most of the time. But nearly all reporters have been luckier. Getting the most out of the off-piste means hiring a guide. We used Hokkaido Powder Guides one day and went to the tiny resort of Kamui where they found us the legendary waist-deep powder at last. A 2015 reporter was very happy with Black Diamond Tours.

Niseko is made up of three areas of slopes – Grand Hirafu (Hirafu and Hanazono), Annupuri and Niseko Village. All except Hanazono open until 8pm or 8.30pm thanks to one of the world's largest – and most heavily used – night skiing operations. The

← There are lots of resorts on the main island of Honshu – only the better-known ones are shown on our map. But the best snow is on Hokkaido

Japan is famous for its tree skiing. Don't worry, they are not all as tight as these ➔

TANYA BOOTH

KEY FACTS

Niseko		
Slopes	300-1200m	
	980-3,940ft	
Lifts		29
Pistes		55km

Rusutsu		
Slopes	400-995m	
	1310-3,260ft	
Lifts		18
Pistes		42km

Furano		
Slopes	250-1200m	
	820-3,940ft	
Lifts		9
Pistes		30km

More information
To really get to grips with the resorts on offer in Japan, spend some time delving into this site:
www.snowjapan.com

TOURIST OFFICES

Niseko
www.nisekotourism.com
www.niseko.ne.jp/en/index.html
Hirafu
www.grand-hirafu.jp/winter/en/
Niseko Village
www.niseko-village.com
Annupuri
www.annupurivillage.com
Rusutsu
www.rusutsu.co.jp
Furano
www.furanotourism.com

three are linked, but not as efficiently as you might wish. There are some modern lifts, but also lots of old chairs – including three ancient singles.

The biggest and most popular area, Grand Hirafu, has an eight-seat gondola from the base and a smart day lodge and restaurant.

Go Snow does lessons and guiding – 'instructors were great and spoke English' said a 2015 reporter. There are modern rather isolated ski-in/ski-out hotels (but little else) at the Annupuri and Niseko Village bases. We (and a reporter) stayed happily at The Green Leaf in Niseko Village in 2013 – lovely onsen (see below), good buffet food, friendly staff. The Hilton Niseko Village has spectacular views from most rooms and its own onsen.

Or you can stay in the little town of Hirafu which has varied architecture – ancient and modern; a bit ramshackle but with a very friendly feel with lots of small bars and restaurants serving excellent traditional Japanese food as well as burgers and the like, many quite lively and busy. We enjoyed the Tamashii bar – full of Australians, with music, dancing, pool and dartboards. A 2015 visitor praised Wild Bill's. There are some good modern apartments alongside traditional pensions and lodges. Beware of the pavements – they are often icy and treacherous.

Free shuttle-buses run between the lift bases every 20 minutes, but they were oversubscribed on our visit and they stop at 8.30pm. Taxis from Hirafu to Niseko Village cost 3,000 yen.

Rusutsu is about half an hour from Niseko, and makes a viable day trip. The slopes, over three interlinked mountains, are slightly more limited but have a much better lift system (four gondolas and seven fast chairs). The snow here can be as good as in Niseko (though it doesn't fall in quite the same quantity), and it doesn't get tracked out so quickly. But they blast out pop music from speakers on the lift pylons which spoils the charm of the surroundings. The Side Country Park has wooden obstacles in the

trees; there's a half-pipe too. The vast Rusutsu Resort Hotel complex is quite bizarre to western eyes, with a huge summer roller coaster and big wheel outside. Inside there are surreal touches such as life-size dummies playing jazz and a huge carousel for kids to ride. None of the bars open till 5pm so there is a distinct lack of après-ski. There's a wide choice of restaurants serving good Japanese food. The Pension Clydesdale, a few kilometres away, was recommended by a recent reporter.

Furano is four to five hours from Niseko and offers a tad more vertical, over two linked sectors. But the ski area is half the size, the slopes are easy and there are a lot of old lifts. You can visit other nearby resorts such as Kamui and also go with a guided group to the lift-served but ungroomed Asahidake mountain (a live volcano, around an hour away). The Furano Prince is a vast modern, isolated hotel at the foot of the slopes and a 10-minute bus ride from town.

The largest ski area in Japan is on the main island of Honshu: **Shiga Kogen**, comprising 21 interlinked resorts and a huge diversity of terrain. It was the site of several major events in the 1998 Winter Olympics. **Hakuba** is a group of nine resorts accessing more than 200 runs.

Japan

671

THE ONSEN EXPERIENCE

Onsen are complexes of hot baths to soak in, showers and communal volcanic thermal pools; they are a key part of Japanese culture and a major part of après-ski. All onsen are basically set up in the same way: men and women shower and bathe in their separate areas. Then, if they wish, they can congregate to soak and have a drink in a communal thermal pool, which more often than not will be outside and surrounded by snow.

RESORT DIRECTORY / INDEX

This is an index to the resort chapters in the book; you'll find page references for about 400 resorts that are described in those chapters (note that if the resort you are looking up is covered in a chapter devoted to a bigger resort, the page reference will be to the start of the chapter, not to the exact page on which the minor resort is described). You'll also find here brief descriptions of around 1,000 other resorts, most of them smaller than those we've covered in full.

Key

🚡 *Lifts*
🎿 *Pistes*

49 Degrees North USA
Inland area with best snow in Washington State, including 120-acre bowl reserved for powder weekends.
1195m; slopes 1195–1760m
🚡 *5* 🎿 *780 acres*

Abetone Italy
Resort in the exposed Apennines, less than two hours from Florence and Pisa.
1400m; slopes 1200–1940m
🚡 *25* 🎿 *70km*

Abtenau Austria
Sizeable village in Dachstein-West region near Salzburg, on large plain ideal for cross-country.
710m; slopes 710–1190m
🚡 *7* 🎿 *12km*

Achenkirch Austria
Unspoiled, low-altitude Tirolean village close to Niederau and Alpbach. Beautiful setting overlooking a lake.
930m; slopes 930–1800m
🚡 *30* 🎿 *50km*

Adelboden 454

Les Aillons-Margériaz France
Traditional village near Chambéry. Nicely sheltered slopes.
1000m; slopes 1000–1900m
🚡 *21* 🎿 *40km*

Alagna 416
Small resort on the east fringe of the Monterosa Ski area.

Alba Italy
Picturesque Trentino village with a small, quiet area; access to the Sella Ronda at nearby Canazei.
1515m; slopes 1515–2428m
🚡 *6* 🎿 *15km*

Alberschwende 104
Village in Bregenzerwald.

Albiez-Montrond 265
Authentic old French village in Maurienne valley.

Alleghe Italy
Dolomite village near Cortina in a pretty lakeside setting close to numerous areas.
1000m
🚡 *24* 🎿 *80km*

Les Allues 282
Rustic village on the road up to Méribel.

Alpbachtal-Wildschönau – Ski Juwel 93

Alpe-d'Huez 196

Alpe-du-Grand-Serre France
Small resort close to Grenoble, off road to Alpe-d'Huez and Les Deux-Alpes. 800m vertical, split between a broad open bowl above the treeline and a worthwhile sheltered sector below it. Mainly blue and red slopes served by draglifts.
1370m; slopes 1370–2185m
🚡 *14* 🎿 *55km*

Alpendorf Austria
Outpost of St Johann im Pongau, at one end of an extensive three-valley lift network linking via Wagrain to Flachau – all part of the Salzburger Sportwelt area. Good intermediate runs.
850m; slopes 800–2185m
🚡 *64* 🎿 *200km*

Alpenglow USA
Alaskan ski resort.
762m; slopes 2500–3900m
🚡 *4* 🎿 *320 acres*

Alpenregion Bludenz Austria
Area centred on the medieval town of Bludenz, in the west of Austria, bordering Switzerland. Two main ski areas: Brandnertal to the west and Sonnenkopf in the Klostertal to the east, covered by the Arlberg ski pass.

Alpika Service Russia
One of the venues for the Sochi Winter Olympics in 2014.
560m; slopes 940–2320m
🚡 *13* 🎿 *72km*

Alpine Meadows USA
Squaw Valley's neighbour – and covered on the same lift pass – with similar, lightly wooded terrain, an impressive snow record and runs of all classifications; excellent beginner slopes and mostly uncrowded. The resort boundary is open – expeditions require guidance. There's no resort in the European sense, but there's lots of lodgings close by in lakeside Tahoe City.
2085m; slopes 2085–2635m
🚡 *13* 🎿 *2400 acres*

Alps Resort South Korea
Korea's most northerly, snow-reliable resort, about five hours from Seoul. 🚡 *5*

Alta 586

Alta Badia 429
Part of the Sella Ronda circuit.

Radstadt-Altenmarkt Austria
Unspoiled village, well placed just off the Salzburg-Villach autobahn for numerous resorts including snow-sure Obertauern and those in the Salzburger Sportwelt.
855m; slopes 855–1570m
🚡 *8* 🎿 *20km*

Alto Campoo Spain
Barren, desolate place near Santander, with undistinguished slopes, but magnificent wilderness views.
1650m; slopes 1650–2130m
🚡 *13*

Alt St Johann Switzerland
Old cross-country village with Alpine slopes connecting into Unterwasser area near Liechtenstein.
900m; slopes 900–2260m
🚡 *17* 🎿 *60km*

Alyeska USA
Alaskan area 60km from Anchorage, with luxury hotel.
75m; slopes 75–1200m
🚡 *9* 🎿 *785 acres*

Aminona 465
Purpose-built resort in the Crans-Montana network.

Andalo Italy
Trentino village not far from Madonna.
1050m; slopes 1035–2125m
🚡 *16* 🎿 *60km*

Andelsbuch 104
Village in Bregenzerwald.

Andermatt 457

Andorra la Vella 76
Andorra's capital.

Angel Fire USA
Intermediate area near Taos, New Mexico. Height usually ensures good snow.
2620m; slopes 2620–3255m
🚡 *5* 🎿 *455 acres*

Les Angles 317

Ankogel Austria
Limited but varied area in the Hohe Tauern region in Carinthia; close to the Molltal Glacier and Slovenia. Mostly red and black runs; longest is 7km. Lift station a short drive from Mallnitz village.
1050m; slopes 1300–2635m
🚡 *7* 🎿 *35km*

Annaberg-Lungötz Austria
Peaceful village near Filzmoos in a pretty setting, sharing a sizeable area with Gosau.
775m; slopes 775–1620m
🚡 *33* 🎿 *65km*

Annupuri 670
Interlinked area in Niseko, Japan.

Antagnod Italy
Day-trip area near Champoluc, above Aosta valley. Great views to Monte Rosa. No village, but family oriented with quiet nursery slopes and a handful of runs.
1710m; slopes 1710–2305m
🚡 *4* 🎿 *14km*

Anthony Lakes USA
Small area in Oregon with one chair and two beginner lifts.
2165m; slopes 2165–2435m
🚡 *3* 🎿 *21trails*

Resort directory / index

Anzère Switzerland
Sympathetically designed
modern resort on a sunny
balcony near Crans-Montana,
with uncrowded slopes suited
to leisurely intermediates.
Lots of old, slow lifts but the
area is very much a family
resort, with village nursery
slopes and spa centre. Little
to challenge experts except
the 5km Pas de Maimbre
black run, an itinerary and
some gentle off-piste. There's
a terrain park. For a small
place there is a reasonable
choice of restaurants and
bars. Lots of marked walks
and a 3km toboggan run.
1500m; slopes 1500–2420m
⛷ 14 🚠 58km

Aosta Italy
Historic valley town with a
long gondola ride up to
mountain resort of Pila. Aosta
is a real working town with
people in suits rather than
skiwear. It has good-value
accommodation, a lot more
bars and restaurants than
Pila, and a lovely traffic-free
centre. Other resorts in the
Aosta valley are within day-
trip distance and are covered
by the lift pass.
1800m; slopes 1550–2750m
⛷ 14 🚠 70km

Aosta valley Italy
Region north of Turin with
Italy's highest skiing and
dominated by Monte Bianco
(Mont Blanc). Lots of resorts
covered by the Valley pass.

Apex Canada
Small, friendly, rather isolated
modern village. Well worth
stopping off here for a night
or two on a tour of western
BC resorts. Varied terrain that
suits confident intermediates
best, but also excellent
beginner slopes.
1575m; slopes 1575–2180m
⛷ 4 🚠 1112 acres

Aprica Italy
Ugly, straggling village
between Lake Como and the
Brenta Dolomites, with bland
slopes and limited facilities.
1180m; slopes 1180–2300m
⛷ 18 🚠 50km

Arabba 429
Village in the Sella Ronda.

Aragnouet-Piau France
Purpose-built mid-mountain
satellite with lifts up from the
old valley town too. Best
suited to families, beginners
and early intermediates.
1850m; slopes 1420–2500m
⛷ 12 🚠 65km

Arapahoe Basin USA
Developing, exceptionally high
day-skiing area near Keystone.
Excellent snowfall record and
very long season. Good mix of
open and wooded runs of
every standard, plus serious
steeps.
3285m; slopes 3285–3800m
⛷ 7 🚠 900 acres

Araucarias Chile
Exotic area in central Chile,
around and below a mildly
active volcano in the
Conguillio National Park.
1500m
⛷ 4 🚠 350 hectares

Arcalis 76
Isolated ski area in Andorra.
1940m; slopes 1940–2625m
⛷ 13 🚠 28.5km

Les Arcs 206

Ardent 216
Quiet hamlet with quick
access to Avoriaz.

Åre 661

Arêches-Beaufort France
Secluded little village 25km
from Albertville, with mostly
intermediate terrain on two
areas 3km apart. The slopes
of both Les Saisies and Les
Contamines are less than
25km away.
1080m; slopes 1080–2300m
⛷ 12 🚠 55km

Argentière 223
Village beneath Chamonix's
Grands Montets.

Arinsal 78

Arizona Snowbowl USA
Small but interesting ski area
just outside the pleasant town
of Flagstaff. Worth a visit if en
route to the nearby Grand
Canyon in winter. Low
snowfall despite the high
altitude is a drawback.
slopes 2690–3290m ⛷ 4

Arnoldstein / Dreiländereck
Austria
One of several little areas
overlooking the town of
Villach.
68om; slopes 680–1455m
⛷ 7 🚠 17km

Arolla Switzerland
Tiny village in pretty riverside
setting south of Sion in the
Val d'Hérens. Main attraction
is heli-skiing. Wonderful
descents from 3800m.
2000m; slopes 2000–2890m
⛷ 6 🚠 47km

Arosa 459

Arrowhead 559
Slope-side hamlet next to
Beaver Creek.

Artesina Italy
Purpose-built Piedmont resort
south of Turin, lacking
character and atmosphere.
Part of Mondolé ski area with
Prato Nevoso.
1300m; slopes 1320–2100m
⛷ 23 🚠 130km

Ascutney Mountain USA
Family resort in Vermont 6okm
from Killington, 200km from
Boston.
⛷ 6 🚠 200 acres

Asiago Italy
Sizeable resort close to
Verona, but at low altitude
and with limited vertical.
1000m; slopes 1000–1380m
⛷ 8 🚠 12pistes

Aspen 552

Attitash USA
One of the biggest ski areas
in eastern US. Uncrowded
slopes. Lodging in nearby
North Conway, and other New
Hampshire areas close by.
slopes 180–715m
⛷ 12 🚠 280 acres

Au 104
Village in Bregenzerwald.

Auffach 93
Small village in Ski Juwel
(Alpbachtal-Wildschönau).

Auris-en-Oisans 196
Quiet hamlet linked to Alpe-
d'Huez.

Auron France
Pleasant, family-oriented
resort with varied, sheltered,
intermediate slopes; a stark
contrast to nearby Isola 2000.
Good choice of mountain
restaurants.
1600m; slopes 1150–2450m
⛷ 20 🚠 135km

Auronzo di Cadore Italy
Sizeable village that's a
cheaper base for visiting
Cortina. Its own slopes are of
negligible interest.
865m; slopes 865–1585m
⛷ 5 🚠 7km

Aussois 265
Charming rustic working
village in the Maurienne
valley.

Autrans France
Major cross-country village,
close to Grenoble. Two limited
areas of downhill slopes.
1050m; slopes 1050–1650m
⛷ 12 🚠 20km

Avon USA
Small town only a couple of
miles from Beaver Creek.
Inexpensive base from which
to ski Beaver Creek, Vail and
Breckenridge.

Avoriaz 216

Axamer Lizum Austria
Mountain outpost of the Inn-
side village of Axams. A
simple ski station and nothing
more, but it does have some
good slopes and reliable
snow conditions. Covered by
standard Innsbruck pass.
1580m; slopes 830–2340m

Axams Austria
Quiet village in Innsbruck
area, at bottom of the Axamer
Lizum ski area.
880m

Ax-les-Thermes 317

Bad Gastein 96

Badger Pass USA
Base for 350 miles of superb
backcountry touring in
Yosemite National Park.
Spectacular views.
2195m; slopes 2195–2435m
⛷ 5 🚠 90 acres

Bad Hofgastein 96
Relaxed and spacious spa
resort in the Gastein Valley.

Badia (Pedraces) 429
Roadside village linked via La
Villa to the Sella Ronda.

Bad Kleinkirchheim 99

Banff 616

Bansko 662

Baqueira-Beret 655

Barboleuse 515
Quiet base for skiing the
Villars slopes.

Bardonecchia Italy
Sizeable railway town set in
an attractive valley near the
entrance to the Fréjus road
tunnel; overlooked until the
2006 Turin Winter Olympics
brought investment and
raised its profile as a good-
value intermediate
destination. What it lacks in
classic mountain charm, it
gains in a fairly extensive area
of slopes on two separate
mountains linked by free bus.
There are plenty of hotels,
and the former Olympic
village residence has spacious
apartment accommodation.
The resort's easy road and rail
links mean it is popular with
weekenders from Turin, but
otherwise fairly quiet during
the week with plenty of
leisurely cruising on
uncrowded pistes – worth
considering as a base for
touring other nearby French
and Italian resorts too. Snow
reliability isn't particularly
great though and, coupled
with the large number of
awkward draglifts, may deter
some visitors.
1310m; slopes 1290–2695m
⛷ 23 🚠 100km

Barèges 317

Bariloche (Catedral)
Argentina
The place to stay when skiing
Cerro Catedral, this was once
a quaint lakeside town, but is
now a substantial resort –
including the Llao Llao Resort
and Spa. The slopes at
Cathedral are 20 minutes by
shuttle-bus.
slopes 1030–2180m
🚠 39 ⛷ 103km

Les Barzettes 465
Smaller base along the road
from Crans-Montana.

Bayrischzell Germany
Bavarian resort south of
Munich and close to Austrian
border.
800m; slopes 1090–1563m
🚠 25 ⛷ 40km

Bear Mountain USA
Southern California's main
area, in the beautiful San
Bernardino National Forest
region. Full snowmaking.
slopes 2170–2685m
🚠 12 ⛷ 195 acres

Bears Town South Korea
Modern resort with runs cut
out of thick forest. Biggest
resort near Seoul (only an
hour's drive), so it can get
very crowded.
🚠 9

Bear Valley USA
Resort in northern California,
between Lake Tahoe and
Yosemite.
2010m; slopes 2010–2590m
🚠 10 ⛷ 1280 acres

Beaulard Italy
Little place just off the road
between Sauze d'Oulx and
Bardonecchia.
1215m; slopes 1215–2120m
🚠 6 ⛷ 20km

Beaver Creek 559

Beaver Mountain USA
Small Utah area north of Salt
Lake City, too far from Park
City for a day trip.
2195m; slopes 2195–2680m
🚠 3 ⛷ 525 acres

Beitostølen Norway
Small family resort in
southern Norway (east of
Bergen), with lots of cross-
country in the region.
900m
🚠 9 ⛷ 25km

Belleayre Mountain USA
State-owned resort near
Albany, New York State. Cheap
but old lifts and short runs.
775m; slopes 775–1015m
🚠 7 ⛷ 170 acres

Bellwald Switzerland
Traditional Rhône valley resort
near Fiesch, Riederalp and
Bettmeralp. Part of the Goms
Valley region.
1600m; slopes 1600–2560m
🚠 5 ⛷ 30km

Ben Lomond Australia
Small intermediate/beginner
area in Ben Lomond National
Park, Tasmania, 260km from
Hobart.
1450m; slopes 1460–1570m
🚠 6 ⛷ 14 hectares

Berchtesgaden Germany
Pleasant old town close to
Salzburg, known for its Nordic
skiing but with several little
Alpine areas nearby.
550m

Bergün Switzerland
Traditional, quiet, unspoiled,
virtually traffic-free little family
resort on the rail route
between Davos and St Moritz.
5km toboggan run.
1375m; slopes 1400–2550m
🚠 3 ⛷ 23km

Berkshire East USA
Resort in Massachusetts,
southern New England, near
the Mohawk Trail.
slopes 165–525m
🚠 5 ⛷ 200 acres

Berwang Austria
Quiet village in a spacious
valley close to Lermoos. It
claims the most skiing of the
region too (36km) – though
many runs are short and easy.
The Zugspitz Arena lift pass,
to which our figures relate,
covers these and the other
resorts of the valley. The
village enjoys a splendid
winter-wonderland setting,
with lifts rising on two sides.
There is a good mix of sunny
and shady slopes, shared with
Bichlbach; some of these give
over 500m vertical to the lift
station. There are good cross-
country loops at altitude,
plenty of huts and a long
toboggan run.
1340m; slopes 990–2960m
🚠 52 ⛷ 147km

Bessans France
Old cross-country village near
Modane well placed for
touring Maurienne valley
resorts.
1710m; slopes 1740–2200m
🚠 2 ⛷ 3km

Besse France
Charming old village built out
of lava, with purpose-built
slope-side satellite Super-
Besse. Beautiful extinct-
volcano scenery.
1050m; slopes 1300–1850m
🚠 23 ⛷ 43km

Bethel USA
Pleasant, historic town very
close to Sunday River, Maine.
Attractive alternative to
staying in the resort.

Le Bettex 269
Small base above St-Gervais,
with links to Megève.

Bettmeralp Switzerland
Central village of the sizeable
Aletsch area near Brig, high
above the Rhône valley, amid
spectacular glacial scenery.
Reached by cable cars from
the valley.
1950m; slopes 1925–2870m
🚠 35 ⛷ 100km

Beuil-les-Launes France
Alpes-Maritimes resort closest
to Nice. Medieval village
which shares area with
Valberg.
1460m; slopes 1400–2011m
🚠 26 ⛷ 90km

Bezau 104
Bregenzerwald village.

Biberwier Austria
Village near Lermoos, with
mainly shady local slopes
more or less spilt equally into
red and blue runs. Makes a
quiet base from which to
access the rest of the Zugspitz
Arena (to which our figures
relate). The main lift from the
valley is a six-pack, and there
are quiet nursery slopes at
the base – with a very long
moving carpet. There is a
terrain park, half-pipe and
snowcross course. There are a
couple of pleasant restaurants
and bars. Like Lermoos, the
village benefits from a tunnel
to remove traffic from the
centre.
990m; slopes 990–2960m
🚠 52 ⛷ 147km

Bichlbach Austria
Smallest of the Zugspitz Arena
villages, sharing slopes with
Berwang. Austria's first
chondola lift starts here. An
unspoiled base for visiting the
rest of the area.
1080m; slopes 990–2960m
🚠 52 ⛷ 147km

Bielmonte Italy
Popular with day trippers from
Milan. Worthwhile on a bad-
weather day.
1200m; slopes 1200–1620m
🚠 9 ⛷ 20km

Big Powderhorn USA
Area with the most 'resort'
facilities in south Lake
Superior region – and the
highest lift capacity too. The
area suffers from winds.
370m; slopes 370–560m
🚠 10 ⛷ 250 acres

Big Sky 600

Big White 622

Bischofshofen Austria
Working town and mountain
resort near St Johann im
Pongau, with very limited
local runs and the main
slopes starting nearby at
Muhlbach (Hochkönig area).
545m; slopes 545–1000m
🚠 1 ⛷ 2km

Bivio Switzerland
Quiet village near St Moritz
and Savognin, with easy
slopes.
1770m; slopes 1780–2560m
🚠 4 ⛷ 40km

Björkliden Sweden
538m vertical. Feb-to-May
Arctic Circle area. Ultra snow-
reliable. You can even ski in
caves – beautiful ice
formations. Magnificent
Lapland views.
🚠 5 ⛷ 15km

Björnrike Sweden
20 minutes from
Vemdalsskalet (same pass).
385m vertical.
🚠 9 ⛷ 15km

Black Mountain USA
New Hampshire area with
lodging in nearby Jackson.
🚠 4 ⛷ 143 acres

Blatten Switzerland
Mountainside hamlet above
Naters, beside the Rhône near
Brig. Small but tall Belalp ski
area, with larger Aletsch area
nearby.
1320m; slopes 1320–3100m
🚠 9 ⛷ 60km

Bled 666
Lakeside base in Slovenia.

Blue Cow Australia
Part of Perisher resort,
Australia's highest and
expanding ski area. Accessible
only by tube train. Nearest
town is Jindabyne. Six hours
from Sydney.
1890m; slopes 1605–2035m
🚠 47 ⛷ 3075 acres

Blue Mountain Canada
Largest area in Ontario, with
glorious views of Lake Huron.
High-capacity lift system and
100% snowmaking.
230m; slopes 230–450m
🚠 15 ⛷ 275 acres

Blue River Canada
Base of world-famous Mike
Wiegele heli-ski operation in
Cariboo and Monashee
mountains.

Bluewood USA
Particularly remote area even
by American north-west
standards. Worth a visit if
you're in Walla Walla.
1355m; slopes 1355–1725m
🚠 3 ⛷ 530 acres

Bogus Basin　　　USA
Sizeable area overlooking
Idaho's attractive, interesting
capital, Boise. Limited
accommodation at the base.
1760m; slopes 1760–2310m
🚡 8 ⛷ 2600 acres

Bohinj　　　Slovenia
Lakeside village near Bled set
in a beautiful valley, with
lovely views from its plateau
area of short runs high above.
540m; slopes 540–1480m
🚡 6 ⛷ 23km

Bois-d'Amont　　　France
One of five resorts that make
up Les Rousses area in Jura
region on the Franco-Suisse
border.
1050m; slopes 1120–1680m
🚡 40 ⛷ 50km

Boi Taull　　　Spain
A typical Pyrenean resort set
high above the Boi Valley,
close to the stunning Aigues
Tortes National Park. Good
intermediate terrain.
slopes 2020–2750m
🚡 15 ⛷ 44km

Bolognola　　　Italy
Tiny area in Macerata region
near the Adriatic Riviera.
1070m; slopes 1070–1845m
🚡 5 ⛷ 8km

Bolton Valley　　　USA
Resort near Stowe with mostly
intermediate slopes.
465m; slopes 465–960m
🚡 6 ⛷ 155 acres

Bonneval-sur-Arc　　265
Unspoiled, remote old village
in the Haute Maurienne valley.

Bons　　248
Rustic, unspoiled old hamlet
linked to Les Deux-Alpes.

Boreal　　　USA
Closest area to north Lake
Tahoe town, Truckee. Limited
slopes, best for novices.
2195m; slopes 2195–2375m
🚡 9 ⛷ 380 acres

Bormio　　　Italy
An attractive old spa town,
distinctly Italian and within
day-trip distance from Livigno
and Santa Caterina. The main
slopes are a 15-minute walk
from the centre, where a
gondola goes to the hub at
Bormio 2000, with fast lifts to
the high point at 3010m. The
mountain is confined, long
(vertical of 800m) and narrow
– mainly suited to
intermediates. The men's
downhill course is a tough
red. The nursery slopes are
snow-sure, but there are few
progression runs. There's a
good terrain park and ample
mountain huts. There are
more slopes in a separate
area, with fast lifts from Le

Motte or Isolaccia, on the
other side of town. The resort
has over 40 hotels, plus a
wide choice of restaurants.
Après-ski is quite lively.
1225m; slopes 1225–3010m
🚡 35 ⛷ 110km

Borovets　　662

Bosco Chiesanuova　　Italy
Weekend day trippers' place
near Verona. A long drive from
any other resort.
1105m; slopes 1105–1805m
🚡 18 ⛷ 20km

Bosco Gurin　　Switzerland
Highest ski area in Ticino. The
only German speaking village
in the Italian canton.
1500m; slopes 1480–2400m
🚡 6 ⛷ 30km

Les Bottières　　　France
Hamlet at the edge of the
Sybelles area, with limited
infrastructure and poor access
to the main network – it takes
three lifts to reach La
Toussuire, before setting off
for L'Ouillon.
1300m

La Bourboule　　　France
Spa and cross-country village
with the Alpine slopes of Le
Mont-Dore nearby. Spectacular
extinct-volcano scenery.
850m; slopes 1050–1850m
🚡 17 ⛷ 42km

Bourg-d'Oisans　　　France
Pleasant valley town on main
Grenoble-Briançon road.
Cheap base for visits to Alpe-
d'Huez and Les Deux-Alpes.

Bourg-St-Maurice　　206
French valley town with a
funicular to Les Arcs.

Bovec　　666
Town linked to Kanin-Sella
Nevea on the Italian border.

Boyne Highlands　　　USA
Area with impressive, high-
capacity lift system for
weekend Detroit crowds.
Fierce winds off Lake Michigan
a major drawback.
225m; slopes 225–390m
🚡 10 ⛷ 240 acres

Boyne Mountain　　　USA
Popular with weekend Detroit
crowds. Not as windy as sister
resort Boyne Highlands.
190m; slopes 190–340m
🚡 12 ⛷ 115 acres

Bozel　　　France
Small town that, in good
snow conditions, you can ski
down to off-piste from
Courchevel and catch a bus
back. Also near access road
for Champagny-en-Vanoise (La
Plagne ski area).
860m

Bramans　　　France
Old cross-country village near
Modane. Well placed for
touring numerous nearby
resorts such as Val Cenis and
Valloire.
1200m
🚡 1 ⛷ 3km

Bramberg　　　Austria
Village near Pass Thurn
(Kitzbühel area). Shares
slopes with Neukirchen.
820m; slopes 820–2150m
🚡 15 ⛷ 55km

Brand　　102
Family resort in the
Brandnertal
1035m; slopes 890–1920m
🚡 14 ⛷ 55km

Brandnertal　　102

Les Brasses　　　France
Collective name for six
traditional hamlets with some
of the closest slopes to
Geneva, but best known for
cross-country.
900m; slopes 900–1600m
🚡 14 ⛷ 50km

Braunwald　　Switzerland
Sunny but limited area near
Zürich, a funicular ride above
Linthal.
1255m; slopes 1255–1900m
🚡 9 ⛷ 32km

Breckenridge　　561

Bregenzerwald　　104

Brentonico　　　Italy
Little resort just off Verona-
Trento motorway, with linked
slopes of La Polsa and San
Valentino above.
1160m; slopes 1160–1520m
🚡 15 ⛷ 35km

Bressanone　　　Italy
Valley town 20 minutes by
free ski-bus from the lift base
of Plose.
565m

La Bresse　　　France
Largest resort in the northerly
Vosges mountains near
Strasbourg. Three separate
downhill areas (with a lot of
snowmaking), but also
extensive ski de fond and lots
of other activities.
900m; slopes 900–1350m
🚡 24 ⛷ 220 hectares

Briançon　　327
Part of the Grand Serre
Chevalier region.

Brian Head　　　USA
Utah area south of Salt Lake
City, too far from Park City for
a day trip.
2925m; slopes 2925–3445m
🚡 10 ⛷ 500 acres

Brides-les-Bains　　282
Quiet spa town in valley
below Méribel.

Bridger Bowl　　599
Day-trip resort near Big Sky,
Montana.
1855m; slopes 1855–2460m
🚡 7 ⛷ 1200 acres

Brigels-Andiast Switzerland
In the same valley as Laax-
Flims. Access from two sunny
villages. Mostly red runs.
1300m; slopes 1100–2420m
🚡 7 ⛷ 75km

Brighton　　　USA
Linked with Solitude. Total
acreage is half that of Alta-
Snowbird (in the next valley),
but attracts fewer people so
the powder doesn't get
tracked out in hours. Four fast
chairs, including one serving
the resort's maximum vertical
of 530m on Clayton Peak. This
and the slightly lower Mt
Millicent are almost all expert
terrain, but other lifts serve a
wide spectrum of runs. The
resort's boundaries are open,
and there are excellent
backcountry adventures.
Accommodation is in the
slope-side Brighton Lodge
and some cabins.
2670m; slopes 2435–3200m
🚡 13 ⛷ 2250 acres

Brixen im Thale　　167
Grossraum village that shares
slopes with Söll and Ellmau.

Bromley　　　USA
New York City weekend
retreat, reputedly the warmest
place to ski in chilly Vermont.
595m; slopes 595–1000m
🚡 9 ⛷ 300 acres

Bromont　　　Canada
Purpose-built resort an hour
east of Montreal, with one of
the best small areas in
eastern Canada, popular for
its night skiing.
slopes 405–575m
🚡 6 ⛷ 135 acres

Bruck am Grossglockner
　　　Austria
Low beginners' resort, but
also a quiet base from which
to visit Zell am See.
755m

Brundage Mountain　　USA
Remote, uncrowded Idaho
area with glorious views
across the lake towards Hell's
Canyon. Mostly intermediate
slopes. Also has a snowcat
operation.
1760m; slopes 1760–2320m
🚡 5 ⛷ 1300 acres

Bruneck　　　Italy
Town with gondola link into
the Plan de Corones/Kronplatz
area. Italian name is Brunico.

Brunico　　　Italy
Town with gondola link into
the Plan de Corones/Kronplatz
area. Bruneck in German.

Bruson 505
Relaxing respite from Verbier's crowds.

Brusson Italy
Major cross-country village in the Aosta valley, near Antagnod. Sunny downhill slopes up a side valley at Estoul (Palasinaz ski area).
1330m
🚡 3 ⛷ 17km

Les Bugnenets–Savagnieres Switzerland
Very small area in the Jura mountains, north of Neuchatel. Short runs served by drag lifts. Valid with the Valais Ski Card.
slopes 1090–1440m
🚡 7 ⛷ 30km

Bukovel Ukraine
Ukraine's second highest resort.
slopes 900–1370m
🚡 14 ⛷ 50km

Burke Mountain USA
Uncrowded, isolated family resort in Vermont with mostly intermediate slopes. Great views from the top.
385m; slopes 385–995m
🚡 4 ⛷ 130 acres

Bürserberg 102
Valley town in the Brandnertal.
890m; slopes 890–1920m
🚡 14 ⛷ 55km

CairnGorm Mountain 669
Scottish ski resort.
slopes 550–1100m
🚡 11 ⛷ 35km

Caldirola Italy
Genoese weekend day-tripper spot in a remote region off the motorway to Turin.
1010m; slopes 1010–1450m
🚡 3 ⛷ 4km

Cambre-d'Aze France
Quiet ski area in the Pyrenees with few British visitors. Good beginner and intermediate terrain. Forms part of the Neiges Catalan (10 resorts on one pass).
1640m; slopes 1640–2400m
🚡 17 ⛷ 35km

Camigliatello Italy
Tiny area on the foot of the Italian 'boot' near Cosenza. Weekend/day-trip spot.
1270m; slopes 1270–1750m
🚡 4 ⛷ 6km

Campitello 429
Village in Val di Fassa.

Campitello Matese Italy
The only slopes near Naples. Surprisingly large area when snow-cover is complete. Weekend crowds.
1440m; slopes 1440–2100m
🚡 8 ⛷ 40km

Campo di Giove Italy
Highest slopes in L'Aquila region east of Rome.
1070m; slopes 1145–2350m
🚡 15 ⛷ 21km

Campodolcino Italy
Valley town with funicular up to Madesimo's slopes.
1070m; slopes 1545–2880m
🚡 6 ⛷ 8km

Campo Felice Italy
Small resort in Abruzzo, east of Rome. Shares a lift pass with equally small Ovindoli, nearby.
1410m; slopes 1400–2065m
🚡 15 ⛷ 30km

Campo Imperatore Italy
One of the best of the areas east of Rome in L'Aquila.
1980m
🚡 8 ⛷ 20km

Canazei 429
Lively rustic village in the Sella Ronda.

Candanchu / Astún Spain
French border resort on Pau road set in some of the Pyrenees' most stunning scenery. Almost exclusively challenging open slopes.
1450m; slopes 1560–2400m
🚡 24 ⛷ 80km

Canillo 80
Small, quiet village linked to Soldeu.

Canmore Canada
Old frontier town on the way to Nakiska/Fortress, well placed for touring the region and an attractive alternative to staying in Banff.

Cannon Mountain USA
One of several small New Hampshire resorts scattered along the Interstate 93 highway; a ski area and nothing more. High, steep mountain by eastern standards.
605m; slopes 605–1260m
🚡 9 ⛷ 165 acres

Canyons 588

Cardrona New Zealand
Three large basins with slopes for all standards. Good snow record and childcare facilities. Super value. An hour from Queenstown.
1650m; slopes 1260–1860m
🚡 8 ⛷ 345 hectares

Carezza Italy
Dense network of short lifts close to Val di Fassa, also called Passo Costalunga.
🚡 16 ⛷ 40km

Les Carroz 221

Caspoggio Italy
Attractive, unspoiled village north-east of Lake Como, with easy slopes (and more at nearby Chiesa).
1100m; slopes 1100–2155m
🚡 8 ⛷ 22km

Castelrotto Italy
Picturesque village west of Sella Ronda circuit with small sunny Alpine area and good cross-country trails.
1060m

Castel S Angelo Italy
Tiny area in Macerata region near Adriatic Riviera.
805m
🚡 4 ⛷ 2km

Castle Mountain Canada
Remote resort south of Calgary. Good proportion of intermediate and advanced terrain. Area on Haig Ridge provides beginner and intermediate terrain.
1410m; slopes 1410–2270m
🚡 6 ⛷ 1750 acres

Catedral (Bariloche) Argentina
One of South America's most developed resorts, linked with Lado Bueno and 19km from San Carlos de Bariloche. Sheltered intermediate slopes, but very crowded in peak season. Base-side luxury lodgings available.
slopes 1030–2180m
🚡 39 ⛷ 103km

Cauterets 317

Cavalese Italy
Unspoiled medieval town in Val di Fiemme with pretty slopes at Alpe Cermis.
1000m; slopes 975–2265m
🚡 9 ⛷ 70km

Caviahue Argentina
Mountain village at the foot of the Copahue Volcano, 357km from Neuquén City.
1645m; slopes 1645–2045m
🚡 8 ⛷ 37km

The Cedars Lebanon
The largest of Lebanon's ski areas, 130km inland from Beirut. Good, open slopes; a surprisingly long season.
1850m; slopes 2100–2870m 🚡 6

Ceillac France
Tight cluster of rustic old buildings near Serre-Chevalier. Not far from the highest village in Europe, St-Veran.
1600m; slopes 1600–2450m
🚡 7 ⛷ 25km

Celerina 494
Quiet village with links to St Moritz's slopes.

Cerkno Slovenia
Modern, family resort 50km from Ljubljana. Lifts include three fast chairs.
900m
🚡 8 ⛷ 18km

Cerler Spain
Very limited, purpose-built resort with a compact ski area similar to that of nearby Andorra's Arinsal.
1500m; slopes 1500–2630m
🚡 18 ⛷ 76km

Le Cernix France
Hamlet near Megève where Les Saisies' slopes link to those of Crest-Voland, part of the Espace Diamant to which our figures relate.
1250m; slopes 1000–2070m
🚡 84 ⛷ 179km

Cerrato Lago Italy
Very limited area near the coastal town of La Spezia.
1270m; slopes 1270–1890m
🚡 5 ⛷ 3km

Cerro Bayo Argentina
Limited area amid stunning scenery 10km from La Angostura, and 90km from San Carlos de Bariloche.
slopes 1050–1780m
🚡 12 ⛷ 200 hectares

Cerro Castor Argentina
The most southern ski runs in the world, on Tierra del Fuego. Lodgings are in Ushuaia, the southernmost city in the world. Also plenty of cross-country skiing on the island.
195m; slopes 195–1057m
🚡 11 ⛷ 24km

Cerro Mirador Chile
Chile's most southerly snow-zone, located 8km outside Punta Arenas. Tiny but attractive woodland runs. No base lodging.
600m 🚡 2

Cervinia 391

Cesana Torinese Italy
Little Italian village linking the Sauze d'Oulx, Sestriere and Sansicario side of the Milky Way to the Clavière, Montgenèvre side.
1350m

Le Châble 505
Small village below Verbier.

Chaillol France
Cross-country base on the edge of the beautiful Ecrins National Park, near Gap. Small Alpine area, lots of snowmakers.
1600m; slopes 1450–2000m
🚡 10 ⛷ 13km

Chamois Italy
Small area above Buisson, a few miles down the road from Valtournenche (near Cervinia) - worth a look on bad-weather days.
1815m; slopes 1815–2270m
🚡 9 🚠 20km

Chamonix 223

Champagny-en-Vanoise 305
Charming village linking to the La Plagne network.

Champéry 462

Champex-Lac Switzerland
Lakeside hamlet tucked away in the trees in Ski St-Bernard area near Verbier. A quiet, unspoiled base from which to visit Verbier's area. Small area of slopes due to open again after being closed by a fire.
1480m; slopes 1480–2220m
🚡 4 🚠 15km

Champfèr 494
Lakeside hamlet between St Moritz and Silvaplana.

Champoluc 416
Unspoiled village at one end of the Monterosa Ski area.

Champorcher Italy
Small village south of Aosta valley with tall but narrow ski area, mostly red runs on open slopes, with one black through the trees to the lift base at Chardonney.
1430m; slopes 1430–2500m
🚡 5 🚠 21km

Champoussin 462
Quiet village with links to the rest of the Champéry slopes.

Chamrousse France
Functional family resort near Grenoble, with good, sheltered slopes. Chairlifts and a cable car from three bases serve largely beginner and intermediate slopes.
1650m; slopes 1400–2250m
🚡 19 🚠 90km

Chandolin 501
Village in the Val d'Anniviers.

Chantemerle 327
One of the villages making up Serre-Chevalier.

Chapa Verde Chile
60km north-east of Rancagua and 145km from Santiago.
1200m; slopes 1200–2500m
🚡 4 🚠 1200 hectares

Chapelco Argentina
Small ski area with full infrastructure of services 19km from sizeable town of San Martin de Los Andes. Accommodation in hotels 11km from the slopes.
slopes 1250–1980m
🚡 10 🚠 140 hectares

La Chapelle-d'Abondance 233
Unspoiled village 5km down the valley from Châtel.

Charlotte Pass Australia
Oldest and most remote resort in NSW, on a charming Alpine pass near Mt Kosciusko. Reached only by snowcat from Perisher. Scenic chalets and five lifts. Nearest town Jindabyne. 6.5 hours from Sydney.
1765m; slopes 1850–2000m
🚡 5 🚠 123 acres

Chastreix Sancy France
Small family ski area near Mont Dore and Super-Besse. Limited but varied terrain. All draglifts.
1400m
🚡 7 🚠 16km

Château d'Oex Switzerland
Pleasant French-speaking valley town sharing a lift pass with neighbouring, but unconnected, Gstaad. Good rail links to other sectors. Low slopes. Famous for its Alpine Balloon festival.
950m; slopes 890–1630m
🚡 8 🚠 30km

Châtel 233

Le Chatelard France
Small resort in remote Parc des Bauges between Lake Annecy and Chambéry.

Le Chazelet France
Tiny hamlet 5km above La Grave, useful on bad-weather days.
1800m; slopes 1800–2300m
🚠 6km

Chiesa Italy
Attractive beginners' resort with a fairly high plateau of easy runs above the resort.
1000m; slopes 1700–2335m
🚡 16 🚠 50km

Le Chinaillon France
Chalet-style village at lift base above Le Grand-Bornand.
1300m; slopes 1000–2100m
🚡 29 🚠 90km

Chiomonte Italy
Tiny resort on the main road east of Bardonecchia and Sauze d'Oulx. A good half-day trip from either.
745m; slopes 745–2210m
🚡 6 🚠 10km

Chsea Algeria
Largest of Algeria's skiable areas, 135km south-east of coastal town of Alger in the Djur Djur mountains.
1860m; slopes 1860–2510m 🚡 2

Chur–Brambruesch Switzerland
Chur's local ski area, a cable car and gondola ride from the town.
595m; slopes 1170–2200m
🚡 6 🚠 25km

Churwalden Switzerland
Hamlet on fringe of Lenzerheide-Valbella area, linked via a slow chair. Four short local runs served by a quad and steep drag.
1230m; slopes 1230–2865m
🚡 35 🚠 155km

Claviere 291
Village linked to Montgenèvre and the Milky Way ski area.

La Clusaz France
Genuine mountain village near Geneva that exudes rustic and Gallic charm. Attracts a lot of weekend visitors, so can be crowded. Buses also link with Le Grand Bornand. Together they offer over 200km slopes – covered by the area lift pass. The local slopes sprawl over five attractively wooded and varied sectors. All are below 2500m, so snow conditions are unreliable; but there is a lot of snowmaking. Good steep blacks and bumps on La Balme (the highest sector), as well as decent off-piste when conditions permit. There are challenging but wide blues, as well as gentle cruises and nursery slopes up the mountain. But there are still a lot of old chairs and drags. There's a park and pipe, plentiful rustic huts, and a few lively bars.
1100m; slopes 1000–2600m
🚡 52 🚠 132km

Les Coches 305
Purpose-built village, linked to the La Plagne ski area.

Cogne Italy
One of Aosta valley's larger villages. Main resort in the Gran Paradiso national park. Worth a visit from nearby Pila. Limited, mostly red slopes. Major cross-country centre, with 70km trails.
1535m; slopes 1530–2250m
🚡 4 🚠 9km

Colfosco 429
Smaller, quieter satellite of Corvara in the Sella Ronda.

Colle di Tenda Italy
Dour, modern resort that shares a good area with much nicer Limone. Not far from Nice.
1400m; slopes 1120–2040m
🚡 33 🚠 80km

Colle Isarco Italy
Brenner Pass area – and the bargain-shopping town of Vipiteno is nearby.
1095m; slopes 1095–2720m
🚡 5 🚠 15km

Le Collet-d'Allevard France
Ski area of sizeable summer spa Allevard-les-Bains in remote region east of Chambéry-Grenoble road.
1450m; slopes 1450–2140m
🚡 11 🚠 35km

Collio Italy
Tiny area of short runs in a remote spot between lakes Garda and d'Iseo.
840m; slopes 840–1715m 🚡 14

Les Collons 505
Near Thyon 2000 in the Verbier area.

Combloux 269
Quiet, unspoiled alternative to linked Megève.

Les Contamines France
Largely unspoiled but sprawling chalet resort close to Megève and Chamonix, with a fair-sized intermediate area and a good snow record for its height. The main access lift is a shuttle-bus ride from the centre, with a few lodgings at its base. Most of the slopes are above the treeline and on both sides of the Col du Joly – from where a long red run descends over 1000m vertical. There's a good mix of blue and red runs, and substantial off-piste opportunities. Complete beginners are better off elsewhere though. Reports of the school are mixed too. The village is quiet with few amenities, but there are other sporting activities.
1160m; slopes 1160–2485m
🚡 24 🚠 120km

Copper Mountain 566

Le Corbier 265
Purpose-built tower-block resort centrally placed in the Sybelles area.

Cordon France
Traditional little family resort near Megève. 'Ideal for a relaxing ski before catching an early evening flight' says a visitor.
870m; slopes 1000–1600m
🚡 6 🚠 11km

Corno alle Scale Italy
Small resort in the Emilia Romagna region of the Apennines.
1355m; slopes 1355–1945m
🚡 9 🚠 36km

Coronet Peak New Zealand
Closest area to Queenstown (20 minutes). Good mix of bowls, chutes, varied level pistes. Biggest vertical is 462m. Relies on large snowmaking facility for good snow-cover. Splendid views.
1230m

Corrençon-en-Vercors France
Charming, rustic village at foot of Villard-de-Lans ski area. Good cross-country, too.
1160m; slopes 1145–2170m
⛷ 25 ↟ 125km

Cortina d'Ampezzo 397

Corvara 429
Lively village at the junction of the Alta Badia and the Sella Ronda circuit.

Courchevel 238

Courmayeur 402

Cranmore USA
Area in New Hampshire with attractive town/resort of North Conway. Easy skiing. Good for families.
150m; slopes 150–515m
⛷ 9 ↟ 190 acres

Crans-Montana 465

Crested Butte USA
One of the cutest old Wild West towns in Colorado, and the steep, gnarly terrain enjoys cult status among experts. It's a small area, but it packs in an astonishing mixture of perfect beginner slopes, easy cruising runs and expert terrain. Snowfall is modest by Colorado standards, but for those who like steep, ungroomed terrain, if the snow is good, it's idyllic. You can stay there or at the mountain, a couple of miles away, with its modern resort 'village'.
2860m; slopes 2775–3620m
⛷ 15 ↟ 1547 acres

Crest-Voland France
Attractive, unspoiled traditional village near Megève and Le Grand Bornand with wonderfully uncrowded intermediate slopes linked to Les Saises and beyond to Praz sur Arly, as part of the Espace Diamant region – to which our figures relate.
1035m; slopes 1000–2070m
⛷ 84 ↟ 179km

Crissolo Italy
Small, remote day-tripper area, south-west of Turin. Part of the Monviso ski area.
1320m; slopes 1745–2340m
⛷ 4 ↟ 20km

La Croix-Fry France
On the pass to La Clusaz. Couple of hotels and good gentle slopes.
1480m

Les Crosets 462
Micro-resort above Champéry in the Portes du Soleil.

Crystal Mountain USA
Area in glorious Mt Rainier National Park, near Seattle. Good, varied area given good snow/weather, but it's often wet. Lively at weekends.
1340m; slopes 1340–2135m
⛷ 9 ↟ 2300 acres

Cuchara Valley USA
Quiet little family resort in southern Colorado, some way from any other ski area.
2800m; slopes 2800–3285m
⛷ 4 ↟ 250 acres

Cutigliano Italy
Sizeable village near Abetone in the Apennines. Less than two hours from Florence and Pisa.
1125m; slopes 1125–1850m
⛷ 9 ↟ 13km

Cypress Mountain Canada
Vancouver's most challenging area, 20 minutes from the city and with 40% for experts. Good snowfall record but rain is a problem.
920m; slopes 910–1445m ⛷ 5

Daemyeong Vivaldi Resort South Korea
One of the less ugly Korean resorts, 75km from Seoul.
⛷ 10

La Daille 360
Ugly apartment complex at the entrance to Val d'Isère.

Daisen Japan
Western Honshu's main area, four hours from Osaka.
800m; slopes 740–1120m ⛷ 21

Damüls 104
Village in Bregenzerwald.

Davos 467

Deer Mountain USA
South Dakota area close to 'Old West' town Deadwood and Mount Rushmore.
1825m; slopes 1825–2085m
⛷ 4 ↟ 370 acres

Deer Valley 590

Les Deux-Alpes 248

Les Diablerets Switzerland
Spacious chalet resort towered over by the Diablerets massif, with two areas of local slopes, plus Glacier 3000. A high-speed quad followed by a slow chair lead up to the red runs of the Meilleret area and the link to Villars. A gondola in the centre of town takes you to Isenau, a mix of blues and reds served by draglifts. From Isenau there's a red run down to Col du Pillon and the cable car to and from the glacier. On Glacier 3000, you'll find blue runs at over 3000m, stunning views and the long, black Combe d'Audon – a wonderful, usually quiet, run away from all the lifts with sheer cliffs rising up on both sides. Snow reliability away from the glacier is not great – especially on sunny Isenau.
1150m; slopes 1115–3000m
⛷ 44 ↟ 125

Diamond Peak USA
Quiet, pleasant, intermediate area on Lake Tahoe, with lodging in Incline Village five minutes' drive away. Its narrow area consists of a long ridge served by one fast chair; there are great lake views from the run along the ridge and from the terrace of Snowflake Lodge. There are black runs off the ridge, but nothing seriously steep.
2040m; slopes 2040–2600m
⛷ 6 ↟ 655 acres

Dienten 128
Quiet village at the heart of the Hochkönig area.

Dinner Plain Australia
Attractive resort best known for cross-country skiing. Shuttle to Mt Hotham for Alpine slopes. Four hours from Melbourne.
1520m; slopes 1490–1520m

Discovery Ski Area USA
Pleasant area miles from anywhere except Butte, Montana, with largely intermediate slopes but double-black runs on the back of the mountain – and the chance of seriously good snow. Fairmont Hot Springs (two huge thermal pools) nearby.
1975m; slopes 1760–2485m
⛷ 8 ↟ 2200 acres

Disentis Switzerland
Unspoiled old village in a pretty setting on the Glacier Express rail route near Andermatt. Scenic area with long runs.
1125m; slopes 1150–2830m
⛷ 10 ↟ 60km

Dobbiaco Italy
One of several little resorts in the South Tyrol near the Austrian border; a feasible day out from the Sella Ronda. Toblach is its German name.
1250m; slopes 1250–1610m
⛷ 5 ↟ 15km

Dodge Ridge USA
Novice/leisurely intermediate area north of Yosemite. The pass from Reno is closed in winter, preventing crowds.
2010m; slopes 2010–2500m
⛷ 12 ↟ 815 acres

Dolonne 402
Quiet suburb of Courmayeur.

Donnersbachwald Austria
Small area in the Dachstein-Tauern region.
950m; slopes 950–1990m
⛷ 4 ↟ 25km

Donner Ski Ranch USA
One of California's first ski resorts, still family owned and operated.
2140m; slopes 2140–2370m
⛷ 6 ↟ 460 acres

Dorfgastein 96
Quieter, friendlier alternative to Bad Gastein.

Doucy-Combelouvière France
Quiet hamlet tucked away in the trees at the foot of Valmorel's slopes, linked by easy green pistes, a fast chair and draglifts into the main sector.
1250m

Dundret Sweden
Lapland area 100km north of the Arctic Circle with floodlit slopes open through winter when the sun barely rises.
slopes 475–825m
⛷ 7 ↟ 15km

Durango Mountain Resort USA
Not a resort to cross the Atlantic to visit – it's a small area even by US standards. Directly above the resort is a steepish slope with a slow double chair off to the right serving gentle green runs. All link to the shady slopes that form the main part of the area, served by a row of three chairs with a vertical of not much over 350m. Snowcat skiing is said to operate from the top. The heart of the resort is Purgatory Village, a modern, purpose-built affair. Evening options in the 'village' are extremely limited. The city of Durango is worth visiting.
2680m; slopes 2680–3300m
⛷ 11 ↟ 1200 acres

Eaglecrest USA
Close to Yukon gold rush town Skagway. Family resort famous for its ski school.
365m; slopes 365–790m
⛷ 3 ↟ 640 acres

Eben im Pongau Austria
Part of Salzburger Sportwelt
Amadé area that includes
nearby St Johann, Wagrain,
Flachau and Zauchensee.
855m; slopes 855–2185m
⛷ 100 ⛷ 350km

Egg 104
Village in Bregenzerwald.

Ehrwald Austria
Pleasant village with easy
access to three small and
varied ski areas, notably the
Zugspitze glacier. Access to
the slopes there is by cable
car a couple of miles outside
the resort at Obermoos. There
are gentle nursery slopes and
good open intermediate
terrain – including a couple of
genuine reds. Most are of
limited extent. There's a half-
pipe and three restaurants.
Après-ski is fairly lively. The
Zugspitz Arena lift pass covers
all three sectors, plus the
other resorts of the valley.
1000m; slopes 990–2960m
⛷ 52 ⛷ 147km

El Colorado / Farellones Chile
Scattering of accommodation
around a base station 40km
east of Santiago, sharing Valle
Nevado's ski area (to which
our figures relate).
slopes 2430–3670m
⛷ 43 ⛷ 113km

Eldora Mountain USA
Day-visitor resort with varied
terrain (including plenty of
steep stuff) close to Denver
Boulder (45min by regular
scheduled bus). All forest
trails, but with some good
glade areas. Crowded at
weekends.
2795m; slopes 2805–3230m
⛷ 12 ⛷ 680 acres

Elk Meadows USA
Area south of Salt Lake City,
more than a day trip from
Park City.
2775m; slopes 2745–3170m
⛷ 6 ⛷ 1400 acres

Ellmau 106

Elm Switzerland
One hour from Zürich, at the
head of a quiet, isolated
valley. Good choice of runs
including a long black to the
valley.
1020m; slopes 1000–2105m
⛷ 6 ⛷ 40km

Encamp Andorra
Traffic-choked town, with a
gondola link to the Pas de la
Casa slopes. Popular for its
nightlife and low prices.

Enego Italy
Limited weekend day-trippers'
area near Vicenza and Trento.
1300m; slopes 1300–1445m
⛷ 7 ⛷ 30km

Engelberg 474

Entrèves 402
Cluster of hotels at the lift up
to Courmayeur's slopes.

Escaldes Andorra
Central valley town, effectively
part of Andorra la Vella.

Estoul Italy
Village in the Aosta valley up
a side valley near Brusson.
Sunny, easy red slopes.
1800m; slopes 1800–2235m
⛷ 2 ⛷ 9km

Etna Italy
Scenic, uncrowded, short-
season area on the volcano's
flank, 20 minutes from
Nickolossi.
1800m; slopes 1800–2350m
⛷ 5km

Evolène Switzerland
Charming rustic village in the
Val d'Hérens. Small ski area in
unspoiled, attractive setting
south of Sion. Area lift pass
gives access to the 4 Valleys.
1370m; slopes 1405–2680m
⛷ 7 ⛷ 42km

Faak am See Austria
Limited area, one of five
overlooking town of Villach.
560m; slopes 560–800m
⛷ 1 ⛷ 2km

Fai della Paganella Italy
Trentino village near Madonna
that shares its slopes with
Andalo.
1000m; slopes 1035–2125m
⛷ 16 ⛷ 60km

Fairmont Hot Springs Canada
Major luxury spa complex
ideal for a relaxing holiday
with some gentle skiing
thrown in.
⛷ 2 ⛷ 60 acres

Faistenau Austria
Cross-country area close to
Salzburg and St Wolfgang.
Limited Alpine slopes.
785m; slopes 785–1000m
⛷ 3 ⛷ 3km

Falcade Italy
Trentino village south of the
Sella Ronda with lifts up to
slopes at San Pellegrino.
1150m; slopes 1150–2245m
⛷ 19 ⛷ 75km

Falera 482
Village with access to ski area
shared by Flims and Laax.

Le Falgoux France
One of the most beautiful old
villages in France, set in the
very scenic Volcano National
Park. Several ski areas nearby.
930m; slopes 930–1350m

Falkertsee Austria
Base area rather than a
village, with bleak, open
slopes in contrast to nearby
Bad Kleinkirchheim.
1850m; slopes 1690–2310m
⛷ 5 ⛷ 15km

Falls Creek Australia
Alpine-style modern family
resort, 5 hours from
Melbourne, near Mt Hotham.
Fair-sized area of short
intermediate runs. Access by
snowcat to Mt McKay's steep
slopes. Lavish spa resort
nearby.
1600m; slopes 1500–1780m
⛷ 14 ⛷ 1115 acres

La Feclaz France
One of several little resorts in
the remote Parc des Bauges.
Popular cross-country ski
base.
1165m

Feldberg 382
Small resort in the Black
Forest.
⛷ 31 ⛷ 55

Fernie 624

Fieberbrunn 152
Pretty, jolly Tirolean resort
now linked to Saalbach.

Fiesch Switzerland
Traditional Rhône valley resort
near Brig, with a lift up to
Fiescheralp (2220m) part of
the lovely Aletsch area;
includes Bettmeralp to
Riederalp.
1050m; slopes 1925–2870m
⛷ 35 ⛷ 100km

Fiescheralp Switzerland
Mountain outpost of Fiesch,
down in the Rhône valley. At
one end of the beautiful
Aletsch area extending across
the mountain via Bettmeralp
to Riederalp.
2220m; slopes 1925–2870m
⛷ 35 ⛷ 100km

Filzmoos Austria
Charming, unspoiled, friendly
village with leisurely slopes
that are ideal for novices.
Good snow record for its
height. Quiet pistes, good
grooming and decent nursery
slopes.
1055m; slopes 1055–1645m
⛷ 8 ⛷ 32km

Finkenberg 109
Village between Mayrhofen
and Hintertux.

Fiss Austria
Nicely compact, quiet,
traditional village sharing an
extensive, sunny area with
bigger Serfaus.
1435m; slopes 1200–2750m
⛷ 70 ⛷ 190km

Flachau Austria
Quiet, spacious village in a
pretty setting at one end of
an extensive three-valley lift
network linking via Wagrain to
Alpendorf. Central to an
impressive lift system. On the
Salzburger Sportwelt lift pass.
925m; slopes 800–2185m
⛷ 64 ⛷ 200km

Flachauwinkl Austria
Tiny ski station beside Tauern
autobahn. Centre of an
extensive three-valley lift
network linking Kleinarl to
Zauchensee. Near similarly
sized Flachau. All these
resorts are covered by the
Salzburger Sportwelt ski pass.
930m; slopes 800–2185m
⛷ 15 ⛷ 65km

Flaine 254

Flims 482
Long-established resort
sharing an area with Laax.

Flumet France
Surprisingly large traditional
village, the main place from
which to ski the Espace
Diamant area, linked through
to Les Saisies/ Crest Voland.
Near Megève.
1000m; slopes 1000–2070m
⛷ 84 ⛷ 179km

Flumserberg Switzerland
Collective name for the
villages sharing a varied area
an hour south-east of Zürich.
Part of the wider Heidiland
region. Mostly red and black
runs, served by good network
of fast lifts.
425m; slopes 1220–2220m
⛷ 16 ⛷ 65km

Folgaria Italy
Sizeable area east of Trento.
1165m; slopes 1185–2005m
⛷ 22 ⛷ 74km

Folgarida 411
Small Trentino village linked
to Madonna di Campiglio.

Foncine-le-Haut France
Major cross-country village in
the Jura Mountains with
extensive trails.

Fonni Gennaragentu Italy
Sardinia's only 'ski area' – and
it's tiny.
⛷ 1 ⛷ 5km

Font-Romeu   317

Foppolo   Italy
Relatively unattractive but user-friendly village, a short transfer from Bergamo.
1510m; slopes 1610–2160m
🚠 9 ⛷ 47km

Forca Canapine   Italy
Limited area near the Adriatic and Ascoli Piceno. Popular with weekend day-trippers.
1450m; slopes 1450–1690m
🚠 11 ⛷ 20km

Formazza   Italy
Cross-country base with some downhill slopes.
1280m; slopes 1275–1755m
⛷ 8km

Formigal   655

Formigueres   France
Small downhill and cross-country area in the Neiges Catalanes. There are 110km cross-country trails.
slopes 1700–2350m
🚠 8 ⛷ 19km

Le Fornet   360
Rustic old hamlet 3km up the valley from Val d'Isère.

Forstau   Austria
Secluded hamlet above Radstadt–Schladming road. Very limited area (Fageralm) with old lifts, but nice and quiet.
930m; slopes 930–1885m
🚠 7 ⛷ 14km

La Fouly   Switzerland
Small area in Ski St-Bernard area near Verbier, with west-facing slopes, 10km of cross-country trails and a floodlit toboggan run. Good base for ski touring. Hotel Edelweiss serves excellent food.
1600m; slopes 1600–2200m
🚠 3 ⛷ 20km

La Foux-d'Allos   France
Purpose-built resort that shares a good intermediate area with Pra-Loup (Val d'Allos ski area).
1800m; slopes 1800–2600m
🚠 51 ⛷ 180km

Frabosa Soprana   Italy
One of numerous little areas south of Turin, well placed for combining winter sports with Riviera sightseeing.
850m; slopes 860–1740m
🚠 7 ⛷ 40km

Frisco   561
Small town down the valley from Breckenridge.

Frontignano   Italy
Best lift system in the Macerata region, near the Adriatic Riviera.
1340m; slopes 1340–2000m
🚠 8 ⛷ 10km

Fucine   Italy
Old Trentino valley village near Marilleva/Folgarida.
980m

Fügen   Austria
Unspoiled Zillertal village with road up to satellite Hochfügen – part of fair-sized Ski Optimal area, along with Kaltenbach.
550m

Fulpmes   183
Village in the Stubai valley.

Furano   670
Resort on Hokkaido island, Japan.

Fusch   Austria
Cheaper, quiet place to stay when visiting Zell am See. Across a golf course from Kaprun and Schuttdorf.
805m; slopes 805–1050m
🚠 2 ⛷ 5km

Fuschl am See   Austria
Attractive, unspoiled, lakeside village close to St Wolfgang and Salzburg, 30 minutes from its slopes. Best suited to part-time skiers who want to sightsee as well.
670m

Gålå   Norway
Base for downhill and cross-country skiing, an hour's drive north of Lillehammer.
930m; slopes 830–1150m
🚠 7 ⛷ 20km

Gallio   Italy
One of several low resorts near Vicenza and Trento. Popular with weekend day-trippers.
1100m; slopes 1100–1550m
🚠 11 ⛷ 50km

Galtür   114
Charming traditional village near Ischgl.

Gambarie d'Aspromonte   Italy
Italy's second most southerly ski area (after Mt Etna). On the 'toe' of the Italian 'boot' near Reggio di Calabria.
1310m; slopes 1310–1650m 🚠 3

Gantschier   Austria
No days of its own but particularly well placed for visiting all the Montafon areas.
700m

Gargellen   Austria
Quiet, tiny and secluded village tucked up a side valley in the Montafon area, with a small but varied piste network of blues and reds on Schafberg that is blissfully quiet. For experts there is lots of off-piste terrain plus ski routes, and there is a special day tour of Madrisa (Klosters). Snowmaking on the valley

pistes is good, and you can ski to the door of some hotels.
1425m

Garmisch-Partenkirchen 384

Gaschurn   Austria
A pleasant village in the Montafon area, bypassed by the valley traffic, with a gondola to the Nova area of slopes – the valley's largest, with 114km of pistes. This is generally the most challenging area in the valley, with many red runs, and blues that are not entirely easy. Most of the slopes are above the treeline, typically offering a very modest 300m vertical. There is lots of off-piste potential, including steep (and quite dangerous) slopes down into the central valley. Snowmaking covers almost half the area, including runs down to the valley. The NovaPark terrain park features a half-pipe and snowcross course. There are lots of mountain restaurants. It also links to the Hochjoch ski area (see St Gallenkirch).
1000m

Gaustablikk   Norway
Small snow-sure Alpine area on Mt Gausta in southern Norway with plenty of cross-country. ⛷ 15km

Gavarnie   France
Traditional village and fair-sized ski area, with the longest green run in the Pyrenees. Grand views of the Cirque de Gavarnie.
1400m; slopes 1850–2400m
🚠 11 ⛷ 45km

Gazprom Laura   Russia
One of the venues for the Sochi Winter Olympics in 2014.
560m; slopes 940–2320m
🚠 13 ⛷ 72km

Geilo   Norway
Small, quiet, unspoiled community on the railway line from Bergen, on the coast, to Oslo. It provides all the basics of a resort – a handful of cafes and shops around the railway station, a dozen hotels more widely spread around the wide valley, children's facilities and a sports centre. Geilo is a superb cross-country resort. It's very limited for downhillers, and none of the runs is very difficult, but it does claim to have Scandinavia's only super-pipe.
800m; slopes 800–1180m
🚠 18 ⛷ 35km

Gérardmer   France
Sizeable lakeside resort in the northerly Vosges mountains near Strasbourg, with plenty of amenities. Limited downhill slopes nearby include one of almost 4km. Extensive ski de fond trails in the area.
665m; slopes 750–1150m
🚠 20 ⛷ 40km

Gerlitzen   Austria
Carinthia's central ski area. A worthwhile outing from Bad Kleinkirchheim. Gondola ride from the valley near Villach, with good views and varied but short runs.
500m; slopes 1000–1910m
🚠 15 ⛷ 26km

Gerlos   138
Village in the Zillertal Arena.

Gerlosplatte   Austria
Inexpensive but fairly snow-sure area above the village of Krimml, linked to Königsleiten, Gerlos and Zell am Ziller to form a fair-sized intermediate area.

Les Gets   261

La Giettaz   269
Tiny village between La Clusaz and Megève.

Gitschtal / Weissbriach   Austria
One of many little areas near Hermagor in eastern Austria, close to Italian border.
690m; slopes 690–1400m
🚠 4 ⛷ 5km

Glaris   Switzerland
Hamlet base station for the uncrowded Rinerhorn section of the Davos slopes.
1460m; slopes 1460–2490m
🚠 5 ⛷ 30km

Glencoe   669
Scottish ski resort.
305m; slopes 305–1110m
🚠 7 ⛷ 20km

Glenshee   669
Scottish ski resort.
610m; slopes 610–1070m
🚠 22 ⛷ 40km

Going   106
Small area near Ellmau, linked to the huge SkiWelt area.

Goldegg   Austria
Year-round resort famous for its lakeside castle. Limited slopes but Wagrain (Salzburger Sportwelt) and Grossarl (Gastein valley) are nearby.
825m; slopes 825–1250m
🚠 4 ⛷ 12km

Golden   Canada
Small logging town, the place to stay when visiting Kicking Horse resort 15 minutes away. Also the launch pad for Purcell heli-skiing.

Golte   Slovenia
Ski area in the East Karavante mountains, above Mozirje. Gondola to the slopes from Zekovec village. Mostly advanced runs.
⛷7 🚡18km

Gore Mountain   USA
One of the better areas in New York State. Near Lake Placid, sufficiently far north to avoid worst weekend crowds. Intermediate terrain.
455m; slopes 455–1095m
⛷9 🚡290 acres

Göriach   Austria
Hamlet with trail connecting into one of the longest, most snow-sure cross-country networks in Europe.
1250m

Gornaya Karusel   Russia
One of the venues for the Sochi Winter Olympics in 2014.
560m; slopes 940–2320m
⛷13 🚡72km

Gortipohl   Austria
Traditional village in the pretty Montafon valley.
920m; slopes 900–2395m
⛷61 🚡243km

Gosau   Austria
Family-friendly resort, with straggling village. Plenty of pretty, if low, runs. Fast lifts mean queues are rare. Snow-sure Obertauern and Schladming are within reach.
755m; slopes 755–1800m
⛷37 🚡80km

Göstling   Austria
One of Austria's easternmost resorts, between Salzburg and Vienna. A traditional village in a wooded setting.
530m; slopes 530–1880m
⛷8 🚡18km

Götzens   Austria
Valley village base for Axamer Lizum and Mutters, near Innsbruck. Gondola from village to Mutteralm and red run back down.
870m; slopes 830–2100m
⛷4 🚡15km

Gourette-Eaux-Bonnes   France
Most snow-sure resort in the French Pyrenees. Very popular with local families, so best avoided at weekends.
1400m; slopes 1400–2400m
⛷14 🚡30km

Grächen   Switzerland
Charming chalet-village reached by tricky access road off the approach to Zermatt. A small area of open slopes, mainly above the trees and of red-run difficulty, reached by two gondolas – one to Hannigalp (2115m), the main

focus of activity with a very impressive children's nursery area. The village has almost a score of hotels, mostly 3-star; most of the accommodation is in chalets and apartments.
1615m; slopes 1615–2865m
⛷9 🚡42km

Le Grand-Bornand   France
Covered by the Aravis lift pass, and much smaller and even more charming than La Clusaz. The slopes can be accessed from either the outskirts of the village or from the satellite village of Le Chinaillon. There are worthwhile shady black runs on Le Lachat, and on the lower peak of La Floria. There are plenty of good cruising blue and red intermediate runs, and also good beginner slopes. And there are extensive cross-country trails in the Vallée du Bouchet and towards Le Chinaillon.
1000m; slopes 1000–2100m
⛷29 🚡90km

Grand Targhee   **599**
Powder skiing paradise an hour from Jackson Hole.
2439m; slopes 2260–3005m
⛷5 🚡2100 acres

Les Granges   **206**
Hamlet at the mid-station of the funicular up from Bourg to Les Arcs.

Grangesises   Italy
Small satellite of Sestriere, with lifts up to the main slopes.

Granite Peak   USA
One of the oldest areas in the Great Lakes region, and now one of the largest. New base village. Good selection of black runs on the upper mountain.
⛷7 🚡400 acres

Grau Roig   **80**
Mini-resort between Pas de la Casa and Soldeu.

La Grave   **263**

Great Divide   USA
Area near Helena, Montana, best for experts. Mostly bowls; plus near-extreme Rawhide Gulch.
1765m; slopes 1765–2195m
⛷6 🚡720 acres

Gresse-en-Vercors   France
Resort south of Grenoble. Sheltered slopes worth noting for bad-weather days.
1250m; slopes 1600–1750m
⛷13 🚡18km

Gressoney-la-Trinité   **416**
Village in Monterosa Ski area.

Gressoney-St-Jean   Italy
Larger and lower of the two villages in the central valley of the Monterosa Ski area. Good for cross-country as well as downhill. Varied slopes and well-equipped nursery area.
1390m

Grimentz   **501**
Village in the Val d'Anniviers.

Grindelwald   **476**

Grossarl   **96**
Secluded village in the Gastein valley.

Grossglockner area   Austria
Two linked areas near Heiligenbluit, above the villages of Kals and Matrei. Remote position west of Bad Gastein. Uncrowded, fairly extensive slopes. Some long, varied runs.
1000m; slopes 1000–2620m
⛷15 🚡110km

Grosskirchheim   Austria
Area near Heiligenblut, not linked but access to 55km slopes.
1025m; slopes 1025–1400m

Grouse Mountain   Canada
The Vancouver area with the largest lift capacity. Superb city views from mostly easy slopes; night skiing.
880m; slopes 880–1245m
⛷11 🚡120 acres

Grünau   Austria
Spacious riverside village in a lovely lake-filled part of eastern Austria. Nicely varied area, but very low.
525m; slopes 620–1600m
⛷15 🚡40km

Gryon   **515**
Village below Villars.

Gstaad   Switzerland
Despite its exclusive reputation, an attractive, traditional village where anyone could have a relaxing holiday. Of the four sectors, the largest is above Saanenmöser and Schönried, reached by train. Snow-cover can be unreliable except on the Glacier des Diablerets, 15km away. Few runs challenge experts. Black runs rarely exceed red or even blue difficulty. There is off-piste potential. Given good snow, this is a superb area for intermediates, with long, easy descents in the major area. The nursery slopes at Wispile are adequate, and there are plenty of runs to progress to. Time lost on buses or trains is more of a problem than queues.
1050m; slopes 950–3000m
⛷53 🚡220km

Gunstock   USA
One of the New Hampshire resorts closest to Boston, popular with families. Primarily easy slopes. Lovely Lake Winnisquam views.
275m; slopes 275–700m
⛷8 🚡220 acres

Guthega   Australia
Australia's most challenging and diverse slopes (at Perisher). Comfortable accommodation in the resort's only commercial lodge. Free shuttle from Jindabyne. 6.5 hours from Sydney.
1640m; slopes 1605–2035m
⛷47 🚡3075 acres

Guzet   France
Charming cluster of chalets set in a pine forest at Guzet 1400. Three main sectors offer slopes for all levels.
1400m; slopes 1100–2100m
⛷14 🚡40km

Hafjell   Norway
Main ski area for Lillehammer.
⛷12 🚡33km

Haider Alm   Italy
Area in the Val Venosta in the South Tyrol close to Nauders. Malda Haider is its Italian name.

Hakuba   **670**
European-style resort four hours from Tokyo.

Harper Mountain   Canada
Small, family-friendly resort in Kamloops, British Colombia.
1100m; slopes 1100–1525m
⛷3 🚡400 acres

Harrachov   Czech Republic
Closest resort to Prague, with enough terrain to justify a day trip. No beginner area.
650m; slopes 650–1020m
⛷4 🚡8runs

Hasliberg   Switzerland
Four rustic hamlets on a sunny plateau overlooking Meiringen and Lake Brienz. Two of them are the bottom stations of a varied intermediate area.
1050m

Haus   **158**
Village next to Schladming.

Haystack   USA
Minor satellite of Mount Snow, in Vermont, but with a bit more steep skiing.
580m; slopes 580–1095m
⛷26 🚡540 acres

Heavenly   **539**

Hebalm   Austria
One of many small areas in Austria's easternmost ski region near Slovenian border. No major resorts in vicinity.
1350m; slopes 1350–1400m
⛷6 🚡11km

Heiligenblut   Austria
Picturesque village in beautiful surroundings at the foot of the Grossglockner, west of Bad Gastein. Quiet, mainly red runs in two main areas. Lifts include three gondolas and a fast chair.
1300m; slopes 1300–2910m
🚠 12 ⛷ 55km

Heiterwang   Austria
Small lakeside village with access to Berwang's slopes in the Zugspitz Arena. Bus ride to the lift station. Couple of local downhill slopes and popular cross-country venue.
995m
🚠 2 ⛷ 2km

Hemlock Resort   Canada
Area 55 miles east of Vancouver towards Sun Peaks. Mostly intermediate terrain and with snowfall of 600 inches a year. Lodging is available at the base area.
1000m; slopes 1000–1375m
🚠 4 ⛷ 350 acres

Hemsedal   659

Heremence   Switzerland
Quiet, traditional village in unspoiled attractive setting south of Sion. Verbier's slopes are accessed a few minutes' drive away at Les Masses.
1250m

Hermagor   Austria
Main village base for the Nassfeld ski area in Carinthia.
600m; slopes 610–2000m
🚠 30 ⛷ 100km

High 1 Resort   South Korea
Small ski area at the High 1 leisure complex, 250km from Seoul by train. ⛷ 21km

Hinterglemm   152
One of the villages making up Saalbach-Hinterglemm.

Hintermoos   Austria
Tiny village east of Saalbach and part of the large, low-altitude Hochkönig area that spreads impressively over a series of gentle peaks linking Maria Alm to Mühlbach.

Hintersee   Austria
Easy slopes very close to Salzburg. Several long top-to-bottom runs and lifts, so size of the ski area is greatly reduced if the snowline is high.
745m; slopes 750–1470m
🚠 9 ⛷ 40km

Hinterstoder   Austria
A very quiet valley village – neat but not overtly charming – spread along the road up the dead-end Stodertal in Upper Austria. The local Höss slopes are pleasantly wooded, less densely at the top, with splendid views. It's a small

area, but has a worthwhile vertical of 1250m, and 450m above mid-mountain. A gondola from the main street goes up to the flat-bottomed bowl of Huttererböden (1400m), where there are very gentle but limited nursery slopes and lifts up to higher points. Most of the mountain is of easy red steepness. The run to the valley is a pleasant red with one or two tricky bits where it takes a quick plunge; it has effective snowmaking.
600m; slopes 600–1860m
🚠 14 ⛷ 36km

Hinterthal   Austria
One of five villages in the varied Hochkönig area that spreads over a series of gentle peaks from Maria Alm to Mühlbach. The village is small – little more than a few four-star hotels and chalets, shops and bars – but it connects well with the main area via a newish gondola. There are good nursery slopes and some challenging reds.
990m

Hintertux / Tux valley   109

Hippach   138
Hamlet near a crowd-free lift into Mayrhofen's main area.

Grand Hirafu   670
Interlinked area in Niseko, Japan.

Hittisau   104
Village in Bregenzerwald.

Hochfügen   Austria
High-altitude ski-station outpost of Fügen, part of Ski Optimal area linked with Kaltenbach. Best suited to intermediates.
1500m; slopes 560–2500m
🚠 35 ⛷ 155km

Hochgurgl   144
Quiet village with connection to Obergurgl's slopes.

Hochkönig   Austria
Varied area that spreads over four linked mountains from Maria Alm via Hinterthal and Dienten to Mühlbach.
800-1070m; slopes 800–1900m
🚠 33 ⛷ 120km

Hochpillberg   Austria
Hamlet with fabulous views towards Innsbruck and an antique chairlift into varied terrain above Schwaz with good vertical of 1000m. Wonderfully safe for children; all accommodation within two minutes of lift.
1300m; slopes 1300–2100m
🚠 5 ⛷ 10km

Hochsölden   162
Satellite above Sölden.

Hoch-Ybrig   Switzerland
Purpose-built complex only 64km south-east of Zürich, with facilities for families.
1050m; slopes 1050–1830m
🚠 12 ⛷ 50km

Hochzillertal   Austria
Along with Hochfugen forms the large Ski Optimal area above the valley village of Kaltenbach. Best suited to intermediates – but there is plenty of potential for off-piste too.
1500m; slopes 560–2500m
🚠 35 ⛷ 155km

Holiday Valley   USA
Family resort in New York State, an hour's drive south-east of Buffalo.
slopes 485–685m
🚠 12 ⛷ 270 acres

Hollersbach   Austria
Hamlet near Mittersill, over Pass Thurn from Kitzbühel, with a gondola up to the Resterhöhe above Pass Thurn.
805m; slopes 805–1000m
🚠 2 ⛷ 5km

Homewood   USA
Uncrowded area near Tahoe City with the most sheltered slopes in the vicinity. Apart from one fast quad, most slopes are served by slow chairlifts, and the views are as much of an attraction as the slopes. Set right on the western shore of the lake, so access is quick and easy. The notably quiet slopes include plenty of short black pitches as well as cruisers.
1900m; slopes 1900–2400m
🚠 7 ⛷ 1260 acres

Hoodoo Ski Bowl   USA
Small area in Oregon with short runs and limited vertical of around 300m. Some 65km from Bend (see Mount Bachelor).
1420m; slopes 1420–1740m
🚠 5 ⛷ 800 acres

Hopfgarten   167
Small chalet village with lift link into the SkiWelt area.

Horseshoe Resort   Canada
Toronto region resort with high-capacity lift system and 100% snowmaking. The second mountain – The Heights – is open to members only.
310m; slopes 310–405m
🚠 7 ⛷ 60 acres

Les Houches   223
Varied area at the entrance to the Chamonix valley.

Hovden   Norway
Big, modern luxury lakeside hotel in wilderness midway between Oslo and Bergen. Cross-country venue with some Alpine slopes.
820m; slopes 820–1175m
🚠 5 ⛷ 14km

La Hoya   Argentina
Small uncrowded resort 15km from the town of Esquel.
slopes 1350–2150m
🚠 9 ⛷ 22km

Huez   196
Charming old hamlet on the road up to Alpe-d'Huez.

Hunter Mountain   USA
Popular New Yorkers' area so it gets very crowded at weekends.
485m; slopes 485–975m
🚠 14 ⛷ 230 acres

Hüttschlag   Austria
Hamlet in a dead-end valley with lifts into the Gastein area at nearby Grossarl.
1020m; slopes 1020–1220m 🚠 1

Hyundai Sungwoo Resort   South Korea
Modern high-rise resort, 140km from Seoul. Host to the 2009 World Snowboard Championships. 🚠 9

Idre Fjäll   Sweden
Collective name for four areas 490km north-west of Stockholm.
slopes 590–890m
🚠 30 ⛷ 28km

Igls   Austria
Almost a suburb of Innsbruck – the city trams run out to the village – but it is a small resort in its own right. Its famous downhill race course is an excellent piste.
900m

Iizuna   Japan
Tiny area 2.5 hours from Tokyo.
slopes 1080–1480m 🚠 7

Incline Village   USA
Large village on northern edge of Lake Tahoe – it is a reasonable stop-off if you are touring.

Indianhead   USA
South Lake Superior area with the most snowfall in the region. Winds are a problem.
395m; slopes 395–585m
🚠 12 ⛷ 195 acres

Inneralpbach   Austria
Small satellite of Alpbach, 3km up the valley.
1050m

Inner-Arosa   Switzerland
The prettiest part of Arosa, with lifts into the slopes and a quiet, 'gentle' children's area.
1800m

Innichen Italy
Small resort in South Tyrol. San Candido in Italian.
1175m; slopes 1175–1580m
🚠 4 🚡 15km

Innsbruck Austria
Lively and interesting former Olympic city at Alpine crossroads, surrounded by small areas, each ideal for a day trip. Among them is the Stubai glacier. Area pass available.
575m; slopes 860–3210m
🚠 83 🚡 266km

Interlaken Switzerland
Large lakeside summer resort at entrance to the valleys leading to Wengen, Grindelwald and Mürren.

Ischgl 114

Ishiuchi Maruyama-Gala-Yuzawa Kogen Japan
Three resorts with a shared lift pass 90 minutes from Tokyo by bullet train and offering the largest ski area in the central Honshu region.
255m; slopes 255–920m 🚠 52

Isola 2000 France
A compact purpose-built resort 90km from Nice, which makes it great for short breaks and very convenient. The doorstep snow, high slopes and an improving range of amenities make it equally appealing to families and beginners; there are some excellent nursery slopes near the base. But the core of the resort village isn't pretty: mostly block-like and tatty apartment buildings. The slopes spread across three main sectors, with varied runs suiting confident intermediates best; most are above the treeline and often sunny, but the resort's southerly aspect means that the area can have masses of snow when it is in shorter supply elsewhere in the French Alps. And most slopes keep their snow well.
2000m; slopes 1840–2610m
🚠 20 🚡 120km

Iso Syöte Finland
Finland's most southerly fell region, 150km south of the Arctic Circle but receiving the most snow in the country. A family-friendly resort that suits beginners and intermediates best, since there are only two black runs. But there are two freeride areas. Most runs are short, with the longest 1200m and a maximum vertical of less than 200m. And all the lifts are drags. There's a terrain park, expanded children's nursery area, tubing, tobogganing, and igloo hotel.

Cross-country is big here, with 120kms of trails. There's a choice of hotels and cabins.
430m; slopes 240–430m
🚠 9 🚡 21km

Itter 167
Next to Söll.

Jackson USA
Classic New England village, and a major cross-country base. A lovely place from which to ski New Hampshire's Alpine areas.

Jackson Hole 605

Jasná Slovakia
Largest ski area in Slovakia, in the Low Tatras mountains. Big children's area, terrain park, night skiing. Several tough 'freeride zones'.
slopes 940–2005m
🚠 26 🚡 36km

Jasper Canada
Set in the middle of Jasper National Park, this low-key, low-rise little town appeals more to those keen on scenery and wildlife (and cross-country skiing) rather than piste miles. Could combine a stay with Whistler, Banff or Lake Louise. Snowfall is modest by North American standards and there is lots of steep terrain that needs good snow to be fun. Keen piste-bashers will cover all the groomed runs in half a day. There are excellent nursery slopes. Visitors have commented on few crowds and queues. There are 300km of cross-country trails. Most accommodation is out of town or on the outskirts and the local slopes are a 30-minute drive.
1695m; slopes 1695–2610m
🚠 8 🚡 1675 acres

Jay Peak USA
Vermont resort near Canadian border with best snowfall record in the east. Tree-lined intermediate/advanced slopes – as many classified black as blue. Experts also have access to hike-in/out terrain in West bowl.
550m; slopes 550–1205m
🚠 8 🚡 385 acres

Jochberg 121
Straggling village, 8km from Kitzbühel.

La Joue-du-Loup France
Slightly stylish little purpose-built place a few km north-west of Gap. Shares a fair-sized intermediate area with Superdévoluy. A ski-in/ski-out, family-oriented resort; all accommodation in good-value apartments and chalets; good choice of affordable

restaurants. Easily reached using budget flights to Marseille.
1450m; slopes 1450–2450m
🚠 22 🚡 100km

Jouvenceaux 424
Less boisterous base near Sauze d'Oulx.

Jukkasjärvi Sweden
Centuries-old cross-country resort with unique ice hotel rebuilt every December.

June Mountain USA
Small area a half-hour drive from Mammoth and in same ownership.
2300m; slopes 2300–3090m
🚠 8 🚡 500 acres

Juns 109
Small village between Lanersbach and Hintertux.

Kals am Grossglockner Austria
Remote valley village north of Lienz. Now linked to Matrei.
1325m; slopes 975–2620m
🚠 15 🚡 110km

Kaltenbach Austria
Valley village with one of the larger, quieter Zillertal areas, with plenty of high-altitude slopes, mostly above the treeline. Ski Optimal is the name given to the area and slopes of the Hochzillertal-Hochfügen above the resort. The pistes suit intermediates best – but there is plenty of potential for off-piste, too.
560m; slopes 560–2500m
🚠 35 🚡 155km

Kamui Ski Links Japan
Small area on Hokkaido with excellent powder reputation and access to it allowed more than in many other resorts. Easy day trip from Furano.
slopes 150–750m 🚠 6

Kananaskis Canada
Small area near Calgary, nicely set in woods, with slopes at Nakiska.
slopes 1525–2465m
🚠 12 🚡 605 acres

Kandersteg Switzerland
Good cross-country base set amid beautiful scenery near Interlaken. Easy, but limited, slopes. Popular with families.
1175m; slopes 1175–1900m
🚠 7 🚡 14km

Kanin Slovenia
Area near Bovec with uncrowded intermediate slopes that are Slovenia's highest, offer the biggest vertical (1150m) and are linked to nearby Sella Nevea in Italy. Sadly it was closed

during the 2013/14 season and did not reopen for the 2014/15 season.
460m; slopes 1140–2290m
🚠 9 🚡 30km

Kappl Austria
A 15-minute bus ride down the valley from Ischgl, and worth a visit. Both the village and the slopes are family-oriented, and delightfully quiet compared with Ischgl. The village, with a couple of dozen hotels and guest-houses, sits on a shelf 100m above the valley floor. The slopes – served by an access gondola from the roadside and fast quads above it – offer plenty of variety, with several tough reds. Most of the slopes are open, but the run down the gondola offers some shelter for bad-weather days.
1260m

Kaprun 185
Classic Austrian charmer near Zell am See.

Les Karellis 265
Resort in the Maurienne valley near better-known Valloire.

Kastelruth Italy
German name for Castelrotto.

Kasurila Finland
Siilinjarvi ski area popular with boarders. 🚠 5

Katschberg Austria
Cute hamlet above the road pass from Styria to Carinthia, by-passed by Tauern motorway. Non-trivial area of high intermediate slopes. Popular with families.
1640m; slopes 1065–2220m
🚠 16 🚡 70km

Keystone USA
Sprawling condo-dominated resort below three varied mountains; the nearest thing to a proper village is a handy development near the gondola. Evenings are quiet, with limited restaurants/bars. The lift pass covers Breckenridge and nearby Arapahoe Basin. Fast lifts link all three mountains, with varied terrain including ungroomed steep bowls, forest glades and cat skiing. There's a beautifully groomed network of tree-lined blues and greens, and good nursery slopes. Reporters praise the school for small classes. There's a huge terrain park and super-pipe, floodlit skiing and tubing. A favourite hut is the table-service Alpenglow Stube.
2830m; slopes 2830–3780m
🚠 20 🚡 3148 acres

Kicking Horse 629

Killington 610

Kimberley Canada
Mining town turned twee mock Austro-Bavarian/English Tudor resort scenically set 2 hours from Banff. The terrain offers a mix of blue and black runs (and occasional green) and a vertical of 750m. The mainly forested runs are spread over two rather bland hills. There are only a few short double diamonds, but classification tends to understate difficulty, and many of the single diamonds are quite challenging. It has a reputation for good powder, although it doesn't get huge amounts by the standards of this region. 'Superb grooming and the off-piste doesn't ski out if you are lucky enough to get a powder day,' says a 2014 visitor.
1230m; slopes 1230–1980m
🚡 5 🚠 1800 acres

Kirchberg 121
Lively town close to Kitzbühel.

Kirchdorf Austria
Attractive village a bus ride from St Johann in Tirol, with good local beginner slopes.
640m

Kirkwood USA
Renowned for its powder, and has a lot to offer experts and confident intermediates, but it's limited for intermediates who are not happy to tackle black runs. It makes a great outing from South Lake Tahoe, though heavy snowfall may close the high-level passes to get there. Deep snow is part of the attraction, often reportedly better than Heavenly.
2375m; slopes 2375–2985m
🚡 14 🚠 2300 acres

Kitzbühel 121

Kleinarl Austria
Secluded traditional village up a pretty side valley from Wagrain, part of the three-valley lift network linking Flachauwinkl to Zauchensee – our figures relate to this area.
1015m; slopes 800–2185m
🚡 15 🚠 65km

Kleinwalsertal 382
Area in the German Alps.

Klippitztörl Austria
One of many little areas in Austria's easternmost ski region near Slovenian border.
1550m; slopes 1460–1820m
🚡 6 🚠 25km

Klösterle Austria
Valley village at the base of the Sonnenkopf ski area a few km west of the Arlberg pass – and covered by the Arlberg ski pass.
1100m; slopes 1100–2300m
🚡 10 🚠 39km

Klosters 480

Kobla 666
Slovenian village a bus ride from Vogel.

Kolasin 1450 Montenegro
Small ski area on Bjelasica Mountain above the town of the Kolasin, where you stay.
1450m
🚡 5 🚠 20km

Kolsass-Weer Austria
Pair of Inn-side villages with low, inconvenient and limited slopes.
555m; slopes 555–1010m
🚡 3 🚠 14km

Königsleiten 138
Quiet resort sharing area with Gerlos in the Zillertal Arena.

Konjiam South Korea
Purpose-built resort 40 minutes north of Seoul. The slopes suit beginners best, and offer the area's longest run at 1.8km. The base area has over 400 condos, a restaurant and spa, Popular with families.
🚡 3 🚠 11runs

Kopaonik Serbia
Modern, sympathetically designed family resort in a pretty setting.
1770m; slopes 1110–2015m
🚡 23 🚠 60km

Koralpe Austria
Largest and steepest of many gentle little areas in Austria's easternmost ski region near the Slovenian border.
1550m; slopes 1550–2050m
🚡 10 🚠 25km

Korea Condo South Korea
A single condo complex built some way from the three slopes. 🚡 2

Kössen Austria
Village near St Johann in Tirol with low, scattered and limited local slopes.
600m; slopes 600–1700m
🚡 9 🚠 25km

Kötschach-Mauthen Austria
One of many little areas near Hermagor in eastern Austria, close to the Italian border.
710m; slopes 710–1300m
🚡 4 🚠 7km

Kranjska Gora 666

Krimml Austria
Sunny area, high enough to have good snow usually. Shares regional pass with Wildkogel resorts (Neukirchen).
1075m; slopes 1640–2040m
🚡 9 🚠 33km

Krippenstein Austria
A mainly freeride resort on Dachstein glacier near Salzburg. Cable car from Obertraun in the valley. 30km off-piste routes and 11km long blue/red run. Shares lift pass with Annaberg-Gosau region.

Krispl-Gaissau Austria
Easy slopes very close to Salzburg. Several long top-to-bottom lifts mean the size of the area is greatly reduced if the snow line is high.
925m; slopes 750–1570m
🚡 11 🚠 40km

Kronplatz Italy
Distinctive ski area in South Tyrol, with amazingly efficient lifts from Brunico and San Vigilio de Marebbe. Plan de Corones is its Italian name.
1200m; slopes 1200–2275m
🚡 32 🚠 114km

Krvavec 666

Kühtai Austria
A collection of comfortable hotels beside a high road pass only 25km from Innsbruck – higher than equally snow-sure Obergurgl or Obertauern, but cheaper than either. Covered also by the standard Innsbruck pass. A modern gondola, three fast quads and a handful of drags serve red cruisers of about 500m vertical on either side of the road, plus some token black runs; not ideal for novices – few easy blues to graduate to. Very quiet in the week, but liable to weekend crowds if lower resorts around Innsbruck are short of snow. Limited mountain huts. Quiet in the evening, but for its size a reasonable selection of hotels.
2020m; slopes 800–2620m
🚡 12 🚠 44km

Kusatsu Kokusai Japan
Attractive spa village with hot springs, three hours from Tokyo.
slopes 1250–2170m 🚡 13

Laax 482

Le Lac Blanc France
Mini-resort with six-pack in the northerly Vosges mountains near Strasbourg. Extensive ski de fond trails.
830m; slopes 830–1235m
🚡 9 🚠 14km

Laces Italy
Village in the Val Venosta in the South Tyrol covered by the Ortler Skiarena pass.

Lachtal Austria
Second largest ski resort in the Styrian region NE of Salzburg.
1600m; slopes 1600–2100m
🚡 8 🚠 29km

Ladis Austria
Smaller alternative to Serfaus and Fiss, with lifts that connect into the same varied ski area.
1200m; slopes 1200–2750m
🚡 70 🚠 190km

Lagunillas Chile
83km south-east of Santiago. 🚠 494 acres

Le Laisinant 360
Tiny hamlet down the valley from Val d'Isère.

Lake Louise 631

Lake Tahoe USA
Collection of 14 ski areas spectacularly set on California-Nevada border - Heavenly and Squaw Valley best known in Britain.

Lamoura France
One of four villages that makes up the Les Rousses area in the Jura.
1120m; slopes 1120–1680m
🚡 40 🚠 40km

Landeck–Zams Austria
Small ski area in the Tirol region.
780m; slopes 816–2210m
🚡 7 🚠 22km

Lanersbach 109
Attractive village near Hintertux.

Lans-en-Vercors France
Village close to Villard-de-Lans and 30km from Grenoble. Highest slopes in the region; few snowmakers.
1020m; slopes 1400–1805m
🚡 16 🚠 24km

Lanslebourg 357
One of the villages that make up Val Cenis.

Lanslevillard 357
One of the villages that make up Val Cenis.

Laterns Austria
Small, low altitude resort in the Vorarlberg near Friedrichshafen. Two fast chairs serve mainly red runs and some ski routes.
900m; slopes 900–1785m
🚡 6 🚠 27km

Lauchernalp-Lötschental
Switzerland
Small but tall and challenging slopes reached by cable car from Wiler in the secluded, picturesque, dead-end Lötschental, north of Rhône valley. Glacier runs above 3000m.
1970m; slopes 1420–3110m
🚡 6 ⛷ 33km

Lauterbrunnen 485
Valley town with rail connection up to Mürren.

Le Lavancher 223
Quiet village between Chamonix and Argentière.

Lavarone Italy
One of several areas east of Trento, good for a weekend day trip.
1195m; slopes 1075–1555m
🚡 13 ⛷ 12km

Leadville USA
Old mining town full of historic buildings. Own easy area (Ski Cooper) plus snowcat operation. Picturesque inexpensive base for visiting Copper Mountain, Vail and Beaver Creek.

Lech 129

The Lecht 669
Scottish ski resort.
640m; slopes 610–825m
🚡 13 ⛷ 20km

Lélex France
Family resort with pretty wooded slopes between Dijon and Geneva.
900m; slopes 900–1680m
🚡 29 ⛷ 50km

Las Leñas Argentina
European-style resort, 400km south of Mendoza, with varied, beautiful terrain and extensive off-piste. But it's a stormy place that can close the lifts for days. Lodgings at the foot of the slopes.
2240m; slopes 2240–3430m
🚡 14 ⛷ 64km

Lenggries-Brauneck 382
Bavarian resort south of Munich.
68om; slopes 700–1710m
🚡 18 ⛷ 34km

Lenk Switzerland
Traditional village sharing a sizeable area with Adelboden, and with its own separate slopes at Betelberg. Buses to lifts at Rothenbach, or to the six-pack from Buhlberg.
1070m; slopes 1070–2360m
🚡 56 ⛷ 185km

Lenzerheide 459
Spacious village whose slopes are linked with Arosa's.

Leogang 152
Quiet village with link to Saalbach-Hinterglemm.

Lermoos Austria
Pleasant little village with 30km of shady intermediate slopes on Grubigstein, and a pass giving access to a variety of other areas in the locality, including the towering (and glacial) Zugspitze, on the border with Germany. The slopes offer splendid views of the mountain. The village is compact, with good family-friendly hotels. Fast lifts go from both ends, serving some worthwhile descents - including a fine black run and an area of ready-made moguls. The runs below mid-mountain are worthwhile blues and reds, with good nursery slopes at village level. Lots of cross-country trails along the flat valley.
1005m; slopes 990–2960m
🚡 52 ⛷ 147km

Lessach Austria
Hamlet with trail connecting into one of the longest, most snow-sure cross-country networks in Europe.
1210m 🚡 1

Leukerbad Switzerland
Major spa resort of Roman origin, spectacularly set beneath towering cliffs, which are scaled by a cable car up to high-altitude cross-country trails. The downhill slopes are on the opposite side of the valley, mainly above the treeline and of red gradient, though there are a couple of blacks including a World Cup downhill course, which descends from open slopes into the woods. Lifts include a six-pack.
1410m; slopes 1410–2700m
🚡 10 ⛷ 52km

Leutasch Austria
Traditional cross-country village with limited slopes but a pleasant day trip from nearby Seefeld or Innsbruck.
1130m; slopes 1130–1605m
🚡 3 ⛷ 6km

Levi 657

Leysin Switzerland
This is a spread-out village, climbing up a wooded hillside. The lifts are to the east of the village and take you to a pretty mix of mainly red and blue runs. Itineraries from the top of Chaux de Mont provide the best options for experts, along with a heli-operation. There are nursery slopes at village level. The revolving Kuklos restaurant at La Berneuse has stunning views.
1250m; slopes 1300–2200m
🚡 14 ⛷ 60km

Lienz Austria
Pleasant town in pretty surroundings.
675m; slopes 730–2280m
🚡 17 ⛷ 40km

Lillehammer Norway
Cultural fjord-side town, 2 to 3 hours north of Oslo by train/car, with its two Olympic areas 15 and 35km away, poorly served by bus.
200m; slopes 200–1030m
🚡 10 ⛷ 25km

Limone Italy
Pleasant old town not far from Turin, with a pretty area, but far from snow-sure.
1010m; slopes 1030–2050m
🚡 15 ⛷ 80km

Lincoln USA
Sprawling New Hampshire town from which to visit Loon mountain.

Lindvallen-Högfjället
Sweden
Two of the mountains that make up the four unlinked ski areas of Sälen.
800m; slopes 590–890m
🚡 46 ⛷ 85km

Le Lioran France
Auvergne village near Aurillac with a purpose-built satellite above. Spectacular volcanic scenery.
1160m; slopes 1160–1850m
🚡 24 ⛷ 60km

Livigno 407

Lizzola Italy
Small base development in remote region north of Bergamo. Several other little areas nearby.
1250m; slopes 1250–2070m
🚡 9 ⛷ 30km

Loch Lomond Canada
Steep, narrow, challenging slopes near Thunder Bay on the shores of Lake Superior. Candy Mountain is nearby.
215m; slopes 215–440m
🚡 3 ⛷ 90 acres

Lofer Austria
Quiet, traditional village in a pretty setting north of Saalbach with a small area of its own, and Waidring's relatively snow-sure Steinplatte nearby.
640m; slopes 640–1745m
🚡 10 ⛷ 46km

Longchamp France
Dreary purpose-built resort with little to commend it over pretty Valmorel, with which it shares its ski area.
1650m

Loon Mountain USA
Small, smart, modern resort just outside Lincoln, New Hampshire. Mostly intermediate runs.
290m; slopes 290–910m
🚡 10 ⛷ 275 acres

Lost Trail USA
Remote Montana area, open only Thursday to Sunday and holidays. Mostly intermediate slopes.
2005m; slopes 2005–2370m
🚡 6 ⛷ 800 acres

Loveland USA
Exceptionally high and snowy slopes right next to highway I70, just east of the Continental Divide, easily reached from other Colorado resorts, especially Keystone.
3230m; slopes 3230–3870m
🚡 9 ⛷ 1365 acres

Luchon France
Sizeable village with plenty of amenities, with gondola (eight minutes) to its ski area at purpose-built Superbagnères.
630m; slopes 1440–2260m
🚡 16 ⛷ 35km

Lurisia Italy
Sizeable spa resort, a good base for visits to surrounding little ski areas and to Nice.
750m; slopes 800–1800m
🚡 8 ⛷ 35km

Lutsen Mountains USA
In Minnesota, the largest ski area in between Vermont and Colorado, with panoramic views of Lake Superior. Four small linked hills offer surprisingly good and extensive terrain. 8om; slopes 80–335m
🚡 9 ⛷ 1000 acres

Luz-Ardiden France
Spa village below its ski area. Cauterets and Barèges nearby.
710m; slopes 1730–2450m
🚡 15 ⛷ 60km

Macugnaga Italy
Two quiet, pretty villages dramatically set at the head of a remote valley, over the mountains from Zermatt and Saas-Fee. Lifts run up to the foot of the Belvedere glacier. A chairlift rises very slowly from the village to Burky, in the middle of the small, woody area of gentle runs. There is an excellent nursery slope beside the village and a two-stage cable car going over sunny slopes to the Swiss border. Good, varied red runs down the 1100m vertical of the top cable car, and considerable off-piste possibilities given good snow.
1325m; slopes 1325–2800m
🚡 11 ⛷ 35km

Madesimo Italy
Lots of fast lifts but limited extent of slopes. Not ideal for a week, but the mountain has something for everyone and the system copes well with weekend visitors– it's a couple of hours from Bergamo or Milan. The village spreads along both sides of a river; a random mix of traditional buildings and narrow streets on one side and more modern development on the other, but with a good choice of mid-priced hotels. The slopes have an almost equal share of blue and red runs that make great intermediate territory, though there are a few notable challenges – including the classic Canalone ski route. For a resort with a respectable altitude and a generally quiet and queue-free mountain, it is worth considering.
1550m; slopes 1550–2945m
🚡 12 ☂ 60km

Madonna di Campiglio 411

Mad River Glen USA
Cult resort, co-operatively owned, with some tough ungroomed terrain, a few well-groomed intermediate trails and antique lifts. Snowboarding is banned.
485m; slopes 485–1110m
🚡 4 ☂ 115 acres

La Magdelaine Italy
Close to Cervinia, and good on bad-weather days.
1645m; slopes 1645–1870m
🚡 4 ☂ 4km

Maishofen Austria
Cheaper place to stay when visiting equidistant Saalbach and Zell am See.
765m

Malbun Liechtenstein
Quaint user-friendly little family resort, 16km from the capital, Vaduz. Limited slopes and short easy runs.
1600m; slopes 1595–2100m
🚡 6 ☂ 21km

Malcesine Italy
Large summer resort on Lake Garda with a fair area of slopes, served by a revolving cable car.
1430m; slopes 1430–1830m
🚡 8 ☂ 12km

Malga Ciapela Italy
Resort at the foot of the Marmolada glacier massif, with a link into the Sella Ronda. Cortina is nearby.
1445m; slopes 1445–3270m
🚡 8 ☂ 18km

Malga Haider Italy
Small area in Val Venosta, close to Austrian border. Haideralm is its German name.
🚡 5 ☂ 20km

Mallnitz Austria
Village in a pretty valley close to Slovenia, with two varied areas providing a fine mix of wooded and open runs. Closest is Ankogel. The snow-sure Molltal Glacier is nearby, above Flattach.
1200m
🚡 15 ☂ 88km

Mammoth Mountain 544

Manigod France
Small valley village, sharing quiet, wooded slopes with La Clusaz - over the Col de la Croix-Fry.
1100m ☂ 132km

Marble Mountain Canada
Tiny area in the Humber Valley on Newfoundland. Good snow record by east coast standards. Splendid base lodge, and some slope-side lodging. Blomidon Cat Skiing operates nearby.
85m; slopes 10–545m
🚡 5 ☂ 175 acres

Les Marecottes Switzerland
Small area in Ski St-Bernard area near Verbier and 15 minutes from Martigny. Good views. Popular with families and freeriders.
1100m; slopes 1720–2200m
🚡 4 ☂ 25km

Maria Alm 128
Charming village at one end of the Hochkönig area.

Mariapfarr Austria
Village at the heart of one of the longest, most snow-reliable cross-country networks in Europe. Sizeable Mauterndorf-St Michael Alpine area and Obertauern area are nearby.
1120m
🚡 5 ☂ 30km

Mariazell Austria
Traditional Styria village with an impressive basilica. Limited slopes.
870m; slopes 870–1265m
🚡 5 ☂ 11km

Maribor-Pohorje 666

Marilleva 411
Small Trentino resort linked with Madonna di Campiglio.

Le Markstein France
Long-standing small resort in the northerly Vosges region near Strasbourg, which has hosted World Cup slalom races. Extensive Nordic trails.
slopes 770–1270m 🚡 10

Masella Spain
Friendly Pyrenean village linked with the slopes of La Molina to form the Alp 2500 area. Weekend crowds.
1600m; slopes 1600–2535m
🚡 31 ☂ 121km

La Massana Andorra
Pleasant valley town linked by gondola to the Arinsal/Pal slopes and fairly convenient for trips to Arcalis.
slopes 1550–2563m
🚡 31 ☂ 63km

Les Masses 505
A hamlet below Les Collons in the Verbier ski area.

Le Massif Canada
One of several small but developing areas near historic Québec City, dramatically set in a UNESCO World Bio Reserve overlooking the St Lawrence river; the views of the ice floes from the summit lodge are stunning. The varied but limited tree-lined slopes offer Eastern Canada's biggest vertical at 770m – including a couple of steep double-black-diamond runs and some good intermediate cruising.
35m; slopes 35–805m
🚡 6 ☂ 406 acres

Matrei in Osttirol Austria
Large market village south of Felbertauern tunnel. Mostly high slopes, linked to Kals on the other side of the hill.
1000m; slopes 975–2620m
🚡 15 ☂ 110km

Maurienne valley 265

Mauterndorf Austria
Village near Obertauern with tremendous snow record.
1120m; slopes 1075–2360m
🚡 10 ☂ 35km

Maverick Mountain USA
Montana resort with plenty of terrain accessed by few lifts. Cowboy Winter Games venue – rodeo one day, ski races the next.
2155m; slopes 2155–2800m
🚡 2 ☂ 500 acres

Mayens de Riddes Switzerland
Hamlet at the base of lifts on the back of Verbier's Savoleyres sector, more often referred to as La Tzoumaz.
1500m

Mayens-de-Sion Switzerland
Tranquil hamlet off the road up to Les Collons – part of the Verbier area.
1470m

Mayrhofen 138

Méaudre France
Small resort near Grenoble with good snowmaking to make up for its low altitude.
1000m; slopes 1000–1600m
🚡 10 ☂ 18km

Megève 269

Meiringen Switzerland
An old town in the broad Haslital valley, a good outing from the nearby Jungfrau resorts or Interlaken and 90 minutes' drive from Zürich or Bern. High-speed lifts take you into the slopes, which are on a broad, sunny mountainside spread across two main sectors. The area is particularly suitable for beginners and confident intermediates – experts will find little to challenge them and early intermediates will find a lack of blue runs. The area is popular with boarders but there are some flat sections. There's a good choice of mountain restaurants, and the resort is great for families with kids' snow gardens, special restaurants and fun areas. There's a choice of hotels and plenty of apartments; most of the restaurants are hotel-based. Après-ski is lively up the mountain but quiet and relaxed in town later on. There's plenty to do off the slopes – including visiting the Sherlock Holmes museum, of course.
600m; slopes 1060–2435m
🚡 14 ☂ 60km

Melchsee-Frutt Switzerland
Limited, but high and snow-sure bowl above a car-free village. Family-friendly.
1920m; slopes 1080–2255m
🚡 10 ☂ 32km

Mellau 104
Village in Bregenzerwald.

Les Menuires 276

Merano 2000 Italy
Small ski area just outside Merano, with main lift base at Falzeben above Avelengo/ Hafling.
2000m; slopes 2000–2240m
🚡 7 ☂ 40km

Méribel 282

Métabief-Mont-d'Or France
Twin villages in the Jura region, not far from Geneva.
900m; slopes 880–1460m
🚡 22 ☂ 42km

Methven New Zealand
Nearest town/accommodation to Mt Hutt, and helicopter base for trips to Arrowsmith range – good for intermediates as well as advanced.

Mieders Austria
An unspoiled village with a small selection of hotels and guest houses at the entrance to the Stubai valley. Its own area of slopes at Serles is tiny, just four runs – two blue, two red. But there are extensive cross-country trails at altitude.
980m

Mijoux France
Pretty wooded slopes between Dijon and Geneva. Lélex nearby.
1000m; slopes 900–1680m
⛷ 29 🚡 50km

Mission Ridge USA
Area in dry region that gets higher-quality snow than other Seattle resorts but less of it. Good intermediate slopes.
1390m; slopes 1390–2065m
⛷ 6 🚡 300 acres

Misurina Italy
Tiny village near Cortina. A cheap alternative base.
1755m; slopes 1755–1900m
⛷ 4 🚡 13km

Mittenwald 382
Cute town in the Bavarian Alps.
915m

Mittersill Austria
Valley-junction village south of Pass Thurn. A gondola runs from Hollersbach up to the Resterhöhe sector above Pass Thurn.
790m; slopes 1265–1895m
⛷ 15 🚡 25km

Moena Italy
Large village between Cavalese and Sella Ronda resorts, ideally located for touring the Dolomites area.
1200m; slopes 1200–2500m
⛷ 8 🚡 35km

La Molina Spain
Cheap, basic resort near Andorra, sharing a fair-sized, varied area with Masella to form Alp 2500.
1400m; slopes 1400–2535m
⛷ 31 🚡 121km

Mölltal Glacier Austria
Little-known high glacier slopes above Flattach on the other side of the Tauern tunnel from Bad Gastein. Varied runs and fast lifts. Worthwhile excursion when the snowline is high. Summer skiing available.
2570m; slopes 695–3120m
⛷ 8 🚡 53km

Molveno Italy
Lakeside village on the edge of the Dolomites, with a couple of lifts – but mostly used as a base to ski nearby Andalo.

Monarch USA
Wonderfully uncrowded area, a day trip from Crested Butte. Great powder. Good for all but experts.
3290m; slopes 3290–3645m
⛷ 5 🚡 800 acres

Monesi Italy
Southernmost of the resorts south of Turin. Close to Monaco and Nice.
1310m; slopes 1310–2180m
⛷ 5 🚡 38km

Le Monêtier 327
Quiet little village with access to Serre-Chevalier's slopes.

La Mongie 317

Montafon Austria
The 40km-long Montafon valley contains eleven resorts and four main lift systems. The valley is well worth a look. The biggest is the Nova area (linking Gaschurn and St Gallenkirch) and this is now linked to the Hochjoch area and Schruns. Gargellen and Golm are smaller ski areas in the valley.
655-1425m; slopes 655–2395m
⛷ 61 🚡 219km

Montalbert 305
Traditional village with access to the La Plagne network.

Mont Blanc Canada
Small locals' hill near Tremblant, with only 300m of vertical and no resemblance to the Franco-Italian item.
⛷ 7 🚡 36

Montchavin 305
Attractive village on the fringe of La Plagne.

Mont-de-Lans 248
Low village near Les Deux-Alpes.

Le Mont-Dore France
Attractive traditional small town, the largest resort in the stunningly beautiful volcanic Auvergne region near Clermont-Ferrand.
1050m; slopes 1350–1850m
⛷ 17 🚡 42km

Monte Bondone Italy
Trento's local hill.
1300m; slopes 1185–2090m
⛷ 5 🚡 20km

Monte Campione Italy
Tiny purpose-built resort, spread thinly over four mountainsides; 80% snowmaking helps to offset the low altitude.
1100m; slopes 1200–2010m
⛷ 16 🚡 80km

Monte Livata Italy
Closest resort to Rome, popular with weekenders.
1430m; slopes 1430–1750m
⛷ 8 🚡 8km

Monte Piselli Italy
Tiny area with the highest slopes of the many little resorts east of Rome.
2100m; slopes 2100–2690m
⛷ 3 🚡 5km

Monte Pora Italy
Tiny resort near Lake d'Iseo and Bergamo. Several other little areas nearby.
1350m; slopes 1350–1880m
⛷ 11 🚡 30km

Monterosa Ski 416

Mont Gabriel Canada
Montreal area with runs on four sides of the mountain, though the south-facing sides rarely open. Two short but renowned double-black-diamond bump runs. ⛷ 9

Montgenèvre 291

Mont Glen Canada
Least crowded of the Montreal areas, so a good weekend choice.
680m; slopes 680–1035m
⛷ 4 🚡 110 acres

Mont Grand Fonds Canada
Small area sufficiently far from Québec not to get overrun at weekends.
400m; slopes 400–735m ⛷ 4

Mont Habitant Canada
Very limited area in the Montreal region but with a good base lodge. ⛷ 3

Mont Olympia Canada
Small, two-mountain area near Montreal, one mostly novice terrain, the other best suited to experts. ⛷ 6

Mont Orford Canada
Cold, windswept lone peak (no resort), worth a trip from nearby Montreal on a fine day.
slopes 305–855m
⛷ 8 🚡 180 acres

Mont-Ste-Anne Canada
Quebec City's biggest and most varied local ski area. Wide choice of amenities at the base. The slopes are limited, but the vertical is a decent 625m. A gondola goes to the top, from where slopes span north and south sides of the mountain. The views are spectacular. Over a third of the area is classified black or double-black, so it's a good place for experts. The Beast (double black diamond) has one of the steepest pitches in the east at 65%. But there are decent intermediate trails too, adequate nursery slopes and

an easy top-to-bottom green run. The Dual mountain lift pass is valid at Stoneham.
175m; slopes 175–800m
⛷ 7 🚡 530 acres

Mont-St-Sauveur Canada
Perhaps the prettiest resort in Canada, popular with Montreal (60km) day trippers and luxury condo owners.

Mont Sutton Canada
Varied area with some of the best glade skiing in eastern Canada, including some for novices. Quaint Sutton village nearby.
⛷ 9 🚡 175 acres

Moonlight Basin 600
Quiet area of slopes linked to Big Sky, Montana.

Morgins 462
Resort on the Swiss side of the Portes du Soleil circuit.

Morillon 254
Valley village in the Flaine network.

Morin Heights Canada
Area in the Montreal region with 100% snowmaking. Attractive base lodge. ⛷ 6

Morzine 296

Les Mosses Switzerland
Peaceful scenic resort and area, best for a day trip from Villars or Les Diablerets. There's a terrain park, a few chalet-style hotel-restaurants, shops and a rather fine church. There are only draglifts to access the mainly red and blue runs. Prides itself on the number of activities on offer – such as ice-diving, a natural ice rink and an international dog-sled track.
1500m; slopes 1500–2200m
⛷ 14 🚡 60km

Mottaret 282
Purpose-built but reasonably attractive part of Méribel.

Mottarone Italy
Closest slopes to Lake Maggiore. No village – just a base area.
1200m; slopes 1200–1490m
🚡 25km

Les Moulins Switzerland
Village down the road from Château d'Oex with its own low area of slopes, part of the big Gstaad lift-pass area.
890m; slopes 890–3000m
⛷ 58 🚡 250km

Mount Abram USA
Small, pretty, tree-lined area in Maine, renowned for its immaculately groomed easy runs.
295m; slopes 295–610m
⛷ 5 🚡 170 acres

Mountain High USA
Best snowfall record and highest lift capacity in Los Angeles vicinity – plus 95% snowmaking. Mostly intermediate cruising.
2010m; slopes 2010–2500m
🚡12 🎿 220 acres

Mount Ashland USA
Arty town in Oregon renowned for Shakespeare performances. Tiny ski area best for experts run by local charity.
1935m; slopes 1935–2285m
🚡4 🎿 200 acres

Mount Bachelor USA
Extinct volcano in Oregon with a big ski area and runs on all sides. Higher elevation means better chance of good snow than many other resorts in north-west USA and average annual snowfall of 370 inches is more than any major Colorado resort. Good cruising and beginner terrain lower down and plenty to occupy experts, including tree-lined blacks and steep terrain on the south-facing slopes. No lodging at the base; stay 30 mins away at Sunriver Resort – a big lodge with bar, restaurant, chalet lodging and excellent spa – or in Bend, an attractive small town served by free shuttles.
1920m; slopes 1755–2765m
🚡13 🎿 3680 acres

Mount Baker USA
Almost on the coast near Seattle, yet one of the top resorts for snow (averages 600 inches a year). Plenty of challenging slopes. Known for spectacular avalanches.
1115m; slopes 1115–1540m
🚡9 🎿 1000 acres

Mount Baldy Canada
Tiny area, but a worthwhile excursion from Big White. Gets ultra light snow – great glades/powder chutes.
slopes 1705–2150m
🚡2 🎿 150 acres

Mount Baldy USA
Some of the longest and steepest runs in California. Only an hour's drive from Los Angeles so a day trip is feasible, but 20% snowmaking and antiquated lifts are major drawbacks.
1980m; slopes 1980–2620m
🚡4 🎿 400 acres

Mount Baw Baw Australia
Small but entertaining intermediate area in attractive woodland, with great views. Closest area to Melbourne (150km).
1450m; slopes 1450–1560m
🚡7 🎿 35 hectares

Mount Buffalo Australia
Site of Australia's first ski lift. Plateau area best suited to beginners. Short season. On-mountain accommodation. four hours from Melbourne.
1400m; slopes 1455–1610m
🚡8 🎿 66 acres

Mount Buller Australia
Three hours from Melbourne and Victoria's largest ski area. Proper resort village, with a 360-degree network of short runs on its isolated massif. Luxury hotel and spa.
1600m; slopes 1600–1790m
🚡22 🎿 80km

Mount Dobson New Zealand
Mostly intermediate slopes in a wide, treeless basin near Mt Cook, with good snow-cover. Accommodation in Fairlie, 40 minutes away.
1610m; slopes 1610–2010m
🚡3 🎿 990 acres

Mount Falakro Greece
Area two hours' drive from Salonica in northern Greece; almost as big as Parnassos, uncrowded and with good views. Has a fast quad.
1720m
🚡8 🎿 22km

Mount Hood Meadows USA
The biggest and most varied ski area on Mt Hood in Oregon served by 11 lifts including five fast quads. Good beginner area, intermediate cruising, single-black-diamond runs in the centre of the main ski area and a big area of double-black-diamond runs roped off and entered through gates. Up to six terrain parks, depending on snow conditions. No accommodation at the base – stay at Timberline (see separate entry) half an hour away or Government Camp (near Mount Hood Skibowl, which also gets its own entry) 20 minutes away.
1635m; slopes 1375–2225m
🚡11 🎿 2150 acres

Mount Hood Skibowl USA
Small area of mainly tough gladed runs, offering the steepest and most extreme slopes in the Mount Hood area. Claims to be America's largest night skiing area with a lot of runs open up to 10/11pm nightly. Two floodlit terrain parks, tubing hills, snow bikes and snowmobiles. Just below Timberline ski area; stay there or in Government Camp at the foot of Skibowl's slopes, a sizeable settlement

with a choice of lodgings and restaurants. Other local ski area is Mt Hood Meadows.
1075m; slopes 1075–1530m
🚡7 🎿 960 acres

Mount Hotham Australia
Australia's highest ski village. Built on a ridge above the slopes. Intermediate and advanced skiing. Good snow record. Nearest town Bright, four hours from Melbourne.
1750m; slopes 1450–1845m
🚡13 🎿 30km

Mount Hutt New Zealand
Steepest, most snow-sure area in NZ, with ocean views, but prone to bad weather; 100km from Christchurch, a tricky drive up from Methven.
slopes 1405–2085m
🚡4 🎿 365 hectares

Mount Lemmon USA
Southernmost area in North America, close to famous Old West town Tombstone, Arizona. Reasonable snowfall.
2500m; slopes 2500–2790m
🚡3 🎿 70 acres

Mount McKay Australia
Australia's steepest skiing accessed from Falls Creek, with genuine black-diamond terrain and snowcats.
1600m

Mount Pilio Greece
Pleasant slopes cut out of dense forest, only 15km from the holiday resort of Portaria above town of Volos.
1500m 🚡3

Mount Rose USA
Much the highest base elevation in the Tahoe area – a good 600m above the lake – and with an annual snowfall average of 400 inches. The Chutes is a shady bowl mainly of serious double-diamond gradient on the front face of the slopes. But there are blue and easy black runs to the base and a wider, gentler, lightly wooded area. The slopes have a lot to offer, especially if staying in Heavenly – where the groomed stuff may be too dull and the ungroomed stuff too challenging.
2520m; slopes 2410–2955m
🚡6 🎿 1200 acres

Mount Shasta Ski Park
USA
Californian resort 300 miles north of San Francisco.
🚡4 🎿 425 acres

Mount Snow USA
A one-peak resort, with a long row of lifts on the front face (two fast quads among them) serving easy and intermediate runs of just over 500m vertical. Separate area of

black runs on the north face – including a couple of short but serious double blacks – served by a triple chair and a six-pack. And on the opposite side a small area of intermediate runs above Carinthia base, accessed by a third fast quad. Reputed to have some of the best terrain parks in the east. Lodgings at the base include a Grand Summit hotel.
580m; slopes 580–1095m
🚡19 🎿 590 acres

Mount Spokane USA
Little intermediate area near Spokane (Washington State).
1160m; slopes 1160–1795m
🚡5 🎿 350 acres

**Mount St Louis /
Moonstone** Canada
Premier area in Toronto region, spread over three peaks. Very high-capacity lift system and 100% snowmaking.
🚡13 🎿 175

Mount Sunapee USA
Area in New Hampshire closest to Boston; primarily intermediate terrain.
375m; slopes 375–835m
🚡10 🎿 230 acres

Mount Vermio Greece
Oldest ski base in Greece. Two areas in central Macedonia 60km from Thessaloniki. Barren but interesting slopes.
slopes 1420–2000m 🚡7

Mount Washington Resort
Canada
Scenic area on Vancouver Island with lodging in the base village. Impressive snowfall record but rain is a problem.
1110m; slopes 1110–1590m
🚡6 🎿 970 acres

Mount Washington Resort
USA
One of several small resorts in New Hampshire scattered along the Interstate 93 highway. The slopes are on a single mountain face but highly rated, particularly by families, who relish the top-to-bottom easy trails on the main peak, Mt Rosebrook. There is a good mix of terrain, with West Mountain consisting mainly of double-diamond slopes. Snowmaking is comprehensive. There's a terrain park, half-pipe and snowcross. There are a few places to stay near the base, with the grand old Mount Washington hotel five minutes away.
480m; slopes 480–940m
🚡8 🎿 435 acres

Mount Waterman USA
Small Los Angeles area where children ski free. The lack of much snowmaking is a drawback.
2135m; slopes 2135–2440m
♦ 3 ♦ 210 acres

Mühlbach 128
Village in the Hochkönig area.

Mühltal Austria
Small village halfway between Niederau and Auffach in the Wildschönau. No local skiing of its own.
780m; slopes 830–1905m
♦ 25 ♦ 70km

Muhr Austria
Village by Katschberg tunnel well placed for visiting St Michael, Bad Kleinkirchheim, Flachau and Obertauern.
1110m

Muju Resort South Korea
Largest area in Korea and with a fair amount of lodging. Though it is the furthest resort from Seoul (four hours south) it is still overcrowded.
♦ 14

Mürren 485

Mutters Austria
Charming rustic village near Innsbruck, at the foot of long slopes of 900m vertical that extend along the Götzens valley to Axamer Lizum. Good for families and beginners.
830m

Myoko Suginohara Kokusai Japan
A series of small resorts two or three hours from Tokyo, which together make up an area of extensive slopes with longer, wider runs than normal for Japan. ♦ 15

Naeba Japan
Fashionable resort with lots of accommodation two hours north of Tokyo. Crowded slopes.
900m; slopes 900–1800m ♦ 30

Nakiska Canada
Small area of wooded runs between Banff and Calgary, with emphasis on downhill speed. Unreliable snow, but state-of-the-art snowmaking and pancake-flat grooming.
1525m; slopes 1525–2260m
♦ 5 ♦ 230 acres

Nasserein 174
Quiet suburb of St Anton.

Nassfeld Ski Arena Austria
Carinthia's biggest: scenic and sunny area on the Italian border. Good intermediate slopes. Stay in Tröpolach, by the gondola, or larger Hermagor, further east.
1500m; slopes 610–2195m
♦ 30 ♦ 110km

Nauders Austria
Spacious, traditionally Tirolean village tucked away only 3km from the Swiss border and almost on the Italian one. Its slopes start 2km outside the village (free shuttle-bus) and are mainly high and sunny intermediate runs spread over three areas. Lots of snowmaking. Not ideal for experts, though there is a lot of off-piste terrain. Not ideal for complete beginners either – the village nursery slopes are some way out. There are five cross-country trails amounting to 40km in all.
1400m; slopes 1400–2850m
♦ 24 ♦ 120km

Nax Switzerland
Quiet, sunny village in a balcony setting overlooking the Rhône valley. Own little area and only a short drive from Veysonnaz. Handful of red and blue runs.
1300m
♦ 6 ♦ 35km

Nendaz 505
A sizeable family resort linked in to the Verbier ski area.

Neukirchen Austria
Quiet, pretty resort sharing slopes with Bramberg. Fairly snow-sure plateau at the top of its mountain.
855m; slopes 855–2150m
♦ 15 ♦ 50km

Neustift 183
Village in the Stubai valley.

Nevegal Italy
Weekend place near Belluno, south of Cortina.
1030m; slopes 1030–1650m
♦ 14 ♦ 30km

Nevis Range 669
Scottish ski resort.
90m; slopes 655–1220m
♦ 11 ♦ 35km

Niederau 93
Village in Ski Juwel (Alpbachtal-Wildschönau).

Niederdorf Italy
Cross-country village in South Tyrol. Villabassa is its Italian name.

Niseko 670
Resort on Hokkaido island, Japan.

Niseko Village 670
One of Niseko's three interlinked areas.

Nockberge Innerkrems Austria
Area just south of Katschberg tunnel. 1500m; slopes 1500–2020m
♦ 10 ♦ 33km

Nordseter Norway
Cluster of hotels in deep forest north of Lillehammer. Some Alpine facilities but best for cross-country.
850m; slopes 1000–1090m
♦ 2 ♦ 2km

Norefjell Norway
Norway's toughest run, a very steep 600m drop. 120km north-west of Oslo.
185m; slopes 185–1185m
♦ 10 ♦ 23km

La Norma 265
Traffic-free, purpose-built resort near Modane in the Maurienne.

Norquay 616
Banff's quiet local hill.

North Conway USA
Attractive factory-outlet-shopping town in New Hampshire close to Attitash and Cranmore ski areas.

Northstar-at-Tahoe USA
Classic US-style mountain, with runs cut through dense forest and a pleasant base village that is still growing. The whole area is very sheltered and good for bad-weather days. A gondola and a fast quad go up to a lodge at Big Springs, only 160m above the village. From this point three fast chairs radiate to serve a broad bowl with some short steep pitches at the top, with easier blue runs lower down and around the ridges. From the ridge you can access the Backside, a steeper bowl with a central fast quad chair serving a row of easy black runs. Lookout Mountain has more black runs and a modest vertical of 390m.
1930m; slopes 1930–2625m
♦ 19 ♦ 3000 acres

Nôtre-Dame-de-Bellecombe France
Pleasant 'very French' village spoiled by the busy road. Inexpensive base from which to visit Megève, though it has fair slopes of its own. Queues and slow lifts can be a problem now it is linked to Les Saisies. Free bus to/from Crest Voland.
1150m; slopes 1035–2070m
♦ 84 ♦ 175km

Nova Levante Italy
Village close to Bozen/Bolzano with lifts up to small network around Passo di Costalunga.
1200m
♦ 16 ♦ 40km

Nozawa Onsen Japan
Spa village with good hot springs three hours from Tokyo. The runs are cut out of heavy vegetation.
500m; slopes 500–1650m ♦ 21

Nub's Nob USA
One of the most sheltered Great Lakes ski areas (many suffer fierce winds). 100% snowmaking; weekend crowds from Detroit. Wooded slopes suitable for all abilities.
275m; slopes 275–405m
♦ 8 ♦ 245 acres

O2Resort South Korea
Built up the mountain in Gangwon province and with Korea's best snow. Slopes suit all levels and include a 3.2km long run. Facilities include: condos, youth hostel, fitness centre, spa and restaurants.
1420m ♦ 16runs

Oberammergau 382
Village in the Bavarian Alps.
835m

Oberau 93
Pretty village in the Ski Juwel (Alpbachtal-Wildschönau) area.

Obereggen Italy
Tiny resort close to Bozen/Bolzano with modest area of slopes also accessible from Predazzo in Val di Fiemme.
1550m; slopes 1550–2200m
♦ 6 ♦ 10km

Obergurgl 144

Oberjoch–Hindelang Germany
Small, low-altitude resort, particularly good for beginners.
850m; slopes 1140–1520m
♦ 12 ♦ 32km

Oberlech 129
Car- and crowd-free family resort alternative to Lech.

Oberndorf Austria
Quiet hamlet with beginners' area and a chair connecting it to St Johann's undemanding ski area.
700m

Oberperfuss Austria
Small village west of Innsbruck, with tall but limited slopes. On the Innsbruck lift pass.
820m

Obersaxen-Mundaun-Lumnezia Switzerland
Several quiet villages above Ilanz, in the Vorderrhein Valley, near Laax. Sizeable area of mainly red and blue runs on four linked mountains. The main lifts are fast chairs.
1300m; slopes 1200–2310m
♦ 18 ♦ 120km

Oberstaufen   Germany
Three small areas: Steibis; Thulkirchdorf and Hochgrat. Within an hour of Friedrichshafen.
600m; slopes 860–1880m
⛷ 30 🚡 45km

Oberstdorf   **382**
Town in the German Alps near the Austrian border.
815m; slopes 800–2220m
⛷ 31 🚡 30km

Obertauern   **150**

Ochapowace   Canada
Main area in Saskatchewan, east of Regina. It doesn't get a huge amount of snow but 75% snowmaking helps.
⛷ 4 🚡 100 acres

Ohau   New Zealand
Some of NZ's steepest slopes, with great views of Lake Ohau 9km away (where you stay). 320km south of Christchurch.
1500m; slopes 1425–1825m
⛷ 3 🚡 310 acres

Okemo   USA
Worthwhile and nicely varied intermediate area above the old Vermont town of Ludlow. Family oriented, with good child care. Comprehensive snowmaking and highly rated grooming.
345m; slopes 345–1020m
⛷ 18 🚡 624 acres

Oppdal   Norway
One of the larger Norwegian resorts, but very far north. Many runs are quite short.
715m; slopes 715–1020m
⛷ 17 🚡 60km

Orcières-Merlette   France
High, convenient family resort a few km north-east of Gap, Merlette being the ugly, purpose-built ski station above the village of Orcières (1450m). Snow-sure beginner area. Slopes have a good mix of difficulty spread over several mountain flanks.
1850m; slopes 1850–2725m
⛷ 28 🚡 100km

Ordino   Andorra
Rustic valley village near La Massana, on the way up to Andorra's best snow at Arcalis.

Orelle   **372**
Village in the Maurienne with access to Val Thorens.

Oropa   Italy
Little area just off the Aosta–Turin motorway. An easy change of scene from Courmayeur.
1180m; slopes 1200–2390m 🚡 15km

Les Orres   France
Friendly modern resort with great views and varied intermediate terrain, but the snow is unreliable, and it's a long transfer from Lyon.
1550m; slopes 1550–2720m
⛷ 23 🚡 62km

Orsières   Switzerland
Traditional winter resort near Martigny. Close to Grand St Bernard resorts, including Champex-Lac. Well-positioned base from which to visit Verbier and the Chamonix valley. *900m*

Ortisei   **437**
Market town in Val Gardena.

Oslo   Norway
Capital city with cross-country ski trails in its parks. Alpine slopes and lifts in Nordmarka region, just north of city boundaries.

Otre il Colle   Italy
Smallest of many little resorts near Bergamo.
1100m; slopes 1100–2000m
⛷ 7 🚡 7km

Ötz   Austria
Village at the entrance to the Ötz valley with an easy/intermediate ski area of its own and access to the Sölden, Kuhtai (sharing a lift pass) and Niederau areas.
820m; slopes 820–2200m
⛷ 11 🚡 34km

Oukaimeden   Morocco
Slopes 75km from Marrakech with a surprisingly long season.
2600m; slopes 2600–3260m
⛷ 7 🚡 15km

Ovindoli   Italy
Small area in Abruzzo, east of Rome, claiming the distinction of Europe's longest magic carpet lift. The town is about 3km from the slopes. Shares a lift pass with equally small Campo Felice, nearby.
1375m; slopes 1470–2055m
⛷ 11 🚡 30km

Ovronnaz   Switzerland
Pretty village set on a sunny shelf above the Rhône valley, with a good pool complex. Limited area but Crans-Montana and Anzère are close.
1350m; slopes 1350–2080m
⛷ 8 🚡 30km

Owl's Head   Canada
Steep mountain rising out of a lake, in a remote spot bordering Vermont, away from weekend crowds.
⛷ 7 🚡 90 acres

Oz-en-Oisans   **196**
Old village with satellite at the lifts into Alpe-d'Huez.

Pajarito Mountain   USA
Los Alamos area laid out by nuclear scientists. Atomic slopes too – steep, ungroomed. Open Fridays, weekends and holidays. Fun day out from Taos.
2685m; slopes 2685–3170m
⛷ 6 🚡 220 acres

Pal   **78**
Prettily wooded mountain linked with slopes of Arinsal.

Palandöken   Turkey
Varied skiing area, transformed by three big hotels, overlooking the Anatolian city of Erzurum.
slopes 2150–3100m 🚡 4

Pampeago   Italy
Trentino area convenient for a trip from Milan.

Pamporovo   **662**

Panarotta   Italy
Smallest of the resorts east of Trento. At a higher altitude than nearby Andalo, so worth a day out from there.
1500m; slopes 1500–2000m
⛷ 6 🚡 7km

Panorama   Canada
Home to one of North America's biggest verticals (1220m), with something for everyone on its quiet, wooded mountain. Small, purpose-built place at the foot of the slopes and on two levels. The upper 'village' is centred on a hot-pool complex, while the mostly condo accommodation in the lower area. The slopes rise steeply above the resort, but steepest at the top – with genuine blacks and two expert bowls (Taynton and Extreme Dream). Excellent terrain for adventurous intermediates too. More limited for novices. Heli-ski trips are available. There's a big park, pipe and floodlit mini-park. The school is 'very professional' and facilities for families good.
1160m; slopes 1150–2375m
⛷ 10 🚡 2847 acres

Panticosa   Spain
Charming old Pyrenees spa village near Formigal with limited but varied slopes.
1500m; slopes 1500–2220m
⛷ 16 🚡 35km

Paradiski   **303**

Park City   **592**

Parnassos   Greece
Biggest and best-organised area in Greece, 180km from Athens and with surprisingly good slopes and lifts.
slopes 1600–2300m
⛷ 9 🚡 14km

Parpan   Switzerland
Pretty village linked to the large intermediate area of Lenzerheide.
1510m; slopes 1230–2865m
⛷ 35 🚡 155km

Partenen   Austria
Traditional village in a pretty setting at the end of the Montafon valley. The slopes start at Gaschurn, and there are lots more in the vicinity.
1100m

La Parva   Chile
Only 50km east of Santiago and condoville for the capital's elite. A collection of apartments occupied mostly at weekends, linked with Valle Nevado and El Colorado (no area pass).
2750m; slopes 2430–3630m
⛷ 43 🚡 113km

Pas de la Casa   **80**
Sprawling mess popular with French duty-free shoppers, in a bleak setting with Andorra's largest, highest skiing.

Passo Costalunga   Italy
Dense network of short lifts either side of the road over a pass, close to Val di Fassa, with links up from Nova Levante.

Passo Lanciano   Italy
Closest area to Adriatic. Weekend crowds from nearby Pescara when the snow is good.
1305m; slopes 1305–2000m ⛷ 13

Passo Rolle   Italy
Small group of lifts either side of the road over a high pass just north of San Martino di Castrozza.

Passo San Pellegrino   Italy
Smallish ski area south of the Sella Ronda, with lifts each side of the pass road and links with the valley village of Falcade.
1920m; slopes 1150–2245m
⛷ 19 🚡 75km

Passo Tonale   **422**

Pass Thurn   **121**
Road-side lift base for one of Kitzbühel's ski areas.

Passy-Plaine-Joux   France
Small, quiet village 25km from Chamonix. Draglifts serve woody slopes best suited to novices.
1340m
⛷ 6 🚡 12km

Pebble Creek   USA
Small area on Utah-Jackson Hole route. Blend of open and wooded slopes.
1920m; slopes 1920–2530m
⛷ 3 🚡 600 acres

Pec Pod Snezku
Czech Republic
Collection of hamlets spread along the valley road leading to the main lifts and the very limited ski area.
770m; slopes 710–1190m
⛷ 10 ⛷ 9km

Peisey 206
Small village linked to Les Arcs.

Peisey-Vallandry 206
Group of villages linked to Les Arcs and Paradiski area.

Pejo Italy
Trentino spa resort near Madonna. New cable car now serves slopes to 3000m.
1400m; slopes 1400–3000m
⛷ 7 ⛷ 15km

Penitentes Argentina
180km from Mendoza. Accommodation at the base.
⛷ 10 ⛷ 300 hectares

Perelik Bulgaria
Development aiming to link Pamporovo with Mechi Chal.

Perisher / Smiggins
Australia
Expanding resort with slopes on seven mountains, which between them offer plenty of short, intermediate runs. 30km from Jindabyne town, six hours from Sydney.
1640m; slopes 1680–2035m
⛷ 47 ⛷ 3075 acres

Pescasseroli Italy
One of numerous areas east of Rome in L'Aquila region.
1250m; slopes 1250–1945m
⛷ 6 ⛷ 25km

Pescocostanzo Italy
One of numerous areas east of Rome in L'Aquila region.
1395m; slopes 1395–1900m
⛷ 4 ⛷ 25km

Pettneu Austria
Snow-sure beginners' resort with an irregular bus link to nearby St Anton.
1250m; slopes 1230–2020m
⛷ 4 ⛷ 15km

Petzen Austria
One of many little areas in Austria's easternmost ski region near the Slovenian border.
600m; slopes 600–1700m
⛷ 5 ⛷ 16km

Peyragudes 317

Pfelders Italy
Resort near Merano in the South Tyrol covered by the Ortler Skiarena pass.
⛷ 4 ⛷ 5km

Pfunds Austria
Picturesque valley village with no slopes but quick access to several resorts in Switzerland and Italy, as well as Austria.
970m

Phoenix Park South Korea
Golf complex with 12 trails in winter. Two hours (140km) from Seoul.
slopes 650–1050m ⛷ 9

Piancavallo Italy
Uninspiring yet curiously trendy purpose-built village, an easy drive from Venice.
1270m; slopes 1270–1830m
⛷ 17 ⛷ 45km

Piani delle Betulle Italy
One of several little areas near the east coast of Lake Como.
730m; slopes 730–1850m
⛷ 6 ⛷ 10km

Piani di Artavaggio Italy
Small base complex rather than a village. One of several little areas near Lake Como.
875m; slopes 875–1875m
⛷ 7 ⛷ 15km

Piani di Bobbio Italy
Largest of several tiny resorts above Lake Como.
770m; slopes 770–1855m
⛷ 10 ⛷ 20km

Piani di Erna Italy
Small base development – no village. One of several little areas above Lake Como.
600m; slopes 600–1635m
⛷ 5 ⛷ 9km

Piau-Engaly France
User-friendly St-Lary satellite in one of the best Pyrenean areas.
1850m; slopes 1420–2530m
⛷ 17 ⛷ 65km

Piazzatorre Italy
One of many little areas in the Bergamo region.
870m; slopes 870–2000m
⛷ 5 ⛷ 25km

Pichl 158
Hamlet outside Schladming.

Pico USA
Low-key little family area (no resort village) close to Killington.
605m; slopes 605–1215m
⛷ 9 ⛷ 160 acres

Piesendorf Austria
Cheaper, quiet place to stay when visiting Zell am See. Tucked behind Kaprun near Niedernsill.
780m
⛷ 3 ⛷ 3km

Pievepelago Italy
Much the smallest and most limited of the Apennine ski resorts. Less than two hours from Florence and Pisa.
1115m; slopes 1115–1410m
⛷ 7 ⛷ 8km

Pila Italy
Modern, purpose-built, car-free resort that's popular with families and school groups and is set above the old Roman town of Aosta – a 15-minute gondola ride away or reached by a 30-minute drive on a winding road. Chairlifts (some fast, most slow) and a cable car fan out to serve a fair-sized and interesting mix of well-groomed, snow-sure slopes. The treeline is high, at about 2300m, and most runs are below it, making this an excellent bad-weather resort. From the top heights there are grand views to Mont Blanc in the west and the Matterhorn in the east. There are runs for all standards, but mostly they are reds. The few blacks, above the treeline at the top of the area, don't amount to much, but there is quite a bit of off-piste. There are two short beginner lifts, but progression to longer runs means using a central run, which when the resort is busy is unpleasant. Like so many other Aosta Valley resorts, Pila is pretty quiet during the week but can be hectic at weekends – and it does attract lots of British school groups. 'A good day trip,' says a 2014 visitor.
1800m; slopes 1800–2750m
⛷ 15 ⛷ 70km

Pinzolo 411
Trentino resort near Madonna.

Pitztal Austria
Long valley with good glacier area at its head, accessed by underground funicular.
1680m; slopes 880–3440m
⛷ 12 ⛷ 68km

Pla-d'Adet France
Limited purpose-built complex at the foot of the St-Lary ski area (the original village is further down the mountain).
1680m; slopes 1420–2450m
⛷ 32 ⛷ 80km

La Plagne 305

Plan de Corones Italy
Distinctive ski area in South Tyrol, with amazingly efficient lifts from Brunico and San Vigilio di Marebbe. Better known by its German name, Kronplatz.
1200m; slopes 1200–2275m
⛷ 32 ⛷ 103km

Plan-Peisey 206
Small development with link to Les Arcs.

Plose Italy
Varied area close to Bressanone, with the longest run in the South Tyrol.
560m; slopes 1065–2500m
⛷ 11 ⛷ 40km

Poiana Brasov 665
Cheap, informal resort in Romania.
1020m; slopes 1020–1775m
⛷ 10 ⛷ 24km

Pomerelle USA
Small area in Idaho on the Utah–Sun Valley route.
2430m; slopes 2430–2735m
⛷ 3 ⛷ 300 acres

Pontechianale Italy
Highest, largest area in a remote region south-west of Turin. Day-tripper place.
1600m; slopes 1600–2760m
⛷ 8 ⛷ 30km

Ponte di Legno 422
Attractive sheltered alternative to Passo Tonale.

Pontresina Switzerland
Small, sedate, sunny village with one main street, rather spoiled by the sanatorium-style architecture. All downhill skiing involves travel by car or bus, except the single long piste on Pontresina's own hill, Languard. It's cheaper to stay here than St Moritz.
1805m; slopes 1730–3305m
⛷ 54 ⛷ 350km

Port-Ainé Spain
Small but high intermediate area in the Spanish Pyrenees near Andorra. Lifts include a six-pack; eponymous 3-star hotel at base.
1975m; slopes 1650–2440m
⛷ 8 ⛷ 44km

Port del Comte Spain
High resort in the forested region of Lleida, north-west of Barcelona. The slopes spread across three linked sectors: El Sucre, El Hostal and El Estivella.
slopes 1700–2400m
⛷ 15 ⛷ 40km

Porté Puymorens France
Little-known Pyrenean area close to Pas de la Casa in Andorra.
slopes 1600–2470m
⛷ 12 ⛷ 45km

Porter Heights New Zealand
Closest skiing to Christchurch (one hour). Open, sunny bowl offering mostly intermediate skiing – with back bowls for powder.
1340m; slopes 1340–1950m
⛷ 5 ⛷ 200 acres

Portes du Soleil 316

Portillo Chile
Luxury hotel 150km north-east of Santiago. Quiet snow-sure slopes used for training by US national ski team. Suits experts best.
2880m; slopes 2450–3310m
⛷ 14 ⛷ 1235 acres

Powderhorn USA
Area in west Colorado perched on the world's highest flat-top mountain, Grand Mesa. Sensational views. Day trip from Aspen.
2490m; slopes 2490–2975m
⛷ 4 ⛷ 300 acres

Powder King Canada
Remote resort in British Columbia, between Prince George and Dawson City. As its name suggests, it has great powder. Plenty of lodging.
880m; slopes 880–1520m
⛷ 3 ⛷ 160 acres

Powder Mountain USA
Massive Utah area sprawled over six ridges, an hour and a quarter's drive from Salt Lake City. An ample 2,800 acres of its terrain is lift served, a mix of mainly north-facing slopes with enough green, blue and black runs to satisfy all abilities. You access the rest by snowcat or snowmobile tow, buses and hiking. It is the abundance of intermediate freeride terrain that makes it special. You can also stay in Ogden, 32km away.
2100m; slopes 2100–2740m
⛷ 7 ⛷ 2800 acres

Pozza di Fassa Italy
Pretty Dolomite village with its own slopes, three other small areas close by, and access to the Sella Ronda at Campitello.
1320m; slopes 1320–2428m
⛷ 7 ⛷ 16km

Pragelato 444
Inexpensive base, linked by cable car to Sestriere. Its own area is worth a try for half a day.

Prägraten am Grossvenediger Austria
Traditional mountaineering/ski touring village in lovely setting south of Felbertauern tunnel. The Alpine ski slopes of Matrei are nearby.
1310m; slopes 1310–1490m
⛷ 2 ⛷ 30km

Prali Italy
Tiny resort east of Sestriere – a worthwhile half-day trip.
1450m; slopes 1450–2500m
⛷ 7 ⛷ 25km

Pralognan-la-Vanoise France
Unspoiled traditional village overlooked by spectacular peaks. Champagny (La Plagne) and Courchevel are close by.
1410m; slopes 1410–2355m
⛷ 14 ⛷ 30km

LAGRANGE Prestige

High-standard Self-catering Apartments

020 7371 6111
lagrange-holidays.co.uk

Pra-Loup France
Convenient, purpose-built family resort with an extensive, varied intermediate area linked to La Foux-d'Allos (Val d'Allos region).
1500m; slopes 1500–2600m
⛷ 51 ⛷ 180km

Prati di Tivo Italy
Weekend day-trip place east of Rome and near the town of Teramo. A sizeable resort by southern Italy standards.
1450m; slopes 1450–1800m
⛷ 6 ⛷ 16km

Prato Nevoso Italy
Purpose-built resort with rather bland slopes. Part of Mondolé ski area with Artesina.
1500m; slopes 1500–1950m
⛷ 25 ⛷ 90km

Prato Selva Italy
Tiny base development (no village) east of Rome near Teramo. Weekend day-trip place.
1370m; slopes 1370–1800m
⛷ 4 ⛷ 10km

Le Praz 238
Lowest of the Courchevel resorts.

Les Praz 223
Quiet hamlet near Chamonix.

Praz-de-Lys France
Small family resort close to Geneva with slopes fanning out in all directions. Short runs and old lifts, but nicely varied skiing, and its snow-pocket location means it can have better conditions than neighbouring resorts such as La Clusaz. A good day out.
1450m; slopes 1240–1965m
⛷ 23 ⛷ 60km

Praz-sur-Arly France
Traditional village in a pretty, wooded setting just down the road from Megève ('but without the price tag!' says a 2014 visitor). Shares slopes with Notre Dame de

Bellecombe and beyond to Crest Voland / Les Saises, to form the Espace Diamant.
1035m; slopes 1035–2070m
⛷ 84 ⛷ 175km

Predazzo Italy
Small, quiet place between Cavalese and the Sella Ronda resorts, with lift into modest area of slopes above Obereggen.
1015m; slopes 995–2205m
⛷ 8 ⛷ 17km

Premanon France
One of four resorts that make up Les Rousses area in Jura region.
1050m; slopes 1120–1680m ⛷ 40

La Presolana Italy
Large summer resort near Bergamo. Several other little areas nearby.
1250m; slopes 1250–1650m
⛷ 6 ⛷ 15km

Les Prodains 216
Village at the foot of the cliffs on which Avoriaz sits.

Pucón Chile
Ski area on the side of the active Villarrica volcano in southern Chile, 800km south of Santiago. Lodgings are at Pucón village, 30 minutes away from the slopes.
1200m; slopes 1200–2440m
⛷ 9 ⛷ 20runs

Puigmal France
Resort in the French Pyrenees with accommodation in nearby villages.
1830m; slopes 1830–2700m
⛷ 12 ⛷ 34km

Puy-St-Vincent France
Modern apartment complex above an old village south of Briançon; convenient access to an area of slopes that are limited in extent but offer a decent vertical and a lot of variety, including a bit of steep stuff. Most accommodation is in self-catering apartments at the foot of the slopes. It is relatively inexpensive and makes an attractive choice for a family not hungry for piste miles.
1400-1600m; slopes 1250–2700m
⛷ 12 ⛷ 75km

Pyhä Finland
Expanding resort 150km north-east of Rovaniemi. Much of the area is in a National Park, with the 14 slopes on two sides of a part-wooded hill. Vertical is only 280m and there's no steep terrain but good off-piste. The best powder runs are on both sides of a long T-bar on the north side. Most pistes open

for floodlit skiing. There's a well-developed terrain park, hosting regular competitions.
220m ⛷ 8

The Pyrenees 317

Pyrenees 2000 France
Tiny resort built in a pleasing manner. Shares a pretty area of short runs with Font-Romeu. Impressive snowmaking.
2000m; slopes 1750–2250m
⛷ 32 ⛷ 52km

Québec City Canada
French-speaking capital and old city with a number of ski areas a short drive away.

Queenstown New Zealand
South Island's outdoor adventure capital, in a stunning lakeside setting. Two local resorts: the Remarkables and Coronet Peak. Treble Cone and Cardrona are easily reached by car. Typically commercialized but lively and relaxed, and where most people stay. The slopes are a 30-40 minute drive away. The Remarkables appeals mainly to families and beginners, while Coronet Peak is more satisfying to intermediates. Both resorts have challenges for experts too.
310m; slopes 1170–1650m
⛷ 8 ⛷ 280 hectares

Radium Hot Springs Canada
Summer resort offering an alternative to the purpose-built slope-side resort of Panorama.
slopes 975–2155m
⛷ 8 ⛷ 300 acres

Radstadt Austria
Unspoiled medieval town near Schladming, with its own small area and the Salzburger Sportwelt slopes accessed from nearby Zauchensee or Flachau.
855m; slopes 855–2185m
⛷ 100 ⛷ 350km

Ragged Mountain USA
Family-owned ski area in New Hampshire.
⛷ 9 ⛷ 200 acres

Rainbow New Zealand
Northernmost ski area on South Island. Wide, treeless area, best for beginners and intermediates. Accommodation at St Arnaud.
1440m; slopes 1440–1760m
⛷ 5 ⛷ 865 acres

Ramsau am Dachstein Austria
Charming village overlooked by the Dachstein glacier. Renowned for cross-country, it also has Alpine slopes locally, on the glacier and at Schladming.
1200m; slopes 1100–2700m
⛷ 18 ⛷ 30km

Ramundberget Sweden
Small, quiet, ski-in/ski-out family resort with very limited pistes but lots of cross-country. ⛷ 22km

Rasos de Peguera Spain
The only resort in the Barcelona province. 14km from Berga. Ten pistes, mostly red classified.

Rauris Austria
Small village in a quiet, dead-end valley south-east of Zell, about 25km by road. Across the valley road from the village are nursery draglifts and a gondola accessing intermediate slopes with a vertical of 1250m. Good for an all-round winter holiday as there are lots of activities to try, all set within the beautiful Hohe Tauern National Park.
950m; slopes 950–2175m
⛷ 10 ⛷ 30km

Ravascletto Italy
Resort in a pretty wooded setting near Austrian border, with most of its terrain high above on an open plateau.
920m; slopes 920–1735m
⛷ 12 ⛷ 40km

Reallon France
Traditional-style village, with splendid views from above Lac de Serre-Ponçon.
1560m; slopes 1560–2115m
⛷ 6 ⛷ 20km

Red Lodge USA
Picturesque Old West Montana town. Ideal for a combined trip with Big Sky or Jackson Hole.
1800m; slopes 2155–2860m
⛷ 8 ⛷ 1600 acres

Red Mountain Resort Canada
Up there with the likes of Fernie as a cult resort for expert skiers who can handle its steep terrain, wide glades and powder-filled bowls. While not big in European terms, it packs a lot of tough stuff into its mountains. If that's your scene, get there quickly as the ski area has been developing. For the 2013/14 season the ski area was hugely expanded by a new quad chair up Grey Mountain, adjacent to its existing Granite Mountain terrain, adding some more

intermediate runs to its existing mainly gnarly black runs through the trees. But it's still the black and double-black stuff that is the real attraction; it's marked on the map, but not on the mountain – so a guide may be necessary to explore it fully. There is good cat-skiing here too – and another 200 acres was added for 2014/15. Accommodation has recently been built at the base, but otherwise you stay at the small old mining town of Rossland just 4km away.
1185m; slopes 1185–2075m
⛷ 7 ⛷ 2957 acres

Red River USA
New Mexico western town – complete with stetsons and saloons – with intermediate slopes above.
2665m; slopes 2665–3155m
⛷ 7 ⛷ 290 acres

Reichenfels Austria
One of many small areas in Austria's easternmost ski region near the Slovenian border.
810m; slopes 810–1400m

Reinwald Italy
Resort near Merano in the South Tyrol covered by the Ortler Skiarena pass.

Reit im Winkl Germany
Southern Bavarian resort, straddling the German-Austrian border. Winklmoos ski area is best suited to intermediates.
750m; slopes 750–1800m
⛷ 7 ⛷ 40km

The Remarkables New Zealand
Three bleak basins with great views of 'remarkable' jagged alps, 45 minutes from Queenstown. Popular with families and beginners, but some tougher terrain too. Big terrain park.
1580m; slopes 1580–1945m
⛷ 6 ⛷ 545 acres

Rencurel-les-Coulumes France
One of seven little resorts just west of Grenoble. Unspoiled, inexpensive place to tour. Villard-de-Lans is the main resort.

Reschenpass Austria
Area in the Tirol right on the Swiss border; includes Schöneben and Haider Alm in Italy. Nauders is the main resort.
1520m

Rettenberg Germany
Small resort near Austrian border.
750m; slopes 820–1650m
⛷ 15 ⛷ 40km

Reutte Austria
500-year-old market town with many traditional hotels, and rail links to nearby Lermoos.
855m; slopes 855–1900m
⛷ 9 ⛷ 19km

Revelstoke 636

Rhêmes Notre Dame Italy
Unspoiled village in the beautiful Rhêmes valley, south of Aosta. Courmayeur and La Thuile within reach. Handful of hotels and tiny amount of downhill – including two black runs.
1725m; slopes 1625–3605m
⛷ 4 ⛷ 5km

Riederalp Switzerland
Pretty, car-free village high above the Rhône valley near Brig; part of the Aletsch Arena. Cable car or gondola from the valley village of Mörel. Quiet, friendly, uncrowded slopes.
1925m; slopes 1050–2870m
⛷ 35 ⛷ 100km

Riefensberg 104
Village in Bregenzerwald.

Rigi-Kaltbad Switzerland
Resort on a mountain rising out of Lake Lucerne, with superb all-round views, accessed by the world's first mountain railroad.
1440m; slopes 1195–1795m
⛷ 4 ⛷ 9km

Riihivuori Finland
Small area with 'base' at the top of the mountain. 20km south of the city of Jyväskylä.
⛷ 5

Riksgränsen Sweden
Unique Arctic Circle Alpine area not open until late February. You can use the slopes under the midnight sun (lift-served) from mid-May to June. 20 hours by train from Stockholm.
600m; slopes 600–910m
⛷ 6 ⛷ 21km

Riscone Italy
Dolomite village sharing a pretty area with San Vigilio. Good snowmaking. Short easy runs.
1200m; slopes 1200–2275m
⛷ 35 ⛷ 40km

Risoul 379
Small, convenient family resort linked with Vars to form a sizeable skiing area.

Rittner Horn Italy
Resort near Merano in the South Tyrol covered by the Ortler Skiarena pass.
⛷ 3 ⛷ 15km

Rivisondoli Italy
Sizeable mountain retreat east of Rome, with one of the better lift systems in the vicinity.
1350m; slopes 1350–2050m
⛷ 7 ⛷ 16km

Roccaraso Italy
Clearly largest of the resorts in Abruzzo, east of Rome, with lodgings in the town of Roccaraso and at three lift bases on the mountain.
1280m; slopes 1325–2140m
⛷ 24 ⛷ 110km

Rohrmoos 158
Suburb of Schladming, with vast area of nursery slopes.

Rosa Khutor Russia
One of the venues for the Sochi Winter Olympics in 2014.
560m; slopes 940–2320m
⛷ 13 ⛷ 72km

La Rosière 321

Rossland Canada
Remote little town 5km from cult powder paradise Red Mountain.

Rougemont Switzerland
Cute rustic hamlet just over the French/German language border near Gstaad, with local slopes and links to Gstaad's Eggli sector.
990m; slopes 950–3000m
⛷ 58 ⛷ 250km

Les Rousses France
Group of four villages – Les Rousses, Premanon, Lamoura and Bois d'Amont – in the Jura mountains, 50km from Geneva airport.
1120m; slopes 1120–1680m
⛷ 40 ⛷ 40km

Ruka Finland
80km south of the Arctic Circle, close to Kuusamo airport and the Russian border, in a region known for abundant and enduring snow. Lively, upbeat resort with a newly developed pedestrian village. Good but widely spread cabin lodging served by the ski bus. Slopes on two sides of a single low hill, with a mix of open and forest terrain, most floodlit and with snowmaking. None is particularly steep and the vertical very modest – but there is a new FIS racing piste. There's a terrain park and snowcross course. The cross-country scope is vast: 500km, of which 40km are floodlit.
200m
⛷ 20 ⛷ 20km

Russbach Austria
Secluded village tucked up a side valley and linked into the Gosau-Annaberg-Lungotz area. The slopes are spread over a wide area.
815m; slopes 780–1620m
🚡 *33* 🚠 *65km*

Rusutsu 670
Resort on Hokkaido, Japan.

Saalbach-Hinterglemm 152

Saalfelden Austria
Town ideally placed for touring eastern Tirol. Lift networks of Maria-Alm and Saalbach are nearby.
745m; slopes 745–1550m
🚡 *3* 🚠 *3km*

Saanen Switzerland
Cheaper and more convenient alternative to staying in Gstaad – but much less going on.
slopes 950–3000m
🚡 *58* 🚠 *250km*

Saanenmöser Switzerland
Small village with rail/road links to Gstaad. Scenic and quiet local slopes, with good mountain restaurants.
1270m; slopes 950–3000m
🚡 *58* 🚠 *250km*

Saas-Almagell Switzerland
Compact village up the valley from Saas-Grund, with good cross-country trails and walks, and a limited Alpine area.
1670m; slopes 1670–2400m
🚡 *7* 🚠 *12km*

Saas-Fee 489

Saas-Grund Switzerland
Sprawling valley village below Saas-Fee, with a separate small but high Alpine area.
1560m; slopes 1560–3200m
🚡 *8* 🚠 *35km*

Saddleback USA
Small area between Maine's premier resorts. High slopes by local standards.
695m; slopes 695–1255m
🚡 *5* 🚠 *100 acres*

Sahoro Japan
Ugly, purpose-built complex on snowy northern Hokkaido island, with a limited area.
610m; slopes 610–1030m
🚡 *8* 🚠 *15km*

Les Saisies France
Traditional-style cross-country venue, surrounded by varied four-mountain Alpine slopes. Now part of Espace Diamant. Easy runs, but some lift queues at peak times.
1650m; slopes 1035–2070m
🚡 *84* 🚠 *175km*

LAGRANGE Prestige
High-standard Self-catering Apartments
020 7371 6111
lagrange-holidays.co.uk

Sälen Sweden
Well-developed family resort with extensive lift system, and some good off-piste for experts.
550m; slopes 550–950m
🚡 *101* 🚠 *144km*

Salt Lake City USA
Underrated base from which to ski Utah. 30 minutes from Park City, Deer Valley, The Canyons, Snowbird, Alta, Snowbasin. Cheaper and livelier than the resorts.

Salzburg-Stadt Austria
A single, long challenging run off the back of Salzburg's local mountain, accessed by a spectacular lift-ride from a suburb of Grodig.
425m

Samedan Switzerland
Valley town, just down the road from St Moritz. A run heads back to base from Corviglia-Marguns.
1720m

Samnaun 114
Shares large ski area with Ischgl.

Samoëns 324

San Bernardino Switzerland
Pretty resort south of the road tunnel, close to Madesimo.
1625m; slopes 1600–2525m
🚡 *8* 🚠 *35km*

San Candido Italy
Resort on the border with Austria on the road to Lienz. Innichen is its German name.
1175m; slopes 1175–1580m
🚡 *4* 🚠 *15km*

San Carlos de Bariloche Argentina
Year-round resort, with five areas nearby and the place to stay when skiing Cerro Catedral – 20 minutes away by bus. Once a quaint lakeside town, but now a substantial resort.
slopes 1030–2180m
🚡 *39* 🚠 *103km*

San Cassiano 429
Quiet village linked via the Alta Badia to the Sella Ronda circuit.

Sandia Peak USA
The world's longest lift ride ascends from Albuquerque. Mostly gentle slopes; children ski free.
slopes 2645–3165m
🚡 *7* 🚠 *100 acres*

San Grée di Viola Italy
Easternmost of resorts south of Turin, surprisingly close to the Italian Riviera.
1100m; slopes 1100–1800m 🚠 *30km*

San Martin de los Andes Argentina
Sizeable town with accommodation, 19 km from the Chapelco ski area.

San Martino di Castrozza Italy
Trentino village south of Val di Fassa.
1465m; slopes 1465–2610m
🚡 *20* 🚠 *50km*

Sansicario 424
Small, stylish resort in the Milky Way near Sauze d'Oulx.

San Simone Italy
Tiny development north of Bergamo, close to unappealing Foppolo area.
2000m; slopes 1105–2300m
🚡 *9* 🚠 *45km*

Santa Caterina Italy
Pretty, user-friendly village near Bormio, with a snow-sure novice and intermediate area.
1740m; slopes 1740–2725m
🚡 *8* 🚠 *25km*

Santa Cristina 437
Quiet village in Val Gardena.

Santa Fe USA
Interesting area only 15 miles from beautiful Santa Fe town. A tree-filled bowl with a good variety of terrain crammed into its small area. Ideal stopover en route from Albuquerque airport to Taos.
3145m; slopes 3155–3680m
🚡 *7* 🚠 *550 acres*

Santa Maria Maggiore Italy
Resort south of the Simplon Pass from the Rhône valley, and near Lake Maggiore.
820m; slopes 820–1890m
🚡 *5* 🚠 *10km*

San Vigilio di Marebbe / Kronplatz Italy
Pretty village in South Tyrol with lifts on two mountains, one being the quite impressive Plan de Corones / Kronplatz.
1200m; slopes 1200–2275m
🚡 *31* 🚠 *116km*

San Vito di Cadore Italy
Sizeable, alternative place to stay to Cortina. Negligible local slopes, though.
1010m; slopes 1010–1380m
🚡 *9* 🚠 *12km*

Sappada Italy
Isolated resort close to the Austrian border below Lienz.
1215m; slopes 1215–2050m
🚡 *17* 🚠 *21km*

Sappee Finland
Resort within easy reach of Helsinki, popular with boarders and telemarkers. Lake views. 🚡 *7*

Sarnano Italy
Main resort in the Macerata region near Adriatic Riviera. Valley village with ski slopes accessed by lift.
540m
🚡 *9* 🚠 *11km*

Le Sauze France
Fine area near Barcelonnette, sadly remote from airports.
1400m; slopes 1400–2440m
🚡 *23* 🚠 *65km*

Sauze d'Oulx 424

Savognin Switzerland
Pretty village with a good mid-sized area; a good base for the nearby resorts of St Moritz, Davos/Klosters and Laax.
1200m; slopes 1200–2715m
🚡 *10* 🚠 *80km*

Scheffau 106
Rustic village not far from Söll.

Schia Italy
Very limited area of short runs – the only ski area near Parma. No village.
1245m; slopes 1245–1415m
🚡 *7* 🚠 *15km*

Schilpario Italy
One of many little areas near Bergamo.
1125m; slopes 1125–1635m
🚡 *5* 🚠 *15km*

Schladming 158

Schnalstal Italy
Valley and high ski area, in the Dolomites near Merano. Val Senales is its Italian name.
3210m; slopes 2110–3210m
🚡 *12* 🚠 *35km*

Schöneben   Italy
Area in the Val Venosta in the South Tyrol, close to Austrian border and Nauders.
1520m

Schönried   Switzerland
A cheaper and quieter resort alternative to staying in Gstaad.
1230m; slopes 950–3000m
🚡 *58* 🎿 *250km*

Schoppernau   **104**
Village in Bregenzerwald.

Schröcken   **104**
Bregenzerwald village linked to Lech Zürs.

Schruns   Austria
Pleasant little working valley town with a car-free centre at the heart of the Montafon region, with access to both the Hochjoch area (see St Gallenkirch) from a cable car near the centre of town and the Golm ski area (a few km away). At Golm four chairs and a drag serve easy blue and red slopes above the trees. A six-pack goes to the top of the area, linked via a ski tunnel to slopes on the back of the hill, including the Diabolo black run (the steepest in the valley). Snowmaking covers many of the upper slopes and the run to the valley. Ernest Hemingway ensconced himself in Schruns in 1925/26, and his favourite drinking table in the hotel Taube can be admired. Après-ski is not the big deal it is in many Austrian resorts, but a few places get quite lively. There's a big sports centre.
700m

Schüttdorf   **185**
Ordinary dormitory satellite of Zell am See, with easy access to the shared ski area. Kids' area and nursery slopes at the base.

Schwarzach im Pongau   Austria
Riverside village with rail links. There are limited slopes at Goldegg; Wagrain (Salzburger Sportwelt) and Grossarl (Gastein valley) are also nearby.
600m
🚡 *4* 🎿 *12km*

Schwarzenberg   **104**
Village in Bregenzerwald.

Schwaz   Austria
Valley town beside the Inn with a lift into varied terrain shared with the village of Pill and its mountain outpost, Hochpillberg.
540m; slopes 540–2030m
🚡 *6* 🎿 *10km*

Schweitzer   USA
Family-friendly resort in northern Idaho, 85 miles from Spokane (Washington state) and 45 miles from Canada. 'Excellent childcare,' says a 2014 visitor.
1220m; slopes 1229–1950m
🚡 *10* 🎿 *2900 acres*

Schwemmalm   Italy
Resort near Merano in the South Tyrol covered by the Ortler Skiarena pass.
🚡 *5* 🎿 *18km*

Scopello   Italy
Low area close to the Aosta valley, worth considering for a day trip in bad weather.
slopes 690–1700m
🚡 *6* 🎿 *35km*

Scuol   Switzerland
Year-round spa resort close to Austria and Italy, with an impressive range of terrain.
1225m; slopes 1225–2780m
🚡 *15* 🎿 *80km*

Searchmont Resort   Canada
Ontario area with modern lift system and 95% snowmaking. Fine Lake Superior views.
275m; slopes 275–485m
🚡 *4* 🎿 *65 acres*

Sedrun   Switzerland
Sizeable roadside village east of the Oberalp Pass, and covered along with Andermatt by the Gotthard Oberalp lift pass. The most extensive piste skiing in the area. There's a good choice of red runs, a rewarding black and a 'freeride' route, plus plenty of scope for off-piste. At Milez there's a terrain park and family restaurant area. Spa centre.
1450m; slopes 1450–2350m
🚡 *10* 🎿 *50km*

Seefeld   Austria
Classic winter holiday resort, well designed in traditional Tirolean style, with a large pedestrian-only centre and lots of upmarket hotels (including three 5-stars). Lots of people come here to enjoy the superb cross-country trails and off-slope activities rather than the downhill skiing, but there are two main downhill sectors on the outskirts – Gschwandtkopf and Rosshütte – the latter served mostly by fast lifts. Both areas have intermediate runs of decent vertical; Rosshütte is more extensive, with a cable car across to the separate peak of Härmelekopf, and some worthwhile challenges for experts. There's a good long red run back to village level and a gentle nursery area too. But overall the terrain is far too limited to keep most folk

entertained for a week's stay. You can always make excursions to Innsbruck, not far away and easily reached by train, or to the Stubai and Zugspitze glaciers.
1200m; slopes 1200–2065m
🚡 *30* 🎿 *37km*

See im Paznaun   Austria
Small family-friendly area in the Paznaun Valley, near Ischgl, with rustic old village set quietly 100m above the valley floor and main road.
1050m

Le Seignus-d'Allos   France
Close to La Foux-d'Allos (which shares large area with Pra-Loup) and has own little area, too.
1400m; slopes 1400–2425m
🚡 *13* 🎿 *47km*

Seis   Italy
German name for Siusi.

Sella Nevea   Italy
Limited but developing resort in a beautiful setting on the Slovenian border, and now linked to Bovec-Kanin. Summer glacier nearby.
1140m; slopes 1190–2300m
🚡 *12* 🎿 *30km*

Sella Ronda   **429**

Selva / Val Gardena   **437**

Selvino   Italy
Closest resort to Bergamo.
960m; slopes 960–1400m
🚡 *9* 🎿 *20km*

Selwyn Snowfields Australia
Popular with beginners and families. 6 hours from Sydney. Good lift system and cheaper passes than the major Oz resorts.
1520m; slopes 1490–1615m
🚡 *10* 🎿 *111 acres*

Semmering   Austria
Long-established winter sports resort set in pretty scenery, 100km from Vienna, towards Graz. Mostly intermediate terrain.
1000m; slopes 1000–1340m
🚡 *5* 🎿 *14km*

Semnoz   France
Small, family and beginner focused resort above Lake Annecy with views of the lake and Mont Blanc.
1705m
🚡 *11* 🎿 *18*

Les Sept-Laux   France
Improving family resort near Grenoble. Modern lift system – 90% of lifts having been replaced in recent years. Pretty slopes.
1350m; slopes 1350–2400m
🚡 *21* 🎿 *120km*

Serfaus   Austria
Virtually unknown in the UK, but it is a charming village of chalet-style buildings set on a sunny shelf and kept largely traffic-free by an underground railway to the lifts. Most of the accommodation is in hotels, frequented by well-heeled German families. It shares with Fiss and Ladis a broad area of high slopes, with long runs spanning several ridges – well-suited to mixed-ability parties and especially good for families. The vast kids' facilities at mid-mountain level and ample nursery slopes are key attraction. A lack of English speakers may be a drawback though.
1430m; slopes 1200–2830m
🚡 *67* 🎿 *212km*

Serrada   Italy
Very limited area near Trento.
slopes 1250–1605m 🚡 *5*

Serre-Chevalier   **327**

Sesto   Italy
Dolomite village off the Alta Val Pusteria, surrounded by pretty little areas. Sexten is its German name.
1310m; slopes 1130–2200m
🚡 *31* 🎿 *50km*

Sestola   Italy
Apennine village a short drive from Pisa and Florence with its pistes, some way above, almost completely equipped with snowmakers.
900m; slopes 1280–1975m
🚡 *23* 🎿 *50km*

Sestriere   **444**

Seven Springs Mountain USA
Pennsylvania's largest resort.
slopes 220–2995m
🚡 *18* 🎿 *494 acres*

Sexten   Italy
Dolomite village off the Hochpustertal, surrounded by pretty little areas. Sesto is its Italian name.
1310m; slopes 1130–2200m
🚡 *31* 🎿 *50km*

Shames Mountain Canada
Remote spot inland from coastal town of Prince Rupert and with impressive snowfall record. Deep powder.
670m; slopes 670–1195m
🚡 *3* 🎿 *183 acres*

Shawnee Peak   USA
Small area near Bethel and Sunday River renowned for its night skiing. Spectacular views. Mostly groomed cruising.
185m; slopes 185–580m
🚡 *5* 🎿 *225 acres*

Shemshak   Iran
Most popular of the three
mountain resorts within easy
reach of Tehran (60km).
3600m; slopes 2550–
3050m ♨ 7

Shiga Kogen   670
Largest area in Japan.

Showdown   USA
Intermediate area in Montana
forest north of Bozeman.
50km to the nearest hotel.
2065m; slopes 2065–2490m
♨ 4 ♙ 640 acres

Sierra-at-Tahoe   USA
A Colorado-style resort, with
runs cut on densely wooded
slopes. It claims an impressive
average of 420 inches of
snow. The slopes are spread
over two flanks of Huckleberry
Mountain. The fronts of both
offer good intermediate
cruising plus some genuine
single-diamond blacks. The
backside of Huckleberry has
easier blue and green slopes.
This is a natural day trip for
those staying in South Lake
Tahoe.
2210m; slopes 2025–2700m
♨ 14 ♙ 2000 acres

Sierra Nevada   655

Sierra Summit   USA
Sierra Nevada area accessible
only from the west. 100%
snowmaking.
2160m; slopes 2160–2645m
♨ 8 ♙ 250 acres

Silbertal   Austria
Low secluded village in the
Montafon valley, linked to
Schruns. A good base for
touring numerous areas.
890m

Sillian   Austria
A gondola and two fast quads
serve this varied area in
Austria's Hochpustertal region.
1100m
♨ 6 ♙ 45km

Sils Maria   494
Lakeside village linked to the
St Moritz Corvatsch slopes.

Silvaplana   494
Pretty village near St Moritz.

Silver Mountain   USA
Northern Idaho area near
delightful resort town of
Coeur d'Alene. Best for
experts, but plenty for
intermediates too.
1215m; slopes 1215–1915m
♨ 6 ♙ 1500 acres

Silver Star   639

Silverthorne   USA
Factory outlet town on main
road close to Keystone and
Breckenridge. Good budget
base for skiing those resorts
plus Vail and Beaver Creek.

Silverton   USA
Expert-only area in southern
Colorado that used to be heli-
ski country. Served by one lift.
Avalanche transceiver, shovel
and probe compulsory.
3170m; slopes 3170–3750m ♨ 1

Sinaia   Romania
Dreary main-road town with a
modest, open area of slopes.
Recent investment in new
lifts, included a gondola.
795m; slopes 795–2030m
♨ 10 ♙ 20km

Sipapu   USA
Great little New Mexico area,
with mostly treelined runs.
Snow unreliable, but 70%
snowmaking. Nice day out
from Taos when conditions
are good.
slopes 2500–2765m
♨ 4 ♙ 70 acres

Siusi   437
Village west of the Sella
Ronda circuit; Seis in German.

Siviez   505
A quieter, cheaper base for
Verbier's Four Valleys circuit.

Sixt-Fer-a-Cheval   254
Village near Samoëns.

Sjusjøen   Norway
Cluster of hotels in deep
forest close to Lillehammer.
Some Alpine facilities but
better for cross-country.
885m; slopes 1000–1090m
♨ 2 ♙ 2km

Ski Apache   USA
Apache-owned area south of
Albuquerque noted for
groomed steeps. Panoramic
views. Nearest lodging in
charming Ruidoso.
2925m; slopes 2925–3505m
♨ 11 ♙ 750 acres

Ski Cooper   USA
Small area close to historic
Old West town of Leadville.
Good ski/sightseeing day out
from nearby Vail, Beaver Creek
and Copper Mountain.
slopes 3200–3565m ♨ 4

Ski Windham   USA
Two hours from New York City
and second only to Hunter for
weekend crowds. Decent
slopes by eastern standards.
485m; slopes 485–940m
♨ 7 ♙ 230 acres

Smugglers' Notch   USA
French-style purpose-built
family resort with sympathetic
instructors, comprehensive
childcare, child-friendly layout
and long, quiet, easy runs.
There are varied and
satisfying slopes, spread over
three hills, with a worthwhile
vertical of 800m. It's a great
area for beginners, but
mileage-hungry intermediates
should go elsewhere.

Snowboarding is encouraged,
and there are three impressive
terrain parks and an Olympic-
size super-pipe.
315m; slopes 315–1110m
♨ 8 ♙ 1000 acres

Snowbasin   USA
Underrated hill, usually with
very good snow. No base
village, but a worthwhile day
out from Park City. The crowd-
free slopes cover a lot of
pleasantly varied terrain. This
is a great mountain for
experts – the Grizzly Downhill
course drops 885m and is
already claimed to be a
modern classic. Between the
race course and the area
boundary is a splendid area
of off-piste wooded glades
and gullies. Middle Bowl is
great terrain for the
adventurous, with a complex
network of blues and blacks.
You have to stay in the town
of Ogden on the Salt Lake
plain in the backwater of
Huntsville. 'Well worth the
drive to visit for a day –
fabulous views and
exceptional lodges,' says a
2014 visitor.
1965m; slopes 1965–2850m
♨ 11 ♙ 3000 acres

Snowbird   597

Snowbowl (Arizona)   USA
One of America's oldest areas,
near Flagstaff, Arizona, atop
an extinct volcano and with
stunning desert views. Good
snowfall record.
2805m; slopes 2805–3505m
♨ 5 ♙ 135 acres

Snowbowl (Montana)   USA
Montana area renowned for
powder, outside lively town of
Missoula. Intermediate pistes
plus 700 acres of extreme
slopes. Grizzly Chute is the
ultimate challenge.
1520m; slopes 1520–2315m
♨ 4 ♙ 1400 acres

Snowmass   568

Snow Park   New Zealand
Dedicated terrain park across
the valley from Cardrona.
Features galore, including
new 7m pipes. Budget lodging
at the base.
1530m ♨ 1

Snow Summit   USA
San Bernardino National
Forest ski area near Palm
Springs. Lovely lake views.
100% snowmaking. High-
capacity lift system for
weekend crowds.
2135m; slopes 2135–2500m
♨ 12 ♙ 230 acres

Snow Valley   USA
Area quite near Palm Springs.
Fine desert views. High-
capacity lift system copes with
weekend crowds better than
nearby Big Bear.
2040m; slopes 2040–2390m
♨ 11 ♙ 230 acres

Sochi   Russia
Host of the 2014 Winter
Olympic Games. Three
developing areas: Gasprom,
Rosa Khutor and Mountain
Carousel.
520m
♨ 19 ♙ 100km

Solda   Italy
The other side of the Stelvio
Pass from Bormio. Very long
airport transfers. Sulden is
German name.
1905m; slopes 1905–2625m
♨ 10 ♙ 40km

Sölden   162

Soldeu   80

Soldier Mountain   USA
Family resort in Central Idaho;
backcountry snowcat tours.
slopes 1770–2195m
♨ 4 ♙ 670 acres

Solitude   USA
Smart, car-free mini-village
linked with Brighton in the
valley next to Alta and
Snowbird. Most (not all) of
the slopes are easy or
intermediate, including a wide
area served by the one fast
quad. When open, the top lift
accesses lots of steeps in
Honeycomb Canyon, on the
back of the hill, with a short
quad to bring you back to the
front face. Headwall Forest
and Eagle Ridge also have
good blacks. The resorts'
boundaries are open, and
there are good backcountry
adventures to be had. 'An
appropriately named resort as
it was all but empty on our
visit,' says a 2014 visitor.
Taken over by Deer Valley
resort in April 2014 and
improvements are planned.
2490m; slopes 2435–3200m
♨ 13 ♙ 2250 acres

Söll   167

Solvista   USA
Child-oriented resort close to
Winter Park. Low snowfall
record for Colorado.
2490m; slopes 2490–2795m
♨ 5 ♙ 250 acres

Sommand   France
Purpose-built base that shares
area with Praz-de-Lys.
1420m; slopes 1200–1800m
♨ 22 ♙ 50km

Sonnenkopf   Austria
Ski area above Klösterle a few
km west of the Arlberg pass –
and covered by the Arlberg ski
pass. 'Good range of runs for
a small area,' says a reporter.
slopes 1100–2300m
🚡 9 ⛷ 30km

Sorenberg   Switzerland
Popular weekend retreat
between Berne and Lucerne,
with a high proportion of
steep, low runs.
1165m; slopes 1165–2280m
🚡 16 ⛷ 50km

South Lake Tahoe   USA
Tacky base for skiing
Heavenly, with cheap lodging,
traffic and gambling.

Spindleruv Mlyn
           Czech Republic
Largest Giant Mountains
region resort but with few
facilities serving several little
low areas.
715m; slopes 750–1310m
🚡 16 ⛷ 25km

Spital am Pyhrn   Austria
Small village near Hinterstoder
in Upper Austria, a bus ride
from its limited intermediate
slopes at Wurzeralm.
650m; slopes 810–1870m
🚡 8 ⛷ 20km

Spittal an der Drau Austria
Historic Carinthian town with
a limited area at Goldeck
starting a lift-ride above it. A
good day trip from Bad
Kleinkirchheim or from
Slovenia.
555m; slopes 1650–2140m
🚡 8 ⛷ 30km

Spitzingsee   Germany
Beautiful small lake (and
village) an hour from Munich.
🚡 18 ⛷ 25km

Splugen Reinwald
           Switzerland
Small intermediate area south
of Chur.
1485m; slopes 1455–2215m
🚡 6 ⛷ 30km

Sportgastein   96
Remote, high ski area at the
top of the Badgastein valley.

Squaw Valley   549

Stafal   416
Isolated village with access to
the Monterosa Ski area.

St Andra   Austria
Valley-junction village ideally
placed for one of the longest,
most snow-sure cross-country
networks in Europe. Close to
the Tauern pass and to St
Michael.
1045m

St Anton   174

Starhill Resort South Korea
Purpose-built resort formerly
called Cheonmasan, 30km
north-east of Seoul. 🚡 8

Stari Vrh   Slovenia
About 30 minutes from
Ljubljana airport. Runs include
a never-groomed black, three
interesting reds and a winding
blue virtually from top to
bottom.
slopes 580–1200m
🚡 5 ⛷ 12km

Stary Smokovec   Slovakia
Spa town in the High Tatras
mountains, with three small
areas – Tatransky Lomica is
the biggest. Funicular railway
and snowmaking facilities.
1480m; slopes 1000–1500m
🚡 8 ⛷ 4km

St Cergue   Switzerland
Limited resort in the Jura
mountains, less than an hour
from Geneva and good for
families with young children.
1045m; slopes 1045–1680m
🚡 16 ⛷ 21km

St Christoph   174
Small village on Arlberg pass
above St Anton.

St-Colomban-des-Villards
           France
Small resort in next side
valley to La Toussuire. Series
of drags link to the rest of the
area, with a pretty run to
return.
1100m

Steamboat   570

Ste-Foy-Tarentaise   336

Steinach   Austria
Pleasant market town with
small area of slopes in
picturesque surroundings, just
off the autobahn up to the
Brenner Pass, south of
Innsbruck.
1050m; slopes 1050–2200m
🚡 6 ⛷ 25km

Stevens Pass   USA
A day trip from Seattle, and
accommodation 60km away in
Bavarian-style town
Leavenworth. Mostly
intermediate slopes, with long
expert runs on backside. Busy
at weekends Jan to March.
1235m; slopes 1235–1785m
🚡 14 ⛷ 1125 acres

St-François-Longchamp 370
Sunny ski area linked to
Valmorel.

St Gallenkirch   Austria
Village in the Montafon strung
along the main road and
spoiled by traffic. A gondola
goes up to Valisera on the
west ridge of the Nova ski
area (see Gaschurn) and a
blue run comes back down to

the gondola base. From the
2011/12 season a new gondola
from the same area as the old
one goes up the opposite
side of the valley to Grasjoch
on the Hochjoch ski area –
but there is no piste back.
Hochjoch is a fair-sized area
of easy blue runs, with
occasional red alternatives.
Apart from the new gondola
and one eight-pack, the lifts
are slow chairs and drags. The
blue/red run from Kreuzjoch
down to Schruns is a notable
12km long and 1700m vertical
(and includes a section
through the longest ski tunnel
in the world – 473m).
Snowmaking covers almost
half the runs.
900m

St-Gervais   269
Small town sharing its ski
area with Megève.

St Jakob am Arlberg
           Austria
Quiet St Anton village, beyond
Nasserein. Depends on
shuttle-bus to the slopes.
1295m

St Jakob in Defereggen
           Austria
Unspoiled traditional village in
a pretty, sunny valley close to
Lienz and Heiligenblut, and
with a good proportion of
high-altitude slopes.
1400m; slopes 1400–2525m
🚡 7 ⛷ 52km

St Jakob in Haus   Austria
Snowy village with its own
slopes (Buchensteinwand).
Fieberbrunn, Waidring, St
Johann are nearby.
855m; slopes 855–1500m
🚡 8 ⛷ 19km

St-Jean-d'Arves   France
Small, scattered community
with 'friendly locals', set in
the Sybelles area. The original
old village, with the usual
ancient church, is set across
the valley from the slopes,
which are at the mid-
mountain hamlet of La Chal.
Here, where a tasteful
development of chalet-style
buildings has been expanding,
there are nursery slopes and
the lift link to and piste back
from Le Corbier. Not the best
base to exploit the whole
area, given the slow chair to
Le Corbier, but a bus goes to
St-Sorlin-d'Arves.
1550m

St Jean d'Aulps   France
Small village in Portes du
Soleil area, not part of main
circuit but with its own
interesting slopes consisting
of two small areas - Domaine

Chèvrerie and Domaine
Grande Terche. 'A little gem,'
says a 2014 visitor.

St-Jean-de-Sixt   France
Traditional hamlet, a cheap
base for La Clusaz and Le
Grand-Bornand (3km to both).
960m

St-Jean-Montclar   France
Small village at the foot of
thickly forested slopes. Good
day out from nearby Pra-Loup.
1300m; slopes 1300–2500m
🚡 18 ⛷ 50km

St Johann im Pongau
           Austria
Bustling, lively working town
with its own small area. An
extensive three-valley lift
network starts 4km away at
Alpendorf, linking via Wagrain
to Flachau – all part of the
Salzburger Sportwelt ski pass
area.
650m; slopes 800–2185m
🚡 64 ⛷ 200km

St Johann in Tirol   Austria
Friendly valley town, an
attractive place for beginners
and leisurely part-timers –
keen piste-bashers will ski all
the local slopes in a day and
need to go on to explore
nearby resorts covered by the
Kitzbüheler Alpenskipass as
well. There is nothing here to
challenge an expert. The main
access lift is a 10-minute walk
from the centre. It gets more
snow than neighbouring
Kitzbühel and the SkiWelt,
and also has substantial
snowmaking. Given good
snow, St Johann is one of the
best cross-country resorts in
Austria – trails total 275km.
'Some horrid slow lifts, but
great for a day out from
Kitzbuhel – and it's included
in the All Star pass,' says a
2014 visitor.
650m; slopes 660–1605m
🚡 17 ⛷ 43km

St Lary Espiaube   317
Satellite of St-Lary-Soulan in
the Pyrenees.

St-Lary-Soulan   317
Well preserved old stone
Pyrenean village, a lift-ride
below its fine intermediate
area.

St Leonhard in Pitztal
           Austria
Village beneath a fine glacier
in the Oetz area, accessed by
underground funicular.
1250m; slopes 880–3440m
🚡 12 ⛷ 68km

St Luc   501
Village in the Val d'Anniviers.

St Margarethen Austria
Valley village near Styria/
Carinthia border, sharing
slopes with higher Katschberg.
1065m; slopes 1065–2210m
🚠 16 ⛷ 70km

St Martin bei Lofer Austria
Traditional cross-country
village in a lovely setting
beneath the impressive
Loferer Steinberge massif.
Alpine slopes at Lofer.
635m; slopes 640–1745m
🚠 10 ⛷ 46km

St-Martin-de-Belleville 339
St Martin in Tennengebirge
Austria
Highest village in the
Dachstein-West region near
Salzburg. It has limited slopes
of its own but nearby
Annaberg has an interesting
area.
1000m; slopes 1000–1350m
🚠 4 ⛷ 5km

St-Maurice-sur-Moselle
France
One of several areas near
Strasbourg. No snowmakers.
550m; slopes 900–1250m
🚠 8 ⛷ 24km

St Michael im Lungau
Austria
Quiet, unspoiled village in the
Tauern pass snowpocket with
an uncrowded but disjointed
intermediate area. Close to
Obertauern and Wagrain.
1075m; slopes 1065–2220m
🚠 16 ⛷ 70km

St Moritz 494
St-Nicolas-de-Véroce 269
Small hamlet in the Megève
network.

St-Nicolas-la-Chapelle
France
Small village close to larger
Flumet, in the Val d'Arly.
1000m; slopes 1000–1600m
🚠 10 ⛷ 40km

St-Nizier-du-Moucherotte
France
Unspoiled, inexpensive resort
just west of Grenoble with no
lifts of its own. Villard-de-Lans
is the main resort.

Stoneham Canada
The closest resort to Québec
City, around 20 minutes away.
It also has its own small base
'village', with condo
accommodation and an
impressive lodge that has its
own lively après-ski bar,
restaurant and spas. But night
owls should probably head for
the city as the evenings are
generally quiet in resort. Like
most resorts in this region,
the ski area is small. The
slopes spread across several
linked peaks, with mainly

sheltered intermediate and
beginner pistes. It suits
families well and has a special
nursery area equipped with a
moving carpet. A key
attraction is the resort's four
terrain parks and half-pipe,
regularly revamped. They
hosted the 2013 Snowboard
World Championships.
210m; slopes 250–595m
🚠 7 ⛷ 32km

Stoos Switzerland
Small, unspoiled village an
hour from Zürich. Weekend
crowds. Splendid views of
Lake Lucerne.
1300m; slopes 500–1935m
🚠 7 ⛷ 35km

Storlien Sweden
Small family resort amid
magnificent wilderness
scenery, one hour from
Trondheim, 30 minutes from
Åre.
600m; slopes 600–790m
🚠 7 ⛷ 16km

Stowe 610
St-Pierre-de-Chartreuse
France
Locals' weekend place near
Grenoble. Unreliable snow.
900m; slopes 900–1800m
🚠 14 ⛷ 35km

Stratton USA
Something like the classic
Alpine arrangement of a
village at the foot of the lifts:
a smart, modern development
with a car-free shopping
street. The slopes are mostly
easy and intermediate, with
some blacks and some short
double-black pitches, spread
widely around the flanks of a
single peak, served by
modern lifts. Stratton calls
itself the 'snowboarding
capital of the east', with no
fewer than five terrain parks.
The Suntanner Park has a
super-pipe.
570m; slopes 570–1180m
🚠 14 ⛷ 660 acres

Strobl Austria
Close to St Wolfgang in a
beautiful lakeside setting.
There are slopes at nearby St
Gilgen and Postalm.
545m; slopes 545–1510m
🚠 7 ⛷ 12km

St-Sorlin-d'Arves France
A refreshing contrast to the
stark, functional resorts of Le
Corbier and La Toussuire, with
which it shares the extensive
Les Sybelles ski area. And the
resort accesses some of the
most interesting slopes. The
village is a picturesque
collection of traditional
buildings, alongside a more
modern development that
spreads out along the main

road and has attracted some
major tour operators. The
local slopes form the biggest
single sector of the linked
network, with lifts serving two
distinct mountains. Some of
the most varied slopes in the
whole area are here, and
reached by fast quads to Les
Perrons – which also has
some of the best off-piste
opportunities. There are
leisurely cruising runs on La
Balme.
1600m

St Stephan Switzerland
Unspoiled old farming village
at the foot of the largest
sector of slopes in the area
around Gstaad.
1000m; slopes 950–3000m
🚠 58 ⛷ 250km

Stubai valley 183
Stuben 174
Small, unspoiled village linked
to St Anton.

St Veit im Pongau Austria
Spa resort with limited slopes
at Goldegg; Wagrain
(Salzburger Sportwelt) and
Grossarl (Gastein valley) are
nearby.
765m
🚠 4 ⛷ 12km

St-Veran France
Said to be the highest 'real'
village in Europe, and full of
charm. Close to Serre-
Chevalier and the Milky Way.
Snow-reliable cross-country
skiing.
2040m; slopes 2040–2800m
🚠 15 ⛷ 30km

St Wolfgang Austria
Charming lakeside resort near
Salzburg, some way from any
slopes, best for a relaxing
winter holiday with one or
two days on the slopes.
540m; slopes 665–1350m
🚠 9 ⛷ 17km

Sugar Bowl USA
Exposed area north of Lake
Tahoe with highest snowfall in
California, best for experts.
Lodging in Truckee but Squaw
Valley nearby.
2100m; slopes 2100–2555m
🚠 8 ⛷ 1500 acres

Sugarbush USA
Dynamic resort in upper
Vermont, with two mountains
linked by fast chair, and
something resembling a
village at the foot of one of
them. Good range of runs,
including some real
challenges.
480m; slopes 450–1245m
🚠 16 ⛷ 508 acres

Sugarloaf USA
Developing Maine resort, 5
hours from Boston, with the
Eastern US's best open
terrain.
430m; slopes 405–1290m
🚠 15 ⛷ 1410 acres

Sulden Italy
The other side of the Stelvio
Pass from Bormio. Very long
airport transfers. Solda is its
Italian name.
1905m; slopes 1905–2625m
🚠 10 ⛷ 40km

Summit at Snoqualmie USA
Four areas – Summit East,
Summit Central, Summit West
and Alpental – with interlinked
lifts. Damp weather and wet
snow are major drawbacks.
slopes 915–1645m
🚠 24 ⛷ 2000 acres

Sun Alpina Japan
Collective name for three ski
areas four hours away from
Tokyo. 🚠 21

Sundance USA
Robert Redford-owned,
tastefully designed family
resort set amid trees in snow-
sure Utah. It's a small, narrow
mountain but the vertical is
respectable, the setting is
spectacular and there is
terrain to suit all abilities. The
lower mountain is easy-
intermediate, the upper part
steeper. There are 17km of
cross-country trails, of varying
difficulty.
1860m; slopes 1860–2515m
🚠 4 ⛷ 450 acres

Sunday River USA
One of the more attractive
resorts in the East, four hours
from Boston, best for
intermediate cruisers. The
slopes spread across eight
peaks, but it's a small area.
Only four of the chairs are
fast quads but queues are not
a problem – midweek, the
resort is very quiet. Cross-
country is big around here.
245m; slopes 245–955m
🚠 15 ⛷ 870 acres

Sunlight Mountain Resort
USA
Quiet, small area 10 miles
south of Glenwood Springs.
Varied terrain with some
serious glades.
2405m; slopes 2405–3015m
🚠 3 ⛷ 470 acres

Sun Peaks 641
Sunrise Park USA
Arizona's largest area,
operated by Apaches. Slopes
are spread over three
mountains; best for novices
and leisurely intermediates.
2805m; slopes 2805–3500m
🚠 12 ⛷ 800 acres

Sunshine Village 616
One-hotel mountain station in Banff's ski area.

Sun Valley 599
Purpose-built resort in Idaho.
1750m; slopes 1750–2790m
⛷ 18 ⛰ 2154 acres

Suomu Finland
A lodge (no village) right on the Arctic Circle with a few slopes but mostly a ski-touring place.
140m; slopes 140–410m ⛷ 3

Superbagnères France
Little more than a particularly French-dominated Club Med; best for a low-cost, low-effort family trip to the Pyrenees. Said to have good off-piste if the snow is good.
1880m; slopes 1440–2260m
⛷ 16 ⛰ 35km

Super-Besse France
Purpose-built resort amid spectacular extinct-volcano scenery. Shares area with the spa town of Mont-Dore. Limited village.
1350m; slopes 1300–1850m
⛷ 22 ⛰ 43km

Superdévoluy France
Purpose-built but friendly family resort in a remote spot near Gap, with huge apartment blocks plus traditional chalets. Sizeable intermediate area shared with more appealing La Joue-du-Loup.
1450m; slopes 1450–2450m
⛷ 22 ⛰ 100km

Super Espot Spain
Small area on the eastern edge of the Aigues Tortes National Park, close to the valley town of Sort.
slopes 1500–2500m
⛷ 8 ⛰ 28km

Supermolina Spain
Dreary, purpose-built satellite of Pyrenean resort of La Molina, with a reasonable sized area of its own and linked to the slopes of Masella to form an area called Alp 2500.
1700m; slopes 1600–2535m
⛷ 31 ⛰ 121km

Les Sybelles 265
A group of linked ski resorts in the Maurienne massif, forming an impressively large network.

Tahko Finland
Largest resort in southern Finland. Plenty of intermediate slopes in an attractive, wooded, frozen-lake setting.
⛷ 9

Tahoe City USA
Small lakeside accommodation base for visiting nearby Alpine Meadows and Squaw Valley.

Talisman Mountain Resort
Canada
One of the best areas in the Toronto region, but with a relatively low lift capacity. 100% snowmaking.
235m; slopes 235–420m ⛷ 8

Tamsweg Austria
Large cross-country village with rail links in snowy region close to Tauern Pass and St Michael.
1025m

La Tania 342

Taos 599
Isolated resort in New Mexico.
2805m; slopes 2805–3795m
⛷ 15 ⛰ 1294 acres

Tärnaby-Hemavan Sweden
Twin resorts in north Sweden, offering downhill, cross-country and heliskiing. Own airport.
slopes 465–1135m
⛷ 13 ⛰ 44km

El Tarter 80
Relatively quiet, convenient alternative to Soldeu.

Tarvisio Italy
Interesting, animated old town bordering Austria and Slovenia. A major cross-country base with fairly limited Alpine slopes.
750m; slopes 750–1860m
⛷ 12 ⛰ 15km

Täsch 522
The final road base on the way to car-free Zermatt.

Tatranská Lomnica Slovakia
Second largest resort in Slovakia, set in the High Tatras mountains.
890m; slopes 890–2635m
⛷ 7 ⛰ 11km

Tauplitz Austria
Traditional village at the foot of an interestingly varied area north of Schladming. Few queues and decent lift system, including some fast chairs.
900m; slopes 900–2000m
⛷ 18 ⛰ 40km

Telluride USA
An isolated resort in south-west Colorado, but a beautifully renovated old mining town with great Wild West charm and fairly dramatic mountain scenery. It's a friendly, small-scale resort, with a smartly developing slope-side base above it. Both have lifts into the ski area. Mountain Village has new luxury hotels and spa facilities. The slopes are limited in overall extent, but quite varied and with recently expanded expert terrain. Most runs are below the treeline, but the top lifts and bowls give great views. Queues are rarely a problem. Experts have some truly challenging terrain to play such as the Gold Hill Chutes, while there are splendid blue and greens runs for intermediates and beginners too – but it's not a resort for keen piste bashers. There are three terrain parks. Nightlife revolves around the bars.
2665m; slopes 2660–3830m
⛷ 18 ⛰ 2000 acres

Temù Italy
Sheltered hamlet near Passo Tonale. Worth a visit in bad weather.
1155m; slopes 1155–1955m
⛷ 4 ⛰ 5km

Tengendai Japan
Tiny area three hours by train and bus from Tokyo. One of Japan's best snow records, including occasional powder.
920m; slopes 920–1820m ⛷ 4

Termas de Chillán Chile
Ski and spa resort 400km south of Santiago. Base village has lodgings or you can stay at Las Trancas a few minutes' drive away.
1650m; slopes 1600–2700m
⛷ 9 ⛰ 35km

Termignon 357
Rustic village 6km from Lanslebourg and the linked slopes of Val Cenis.

Terminillo Italy
Purpose-built resort 100km from Rome with a worthwhile area when its lower runs have snow-cover.
1500m; slopes 1500–2210m
⛷ 15 ⛰ 40km

Teton Village 605

Thollon-les-Mémises France
Attractive base for a relaxed holiday. Own little area and close to Portes du Soleil.
1000m; slopes 1600–2000m
⛷ 19 ⛰ 50km

Thredbo Australia
Oz's best, 6 hours from Sydney; with uncharacteristically long (and, in places, testing) runs, snowmaking, lots of accommodation and active nightlife.
1365m; slopes 1365–2035m
⛷ 14 ⛰ 480 acres

Three Valleys 346

La Thuile 446

Thyon 2000 505
Mid-mountain resort above Veysonnaz in the Verbier area.

Tignes 348

Timberline (Palmer Snowfield) USA
Fair-sized area of largely intermediate slopes served by six lifts including four fast quads on Mt Hood in Oregon.
1800m; slopes 1510–2600m
⛷ 6 ⛰ 1430 acres

Toblach Italy
Small resort in South Tyrol. Dobbiaco is its Italian name.
1250m; slopes 1250–1610m
⛷ 5 ⛰ 15km

Togari Japan
One of several areas close to the 1998 Olympic site. Nagano, 2hr30 from Tokyo.
slopes 400–1050m ⛷ 9

Torgnon Italy
Small village off the road up to Cervinia, good for bad-weather days. Some good cross-country loops.
1500m; slopes 1500–1965m
⛷ 7 ⛰ 6km

Torgon Switzerland
Old village in a pretty wooded setting, with a connection to the Portes du Soleil. Still some steep draglifts.
1150m; slopes 950–2300m
⛷ 197 ⛰ 650km

Le Tour 223
Charming hamlet at the head of the Chamonix valley.

La Toussuire 265
One of the central resorts of the Sybelles area.

Trafoi Italy
Quiet, traditional village in the Val Venosta in the South Tyrol covered by the Ortler Skiarena pass.
1570m; slopes 1570–2550m
⛷ 4 ⛰ 10km

Treble Cone New Zealand
Plenty of good skiing opened up by two main lifts. Varied open terrain suitable for all levels. Great powder bowls. Nearly 2 hours from Queenstown.
1260m; slopes 1260–1960m
⛷ 4 ⛰ 550 hectares

Tremblant 653

Trentino Italy
Fabulously scenic area of the Dolomites, with a great many small ski areas that you won't have heard of, as well as a few large ones that are better known – Madonna di Campiglio chief among them.

Troodos Cyprus
Ski area on Mt Olympus, a 70-minute drive from Nicosia. Pretty, wooded slopes and fine views.
slopes 1730–1950m
⛷ 4 ⛰ 5km

Tröpolach Austria
Small village at base of access gondola for Nassfeld ski area.
610m; slopes 610–2195m
⛷ 30 🚡 110km

Trysil Norway
Extensive area, some distance from the town, spread around the conical Trysilfjellet, with some good, long runs of up to 4km. On the border with Sweden.
350m; slopes 350–1100m ⛷ 24

Tryvann Norway
Small area close to Oslo and popular with ocals. Vertical of 380m – are served by two drags and two chairs, one of them fast. ⛷ 6

Tschagguns Austria
Village the Montafon valley – effectively a suburb of Schruns.
700m; slopes 700–2100m
⛷ 13 🚡 32km

Tsugaike Kogen Japan
Sizeable resort four hours from Tokyo, three hours from Osaka. Helicopter service to the top station.
800m; slopes 800–1700m ⛷ 26

Tulfes Austria
Hamlet on mountain shelf close to Innsbruck, with small main area above the trees and long runs back to base.
920m; slopes 920–2305m
⛷ 7 🚡 22km

Turoa New Zealand
On the south-western slopes of Mt Ruapeha, with NZ's biggest vertical. Shares lift pass with Whakapapa. Mix of open, gentle and steeper runs. Good scope for off-piste.
slopes 1600–2320m
⛷ 23 🚡 2590 acres

Turracherhöhe Austria
Tiny, unspoiled resort on a mountain shelf, with varied intermediate slopes above and below it. A good outing from Bad Kleinkirchheim.
1765m; slopes 1400–2205m
⛷ 14 🚡 38km

Tyax Mountain Lake Resort Canada
Heli-skiing operation in the Chilcotin mountains – transfers from Whistler or Vancouver.

La Tzoumaz 505
Hamlet in Verbier's ski area.

Uludag Turkey
Surprisingly suave, laid-back, well-equipped, purpose-built resort near Bursa, south of Istanbul.
1750m; slopes 1750–2322m
⛷ 14 🚡 15km

Unken Austria
Traditional village hidden in a side valley. Closest slopes to Salzburg.
565m; slopes 1000–1500m
⛷ 4 🚡 8km

Untergurgl 144
Valley-floor alternative to staying in Obergurgl.

Unternberg Austria
Riverside village with trail connecting into one of the longest, most snow-sure cross-country networks in Europe. St Margarethen slopes close by.
1030m

Unterwasser-Toggenburg Switzerland
Old but not especially attractive resort 90 minutes from Zürich. Fabulous lake and mountain views. The more challenging half of the Toggenburg area shared with Wildhaus.
910m; slopes 900–2260m
⛷ 17 🚡 60km

Uttendorf-Weiss-See Austria
Astute alternative to crowded Kaprun when the snowline is high.
805m; slopes 1485–2600m
⛷ 8 🚡 23km

Vail 573

Valbella 459
Convenient village sharing Lenzerheide's area, now linked to Arosa's.

Valberg France
Large Alpes-Maritimes resort (bigger than better-known Isola 2000) close to Nice.
1650m; slopes 1430–2100m
⛷ 26 🚡 90km

Val Cenis Vanoise 357

Val d'Anniviers 501

Val di Fassa 429
Valley area of Campitello and Canazei – part of the Sella Ronda circuit.

Val d'Illiez 462
Peaceful, unspoiled village near Champéry.

Val d'Isère 360

Val Ferret Switzerland
Old climbing village near Martigny, with spectacular views. Own tiny area.
1600m
⛷ 3 🚡 20km

Valfréjus 265
A small, quiet and modern resort in the Maurienne valley.

Val Gardena 437
Valley area of Selva, Ortisei and Santa Cristina.

Valgrisenche Italy
Small, peaceful village on the southern side of the Aosta valley. Established heli-ski centre – about 20 drop points on the local peaks. A couple of intermediate runs, nursery area and a few cross-country loops.
1665m
⛷ 4 🚡 12km

Vallandry 206
Satellite of Les Arcs.

Valle Nevado Chile
Developing purpose-built resort 46km east of Santiago. Varied, intermediate terrain.
3025m; slopes 2860–3670m
⛷ 14 🚡 2200 acres

Valloire 265
Old village above the Maurienne valley.

Vallorcine 223
Backwater on road between Chamonix and Switzerland.

Vallter 2000 Spain
Small resort on the far eastern fringes of the Pyrenees, close to the Costa Brava.
slopes 1960–2535m
⛷ 10 🚡 420 acres

Valmeinier 265
Quiet, old mountain village in the Maurienne region.

Valmorel 370

Val Senales Italy
Top-of-the-mountain hotel, the highest in the Alps, in the Dolomites near Merano.
3210m; slopes 2110–3210m
⛷ 12 🚡 35km

Val Thorens 372

Valtournenche 391
Cheaper alternative to Cervinia.

Vandans Austria
Sizeable working village well placed for visiting all the Montafon areas. A gondola goes up directly from here into the Golm area.
655m

Vars / Risoul 379

Vasilitsa Greece
Resort in northern Greece, in the Pindos range, offering intermediate skiing.
1780m ⛷ 8

Vaujany 196
Tiny village in the heart of the Alpe-d'Huez ski area.

Las Vegas Ski Resort USA
Tiny area formerly known as Lee Canyon, cut from forest 50 minutes' drive north-west of Las Vegas.
2595m; slopes 2595–2855m
⛷ 4 🚡 200 acres

Velka–Raca Slovakia
Small resort near Oscadnica, with a modern lift system, including a 'chondola'.
630m; slopes 630–1050m
⛷ 6 🚡 14km

Vemdalen Sweden
Twin areas of Björnrike and Vemdalsskalet (same pass) 20 minutes apart. 385m vertical.
⛷ 18 🚡 28km

Vemdalsskalet Sweden
20 minutes from Björnrike (same pass). 385m vertical. Said to have hottest après-ski in Sweden.
⛷ 18 🚡 28km

Venosc France
Captivating tiny village of cobbled streets, ancient church and craft shops with fast gondola to Les Deux-Alpes.

Vent Austria
High, remote Oztal village known mainly as a touring base, with just enough lift-served skiing to warrant a day trip from nearby Obergurgl.
1900m; slopes 1900–2680m
⛷ 4 🚡 15km

Ventron France
Small village near La Bresse in the northerly Vosges mountains near Strasbourg, with more ski de fond than downhill terrain.
630m; slopes 900–1110m
⛷ 8 🚡 15km

Verbier 505

Vercorin 501
Cluster of chalets in the Val d'Anniviers.

Verditz Austria
One of several small, mostly mountain-top areas overlooking the town of Villach.
675m; slopes 675–2165m
⛷ 5 🚡 15km

Vex Switzerland
Major village in unspoiled, attractive setting south of Sion. Verbier slopes accessed nearby at Mayens-de-l'Ours.
900m

Veysonnaz 505
Little old village within Verbier's Four Valleys network.

Vichères–Liddes Switzerland
Small area near Verbier that is popular with families. Good off-piste down to near La Fouly to be explored with a guide.
1350m; slopes 1600–2270m
⛷ 4 🚡 15km

place, both on and off the slopes. Its 3,000 acres embrace a wide range of slopes that are not only impressively snowy but also blissfully devoid of people. There's easy cruising in dense forest around the base area, and steeper stuff higher up on 'gladed' slopes. There are two good terrain parks. There's lodging at the base and you can stay in the small town of Whitefish, a few miles away.
1360m; slopes 1360–2135m
🚡 13 🎿 3000 acres

White Pass Village USA
Closest area to Mt St Helens. Remote and uncrowded during the week, with a good snowfall record. Some genuinely steep, expert terrain, as well as intermediate cruising.
1370m; slopes 1370–1825m
🚡 5 🎿 635 acres

Whitewater Canada
Renowned for powder (40% off-piste), food and weekend party atmosphere. Accommodation in the historic town of Nelson or a great day out from nearby Red Mountain.
1640m; slopes 1640–2040m 🚡 3

Wildcat Mountain USA
New Hampshire area infamous for bad weather, but one of the best areas on a nice day. Lodging in nearby Jackson and North Conway.
slopes 600–1250m
🚡 4 🎿 225 acres

Wildhaus Switzerland
Undeveloped farming community in stunning scenery near Liechtenstein; popular with families and serious snowboarders. Shares its slopes with Unterwasser.
1050m; slopes 900–2260m
🚡 17 🎿 60km

Wildschönau 93
Part of the Ski Juwel (Alpbachtal-Wildschönau) area.

Willamette Pass USA
Set in national forest near beautiful Crater Lake, Oregon. Small area of varied slopes. An average of 430 inches of snow a year – that's up there with Utah.
1560m; slopes 1560–2035m
🚡 6 🎿 550 acres

Williams USA
Tiny area above the main place to stay for the Grand Canyon.
slopes 2010–2270m
🚡 2 🎿 50 acres

Willingen Germany
Resort in Sauerland, east of Düsseldorf. 🚡 8

WindhamMountain USA
Boutique resort in the Catskill Mountains 2.5 hours from New York.
455m; slopes 455–945m
🚡 10 🎿 269 acres

Windischgarsten Austria
Large working village in Upper Austria with cross-country trails around and downhill slopes at nearby Hinterstoder and Spital am Pyrhn.
600m

Winterberg Germany
Resort in Sauerland, east of Düsseldorf. 🚡 24

Winter Park 580

Wolf Creek USA
Remote area on a pass of the same name, with 'the most snow in Colorado' – 465 inches a year. One-third of the terrain is standard American trails through the trees; two-thirds is 'wilderness', served by a single lift. Great stop en route between Taos and Telluride. Stay in Pagosa Springs to the west, or South Fork to the east.
3140m; slopes 3140–3630m
🚡 6 🎿 1600 acres

Wolf Mountain USA
Utah area close to Salt Lake City, due to be expanded and renamed Skyline Mountain Base for 2014/15.
🚡 3 🎿 100 acres

Xonrupt France
Cross-country venue only 3km from nearest Alpine slopes at Gérardmer.
715m

Yangji Pine Resort South Korea
Modern resort an hour (60km) south of Seoul, with runs cut out of dense forest. Gets very crowded. 🚡 6

Ylläs 657

Yong Pyong Resort South Korea
200km east of Seoul, close to the east coast, also known as Dragon Valley. The self-contained purpose-built resort village is centred on 200-room Dragon Valley Hotel. Modern lifts serve a small, mainly wooded slope area, with snowmaking on all its runs.
750m; slopes 750–1460m
🚡 15 🎿 20km

Zakopane Poland
An interesting old town 100km south of Kraków on the Slovakian border. Mostly intermediate slopes, branded as 14 small and fragmented

sectors. Reported to have renovated its 70-year-old cable car.
830m; slopes 1000–1960m
🚡 60 🎿 60km

Zao Japan
Big area with unpredictable weather, four hours from Tokyo by train. Known for 'chouoh' – pines frozen into weird shapes. Hot springs.
780m; slopes 780–1660m 🚡 42

Zauchensee Austria
Purpose-built resort part of big three-valley lift network linking it via Flachauwinkl to Kleinarl – which our figures relate too. Also on the Salzburger Sportwelt ski pass. 'Attractive, compact village, shops limited to ski kit, no nightlife, dining only in hotels, relatively easy family-friendly skiing'.
855m; slopes 800–2185m
🚡 15 🎿 88km

Zell am See 185

Zell im Zillertal 138
Sprawling valley town with slopes on two mountains.

Zermatt 522

Zillertal Austria
Valley of ten ski resorts, of which the most well known is Mayrhofen.

Zinal 501
Village in the Val d'Anniviers.

Zug 129
Tiny village with Lech's toughest skiing.

Zugspitz Arena Austria
The name of Germany's highest mountain, and part of Austria's Zugspitz Arena over the border – a collection of small, gentle but low ski areas, with pretty villages.
990–1340m; slopes 990–2960m
🚡 55 🎿 148km

Zuoz Switzerland
An unspoiled village in a sunny setting just down the valley from St Moritz, with gentle slopes at village level and some more challenging runs higher up.
1715m; slopes 1720–2465m
🚡 5 🎿 15km

Zürs 129
High village on road to Lech.

Zweisimmen Switzerland
Limited but inexpensive base for slopes around Gstaad, with its own delightful little easy area too.
965m; slopes 950–3000m
🚡 58 🎿 250km

You'll appreciate the lengths we go to to find you a dream ski holiday

Ski*line*.co.uk

The skiers' travel agent

We search the whole ski market so you don't have to

Call 020 8313 3999

ABTA No. L6436